Index to the Deaths Found in

The New Yorker Volks-Zeitung

1878–1920

Thomas Reimer

HERITAGE BOOKS
2011

HERITAGE BOOKS
AN IMPRINT OF HERITAGE BOOKS, INC.

Books, CDs, and more—Worldwide

For our listing of thousands of titles see our website
at
www.HeritageBooks.com

Published 2011 by
HERITAGE BOOKS, INC.
Publishing Division
100 Railroad Ave. #104
Westminster, Maryland 21157

Copyright © 2000 Thomas Reimer

This book was previously published as a two-volume set

All rights reserved. No part of this book may be reproduced or transmitted in any form or by any means, electronic or mechanical, including photocopying, recording or by any information storage and retrieval system without written permission from the author, except for the inclusion of brief quotations in a review.

International Standard Book Numbers
Paperbound: 978-0-7884-1684-2
Clothbound: 978-0-7884-8765-1

FOREWORD

This is an index of about 27,000 obituaries, death notices, reported deaths and other biographical material found in the New Yorker Volks-Zeitung, or NYVZ, from January 28, 1878 to December 31, 1920.

Published from Jan. 28, 1878 to Oct 12, 1932, the daily NYVZ and its successor, the weekly Neue Volks-Zeitung (December 17, 1932 to August 6, 1949), catered to the German-speaking union members and people affiliated with the Socialist movement. Circulation was moderate, with the daily's and its Sunday edition selling 4,000 copies in 1878, 10,200 in 1880 and from 18,000 to 23,000 between 1900 and 1930. Not included in this index was its weekly edition Vorwaerts (not to be confused with the Jewish Vorwaerts, also affiliated with the socialist movement). The NYVZ is of interest to genealogists but also to social and labor historians looking for middle-level labor leaders and members whose deaths were not noted by the New York Times. For easier identification and to allow the creation of sample groups, I noted information usually not highlighted in an obituary index, such as unionization and membership in a socialist party.

For the years 1894 to 1920 I used the microfilm holdings of the New York Public Library, which generally included the Sunday edition. For the years 1878 to 1893, I used the microfilms of the Rand School of Social Research and of the Library of Congress. These often did not include the Sunday edition, the Sonntagsblatt, and are incomplete. Missing, for instance, in 1886 were the issues of August 27, August 30 to September 6, September 10 to 14, and September 16. The paper used to film certain reels was badly decayed, such as the year 1889, making the microfilm very difficult to read.

Several microfilm sets of the NYVZ exist but it may still be difficult to get the year you need. If you can, consider purchasing a copy from the New York Public Library, and donating it to your local library for the benefit of other genealogists and historians.

More information about the New Yorker Volks-Zeitung and its world can be found in:

Arndt, Karl and May Olson. German–American Newspapers and Periodicals: History and Bibliography. Heidelberg: Quelle & Meyer 1961, vol. I, p. 385, 396, 406

Hoerder, Dirk, and Christiane Harzig. The Immigrant Labor Press in North America. New York: Greenwood Press 1987, 3 vols., vol. 3, p. 309-558.

Shore, Elliott, et alii. The German-American Radical Press. Urbana, IL: University of Illinois Press 1992.

ABBREVIATIONS AND SYMBOLS, PART I:

@ see summary entry for specific catastrophes at beginning of the index. Rather than repeat a great deal of entries after each victim's name (Slocum catastrophe, notably), a summary was created.
SS steamship, i.e. SS General Slocum
\# picture included
b. born—maiden name
exec. executed
* born in
fr The notice states that he/she came from there
% married see also reference
= burial/cremation
fam. family card of thanks
mem. memorial ad
wd widow
War 1 died as member of the armed forces of a country
War 2 died of war-related causes as civilian, often of anguish because of the war

ABBREVIATIONS AND SYMBOLS, PART II:

ATB Arbeiterturnerbund (Workers' Gymnastic Federation)
AKK Arbeiterkrankenkasse (Workmen's Benefit Fund)
CH Switzerland
F France
GV Gesangverein
Gy Germany

'48er Veteran of the 1848–49 German Revolution
LI Long Island
MdL Mitglied des Landtags. Member of a state legislature
MdR Mitglied des Reichstags (Germany), des Reichsraths (Austria) Member of the national parliament
MGV Maennergesangverein
NYC-Bx New York City-Bronx
NYC-B New York City-Brooklyn
NYC-M New York City-Manhattan
NYC-SI New York City-Staten Island
NYC-Q New York City-Queens
NYSZ New Yorker Staats–Zeitung
NYVZ New Yorker Volks–Zeitung
SDP Member of the Social-Democratic Party. Occasionally, party affiliations were ambiguous, and it is quite possible that I listed SDP members as SLP and vice-versa.
? When followed by ?, the entry was not clear—e.g. the departed was a member of the Socialist Gymnastic Society, but not specifically described as party member, or the age was difficult to read, etc.
SLP member Socialist Labor Party
SP member of the Socialist Party
TV Turnverein (Gymnastic Society)
un. unionized

BIOGRAPHICAL INFORMATION FOUND IN THE NYVZ

The NYVZ index includes news about the following groups of people:

Members of the German American labor and Socialist movements in the Greater New York area, including New Jersey. German in the 19th century referred to all Germans by ethnicity, not only those from the Second German Empire founded in 1871. Occasionally, the NYVZ noted the deaths of militants in other parts of the United States. A small number of marriages, births, birthdays and jubilees, such as Silver Weddings, whether to one's spouse or to the Socialist cause, were found and included in the index.

Not all local people whose deaths were recorded by the paper were members of the labor movement, some were simply people known to the neighborhood. This included a few mobsters and ladies of the night.

Occasionally, the NYVZ noted the deaths of militants from Europe, especially from the German and German-Austrian labor movement, with which the paper's editors and readers retained close ties.

The NYVZ reported the deaths of public figures in the United States and abroad, like any other daily. But not everyone whose death was found worthy of comment in the middle-class press was noted in the NYVZ, and NYVZ obituaries often also had a distinctive slant. Those of Andrew Carnegie or Russell Sage, for instance, were scathing denunciations, while those of Patrick O'Donnell and William O'Donovan, executed in the 1880s for attacking British occupation officials in Ireland, praised them as selfless freedom fighters. This lead to a difficult decision concerning their description in this index, which may startle some readers. There were probably hundreds of men called William O'Donovan and Patrick O'Donnell who died in the 1880s, hence they had to be described more specifically. Since this is an index to the NYVZ, I decided to use the descriptions written by the NYVZ editors, though I did not always share their judgment.

The paper also covered executions, which are included in this index when in the North East of the United States, or nationwide if a German-American was involved. The paper also reported extensively and sharply condemned the gruesome lynching of Negroes that overshadowed these decades. These are listed in this index, too.

The amount of information found in the obituaries and death notices varies greatly. In general, as other newspapers at the time, the NYVZ did not include birthplaces. Deaths were reported within a day or two, which helps researchers to check the relevant files at the New York Municipal Records Office. In general, a worker would receive a death ad from his family and another from his union. For militants, the paper also reported their burials or cremations, and reprinted parts of the eulogy. For people in the community who were not members of the movement, the paper often only gave name, age, place of residence, and details about the manner of death if that was the news-item. Quite a number of workers listed here chose their moment of death. Those who wonder why may want to read the NYVZ editorials "Eine bezeichnende Thatsache" (27 Mr 1909:4b, 28 Mr:6a-c), "Leider kein Phantasiegebilde," (1 Sept 1913:8e) and "Verhungernde Alte" (22 Jan. 1913:4a) about what it meant to be an old immigrant worker before Social Security.

The paper filed death notices for New York City by borough, but not always consistently. Borough designations for the rapidly developing boundary areas of Brooklyn and Queens in the 1880s and 1890s seem occasionally wrong, while the South Bronx was filed under Manhattan until 1898. I have checked street addresses to identify, whenever possible, in which of the five boroughs the deceased lived because the indices to New York City civil records are organized that way. However, mistakes are likely to have occurred. *It is always better to first get a copy of your ancestor's death notice in the NYVZ before contacting City Hall for a copy of the death records.*

The index gives name, place of residence/death, date and page/ column of the notice, and if given, date of death and of the funeral. It also notes occupation, membership in an union, maiden names and city/area of birth.

When an occupational title can have different meanings–painter, for instance–the labor meaning is always implied. The few art painter are listed as artist (painter). Also, a "brewer" (Brauer) is always a brewery worker, whether skilled or not; Owners/managers are specified as such. For people in public life, I have cited only the page, since researchers will hardly turn to the NYVZ to get biographical details about Alexander III of Russia, for instance.

Crowned heads are indexed under the name of their country, not their first names. Alexander III of Russia is found under Russia, not under Alexander. Surnames with prefixes such as de, von, van are indexed under their main part, e.g. von Alvensleben under Alvensleben, von. Often, the prefix was the first part of the name to be dropped by immigrants.

Place names: The NYVZ used the German names of cities, whether this was their official name (in the Second German Empire or the Austrian Empire), or their traditional name, e.g. Pressburg instead of Poszony in the old Kingdom of Hungary (called nowadays Bratislava in Slovakia). I have not upated the names, for looking up their present designation and learning about their history is an interesting part of ancestry–hunting. Assuming that people searching for German ancestors have some basic knowledge about Germany, I did not always add "Germany" after Bavaria etc. The Elsass area was called that instead of the French term Alsace, reflecting both the legal usage of that time and that of its native Germanic population.

Birthdates are given day/month/year. Newspaper issues are listed by year/month/day/page/column counted from the left. Closely following dates do not repeat year and month, as in the following example:

BARTSCH, Gustav, 57, un. printer, SLP, *Koenigsberg/East Prussia, NYC-B – 1894/07/24:1g, 4a, =26:4c

The latter date, 26:4c, is of course the 26th July. If the burial was in a different month from the death, the month is also given.

NAME CHANGES, VARIANTS, UMLAUTS and ß:

Small changes, such as dropping double consonants, e.g. from –mann to –man, the umlaut, from Böse to Boese to Bose, or altering –meier (also mayer, meyer, maier) into myer or myre still allows to recognize the name. This can be more difficult if the name was altered drastically or translated, e.g. from Grün to Green. Generally, *see also* references to related names were not given. When looking for Hortstmann, think also of Hortstman, for Hoffmann, think of Hoffman, Hofmann, Hofman. As a rule, browse. Your local phone book contains useful *see also* references, including for German names. Quite often, names will be spelled slightly differently in the ads given by the family and the trade union the departed belonged to, one using –man and the other –mann, for instance. Children may spell their names differently from their parents or from their siblings. In addition to intentional name variants, names could also be unintentionally misspelled by the typesetter, or the person reporting the death. Also, I may have misread the small type fraktur.

The letter ß, a sharp s sound always preceded by a vowel, was spelled –ss. Umlauts were transcribed as ae, ue, oe and indexed as such, which is the traditional way and would have been used by the immigrants themselves. So, for instance, for Weiß, see Weiss.

I hope that my modest booklet will be useful to many. I wish to dedicate it to my grandmothers, Martha Reimer, b. Cyllies, and Marta Alexy, b. Böhm, from whom I learned to respect the past, and my wife Yayin Chu–Reimer, whose understanding sustained me during this project.

Thomas Reimer, PhD
Albany, New York

AANTEE, Hermann, Newark, NJ - 1918/03/11:6a
AARONSON, Philip, stoker, NYC-M - 1911/01/18;1f
ABBATO, Francesco, exec. Camden, NJ - 1900/05/11:4b
ABBE, Anna, 41, SP, NYC-B - 1913/07/11:2c, 6a, 13:6a, =14:2c, fam. 20:7a
ABBE, Ernst, Dr., German industrialist - 1905/02/05:7b, monument in Jena 12 Aug. 1911:4d
ABBOTT, George H., see Almy, Frank
ABBOTT, Josef, exec. Elmira, NY - 1882/01/07:1f
ABEL, Anna, 20, NYC-M, + New Haven, CT - 1899/09/01:1d
ABEL, Annie, b. Metzner, 59?, NYC-Q - 1918/01/16:6a
ABEL, Carrie, NYC-Q see Frederick Sigmund
ABEL, Christian W., NYC-M - 1892/07/07:4a
ABEL, Daniel, un. carp., NYC-M - 1902/03/02:5a
ABEL, Sarah, 80, NYC-M - 1881/09/08:4b
ABEL, William, 39, exec. Philadelphia, PA - 1914/12/04:1g
ABELTEIN, Abel, 33, Hoboken, NJ - 1896/08/11:1d
ABENDSCHEIN, Mary, 32, NYC-M, + on @ SS Genl Slocum - 1904/06/17:3b
ABENDSCHEIN, Wilhelmina, 21, NYC-M - 1902/10/18:4a, fam. 26:5a; mem. 17 Oct 1904:4a
ABERG, Frederick, 22, el. RR employee, NYC-M - 1891/04/03:2f
ABERGAST, John, 66, NYC-M - 1891/07/17:4a
ABERLE, Gustav, 40, upholsterer, NYC-M - 1883/01/11:1f
ABERS, Elias, Kenville, NJ - 1898/04/29:3f
ABERSTEIN, Julia, @Triangle Shirtwaist Co. fire, NYC - 1911/03/27:1d
ABLE, Christian, Union Hill, NJ - 1902/05/11:5a
ABLOWICH, Julie, NYC-M - 1880/04/05:1e, 6:1e
ABMAIER, Conrad, 69, Creedmore, LI - 1919/09/17:6a
ABRAHAM, Ike, NYC-M, + @ SS Genl Slocum - 1904/06/26:5c
ABRAHAMS, A., 52, NYC-M - 1894/02/01:4a
ABRAHAMS, Bertha, 24, NYC-M - 1904/07/28:3g
ABRAMOFF, Cossack officer who raped Maria Spiridowna, + by patriots - 1906/04/19:4c
ABRAMOWITZ, Jacob Scholem, 82, writer, + Odessa/Ukraine - 1917/12/17:2e
ABRAMOWITZ, Louis, 60, manuf., NYC-B - 1915/11/16:2d
ABRAMS, B.P., 45, NYC-M - 1893/10/25:4a
ABRAMS, Dora, 62, and Charles, 23, Sadie, 22, Carrie, 20, Anna, 16, NYC-B - 1908/05/04:1e
ABRAMS, George, 65, NYC-Q - 1916/02/05:6b
ABRAMS, J., musician, NYC-M, + @ SS Genl Slocum - 1904/06/24:1c

ABRIE, Maria, West New York, NJ – 1880/09/18:3c
ABROMEIT, John, iron worker, SP, *4 Ap 1852 Memel/Gy, USA 1870, NYC-M – 1908/10/18:7c,e, 19:6a, =20:1d, fam. 23:6a
ABT, John, 40, NYC-B – 1893/07/18:4a, 19:4a, fam. 23:5a
ABT, Michael, machinist, fr Elsass, NYC-M – 1890/12/05:1h, 6:2g
ACH, Michael, 29, West New York, NJ - 1918/10/18:6a
ACHARD, Louis, 63, NYC-M – 1891/03/09:4a
ACHELIS, Friedrich, pres. Chamber of Commerce in Bremen/Gy – 1917/05/23:2d
ACHTMANN, Georg, 52, USA 1881, NYC-M – 1882/04/06:1g, 7:4c
ACKER, Christian, 48, NYC-M – 1890/02/25:1g
ACKER, Philipp, 32, SLP, un. arch. iron worker, NYC- M – 1898/08/28:5e, 30:3f, fam. 2 Sept:4a
ACKER, William, 64, carp., NYC-M – 1907/09/24:2f
ACKERBERG, Catherine, 55, NYC, + Atlantic City, NJ - 1916/02/01:2b
ACKERBLUM, Fannie, 31, NYC-Q – 1912/02/16:1f
ACKERMAN, Jane L., 19, NYC-M – 1898/12/27:1h
ACKERMANN % Flick
ACKERMANN, Bertha, b. Fuchs, Washingtonville, NY – 1891/06/23:4a
ACKERMANN, Franz, 52, carp., NYC-M – 1896/05/06:1d
ACKERMANN, Karl Heinrich, 59, SP, plasterer, 1882 fr Wiesbaden/Gy, NYC-Bx – 1911/04/23:7a, =30:7a
ACKERMANN, Karl Gustav, Dr., ex-MdR fr Saxony – 1901/03/25:2e-f
ACKERMANN, Louis, un. cloth cutter, SLP, NYC-B – 1890/10/01:4a, 2:4a, = 4:4e
ACKERMANN, Lucas, 16, Newark, NJ – 1893/06/20:4f
ACKERMANN, Mary, 70?, fr Gy, NYC-M – 1909/06/09:1d
ACKERMANN, Millie's 1 yr old child, NYC-M – 1897/07/28:1g
ADAM % Michel
ADAM, Carl, NYC-M – 1907/11/11:6a
ADAM, Charles A., 64, NYC-B – 1890/10/20:4a
ADAM, Georg, NYC-M? – 1890/01/01:4a
ADAM, George, 14 months, NYC-M – 1890/09/27:4a
ADAM, John, 35, un. printer, NYC-M - 1895/10/18:4a
ADAM, Louis, 52, NYC-B – 1913/06/25:6a
ADAM, Rada, grain mill owner in Weiskirchen/Hungary, exec. 8 Sept. – 1914/11/15:3c
ADAMETZ, Stefan, 54, un. baker, NYC-M - 1916/11/18:6a, 19:7a
ADAMS, Al, gambler, NYC-M – 1906/10/02:2e, 3:2e
ADAMS, Georg, 46, SP, Lakeview, NJ – 1917/04/04:6a

ADAMS, Henry, 47, publ. NYC Belletristisches Jr – 1883/12/11:4e
ADAMS, John, anarchist,*Russia, USA 1906, # NYC meeting for his freedom – 1910/04/10:1c,7e, freed fr police jail 29:2d
ADAMS, John, chief of police, Newark, NJ – 1907/04/16:3c
ADAMS, Robert, Congressman, Philadelphia – 1906/06/02:1d
ADAMS, Sam, 18, Negro, lynched in Pass Christian, MI – 1903/11/07:1e
ADAMS, Susanne, un. cigar maker, NYC-M – 1886/01/04:2f
ADAMS, Wolf, 61, NYC-M - 1878/09/19:4c, 20:4b, 23:5e
ADAMSON, Jessie, 19, sales girl, NYC-M – 1890/11/25:1g
ADANK, Peter, NYC-M – 1909/07/06:6a
ADDICKS, Margaret, 12, NYC-M, + @ SS Genl Slocum – 1904/06/18:3c
ADE, Anna, 50, NYC-M - 1918/03/06:6a
ADE, Emil, NYC-M – 1910/08/10:6a
ADELHOFER, Leopold, un. painter, NYC-M – 1910/03/07:6a
ADELHOFF, Herman, 40, worker, NYC-M – 1896/08/12:1a
ADELMAN, Jacob, 47, flour dealer, NYC-B - 1916/08/13:1f
ADELMANN, Frederick, 20, NYC-M – 1891/09/20:5f
ADELMANN, Johann, 66?, NYC-M – 1891/09/19:4a
ADINKES, John, 15, NYC-M, + @ SS Genl Slocum – 1904/06/23:1b
ADLER, Adolph, 44, NYC-B – 1890/10/21:4a
ADLER, Albert, NYC-M – 1892/11/22:4a
ADLER, Bernhard, tailor, 24, NYC-M – 1893/11/30:1h
ADLER, Caroline, b. Guenther, 48, NYC-M – 1890/04/08:4a
ADLER, Constantin, un. printer, NYC, + Denver, CO - 1894/11/21:4a
ADLER, E., 60, NYC-M – 1893/10/25:4a
ADLER, Fanny, 22, NYC-M – 1880/04/13:4b-c
ADLER, Felix, Prof., 29, Ethical Culture, married Nellie Goldmark, 21, NYC-M – 1880/05/24:2a
ADLER, Fred, locksmith, NYC-M – 1892/07/12:2d
ADLER, Henry, 65, brewer, War 2, NYC-M? - 1915/07/24:2e
ADLER, Hermann, 50, NYC-B – 1905/05/02:3d
ADLER, Hugo & Isaac, toddlers, NYC-M – 1882/05/14:5e
ADLER, Ignatz, NYC-Bx – 1919/11/18:6a
ADLER, Johanna, 83, mother of SP leader Viktor, + Vienna – 1910/03/13:3c
ADLER, Joseph, un. bricklayer, NYC-Bx – 1911/01/07:6a
ADLER, Josephine, NYC-M – 1913/10/30:6a
ADLER, Lizzie, 24, @Triangle Shirtwaist fire, NYC-M – 1911/03/27:1d
ADLER, Pauline, b. Hirschkind, NYC-M – 1892/09/05:4a
ADLER, Reinhold, Union Hill, NJ - 1918/03/13:6a, 14:6a
ADLER, Samuel, businessman, NYC-M – 1893/06/19:2d, 3 Oct:1g

ADLER, Tilly, servant, NYC-B - 1918/11/15:2g
ADLER, Viktor, SP leader Vienna,#, 50th birthday – 1902/07/13:4d-e;
 + 1918/11/13:4c, 14:1b, obit. by Josef Jodlbauer 24:6c-e, 1 Dec., 6c-e,
 more 29 Dec.:4c, mem. 1919/02/21:4e
ADLER, Viktor, Dr., SP Vienna – 1910/03/13:3c
ADLER, William, 32, haberdasher, NYC-B – 1911/06/01:2e
ADOLF, Hans, un. butcher, NYC-M - 1916/08/27:7a
ADOLFF, Margarethe, 3, NYC-M – 1899/01/30:4a
ADOLPH, Elizabeth, NYC-B - 1916/03/15:6a
ADRIAN, Phil., NYC-M – 1904/04/25:4a
AEGERTER, Julia, b. Hollenbach, 57, NYC-Q – 1920/03/25:6a, fam. 30:6a
AERENTHAL, L. von, ex-foreign min. of Austria, crit. obit – 1912/02/18:1b, 6 Mr:4e
AERNOULT, drafted French un. worker, + 1900 military jail, reburial in Paris 11 Fb. powerful demonstr. vs French militarism – 1912/02/24:4e-f
AEROBOE, Ernst, 61, SP, un. cigarmaker, fr Hamburg/Gy, USA 1879, NYC-M – 1916/09/15:2b,6a, =19:2f
AEROBOE, Georg, NYC-Q – 1901/07/21:5a, 22:4a, fam. 28:5a
AEROBOE, Wilhelmine, NYC-Q - 1914/05/26:6a
AESCH, Ernst von, West New York, NJ – 1911/10/10:6a
AESCH, L. J. von, Swiss?, NYC-M – 1881/07/13:3c
AEX, VON % Lau
AGESEN, Charles' wife, Jersey City Heights, NJ – 1883/03/14:3c
AGSTER, Alfred Emil, MdR for SPD, + Stuttgart/Gy – 1904/01/12:1b
AHEARN, Maurice, New Rochelle, NY police – 1903/06/21:1g, 28:1c
AHL, Friedericke, Hoboken, NJ – 1906/06/21:2c
AHLERS, Herman, un. carpenter, NYC-B - 1896/04/01:4a
AHLMANN, Otto, 55, banker, * Kiel/Gy, NYC-M – 1904/01/01:1d
AHLSTROM, Christopher, Dr. med, NYC-M – 1900/11/16:1f-g
AHLWARDT, Hermann, MdR, crit obit - 1914/04/18:3d, 20:4c
AHNE, Henry, soda water store, NYC-M – 1898/09/28:1f
AHO, Auro, 30, NYC-M - 1919/01/03:6a
AHREND % See
AHREND, Siegmund, 47, dry goods clerk, NYC-M - 1895/01/16:1b
AHRENS, Anna, 72, NYC-M – 1893/12/27:4a
AHRENS, Annette, 77, NYC-M – 1892/12/31:1d
AHRENS, August, un. carp., NYC-M – 1889/09/19:4a
AHRENS, Babette, b. Kaufmann, NYC-M – 1892/06/19:5c
AHRENS, Caroline, NYC-M – 1900/05/06:1e
AHRENS, Chr., 30, NYC-B – 1893/01/10:4a
AHRENS, Dora, 22, NYC-M – 1892/08/20:4a

AHRENS, Elise D., b. Ma....(unreadable), 64, NYC-M – 1890/04/08:4a
AHRENS, Emma Rosa, b.Engelbach, 33, NYC-M – 1892/07/06:4a
AHRENS, Henry, salesclerk, +during Brooklyn Trolley Car strike – 1895/01/24:1a, 25:1c
AHRENS, Hermann, NYC-Bx – 1910/11/08:6a
AHRENS, William, NYPD, a hero (dying) – 1900/08/28:2h
AHRENS, William, 79, NYC-Bx – 1908/02/24:6a
AHRENSDORF, (or –berg), Alex, 16, NYC-M – 1891/06/07:1g 13:2g
AHRINGER, Andrew, 54, innkeep, NYC-B – 1887/09/23:2d
AHRMANN, Max, 70, un. waiter, NYC-M – 1894/05/07:4a
AHRWEILER, Rudolf, 29, NYC-M – 1892/09/23:4a
AHSKAR, Christian J., 59, NYC-B – 1891/04/05:5a
AICHBICKLER, Josef, MdR 1884-1906 for Catholic Center Party in Gy – 1912/04/28:3a
AICHELE, Charles, 8, NYC-M – 1891/04/21:4a
AICHELE, P., Newark, NJ – 1903/07/02:4a
AICHMANN, Louis, 57, NYC-M – 1900/06/20:4a
AIDAG, H., NYC-M – 1914/01/06:6a
AKONLIUS, L., un. baker, NYC-M – 1911/07/02:7b
AKUNIAN, Ilse, b. Frapan, German poet married to Armenian poet Akunian, – 1908/12/23:4e-f
ALAFBERG, Lydia, child, NYC-B – 1891/02/19:4a
ALBANO, Angelo, lynched Tampa, FL – 1912/09/22:1b
ALBEKE, Ferdinand, 37, music director of Brooklyn Saengerbund,
 * Lippe-Detmold/Gy, USA 1899, NYC-Bx – 1917/12/06:1e
ALBER, Gustav, 44, fr Esslingen/Wuertt., NYC-M – 1889/07/17:4a
ALBERS, William, 37, baker, NYC-Bx – 1910/06/13:6a, 14:6a
ALBERT, A., NYC-B – 1893/03/31:4a
ALBERT, Bertha, 2, Jersey City Heights, NJ – 1882/06/12:3b
ALBERT, Christiane, 64, NYC-Q – 1882/07/02:8a
ALBERT, Clara, 17, NYC-M – 1901/12/10:4a
ALBERT, Florian, un. carp., fam. – 1888/02/15:3a
ALBERT, George, brewer or cooper, NYC-M – 1902/01/28:4a
ALBERT, George, NYC-Bx - 1914/01/29:6a
ALBERT, Harris, peddler, 30, NYC-M – 1897/08/11:1e
ALBERT, Jennie, fr Kiew/Ukr., War 2, Philadelphia, PA – 1915/10/25:2d
ALBERT, Joseph, So. Newark, NJ - 1918/11/26:6a
ALBERT, Karl, 1, NYC-B – 1890/08/15:4a
ALBERT, Leonhard, 36, NYC-M – 1892/06/20:4a
ALBERT, Rudolf, NYC-B – 1911/10/20:6a
ALBERT, Sylvester, 55, Newark, NJ – 1906/08/02:3c
ALBINGER, August, NYC-M – 1903/03/06:4a

ALBINGER, Augusta, b. Jorns, 68, fr Braunschweig?, NYC-Bx – 1914/11/12:6a, 13:6a
ALBINGER, Peter, SPD Bremen/Gy -1915/11/14:3a
ALBINUS, John, NYC-M – 1903/09/30:4a, 1 Oct:4a, fam. 26:4a
ALBRECHT, A., NYC-B - 1918/05/14:6a
ALBRECHT, Alma, NYC-B – 1890/08/10:4a
ALBRECHT, Bernhard, 41, NYC-M – 1906/08/07:1e
ALBRECHT, Carl, 59, NYC-B – 1900/04/14:4a
ALBRECHT, Charles, 69, NYC-B – 1891/07/07:4a
ALBRECHT, G., NYC-M – 1893/01/20:4a
ALBRECHT, Heinrich's wife, NYC-M – 1880/09/10:3d
ALBRECHT, Hermann, un. painter, NYC-M - 1916/09/15:6a
ALBRECHT, Horst, 42, NYC-M – 1891/07/18:4a
ALBRECHT, Ida, b. Schumann, NYC-B – 1881/03/02:3b
ALBRECHT, Ida, NYC-M - 1917/08/07:6a
ALBRECHT, Jacob, 50, un. bricklayer, NYC-B – 1892/07/15:4a
ALBRECHT, Johann, 30, NYC-M, fr Eisenach/Thueringia – 1878/07/20:3a
ALBRECHT, Lorenz, NYC-M - 1915/05/28:6a
ALBRECHT, Magdalena, 48, NYC-B - 1919/02/15:6a
ALBRECHT, Margarethe, ~20, Newark, NJ – 1887/01/20:2f, 22:2g, 21:3d, inquest 27:2e, 29:2d, 14 Fb:1f, murderer found 28 Fb:1g
ALBRECHT, Margherita, b. Pult, 48, NYC-M – 1890/03/30:5b
ALBRECHT, Mary, NYC-B – 1901/07/01:4a
ALBRECHT, Peter, 69, NYC-M – 1890/03/19:4a
ALBRECHT, Robert, 72, engraver, NYC-M – 1888/11/29:1h
ALBRECHT, Selma, NYC-M, + @ SS Genl Slocum – 1904/06/16:1c, 17:3b
ALBRECHT, William Jacob, un. carp., NYC-M – 1905/03/08:4a, 9:4a
ALDAG, Herman, un. cigar maker, NYC-M – 1897/03/30:4a
ALDEN, Charles, 76, US condensed milk inventor – 1887/06/29:6b
ALDHAUS, Julie, NYC-M – 1882/08/20:5e, 21:1g
ALDRICH, Nelson, US Senator - 1915/04/17:1e
ALEICHEM, Sholem, (Sol Rabinowitz), Jewish writer, NYC – 1916/05/14:11a, =15:1f, 16:2d
ALEKSIEJEW, Peter, Russian labor leader, + Sibiria – 1892/03/04:2b
ALEX, Julius, 69, SPD Neuendorf/East Prussia/Gy – 1904/12/05:2c
ALEXANDER, Aaron, 27, NYC-M - 1894/07/07:4d
ALEXANDER, Frederick, 32, silk weaver, Paterson, NJ – 1912/04/23:2e
ALEXANDER, Frederick, Negro, lynched Leawenport, KS – 1901/01/16:1h
ALEXANDER, George, 40, iron-worker, NYC-B – 1901/04/13:3b

ALEXANDER, Henry, 19, NYC-B – 1890/07/03:2f
ALEXANDER, Joseph, 46, NYC-M – 1890/03/22:4a
ALEXANDER, Olga, 18 months, NYC-M – 1907/05/10:6a
ALEXANDROWITZ, Rose, 22, Newark, NJ – 1910/03/22:3b
ALEXANDROWSKI, S.A.,governor of Pensa/Russia, killed by revol. – 1907/02/09:1d
ALEXIS, Nord, Haiti president, 1910/05/02:1c
ALEXIS, Gustav, Rev., missionary to local Czechs, NYC-M – 1880/01/4c
ALFARTH, Gottwald, SP, un. carp., * Reichenbach/Saxony, USA 1884, Lawrence, MA - 1918/08/16:2f
ALFELD, Anna, 45, & Tillie, 16, NYC-M, + @ Genl Slocum – 1904/06/17:3b, 22:1d
ALIKHANOW, Gov. of Kutais/Russia, + by revol. – 1907/07/17:1c
ALIS, Karl, NYC-M - 1917/02/04:7a
ALLEMAN, Bernhardt, NYC-M - 1915/09/12:7a
ALLEMANN, A. Katherina, NYC-M - 1914/02/16:6a
ALLEMANN, Hermann, NYC-M – 1893/10/17:4f
ALLEN % Grunzig
ALLEN, Claude & Floyd, exec. Richmond, VA – 1913/03/29:3d-e, 1 Apr:2d
ALLEN, Irish patriot, exec. with O'Brien & Larkin, Brooklyn Irish had memorial meet. – 1883/11/24:2g
ALLEN, Richard, Negro, lynched Watkinsville, GA – 1905/06/30:1h
ALLESANDRO, Desiderio, striking worker at Armour & Co, Roosevelt, NJ - 1915/01/20:1a, =24:1g
ALLGAEUER, Urban Ferd., 74, SP,un. metal worker, *Feldkirch/Tirol, US 1877 NYC-M – 1919/08/6:2f,6a,7:6a,b-c,=9:2e, n. 19 Nov:2f
ALLGEIER % Velten
ALLGEIER, A., tailor, Carmel, NJ – 1899/01/11:4a
ALLGEIER, Anton, NYC-B - 1918/03/12:6a, 13:6a
ALLGEIER, Frank J., 44, innkeep, NYC-B – 1910/08/27:2b, 28:7f, 30:6a
ALLGEIER, John, 48, NYC-M – 1892/08/21:5b
ALLGEIER, John, 50, NYC-Q – 1900/08/20:1e
ALLGEIER, Joseph, watchman, Perth Amboy, NJ – 1912/06/15:1g
ALLJES, Andrew, 62, un. carp., NYC-M – 1906/12/18:6a
ALLMANN, Jacob, 65, NYC-B – 1904/04/25:3b
ALLMENDINGER, Friedrich Wilhelm, un. printer, NYC-B – 1917/05/28:6a
ALLMENDINGER, G..A., NYC-Bx – 1907/01/13:7b
ALLMENDINGER, Louise, b. Oesterreicher, NYC-B – 1892/03/21:4a
ALLMENDINGER, Mrs, NYC-M – 1905/10/05:4a
ALLMENDINGER, William, un. typesetter, NYC-B – 1905/07/21:4a

ALLMERS, Hermann, German poet, + 10 Mr – 1902/03/30:7a-c
ALLMEYER % Bohl
ALLRICH, Anna, NYC-M - 1894/01/21:5d
ALMEREYDA, Miguel, ed. pacifist Bonnet Rouge, + in jail, Paris – 1917/08/19:11b, 2 Sept:11e
ALMY, Frank L., (Geo. H. Abbott), exec. Concord, NH – 1893/05/17:1b
ALPER, Isidor, 8, NYC-Q - 1916/01/06:6b
ALRATH, William, 45, silk weaver, Newark, NJ - 1894/10/23:4a
ALS, Jacob, 52, butcher, NYC-B – 1899/05/06:1e
ALSCHER, Karl, 40, SP Vienna/Austria, * Badewitz/Silesia, leader barber union – 1908/07/26:3d
ALSDORFER, George, NYC-M – 1892/06/22:2e
ALSINA, Spanish anarchist, exec. Barcelona – 1897/05/22:2d
ALSLEBEN, Friederike, b. Wageler, 75, Kingsland, NJ – 1911/11/01:6a
ALT, Charles, Newark, NJ – 1897/03/27:3c
ALT, Henry Christian, 27, US Navy, NYC-B - 1919/01/04:6a
ALT, John, un. carp., NYC-M – 1892/09/18:5e, fam. 26:4a
ALT, Martin, un. carp., NYC-M – 1908/12/06:7c
ALT, Samuel, 62, butcher, NYC-M – 1881/08/04:1f
ALTEMEYER, Louise, cigar maker, NYC-M – 1896/09/20:1d
ALTENBERG, William, 66, tailor, fr Gy, NYC-B - 1895/07/09:4a
ALTENBERGER, Bernhard, tailor,* 11 Aug. 1873 Hagenheim/Baden, exec. Jersey City for killing Kaethe Rupp - 1894/09/07:3d
ALTENDORF, Paul, Dr., * Posen, alleged triple agent, perhaps + Mexico - 1920/08/15:1e
ALTENKIRCH, Max, hotelier, NYC-B - 1916/05/12:6b
ALTER, Sofia, 16, NYC-M, + @ SS Genl Slocum – 1904/06/18:3c
ALTERMANN, Peter, brewer, NYC-B – 1906/06/22:6a
ALTGELD, John Peter, Illinois Gov., note 1897/01/08:2b, 13:1b
ALTGELD, John Peter, ex-gov. of Illinois, * 30 Dec 1847 Niederselters/ Prussia, + Joliet, IL – 1902/03/13:1a-b, 2a-b, NYC grieves 20:2h, obit by Julius Vahlteich 23:9a-c, NYC mem. 30:1e, 3 Apr:1f, rev. 4:1a, 6:4b-c, rev. New Haven, CT mem. 14 Apr 1902:1c; Memory honored #, a.e. with speeches by John Geo. Frederick. Williams of MA – 1910/09/05:1c-d
ALTHER, John, un. carp., NYC-Q – 1903/09/12:4a
ALTHMEYER, Lena, 39, NYC-B – 1913/01/22:2a
ALTHOF, Hermann, 20, clerk, NYC-M – 1885/04/10:3c
ALTHOFF, Alphons, musician, NYC-B - 1916/08/25:2b
ALTMAN, striking coalminer, killed by militia in Oakley, W.Va – 1912/09/09:2b
ALTMAN, Anne, 16, @Triangle Shirtwaist Co. fire,NYC – 1911/03/27:1d

ALTMAN, Benjamin, NYC Dept Store owner, crit. edit on his will - 1913/10/16:4b-c
ALTMANN, A.D., 45, engineer, NYC-B – 1904/06/10:4b
ALTMANN, Annie, 30, servant, (dying), NYC-M – 1890/07/01:4c
ALTMANN, Ernst, un. carp., NYC-M – 1888/06/02:3b
ALTMANN, Heinrich, SPD, Frankfurt-Sachsenhausen, War 1 - 1914/11/01:3b
ALTMANN, Helena, b. Weilenbroenner, 60, NYC-B - 1914/07/06:6a
ALTMANN, W., un. painter, NYC-M – 1891/10/07:4a
ALTMAYER, Heinrich, NYC-M – 1893/03/27:4a
ALTMEYER, Aaron, 73, NYC-M - 1895/06/27:1h
ALTREIN, Claus, West New York, NY - 1915/01/02:6a
ALVANUS, Carl L., 36, NYC-M – 1912/03/27:6a
ALVARY, Max, (born Max Aschenbach), 41, German opera singer – 1898/11/09:3f
ALVENSLEBEN, Freiherr (Baron) von, ex-ofc Prussian guard regiment, here bartender under alias Reinhold Bergholz, NYC-M – 1887/07/15:4c
ALZMONEIT % Closa
AM ENDE, Karl, 43, waiter & alderman, SPD Goerlitz/Gy – 1911/12/10:3b
AMANN, Frank, 53, tailor, NYC-M – 1897/02/28:1c
AMANN, George, 48, un. machinist, NYC-M - 1918/08/13:6a
AMBACH, William, 48, NYC-M – 1890/01/22:4a
AMBACHER, Christian, NYC-B – 1910/02/01:6a, 2:6a, fam. 5:6a
AMBERG, Johann, 64, NYC-M – 1890/07/10:4a
AMBERG, Maurice, SP, NYC-Bx - 1920/12/20:1d
AMBOS, Max, 54, merchant, NYC-M – 1905/08/17:1b
AMBROSIUS, Johanna, 50, German poet fr Lengwethen/East Prussia, her birthday – 1907/02/10:20b-d
AMELUNG, Henry, 25, NYC-B – 1898/10/19:4b
AMEND, Barbara, 84, NYC-M – 1892/10/31:4a
AMEND, Josephine, b. Benser, Jersey City or NYC - 1914/01/27:2f
AMICIS, Edmondo, 62, Italian writer – 1908/03/26:4f, 5 Apr:5f-g
AMMAN % Steenbock
AMMAN, Julius A., 55, NYC-M - 1915/01/24:7b
AMMANN, Johann, un. baker, NYC-M – 1908/06/24:6a
AMMER, Mariana, 38, NYC-M - 1919/01/03:6a
AMMERMANN, Erastus P., clerk, NYC-B – 1904/09/12:3c
AMMERMANN, Maria, 78, NYC-Q - 1914/10/04:7d
AMMON, Anna S., 50, NYC-B – 1891/09/06:5a
AMON, Barbara, b Henneberger, 23, NYC-M – 1892/03/11:4a
AMON, Barbara, NYC-B – 1891/04/11:4a

AMON, Sophie, 44, cook, NYC-B - 1895/11/11:3g
AMOS, Jacob, treas. Cigarmakers' Union, + St Paul, MN - 1897/11/01:1g
AMOUROUX, Charles, French hat maker & communist, + Paris
 - 1885/05/26:1d
AMREIN, John, NYC-M - 1915/06/27:7a
AMTMANN, G., NYC-B - 1909/08/18:6a
ANDARRESE, John T., heroic fireman, NYC-M - 1903/02/27:1e
ANDEL, Michael, NYC-M - 1897/06/25:4a
ANDERES, Philipp, 50, un. stone cutter, NYC-M - 1904/06/21:4a
ANDERS, Bertha, active in Free German School, NYC-B - 1885/02/07:4e
ANDERS, Marie, 59, NYC-M - 1896/08/21:4a
ANDERS, William, un. carp., NYC-M - 1901/05/04:4a
ANDERSEN, Hans, shoemaker, Swede, on SS Britannic - 1881/02/01:1f
ANDERSEN, Igwer, NYC-M - 1903/09/02:4a
ANDERSEN, Jacob, 60, NYC-M - 1896/09/11:4a
ANDERSON, Adolph, 43, tailor, NYC-M - 1903/11/17:2h
ANDERSON, Adolph, construction worker, Elizabeth, NJ - 1915/01/22:2e
ANDERSON, Andrew, 45, sculptor, NYC-B - 1911/03/09:3b
ANDERSON, Anna, b. Cobden, English soc., #, (not +), her life
 - 1909/02/28:20:d-e
ANDERSON, Annie, servant, Trenton, NJ - 1896/05/10:1d
ANDERSON, Carrie, 3, NYC-B - 1899/04/19:1d
ANDERSON, Charles, NYC-Q - 1914/06/22:6a
ANDERSON, Christian, 15, NYC-B - 1899/10/26:3b
ANDERSON, Conrad, candy store, NYC-B - 1901/03/27:2h
ANDERSON, Elsie, 28, cook, NYC-M - 1907/02/15:5f
ANDERSON, Gustav, 26, NYC-Q - 1901/05/22:3d
ANDERSON, Gustave, carp., NYC-B - 1908/11/21:1a
ANDERSON, Harry, 38, striking leather worker, NYC-B - 1916/12/08:6b
ANDERSON, John, exec. Norfolk, VA - 1898/12/10:1d
ANDERSON, John, NYC-M - 1898/02/18:1b
ANDERSON, John, tailor, NYC-B - 1904/08/01:3d
ANDERSON, Louise, b. Guendthardt, 52, NYC-M - 1892/07/25:4a
ANDERSON, Maria, b. Bading, NYC-M - 1906/09/04:6a
ANDERSON, Mary, 23, NYC-M - 1880/05/07:1g
ANDERSON, Michael, 54, printer, NYC-M - 1917/05/25:2f
ANDERSON, Richard, 40, Jersey City, NJ - 1904/06/19:1e
ANDERSON, Sam, Negro, lynched Atlanta, GA - 1909/08/02:1e
ANDERSON, Stephen P., 42, architect, NYC-M - 1899/12/13:1e
ANDKIER, Gustav E.,salesman, *Denmark, NYC-M - 1895/09/17:1d
ANDORF, Jakob, German labor poet & SPD member, #, * 1 Aug. 1835
 Hamburg, + Hamburg - 1898/06/23:1d, 2c, = 11 Jy:3c-d

ANDRASSY, Anna, b. Bozogany, NYC-B – 1891/02/27:4a
ANDRASSY, Julius, Hungarian statesman – 1890/02/19:1a
ANDREAS, John, un. carp., NYC-M – 1906/12/05:6a
ANDREE, Franz, 48, NYC-B – 1917/06/05:6a, mem. 4 June 1918:6a
ANDREE, Max, Dumont, NJ – 1916/11/08:6a, 10:6a
ANDREES, Henry, NYC-Bx – 1908/02/23:10b
ANDREJANOW, Michael, 28, Russian poet, + Davos/Switz., 1908/02/24:4f, 7 Mr:2c
ANDRES, comrade, Swiss soc. & artist, + Luzern, - 1920/04/08:4g-h
ANDRES, Emil, 61, SP, NYC-Bx - 1918/08/27:6a
ANDRES, Heinrich Theodor, NYC-M – 1890/01/30:4a
ANDRES, Ludwig, 53, NYC-M – 1907/04/13:6a
ANDRES, M., b. Nicolai, 38, NYC-M – 1892/08/03:4a
ANDRESJOHN % Haarbauer
ANDRESSEN, John, brewer or cooper, NYC-M – 1898/12/02:4a
ANDREWS, George, exec. Belvedere, NJ - 1895/06/14:4a
ANDREWS, Judd W., Negro, lynched Princess Ann, MD – 1897/06/10:1f
ANDRIESSE, Gretchen, NYC-M – 1891/01/04:5a
ANDROSKOVY, Gisela, 17, NYC-M – 1882/09/15:1g
ANDRUJUSCHENKO, Russia rev., exec. with Lenin's brother for March 13 attentate on Czar– 1887/05/26:5b, 30:2f, + 10 June:5b, note 17:5e
ANDRUS, Hamlin, manuf. of explosives, Yonkers, NY – 1896/10/22:1c, 23:1e, 24:1c, 25:1h, 14 Nov:1c
ANDRUSS, Helen, 20, Vassar College, Poughkeepsie, NY – 1916/04/25:2f
ANETTE, Willy, Negro, lynched Newton, GA – 1903/06/27:1a
ANGEMEIER, Andrew, un. carp., NYC-M – 1891/07/14:4a
ANGEMEIER, George, mgr Alcohol Chem Co, Jersey City, NJ – 1902/06/22:5d
ANGER, Karl, NYC-M, + @ SS Genl Slocum – 1904/06/17:3b
ANGER, Rosalia, b. Merz, NYC-M – 1891/05/31:5d
ANGERBAUER, Johanna, 65, West Norwood, NJ – 1906/11/11:7b 12:6a
ANGERER, Johann, miner, SLP, Latrobe, PA – 1898/07/17:12a
ANGERHOFER, 61, SPD alderman Kaufbeuren/Bav. - 1913/06/22:3b
ANHALT, Georg, NYC-M – 1893/09/02:4a
ANISHAEUSLI, Emil, weaver?, NYC-Bx – 1909/12/16;6a, 17.6a
ANKOWITZ, Michael, NYC-B - 1915/04/10:6a
ANLAUF, comrade, SPD Leipzig, + Halle/Gy – 1881/08/08:2c
ANNEMANN, Adam, un. typesetter, NYC-B – 1898/01/30:5d
ANNIS, William E., 33, publ., NYC-M – 1908/08/16:1c, 18:2d-e, 19:1g
ANSBACHER, Simon, 78, NYC-M – 1890/08/11:4a

ANSCHUETZ, Ottomar, 62, manuf. Of photographic machines, Berlin/Gy – 1907/06/16:8c
ANSEL, Louise, 28, NYC-M, + on SS Genl Slocum – 1904/06/17:3b
ANSINGER, Ignaz, Newark, NJ – 1901/07/04:3b
ANSION, Erasmus,Rev., Polish Natl Church, Newark, NJ – 1909/03/11:1e, 13:1c,= 14:1d, 17:3c, note 11 Apr:7d
ANSPACH, Jacob W., 37, optician, NYC-M – 1905/09/12:1a
ANSPACH, Rudolph, 30, NYC-M – 1906/09/09:7a, fam. 12:6a
ANSTEDT, Karl, un. brewery worker, NYC-M - 1895/04/12:4a
ANTEM, Elizabeth, NYC-M – 1900/12/09:5b
ANTES, Martin, un. carp., NYC-Bx – 1912/07/31:6a
ANTES, Simon, un. carp., NYC-M – 1901/02/28:4a
ANTHES, Friedrich, NYC-M – 1890/08/30:4a
ANTHONY, Julia, NYC-M – 1907/12/24:6a
ANTHONY, Susan B., 86, US Feminist – 1906/03/18:4b-c; mem. By Eugene Debs, #, 28 Fb 1909:19e-g
ANTIGNA, Alexandre, French genre painter - 1878/03/28:2f
ANTON, E., NYC-B – 1904/07/29:4a
ANTONI, Mathias, un. carp., NYC-M – 1904/06/19:5a
ANTONI, Michael, SLP, NYC-M – 1891/09/13:5b
ANTZER, Ludwig, janitor, NYC-M – 1897/04/29:1h
ANUSEWITZ, Ida, 18,stenographer,NYC-M - 1913/12/13:1e, 14:1f
ANVERMANN, John, Elizabeth, NJ - 1913/11/16:7a
ANZENGRUBER, Ludwig, Viennese poet – 1890/01/12:7f, note 11 May:1e
APEL, Joseph, un. carp., NYC-M - 1913/12/19:6a, 20:6a,21:7c
APEL, Julius, innkeep, Paterson, NJ – 1910/07/19:3c
APFEL, Else, b. Hauch, 54, NYC-M – 1890/03/09:5c
APFEL, Henry, boxer, NYC-B – 1899/11/17:3a
APITZSCH, Carl Theodor, 39, NYC-B – 1899/09/01:4a
APITZSCH, Karl Julius, engineer, NYC-B – 1887/05/10:2-d, fam. 10:3c
APPEL % Ross
APPEL, Barbara, NYC-M – 1889/01/16:1f, 17:4a, inquest 23:1h
APPEL, Bertha, 46, NYC-M - 1920/11/26:6a
APPEL, Frederick, driver, NYC-B – 1890/09/14:5b
APPEL, John, NYC-M – 1905/01/04:4a
APPEL, Mary, 59, NYC-M – 1902/10/07:4a
APPEL, Morris, fr Russia, USA 1904, NYC-M – 1905/02/14:1g
APPEL, Philip, 53, NYC-M – 1893/10/30:4a
APPEL, William Albert, innkeep, NYC-M – 1887/07/28:3c
APPELBAUM, Anna, NYC-B – 1889/10/17:4a

APPELSLEBEN, Max, 26, poet & writer, USA 1911, Newark, NJ
 – 1912/02/19:2f
APPUHN, Ernst, 18, Newport, NJ – 1912/03/05:6a
APRATH, Clara, West Newark, NJ – 1907/03/15:6a
APREMONT, Marguerite d', French Countess, NYC? – 1881/01/12:4b
ARATA, Don, Italian, lynched Denver, CO – 1893/07/28:1b
ARBOR, Gustav, un. printer, NYC-B - 1916/05/01:2e
ARCHIBALD, James P., un. paper hanger & local AFL leader, *Ireland, NYC-M - 1913/09/09:2a
ARCHNER, Kath., 22, NYC-M – 1891/08/15:4a
ARCULARIUS, Benjamin F., 54, NYC-B – 1905/06/08:3d
ARENDT, Julius, carp., SLP, NYC-M – 1891/04/19:1h
ARGYRIADES, Panagiutis, 49, Macedonian-born French soc., + Paris
 – 1901/12/11:2d
ARLINGTON, Georgie, 18, fr New Orleans, NYC-M – 1891/05/04:1g
ARM, Gottlieb, 52, West Hoboken, NJ - 1917/10/20:6a, fam. 25:6a
ARMAC, Edward, 7, see Madeline Hanger
ARMANN, Felix, ?37, SLP, ex-activist in Carlstadt, NJ, NYC-B –
 1900/03/21:3b
ARMAUER, Phillipine, 11, NYC-M – 1896/04/27:1h
ARMBRUST, Barbara, 46, NYC-M, + @ SS Genl Slocum –
 1904/06/17:3b
ARMBRUSTER, Anton, 68, un. wheelwright, SLP, NYC-M –
 1889/03/01:4a, 2:4a, 3:5b, =4:4c, fam. 5:4a
ARMBRUSTER, Frederick C., 48, suitcase maker, NYC-B –
 1887/01/22:2f, 21:3c
ARMBRUSTER, John, 60, NYC-Bx - 1913/10/01:2c
ARMBRUSTER, Karl, 69, Jersey City, NJ – 1892/12/02:4a
ARMBRUSTER, Katherine, b. Nies, NYC-B – 1890/11/13:4a
ARMBRUSTER, Otto, married Anna Kratschlik, NYC-M –
 1881/08/04:1c
ARMBRUSTER, Theo., 50, machinist, NYC-Bx – 1910/10/11:6a
ARMBRUSTER, Wilhelm, 76, NYC-B - 1894/01/19:4a
ARMGART, August, 32, un. cigar maker, SLP, NYC-M – 1890/03/06:4a,
 =7:1g, fam. 8:4a
ARMOUR, Philip D., 68, US butcher king, + Chicago, crit. obit –
 1901/01/06:1g
ARNBERG, Jakob, 33, bricklayer, NYC – 1899/09/07:1d
ARNDT, Eva, NYC-M – 1902/08/29:1f
ARNDT, Johann Gottfried, 70, a 48'er, Newark, NJ – 1879/04/14:4e
ARNDT, Rosa, b. Mertens, NYC-M – 1887/11/22:1c
ARNDT, Vera, 16, NYC-M - 1917/12/22:6a

ARNEMANN, Gesine, NYC-M – 1892/09/28:1h
ARNEMANN, Martin, USA 1863 fr Gy, innkeep, NYC-M – 1889/08/29:4e
ARNETT, Elisabeth, 76, NYC-M – 1904/09/24:2h
ARNHARDT, Henry, 23, fr Hessen-Cassel, USA 1890?, NYC-M or Bx – 1890/09/11:1h
ARNHEIM, Lena, b. Bauder, 54, SP, active Bronx Free German School, husband Ludwig active in SPD in Posen/Gy 1870s – 1906/01/18:1h, body fd 25 Apr:1d,4a
ARNHEIM, Lena, b. Davis, NYC-M – 1903/04/26:1d
ARNHEIM, Salo, un. typesetter, NYC-M – 1888/05/01:3a
ARNHOLD, Georg, infant, NYC – 1882/07/11:3c
ARNHOLD, William F., NYC-M – 1915/06/14:6c
ARNIM, Clara, 28, Hoboken, NJ - 1894/08/30:4a
ARNOLD % Schleth
ARNOLD, Albert, 30, NYC-M – 1888/02/16:3a
ARNOLD, B., pol. detec. + strike, NYC-Q – 1892/03/28:1g, 29:1g, 30:1d
ARNOLD, Babette, NYC-M – 1903/12/28:4a
ARNOLD, Carl, 56, un. cigar maker, * 27 June 1848 Stoetteritz/ Saxony, USA 1882, SP, NYC-M – 1904/02/19:4a, 20:4a, =22:2h
ARNOLD, Carl, 23, & Florence, 20, NYC-M – 1901/02/08:1d
ARNOLD, Charles, 66, NYC-B - 1916/01/24:6a
ARNOLD, Charles, un. carp., NYC-B - 1915/01/17:7c
ARNOLD, Ernst, NYC-M – 1910/03/04:6a
ARNOLD, Friedrich, un. carpenter, NYC-M - 1895/12/07:4a
ARNOLD, Gustav, 4, NYC? – 1884/12/14:5f
ARNOLD, Harry, NYC-M - 1916/10/10:6a
ARNOLD, Henry, 47, innkeep, Newark, NJ - 1917/02/28:2f
ARNOLD, Joseph, NYC-M – 1907/06/21:6a
ARNOLD, Julius, NYC-B – 1902/06/21:4a
ARNOLD, Karl, NYC-B - 1918/11/26:6a
ARNOLD, Katherina, 17, raped & killed by French soldiers in Ludswigshafen/Gy – 1919/11/16:7g
ARNOLD, Louis, laborer, Portchester, NY - 1913/12/17:11d
ARNOLD, Ludwig W., *10 May 1852 Dresden/Gy, merchant, + visiting NYC-M – 1880/10/23:4d, 24:5c
ARNOLD, M., NYC-M – 1893/03/28:4a
ARNOLD, Maggie, 1, NYC-M – 1907/07/18:1f
ARNOLD, Martin, 66, & wife Sophie, 64, NYC-B – 1900/05/09:1g
ARNOLD, Mrs, 52, NYC – 1881/04/19:3c
ARNOLD, Philip, 52, chauffeur, Newark, NJ - 1917/12/01:2c
ARNOLD, Rudolf, 17, NYC-B – 1887/06/17:2d

ARNOLD, William A., 63, SP, un. printer, sheriff of Milwaukee County 1911-13, + Milwaukee - 1920/06/24:2f
ARNOLD, William, 27, NYC – 1912/06/17:6a, 18:6a
ARNOLD, William, 31, NYC-M - 1914/04/06:6a
ARNOLD, William, Elizabeth, NJ – 1908/08/09:7b
ARNOLD, William, Elizabeth, NJ – 1910/04/26:6a
ARNOLD, William, NYC-M – 1882/04/19:1e
ARNOLDI, Ella, 11, NYC-M, +@ SS Genl Slocum – 1904/06/26:1c
ARNOLDI, Karl, 64, un. cigar maker, NYC-M – 1905/09/05:4a
ARNOUX, Jacques, 32, fr Elsass, nurse, NYC-M – 1893/01/19:1h
ARNOUX, Joseph, NYC-M – 1893/11/01:1g
ARNREITER, Louis, 77, USA fr Gy 1863, restaurant owner & aviation pioneer, Jersey City, NJ - 1918/03/12:3e
ARNSON, Estelle, NYC-M - 1878/01/28:3d
ARNSPERBERG, John S., 75, ret. fr Brooklyn Navy Yard, & wife, 74, NYC-B - 1914/01/27:2c
ARNST, Mary, 48, NYC – 1912/07/12:1g
ARON, Martin, 72, SP,un. typesetter, *15.08.1842 Schwerin/ Mecklenburg,USA 1865, NYC-M - 1915/03/05:2f, 6a, 6:6a,=#8:2d
ARONOWITZ, Katie, 80, NYC-M – 1907/09/05:1f
ARONSON, Alexander, Dr., 37,NYC-M - 1895/06/25:1h
ARONSON, Max, grocer, NYC-M – 1886/10/04:1e
ARRACK, Rudolf, Wilkesbarre, PA, War 2, beaten to death by patriotic thugs for saying Germans human beings, too - 1919/07/11:1g
ARRAS, Emma C., 31, NYC-M – 1893/09/14:4c, 15:2d
ART, Emil, 55, Jersey City, NJ – 1912/08/16:2e
ARTEBISE, Yvonne, modiste, French, NYC-M – 1903/09/09:3d
ARTHUR, Chester A., US pres., 1886/11/19:1a-b, = 20:2e, 22:1c, rev. 23:2f
ARTHUR, Herman & Irving, Negroes, lynched Roxboro, NC – 1920/07/08:1b
ARTHUR, Peter M., * Scotland, lived Schenectady, NY, head of Brotherhood Locom. Eng., + Winnipeg, Manitoba – 1903/07/18:1f, 2c
ARTUS, Achatius, NYC-B – 1891/04/21:4a
ARTZ, Adolph, 72, ex-innkeep, Stryker's Farm, NYC – 1908/09/29:5e
ARVIDSEN, Gustav, un. engineer, SP?, NYC-M – 1908/01/25:6a, fam. 4 Fb:6a
ARZBERGER, Kaethe, 18, NYC-M – 1887/06/22:3a, 23:3c
ARZBERGER, Sebastian, 40, NYC-M – 1890/04/28:4a
ARZMONEIT % Closa, Hencke
ASAM, Anna, 29, NYC-M - 1918/12/28:6a
ASCHBACH, Herman D., 40, barber, Hoboken, NJ – 1907/12/09:3b

ASCHENBRAND, Louis, NYC, + St Joseph, MO - 1878/07/19:3c
ASCHENTRUP, Wilhelmina, NYC-B -- 1908/09/15:6a
ASCHER, Albert, musician & music teacher, studied in Munich, Hoboken, NJ - 1908/12/10:6d
ASCHER, Charles, 56,un. painter, NYC-M - 1917/01/15:6a, 16:6b
ASCHERI, Spanish anarchist, exec. Barcelona -- 1897/05/22:2d
ASENDORF, Hermann C., 45, wine dealer, NYC-Q - 1916/04/29:5c
ASH, Lewis, 58, NYC-M -- 1892/08/15:4a
ASHLEY, Alfred, labor journalist, NYC-M -- 1893/08/28:1f
ASHLEY, Jessie, SP, lawyer, NYC-M - 1919/01/21:1f, =27:2f
ASKEW, Negro, lynched near Mississipi City, LO -- 1900/06/11:1c
ASKEW, Robert, Negro, lynched Henderson,TX -- 1905/11/13:1d
ASMUS, August, un. typesetter & SPD Braunschweig/Gy -- 1899/04/23:13c
ASMUS, Chas A., un. painter, NYC-M - 1916/06/22:6a
ASMUS, Emma, 27, NYC-M -- 1889/05/12:5b
ASMUS, Otto, 21, butcher, NYC-M -- 1897/08/18:4a
ASPLUND, Gustav, clockmaker, Swede?, NYC-M -- 1892/08/02:2e
ASSEL, John, NYC-M -- 1892/07/14:4a
ASSING, Ludmilla, 59, niece of Varnhagen von Ense, + Florence/Italy -- 1880/04/25:4g
ASSMANN, Charles, 32, NYC-B - 1916/09/24:7a
ASSMANN, Louis, 38, brewery worker, NYC-M - 1917/12/22:1g, 23:7a
ASSMANN, Max, 35, musician, NYC-M -- 1882/04/02:5e
ASSMANN, Paul, 52, SP, NYC-B -- 1908/07/18:6a, 19:7e, fam. 21:6a
ASTER, Laura, NYC-M -- 1899/09/17:1c
ASTON, Louise, b. Hoche, German writer & feminist, * 26 Nov. 1815 Groeningen/Halberstadt, + Wanen/Bodensee -- 1903/09/13:16b-c
ASTOR, Charlotte, her will -- 1887/12/29:4d
ASTOR, Johann Jacob Sr., 60, grandson of fdr, NYC -- 1890/02/23:1h
ASTOR, John, + on Titanic, very crit. notes -- 1912/05/09:4c-d
ASZMONEIT, Elisabeth, NYC-Bx - 1918/12/20:6a
ATKINSON, Edward, US economist, + Boston -- 1905/12/13:2d
ATTE, Paul, NYC-M -- 1909/08/12:6a
ATTINGER, Adolph, 61, un. painter, NYC -- 1919/08/01:6a
ATTINGER, Adolph, un. painter, NYC-M - 1919/08/01:6a
ATZGERSTORFER, Johann, NYC-M -- 1901/09/04:4a
AUBERT, Henry, 58, & wife, NYC-M -- 1897/08/03:1e
AUBON, Marie, servant, fr Austria, War 2, Metuchen, NJ - 1915/06/17:6c
AUCHTER, George, 52, tailor, NYC-M -- 1879/09/01:1f
AUEN, John, 59, Yonkers, NY - 1913/05/21:6a
AUER, Bernhard, 49, NYC? - 1913/05/06:6a

AUER, Franz, 55, SP Vienna & AKK off., + near Vienna – 1911/08/13:3d
AUER, George, 49, Swiss?, SP, NYC-B – 1908/04/25:6a, 26:7b
AUER, Henry, un. carp., NYC-M – 1907/10/27:7b
AUER, Ignaz, 61, SPD polit., MdR for Glauchau-Meerane, * 19 Apr 1846 Dommelstadt/Passau, + Berlin/Gy, 1907/04/11:1a,2b,4a, 14:1b, 15:4b-c, =16:1b, 19:4b-c, more 27:4d-g, 29:4d, 2 May:4g, on feminism 12 May:20d, opposed Johann Most 2 June:15g; grave monument planned 1908/01/05:3b, unveiled 1908/05/15:4e-f
AUER, Julius, Dr., brother of German novelist Berthold Auerbach; USA 1850s, NYC-B - 1878/08/29:1e, 30:4d
AUER, Katherina, 54, NYC-B – 1892/06/28:4a
AUER, Peter, NYC-B – 1912/01/02:6a
AUERBACH, Berthold, German writer - 1882/02/05:5a-b, 12:4g-5d, 19:2a-d, 12 Mr:7b-c
AUERBACH, Emil, SLP, Adams, MA – 1898/09/13:1e
AUERBACH, Hermann, 49, ex-candymaker, realtor, wife Claire, b. Levy, 34, & 2 daughters, NYC-M - 1915/02/01:1d
AUERBACH, Jacob, merchant fr Pinto, Montana, + NYC – 1880/06/29:1e, 8 June:4e
AUERBACH, Max, 50, NYC-M - 1894/01/12:4a
AUERBACHER, Herbert, 31, millionaire, NYC-SI – 1907/07/27:2c
AUGENSTEIN, August, 55, SLP, Meriden, CT – 1897/03/30:1c, 2 Apr:2d
AUGER, Charles, 32, & Minnie, 28, & Rose, NYC-M, + @SS Genl Slocum – 1904/06/17:3b
AUGUSTIN, Lina, NYC-B – 1891/05/31:5d
AUGUSTIN, Richard, innkeep, SPD alderman in Berlin/Gy, 1909/07/04:3b, =11:3b
AUHL, Charles, 25, worker, NYC-B – 1899/10/20:1g
AUKAMP, Anton, 40, NYC-M, cigarmaker?,USA 1859, first Baltimore, then NYC - 1878/08/06:4d
AULT, Harold H., Newark, NJ - 1915/05/17:1f
AUMANN, Andreas, un. worker, NYC-M – 1895/01/21:4a
AUMUELLER % Hayn
AUMUELLER, Anna, servant, NYC-M, murdered by Rev. Hans Schmidt - 1913/09/15:1g, 16:1f,2a,4a-b,17:1f,2a,4a-b, 18:2a,4a-b, 19:1e,20:1d; Notes 1915/08/26:2a, 4 De:1d
AUMUELLER, Josef, 57, NYC-M – 1890/08/10:4a
AURBACH, Isabella, 19, fr South America, NYC-B – 1911/10/24:3a
AURINGER, Erhard, NYC-M – 1910/09/12:6a
AURIS, Anna, NYC-M – 1912/12/11:6a
AURIS, Richard, 60, un. cigarmaker, NYC-M - 1917/08/09:6a
AUSLANDER, Helen, 25, servant, NYC-B – 1913/09/06:3b

AUSSENEK, Frederick, 4, (+ 2 Jan. 1918), NYC-M, mem. –
 1919/01/02:6a, 1920/01/02:6a
AUST, Karl, 58, Ravenswood, L.I. - 1916/05/19:6a
AUSTIN, Alfred, British poet - 1913/06/03:1e
AUSTIN, Bob, Negro, lynched Marion, AK – 1910/03/19:1d
AUSTRIA-HUNGARY, Elisabeth, Empress-Queen of, killed by anarchist
 Luccheni – 1898/09/11:1a-b, 12:2a, 13:1a-b, 2a-b, 14:1h, 2a-b, 15:1h-2a,
 16:1a, 2a, 18:4a-b, Luccheni rec life 29 Nov:1f
AUSTRIA-HUNGARY, Franz Ferdinand, crown prince, + in Sarajevo –
 1914/06/29:1a, "Ein Schuss ins Schwarze":4a, 30:1a-b, 4d, 2 Jy:1a,3:4d,
 5:1c, 14:4f-g, 16:4e-f, war threatens 25:4a-b
AUSTRIA-HUNGARY, Franz-Josef, Emperor-King of, crit. Notes on 80th
 birthday 1910/08/18:4c, + 1916/11/22:1d, 23:1c,4a-b, 24:3c, 25:2a, 1
 Dec:4a, =2:2c
AUSTRIA-HUNGARY, Rudolf, Crown Prince, + anniv.– 1899/06/25:1d
AUTEM, John, NYC-M - 1919/01/22:6a
AUTENRIETH, Christoph, 43, SDP, NYC-B – 1904/10/12:4a, =14:2e
AUTENRIETH, J. F., 79, SPD Offenburg/Gy, 1908/06/07:3a
AUTENRIETH, Wilhelm, NYC-B – 1904/08/28:5a
AUTHENRIETH, Christine, NYC-B – 1920/05/27:6a
AVELING, Eduard, Dr., + London – 1898/08/24:2e
AVELING, Eleonor, b. Marx, + London – 1898/04/03:1e-f, note 16:2d,
 =24:4f-g, note by Eduard Bernstein 3 May:2d, by Robert Banner 14
 May:2d-e, 25 June:2e, 24 Jy:9c-h,
AVELING, Henry (Anderson), actor, NYC-M – 1891/03/20:1h
AVERY, John, Negro, lynched Cordova, AL – 1904/08/22:3c
AXE, Fritz, alias Frank Braun, burglar, Jersey City, NJ – 1883/07/14:3a-b,
 =16:4b
AXELRODE, Annie, 31, NYC-B - 1914/04/21:6c
AXELSON, Carl, foreman, NYC-M – 1892/08/23:4f
AXMACHER, Hugo, 63, * Koeln, NYC-Flushing - 1915/04/11:7c
AXTEROTH, Bernard, 28, painter, NYC-M - 1894/07/21:1h
AYEN, Adolf, butcher, NYC-B – 1880/07/29:1g, 30:4c
AZEW, Eugen's wife, Russian soc., chose death after learning husband
 works as police informer – 1910/01/05:2d, 19:4d-e
BAAB, Robert, secy AKK 27, Elizabeth, NJ - 1914/02/11:6a
BAADER, Carl, 63, typesetter, SP?, NYC –
 1913/01/ 31: 2c, 6a,1 F:6a, =3:1c, fam. 7:6a
BAADER, Rosine, b. Lipps, NYC-Bx - 1913/11/21:6a
BAAKE, Charles A., 50,lawyer,Atlantic City, NJ – 1914/01/30:2b
BAALMANN % Pfeil
BAARSCH, Rudolph, NYC-M – 1912/06/09:6a

BABENDREIER, Wilhelm, pianomaker?, Orange, NJ – 1888/06/16:3b
BABIAK, John, NYC-M - 1917/03/24:6a
BABICK, Josephine, 60, paper shop, fr Austria, NYC-M – 1909/05/31:2d
BACATE, Paul, 56, SP?, un. carp., NYC-M - 1920/06/22:6a
BACCHIOCHI, striking worker, killed in Hopesdale, PA – 1913/04/25:6c
BACH % Burghardt
BACH, Barbara, NYC-B – 1914/03/29:7c
BACH, Christian, 13, NYC-M – 1885/07/11:1d
BACH, Ernst, *Emmendingen/Baden, USA 1842, 99th birthday, Newark, NJ – 1912/12/30:2d
BACH, Frederick, NYC-M – 1919/11/16:12a
BACH, Henriette, NYC-M – 1890/07/02:4a
BACH, James Ernst, ret. clothing manuf., * Baden Prov., Newark, NJ – 1918/10/31:2f
BACH, John, NYC-B– 1915/01/03:7d
BACH, Louis G., 23, NYC-B – 1899/11/30:2g
BACH, Richard, 82, SLP, NYC-M – 1891/08/13:4a, =15:1g
BACH, Thomas, 50, NYC-B – 1896/04/22:4a
BACH, Wilhelm, 50, un. typesetter, NYC-B – 1903/05/03:5a, 4:4a
BACH, Wilhelm, NYC-M – 1912/02/27:6a
BACHEN, August, 68, accountant, War 2, NYC-B - 1917/10/19:3f
BACHENBERGER, John, 38, diamond worker, NYC-B – 1908/04/22:3b
BACHER, Ludwig, 70, NYC-M – 1890/05/16:4a
BACHERACH, Joseph, merchant, NYC-M – 1900/11/02:1e
BACHFELD, Diedrich, John & Henry, NYC – 1890/03/28:1h
BACHMAN, Margaret, NYC-M, + @ Genl Slocum – 1904/06/17:3b
BACHMANN % Graf
BACHMANN, Anna, b. Wossner, 75, NYC-M? – 1915/01/28:1f
BACHMANN, Bertha, fr Bielefeld?, NYC-M – 1883/03/28:3d
BACHMANN, Charles, 50, NYC-M – 1904/11/02:3d
BACHMANN, Emil, carp., NYC-B – 1908/11/21:1a
BACHMANN, J., 69, NYC-B – 1911/07/12:1f
BACHMANN, J.A., 52, NYC-B – 1892/08/08:4a
BACHMANN, Maria, NYC-M   1897/04/16·4a
BACHMANN, Max, 22, artist, fr Russia, NYC-M – 1905/02/07:3b
BACHMANN, Robert, 61, NYC-M– 1917/01/25:6a
BACHOFEN, Heinrich, machinist, NYC-M – 1903/03/01:5a
BACHTLER, Friedrich, NYC-B – 1908/01/28:6a
BACKERT, Dora, b. Gerner, NYC-M – 1893/10/31:4a
BACKES, Adam, 43, NYC-M – 1893/08/27:5a
BACKHAUS, comrade, un. painter, SPD Elberfeld/Gy – 1912/06/02:3c
BACKS, Franz, un. cigarmaker, NYC-M – 1885/03/08:8a

BACKSTEIN, Karl, 72, SPD Berlin, innkeep – 1913/07/06:3a
BACKSTETTER, Teresa, 26, & daughter Teresa, 8, & infant son, NYC-M – 1916/03/20:1e
BACMEISTER, Alfred, West New York, NJ – 1919/10/02:6a
BACON, Augustus O., US Senator, Georgia – 1914/02/15:1d
BACON, Francis, 79, English judge, laudat. note – 1911/06/29:4e-f
BADE, Henry, un. carp., NYC-M – 1910/03/08:6a
BADEN, Anna, 80, No. Bergen, NJ– 1914/02/04:3c
BADENHAUSEN, Rudolph, 51, cashier of G-A Amberg Theatre, NYC-M – 1892/04/22:1e
BADENHOP, Karl, 43, NYC-M - 1895/02/24:5b
BADER, Annie, 17, NYC-B – 1887/07/12:1c, 13:2g, 14:2d
BADER, Charles, NYC-Q – 1906/05/05:4a
BADER, Chr., un. carpenter, NYC-M – 1904/10/17:4a
BADER, George, 55, tailor, fr Wiltshire/GB, Philadelphia - 1920/02/14:2d
BADER, Henry, NYC-Bx – 1911/09/22:6a
BADER, John, 45, stoker at Havemeyer's, NYC-B – 1898/01/02:5e
BADER, John, un. cigar maker, NYC-M – 1889/09/03:4a
BADER, Lena, NYC-M – 1906/01/13:4a
BADER, Richard, weaver, Paterson, NJ – 1913/04/26:6a
BADERMANN, Nathan, 35, & wife, Philadelphia - 1920/05/11:2d
BADING % Anderson
BADING, Albertine, NYC-M – 1888/04/23:3a
BADING, Anna, b. Bosse, Jersey City, NJ – 1898/08/09:4a
BADING, Carl, NYC-M? – 1911/11/03:6a
BADING, Maria, b. Schlueter, NYC-M – 1900/06/18:4a
BADSTEIN, Dora, 22, NYC-M – 1889/02/18:4a
BAECKER, Henry, 30, USA 1890, NYC-M – 1893/06/04:1f
BAECKER, Henry, West New York, NJ - 1915/11/19:6a
BAEDEKER, Karl, travel publ., Esslingen/Wuertt., – 1911/05/13:2d
BAEDER, Jacob, un. carp., NYC-M – 1904/12/14:4a
BAEHR, Julius, 67, bakery items salesman, NYC-M – 1912/03/31:1f
BAEHR, K., 63, NYC-B – 1893/10/25:4a
BAENKE, Robert, NYC-B – 1898/06/30:4b
BAER, Amelia, 24, NYC-M – 1880/03/07:5d, 8:1f
BAER, Andreas, NYC-Q - 1917/12/22:6a
BAER, Bertha Alma, b. Ollmann, NYC-M – 1904/09/11:5a
BAER, Daniel, 44, shoemaker, NYC-B - 1894/05/02:4f
BAER, Frank, NYC-B - 1913/05/17:6a
BAER, Isidor, 38, un. cigarmkr, NYC-M – 1892/09/30:4a, fam. 4 Oct:4a
BAER, Louis D., upholsterer, 53, USA 1867, NYC-M – 1893/01/08:5e
BAER, Peter, carp., Newark, NJ – 1900/01/24:4a

BAER, Philipp, 28, salesman, NYC-M – 1888/11/10:2h, 9:1g
BAER, Samuel L., 62, insurance agent, NYC-M – 1907/06/11:2f
BAERE, Josef, NYC-M – 1893/02/24:1g
BAERMANN, Jacob B., NYC-M – 1917/06/13:6a
BAERST, Eleonora, 29, NYC-B – 1902/06/22:5a
BAESSLER, August, NYC-M – 1903/10/25:5a
BAETCKE, F. H. Karl, 23, cigarmaker & SPD activist expelled fr Berlin via Altona, arrived NYC – 1880/12/18:1g, + NYC 30 Apr 1882:5e,f
BAETHKE, R., NYC-M – 1903/07/17:4a
BAETZ, Hermann, 35, pianomaker, NYC-M – 1891/07/12:5d
BAEUERLE, George, un. brewer, NYC-M – 1907/03/10:7a, 11:6a
BAEUSCHER, Theo.,63,NYC-B – 1913/12/11:6a,12:6a
BAEYER, Adolf von, 82, German chemist, 1905 Nobel Prize, + Starnberg – 1917/08/25:5f
BAFF, Barnett, chicken dealer, killed during labor dispute, NYC-M – 1914/11/25:1g, 26:2d, 27:2d, 3 De:1e, 24:2b, 25:1a, 27:11a, 30:2f
BAGAR, Anton, fr Austria, NYC-Q – 1882/08/06:5f
BAGNELL, Mary, NYC-B – 1888/07/26:4f, 27:1b
BAHERY % Somsack
BAHLBURG, John, 59, un. carp., Hoboken, NJ – 1897/11/21:5a
BAHLBURG, Margarethe, Hoboken, NJ – 1892/12/06:4a
BAHNSEN, Mathilde, 37, Hoboken, NJ – 1900/11/07:4b
BAHR, Bertha, 67, NYC-B - 1914/10/30:6a
BAHR, Gustav, 82, NYC-M – 1911/01/25:6a
BAHR, Ida, 12, NYC-M, +@ Genl Slocum – 1904/06/17:3b
BAHR, Jacob, 56, merchant, NYC-B – 1907/09/29:7e
BAHR, Julius, SPD Berlin – 1909/06/06:3c
BAHR, Lillie, 7, NYC-M, +@ Genl Slocum – 1904/06/23:1b
BAHR, Moritz, 70, carpenter, NYC-SI? – 1916/01/15:2e
BAHR, Mrs see Berry.
BAHRNMUELLER, John, 34, innkeep, & wife, 32, NYC-B – 1907/10/05:3a
BAIER see also Beier, Beyer and other variant spellings
BAIER, August, 67, un. printer, NYC-Bx – 1919/01/31:2d,6a, 1 Feb.:6a
BAIER, August, box manuf., NYC-B – 1916/03/15:6a
BAIER, Charles G., 33, NYC-Bx - 1918/09/05:6a
BAIER, Konrad, 58, NYC-M - 1920/05/10:6a, 11:6a
BAIER, Robert, 54, Bergen, NJ – 1881/09/02:3c
BALSKY, Charles, NYC-M – 1881/05/26:1e, 27:1e
BAIER, Willie, 7, NYC-M – 1901/03/05:4a
BAIL, Gustave, NYC-Q – 1920/03/21:12a
BAILER, Emil, machinist, NYC-B – 1906/11/26:6a

BAILEY, Edwin, ex-US Senator, Patchogue, NY - 1914/07/09:3c
BAILEY, Frank, Negro, lynched Osage, OK – 1907/07/18:1d
BAILEY, John, Negro, lynched Marietta, GA – 1900/03/19:3a
BAINIK, Senare, fr Hungary, worked West VA., + NYC on way home – 1908/02/13:1d
BAIST, Lillian, 10, NYC-M, +@Genl Slocum – 1904/06/25:1d
BAITER, Kate E., NYC-M – 1898/10/28:4a
BAITHER, Christian, NYC-Q – 1902/10/24:4a
BAJINSKY, Betsy, 12, NYC-M – 1880/08/02:1g
BAJZEK, Stephan & Marie, USA 1901 fr near Prague, NYC-M – 1906/09/17:1g
BAKENSKY, Joseph & Virginia, Passaic, NJ - 1917/09/03:3e
BAKER, Albert, Negro, lynched Waycross, GA – 1908/06/29:5f
BAKER, Frazer B., Negro, Lake City, SC, lynched – 1898/02/23:1e
BAKER, George, Negro, lynched Steele, ND – 1912/11/09:6a
BAKER, Joseph, basket-weaver, NYC-M - 1918/04/03:6a
BALAGE, John, NYC-Q - 1920/02/04:6a
BALBACH, Edward Sr., NYC? – 1890/10/20:4a
BALBO, Pietro, 23, exec. NYC, 1880/07/28:1f, 2 Aug:1d, 3:1f, 4:1e, 5:1f, done 6:1e, 7:1d, =8:5c
BALDACH % Ruhn
BALDEN, Hubert, miner, + Blockton, AL – 1897/10/02:1d, 3:4b
BALINT, Albert, US army, Syracuse, NY, War 2 – 1917/10/14:11e
BALKAM, Howard, 54, un. painter,*Irel., 1896 gov. cand. SLP, NYC-B – 1901/05/02:1e, 4a, 3:4a
BALKE, Hermine, NYC-M – 1905/05/16:4a
BALL, Adam, Woodside, NJ – 1908/07/31:6a
BALL, Arthur T., 21, boxer, Newark, NJ – 1899/10/30:1d
BALLAUF, Paul, Rev., NYC-B, + Auburn State Jail – 1895/04/03:4b
BALLESTREM, Franz Xaver, Count, 76, MdR crit obit – 1910/12/25:1b
BALLIN, Albert, German shipping magnate, War 2 - 1918/11/12:1c, 13:1b
BALLIN, J., realtor, brother of German shipping magnate – 1907/11/16:1b
BALLING, Anthony, innkeep, NYC-B – 1896/09/04:4b
BALLING, Charles, cabinetmaker, NYC-M - 1879/02/08:4d
BALLING, Charles, NYC-B – 1898/11/03:4a
BALLING, Francis, NYC-M – 1880/05/03:3a
BALLING, Philip, NYC-B – 1880/08/04:3a, fam. 9:3a
BALLINGER, Joseph, 51, un. cabinetmaker, NYC-M – 1894/02/14:4a
BALLINGER, Ludwig, NYC-Q – 1915/09/28:6a
BALLMER, infant son of Joseph, NYC-M, + @ SS Genl Slocum – 1904/06/16:1c
BALLOK, Peter, NYC-B – 1887/12/24:2d

BALLSCHMIEDER, (Mr), NYC-Bx – 1883/03/07:3c
BALMER, Mabel, 10, NYC-B - 1913/05/13:3a
BALMES, John, 66, cook, NYC-M – 1893/01/10:4e
BALOTSCHIN, Meta, 35, NYC-M – 1902/08/20:1h
BALSCHENEFF, Russian revol. who killed interior minister Sipjagin, see Sipjagin.
BALTCHEFF, Bulgarian finance-minister, murdered – 1891/03/31:1a
BALTHAUPT, Franz Joseph, baker, Newark, NJ - 1878/07/22:4e
BALTZ % Miller; BALZ % Schanzenbach
BALZ, Heinrich, NYC-M – 1891/04/02:4c
BALZER, Alvine, NYC-Bx - 1914/10/01:6a
BAMBACH, Adam, East Rutherford, NJ - 1918/10/29:1f
BAMBACH, Peter J., un. bricklayer, NYC? – 1892/12/07:4a
BAMBERG, James, 36, laborer, NYC-M – 1897/08/18:1g
BAMBERG, Philip, un. cigarmaker, NYC-M - 1896/02/23: 5a
BAMBERGER, Edward, 40, NYC-M – 1898/09/07:1f
BAMBERGER, Emilie, b. Scharff, ?52, NYC-M – 1890/04/19:4a
BAMBERGER, Ludwig, 76, ex-MdR & German liberal – 1899/03/15:1d
BAMBRICK, Thomas, exec. Ossining, NY - 1916/10/08:7d
BANDER, Josephine, b. Binder, +1913, mem. - 1914/02/12:6a
BANDISCH, John, 54, un. tailor, Buffalo, NY - 1895/08/28:4a, 29:4a
BANDLOW, Robert, 59, SP, *Waldeck/Gy, un. typesetter, co-publ. Cleveland Citizen, Cleveland, OH – 1911/02/02:1f, 4:4b, letter 5:13d, =4:2e, note 8:2e
BANDONIER, Ernest, NYC-M - 1920/12/22:6a
BANDSACK, John, worker, killed in strike, Buffalo, NY – 1919/09/24:1f
BANG, Gustav, Dr., Danish soc., + Hornbek - 1915/02/26:4f
BANGA, John, Union Hill, NJ – 1903/03/07:4a
BANGE, Jakob, 26, NYC-B – 1890/11/06:4a, fam. 10:4a
BANGERT % Taake
BANGERT, Friedrich, NYC-M - 1919/03/07:6a
BANGERT, Phillip, 38, un. framer, NYC-B - 1916/12/20:6a
BANKELOW, Martha, 17, NYC-B – 1891/07/05:5a
BANKERT, Frederick, 30, Amsterdam, NY – 1901/11/03:1h
BANNER, Julius, 45, & wife Henriette, Elizabeth, NJ - 1913/10/13:3c
BANNER, Victor, merchant, fr San Francisco, + NYC-M – 1903/11/29:1g
BANNERT, Gustav, NYC-Q – 1908/10/22:6a
BANSE, A., SP, Newark, NJ - 1915/02/07:7b
BANSEMER, Herman, painter, treas. Luth. Zion, 84th East, NYC-M – 1896/04/17:1g, 19:1e, 23:4e
BANTA, James N., Chicago RR worker – 1907/08/08:4c
BANTKE, Rudolf, NYC-M – 1903/07/16:4a

BANUSIK, Frank, exec. Newark, NJ – 1907/02/08:3c
BANZHOF, David, NYC-M – 1892/09/01:4a
BANZHOF, Fritz, un. carp., NYC-Bx – 1905/12/25:4a
BAPTIST, Michael, pocketbook mkr, fr Hungary, NYC-M – 1892/07/07:4c
BARADINA, Madezka, Russian Revol., + St Petersburg – 1907/05/01:1g
BARBATO, Mary, 8, NYC-B – 1912/07/28:11d, 29:1e
BARBER, D. Allen, millionaire & congressman for Wisconsin, crit. Notes – 1881/06/30:2d
BARDENKOW, child, NYC-M, + on @ SS Genl Slocum – 1904/06/18:3b
BARDENSKI, August, 51, NYC-B - 1920/08/18:6a
BARDES, Christian, 65, feed store owner, *Gy, USA 1860s, NYC-SI - 1917/11/26:2f
BARDINA, Sophia Lanonowna, Russian labor organizer, + in exile in Geneva, Switz. – 1883/06/01:2e
BARDOFF, Mary, 15, servant, fr Gy in June, W. Hoboken, NJ – 1905/06/24:1c
BARDORF, Christian, NYC-B see also Caroline Mayer
BAREIS, Gottlieb, NYC-M - 1913/10/18:6a
BARENSTEIGER, David, un. miner & SLP, Scottsdale, PA – 1899/03/06:1e
BARENZ, Franziska, NYC-M – 1900/06/12:4a
BARFUS, France, Jersey City, NJ – 1909/06/04:3b
BARISCH, John, un. baker, NYC-M – 1910/09/21:6a, fam. 24:6a
BARKDALE, Annie, 30, Negro, lynched Vienna, GA – 1912/06/26:1b
BARKER, Adeline, NYC – 1913/12/16:3e
BARKER, John Henry, White Plains, NY, exec. Ossining, NY – 1897/07/07:1d
BARKLUNS, Gustav, un. carp., NYC-M – 1903/02/05:4a
BARKNER, Max, ship steward, @ 1900 dock fire, Hoboken, NJ 1900/07/03:1c
BARLEBEN, Rudolph, NYC-M - 1914/05/07:6a
BARLING, Otto, NYC-M – 1898/09/06:1c
BARLOW, Louise, NYC-B – 1883/07/11:1g
BARNA, Henry, 43, SP, NYC-B – 1911/02/16:6a
BARNARD, Frank, gym teacher 23rd Regt NYNG, & his family, NYC-M – 1911/02/09:1e
BARNARD, George G., judge, NYC-M - 1879/04/29:2b
BARNES, Lue, 16, Negro, lynched Clarendon County, S.C. – 1880/12/12:5b, 16:2c
BARNES, Thomas, exec. NYC – 1911/06/09:6d, 13:3e-f

BARNEY, Charles T., ex-pres. Knickerbocker Trust Co., NYC-M – 1907/11/15:1e
BARNGESER, Christine, NYC-M – 1885/06/11:3d
BARNUM, Eugene E., secy of Prof. Adler's Coop. Colonization Society – 1880/04/06:2c
BARNUM, P. T., Circus bus., 1891/04/08:1c, will 12 Apr:1b
BAROBUTO, John, exec. Ossining, NY – 1910/01/04:1b
BAROSTOCK, Samuel, 37, worker, NYC-M – 1913/05/30:3b
BARRATT, Leon, 41, French merchant, * Lyon, NYC-M – 1880/04/24:1e
BARRETT, Elisabeth, b. Mock, 74, NYC-M – 1882/07/30:8a
BARRETT, George H., 69, NYS Supr Ct judge, crit obit – 1906/06/08:2h
BARRETT, Isaac, Negro, lynched near Orangedale, FL – 1897/06/06:7h
BARRIE, Maltman, Engl. Socialist, + London – 1909/04/23:4c
BARRIN, Joseph, 26, butcher, NYC-B – 1911/01/02:3a
BARRISON, Cyrus, Danish variete artist, NYC-M – 1905/04/07:1g
BARSCHOW, William, 4, NYC-M – 1881/12/09:3a
BARSENECK, Barbara, 24, NYC-M – 1891/08/12:4a
BARSUTO, Mary, see BARBATO, Mary
BART, Johann, + 9 Mr 1887, mem. – 1888/03/09:3b
BARTEL % Becker
BARTEL, August, NYC-M – 1915/12/25:2b
BARTEL, Charlotte, Seaford, NY – 1914/06/27:6a
BARTEL, Robert, 27, carp., NYC-B – 1903/08/06:1c
BARTELINEZ, Theodor, 48, NYC-M – 1892/07/19:4a
BARTELS, Conrad, un. painter, NYC-Q – 1914/03/14:6a
BARTELS, Eleonore, 71, NYC-B – 1900/07/20:4a
BARTELS, Frederick, 70, NYC-M – 1907/07/14:7b
BARTELS, Frederick, NYC-M – 1917/08/30:6a
BARTELS, Heinrich, infant, NYC – 1912/03/17:7c
BARTELS, Heinrich, NYC-Bx – 1913/04/27:11a
BARTELS, Henry, 24, bartender, NYC-M – 1891/08/05:4f
BARTELS, Karl, 43, un. waiter, NYC-B – 1895/11/29:4b
BARTELS, Wilhelm, NYC-M – 1907/07/14:7b
BARTELS, William, 34, SP, un. butcher, agent for local 174, USA 1901,NYC-M – 1914/07/20:2g,#21:2c,6a,=22:6d,fam. 24:6a, mem. 1915/07/19:6a
BARTELS-KOCH, Emma, NYC-M – 1916/05/13:6a
BARTFELD, Heinrich, un. waiter, NYC – 1886/03/08:3c
BARTH % Mauerer
BARTH, Anna, b. Laibler, NYC-M – 1895/06/06:4e
BARTH, Franz Ed., 64, Yonkers, NY – 1920/03/09:6a

BARTH, Henry, 5, NYC-B – 1901/08/28:4a
BARTH, Ignatz, 63, NYC-B - 1920/05/18:6c
BARTH, John, 23, NYC-M – 1887/03/11:3d, fam. 15:3e
BARTH, Joseph, glass cutter, MdR for Gablonz/Bohemia – 1910/05/31:4d
BARTH, Linus, 42, un. carp., NYC-M - 1919/04/25:6a
BARTH, Maria, NYC-B – 1891/04/06:4a
BARTH, Mary, NYC-SI – 1880/01/29:3a
BARTH, Pauline, fam., – 1896/04/19:5a
BARTH, Philipp, un. carp., NYC-M – 1888/11/24:3c
BARTH, Robert L., 68, clothes dealer, NYC-M – 1880/08/26:1e
BARTHEL, Valentin, Newark, NJ - 1916/04/01:6a
BARTHELME, Anna, 46, NYC-B – 1908/08/14:6a
BARTHELME, Carolina, 19, NYC-M – 1906/08/05:7a
BARTHELMES, J. F., 61, NYC-M – 1892/07/28:4a
BARTHELMES, J. G. W., carpenter fr Detter/Franconia, searched for by his brother? in Jersey City, NJ – 1881/04/24:5f
BARTHELMES, John W. G., 65, NYC-M – 1886/10/09:3c
BARTHELOT, Marcelin, French scientist – 1901/12/08:12g-h, 13a
BARTHELS, E. Adolf, Jersey City Heights, NJ – 1898/05/21:4a
BARTHELS, Robert, SLP, *23 Mr 1860 Tiegenhoff/Westprussia, Cleveland, OH – 1900/06/02:2h
BARTHEN, Friedericke Auguste, b. Ehrichs, ?73, NYC-M – 1889/08/31:4a
BARTHEN, Theodor, 73, SLP, un. printer for NYVZ, * Hannover/Gy, US 1849, NYC-M - 1895/04/11:4a, = 13:1g
BARTHOLD, Friedrich, 60, NYC-M - 1894/01/28:5d
BARTHOLDI, Frederick August, Alsatian artist, *2 Ap 1834 Kolmar, designed Statue of Liberty, + Paris – 1904/10/05:1b
BARTHOLDI, Frederick, 25, un. types., NYC-M – 1900/08/15:4a, 16:4a
BARTHOLDI, Henry, 42, worker, NYC-M – 1898/09/18:1c
BARTHOLDI, Lena, b. Schaaf, 39, NYC-B – 1906/12/02:7c
BARTHOLDI, Magdalena, b. Wendel, 78, NYC-M – 1891/06/19:4a
BARTHOLDT, Mathilde, 22, NYC-B – 1897/01/18:4a
BARTHOLDUS, H., un. cigarmaker, NYC-M – 1905/09/06:4a
BARTHOLF, Samuel Jr, fr Bingen/Rhine, hotel owner, Guttenberg, NJ - 1878/11/18:4a
BARTHOLOMAEUS % Wilhelm
BARTHOLOMEE, infant son of Robert, NYC? – 1880/09/20:3c
BARTHOLOMOES, Clara, infant, NYC-M - 1878/07/17:3c
BARTINGER, Matthew, 70, fr Austria, NYC-B – 1913/01/28:3b
BARTLETT, Dorothea, b. Fleck, 29, NYC-M – 1885/02/12:1f, fam. 22:8a
BARTLETT, Fritz, 34, un. painter, SLP, * Memel/Gy, USA ~1869, NYC-M – 1884/09/13:1f,3e, 14:8a, =15:1f

BARTLING, Henry, 67, NYC-M – 1892/07/06:4a
BARTMANN, Elizabeth, b. Hartmann, 39, NYC-B – 1908/08/03:6a
BARTMANN, George, 49, NYC-B – 1909/07/01:6a
BARTMETTKER, Joseph, 37, shoemaker, Newark, NJ – 1886/06/11:2g
BARTNIK % Schwacha
BARTOLITS, Elizabeth, 55, NYC-M - 1917/09/02:7a
BARTON, Clara, 91, fdr US Red Cross – 1912/04/13:1d
BARTOW, Frances, NYC-B - 1916/03/23:6b
BARTSCH, Alfred, painter, NYC-M – 1897/08/19:4a
BARTSCH, Charles F., 38, NYC-B – 1911/02/26:11c, 1 Mr:3a
BARTSCH, Gustav, 57, SLP, printer, * Koenigsberg/East Prussia, NYC-B – 1894/07/24:1g,4a, =26:4c
BARTSCH, Maria, NYC-M – 1891/04/05:5a
BARTSCH, Robert George, NYC-B – 1891/08/26:4a
BARTSCH, Susanna, fr Ofen/Hungary, NYC-M – 1893/07/12:1h
BARTSCH, Theodore, Dr., German writer & left-lib MdR – 1909/06/04:1b
BARZ, Georg, NYC-B - 1917/01/19:6a
BASCHT, Jacob, 18, bookbinder, dying, NYC-M – 1911/07/24:7c
BASEDOW, Heinrich, NYC-B – 1896/08/08:4a
BASEL % Schneider
BASEL, Margaretha, b. Feser, NYC-Bx – 1911/07/28:6a
BASS, Philipp, gardener, Hempstead, NY - 1916/04/27:2e
BASSEN, Hinrich C., 3, NYC-M - 1878/09/21:3a
BASSEUR, Joseph, 30, French soldier, NYC-M - 1917/11/05:2e
BASSING, John, un. carp., NYC-M – 1907/12/25:6a
BASSINGER, Ernst, un. machinist, SP?, NYC-M – 1904/02/11:4a
BASSLER, Albert, 18, NYC-B – 1899/12/01:1e, 4:4a
BASTA, Giuseppe, + during strike, Syracuse, NY - 1913/05/08:2b
BATAL, Sophie, 17, fr Bohemia 1902, + Chicago, IL – 1902/05/28:3c
BATH, Ludwig, NYC - 1914/04/01:6a
BATHAUER, Henry, un. machinist, NYC-Bx - 1914/10/06:6a
BATHJE, Elise A., 72, NYC-M – 1899/08/27:1d
BATTERMAN, Henry, 62, banker & dept store owner, *NYC-B fr parents fr Hannover, NYC-B – 1912/01/11:3e-f, will 1912/01/17:2d
BATTISTE % Jeschke
BATTISTI, Cesare, Dr., ex-SP MdR for Trentino, turned Italian nationalist, crit. obit - 1916/07/17:4c-d
BATUN, Georg, 83, NYC-M - 1916/01/15:2f
BATZ, Michael, NYC-M - 1916/01/08:6a
BAUBEL, Harry A., 45, barber, NYC – 1904/05/04:4c
BAUCH, Emil F., 33, SLP, un. tailor, NYC-M – 1890/07/19:4a, 20:5a, =21:4f, fam. 23:4a

BAUDACH, Heinrich, stone cutter, SPD Striegau/Gy – 1908/07/12:3c
BAUDER % Arnheim, % Hanke
BAUDER, Chr. M., 4, NYC-M – 1888/01/09:3a
BAUDER, Josephine, b. Binder, 74, NYC-M – 1913/02/13:6a
BAUDER, Josephine, NYC-M – 1881/07/26:3b, 30:3c
BAUDER, Maria Eva, 4, NYC-M – 1881/07/17:5g
BAUDER, Theobald, 73, SP, tailor, fr Palatine area/Gy to USA 1860, NYC-M - 1913/07/29:3e,6a, 30:6a, =31:2b
BAUDERLOW, Louise, NYC-M, + on @Genl Slocum – 1904/06/17:3b
BAUER % Bethon, % Engesser, % Frey, % Kirchner, % Oehlecker
BAUER, Adolph, 48, Fire Dept., Elizabeth, NJ – 1899/05/07:1d
BAUER, Alwina, 43, NYC-B – 1900/05/31:1g
BAUER, Anna, NYC-Q - 1916/12/17:11e
BAUER, Annie, in @Turnhalle-fire, NYC-M – 1880/01/06:1a-c, 7:1e, =8:1g, 3a, 9:1e-f, 11:8a, inquest 3 Fb:1g
BAUER, Anton, butcher, NYC-M – 1881/07/21:1f
BAUER, Anton, NYC – 1912/09/30:6a
BAUER, Anton, SP org.,Littmitz/Sudeten, War 1 - 1915/05/02:3d
BAUER, August, un. painter, NYC-M – 1906/10/18:6a
BAUER, Barbara, 60, NYC-B - 1878/10/15:4d
BAUER, Bruno, German theologian, + Berlin in April – 1882/05/21:3a-b
BAUER, Carrie, 49, NYC-M, +@Genl Slocum – 1904/06/23:1b
BAUER, Catherina, b. Muskopf, 55, NYC-B – 1882/05/10:3c
BAUER, Emil, carp., NYC-M – 1880/06/22:1f
BAUER, Frank's wife, Hackensack, NJ - 1915/10/11:2d
BAUER, Georg, teacher at German Free School, Hoboken, NJ – 1907/07/28:7b
BAUER, Harry, 67, violinist, NYC-M – 1899/12/31:1b
BAUER, Henrietta, NYC-M – 1891/04/11:4a
BAUER, Henry J., 37, NYC-M – 1881/04/22:1f
BAUER, Henry, 42, NYC-B – 1906/03/31:4a, 1 Apr:5a
BAUER, Henry, 58, stonecutter, Jersey City, NJ – 1909/04/21:3b
BAUER, Henry, 67, Newark, NJ – 1904/06/06:3d
BAUER, Henry, NYC-Q - 1914/09/19:6a
BAUER, Henry, un. baker, NYC-M – 1901/12/09:4a
BAUER, Henry, un. carp., NYC-M – 1891/09/06:5a
BAUER, Hermann, un. typesetter, Hoboken, NJ – 1890/01/03:4a, 4:4a
BAUER, Hugo, 55, un. cigarmaker, sister in Breslau/Gy, NYC-M – 1902/02/14:3c, 4a
BAUER, Jacob, NYC-Q - 1920/02/06:6a
BAUER, Johann, NYC-M – 1891/02/27:4a
BAUER, John, 49, NYC-M – 1892/08/16:4a

BAUER, John, 64, Newark, NJ – 1897/09/15:3c
BAUER, John, 68, NYC-M – 1905/12/21:4a
BAUER, John, X-Ray equipment manuf., Hartford, CT – 1908/11/12:1f
BAUER, Joseph, 17, NYC-M – 1881/06/02:4c, 3:1f
BAUER, Joseph, 25, brewer, NYC-B? - 1915/03/16:2b
BAUER, Joseph, Newark, NJ – 1910/11/18:6a
BAUER, Joseph, un. furniture maker, NYC-M – 1890/04/20:5a, fam. 28:4a
BAUER, Joseph, un. painter, NYC-M – 1907/01/12:6a
BAUER, Josephine, NYC-M – 1907/01/02:6a
BAUER, Josephine, 15, daughter of Mrs E. Steiner of Chicago, + grandfather Boehm's place, NYC-Bx - 1915/03/18:6a
BAUER, Julius, 23, pianomaker, NYC-B - 1915/12/25:6b
BAUER, Leopold, 57, NYC-B – 1900/04/27:4c
BAUER, Margaret, 37, NYC-B – 1911/02/28:2e
BAUER, Marie, 23, NYC-B – 1883/05/29:3a
BAUER, Marie, 25, NYC-B - 1918/05/22:6b
BAUER, Mary, 18, wife of owner of Germania Hall, NYC-B – 1883/07/19:2g
BAUER, Mary, b. Bosseler,49, SP,NYC-Q- 1915/06/17:6a,18:6a,=21:2e
BAUER, Max, 21, waiter, NYC-M – 1889/10/24:2g
BAUER, Moses G., fr Schothen?/Hessen-Darmstadt/Gy, NYC-M – 1889/02/16:4a
BAUER, Nicolaus, NYC-B – 1911/12/28:6a
BAUER, Oscar, NYC-M – 1902/01/02:4a
BAUER, Otto, un. spec. chair cloth weaver, SLP, NYC-B – 1886/07/27:3b, 28:3b,c, =29:2d, fam. 30:3d
BAUER, Paul, hotelier in Coney Island, +NYC-M – 1889/01/03:2c
BAUER, Phil., un. butcher, NYC-B – 1907/03/09:6a
BAUER, Rudolph, 54, Swiss fr Canton Bern, waiter, NYC-M – 1893/09/07:1h
BAUER, Sophie, b. Straeter, wd of printer Johannes B. +1872 Dortmund/Westfalia, + Hoboken, NJ - 1896/03/01:5a
BAUER, Susanna, b. Robst, 63, NYC-M – 1891/04/09:4a
BAUER, William, NYC-B - 1915/12/11:6a
BAUERLEIN, Francis, infant, NYC-B – 1901/07/04:1e
BAUERMANN, Margaret, 69, NYC-B - 1915/05/11:2f
BAUERMEISTER, Karl, 59, NYC-Q - 1920/02/28:8a
BAUERNSCHMIDT, Eberhardt, NYC-M - 1913/07/19:6a
BAUERNSCHMIDT, Joseph, un. cigarmaker, NYC-B – 1911/01/17:6a
BAUERSFELD, Carl, 54, un. cigarmaker, NYC-B – 1913/12/07:7a
BAUES, Ferdinand, 46, NYC-B - 1913/12/06:6a
BAUGHEY, Elizabeth, 70, NYC-M - 1915/04/21:6a

BAULE % Kroll
BAUM, Adam, 48, SDP, NYC-B – 1902/10/17:4a
BAUM, Archibald, Negro, lynched near Tompkinsville, KY –
 1898/10/23:5e
BAUM, August, un. carpenter, NYC-M – 1889/12/07:4a
BAUM, Charles, NYC-Q – 1910/09/24:6a
BAUM, Conrad, 54, un. cigar maker, NYC-M – 1897/04/29:4a
BAUM, Eva, 59, NYC-M – 1904/08/15:4a
BAUM, George, 60, Newark, NJ – 1900/05/13:5d
BAUM, Henry S., sailor on USS Maine, + Havana/Cuba, NYC-M –
 1898/02/18:1b
BAUM, Henry's wife, NYC-B – 1882/01/04:3b
BAUM, Isidor, 16, Newark, NJ – 1908/09/30:1d
BAUM, Jacob, NYC-Q - 1920/03/04:6a
BAUM, Max, 58, clothes dealer, NYC-M – 1908/01/14:1g
BAUM, Meyer, jeweler, NYC-M – 1906/01/17:3b
BAUMAN, Magdalena, 30, NYC-M, + @ Genl Slocum – 1904/06/17:3b
BAUMAN, Magdalene, 13, NYC-M, + @ Genl Slocum – 1904/06/18:3b
BAUMANN % Heim, % Kunniantz, % Thiel
BAUMANN, A., ~55, language teacher in Galveston, TX, + NYC-M –
 1907/08/05:1f
BAUMANN, Adam, un. carp., NYC-Bx – 1908/01/31:6a
BAUMANN, August, typesetter, *29 Dec 1841 Erlangen/Gy, SPD activist
 expelled from Berlin/Gy, arrived NYC – 1880/12/18:1g, + NYC-M
 – 1900/03/18:5a, 19:3e, 21:4a, =22:4c
BAUMANN, Auguste, 63, NYC-B - 1915/12/21:2b
BAUMANN, Dora, 36, NYC-M - 1895/10/28:1e
BAUMANN, Ernst, machinist, NYC-M – 1903/06/02:4a
BAUMANN, Franz, 49, un. baker, NYC-Bx – 1919/11/18:6a
BAUMANN, Franz, NYC-M - 1917/07/22:7a
BAUMANN, Gustav, 61, owner Biltmore Hotel, *St Gallen/CH, NYC-M -
 1914/10/15:1d
BAUMANN, Heinrich, un. painter, NYC-M - 1914/06/27:6a
BAUMANN, Jacob, 64, un. cornicemaker, NYC-Q – 1909/02/17:6a
BAUMANN, Jakob, 55, Carlstadt, NJ – 1890/09/24:3b
BAUMANN, Jakob, 63, SPD Berlin/Gy – 1908/06/28:3c
BAUMANN, John, Swiss, NYC-M – 1890/12/29:4a
BAUMANN, John, un. carp., NYC-M – 1891/04/23:4a
BAUMANN, Julius F. W., 58, NYC-M – 1904/11/06:5b
BAUMANN, Katharina, 66, NYC-Q – 1912/10/31:6a, 2 Nov:6a
BAUMANN, Ludwig, 60, furniture manufacturer, un. mason –
 1904/02/21:1d

BAUMANN, Margaret, 6, NYC-M, +@Genl Slocum – 1904/06/23:1b
BAUMANN, Martin, brewer or cooper, NYC-M – 1903/06/13:4a
BAUMANN, Michael, 69, un. baker, Jersey City, NJ - 1920/12/07:6a
BAUMANN, P., 13, NYC-B – 1911/07/05:2b
BAUMANN, Peter, Dr., 53, physician, NYC-M - 1894/04/05:1g
BAUMANN, William, 30, Philadelphia, PA - 1919/06/07:6a
BAUMANN, William, 53, un. carp., NYC-B – 1888/07/14:3b
BAUMEISTER % Froemmchen
BAUMEISTER, Ernst's wife, NYC-M – 1904/04/08:4a
BAUMEISTER, George, 18, grocery clerk, NYC-B – 1889/11/07:2d
BAUMEISTER, Harry, 18, NYC-M – 1901/01/24:1d
BAUMEISTER, Heinrich, un. carp., NYC – 1883/06/12:3a
BAUMEISTER, William, West New York, NJ - 1920/12/20:6a
BAUMERT, Katherina, 60, NYC-M - 1920/03/18:6a
BAUMFELD, Maurice, Dr., G-A writer & theater manager, * 6 Oc 1868
  Vienna, NYC-M – 1913/03/05:1d,4c, =6:2e,7:2e,3b, ashes to be buried
  in Schreiberhau 8:3c
BAUMGAERTNER, Anna, b. Jaschke, 30, NYC-M – 1892/07/12:4a
BAUMGAERTNER, Anna, NYC-M – 1907/11/09:6a
BAUMGAERTNER, Dominik, un. carp., NYC-M – 1902/05/21:4a
BAUMGART % Thomas
BAUMGART, Gustav, 31, SP, weaver, Pawtucket, R.I., + NYC -
  1916/03/03:6c, 5:6a-b
BAUMGARTEN, Charlotte, b. Delorme, 72, NYC-M – 1908/08/12:6a
BAUMGARTEN, Henry, 22, waiter, fr Bavaria, NYC-B – 1893/08/15:2b
BAUMGARTEN, Morris, 5, NYC-M – 1897/06/09:1e
BAUMGARTEN, Oskar, NYC-M - 1894/02/24:4a
BAUMGARTEN, Walter, 11, NYC-M - 1915/07/22:6a
BAUMGARTH, Hermine, b. Reyher?, NYC-M – 1891/05/20:4a
BAUMGARTH, Jakob, 48, un. carp., NYC-M – 1887/08/29:2g
BAUMGARTNER, C., 28, NYC-B – 1891/01/12:4a
BAUMHARDT, August, 47, NYC-B - 1894/07/23:2c
BAUMLE, Anna, 103, *Kurschin/Austria?, Newark, NJ – 1900/09/16:1f
BAUMLER, August, 40, shoemaker, West Hoboken, NJ – 1909/06/03:1f
BAUMLER, Margarethe, 43, Anna, 12, Charles, 10, Amelia, 15, NYC-M, +
  on @SS Genl Slocum – 1904/06/17:3b, 18:3b, 25:1d
BAUMUELLER, Andrew, 37, theater business, NYC-Q - 1917/01/07:11b
BAUR, Julius, 45, NYC-B - 1878/08/07:3a
BAUR, Leo, un. carpenter, Wallington, NJ - 1919/03/11:6a
BAURIEDL, John Hermann, 48, SP?, Jersey City Heights, NJ –
  1906/02/24:4a, fam. 28:4a
BAUS % Elsaesser

BAUSBACH, Fr., 38, Newark, NJ – 1882/03/11:3b
BAUSCH, Adam, 61, SP, un. machinist, USA 1881 fr Mannheim/Gy, Jersey City, NJ - 1919/03/30:2g, mem. 1920/03/28:12a
BAUSCH, Mary, NYC-M, + @SS Genl Slocum – 1904/06/17:3c
BAUSCHER, Carl, 29, Hoboken, NJ – 1901/04/22:4a
BAUSENBACH, Gustav A., 64, accountant, NYC-SI – 1913/04/30:6d
BAUSMANN, Peter, innkeep, USA ~1860, NYC-M – 1900/08/16:4c
BAUST, Annie, 21, NYC-B – 1898/09/09:4b
BAUST, Friedrich, Newark, NJ - 1917/03/01:6a
BAUST, Henry, NYC-M – 1892/01/16:4a
BAUST, Otto, 67, NYC-B - 1894/02/03:4a
BAUTZ, Emil, Union Hill, NJ - 1913/10/09:6a
BAUWENS, Auguste, b. Flemming, 60, NYC-Q – 1900/09/23:5a
BAUWENS, Peter, un. cigarmaker, NYC-M – 1890/04/01:4a
BAVARIA, Karl Theodor, Duke of, humanist –1909/12/01:1a, 20:4g
BAVARIA, Ludwig II, King of, + 1886/06/15:1a-c, 2b, 16:1a-b, 17:6b-c, 18:1a, 22:1c, 29:4d, 30:5b-c
BAVARIA, Luitpold, Prince-Regent of, 91, 1912/12/13:1b, =20:1e
BAVARIA, Otto, King of Bavaria - 1916/10/13:1a
BAY, August, 59, innkeep, NYC-Bx - 1916/03/03:2e,6a
BAY, Francis Marie, NYC-M – 1892/03/01:4a
BAY, Thomas, SP, NYC-Q, & wife, 25th Wedding Anniversary – 1912/12/24:5f
BAYER % Nolte
BAYER, Charles H., 44, pres. ad agency Bayer & Stroud, & wife, NYC-M - 1918/09/23:3e-f
BAYER, Charles Hermann, typesetter, NYC-M - 1878/12/06:4c
BAYER, Christian, NYC-Q – 1909/07/12:6a
BAYER, Christian, NYC-Q - 1915/04/03:6a
BAYER, Gottfried, since a few months in USA, + West New York, NJ – 1883/10/12:4e
BAYER, John, un. carp., NYC-Bx – 1913/01/24:6a
BAYER, Mary, 45, servant, NYC-M - 1915/08/18:2c
BAYER, Oskar, 17, NYC-M – 1905/04/20:3c
BAYER, Peter, 47, un. baker, NYC-M - 1915/08/15:7a
BAYER, Robert, 35, NYC-M – 1891/08/12:4a
BAYER, Willy, 7, NYC-M - 1878/07/30:3d
BAYERLE, George, un. carp., NYC-M - 1917/10/06:6a
BAYERSDORFER, Lina, b. Hofmann, NYC-M – 1891/03/30:4a
BAYH, William, NYC-Bx – 1906/10/31:6a
BAYRA % Oberkrieser,
BAYS, Glenco, Negro, lynched Crossett, AK – 1904/02/20:1d, 22:2c

BEACH, Charles F., un. cigarmaker, NYC-M - 1915/06/27:7a
BEACH, William, Negro, lynched Arilby, FL - 1915/08/07:5d
BEADLES, Charles H., 54, un. painter & labor org., NYC-M – 1892/07/14:1g
BEAR, Bernard De, 69, merchant, fr Netherlands, NYC-M – 1882/02/23:1f
BEARTH, Adolf, gardener, Harrison, NJ – 1910/09/17:3b
BEATTIE, Richard, un. painter, NYC-Bx - 1916/02/11:6a
BEBEL, Ferdinand August, SPD patriarch, 69th birthday celebr in Berlin 11 Mr 1909:4d-f, 13:3a-b, 15:4f; 70th anniv. in NYC 10 Fb 1910:5f, 12:4f, 20:4a-f, 15a-d, 20a, by Russian Soc. 21 Fb 1910:2c, by G-A 22:4a-b, 23:1g, 2a,e, Bebel thanks 27:18c-d
+Zuerich/Switz.,6# 1913/08/14:1a-g, 2a-g,4a-f; >40,000 at cremation 16 Aug.:1b, 17:1a,6a-g, 18:1a-b; more 25:1g,3a-f, 26:4e, 27:4c-d,more on cremation 28:3a-f, 4ab-c, 29:4d, rev. mem. meeting in Prague 31:3a, Italy 1 Sept:4f, speeches at the cremation 1 Sept:5b-e, in London 3:4d, his life 7:3c-d, views on trade unions 8:4d-e, his life 14:3b-c,5a-c, SPD memorial at Jena party convention 24:4d-g, on his memoirs 25:4c, mem. meeting in Japan, rev. 2 Oct:4d, reaction German Catholic and Protestant press 14:4f, his will 17:4e, Bebel & the theater, by Heinz Gordon 26 Oct:4d-e, mem. meetings in Russia 7 Nov:4d, Bebel on women 30 Nov:20e-f, Paris soc. want local street named for him 2 Dec:4f. US reactions: by Julie Romm 17 Aug:6c-e, 20a, by Morris Hillquit :8a-c, poem by Georg Biedenkapp :9b; Mem. meetings: Manhattan 14 Aug.:5b, 15:1c, rev. 21:1g, 22:2b; Manhattan-Harlem, prep. 23:6d, rev. 25:6c; Bronx, 19 Aug.:1f,2g, rev. 23:2d-e; Brooklyn 19:2b-c,23:6c, rev 25:6c-d; Queens 23:1c,rev. 26:2f; New Haven,CT 19 Aug:2g, 21:3a; Haledon,NJ rev. 19:2c; Hoboken, NJ rev. 19:2c, Cincinatti,OH rev. 21 Aug:3b, Dover, NJ rev. 23:3a, Newark, NJ prep 23:1c, rev. 26:3c-d; Pittsburgh,PA prep 23:2e, US mem. meetings in genl 24:4c, Chicago rev. 25:1b, Boston prep 1 Sept:6d, Cleveland, OH rev. 4:3f, Erie,PA rev 11:2f, Schenectady, NY rev 14:7c, grief at NYC SP convention 13 Oct:1c-d, newsreels of cremation shown NYC 16:1c. Memory - 1914/09/03:3a-c
BEBEL, Julie, wife of SPD leader F. August Bebel, 1910/11/26:4b; note 1 Jan 1911:20d-f
BECHAMP, Maria, b. Goss, 49, NYC-M – 1892/05/16:4a
BECHER, infant girl, NYC-B – 1890/01/22:4a
BECHER, Theodore, un. cigarmaker, *18 Oct 1840 Zeitz/Saxony, USA 1881, SP, NYC-M – 1906/05/21:4b, 25:3e, fam. 25:4a
BECHLE, John, 37, carp., & wife Emily, NYC-B – 1905/05/30:3c
BECHSTAEDT, Rosa, b. Schmidt, NYC-M – 1881/04/24:5e
BECHSTEIN, Franz, un. butcher, NYC-B - 1917/05/23:6a
BECHSTEIN, Henry, NYC-M - 1916/03/01:6a

BECHTEL, Jacob, NYC-M? - 1913/12/05:6a
BECHTEL, John F., brewery agent, NYC-M - 1904/07/16:1e
BECHTEL, Peter, 55, NYC-B - 1900/04/29:5c
BECHTER % Spinnler
BECHTER, Elise, b. Herrich, fr Trier/Mosel, NYC-B - 1878/06/08:3a
BECHTLE, Fritz, 42, un. baker, NYC-M - 1918/07/14:12a
BECHTOLD, Barbara, 63, NYC-B - 1895/12/10:4a
BECHTOLD, Charles F., 48, un. brewer, SP, *Ladenburg/Baden, USA 1877, NYC-M - 1908/12/28:1e,29:6a, 30:6a, =31:2d, fam. 4 Jan 1909:6a
BECHTOLD, Charles, NYC-Q - 1919/10/30:6a
BECHTOLD, Conrad, 43, NYC-B - 1878/01/28:3g
BECHTOLD, Eddie, 4, NYC-B - 1889/04/15:4a
BECHTOLD, Else, 4, NYC-B - 1888/09/17:4g
BECHTOLD, Leopold, NYC-Q - 1915/01/08:6a
BECK, Adam, 30, stonecutter, NYC-M - 1893/10/12:4a
BECK, Adam, un. baker, NYC-M - 1908/05/29:6a
BECK, Alice Wilhelmine, 19, NYC-M - 1915/05/19:6a
BECK, Anna F. McCarthy, NYC-B - 1920/03/02:6a
BECK, Barbara, NYC-B - 1907/11/09:6a
BECK, Charles, 50, NYC-M - 1897/07/24:1f
BECK, Charles, Newark, NJ - 1904/05/04:4a
BECK, Christian, NYC-M - 1912/03/14:6a
BECK, Christina, 57, NYC-M, + on @SS Genl Slocum - 1904/06/18:3b
BECK, Emil, German soc., *11 Jy 1848 near Waldshut, + Zuerich/CH - 1896/08/07:1f
BECK, Fritz, 32, killed during Pittsburgh, PA strike - 1913/01/29:2b
BECK, Fritz, 65, Union Hill, NJ - 1910/05/31:6a
BECK, George, ~30, cigar maker, fr Wenglingen/Switz., NYC-Q - 1880/02/10:1g, 12:1d
BECK, George, 57,un. cigarm.,NYC-Bx - 1912/09/22:7b, 23:6a, fam. 27:6a
BECK, George, NYC-B - 1911/12/22:6a
BECK, George, NYC-M - 1895/11/09:4a
BECK, Heinrich J., 85, NYC-B - 1891/08/12:4a
BECK, Henry, baker, Watsessing, NJ - 1891/02/28:2f
BECK, Hugo, un. carpenter, NYC-M - 1918/02/08:2g
BECK, Ignatz, 40, Newark, NJ - 1878/11/02:4e
BECK, Jacob, 61, NYC-M - 1890/10/19:5b
BECK, Johann Chr., NYC-M - 1892/07/10:5c
BECK, John T., 78, NYC-M - 1891/07/29:4a
BECK, Karl, 1817-1879, German-Hung. poet, life - 1917/06/11:4f-g
BECK, Katrina, 40, & niece Ms Bauer, 12, Dumont, NJ - 1912/01/30:1f
BECK, L., NYC-Bx - 1911/10/22:7a

BECK, Lina, b. Stengel, 69, NYC-B - 1920/02/04:6a
BECK, Louise, b. Biesinger, 60, NYC-B – 1885/01/12:3b
BECK, Ludwig's wife, NYC-M – 1909/07/03:6a
BECK, M., NYC-M – 1919/08/24:6a, 12a
BECK, Marie, & baby Frederick, NYC-M – 1886/03/20:1d, 22:5e, 31:3a
BECK, Mary, 75, nurse, NYC-M – 1910/12/27:1b
BECK, Mary, NYC-B – 1892/07/08:4a
BECK, Max, 68, edit. Reading Adler, * Michelstadt/Hessen, USA 1827, + Reading, PA – 1881/05/24:2e-f
BECK, Michael, 63, SP?, un. cigarmkr, NYC-M - 1914/12/17:6a
BECK, Mrs, Philadelphia, + California in July (scandal) – 1880/09/02:1e
BECK, Theodor, ex-secy Yorkville Free German School, NYC-Bx - 1918/01/16:6a, 17:6a
BECKER % Gerner, % Nueske, % Oberlies, % von Elterlein
BECKER, Adolf, 74, SPD org. in Berlin-Tegel, tailor - 1915/04/04:3c
BECKER, Anton, NYC-Bx – 1912/08/10:6a
BECKER, August, 27, NYC-M – 1911/07/12:6a
BECKER, August, exec. Chicago, IL – 1899/11/11:4a
BECKER, August, German-b. Communist, 1812-1875, Cincinatti, mem. 1902/03/30:4c-f, 6 Ap:4c-f
BECKER, August, NYC-M - 1879/11/15:4e
BECKER, Auguste, b. Bartel, 39, NYC-M – 1890/02/20:4a
BECKER, Benedict, 41, NYC-M – 1892/12/14:1b
BECKER, Bernhard, German labor leader, + Jan. 1882, mem. 1891/11/12:2c
BECKER, Carl, 63, carp., NYC-M – 1892/06/04:1f
BECKER, Catherine, NYC-M, + @ Genl Slocum – 1904/06/18:3b
BECKER, Charles, NYPD capt, mother + 1913/12/20:1e, exec. Ossining, NY - 1915/07/30:2c,31:1g, 1 Aug:6a-b,2:3c,3:1c
BECKER, Charles, 52, carpenter, NYC-B – 1899/09/01:3c
BECKER, Charles, 65, NYC-Bx - 1914/12/13:1d
BECKER, Charles, movie theater mgr, NYC-Bx - 1914/10/31:6d
BECKER, Christina, NYC-M - 1915/02/22:7a
BECKER, Clara, 22, NYC-B – 1909/09/05:1e, 7:3b
BECKER, Elise, NYC-Q – 1909/07/31:6a
BECKER, Elizabeth, 37, NYC-Q – 1902/05/03:4a
BECKER, Frank, un. butcher, NYC-SI – 1911/11/11:6a
BECKER, Franz, 4, NYC-Q – 1882/05/01:3b
BECKER, Frederick, 20, NYC-B – 1897/05/14:1b
BECKER, Friedrich, 31, NYC-M – 1895/12/19:4a
BECKER, Fritz, 62, machinist, NYC-Q – 1911/03/23:2d
BECKER, Fritz, driver, NYC-Q - 1913/12/28:11d

BECKER, Fritz, son of former mayor of Cologne, + Milwaukee –
   1885/12/18:6c
BECKER, Gabriel, 24, shirtmaker, NYC-M – 1897/09/29:4a
BECKER, Georg, 50, Gayhead, Greene Co., NY - 1915/03/06:6a
BECKER, Gustav, typesetter, SPD Stoetteritz/Leipzig, Gy, + Dresden –
   1902/02/08:2c
BECKER, Helen, 3, NYC-B - 1913/10/08:3b
BECKER, Henry, 42, Hoboken, NJ – 1904/07/11:1a, 12:1f
BECKER, Hulda, NYC-B – 1892/09/30:4a
BECKER, Jacob, 52, NYC-M – 1881/05/07:3a
BECKER, Jacob, 58, un. painter, NYC-M - 1920/02/20:6a
BECKER, Johann Philipp, '48er, * 1809 Frankenthal/Pfalz, +
   Geneva/Switz. – 1886/12/29:5c-d, 3 Jan. 1887:4c, 5:5c
BECKER, Johanna, 57, NYC-M – 1891/03/15:5b
BECKER, Johanna, b. Dietrich, 58, NYC-B – 1900/01/14:5a
BECKER, John, NYC-M – 1891/01/23:4a
BECKER, Joseph, 30, chauffeur, NYC-M - 1917/11/11:11e
BECKER, Joseph, NYC-Bx – 1911/05/04:6a
BECKER, Joseph, un. brewer, NYC-Bx - 1914/02/05:6a
BECKER, Julia, NYC-Bx – 1907/03/03:9f
BECKER, Julie, b. Philippe, 52?, SLP, NYC-M – 1891/07/31:4a
BECKER, Karl, NYC-M – 1881/11/23:3b
BECKER, Karl, SLP, weaver, fr Berlin/Gy, NYC-M – 1892/01/09:4a,
   10:5c, fam. 12:4a
BECKER, Katherina, Greenville, NJ – 1905/01/02:4a
BECKER, Lena, 9, NYC-M, + in @1883 Manhattan school fire.
BECKER, Louis, 39, machinist, NYC-M – 1882/04/28:1g
BECKER, Louis, 86, chemist, *Westfalia, + Philadelphia, PA –
   1901/03/06:3h
BECKER, Marie, b. Behrens, 30,NYC-M - 1878/04/19:3b
BECKER, Mary, b. Kitzing, 45, NYC-B - 1894/04/04:4a
BECKER, Max, 37, un. waiter, fr Breslau/Gy, & wife Emma, 30, NYC-M –
   1896/12/27:1f, =28:1e, 29:1g
BECKER, Max, NYC? – 1885/07/03:3c
BECKER, Michael, 64, NYC-M – 1892/08/04:4a
BECKER, Nicholas, NYC-B – 1912/08/08:6a
BECKER, Peter, Harrison, NJ – 1906/10/28:7b
BECKER, Philipp, fr Meisenheim area/Gy, NYC-M – 1888/05/17:3a, 16:2f
BECKER, Robert, Guttenberg, NJ - 1915/01/15:6a
BECKER, Sebastian, un. baker, NYC-Bx - 1915/05/06:6a
BECKER, Theodore, 3, NYC-M, + @Genl Slocum – 1904/06/17:3b
BECKER, Theodore, 53, NYC-M – 1910/07/05:6a

BECKER, W. F., un. carp., NYC-M – 1901/02/27:4a
BECKER, W., NYC – 1888/08/04:3b
BECKER, Wilhelm, NYC-Q – 1911/10/17:6a
BECKER, Wilhelm, USA 1894, NYC-M - 1895/02/07:3c, 8:1g, 15:3f. S.a. Carl Fesecke.
BECKER, William, Jersey City Heights, NJ – 1903/02/14:4a
BECKERICH, Johann J., un. carp., NYC-M – 1886/11/20:2f, fam. 14 Dec:2g
BECKERMANN, Rebekka, 60, NYC-M – 1892/06/28:4a
BECKMANN, Carl's wife, NYC-M – 1881/03/29:3c
BECKMANN, Joseph, 40, innkeep, NYC-M – 1884/09/30:1f
BECKMANN, Otto, 50, manufacturer, NYC-B - 1920/07/03:1b
BECKMANN, Theodor, 26, NYC-B – 1892/08/08:4a
BECKWITH, Oskar, 80, exec. Hudson, NY – 1888/03/02:1b
BECKX, Peter Johann, 93, Jesuit leader 1853-84, + Frascati/Italy – 1887/03/29:6a-c, 30:5c-d
BECQUEREL, Henry, French scientist – 1908/09/20:16b-c
BEDACHT, John, innkeep, NYC-M - 1878/01/28:3d, Feb. 1:4d, Apr 3:4b
BEDARF % Kalinofsky
BEDELL, Marie, 31, NYC-B - 1894/07/18:4a
BEDINGER, Elisabeth, b. Berges, 58, fr Heiler/Gelnhausen/Gy, NYC-M - 1878/05/07:3b
BEDLER, Maria, cook, NYC-M – 1892/12/27:1g
BEECHER, F., Bayonne, NJ - 1913/09/24:6a
BEECHER, Henry Ward, negat. Obit – 1887/03/07:1c-e, 9:1f, =10:2e, notes 11:2d, 12:2d, Sarcastic mem. notes 25 June 1891:1g
BEECHER-STOWE, Harriet, abol. Writer, noted 1888/09/08:2h, + Hartford, CT 1896/07/02:1c,2a, 15th anniv. + 1911/07/16:20d-e
BEEH, Eugene, un. carp., NYC-M – 1902/07/22:4a
BEEKMANN, Anna, infant, NYC-M, + @ Genl Slocum – 1904/06/17:3b
BEENK, John, NYC-M - 1920/05/29:6a
BEER, Betty, 58, NYC-M – 1891/12/03:1c
BEER, Georg, brewer, SDP?, Butte, Montana – 1901/06/17:4a
BEER, Johanna, NYC-M – 1901/06/30:5a
BEER, Louis, NYC-B 1892/06/20:4a
BEER, Marie, 3, NYC-M – 1888/01/17:4a
BEERMANN % Volkmar
BEERS, Joseph, 14, Madison, NJ – 1880/03/29:1c
BEERSTECHER, Maria K., 48, NYC-B – 1919/01/12:12a
BEESLYS, Edward Spencer, Engl. historian & econ. - 1915/07/30:4b-c
BEGAS, Reinhold, 81, German sculptor, friend of Lasalle – 1911/08/22:4f
BEGASSE, John, NYC-Bx – 1912/02/18:7c

BEGIEBING % Jahn
BEGLEY, J., b. Klein, killed in Chicago by Pinkertons, inquest –
   1886/10/28:5e, 2 Nov:2a-b
BEHL, Peter, un. innkeep, NYC-M – 1891/06/11:4a
BEHLER, Catherina, NYC-B – 1881/07/26:3b
BEHLER, Peter, 19, brewery worker, 1881 fr Bavaria, NYC-M –
   1882/05/09:1f
BEHLERT, Katie, 15, NYC-M – 1885/08/01:3d
BEHLUNG, Ernst, hotelier, NYC-M – 1903/03/21:1b
BEHM, Paul, NYC-M – 1908/11/25:6a
BEHMANN, Otto, 45, tailor, NYC-M – 1891/06/29:4e
BEHME, Fred., exec. McLeansboro, IL – 1896/12/05:4c
BEHNCKE, Anna Christine, 73, NYC-Bx – 1914/08/09:7b
BEHNCKE, Christine, 18, NYC-Bx – 1908/06/30:6a
BEHNKE % Breimann
BEHNKE, Charles, 65, SLP, un. waiter, NYC-M – 1917/12/24:6a
BEHNKE, Friedrich August, Dr., 45, * Stavenhagen/Mecklemburg-
   Schwerin/Gy, USA 1885, NYC-M – 1885/10/16:1f
BEHR, Louis, NYC-M – 1901/04/30:4a
BEHREN, Annie von, actress, + Cincinatti – 1882/12/01:1e
BEHREND, Paul, music teacher, NYC-M – 1891/04/21:4d, 22:1h
BEHRENDS % Becker, % Finke, % Mahnken
BEHRENDS, Albert, fr Warin/Mecklemburg/Gy, NYC-M – 1909/04/19:2e
BEHRENDS, Joseph, 17, NYC-B – 1895/11/02: 4b
BEHRENDS, Wilhelm, 29, Hoboken, NJ – 1891/07/06:4a
BEHRENET, Laura & Lizzie, NYC-M, + @ Genl Slocum – 1904/06/17:3b
BEHRENS % Becker
BEHRENS, Augusta, 57, & Alice, 16, Hoboken, NJ, +@ Genl Slocum –
   1904/06/18:3b
BEHRENS, Catherina,60, NYC-M – 1894/01/18:4a
BEHRENS, Charles, NYC-B – 1909/04/23:6a
BEHRENS, Charles, NYC-Q – 1912/09/06:6a
BEHRENS, Claus, fr Schleswig-Holstein?, NYC – 1887/08/29:2g
BEHRENS, Emil, un. painter, NYC-M – 1918/02/11:6a, 17:7a
BEHRENS, Ernst, Prof., 38, Reading, PA – 1900/05/23:1b
BEHRENS, Friedrich, 18, NYC-M – 1882/04/15:1g
BEHRENS, Heinrich, 23, stoker, fr Hannover/Gy, NYC – 1891/01/20:2e
BEHRENS, Hermann, 49, NYC-M – 1887/11/03:2g
BEHRENS, Hinrich, 48, NYC-B – 1878/05/02:3b
BEHRENS, John, 32, un. beerdriver, SP, *Oldenburg/Gy, NYC-M –
   1910/04/13:1d, 14:6a, =16:2b, 24:13a-b
BEHRENS, John, 50, NYC-B – 1906/05/14:3c
BEHRENS, Louisa, NYC-Q – 1914/07/09:6a

BEHRENS, Mary, & son Peter, 12, NYC-B – 1906/06/22:1g
BEHRENS, Meta F., Newark, NJ – 1911/01/13:2e
BEHRENS, Nicolas, 40, Hoboken, NJ – 1900/06/12:3b
BEHRENS, Siegfried, 73, Hamburg-born US conductor, Philadelphia, PA – 1912/11/06:2b
BEHRENTZ, Gesine, 27, servant, fr Gy, NYC-B - 1895/03/25:2d
BEHRING, Emil von, German scientist - 1917/04/03:2d,05/27:9b-c
BEHRING, Frederick NYC-B – 1908/05/18:6a
BEHRING, Frederick, un. painter, NYC-M – 1906/11/05:6a, 6:6a, fam. 8:6a
BEHRING, John, NYC-B – 1910/12/21:6a
BEHRING, Louise, 85, NYC-M - 1914/02/10:6a
BEHRINGER, Lille F., 39, Mt Vernon, NY - 1915/06/26:4d
BEHRMANN, Anna, 79, NYC-Q - 1916/03/30:2g
BEHRMANN, Henry, 38, NYC-B – 1893/11/24:4a
BEHRMANN, Sophia, NYC-B – 1892/02/20:4a
BEICHEL, Karl, NYC-Q – 1907/08/06:6a
BEICHEL, Maude, NYC-B – 1903/07/04:3c
BEICHT, L., 43, un. carp., NYC-M – 1890/12/03:4a
BEIDLICH, Robert, waiter, NYC-M – 1903/02/04:1e
BEIER s.a. Baier, Beyer and other spelling variants
BEIER, Emil, NYC-M - 1895/08/23:4a
BEIERLE, John, 27, worker at Doelger's Brewery, NYC-M – 1881/01/07:1a, =8:1e-f, notes 9:5f, 4e, 10:2a-b, inquest 8 Fb:1f, 9:1e-f, 10:1e-f
BEIERLEIN, Frank, painter, NYC-B – 1897/10/14:1g
BEIL, Charles, innkeep, NYC-M – 1898/03/21:1e
BEIL, Josef, NYC-M – 1891/05/21:4a
BEILFUSS, Ottilie, 27, NYC-B – 1899/12/ 11:4a
BEILHAUER, Rudolph, innkeep, NYC-M – 1891/07/04:1b
BEILICH, Heinrich, SPD Loebtau/Saxony – 191/04/02:3b
BEILLER, Otto, 32, shoemaker, NYC-M – 1892/08/27:4d
BEILMANN % Berg
BEIMANN, Georg, baker, NYC-M – 1885/10/26:1g
BEIN, John, 35, NYC-M – 1887/12/08:1f
BEIS, A., NYC-B - 1916/04/23:7c
BEISEL, John, 60, NYC-B – 1909/09/08:3b
BEISSNER, Christian, NYC-Bx - 1915/06/09:6a
BEISSWENGER, Walter, 2, NYC-M – 1908/06/23:6a
BEITELROCK, L., NYC-Q – 1911/12/14:6a
BEITH, John, 50, NYC-M – 1891/03/29:5a
BEITUNEK, Frank, beerdriver, fr Austria, & wife, NYC-M – 1904/02/16:1d
BEITZ, Edith, 28, & Edith, 2, NYC-M, +@Genl Slocum – 1904/06/23:1b

BEITZ, Kate, 33, NYC-M – 1893/09/07:1h
BEKMANN, Berthold, + 24 Jan. 1888 in Reptich/Hessen. Ex-NYC, SLP? –
  1888/02/15:3a
BELGIUM, Leopold II, King of, scathing obit – 1909/12/17:1d,2d,4d,
  18:1a, =20:2d, 22:4a-b, 23:4b, 25:4c
BELITZ, Henry, 56, un. cigarmaker, NYC-M – 1885/01/11:5e, 13:3b, 14:3b
BELL, Charles, Dr., Perth Amboy, NJ – 1911/12/24:1e
BELL, Margaret, 80, NYC-B – 1912/10/20:1f
BELLAMY, Edward, 48, US philosopher – 1898/05/23:1g, 2a
BELLES % Kerfs
BELLING, Tom, 58, famous German clown, + Berlin – 1900/03/26:2f
BELLINGER % Heffner
BELMONT, August, 74, the banker, "not worse than other millionaires,"
  NYC – 1890/11/25:4a
BELMONT, Raymond, son of the banker, NYC-M – 1887/02/01:3a
BELSCHNER, George, NYC-M – 1907/03/24:7c
BELSER, Charles, 58, SP, shoemaker, * Wuerttemberg/Gy, NYC-B –
  1919/11/26:6a, 27:6a, 29:3d; mem - 1920/11/24:6a
BELTE, Elisabeth, b. Von der Schmidt, 62, NYC-M – 1892/08/07:5a
BELTSCH, Oskar, 18, cook, fr Berlin, on ship Teuton – 1881/09/22:2f
BELTZER, Charles, 37, NYC-B – 1899/11/20:4a
BELZ, Gustav, 31, fr Bockenheim/Frankfurt, SLP Chicago, + in Gy –
  1888/10/13:2c
BELZ, Julia, NYC-M – 1892/07/10:5d
BEMIS, Lena, 45, teacher, NYC-M – 1920/07/05:1e
BENCKE, Harry, 19, Hoboken, NJ – 1905/06/20:3g
BENDEEL, Bernard,60, silk manuf., Paterson, NJ - 1913/09/06:3c
BENDEL, A., NYC-Bx - 1917/04/03:6a
BENDER % Fahler, % Kunz
BENDER, Bertha, 24, NYC-B - 1914/07/01:6a
BENDER, Edward, 50, NYC-M – 1898/07/01:2f
BENDER, Eva, 67, NYC-M - 1918/04/23:1b
BENDER, Eva, 76, * in Baden Prov., NYC-B – 1887/11/05:2c
BENDER, Frederick H., 35, New Rochelle, NY – 1911/10/03:2d
BENDER, Georg, machinist, NYC-B – 1908/08/08:6a
BENDER, Henry, un. carp., NYC-Bx – 1906/04/15:5a
BENDER, Herman, Dr., 54, *Karlsruhe/Gy, NYC-B - 1911/08/16:1e, 17:3a
BENDER, John, NYC-B – 1904/06/09:3c
BENDER, Katherine, b. Uhl, 72, NYC-B – 1907/09/05:6a
BENDER, Lorenz, un. carp., NYC-M – 1905/06/01:4a
BENDER, Ludwig, 57, un. brewer, NYC-B – 1911/12/22:6a
BENDER, Margarethe, 79, White Plains, NY – 1909/02/23:6a

BENDER, Peter, 56, NYC-M - 1918/07/21:12a
BENDER, Sebastian, NYC-B - 1914/10/29:6a
BENDFELD, William, 60, fr Gy, NYC-M - 1894/04/28:1f
BENDLAGE, Gustave, 50, coopersmith, NYC-B - 1909/04/05:3b
BENDLER, Lizzie, b. Heusler, 23, NYC - 1881/09/05:3b
BENDRICHS, Sam, 35, NYC-M - 1891/07/23:4a
BENDT, Rose, & husband, Newark, NJ - 1908/04/15:3b
BENEDEK, Louis von, Austrian general, + Graz - 1881/04/28:1a
BENEDETTI, Vincent Count, French amb. in Berlin 1870, + Paris - 1900/03/29:1h
BENEDICKS, Max F., NYC-M - 1891/06/28:5c
BENEDICT, John, tailor, NYC-M - 1891/04/25:2g
BENEDIKTEWA, Anna, Russian student & patriot, exec. Kronstadt fortress 30 Oct - 1906/11/03:1a, praised 3 Dec:4d
BENEDIX, prosecutor in Berlin, famous for anti-labor slogans - 1904/06/13:2c
BENEDUM % Neu
BENEKE, Mary, 30, NYC-M, + @on Genl Slocum - 1904/06/21:1f
BENES, Georg, 59, Czech, NYC-M - 1913/06/22:1f
BENESCH, John, 60, SP?, un. carp., NYC-Bx - 1918/10/11/6a
BENGEL, (Mr.), NYC?, fam. 1892/01/10:5a
BENGSTON, August, tailor, fr Sweden, NYC-M - 1897/01/01:1d
BENISCH, Charles S., NYC-B - 1914/03/05:6a
BENISCH, Florentine, NYC-M - 1900/11/23:4a, 24:4a, fam. 26:4a
BENISCH, Heinrich, Union Hill, NJ - 1909/12/23:6a
BENJAMIN, Hermann, 38, un. cigarmaker, NYC-M - 1897/05/18:4a
BENJES, Theodore, barber, Philadelphia, PA, + NYC-M - 1896/07/14:1f
BENKARD % Strecker
BENKERT, George, NYC-M - 1911/11/30:6a
BENKERT, John, NYC-Q - 1914/04/04:6a
BENKLER, Ferdinand, 56, NYC-M - 1894/01/17:4a
BENNER, Amandus, hotelier, W. Hoboken, NJ - 1908/08/21:3c
BENNETT, Carrie, 30, NYC-B - 1894/01/16:4a
BENNETT, Henry H., Pittsburg/PA millionaire, his will - 1902/09/27:1f-g
BENNETT, Mortimer de Robique, Dr., free-thinker & publisher of Truth-Seeker - 1882/12/08:1f
BENNEWITZ, Abraham, 30, @1911 Triangle Shirtwaist Fire, NYC - 1911/03/27:1d
BENNEWITZ, Wilhelm, 27, Union Hill, NJ - 1891/07/06:4a
BENNING, Henry A., NYC? - 1908/09/04:6a
BENNING, Karoline, b. Feckenstedt, 42, No. Bergen, NJ - 1902/05/02:4a
BENNINGSEN, Rudolf von, German politician - 1902/08/09:1d

BENSCH, John, pianomaker, dying, NYC-M – 1911/07/14:1f
BENSER % Amend
BENT, Friedrich W., NYC-M - 1915/04/16:2c
BENTHEIM, Samuel, 72, salesman, NYC-M – 1888/01/11:4f
BENTSON, Bent M., 59, un. metal worker, SLP, *19 Fb 1840 Kopenhagen/DK, USA 1867, NYC-M – 1899/12/16:3d, 17:5a, 9g, 14a
BENTZ, Arthur, NYC-M, + on @Genl Slocum – 1904/06/17:3c
BENTZIG, Andreas, NYC-Q – 1909/06/01:6a
BENZ, Anton, Union Hill, NJ – 1908/06/21:7a
BENZ, August, Newark, NJ - 1919/03/02:12a
BENZ, Katherina, NYC-B – 1908/11/26:6d
BENZ, Max, 50, baker, fr NYC or New Haven, CT – 1892/04/10:1b
BENZ, William, Jersey City Heights, NJ – 1912/05/02:6a
BENZENBERG, Gustav F., 75, NYC-B – 1919/10/09:6a
BENZENBERG, Karl, 7, NYC-Bx – 1911/06/03:6a
BENZIN, August, 34, un. tailor, SLP, NYC-M – 1888/04/09:3a, =10:1h
BENZINGER, Friedrich, 24, NYC-M – 1886/01/09:3c
BERARD, Reinhard, SPD Hamburg, journalist & alderman 1907-1913, + Hamburg - 1915/07/11:3a
BERBESKY, J., b. Sponberg, 28, Swede, NYC-M – 1901/12/31:2e
BERCHTOLD, Susan, NYC-B - 1894/01/28:5d
BERDITSCHEWSKAYA, Maria Lwowna, 26, Russian revol., + 23 Jan. – 1905/03/19:16c
BERECK, Cath., 70, NYC-B – 1919/11/27:5e
BERENBROICK, Louis, 44, Hoboken, NJ – 1891/03/19:4a
BERENDSEN, Fanny, SDP?, NYC-B – 1903/08/03:4a
BERENSTEINER, Emil, 25, fr Austria, NYC-B – 1903/09/14:3b
BERES, Georg, SP Temesvar/Hung. - 1915/02/28:3c-d
BERG % Zeller
BERG, Adolf, 48, liquor dealer fr Marshall, MO, + NYC-M – 1891/04/25:2g
BERG, Anna Mathilda, 27, NYC-B – 1910/03/31:6a
BERG, Augusta, Swede, painter?, USA 11/1890, NYC-M – 1891/02/11:1g
BERG, Carl, US anarchist, NYC - 1914/07/09:1e, 12:1e
BERG, Eduard, USA 1899, NYC – 1899/09/11:1d
BERG, Eva, 53, NYC-M – 1908/05/08:1c
BERG, Gottlieb, SPD Gelsenkirchen/Gy – 1908/07/12:3c
BERG, Gustav, 41, & wife, daughter, 12, & mother-in-law Mrs Krause, NYC-M – 1888/08/09:1a, 10:1a
BERG, Hattie, 22, NYC-B – 1907/01/26:6a
BERG, John, NYC-M - 1918/04/07:7a
BERG, Lorenz, 70, SPD Offenbach/Hessen, ivory cutter – 1912/08/11:3a

BERG, Louise, b. Demuth, 19, NYC-M - 1878/05/11:3a, 14:3c
BERG, Margareth, 52, NYC-M – 1891/07/29:4a
BERG, Regina, 92, Paterson, NJ – 1891/03/30:4a
BERG, Regina, b. Beilmann, 31, NYC-B - 1918/11/02:6a, 4:6a
BERGE, Christoph, NYC-Bx - 1917/04/06:6a
BERGEL, Otto & wife, SP, NYC-Q, Silver Wedding - 1920/10/28:5f
BERGEL, Otto, 16, NYC-B - 1914/04/20:6a, fam. 24:6a
BERGELT, Clemens, NYC-M – 1900/05/06:5f
BERGELT, Emil, NYC-M - 1915/01/30:6a
BERGEN, Bernhard A., NYC-M - 1914/10/20:6a
BERGEN, Bessie, 24, servant, NYC-B – 1896/08/24:2e
BERGEN, Georg Von, un. cigar maker, NYC-M – 1892/01/12:4a
BERGER, Albin, SPD Meerane/Sax., alderman - 1915/10/10:3b
BERGER, Anton, un. carp., NYC-M – 1900/12/13:4a
BERGER, August, 22, NYC-B – 1905/09/15:4a, fam. 21:4a
BERGER, August, brewer, San Jose, CA – 1900/07/25:3e
BERGER, August, painter, NYC – 1912/01/12:1e
BERGER, C., b. Palte, ~35, NYC-M – 1908/04/14:1c
BERGER, Charles, un. painter, NYC-M - 1917/01/27:6a
BERGER, Charles,50,SLP, un. surgical instrument maker, *Solingen/Gy, NYC-B - 1895/07/16:1d,4c
BERGER, Emil, 55, NYC-B - 1915/02/01:6a
BERGER, Emil, NYC-Bx – 1907/08/29:6a
BERGER, Franz X., 55, liquor dealer, NYC-B - 1915/04/23:6a, 24:6a
BERGER, Friedericke, b. Lick, NYC-B – 1891/04/27:4a
BERGER, Fritz, un. printer, NYC-Bx - 1919/08/15:6a
BERGER, George, 27, NYC-M – 1893/01/23:4a
BERGER, Gustav, 65, Hoboken, NJ – 1911/11/04:6a, 5:7a, fam. 8:6a
BERGER, Hermann, married Alvina SEIDEN, in NYC-M – 1896/10/15:3f
BERGER, Jenny, b. Burgess, NYC-B – 1891/03/12:4a
BERGER, Josef, NYC-M – 1902/10/20:4a
BERGER, Joseph, 13, NYC-M – 1887/10/25:1e
BERGER, Lillie, 24?, NYC-M – 1892/06/12:1f
BERGER, Ludwig, un. carp., NYC-B – 1901/03/12:4a
BERGER, Lukas, 40, * Furtwangen/Baden, SPD Frankfurt/Main/Gy – 1908/07/19:3a
BERGER, Mary, ~40, NYC-B – 1902/02/14:4a
BERGER, Maurice, 22, US Army, NYC-Bx – 1913/01/01:2f
BERGER, Otto, from Baden/Gy, + 9 Aug. 1878 NYC, = only now fr morgue – 1880/10/29:4b
BERGER, Otto, New Rochelle, NY – 1903/05/10:5a
BERGER, Pauline, 5, NYC-M, + @ Genl Slocum – 1904/06/18:3b

BERGER, Peter, 58, un. waiter, NYC-M - 1917/01/17:6a
BERGER, Rose, NYC-M - 1917/05/18:6a
BERGER, Sophie, 51, NYC-M - 1917/11/24:1e
BERGER, Wilhelmina, 55, NYC-B - 1912/03/17:7c, fam. 20:6a
BERGES % Bedinger,
BERGH, Henry, animal rights activist, his = 1888/03/17:1g
BERGHAUSEN, Andreas, NYC-M - 1904/12/26:4a
BERGHAUSEN, Hans, un. carp., NYC-Bx - 1905/08/29:4a, 30:4a
BERGHAUSEN, Henrietta, NYC-M - 1905/02/13:4a
BERGHOLD, Rebecca, NYC-M, + Chicago, IL - 1893/05/03:4e
BERGHOLZ, Reinhold, + 1887 see ALVENSLEBEN
BERGHORN, Wilhelm, 26, un. longshoreman, Hoboken, NJ - 1909/10/30:6a
BERGHORN, William, 30, railroad empl., NYC-Q - 1919/06/15:7e
BERGIN, Martin, Molly Maguire, exec. Pottsville, PA - 1879/01/17:1c
BERGMAN, August, exec. Morristown, NJ - 1895/06/21:4c
BERGMANN % Schroeder
BERGMANN, Alfred, NYC-M - 1905/06/01:2h
BERGMANN, Carl, 42, NYC-M - 1900/02/17:4a, 18:5a
BERGMANN, George, Rabbi, fr Austria, USA ~ 1899, NYC-M - 1909/10/12:1b
BERGMANN, Henry, 55, clothing store mgr, NYC-M - 1892/07/27:2g
BERGMANN, Lena, NYC-M - 1891/11/01:5a
BERGMANN, Minna, b. Wanflug?, 31, NYC-M - 1891/04/14:4a
BERGMANN, Paul, machinist, + Pittsfield, MA - 1905/05/02:4a
BERGMANN, W., 39, NYC-M - 1893/09/30:4a
BERGMEISTER, J.N., Elisabeth, NJ - 1919/11/22:6a
BERGNER, Friedrich, 80, cellist at NY Philharmonic, *1 Fb 1827 Donaueschingen/Gy, USA 1847, NYC-M - 1907/04/04:2c
BERGNER, Mary, Newark, NJ - 1897/12/27:3d-e
BERGS % Blendau
BERGSTROM, Oscar, gardener fr Mt Kisco, exec. Ossining, NY - 1904/06/14:4d
BERHUSEN, Sophia, 33, NYC-B - 1880/04/29:1e, 6 May:1e
BERINGER, Charles, NYC-M - 1916/12/31:7a
BERKA, Franz, 56, Czech laborer, exec. for sedition in Maehrisch-Truebau/Moravia - 1915/07/31:4d, 9 Aug.:4d
BERKA, Thomas, un. carp., NYC-M - 1911/07/13:6a, 14:6a
BERKER, George, 50, NYC-B - 1918/07/10:6b
BERKOWITZ, Hyman, 42, fruit peddler, & family, Philadelphia, PA - 1911/02/13:1a
BERKOWITZ, Yetta, 18, NYC-M - 1904/09/09:1b

BERLA, Jacob, 57, NYC-M - 1894/01/19:4a
BERLIN, Elizabeth, 70, NYC-M – 1911/05/12:3e
BERLIN, Max, 45, Newark, NJ - 1915/08/13:2b, 14:6a
BERLINER % Honig
BERLINER, Henry, 76, tailor, NYC-M – 1893/10/25:4e
BERLINER, Ida, NYC-M – 1893/12/29:4a
BERLINGER, Louisa, 56, NYC-M – 1901/02/20:4a
BERLINGER, Martha, 3, NYC-M – 1897/08/31:1d
BERLINGHOF, Barbara, NYC-M – 1890/03/13:1g
BERLINHOFF, Charles F., un. cigarmaker, NYC-M – 1880/05/27:3b
BERLITZ, Abraham, baker, NYC? – 1910/12/20:3e
BERMAN, Benjamin, 39, NYC-B - 1916/06/16:6b
BERMAN, Frank, NYC-M - 1914/05/06:6a
BERMAN, Harry, 25, Brownsville, NYC? - 1914 /12/04:2b
BERMAN, Ignatz, 64, NYC-M – 1890/07/06:5a
BERMEL, John, SLP Bergen County, NJ – 1900/02/16:4a
BERNARD, Ethel, ~20, NYC-M – 1910/02/05:2d
BERNARD, Jacob, NYC-Bx - 1913/11/29:6a
BERNARD, Morris, NYC-M – 1901/02/16:2g
BERNATZ, F., West Hoboken, NJ - 1917/06/27:6a
BERNAYS, Carl Ludwig, 64, 48er, St Louis, MO 1849, U.S. consul Zuerich/Switz, & G-A journalist, + 20 June - 1879/06/27:2b
BERNDT % Faust
BERNDT, Anna G., b. Schaefer, 76, NYC-M – 1891/07/05:5a
BERNDT, Ferdinand, NYC-M - 1915/12/30:6a
BERNER, Paul, NYC-M – 1902/03/18:4a
BERNERT, Gustav, fr Steiermark?, NYC-M - 1914/11/27:6a
BERNET, Friedrich, 64, NYC-M – 1898/01/27:4a
BERNET, Philip, 64, NYC-M - 1894/04/03:4a
BERNHARD, Bertha, 7, NYC-M
BERNHARD, Elisabeth, cook, NYC-M – 1892/10/16:1h
BERNHARD, Gustav, fresco-painter, NYC-M – 1893/06/21:4a
BERNHARD, James, NYC-M – 1901/12/23:4a
BERNHARD, Joseph, 47, brewery worker, NYC-M – 1893/11/01:1g
BERNHARD, Martin, 49, SPD Frankfurt/Main, alderman 1908-14 - 1915/03/21:3c
BERNHARDI, Annie, 5, NYC-M, + on @Genl Slocum – 1904/06/17:3b
BERNHARDT, Celia, 57, NYC-M – 1899/07/23:5a
BERNHARDT, Daniel, 50, NYC-B – 1913/01/23:2a
BERNHARDT, Engelke, un. cigarmaker, NYC-M – 1896/05/23:4a, 24:5a, fam. 26:4a

BERNHARDT, Friedrich, fr Ittlingen/Baden, USA 1880, ad searching for his brother – 1880/12/13:3b
BERNHARDT, Louise, 83, NYC-M – 1903/01/21:4a
BERNHARDT, Maria, 60, NYC-M – 1889/03/12:4a
BERNHARDT, Minna, b. Buermann, 32, NYC-M – 1884/09/18:3d
BERNHEIMER, Emmanuel, 79, NYC-M – 1890/03/31:4a
BERNHEIMER, Martin,32, carpenter, fr Bechtoldsheim/Hessia, NYC - 1878/06/03:4e
BERNHEIMER, Max, 58, pres. Bernheimer & Schwartz Brewery, NYC-B - 1913/09/26:2b
BERNHEIMER, Otto, 28, cotton dealer, NYC-M – 1905/07/26:3c
BERNHEIMER, Simon E., head of Bernheimer & Schwarz Brewing Co., NYC-M – 1911/07/26:3f, will probated 1913/03/30:11b
BERNINGER, John, un. typesetter, NYC-M – 1891/11/11:4a
BERNINS % Lutz
BERNIUS, Katherina, NYC-B – 1910/03/05:6a
BERNNAT, Uriah C., 66, dry goods dealer, NYC-B – 1900/12/09:5a
BERNREUTHER, Joseph, 34, un. machinist, NYC-M – 1882/10/11:3c
BERNSTADT, Annie, NYC-M, + @ Genl Slocum – 1904/06/17:3c
BERNSTEIN, Albert, fair booth owner, NYC-M – 1901/03/01:4b
BERNSTEIN, Benjamin, 27, lawyer, NYC-M – 1903/05/28:3c
BERNSTEIN, children of Adler Bernstein, fr Russia, NYC-M – 1893/03/04:4c
BERNSTEIN, Essie, 19, +@ Triangle Shirtwaist Fire, NYC-M – 1911/03/28:1b
BERNSTEIN, Fr., sailor on ship Samarand, NYC – 1880/06/21:2g
BERNSTEIN, Henriette, NYC-B - 1895/02/01:4a
BERNSTEIN, Hermann, 40, laundry worker, NYC-M - 1920/08/15:1c
BERNSTEIN, Hermann, clerk, NYC-M – 1892/05/29:5e
BERNSTEIN, Jacob, +@Triangle Shirtwaist Fire, NYC-M – 1911/03/27:1d
BERNSTEIN, Karl Max, NYC-Q - 1920/10/07:6a
BERNSTEIN, Michael, SP, * Poland, Jersey City, NJ - 1920/02/25:6a, 26:3g,6a
BERNSTEIN, Morris, 19, +@Triangle Shirtwaist Fire, NYC-M – 1911/03/27:1d
BERNSTEIN, Morris, 41, furniture salesman, fr Russian Poland, NYC-M – 1889/05/11:1e
BERNSTEIN, Samuel, 40, baker, NYC-B – 1905/08/03:3c
BERNWELLY % Morian
BERRY, Ed., Negro, lynched Shawnee, OK - 1915/08/07:5d
BERRY, Robert F., & wife & mother-in-law Mrs Bahr, War 2, Yonkers, NY - 1917/04/23:1e, 24:2b

BERSIN, Samuel, painter (artist) – 1909/06/21:3c, 18:2b, 19:2c, 24:1f
BERST, M., NYC-Bx - 1915/05/04:6a
BERT, Paul, French scientist – 1887/02/14:6b-c
BERTCHE % Hageloch
BERTHELOT, Marcelin, Dr., French chemist & polit., – 1907/04/07:8e-g
BERTINE, Louis E., Dr., Mt Vernon, NY – 1898/05/31:1e
BERTRAM % Winkler
BERTRAM, August, 29, ice & coal dealer, NYC-B – 1901/07/04:1e
BERTRAM, Charles N., 43, theater agent, NYC-M – 1900/05/16:1h
BERTRAM, Elizabeth, NYC-B – 1906/12/08:6a
BERTRAM, Ida, 53, un. cigarmaker?, NYC-M – 1901/02/12:4a, fam. 15:4a
BERTRAND, Charles, 32, NYC-B – 1901/05/22:4a
BERTRAND, Francis Joseph, 43, un. cigar packer, SLP, * Koblenz/Gy, USA ~1863, NYC-M – 1881/12/30:1g, 31:3a, = 2 Jan. 1882:1g, collection for family 10 Jan:3b
BERTRAND, Lizzie, 47, NYC-M, + @ Genl Slocum – 1904/06/21:1f
BERTRON, Adolphe, 84, eccentric Parisian liberal politician – 1887/02/18:6c
BERTSCH, Gregor, NYC-Bx – 1910/05/04:6a
BERTSCH, Hubert, 59, SP, NYC-B - 1918/05/14:6a
BERTSCHIE, Adolph, exec. Trenton, NJ – 1909/08/05:2e, done 11:3b
BERTUN, Louis, un. cigar maker, NYC-M – 1885/11/19:3a
BERWALD, Moritz, 18, NYC-M – 1882/11/27:1e, 28:1g
BERWALDT, Theo., 64, NYC-M – 1898/03/05:4a
BERWIG, Paul, Dr., SLP, + Milwaukee, WI – 1888/08/28:2c
BESCHEL, William, NYC-M – 1908/06/04:6a
BESCHER, Louise, b. Schwarz, NYC-M – 1891/06/28:5c
BESCHOLL, Barbara, 10, +@ 1883 NYC-M School Fire.
BESELER, Fr., fr Schleswig?, NYC-M – 1887/09/24:3a
BESENER, William, NYC-B - 1916/05/26:6a
BESKELL, John, cooper fr Bohemia, notice that his 4-yr old boy given over to Gerry Society becz of family's poverty, NYC-M – 1896/11/27:1c
BESSENBACHER, Joseph, NYC-M – 1904/06/08:4a
BESSENDORF, Georg, fr Bavaria, typesetter N.J. Freie Presse, Jersey City, NJ - 1885/10/05:1o f
BESSER, Baruch, 18, barber, NYC-B – 1908/10/22:3b
BESSLER, Caroline, 81, NYC-B – 1900/10/08:3b
BESSLER, Eleonore, 24, NYC-M – 1892/03/11:4a
BEST, Andrew T., ex-KoL, Brooklyn labor leader, +Washington, DC – 1899/08/15:3f
BEST, Katie, 27, NYC-B – 1893/12/30:4a
BEST, L., NYC-Q – 1913/12/03:6a

BESTER, William, NYC-M – 1883/09/09:8a
BETHON, Karl, 83, NYC-B - 1878/03/23:3a 25:3a
BETHON, Rosina, b. Bauer, 78, NYC-B - 1878/03/25:3a
BETSCH, Georg, Union Hill, NJ – 1901/05/27:4a
BETSCH, Jacob, brewer or cooper, NYC-M – 1898/11/10:4a
BETSCH, Katherina, 53, West New York, NJ – 1900/12/24:4a
BETSCHIK, Georg, 64, worker, NYC-M - 1878/03/21:1e
BETT, Johann Georg, NYC-M – 1892/07/01:4a
BETTINGER, Charles, NYC-B – 1911/09/12:6a
BETTINGER, Jacob, Elizabeth, NJ - 1914/01/20:6a
BETTINGER, Kathie, b. Boelker, NYC-B – 1905/06/07:4a
BETTNER, Wilhelmine, 64, NYC-M – 1893/12/29:4a
BETZ % Spahn
BETZ, Emily, NYC-B – 1912/03/29:3a
BETZ, John Martin, 64, NYC-M - 1913/09/28:7b
BETZ, Joseph, NYC-M -1905/09/25:4a
BETZ, Martin, 50, carp., NYC-B – 1880/08/04:1g
BETZ, Valentin, 58, NYC-M – 1882/02/11:1g
BEUKER, Annie, 75, NYC-M – 1901/07/03:1d
BEULER, Gustav, 8, NYC-M – 1889/11/23:5a
BEULINSKI, Ludwig, 32, carp., NYC-Q – 1912/10/14:2e
BEUSCHER, Jacob, 75, Newark, NJ – 1912/07/04:3b
BEUSCHER, Maria, b. Fuchs, 34, NYC-B – 1891/04/02:4a
BEUSCHER, Theodor see Baeuscher, Theodor
BEUTEL, John, 42, bookkeeper, NYC-M – 1892/05/31:4c
BEUTER, Julius, 55, NYC-B – 1910/01/09:7c
BEUTH, William, NYC-B – 1884/07/18:2g
BEUTINGER, Christopher, Swiss?, coal-dealer, Caldwell, NJ - 1916/07/12:2d
BEVEREN, VAN, Edmond, Belgian SP, + Ghent, 1897/12/21:2c
BEVERS, Adolph, 60, salesman, NYC-M - 1895/03/06:2e
BEWALDER, Charles, 43, un. metal polisher, NYC-B – 1910/02/18:6a
BEYER, Adolf, 67, SP, NYC-B - 1919/02/08:6a
BEYER, Barney, NYC-M - 1920/01/07:6a
BEYER, Bertha, NYC-B – 1910/04/06:3a
BEYER, Emil, NYC-M – 1901/07/03:1d
BEYER, Fannie, 26, NYC-M – 1897/07/30:1g
BEYER, Frederick, child of Mrs Christina Kunkel, NYC – 1913/01/01:3b
BEYER, George, 23, machinist, NYC-B – 1911/04/04:3b
BEYER, Heinrich W., 25, NYC-M – 1886/02/13:3f
BEYER, Heinrich, 55, un. carp., NYC-M – 1886/10/13:3b
BEYER, Richard, 55, SPD Leipzig/Gy, un. bricklayer - 1914/02/01:3d

BEYER, Stephen, tailor, NYC-B – 1899/11/17:3a
BEYER, W. F., un. cigarmaker, NYC-M – 1901/07/04:4a
BEYER, William, carp., Elizabeth, NJ – 1887/01/18:2f
BEYERLE, Florian, 23, NYC-M - 1879/06/28:4a
BEYERS, Christian Fred., general, Boer patriot, War 1 - 1914/12/10:1d
BEYL, Christoph, 75, NYC-Bx – 1901/05/02:1e
BEYLE, Ernst F., 35, Orange, NJ – 1886/10/04:3b
BEYLICH, Theo., NYC-B - 1894/01/18:4a
BEYRICH, Edward, un. carp., SLP, *Stoetteritz/Leipzig, USA 1880, NYC-Q – 1884/11/19:1e, 20:1e
BIANCA-MASSA, Ludwig, 19, baker, fr Tessin/Switzerland to USA Jy 1879, NYC – 1880/01/28:1f
BICKEL, George, 45, NYC-M - 1878/01/28:3d
BICKEL, Lina, 41, NYC-B – 1893/05/30:4a
BICKELHAUPT, Frederick, 32, elevator operator, NYC – 1900/10/12:4c
BICKER, H. C., Schleswig-Holstein?, NYC-M - 1879/10/09:3a
BICKERMANN, Simon, 63, un. carp., NYC-M – 1901/08/24:4a, 23:4a
BICKHARDT, Peter, 11, NYC-Bx – 1908/12/06:7c (s.a. :7c bottom)
BICKING % Klein
BICKMEYER, Farina, 71, NYC-Q – 1908/07/10:6a
BICOM, Margaret, 19, NYC-M, + @ Genl Slocum – 1904/06/17:3c
BIDEAU, Wilhelm, NYC-Q - 1914/09/04:6a
BIDERMANN, Gustav F., NYC-M - 1913/09/13:6a
BIDLINGMAIER, Clara, b. Krueger, 24, NYC-M - 1878/06/27:3a
BIDLINGMEYER, Paul, 60, NYC-M - 1916/07/21:6a
BIEBER, E.H., 42, NYC-M – 1888/03/10:3a
BIEBER, Philip C., musician, NYC-M – 1884/09/01:4b
BIEBERSTEIN, Anton, von, 29, East Prussian baron, in Hoboken, NJ, riding teacher, then ship steward, + Port-au-Prince, Haiti – 1907/11/30:2a
BIEBERTHALER, John, NYC-M – 1892/09/03:4a
BIECK, Joseph, NYC-Q – 1906/09/15:6a
BIEDENFELD, T., 50, druggist, NYC-M – 1888/01/09:1d, 10:1g, 14:1f-g, 17:4e
BIEDENKAPP, Anna, Jersey City Heights, NJ – 1889/11/10:5a
BIEDENKAPP, Georg, G-A labor poet, NYC-Q – 60th birthday 1903/05/27:2h, home burned down 26 Fb 1908:3d, benefit 4 Fb 1912:13c, 9:5e, 18:1a, rev 19:2e-f, 70th anniv. celebr. 11 June 1913:6c, 15:4c, 74th anniv., NYC-Q - 1916/06/11:11d
BIEDENKAPP, Katherina, NYC-Q – 1909/02/20:6a, =22:5f, fam. 25:6a, 28:13d
BIEDERDICK, Louis B., 3, NYC-B – 1890/10/19:5b

BIEDERMANN, Adam, shoemaker, * near Bayreuth/Gy, NYC-B – 1897/07/02:4a
BIEDERMANN, Carl, 37,un.baker,Jersey City,NJ - 1914/05/19:6a
BIEDERMANN, Karl, Prof., German historian – 1901/03/07:2c
BIEDERMANN, Michael, furrier, 53, NYC-M – 1900/01/12:1d
BIEG, (Mr), NYC-M – 1887/01/05:3b
BIEG, Georg, 26, NYC-M - 1878/08/14:3d,4e
BIEGEMANN, Emil, 40, un. cigar maker, Hoboken, NJ – 1901/03/02:4a
BIEGERT, Michael, Elizabeth, NJ - 1914/01/20:6a
BIEGLER, Wilhelm, 37, un. brewer, *Freiburg/Baden, SLP, NYC-M – 1891/03/16:4a, 17:4a, 4e, =18:4d, fam. 18:4a
BIEHER, Rudolph, 21, grocery clerk, NYC-Bx – 1910/08/13:5e
BIEHL, Friedrich, un. cigarmaker, NYC-M – 1898/04/06:4a
BIEHLER % Neven
BIELAS, Gustav, un. cigarmaker, NYC-Q – 1911/04/01:6a
BIELAS, Ottilie, b. Voelker, 70, NYC-Q - 1915/08/27:6a
BIELECKI, Marjan, 32, Polish Socialist, on ship to Europe – 1912/11/19:4d
BIELEFELD, Charles, 19, NYC-M - 1914/09/21:6a
BIELING, Otto, Elizabeth, NJ - 1920/01/27:8a
BIENENSTEIN, Jacob, un. carp., NYC-B - 1915/05/23:11f
BIENZ, Minna, NYC-M – 1889/09/18:4a
BIERBACH % Fritz
BIEREGGE, George, Hoboken, NJ - 1917/04/27:6a
BIERER, Frank, un. painter, NYC-M – 1909/08/24:6a
BIERHOFF, Josef, 75, malter, NYC-M - 1913/06/05:2d
BIERMAN, Prof. Henry, HS teacher, NYC-Bx - 1917/10/28:11c
BIERMANN, Gussie, 22, @1911 Triangle Shirtwaist Fire, NYC-M – 1911/03/27:1d
BIERMANN, Paul, 46, engineer, NYC-M - 1895/03/02:4a
BIERMEIER, Marie, 72, NYC-M – 1912/05/17:6a
BIERSCH, Fritz's wife, NYC-M – 1898/02/05:4a
BIERSCHENK, Charlotte, 16, NYC-B – 1919/08/02:6b, 3:2e
BIESBIER, William, 28, barber, NYC-B – 1901/01/05:2g
BIESEL, Maria, NYC-B – 1909/01/23:6a
BIESENTHAL, Isaac, NYC-M – 1894/01/25:4a
BIESINGER % Beck
BIESINGER, Magdalene, NYC-M – 1918/11/16:6a
BIHLER, Chr., NYC-M – 1907/03/22:6a, fam. 25:6a
BILAS, Theodor, 52, Winfield, LI – 1899/10/28:4a, fam. 31:4a
BILGENROTH, Anna, Greenville, NJ - 1920/02/19:6a
BILGENROTH, Frederick, Jersey City, NJ – 1908/10/16:6a
BILKERSWERTH, August, 24, Swede, engineer, NYC-B – 1880/11/29:1e

BILLEB, Ernst, NYC-B – 1903/03/05:4a
BILLEZICK, Stephan, 47, un. machinist, NYC-M – 1913/02/24:6a, 25:6a
BILLIG, Christian H., 56, NYC-M – 1892/06/08:4a
BILLIGMEYER, Barbara, NYC-M - 1894/01/08:4a
BILLSTEIN, Peter, 76, un. weaver, SPD Muehlheim/Rhine – 1911/02/19:3d
BILNSTIEL, Albert, 60, NYC-M – 1912/05/11:6a
BILSE, Benjamin, 85, conductor Royal Orchestra, London, *17 Aug 1816 Liegnitz/Gy – 1902/07/27:16f-g
BINDER % Bander, % Bauder
BINDER, Charles A., 35, ex-NYS Assembly, NYC – 1891/05/18:4c
BINDER, Heinrich, 70, G-A journalist, *Austria, '48er, co-fdr orig. Puck, then Detroit Abendpost, at new Puck, NYC-M – 1901/01/12:1b, 14:4a
BINDER, Henry, NYC-M – 1904/03/16:4a
BINDER, John, NYC-Q - 1914/10/12:6a
BINDER, Julius, NYC-M – 1898/04/12:4a
BINDER, Kate, 23, servant, NYC-M – 1909/03/19:1f
BINDER, Maria, b. Schrenz, 59, NYC-M – 1892/07/15:4a
BINDER, Mary, 60, NYC-M – 1910/03/15:6a
BINDER, Mary, 60, NYC-M – 1910/03/16:6a
BINDERNAGEL, Julius, 57, cigarmaker, NYC-M – 1893/10/22:1f, 23:4a
BINDNAGEL, Lena, 10, NYC-M, + @1883. See School Fire, NYC-M
BINECH, Martha, NYC-M - 1916/04/07:6a
BINESS, Joseph L., 75, NYC-M? – 1910/02/01:6d
BING, Frederick W., 55, NYC-M – 1882/06/08:3b
BINGE, Ida, 63, NYC-M – 1907/02/07:1d, 18:3d, 19:1e, 21:1f, 22:1d, 28:2e, 6 Mr:3e
BINGEL, Heinrich, un. cigarmaker, NYC-M - 1878/08/25:8b
BINGEL, Karl, NYC-M – 1892/10/14:4a
BINGER, Caroline, 73, NYC-M - 1916/07/27:6a
BINGER, Joseph, 73, NYC-M - 1916/05/18:6a
BINGHAM, Henry, Negro, lynched Palmetto, GA – 1899/03/17:2h
BINGOLD, John, un. carp., NYC-M – 1901/06/14:4a, 15:4a, fam. 18:4a
BINTHARSCH, Carl, un. piano maker, NYC-M – 1890/05/17:4a
BIOHL, Georg, 43, NYC-M – 1882/08/19:3c
BIRCHALL, exec. Woodstock, NY – 1890/11/15:1c
BIRCHLER, John, NYC-Bx - 1913/12/12:6a
BIRCHLER, Rudolph, un. locksmith, NYC-M – 1890/06/21:4a, fam. 27:4a
BIRGIN, Conrad, NYC-M - 1914/05/22:6a
BIRINGER, John A., 46, Elizabethport, NJ – 1910/09/21:6a
BIRK % Jann
BIRK, Augusta, 53, West NY, NJ – 1907/04/21:7c
BIRK, Frank F., Greenville, NJ – 1905/05/28:5a

BIRK, Franz, 38, un. furniture maker, * Wien/Austria, dying, NYC-M – 1890/09/17:2f, 18:1f, note? 25 June 1891:1g
BIRK, Joseph, NYC-B – 1899/05/18:4a
BIRKE, Katharina, 17, NYC-B – 1909/03/28:7b
BIRKEL, Ernst, 26, un. bricklayer, SP?, NYC-M – 1902/03/15:4a, fam. 17:4a
BIRKENBAUM, Bertha, 1899 fr Poland, NYC-M – 1900/01/02:1g
BIRKER, Mathias, NYC-B – 1911/07/22:6a
BIRKHOLZ, William, 53, painter, NYC-B – 1907/08/15:3a
BIRLER, Maria, NYC-M – 1906/05/12:4a
BIRMINGHAM, H., & Katherine, 65, NYC-M, + @Genl Slocum – 1904/06/17:3b
BIRMINGHAM, Thomas, Chicago policeman in 1886 Haymarket martyrs, + Chicago, IL – 1912/09/28:1e
BIRNBACH, Eva Marie, b. Scherer, 65, NYC-M – 1892/08/30:4a
BIRNBAUM, August, un. typesetter, NYC-B – 1908/12/29:6a, fam. 2 Jan. 1909:6a
BIRNBAUM, Gustav, 48, NYC-M – 1886/11/10:1e
BIRNBRAEUER, Anton, un. butcher, NYC-B – 1908/08/24:6a, 25:6a
BIRRIOLO, Isaac, exec. Wellsboro, PA – 1900/11/17:1a
BIRTNER, Charles, butcher, NYC-B – 1887/08/04:2c
BISCH, Bernhard, NYC-M – 1892/06/19:5c
BISCHERT, Gustav, un. carp., NYC-M – 1903/06/03:4a
BISCHOF, Annie, 23, USA 1 week, NYC-B – 1883/08/02:3a
BISCHOF, Henry, 75, banker, NYC-M – 1902/03/08:3b
BISCHOF, Herman, 34, cook, NYC-B – 1912/10/15:6c
BISCHOFBERGER, Alois, White Plains, NY – 1908/01/10:6a
BISCHOFF, Adam, 78, NYC-Q - 1914/12/04:2e
BISCHOFF, Henry, NYS Supr Ct judge, active G-A soc., *16 Aug 1852 NYC, NYC-M – 1913/03/29:1f
BISCHOFF, Martin, NYC-M– 1897/06/09:4a
BISCHOFF, Pauline, >80, NYC-B - 1920/02/27:6a
BISCHOFF, Susanna,75,& son William,38, NYC-B - 1917/12/06:2d
BISGEN, Frank, 75, NYC-M – 1892/08/20:4a
BISHOP, George, exec. Ossining, NY – 1913/02/11:1f
BISIG, Joseph, SP, NYC-Q - 1916/10/17:6a
BISMARCK, Otto von, German chancellor, crit. Obit, 1898/07/30:1h, 5a-e, 1 Aug:1e, 2a-b, 2:1e, crit.poem :2c, =3:1e, 4:1h, 2a-b, on reactions 6:2c, 8:1g, crit NYC G-A for grieving 9:3g, 10:3f, 12:2c-e, 20b-c, 24 Aug:2b, 30:2e-f, 31:2g, 2 Oct:15a-d, 7:2c-d, 9:5d, 14:2d, 20:2c, 28:1c; 11 Dec:3f-g, 17:2c-e. Monument in Berlin 1901/06/29:2d-e. NYVZ crit. that he

treated Austrian Germans like foreigners 1904/02/06:2b. 100th anniv.,
  crit. notes 1915/04/01:4a-b, 2:4d, 3:4c
BISSEGGER, Ferdinand, 46, Swiss?, NYC-M – 1885/12/31:2f
BISSER, Cornelius, NYC-M - 1915/05/02:7e
BISSIER, Alexander, un. carp., NYC-M – 1888/10/18:3b
BISSINGER, Joseph, '48er, * Muehlhausen/Baden, Hoboken, NJ –
  1886/08/25:2e
BITELLI, Ines, Italian Socialist - 1914/06/08:4d
BITTER, Karl T.F.,47, sculptor, * Vienna, USA 1889, NYC-M -
  1915/04/11:11f, 7:1d, 12:2c
BITTMANN, Heinrich, un. carp., NYC-M – 1884/11/25:3b
BITTMANN, John, NYC-B – 1913/02/08:6a
BITTNER, Jacob, 49, varnisher, NYC-M – 1886/03/22:3c
BITTROLSS, Jacob, 69?, NYC-B – 1891/04/07:4a
BIVIRSI, John, un. carp., NYC-M – 1902/04/18:4a
BJOERNSON, Bjoernsterne, Norwegian poet – 1910/04/27:2c, 28:4c, 13
  May:4f-g, 22:3e-g, 22:4a 28:20b-c
BLACK, Joe, Negro, lynched Lenoir County, NC - 1916/04/06:2a
BLACK, Paul, NYC-M – 1901/02/23:4a, 24:5a
BLACK, William Perkins, 74, Chicago, IL, lawyer who defended
  Haymarket socialists in 1886 - 1916/01/06:1f
BLACKNICK, Math., brewer/cooper, NYC-M – 1905/07/21:4a
BLACKWELL, Elizabeth, Dr., 90, US feminist – 1910/06/19:20a-c
BLACKWELL, Henry, 84, US feminist, ed. Women's Journal, Dorchester,
  MA – 1909/09/09:2e
BLACKWELL, Homer, Negro, lynched Argenta, AK – 1906/10/09:1d
BLADA, Laura, & John, 10, Irene, 2, Paul, 2, NYC-Q - 1920/05/20:2f
BLAETTLER % Kremer
BLAETTLER, Margarethe, b. Link, 64, NYC-Q – 1908/03/21:6a
BLAETTLER, Richard, 32, NYC-Q – 1910/06/15:6a
BLAHA, Frank, 40, butcher, NYC-Q – 1907/01/10:3a
BLAIKIE, Charlotte, b. Buechner, 32, West Hoboken, NJ - 1914/04/21:6a
BLAINE, James G., US politician, crit. Obit, 1893/01/28:1c,2a, =31:4f
BLAINE, R.J., IWW martyr, + Sacramento, CA, jail 1919/08/21:2b-c
BLAIR, Montgomery, 70, Kentucky politician, honest 1883/07/28:1b,2d
BLAKE, Emily, 22, exec. Brandon, Manitoba – 1899/12/28:1e
BLANC, Louis, 69, French socialist, + Cannes - 1882/12/07:2a-b
BLAND, Valentin, butcher, fr Worms/Gy, USA 1881, NYC-M -
  1896/01/05:3d
BLANK, Andrew, NYC-B – 1909/10/23:6a
BLANK, Charles, janitor, NYC-M – 1908/05/17:7f
BLANK, Fr., NYC-M – 1893/04/02:5a

BLANK, Friedrich, 45, foreman, NYC-M - 1918/01/03:6a
BLANK, Howard, worker, Paulsboro, NJ, & 5 others at Du Pont Powder, Gibbstown, NJ - 1913/12/09:1b
BLANK, John, NYC-Q - 1919/07/30:6a
BLANK, Joseph, fisherman, Elizabethport, NJ – 1898/01/30:1e
BLANK, Louisa, (maiden name, married name not given), NYC-B – 1902/09/24:4a
BLANK, Marie, b. Billard, 60, NYC-M - 1917/01/17:6a
BLANK, Marie, b. Brinkmann, 28, NYC-M – 1892/08/20:4a
BLANK, William, 29, worker, NYC-B - 1918/06/29:6a
BLANKENBERGER, Frank, NYC-M - 1917/02/27:6a
BLANKENBERGER, Katherina, NYC-M - 1916/08/04:6a
BLANKENBURG, Rudolf, 75, Philadelphia mayor 1911-15, * Hannover/Gy, USA 1865, + Germantown, PA - 1918/04/13:6a
BLANKENNAGEL, Emil, silk weaver, Passaic,NJ - 1914/01/09:2e
BLANQUI, Louis Auguste, 75, French socialist, + Paris – 1881/01/01:1c-d, =24:2e, life 30:5b-c, 6 Fb:4a-5b. Praise 2 Jan. 1885:2b-c; 5th anniv. of death 20 Jan. 1886:2d-e. 100th anniv. 26 Fb 1905:9g-h
BLANQUI, sister of Louis, praising obit – 1880/06/05:2a
BLASCHEK, Jakob, ex-SLP, carp., NYC-M – 1883/01/25:4d, 26:4e
BLASCHEK, John, un. baker, NYC-M - 1918/07/24:6a
BLASCHKE, Mary, 18, NYC-B, mother Mary Dietrich in Albany, NY – 1911/03/23:3a
BLASI, Leopold, 49, NYC-M – 1891/08/08:4a
BLASIUS, Auguste, 55, NYC – 1885/05/06:3b
BLASS, Anna, Newark, NJ - 1918/02/24:1f
BLASS, John, NYC-M – 1896/05/10:5a
BLASSMANN, Auguste, b. Ellenberg, NYC-Q – 1913/03/30:7b
BLATT, Fritz, un. pianomaker, NYC-M – 1881/12/18:5e
BLATTMACHER, Leopold, 50, butcher, NYC-B -1895/10/23:2d
BLATTMACHER, Matilda, 36, NYC-Q - 1913/06/21:3a
BLATZ, Anton, NYC-M - 1914/08/20:6a
BLAU, John, 40, baker, NYC-B – 1902/02/27:4b
BLAUSCH, Catherine, +@ Genl Slocum, NYC-SI – 1904/06/20:1b
BLAUT, Abraham, 19, butcher, fr Austria, NYC-B – 1902/07/15:4a
BLAUVELT, Frank, NYC-Bx - 1915/03/28:7c
BLAYER, Thimian, tailor, * 28 Dec 1856 Wyl/Baden, NYC-B – 1880/07/16:1g
BLECH, William, 14, NYC-M?, + visiting grandparents in Neuhaus/Hannover Province - 1878/09/09:3a
BLECHINGER, Joseph, 68, hatmaker, Newark, NJ – 1912/08/02:3b

BLECHSCHMIDT, Oscar, stonecutter, *& Fb 1877 Glauchau/Saxony, SLP, W. Hoboken, NJ – 1899/05/29:3d, 4a, 30:4a, =1June:3b, fam. 1:4a
BLEIBEL, Emil, 27, un. typesetter, NYC-B – 1896/05/05:4a
BLEIBINHAUS, A., 54, SPD Munich/Gy – 1908/04/05:3a
BLEICHERT % Sponheimer
BLEICHROEDER s.a. Von Bleichroeder
BLEICHROEDER, Hans von, 64, banker, + Berlin - 1917/01/12:2d
BLEISTEINER, John, brewer, NYC-M – 1898/02/27:5c
BLENCK, Wilhelm, un. structural iron worker, NYC-M – 1903/05/05:4a
BLEND, Susan, 45, NYC-M – 1891/02/27:4a
BLENDAU, Christiane, b. Bergs, NYC-M – 1888/07/14:3b
BLENDERMANN, John C., 31, constable, NYC-B – 1881/03/26:4d
BLENGE, William, un. baker, NYC-Bx - 1915/04/15:6a
BLESCH, Clara, 32, NYC-M - 1878/09/07:3b,4f
BLESSING, Mary, 10, NYC-B – 1908/04/05:7b
BLETSCH, Mathaeus, 63, un. carp., NYC-M – 1893/08/20:5b
BLEY, William, musician at Hammerstein Theater, NYC-M – 1911/06/17:1f, 24:3d
BLEYER, Georg, un. carp., NYC-M – 1887/09/22:2g
BLICK, Edward H., un. tailor, NYC-M – 1900/06/03:5a
BLICK, Johann, 51, un. tailor, NYC-M – 1882/06/17:3b
BLICK, Maria Ann, 58, Jersey City Heights, NJ – 1892/03/23:4a
BLICKER, William, un. baker, NYC-M - 1917/10/29:6a
BLIE, Arthur, un. carp., NYC-M – 1900/09/22:4a
BLIE, Ignatz, NYC-M – 1903/08/05:4a
BLIESMANN, Fritz, un. carp., Jersey City Heights, NJ – 1890/06/01:5a
BLINKE, Herman, 32, baker, NYC-M – 1896/07/25:1e
BLISS, Evelina, NYC, trial of daughter Marie Alice Fleming – 1896/05/12:1e-f, 13:1d, 15:4b, 19:1h, 22:1f, 25:4a, 26:1h, 27:1a-b, 28:1c-d, 31:4b-c, 3 June:1c-d, 4:1f-g, 5:1f-g, 6:1f-g, 7:1e, 8:3f, 10:1c, 11:1c, 13:1f-g, edit on this social scandal 14:4a-b, 16:1c-d, 17:1d-e, 18:1f-g, 19:1f-g, 20:1h, 23:1f-g, Mrs Fleming found not guilty 24:1f-g, notes 25:1d,f-g, 26:1h,3e, 27:1f, concl. 28:4a-b, 8 Jy:1e
BLOCH, Arthur, 55, painter & anarchist, NYC-B – 1898/08/10:3f
BLOCH, Helena, 35, NYC-M – 1891/10/03:4a
BLOCH, Jacob, un. brewer, NYC-M – 1907/02/19:6a
BLOCH, Katherina, 86, *Vienna, SDP vet, NYC-M – 1902/02/25:1e, 26:3b,4a, 27:4a, =28:3b
BLOCH, Louise, NYC-M – 1892/07/10:5c
BLOCK, Henry, 35, driver, NYC-M? – 1896/10/12:3g
BLOCK, Hermann, 54, NYC-M – 1903/02/18:4a
BLOCK, Jacb, 55, brewery worker, NYC-M – 1893/06/07:1h

BLOCK, John Oscar P., 19,bookkeeper, NYC - 1914/01/08:1f
BLOCK, Margarethe, NYC - 1914/03/27:1f
BLOCK, Mary, 12, Hoboken, NJ - 1918/07/08:2e
BLOCK, O., 51, butcher, NYC-M – 1902/02/26:3b
BLOCKHAUS, Henriette, NYC-M – 1892/06/26:5c
BLOECHLE, John, 48, laborer, NYC-M - 1894/06/22:2c
BLOEHS Jr., Bernard, 26, un. carp., NYC-Bx - 1914/08/07:6a
BLOEHS, Minnie, 57, NYC-M - 1920/11/10:6a
BLOHM % Schaefer
BLOHM, August, 42, NYC-M - 1894/01/13:4a
BLOHME, Elisabeth, 69, NYC-B - 1894/01/21:5d
BLOMBERG, Gotthard, 61, Harrison, NJ - 1917/05/16:6a
BLOOM, Anna, 50, NYC-M, +@Genl Slocum – 1904/06/17:3c
BLOSS, Gabriel, 50, laborer, NYC-M - 1894/05/02:4d
BLUECHER, ?, ensign on interned ship Kronprinz Friedrich Wilhelm, Philadelphia - 1916/12/07:1d
BLUECHER, Graf von, NYC-M – 1892/02/14:1f
BLUEMEL, J., 52, NYC-M – 1893/03/29:4a
BLUEMLER, Emilie, NYC-M - 1918/02/26:6a
BLUM % Diehl, % Ufert
BLUM, Eva, 56, cashier, NYC-M – 1892/01/15:1e
BLUM, Gustav, wholesale jewelry, NYC-M – 1891/07/15:1h
BLUM, Hans, MdR for Leipzig, son of Robert Blum, crit obit of enemy of SPD – 1910/02/20:3b-c
BLUM, Henriette, Phila, NJ – 1919/11/13:2c
BLUM, Jacob, 26, NYC – 1892/07/29:4b
BLUM, John, 68, NYC-B – 1892/07/21:4a
BLUM, Michael, 70, & Betta, 66, Irvington, NJ - 1913/09/28:1d
BLUM, Otto, 40, SP, fr Thueringia., Rochelle Park, NJ - 1915/12/03:2f,6a, = 5 Dec.:7d
BLUM, Paul, + 3 Apr, NYC-M - 1916/04/27:6a
BLUM, Paul, 47, embroiderer, NYC-Bx - 1916/04/24:1f
BLUM, Robert, 50th anniv. of exec. comm. NYC 1898/11/13:7a-c, 20:4b, 7a-e, his grave 3 Dec:98:2c-d, poem by Ida Blum 4:7a-c, his mon. 11:7h, grave decorated by Viennese workers – 1908/11/28:4e-f
BLUM, Robert, 68, locksmith, Hungarian SP, co-fdr Temesvar Volksstimme – 1908/07/05:3d
BLUM, Samuel, *Tauberbischofsheim/Gy, '48er, USA 1848, & wife Caroline, b. Adler, *Eberstadt, 55th wedding anniversary, NYC-B? – 1906/01/23:3d
BLUM, Victoria, 61, NYC-M – 1892/09/18:5e
BLUM, Wilhelm, 47, engineer?, NYC-B - 1914/11/30:6a

BLUM, William, 28, *Mannheim/Gy, SP, USA 1902, Newark, NJ – 1907/12/21:6a, 22:7e
BLUMBERG, Simon, 45, SLP, Newark, NJ – 1896/09/30:4a
BLUME, Arthur, 23, NYC-M - 1920/07/10:2e
BLUME, Frank A., 49, machinist, NYC-M - 1895/08/24:4a,26:4a
BLUME, Hermann, un. cigarmaker, NYC-M - 1879/01/13:3c
BLUME, Solomon, 3, NYC-B – 1903/07/04:3c
BLUMENBERG, Adolf, 16, NYC-B - 1918/09/20:6a
BLUMENBERG, August, NYC-B – 1903/09/27:5a
BLUMENBERG, Frank, 19, NYC-M - 1913/05/25:7b
BLUMENBERG, Fritz, SP, NYC-B – 1909/11/28:7c, 29:6a
BLUMENBERG, Sophie, 81, NYC-B – 1907/06/14:6a
BLUMENFELD, Nettie, 18, NYC-B – 1897/12/11:1h
BLUMENKRANZ, Annie, 29, NYC-M, +@Genl Slocum – 1904/06/22:1d
BLUMENSTOCK, Philip, 38, NYC-B - 1878/04/22:1f
BLUMENTHAL, Charles, Dr., NYC-M – 1883/10/15:4c
BLUMENTHAL, Elkan, 52, NYC-M – 1892/06/12:4a
BLUMENTHAL, Oskar, 65, German comedy writer, + Berlin, - 1917/05/23:2b, 27:18g
BLUMENTRITT-SCHNORR % Hoffmann
BLUMER, Harry, 5, NYC – 1885/05/11:4e
BLUMRATH, Paul, un. wood carver, NYC-M - 1903/04/12:5a
BLUNT, Andy, Negro, lynched Chattanoga, TN – 1893/02/16:1b
BLYN, Jacob, 21, NYC-M – 1889/11/22:4a
BLYNN, Lehmann, 69, NYC-M – 1893/08/15:4a
BOAS, Emil L., director US branch HAPAG shipping line, *15 No 1854 Goerlitz/Gy, + Greenwich, NY – 1912/05/04:2c
BOBB, Joseph, un. sheet metal worker, NYC-M - 1914/02/05:6a
BOBENREITH, Valentin, 23, machinist, NYC-B – 1916/09/27:6c
BOBLER, Elizabeth, 55, NYC-M - 1914/08/23:7c
BOBORYKIN, Peter Dimitriwitsch, Russian writer – 1919/09/30:4f-g
BOBRIKOFF, General, gov. of Finland, + by revol. Schaumann – 1904/06/18:1h, 21:2c, 1 Jy:2c, on Schaumann's family 17 Sept:2d, Schauman's father to be tried 27 Oct:1g
BOCH, Emma, lady of the night,NYC-M – 1888/11/29:1f, −30:1d, 6 Do:2c
BOCHDAM, Lena, 46, NYC-M – 1896/12/21:4a
BOCHERT, Arthur, 31, NYC-Bx - 1918/10/15:6a
BOCHMAN, Camillo, un. cigarmaker, SP, NYC-M – 1911/06/11:1b, 7b, =13:5e
BOCHMANN, Hulda, 74, NYC-M – 1909/07/25:7a,b
BOCK % Haag, % Sudheimer
BOCK, Alexander, univ. student, NYC-M - 1913/10/08:1d

BOCK, Annie, 23, NYC-M – 1896/08/05:1c, 7:1h, 8:1e
BOCK, August, un. turner, SPD Giessen, Gy – 1910/01/30:3d
BOCK, Christina, 57, NYC-M, + @ Genl Slocum – 1904/06/17:3b
BOCK, John, NYC-B - 1917/02/11:7a
BOCK, Marie Louise, NYC-B, +@Genl Slocum – 1904/06/25:1d
BOCK, Theodor, 37, un. bricklayer, USA 1882, NYC-M – 1887/11/05:4c
BOCK, William, un. musician, NYC-Bx – 1919/09/30:6a
BOCKE, Charlotte, b. Mueller, 38, NYC-M – 1883/08/19:8a
BOCKELMANN, Frederick, 37, NYC-M – 1892/10/07:4a
BOCKHAHN, Sophie, Hoboken, NJ - 1915/09/25:6a
BOCKHARDT, George, 25, NYC, USA 1885 – 1889/08/24:1h, 29:1h
BOCKHOLDT % Ludwig; BODDE % Seidel
BODE, Elizabeth, SP, * Ilzen/Gy, NYC-B - 1915/05/04:6a, =6:2e
BODE, Louis T., 40, Newark, NJ – 1900/11/14:4a
BODE, Mary, janitor, NYC-M – 1903/06/24:4c
BODE, Theodor, NYC-M – 1910/07/07:6a
BODE, William F., 7, NYC-M – 1899/06/09:1g
BODEI % Utz
BODELSCHWINGH, Friedrich von, Rev., 80, fdr of Bethel, laudat obit – 1910/04/17:3b
BODENBERG, Louis, tailor, NYC-Bx – 1905/08/09:4d
BODENBERGER, Jacob, un. carp., NYC-B – 1889/04/14:5b
BODENHEIM, Ernst, 44, French vice-consul in Kassel/Gy, + Chicago, IL – 1913/01/11:b
BODENHEIMER % Freeman
BODENREICH, Joseph, 43, NYC-M – 1906/08/07:1e
BODER, Charles, 89, shoemaker, USA 1830s, NYC-Bx – 1910/05/24:1f
BODERBERG % Steen
BODNER, Georg, 23, machinist at Doelger's Brewery, NYC-M – 1906/12/21:1d
BOE, Anna, b. Seedorf, 57, NYC-B - 1915/12/03:6a
BOEBBERT, Albert, 65, un. machinist, Irvington, NJ - 1919/08/25:6a
BOEBERT, Anna, b. Reineck, Irvington, NJ – 1910/05/31:6a
BOECHEL, Erwin A., 15, NYC-B – 1891/03/30:4a
BOECKEL, John C., 83, NYC-B – 1891/04/09:4a
BOECKEL, Louis L., 20, NYC-B – 1881/01/07:2g
BOECKER, Fritz, SLP, tailor, * near Dortmund/Gy, NYC-M – 1893/08/26:4a, 27:1g,5a, = 28:1f, fam. 29:4a
BOECKER, Louise, b. Fuchs, 68, NYC-B - 1913/12/09:6a
BOECKLE % Vogel
BOECKLER, Charles, 52, un. carp., SP, *Grienberg/Gy, NYC-M – 1903/03/19:3d, 4a, 20:4a, fam. 25:4a

BOECKLER, George, 21, SLP, furnit.-maker, * Gruenberg/Hessen, USA 1872, , NYC-M - 1879/12/12:3a, 4a
BOECKMANN, Karl von, 32, painter, NYC-M - 1902/07/08:1f
BOEDDICHER, Dorothea, 64, NYC-M - 1891/03/25:4a
BOEGER, Florence, 3, NYC-B, +@ Genl Slocum - 1904/06/16:1c, 17:3b
BOEGER, Henry, NYC-M - 1914/08/01:6a
BOEGER, Louis, 28, un. typesetter, NYC-M - 1886/08/18:3c
BOEGER, Susan L., 32, NYC-B, +@Genl Slocum - 1904/06/22:1d
BOEGLE, Martin, un. carp., NYC-B - 1892/06/14:4a, 16:4a
BOEHLAU % Ufert
BOEHLE, Barbara, NYC-Q - 1904/08/16:4a
BOEHLER, Jonas, NYC-M - 1891/04/11:4a
BOEHLER, Josef, un. painter, NYC-M - 1916/01/07:6a
BOEHLERT, Henry, infant, NYC-B - 1901/07/04:1e
BOEHM % Greifen
BOEHM, Benjamin, 45, NYC-M - 1920/01/20:8a
BOEHM, Christian, 73, NYC-M - 1893/12/10:5a
BOEHM, Edward, 37, innkeep, NYC-M - 1886/05/13:4b, 12:4d, note 15 Nov 1887:2d
BOEHM, Ferdinand, 45, NYC-M - 1894/01/09:4a
BOEHM, Friedrich, 23, tailor, NYC-M - 1890/12/20:2f
BOEHM, George, un. beer driver, NYC-M - 1895/08/21:4a
BOEHM, Henry, 40, artist-painter, + Briarcliffe, NY - 1914/02/02:1f
BOEHM, Jacob, 36, clerk, NYC-B - 1905/02/15:3b
BOEHM, Jakob, 66, SLP, *Flensburg/Schleswig, NYC-M - 1891/09/28:4a,c, 29:4a, fam. 1 Oct:4a
BOEHM, Johann, un. upholsterer, NYC-M - 1892/03/09:4a, fam. 13:5a
BOEHM, Lizzie, 14, NYC-B - 1885/01/29:3d
BOEHM, Max, 60, un. brewer, Jersey City, NJ - 1914/10/04:7b
BOEHM, Otto, SP, un. bricklayer, NYC-M - 1918/09/02:6a
BOEHM, Robert, 40, painter, NYC-B - 1913/05/15:3a
BOEHM, Wilhelmine, b. Illge, 65, NYC-M - 1890/08/15:4a
BOEHME, Arthur, NYC-M - 1910/07/11:6a, 12:6a
BOEHME, Emil, 7, NYC-B - 1915/05/15:6a
BOEHME, Hermann, un. cigar maker, fr Braunschweig?/Gy, NYC-M - 1886/04/19:5f, =22:3b
BOEHMER % Boye
BOEHMER, Marie, 53, NYC-M - 1919/10/04:6a
BOEHNING, Julius, machinist, NYC-M - 1896/12/05:4a
BOEHNLEIN, Annie, 21, NYC-B - 1909/04/13:6a
BOEHRINGER, Albert, 43, SP, NYC-B - 1914/08/02:7c, fam. 6:6a, mem. 1915/07/31:6a, 1916/07/31:6a, 1917/07/31:6a

BOEHRINGER, Anna, 15, NYC-B - 1918/10/22:6a
BOEHRINGER, Emilie, 42, NYC-B - 1909/10/11:6a
BOEHS, Louis, un. brewery worker, NYC-M - 1894/07/27:4a
BOEKENMEIER, Margaretha, NYC-M - 1899/03/05:5a
BOEKER, Alma L., 2, NYC-M - 1882/04/08:3a
BOELINGER, Herman,43,fr Middletown,NY, NYC-M - 1915/12/10:3f
BOELKER % Bettinger
BOELKER, Charles, un. brewer, Jersey City, NJ - 1918/03/16:6a
BOELKER, Karl, NYC-M - 1906/05/11:4a
BOELL, August, 28, Jersey City Hgts, NJ - 1893/04/02:5a
BOELLER, Johannes, 62, NYC-M - 1893/12/29:4a
BOEMELBURG, Theodor, SPD Hamburg, ex-MdR - 1912/10/29:4d, 30:4e, =3 Nov:3a
BOENNER, Nathan, 12, NYC-B - 1893/12/27:2d
BOENNING, Heinrich, NYC-M - 1891/01/17:4a
BOER, Charles, un. baker, NYC-M - 1910/06/17:6a
BOERCHERT, Adolphe, 61, housepainter, USA 1846, NYC-M – 1878/05/22:4e (missing, probably dead)
BOERGER, Alois, un. carp., NYC-Bx - 1916/11/09:6a
BOERISCH, Adam, NYC-M - 1903/10/29:4a
BOERKE, William C., 44, NYC-B - 1895/02/12:4a
BOERNER, Helene, 24, NYC-M - 1881/10/24:3a
BOES, A., NYC-Q - 1910/01/21:6a
BOESCH, August, NYC-B - 1903/04/10:4a
BOESCH, Franz, 43, un. tailor, NYC-M - 1891/09/23:4a
BOESCH, Rudolf, NYC-M - 1891/06/13:4a
BOESCH, Wilhelm, 32, NYC-M - 1878/04/09:3b
BOESCHE, Heinrich, 73, NYC-Q, SP - 1914/02/24:6a
BOESCHER, Dorothea, b. Kugler, 65, NYC-M - 1891/03/23:4a
BOESE, Henry, 73, fr Elsass, NYC-M - 1897/01/02:1d
BOESICK, Annie, 25, fr Bohemia, NYC-M - 1901/08/22:1b
BOETJER, Henry, SP, NYC-M - 1918/02/26:6a
BOETSCH, Joseph, 70, NYC-B - 1917/05/29:3d
BOETTCHER % Nordbruch; % Wegener
BOETTCHER, August, 54, SPD Frankenhausen/Thueringia – 1910/07/31:3c
BOETTCHER, Dr., G-A journalist, NYC-M - 1883/09/16:4a
BOETTCHER, Friedrich, machinist, NYC-M - 1902/01/01:4a
BOETTCHER, Polychlaus, 71, saddlemaker, Newark, NJ - 1897/05/06:3c
BOETTCHER, Theodor, 68, NYC-Bx - 1919/05/30:6a
BOETTGER, John, broker, NYC-M - 1890/03/13:1g
BOETTGER, NYC-Q - 1909/02/17:6a

BOETTGER, Oswald, 56, machinist, SP, Elizabeth, NJ – 1911/02/28:6a, = 1 Mr:6a, fam. 4:6a
BOETTICHER, F., 74, Jersey City Heights, NJ – 1902/06/08:5f
BOETTICHER, Richard, 57, fr Pomerania, G-A journalist, a.e. NYSZ, NYC-Bx - 1913/11/12:2d, 6a
BOETTINGER, Charles, NYC-M – 1906/06/05:4a
BOETTKE, Gustav, 56, tailor, War 2, Elizabeth, NJ - 1917/06/13:1f
BOETZ, Charles William, 10, NYC-B – 1904/05/03:4a
BOETZKOW, Friederike, b. Bail, 75, NYC-B - 1896/03/02:3a
BOETZOW % Faust
BOGBY, John, Negro, lynched Palmetto, GA – 1899/03/17:2h
BOGDANOWITSCH, Juri, Russian revol., exec. for killing Alex II – 1883/04/24:2c-d
BOGEN, Elizabeth, 67, NYC-B – 1912/05/03:2d
BOGENHARD, Amelia, NYC-M, + @ Genl Slocum – 1904/06/17:3c
BOGENITZ, Friedrich, *1854, cigar maker & SPD activist expelled from Wandsbeck/Gy, arrived NYC – 1880/11/30:1d-e, 2 Dec:2a-b, 6:1d-e. SP, + New Haven, CT 8 Apr 1917:2d, 7a, fam. 15:7a
BOGERT, Benjamin, treasurer Mercantile Exchange, Hackensack, NJ – 1880/01/10:1e, =13:4a, 14:1e,2b
BOGGIANO, Nelson, Buffalo, NY, exec. Auburn, NY – 1904/12/14:3f
BOGGS, Walter D.C., 53, dem. alderman, NYC-M - 1878/02/04:1f
BOGLER, Andrew, NYC-M – 1902/04/15:1e
BOGNERD, E., 38, waiter, NYC-M – 1902/07/26:2h
BOGOSAVLEVIC, Adam, Serbian socialist, + in Serbian Jail – 1880/04/23:2d
BOGROFF, Dmitri, Russian revol. who killed Stolypin, exec. Kiew – 1911/09/26:1f
BOGUMIL, Helene, b. Flart, 49, NYC-M – 1902/03/14:4a
BOGUMIL, Hermann, 67, un. carp., NYC-M - 1917/11/28:6a, mem. 1918/11/26:6a, 1919/11/25:6a
BOGUSCHEWSKI, Karl, NYC-M – 1904/02/06:8a
BOHL, Louis' wife, un. cigarmaker, NYC-B – 1882/12/17:8b
BOHL, Therese, b Allmeyer, NYC-M – 1893/11/23:4a
BOHL, William, 20, driver, NYC-M – 1891/01/28:2g
BOHLE, August, NYC – 1887/01/26:1g, 27:1g, 28:1e, 31:1a-b, 2 Fb:2f. Trial of murderer 12 Fb:1g, 16:1e-f, 17:1e-f, 19:1c-d, rec. 20 yrs 22:4c
BOHLEBEN, John, 71, NYC-B – 1896/07/16:4b
BOHLEN, Katherina, 40, NYC-B – 1881/09/09:3c
BOHLER, Susan, 57, NYC-B – 1897/01/08:4b
BOHLERT, John, 59, NYC-Q – 1908/02/28:3b
BOHLES, Annie, 35, Newark, NJ – 1900/07/10:4b

BOHLINGER, Charles P., 56, machinist, NYC-M - 1920/04/15:4a
BOHLMANN, Herman, coal-dealer, NYC-M - 1881/08/07:4e
BOHLMANN, John E., NYC-B - 1902/07/04:4a
BOHLMANN, John, NYC-M - 1920/07/31:6a
BOHLMANN, Maria, 36, NYC-M - 1892/06/11:4a
BOHM, August, 40, NYC-B - 1907/11/15:3a
BOHM, Catherine, 83, NYC-Bx - 1918/03/28:6a
BOHM, Ernest, Jr., 23, NYC-Bx - 1907/02/03:7a
BOHM, Gertrude, 28, NYC-M - 1893/07/08:4a
BOHM, William, 50, NYC-B - 1917/12/20:3b
BOHN % Rauscher
BOHN, Anna, NYC-B - 1895/07/24:4a
BOHN, Edward, sailor, NYC-B, + New Haven, CT - 1915/03/16:6c
BOHN, Heinrich, 57, * Pinneberg/Holstein, USA 1873, furnit. Maker, SLP, NYC-B - 1890/01/13:1e,4a,14:4a
BOHN, Joseph, sailor, NYC-B, + New Haven, CT - 1915/03/16:6c
BOHN, Thomas, ~35, + Chicago, NYC-M - 1893/09/12:1d
BOHN, William, 33, un. waiter, NYC-M - 1897/04/16:4a
BOHNACKER, Louis, machinist, NYC-B - 1907/07/31:6a
BOHNE, Henry, 22, NYC-M - 1893/01/07:4a
BOHNE, Henry, tailor, NYC-B - 1878/09/16:1f
BOHNE, Meta, b. Gartelmann, 66, NYC-Bx - 1910/03/29:6a
BOHNEN, George K., 57, Central Org. un. Carp. & Joiners, NYC-M - 1912/09/11:2f
BOHNENBERGER, Karl, 40, Newark, NJ - 1914/09/02:2f
BOHNER, John, East St Louis, MO, worker, killed during strike - 1886/04/10:1b, =12:1a, 13:1e-f etc
BOHNHORST, H., NYC-M - 1905/03/08:4a
BOHNSOHN, Henry, 53, feed merchant, NYC-B - 1913/05/13:3b
BOHR % Herrmann
BOHR, Charles, 62, Jersey City, NJ - 1920/06/17:6a
BOHRME, Frederick, 65, killed during RR strike, St Louis, MO - 1900/06/11:1f
BOHYMANN, Christian, 38, @1900 dock fire, Hoboken, NJ 1900/07/03:1c
BOINAY, Charles A., exec. Hartford, CT - 1898/04/15:1e
BOIRKE, Caroline, b. Lieske, NYC-M - 1894/10/15:4a
BOISSIER % Schledorn
BOLAK, Michael, 35, exec. Belvidere, NJ - 1889/07/17:4e
BOLANDER, Michael, foreman,* Weissenburg/Elsass, NYC-M - 1879/07/25:1f, 29:1f
BOLD, Carl, 53, NYC-M - 1905/12/13:4a
BOLD, Theodor, 24, SLP Meriden, CT - 1899/09/08:3c

BOLDEMANN, Charles, 78, un. carp., NYC-B – 1911/05/15:6a
BOLDOGHY % Schufflay
BOLDT, Friedrich, 53, NYC-M – 1891/03/29:5a
BOLGER, Friedrich C. H., NYC-M – 1900/11/23:4a
BOLGHMANN, Christian, sailor, @1900 dock fire, Hoboken, NJ 1900/07/02:1g
BOLKE, Emil, 17, NYC-Q – 1899/01/04:4b
BOLKERT, Charles, 21, bookkeeper, NYC-B – 1909/02/27:2c
BOLL, Anna, 20, NYC-M - 1894/01/29:4a
BOLLAU, Rebecca, 58, NYC-M, + @ Genl Slocum – 1904/06/16:1c
BOLLE, Henry, NYC-M – 1883/10/01:1f
BOLLERMAN, Edward, 29, painter, W. Hoboken, NJ – 1899/09/28:4a
BOLLES, Elisabeth, NYC-M – 1881/06/03:3b
BOLLHOEFER, Simon, 29, SLP?, NYC-M – 1885/10/27:3a
BOLLIER, Albert, NYC-B – 1909/11/02:6a
BOLLIN, Klara, b. Mueller, NYC-M – 1904/01/17:5c
BOLLINGER, Bertha, 38, NYC-M – 1900/04/02:4a
BOLLINGER, Ferdinand, 38, traveling salesman, NYC-M – 1898/04/07:1c
BOLLINGER, John, 14, Newark, NJ – 1897/09/22:3d
BOLLMANN % Cramer
BOLLMANN, Ph., un. carp., NYC-M – 1907/02/13:6a
BOLLMEYER, Anton, un. cigarmaker, NYC-M – 1900/06/01:4a, 2:4a
BOLLSTEDTER, Clemens, 58, *Saulgau/Wuertt., Gy, NYC-M – 1902/10/28:4a
BOLLTEN % Huisberg
BOLLWEBER, Joseph, 48, boos-baker, in New Jersey – 1900/08/18:4a
BOLLWEBER, Samuel, 49, NYC-Q – 1912/07/24:6a
BOLLWEBER, Wendelin, un. carp., NYC-M - 1915/05/02:7e, 3:6a
BOLO PACHA, Paul, European patriot, secretly exec. in Paris 17 Apr 1917 for promoting a negotiated peace to end the senseless slaughter – 1918/04/18:1b, note 25 Oct 1919:1b
BOLSER, John, 23, carp., NYC-Q - 1915/01/18:2e
BOLSTEIN, Fanny, 49, NYC-B – 1910/01/21:3a
BOLT, Friedrich, 21, NYC-M – 1885/11/09:4c
BOLTE, Christopher, 56, driver, NYC-M – 1888/01/16:2e
BOLTEN, Jennie, b. Traub, NYC-B – 1892/07/12:4a
BOLTZ, Frederick, 60, NYC-M – 1880/06/25:4b
BOLTZ, Rose, b. Klotz, 73, NYC-B - 1916/09/26:6a
BOLZ, Anthony F., 54, NYPD, NYC-M - 1915/11/24:6c
BOLZ, Haennchen, 7, NYC-B – 1883/12/20:3a
BOMBIADI, Anna, 52, wife of August, un. machinist, NYC? - 1917/12/10:6a

BOMM, Ernest, 48, janitor, NYC – 1908/11/20:5e
BONAPARTE, Jerome, London? – 1891/03/19:4d
BONAPARTE, Susanna May, widow of Jerome Bonaparte, + Baltimore, MD – 1881/09/16:1b
BONAVENTURA, Eugene, NYC-M, +Michigan – 1902/08/30:4a
BONCELET, Peter, Hoboken, NJ – 1891/06/26:4a
BONEKAMP, Elisabeth, b. Schwarz, 51, NYC-M – 1892/07/29:4a
BONGART % Post
BONHAG, John, un. brewer, NYC-M – 1904/12/12:4a
BONHARD, Amalie, NYC-Bx - 1916/01/06:6a
BONHEIM, I, NYC-M – 1901/07/03:1d
BONHORST, Leonhard von, technician, early SPD activist, *Caub/Rhein, + 30/4/1915 Ravensburg - 1915/12/09:4e-f
BONIFACE, Louis, un. cigarmaker, NYC-M – 1882/03/18:3b
BONIG, Henry, NYC-Q – 1910/02/24:6a
BONKER, Jacob, RR worker, NYC-M – 1891/10/13:1h
BONNEFORD, Jean Noel, 71, fr Burgundy/France, cook, NYC-M – 1884/07/06:5e
BONNEL, Edmond, 75, French historian - 1915/10/20:2b
BONNER, William, textile worker, Bordentown, NJ - 1913/12/20:2e
BONNOT, French anarchist, + Paris – 1912/04/29:1a
BONSEL, Engelbert, 65, SP, un. carp., * Westfalia, USA 1880, NYC-Q - 1915/08/03:2f,6a, 4:6a
BONSKY, Hugo, riding teacher, NYC-M – 1891/10/19:4e
BONTOUX, Eugene, French speculator in RR stocks, + Cannes – 1904/06/03:2h
BONWITSCH, Fritz, un. baker, NYC-M – 1899/04/13:4a
BOOK, Johannes, SLP, un. cigarmaker in NYC-M, *Schleswig/Gy, +Rowlands,PA - 1894/09/14:1b,4a
BOOKBINDER, John, sailor on USS Maine, + Havana/Cuba, NYC-B – 1898/02/18:1b
BOOKSTAEVER, Otto, 9, NYC-M – 1896/12/06:1h
BOOLE, Emily R., 30, teacher, NYC- - 1918/07/08:6a
BOORMANN, Anna, b. Dunkel, 26, NYC-M – 1891/04/05:5a
BOOS, John, Yonkers, NY – 1909/08/14:6a
BOOS, Philip, 45, NYC-M - 1879/11/03:3g
BOOTH, William, Salvation Army fdr, crit. Obit – 1912/08/22:4a-b
BOOTHE, Theodore, Negro, lynched Allentown, GA – 1901/11/06:3h
BOOTH-TUCKER, Emma, head of US branch Salvation Army – 1903/10/30:1e
BOPP, Charles, 56, bookkeeper at Ehret brewery, NYC-M – 1881/10/15:1e
BOPP, Frederick, 34, NYC-M – 1892/10/25:4a

BOPP, Friedrich, NYC-Bx – 1910/07/28:6a
BOPP, Philip, 19, NYC-B – 1897/07/09:4b
BOPPE, G. Hermann, 57, editor of Freidenker & N.-A. Turnerzeitung, *Wettingen/Switz., USA 1861, + Milwaukee 1899/01/14:2h
BORCHARDT, Albert, 43, NYC-B – 1892/07/08:4
BORCHARDT, George, 27, machinist, Jersey City, NJ – 1904/03/23:4a
BORCHER, William, 32, NYC-B – 1890/11/17:2f
BORCKEL, George, 76, polierer, NYC-B - 1914/02/09:2d
BORDAS, Madame, French polit. chanteuse, + Algiers – 1901/06/28:3h
BORDEN, A.J., Falls River, MA (Lizzie Borden case) – 1892/08/07:1c, 12:1b, etc, 14:1g, 31:1e. Trial 9 June 1893:1b, 10:1f, 12:1b, 13:1b, 14:1b, 15:1b, 16:1h, 17:1d, 20:1c-d, 21:1d-e,
BORDEN, Ella, 43, NYC-B, +@Genl Slocum – 1904/06/23:1b
BORDOLLO, Caecilie, b. Buesch, NYC-M – 1889/06/05:4a
BORDOLLO, Julius, 65, SP, former business mgr of NYVZ, NYC-M - 1917/11/09:2c,6a
BORDOLLO, Lina, NYC-M - 1916/07/14:6a
BORDSMANN, Hermann Georg, 42, NYC-B – 1891/09/19:4a
BOREL, Louis, 26, Swiss, waiter, NYC-M – 1886/01/07:1f
BORG, Charles, 53, un. machinist, NYC-M – 1910/08/11:6a
BORG, Dietrich, un. carp., NYC-M – 1911/05/23:6a
BORG, Emma, 26, NYC-M – 1910/03/21:6a
BORGAS % Hildebrandt
BORGEMANN, Carl, 44, NYC-M – 1882/07/28:4d
BORGER, Friedrich, 8, NYC-M – 1883/03/13:1d
BORGMANN, Anton H., NYC-M – 1892/12/19:4a, 20:4a
BORHEK, Christian, un. carpenter, NYC-Q - 1918/06/14:6a
BORKES % Fritz
BORLAND, Clara, 21, NYC-M – 1906/08/01:6b
BORLE, Adolph E., 71, navy secy under Grant – 1880/02/06:1c
BORLE, Frederick, & Albert, & Charles Jr, Camden, NJ – 1887/03/14:2e-f
BORM, Eduard, NYC-M – 1882/01/24:3c
BORMANN, Mathilde, 3, NYC-M – 1881/01/07:3c
BORN, Emil, 61, un. cigarmaker, NYC-M - 1918/02/12:6a
BORN, Friedericka, 56, NYC-Bx – 1906/01/21:5b
BORN, George, un. cigarmaker, NYC-Q – 1912/11/06:6a
BORN, William, NYC-M – 1888/07/23:3c
BORNAUD, Louis, 52, music instrument maker, & wife, Linden, NJ – 1904/09/25:1h
BORNBERGER, George, 48, SDP, un. cigarmaker, USA 1878,
 * Wuerzburg/Gy, Detroit, MI – 1904/12/06:1d

BORNEMANN, Frederick, 78, singer & conductor for singing societies, NYC – 1911/12/28:6c
BORNEMANN, Friedrich, NYC-B – 1891/04/07:4a, 8:4a
BORNEMANN, Gustav, 53, NYC-Q - 1917/05/09:2b
BORNGESSER % Hoppel
BORNGESSER, Heinrich, un. cigar maker, NYC-M – 1880/06/11:4e
BORNGRAEBER, Otto, 42, poet, + Lugano/CH - 1916/11/19:6c-d
BORNHECK % Raab
BORNHORST, John, 48, NYC-B – 1891/02/27:4a
BORNKESSEL, Martin, 52, cigar packer, NYC-M – 1890/07/24:2e
BORNSCHEUER, Fritz, 11, NYC-M – 1886/07/27:3b
BORNSCHEUER, Karl, un. brass worker, NYC-M – 1890/03/30:5b, 31:4a
BORODOW, David Ber, 36, Zionist leader, + St Petersburg/Russia - 1917/12/21:2e
BOROWSKY, August, 59, NYC-M – 1891/08/08:4a
BOROWSKY, Marie, 53, NYC-M – 1909/06/10:6a
BORRHEIMER, Frederick, 11, NYC-M, +@Genl Slocum – 1904/06/17:3b
BORRIES, Hermann, NYC-Bx – 1913/03/22:6a
BORRS, Charlotte, b. Loose, 62, NYC-M - 1914/05/04:6a
BORST, Adam J., NYC-B – 1893/08/27:5a
BORST, Charles, superintendent, NYC-M? – 1890/08/25:4a
BORST, Emilie, 4 mo., NYC-M – 1890/02/22:1f
BORTH, Christian, 24, NYC-M – 1889/07/30:4a
BORTOLICIUS, Paul, NYC, fam. 1904/06/12:5b
BORZIK, Valentine, 57, laundry owner, NYC-B – 1909/11/26:3a
BOSACH, Joseph, infant, NYC-M – 1900/05/28:1d
BOSCH, Anna, b. Overson, 42, NYC-M – 1891/02/10:4a
BOSCH, Dorette, 21, NYC-M – 1892/06/23:4a
BOSCH, Henry, mason, Hoboken, NJ – 1881/05/14:1e
BOSCH, John H., 70, grocer, Newark, NJ - 1918/02/05:2a
BOSCH, Mary, 29, stenorapher, NYC-M – 1896/09/02:1f
BOSCHAU, Ida, NYC-M – 1889/01/07:3c
BOSCHE, Frances, 41, NYC-M – 1892/06/23:4a
BOSCHEITER, Jennie, 19, worker, murd. by 4 middle-class boys, Paterson, NJ – 1900/10/20:1h, 21:1h, 23:1h, 24:1f-g, 25:1c, 2a-b, 26:1f-g, 27:1f-g, 28:1f-g, 29:1h, 30:3e, 31:2b, 1 Nov:1d, 7:4b, 12:1b, 13:1g, 17:1c, 22:4b, 23:4e, trial 2 Jan 1901:4a, 8:3b, 9:3b, 14:1e, 15:1f-g, 16:1c-d, 17:1c-d, 18:1f-g, 19:1c-e, fd guilty but get 30 yrs only, if working class boys had done this to a middle-class lady, they'd hang 20:4a-b, 30:1f-g, 31:1g, 2 Fb:1h, 3d, Notes 27 Apr 1902:5g
BOSCHEN, Maria A., NYC-B – 1891/04/11:4a
BOSCHENS, Henry, un. cigar maker, NYC-B – 1886/01/15:2g

BOSCHERT, George, un. typesetter, NYC-M – 1896/11/15:5a
BOSCHIETER, Jennie, see Boscheiter
BOSCHWINEN, Frank, 48, tailor, * Duesseldorf/Gy, Mt Vernon, NY - 1917/11/20:2d
BOSE, Emily, 19, NYC-M, +@Genl Slocum – 1904/06/22:1d
BOSS, Angus, 45, NYC?, + Del Norte, CO – 1883/03/04:8a
BOSS, Carl, 52, un. carp., NYC-M – 1886/10/30:2g, fam. 3 Nov:3c
BOSS, Frederick, 35, brewer, NYC-B - 1915/02/13:6a
BOSS, Helene, NYC-B – 1892/01/24:4a
BOSS, Hermine, b. Boehmer, Carlstadt, NJ – 1883/08/14:3c
BOSS, Louis, 25, NYC-B – 1902/01/01:1c
BOSSARD, Anna, 67, Swiss, NYC-M - 1895/05/15:1g
BOSSE % Bading
BOSSE, Emil, 28, painter, * 13 IV 1864, fr France, NYC-M – 1892/05/27:1e
BOSSE, Henry, 42, NYC-B – 1911/07/14:2c
BOSSE, Rudolf, un. carp., NYC-M – 1909/03/27:6a, fam. 30:6a
BOSSEIR, Barbara, b. Leopold, Hartford, CT – 1891/03/09:4a
BOSSELER % Bauer
BOSSELMANN, Charles, 54, NYC-B - 1913/09/07:7c, 8:6a
BOSSELMANN, Karl, 7, NYC-B – 1898/06/01:4a
BOSSENZ, Will, NYC-M – 1907/01/30:6a
BOSSERT, Andrew, 41, painter, NYC-B – 1898/03/30:1g
BOSSERT, Friedrich, NYC-Metropolitan – 1907/06/01:6a
BOSSERT, George, un. carp., NYC-M – 1897/03/09:4a
BOSSERT, Henry, 22, athlete, Paterson, NJ - 1913/08/16:6c
BOSSERT, Jacob, un. carp., NYC-M – 1903/11/14:4b, 15:5a
BOSSERT, Jennie, 53, landlady, NYC-M - 1895/10/18: 1g
BOSSERT, Louis, lumbermill owner, NYC, + San Fransisco, crit. obit – 1913/01/31:3e, 15 Fb:3d
BOSSHAMMER, August, 58, *Kassel/Hessen, USA as young man, SP, NYC?, + Guanajuato/Mex. – 1907/10/22:6d
BOSSHARD, John, 42, NYC-B – 1901/09/12:4a
BOSSLER, Charles, 7, NYC-M – 1899/02/26:5f
BOSSNECKER, William, baker, Trenton, NJ – 1896/05/01:2o
BOSTACK, Frank, animal trainer in Coney Island, NYC, + Boston, MA – 1912/10/09:5e
BOSTEL, Louis, Elizabeth, NJ – 1906/12/02:7c
BOSTELMANN, William E., 45, clerk, NYC-M - 1914/11/22:11e
BOTH, E., Dr., + Niagara, NY – 1881/07/23:4d
BOTH, John, 57, SP, un. brewer, * Vorarlberg prov./AU, US late 1880s, Union Hill, NJ - 1915/12/04:6a, 5:7d, =6:6b, family 13:6a

BOTHUR, Elizabeth, NYC-M - 1920/03/24:6a
BOTT, August, Union Hill, NJ – 1901/07/04:3b
BOTT, John, NYC? – 1888/12/15:3c
BOTTENMEIER, John, NYC-B - 1918/02/11:6a
BOTZER, Moritz, 25, worker, NYC-B? - 1913/08/02:3d
BOTZUM, H., NYC-M – 1889/03/29:4a
BOUBAL, Matthaeus, NYC-Q - 1915/06/03:6a
BOUCHEAUX, Reinhard, 52, SP, NYC-M – 1913/02/14:6a, 15:6a, 16:7c, fam. 23:7b
BOUCHER, William H., journalist fr Social Economist, NYC-M – 1892/05/20:1f
BOUCICAULT, Aristide 67, fdr Bon Marche Dept. Store, + Paris/France - 1878/02/07:3f
BOUDIN, Leah, SP, NYC-B, + Liberty, NY – 1906/12/19:2b
BOUHEY-ALEX, comrade, 58, French Soc. Deputy - 1913/08/18:4d
BOUR, Joseph, 74, NYC-M – 1891/04/05:5a
BOURBAKI, French general – 1897/09/23:1a
BOURBONUS, Philipp, 33, NYC-M – 1880/02/29:5g
BOURESSI, Frank, mover, fr Elsass, NYC-M - 1896/01/14:1g
BOURSEUIL, M. French telephone pioneer - 1913/07/22:2e
BOUVERAT, Louise, 54, NYC-M - 1879/05/29:1g,30:4a
BOUVIER, Leopold, 48, patent agent & inventer, * Guadeloupe/Caribbean, NYC-M – 1881/12/21:4c
BOVEGEL % Schreiber
BOY, Reinhold, NYC-M – 1905/02/04:4a
BOYCOTT, Capt., for whom "boycott" was coined, + Ireland – 1897/06/25:2c
BOYD, Willis, Negro, lynched near Silver City, GA – 1899/03/24:1d, 25:1c
BOYE, Anna, b. Wrocklage, 33, NYC-M – 1882/06/07:3b
BOYER, August, 64, un. music instr. Maker, Swiss?, Jersey City Heights, NJ – 1911/07/11:6a
BOYESON, Thomas, 46, steam fitter, NYC-M - 1895/05/03:1g
BOYLAN, Viola, 8, NYC-M – 1907/06/28:1e
BOYLI, John, 62, SP, NYC-M – 1913/04/01:6a, 2:6a
BOYSON, Charles, NYC-B – 1910/09/12:6a
BOYSON, Johann, 28, sailor, on ship "Otto", NYC-M – 1897/10/13:3f
BOZOGANY % Andrassy
BRAASCH, Heinrich, 70, NYC-M – 1893/04/26:4a
BRAAZ, Katherina, b. Tromerhausen, 43, NYC-M – 1890/10/19:5b, 21:4a
BRACH, John, NYC-Q - 1916/12/11:6a
BRACHT, Bernard, 66, NYC-M – 1887/02/04:3d
BRACHVOGEL, Julius, NYC-M – 1892/04/18:4a

BRACHVOGEL, Udo, writer & journalist for G-A media, *26 Sp 1835 Herren-Greben/Danzig, USA 1867, NYC-M – 1913/01/31:2d, 1 F:4c
BRACKE, Wilhelm, 38, + Braunschweig/Gy, SPD MdR – 1880/03/26:2c, =17 Apr:1b, 2a-b, 18:2d
BRADFORD, Allan, NYC-M, exec. Ossining, NY - 1916/08/05:5f
BRADLAUGH, Charles, 68, British liberal MP – 1891/01/31:2b-c
BRADLEY, Eduard, 35, NYC-Bx - 1917/07/31:6a
BRADT, Ch., 24, Jersey City, NJ – 1909/02/19:6a
BRADY, Anthony N., Albany millionaire, crit. obit. - 1913/08/07:4d
BRADY, Edward, member Freiheit GV, NYC-M – 1903/04/04:4a
BRADY, Joseph, Irish patriot, exec. Dublin for Phoenix Park attack – 1883/05/15:1a
BRAEKLE, R., un. cornicemaker, NYC-M – 1898/01/17:4a
BRAENDLE, Wendelin, 32, NYC-B – 1892/07/31:5c
BRAEUER, W., NYC-M – 1893/05/14:5b
BRAEUNERT, Julius, NYC-M – 1906/11/10:6a
BRAEUNLICH, Anna M., 46, NYC-B - 1894/01/15:4a
BRAEUNLICH, Gustav, NYC-M - 1894/10/16:4a
BRAEUNLICH, Richard, NYC-M – 1902/09/08:4a
BRAEUTIGAM % Meyer
BRAEUTIGAM, Mrs, 25, NYC-M - 1895/05/21:4a
BRAEUTIGAM, W.H., NYC-B - 1896/02/04:4a
BRAHMS, Albert de, 32, fr France, conductor, & wife Pauline, 25, NYC-M – 1912/04/30:1f
BRAITLING % Sievers
BRAKE, Mary, 25, NYC-M, +@ Genl Slocum – 1904/06/18:3b
BRAKEN, H. John, businessman, NYC-B – 1888/02/28:2c
BRAMAN, Hedwig, 3, NYC-M - 1887/12/23:3a
BRAMANN, Arthur, 25, NYC-M – 1897/10/10:5a, 12:4a
BRAMANN, Carl, fr Berlin, upholsterer, SLP, NYC-M – 1885/11/26:4a, 28:4a, =30:1g
BRAMANN, Karl, 33, un. typesetter & SPD activist expelled from Berlin/Gy, arrived NYC – 1880/11/30:1d-e, 2 Dec:2a-b, 6:1d-e
BRAMBORA, Charles, 18, NYC-B – 1902/10/06:4a
BRAMBORA, John, NYC-B – 1920/09/01:6a, 2:6a
BRAMBORA, Maria, NYC-M – 1889/01/04:3c
BRAND % Reber
BRAND, Adam, un. carp., NYC-B – 1890/05/06:4a
BRAND, Caecilia, b. Scheidel, 64, NYC-B – 1892/07/28:4a
BRAND, Heinrich, SPD Hamburg-Pinneberg - 1913/06/15:3c
BRAND, Henry, 38, Bavarian?, NYC-B – 1911/09/28:6a
BRAND, Robert, NYC-B – fam. 1882/05/06:3c

BRANDAUER, Frederick. Charles, German-British millionaire, + interned Douglas/Isle of Man - 1918/04/30:2d
BRANDENBERG, Werner, 29, druggist, NYC-Lexington Ave - 1916/04/02:1f
BRANDENBERGER, Lizzie, NYC-Q - 1887/07/28:3a
BRANDENBURG, Henry, hotel in Palissades Park,NJ - 1914/01/14:2e
BRANDENBURG, Paul, NYC-M - 1901/06/12:4a
BRANDENBURG, T. E. B., druggist, NYC-SI - 1902/02/14:3a
BRANDENBURG, Wilhelmine L., 4, NYC-B - 1890/05/16:4a
BRANDENKAUFER, Frederick, waiter, 27, NYC-Q - 1907/10/11:3b
BRANDENSTEIN, Sarah, 47, wife of Rabbi G. Brandenstein, NYC-B - 1878/04/07:8b
BRANDES % Gasler, Wyssmann
BRANDES, Charles A., 27, NYC-M - 1899/01/19:1g
BRANDES, Christian, 18, NYC-M - 1891/03/30:4a
BRANDES, Doris, b. Rohwelt, 19, NYC-M - 1891/03/11:4a
BRANDES, Georg, 36, fr Hannover, NYC-B - 1892/07/15:4a
BRANDES, Johanna, 55, NYC-M - 1892/04/02:4a
BRANDES, Louise, 16, Union Hill, NJ - 1892/04/17:5c
BRANDHOFF % Fechner
BRANDIS, Anna Hedwig, 10 months, NYC-M - 1878/05/25:3b
BRANDLOS, Fannie, 79, NYC-M - 1891/03/19:4a
BRANDMEIER, Agnes, b. Hummel, 45, NYC-Q - 1914/12/21:6a
BRANDORFF, Henrietta, 17, servant, NYC-M - 1881/02/13:5f
BRANDRETH, Benjamin, Dr., nostrum manuf. Ossining, NY, decent employer - 1880/02/24:4a, 27:1f
BRANDT % Mueller, % Tank
BRANDT, A.A., 30, NYC-M - 1894/07/18:4a
BRANDT, Anton, NYC-B - 1909/08/01:7b
BRANDT, Charles, Newark, NJ - 1898/09/06:1d
BRANDT, Daniel R., 65, haberdasher, NYC-B - 1889/09/23:1h
BRANDT, Emil, US Army, + Hongkong/China - 1898/05/26:3g
BRANDT, Ferdinand, West New York, NJ - 1920/08/30:12a
BRANDT, Friedrich, 45, astrologer, NYC-M - 1904/11/2h,c
BRANDT, Friedrich, un. carp., NYC-M - 1910/11/29:6a
BRANDT, Fritz, 61, un. bricklayer, NYC-Q - 1900/05/26:4b-c, 27:5a
BRANDT, George, NYC-M - 1911/04/05:6a, mem. 1912/04/04:6a
BRANDT, Gustav, NYC-M - 1881/05/17:3c
BRANDT, Gustav, NYC-M - 1904/04/17:5b
BRANDT, Henry, 24, Hoboken, NJ - 1887/09/07:4e
BRANDT, Henry, plumber, NYC-M - 1888/02/15:4d
BRANDT, Israel, exec. Lebanon, PA - 1880/05/14:1b

BRANDT, John, or Jonas, 69, pianomaker, NYC-Bx – 1911/07/15:1d, 6a
BRANDT, Julius, construction worker, NYC-M – 1891/04/15:4d
BRANDT, Kaethe, actress, NYC, to be = in Gy – 1902/01/18:3b
BRANDT, Kaethe, b. Schmidt, 32, NYC-Bx – 1906/05/14:4a
BRANDT, Margareth, b. Klees, 44, NYC-M – 1888/07/06:4f
BRANDT, Mary, 25, NYC-M – 1902/06/28:3c
BRANDT, Oskar, NYC-M – 1891/07/23:4a
BRANDT, Peter, NYC-B – 1901/07/04:1c
BRANDT, Vance, 18, & Julia, 15, Negroes, lynched Clarendon County, S.C. – 1880/12/12:5b, 16:2c
BRANDT, William, 69, SLP, restaurant & bartender NY Labor Lyceum, * Celle/Hannover, NYC-M – 1896/10/10:1h,4a, 11;5a, =12:1d, fam. 12:4a
BRANKE, Fritz, 51, NYC-M – 1900/12/30:1e
BRANNIGAN, Mary, + by @Aaron Halle, NYC – 1900/05/18:1h, 19:3c
BRANSCOMBE, Walter, Jersey City Hgts, NJ, + Great Lakes Navy Station, IL - 1918/11/27:6a
BRANT, Mary, servant, fr Galicia, War 2, NYC-B - 1915/06/30:6c
BRASCH, Frederick, NYC-M – 1913/02/23:7b
BRASCH, Heinrich, un. cigarmaker, NYC-M – 1903/10/16:4a
BRASSEL, William, NYC-Q – 1906/01/07:5b
BRATFISCH, Emil, fam. – 1893/10/22:5a
BRATSCH, Charles, 50, gardener, MT Vernon, NY – 1899/06/10:1c
BRATSCH, Frieda, geb. Held, + 1918, mem. 1919/10/21:6a, 1920/10/21:6a
BRAUCH, Maria, geb. Dick, NYC-B – 1892/07/20:4a
BRAUCKE, Gabriel, NYC-M, + @ Genl Slocum – 1904/06/18:3b
BRAUER, August, 62, un. cigarmaker, NYC 1881-1897, SP, + Hamburg/Gy – 1908/01/31:2e
BRAUER, Margarethe, 33, NYC-M, +@Genl Slocum – 1904/06/23:1b
BRAUER, Willie, 16, Greenbush, NY – 1883/08/23:3c
BRAUMAN, Rebecca, 35, & children, NYC-B – 1912/02/24:3a
BRAUN % Eisleben, % Lowitz, % Mueller, % Schmidt, % Treber
BRAUN, J., 43, NYC-B – 1893/08/27:5a
BRAUN, Adam, brewer, NYC-M – 1900/04/12:4a
BRAUN, Adrian, to hang 1898/06/24:1g, exec. Ossining, NY – 1899/05/28:1c, done 30:3g
BRAUN, Alfred C., 44, NYC-M – 1893/01/24:4a
BRAUN, Alphonse, 13, NYC-M, +@Genl Slocum – 1904/06/25:1d
BRAUN, August, ~45, peddler, NYC-B – 1903/05/16:3c
BRAUN, Catherina, 81, NYC-M – 1891/02/27:4a
BRAUN, Catherina, b. Seidler, 30, NYC-M – 1892/06/15:4a
BRAUN, Charles, smith, NYC-M – 1891/12/02:1g
BRAUN, Charles, un. carp., NYC-Q? – 1889/11/09:4a

BRAUN, Christian, USA 4/1880, carpenter, NYC-B – 1880/05/11:1d
BRAUN, Emma, to USA bef. 1860 fr Gy, NYC-M – 1900/11/24:1d
BRAUN, Frederick, NYC-B - 1916/06/22:6a
BRAUN, Fritz, 35, un. typesetter, NYC-B – 1893/05/03:4a
BRAUN, Georg, West Newark, NJ - 1916/10/15:7a
BRAUN, Henry, 9, NYC-B - 1878/09/26:3c
BRAUN, Henry, Jersey City Heights, NJ – 1912/11/01:6a
BRAUN, Jakob, un. carp., NYC-M – 1901/06/04:4a
BRAUN, John, 20, worker at Doelger's Brewery, NYC-M – 1881/01/07:1a, =8:1e-f, notes 9:5f, 10:2a-b, 4e, inquest 8 Fb:1f, 9:1e-f, 10:1e-f
BRAUN, John, un. brewer, NYC-M – 1907/11/15:6a
BRAUN, Joseph, 45, NYC-B – 1911/07/29:3a
BRAUN, K., Newark, NJ - 1913/10/02:6a
BRAUN, Karl, 73, NYC-Bx – 1892/03/28:4e
BRAUN, Katherine, NYC-B – 1898/03/06:1d, 7:1d-e, 8:3g
BRAUN, Lilly, wife of German SPD leader Heinrich Braun - 1916/08/11:4d
BRAUN, Louis, 39, un. iron molder, NYC-B – 1908/06/17:6a, 18:6a, Mem. 1909/06/16:6a, 1910/06/16:6a, 1911/06/16:6a, 1912/06/17:6a
BRAUN, Louis, 41, No. Bergen, NJ - 1914/05/21:6a
BRAUN, Louis, 44, cigar maker, NYC-M – 1886/05/25:3a
BRAUN, Magdalena, 73, Jersey City, NJ - 1913/05/20:6d
BRAUN, Margarethe, 33, NYC-B - 1894/01/21:5d
BRAUN, Martin, 56, laborer, fr Austria, NYC-M – 1891/04/07:1f
BRAUN, Morris, secy cigarmakers' union, local 144, NYC-M, - 1920/05/14:2c
BRAUN, Richard, 70, brewer, Cincinatti, OH - 1918/08/12;1b
BRAUN, Walter, 6, Elise, 9, NYC-M, +@Genl Slocum – 1904/06/23:1b
BRAUN, Werner, 61, grocer, NYC-M - 1878/08/04:8b
BRAUN, Wilhelm, 55, ex-navy captain, NYC-M – 1900/08/13:1b
BRAUN, William, cooper, NYC-M - 1913/07/19:6a
BRAUN, Willie, 3, NYC-M – 1897/08/22:11f
BRAUNE, Bodo, 55, SP, exile in Paris bef. coming to US, NYC-M - 1918/01/19:6a, = 22:3e
BRAUNE, Max Paschky, 2, NYC-M - 1894/01/13:5c
BRAUNE, Minnie, 52, NYC-M – 1911/04/12:6a
BRAUNING, Ludwig, West New York, NJ - 1919/03/26:6a
BRAUNLEDER, Sigismund, 57, who + 10 Jy, NYC-B – 1907/09/17:3a
BRAUNSCHWEIG, Duke of, – 1884/10/22:1a, 23:1a, 26:1a, etc
BRAUNSCHWEIGER, Samuel, 25, traveling salesman, NYC-M – 1898/05/12:3d
BRAUNSTEIN, Ernst, 31, un. furrier, NYC-M – 1897/02/01:4a

BRAUNSTEIN, Samuel, paperhanger, NYC-M – 1899/01/22:5g
BRAUNWART, David, NYC-M – 1909/04/19:6a
BRAUT, Mathias, NYC-B – 1910/09/28:6a
BRAUTSCHECK, Leopold, NYC-B – 1900/04/20:4a
BREBCER, John, NYC-M - 1914/06/09:6a, 10:6a
BRECHENMACHER, Andreas, NYC-M – 1912/07/13:6a
BRECHINSKI, Tillie, 20, servant, fr Austria, War 2, Newark, NJ - 1914/10/23:2f
BRECHT, Felix, 59, NYC-B – 1906/07/03:6a
BRECHT, Margareth, 8, NYC-M, + @1883 Manhattan School Fire.
BRECHTEL, Philipp, NYC-M – 1907/07/06:6a
BRECHTER, Heinrich, NYC-M – 1882/04/02:8a
BRECKA, John, West Newark, NJ - 1917/09/08:6a
BRECKER, Tillie, 11, NYC-M - 1916/10/11:2d
BRECKOW, Aurelia, 35, NYC-B - 1919/07/12:2c
BREDE, Georg, 21, NYC-M – 1893/05/04:4a
BREDEHORST, Anna Margarethe, b. Piate?, 27, NYC-M – 1882/05/23:3b
BREDEN, Ida, 49, NYC-B – 1909/03/10:2d
BREDER, Bernhard, 60, rental stable owner, NYC-B – 1880/04/06:1e
BREDERHOFT, John, ?54, NYC-M – 1890/10/18:4a
BREDOW, Hugo, NYC-B - 1913/06/18:6a
BREEN, James, 23, NYC, exec. Ossining, NY – 1905/07/18:1e
BREGENZER, Barbara, 8, NYC-M, + @1883 Manhattan School Fire
BREHM, Johann Franz, un. carpenter, NYC-M - 1895/10/19: 4a
BREHMER, Hermann, Dr., 1826-89, TB-specialist, '48er & SPD in Goerbersdorf/ Silesia/Gy, grave monument 1908/02/09:3d, memory 15 Apr 1908:4f-g
BREHMER, Julius, 54, un. bricklayer, *Breslau/Silesia,NYC-M - 1913/08/30:6a, 31:7b, = 1 Sept:8d, fam. 2:6a
BREHMEYER, Heinrich, 73, SP, USA mid-1880s, silkworker, Princeton, NJ - 1916/01/12:3g,6a
BREIDENBACH, Conrad, 65, NYC-M - 1894/01/18:4a
BREIDENBACH, John, 48, NYC-Q – 1912/02/12:6a
BREIMAIER, John, un. brewer, NYC-Q – 1912/02/17:6a
BREIMANN, Frederick Emil, 30, * Breunsdorf/Gy, NYC-M – 1880/05/27:1e
BREIMANN, Johanna, b. Behnke, 25, NYC-M – 1880/05/23:5d-e, 24:1g
BREIMEIER, Anton, un. brewer, 32?, fr Angelfingen/Wuertt., NYC-M – 1891/06/07:5a
BREINOESSE, Anton, un. butcher, Jersey City Heights, NJ – 1909/02/26:6a, 27:6a
BREISER, George, 58, restaurant, NYC – 1911/10/02:2c, 3:2f

BREITAG, Mathilde see Freitag, Mathilde
BREITE, August, 76, SP, glasmaker, ex-NYC, San Francisco, CA – 1915/04/12:6a
BREITENBACH, Charles, Hoboken, NJ – 1911/10/17:6a
BREITENFELD, Oscar, clockmaker, fr Rumania, War 2, NYC-B – 1915/01/09:2e
BREITENSTEIN, Augusta, b. Schlem, 28, *Bremen/Gy, NYC-M – 1895/04/12:3b
BREITENSTEIN, Frank, NYC-Bx – 1911/08/29:6a
BREITHACK, Elise, b. Willfarth, NYC-B – 1907/03/30:6a
BREITHAUPT, Lena, servant, NYC-M – 1882/12/12:1f
BREITHAUPT, Philip, 30, printer, NYC-Ditmars St (B?) - 1916/11/19:11e
BREITKOPF, Wilhelm, 66, worker, & Marie, 71, NYC-M – 1891/05/29:2h
BREITNER, Charles, 27, NYC-M – 1891/08/27:1d
BREITSAMER, Anton, 35, NYC-M - 1916/07/20:6a
BREITUNG, Amand, 27, un. typesetter, NYC-M – 1883/08/03:3c
BREITWIESER, Eliza, 44, NYC-M - 1894/01/21:5d
BREIWISCH, Anna, 51, NYC-SI - 1918/01/04:2c
BRELLENTHIN, William, NYC-B – 1908/03/11:6a
BRELLENTHINE, Marie, 60, NYC-B – 1897/08/15:5a
BRELLER, Karl, 54, publ. Freie Presse, Atlantic City, NJ – 1908/09/28:1d
BREMEN, Ida, 19, seamstress, + during strike, Rochester, NY – 1913/02/07:2b
BREMER, Carolina, 11, Verona, NJ – 1900/08/25:1g
BREMER, Friedrich, 51, Union Hill, NJ - 1917/06/06:6a, fam. 9:6a
BREMER, William, 47, *Seesen/Gy, fdr of Bremerton, WA – 1911/01/09:2f
BREMERMANN, August William, innkeep, NYC- M - 1878/08/27:4d, 28:4e, 09/10:4a
BREMMER, A. W., NYC-M – 1897/08/08:1e
BREMMER, John, '48er, USA 1849, publ. of Freischuetz, SLP?, innkeep, NYC? – 1896/12/02:1d
BREMMER, Phillip, SP, NYC-M – 1908/07/08:6a
BRENDEKE % Moltmann
BRENDEL, August, NYC-M – 1911/08/06:7a
BRENDEL, Edward, 41, Newark, NJ - 1916/07/07:6a
BRENDEL, Franz, 71, NYC-B - 1919/07/12:6a, 14:6a
BRENDEL, John, un. carp., NYC – 1912/04/05:6a
BRENDEL, John, un. carp., NYC-M – 1900/03/25:5a
BRENDEL, John, West New York, NJ - 1914/06/19:6a
BRENDEL, M., Mrs, NYC-M – 1919/10/15:6a
BRENDEL, Rose, 68, NYC-B - 1913/07/14:6a

BRENDLIN, Georg, infant, NYC-M – 1893/09/15:4a
BRENFLECK, Emma, 17, NYC-M - 1918/11/01:6a
BRENFLECK, M., NYC-M - 1918/11/14:6a
BRENGEL, Daniel, un. carp., NYC-Q – 1910/10/29:6a
BRENNAN, Philip, ex-fire comm. & local polit., NYC-B – 1888/03/02:4c
BRENNECKE, Anna, b. Schroeder, 42, NYC-M – 1904/10/20:4a
BRENNECKE, Robert, cigarmaker, New Haven, CT – 1909/09/12:7c
BRENNER, Adam, Newark, NJ - 1916/01/02:11f
BRENNER, Adolph, 22, pen maker, NYC-B - 1894/08/02:4a
BRENNER, Joseph, 58, NYC-M - 1894/01/27:4a
BRENNER, Richard, SPD Braunschweig/Gy, edit. at local Volksfreund, War I - 1914/10/31:4d
BRENNER, Simon, 78, ret. Haberdasher, USA 1854, NYC-M – 1898/09/07:4b
BRENNFLECK, Charles, SP, Newark, NJ – 1896/10/18:5a
BRENNFLECK, Karolina, 38, Jersey City Heights, NJ – 1891/12/12:4a
BRENNINK, Henry, NYC-M – 1905/03/10:4a
BRENSINGER, George, comptroller of Jersey City, NJ - 1917/09/12:2e
BRENTANO, August, NYC, * Tyrol Prov., German bookstore, + Chicago – 1886/11/04:4a
BRENZEL, Karl, brewer, NYC-M – 1898/10/07:4a
BRESCH, Christoph, smith, NYC-M – 1881/06/21:1e
BRESCHKOWITZSKAJA, Katherine, Russian revol., her life # – 1910/03/27:20c-e
BRESCI, Gaetano, who killed King Umberto of Italy (see there), notes 19 Aug 1900:1g, got life 30:1b, 2 Sept:1b, 13 Sept:2c-d; + in jail 24 May 1901:1f, 26:5a, NYC anarchists grieve 2 June:1h, 11:2d, Paterson, NJ anarchists mem. svce 29 Jy:1d, 30:1f, rev. 9 Ag:1e,
BRESKA, Andreas, 42, NYC-B – 1882/04/20:3a
BRESLAU, Charles, 42, dying, NYC-M – 1880/06/16:4c
BRESLIN, Jacob, clock maker, NYC-M – 1896/12/17:1e
BRESLIN, John J., New York polit., who in 1875 took part in daring Fenian raid on ship Catalpa that freed 7 Irish patriots from Australian labor camp – 1887/11/19:1e
BRESLIN, John, 75, NYC-B – 1899/07/31:3b
BRESTALD, Rudolph, 18, druggist, NYC-SI – 1911/07/10:3a
BRET, Harte, lauded by Alfred Semerau – 1902/08/03:15c-e
BRETEL, Philip, un. carp., NYC-M – 1906/02/06:4a
BRETHAUER, Otto, '48er, G-A journalist, NYC-M – 1880/02/23:4d, =24:2g, benefit for his kids 28:4a, 29:4d, 5 Mr:4d 7:4e, rev. 9:4c, his widow + 3 Apr:2g
BRETOW, William, Dr. 45, NYC-B - 1919/07/10:6a

BRETTERMANN, Hermann, butcher, NYC-B – 1909/05/05:3a
BRETTHAUER, August, 64, newsdealer, NYC-M – 1892/08/06:1e, 7:4a
BRETTHAUER, Charles, 47,NYC-M – 1919/02/01:6a, fam. 3:6a
BRETTHAUER, Charles, NYC-B – 1920/02/17:8a
BRETZ, Eddie, 12, NYC-M – 1908/01/20:6a
BRETZ, Edith, 2, NYC-M, +@Genl Slocum – 1904/06/23:1b
BRETZ, Eleonore, 40, NYC-M – 1913/12/12:6a
BRETZ, Fredie, 6, NYC-M – 1907/08/18:7b
BRETZ, Marie, & infant kid, & Edna, 3, NYC-M, +@Genl Slocum – 1904/06/17:1b
BRETZ, Samuel, un. carp., fr Zips/Hungary?, NYC-M – 1911/10/02:6a, 3:6a, fam. 10:6a
BRETZIUS, Michael, labor leader in Chicago, IL, + Denver, CO – 1900/12/25:1c
BRETZON, Elizabeth, NYC-B – 1901/09/21:1b
BREUER, Kunigunde, b. Fichenscher?, NYC-M – 1892/07/30:4a
BREUER, William, 55, innkeep, Paterson, NJ – 1896/12/02:4a
BREUHAUS, Carl, SP?, Newark, NJ – 1919/03/15:6a
BREUNIG, Andreas Sr., 62, NYC-B – 1917/01/07:7a, 8:6a
BREUNIG, Friedrich, 17, NYC-B – 1903/03/01:5a
BREUNIG, Julius, New Haven, CT – 1903/05/21:4a
BREUNIG, Margaret Eva, 25, NYC-Q – 1916/01/07:6a
BREUSCH, Caroline, b. Fuchs, 49, NYC-Q – 1914/07/20:6a
BREWER, Leo. R., 55, shoe salesman, NYC-M – 1908/02/14:1b
BREYER, Karl, spinner & peddler, *14 De 1846 Zschopau/Saxony, SP, +Holyoke, MA – 1909/03/19:2f
BREYER, Wilhelmine, b. Roth, 51, NYC-M – 1892/06/14:4a
BREZOWSKY, Franz, Union Hill, NJ – 1918/01/14:6a
BRIAN, Jacobine, 52, NYC-Bx – 1915/07/26:6a
BRICKHARDT, Adam, NYC-Bx – 1908/03/07:6a
BRICKMAN, Heinrich, un. cigarmaker, NYC-M – 1916/12/09:6a
BRICKNER % Gaebel
BRIDGES, J. J., alderman, NYC-B – 1902/08/09:4a
BRIEGEL, Louis, 40, tailor, fr Austria, NYC-M – 1897/08/05:1g
BRIEGER, Richard, NYC-M – 1902/04/14:4a
BRIESE, Emilie, NYC-B – 1902/12/28:5b
BRIESE, Louise, NYC-B – 1916/05/01:6a
BRIESE, Robert, NYC-M – 1890/08/06:4a
BRIESEN, Franz von, 65, patent lawyer, NYC-M – 1918/12/31:3g
BRIGGS, Frank O., ex-US Senator, Trenton, NJ – 1913/05/09:6c
BRILL, Anton, 47, Hoboken, NJ – 1891/09/19:4a
BRILL, Carl, 49, un. amber & meerschaum cutter, NYC-M –1881/08/10:3c

BRILL, Jacob, NYC-B - 1916/02/08:6a
BRILL, Max, 53, lawyer, NYC-B – 1900/10/17:4a
BRILL, William E., 75, civil war vet, NYC-B - 1916/05/29:2b
BRILLA, Paulina, 50, NYC-Bx - 1916/04/18:6a
BRINCKERHOFF, Phil. M., circus clown, + Chicago - 1915/05/04:2e
BRINGEZU, Fritz, un. carp., NYC-M – 1901/11/05:4a
BRINGOLF, Jakob, 20, cook, Swiss, NYC-M - 1894/04/05:1g
BRINK, Ida, 11, NYC? – 1886/10/01:4a, inquest 10 Dec:3a
BRINKER, Emil, smith, NYC-M – 1897/12/22:2e
BRINKERHOFF, John, book agent, NYC-M – 1906/01/12:3b
BRINKMANN % Blank
BRINKMANN, Heinrich, 69,SPD Kassel/Gy, carp. - 1913/05/25:3c
BRINKMANN, Henry, NYC-M – 1908/06/17:6a
BRINKMANN, John, 40, secy Natl Carriagemakers' Union, + NYC –
    1910/08/21:1g
BRINKMANN, Meta, b. Odemann, NYC-M – 1904/04/08:4a
BRINKMANN, Ph., 42, un. carpenter, NYC-B - 1878/07/13:1f,3a
BRINKMANN, Theo, 43, NYC-M – 1893/03/28:4a
BRINN, Mrs, NYC-M, +@ on Genl Slocum – 1904/06/16:1c
BRINSKELE, Ernst, NYC-Q – 1912/12/02:6a
BRINZER, Julius, 53, SP, NYC-B – 1911/06/12:6a, 13:6a
BRISLIN, John, 73, whose inventions made Carnegie Steel possible, +
    Pittsburgh – 1907/04/01:4d
BRISSON, Henri, French politician – 1912/04/15:1b
BRITSCH, Charles, 48, electrician, NYC-M – 1898/06/08:1e
BRITTING, Mathilde, & infants George and Grace, Millbrook, NJ –
    1907/04/01:1g
BRITZELMAYR, John, 29, NYC-B – 1918/08/30:6a
BRITZLMAYER, Robert, 25, US vet, NYC-B - 1920/10/03:2a
BRIXUS, John, 20, Newark, NJ – 1883/08/01:4d
BROADHURST, Henry, English politician, crit notes – 1911/10/12:4a-b
BROCA, Paul, Dr., French scientist & socialist, Senotor – 1880/07/19:2d
BROCH, Anna Elisabeth, SLP, co-fdr local Socialist Women's Assoc.,
    Newark, NJ – 1885/01/02:3c, 4c, 4:8a, =6:3a, 8:4d-e
BROCKARB, Maria, 18, NYC-B – 1888/02/04:3b
BROCKARD, Rose, 10, NYC-B – 1882/11/06:3a
BROCKELMANN, George, 47, NYC-M – 1885/12/15:1d
BROCKER, John, NYC-Bx - 1920/01/30:8a
BROCKLE, James, striker at Standard Coke Works, Morewood near Mt
    Pleasant, PA, + by Police – 1891/04/03:1b, =4:1a-b, 5:1f, 4a
BROCKMAN, Margarethe, 80, NYC-M - 1895/02/07:1b

BROCKMANN, Hermann,*5 No 1845 Bremen,typesetter, Cleveland, OH,his life (not +) – 1910/08/08:2a
BROCKMANN, Wilhelm, 72, USA 1850 fr Gy, SLP, Hoboken, NJ – 1896/07/11:1c,4a
BROCKMEIER, John, 70, NYC-B - 1895/07/11:4a
BROCKMEYER, Christian, un. cigarmaker, NYC-B – 1882/12/10:8a
BROCKS % Caprano
BROCKS, Margaret, 11, NYC-M, +@Genl Slocum – 1904/06/18:3b, 21:4a
BROCKSTADT, Henry, stevedore, NYC-M – 1902/10/08:1h
BROCLIE, Karl, NYC-B - 1918/01/31:6a
BRODA, Karl, 36, un. painter & SPD activist expelled from Berlin/Gy, arrived NYC – 1880/11/30:1d-e, 2 Dec:2a-b, 6:1d-e
BRODBECK, Bernhardt, NYC-M – 1896/09/07:1d
BRODERICK, Annie, 26, & her 3 kids, NYC-M – 1892/07/08:1g
BRODESSER, Christian, Elisabeth, NJ – 1912/05/03:6a
BRODESSER, Louise, NYC-M – 1905/01/19:4a, fam. 21:4a
BRODESSER, Theodor, un. pattermaker, NYC-M - 1914/11/03:6a, fam. 4:6a
BRODHUBER, Johann, 38, steel worker, SP St Georgen/Traismauer, Austria – 1909/12/19:3c
BRODKOPF, Hieronymus, 37, NYC-M – 1881/05/23:4c
BRODMERKEL, Anna M.K., child, NYC-M - 1895/09/08: 5a
BRODMERKEL, George William, 15, NYC-M – 1905/08/23:4a, fam. 3 Sept:5b mem. 1906/08/21:6a, 1907/08/21:6a
BRODMERKEL, Thomas, 62, West New York, NJ – 1912/08/22:6a
BRODSKI, Frank, RR worker, + Jersey City, NJ – 1898/11/19:1f
BRODSKY, Ida, 15, & Sarah, 21, @1911 Triangle Shirtwaist Fire, NYC-M – 1911/03/28:1b
BROEKSMAN, Dr., Boer patriot, POW, shot by British in Pretoria – 1901/10/03:1a
BROESLER, W., SLP, NYC-M - 1879/11/22:4e
BROESSEL, Felix, 30, technical drawer, fr Elsass, NYC-M – 1889/11/21:2e, 20:1e
BROGER, Philip, 9, NYC-M, +@Genl Slocum – 1904/06/22:1d
BROGLIE, Jacques de, 80, French Duke & react. Politician – 1901/01/20:1b
BROGUS, Charles, NYC-B – 1900/04/18:4a
BROHM, Barbara, b. Drabold, 53, NYC-M – 1885/01/29:3d
BROHM, Fritz, NYC-M – 1900/09/16:5a
BROHMER, Bertha, 63, NYC-M - 1894/02/12:4a
BROHMER, Friedrich, ?57, NYC-M – 1890/01/03:4a
BROMBACH, Albert, Paterson, NJ – 1906/08/24:6a

BROMBACHER, Helene, b. Daettmann, NYC-M – 1910/06/01:6a, 2:6a
BROMBACHER, Louis, 79, SP, un. tailor, fr Loerrach/Baden, USA ca. 1890, NYC-M - 1920/02/05:6a, 6:3e,6a
BROMBERG, Hannah, NYC-M - 1894/09/26:4c
BROMHORST, George, NYC-M – 1885/07/31:3a
BROMMER, Friedrich, 57, fr Hanau/Gy, SLP, Newark, NJ – 1890/12/14:5b
BROMMER, Louise, b. Enzen, 68, NYC-M – 1891/03/23:4a
BRONINAU, Louise, 30, servant, NYC-M – 1907/09/05:6a
BRONNER, Eva, War 2, NYC-B - 1918/03/20:2e
BRONSON, James M., 35, SP, barber, SP of Delaware - 1913/07/09:2e, 13:6a-b
BROOKE, Charles W., lawyer, NYC-SI – 1897/02/08:1d, 11:2f, 16:4e
BROOKFIELD, Charles,60, London actor & critic - 1913/11/08:4f
BROOKS, Allen, Negro, lynched Dallas, TX – 1910/03/04:1c
BROOKS, Carl, un. cigarmaker, NYC-M – 1909/04/18:7b
BROOKS, D., NYC-Bx – 1910/06/25:6a
BROOKS, Margaret, NYC-M, +@on Genl Slocum – 1904/06/17:3b
BROOKS, Marie, b. Osterndorf, 26, NYC-M - 1878/03/31:8b
BROOKS, Mary, lady of the night, NYC-M – 1880/01/29:4a
BROOKS, Tom, Negro, lynched Somerville, TN - 1915/04/29:2c
BROOKS, Walter S., 20, clerk, NYC-M – 1902/02/16:1h, 19:1e, 20:1e, 21:3b, 27:1f-g, 19 Mr:3b, 24 Mr:2c, 21 May:2h
BROSCHECK, Peter, (also Brozek) worker at Singer's, Elizabeth, NJ – 1903/05/14:4a, fam. 19:4a
BROSE, Henry, stoker on SS Newport – 1881/11/29:4a
BROSI, Frank, NYC-Q 1918/03/16:6a
BROSIUS, Georg, 81, ex-NYC, gymnastics pioneer, co-fdr 1889 NYC Central Turnverein (East 67th St) + Milwaukee, WI - 1920/03/24:2a
BROSSMANN, Hermann, 50, bookdealer, SPD Leipzig/Gy –1909/12/19:3b
BROTBECK, Frederick, un. typesetter, Jersey City Heights, NJ – 1906/10/18:6a
BROUGEWITSCH, Louis, 14, striking miner, killed near Scranton, PA – 1912/05/12:1g
BROUSKER, Albert, 35, cigar dealer, NYC-M – 1881/05/09:1e
BROUSSE, Paul, 68, French socialist, 1912/04/18:4d
BROWER, Jeanette, 6, NYC-M, +@Genl Slocum – 1904/06/25:1d
BROWN, exec. Ossining, NY – 1911/11/21:4d
BROWN, Abe, Negro, lynched near Goliad, TX – 1899/07/16:1h
BROWN, Corinne Stub, SP, feminist, ex-NYC, + Chicago, IL - 1914/03/17:2d
BROWN, Edward, exec. Freehold, NJ – 1906/06/30:2b
BROWN, Emma, 29, Sullivan Co., NY, + @ Genl Slocum – 1904/06/21:1f

BROWN, Erastus, Negro, lynched Union, MO – 1897/07/11:1b
BROWN, George's wife,, ex-SP, NYC-M – 1913/01/18:2b
BROWN, Grace, Cortland, NY, killed by Chester Gillette – 1906/07/15:1e
BROWN, Henry H., Koltes Post 32, NYC-M – 1882/06/14:3b
BROWN, James K., exec. Jersey City, NJ – 1900/02/10:1e
BROWN, John, abolitionist, meeting in memory of 22nd anniv. Of his execution, in NYC Turnhalle – 1881/12/02:2a-b, 3:4a, 4:4e-5a, 42nd Anniv. 1901/12/23:1c-f, 50th anniv. – 1909/12/02:4a-b
BROWN, Seymour A., NYC-M - 1916/11/03:6a
BROWN, Ted, Negro, lynched Palmetto, GA – 1899/03/17:2h
BROWN, William, Negro, lynched Lincolnton, GA – 1919/10/07:1c, 8:4c
BROWN, William, Negro, lynched Omaha, NE – 1919/09/30:2c, 1 Oct:4a
BROWNE, Carl, 66, labor activist, + Washington, DC - 1914/01/17:1e
BROZEK, Peter see Peter Broscheck
BRUCH, Bernhard, NYC-M - 1916/02/05:6a
BRUCH, Max, 82, German composer, + Berlin - 1920/10/05:5e
BRUCHMUELLER, Max, NYC?, fam. - 1914/04/18:6a
BRUCHNOWSKY, Johann, 38, NYC-M – 1892/06/26:5c
BRUCKER, Edward,, gardener, Summit, NJ – 1883/03/27:4c
BRUCKER, Helene, 4, Carlstadt, NJ – 1908/10/20:3c
BRUCKHEIMER, Leopold, pawnbroker, NYC-M – 1908/05/07:2d
BRUCKNER % Grundlach
BRUECHHERT, Anna, 69, NYC-M, + @on Genl Slocum – 1904/06/17:3c
BRUECK, Susanna J., 28, NYC-B – 1892/04/26:4a
BRUECKEL, Henrietta, b. Menk, NYC-M – 1892/06/10:4a
BRUECKHAUSER, Kath., 18, servant, USA 1881 fr Bremen, NYC-M – 1882/05/17:4f
BRUECKL, Georg, un. butcher, NYC-M - 1914/11/17:6a
BRUECKMANN, Anna Margareth, NYC-M – 1904/07/17:5b, 18:4a
BRUECKMANN, Engelbert, *24 Dec. 1843 Duesseldorf/Gy, un. cigar-maker & SPD activist expelled from Altona/Gy, arrived NYC – 1880/11/30:1d-e, 2 Dec:2a-b, 6:1d-e. SLP, #, + NYC-M – 1897/04/25:1f,5d, 26:4a, 27:4a, =28:1f, fam. 28:4a
BRUECKMANN, Wilhelm, 71, NYC-M – 1890/08/22:4a
BRUECKNER, Carl, 76, fr St Wendell, Gy, USA 1860s, NYC-B – 1909/01/24:1f
BRUECKNER, Ephraim, pretzel-baker, NYC-M – 1880/03/11:4a, 12:4a
BRUECKNER, Michael, 39, shoemaker, NYC-M - 1895/05/12:5b
BRUECKNER, Therese, 33, NYC-M – 1891/09/20:5f
BRUEDERLE, Babette, b. Krell, 43, Jersey City Heights, NJ – 1907/12/13:6a

BRUEDERLE, Leo, 38, SDP, un. brewer, Union Hill, NJ – 1902/04/28:4a, =3 May:2g
BRUEDERLEIN, Louise M., b. Schwab, NYC-M - 1914/09/29:6a
BRUEDERLEIN, Wilhelm, un. furrier, NYC-M – 1891/09/02:4a
BRUEGGE, Joachim, SPD, weaver, Neumuenster/Prussia, + Hamburg - 1915/07/04:3c
BRUEGGEMANN, Henry & Emily, SLP?, celebrated Silver Wedding, NYC-B – 1881/03/01:3a
BRUEGGEMANN, Hermann, 68, NYC-M – 1898/10/12:4a
BRUEGGEMANN, Sophie, b. Walleward, 68, NYC-M – 1902/12/01:4a
BRUEGGER % Zinz
BRUEGMANN, Anna, NYC-B - 1919/02/03:6a
BRUEGMANN, Henry, 43, * Thueringia?, NYC-B - 1920/10/15:6a
BRUEHL, Christopher, 60, NYC-B – 1892/07/31:5c
BRUEMER, Henry, NYC-M – 1913/04/19:6a
BRUEMMER % Schulenburg
BRUEMMER, Mary, NYC-M – 1893/11/27:4a
BRUEMMER, Willie, 1, NYC-M – 1885/07/13:4g
BRUENING, William C. C., saddle maker, Passaic, NJ – 1880/03/05:1g
BRUENJAS, Otto Martin, NYC-M – 1891/06/26:4a
BRUESSEL, Adolph, 87, NYC-M – 1891/03/15:5b
BRUETISAUER, John, NYC-M – 1892/02/14:5c
BRUETLING, Thomas, brewer or cooper, NYC-M – 1902/02/08:4a
BRUGGEMANN, Albert, NYC-M – 1908/09/30:6a
BRUGGER % Heinrich
BRUGGER, Fannie, 82, NYC-Bx - 1920/12/08:6a, 9:6a, fam. 14 Dec:6a
BRUGGMANN, Jules, USA 1900 fr Switz., NYC-M – 1906/12/01:1f
BRUHN, Sophie, NYC-M – 1886/03/08:3c
BRUHNS, Christian, 59, worker, Newark, NJ – 1910/12/18:11a
BRUMM, Christian, un. carp., NYC-M – 1906/02/24:4a
BRUMM, Jacob, NYC-M - 1915/12/06:6a
BRUMMER, Auguste, 71, NYC-M – 1893/02/18:4a
BRUMMER, Henry, flour salesman, NYC-B – 1910/02/22:3a
BRUNCKEN, Gustav, NYC-Q – 1910/04/13:6a
BRUNEMER, Louisa, 17, NYC-B - 1894/01/17:4a
BRUNERT, Julius, 45, NYC-M – 1892/07/16:4a
BRUNING, Anna G., 69?, NYC-B – 1891/08/16:4a
BRUNING, Annie, 43, NYC-M, +@ on Genl Slocum – 1904/06/17:3c
BRUNING, Herman, 39, Jersey City, NJ – 1909/04/06:6a
BRUNJES, J. M., 45, NYC-M – 1893/03/29:4a
BRUNK, Max, child, New Haven, CT – 1906/10/26:6a
BRUNKEN, Hermann, grocer, Hoboken, NJ - 1879/12/05:4d

BRUNN, Arnim, Dr. vet., 49, South Woodstock, CT – 1909/10/01:2d
BRUNN, Frieda, 40, South Woodstock, CT – 1909/10/01:2d
BRUNN, Konstantin, businessman, NYC-B – 1909/10/01:2d
BRUNN, Max, boxer, NYC-B - 1913/10/31:6c
BRUNNENGRAEBER, NYC-Q - 1914/09/03:6a
BRUNNENKAND, Wilhelm, NYC-M – 1882/12/18:3a
BRUNNER % Riedel
BRUNNER, Bernard's wife, NYC-M – 1883/09/02:8a
BRUNNER, Chas W., Dr., NYC-B - 1915/01/23:6a
BRUNNER, Emil, 45, Newark, NJ – 1911/07/11:1e
BRUNNER, Frank, un. beer driver, NYC-M – 1902/02/27:4a
BRUNNER, Heinrich, miller, fr Wahlhausen/Allendorf, USA 1881, Baltimore, MD – 1881/08/26:1d
BRUNNER, John, 21, W. Hoboken, NJ – 1904/05/21:4c, 24:3d
BRUNNER, Marcus F., un. typesetter, Newark, NJ – 1901/05/07:4a
BRUNNER, Peter, NYC-B – 1906/08/27:2d
BRUNNER, William, Swiss, embroiderer, NYC-M - 1894/02/01:1g, 02:4d
BRUNNING, Charles, 42, NYC-M – 1903/09/08:3d
BRUNNQUELL, Elizabeth, NYC-M – 1905/04/12:4a
BRUNNQUELL, Joseph, 43, NYC-B – 1908/11/17:6a
BRUNO, Charles, 67, music instrument manuf., NYC-M – 1912/04/18:3d-e
BRUNS, Catherina, b. Wellmann, 54, NYC-B – 1887/06/15:3b
BRUNS, Conrad, 61, New Haven, CT - 1916/06/22:6a
BRUNS, Frederick Charles, 65, NYC-M – 1881/12/17:1g
BRUNS, Gustav, NYC-B – 1909/02/20:6a
BRUNS, John, Elizabeth, NJ – 1919/09/03:6a
BRUNS, Katherine, NYC-B – 1903/11/16:3c
BRUNS, Marie, b. Koelling, NYC-M – 1899/11/03:4a, fam. 6:4a, 7:4a
BRUNSWICK, John, NYC – 1912/08/26:3a, 6a
BRUST, Charles C., NYC-B - 1914/01/19:1b
BRUST, Eliza, 48, NYC-B – 1909/05/14:1e
BRUST, Frederick. W., 63, West Stockbridge, MA – 1919/08/31:7a, 1 Sept:6a, fam. 4:6a
BRUSWITZ, William, NYC-B – 1902/07/26:4a
BRYANT, Ben, Negro, lynched Redwood, LA – 1903/05/04:1b
BRYANT, James, member of Tweed Ring, NYC – 1899/02/13:1g
BRYANT, Royal, Negro, lynched near Clinton, VA – 1881/01/23:5d
BRYER, Benedikt, un. cigarmkr, NYC-M - 1914/09/25:6a
BUBACH, Anton, 27, NYC-M – 1889/03/04:4a
BUBACH, Charles, 27, cigarpacker, NYC-M – 1880/07/04:5f, 5:1g
BUBECK, Sophia, 28, NYC-M – 1892/08/16:4a
BUBISCH, Frank, un. baker, NYC - 1913 /12/18:6d

BUCH, Frieda, 56, NYC-M - 1917/07/29:7a
BUCHANAN, Robert W., Dr., NYC, exec. Ossining, NY - 1895/07/02:1h
BUCHEGGER, Henry, NYC-M - 1902/01/21:4a
BUCHENSCHEIT, Joseph, un. stone cutter, NYC-B - 1904/06/02:4a
BUCHER, Lothar, German politician, friend of Lassalle & Bismarck, crit. obit - 1892/10/14:2b, 5 Nov:4b
BUCHERT, Henry, 46, NYC-B - 1916/12/19:6a
BUCHHOLZ, Charles, 40, NYC-M - 1892/07/27:4a
BUCHHOLZ, Conrad, 48, NYC-M - 1891/03/29:5a
BUCHHOLZ, John, SLP, NYC-M, 50th anniv. as printer - 1888/05/07:1b; + 70 yrs old - 1895/03/18:4a,= 21:4d
BUCHHOLZ, William, see SCHULTE
BUCHLER, Rosa, infant, Newark, NJ - 1899/06/09:1g
BUCHMUELLER, Annie, 27, NYC-B +@Genl Slocum - 1904/06/23:1b
BUCHNAN, Bertha, NYC - 1912/07/06:6a, 7:7a
BUCHNER, Bernard, 39, laborer, NYC-M - 1891/09/26:2f
BUCHNER, Karl, 36, un. cigarmkr, NYC-M - 1893/01/29:5c, 30:4a
BUCHS, Akino, 42, worker, + in sweatshop fire, NYC-M - 1893/06/14:1e
BUCHS, Katharina, 95, NYC-M - 1898/02/26:4a
BUCHSBAUM, Charles, 49, cigar maker, NYC-B - 1885/05/12:2g
BUCHTERKIRCH, Heinrich A., un. typesetter, NYC-M - 1885/11/09:4c, = Rochester 11:3a
BUCHWALD, Edmund, 65, SPD Altenburg/Thuer., MdL - 1913/10/05:3a
BUCHWALTER, Albert, 28, NYC-B - 1893/05/14:5b
BUCKEL, Albert, 26, NYC-Bx - 1918/07/12:6a
BUCKEL, Frederick, 23, NYC-Bx - 1908/11/21:6a
BUCKEL, Jacob J., NYC-M - 1898/01/08:4a
BUCKER, Jennie, 21,laundress,*Austria, NYC-M - 1894/07/19:1g
BUCKERT, Frank, 54, NYC-Q - 1915/01/17:11d
BUCKLEY, Daniel, 80, NYC-M - 1892/11/07:4a
BUCKOW, Gustav, un. carp., NYC-Bx - 1911/11/18:6a
BUCKSATH, Wilhelm, 50, Union Hill, NJ - 1908/10/24:6a
BUDD, Thomas E., Dr. vet., 75, Orange, NJ - 1912/09/14:3a
BUDDE, Gustav, Union Hill, NJ - 1917/04/26:6a
BUDDENHAGEN, Minnie, NYC-M - 1891/02/26:4a
BUDDIN, Heinrich, 57, porter at St Michael's Hospital, Newark, NJ - 1918/01/03:2d
BUDDIN, John, 32, cigar shop, USA ~1872, NYC-M - 1882/03/22:1g
BUDENBENDER, William C., 63, ex-Justice of the Peace, Hoboken, NJ - 1909/11/21:1d
BUDZEWITSCH, Juri, Polish revol., exec. for killing Czar Alex II - 1883/04/24:2c-d

BUECHE, Arnold, 41, un. embroiderer, Swiss?, West Hoboken, NJ - 1895/04/05:4a
BUECHKERT, Mrs, NYC-M, + @on Genl Slocum – 1904/06/16:1c
BUECHLEIN, Katherine, (or Buechling) 52, NYC-B – 1903/07/10:1f
BUECHLER, Hedwig, b. Simon, NYC-B - 1919/07/19:6a, fam. 23:6a
BUECHLER, Ludwig, Jersey City Heights, NJ – 1908/07/08:6a
BUECHLER, Margaretha, West Hoboken, NJ – 1903/12/14:4a
BUECHLING, Katherine s.a. Buechlein
BUECHNER % Blaikie
BUECHNER, August, West Hoboken, NJ - 1917/03/14:6a, 15:6a, fam. 17 April:6a
BUECHNER, Georg, 70th ann. Death of the German revol. Poet – 1907/03/17:4a-b
BUECHNER, Klara, 19, West Hoboken, NJ – 1911/03/04:6a
BUECHNER, Lina, 40, NYC-M – 1897/02/21:5a
BUECHNER, Lorenz, 58, NYC-M – 1883/11/30:3b
BUECHNER, Ludwig, 70, German physician & writer – 1899/05/02:3d, naïve idealist who refused to admit necessity of class warfare 21 May 1895:9c-e, 23:2d-e
BUECHNER, Mrs, Milwaukee, Wisc. – 1893/08/02:4a
BUECHNER, Richard, 40, NYC-M – 1891/09/03:4c
BUEGLER, Georg, NYC-B – 1906/01/08:4a, 9:4a
BUEGLER, Maria, b. Diehlmann, NYC-B – 1904/11/20:5b
BUEHL, Caroline, 74, NYC-M – 1891/06/21:5a
BUEHL, Charles, 35, NYC-B - 1917/05/14:6a
BUEHLEN, John Jakob, 46, NYC-M – 1881/07/12:3c
BUEHLER, Anna, NYC-M - 1916/11/08:6a
BUEHLER, Carl, 50,grocer, NYC-M - 1894/07/28:4c
BUEHLER, Carrie, 56, NYC-SI – 1905/10/17:1d
BUEHLER, Ch., NYC-B – 1887/02/08:3d
BUEHLER, Charles, War 2, NYC-B - 1914/08/19:6c
BUEHLER, Dorothea, 37, Newark, NJ – 1906/07/14:6a
BUEHLER, E., NYC-Q - 1913/12/16:6a
BUEHLER, Fritz, Passaic, NJ - 1916/05/30:6a
BUEHLER, G., un. brewer, SP, Newark, NJ, married Louise, wd Kiefer, b. Mersfolder – 1906/11/25:9e
BUEHLER, George, West Newark,NJ,+ Whippong,NJ - 1914/12/29:6a
BUEHLER, Gottlieb, 30, cigardealer, NYC-M – 1905/06/20:3e
BUEHLER, Jakob, un. beer driver, NYC-M – 1893/03/08:4a, 9:4a
BUEHLER, Lizzie, 22, NYC-Q – 1892/07/03:1h, 5:4b, 6:2d, 9:2c-d
BUEHLER, Martin, Union Hill, NJ – 1904/12/17:4a
BUEHLER, Mathias, Elizabeth, NJ - 1913/08/19:6a

BUEHLERT, Lorenz, NYC-B – 1908/04/13:6a
BUEHNER, Ernst F., 68, un. surgical instrument maker, NYC-B - 1913/11/23:7c
BUEHREN, George von, NYC-M – 1906/07/11:6a
BUEHREN, George, NYC-B – 1891/04/06:4a
BUEHRER, G., NYC-B - 1915/05/24:6a
BUEHRER, Oscar, Swiss?, NYC-M - 1920/08/07:6a, fam 13:6a
BUEHRIG, Herman, Jersey City, NJ – 1912/10/23:6a
BUEHRIG, Johanna, W. Hoboken, NJ – 1898/06/10:4a
BUELL, Otto, 44, NYC-B - 1915/02/28:7f
BUELOW, Max von, Globe Trotter, + Reno, NV – 1912/12/28:1f
BUENTE, Carl, 45, un. cigarmaker, NYC-M – 1881/06/21:3a
BUENZ, Henry, 50, brother of Alfred Buenz, German consul-genl in Chicago, NYC-B - 1896/02/03:2d
BUER, Fritz, 51, NYC-B – 1892/07/07:4a
BUERCK, Balthasar, 31, tailor, *Ladenburg/Mannheim, USA 1868, NYC-M - 1879/11/16:1a, 18:1e
BUERGER, Martin, 71, SPD Dortmund, *Kassel - 1915/01/24:3b
BUERKLE % Roth
BUERKLE, George John, 61, NYC-B – 1890/03/31:4a
BUERKLE, Gottfried, 63, un. carp., NYC-M – 1911/02/24:6a
BUERKLI, Karl, 78, Swiss liberal polit., Zuerich/Switz. – 1901/11/02:2d
BUERMANN % Bernhardt
BUERNER, Andreas, 45, silk weaver, Paterson, NJ – 1896/09/08:1f
BUESCH % Bordollo
BUESE, Frederick, butcher, NYC-B – 1887/11/25:4c
BUESENER, Herman, NYC-B - 1916/04/27:6a
BUETHE, Louis, 4, NYC-M - 1878/07/27:3c
BUETOW, William, un. carp., NYC-B – 1903/11/27:4a
BUETTNER, A., Orange, NJ – 1887/04/11:2d
BUETTNER, August, USA 1885, printer, NYC-M – 1885/12/05:1g
BUETTNER, Barbara, b. Zeidler, NYC-Q – 1906/10/31:6a, 1 Nv:6a
BUETTNER, Johann, 49, NYC-M - 1878/11/16:3a
BUETTNER, Paul, NYC-B – 1912/04/02:6a
BUFFLER, L., NYC-B – 1916/02/07:6a
BUGE, Johanna Alwine, (or RUGE) 3, Jersey City Heights, NJ – 1891/04/23:4a
BUHL, Jacob, 57, musician, NYC-M – 1915/11/16:6a
BUHR, Bruno, machinist, NYC-M – 1901/04/30:4a
BUHRBANK, John, NYC-M – 1885/06/26:3c
BUHRER, Charles, 22, mason, NYC-B – 1898/03/24:1f
BUKOFZER, Moritz, 58, un. cigarmaker, NYC-M – 1917/04/07:6a

BUKOFZER, Pauline, NYC-M – 1913/01/19:7b
BUKOFZER, Rosa, daughter of Moritz, NYC-M - 1913/10/19:7b
BUKOWSKY, Carl, 51, un. carp., NYC-Q – 1902/02/15:4a
BULEMEYER, Frederick, 38, engineer, NYC-B - 1917/12/24:2a
BULENSKI, Mary O., 25, Newark, NJ – 1913/04/11:1f
BULGARIA, Eleonore, Queen of,, crit. obit. - 1917/09/24:4c
BULL, Ole, 70, violinist, * Bergen/Norway – 1880/08/22:4d
BULL, William Tillinghast, Dr., cancer researcher, ex-NYC, + Womberly, GA – 1909/02/23:2b
BULLING, Elizabeth, 68, NYC-M – 1891/05/30:1f
BULLWINKEL, Henry, NYC-M - 1916/08/22:1f
BULZER, Henry, cook, NYC-M – 1901/08/22:1b
BUMB % Thaler
BUMBE, Hans, 19, War 2, NYC-M - 1914/08/13:5f
BUMILLER, William, NYC-M - 1917/04/13:6a
BUMKE, Rudolph, Hoboken, NJ – 1893/08/09:4a
BUNCE, Arthur J., smith, killed during RR strike, St Louis, MO – 1900/05/28:1c
BUNDIG, Karl, 21, German navy, POW in England, + 24 Aug. 1915, his burial 1915/12/10:4f
BUNDSCHUH, William E., 50, Irvington, NJ – 1911/03/27:3c
BUNNER, Henry C., editor of English lang. Issue of Puck & enemy of labor, NYC – 1896/05/13:2c, 17:4b
BUNSCHROW, Florence, 16, NYC-Bx - 1915/02/10:6c
BUNSEN, Robert W., German scientist, + 17. Aug – 1899/09/24:3e-h, 13b, 1st anniv. of his + 1900/06/24:4a-d
BUNTE, Friedrich, un. miner & SPD Dortmund/Gy – 1910/05/15:3c
BUNTHER, Louise, 27, fr Gy, + on ship "Bohemia" – 1890/02/21:2f
BUNTING, Annie, 14, NYC-B - 1917/03/06:6d
BUNTZ, Frank, 25, musician fr Philadelphia, + NYC-B – 1899/08/17:2h
BUNZEL, Karoline, b. Feldman, NYC-M – 1903/05/12:4a
BUR, Friedericke, b. Kessler, 51, NYC-M – 1911/05/25:6a
BURBACH, William, 60, innkep, NYC-Bx – 1902/10/07:1g
BURCHARD, Annie, NYC-M, +@ Genl Slocum – 1904/06/16:1c,d,17:3c
BURCHARD, Julia, 45, NYC-Q – 1898/09/04:1d
BURCHARD, Richard, teacher at Free German School, Jersey City Hghts, NJ - 1917/12/18:6a, mem. 1918/12/16:6a
BURCHEIMER, Henry, 58, fish dealer, NYC-M – 1887/11/30:4c
BURCKARDT, Anton, NYC-Q - 1918/05/11:6a
BURCKEL, Martin, NYC-Q - 1916/02/14:6a
BURCKHARDT, Johannes, 66, NYC-M – 1912/03/24:7c
BURCKHARDT, John, 66, tool maker, Mt Vernon, NY – 1908/10/02:2b

BURDYCK, Anton, SP?, NYC-Bx - 1919/07/15:6a, fam. 18:6a
BUREN, VAN % Dutcher
BURFEIND, Dora, 22, Kate, 21, Mary, 2, Dora & John T., infants, NYC-M, +@ Genl Slocum – 1904/06/17:3c, 18:3b, 22:1d, 27:1h
BURG, Maria, NYC-M – 1891/03/24:4a
BURGDORF % Eisner
BURGEMEISTER, Philip, 71, NYC-B - 1916/05/21:1g
BURGER, Adam, NYC-M - 1919/04/29:6a
BURGER, Elise, b. Fuhrer, NYC-M – 1908/08/15:6a
BURGER, George, 46, un. brewer, NYC-Bx – 1886/06/14:2f
BURGER, Jacob, 48, un. brewer, NYC-Bx – 1904/07/05:4a, 7:4a
BURGER, Margarethe, b. Emeld, NYC-M – 1891/06/22:4a
BURGER, Theodor, cooper, NYC-M - 1879/07/09:1e
BURGESS % Berger
BURGESS, Charles, exec. Auburn, NY – 1897/12/08:1h
BURGHARD, George, NYC-M – 1892/07/29:4a
BURGHARDT, Franziska, b. Bach, 60, NYC-B – 1888/03/10:3a
BURGHARDT, George, 42, NYC-M - 1918/09/27:5g
BURGHER, Katherine, 41, NYC-Q – 1908/11/11:6a
BURGHOLZ, Bernhard, Elizabeth, NJ - 1920/12/21:6a
BURGLER, Leonhard, SLP, un. hatmaker, * Schwyz/Swit., NYC-M - 1894/10/15:4a, =17:3e
BURGMEYER, Elise M., 22, servant, Jersey City, NJ, family in Farnwood, NJ - 1879/11/25:4e
BURGTORF, Theodore, Dr., 55, & wife Anna, NYC-Bx – 1910/11/15:1c, 2b, 16:3d
BURIAN, George, NYC-B – 1912/11/28:6a
BURIAN, John, un. baker, NYC-M - 1920/11/17:6a
BURK, Carl, NYC-M – 1892/10/01:4a
BURK, Lena, b. Kobberger, 19, NYC-B – 1886/03/22:5e
BURKARD, Barbara, b. Knoepfle, 32, NYC-B – 1898/12/20:4a
BURKARD, Joseph, NYC-B – 1906/03/14:4a
BURKARDT, Gustav, NYC-M - 1916/05/08:6a
BURKART, Theodor, un. baker, Jersey City, NJ – 1910/10/14:6a
BURKE, Ottilie, (Burg?), 29, servant, fr Gy, Newark, NJ - 1878/11/28:4e
BURKHARD, Conrad, (orig. Burkhardsmeier), innkeep, NYC-M – 1888/12/07:1e
BURKHARDT, Albertina, 39, NYC-M, +@Genl Slocum – 1904/06/22:1d
BURKHARDT, Andreas, 46, NYC-Q – 1907/04/10:6a
BURKHARDT, Anna, b. May, 26, NYC-Bx – 1910/07/31:7c, 1 Aug:6a
BURKHARDT, Carl, NYC-M – 1908/09/13:7a
BURKHARDT, Christian, SP, * Pforzheim/Gy, NYC-M – 1903/12/24:1g

BURKHARDT, Edward, RR car driver, + during strike, St Louis, MO – 1900/06/11:1f
BURKHARDT, Elizabeth, b. Miller, NYC-M - 1916/10/03:6a
BURKHARDT, Jonathan, NYC-Q – 1908/08/22:6a, fam. 26:6a
BURKHARDT, Louis, 45, SLP, salesman, sister in Buchholz/Gy, NYC-B - 1895/04/03:4c
BURKHARDT, Maria, NYC-Q – 1905/08/06:5b, 7:4a
BURKHARDT, Minnie, Hoboken, NJ – 1901/02/09:1g
BURKHARDT, Tillie, 22, Newark, NJ – 1907/09/24:3c
BURKHART, John, un. carp., NYC-M - 1913/06/15:7b
BURKLE, Herman, 37, SP?, Hopkins, MN, sister in NYC - 1913/07/29:6a
BURMEISTER, Bertha, grocer, NYC-M – 1892/07/04:1e,4a, 5:1b
BURMEISTER, Charles, NYC-M – 1883/02/28:3c, 1 Mr:3c
BURMEISTER, Emil, capt of SS Hamburg, + Newark, NJ? – 1910/01/12:2b
BURMEISTER, Georg, grocer, fr Gy, NYC-B - 1894/02/03:3c
BURNESS, Frank H., exec. Ossining, NY for + George B. Townsend – 1904/06/28:4a
BURNHAM, Frederick A., ex-pres. Mutual Reserve Life Ins. Co., NYC-M – 1908/12/24:3d-e
BURNS, Ed, IWW martyr, + Sacramento, CA jail – 1919/08/21:2b-c
BURNS, John, life of the English labor leader – 1889/11/17:4d-e, his 32nd birthday # 24 Nov 1890:1c-d
BURNS, Robert, Scottish writer, on his 100th anniv. – 1896/08/09:4b-e
BURNS, William H., SP county secy, NYC-Q – 1908/03/06:2e, 6a
BUROW, Hermann, SLP?, NYC-M – 1891/01/15:4a, 17:4a, =19:1c, fam. 21:4c
BURR, John, NYC-M - 1915/02/05:6a
BURRI, Marie A., 57, NYC-M - 1917/03/20:6a
BURRIS, William, NYC-B – 1900/06/11:3c
BURRITT, Elihu, 69, abolitionist & pacifist - 1879/03/08:2b
BURROWS, Peter, 65, Irish-Am. SP, NYC-M – 1909/12/11:3b, =13:5e
BURSHAK, Stephan, 40, striking worker, Perth Amboy, NJ – 1912/06/15:1g
BURTAMP, Karl, *Gehlendeck/Westfalia, NYC – 1910/05/24:6a
BURTON, Murray, Negro, lynched Ellisville, GA – 1911/04/09:1f
BURTON, Reddick, Negro, lynched Hempstead, TX – 1902/10/22:3c
BUS, Edward, 9, NYC-B - 1920/07/28:6a
BUSCH % Mark
BUSCH, Adolph, pres. Anheuser-Busch brewery, St Louis, MO, *10 Jy 1837 Mainz/Gy, USA 1857, + in Gy – 1913/10/11:2c, notes 15:2d, 22:1g, will 31:2f, crit 1 Nov:4d

BUSCH, Annie, 18, Newark, NJ – 1891/09/26:1h
BUSCH, Annie, NYC-M – 1906/04/30:4a
BUSCH, Carl, un. carp., NYC-B – 1887/11/15:2g
BUSCH, Charles, 33, machinist, NYC-B – 1906/05/05:3d
BUSCH, Christian, NYC-M - 1914/09/10:6a
BUSCH, Emilie, b. Pfannstiel, 56, NYC-M – 1901/07/23:4a
BUSCH, G.F., Newark, NJ - 1916/04/13:6a
BUSCH, Hermann D., hotelier, Hoboken, NJ – 1886/09/27:2g, 3a
BUSCH, Isidor, NYC-M – 1892/07/25:4a
BUSCH, Johann C., 60, NYC-M – 1890/03/22:4a
BUSCH, John, 40?, fr Holstein/Gy, NYC-M – 1890/09/15:4a
BUSCH, Josephine, NYC – 1901/03/17:5g
BUSCH, Julius Moritz, German writer – 1899/11/17:1b
BUSCH, Lizzie, 17, NYC-M – 1889/02/04:4a
BUSCH, Paul VAN DER, fr Belgium, old inventor, NYC-M – 1890/02/05:2g
BUSCH, Robert, NYC-College Point - 1916/09/20:6a
BUSCH, S., NYC-Bx - 1917/04/03:6a
BUSCH, S.F., 42, woolstuff importer, NYC-M - 1895/11/09:1c
BUSCH, Walter, NYC-M – 1909/07/05:6a
BUSCH, Wilhelm, German humorist, 75th anniv. – 1907/04/28:6f-g
BUSCH, Wilhelm, NYC-M – 1909/03/31:6a
BUSCHAUER, Josef, un. baker, NYC-M – 1912/05/05:7a
BUSCHBAUM, Jacob, un. carp., NYC-M – 1902/03/23:5a
BUSCHER, Ph., SLP, NYC-B, sick, call for a benefit – 1893/01/01:5f
BUSCHIRI, rebel leader in German East Africa, exec. – 1890/01/06:2b-c
BUSCHMANN, Bruno, innkeep, SPD Chemnitz/Gy – 1908/06/14:3c-d
BUSCHMANN, Eduard, 70, USA ~1853, to Orange County, NY, NYC-M – 1885/05/02:1g
BUSCHMANN, Edward, 70, NYC-M – 1885/05/02:1g
BUSCHMANN, Fernande, exec. by French during the war as alleged German spy, noted - 1920/04/10:4
BUSCHMANN, Joseph, 66, NYC-Q - 1894/01/23:4e
BUSCHWALD, Anton, 17, Newark, NJ – 1906/08/01:2e
BUSER, Adam, 67,fr.Froschhausen/Hessia,NYC-M - 1895/06/22:3e
BUSER, John,52, innkeep?, Swiss?, Union Hill,NJ - 1896/03/21:4a
BUSH % Polack
BUSHMAN, Charles, NYC-B – 1910/01/25:6a
BUSHROD, Raymond, 20, Negro, lynched Hawesville, KY – 1897/09/27:1e
BUSIAN, J.J., Dr., NYC-M – 1890/01/02:4a

BUSIGNI, Spanish peasant, exec. for anarchism in Xerez de la Frontera – 1892/02/11:1a-b, 12:1a, NYC Soc. protests 19:1g
BUSKING, W., Manhattanville, - 1896/02/23:5a
BUSKO, Victoria, 24, NYC-B – 1892/04/26:4a, fam. 1 May:5b
BUSOLD, Heinrich, SPD, ex-MdL Hessen/Gy, + Friedberg/Hessen - 1915/09/05:3a
BUSSANICH, James, Secaucus, NJ – 1912/08/11:1b
BUSSE, Ernst, Union Hill, NJ – 1900/03/29:4a
BUSSE, Hermann, un. cigar maker, NYC-M – 1886/03/16:3a
BUSSE, Mary, 74, NYC-B – 1910/10/08:2b
BUSSE, Sadie, musician, NYC-M - 1917/11/23:5f
BUSSER, Joseph, 44, cooper, NYC-M – 1891/09/17:4c
BUSSERT, L.E., 24, NYC-M - 1894/02/01:4a
BUSSINGER, Henry, 43, weaver?, Hoboken, NJ – 1909/07/10:6a
BUSSMANN, Magdalena, b. Schmitt, 62, NYC-M – 1889/02/01:4a
BUSZKOWSKA % Wallstrom
BUTCHEROFF, Bertha, 42, NYC-M – 1891/07/23:4a
BUTENSCHOEN, K., NYC-M – 1893/08/27:5a
BUTKEREIT, Emma, NYC-B - 1919/05/03:6a
BUTLER, Benjamin F., US genl & populist polit., – 1893/01/12:1b, = 17:1d
BUTLER, Michael, hotelier & politician, NYC-Bx – 1906/11/20:3b
BUTLER, Michael, undercover cop, killed during building workers' strike, NYC-M – 1906/07/12:1e, 13:4a-b, 25:1g, 27:1g,2a, 26:1e
BUTLER, William, Negro, lynched Paris, TX – 1893/02/09:1b
BUTLER-HEIMHAUSEN, Viktoria, Countess, 92, friend of SPD, + Munich – 1902/02/20:2d
BUTTELMANN, Ernst, 62, NYC-B – 1904/08/01:4a, 3:4a
BUTTELMANN, Marie, b. Esser, NYC-Q – 1909/12/18:8a
BUTTELMANN, Theodor, infant, NYC-M - 1878/09/11:3a
BUTTLE, Joseph, 83, journalist & alderman, SPD Mannheim/Baden – 1911/04/09:3a
BUTTLER, Ludwig, un. painter, NYC-Bx – 1907/11/04:6a
BUTTS, Arthur C., 65, Police Court Judge, NYC-Bx - 1913/10/13:2f
BUTZIGER, Franz, NYC-M – 1893/02/03:4a
BUTZKI, August, tailor, Swedish Socialist pioneer, 50th birthday – 1899/03/03:2c
BUZZELL, Joseph R., exec. Concord, N.H. - 1879/07/11:1c
BYCHAWER, Julius, SP, ex-bus. mgr of Jewish Vorwaerts, NYC-B – 1913/04/25:6c
BYRNES, Thomas F., NYC Police Chief, negat obit – 1910/05/09:4c

CABONERO, John, SP, un. machinist, NYC-Q - 1918/12/04:6a
CABRILOVIC, Veljko, one of the murderers of Archduke Franz Ferd. of Austria,exec. Sarajewo – 1915/03/02:4d, 18:3d-e
CACKOWSKI, Augusta, 51, NYC-M – 1920/10/02:6a, 3:2a
CACKOWSKI, Hermine, wd Schulz, NYC-M - 1919/02/14:6a
CADE, William, un. cigarmaker, NYC-B – 1894/05/01:4a
CADET, Santa, 71, vet. 1848 Rome revol., NYC? – 1889/05/04:2c
CADORE, Norman, Negro, lynched Baton Rouge, LA – 1912/12/24:2c
CAESAR, Catharina, NYC? – 1888/10/08:3a
CAFFREY, John, 76,tailor,*Norfolk/Eng., NYC-M - 1878/12/19:1f
CAHAN, Abraham, SP, chief ed. Jewish Vorwaerts, rev. 50th birthday, NYC-M – 1910/11/12:2c
CAHILL, Annie, 21, NYC-M, + @SS Genl Slocum – 1904/06/17:3b
CAHILL, John, NYPD - 1913/07/22:3b, 26:3a, 29:1f, 1 Aug:6c, 2:2a, 3:1d, 5:3b
CALFER, Joseph, 19, cafe musician, NYC-M - 1913/11/26:2c
CALI, Lorenzo, NYC, exec. Ossining, NY – 1912/08/13:1e, 14:3e-f, 15:2d
CALM, Anna, b. Ermeling, NYC-M – 1893/12/14:4a
CALMETTE, Gaston, chief ed. Paris Figaro, killed by Mrs Caillaux - 1914/03/17:2b, 18:1a, =21:1a,2d, 22:1c, 27:2a
CALSING, Henry, 38, un. iron moulder, NYC-B – 1900/06/09:4a, 10:5a, fam. 13:4a
CALVI, Giusto, 43, Italian soc. Polit. & MP – 1908/07/02:4d
CALVINHAC, Louis, French soc. Deputy for Toulouse – 1902/07/23:2d
CAMERON, Simon, Republ. "Boss" of Pennsylvania, negat. Obit – 1889/06/28:2a
CAMIN, Johannes, (Kamin?) German anarchist, + Halle/Gy, jail – 1897/04/27:2f
CAMMARERI, (Comrade), lawyer for SP Messina, + during earthquake with wife – 1909/02/23:4d
CAMPANELLA, Vinzenzo, NYC, exec. Ossining, NY - 1915/02/27:6b
CAMPBELL, Irving & Richard, Negroes, lynched Rowlette, KY – 1880/12/25:1c
CAMPBELL, John R., un. sheet metal worker, NYC-M – 1911/01/14:6a
CAMPBELL-BANNERMAN, Henry, English polit., 1908/04/23:1a, =28:1b
CAMPERS, Eduard, un. cigarmaker, NYC-M - 1919/03/15:6a
CAMPHAUSEN, Otto, Prussian Finance Minister, crit. obit. – 1896/05/20:2c,4a
CAMPO, un. butcher, NYC-M – 1919/10/07:8a
CAMPOS, Vicerbo de, Portuguese Socialist polit. – 1904/06/23:2c
CAMPRICI, Vincent J., Dr., 35, NYC-B - 1920/03/26:1d

CANALEJAS Y MENDES, Jose, Spanish Prime-Min. – 1912/11/13:1g, 4b
CANDIDA, Salvatore, exec. Ossining, NY – 1912/05/06:6d
CANEHL, Carl, NYC-B – 1912/04/16:6a, fam. 21:7b
CANITZ, Paul, Dr., SP?, NYC-M – 1912/06/20:6a
CANTER, Bernard, butcher, Passaic, NJ – 1902/03/06:4a
CANTINE, Chester, Poughkeepsie, NY, exec. Ossining, NY - 1920/05/15:2g
CANTIUS % Steinen, Von Den
CANTIUS, Florentine, b. Lange, 53, fr Berlin, SLP, NYC-B – 1899/09/16:1c, 3c, 4a, 17:2h,4a, 18:1d,4a, =19:2g, fam. 20:4a
CAPPELS, J. J., un. cigar maker & SP, ex-NYC, Huntingdon, IN, + Chicago – 1906/06/24:7a
CAPRANO, Lena, b. Brocks, NYC-M – 1906/02/08:4a
CAPRIVI, Leo von, ex-German chancellor – 1899/02/07:1f
CARDILLO, Donato, exec. Ossining, NY – 1913/02/11:1f
CAREY, Henry C., US economist - 1879/10/14:2c
CAREY, James, who betrayed the Irish patriots who shot Lord Cavendish in Phoenix Park/Dublin, found + 1883/07/31:1a-b, 1 Aug:1a-b, Carey's killing praised :2a-b, notes 3:1a, 4:2e
CAREY, John H., NYPD, NYC-M – 1892/11/04:4d
CARIELLI, Giuseppe, exec. Ossining, NY – 1912/07/09:1b
CARIUNI, ..., exec. Lancaster, PA – 1907/10/04:1e
CARIUS, Conrad, un. beer drover, NYC-M - 1895/01/02:4a
CARL, C., infant, NYC-M – 1906/08/08:2c
CARL, Conrad, 60, NYC-B – 1890/08/15:4a
CARL, Pauline, NYC-M – 1886/03/23:3d
CARLESON, John, 27, carp., fr Sweden, NYC-M – 1898/11/07:1g
CARLIN, Bernard, 22, to be exec. In Aug. – 1908/07/07:1e-f
CARLIN, Martin, exec. NYC – 1909/04/14:2e
CARLSEN, Sven M., Swede, NYC-B – 1900/06/02:3b
CARLSON, John, un. painter, fr Russia, Hoboken, NJ – 1900/08/22:3b
CARLSON, Rudolf, 68, un. cigar maker, fr Sweden, Gy 1871-1880, SP, New Haven, CT – 1910/02/06:7a, 7:2f,6a
CARLTON, Henry, NYC-M, to be exec. 5 Dec – 1889/10/18:2g, 5:2d, + 6 Dec:1d,
CARLYSLE, Thomas, 81, English philosopher, + London – 1881/02/14:2f
CARMER-OSTEN, Count von, 66, MdR (conservative), crit. - 1915/07/04:3b
CARMESIN, William, 69, Hoboken, NJ– 1919/05/14:6a
CARNEGIE, Andrew, US industrialist, crit. notes (example) 1901/03/15:2a-b, 17:4a-b, 24:4a-b, 26:3d. +, scathing obit. - 1919/08/12:1c,4c, =15:6a, note 3 Sept:4c-d, lt by Max Baginski 7:6e-g

CARNOT, Sadi, French president – 1894/06/26:2a
CAROLIN, Bridget, NYC-M – 1888/03/16:1g, 11 Apr:1e, husband
 Ferdinand sent. to death 18 Nov:1d, 19:1e, 22 Nov:2h, 4c, exec. 24 Jy
 1889:1h, 23:4e, + 24:2e
CARON, Arthur, US anarchist, + NYC – 1914/07/09:1e, 12:1e
CARPENTER, John K., NYPD, NYC-B - 1914/11/23:6d
CARPENTER, John, to be exec. – 1884/07/02:1g, 1:2c, on 29. Aug. 29
 Jy:3e, on 21 Aug. 1885/07/02:1g, 4:4b
CARPENTER, Matt H., US Sen. For Wisconsin – 1881/02/25:1b
CARPUS, Mathilde, servant, fr Hungary, War 2, Cedarhurst, L.I.–
 1915/09/04:2a
CARR, Royal S., exec. Windsor, VT – 1881/04/30:1d
CARRANZO, Veneziano, Mexican revol. – 1920/05/23:1f,4a-b, 25:1b
CARROLL, Thomas, 46, pres. Stereotypers Union #1, NYC-Bx –
 1916/10/29:11e
CARSTEN, John, 18, grocer, NYC-B – 1880/02/06:1g, 13:4a
CARSTENS, Ernst, infant, NYC-B – 1889/08/22:4a
CARSTENS, John, NYC-B – 1919/11/25:6a
CARSTENS, Joseph, infant, NYC-B – 1896/06/24:4a
CARSTENS, Wilhelmine, b. Zuckeyer, NYC-M - 1915/01/25:6a
CARTER, George, Negro, lynched Paris, KY – 1901/02/12:1b
CARTER, Kath., NYC-Bx – 1919/12/16:8a
CARVE, Heinrich, un. cigar maker, NYC 1880s, SLP, in Gy SPD, +
 Hamburg/Gy – 1900/05/20:1g
CASALI, Secchi di, fdr of NYC L'Eco D'Italia – 1885/06/11:3c
CASE, Leonard, Cleveland, OH millionaire but decent man – 1880/01/08:2d
CASELLA, Daniel A., Dr. med., NYC-M – 1911/01/31:1b
CASEMENT, Roger, Irish patriot, exec. London - 1916/08/04:1a, 2d, 4c,
 5:4a-b
CASH, August P., Harrison, NJ – 1904/12/25:5a
CASIMIR-PERRIER, Jean Paul, ex-French pres., + Paris – 1907/03/13:2b
CASLOW % Nalbach
CASPAR, Rosalie, b. Pietsch, NYC-M – 1889/02/18:4a
CASPARY, J., NYC-M – 1893/06/19:4a
CASPERS, Johanna, 20, NYC-M – 1900/10/03:4a
CASPERS, John, NYC-M - 1918/06/29:6a
CASSEBOHM, Karl J., 54, Hoboken, NJ – 1900/03/17:4a
CASSEL, Adolf, 42, grocer, Booton, NJ – 1912/09/05:3c
CASSEL, Casper, fr Luxemburg, + Chicago – 1892/04/19:1b
CASSELS, John D., exec. Charleston, MD – 1902/05/07:3c
CASSENS, Friedrich, SLP, mechanic, Yonkers, N.Y. – 1894/12/12:3g
CASSIDY, Joseph, 60, Demo. ward politician, NYC-Q - 1920/11/22:2e

CASTILLO, Canovas de, Spanish Prime-Minister, + by anarchists – 1897/
08/09:1a, 10:2a, =11:1h, 12:1a,14:1a, NYC Sp.-Am. mourn 19:1f, 20:1b
CATENESI, comrade, SP youth movement, Rome/Italy, War 1 -
1915/08/28:4d
CATHOR, Peter, un. cement & asphalt worker, NYC – 1913/02/14:6a
CATO, Negro, lynched Statesboro, GA – 1904/08/17:1d, 18:1f,2c, 19:1d
CATTERVE, Henry, Swiss, Chicago goldworker, + NYC-M -
1878/06/28:1g
CAVALOTTI, Felice, Italian polit. – 1898/03/27:9e-f
CAVELL, Edith, nurse, exec. 11 Nov. fr smuggling POWs out of Belgium -
1915/10/20:1d,22:2f, 23:1g, 4a-b, 24:1c, 26:2c, 1 Nov:1e, 9:3b-d
CAVENDISH, Lord, Genl-Secy for Ireland, & his assistant Mr. Burke, + by
Irish patriots in Phoenix Park/Dublin – 1882/05/08:2a-b, 9:1a-c, 10:2e-f,
12:1a-c,2a, meeting in NYC 13:1d-e, 14:4a-b etc, 21:5b-c
CAZENAVE, Albert, 48, & wife Lucie, 42, War 2, NYC-M - 1916/11/24:2a
CECH, Josef, brewer, San Jose, CA – 1900/07/25:3e
CECH, Svatopluk, Czech poet, – 1908/03/15:11a-c, = 29:3e-f
CECIL, Thomas, un. cigarmaker, NYC-M - 1878/09/04:3a
CEDARBAUM, Max, NYC, + Ethical Culture camp, 1906/09/03:2d, 4:6c
CELIA, Mathilde, fr Gy, USA 1873, NYC-M - 1878/09/04:4c
CELLIONE, ..., exec. Lancaster, PA – 1907/10/04:1e
CEMVELES, John, 61, cigarmaker, fr Belgium, War 2, NYC-B -
1916/04/07:6a
CESAR, Maria, 44, NYC-Q – 1899/01/15:5a
CESAR, Mathias, NYC-Q - 1913/09/20:6a
CHACON, Miguel, exec. NYC-M – 1886/07/10:1f
CHALTURIN, Stephan, Russian revol., exec. 3 Apr 1882 Odessa –
1883/08/26:3a-c, 2 Sept:3a-e; Memory 1904/01/17:4c-e
CHAMBERS, comrade (female), SP, Liberty, NY – 1911/10/24:6a
CHAMBERS, Henry, Negro, lynched Annapolis, MD – 1906/12/22:2a
CHAMBORD, Count, Heir French throne, + Paris, crit. Obit –
1883/07/03:1a,2c, 4:1a, 9:2d, his will 26:2f
CHAMPELLIE, Frank, 21, Austrian, NYC – 1915/11/04:6d
CHAMPLIN, Roy, 25, exec. Ossining, NY – 1916/06/03:1e
CHANG, Li Hung, Chinese politician – 1901/11/08:1f
CHANIN, Fanny, fr Russia, NYC-M – 1901/03/21:1g
CHANNING, William Ellery, 100th anniv. fdr of Unitarianism, praise –
1880/04/08:2c
CHANOWITZ, Samuel, watchman, fr Russia, NYC-M – 1900/10/03:1d
CHANTZ, Ch., machinist, NYC-M – 1888/10/06:2h
CHANUTE, SP, New Orleans, LA - 1913/11/10:1b

CHAPMAN, Victor, NYC, US vol. in French airforce, War 1 - 1916/06/25:11g
CHARDON, comrade, SLP, vet 1870 Paris commune, Paterson, NJ - 1879/11/19:2b
CHARLES, Robert, Negro, lynched New Orleans – 1900/07/28:1c
CHARLIER, Johann, stonecutter fr Koeln, USA 1885?, NYC-M – 1889/03/03:5b
CHARLOTTE, May, 51, NYC-M, + @ SS Genl Slocum – 1904/06/17:3b
CHARRIER, George, 62, Steinway worker, NYC – 1884/10/25:3b
CHARRON, Ed., 11, NYC-B – 1911/01/19:1d
CHARTLAS, Louisa, 24, 1908 fr Switzerland, NYC-M – 1908/05/13:2b
CHARWAT, Johann, SP Vienna/Austria – 1908/03/01:3e
CHASE, Edna May, 22, teacher at PS 16, NYC-B – 1898/01/30:1g
CHASE, Nathan, 26, salesman - 1913/12/05:1e, 6:2b
CHASEN, Bertha, 50, NYC-Q – 1909/11/08:6a
CHAUVIERE, Emanuel, 60, French soc. & MP – 1910/06/14:4d-e
CHEKA, Frank, Harwood, PA, coal-miner, killed by militia in @Latimer – 1897/09/12:1b
CHENEY, US consul in Messina, = after earthquake 1909/01/30:2e
CHERNOCK, Harry, 30, tailor, fr Russia, NYC-M – 1907/09/26:1d
CHESLOK, Michael, Harwood, PA, coal-miner, killed by militia in @Latimer – 1897/09/12:1b
CHESTER, Michael, 45, knitted goods manuf., War 2, NYC-B - 1915/05/06:6c
CHEVALIER, Francois, fdr Swiss Benevolent Soc, Hoboken, NJ – 1881/04/07:3a
CHEZANOWSKI, Julian, 27, + during strike, NYC-B – 1910/08/18:1f
CHICKERING, Charles, Congressman (Republ) fr Lewis County, NY – 1900/02/14:4c
CHIESA, Pietro, Italian socialist & member of parliament, - 1916/01/14:4f
CHILACK, Anderusia, fr Bohemia, NYC-M – 1882/09/13:1g
CHILDS, Geo. W.,65,publisher & social reformer - 1894/02/04:1d
CHINA, Emperor of, + 1898/10/02:1c
CHINA, Tsu Hi, Empress of, 1908/11/29:20c
CHINN, S. O., IWW member, killed by Spokane police – 1910/03/25:1f,
CHISHOLM, John, exec. Newark, NJ – 1883/11/22:2g, 23:4e, his will 4 Dec:2g
CHITEL % Schaefer
CHMELIK, Johann, NYC-M – 1892/07/10:5c
CHMILEWSKI, Casimir, un. carp., NYC-Bx – 1912/02/09:6a
CHOATE, Joseph H. Sr, 85, US diplomat, hon. pres. National Security League, obit. crit. his war-mongering, NYC-M - 1917/05/16:6c

CHODORA, Josef, SP, West Hoboken, NJ – 1909/04/04:7c
CHOWOGEE, Mindec, Negro, lynched Marshall, MO – 1900/04/30:1d
CHRIST, (Mr.), Oneida, NY – 1901/01/22:4a
CHRIST, Arthur, 47, NYC-Q – 1911/11/23:2e
CHRIST, Bernhard, un. carp., NYC-M – 1891/06/24:4a
CHRIST, John, 16, NYC-B – 1901/02/09:4a
CHRIST, Karl, NYC-M – 1893/06/11:5b
CHRIST, Paul, 10, Frankfurt/Main, killed by car driven by prince Henry of Netherlands – 1913/03/23:3c
CHRISTEN, Dorothea, b. Gerber, 60, NYC-M – 1883/04/08:8a
CHRISTEN, Wilhelm, 20, NYC-M – 1892/06/19:5c
CHRISTENSEN, Carl Adolph, 56, Bogota, NJ - 1917/11/26:6a
CHRISTENSEN, Jens – 1902/07/19:2h, 28:2e, 12 Aug:2d, 18:2d
CHRISTENSEN, Jens, lawyer, at Chicago Arbeiter-Zeitung, SDP, * Schleswig, USA 1888, + NYC
CHRISTENSEN, Peter, 25, sailor, NYC – 1904/01/24:5f
CHRISTENSEN, Waldemar, 66, SP, un. carp., * Aalborg, USA 1884, NYC-Bx - 1917/08/08:6a, = 10:2d
CHRISTIAN, Juergens, un. carp., NYC?, + in "Heimath" – 1884/09/18:3d
CHRISTIANSEN, Asmund, NYC-Q - 1914/11/04:6a
CHRISTIANSEN, Caroline, 22, NYC-M – 1891/03/22:1c
CHRISTIANSEN, Hans P., 53, un. carp., Jersey City Heights, NJ – 1902/02/09:5a, 11:4a
CHRISTIANSEN, Mary Christine, 19, NYC-M – 1896/11/01:5a
CHRISTLER, Adam, 60, NYC-B – 1911/10/24:3a
CHRISTMANN, Heinrich, 47, un. carp., NYC-M – 1906/01/29:4a, 31:4a
CHRISTMANN, Henry, 29, box maker, NYC-M – 1880/11/04:4c, 9:1c
CHRISTMANN, Philipp, 60, NYC-B – 1887/01/03:2e
CHRISTMANN, Philippina, 73, NYC-M - 1878/08/30:3a
CHRISTMANN, Rudolf, NYC-Bx – 1912/10/15:2d
CHRISTOCK, Joseph, ex. Pottsville, PA – 1911/03/31:3d
CHRISTOPH, Wilhelm, 24, NYC-M – 1892/08/11:4a
CHRISTOPHCSAKS, Stephan, 48, artist fr Hungary, NYC-B – 1912/10/01:2a
CHRISTOPHER, John, grocer, * Amt Hagen/Hannover, NYC-M - 1878/08/05:4b
CHRISTOPHER, Joseph, 30, cigar salesman, French, NYC-M – 1908/04/15:2c
CHRISTOPHERS, M.H., 62, NYC-B - 1894/01/28:5d
CHRISTY, John, stevedore, fr Austria, NYC-M – 1901/06/20:2b
CHROMETZKA, Paul, 54, un. carp., NYC? – 1907/12/30:7a, = 1 Jan. 1908:5f

CHURCH, Sanford E., NYS judge, posit. Obit – 1880/05/15:1d, 17:2c
CHURCHILL, Lord Randolph, British polit. – 1895/01/25:2c
CIPRIANI, Amilcar, + Paris, vet 1870 Commune – 1918/05/30:4c
CIROSICI, Frank, exec. Ossining, NY – 1914/04/14:1g,2a-b,4a
CITRON, Isaak, 60, NYC-M – 1890/07/02:4a
CLAAR, Henry, NYC-M? – 1900/06/21:4a
CLAAS, Wilhelmina, 37, NYC-M – 1904/10/30:5d
CLAASSEN, Henry, un. mechanic, NYC-B – 1894/11/05:4a
CLARA, J., Newark, NJ – 1904/03/31:4a
CLARK, Billy, 8, murdered near Albany, NY – 1916/04/16:1f
CLARK, Jumbo, Negro, lynched High Springs, VA – 1904/01/16:1b
CLARK, Samuel, Negro, lynched near Trail Lake, Miss., – 1904/06/04:3f
CLARKE, Thomas J., Irish patriot, exec. – 1916/05/04:1a-b,4d
CLAUBERG, Hermann, 44, Newark, NJ – 1904/07/13:4a
CLAUS, Charles Theodor, machinist, NYC-M – 1907/11/13:6a
CLAUS, Friedrich, innkeep, SPD Hamburg/Gy – 1909/02/21:3a
CLAUS, Henry Christian, SLP, NYC-M – 1892/05/26:4a
CLAUSEN, A., '48er, fr Schleswig, Orange, NJ – 1886/08/25:2e
CLAUSEN, Dietrich, 38, laborer, NYC-M – 1906/02/11:1e
CLAUSEN, Franz, 30, NYC-M – 1892/11/06:5c
CLAUSEN, Frederick., innkeep, NYC-M? – 1892/07/30:1e
CLAUSEN, Henry Jr., 56, NYC-M – 1893/12/30:4a
CLAUSNER, Ehrhardt, 48, SP, foreman, NYC-B – 1907/03/16:2c, 25:3a,6a, fam. 28:6a
CLAUSNITZER, Carl Moritz, surgical instrument maker, NYC-B – 1894/12/02:5a
CLAUSS, Jacob, 50, NYC-M – 1882/06/05:3g
CLAUSSEN, August, un. cigarmaker, 45, NYC-Bx – 1893/06/14:4a
CLAUSSEN, Diedrich, 59, NYC-Bx – 1913/02/12:6a
CLAUSSEN, Heinrich, 45, USA 1903, bus. Agent for Hamburg sock manuf., NYC-M – 1907/11/30:6c
CLAUSSEN, Hermann C., 46, NYC-M – 1891/08/28:4a
CLAUSSEN, Louise, b. Rippstein, fr Hamburg/Gy, NYC-M – 1893/05/22:4a
CLAWSON, Elmer, 18, exec. in Somerville, NJ – 1897/05/12:2f, 13:1f
CLEARY, James, politician, + by police chief Cash, NYC-Bx – 1893/05/28:1h, 29:1g, 30:1c-d, 3 June:2d
CLEAVE, J. W. Van, chair Natl Manuf Assoc., very crit. obit, + St Louis, MO – 1910/05/16:1d
CLEBOWSKY, Stephen, 31, NYC-B – 1917/10/03:6c
CLEFF, Louise, b. Zuberer, NYC-M – 1917/05/17:6a
CLEMENS, Emile, 60, silkflower dyer, French, NYC-M – 1894/02/26:1f

CLEMENS, Jean, daughter of Mark Twain, Redding, CT – 1909/12/25:1b
CLEMENS, Rudolf, 48, NYC-M – 1901/10/29:4a
CLEMENT, Constantin, cigarmaker, NYC-M - 1878/03/23:4a
CLEMM, Dr., BASF founder & MdR (natl-lib) – 1899/03/19:12f
CLEMM, George, 69, locksmith, Newark, NJ – 1900/07/29:5c
CLEMMER, James A., exec. Norristown, PA – 1899/05/19:1f
CLERGET, Max, NYC-M – 1892/07/02:2f
CLEVELAND, Grover, US pres., crit. obit – 1908/06/25:1g,2a, 4a-b, 26:4a-b, =27:2c, note 28:4a-c
CLEVER % Klingelhoeffer
CLEW, Robert, un. carp., NYC-B – 1902/10/13:4a
CLEYRE, Voltairine De, US socialist & feminist, IWW org. – 1912/06/27:1d
CLIFFORD, Edward, exec. Jersey City, NJ – 1900/05/09:4b
CLIFFORD, Stephan, actor, NYC-Q – 1916/10/17:1f
CLOSA, Susanna, b. Hencke, wd Alzmoneit?, NYC-Bx - 1916/12/20:6a
CLOSE, David, 60, hatmaker, Newark, NJ – 1886/10/08:2f
CLOUST, Minnie, (Clusth?), 13, NYC-M, + @SS Genl Slocum – 1904/06/18:3c
CLOW, Margaret, 35, NYC-M, + @ SS Genl Slocum – 1904/06/17:3b
CLUBOCK, Clara, fr Texas, War 2 NYC-M - 1917/08/01:2f
CLUNDT, Christian, NYC-M – 1889/06/06:4a
CLUNDT, Concordia, b. Vogt, 60, fr Bad Horb/Bav., NYC-Bx – 1906/04/16:4a
CLUSERET, Gustav Paul, 77, French communard & MP for Toulon after amnesty – 1900/08/24:1c
CLUSTH, Kate, 25, NYC-M, + @SS Genl Slocum – 1904/06/22:1d
CLUTE, Jacob W., ex-mayor Schenectady, NY – 1911/04/13:1d
COBBE, William Rosser, ret. Professor, NYC? – 1907/01/02:6c
COBBES, Charles, brewer or cooper NYC-M – 1890/01/16:4a
COBDEN % Anderson
COBELSKY, Ida, servant, 23, NYC-M – 1889/02/06:2g
COESTER, H. F., NYC-M – 1896/08/06:4a
COHEN % Oppenhym
COHEN, Alex, Elizabeth, NJ – 1909/01/02:3b
COHEN, Anna, 25, NYC-B, @Triangle Shirtwaist Co fire – 1911/03/27:1d
COHEN, Aziel, 80, NYC-M – 1891/08/12:4a
COHEN, Charles, NYC-M – 1898/09/04:1c
COHEN, David, 40, tailor, & family, NYC-M – 1903/01/03:1g
COHEN, Eliza, 57, NYC-M – 1881/01/25:1d
COHEN, Esther, 38, & children, NYC-M – 1901/03/31:1h
COHEN, Fannie, 57, NYC-B – 1911/07/22:3a

COHEN, Gussie, 24, fr Poland, War 2, NYC-M - 1916/02/08:6e
COHEN, Harry, mobster, NYC-M - 1918/04/02:1d, 3:1g, 6:6a
COHEN, Hermann, 25, fr Russia, NYC-M - 1890/02/15:1g
COHEN, Jennie, 68, NYC-B - 1908/05/04:1e
COHEN, Joseph, 56, Newark, NJ - 1902/01/01:1c
COHEN, Louis, innkeep, NYC-B - 1900/03/24:1e
COHEN, Louise, 45, NYC-M - 1893/01/23:4
COHEN, Max, 19, mobster, member of Galaxy Gang, NYC-M - 1913/11/30:1f
COHEN, Michael, 79, NYC-M - 1890/03/30:5b
COHEN, Morris & family, NYC-M - 1893/02/04:1g
COHEN, Morris, cloak cutter, NYC-M - 1898/12/29:2h
COHEN, Nathan, 1912 fr Brazil, + NYC = 1916/03/06:6d
COHEN, Rebecca, & son Karl, infant, NYC-B - 1896/05/06:4b
COHEN, Sadie, 23, un. blouse maker, NYC-M - 1909/12/07:2e
COHEN, Salomon, 3 months, NYC-M - 1895/04/10:4a
COHEN, Samuel, worker, NYC-B - 1886/06/09:2c
COHEN, Sophia, 19, NYC-M - 1907/07/26:1d
COHEN, Wilhelm, 20, NYC-M - 1914/08/10:2f, 11:2d
COHEN, Wolf, 21, shoe maker, NYC-M - 1897/06/03:4d
COHEN, Wolf, 26, coal-dealer, NYC-M - 1894/04/25:1d
COHEN, Yetta, 42, NYC-M - 1901/11/26:3c
COHN, Charles, *24 Jan. 1825 Breslau, G-A Journalist, NYC-M - 1886/02/16:1e, 18:1f
COHN, Elias, 62, landlord, NYC-M - 1888/09/01:1h
COHN, Estelle, 50, madam, Hackensack, NJ - 1914/01/02:3c
COHN, Esther, NYC-B - 1918/04/16:6a
COHN, Henry, un. painter, NYC-Bx - 1919/04/28:6a
COHN, Ida, 11, NYC-M - 1892/07/18:1g
COHN, Isidor, un. cigarmaker, NYC-M - 1897/11/29:4a
COHN, Joseph, 55, tailor, NYC-M - 1902/11/12:3d
COHN, Joseph, 86, NYC-M - 1892/02/14:5d
COHN, Louis M., 62, NYC-M - 1892/06/21:4a
COHN, Louis, 89, old leader of SPD Breslau/Gy - 1911/07/28:2c, =30:3b
COHN, Louisa, 27, NYC-M - 1892/04/02:4a
COHN, Nathan S., 50, bus mgr N.Y. Morgenjournal, NYC-M - 1906/03/27:3d
COHN, Regine, b. Kanter, 47, NYC-M - 1910/03/08:6a
COHN, Samuel, 24, NYC-M - 1892/11/30:4a
COHN, Siegfried, NYC-M - 1897/09/25:4a
COHNEN, Francis William, NYC-M - 1888/04/10:3a
COHNEN, Salomon, 62, NYC-M - 1894/01/28:5d

COHR, Anna, 59, NYC-M – 1893/11/26:5d
COHRS, Frieda, 26, & daughter Frieda, NYC-M, +@SS Genl Slocum – 1904/06/17:3b, 26:1c
COHS, Albert, NYC-M – 1904/07/26:4a
COKER, Frederick, Negro, lynched Springfield, MO – 1906/04/16:1c-d, 17:1d
COLBERG, Ferdinand, 43, NYC-B – 1892/06/28:4a
COLDITZ, August, 78, SPD Crimmitzschau/Saxony, ex-MdL – 1912/01/14:3c
COLE, Henry A., un. carp., NYC-B - 1918/08/02:6a
COLELL, C.H., NYC-B - 1914/05/03:7a
COLEMAN, Richard, Negro, lynched Maysville, KY – 1899/12/07:1h, 11:2b
COLFAX, Schuyler, Indiana polit. & vice-president – 1885/01/14:2c
COLIN, John B., 60, florist, fr France 1870s, NYC-M – 1898/12/20:3b
COLIOS, Frieda, NYC-M, + @SS Genl Slocum – 1904/06/18:3c
COLLENBURG, Amalie, NYC-M – 1898/08/04:4a
COLLENBURG, C. E., 68, NYC-M – 1902/11/16:5a
COLLIER, Peter Fenelon, publ. Colliers Weekly – 1910/07/16:4d
COLLIER, Robert J., publ. Collier's Magazine, obit. crit. rabid prohibitionist, NYC-M - 1918/11/11:4d
COLLINS, Anna, b. Sturm, NYC-M - 1918/10/26:6a
COLLINS, J.C., Negro, lynched Mondale, Montana – 1913/04/06:9g
COLLINS, John, NYC, exec. Ossining, NY – 1912/08/13:1e
COLLINS, Margarethe, b. Strehl, 65, NYC-M – 1892/06/16:4a
COLLINS, Thomas, Negro, lynched Bunkie, LA - 1915/07/17:1c
COLLOSENS, Georg, sculptor, NYC-M – 1895/07/24: 4a
COLYER, Samuel, lithographer, NYC-B – 1880/03/19:1g
COMM, Franz, NYC-M - 1917/08/30:6a
COMOLLI, Martin, 48, NYC-M – 1909/08/08:7b
CONA, Vincenzo, NYC, exec. Ossining, NY – 1912/08/13:1e, 14:3e-f, 15:2d
CONKLING, Alfred R., 67, Rep. polit. NYC-M - 1917/09/19:1f
CONNELLY, Joseph, NYC-B – 1919/01/11:6a
CONNER % Wetzel
CONNOLLY, James, Irish patriot & Soc., exec. by the British in Dublin - 1916/05/04:1a-b, 4d, 7:7c, done 13:1c,2c, NYC SP mem. meeting 27:2b, NYC Irish mem. Meeting 11 June:1c, 12:4d, notes 7 Aug:1e
CONNOLLY, Richard B., NYC comptroller under Boss Tweed – 1880/06/02:2c
CONNORS, Julia, (also O'Connors), 11, NYC-Bx – 1912/07/08:1d, 9:1e, 14:6b, 16:2b-c, 17:1c

CONNORS, Sarah Victoria,18,+ 28 Ju,NYC-M - 1878/10/02:1f,4:1g
CONRAD % Rohling
CONRAD, Elizabeth, 58, NYC-B - 1911/05/16:6a
CONRAD, Ernst, treas. D-A Schuetzenbund, NYC-M - 1890/01/09:4a
CONRAD, Gottfried H., NYC-M - 1891/07/17:4a
CONRAD, Heinrich, 1, NYC-M - 1878/08/17:3e
CONRAD, Jacob, 46, billard-ball maker, * Gy, NYC-M - 1894/08/26:5f
CONRAD, John H., NYC-B - 1880/02/03:2g
CONRAD, Joseph, NYC-M - 1892/07/29:4a
CONRAD, Lizzie, b. Gscheidle, NYC-M - 1918/10/15:6a
CONRAD, Maria, b. Riethe, 32, * Neuenstein/Oehringen/Gy, NYC-M - 1887/03/29:3d
CONRAD, Mary, 46, NYC-M - 1900/06/19:4a
CONRAD, Ms, 19, NYC-M - 1909/04/25:7c
CONRAD, Wilhelm, NYC-Q - 1907/03/30:6a
CONRAD, Wilhelm?, SP, NYC-Q, (not +), needs help - 1907/03/06:6c
CONRADY, Henry, 40, NYC-B - 1898/11/19:4d
CONRATH, John Peter, 57, carp., NYC-Q - 1911/06/01:2e
CONROY, J., labor informer, NYC? - 1911/12/18:1d
CONTERNO, Louis, 62, conductor 14th regt NYNG band - 1910/12/25:7c
CONWAY, Charles W., NYC-M? - 1891/01/15:4a
CONWAY, James J., NYPD, NYC-Q? - 1916/06/30:2b
CONZETT, Adolf, son of late editor Chicago Arbeiter-Zeitung, Boer army volunteer, + fighting against British imperialism near Ladysmith/South Africa - 1900/01/11:2c
COOK, Adolph, 28, tailor, NYC-B - 1882/07/20:4e
COOK, Henry, 57, Hoboken, NJ - 1900/06/14:4a
COOK, Robert, 45, NYC-M - 1917/03/15:6a
COOKE, Henry D., ex-gov. District of Columbia - 1881/02/25:1b
COOMBS, Cornelius, Negro, exec. Pittsburgh, PA - 1906/09/07:1b
COON, George, 52, NYC-M - 1894/01/21:5d
COOPER, Ella, artist (painter), NYC-M - 1897/04/13:3f
COOPER, Peter, 86, NYC philanthropist, 1883/04/05:1e, 2a, 6:1g, 7:1g, =8:1f, 4a-b, his will 12:1d, monument, plans 1883/09/16:4b, 1886/12/29:2f, 1888/09/29:1d,
COPELAND, ..., Negro,lynched Springfield, MO - 1906/04/16:1c-d, 17:1d
COPLER, W., 60, NYC-B - 1902/07/30:4b
COPPEE, Francois, French writer, + Paris - 1908/05/24:7e
CORBACH, William, 49, un. cigarmaker, NYC-M - 1893/09/20:4a, mem. 24 Nov:4a; 1894/09/29:4a

CORBEDDU, Salis Giovanni, famous Sardinian highway robber, 1898/09/23:2c-d
CORBIN, Austin, crit. obit of the millionaire – 1896/06/07:4a-b
CORCORAN, Daniel, un. tool maker & KoL official, NYC-M – 1900/07/16:3b
CORCORAN, John, un. architect. Iron worker, NYC-M – 1901/10/11:4a
CORDES, Anna E., b. Faatz, 52, Mt Vernon, NY – 1886/09/06:3c
CORDES, Bertha, 31, NYC-B – 1912/09/06:2d
CORDES, Caroline, b. Warnken, NYC-M – 1888/01/14:3a
CORDES, Chas W, NYC-M – 1892/07/08:4a
CORDES, Elise M. L., NYC-M – 1891/11/11:4a
CORDES, Frieda, 6, NYC-M, +@ SS Genl Slocum – 1904/06/18:3c
CORDES, H.F.,39, grocer, fr Amt Rotenburg/Hannover?, NYC-B - 1878/04/03:4f, 4:3a
CORDES, Henrietta A., NYC-M – 1891/06/25:4a
CORDES, Hermine, 10, & Hermann, 2, NYC-B – 1889/02/04:4a
CORDES, John F., NYC-B – 1890/05/25:5a
CORDES, John Henry, 76, NYC-M – 1889/09/03:4a
CORDES, Marjorie, b. Holzenthal, NYC-M – 1891/07/16:4a
CORDES, Mary, NYC-B - 1918/04/19:6a
CORDES, Meta, 31, & Henrietta, NYC-M, + @SS Genl Slocum – 1904/06/17:3b
CORDES, Wilhelm F., NYC-M – 1892/11/03:4a
CORDTS, Henry W., 64, NYC-B - 1894/01/24:4a
CORDTS, Lena S., stewardess on ship Saale, + fr explosion, Jersey City, NJ – 1900/07/02:1g, 3:1c
CORDUAN, Otto, un. typesetter, NYC-M? – 1893/03/29:4a
CORLEIS, Henry Paul, 5, NYC-B – 1891/03/16:4a
CORNEHL, Catherine, b. Schmidt, 52, NYC-B - 1920/11/25:6a
CORNELISSEN, Maurice de, *23.XII.1862 Paris, French count, & wife, NYC-M – 1893/10/20:1f
CORNELIUS % Marquardt
CORNELIUS, Georg Adam, 32, tinsmith, NYC-M – 1889/12/30:4a, 1 Jan. 1890:4a
CORNELIUS, Jacob, SP, un. metal worker, NYC-B - 1919/02/28:6a, fam. 10 Mr:6a; mem. 1920/02/26:6a
CORNELIUS, Wilhelmina, NYC-B – 1900/08/12:5a
CORNELLY, Philipp, un. carp., NYC-B - 1913/05/22:6a
CORNETTI, Angelo, exec. White Plains, NY – 1883/05/12:1b
CORNILLS, John, 52, NYC-B - 1895/12/07: 4a
CORRIGAN, archbishop, crit. obit – 1902/05/08:2b, =10:1f
CORSSEN, Fritz, un. butcher, NYC-B – 1903/08/25:4a

CORTESE, Robert, 48, Justice of the Peace, Paterson, NJ – 1907/02/09:1d, 11:1b, 18:3b
CORVIN-WIESBITZKI, Otto Julius von, '48er, journalist & historian, * 12 Oc 1812 Gumbinnen, + in Thueringia – 1886/03/18:6b-c
CORYUT, Petrus Von Den, exec. Ossining, NY - 1917/04/22:7f
COSFELD, D., un. cigar maker, NYC-M – 1891/09/02:4a
COSTA, Andrea, Italian Soc., + Imalo – 1910/01/26:4b, =4 Fb:4e-f, note 3 Mr:4e-f
COSTELLO % Schramm
COTTE, Gilbert, 48, leader of French miners, 1905/06/07:2d
COTTER, ..., 27, NYPD - 1913/08/05:2d
COTTIGNEIS, Etienne DE, French, silk worker, War 2, Phillipsburg, NJ - 1914/09/02:2f
COTTO, Jeremiah, exec. Ossining, NY – 1892/03/29:1b
COTTON, Budd, Negro, lynched Palmetto, GA – 1899/03/17:2h
COTTON, T. E., 16, Negro, lynched Columbus, GA – 1912/08/14:2e
COTTRELL, Wilhelmine, b. Roesch?, NYC-B – 1891/07/09:4a
COUCH, Melvin H., ex-D.A., Monticello, NJ - 1913/12/23:1d, 24:1c, 25:2b
COUCHE, Friedrich, 13, Union Hill, NJ – 1892/08/07:1e
COULSON, William H., 35, chemist, Jersey City, NJ – 1896/05/01:2e
COUNARD, Henry, 45, bricklayer, Swiss, Northport, L.I. - 1915/12/06:2e
COURAY, Jean, 1871 Commune vet, NYC-M – 1887/04/11:2e
COURBET, Gustave, French painter - 1878/03/24:7c-e
COUSENS, Leonora, actress, NYC-M – 1896/06/30:1d
COX, Abraham, Negro, lynched Oglethorpe County, GA – 1919/09/11:5e
COX, Chastine, exec. in NYC – 1880/07/13:1f, 14:1e, 15;4d, 16:1f, + 17:1d-e, 2c, 4a
COX, Geo. B., "Boss" of Cincinatti - 1916/05/21:1g
COX, Samuel J., congressman fr Ohio, + NYC – 1889/09/11:4e, 14:3a
COYER, George, exec. Auburn, NY - 1914/09/01:2b
CRADDOCK, Ida, 45, writer & reformer, NYC-M – 1902/10/18:1c
CRAMER, Anna, b. Bollmann, 49, NYC-M – 1892/07/16:4a
CRAMER, Louis, 76, NYC-M – 1892/06/29:4a
CRAMER, Richard, labor poet (as Rudolf Lavant) & journalist for Leipziger Volkstimme, + Leipzig 5 Dec 1915 - 1916/01/30:3d
CRAMER-GREIE, Johanna see Johanna Greie-Cramer
CRANE, Walter, 70, English painter & socialist, + London - 1915/03/17:1e,4a-b, 4 Jy:18e-g
CRANTZ, Frantz, 35, hotelier, Freehold, NJ – 1900/09/17:3c
CRATZ, C., NYC-B – 1918/09/10:2g
CRAVATH, Victor, 30, Fr Desoto, MO, + NYC-M – 1890/02/18:1g

CRAVE, Catharina, NYC boarding house – 1881/01/27:1e, 29:4a, dying 19 Apr:4a, + 7 June:3b, 8:1d, 19:5d, trial of W. Sindram 1881/09/30:1g
CRAVEN, Charles, negro, lynched Leeksburg, VA – 1902/08/01:1h
CRECI, comrade, Cuban socialist, = 1899/11/20:1b
CREDI, Christian, un. cabinet maker, NYC-M – 1892/05/29:5b, 30:4a, fam. 2 June:4a
CREIGHTON, Edith, actress, see Simmons, Edith
CREMER, William Randall, British MP, posit. Note – 1908/07/28:4b-c
CREMIEUX, Isaac, 83, Franco-Jewish polit., – 1880/02/11:1b
CREVIER, William, 20, NYC-M – 1880/09/02:1e, 3:4b
CRILL, Frederick, exec. Newton, NJ – 1880/04/25:5d
CRINKLER, Clar, NYC-B – 1908/05/21:6a
CRISPI, Francesco, ex-prime min. of Italy – 1901/08/12:1b
CROLA, Maria Magdalena, 65, wife of SPD member & NYVZ contrib., + 4 Nov. 1915 Ilsenburg/Harz – 1916/03/19:7b
CROMBURGER, Frederick, 13, NYC-Q – 1897/05/02:9g
CRONIN, Dr., murdered in Chicago, notes – 1893/12/03:1h
CRONJE, Piet, Boer general, + Kliendorp/RSA – 1911/02/05:7e
CRONK, Ida L.,23, servant, Jersey City, NJ - 1879/05/05:4d
CRONSON, F. J., 40, salesman, NYC – 1903/06/13:4a
CROSBY, Ernest H., reformer, + 3 Jan., memorial 1907/03/08:1d
CROSBY, Howard, Dr., reformer, NYC-M – 1891/03/30:4a
CROSBY, Robert, Negro, lynched near Montgomery, AL – 1919/10/01:1e,4a
CROSBY, Warner, songwriter, NYC-M – 1907/04/29:1f
CROTLY, George, NYC-B – 1900/03/27:3b
CRUGER, Frederick, 60, NYC-B - 1915/03/16:6c
CRUGER, Ruth, 17, HS student, vanished 13 Feb., body found, NYC-M - 1917/06/17:1g, 18:1e, killer fd 23:1g, 25:2f, 26:6b, 27:1c, 3 Jy:5f, 4:2c
CRUSIUS, Henry, 25, bartender fr Bremerhaven/Gy, NYC-B – 1887/03/11:2f
CRUTCHFIELD, Dusty, Negro, lynched Hamilton, GA – 1912/01/24:1b
CSILLAG, Sigismund, Dr. med., 60, Hungarian soc. – 1910/03/06:3d
CUCHINER, August, 39, un. tailor, NYC-M – 1882/01/06:3b
CULBERTSON, Cleve, Negro, lynched Williston,ND - 1913/12/17:1d
CULLMANN, Grace A.L., 29, NYC-M – 1892/06/10:4a
CULMISKY, Minnie, infant, NYC-M – 1898/09/07:1f
CUMMINGS, Amos J., congressman & union member – 1902/05/07:4b
CUMMINGS, James, & Ed Hurley, drivers, killed by boss Michael Gallivan over unpaid wages 26 Dec 1890:1d, 27:1h, 28:1f, 30:1h, 31:1h; Gallivan released 14 Jan. 1891:1e, again indicted 28 Feb:2g, 5 Mr:2g, 6:2g, trial 2 Dec. 1891:1e, freed by jury 4:1h

CUNO, Mrs, 35, * Wilmington, DE, actress, played in Leipzig as "Annette Ricca," husband Theodor SLP, NYC? – 1882/07/21:3a
CUNO, Theodor F., ex-NYVZ editor, letter fr commune in Newllano, Vernon Parish, LA - 1920/05/03:2c
CURIE, Pierre, French scientist, + Paris – 1906/04/20:1f
CURLEY, Daniel, Irish patriot, exec. Dublin – 1883/05/19:1b
CURRAN, Peter Francis, British labor leader, MP – 1910/02/16:1b, 4c,
CURSCHMANN, Wilhelmine, b. Guembel, 66, NYC-M – 1906/07/12:6a
CURTIS, William E., 58, chief judge NYC Supr. Ct – 1880/07/08:3a
CUSACHS, Philipp G., newspaper drawer, NYC-M – 1892/03/16:1d
CUSTERS, Anton, NYC-M - 1915/08/06:6a
CUZ, Christiana, 61, NYC-M, +@Genl Slocum – 1904/06/22:1d
CVETKOVICH, Joseph, un. carp., secy local 1164, carp. & joiners - 1918/11/26:6c
CZAGLE, Rudolph V., 28, NYC-M – 1887/07/06:2e
CZECH, Franz, 44, postal clerk & SPO Bruenn/Moravia - 1914/05/10:3a
CZECH, John, 64, exec. Jersey City, NJ - 1895/10/04: 3d
CZERNY, Christoph, 39, SP Austria, * Teplitz/Bohemia, + after 15 years in jail – 1899/12/26:2e-f
CZERWIENSKI, Boleslaw, Polish labor poet, + Lemberg – 1888/05/07:2c
CZOLGOSZ, Leo, American anarchist on trial for killing pres. McKinley (see there). His family 8 Sept 1901:1c, trial 17 Sept:1c, 18:1c-d, 19:1c-d, 22:5c, etc, fd guilty 25:1h,2c, 26:2a-b, 27:1a-b, 28:1a-b, 2a-b, etc, 15 Oct:3c, exec. 29 Oct:1h, 30:1a, 3c-d, notes 21 Nov.:1f, 23:1b, 9 Dec:1e, 13:2a-b; Crit. Czolgosz fans 11 Apr 1902:1e; NYC anarchists mem. 5th anniv. exec., 1906/10/27:1e, 29:1c-d, 4c-d, 1 Nov:4b, 6:4a-b, 7:4b-c
DAAB, Friedrich, carp., Jersey City, NJ – 1892/05/08:1h
DACHOFSAUER, Charles, 60, smith, NYC-M – 1892/07/30:1a
DADARIO, Pasquale, exec. Philadelphia, PA – 1897/07/28:1d
DAEHMEL, Wilhelm, (Dreamel?),74, SP, un. carp., USA 1882, NYC-LI City - 1920/07/18:3a, 12a, 19:6a
DAEHN, William, un. cigar maker, NYC-M – 1889/08/15:4a
DAEMMER, Anna Maria, 60, NYC-M – 1885/11/16:4c
DAEMMER, Karl Friedrich, 62, un. tailor, NYC-M – 1886/01/25:3b, 26:2g
DAEN, Gustav, SLP, un. cigarmaker, NYC-M - 1894/05/19:4a;?2:4c
DAENNER % Hesse
DAERENSTAEDT, Anton, 35, NYC-M – 1889/07/30:4a, 31:4a
DAETSCH, John, 47, NYC-B – 1906/01/29:4a
DAETTMANN % Brombacher
DAEUBLER, Max, NYC-M - 1916/07/31:6a
DAEUMER, Franz, Dr., '48er, St Joseph's Hospital, NJ – 1885/10/07:2g
DAG, Albert, un. carp., NYC-Bx – 1907/06/03:6a

DAGOSTINI, Franz, 68, SP Vienna - 1916/04/02:3d
DAHL, Charles, NYC-B - 1898/09/06:1c
DAHL, Frederick, watchmaker, + Parral/Mexico - 1901/05/07:3f
DAHLMANN, Rudolf, 46, pianomaker, NYC-M - 1915/08/22:1f
DAHLMEIER, Lina, NYC-SI - 1893/05/03:2e
DAHN, Anna, 33, NYC-B - 1894/01/10:4a
DAHN, Felix, 87, German historian, + Breslau/Gy - 1912/01/05:4c
DAIBLE, Karl, Newark, NJ? - 1904/01/02:1f
DAIMINGER, Michael, un. carpenter, NYC-M - 1894/01/22:4a
DAISER, Carl, un. cigar maker, NYC-M - 1891/04/05:5a
DAISS, Charles, butcher, NYC-M - 1878/03/02:4d
DALGLISH, James, un. brushmaker, NYC-B - 1880/03/21:8a
DALHAUSER, Fred, 44, carp., NYC-M - 1896/05/08:1h
DALKOFSKY, Henry, 58, un. mason, NYC-M - 1899/05/07:5b
DALLENDORF, William, 22, NYC-M - 1882/10/27:1g
DALLER, Dr., 78, Bavarian leader (Zentrum) - 1911/03/26:3a
DALLMANN, John N., NYC-B - 1892/08/19:4f
DALLYE, Ernest, 43, NYC - 1888/03/10:3a
DALOU, Jules, French scuptor & Progressive - 1903/07/19:4c-e
DALRYMPLE, Alfred, Essex County, NJ, Republican leader - 1916/05/22:6b
DALY, Edward, Irish patriot, exec. Dublin - 1916/05/06:1c
DAMM, Adam, fireman, NYC - 1907/02/28:3b
DAMM, Anna Von, b. Doscher, 27, NYC-B - 1890/03/21:4a
DAMM, Henry, Newark, NJ - 1915/12/28:6a
DAMM, John, NYC-B - 1910/12/02:6a
DAMM, Julia, NYC-M - 1892/08/08:4a
DAMM, Martha, NYC-M - 1891/08/11:4a
DAMON, "Mother," 61, shoemaker labor org., led March 1860 strike in Lynn, MA - 1901/03/02:1g
DAMPF, Meyer, un. cigarmaker, treas. NYC Central Labor Union - 1895/02/28:3e, 1896/02/01:2e
DAMROSCH, Leopold, conductor, NYC-M - 1885/02/16:1d-e, 17:1g, 18:1g, =19:1c-f, Arion GV plans monument 7 Mr:3c, 8:5c-d, honor crit by Philadelphia Enquirer 31:2f
DANA, Charles A., 78, chief editor N.Y. Sun, - 1897/10/18:3g
DANBACH, Gottlieb, carp., Newark, NJ - 1906/07/09:3c
DANENHAUER, John W., 37, US polar explorer - 1887/04/21:1c
DANGELMANN, Nicholas, 65, cigar maker, NYC-M - 1889/02/02:1d
DANGL, Joseph, un. butcher, NYC-M - 1911/12/22:6a
DANIEL, Mitchell, Negro, lynched near Leeburg, GA - 1899/04/28:4c

DANJUNAS, Nikodemus, 54, SP?, bartender, Hackensack, NJ - 1914/01/18:11e, fam. 21:6a
DANKE, Karl, un. butcher, NYC-M - 1918/07/21:6a
DANNECKER, Elizabeth, NYC-Q - 1916/10/01:7a
DANNEFELDER, Sophia, 40, NYC-M – 1891/08/12:4a
DANNENBERG, Margarete, 22, War 2, Maywood, NJ - 1915/09/19:1f
DANNENBERG, Minna, fam. 1899/08/12:4a
DANNENBERG, Minnie, 47, NYC-M – 1887/07/25:1d, 23:2f
DANNENBERG, William, NYC-M – 1907/04/25:6a
DANNHEIMER, Elsa, NYC-M – 1891/04/21:4d, 22:1h
DANNLER, John, 18, NYC-M – 1891/03/11:4a
DANSNER, Mary, 60, War 2, dying, NYC-B - 1915/04/05:2d
DANY, Philippe, exec. with Edith Cavell for smuggling British POWs out of Belgium - 1915/10/20:1d
DANZEISEN, Charles, 40, un. carpenter, NYC-B - 1894/09/13:4a
DANZEISEN, Christ., un. carp., NYC-B? – 1889/04/28:5c
DANZIGER, Heinrich, 56, NYC-B – 1907/07/11:1d
DANZIGER, Max, 45, builder, & wife Yetta, 42, NYC-B – 1911/10/31:3a
DARDENNE, Marie, b. Hummel, actress at German theaters in USA, *25 Jy 1827 Nuernberg/Gy, + at Marie Drexel Home in Philadelphia - 1915/12/09:2b
DARE, Elisa, 29, NYC-M – 1892/06/12:4a
DARHEIM, Franz, 63, NYC-M - 1914/05/24:11g
DARMSTADT, John, carp., Red Bank, NJ – 1882/06/28:1g, 29:3b
DARMSTADT, Rudolph Louis, druggist, Orange, NJ – 1899/01/12:3b
DARMSTADT, Wilhelm L., 32, NYC-M – 1890/03/22:4a
DARNY, Joe, un. butcher, NYC-B - 1920/02/21:6a
DART, George, 53, druggist, Tuxedo, NJ – 1912/05/23:2d
DARWIN, Charles, English scientist, by Dr. Rachel, 1882/04/21:2b-c, 23:4f-5c, 30:3d-e, 12 May:2d 14:3e-f, 7b, Darwinism & capitalism 4 June:2a-c, by Rudolf Virchow 3 Sept:2c-e & 10:2b-e, by Friedrich Haeckel 15 Oct:3b-f, notes 26 Nov:2e-g. 100th anniv 12 Fb 1909:4b-c, 14:20b, 21:6c, 28:3e-g, 7 Mr:3e-g,4c-e, 6d-g
DASSEL, Fannie von, NYC-M – 1885/12/04:1d
DASSING, Eduard, Newark, NJ – 1908/11/03:6a
DATHE, Wilhelm, 93, NYC-B – 1907/03/24:7c, 25:6a
D'ATTEL, Nicolas, silk flower maker, veteran Paris Commune, NYC-M - 1878/04/24:4d
DATZ, Adam, 32, NYC-M – 1893/05/06:4a, 7:5a, fam. 9:4a
DATZ, Catherina, 48, NYC-M – 1899/06/23:4a
DATZ, John, un. carp., NYC-M – 1912/05/15:6a
DAUB, Louise, NYC-M – 1892/07/31:5c

DAUBE, Agnes, 41, Paterson, NJ – 1897/06/13:5h
DAUBE, Gustav, 61, NYC-B – 1891/06/25:4a
DAUBENSCHMIDT, Dorothy, 29, cabaret singer, Hoboken, NJ – 1919/11/24:2e, 25:2c
DAUBENSCHMIDT, Henry,21, baker, fr Gy, NYC-M - 1895/06/20:1h
DAUBER, Julia D., 1, NYC-B - 1878/07/10:3c
DAUBERT, Louis A., NYC-M – 1910/10/04:6a
DAUBIGNY, Charles Francois, French painter - 1878/04/20:2a
DAUBMANN, Elizabeth, NYC-M – 1909/07/12:6a
DAUBMANN, George, 37, NYC-M – 1905/02/28:4a
DAUBMANN, Lorenz, 47, un. carp., NYC-Q – 1897/10/31:5a
DAUDET, Alphonse, French nationalist writer – 1897/12/17:1b, =20:1a
DAUERNHEIM, Anna, 58, NYC-M, +@ Genl Slocum – 1904/06/18:3b
DAUM, Kathie, 28, NYC-M – 1899/12/09:4a, 10:5a, fam. 12:4a
DAUMER, Georg Fried., German poet, 100th anniv. – 1900/04/22:9g-h
DAUPERN, Louis, un. Machinist, NYC-Bx – 1911/07/23:7a
DAUS, Louis, un. cigarmaker, NYC-M - 1878/07/09:3c
DAUS, Louis, un. cigarmaker, NYC-M - 1879/10/23:3a
DAUSCH, Joseph, un. carp., NYC-M - 1915/01/21:6a
DAUSCH, Katie, 18, NYC-B – 1903/06/16:4a-b
DAUSZ, Marie, b. Knackfus, 46, NYC-M – 1892/08/13:4a
DAUTH, Mathias, un. cigar maker, NYC-M – 1886/12/16:3b
DAUTH, Mathias, un. cigarmaker, NYC-M – 1883/09/30:5e
DAUTZ, Adolph, 26, Newark, NJ – 1903/07/26:5d
DAVID, J. J., Viennese poet from Moravia, + 1906/12/12:4f-g
DAVID, John, un. cigarmaker, NYC-M – 1903/06/18:4a
DAVID, William, NYC-B - 1916/12/04:6a
DAVIDS, Geo. W., 48, NYC industrialist – 1883/04/05:1d
DAVIDSON, Daniel, 64, NYC-M – 1891/06/24:4a
DAVIDSON, John McB., member of Tweed Ring, + Saratoga, NY – 1887/02/02:6c
DAVIDSON, Matilda, b. Evertz, 33, NYC-B - 1920/09/26:9c
DAVIN, Charles, Secaucus, NJ - 1915/10/29:6a
DAVIS % Arnheim
DAVIS, Celia, 28, worker, + in sweatshop fire, NYC-M – 1893/06/14:1e
DAVIS, Dan, Negro, lynched in Tyler, TX – 1912/05/26:1b
DAVIS, David B., Homestead, PA, steelworker killed by Pinkertons – 1892/07/08:1a
DAVIS, Jack, Negro, lynched New Iberia, LA – 1897/07/23:3g
DAVIS, James, Negro, lynched Wilmington, DE - 1913/11/24:2e
DAVIS, Jefferson, ex-CSA pres., – 1889/12/07:1c
DAVIS, Maurice M., 16, NYC-M – 1886/02/24:3d

DAVIS, Richard Harding, NYC journalist, obit crit. his German-bashing - 1916/04/14:4d
DAVIS, Robert P., 68, un. painter & labor org., NYC-B - 1916/10/05:2b
DAVIS, Tom, mobster, NYC-M - 1885/09/01:1f, 2:1e-f, 3:1f, etc., trial 3 Mr 1886:4b, 4:2f-g, etc, 6:1g
DAVIS, Walter, Negro, lynched Marshall, TX - 1903/10/03:1h
DAVISON, Emily Wilding, English suffragette - 1913/06/06:1a, 09:1c, 11:1a, =15:1a
DAVITT, Michael, 60, Irish patriot, + Dublin - 1906/05/31:1b, 15 June:2c-d
DAY, Elizabeth, 38, NYC-M - 1918/02/20:6a
DAYTON, (fed) judge, enemy of labor, - 1920/08/20:4b
DE GRIMM, Malwina, 47, Austrian, NYC-M - 1895/05/31:3f
DE LA REY, Jacob Hendrik, 57, general, Boer patriot, + Johannesburg - 1914/09/17:1f
DE LEON, Daniel, SLP leader, NYC-M, crit. obit - 1914/05/12:1e, 13:4b, 16:1f, 18:1b
DE LUCCIA, Lena, (not +), her 4 children, NYC-M, + @ Genl Slocum - 1904/06/16:1d
DE MARS, Henry W., 90, ret. hotelier, NYC-B - 1915/12/08:3g
DE MOTTE, Paul R., 22, US citizen, killed in German civil war in Ruhrgebiet - 1920/04/14:6a, 15:4a-b, 20:2f
DE PALMA see Palma
DE....With the exception of the above, surnames beginning with "de," or "de la," are indexed under the main element of their name. E. g. Etienne De Cottigneis see Cottigneis, Etienne De
DEACONS, exec. Rochester, NY - 1888/07/11:1g
DEBARA, Max, NYC-B - 1900/01/13:2h
DEBORAH, Sam, 46, NYC-M - 1891/04/06:4a
DEBOY, Gabriel, brewer, NYC-M - 1898/08/25:4a
DEBROVSKY, Julius, banker, fr Hungary, NYC-M - 1911/03/28:6c
DEBRUNNER, Fritz, NYC-Bx - 1911/11/21:6a
DEBS % Selby
DEBS, Anthony, NYPD - 1912/09/27:2e
DEBUS, Tobias, un. baker, NYC-M - 1880/11/29:3a
DECHENT, John, 63, NYC-B - 1886/04/16:3b
DECKE % Huebner
DECKER, Annie, 12, NYC-B - 1896/12/06:1c
DECKER, Bailer's wife, NYC-SI - 1898/05/26:3g. Bailer exec. Ossining, NY - 1899/01/10:1g
DECKER, Charles, NYC-M - 1888/01/30:2h
DECKER, Geo. W., 62, chair Hudson County Republican Co., Jersey City, NJ - 1916/01/30:1d

DECKER, Henry, un. carp., NYC-M – 1904/08/27:4a
DECKER, John, 58, typesetter, NYC-M – 1908/01/20:3a
DECKER, Josephine, 40, NYC-B – 1896/07/21:4a
DECKER, Marie, Elizabeth, NJ - 1920/01/27:8a
DECKER, Theodore, last surviving member of Haymarket jury, + insane asylum – 1904/04/15:2c
DECKER, Walter, 32, RR worker, & wife, 30, Union Hill, NJ – 1905/11/09:3d
DECKER, Walter, musician, * NYC-B, NYC-B - 1918/10/07:3e
DECKERMAN, James, 53, silversmith, NYC-B - 1917/04/09:2b
DECKERT, Johann, NYC?, fam. 1882/09/18:3c
DECKERT, Theodore, 45, Newark, NJ – 1899/04/20:4b
DECKWITZ, Gustav, carp. & SPD Bremen, *Zeitz/Thueringen, 75th birthday – 1912/05/19:3a-b
DEECKE, George, 87, baker?, NYC-M – 1887/07/22:3b
DEFFARGE, Albert, 35, French pharmacist, USA 1865?, butter dealer here NYC-M - 1879/04/25:1e, 26:1f, 30:1g
DEFNET, Gustave, Belgian Socialist, his = Brussels St Gilles – 1904/06/04:2c. Grave monum. Inaug Bxl-St Gilles – 1908/11/18:4f
DEFUISSEAUX, Leon, Belgian Socialist, = 27 Dec – 1907/01/14:4d
DEGE, George F., NYC-M – 1885/12/14:3d
DEGELE, Friedrich, Jersey City Heights, NJ – 1890/10/12:5b
DEGEN % Rebsamen
DEGEN, Charles, Rahway, NJ – 1900/06/13:4a
DEGEN, Dr., 70, SPD Fuerth/Bavaria, – 1911/02/19:3a
DEGEN, Magdalene, 83, NYC-Q – 1902/10/21:4a
DEGENDORF, Edward, 31, typesetter, NYC-B – 1881/05/30:1d, 31:3a
DEGENHARD, Christian, 32, typesetter & SPD militant, *Calw/Wuertt. + near Ludwigsburg – 1886/01/25:5c
DEGENHARDT, Phillipine, b. Fronke?, 44, NYC-M – 1891/04/02:4a
DEGER, Ernestine, 71, NYC-M – 1892/07/30:4a
DEGES, George, Greek restaurant owner, NYC – 1901/01/02:2g, 26 Mr:4a, 27:2g, 28:3b, 30:1h
DEGET, Katharina, NYC-M - 1915/12/17:6a
DEGET, Philip, 65, NYC-M - 1916/11/11:6a
DEGHUCE, Werner Henry, 52, lumber merchant, & wife, NYC-B - 1918/06/05:5e
DEGLMAN, M., NYC-B - 1917/05/17:6a
DEHL, Minna, 63, NYC-B – 1907/01/21:3a
DEHLING, Louisa, NYC-M – 1887/01/15:3c
DEHM, Clemens, NYC-M – 1907/02/10:7a

DEHMEL, Richard, German poet, his works – 1904/03/27:15e-h, his life 13 May 1906:2e-g, + 1920/02/12:6a, 15:5c, 23:3a-d, obit by Carl-Ludwig Schleich - 1920/03/21:10a-g, notes 31:3g, 25 Apr:7a-c
DEHMS, William, SDP, & wife, Silver Wedding, Elizabeth, NJ – 1904/10/25:3d
DEHNA, Paul, 42, NYC-M – 1902/09/07:5b, 8:4a
DEHNART, L., 1, Newark, NJ – 1911/07/11:1e
DEHNKE, Emil, 69, SDP, poet, * 10 Apr 1836 Husum/Gy, USA 1887, NYC-Bx – 1905/01/23:4c
DEHORN, Emma, NYC-M – 1892/11/07:4a
DEHRENS, Hermann, (Behrens?), 40, NYC-Q - 1917/07/08:1b
DEHRLE, Paul, 60, worker, NYC-M – 1880/06/22:1g
DEHSEN, Emilie von, 1, NYC-M – 1889/08/28:4a
DEIB, J., 21, NYC-M – 1893/10/25:4a
DEIBEL, August, 76, NYC-B – 1899/04/09:5b
DEIBEL, Jacob, 47, NYC-M – 1898/04/09:1e
DEICHERT, Christian, Newark, NJ – 1908/05/13:6a
DEICHERT, Samuel, 68, Newark, NJ – 1899/06/09:1g
DEICHLER, Emil, un. cigarmaker, 42, NYC-B – 1902/05/05:1g, 4a
DEICHMUELLER, Wilhelm, 45, printshop laborer & SPD Leipzig/Gy – 1911/08/06:3c
DEICKHOFF, Marie & Edward, NYC-B, + @ Genl Slocum – 1904/06/18:3b
DEIKE, Wilhelm F., NYC-B – 1890/10/11:4a
DEIKLER, John, builder, NYC-Q – 1904/09/01:1f, 2:3b, 9:3c
DEILEN, Henry von, 24, NYC-B – 1889/09/29:5b
DEILETH, Leonhard, un. carp., NYC-M - 1915/10/25:6a
DEIMEL, Celia, NYC-M - 1916/08/25:6a
DEINHART, Ernst, un. woodworker, SPD activist in Berlin – 1909/06/20:3a
DEISINGER, Joseph, stoker, Newark, NJ – 1892/08/31:2e
DEISS, Edward, 32, silkweaver, Paterson, NJ - 1916/04/24:2d, 25:6a
DEISSLER, Charles, West New York, NJ - 1920/02/17:8a
DEITZ, Pauline, b. Meadrach, NYC-M – 1891/05/31:5d
DEITZEL, Philip, 65, & Adelina, 62, NYC-Q – 1909/03/17:2a, 18:3c
DEKENS, John, NYC-Bx – 1908/07/10:6a
DELABAR, August, *20 Jy 1860 Schelingen/Baden, USA 1873, SDP NYC, natl secy Baker Union, s. 1894 innkeep in St Louis, MO – 1905/04/22:4b
DELANEY, William see "Monk" Eastman
DELANGE, Louis, writer & actor, NYC-M – 1906/03/14:1g, 15:1d

DELBRUECK, Rudolf von, ex-Prussian State Secy of Commerce – 1903/02/03:1b
DELERO, exec. Lancaster, PA – 1907/10/04:1e
DELFINO, John, exec. Ossining, NY – 1893/12/04:4f, 5:4a
DELFS, Otto C., butcher, NYC-M – 1898/01/30:1e
DELISLE, John Louis, NYC-M – 1888/11/06:3a
DELIUS % Meyer
DELIUS, Hermann R., un. cigarmaker, Guttenberg, NJ – 1912/01/21:7b
DELKE, Charles, 21, NYC-B – 1890/05/18:5a
DELL'OMO, Matteo, exec. Ossining, NY – 1912/12/17:1e
DELLE, Anna Margaretha, 67, NYC-B – 1893/01/12:4a
DELLE, Bernhard, NYC-B – 1897/01/03:5a
DELLE, Otto, 32, NYC-B – 1909/09/25:6a
DELLE, Otto, 68, un. printer, NYC-B - 1915/03/30:6b, 31:2e,6a, =2 Apr:5f
DELLE, Sophie, 1, NYC? – 1881/09/13:3c
DELLER, Elizabeth, 48, NYC-B – 1902/01/31:4a-b
DELLER, George, 46, NYC-B – 1900/06/11:1f
DELLERMANN, Franz, 50, un. brewer or cooper, NYC-M – 1891/11/26:4a
DELLINGROTH, Eugen, Hoboken, NJ - 1915/12/08:6a
DELLON, Sadie, 13, War 2, NYC-M - 1918/10/28:3f, =31:1c
DELLUTH, Christine, 64, Newark, NJ – 1906/08/07:3c
DELMONICO, Lorenzo, restaurant owner, NYC, his = 1881/09/08:4f
DEMAND % Ezelius
DEMAND, Anton, Hoboken, NJ – 1904/12/20:4a
DEMARZO, Nicholas, exec. Scranton, PA – 1909/07/30:2c
DEMMLER, Adolf, 82, ret. civil servant & SPD member in Schwerin – 1886/01/18:2c-d, =25:2e, 6 Fb:5b, notes 29 Jy:6b, will 1 Sept:5c, 30 Sept:5e. 100th anniv. commemorated – 1905/01/15:9d-g
DEMOLIERE, Fanny, servant, NYC – 1912/05/27:6d
DEMPSEY, Bill, boxer, Fort Hamilton, LI – 1888/01/23:1h
DEMPSEY, James, ex-coroner, NYC-SI – 1880/04/01:4d
DEMUTH % Berg
DEMUTH, Charles, un. wood carver, West New York, NJ – 1901/02/05:4a
DEMUTH, Vincent, 46, NYC-B - 1894/01/22:4a
DENBINSKI, Alfred, NYC-M - 1918/06/25:6a
DENEEN, John, SLP, NYC-M – 1882/11/30:3b, = 1 Dec:4a
DENEKE, John F., 80, NYC-M – 1892/09/19:4f
DENEKE, Rosa, b. Dreyer, NYC-B – 1909/05/20:6a
DENGEL, G., 54, lithographer, NYC-M – 1902/05/16:3b
DENGER % Haefelfinger
DENGLER, Adolph, 4, NYC-M, +@ Genl Slocum – 1904/06/17:3b
DENGLER, Charles, 70, Newark, NJ – 1903/10/13:3d

DENGLER, John "Hans," 60, SP, NYC-M - 1918/07/13:6a, 16:6a, mem. 1919/07/12:6a
DENIG, Marie, b. Huber, 58, NYC-M - 1892/07/30:4a
DENIS, Hector, 71, Dr., Belgian univ. prof. & soc. deputy, + Brussels - 1913/05/23:4d, =26:4d
DENK, John, NYC-M - 1892/10/25:4a
DENKER, Heinrich, un. carp., SLP, NYC-B - 1887/10/26:2g
DENKERT, Eduard, 63, SPD Chemnitz/Gy - 1910/06/26:3e
DENMARK, Christian IX, King of, 1906/01/30:1b, 31:1b
DENMARK, Frederick, King of - 1912/05/16:1c, 17:1e, =25:2b
DENNECKE, Minna, b. Grimm, alias Minna Hampe, 64, NYC-M - 1903/02/10:4a, 11:4a
DENNECKE, William, un. butcher, NYC, married Lina - 1912/03/06:5e
DENNER, (man), fam. 1891/06/14:5b
DENNER, Louis, bricklayer, NYC-M - 1894/10/27:4a
DENNER, Mary, NYC-Q - 1902/06/05:2g
DENNERLEIN, Michael, 30, spec. weaver fr Bavaria, USA 1887, NYC-M - 1890/02/11:2h
DENNING, Charles, sailor on USS Maine, + Havana/Cuba, Newark, NJ - 1898/02/18:1b
DENNINGER, Minnie, 1, NYC-M - 1882/07/29:4c
DENNISON, Henry, machinist, NYC-B - 1907/06/07:6a
DENTON, James M., 48, alderman, Paterson, NJ - 1904/10/03:1d
DENUSKA, William's wife, 30, NYC-M - 1901/11/28:2h
DENZER, George, news dealer, Jersey City Heights, NJ - 1887/07/08:2f
DENZMORE, Jene, Negro, lynched Belgreen, AL - 1891/03/31:4a
DEOBALD, Henry, carpenter, + NYC 3 Jan. 1880, his will probated 1884/07/09:4a
DEPEW, Chauncey W., NYS politico, (not +), negative assessment of his career so far, # - 1890/09/21:1c-e, 22:1h
DEPNER, Anna, 26, fr Greifswald/Gy, Columbia U student, NYC-M - 1908/08/14:1f
DEPP, Henry, 59, tailor, NYC-M - 1903/04/01:4a, 2:3e
DEPPE, Louis, ?37, NYC-B - 1892/08/23:4a
DEPPERT, Agnes, 62, NYC-M, + @Genl Slocum - 1904/06/17:3b
DERENGOWSKI, Roman, un. cigarmaker, NYC-M - 1909/08/07:6a
DERLET, Philipp, 40, smith, NYC-M - 1882/03/03:1g
DERMIGNI, Emil, NYC-Q - 1919/04/02:6a
DERNER, Christoph, watchman, War 2, Hastings, NY - 1915/08/23:2e
DEROSSI, Carl, 66, hatmaker, *Duesseldorf/Gy, SP, NYC-M - 1910/05/31:6a
DEROULEDE, Paul, 68, French monarchist politician - 1914/01/31:1c

DERR, Michael, un. carp., NYC-B – 1909/05/20:6a
DERRINGER, Catherine E., NYC-M – 1891/04/22:4d, 25:1f, trial of husband Philip 26 June:1h, 27:1f,
DERSCH, Elsie, 15, NYC-M, +@Genl Slocum – 1904/06/22:1d
DERSCHEIDT, Katherine, 31, NYC-M – 1899/05/26:4a
DESACK, Hermine, 21, nurse, NYC-Q – 1912/10/10:2e
DESEL, Josephina, b. Reinhardt, 32, NYC-M – 1892/09/05:4a
DESMOND, Katherina, 32, NYC-M - 1918/07/26:6a
DESSART, Marie, b. Gasser, 35, NYC-B – 1893/01/06:4a
DESSAUER, Elizabeth von, NYC-M – 1907/07/11:2a, 13:2d
DESTAT, Philipp, NYC-B – 1910/03/25:6a
DESTER, John, 45, worker, fr Austria, War 2, NYC-B - 1916/07/13:3g
DESUISSEAUX, Alfred, Belgian SP, deputy for Mons – 1901/11/29:2c-d
DETHLOFF, Wilhelm, NYC-B - 1914/01/31:6a
DETLEF, William, NYC-B – 1911/03/11:6a
DETTE, Josephine, b. Richter, 24, NYC-M – 1892/06/12:4a
DETTERLING, John, innkeep, NYC-B - 1896/01/28:2d
DETTINGER, Klara, b. Kaiser, 60, NYC-M – 1891/07/29:4a
DETTMANN, Carl, 49, NYC-M – 1891/09/20:5f
DETTMAR, Alwine, b. Heimann, 52, NYC-M – 1892/10/01:4a
DETTMER, John, 73, baker, NYC-M - 1916/11/09:6c
DETTON, Franz, 38, NYC-M – 1891/03/25:4a
DETZEL, Charles, un. carp., NYC-M – 1908/02/11:6a
DEUBEL, Julius, NYC-Q - 1914/04/04:6a
DEUBERT, Charlotte, NYC-Q – 1901/01/10:4a
DEUBLER, Konrad, Austrian MdR, SP, 20th anniv. + – 1904/07/03:9f-h
DEUSCHL, Franz, NYC - 1914/03/07:6a
DEUTSCH, Eva, NYC-M – 1912/12/26:1f
DEUTSCH, Isaac, ex-alderman 5th ward, Philadelphia, PA - 1919/06/19:2a
DEUTSCH, Josephine, NYC-M – 1890/06/20:4a
DEUTSCH, Julius's wife, NYC-M – 1893/12/08:4a
DEUTSCH, Max, 50, Hoboken, NJ – 1896/08/11:1a
DEUTSCH, Otto, 28, waiter, USA 1890, NYC-M – 1897/05/01:1e
DEUTSCH, Philipp, 25, clerk, NYC-B – 1908/02/23:3g
DEUTSCH, Therese, 64, NYC-M – 1887/07/30:1e, inquest 23 Aug.:1e
DEUTSCHERT % Meinhardt
DEUTSCHMANN % Kraker, also see Forman
DEUTSCHMANN, Friedrich A. H., 42, NYC-Q – 1909/07/21:6a
DEUTSCHMANN, Johanna, NYC-M - 1918/03/08:6a, 9:6a
DEUTSCHMANN, Johanna, s.a. Wanda Forman, b. Kolloff
DEUTSCHMANN, Karl, NYC-Q - 1914/09/14:6a
DEUTZ, Wilhelm, 56, lithographer, NYC-B – 1882/01/20:3a

DEVERELL, Thomas R., 64, musician, NYC-M - 1895/01/08:1e
DEVERY, William S., 65, former chief NYPD, crit. obit., NYC-Q - 1919/06/21:2b
DEVEZ, Hermann, German sailor on ship Ryndam, + Jersey City, NJ - 1912/06/30:1f
DEVLIN, William, 42, NYC Fire Chief, NYC-SI - 1911/09/25:1b
DEWAS, Karl, un. printer, NYC-M - 1913/02/11:6a
DEWES, Hermann's wife, NYC-M - 1888/05/17:3a
DEWES, J., 69, NYC-B - 1893/06/13:4a
DEWES, Michael, un. cigar maker, NYC-M - 1890/01/14:4a, 15:4a
DEWEY, George, US admiral, obit. crit, his role in fostering US imperialism - 1917/01/21:6a, 11f
DEXHEIMER, Rosa, 65, NYC-B - 1903/09/28:3c
DEXTREUX, Henry, pres. Vereinigte Saenger of Philadelphia s. 1899, 1913/04/22:2d
DEYHLE, Christian J., 70, inventor, ex-Philadelphia, NYC-M - 1891/03/09:2e (s.a. 1889/09/20:1g, 23:1h)
DEYN % Staer
DHINGRA, Madar Lal, Indian fr Amritsar, exec for killing an occupation officer - 1909/07/03:1a, deed praised 5 Jy:4a-b, 18:1a, 19:4d, 24:1a; note 4 Sept:4d-e
DI GOIA, Joseph, exec. Auburn, NY - 1914/09/01:2b
DIAMOND, Francis, 4, NYC-M, +@Genl Slocum - 1904/06/22:1d
DIAMOND, Frank, 6, & May, 7, NYC-M, + Genl Slocum - 1904/06/26:1c
DIAMOND, Mary, 8, NYC-M, +@Genl Slocum - 1904/06/23:1b
DIAMOND, Mary, 9, NYC-B - 1886/07/22:2d
DIAMOND, William ," exec. Trenton, NJ - 1913/12/03:6c
DIBRELL, Tucker, Negro, lynched Houston, MS - 1913/02/08:5f, 9:1b
DICHTUNG, Henriette, 46, NYC-B - 1906/05/05:3d
DICK % Brauch, %Drueckel, % Rosskopf
DICK, John, 43, NYC-M - 1890/07/06:5a
DICK, Joseph, Elizabeth, NJ - 1908/09/13:7a
DICKERHOF, Katherina, NYC-B - 1911/05/06:6a
DICKERSON, Ben, Negro, lynched Purcell, OK - 1914/01/28:3d
DICKERT, Anton, 35, philosopher, NYC-M - 1892/11/01:1h
DICKHARD, John, un. bartender, NYC-M - 1889/07/18:4f
DICKHARDT, August, Jersey City Hgts, NJ - 1914/11/11:6a
DICKHAUS, Otto, NYC-B - 1910/07/16:6a
DICKMAN, Ida, 35, NYC-B - 1902/08/01:4a
DICKMANN, Dora, NYC-B - 1912/10/22:6a
DICKMANN, Heinrich, 59, NYC - 1914/02/01:7a
DICKMANN, Julia, 86, NYC-M - 1903/12/28:4a

DIEBESON % Funke
DIECKHOFF, Catherine, 43, Annie, 17, William, 8, ??, 20, Catherine, 14, NYC-B, +@Genl Slocum – 1904/06/17:3b, 23:1b
DIECKHOFF, Hermann H., 59, NYC-Q – 1908/07/27:6a
DIECKMANN, August, 41, fr Hamburg?/Gy, + at sea – 1889/02/02:1e
DIECKMANN, Carl, un. cigarmaker, NYC-M - 1894/07/16:4a
DIEDERICH, Emma, NYC-M, + @on Genl Slocum – 1904/06/17:3b
DIEDRICH % Walker
DIEFENBACH, Charles, 50, shoemaker, NYC-M – 1882/05/17:1f
DIEFENBACH, J., NYC-Q – 1908/04/21:6a
DIEFENBACH, Johann, 89, NYC-M – 1892/07/22:4a
DIEFENBACHER, Catherina, 64, NYC-B – 1892/04/05:4b
DIEFENBACHER, Otto, dying, NYC-M – 1904/04/17:1h
DIEFFENBACH, Katie, 21, NYC-M – 1902/03/06:3a
DIEFFENBACH, Louis, un. machinist, NYC-M - 1895/01/21:4a
DIEFFENBACH, Otto, infant, NYC-M – 1884/07/07:3c
DIEGEL, Jacob, 57, NYC-M – 1892/04/19:4a
DIEHL, Carl, 55, NYC-M – 1889/12/04:4a
DIEHL, Catherine, 58, NYC-Bx, + @Genl Slocum – 1904/06/17:3b
DIEHL, Elisabeth, b. Blum, NYC-M – 1890/10/26:5a
DIEHL, F. W., NYC-M – 1890/02/26:4a
DIEHL, Heinrich, un. cigarmkr, NYC-M – 1892/12/11:5b
DIEHL, J. J., NYC-M – 1890/10/11:4a
DIEHL, Jacob, 45, treasurer of Journeymen's Baker and Confectioners' Union of America, NYC-B, + Orange Lake/Newburgh, NY 1920/07/23:5f,6a, fam. 27:6a
DIEHL, John C., 41, NYC, + Chicago – 1909/08/09:2b
DIEHL, Ludwig, 10, NYC-B – 1897/01/21:4b
DIEHL, Otto, NYC-B – 1898/01/19:1h, notes 16 Fb:2e, 17:4b-c, 24:4a
DIEHL, Theo. W., 38, druggist, NYC-B - 1914/08/12:2e
DIEHLMANN % Buegler
DIEHM, Henry, 56, worker, NYC-B - 1916/02/01:6c
DIEHM, Jakob, 50, NYC-M – 1880/07/08:4a
DIEHM, Samuel, mason, NYC-M – 1880/05/11:1g, 12:1g, 13:4c
DIEM, Albert, Newark, NJ – 1908/06/23:6a
DIEM, Maria Agnes, 60, NYC-M – 1892/07/19:4a
DIEMER, William, NYC-M – 1909/08/25:6a
DIENER, Regine, 66, NYC-M - 1894/01/31:4a
DIERCKS, Frederick, 65, NYC – 1912/03/25:6a, 26:6a
DIEROFF, Emma, (Dierolf?)18, NYC-B – 1908/05/02:6a, fam. 7:6a
DIEROLF, Carl, un. cigarmaker, NYC-M – 1906/11/21:6a, fam. 26:6a

DIEROTT % Fried
DIESBACH, Charles, 50, servant, NYC-B - 1915/08/30:1b
DIESCHBURG, John H., 49, NYC-B – 1912/07/12:6a, 13:6a
DIESEL, Rudolf, Dr., German, inventor of Diesel motor - 1913/10/16:4c, 15:2d, 17:4f, 4 Nov:4f
DIESTELMEIER, Wilhelm, 53, janitor, NYC-M – 1902/11/14:1e
DIESTELZWEIG, Constantine, NYC-Bx – 1888/05/26:3a
DIESTERWEG, Adolph, '48er & educator, + 1866, his life, by Dr. Adolph Kohut – 1890/11/16:7b-c
DIETER, Georg, un. carp., NYC-M – 1881/12/24:1f, 3a, =27:1f
DIETER, Louise, NYC-M – 1910/09/09:6a
DIETERLE, Hector, 62, NYC-M – 1893/02/14:4a
DIETMAIER, Peter, un. carp., NYC-B – 1890/01/06:4a
DIETRICH % Becker
DIETRICH, Anna Maria, 72, NYC-M - 1894/01/15:4a
DIETRICH, Carl, NYC-M – 1908/01/29:6a
DIETRICH, Charles A., NYC? – 1886/09/01:3b
DIETRICH, Conrad & Marie, NYC-B – 1902/05/10:4b
DIETRICH, Conrad, NYC-M – 1882/02/11:3c
DIETRICH, Friedrich, 32, NYC-B – 1900/09/08:4a, 9:5a, fam. 10:4a
DIETRICH, Fritz, un. butcher, NYC-B - 1913/09/05:6a, mem. 3 Sept 14:6a
DIETRICH, Georg B., 27, NYC-M – 1891/07/31:4a
DIETRICH, George, 10, NYC-M, +@ Genl Slocum – 1904/06/27:1h
DIETRICH, H., worker & SPD activist expelled fr Ottensen/Gy, arrived NYC – 1881/06/16:4a
DIETRICH, Heinrich, un. typesetter, NYC-B – 1905/02/03:4a
DIETRICH, John Emil, weaver?, Paterson, NJ – 1913/03/18:6a
DIETRICH, Louis, 85, un. upholsterer, NYC-B - 1915/02/09:6a
DIETRICH, Louis, NYC-M – 1886/04/13:3e
DIETRICH, Maria, 53, NYC-B - 1918/11/20:6a; mem. 1919/11/18:6a
DIETRICH, Rosie, NYC-Q – 1909/10/29:6a; fam. 4 Nov:6a
DIETRICH, Therese, b. Henrich, 54, NYC-M – 1892/07/31:5c
DIETRICH, William, NYC-B – 1910/05/30:6a
DIETSCHER, Edward, 6, NYC-M – 1902/08/30:4b
DIETTRICH, Gustav, carp., SPD Leipzig-Reudnitz/Gy – 1901/04/03:2f
DIETZ, Albert, War 2, Norwich, NY - 1918/05/17:2c
DIETZ, Anna, 52, NYC-B – 1891/04/02:4a
DIETZ, August, Rahway, NJ – 1883/08/25:3a
DIETZ, Bernhard, 24, NYC-B – 1887/01/31:3c
DIETZ, Charles, NYC-M – 1891/03/16:4a
DIETZ, Charles, painter, (dying), NYC-B - 1916/04/30:11b

DIETZ, Charles, painter, (dying), NYC-B - 1916/04/30:11b
DIETZ, Emma, child, NYC-B - 1891/05/19:4a
DIETZ, Frederick, lantern manuf., + 31 Mr, NYC-M - 1915/04/24:2f
DIETZ, George, silk flower manuf., NYC-B - 1909/03/18:3a
DIETZ, Hermann, 34, bookkeeper, & wife Emma, 27, NYC-M – 1909/10/29:1e
DIETZ, Jacob, NYC-B - 1917/08/15:6a
DIETZ, Jane, 65, NYC-M - 1900/01/23:1e
DIETZ, John & Margareth, NYC-B - 1891/04/04:4a
DIETZ, John F., 44, NYC-M - 1891/10/24:4a
DIETZ, John F., SP, arrested after defending himself vs deputy, Camerondam/Wisc. 1910/10/27:4f, 30:7b
DIETZ, John Georg, NYC-Metropolitan - 1909/04/25:7c
DIETZ, Joseph, 39, un. carp., NYC-M - 1893/08/29:4a
DIETZ, Louis, Harrison, NY - 1913/09/03:6a
DIETZ, Louis, owner Metropolitan Park, 49, NYC-B – 1898/01/24:1e
DIETZ, Ludwig, 33, fr Frankfurt/Main. Un. typesetter, NYC-M – 1888/02/16:3a
DIETZ, M. A., NYC-M - 1893/07/30:5a
DIETZ, Ottmar, 47, NYC-M - 1901/12/26:4a
DIETZ, Philip M., NYC-M - 1892/09/03:4a
DIETZ, Rosa, 20, New Haven, CT - 1896/01/31:4a, 02/07:4a
DIETZ, Wilhelm, 45, jeweler, NYC-M - 1901/03/21:4a
DIETZ, William, 50, jeweler, NYC-B - 1917/05/19:1e
DIETZE, Emma, infant, NYC-M - 1884/07/29:3c
DIETZEL, Annie, 26, NYC-M - 1888/12/25:4b
DIETZEL, Oscar, 40, & wife Maggie, 29, NYC-M - 1893/08/28:1e
DIETZEL, Robert, woodworker, NYC-M - 1892/05/18:2f
DIETZEL, Wilhelm, SPD Anspach/Frankfurt, War 1 - 1914/11/01:3b
DIETZGEN, Josef, 67, SLP, * Blankenberg/Koeln, publ. NYC Der Socialist, teacher & writer, + Chicago, IL - 1888/04/17:1c,2b, 19:2d. Mem. by son Eugen - 1895/09/15:4c. 25th an. of + 1913/04/15:4d
DIETZSCH, Jacob, Hoboken, NJ - 1896/06/17:4a
DIETZSCH, Louise, Jersey Hgts, NJ - 1919/01/08:6a
DIEULAFOY, Jane, 65, French archaeologist - 1916/05/28:1b, 7 Jy:4f
DILG, Henry, 50, upholsterer, NYC-B - 1896/08/27:1g
DILIESLE, F. S., 40, Swiss?, NYC-M - 1882/04/02:8a
DILKE, Charles Wentworth, 68, British politician - 1911/01/27:1b
DILKS, Robert, 60, phrenologist, NYC-M - 1879/02/21:4c
DILL % Hardenfelder

DILL, August, *1871, born Ziegler, changed his name to his stepfather's, NYC-B – 1905/09/29:3c
DILL, Otto, 44, brewer or cooper, NYC-M – 1891/05/19:4a
DILLENBERG, Jacob, 66, & wife Anna, 73, NYC-M – 1898/02/22:3f
DILLER, Franz, 74, un. tailor, fr Werneck/Wuerzburg, NYC-B - 1878/10/21:3a
DILLING, Carl, NYC-B – 1904/10/ 29:4c
DILLING, Charles, NYC-Q - 1916/02/29:6a
DILLINGER, Elizabeth, 42, NYC-M - 1913/06/18:6a
DILLMANN, Emma, NYC-B - 1894/10/15:4a
DILSNER, Emma, 65, NYC-M - 1914/05/04:6a
DIMANT, Franz, flight pioneer, NYC-M – 1888/12/01:3b
DIMIG, Katharina, 45, NYC-M - 1913/07/30:6a
DIMITRIEVITS, John, un. baker, NYC-Bx - 1917/02/03:6a
DIMLER % Koetzler
DIMMLER, Amalia, 29, Westchester, NY – 1891/03/25:4a
DIMMLER, Marie A., 67, Weehawken, NJ – 1911/11/03:2d
DINE, VAN, Harvey, Chicago gangster, exec. Chicago, IL – 1904/04/23:1g
DINGELSTEDT, Franz, manager of Hofburg theater, Vienna/Austria – 1881/05/22:4d-e
DINGER Sr., comrade, SP, NYC-B - 1913/08/12:6a
DINGER, Emilie, b. Hoffmann, 40, NYC-M – 1890/01/29:4a
DINGES, Joseph, 37, driver, NYC-M – 1896/11/03:1g
DINGLER, Maria, b. Engelbrecht, NYC-M – 1906/06/14:4a
DINGLEY, Nelson, US Congress for Maine, crit. obit – 1899/01/14:1e, 17:2c
DINKEL, John A., 53, ex-judge, NYC-M – 1893/08/13:1f
DINKELMANN, Alois & Adelheid, NYC-M – 1896/08/17:1f
DINKELMANN, Bernh., NYC-B – 1892/07/12:4a
DINKELSPIEL, Fanny, NYC-M – 1892/07/15:4a
DINKER, Emil, un. butcher, NYC-B - 1917/03/22:6a
DINNINGER, Lena, b. Kronauer, NYC-M – 1889/07/05:4a, fam. 8:4a
DINWIDDIE, Charles, Negro, lynched McKenzie, TN – 1886/11/17:1g
DINYES, Charles, 50, un. tailor, NYC-M – 1885/03/27:3d
DINZLER, George, NYC-M - 1917/05/22:6a
DIPPE, Georg, 34, laborer, NYC-M – 1897/01/08:1e
DIPPERT, Agnes, 62, NYC-M, +@ on Genl Slocum – 1904/06/16:1c
DIPPOLD, John, NYC-B - 1916/06/01:6a
DIRDEN, Monroe, Negro, lynched Shreveport, LA – 1914/12/04:1d
DIRK, Frank, NYC?, + @on Genl Slocum – 1904/06/18:3b
DIRKES, Maria, 87, NYC-M – 1892/06/12:4a
DIRKMANN, Anthony, NYC-M – 1911/11/23:6a

DISCH, Martin, 54, tailor, NYC-M - 1879/05/9:1f
DISQUE, George, 33, exec. Jersey City, NJ - 1887/06/02:1e-f
DISQUE, Marie, Hoboken, NJ - 1885/10/08:1c-d
DISRAELI, Benjamin, Lord Beaconsfield, ex-British premier, 1881/04/20:1a, comment :2b, will 28:1a
DISTELBORST, Fritz, 39, fr Karlsruhe/Gy, NYC-M - 1901/09/02:4a
DISTLER, John, 60, ex-pres Jamaica Saengerbund, NYC-B - 1910/04/20:3a
DITERLIN, Carl Wilhelm,45, Spring Valley, NY - 1894/06/16:3g
DITLER, Lizzie, 47, cigarmaker, NYC-M - 1906/08/07:1e
DITMAR, Charles, NYC-M - 1885/05/11:3a
DITMAR, Charles, NYC-M - 1885/05/11:3a
DITMAR, John, NYC-B - 1880/10/12:1g
DITMARS, William B., architect, NYC-B - 1883/11/02:1g
DITRICHSEN, Christ., un. carp., NYC-M - 1902/06/06:4a
DITTMANN, Caspar, ?47, un. furnit. Maker, NYC-B - 1889/09/09:4a
DITTMAR, August, 50, NYC-M - 1890/07/10:4a
DITTMAR, Franz, 55, Dr., physician, NYC-M - 1879/05/01:1e
DITTMAR, John M., 41,pres. Longshoremen's Assoc. #306, Hoboken, NJ - 1914/04/10:6a, 11:6a, 12;7b, =13:2d
DITTMAR, Mary, NYC-M - 1890/08/21:2f
DITTMER, Adolf, (Dittmann), 74, tobaccoworker & SPD act. in Berlin-Schoenhausen - 1909/10/10:3b
DITTMEYER, Mrs (John), 20, NYC-M - 1900/02/25:1e
DITTMEYER, Rosie, 25, NYC-M - 1896/11/25:1h
DITTON % Garten
DITTRICH, Adolph, 74, un. cigarmaker, NYC-M - 1911/04/01:6a
DITTRICH, Albert, un. baker, NYC-M - 1913/10/18:6a, 19:7b
DITTRICH, Caroline, 66, NYC-B - 1904/10/30:5d
DITTRICH, Charley, 33, West Hoboken, NJ - 1904/03/18:4a, 20:5c
DITTRICH, D., 35, NYC-M, + @on Genl Slocum - 1904/06/17:3b
DITTRICH, Friedrich, 71, SDP, Jersey City Heights, NJ - 1902/05/04:5a
DITTRICH, Henriette, b. Doehlert, Jersey City Heights, NJ - 1887/12/29:2h
DITTRICH, J., NYC-M - 1917/09/14:6a
DITTRICH, John, Prof., 57, conductor Odd Fellow Maennerchor & MGV Liberty, NYC-B - 1917/03/26:6a
DITTRICH, Mrs, SP?, NYC-Q - 1914/07/12:11a
DIVIANT, Henry, Swiss?, NYC-M - 1881/05/20:3c
DIVVER, Patrick, ret. Police court judge, NYC - 1903/01/29:1g
DIX, Dorothea, reformer, 1887/07/21:1f
DJOHNE, Edward, 58, Tompinksville, NJ - 1914/08/15:2e
DJORNKE, Annie, 27, Pole, NYC-B - 1895/10/08:3d

DOBBERT % Miller
DOBERT, Jacob, 61, NYC-B – 1907/04/29:6a
DOBLANDER, Alois, 44, fr Steiermark?, NYC-M - 1920/09/28:6a, fam. 30:6a
DOBLER, Lorenz, 55, NYC-B – 1907/06/18:1f
DOBRINKAT, Fritz, engineer, NYC-M – 1901/07/04:4a
DOBRINKAT, Lina, NYC-M – 1919/09/25:6a
DOBRONYI, Louis, 21, son of NYC SLP member Kate Dobronyi,ran away 1915 to enlist Canadian army, + 29 Oct. 1917 in an English field hospital - 1918/01/06:11g
DOBRONYI, Louis, NYC-M – 1912/04/29:6a
DOBROWOLNY, Jacob, NYC-M – 1919/09/17:6a
DOBSAU % Schmolinska
DOCHTERMANN, Friedrich, innkeep, inquest, killed 16 Dec – 1882/12/19:4c, murderer Martin Hess tried 24 Jan. 1883:1g
DOCK, Lee, member of Hip Sing Tong, NYC, exec. Ossining, NY - 1914/10/29:2, 1915/02/06:1d
DOCKERY, Friedericke, 45, Hoboken, NJ – 1909/07/01:2a
DOCKMAN, Clara, 19, @1911 Triangle Shirtwaist Fire, NYC-M – 1911/03/29:1c
DODD, Frank, Negro, lynched Little Rock, AK - 1916/10/11:1c
DODEL, Arnold, Dr., Prof. Zuerich U/Switz. – 1908/04/24:4f
DODSCH, Lena, 15, servant, NYC-B – 1890/12/03:1g
DOEBBELER, John, SLP, silver wedding in Paterson, NJ – 1880/11/17:4e
DOEBEL, William, Jersey City Heights, NJ – 1890/12/07:5a
DOEBLER, Carl, bookmaker, NYC-M – 1885/03/14:4a
DOEDELE, Elisa, b. Schaffner, 61, NYC-M – 1892/08/09:4a
DOEGER, Richard, 61, un. typesetter, NYC-M – 1902/05/29:4a
DOEHLERT % Dittrich
DOEHRING, John, NYC-Q – 1902/10/13:4a
DOEHRING, Wilhelm, 43, un. butcher, NYC-B - 1916/04/11:6a, fam. 20:6a
DOELFEL, Friedrich, NYC-M – 1883/11/16:3c
DOELGER, Fanny, 35, NYC-M – 1885/09/26:1e
DOELGER, F.'s wife, NYC-M – 1883/01/12:1g
DOELGER, Joseph, 11, NYC-M – 1886/11/04:4a
DOELGER, Joseph, brewery-owner, NYC – 1882/08/12:1d
DOELGER, Maria Magdalena, b. Lambrecht, 39, NYC-M - 1878/06/26:3c, 29:3c
DOELGER, Peter, brewery owner, NYC – 1912/12/26:4c
DOELL, Anna, 80, NYC-B - 1914/04/15:6a
DOELL, August, 52, fr Eisenach/Thueringia, NYC-M - 1878/06/01:3b

DOELL, Caecilie, 69, SP?, co-fdr NYVZ, USA 1870s, NYC-B - 1915/09/11:2b, 6a, fam. 14:6a
DOELL, Georg, NYC-B - 1879/01/28:3a
DOELL, Rudolf, NYC German Society, + Gy - 1883/12/25:2c
DOELL, SPD member in Frankfurt/Main, Gy, grave monument inaug. 1884/07/25:2e
DOELSEL, Carl, NYC-M - 1889/07/30:4a
DOELZ, Augustina, 38, Union, NJ - 1919/07/22:6a
DOENNIGES, VON % Schewitsch
DOEPPER, John Ferdinand, SP, Jersey City Hgts, NJ - 1920/06/16:6a
DOEPPING, Friedericke, b. Wohlfahrt, NYC-M - 1906/01/15:4a
DOEPPING, Wilhelm, un. carp., NYC-M - 1908/03/25:6a
DOERFFLINGER, Henry, 45, silk weaver, NYC-M - 1903/01/27:4a
DOERING, Alfred, 7, NYC-M - 1890/08/30:4a
DOERING, Carl, un. carp., NYC-M - 1917/05/08:6a
DOERING, Herman, lantern manuf., & wife, NYC-Q - 1901/12/13:1f
DOERING, Ida, wife of Rev. Doering, Luth. Immigr. Home, NYC-M, + @Genl Slocum - 1904/06/24:1c
DOERING, Karl, SPD?, Bremen/Gy, War 1 - 1914/11/01:3b
DOERING, Karl, NYC-M - 1910/04/13:6a
DOERING, Louise von, b. Frank, NYC-M - 1891/03/15:5b
DOERING, Theodor, German actor - 1878/09/01:5a-b
DOERR % Hoffmann
DOERR, Joseph, un. brewery worker, NYC-M - 1894/05/21:4a
DOERR, Paul, un. cigar maker, NYC-M - 1897/01/21:4a
DOERRKOEFER, Freda, 18, NYC-M, +Genl Slocum - 1904/06/23:1c
DOES, August, machinist, NYC-M - 1908/08/14:6a
DOES, Christina, b. Poessing, mem. - 1888/05/21:3a
DOESCH, Karl, NYC-Q - 1908/09/02:6a
DOESCHER, Otto, 47, janitor, NYC-M - 1917/01/16:6c
DOEVEL, John, NYC-B - 1878/10/08:3a
DOGGERT, Peter, 30, worker, NYC-M - 1897/08/29:11d
DOHL, Elsie, 17, NYC-B - 1920/10/08:2d, 9:6b
DOHLEN, Christoph von, 60, driver, NYC-M - 1879/04/17:4b
DOHM, Henry E., stoker, NYC-B - 1880/06/01:1g
DOHM, Peter, 43, butcher, NYC-Q - 1916/05/06:3d
DOHMANIK, Paul, striker at Standard Coke Works, Morewood, PA - 1891/04/03:1b, =4:1a-b, 5:1f,4a
DOHMANN, John, lamp cleaner, NYC-M - 1891/02/08:1f
DOHN, Frank, 5, Hoboken, NJ - 1892/04/01:1c
DOHNE, Carl, 28, cigar maker & SPD activist expelled fr Hamburg/Gy, arrived in NYC - 1881/01/19:1g, 20:4c

DOHREN, Adam, 18, NYC-M – 1891/08/27:1d
DOHRMANN, Karl, 28, NYC-M – 1909/12/29:6a
DOHS, Richard, NYC-M – 1891/08/28:4a
DOLAN, John, exec. Trenton, NJ - 1914/08/19:2f
DOLAN, Patrick J., leader Un. Mine Workers, + Pittsburgh, PA – 1910/10/24:1d
DOLGE, fdr Dolgeville, said in 1908 to be +, still alive at 65 in Covina, CA - 1913/06/08:7a
DOLL % Koehl
DOLL, August, un. carp., NYC-M – 1889/07/14:5a
DOLL, John G., 55, NYC-M – 1892/08/19:4a
DOLLACK, Charles, NYC-B - 1914/09/09:6a
DOLLACK, Henry, NYC-B - 1919/05/13:6a
DOLLERMAN, Anton, 79, weaver, NYC-M – 1909/12/31:1b
DOLLMANN, Eva, 6, NYC-M – 1892/07/05:4a
DOLOFF, Carl P., Orange, NJ - 1915/03/09:6a
DOLT, Friedrich Frank, 1, NYC-M – 1887/12/01:3b
DOLWAGEN, Georg, 65, gravedigger, Woodlawn?, NJ – 1893/11/29:2f
DOMACSEK, Esther, + 14 June Schenectady, NY – 1892/07/16:2e
DOMEIER, Wilhelm, 45, SLP?, NYC-B – 1890/10/31:4a, fam. 3 Nov:4a
DOMELION, Therese, 55, NYC-M? – 1880/02/13:3a
DOMIS, Franziska, NYC-M - 1896/01/25:4a
DOMMERS, August, NYC-B - 1913/11/24:6a
DOMSCHITZ, Josef, 50, alderman, SP Hainburg/Austria - 1908/07/12:3d
DOMSCHKY, J. E., un. cigar maker, NYC-B – 1889/09/18:4a
DONAHUE, William J., NYS Assembly, NYC-B – 1907/02/01:3a-b, 2:3b, 3:1d
DONATH, F., NYC-B – 1911/04/21:6a
DONATH, Ottilie, 58, NYC-M – 1901/01/09:4a
DONATH, Wilhelm, 68, NYC-B – 1909/01/23:6a
DONEGAN, Richard, exec. Trenton, NJ – 1909/09/08:2e
DONJES, Oskar, 18, butcher, NYC-B – 1896/07/11:3d
DONNELLY, Dennis, Molly Maguire, exec. Pottsville, PA - 1878/06/12:1c, 2c
DONNELLY, Ignatius, 69, Populist writer, + Minneapolis, MN – 1901/01/03:3d
DONNERSBERG, F.H., 51, un. carp., NYC-M? – 1897/03/08:1d, 9:4a, =11:4d
DONNTER, Julia, washer, NYC-M – 1909/10/09:1d
DONOVAN, Mike, mobster, NYC-M – 1903/09/17:1g, 18:3g, =21:1g
DONZELMANN, Claus, 58, NYC-B – 1892/06/26:5c
DOPPEL, Eva R., NYC-Q – 1908/03/17:3b

DOPPLER, Franz, 63, Viennese composer fr Lemberg – 1883/08/12:4e
DORDAK, Julia, 19, servant, fr Gy, NYC-M – 1907/04/24:3e
DORE, Gustave, French cartoonist, + Paris – 1883/01/24:1c, 2c
DOREMUS, David M., 65, vet. Duryea Zouaves, Mt Vernon, NY – 1909/12/04:3d
DOREMUS, John Myers, exec. Hackensack, NJ – 1888/12/20:1d
DORFMAN, Abe, burglar, NYC-B – 1897/09/07:1h
DORFMANN, W., SP?, NYC-M - 1916/08/12:6a
DORHOEFER, Susanne, 6 mo., NYC-M or –Bx – 1890/08/08:4a
DORMANN, Fannie, 60, fr Russia 1911, NYC-M - 1913/06/26:1a
DORMAUL, E. H., fr Fuerth/Bavaria, NYC-M – 1889/02/12:4a
DORMER, Josephine, 12, NYC-M – 1919/10/07:8a
DORN, George, 34, un. typesetter, SDP?, NYC-M – 1905/04/19:4a
DORN, Lena, 20, NYC-M – 1899/03/07:3c
DORN, Theresa, NYC – 1898/05/26:4c
DORN, Thomas, 42, chemist at Havemeyer Sugar Refining Co., NYC-M – 1906/12/27:3b
DORNBACH, Ferdinand, G-A theatre, + Toledo, OH during tour – 1883/02/03:3b
DORNHACKEL, Johann, glass worker, labor org., Hermanshuette/ Bohemia, War 1 - 1915/02/21:3b
DORNHEIM, Amelie, ~50, NYC-M – 1887/07/28:1g
DORNHEIM, Theodor, NYC-B – 1901/02/13:4a
DORNLEY, Catherine, 36, NYC-M – 1893/03/12:1h
DOROWSKI, Julius, 79, SPD Danzig/Gy, un. carp. - 1914/02/22:3a
DORR % Feidner
DORR, Louis, 63, mason, NYC-M – 1903/06/22:4a
DORSAM, George, NYC-B - 1920/02/15:12a
DORSCH, Anna, 35, NYC-B – 1899/06/19:1d, 18:1d, 22:4c, 6 Dec:3b
DORSCH, Charles, 32, un. upholsterer, SLP, NYC-B – 1892/02/16:4a
DORSCH, Michael, un. packer, NYC-B – 1903/05/16:3c
DORSCHEL % Schwaise
DORSCHEL, Oskar, 48, NYC-M - 1894/02/01:4a
DORSEMENT, Henri, 61, candy store, French, NYC-M - 1894/08/07:4a
DORSH % Trauth
DORSHEIMER, William, NYS Lt Gov 1874-78 – 1888/03/28:4d
DORST, Charles, NYC-M - 1918/01/15:6a
DORT, Maria, 78, NYC-M – 1892/08/01:4a
DORTUE, Max, '48er, memorial plaque in Freiburg/Gy – 1912/09/08:3a
DORUFF, Hermann, former quartermaster on SS Nuernberg, married Dorothea Happenberg, NYC-M – 1881/06/23:4c
DOSCH, Babette, 30, NYC-M – 1888/02/09:3a

DOSCH, Ch., NYC-B – 1908/06/16:6a
DOSCHER % von Damm
DOSCHER, Ahrend, 86, NYC-B – 1892/07/02:4a
DOSCHER, Henry & Willi, NYC-B – 1889/06/16:5d
DOSCHER, Henry, 42, NYC-M – 1892/07/25:4a
DOSER, Engelbert, NYC-M – 1907/03/01:6a
DOSKOPIL, Emil, un. carpenter, NYC-M – 1911/08/22:6a
DOSSET, Moe, Negro, lynched near Mobile, AL – 1907/09/23:1f
DOSTOJEWSKI, Michael Fedorowitsch, Russian poet & friend of the people, + St Petersburg/Russia – 1881/03/13:4b-d
DOTTERER, Emma, Guttenberg, NJ - 1915/04/15:6a
DOTTERWEICH, Margarethe, 100, * Bavaria 20 Fb 1780, Paterson, NJ – 1880/01/21:4d
DOUAI, Adolf, SLP leader, 69, NYC-M – 1888/01/23:1h, 2g, =24:1d, 3a, 25:1a-d,2a,g, 26:1d, fam. 26:2a, notes 15 Fb:2e, cremated now 1890/04/11:2c, 20:1h. 90th anniv. Birth comm.. 21 Fb 1909:3d-g. His life in Texas 1850s, repr fr Dr. Th. Hertzberg 1887 – 1910/05/15:3b-g
DOUAI, Agnes, 79, wd of Adolf Douai, NYC-B – 1898/12/16:4a, 17:4a
DOUAI, Antoinette, 15, NYC-M – 1889/09/07:4a
DOUAI, Katherina, b. Hackel, NYC-B – 1892/09/09:4a
DOUAI, Max A., un. printer, NYC-B - 1913/08/12:6a, 13:6a
DOUGALL, John, 78, editor N.Y. Witness, NYC-Flushing – 1886/08/20:3b
DOUGLAS, James, Dr., 81, chair of Phelps-Dodge Co., crit. obit., NYC-B - 1918/06/26:3f, 27:4c
DOUGLAS, Robert, police sergeant, +White Plains, NY – 1900/05/08:1c
DOUNIK, Kalman, 24,@1911 Triangle Shirtwaist Fire, NYC-M – 1911/03/27:1d
DOWD, Dennis, Seacliff,L.I., vol. French airforce, War 1 - 1916/08/15:2f
DOWIE, John Alex, fd Zion City,+ Chicago – 1907/03/10:1e, 13:1c, 16:4a
DOWLEY, Annie, 23, lady of the night, NYC-M – 1880/01/18:5d-e, 19:1e, 20:1g
DOWNING, David L., musician – 1880/08/20:1d
DOZIER, Gustav, NYC-B – 1903/02/20:1f
DRABOLD % Brohm
DRACHMANN, Holger, Danish poet, with # – 1908/02/23:15f, 19a-c
DRACK, Albert, NYC-Q – 1906/03/17:4a
DRAECKERT, Bernhardt, un. brewer, NYC-B – 1897/01/01:1d
DRAHEIM, August, 63, janitor, NYC-M – 1889/09/26:4e
DRAKE, Joe, Negro, lynched near Ripley, TN – 1903/12/20:5e
DRANISWICZ, Karol, exec. Ossining, NY - 1915/08/28:1b
DRAPER, John W., 70, US scientist, good obit – 1882/01/05:2c
DRAPER, Prof. Henry, 45, US scientist – 1882/11/21:2c

DRASKOVITZ, Gottlieb, 50, NYC-Q - 1919/07/19:6a, fam. 27:12a
DRASKOWITZ, Elsa, child, NYC-B - 1917/04/16:6a, fam. 21:6a
DRASZIK, Rudolf, SP Steinau/Teplitz/Bohemia, War 1 - 1915/05/30:3d
DRATHSCHMIDT, August, Yonkers, NY - 1914/12/16:6a
DRAUTZ % Lochhaus
DRAY, Anna, 53, (> Frederick. Schaeffer), NYC-Q - 1915/12/16:1g
DREBINGER, Charles, un. printer, NYC-B - 1895/05/28:4a
DRECHSLER, Georg, 74, '48er, +Grosskarlbach/Rheinpfalz - 1899/06/11:12g
DRECHSLER, John, NYC-M - 1904/01/10:5a
DREDA, Minnie, NYC-M, + @ Genl Slocum - 1904/06/17:3b
DREESBACH, August, carp., SPD MdR for Mannheim - 1906/12/10:4e-f, =15:4e-f, 24:4g
DREHER % Winker
DREHER, Herman, un. carp., NYC-M - 1911/05/11:1f, 12:6a
DREHER, Katherine, 11, John, 1, & Annie, NYC-M, +@ Genl Slocum - 1904/06/17:3b, 18:3b
DREHER, Louis, 50, & wife Pauline, 40, Newark, NJ - 1909/02/09:2b, 10:6a, 11:3b,6a
DREHER, Matthias, 55, NYC-M - 1913/06/09:6a, 10:6a
DREHER, Otto L., butcher, Mt Vernon, NY - 1913/12/03:1e
DREIER, George, NYC-B - 1913/02/21:6a
DREIER, Henriette, 17, servant, + with Mrs Horn of food poisoning, NYC-B - 1879/03/14:1e
DREISCH, Valentin, 47, worker, NYC-M - 1885/12/30:3c
DREISER, Philip, NYPD, NYC-M - 1900/05/13:1g
DRELLMANN, Franz, un. cigar maker, Jersey City, NJ - 1888/11/02:3b
DRESBOLD, Liebschmuel, ~60, glass worker, NYC-Bx - 1904/11/04:1h
DRESCHER % Vogt
DRESCHER, Amanda, NYC-M - 1915/04/21:6a
DRESCHER, Christian, 62, elevator repair, NYC-M - 1889/02/07:4d, 8:4a
DRESCHER, Emil, 78, active in German singing, NYC-B - 1915/01/27:2a
DRESCHER, Franz, 26, machinist, Newark, NJ - 1916/06/22:6a, 23:6a
DRESCHER, Friedrich, SLP, un. machinist, * Remscheid/Ruhr, USA 1891,1895/07/22: 4b = 24: 2d
DRESCHER, Karolina, NYC-M - 1878/08/02:3c
DRESCHER, Katherina, 67, NYC-B - 1891/04/05:5a
DRESCHER, Louis, Dr., Newark, NJ - 1904/05/02:3c
DRESCHER, Martin, 57, G-A poet, * May 1863 Thueringen, law student in Gy, worker & journalist in USA, NYC-Q - 1920/03/09:1f, 4g, 6a, 10:2b,6a, = 11:6c, poem 13:7d, obit by Martin Baginski 21:8d-g
DRESDEN, Beatrice von, 17, balloon racer,+ Buffalo, NY - 1894/10/08:1c

DRESEN, Emilie, NYC-M? – 1882/05/06:3b
DRESSEL, Ann, 32, NYC-M – 1908/10/24:1c
DRESSEL, Elmer, Newark, NJ – 1909/02/03:3c
DRESSEL, Frank, 32, postal clerk, NYC-M – 1908/08/15:1d
DRESSEL, William G., NYPD, NYC-B – 1900/02/23:4a
DRESSER, Frederick., 35, fr NJ, worker at Aqueduct Tunnel near Ossining, NY – 1885/12/08:1e, =9:1f
DRESSER, Kate, b. Hart, 68, Peekskill, NY - 1916/05/03:2c
DRESSLER, Edward, worker, Jersey City, NJ - 1913/05/15:3a
DRESSLER, Elsa, infant, NYC-M – 1890/10/26:5a
DRESSLER, Gottfried, NYC-Bx – 1911/02/23:6a, 24:6a
DRESSLER, Gustav, sailor on USS Maine, + Havana/Cuba, NYC-M – 1898/02/18:1b
DRESSLER, John A., un. cigar maker, NYC-M – 1886/07/01:3b
DRESSLER, Louis, 38, NYC-M – 1892/07/29:4b
DRESSLER, William, innkeep, Wallington, NJ – 1903/06/27:3c
DRESSLER, William, NYC-Q - 1919/04/02:6a
DREVERMANN, Max, NYC-B – 1907/10/06:7a
DREW, Thomas, porter, NYC-M – 1880/04/13:1g
DREWS, August, un. cigarmaker, NYC-Bx – 1906/03/28:4a, 29:4a
DREWS, Catherine, 68, NYC-M, + on Genl Slocum – 1904/06/17:3b
DREXEL, Joseph W., banker & philanthropist, NYC-M – 1888/03/27:3a
DREXLER, Herman, Union Hill, NJ - 1918/02/06:6a
DREY, John, 28, worker, Whippany, NJ – 1909/11/17:3b
DREYER % Deneke
DREYER, Clara, 19, NYC-B – 1892/10/12:4a
DREYER, Julie, 16, NYC-M – 1882/03/01:1e
DREYER, Julius, 65, NYC-M – 1892/07/28:4a
DREYER, Margarethe, b. Schwich, NYC-M – 1890/03/21:4a
DREYER, Otto,45, plumber, NYC-M - 1894/05/02:4d
DREYER, W., un. stonemason, NYC-M – 1892/01/11:4a
DREYER, Wilhelm, 65, SPD Stockelsdorf/Luebeck/Gy – 1912/06/02:3a
DREYFUS, Capt., notes on sentence, 1896/11/28:2d-e
DRIESEN, Franz, 40, upholsterer, Hoboken, NJ – 1900/12/12:1d, 13:3b
DRIGGS, Andrew, Negro, lynched Larksville, AL – 1903/07/01:3b
DRINKEL, Minnie, 19, nanny, NYC – 1900/05/03:4b
DRISCOLL, Dan, exec. – 1888/01/14:4e, 17:1h, 18:2e, 19:1f, 20:1f, 21:1f-g, 23:1h, 24:1f, =25:4a
DROEGE, Mathilde, NYC-Q – 1908/02/11:3a
DROLLE, Herman, un. butcher, NYC-M - 1914/05/19:5f, 6a
DROLLINGER, Magdalene, 52, NYC-B – 1898/04/17:5e

DROMMER, Emil, 22, SP, un. textile worker, fr Saxony, USA 1912, Dover, NJ, + Philadelphia, PA - 1913/07/09:6a
DROSIHN, Charles, NYC-M - 1910/07/17:7b
DRUCKER, Adolph, British millionaire, + NYC - 1903/12/16:1h, 17:3c
DRUCKER, Charles, NYC-Metropolitan - 1910/05/24:6a
DRUCKER, Georg, 40, mason, NYC-M - 1892/06/22:1e
DRUCKER, Hermann, 60, cigar maker & SPD veteran, = Berlin/Gy - 1889/04/02:2d
DRUCKER, Julia E., NYC-M - 1908/07/31:1d
DRUCKEREY, Friedrich, 37, un. carp., NYC-M - 1889/11/04:4a
DRUECKEL, Maria, b. Dick, NYC-M - 1891/03/24:4a
DRUESICKE, Louis, 38, locksmith, NYC-M - 1887/07/26:3b
DRUMM, Louise, Jersey City Heights, NJ, fam. 1885/02/03:3b
DRUMM, Ludwig, NYC-Bx - 1909/03/02:6a
DRUNK, Adam, driver, Metropolitan, LI - 1907/07/28:7b, 26:3c
DRUNSKO, Michael, 43, worker, & daughter, 12, NYC-M? - 1912/08/12:2a
DRUSE, Roxaline, exec. Herkimer, NY - 1887/02/28:1f, 1 Mr:1c,2c
DRUX, Franz Wilhelm, 70, veteran & SPD, + streets of Berlin/Gy becz of bureaucracy– 1912/08/08:4e-f
DRYER, VAN DEN, Wilhelm,un.cigarmaker, NYC-M - 1919/03/16:12a
DRYFUS, Arthur, Dr. med., 42, NYC-M - 1918/08/23:2c
DSCHAPARIDSE, Arschill, 30, Georgian Soc., 2nd Duma member, + 29 Dec in jail – 1909/02/28:15d
DUBENKOPF, August, 54, un. cigarmaker, NYC-M - 1899/04/05:4a, 3f
DUBON, Friedericke, Newark, NJ - 1918/07/11:6a
DUBON, Friedrich, SP, Newark, NJ – 1913/02/04:6a, 6:3b-c
DUBON, Pauline, Newark, NJ – 1912/09/08:7b
DUBOURGNE, Virgile, 75, French, NYC-M - 1882/02/16:4c
DUBRA, Samuel, Slovak RR worker, + Roseville, NJ – 1910/04/15:1a
DUBROWSKY, Demetrius, Russian student in Berlin, + 1911/05/24:4e-f
DUCEY, Rev., spiritual advisor to Terence Powderly, KoL, crit obit – 1909/08/25:4c
DUCIMETIERE, Emilienne Rose, 19, servant, killed by French for alleged spying - 1917/04/27:6b
DUCKER, John, 11, NYC-M, +@ Genl Slocum – 1904/06/17:3b
DUDAS, Joseph, un. carp., NYC - 1914/03/13:6a
DUDEN, August, 38, painter, NYC-M – 1892/03/29:1c
DUDLEY, Albert, Negro, lynched Olatha, KS - 1916/09/22:1e
DUDLEY, Carl, Negro, lynched Lawton, OK - 1916/04/11:2a
DUEFER, Daniel, NYC-Bx – 1912/04/28:7a
DUEFER, William, 52, NYC-Bx - 1918/10/22:6a

DUEMMKE, Heinrich A., Westbrook, CT – 1911/08/18:6a
DUENKEL, Georg, 42, West Hoboken, NJ – 1908/05/17:7c
DUENKEL, Louis C., Jersey City Heights, NJ – 1891/03/11:4a
DUENSING, George, 55, un. carp., NYC-Q – 1912/10/25:6a, 26:6a, fam. 29:6a
DUEPPEL, Friedrich, un. carp., Paterson, NJ – 1911/01/03:6a
DUER, Barbara, NYC-M – 1902/03/23:5a, fam. 26:4a
DUER, Margaret, 52, NYC-M – 1902/07/30:2f
DUERFLER, Isaac, 58, NYC-B - 1916/02/03:6d
DUERING, A. von, Dr., 57, *Hamburg/Gy, physician, NYC-Bx – 1909/02/11:2f
DUERR, Albert, un. ironworker, NYC – 1896/04/23:4a
DUERR, Andreas, NYC-M – 1893/03/27:4a
DUERR, Christian, Philadelphia, PA – 1919/12/11:2d
DUERR, Frank, 75, NYC-B – 1900/11/12:3b
DUERR, Fridolin, 52, SP, un. turner, *Burkheim/Baden, NYC-B – 1910/02/27:7c,g, 28:6a, =2 Mr:3d, fam. 5:6a
DUERR, Jacob, 43, un. carp., NYC-M – 1905/06/04:5b
DUERR, John, 63, NYC-M – 1896/06/03:3f
DUERRKOP, Johann, 55, mason & SPD activist in Luebeck/Gy – 1907/07/18:3a
DUEVEL, Fritz, 38, SPD Berlin, active in party media – 1911/08/11:4d
DUFFER, Justus, un. baker, NYC-Bx - 1920/11/25:6a
DUFFY, P. J., Rev., RC Sacred Heart, Port Jervis, NY – 1900/03/23:3d
DUGGAN, Dr., his killer George Weidler tried 30 Nov 1887:4d, 1 Dec:2c, 2:2d, jail 3:1g, 10:2c, 17:2f
DUGGAN, Edward H., Dr., 48, NYC-B – 1887/06/25:1g, 28:2d
DUGRO, Antony, = NYC – 1884/10/14:1f
DUHNKE, William, 58, shoe manuf. fr Minneapolis, MN, + NYC – 1887/01/04:2e
DUHNKRACK, Heinrich, 57, Weehawken, NJ – 1907/01/30:6a
DUICK, Mary, 16, NYC-B, + @ Genl Slocum – 1904/06/17:3b
DUK, Pauline, NYC-M, + @Genl Slocum – 1904/06/18:3b
DULEWEIT, Hermann, un. sailor, + on SS Hamburg, =Hoboken, NJ – 1909/12/29:6c
DULK, Adalbert, Dr., Stuttgart/Gy, labor-friendly liberal – 1884/11/18:2f
DULTGEN, August, 71, SP, NYC-B – 1916/05/18:6a
DUMAS, John, weaver?, NYC - 1914/04/06:6a
DUMB, Frank, NYC-M – 1903/12/30:4a
DUMBERGER, John, un. carp., NYC-Bx - 1914/10/05:6a
DUMIZINSKY, Karl, un. shoemaker, NYC-B – 1881/01/15:4f
DUMMBACH % Mohnkorn

DUMPKE, August, NYC-B - 1917/04/20:6a
DUMROSE, Max NYC-Bx - 1909/10/11:6a, 12:6a
DUNANT, Henri, 82, fdr Red Cross -- 1910/11/17:4f
DUNCAN, Horace, Negro, lynched Springfield, MO -- 1906/04/16:1c-d, 17:1d
DUNHAM, George, exec. Woodbury, NJ – 1888/04/27:2e
DUNKEL % Boormann
DUNKHASE, Claus, 48, NYC-B – 1892/06/16:4a
DUNN, David, 20, exec. Auburn, NY - 1915/07/03:2a
DUNN, Dennis, 45, NYC-M – 1897/09/25:4a
DUNN, John E., un. brass worker & labor activist, NYC-M -- 1893/08/14:1b
DUNN, Julia, 29, & Arthur, 4, NYC-M?, +@ Genl Slocum – 1904/06/17:1b, 3b, 18:1c, 3b
DUNSER, Jacob, smith, NYC-M – 1881/06/25:4c
DUNST % Rausch
DUNST, Mathilde, b. Orth, 36, NYC-Q – 1887/03/10:3d
DUNTZ, Hermann, NYC-Q – 1906/09/16:7c
DUPERTUIS, Marie, governess, Swiss, NYC-M – 1902/12/01:1g
DUPKA, Ignatz, tailor, fr Russia, NYC-M – 1896/09/30:3f
DUPOND, Anna, (s.a. Martin) NYC-M – 1903/07/25:4a
DUPREE, Frank, 21, Negro, lynched Long Leaf, LA – 1903/06/14:5d
DURFEE, Joe, Negro, lynched Angleton, TX - 1914/10/15:2c
DURLACH, Elias, merchant, NYC-B – 1901/05/21:2h
DUROFF, Russian Revolutionary working as circus clown, his heroic death in St Peter & Paul Prison/St Petersburg/Russia – 1893/03/25:2c
DURR, Christian's wife, 20, NYC-B – 1899/11/06:3b
DURR, Louis, '48er, gold & silver refiner, fr Baden, NYC-M – 1880/04/05:1e
DURR, Louise, 25, NYC-B – 1911/11/22:6a
DURRANT, Theodore, exec. St Quentin, CA – 1898/01/08:1c-d
DURSCH, Herman, 46, NYC-B - 1916/06/10:6a
DURST, Henry, NYC-M – 1885/05/06:1c-d, 2a, 7:1c, 8:1d, inquest 16:2e-f, 23:2g
DURST, Rudolph, 40, un. waiter, NYC-M – 1891/01/12:4a, 13:4a
DURST, Wilhelm, carp., * 4 Feb. 1872 Esslingen/Stuttgart, USA 1894, Philadelphia - 1918/03/07:6c
DURYEA, Chester, US genl, NYC-M - 1914/05/06:1c
DURYEA, George, Tweed Ring member, NYC – 1887/06/09:2d
DUSCH, Elizabeth, 61,NYC-M - 1916/05/17:6a;mem 1917/05/15:6a
DUSCH, Henry, NYC-M – 1893/02/23:4a
DUSS, H., 63, NYC-Q - 1915/08/27:6a

DUSTROW, Alfred, St Louis millionaire, exec. Union, MO – 1897/02/17:1c
DUTCHER, Hattie, b. Van Buren, 30, NYC-M – 1880/04/06:1g, 7:1e, 8:1e, 13:2g, 6 May:1f
DUTERSTADT, Christian, un. cigarmaker, NYC-M - 1879/02/05:8b
DUTKO, Michael, innkeep, NYC-M – 1891/08/11:2e, inquest 25 Aug.:2f; notes 1 Jy 1892:1f
DUTTGE, Friedrich Theodor, + 30.01.19, mem. - 1920/01/30:8a
DUTTGE, Gottfried, + 1.10.19, mem. - 1920/10/01:6a
DUTTGEN, Gertrude, 12, NYC-B – 1897/06/10:4a
DUTTJE, Theodore Gotthold, 53, un. painter, NYC-M – 1919/10/03:6a, fam. 7:8a
DUTTON, Ira Barnes, Rev., head Malokai/Hawaii Leprosy Colony – 1913/01/20:2e
DUVAL, M., European patriot, exec. by French govt 17 Jy 1918 for wanting peace of understanding (Caillaux Affair) – 1919/10/25:1b
DUVORSAK, Rudolph, infant, NYC-M – 1881/02/26:3d
DUZER, VAN, Tillie, 13, NYC-M, + @Genl Slocum – 1904/06/27:1h
DVORAK, Albrecht, Czech Socialist, leather worker & mgr of Delnicke Listy, * Trebitsch/Moravia, + Vienna - 1914/10/04:3e
DVORAK, Marie, 20, Czech, NYC-M – 1898/10/15:1f
DWYER, Matthew, stoker, +during strike, Buffalo, NY – 1909/09/01:2c
DYKE, VAN, Wm. S., furniture dealer, NYC-M - 1878/10/04:1e
DYRENDAHL, H., Dane, dyer?, NYC – 1880/04/24:1f
DYROTT, Adam, NYC-M - 1916/02/20:7a; mem. 1917/02/17:6a, 1918/02/17:7a
EAGAN, James J., exec. Montrose, PA – 1900/01/10:2h
EARLE, general, British, killed in Sudan, comment 1885/02/13:1a-c
EASTMAN, "Monk," (Wm Delaney), NYC mobster who became good, on his parole 1909/06/22:4b-c, + NYC-B - 1920/12/27:1e,
EATON, George H., ex-pres. Buffalo Typograph. Union – 1885/09/21:1g
EATON, William, + saving 2 boys fr drowning, NYC-M – 1907/09/23:1a
EBBECKE, Bernhard, NYC-Bx – 1909/02/14:7c
EBBECKE, Carl W., un. musician, Newark, NJ – 1900/05/04:4f
EBBECKE, Katherine, child, NYC-M – 1882/09/01:3b
EBBRECHT, Philip, un. lithographer, NYC-Q – 1910/07/01:6a, 2:6a, =6:2d, fam. 6:6a
EBEL, August, 61, machinist, NYC-B – 1902/03/24:4a
EBEL, Henriette, 29, NYC-B – 1909/02/08:3e
EBEL, Louise Wilhelmina, b. Stitz, NYC-M – 1903/03/17:4a, fam. 21:4a
EBEL, Wilhelm, 2, NYC-M – 1906/06/11:4a
EBELING, Emilie, + Kopenhagen/DK – 1888/05/23:3a

EBELING, George H., Newark, NJ – 1881/09/01:1g
EBELING, William, NYC-M – 1907/02/24:7d
EBELT, Augusta, 22, Mt Vernon, NY – 1903/07/27:1b, 29:1a-b
EBELT, Martin, exec. Ossining, NY – 1905/04/07:1e, 10:1c, done 11:3b
EBENHOCH, Ernst, 43, un. waiter, NYC-B - 1894/08/13:4a
EBERBACH, Mary, 35, Paterson, NJ – 1899/04/10:3b
EBERBACHER, Charles, 23, West Hoboken, NJ - 1917/12/21:2d
EBERENZ, Katherina, b. Rupp, 55, NYC-B - 1920/03/09:6a
EBERHARD, Elizabeth, NYC-M – 1901/10/14:4a, 16:4a
EBERHARD, Jakob, NYC-B – 1910/01/24:6a
EBERHARD, Ophelia? Ottilie?, 45, Coalberg?, NJ – 1908/07/20:1d, 21:1g, 22:2a, 24:1c, her killer rec 30 yrs 24 Sept:1g
EBERHARDT % Loos
EBERHARDT, ..., 45, porter Customs House, NYC-M – 1882/05/06:3a-b
EBERHARDT, Auguste, NYC-M - 1917/06/03:7a
EBERHARDT, Dietrich, 45, NYC-M – 1892/01/12:4a
EBERHARDT, Georg, 24, plumber, NYC-M – 1899/01/25:1f-g, 27:1f
EBERHARDT, Henry, 73, NYC-B - 1920/05/07:6a
EBERHARDT, Ida, NYC-M – 1890/06/29:4a
EBERHARDT, John, 18, baker, NYC-M – 1887/03/01:1b
EBERHARDT, John, 43, NYC-B – 1906/12/03:3a
EBERHARDT, John, un. cigarmaker, NYC-M – 1880/06/22:3a
EBERHARDT, Martin, un. cigarmaker, NYC-M – 1902/02/02:5a
EBERHARDT, Wilhelmine, b. Hackbarth, 32, NYC-M – 1892/05/16:4a
EBERHART, Kathie, 12, NYC-M – 1888/01/02:3a
EBERL, Martin, un. printer, NYC-B - 1918/05/10:6a
EBERLE % Rehfeld
EBERLE, Barbara, 17, NYC-M – 1888/09/12:1f
EBERLE, Christian, NYC-M - 1919/06/13:6a
EBERLE, Henry, 63, NYC? - 1914/08/14:6a
EBERLE, John, 37, NYC - 1914/02/25:6a
EBERLE, Leonhardt, 20, NYC-Bx – 1912/01/29:6a
EBERLE, Philipp, 17, NYC-B – 1891/08/27:1d
EBERLE, R., NYC-Bx - 1914/05/18:6a
EBERLEIN, Ludwig, 13, NYC-M – 1888/09/17:3a
EBERLI, Rosi, 24, NYC-M – 1891/08/10:4a
EBERLING, Carl, un. typesetter, NYC-B – 1909/07/29:6a
EBERLOH, Anna, NYC-M – 1891/06/26:4a
EBERLY, John, 35, fish dealer, NYC-M – 1891/08/15:4e
EBERS, Joseph, 65, carp., NYC-B – 1897/11/02:4c
EBERT, Emil, 55, frame manuf., NYC-M – 1889/06/20;1h
EBERT, Frieda, 12, Glen Cove, NY – 1900/08/17:3b

EBERT, H., NYC-B – 1912/12/31:6a
EBERT, Henry, 50, homeless, NYC-Q – 1914/12/03:1d
EBERT, Henry's wife, West Hoboken, NJ – 1887/11/29:2e, = 2 Dec:4f, Henry tried 9 May 1888:2e, 12 May:2e, exec. Hoboken 18 Jy:2h, 19:1c
EBERTH, Walter, NYC-B – 1891/03/23:4a
EBERWEIN, Ch., NYC-M – 1889/07/06:4a
EBERWEIN, William's wife, 65, Philadelphia, PA - 1914/01/21:1e
EBETSCH, Fredericka, NYC-B – 1907/07/27:6a
EBITSCH, Casper, un. carp., NYC-M - 1916/07/22:6a
EBLE, Christian, 18, NYC-B – 1887/08/02:2d
EBLE, Frank, 15, worker, NYC-M – 1890/05/17:2e
EBLE, John, 49, un. carp., NYC-M – 1900/12/29:4a, 30:5a
EBLING, John, Dr., druggist, Pine Ridge, NJ – 1905/08/22:1h
EBNER, Johann, 63, SPD Meerane/Saxony – 1886/01/25:4f
EBNER, Josef, un. carp., NYC-M – 1889/02/07:4a
EBNER-ESCHENBACH, Marie von Dubsky, Austrian writer & humanitarian, *Moravia, 80th birthday – 1910/09/11:11a-c, + Vienna - 1916/03/15:2e
EBSTEIN, Henry, 45, bookkeeper, NYC-M – 1908/10/22:5f
ECHTLER, Jacob, NYC-B - 1894/12/01:4a
ECK, George, 21, NYC-M – 1900/04/09:2h, 11:2h
ECK, Jacob, NYC-B – 1906/12/01:6a
ECK, William J. NYC-New Brooklyn - 1920/02/20:6a
ECKARDT, Fritz, SPD, un. cigarmaker & MdL Sachsen-Meiningen s. 1895, + Salzungen - 1913/09/14:3b
ECKEL, Carl, NYC-M – 1893/04/22:4a
ECKEL, Peter J., mailman, NYC-B – 1893/01/06:2d, 24 My:2d
ECKELMAN, Herman C., 45, dock employee, War 2, Hoboken, NJ - 1914/12/15:2d
ECKELMANN, Alexander, 62, NYC-M - 1894/02/03:4a
ECKELS, Gustav, 19, NYC-M – 1893/05/05:4a
ECKERLEIN, Mary, 39, NYC-M - 1895/01/22:4a, 25:4a
ECKERLIN, Louis, NYC-Q - 1914/06/24:6a
ECKERN, August von, Jersey City Heights, NJ – 1909/04/10:6a
ECKERT % Zeltlager
ECKERT, Agnes, b. Gieselbach, 45, SP, NYC-M – 1909/04/16:6a, 17:2b,6a, fam. 18:7b
ECKERT, Benedict, 50, carp., NYC-Bx – 1906/04/24:4c
ECKERT, Ernest, 71, NYC-B - 1917/10/26:6a
ECKERT, Ernst, un. carp., NYC-M – 1908/02/04:6a
ECKERT, Frederick, NYC-B – 1909/08/26:6a
ECKERT, George, 50, butcher, Paterson, NJ – 1904/06/03:3e

ECKERT, Gottlieb, un. archit. iron worker, NYC-M – 1901/02/18:4a
ECKERT, Jacob, 35, NYC-Bx – 1910/10/17:6a
ECKERT, Johann, 40, NYC-M - 1894/01/28:5d
ECKERT, Joseph, un. carp., NYC-M – 1890/08/26:4a
ECKERT, Julia, child, NYC-Bx - 1918/08/06:2g
ECKERT, Julius, 40, florist, NYC-M – 1880/11/10:1f
ECKERT, Louis, 57, band leader, Jersey City Heights, NJ – 1905/05/18:3b
ECKERT, Louisa, 83, NYC-B – 1907/02/28:3b
ECKERT, Maria, b. Kaiser, 78, NYC-B - 1918/07/25:6a
ECKERT, Max, NYC-Q – 1911/05/13:6a
ECKERT, Rosa, 50, NYC-B - 1913/11/06:6a
ECKERT, Sophie, b. Schmid, NYC – 1912/01/04:6a
ECKHARDT, Emil, 35, NYC, + Buffalo, NY – 1903/01/29:1g
ECKHARDT, Ernst, 37, salesman, NYC-B – 1907/05/09:1a
ECKHARDT, Francis's wife, 70, Elizabethport, NJ – 1898/08/25:4c
ECKHARDT, Georg, 42, un. baker, NYC-M - 1920/05/03:6a
ECKHARDT, Henry, Hoboken, NJ – 1880/11/22:1g
ECKHARDT, William, 33, tramway conductor, NYC-M – 1900/05/24:2h
ECKS, Henry, SP, cigar dealer, NYC-Bx, veteran 1872 Berlin cigarmkr strike,70th birthday 1906/06/11:3f, 75th birthday 1911/05/23:6c 80th birthday, 1916/05/18:2e, + 1917/01/03:2e, 4:6a, =6:5c
ECKS, Mathilde, Killington, VT – 1912/09/12:6a
ECKSTEIN, Blanche, 2, NYC-M – 1880/04/05:1g
ECKSTEIN, E.'s wife, NYC-B – 1912/05/19:7a
ECKSTEIN, Eddie, 4?, NYC-M – 1893/05/07:5a
ECKSTEIN, Erhard, un. carp., NYC-M – 1906/10/29:6a, fam. 4 Nov:7b
ECKSTEIN, Frank, 70, barber, NYC-B – 1903/10/05:2h, 6:3c
ECKSTEIN, Georg, 52, un. carp., NYC-M – 1904/08/17:4a
ECKSTEIN, Georg, child, NYC-M – 1888/06/07:3b, 8:3c
ECKSTEIN, Gustav, Dr., 41, Austrian marxist theoretician, + Zuerich/Switz. - 1916/08/18:4c-d
ECKSTEIN, Henry F., 23, NYC-M – 1902/02/17:4a
ECKSTEIN, Joseph, lumber dealer, Englewood, NJ – 1907/11/19:1d, 25:3b
ECKSTEIN, Rudolf, un. brewer, NYC-M – 1906/11/19:6a
EDDY, Mary, b. Baker, Christian Scientist, will discussed 1910/12/15:1e
EDELE, Louis, brass worker, NYC-M – 1905/09/12:4a
EDELHAEUSER, Rosa, 56, NYC-Bx - 1919/02/26:6a
EDELHOFF, Frederick, 53, NYC-B – 1909/04/14:2b
EDELING, Julius, SPD Halle/Thuer., - 1914/05/17:3c
EDELMANN, Isaac, 3, NYC-M - 1895/06/19:1d
EDELMANN, John G., 48, architect & radical socialist, NYC-M – 1900/07/14:2h

EDELMANN, Leo, 55, NYC-B - 1915/08/12:6a, 13:6a
EDELMANN, Max, 17, NYC-M - 1905/02/03:3e
EDELMANN, Morris, butcher, NYC-B? - 1914/01/09:3b
EDER, Erhart, 51, NYC-M or Bx - 1891/04/14:4d
EDERER, Anna Maria, NYC-Q - 1916/01/22:6a, mem. 1917/01/20:6a, 1918/01/20:7a, 1919/01/20:6a, 1920/01/21:6a
EDERLE, Pauline, SP, Jersey City Heights, NJ - 1912/01/30:6a, 31:6a
EDINGER, Henry, 53, brewer, NYC-B - 1914/02/18:6a
EDITZKY, Anton, 48, butcher, NYC-M - 1894/08/29:4d
EDLICH, Ernst, 75, Philadelphia, PA - 1919/09/09:2d
EDSON, Henry Townsend, NYC-M - 1903/09/03:1f-g
EDWARDS, B. F., SP?, NYC-B - 1896/06/28:1d
EDWARDS, Bob, 19, Negro, lynched Culling, GA - 1912/09/11:2f
EDWARDS, Enoch, 60, pres. British Miners' Union - 1912/07/16:4e
EDWARDS, Josephine, b. Ochs, NYC-B - 1909/11/21:1e, 22:3a, 23:3b
EDWARDS, Kate, to be exec. 1905/02/10:1c, 14:1h,15;1b, postp. 16:4c
EDZARDS, Edward, un. carp., NYC-B - 1919/01/28:6a
EFFINGER, Ignaz, un. machinist, NYC-Bx - 1912/06/15:6a
EFFTINGER, Joh., 45, bricklayer, SPD & alderman in Wandsbeck/Gy - 1909/09/05:3c, 19:3b
EGAN, John, NYC, exec. Ossining, NY - 1920/08/27:2f
EGENBERGER, Joseph A., 70, NYC-M - 1891/06/23:4a
EGENTER, Josef, Swiss Soc., adm. Berner Tagwacht - 1919/09/10:4d
EGER, Elsie, 4, Elizabeth, NJ - 1915/11/07:1d
EGER, Johann Wilhelm, * 2 Fb 1820 Bavaria, baker, USA 1861, NYC - 1886/11/22:3b, will 23:2e, 27:1b
EGGEN, Wilhelm, 33, SPD leader in Lippe/Gy, + 28 Oct. in Detmold - 1913/11/16:3c
EGGENSCHWILER, Jakob, Swiss?, NYC-M - 1889/02/11:4a
EGGER, John, NYC-Q - 1920/12/20:6a
EGGER, John, un. carp., NYC-M - 1890/06/28:4a
EGGERS, Albert, cigar maker, NYC-M - 1889/12/14:4a, 15:5a
EGGERS, Minna, Jersey City Heights, NJ - 1906/12/17:6a
EGGERT, Christopher, 69, * Strassburg/Elsass, NYC-M - 1897/07/22:1f
EGGERTE, Fritz, un. painter, NYC-M - 1897/01/15:5c
EGLAU, Max, Dr., killed Feb. 10, NYC - 1896/04/01:1h
EGLE % Schober
EGLOFF, August, un. butcher, NYC-M - 1904/07/07:4a
EGLOFF, Jacob, 66, NYC-B - 1894/05/02:4e
EGNER % Wisch
EGSTEIN, Philip, SP, Kingston, NY - 1918/08/09:2f,6a
EHINGER, Gottlieb, 76, un. carp., SLP, NYC-M - 1896/07/14:4a, =16:4b

EHLENBERGER % Michel
EHLENBERGER, Max, 56, Yonkers, NY - 1913/06/06:6a
EHLER, Christian, 56, NYC-M – 1907/03/21:6a
EHLER, Henry, driver, NYC-B – 1900/11/11:5f
EHLERS % Meyer
EHLERS, Antoinette, 63, NYC-M - 1913/11/18:6a, 19:6a
EHLERS, Bernhard, NYC-M – 1906/09/05:6a
EHLERS, Emma, NYC-B - 1913/12/10:6a
EHLERS, Heinrich, un. carp., NYC-M – 1902/01/19:5a
EHLERS, Julius, 45, un. upholsterer, NYC-M – 1891/04/12:5e, 13:4a, 14:4a, =15:1g, fam. 16:4a
EHLERS, Martin, 28, NYC-B – 1892/06/22:4a
EHMANN, Carl, un. carp., NYC-Bx – 1910/09/07:6a
EHMANN, Jakob, un. carp., NYC-B – 1910/01/08:6a
EHNHUS, Hermann, 42, NYC-M – 1891/09/03:4a
EHNI, Gottlieb, NYC? – 1881/07/13:3c
EHRENBERG, Charles, NYC-B – 1912/12/06:6a
EHRENFELD, Adolf, 36, SP, carpenter, fr Nagyvarad/Bihar, officer of Nepszava - 1915/06/13:3d
EHRET, R., NYC-Bx – 1919/12/11:6a
EHRET, William F., 72, SP, un. carp., ex-treasurer New York Call, NYC-M - 1918/12/15:11f, 16:4c,a, 17:2g,6a,fam. 25:6a. mem. – 1919/12/14:3a
EHRHARDT, Theresa, servant, NYC-M – 1880/01/06:1a-c, 7:1e, =8:1g, 3a, 9:1e-f, 11:8a, inquest 3 Fb:1g
EHRHARDT, Christian, 61, un. cigarmaker, NYC-M - 1917/11/23:6a, 24:6a
EHRHARDT, Elizabeth, 2, NYC-M, +@Genl Slocum – 1904/06/22:1d
EHRHARDT, Franz Joseph, 55, paperhanger & SPD MdR for Ludwigshafen/Gy – 1908/07/29:4d, 6 Ag:4f
EHRHARDT, Frederick, 47, West Hoboken, NJ - 1917/12/13:6a
EHRHARDT, Johanna, 4, NYC-Jamaica - 1914/08/10:2f
EHRHARDT, Minnie, 13, NYC-M, +@ Genl Slocum – 1904/06/17:3b
EHRHARDT, Stephan, 43, NYC-M – 1891/07/23:4a
EHRHART, Maggie L., 14, NYC-Flushing – 1898/10/14:4a
EHRICH, Moses, 59, jeweler, NYC-M – 1886/11/30:4d
EHRICHS % Barthen
EHRLES, Heinrich, 65, NYC-B – 1911/08/05:6a
EHRLICH, Etta, 42, NYC-B - 1917/09/06:6b
EHRLICH, Paul, Dr., German scientist, 1908 Nobel Prize in Chemistry - 1915/08/22:11e
EHRMANN, Frederick, hotel clerk, NYC-M – 1903/08/23:5a
EHRMANN, Minnie, 4, NYC-B – 1896/06/01:4c

EHRMANN, Rudolph, un. bricklayer, NYC-M – 1900/06/13:3g
EHSEN, August's wife, NYC-M – 1890/05/07:4a
EHSER Jr., August, Guttenberg, NJ - 1914/11/12:6a
EIBEL, Charles, 72, NYC-M – 1890/02/23:5b
EIBEN, Annie, 22, NYC-M – 1911/08/04:1f
EIBL, Johann, SPD Munich/Gy– 1901/12/17:2c
EICH, Meier, 8, NYC-B – 1903/07/11:1f
EICHE, Charles F., 56, West Hoboken, NJ – 1901/05/14:3b
EICHE, Maggie, 60, nurse, NYC-B – 1897/07/07:1d
EICHELDORFER, Charles, un. typesetter, Newark, NJ – 1887/09/09:3b
EICHELE, Christoph, 60, gold worker, NYC-M – 1900/09/19:1d
EICHELE, Mary, SP, Newark, NJ – 1912/01/19:3d, 6a, fam. 23:6a
EICHENAU, Eduard von, 36, Austrian nobleman, barber here, NYC-M – 1882/03/16:1e-f, =18:1g, notes 19:5e-f, 21:4e, inquest 7 Apr:1d-e,
EICHENAUER, Charles, Union Course, LI – 1910/02/14:6a
EICHENRODT, Henry, US Navy musician, & wife Clara, b. Petzold, 26, Paterson, NJ – 1905/06/27:3f
EICHHORN, Georg, 15, office boy, NYC-M – 1896/10/25:5b
EICHHORN, Minnie, b. Pfeifer, NYC-M – 1900/03/04:5a
EICHHORST, Alfred, 3, NYC-M – 1901/06/28:4a
EICHLE, Philip, 35, NYC-Q – 1897/07/12:1e
EICHLER, Frederick., NYC-M – 1892/07/26:4a
EICHLER, John, brewery owner, b. 20 Oct. 1829 Rottenburg/Wuertt./Gy, USA 1853, NYC-Bx – 1892/08/05:1c
EICHLER, Margaret, 22, NYC-B – 1910/07/23:3a
EICHLER, Rose, 23, & Rebecca, 3, NYC-M – 1904/09/05:1e, 6:2b
EICHMAN, John, 33, tailor, NYC-B - 1895/04/30:4c
EICHMANN, Robert W., 44, carpenter, Jersey City, NJ - 1917/12/08:1b
EICHORN, George, 70, Newark, NJ – 1907/11/25:3b
EICKHOFF, William, 20, NYC-M, + @Genl Slocum – 1904/06/17:3b
EID, Marie, NYC-M - 1896/04/02:4a
EIDEL, Adam, NYC-M - 1920/11/04:6a
EIERMANN, Ferdinand, NYC-B – 1911/05/17:6a
EIFERT, George, un. marble cutter helper, union official, NYC-M – 1898/06/12:1d
EIFFLER, Karl, NYC-M – 1881/07/16:1d, 3b
EIFLER, Karl, NYC-M – 1888/06/10:3b
EIGENBRODT, Mary, NYC-M – 1898/02/04:1b
EIGNER, Maria Susanna, b. Mueller, 45, NYC-M – 1882/09/11:3b
EILER, John, NYC-M – 1888/03/19:3b
EILERS, Frederick, ship's cook, @1900 dock fire, Hoboken, NJ 1900/07/03:1c

EILES, Albert, clerk, NYC-M – 1887/07/14:1g
EIMANN, Henry, 40, worker, fr Baden, NYC-M – 1891/06/10:1f
EIMER, Barbara, NYC-M – 1893/12/27:4a
EIMER, Georg, Karl, Kate, NYC-B, +@ Genl Slocum, fam. 1904/06/17:3b, note 24:4a
EIMER, Kath. Dorothea, b. Pfeifer, 45, NYC-B – 1912/04/19:6a, 21:7b
EINBIGLER, W., NYC-M – 1885/11/16:4c
EINERT, Andreas, 49, NYC-B – 1886/02/17:3d
EINFELD, Gustav, NYC-M – 1888/11/21:3b, fam. 27:3b
EINFELD, Minna, NYC-M – 1888/12/18:3b
EINHART, Matilda E., 29, Dutch Kills, LI – 1886/10/22:3b
EINHORN, Martin, Elizabeth, NJ – 1910/01/25:6a
EISBERG, William, 24, NYC-M – 1900/03/09:1d
EISCHNER, Pauline, b. Alte, 78, NYC-M – 1889/01/25:4a
EISELE, Florenz, NYC-M - 1914/04/22:6a
EISELE, Gottlob, NYC-M – 1905/03/28:4a
EISELE, Karl, 64, Grantwood, NJ - 1915/11/19:6a
EISELE, Kath., b. Enzer?, NYC – 1891/03/24:4a
EISEN, Johann, 74, NYC-B – 1891/03/27:4a
EISEN, Lorenz, 33, * Berlin, sailor, USA 1901, SP, NYC-B – 1908/05/17:7c, =24:7e
EISEN, Nicholas, 50, driver, NYC-B – 1911/12/23:2a
EISEN, Sadie, 29, NYC-M – 1900/09/14:4a
EISENACH, Mrs, Schenectady – 1906/04/19:2h
EISENBACH, Jacob, 62, NYC-B – 1905/03/13:3b
EISENBART, Laura, NYC-M - 1915/12/13:6a
EISENBARTH % Gescheidt
EISENBERG, Henry, NYC-Bx - 1920/11/19:6a
EISENBERGER, H., NYC-M – 1900/08/28:4a
EISENER, Franz, NYC – 1912/07/23:6a, 24:6a
EISENER, Frederick, 72, un. carp., NYC-Bx - 1916/03/05:7a, 7:6a
EISENER, Paulina, NYC-M - 1895/08/18: 5a
EISENGREEN, Adam, NYC-Bx - 1919/07/05:6a
EISENHARDT, Christian, + 10 Nov., inquest, NYC-M – 1885/11/26:2d-e
EISENHART, Henry, Newark, NJ – 1902/03/20:4a
EISENHAUER, Elsie, b. Forker, NYC-B - 1920/12/25:6a
EISENKOLB, Isidor, un. chinamaker & labor org. in Karlsbad/Bohemia, War 1 - 1914/10/04:3e
EISENMANN, Adolf, tobacco store, NYC-M – 1880/06/11:1f-g, =12:4b, inquest 19:4a
EISENRING, Barbara, NYC-M – 1880/06/29:3b
EISENRING, Mathias, un. typesetter, NYC-Bx – 1891/12/10:4a

EISENSCHMIDT, Charles, 78, Morristown, NJ – 1901/03/29:4b
EISENSTADT, Lubie, Soc. fr Russia, USA 1903, NYC-M – 1903/07/13:1e
EISENSTEIN, Dora, 21, NYC-M – 1896/08/31:1e, 1 Sept:1g
EISERHOLT, Mary, 52, NYC-B – 1903/07/11:1f
EISKANT, Josef, un. carp., NYC-M – 1901/05/11:4a
EISLEBEN, Leopoldine, b. Braun, NYC-M – 1888/01/25:3a
EISLEIN, Bernhard, un. cabinetmaker, NYC-B - 1894/05/06:5e
EISLER, Jacob, Paterson, NJ – 1887/08/22:2g
EISNER, Antonia, b. Burgdorf, NYC-M - 1894/12/27:4a
EISNER, August, 57, musician, former conductor of Montauk Theater orchestra, NYC-B - 1916/01/12:6c
EISNER, Kurt, ex-editor Berlin Vorwaerts, + Munich, 1919/02/22:1a, =28:2b, 14 Mr:1f, 4f-g,6a-c, 13 Apr:6b. Note 1920/01/14:4f
EISNER, Louis, 55, SP, ex-NYC, + Everett, MA – 1908/08/23:1a
EISSLER, Emma, NYC-M – 1905/07/21:4a
EISSLER, Heinrich, un. brewer, NYC-M - 1917/11/22:6a
EITL, John, NYC-B – 1910/06/29:6a
EITNER, Edward, un. carp., NYC-Bx - 1914/03/03:6a
EITNER, Emma, NYC-M – 1910/05/24:6a
EITNER, Louise, Valley Cottage, NY – 1912/07/23:6a, 24:6a, =25:2b
ELAUSS, Paul, Hoboken, NJ – 1899/10/03:4a
ELBERT, Florian, 36, NYC-M – 1887/12/29:2h
ELBERT, Henry Otto, infant, NYC-M – 1880/07/13:3b
ELBERT, Henry, un. carp., NYC-M – 1904/10/06:4a
ELBING, Friedrich, Baltimore, MD, + Plainfield, NJ – 1882/05/07:5e, 6:2g
ELBTHAL, M., Westchester, NY - 1920/10/02:6a
ELDER, Ch., NYC-M – 1900/06/02:4a
ELDER, Claude, Negro, lynched Watkinsville, GA – 1905/06/30:1h
ELDER, James, Negro, lynched Springfield, TN, with 4 others – 1881/02/20:5c
ELFLEIN, Philip, SP, NYC-SI - 1917/06/12:6a, fam. 16:6a
ELIAS, Henry, 37, brewer, NYC-M - 1894/12/11:3f, 13:3e
ELICK, Lizzie, NYC-M, +@ Genl Slocum – 1904/06/17:3b
ELION, Louisa, & children Louise, 8, Rosa, 7, NYC-M – 1904/01/21:1c
ELK, Francis, 2, NYC-M, +@Genl Slocum – 1904/06/22:1d
ELK, Matilda, 39, NYC-M, +@Genl Slocum – 1904/06/22:1d
ELKINS, Samuel, 44, ex-cigar maker & janitor, NYC-M – 1885/11/25:1g
ELL, Carl, un. sheet metal worker, NYC-M – 1899/04/28:4a
ELLENBERG % Blassmann
ELLENBERG, Mrs, Hoboken?, NJ, fam. 1892/05/06:4a
ELLENBROCK, Henry, 29, NYC-M – 1900/09/15:4b, 16:5a, fam. 20:4a
ELLENBUSCH, Hermann, ~60, tailor, NYC-M – 1896/09/08:1d

ELLENSOHN, Andreas, un. carp., NYC-M – 1886/10/16:3b
ELLER, Elsie, NYC-M, + @ Genl Slocum – 1904/06/16:1c
ELLER, Joseph's wife, NYC-M, +@ Genl Slocum – 1904/06/16:1c
ELLERHORST, Catherine, b. Heins, 26, NYC-B – 1892/06/09:4a
ELLERS, John, 68, un. painter, NYC-Bx - 1918/04/03:2g
ELLERS, Lillie, 23, West Hoboken, NJ - 1918/12/20:6a
ELLERT, Albert, NYC-M – 1908/08/01:1b
ELLGASS, C. L. H., NYC-M – 1891/01/02:4e
ELLING, Heinrich, 3, NYC-M – 1888/10/04:3a
ELLING, Heinrich, 42, NYC-M – 1880/08/09:3a
ELLINGER, Georg, Dr., NYC-M, has kin in Philadelphia - 1878/03/01:1g
ELLINGHAUS, Emma, 18, NYC-M – 1896/10/11:5a, fam. 14:4a
ELLIOTT, Walter, Negro, lynched Louisburg, NC – 1919/08/22:3d
ELLIS, Anderson, Negro, lynched Rockwell, TX – 1909/03/09:2f
ELLIS, Clara, NYC-M – 1891/07/18:4a, 17:4a
ELLISON, Anna, b. Tiefenthaler, 30, ex-Chicago, Philadelphia, PA - 1920/05/01:2a
ELLMAN, Richard, 19, NYC-Q - 1913/12/02:3a
ELLMANN, Karl, ATB activist, Munich/Bavaria, War 1 - 1914/11/01:3b
ELLMER, Therese, b. Goeggel, 42, NYC-M – 1910/01/24:6a
ELLNER, comrade, 72, ex-secy of Ferdinand Lassalle, +Paris/France – 1910/06/27:4e
ELLOR, Matilda, 46, & Elise, NYC-M, +@ Genl Slocum – 1904/06/18:3b
ELLWEIN, John, NYC-M – 1892/07/31:5c
ELM, Adolf von, SPD, cigar worker & labor org., ex-MdR - 1916/10/14:4d
ELMENDORF, Oscar, 45, machinist, 45, NYC-Q – 1913/01/19:1d
ELROSE, Julia, NYC-M – 1897/07/24:1e
ELS, Hugo, 60, bookkeeper, fr Denmark, NYC-M – 1909/01/13:3b
ELSAESSER, Elizabeth, b. Baus, 81, NYC-M – 1892/08/05:4a
ELSAESSER, Katrin, b. Hasner, 62, NYC-B - 1918/04/09:6a
ELSEMILLER, R., NYC-M - 1895/10/10: 4a
ELSER, Ida, child, NYC-M - 1895/12/08: 5c
ELSEY, John, 71, fishmonger, Jersey City, NJ – 1912/07/06:2d
ELSING, Henry, +21 Jan. Hoboken, NJ – 1901/02/28:3b
ELSINGER, Mary, 60, NYC - 1913/12/08:6a
ELSNER, NYC-B – 1906/04/18:4a
ELSTER, Kristian, Norwegian poet, + 1881, by Georg Brandes 1882/09/17:2c-d, 10:3c-d
ELSTERMANN, Emma, 51, fr Berlin/Gy, USA 1868, NYC-M - 1895/10/04: 1f
ELSTERMANN, Ferdinand, 42, un. typesetter?, NYC-M – 1901/01/08:4a

ELTERICH, Otto, 42, Swiss, engineer, NYC, + London/Engl. – 1907/06/08:1d
ELTERLEIN, Julia von, b. Becker, NYC-M - 1895/03/10:5a
ELTZ +, burglar Constantin Steiger alias Fritz Meyer arrested 1897/10/28:1g, 29:1h, 31:1e, 4 Nov:1h, 5:1h, 9:1h, 11:1g, 12:1c, 13:1c, 17:1c, 18:1f, 19:1f-g, 20:1c-d, to die 24:1f; postp 1/1/98:1e,
ELVERS, Wilhelm, Elizabeth, NJ – 1904/04/16:4a
ELZE, Carl, 66, NYC-B – 1904/05/26:4a
ELZE, Catherine M., 72, NYC-B – 1913/02/15:6a, 16:7c
ELZENBERGER, Philip, 16, NYC-SI - 1914/12/09:2b
ELZER, Franz, NYC-M – 1907/09/14:6a
EMDE, Henry Von Der, 38, druggist, NYC-M – 1896/08/14:1f
EMDE, Therese, b. Grimm, NYC-M - 1894/10/27:4a
EMELD % Burger
EMERICH, Johann, un. cigar maker, NYC-B – 1887/02/23:3c
EMERSON, Ralph Waldo, 79, US poet, 1882/04/28:1f, =1 May:1b
EMIG, Babette, 43, NYC-B - 1919/03/08:6a
EMIN PASCHA – 1893/09/05:4b, 6:1a, 8 Dec:1h (+ confirmed)
EMMEL, Leopold, German Soc., SPD MdR for Elsass – 1919/12/18:4e
EMMERICH, A., NYC-M - 1917/08/27:6a
EMMERICH, Charles, NYC-B – 1907/10/23:6a
EMMERICH, John, 23, plumber, fr Hungary, NYC-M – 1889/03/02:1c,d
EMMERICH, William, 29, carriage maker, NYC-M – 1903/08/03:1b
EMMET, Georgie, 6?, NYC-M – 1891/04/14:4a
EMMINGER, Charles R., plumber, NYC? - 1913/12/12:2f
EMMOLD, Frederick, 17, Hoboken, NJ - 1913/10/25:3b
EMRICH, Barbara, 36, NYC-M – 1892/09/18:5e
EMRICH, Harry, 13, NYC-M – 1903/06/13:4a
EMRICH, Henry, 59, SDP?, NYC-M – 1905/02/07:1e, 8:4a, 9:4a, =10:3b, fam. 10:4a
ENBERLIN, Frederick, 23, NYC-B - 1913/08/07:3d
ENDE, Heinrich VON, SLP, son Hessian defense minister, USA 1871, journalist., + Chicago - 1879/09/30:2a,1 Oc:2e,10:2e
ENDE, Mrs (Ch.) VON, West Newark, NJ – 1907/02/17:7b
ENDERLE, Henry, 40, engineer, White Plains, NY – 1901/02/15·1d
ENDERLIN, Henry, NYC-M - 1920/02/03:8a
ENDERS, Charles, 33, NYC-B - 1919/08/08:6a
ENDRES, Charles, 33, NYC-B – 1919/08/09:6a
ENDRES, Fried. M., NYC-B – 1891/02/20:4a
ENDRES, L., NYC-B – 1905/08/31:4a
ENDRESS % Roehl
ENGAISKI, Elsie, 18, NYC-M – 1912/06/28:1b

ENGBERT, Andrew, 60, NYC-B – 1899/12/12:3b
ENGEL, (Mrs), NYC-B, on ship "Mystery" – 1887/07/12:1c, 13:2g, 14:2d
ENGEL, Adam, NYC-Q – 1903/12/18:4a
ENGEL, Adolph, waiter, NYC-M – 1913/04/27:1f
ENGEL, Anna, 21, telephonist, NYC-M – 1919/10/26:3b
ENGEL, Anna, Jersey City Heights, NJ – 1901/08/12:4a
ENGEL, Anton, un. carp., NYC-M – 1909/01/28:6a
ENGEL, August, un. carp., NYC-Bx – 1907/01/12:6a
ENGEL, Carl Jacob, un. typesetter, NYC-B – 1896/10/07:4a
ENGEL, Charles, NYC-M - 1919/03/04:6a
ENGEL, Charles, 19, clerk, NYC-M – 1897/09/02:1b
ENGEL, Charles, deli-owner, Hoboken, NJ – 1891/05/26:4c, 27:2f
ENGEL, commissar, 70, persecutor of SPD – 1910/08/05:4e-g
ENGEL, Edward, 25, NYC-Q – 1898/06/12:5c
ENGEL, Frank, un. painter, NYC-Bx - 1915/11/20:6a
ENGEL, Franz, un. baker, NYC-M – 1907/08/31:6a
ENGEL, Frederick. W., SP?, Silver Wedding, NYC-M – 1919/10/06:5f-g
ENGEL, G., 35, bookkeeper & ward polit., NYC-B – 1902/06/08:1f
ENGEL, George @1886 Haymarket
ENGEL, George E., 72, wholesaler, NYC-B – 1903/10/06:3b
ENGEL, Harry, 19, NYC-B - 1913/08/05:3a
ENGEL, Henry, Greenville, NJ - 1916/11/22:6a
ENGEL, Hermann, fr Schleswig-Holstein, NYC-M – 1885/12/09:3b
ENGEL, Jacob, 48, NYC-M – 1909/07/15:6a
ENGEL, Jakob, butcher, NYC-M – 1885/08/17:4a
ENGEL, John, 50, innkeep, Jersey City, NJ – 1901/05/20:3d
ENGEL, John, 72, postmaster, Civil War vet (Duryea Zouaves) Hackensack, NJ - 1917/01/09:6b
ENGEL, John, NYC-Q - 1916/04/13:6a
ENGEL, Joseph, 24, NYC-M - 1895/06/18: 4a
ENGEL, Joseph, Union Hill, NJ - 1913/10/28:6a
ENGEL, Josephine, 15, cigarmaker, NYC-M – 1899/08/24:1f-g
ENGEL, Katherina Rosie, 10, NYC-M – 1893/02/23:4a
ENGEL, Kunigunde, b. Kedl, NYC-M – 1907/01/01:6a
ENGEL, Maggie, NYC-M – 1887/05/24:3c
ENGEL, Marie, NYC-M – 1892/03/14:1e
ENGEL, Martha, NYC-M - 1894/09/02:4a
ENGEL, Martin, chicken dealer, NYC-M – 1891/06/21:1h, 22:1e, 23:4c
ENGEL, Morris, 53, furrier, NYC - 1913/05/23:2d
ENGEL, Peter, NYC-M – 1906/06/18:6a
ENGEL, Sophie, 73, NYC-M - 1919/01/20:6a, 21:6a
ENGELBACH % Ahrens

ENGELBERG, Catherine, 62, NYC-M – 1893/12/29:3c, 31:5c
ENGELBRECHSEN, Caroline, NYC-M - 1917/05/28:6a
ENGELBRECHT % Dingler
ENGELBRECHT, Charles, 43, engineer, NYC-B – 1907/12/31:3a
ENGELBRECHT, Charles, town marshall, Secaucus, NJ – 1902/04/29:1g
ENGELBRECHT, Ernst, 61, SP, NYC-SI – 1908/07/22:6a, fam. 28:6a
ENGELBRECHT, Lina, b. Hotz, NYC-SI – 1907/09/07:6a
ENGELE, Magdalena, servant, fr Gy,Rahway, NJ - 1895/08/06:4a
ENGELHARDT, Alvin, un. cigar maker, NYC-M – 1888/12/29:1g
ENGELHARDT, August, chair manuf. fr Weinsheim/Pfalz/Gy, fled Gy after trying to kill army sergeant who murdered his drafted son, + NYC-M – 1904/10/21:3c
ENGELHARDT, Gustav Bruno, 67, NYC-M – 1919/09/24:6a
ENGELHARDT, Josef, beer driver, NYC-Bx, fam. – 1903/07/04:4a,
ENGELHARDT, Margarethe, 32, NYC-B – 1913/01/02:6c
ENGELHARDT, Philipp, 62, *Baden, USA 1849, NYC-B – 1881/07/19:3b
ENGELHARDT, Wilhelm, 41, Carlstadt, NJ – 1902/07/14:4a
ENGELHART, Amelia, 72, NYC-B - 1915/04/11:2f
ENGELHORN, Friedrich, fdr BASF in Gy – 1902/05/04:2g-h
ENGELKE, D., NYC-Q – 1913/01/ 21:6a
ENGELKERR, Frieda, b. Ronge, Columbia, PA, + NYC-M - 1916/12/01:1f
ENGELMANN, Edna, 5, NYC-M, +@ Genl Slocum – 1904/06/26:1c
ENGELMANN, John, 59, Yonkers, NY - 1919/04/06:12a
ENGELMANN, Lena, 39,NYC-M, +@Genl Slocum – 1904/06/17:3b, 18:3b
ENGELMANN, William A., owner of Brighton Beach track, NYC-B – 1885/02/24:3a
ENGELMANN, William, 6, NYC-M, + @ Genl Slocum – 1904/06/21:1f
ENGELS, Frederick W., artist, NYC-B – 1890/09/24:2f
ENGELS, Friedrich, German socialist, 70th birthday – 1890/11/29:2a-b; + London - 1895/08/07:1a-d, NYC grieves 11: 4c-f,13: 1d,16: 1d; on 25th anniv. + 5 Aug. 1920:1d-e, 4a-d. 10th anniv. Of + – 1905/08/20:4d-e
ENGELS, Johann, SLP, NYC-M – 1899/01/28:4a, 29:5h, =30:3e, fam. 31:4a
ENGELS, Johanna, b. Koch, SLP?, NYC-M – 1892/06/12:4a
ENGELS, Johannes, 28, NYC-M – 1892/08/25:4a
ENGELS, Paul, 76, NYC-B – 1908/09/26:3a
ENGELS, Philippine, b. Meyer, 46, NYC-M – 1886/06/15:3a
ENGELS, Rosalia, NYC-M – 1880/11/08:3a
ENGELSKIRCHEN, Johann, NYC-Bx – 1912/01/30:6a
ENGER, Charles, Hoboken, NJ - 1915/06/02:6b
ENGESSER, Augusta, b. Bauer, 56, Jersey City Heights, NJ – 1911/02/28:6a

ENGESSER, Eva, b. Molitor, NYC-M – 1887/04/07:3e
ENGESSER, Heinrich, 10, Jersey City Heights, NJ – 1893/11/02:4c
ENGESSER, Josef & wife, SP, 25th Wedding anniv., Jersey City Heights, NJ – 1911/04/12:5e
ENGHOLM, Christian, baker, NYC-B – 1895/02/01:4a
ENGLART, Charles, NYC-M – 1918/12/11:6a
ENGLER, Hermann, 43, NYC-M – 1904/02/27:4a
ENGLER, Theresa, NYC-M – 1891/03/17:4a
ENGLER, William A. F., 26, SP, NYC-Bx – 1906/01/18:1h
ENGLER, William, 37, Jersey City, NJ – 1901/07/21:5b
ENGLERT, Franz J., NYC-M – 1890/04/01:4a
ENGLERT, William, Newark, NJ - 1916/02/25:6a
ENGLEY, Eugene, CO State Attney-Genl, laudat obit – 1910/05/03:4c-d
ENGSTROM, Otto, ship captain fr Finland, NYC-M – 1911/12/25:2b
ENKMANN, August, 26, shoemaker, NYC – 1886/06/02:1g
ENNIS, William H., ex-NYPD, NYC-B, exec. Ossining, NY – 1903/12/15:2h
ENS, Charles, 22, Newark, NJ – 1883/01/08:4d
ENSMENGER, George, 5, NYC-B – 1911/10/12:2e
ENSMINGER, Christian, un. baker, SLP, * Muehlhausen/Elsass, NYC-M – 1892/06/18:4a,e, 19:5d, =20:1e, rev. benefit for his family 19 Sept:2d
ENTEMANN, John, NYC-Bx – 1909/08/20:6a
ENTERLEIN, Paul, 40, NYC-B – 1910/09/10:6a
ENTRESS, Kajetan, NYC-M – 1909/01/01:6a
ENTRICH, Andrew, NYC-Bx - 1918/04/25:6a
ENZ, Jacob, 49, NYC-M – 1892/06/19:5c
ENZ, Magdalene, b. Pabst, 40, NYC-B – 1903/01/16:4a, 17:4a, fam. 20:4a
ENZEN % Brommer; ENZER % Eisele
ENZLE, W., NYC-M – 1889/02/13:4a
EPPELL, Christian, Newark, NJ - 1913/11/29:2a
EPPENETTER % Homann
EPPERT, Georg, pres. Local UMW, dying, Mascutah, IL – 1908/12/03:6a
EPPIG, Joseph, 63, brewery owner, fr Bavaria, NYC-B – 1907/09/30:3a
EPPIG, Theo. C., 40, brewery owner & brother-in-law of archbishop Mundelein, NYC-B - 1917/06/29:3f
EPPINGER, Kate, 53, NYC-B – 1912/03/12:2c
EPPLE, Adam's wife, NYC – 1888/04/14:3a
EPPLE, Eugen, 42, un. carp., NYC-M – 1890/07/19:4a, 20:5a
EPPLE, George, NYC-M – 1891/07/15:4a
EPPLE, J. E., un. carp., NYC-M – 1885/05/30:3c
EPPLER, Jacob Pius, NYC-M – 1900/02/10:4a
EPPLER, Martin, 49, NYC-M – 1908/09/22:6a

EPPSTEIN, Michael, 37, NYC-M – 1892/06/19:5c
EPSTEIN, Jacques, 17, NYC-M – 1886/11/06:4d
EPSTEIN, Max, 22, NYC-M – 1911/03/10:3d
EPSTEIN, Morris, fr Russia 1896, NYC-M – 1896/09/11:3e
EPSTEIN, Phillip, 70, SP, * Frankfurt/Main, USA 1865, journalist for G-A media in NYC, San Francisco, Cincinatti, NYC-M - 1915/04/23:6a,c
ERASMUS, Julius, 55, silkweaver & G-A poet, + Philadelphia – 1882/09/22:4d
ERATH, Elisabeth, 23, dying, NYC-M - 1920/07/10:2e
ERB, August, un. carp., NYC-M – 1910/09/10:6a, 11:7c
ERB, Eduard, 56, weaver, Swiss?, NYC-M - 1895/10/27: 5a
ERB, Henry, 54, NYC-M - 1917/04/07:6a
ERB, J., Swiss, NYC-? - 1878/06/24:4a
ERB, Lizzie, b. Weinheimer, NYC-M - 1895/10/02: 1c
ERBERT, Franz, NYC-B – 1898/06/05:5a
ERBS, Adelina, NYC-M – 1893/07/05:4a
ERBS, Sophie, 5, NYC-M – 1891/03/16:4a
ERDLING, Christine, 39, NYC-M – 1899/05/19:1c, 23:4a
ERDMANN % Wehmann
ERDMANN, Alma, 11, NYC-M, +@ Genl Slocum – 1904/06/21:1f
ERDMANN, August, 54, stone cutter, NYC-M – 1885/09/21:3a
ERDMANN, Catherine, 65, Paterson, NJ - 1913/08/06:3e
ERDMANN, Catherine, 69, NYC-B – 1891/04/07:4a
ERDMANN, Charles, lineman, NYC-M – 1889/11/08:1h
ERDMANN, John, NYC-B – 1891/04/07:4a
ERFFTA-WERBURG, Hermann, 67, pres. Prussian Landtag, negat. Obit – 1912/06/11:1a
ERHARD, Pauline, 36, NYC-M, +@Genl Slocum – 1904/06/23:1b
ERHARDT, George, 71, carp., NYC-M – 1901/09/13:4c
ERHARDT, George., NYC-B - 1914/01/28:6a
ERHARDT, Wilhelm, stoker on SS "Kronprinz Wilhelm," + Hoboken, NJ – 1908/06/11:2c
ERICHSEN, Asmus Carl, 4 months, NYC-B – 1894/07/24:4a
ERICKSEN, Augusta, servant, fr Sweden, NYC-M – 1893/03/02:4d, 3:1d
ERICKSON, Magnus, NYC-Q – 1893/08/19:4a
ERICKSON, Mary, 26, servant, fr Finland 1890, NYC-M – 1896/09/04:1f
ERICKSON, Ovedna, 32, fr Norway, NYC-B – 1891/03/28:2d
ERICKSON, Robert, NYC-M – 1908/01/08:1a, 9:2c
ERICSON, John, US ship builder (a.e. Monitor), * Sweden, NYC-M – 1889/03/09:1c, 14:4e, body sent back to Sweden – 1890/08/24:1f
ERK, Max, 39, NYC-M – 1913/02/23:7b
ERK, Rudolph, 54, NYC-M – 1900/02/28:4a

ERKER, Mathias, NYC-B – 1902/10/18:4a
ERLER, Charles, NYC-M – 1886/11/18:2c
ERLTERS, Frederick, stoker,@1900 dock fire, Hoboken, NJ 1900/07/02:1g
ERM, Carl, Elizabeth, NJ – 1907/06/11:6a
ERMELING % Calm
ERMER, Georg, 11, NYC-B, +@Genl Slocum – 1904/06/19:1c
ERMISCH, August, NYC-M – 1881/10/29:3b
ERNE, Gustav A., Jersey City Heights, NJ - 1920/02/23:6a
ERNEST, Hermann, Rev., 44, NYC-Q – 1904/03/06:1e
ERNST, ??, NYC?, + 1878/09/07, letter on - 1879/02/19:3a
ERNST, Alexander, 73, music teacher, NYC-M – 1911/08/13:7f
ERNST, E., NYC-B – 1905/09/08:4a
ERNST, Frederick, 81, NYC-M? – 1908/08/22:5b
ERNST, Frederick, NYC-M - 1915/10/14:6a
ERNST, Gottlieb, 66, un. carp., Swiss?, NYC-Woodhaven – 1912/01/20:2e
ERNST, Heinz, NYC-M – 1892/08/25:4a
ERNST, Julius, 55, butcher, NYC-B - 1917/05/05:2e
ERNST, Lorenz, 81, co-fdr United Carpenters Union, *17 Aug. 1837
   Ungstein/Rheinpfalz, USA 1866, NYC-B - 1919/08/04:5g, 6a, =12:2f
ERNST, Lorenz, 81, un. carp., NYC-B – 1919/08/04:6a, 5:6a, = 12:2f-g
ERNST, Louise, 85, NYC-M – 1899/11/10:1e
ERNST, Margarethe, 72, innkeep, New Haven, CT – 1887/05/13:1e-f
ERNST, Mary, 17, servant, NYC-B – 1888/05/07:2c
ERNST, Mrs, 68, NYC-B - 1917/11/19:6a
ERNST, Nikolaus, NYC-B – 1909/11/06:6a
ERNST, Philipp, 5, & George, 2, NYC-M – 1887/11/30:2h, 1 Dec:3a
ERNST, William, un. carp., NYC-M – 1901/04/29:4a
ERNSTMANN, Joseph, sausage salesman, NYC-M - 1878/01/29:4d
ERRINGER, Anton, NYC-M – 1909/08/31:6a
ERTEL, Christoph, 75, fr Gy 3 mo. Ago, St Louis, MO – 1883/07/04:1d
ERTELT, Emil, NYC-B – 1913/03/24:6a
ERVER, Richard, 28, NYC-B - 1919/03/09:12a
ESCH, Frederick, NYC-M - 1920/12/30:6a
ESCH, Robert, policeman, NYC-M – 1883/01/30:4a
ESCHBACH, Louisa, NYC-B – 1891/04/06:4a
ESCHEN, Henry, 29, coal & ice dealer, * Weimar/Gy, NYC-M –
   1889/07/08:1g
ESCHER, Margarethe, b. Zoelger, NYC-B – 1910/11/08:6a, fam. 12:6a
ESICK, Elisabeth, NYC-M, +@ Genl Slocum – 1904/06/18:3b
ESKILDEN % Schmidt
ESMANN, Albert, 60, vaudeville actor, NYC-B - 1920/05/25:2a
ESSBERGER, August, machinist, NYC-M – 1906/12/08:6a

ESSER % Buttelmann
ESSER, John, 49, baker, Hackensack, NJ - 1915/10/25:2e,27:2g
ESSER, William, well digger, NYC-B - 1915/04/09:2g
ESSLING, Joachim, SPD Hamburg/Gy – 1899/07/16:13b
ESSWEIN, Georg, 62, NYC-M – 1892/07/15:4a
ESSWEIN, Michael, 55, NYC-M – 1891/03/23:4a
ESTEP, Susco, striking miner, killed Holly Grove, W. Va – 1913/02/16:1e
ESTERS, Peter,farm laborer,New Brunswick, NJ - 1896/04/07:4c
ESTROWSKY, Richard, un. carp., Hoboken, NJ – 1901/04/10:4a
ESWEIN, Peter, 69, tailor, fr Gy, USA 1841, NYC-M - 1895/08/01: 4e
ETHERINGTON, Earl, Anti-Saloon League snoop, lynched Newark, OH – 1910/07/10:1e, 11:4b, 12:3c
ETSCHEL, Friedr. L.,56, un. carp., Jersey City, NJ – 1913/04/26:6a, 27:11a
ETTEN, VAN, Ida M., social reformer & journalist, former SLP, member, + Paris/France - 1894/03/07:1g, 8:1b
ETTINGER, Abraham, NYC-M – 1893/03/27:4a
ETTINGER, Charles, 60, SP, writer, Chicago – 1909/06/10:1f
ETTRICH, Julius, un. architec. Iron worker, NYC-B – 1900/09/24:4a
ETZEL, Friedrich, NYC-M – 1890/03/05:4a
ETZLER, Fritz, un. butcher, NYC-B - 1920/02/11:6a
EUCHER, Herman, tailor, NYC-B – 1897/10/01:4b
EUCKELE, Albert, NYC-M, +@ Genl Slocum – 1904/06/23:4b
EULENBERG, Marie, 36, dressmaker, NYC-M - 1894/03/09:1g
EULENBURG, Theodor, Count von, 50, machinist, CSA colonel, ruined by Civil War, NYC-M – 1881/08/27:1g
EULENKAMP, Caspar K., 35, cooper, NYC-M - 1878/03/02:4a
EULER, Charles, baker, NYC-M – 1900/06/11:1f
EULER, Daniel, NYC-M – 1890/11/14:4a
EULER, Henry, NYC-M – 1909/12/09:6a
EULER, Jacob, NYC? – 1881/05/09:3b
EULER, Valentine, 70, NYC-M – 1891/03/29:5a
EULHARDT, H. A., un. cigar maker, NYC-M – 1889/03/16:4a
EULHARDT, Sophie, 60, NYC-M – 1903/03/11:4a
EUSEL, Julia, NYC-M, + @Genl Slocum – 1904/06/18:3c
EUSNER, John, 17, NYC-M – 1891/06/22:4a
EVANS, Charles, Negro, lynched Columbus, SC – 1903/07/02:1f
EVANS, Ella, NYC-M, + @ Genl Slocum – 1904/06/17:3b
EVANS, H.C., IWW martyr, + Sacramento, CA, jail – 1919/08/21:2b-c
EVANS, Hardi & Jerry, Negroes, lynched Hemphill, TX – 1908/06/23:1e
EVERETTS, Ernest, IWW, lynched Centralia, WA – 1919/11/13:2a, 14:1f-g, 4a, 15:1d,4a-b, etc. Notes - 1920/03/08:1g (check year)
EVERS, Emma, 24, NYC-M – 1891/05/21:4a

EVERS, Michael, 67, Jersey City, NJ – 1912/12/31:3a
EVERTZ % Davidson
EWALD, Franz, NYC-M – 1907/04/12:6a
EWALD, Gustav's wife, Hoboken, NJ – 1899/09/14:4a
EWALD, Otto, un. cigar maker, NYC-M – 1889/04/07:5c
EWING, Grace Eaton, SP, labor org. for stenographers, NYC-M - 1915/03/11:2f
EXLER, Anton, 45, NYC-B – 1902/08/06:4a
EXNER, Emil, 54, Bellows Falls, VT, - 1895/10/09: 4a
EXNER, Kunigunde, NYC-M – 1892/10/14:4a
EYBER, Albert, un. cigarmaker, NYC? – 1896/05/20:4a
EYLERS, William, un. machinist, NYC-M - 1915/05/22:6a
EYRING, Dominick, un. carpenter, NYC-M - 1895/01/03:4a
EYSEL, Jennie, 9, NYC-M, +@ Genl Slocum – 1904/06/17:3b
EYSTEIN, Annie, 13, worker, NYC-B – 1886/05/17:2e
EZELIUS, August, un. cigarpacker, NYC-M – 1896/05/26:4a
EZELIUS, Salomea, b. Demand, 32, NYC-M – 1891/10/29:4a
FAATZ % Cordes
FAATZ, Maria Anna, b. Schroeder, NYC-M – 1882/09/08:3b
FABER, Elsa, 2, NYC-B – 1908/03/16:6a
FABER, Friedericke, b. Pfannstiehl, 60, NYC-B – 1912/03/05:6a, 6:6a
FABER, Henry, NYC-B – 1904/05/06:4a
FABER, Hermann, 52, goldsmith & SPD org. in Oberstein/Nahe, +Berlin - 1913/07/27:3a
FABRE, Henri, French scientist, + Orange/France - 1915/10/13:1e
FABRI, Vincent, brewer or cooper, NYC-M – 1900/10/21:5g
FACH, Jacob, 44, NYC-M – 1896/05/06:1e
FACKE, Annie, 17, NYC-M – 1888/01/09:3a
FADEN, Johann Nikolaus, 86, SPD Hamburg/Gy – 1912/02/03:4d-e
FAEH, Gustav, Newark, NJ – 1908/01/14:6a
FAERBER % Grohman
FAES, John Rudolf, SP, >80, silk weaver, fr Basel/CH, USA 1868/69, NYC-Bx - 1917/11/17:6a, 18:7a,11f, fam. 24:6a
FAFF, Gussie, ~30, NYC-M – 1904/08/03:3d
FAGEN, Minnie C., b. Wittkopf, NYC-B – 1892/07/02:4a
FAGEN, Minnie, 39, NYC-M – 1893/05/29:4a
FAHL, Johanna Jacobs, wd Preusse, 50, SP, * Lissa/Posen Prov., NYC-B - 1913/10/08:2e,6a, 9:6a, fam. 11:6a
FAHL, Theodor, 47, NYC-M - 1896/03/31:4a
FAHLAND, Frederick, NYC-M – 1908/11/30:6a
FAHLER, Louis, barber, & Lizzie, b. Bender, NYC-B – 1887/10/31:1e, 1 Nov:2c

FAHNER, George, NYC-M - 1917/02/17:6a
FAHRBACH, Ferdinand, un. brewer, NYC-M - 1898/01/25:4a
FAHRENFELD, Marianne L., Merrick, LI - 1909/02/16:6a
FAHRENHOLZ, Georg, 44, cook, NYC-B - 1915/04/09:2b
FAIFFER, Gottlieb, NYC-M - 1898/08/31:1g
FAIR, Charles L., millionaire, & wife Charlotte, b. Decker, a worker, San Francisco, CA, + near Paris/F - 1902/08/17:1h, 4a-b, will 19:1e, 22:2h
FAIR, Samuel, Negro, lynched near Prosperity, SC - 1881/01/22:1b
FAIS, George, 62, NYC-M - 1903/04/17:4a
FAIST, George, NYC-B - 1888/05/09:3a
FAIX, John, 54, un. carp., NYC-B - 1913/01/02:6a, 3:6a
FAJIN, Hermann, 36, NYC-B - 1905/08/31:4a
FALES, Imogene C., wealthy supporter of SDP, reform, & Irish freedom, NYC - 1902/08/10:1g
FALK, Adalbert, Dr., ex-Prussian min. of culture - 1900/07/08:1c, 14:2b-c
FALK, Arnold, NYC-M - 1891/07/17:4a
FALK, Charles, 4, NYC-M - 1880/05/09:5b
FALKE, August, 43, NYC-B - 1907/07/17:3a-b
FALKE, Charles, NYC-M - 1906/11/10:6a
FALKE, Gregor, NYC-M - 1911/03/23:6a
FALKE, Ida, 23, NYC-M - 1891/08/15:4a
FALKE, Joseph, 63, NYC-B - 1890/03/08:4a
FALKE, Minnie, 45, NYC-M - 1904/04/20:4a
FALKEMANN, Fritz, un. cigarmaker, Hoboken, NJ - 1893/09/02:4a
FALKENSTEIN, Louis, von, 20, fr Bavaria, in NYC messenger boy under the name of "Joseph Seifert," - 1888/06/27:1a, 29:2g
FALKNER, John, SDP, NYC-Bx - 1901/03/18:4a, =20:3b
FALLENBERG, Friedrich, 31, treas. Ale & Porter Union #31, NYC - 1902/11/18:2g
FALLENSTEIN, Peter, + Philadelphia, PA - 1882/01/10:3b
FALLER, Frederick, woodmill worker, NYC-B - 1904/06/13:1e
FALLER, John, 68, * Donau-Eschingen?/Gy, NYC-M - 1889/08/23:4a
FALLER, Theodor, 40, engineer, Jersey City, NJ - 1897/12/25:1h,4b
FALLERT, Joseph, pres. Fallert Brewing Co., * NYC-B, NYC-B - 1919/03/25:3e
FALLETTO, exec. Ossining, NY - 1911/11/21:4d
FALMACH, Annie, 6, NYC-B - 1915/12/16:6b
FALMETER, Lizzie, 40, NYC-M, +@ Genl Slocum - 1904/06/17:3b
FALSCH, Gottlieb, un. carp., NYC-Q - 1906/04/19:4a
FANDREY, Robert, NYC-M - 1920/09/23:6a
FANGBEUEL, Margarethe, 60, NYC-M - 1913/02/07:6a, 8:6a
FARBER, Jacob, NYC-M - 1908/02/02:7b

FARKAS de KISVARDA, Karl, fdr Hungarian section 1st Internatl, + Hungary – 1907/03/06:3e
FARLEY, James, scab leader s. 1880s, NYC, dying - 1913/08/06:2a, 14:6e
FARLEY, John Murphy, Cardinal, oppenent of SP & of labor unions - 1918/09/19:4b
FARLEY, Stephen, 58, mechanic, Passaic, NJ, & wife, 48, War 2 - 1915/01/17:11f
FARMER, Mary, exec. Auburn, NY – 1909/03/29:1f, done 30:1f
FARRELL, Rev., at St Joseph's, a good man, NYC-M – 1880/07/21:2d
FARRENKOPF, Elizabeth, 21, NYC-B – 1889/09/03:4a
FARRENKOPF, Josephine, 18, NYC-M – 1889/01/16:1f, 17:4a, 23:1h
FARRISCH, George, trial begun – 1888/04/05:2f
FARRISH, George, + Blackwell's Island, NYC-M (s.a. Froehlich, Roth) – 1887/05/30:2g, 31:4a, 7 June:3b, 8:1e-f, 14:3a, 15:2g, 30:1d-e, 1 Jy:1g, 6:1g, 7:1f-g
FASS, Bertha, 16, NYC-B – 1909/12/07:3a
FASS, Nicolaus, cooper, NYC-M – 1890/06/08:5b
FASS, Sara, 36, & Samuel, Lena & Morris, NYC-M – 1900/10/18:1h
FASSBERGER, Georg, NYC-Bx – 1909/07/17:6a
FASSBIND, Ignatz, NYC-M – 1883/12/02:5d
FASSELL, Johann, SPD, diamond grinder, Wachenbuchen/Frankfurt, War 1 - 1914/11/01:3b
FASSERT, Ernst, NYC-M – 1883/07/04:3b
FASSNACHT, Lena, NYC-M – 1904/03/06:1d
FATH, Augusta, 54, NYC-M – 1892/10/01:4a
FAUDEL, Carl, NYC-M – 1881/05/29:4a
FAUJRBACH, Barbara, 50, NYC-M – 1891/06/24:4a
FAULHABER, Fritz, 56, un. carp., Jersey City Heights, NJ – 1897/03/29:4a
FAULHABER, Gustav A., NYC? - 1914/12/24:6a
FAULHABER, John, NYC-B - 1916/11/16:6a
FAULHABER, Julie, 34, NYC-M – 1898/08/03:4a
FAULHABER, Julius, 51, un. brass worker & innkeep, SP, *5 Jy 1858 Muehlhausen/Elsass, NYC-M – 1910/11/02:2b, 6a, 3:6a, =4:2b, fam. 6:7a
FAULHABER, Lina, infant, NYC-M – 1892/04/05:4b
FAULHABER, Magdalena, 50, b. Westermann, *Palatinate/Gy, USA 1879, NYC-B – 1909/01/26:2b,6a, 27:6a, 28:6a, =30:2d, fam. 30:6a
FAULHABER, Michael, 70, watchman, NYC-Bx - 1916/05/30:2f,4c
FAULHAMMER, Theresa, 47, NYC-Q – 1906/03/30:4a
FAULTISCH % Hummel
FAURE, Felix, French pres. – 1899/02/17:1d-e, 18:2a, =24:4b; 25 Mr:2d-e
FAURE, Jules C., French reformer, deputy 1858-, foreign minister 1871, obit. Crit. Him for turning nationalist – 1880/01/21:2c

FAUSEL, Elizabeth Mayer, 40, NYC-B - 1915/01/19:6a
FAUSER, Charles, 51, innkeep, Jersey City,NJ - 1914/03/12:6e
FAUSER, Nicolaus, un. tailor, SLP?, NYC-M - 1891/01/25:5a
FAUSER, Oscar, 7, NYC-M - 1882/01/26:3c
FAUST % Seeholzer
FAUST, Anna, cook, NYC-M - 1902/04/15:1e
FAUST, Catherine, b. Berndt, 42, NYC-M - 1889/04/01:4a
FAUST, Christian, un. painter, NYC-Q - 1915/10/18:6a, 19:6a
FAUST, Ferdinand, 47, NYC-B - 1897/03/29:4a
FAUST, Ferdinand, NYC-B - 1904/08/23:3c, 24:4a
FAUST, Ferdinand, married Emilie Boetzow, NYC-B - 1880/02/24:2g
FAUST, Friedrich, un. carp., NYC-Q - 1916/04/28:6a
FAUST, George, un. carp., NYC-M - 1912/02/27:6a
FAUST, Magdalene, 53, NYC-M - 1892/11/27:5d, 28:4a
FAUST, Michael, 50, NYC-M - 1885/11/11:3a
FAUST, Peter, un. carp., NYC-B - 1892/04/19:4a
FAUTH, Mary, NYC - 1914/03/11:6a
FAUTH, Michael, 69, NYC-B - 1917/02/24:6a
FAY, Peter, musician fr Ireland, NYC-M - 1898/10/04:3f
FEATHERSTONE, Bernard, 42, NYC-B - 1915/03/16:6c
FECHNER, Margarethe, b. Brandhoff, 54, NYC-M - 1896/02/03:3a
FECHTENHULZ, Yette, @1911 Triangle Shirtwaist Fire, NYC-M -
    1911/03/29:1c
FECHTER, Charles, actor, + Quakertown, PA - 1879/08/06:1c
FECKENSTEDT % Benning
FECKER, Daisy, 11, NYC-M, + @Genl Slocum - 1904/06/17:3b
FECKNER, Martin, 67, NYC-M - 1891/08/15:4a
FEDDEN, Maria, 7, NYC-M - 1891/07/02:4a
FEDERHART, George, 13, NYC-M - 1900/09/22:4a
FEDERKEIL, Johanna M., NYC-B - 1915/10/15:6a
FEDERLEIN, Sebastian, 62, NYC-M - 1886/07/31:4d
FEDERLI, Carolina, NYC-B - 1918/03/11:6a
FEDZICK, Bertha, 18, NYC-Bx - 1899/10/27:2f
FEGGELER, Frederick, NYC-Q - 1909/12/22:6a, 23:6a
FEHL, Amalia, SDP, Hartford, CT - 1905/08/21:4a-b
FEHLIG, Ernst, un. machinist, NYC-B - 1911/09/23:6a
FEHLING, Ernst, un. cigarmaker, Jersey City, NJ - 1915/11/17:6a
FEHLINGER, Lizzie, 7, NYC-M - 1892/12/25:5b
FEHN, Adam, Hoboken, NJ - 1907/11/03:7d
FEHR, Martin, 80, * Bavaria, shoemaker, SLP, NYC-M - 1896/08/13:1h
FEHR, Matthaeus, SPD, woodworker & union org., Frankfurt 1880s,
    Leutkirch/Allgaeu - 1914/10/25:3d

FEHRENBACH, Albert, 26, NYC-M – 1890/07/03:4a
FEHRING, Fritz, 50, carp., No. Bergen, NJ – 1908/06/23:3c
FEHSENFELD, John, un. baker, NYC-M – 1910/02/12:6a
FEICHTIGER % Gruschka
FEICK, Konrad, NYC-M - 1919/05/28:6a
FEICK, Minnie, NYC-M - 1916/02/06:7a
FEIDELSOHN, Mollie, 60, school candy store, NYC-M - 1915/12/23:1g
FEIDER, Nicholas, 38, NYC-M – 1913/02/13:6a
FEIDNER, Johannes, NYC-B – 1910/07/24:7c
FEIDNER, Margarethe, b. Dorr, NYC-B – 1903/07/12:5a, fam. 15:4a
FEIGE, Charles H., alleged German agent, killed El Paso, TX - 1917/12/24:2a
FEIGELSTOCK, Alois, 55, malt sales agent, NYC-M – 1885/12/25:1f
FEIGENBAUM, Estelle, b. Goodman, 26, SP, teacher at Rand School, * Warsaw/PO, NYC-B, + near Scranton, PA - 1916/08/09:1d, 10:2f, =11;2e
FEIGL, Henry, 18, NYC-B – 1892/08/25:4a
FEIH, Johann Konrad, 58, NYC-Bx – 1907/03/22:6a, mem. 20 Mr 1908:6a
FEIHEL, Charles, 51, un. brewer, SP, fr Hohenzollern/Gy, NYC-M – 1911/12/19:2a, 20:6a, 21:6a
FEIL, Peter, 86, NYC-B – 1897/04/05:4b
FEINGOLD, Fannie, 3, NYC-M – 1896/04/26:1c
FEINLISCH, Rebecca, 18, @1911 Triangle Shirtwaist Fire, NYC-M – 1911/03/27:1d
FEINMAN, Sigmund, 47, Jiddisch actor, played in NY, + Lodsch/Russia – 1909/07/06:3c
FEINS, George, Hoboken, NJ – 1896/08/11:1d
FEINTUCH, Mary, 34, grocer, & Sylvia, 11, Jersey City, NJ - 1919/07/23:2d
FEIS, Henry C., NYC-M – 1892/08/04:4a
FEISEL, Margaretha, b. Naefner, NYC-M? – 1892/08/20:4a
FEISTER, Eugen P., 50, sculptor, NYC-Bx – 1912/01/06:1d
FEITHMEYER, John, 45, Jersey City, NJ – 1904/09/10:3f
FEKETE, Mary, 44, NYC-Bx - 1917/08/17:6a
FELBECK, Ida, b. Jonghaus, NYC-M - 1915/07/02:6a
FELDBOHN, Ernst, 19, NYC-M, +@Genl Slocum – 1904/06/23:1b
FELDER, Joseph, 48, tailor, NYC-B – 1898/01/04:4c
FELDHAUSEN, Mary, 52, NYC-M, + @ Genl Slocum – 1904/06/17:3b
FELDMAN, Helene, b. Hillquist, SP, sister of SP leader Morris Hillquist, NYC-Bx - 1914/12/06:11b
FELDMAN, Lillian, Newark, NJ – 1915/04/02:6b
FELDMANN % Schumacher
FELDMANN, Carolina, b. Schorer, NYC-Bx – 1910/11/10:6a

FELDMANN, Herman, 65, NYC-Bx - 1916/10/08:7a, 10:6a
FELDMANN, Juliana, NYC-Bx - 1912/01/26:6a
FELDMANN, Kathy, b. Graf, NYC-M - 1879/04/16:3a
FELDMANN, Rosalie, 69, NYC-M - 1889/02/01:4a
FELDMANN, Rudolph, 62, NYC-Q - 1916/11/28:6a
FELDNER, Henry, 52, druggist, NYC-M - 1911/07/21:1f
FELDSTEIN, Theodor, 57, NYC-M - 1894/01/28:5d
FELGENTREU, John, Hoboken, NJ - 1900/04/27:3b
FELIX, Wenzel, 32, carp., fr Tauss/Bohemia, USA Spring 1881, NYC-M, married Ms. ?? - 1881/12/20:1e
FELL, Charles, NYC-M - 1908/02/13:6a
FELL, Lawrence T., ex-mayor of Orange, NJ - 1903/04/07:2g
FELLENDORF, Bernhard, NYC-B - 1906/10/28:7b
FELLENDORF, Marie, Seacliff, LI - 1902/05/25:5a
FELLER, Michael, machinist, NYC-M - 1902/10/19:5b
FELLERMEIER, Andreas, ATB, Munich/Bavaria, War 1 - 1914/11/01:3b
FELLGER, Chr., NYC-M - 1907/11/30:6a
FELLGER, Elise Rose, Union Hill, NJ - 1918/10/20:12a
FELLOWS, H., murderer Burns rec life - 1900/12/30:5c
FELLOWS, John R., Distr. Attney, crit. obit., NYC-M - 1896/12/08:4b
FELS % Mierzinsky
FELS, Charlie, 46, un. bartender, NYC-M - 1918/10/23:6a
FELS, Joseph, 61, millionaire & single taxer, Philad., PA - 1914/02/23:1c
FELS, Wilhelmine , b.Wittel, 37, NYC-M - 1879/12/29:3a
FELT, Chauncey M., local Republican politico, NYC-B - 1882/11/10:3b
FELTMETH % Krueck
FELZKE, Elisabeth, NYC-M, + @ Genl Slocum - 1904/06/17:3b
FELZKY, Augusta, 38, NYC-M, +@ Genl Slocum - 1904/06/18:3c
FEMON, Margarete, NYC - 1912/12/17:6a
FENDL, Katherine, 9, NYC-M - 1916/10/14:6a, fam. 21:6a, mem. 1917/10/11:6a, 1918/10/12:6a, 1919/10/11:8a, 1920/10/11:6a
FENDULET, Franz, un. carp., NYC-M - 1892/10/30:5d
FENGEL, K., NYC-M - 1907/06/14:6a
FENGLER, Gustav, un. cigarmaker, NYC-M - 1909/12/14:6a, fam. 17:6a
FENNEBERG, Julius von, NYC-M - 1895/02/21:4a
FENNEL, Conrad, 68, NYC-M - 1879/04/15:3a
FENTSCH, Sophie, b. Moeller, NYC-B - 1913/12/31:6a
FENZ, Emil, Elisabeth, NJ - 1912/03/11:6a
FERBER, Louis, 48, NYC-M - 1888/11/01:3a
FERBER, Matthias, 55, carp., NYC-M - 1891/02/19:1h
FERDINAND, Franz L., 39, NYC-Bx - 1891/07/05:5a

FERGER, Henry, 57, un. cigarmkr, USA 1883 fr Gy, NYC-M - 1914/08/21:6a, 28:2c; mem. 1915/08/19:6a
FERGER, Lilly, b. Lott, NYC-M - 1916/03/27:6a
FERGUSON, William, 38, secy Typo. Union #6, NYC-M - 1897/01/15:1f
FERNAU % Grantz
FERNAU, Gustav, 72, masseur, NYC-M - 1898/09/29:3h
FERNBACH, William, Dr., *12 Jne 1844 Nicolai/Silesia, son local Rabbi, USA 1871, NYC-M - 1878/06/14:4c, 17:3b
FERRAL, John, 82, un. weaver & org. Philadelphia 1830s, + San Francisco - 1882/08/18:2a
FERRARI, Alex, NYC-M - 1900/08/14:4a
FERRARO, Antonio, NYC, exec. Ossining, NY - 1900/02/27:3c
FERRE, Marie, + Paris, her =, old Commune vet, 1882/03/15:2f
FERRER Y GUARDIA, Francisco, *1859, Catalan patriot, sent. to death 1909/10/13:1a, 4c, 14:1a-b, 2a-b, 4a, worldwide protests 15:1a-b, 16:1a-b,2c,4d, 17:1a-b,6a-c, 18:1a-b,e-f, G-A Peace Soc protests 18:2b, 3d,4d-e, 19:1a, 4b-c, 20:1a-c, 2b-c, NYC giant meeting 21:2a, 22:1g,2a, 23:1b, his heroic death 24:1c, 26:1a-b, 2b, 4d,5e, 27:2c, his life 01 Nov:4a-b, 4:2a, 5:4e-f, 6:4c-d, poem 7:16, mon. in Bruessel 16:4d, his will 21 Nov:6d-f, 22:4e, 29:3d, 4g, notes on mass-demo in Berlin Oct 17 1910/01/27:4d.[1]
1st anniv. exec. mem. in NYC 1910/08/12:3c, #4 Sept:4, 11 Oct:1f, rev 14:2a, 16:20a, mon. in Paris 17 Nov:4d. Comm. in NYC Ferrer Modern Sunday School, his life, by James Gorden - 1917/11/18:4c-e
FERRER, Paz, daughter of above, + Paris/France - 1913/05/23:1e
FERRI, Joseph, gardener, Innwood, LI, exec Ossining, NY - 1915/07/01:1f
FERRIS, Joseph, 54, druggist, NYC-M - 1916/07/02:7f
FERRIS, Peter, Homestead, PA, steelworker killed by Pinkertons - 1892/07/08:1a
FERRY, John, NYC, killed during strike in Buffalo, NY - 1913/04/10:1d
FERSCHNEIDER, Joseph, 18, NYC-M - 1886/03/30:3a
FERTIG, Hans K., NYC-M - 1911/06/14:6a
FESECKE, Carl, 32, fr Gy, NYC-M - 1895/02/07:3c, 8:1g, 15:3f
FESENMEYER, Joseph, restaurant, fr Koeln, NYC-M - 1888/12/03:1b
FESER % Basel
FESSLER, Michael, un. carp., NYC-M - 1893/05/08:4a
FESSLER, Rosie Marie, 19, NYC-Q - 1909/05/20:6a
FESTMANN, Christina, NYC-B - 1882/09/28:3a
FESTNER, Bernhard, 65, druggist, NYC-B - 1890/10/21:2e
FETH, Georg, NYC-Q - 1915/07/30:6a
FETT, J.H., un. cigarmaker, NYC-M - 1916/09/01:6a
FETT, Karl, 34, un. cigar maker, SLP, * Koblenz/Rhine, NYC-M - 1886/04/05:1g, 3a, 6:3f, =7:4c, 10:5g

FETT, William, 42, un. cigarmaker, NYC-M – 1892/05/07:4a
FETTE, Hermann, Newark, NJ – 1906/05/05:4a
FETTELI, Adelheid, NYC-Q - 1916/02/23:6a
FETTIG, Christian, 32, NYC-M, +@Genl Slocum – 1904/06/25:1d
FETTIG, Peter, 45, NYC-M, +@Genl Slocum – 1904/06/19:1c
FETTREICH, Joseph, lawyer, NYC – 1912/07/25:1f
FETTUS, John, NYC-M – 1888/12/28:4a
FETZ, Charles, NYC-M – 1901/07/03:1d
FETZEL, Ludwig, 19, driver, NYC-B – 1901/06/29:2g
FETZER, Anna, NYC-M – 1893/08/18:4a
FETZER, John, NYC-M – 1903/11/02:4a
FETZER, Maria, NYC-Q - 1914/08/29:6a
FEUCHTER, Eva, NYC-Bx – 1912/06/13:6a
FEUERBACH, Ludwig, German philosopher, 25th anniv. Of death – 1897/09/30:2e-f. 100th anniv. of birth – 1904/08/07:4f-h, 12:2e
FEUERBERG, Sadie, 46, & Annie, 8, Hermann, 3, Minnie, 5, NYC-M – 1904/09/05:1e, 6:2b
FEUERSTEIN, Alwine, b. Larsen, NYC-M – 1908/12/26:6a
FEUERSTEIN, Benjamin, 67, tailor, NYC-M – 1891/03/09:4f
FEUSS, Friedrich, 48, NYC-M - 1914/12/23:6a
FEY, George C., NYC-M – 1896/05/10:5a
FEY, Gussie, 12, NYC-M – 1890/03/18:4a
FEY, Louise, SLP, NYC-M – 1893/07/18:4a, 19:4a, 27:4e
FEYERABEND, William, NYC-B - 1919/09/28:6a
FEYS, Felix, French sailor, on ship La Bretagne – 1891/06/22:1e
FIALA, Otto, 68, RR ticket agent, NYC-Bx - 1918/11/16:6a, 15:6c
FIBER, Annie, 21, NYC – 1899/04/12:3b
FIBICH, Frank, 62, furrier, NYC-M - 1917/01/18:2b
FICARETTO, Castengo, lynched Tampa, FL – 1910/09/22:1b
FICHENSCHER % Breuer
FICHTE, Fredericka, b. Gulh, 77, NYC-B - 1913/09/06:6a
FICHTE, Herman Raynold, 26, NYC-B – 1907/04/03:6a
FICHTE, Hermann, un. printer, NYC-B - 1918/05/16:2g
FICHTEL, Regina's 2 kids, NYC-B – 1907/08/02:1e, 24 Sept:3a, 1 c:1f
FICHTELMANN, Friedrich, 64, NYC-B – 1891/03/30:4a
FICHTELMANN, John A., 50, barber, NYC-M – 1905/11/22:3h
FICHTER, Balthasar, NYC-M – 1898/02/15:4a
FICHTER, Georg, 34, Jersey City Heights, NJ – 1903/02/14:4a
FICHTMANN, H., un. cigarmaker, NYC-M - 1919/03/19:6a
FICHTNER, Carl, 28, baker, NYC-M – 1907/09/20:1e
FICK, John, innkeep, Jersey City, NJ – 1909/05/04:1e

FICK, Wilhelm, NYC-M – 1892/07/27:4a
FICKBOHN, Marie, 40, & child, 14, NYC-M, + @Genl Slocum – 1904/06/17:3b
FICKE,..., German citizen, exec. 28 Jan. in Casablanca as alleged spy - 1915/03/02:4f
FICKEN, Annie, 18, Egg Harbor, NJ, + @Genl Slocum? – 1904/06/19:5a
FICKEN, Carsten, NYC-M – 1892/07/31:5c
FICKER, John C., 33, liquor dealer, NYC-B – 1887/08/02:2d
FICKERT, Auguste, 55, progr. teacher in Vienna/Austria – 1910/07/03:3d-e
FICKERT, Charles, 77, un. cigarmaker & wife Bertha, 74, NYC-M - 1918/04/28:7b
FIDELMANN, Julia, Dr.med., *Russia, NYC-M – 1904/07/08:1h
FIEBACH % Steinbach
FIEBIG, Otto, un. painter, NYC-B - 1916/02/13:7a
FIEBIG, Rudolf, 33, hotel worker, Hasbrouck Heights, NJ – 1897/08/10:1h
FIEBIGER, Georg, un. furrier, NYC-M – 1883/10/25:3c
FIEBLE, Arthur, US Army, NYC-B – 1898/09/05:1f
FIEDELMEIER, Fritz, *18 May 1843 Hagenau/Elsass, USA 1874, searched for – 1912/03/28:2d
FIEDLER, Adolf, 29, NYC-B – 1901/11/16:4a
FIEDLER, Anna, b. Schlink, 70, NYC-B – 1883/12/08:3b
FIEDLER, F., un. painter, NYC-M – 1889/05/19:5d
FIEDLER, Frederick, 66, shoemaker, NYC – 1898/10/12:2f
FIEDLER, Julius, secy local AKK, SP?, Harrison, NJ – 1910/03/24:6a, 25:6a, 26:6a, fam. 29:6a
FIEDLER, Paul, 65, SPD, coppersmith in Loewen/Silesia - 1914/10/18:3a
FIEDLER, William, 61, NYC-B - 1914/10/19:2c
FIEG, Karl, NYC-Bx – 1906/09/08:6a
FIEGINOW, Mrs, & daughter Bertha, 6, NYC-M – 1902/05/31:1e
FIEGL, Lina, 47, NYC-M - 1916/10/09:6a
FIEGMANN, Henry C., 53, accountant, NYC-B – 1910/12/17:3a
FIEHN, Carl, SLP, NYC – 1898/11/14:3c, 4a, 13:5a, fam. 16:4a, =16:4b
FIEHOEFER, E., 60, NYC-M - 1915/11/19:6a, 20:6a
FIELD, David Dudley, 89, legal scholar, concocted "conspiracy" doctrine vs. trade unions, NYC-M - 1894/04/14:3d
FIELDMAN, Rose, SP activist, courage lauded (not +) 1907/10/20:20a-b
FIELDS, Cyrus W., telegraph manuf., + Ardsley Park, NJ – 1892/07/13:2f
FIELDS, Jumbo, 16, Negro, lynched Shelbyville, KY – 1901/10/03:4c
FIELITZ, R. H., sales clerk, NYC-M – 1890/09/03:2e
FIEN, Fritz, 26, NYC-B, sailor, + on SS Mozart – 1885/08/17:4d
FIESCHE, Ernst, 48, NYC-M – 1891/10/27:4a
FIESELER, Bernhard, NYC-B – 1892/07/30:4a

FIESER, Anna, 2, NYC-M – 1891/04/30:4a
FIETZ, August, 49, musician, NYC-B - 1894/02/27:4a
FIKE, B.C., salesman, Syracuse, NY, + NYC - 1915/08/23:2f
FILBERT, Friedrich, * Darmstadt,/Gy, butcher, NYC-M – 1880/04/30:1g
FILBIG, Michael, SP, Hartford, CT - 1918/11/07:2f
FILIP, Franz, SPD, editor at Reussische Tribuene in Gera/Thuringia, War 1 - 1916/04/02:3c
FILLY, Ferdinand, 72, un. painter, SP, USA 1870s fr Duesseldorf, NYC – 1904/01/03:5f
FILS, John, 54, salesman, NYC-M – 1896/09/14:2d
FINCK, John, 44, silkweaver, NYC-B – 1910/04/16:3a
FINCKEN, Christopher, 22, bartender, NYC-M – 1889/10/24:2g
FINDEISEN, Hugo, 45, US Army, NYC-M – 1881/05/23:4c
FINDEISEN, Theodor, ex-German officer, fr Schmoellen/Thueringen, + St Louis, MO –1881/04/04:1c
FINGER, August, NYC-M – 1903/07/27:4a
FINGER, Frederick, tailor, NYC-M – 1886/04/05:4d
FINGER, Otto, Elizabeth, NJ – 1910/10/18:6a
FINGRATH, Minna, NYC-M – 1892/02/13:4a
FINK % Scheerbarth
FINK, Abraham, 48, NYC-M - 1913/08/03:1e, 5:2b, =4:1c
FINK, Anna, 25, NYC-B – 1893/05/14:5b
FINK, Anna, b. Kohn, NYC-B - 1918/07/05:6a
FINK, Anna, b. Sperb, 71, NYC-B – 1891/02/26:4a
FINK, Barbara, b. Hain, 59, NYC-M - 1878/05/01:3b
FINK, Charles, 11, NYC-M – 1898/09/29:3g
FINK, Christian, NYC-M – 1892/07/10:5c
FINK, Dominick, 69, tailor, NYC-M – 1898/08/11:3g
FINK, George H., lawyer, NYC-M – 1901/04/24:1c
FINK, Henry H., 29, machinist, & wife Alice, 28, NYC-B – 1909/08/29:1g
FINK, Henry, 30, NYC-B – 1893/11/24:4a
FINK, Jeanette, b. Schott, 86, NYC-M - 1916/02/21:6a
FINK, John F., NYC-Bx - 1913/08/06:3f
FINK, Josef, NYC-M - 1914/06/02:6a
FINK, Joseph, NYC?, fam. 1881/05/18:3b
FINK, Margarethe, b. Kaessel, 56, NYC-M – 1892/02/26:4a
FINK, Mathias, 72, un. mason, NYC-M – 1901/01/05:4a
FINK, Tillie, 19, fr Russia, NYC-M – 1901/05/13:1e
FINK, Wilhelm, 56, un. brewer, NYC-B - 1916/08/20:7a
FINK, Wilhelm, SPD Leipzig – 1890/06/09:1f
FINKE, Charlotte, b. Lueneberg, 34, Jersey City, NJ – 1890/04/29:4a

FINKE, Doris Hortense, b. Behrends, wd Harmuth, 44, Jersey City, NJ – 1902/06/30:4a
FINKELSTEIN, Henry, 41, NYC-Q – 1912/12/23:2c
FINKELSTEIN, Isaac, painter, fr Russia, NYC – 1910/01/08:2b, 9:1c
FINKELSTEIN, Isidor's wife, NYC-B, + Nassau, NY – 1911/07/29:1d
FINKELSTEIN, Lazarus, 50, physician & language teacher, dying, NYC-M - 1914/12/17:2b
FINKELSTEIN, Leah, NYC, married Edward ST CLAIRE – 1897/01/21:1g
FINKELSTEIN, Phillip, 10, NYC-B – 1896/08/03:1e
FINKEN, Martin, un. brewer, NYC-B – 1891/04/29:4a
FINKENBERG % Riemer
FINKENSTADT, Anna, b. Hagenau, 68, NYC-M – 1904/06/29:4a
FINKENSTAEDT, Catherina, b. Hall, NYC-M – 1883/07/23:3c
FINKENSTEDT, Heinrich, 3, NYC-M – 1888/05/11:3a
FINKENSTEIN, Joseph, NYC-M – 1890/07/10:4a
FINKER, Rosa, 12, NYC-M – 1896/07/14:1e
FINKERNAGEL, Henry, 47, un. painter, NYC-M – 1905/10/17:4a
FINLEY, Brick, 35,Negro, lynched Paducah, KY - 1916/10/17:1d
FINN, Daniel E., city judge, NYC-M – 1910/03/24:1f
FINN, Jacob L., 18, manufacturer's son, NYC-M – 1886/09/02:1f
FINN, Wilhelm, 44, hatmaker & SPD activist expelled from Altona/Gy, arrived NYC – 1880/11/30:1d-e, 2 Dec:2a-b, 6:1d-e
FINNEISEN, Wilhelm, 57, SP, Jersey City Heights, NJ – 1910/10/28:6a, 29:6a, fam. 2 Nov:6a
FINSTERER, Mary, 58, NYC-M – 1892/08/03:4a
FIORELLI, Doretta b. Ramm, 34, NYC-Bx – 1919/12/04:6a
FIPPINGER % Kalenborn
FIRNBACH, Adam, NYC-M – 1887/03/21:2f
FIRNZES, Jacob, 68, NYC-Q – 1911/10/09:2b
FIRSCHING, Georg, 63, NYC-B - 1918/05/18:6a. S.a. Pfirsching
FISBECK, Charles, SP, student at Rand School, NYC-B - 1916/07/19:6c
FISCH, John, NYC – 1883/12/15:3a
FISCHBACH s.a. Strauss
FISCHBACH, Herman, 50, dyer, NYC-M – 1911/04/16:1e
FISCHBACH, L., NYC-B – 1909/05/15:6a
FISCHBACH, Leopold, Union Hill, NJ - 1917/08/27:6a
FISCHEL, Emanuel, 23, NYC-M – 1884/07/14:4b
FISCHEL, Salomon, Dr., 43, NYC - 1913/10/21:2d
FISCHER % Fuchs, % Habinay
FISCHER, Adam, un. carp., NYC-B – 1903/08/13:4a
FISCHER, Adolf @1887 Haymarket
FISCHER, Albert G., NYC-Bx – 1909/10/28:6a, 29:6a

FISCHER, Albert, NYC – 1911/10/04:6a
FISCHER, Alex, tailor, NYC-M – 1881/09/28:1f, 29:1g
FISCHER, Alfonsa, 7, NYC-M, @1883 School Fire, NYC-M
FISCHER, Alfred, 15, NYC-M – 1897/07/01:1d
FISCHER, Anna, b. Hoepfner, 26, Hoboken, NJ – 1904/09/02:4a
FISCHER, Anna, NYC-M – 1891/02/27:4a
FISCHER, Bernhard, 59, cigar-store owner & realtor, * Saaz/Bohemia, NYC-M - 1879/09/08:1d
FISCHER, Bernhard, un. butcher, NYC-B – 1903/09/09:4a
FISCHER, Caroline, 68, NYC-M – 1908/10/09:2d
FISCHER, Charles C., engineer, fr Vienna 1911, NYC-M – 1912/04/27:2a
FISCHER, Charles J., ?36, un. furnit. Maker, NYC-M – 1890/04/22:4a
FISCHER, Clara, b. Winkler, NYC-M – 1897/01/30:4a
FISCHER, Conrad, stonecutter, NYC-M – 1887/06/08:3b, 9:3c
FISCHER, Eduard, un. cornicemaker, NYC-M – 1893/04/22:4a
FISCHER, Elizabeth, 13, NYC-M – 1896/08/24:1f
FISCHER, Emil, 59, fr Saxony, NYC-SI – 1903/11/11:4a
FISCHER, Emil, Dr., German chemist, Nobel Prize winner - 1919/08/14:4f
FISCHER, Emil, SPD Hamburg, ed. at Hamburger Echo, ex-alderman – 1909/04/18:3a
FISCHER, Emilie, NYC-M – 1891/07/03:4a
FISCHER, Emma, 40, NYC-M, +@Genl Slocum – 1904/06/19:1c, 25:1d
FISCHER, Emma, NYC-M - 1895/07/01: 1b
FISCHER, Ernst, 44, SP, Hoboken, NJ - 1915/09/04:6a,e, 5:7a, =7:2d, fam. 9:6a
FISCHER, Frank, 28, Mt Carmel, NJ – 1899/01/11:4c
FISCHER, Frederick, 45, Newark, NJ - 1914/09/29:6d
FISCHER, Frederick, NYC – 1912/08/21:6a
FISCHER, Friedrich, 45, NYC-B – 1886/11/27:3b, =29:2c
FISCHER, Fritz, NYC-Bx - 1916/01/11:6a
FISCHER, Georg, un. carp., NYC-M – 1882/06/26:3b
FISCHER, George, piano-tuner, NYC-B – 1880/06/15:1g
FISCHER, Heinrich, 1, NYC-B - 1879/04/28:3a
FISCHER, Heinrich, 47, grocer, USA bef. 1862 fr Arnstadt/Gy, NYC-M – 1882/04/07:4c
FISCHER, Henry, 33, NYC-B – 1901/07/03:1d
FISCHER, Henry, innkeep, NYC-M – 1898/12/28:1e, & wife Louise, too, 1 May 1899:1b
FISCHER, Henry, NYC-B - 1915/10/21:6a
FISCHER, Henry, un. butcher, NYC-M - 1920/08/17:6a
FISCHER, Herman, NYC-Q - 1919/04/13:12a

FISCHER, Hermann, 33, SP, NYC-M – 1907/03/14:6a, 15:6a, 16:6a, 17:7c, fam. 21:6a
FISCHER, Hermann, 58, NYC-M – 1892/06/26:5c
FISCHER, Hermann, 60, NYC-M – 1906/01/18:4c
FISCHER, Hugo, 36, fd + near Bound Brook, NJ – 1880/06/18:1d-e
FISCHER, Hugo, 51, NYC-M – 1892/06/11:4a
FISCHER, Jacob, 43, sausage manufacturer, pres. Murray Hill Schwaben KUV, NYC-M - 1916/01/26:2f,6a
FISCHER, Jakob, 41, SLP, un. stone cutter, NYC-M – 1897/03/01:4a
FISCHER, Jakob, 43, NYC-M - 1878/03/08:3c
FISCHER, Jakob, bricklayer, NYC-M - 1878/06/17:1f
FISCHER, John, 52, Lakeview, NJ – 1913/01/19:1f
FISCHER, John, furnit. Dealer, NYC-B – 1880/12/04:1d
FISCHER, John, NYC-M – 1910/03/08:6a
FISCHER, Joseph, 52, NYC-M – 1893/02/02:2f
FISCHER, Joseph, NYC-B - 1878/08/13:2c
FISCHER, Joseph, NYC-M – 1906/03/31:4a
FISCHER, Julius, NYC-Q - 1913/07/01:6a
FISCHER, Karl, 43, NYC-M – 1891/03/23:4a
FISCHER, Karl, NYC-M - 1918/12/09:6a
FISCHER, Karl, SPD Mittweida/Saxony – 1908/02/16:3d
FISCHER, Karl, un. carp., NYC-M – 1881/12/24:1f, 3a, =27:1f
FISCHER, Katharina, b. Petri, 26, NYC-B – 1882/02/28:3b
FISCHER, Lorenz, 53, un. machinist, SP, Harrison, NJ – 1913/03/30:7b, 11b, 31:6a, 1 Ap:6a, fam. 4:6a
FISCHER, Louis, 40, roofer, NYC-B – 1886/01/13:5d
FISCHER, Louis, silk weaver, Paterson, NJ – 1898/06/14:4c
FISCHER, Lucy, West Hoboken, NJ - 1913/09/06:6a
FISCHER, Maria, NYC-M - 1915/05/21:6a
FISCHER, Martin, 47, dye-mixer, NYC-M – 1892/08/02:2e
FISCHER, Mary, 50, NYC-M – 1881/08/09:1g
FISCHER, Mathias, 56, innkeep, NYC-M – 1898/07/14:1g, 15:3d
FISCHER, Minnie, 16, NYC-M – 1897/11/29:4a
FISCHER, Oskar, NYC-M – 1893/10/31:4a
FISCHER, Otto, 60, un. Painter, NYC-M – 1911/07/08:6a, mem. 1912/07/05:6a
FISCHER, Peter J., 60, wine dealer, New Rochelle, NY – 1908/11/23:2f
FISCHER, Peter, NYC-Bx – 1911/08/30:6a
FISCHER, Richard, Guttenberg, NJ - 1915/07/03:6a
FISCHER, Rosa, NYC-M – 1896/09/15:1f, 23:1f
FISCHER, Samuel Friedrich, 87, & wife, 85, 60th Wedding Anniversary, SLP, both fr Kindelbrueck/Wipper, USA 1846, NYC – 1898/01/10:1e

FISCHER, Sophie, 29, NYC-M – 1897/05/12:1b
FISCHER, Valentine's wife, 22, NYC-B – 1899/02/01:1g, 2:1g
FISCHER, Valerie, 28, & her sister Louise Abel, 30, NYC-M – 1904/11/14:1h
FISCHER, Viola, 18, NYC-M – 1900/07/11:3e
FISCHER, Wilhelm, un. carp.,NYC-M - 1917/01/09:6a,fam. 13:6a
FISCHER, William T., ~35, & his common-law wife, NYC? – 1910/02/05:2d
FISCHER, William, 51, NYC-M – 1919/11/11:8a
FISCHER, William, 61, NYC-M – 1891/04/01:4a
FISCHKA, Annie, 36, NYC? – 1912/06/21:2e
FISCHLER, Bertha, 8, NYC-M, +@Genl Slocum – 1904/06/23:1b
FISHER, Carolina, NYC-B – 1885/09/16:1e-f, 17:1f, 18:1e, =23:4e
FISHLER, Anna, 6, NYC-M, + @on Genl Slocum – 1904/06/21:1f
FISSLER, Frank, 45, servant for sport star James R. Keene, NYC-M – 1912/12/27:3e-f
FISTHER, Andreas, Elizabeth, NJ - 1915/09/21:6a
FISTL, John, un. carp., NYC-M – 1888/05/18:3a
FITZELL, J. H., 46, innkeep, NYC – 1912/05/26:1f
FIX, Leopold, Newark, NJ – 1908/10/13:6a
FIX, Vitus, un. painter, NYC-M – 1909/04/20:6a
FLACHMUELLER, Michael, un. furniture maker, NYC-M – 1893/08/12:4a
FLAESCHEL, Minna, 57, NYC-M - 1915/02/03:6a, fam. 6:6a
FLAESCHEL, Paul, un. cigarmaker, SP, NYC?, 50th birthday – 1905/11/09:3f
FLAESCHNER, Mina, NYC-B – 1911/12/12:6a
FLAMMER, Marguerite, 38, NYC-B – 1902/06/06:4a
FLAMMER, Paul, 41, stoker, NYC-M – 1893/04/19:1f
FLANAGAN, Clara, b. Niehaus, NYC-B – 1908/12/30:6a
FLART % Bogumil; FLASCHHAUS % Kempel
FLASCHNER, Wilhelm, 73, NYC-M – 1913/04/15:6a
FLATH, Anton, 58, baker, NYC-B – 1886/07/28:2b
FLATZ, Mrs, NYC?, fam. 1903/05/19:4a
FLAXENBERG, Gottfried, 40, & son Frederick, 3, NYC-B – 1903/02/27:1e
FLECK % Bartlett
FLECK, Anton, 50, NYC-M - 1879/01/06:3a
FLECKENSTEIN, Charles, tailor, & daughter Emma, 9, NYC-B – 1902/04/18:4a
FLECKENSTEIN, Frank, NYC-Q - 1915/03/09:6a
FLECKENSTEIN, John, NYC-B - 1915/04/27:6a
FLECKENSTEIN, Joseph, NYC-B – 1908/08/20:6a

FLEGENHEIMER, Adolph, 68, wine importer, fr Rheinpfalz, NYC-M - 1915/12/26:11e
FLEGENHEIMER, Henry, 53, popular wine importer, ex-alderman, *Ruchheim/Rhine, NYC-SI – 1898/11/19:4c, =21:1e
FLEGENHEIMER, Lena, NYC-B, + @on Genl Slocum – 1904/06/18:3c
FLEGENHEIMER, Moses, fr Ruchheim/Wuerzburg, NYC-B - 1879/06/19:3a
FLEHRE, A. H., 11, NYC – 1902/06/15:1b
FLEIDNER, Louis, NYC-M – 1886/09/04:3a
FLEIG, Anna, NYC-Q - 1913/11/23:7c
FLEIG, Ferdinand, un. carp., NYC-B – 1912/05/12:7b
FLEISCHER, Alex, coat dealer, NYC-B - 1913/10/30:1d
FLEISCHER, Conrad, un. cigarmkr, NYC-M – 1893/01/30:4a
FLEISCHER, Henry, 15, NYC-M, + Genl Slocum – 1904/06/26:1c
FLEISCHER, Wilhelm, Hoboken, NJ – 1911/03/19:7b
FLEISCHHAUER, Marcus, NYC-M – 1892/08/04:4a
FLEISCHHAUER, Robert, NYC-M - 1919/05/31:6a
FLEISCHMANN % Kraemer
FLEISCHMANN, Charles, son of former Cincinatti mayor, US Airforce, War 1 - 1917/08/03:1f
FLEISCHMANN, comrade, SPD militant, + Nuernberg, Gy – 1906/09/14:4d
FLEISCHMANN, George, NYC-M – 1908/04/08:6a, 9:6a
FLEISCHMANN, John, un. carp., NYC-M – 1898/11/20:5a
FLEISCHMANN, Louis, owner of Vienna Bakery & humanitarian, gave daily free bread to homeless w/o asking humiliating questions, *18 Aug. 1836 Austria, NYC-M – 1904/09/26:3e, 4a
FLEISCHMANN, Max, NYC, will, 1900/03/13:2h, 17 April:3a
FLEISCHMANN, Max, principal, NYC? – 1890/09/24:4a
FLEISCHMANN, Otto F.,pres.Fleischmann Vehicle Co. & Fleischmann Baking Co., fr Vienna, NYC-M - 1915/05/13:1g, 14:2b
FLEISS, Joseph, brewer or cooper, NYC-M – 1904/12/19:4a
FLEISSEN, Hermann, 17, baker, NYC-M – 1880/02/04:1e, inquest 10:1f
FLEISSNER, Frank,34, un. bronze worker,NYC-M - 1920/12/24:6a
FLEMING, Thomas, 40, brewer, NYC-M – 1908/01/08:1a, 9:2c
FLEMMING % Bauwens
FLEMMING, Charles F., 21, SP, Fort Lee, NJ - 1918/06/01:6a, fam. 5:6a; mem 1919/05/31:6a
FLEMMING, Karl F., 44, SP, NYC-M – 1909/04/12:6a, 13:6a, mem. 10 Ap 1910:7c
FLESCH, Dr., Liberal alderman Frankfurt/Main - 1915/09/19:3b
FLEUCHAUS, Henry, un. butcher, NYC-M – 1919/09/03:6a

FLEZAK, Frank, tailor, NYC-M – 1903/12/25:1b
FLICK, John J., 68, SP, co-fdr NYVZ, NYC-M – 1909/01/27:1d, 6a
FLICK, Marie Magdalena, b. Ackermann, 56, SLP, NYC-M – 1896/07/08:3e,4a
FLIEGER, Paul, 37, NYC-M – 1905/05/23:4a
FLIGIN, Morris, un. cigarmaker, NYC-M – 1910/04/23:6a
FLINCKER, Elise, child, NYC-M – 1884/07/04:1e
FLINK, Theodor, old, NYC-M – 1905/06/27:2h
FLITTNER, William, NYC - 1914/02/11:6a
FLOCK, Eliza, 78, NYC-B - 1913/06/04:5e
FLOCK, Louis, 49, NYC-Bx - 1916/02/09:6a
FLOECK, John, 48, fr Switzerland?, NYC-M – 1891/11/18:4a, 20:4a
FLOHR % Schrum
FLOHR, Alexander, 68, un. printer, NYC-B - 1895/10/19: 4a
FLOOD, John P., 38, NYPD, NYC-M - 1917/07/04:1f
FLOREN, Adolph, wood worker, NYC-M – 1896/11/27:4a, 28:4a
FLOREN, Louise, 9, @1883 School Fire, NYC-M 1883
FLORENCE, Marie Zeika, b. Von der Wenden, NYC-M – 1893/05/05:4a
FLORENZ, Protas, 46, wall paper maker, NYC-M 1895/05/03:1h
FLORIAN, Julia, 40, worker, NYC-M - 1915/06/20:11g
FLORY, Nikolaus, un. piano maker, NYC-M – 1889/05/13:4a
FLOSSDORF, William, NYC-M – 1890/10/19:5b
FLOTOW, Annie, 27, NYC-M – 1888/06/19:1g
FLOTSCHER, Otto, 32, NYC-M – 1912/06/14:6a
FLOWER, Roswell P., ex-NYS gov., NYC-M – 1899/05/13:1c, 14:1h
FLOYD, Zeb, Negro, lynched Wetumpka Co., AL – 1900/09/11:1d
FLUCH, Henry, NYC-M – 1899/02/15:1h
FLUCKIGER, Rosa, 39, NYC-B - 1901/12/23:1h
FLUEGER, Fritz, 54, un. baker, Jersey City, NJ - 1920/07/22:6a
FLUEGGER, Friedrich, 37, fr Amt Hagen/Schleswig?, NYC-M – 1888/05/04:3b
FLUERSCHEIM, Michael, 68, German iron manuf. & social reformer, + Berlin, Gy – 1912/05/10:4f
FLUES, Conrad, 23, Newark, NJ – 1911/03/13:2e
FLUGRATH, Johanna, b. Haas, 63, NYC-Bx - 1918/10/11:6a
FLUGRATH, John Frederick., 69, NYC-M – 1886/07/03:3a
FLUGRATH, Richard, 30, merchant navy, NYC-M?, +30 Jan. 1920 in Newcastle-upon-Tyne, GB – 1920/05/07:6a
FLUGRATH, William, un. printer, NYC-Bx - 1920/08/03:6a
FLUKINGER, John A., 48, butcher, NYC-M - 1914/11/03:2f
FLUX, Friedrich, un. carp., NYC-B – 1911/01/30:6a
FOCKE, Henry, machinist, NYC-M – 1906/08/08:6a

FOCTSING, Frederick, 8, (misp.?), NYC-M, + @ Genl Slocum – 1904/06/18:3c
FODERS, Max, family thanks 1920/09/14:6a
FODY, Frank, NYC-M - 1918/03/24:7a
FOELIG, Joseph, 20, NYC-B – 1891/08/15:4a
FOELKER, Mrs, 62, NYC-M – 1882/08/27:8a
FOELSING, Henry, NYC-Bx – 1913/02/14:6a
FOERG, Leopold, 36?, NYC-M – 1891/04/14:4a
FOERG, Margarethe, NYC-Bx – 1908/12/18:6a
FOERNSTER, Auguste, b. Heyer, NYC-B – 1910/12/30:6a
FOERNSTER, Katherina, 72, NYC-Bx – 1910/01/13:6a
FOERST, Elizabeth, NYC-B – 1908/06/03:6a
FOERSTE, Lulu, 12, NYC-Valley Cottage – 1910/02/28:6a
FOERSTER % Schere
FOERSTER, Albert, painter, NYC-M, + on trip to Zanesville, OH – 1881/04/18:3a, fam. 7 June:3c
FOERSTER, Clara Bertha, 5, NYC-M – 1884/09/19:3d
FOERSTER, comrade, 57, SPD Lauschau/Thueringia/Gy – 1899/04/30:12c
FOERSTER, Hermann, cigarmaker & SPD MdR for Reuss/Gy, *Zinna, Gy – 1912/12/06:4c, =13:4d
FOERSTER, Maria, NYC-M – 1882/03/06:3b
FOERSTERLING % Kehrbaum
FOERSTNER, Christian, 72, SP?, NYC-M - 1920/01/14:6a, = 16:2f, fam. 20:8a
FOESEL, George, 38, un. carp., NYC-B – 1898/05/09:4a, 10:4a
FOESIG, Gustav, 56, NYC-B – 1910/08/11:6a
FOESIG, Otto, NYC-B - 1920/02/02:6a
FOGARTY, Lancelot Cormac, grocer, Irish, fr Thunlas?, and his family, NYC-M - 1878/04/12:4c-e
FOGINSKY, Franz, 31, miner's union official in Kochlowitz/Gy – 1912/01/07:3b
FOLD, Mrs, NYC-M, + @ Genl Slocum – 1904/06/18:3c
FOLDHAUS, George, 10, NYC-M, +@Genl Slocum – 1904/06/23:1b
FOLGER, George Clark, 26, trolley employee, Maywood, NJ – 1905/01/17:3c
FOLGNER, Anna, b. Urban, 59, NYC-M - 1894/11/01:4a
FOLK, Friedrich, West Hoboken, NJ – 1910/01/11:6a
FOLKE, Anna & Dora, NYC-M, +@Genl Slocum – 1904/06/17:3b, 18:3c
FOLKER, Henry, 64, Jersey City Heights, NJ – 1888/05/08:2f
FOLKERT, Henry, 58, furrier, NYC-M – 1896/11/29:5b
FONFARA, Frieda, NYC-M – 1904/10/21:4a, fam. 24:4a
FORCHT, John Nicholas?, un. baker, NYC-M - 1920/07/16:6a, 17:6a

FORD, Charles, exec. Trenton, NJ – 1913/02/19:2e
FORD, Simon, Negro, lynched Hohenwald, TN – 1905/06/21:3b
FORD, Walter B., 24, SLP, * England, USA 1902, active SLP organizer, Elizabeth, NJ - 1917/12/03:2c, 6a
FOREST, F., Newark, NJ – 1906/10/02:6a
FORGBERT, Fritz, 56, carpenter, fr Breslau/Gy, USA 1882, NYC-M – 1882/09/30:4c
FORKER % Eisenhauer
FORKER, Max, SP activist, active in G-A SP media, *Saxony, USA 1887, + McKees Rocks, PA – 1913/03/29:1g, =2 Apr:3e
FORMAN, Wanda, b. Kolloff, (parents: August & Johanna Deutschmann), NYC-M – 1911/12/30:6a
FORMANCK, Mary, 4, NYC-M – 1892/11/05:4a
FORMANEK, Fritz, infant, NYC-M? – 1893/08/26:4a
FORMANEK, Ignatz, NYC-M – 1906/12/30:7b
FORREST, Reuben, steelworker, Homestead, PA – 1892/07/08:1a
FORSBOURG, Mary, 63, NYC-M – 1882/03/01:1e
FORSCHNER, August, cigarmaker & SPD activist, fr Baden/Gy, expelled from Altona/ Gy, arrived NYC – 1880/11/30:1d-e, 2 Dec:2a-b, 6:1d-e. SP, + 64 yrs old Unionport, NJ – 1904/06/21:4a, =23:1h, fam. 23:4a
FORSCHNER, Margarethe, NYC-M – 1900/03/29:4a
FORST, Adam, 45, North Bergen, NJ – 1905/12/27:3f
FORST, Morris, NYC-Bx – 1909/11/04:6a
FORSTER, Charles, SP?, Newark, NJ – 1903/03/01:5a, fam. 5:4a
FORSTER, Fritz, un. baker, NYC-M - 1919/02/10:6a
FORSTER, Georg, 150th anniv. of the German revolutionary – 1904/11/27:4c-e
FORSTER, George H., NYC politician, NYC-M – 1888/11/09:1d
FORSTER, Heinrich C., NYC-M – 1903/04/21:4a
FORSTER, Jacob, 69, NYC-B – 1892/07/14:4a
FORSTER, Louise, Syracuse, NY, by Ernst Hecht – 1900/05/26:1c
FORSTER, Philipp Jakob, 46, Jersey City Heights, NJ – 1891/03/31:4a
FORTE, Ricardo, exec. Westchester, PA – 1906/09/07:1b
FORTENBACH, Heinrich, 41, un. carp., NYC-M – 1885/03/29:8a
FORTHMANN, C., NYC-Q -1914/09/29:6a
FORTMUELLER, Rosette, 42, NYC-M – 1889/09/06:4a
FOSS, Freeman J., 48, mgr local Swift & Co branch, Jersey City, NJ – 1912/09/14:1b
FOTH, Annie, NYC-M – 1891/07/15:4a
FOTH, Heinrich, 60, un. cabinetmaker, SP, NYC-Bx – 1911/06/17:2a, 6a, fam. 2 Jy:7b. Mem. – 1912/06/15:6a
FOTSCHKY, Valentine, 64, NYC-B - 1918/11/26:6a

FOTTHAUER % Schiller
FOUQUET, Phil., NYC-M – 1911/10/02:6a
FOURIER, Charles, French Utopist, notes on his life – 1881/06/18:2b-c
FOURNIER, Alfred, French scientist, + Paris in June - 1915/09/06:4g
FOURNIER, Ulrich, fr Montreal, + NYC-Bellevue Hosp. – 1908/11/23:2e
FOY, Martin, exec. Dannemora, NY – 1893/10/24:1b
FRAAS, John, 50, un. carp., NYC-Corona - 1917/07/12:6a
FRAEBER, Julius, NYC-M – 1891/12/06:5c
FRANKEL, Leo, goldsmith & SP activist, * Hungary, jailed again –
  1881/03/ 24:1b-c, 27:4g. + Paris/France - 1896/04/01:1d, 2a, =17:2d-e;
  mon. in Paris – 1900/01/03:2e, in Pere Lachaise cem. – 1902/12/02:2d
FRAGESSER % Senger
FRANCK, Adolf, 83, SPD Kiel/Gy – 1911/04/09:3b
FRANK % Doering, % Fuchs
FRANK, Andreas, NYC-M – 1906/12/02:7c
FRANK, Anna, b. Kramer, NYC-Bx - 1915/11/05:6a, mem. 1916/11/02:6a
FRANK, Arnold, Dr. vet., 62, *Breslau/Gy, Hoboken, NJ – 1910/11/14:2d
FRANK, Charles, 40, painter, NYC-B – 1907/03/31:1b
FRANK, Christian, NYC-B – 1891/03/14:1f
FRANK, Ed, NYC, collection for orphans 1882/09/11:3b
FRANK, Emma, b. Satter, 29, NYC-B – 1896/11/22:5a
FRANK, Frederick Charles, 47, Newark, NJ – 1898/05/04:4b
FRANK, Frieda, 10, NYC-B - 1916/02/29:6b
FRANK, Henry, leather dealer,parents in Albany, NYC-M - 1895/11/07: 4d
FRANK, I.F., Irvington, NJ - 1917/03/24:6a
FRANK, John, killed 9 Oct 1879 West Orange, NJ, trial of murderers Mrs
  Meierhoefer & Frank Lammens – 1880/01/20:1d, 21:4d, 22:1f
FRANK, John, 33, NYC-M - 1919/08/07:6a
FRANK, John, secy of NYC German Cigarmakers' Union, NYC-M -
  1879/08/07:3a
FRANK, Joseph, 60, NYC-M – 1919/12/27:6a
FRANK, Julius, NYC – 1880/06/30:1b
FRANK, Karl H., NYC-M - 1896/01/30:4a
FRANK, L., NYC-M – 1893/08/18:4a
FRANK, Leo M., lynched Marietta, GA - 1915/08/18:1f-g, 4a, 20:2c, =
  NYC-B 6 Sept:6e
FRANK, Louis, 14, NYC-M – 1880/12/04:1d
FRANK, Ludwig, Dr., SPD, MdR for Mannheim-Weinheim, *23 May 1874
  Nonnenweier/Baden, War 1 – #1914/09/09:1a, 4c, 24:4f
FRANK, Ludwig Julius, chief ed. N.Y. Morgenjournal, * 19.12.1839
  Berlin/Gy, USA 1864, NYC-M - 1895/03/22:1d
FRANK, Peter, 8, NYC-M – 1889/01/28:4a

FRANK, Philip, 37, mail carrier, NYC-Bx – 1896/08/09:1c
FRANK, Philipp, mail carrier, + 8 Aug. 96, on his widow – 1897/01/18:4d
FRANK, Rosie, 22, USA 1907, NYC-M – 1908/06/26:2c
FRANK, Swenning H., SP, un. cigarmaker, New Haven, CT - 1915/12/11:3f,6a
FRANK, Theodore, 65,un. painter, NYC-M - 1920/09/18:6a,19:2e
FRANK, Tina, 17, @1911 Triangle Shirtwaist Fire, NYC-M – 1911/03/27:1d
FRANK, Vitus, tailor, Newark, NJ NYC-M – 1892/08/19:4f
FRANK, Wilhelmina, 16, servant, NYC?– 1908/04/08:3e
FRANK, William H., brewery owner, NYC-B - 1917/12/02:11d
FRANKAU, Julia, 52, English writer (as Frank Derby) - 1916/03/19:11g
FRANKE, Alois, 64, NYC-M – 1907/07/30:6a
FRANKE, Charles, 44, NYC-B – 1898/06/09:1b
FRANKE, Charles, sailor on USS Maine, + Havana/Cuba, NYC-B – 1898/02/18:1b
FRANKE, Franz, 38, SP, Hoboken, NJ – 1911/04/16:7b
FRANKE, Ida, 24, NYC-M – 1885/11/11:1e, 12:1g
FRANKE, Louis, '48er, SLP, NYC-M – 1885/11/20:1d, 3a, 21:4a, =22:1g, fam. 24:6b
FRANKE, William, 72, hotelier, family in Dresden/Gy, NYC-M - 1915/02/09:1b
FRANKEL, Adolf, porter, ex-German army officer, NYC-M – 1904/06/20:1d
FRANKEL, Leo see Fraenkel, Leo
FRANKEN, Louis, 36, parents in Koeln/Gy, Plainfield, NJ – 1907/02/08:3c
FRANKENSTEIN, John, 65, sculptor, * Ohio, NYC-B – 1881/04/18:1c-d
FRANKLIN, Benjamin, on his 200th anniv. of birth – 1906/01/17:2a-b
FRANKO, Francis, un. waiter, killed during strike, NYC-M – 1912/11/30:3c, =3 Dec:2c
FRANKOWITZ, Albert, un. carp., NYC-M – 1909/08/06:6a
FRANSSEN, Anton A., 14, Newark, NJ – 1911/02/28:6a
FRANTA, Mathias, NYC-Q - 1920/02/19:6a
FRANTZ, Lottie, 22, servant, ex-Passaic, NJ, NYC-M – 1897/01/17:1e
FRANTZ, Maria, 41, NYC-B – 1906/03/09:4a
FRANTZEN, comrade, 52, weaver & SPD Solingen/Gy – 1909/04/04:3b
FRANTZIUS, Fritz von, 62, banker & art critic, USA 1888, Chicago, OH - 1917/01/09:2b
FRANZ % Junckes
FRANZ, Anton, un. butcher, NYC-M - 1918/10/24:6a
FRANZ, Fanny, 42, NYC-B – 1883/03/07:3c
FRANZ, Freddy, 25, NYC-B – 1892/06/24:4a, 25:4a, fam. 28:4a

FRANZ, Friedrich, NYC-B - 1916/03/28:6a
FRANZ, Georg, 31, Union Hill, NJ - 1893/01/14:4a
FRANZ, Henry, 31, Hoboken, NJ - 1909/11/03:6a, fam. 11:6a
FRANZ, Jacob L., 56, SP, typesetter, *Bavaria, journalist for G-A soc. media, NYC-M - 1902/10/03:1e, 4a, 4:4a, 5:5b, fam. 8:4a
FRANZ, Joseph, 13, NYC-M - 1892/11/26:1e
FRANZ, Louis, child, NYC - 1913/03/25:6a
FRANZ, M., NYC-B - 1919/01/22:6a
FRANZ, Martin, NYC-B - 1919/03/14:6a
FRANZ, Otto, 64, Union, NJ - 1899/09/15:4a
FRANZ, Wolfgang, Newark, NJ - 1904/05/31:4a
FRANZEL, Charles, 24, un. carp., NYC-B - 1914/03/27:6d
FRANZON, Albert, formerly Franzonowitz, fr Riga/Russia, bank clerk, NYC-M - 1906/08/02:1c
FRAPAN % Akunian,
FRAUCHT, Charles, 75, Washington, NY - 1904/05/12:1d
FRAUNE, Anton, un. carp., NYC-M - 1903/07/25:4a
FRAUNHOFER, Teresa, 35, kitchen employee, Trenton, NJ - 1913/02/01:2f,
FRECH, Albert, 59, weaver, Union Hill, NJ - 1911/03/15:6a
FRECKEN, Sophie, NYC-M - 1880/12/30:1d
FREDE, Jacob, un. carp., NYC-Bx - 1902/11/16:5a
FREDERICK, Hermann, NYC-M - 1891/08/15:4a
FREDERICKS, Caroline, 47, NYC-M - 1889/01/19:1g
FREDERICKS, Charles, 46, NYC-B - 1905/09/25:3c
FREDERICKS, George, 14, NYC-B - 1900/05/02:3b, 3:1g
FREDERICKS, Jacob, 10, NYC-B - 1913/07/31:3a
FREDERICKS, Pauline, 20, servant, fr Russia 1913, Yonkers, NY - 1913/08/15:1e
FREDERICKS, Theodore, grocer, & family, Yonkers, NY - 1909/12/22:1b
FREDERSCH, Sebastian, NYC-B - 1881/02/17:3a
FREEBEELEIN, Joseph, 79,carp., War 2, NYC-Q - 1915/08/22:11a
FREEMAN, Carrie, b. Bodenheimer, NYC-M - 1892/10/16:5c
FREEMAN, Henry Louis, Jersey City, NJ - 1912/02/10:6a
FREEMAN, Margareth, NYC-M - 1891/06/24:1g
FREEMANN, Max, actor & theater manager, NYC-M - 1912/03/29:1f
FREES, B., 28, NYC-M - 1894/01/31:4a
FREESE, Caroline, b. Roehrig, NYC-M - 1893/09/28:4a
FREESE, Frank, 47, NYC-Bx - 1909/02/04:6a
FREI, Rosa, Union Hill, NJ - 1911/10/06:6a
FREIBERG, Nathan, 23, SP, NYC-M - 1908/03/29:1f
FREIBURGER, Katie, 2, Newark, NJ - 1893/08/19:4f

FREIDENBERG, Christian, 50th anniv. as music instrument maker, NYC-B
– 1880/08/24:4d
FREIERMUTH, E., NYC-B - 1918/06/06:6a
FREIFELD, George, 58, judge, *NYC, NYC-B - 1917/11/18:1b
FREIHALDER, Mary, NYC-M – 1893/12/28:1h, 29:1g
FREILANDER, Golden, Carmel, NJ – 1909/11/19:2b
FREILIGER, Paulina, Union Hill, NJ – 1880/11/19:4e
FREILIGRATH, Ferdinand, poet, on him in 1848 – 1898/08/14:4c-e. Life & work 1906/04/01:9d-f. 100th anniv. #, 1910/06/12:1c-d, 12:3b, 4a-g, 5a-b, 13c-d, his trial 1848 3 Jy:3f-g, 15f-g, NYC mem. 28 Aug:3e-g
FREIMANN % Schnalke
FREIMER, Louis, 53, flower dealer, NYC-B – 1893/07/25:2d
FREIMUTH, Christian, 52, un. carp., NYC-Bx /10/05:7a, 7:6a
FREIMUTH, Dorothea, b. Lieth, 56, NYC-B – 1882/08/25:3b
FREIMUTH, Marie, 94, NYC-B - 1878/02/24:8b
FREISCHLAG, Josef, 7, NYC-M – 1887/07/19:1g
FREISE, August, NYC-Q - 1916/11/01:6a
FREISE, Magda, b. Meyer, 24, NYC-M - 1878/07/25:3b
FREISE, Meta, b. Rodemeyer, NYC-Q – 1911/02/14:6a
FREISENS, Christina, 16, NYC-B – 1903/01/30:4b
FREISINGER, Lucie, 25, actress at Irving Place Theater, *Vienna, NYC-M 1896/02/20:3e, =21:1g
FREITAG % Rauch
FREITAG, A., 50, Newark, NJ – 1903/06/28:5a
FREITAG, Agnes, 34, NYC-M – 1892/06/08:1f
FREITAG, Anton, NYC-M - 1916/01/27:6a
FREITAG, Joseph E's wife., NYC-B – 1900/11/08:4a, husband Joseph rec life -- 1901/02/06:2h
FREITAG, Mathilde, divorced Walker, 40, NYC-M – 1908/12/31:1g
FREITEL, Emil, NYC-M – 1918/12/16:6a
FRELINGHUYSEN, F. T., State Secy, crit. notes on + - 1885/05/22:2b-c
FRENCH, Stephen W., 67, NYC Police Comm., NYC-M - 1896/02/04:1d
FRENTZ, Emil, innkeep, Hoboken, NJ – 1885/12/31:2e
FRENZEL, Emil, un. baker, NYC-M – 1897/07/26:4a
FRENZER, P., NYC-M - 1920/05/23:12a
FREPPEN, Gertrude, 65, NYC-M – 1912/11/12:3a
FRESCH, Peter, *Zuerich/Switz., NYC-M – 1887/02/19:3b
FRESE, Bertha Conrad, 65, NYC-B - 1916/03/05:7a
FRESE, Fritz, 68, NYC-M - 1916/03/04:6a
FRESE, Karolina, 63, NYC-Q – 1912/12/15:7a
FRETZ, Philipp, 49, NYC-M – 1881/01/24:5c
FREUD, Adam, NYC-M – 1911/05/18:6a

FREUD, Heinrich, 69, NYC-M – 1902/09/23:4a
FREUDENTHAL, Wilhelm, NYC-M – 1905/02/22:4a
FREUDIG, Alois, 62, NYC – 1883/01/11:3c
FREUND, Christian, NYC-M – 1891/07/17:4a
FREUND, Clara, 15, fr Gy, NYC-M - 1894/03/06:4e
FREUND, F., NYC-Bx - 1918/01/11:6a
FREUND, Georg, NYC-B – 1906/08/12:7a
FREUND, George, 24, NYC-B – 1893/04/02:5a
FREUND, Henry, 59, NYC-M - 1919/03/02:12a, 4:6a
FREUND, Phillipine, 70, NYC-Q – 1911/06/16:3a
FREUNDLICH, Salomon, un. cigarmaker, NYC-M – 1911/01/25:6a, 26:6a
FREUREN, Emil, Jersey City, NJ – 1898/05/28:4c
FREY % Ruf
FREY, Adam, un. carp., NYC – 1912/08/10:6a
FREY, Adolf, Swiss poet & historian, - 1920/03/29:2f
FREY, Anna, b. Schlesinger, 30, Viennese Socialist, - 1920/03/27:5f-g
FREY, August, weaver, SP, Hoboken, NJ – 1909/03/24:6a, 25:2b, fam. 26:6a
FREY, Bernhard, 61, NYC-M – 1892/08/23:4a
FREY, Caroline, b. Loesch, 45, fr Gross-Rindsfeld/Baden, NYC-B – 1899/09/11:4a
FREY, Conrad H., NYC-M - 1919/01/28:6a
FREY, Conrad Wiegand, 69, NYC-M – 1890/05/02:4a
FREY, Emil, 66, cook, NYC-M - 1916/02/02:2g
FREY, Ferdinand, un. beer driver, NYC-M – 1902/06/15:5a
FREY, George, 65, NYC-M – 1891/03/29:5a
FREY, Gottlieb, 42, innkeep, NYC-M – 1883/12/31:1g
FREY, Gottlieb, SPD Reutlingen/Wuertt., 1910/07/10:3d
FREY, Hermann, ex-NYC?, Garden City, AL – 1906/06/20:6a
FREY, Jacob L., 40, NYC-M – 1892/03/09:4a
FREY, Jacob, 51, NYC-B – 1891/04/11:4a
FREY, Jacob, 66, NYC-Q – 1886/01/15:2g
FREY, Jakob, 60, NYC-M – 1889/02/11:4a
FREY, John, Newark, NJ – 1919/11/08:6a
FREY, Josephine, 36, NYC-Q – 1912/03/30:6a
FREY, Lillie, 34, NYC-M, +@Genl Slocum – 1904/06/25:1d
FREY, Louis, 44, un. typesetter, NYC-B – 1911/04/15:6a, 16:7b
FREY, Manny, NYC-M – 1907/02/14:6c
FREY, Maria, b. Bauer, NYC-M – 1889/08/23:4a
FREY, Michael, 65, Newark, NJ – 1907/01/26:3d
FREY, Nathan, & family, Mt Vernon, NY – 1904/04/07:3e
FREY, Nathan, NYC-M – 1892/02/26:4a

FREY, Walter M., 40, NYC-M – 1892/08/11:4a
FREY, William, 20, photographer, NYC-M – 1901/07/20:1g
FREYBURGER, Sophia M., NYC-M – 1892/09/05:4a
FREYEBERG, Emma, 21, fr Russia, USA 1910, NYC-Bx – 1910/07/03:9c
FREYER, Madeline, NYC-M – 1880/04/18:5d
FREYGANG % Moser
FREYKNECHT, Henry F., 11, NYC-M – 1880/07/16:1g
FREYSENG, Louise, b. Peteler, NYC-SI - 1878/04/18:3b
FREYTAG, Bernhard, 61, lawyer, SPD?, Leipzig/Gy – 1901/06/19:2f
FREYTAG, Emma, 48, NYC-B – 1899/09/16:2g, 15:3d
FREYTAG, Gustav, German writer, + Wiesbaden - 1895/05/01:1b
FREZZI, Italian Soc., + in Italian jail – 1897/05/22:2c-d
FRIAR % Schultz
FRICK, Charles, 4, NYC-M, + @ Genl Slocum – 1904/06/18:3c
FRICK, Friedrich Wilhelm, innkeep & publ. close to SPD, Bremen/Gy – 1900/10/22:2f
FRICK, Henry Clay, US capitalist, crit. Obit. – 1919/12/03:4d, 9:4c
FRICK, Joseph, 59, smith, NYC-B - 1915/08/22:1f, 28:6a, died 27 Oct:2e
FRICK, Joseph, Pittsburg, PA, w. funeral speech by Johann Most – 1891/04/06:1g
FRICK, Otto, machinist, NYC-B - 1915/08/22:1f
FRICK, Sophia, 61, Newark, NJ – 1910/01/03:1c, 4:3c
FRICK, William, un. cabit. maker, NYC-M – 1892/05/30:4a, 31:4a
FRICKE % Kues
FRICKE, Bernhard, un. cigarmkr, NYC-M – 1892/12/01:4a
FRICKE, Carl Emil, NYC-M – 1891/09/20:5f
FRICKE, Christian, Huntingdon, LI - 1916/08/02:6a
FRICKE, Friedericka, un. cigarmkr, NYC-M – 1892/08/11:4a
FRICKE, Sadie, NYC-M - 1920/02/23:6a
FRICKE, William, liquor dealer, +Englewood, NJ – 1880/02/18:1e, 19:1e
FRICKE, William, 67, *Luebeck, photographer, Plattdeutsch poet, NYC-M – 1910/10/18:2e
FRICKHORN, Marie, NYC-M, + @ Genl Slocum – 1904/06/16:1c
FRICKMANN, August, NYC-M – 1885/04/24:3c
FRIEB-BLUMAUER, Minona, actress in Germany – 1886/08/18:6c
FRIEBEL, Karl, un. mechanic, NYC-M – 1894/10/24:4a, =25:1g
FRIECKE % Kues
FRIED, Ferdinand, un. typesetter, NYC-M – 1904/06/20:4a
FRIED, Johann's child, 14, NYC-M – 1891/04/14:4d
FRIED, Joseph, theater machinist, NYC-M – 1890/01/04:1f
FRIEDBERG, Irving, 26, mobster, a.k.a. "Young Jack Zelig," NYC-B - 1914/03/15:7e, 18:3c

FRIEDBERG, Otto, NYC? – 1885/07/14:3b
FRIEDBERG, Samuel, 54, NYC-M – 1919/11/25:6a
FRIEDBERGER, Johann, 60, laundry washer, NYC-M – 1886/01/13:3a
FRIEDEL, August, 75, farm laborer, Hoboken?, – 1898/09/11:1e
FRIEDEL, Dorothea, b. Hunzer, 70, NYC-B – 1882/03/04:3b
FRIEDEL, John, un. carp., NYC-M – 1899/02/12:5a
FRIEDEL, Julius, un. brewer,NYC-M - 1915/02/25:6a,fam. 28:7f
FRIEDEL, Leo, 61, NYC-B – 1904/09/11:5a
FRIEDEL, Mary, 41, & William, 2, NYC-B – 1911/01/25:1d
FRIEDEL, Maurice, 42, Belleville, NJ – 1909/09/01:2c
FRIEDEN, Hulda, 20, dress maker, NYC-B – 1904/06/20:3c
FRIEDENBERG, Edward, 55, butcher-shop, NYC-M – 1891/12/15:2f
FRIEDENCAMP, Stoll, 21, Branchville, NJ – 1880/05/18:1g
FRIEDENHEIT, Estelle, 34, NYC-M - 1913/10/22:1a
FRIEDERICH, John, Dr., 52, ed. Amerikanische Schweizer-Zeitung,
 *Buren/Bern, NYC-B – 1900/03/08:2h, 4a
FRIEDERICHS, Charles, brewer, NYC-M – 1898/05/23:4a
FRIEDHOEFNER, Antoinette, 64, NYC-M – 1893/11/22:4a
FRIEDHOF, Anna, 18, servant, fr Hungary, NYC-M – 1907/08/05:1d, 6:2d
FRIEDHOF, Louise, NYC-B – 1907/02/17:7b
FRIEDL, Franziska, 15, NYC-M – 1892/02/11:4a, 12:4a, fam. 15:4a
FRIEDLAENDER, Benedikt, Dr., German liberal writer – 1908/07/02:4d
FRIEDLAENDER, Isaac, 54, grain wholesaler, * Oldenburg/Gy, USA
 1820s, ex-NYC, + San Francisco - 1878/07/23:1f
FRIEDLAND, Susie, 28, NYC-B – 1908/07/18:3a
FRIEDMAN, Ella, 32, NYC-B – 1909/05/28:1e
FRIEDMAN, Helene, 22, NYC-B – 1912/03/07:3a
FRIEDMAN, Isaac, 30, NYC-M - 1894/01/29:4c
FRIEDMAN, Max, 38, Highland Park, NJ - 1913/06/04:6c
FRIEDMAN, Rose, 18, @1911 Triangle Shirtwaist Fire, NYC-M –
 1911/03/28:1b
FRIEDMANN, Abraham, NYC-M – 1893/03/27:4e
FRIEDMANN, Christian, bakery owner, NYC-B?,will – 1903/05/03:5e
FRIEDMANN, Hydman, 48, car dealer, Paterson, NJ – 1911/01/16:1c
FRIEDMANN, John, collarmaker, NYC-B – 1901/03/26:4a
FRIEDMANN, John, NYC-M – 1892/07/07:4a
FRIEDMANN, Maria, b. Dierott, 24, NYC-M – 1889/11/08:4a
FRIEDMANN, Max, 18, NYC-M – 1885/12/23:1b, 24:1e, 25:1e
FRIEDMANN, Ralph, exec. Auburn, NY – 1912/06/19:1e
FRIEDMANN, Rebecca, 19, NYC-M – 1906/12/11:2d
FRIEDMANN, Robert, 45, civil engineer, * Gy, NYC-M - 1914/03/28:1d
FRIEDMANN, Rudolf, collector, NYC-M – 1888/11/10:2f

FRIEDMANN, Samuel, salesman fr Hannibal, MO, + NYC-M – 1881/05/24:1f
FRIEDMANN, Theodor, guard, NYC-M – 1892/07/30:1e
FRIEDMANN, Xavier, 38, NYC-M – 1892/10/07:4a
FRIEDRICH, Bertha, 68, NYC-B – 1898/12/18:5e
FRIEDRICH, Emil, baker, NYC-Q – 1913/02/05:3a
FRIEDRICH, Emil, merchant marine captain, NYC-B – 1911/10/27:1f
FRIEDRICH, Emmerich, NYC-M – 1893/04/15:4a
FRIEDRICH, Franz, 48, un. carp., NYC-M – 1898/09/04:5a
FRIEDRICH, Franz, language teacher, NYC-M – 1893/03/17:4f
FRIEDRICH, Georg, pianomaker, NYC-M - 1879/12/09:3a
FRIEDRICH, Hilda, child, NYC-M - 1895/04/30:4a
FRIEDRICH, John, un. brewer, NYC-B – 1905/11/18:4a
FRIEDRICH, Karl, 74, NYC-M – 1893/03/28:4a
FRIEDRICH, Ludwig, 75, un. carp., NYC-M - 1916/08/13:6a, fam. 17:6a
FRIEDRICH, Paul, SPD Breslau/Gy - 1913/07/06:3b
FRIEDRICH, Peter, 55, un. carp.,NYC-M - 1913/07/25:2g, 26:6a
FRIEDRICHS % Kresse
FRIEDRICHS, Ernst H., artist supplies, NYC-M - 1894/08/03:2d
FRIEDRICHS, Meta, 17, fr Chemnitz/Saxony, + on way to NYC on SS Markomannia - 1895/05/14:1d
FRIEDRICHSEN, August, NYC – 1913/02/05:6a
FRIEDRICHSEN, Charles, 27, SP?, NYC-M – 1907/06/21:6a
FRIEDSAM, John, machinist, NYC – 1912/12/17:6a
FRIELING, Carl, 61, NYC-M – 1901/04/18:4a
FRIELING, Otto, NYC-M – 1896/07/27:4a
FRIENDT, Louis, NYC-M – 1881/02/24:3b
FRIER, Julie, NYC-M – 1891/07/15:4a
FRIES % Schaefer
FRIES, G., NYC-B – 1904/10/01:4a
FRIES, John, 48, un. engineer, NYC-M - 1920/10/30:8a, 31:12a
FRIES, John, NYC-Bx – 1910/10/03:6a
FRIES, Pauline, infant, NYC – 1888/07/24:4g
FRIESE, Charles, 30, brewery worker, NYC-M – 1889/09/17:4e
FRIESE, Emil's wife, NYC-M – 1902/02/10:4a
FRIESE, John, 65, bookkeeper, NYC-M – 1878/08/07:1d
FRIESE, Karl, 56, German actor, played USA 1886-90, + Dresden, Gy – 1912/05/12:1e
FRIESLEBEN, Bertha, 28, NYC-M – 1911/07/11:2e
FRIETSCHE, Emil, Newark, NJ – 1902/12/23:3c
FRIEWALD, Ferdinand, 46, laborer, NYC-M – 1892/08/21:1h
FRIKE, Otto, 41, SP, NYC-Q – 1914/01/20:6a, 21:6a

FRINGEL, Karl, Union Hill, NJ – 1908/06/14:7c
FRISCH, Caroline, 48, Newark, NJ – 1908/10/28:1f
FRISCH, Nicolaus, 27, un. painter, NYC-B - 1913/05/19:6a
FRISCHE, Henry, NYC-M – 1891/03/23:4a
FRISCHER, Marie Anna - 1894/07/22:5a
FRISKE, Oscar, 13, NYC-M – 1899/05/28:1c
FRITSCH, Joseph, NYC-Q – 1905/10/19:4a
FRITSCHE, Charles, SP, NYC-Q - 1918/02/27:6a
FRITSCHE, Heinrich, 48, NYC-M - 1913/07/28:6a, 29:6a
FRITSCHE, Karl Emil, 40, un. printer, NYC-M - 1895/05/17:4a, 18:4a, 21:4a
FRITSCHE, Marie, b. Gaebelmann, 48, NYC-M - 1918/12/07:6a
FRITSCHLER, Margaret,65, & George, 30, clerk, NYC-B - 1916/12/19:2d
FRITZ % Rieger
FRITZ, (Mr.), 60, NYC-B – 1885/05/30:3c
FRITZ, Alma, 47, NYC-M, +@ Genl Slocum – 1904/06/17:3b
FRITZ, Anna, geb. Borkes?, 44, NYC-B – 1892/07/01:4a
FRITZ, August, NYC-M - 1916/09/29:6a
FRITZ, Catharina, 35, NYC-M - 1878/06/05:3b
FRITZ, Frederick, mechanic, NYC – 1912/04/20:3d
FRITZ, Friedrich, 37, brewery worker, NYC-M – 1893/03/12:1e
FRITZ, Heinrich, 64, SLP, carpenter, * Eschenheim/Frankfurt, NYC-M - 1879/11/28:4c
FRITZ, Joseph, NYC-M – 1907/08/23:6a
FRITZ, Julius, 42, memb. Schwaeb. SB, NYC-Q - 1920/01/24:8a
FRITZ, Katharina, NYC-M – 1912/06/05:6a
FRITZ, Katherina, 44, Jersey City, NJ – 1913/03/08:6a
FRITZ, Lena, servant, Montclair, NJ – 1882/01/22:5c
FRITZ, Lina, b. Bierbach, NYC-M - 1894/05/03:4a
FRITZ, Wilhelmina, b. Kleppert, 38, NYC-Bx – 1912/11/19:6a
FRITZE % Wachsmuth
FRITZE, G., NYC-M – 1892/04/13:4a
FRITZINGER, Peter, 44, NYC-M – 1912/02/04:7f
FRITZSCHE, Friedrich W., * Leipzig/Gy, un. cigarmaker, MdR 1878-1881 for SPD, USA 1881, SLP, Philadelphia, PA 50th anniversary in labor movement – 1896/12/23:1c, + 79 yrs old – 1905/02/07:1c-d, 2b, =14:1f-g
FRODERMANN, Hermann, un. cigarmker, SLP?, NYC-M – 1890/04/10:4a
FROEBEL, Friedrich, German Educator, 100th anniv. – 1882/03/01:2b-c, Coll. in NYC for widow 19 Mr:7d, NYC fest 16 Apr:7e, 21:2a-b, in Brooklyn & St Louis etc 29 Apr:1f, 30:5a-c, 1 May:1d-g, 2d, notes 30:2a-b, 31:4d. Mem. NYC-B 23 Ap 1885:2g-3a. 50th anniv. + 13 Jy 1902:6f-g
FROEHLEIN, Charles, 16, worker, NYC-SI – 1899/02/26:1h

FROTSCHER, Otto Ludwig, 64, musician?, NYC-M – 1910/11/16:6a, fam. 22:6a
FRUECHTNICHT, Bernhard, 53, un. carp., NYC-M – 1899/10/15:5b
FRUECKER, George, baker, NYC-M – 1905/01/01:5f, 2:1e (s.a. Kloppmann, Clara)
FRUEH % Schrank
FRUEH, Stephan, 50, butcher, NYC-M - 1914/10/02:6c
FRUEHLING, Frederick, carp., NYC-B – 1905/05/30:3c
FRUEHLING, Henry, 66, apple-dealer & inventor, * Hamburg/Gy, NYC-M - 1878/09/08:5d, 09:4a
FRYATT, Charles, British merchant navy capt,exec. by Germany for ramming U-boat after surrendering - 1916/07/29:1b,30:11e, 2 Aug.:1b
FUCHAK, Andrew, 42, steel worker, Newark, NJ - 1913/07/30:3e
FUCHS % Ackermann, % Beuscher, % Boecker, % Breusch, % Saevecke
FUCHS, Albert, un. carp., NYC-B – 1904/04/11:4a, 12:4a
FUCHS, Anna Marie, b. Fischer, 25, SLP, USA 1864?, tailor, NYC-B - 1879/06/20:3a, 4d
FUCHS, Armin, banker, New Brunswick, NJ - 1914/11/24:2c
FUCHS, Augusta, b. Frank, 26,husband un. goldworker & Marschner MC, NYC-M - 1878/03/22:3b
FUCHS, Bernhard, 68, fr Schrollbach/Landstuhl/Gy, NYC-Q – 1891/03/05:4a, mem. 4 Mr 1892:4a, 12 May:4e
FUCHS, Charles, 35, cook, NYC-M – 1892/05/11:4e
FUCHS, Charles, 60, Irvington, NJ – 1913/02/21:2f
FUCHS, Engelbertha, NYC-Bx - 1914/07/16:6a
FUCHS, George, 56, NYC-M – 1891/03/30:4a
FUCHS, George, 67, NYC-B – 1891/04/02:4a
FUCHS, Henry, NYC-M - 1915/08/08:11a
FUCHS, Herman, un. carp., Elizabethport, NJ – 1901/05/29:4a
FUCHS, Jacob, 29, NYC-M - 1894/01/10:4a
FUCHS, Jacob, 56, baker, Marion, NJ - 1891/01/30:4e
FUCHS, John G., + 10 May, notes – 1892/07/09:2e, 12:3a
FUCHS, John, 33, NYC-B – 1905/05/24:4a, fam. 27:4b
FUCHS, John, 51, smith, Bayonne, NJ - 1905/02/15:3c
FUCHS, Josef, scissor sharpener, Paterson, NJ - 1879/10/30:1g
FUCHS, Maria b. Neurath, 45, NYC-B – 1892/07/02:4a
FUCHS, Michael, 65, NYC-B - 1918/06/08:6a
FUCHS, Michael's wife, NYC?, fam. – 1885/04/16:3c
FUCHS, Otto, NYC-B – 1892/07/30:1g
FUCHS, Otto, SP, NYC-B – 1911/08/27:7c, 28:6a
FUCHS, Sophia, NYC-B – 1892/06/15:4a
FUCHS, Theresia, 71, NYC-M – 1890/01/13:4a

FROEHLICH % Schwarzer
FROEHLICH, Adam, 35, grocer, NYC-SI – 1893/08/03:1g
FROEHLICH, Alois, un. carp., NYC-M - 1915/10/25:6a
FROEHLICH, Andreas, 62, * Klein-Odernheim/Rheinpfalz, NYC-M - 1878/06/11:3b, poem 23:8b
FROEHLICH, August, NYC-M – 1904/03/02:4a
FROEHLICH, Carl August, 59, NYC-M - 1915/04/30:6a, 1 May:11a
FROEHLICH, Eva Elizabeth, b. Weicker, 54, NYC-B – 1906/03/04:5b
FROEHLICH, Fannie, b. Hoefling, 28, NYC-B – 1905/12/08:1f
FROEHLICH, Georg, 56, un. carp., NYC-M – 1885/10/21:3a
FROEHLICH, John, un. carp., NYC-M – 1891/04/12:5a
FROEHLICH, John, who + 26 Fb in Wards' Island (see also Farrish & Roth), NYC-M – 1887/07/06:1g
FROEHLICH, Loeb, NYC-M - 1894/01/11:4a
FROEHLICH, Louis,62, un. cigarmakers, * Rastatt/Baden, USA 1850, NYC-B - 1895/05/26:5d
FROEHLICH, Moses, 36, manufacturer, NYC-M – 1885/09/11:4a
FROEHNER, Catherine, 35, and Esther, 19, NYC-B - 1920/06/20:1d, 21:2b
FROELICH, Lina, & Carl, 23, NYC-M, + @Genl Slocum – 1904/06/17:3b
FROEMMCHEN, Anna, b. Baumeister, 65, Union Hill, NJ – 1890/03/18:4a
FROENDLE, Gustav, NYC-M – 1901/12/12:4a
FROH, Karl, 69, Schenectady, NY, + NYC – 1910/10/14:3b
FROHUE, Charles, 76, NYC-B – 1904/05/14:3c
FROHWEIN, Gertrud, 16, Emma, 13, Tillie, 8, & cousin Anna Siebeneichen, NYC-M – 1898/08/05:1g, 6:4c
FROMHOLTZ, Henry, engineer, Hoboken, NJ – 1902/06/21:1g
FROMKINA, Mrs, Russian revol., exec. Moscow – 1907/07/26:2e
FROMM, Andrew, 28, printer, NYC-B - 1914/10/22:2f
FROMM, Charles, ex-innkeep, Union Hill, NJ – 1907/01/19:3c-d
FROMM, Jul., NYC-Q – 1909/08/02:6a
FROMME % Kolkschneider
FROMMEL, Oscar, 58, potato dealer & alderman, Hoboken, NJ - 1917/05/25:2g
FROMMLET, Anna, 39, NYC-B – 1900/04/05:4a, =9:2h, fam. 11:4a
FRONKE % Degenhardt
FRONT, Otto, 41, painter, NYC-M - 1895/06/22: 1g
FROSCH, John M., 32, Little Falls, NY – 1905/08/31:4a
FROSS, Otto, shoemaker, NYC-M - 1894/05/02:4d
FROST % Handke
FROST, Charles C., shoemaker & botanist, NYC – 1880/03/29:2c
FROST, Jeremiah C., 72, NYC-M – 1919/04/01:6a

FUCHS, William, 38, un. tailor, SLP, NYC-B – 1885/02/21:3c, 4b
FUECHSEL, Leopold, Greenville, NJ - 1920/05/08:6a,fam. 11:6a
FUEGEN, A., NYC-B - 1920/08/31:6a
FUEGER, Johannes, 55, NYC-M – 1908/01/27:6a
FUELLING, Ludwig, NYC-M – 1901/06/28:4a, 29:4a
FUERDERER, H., NYC-B – 1911/06/21:6a
FUERNKAS, George, 75, SP, NYC-M - 1919/02/26:6a, 27:6a, =4 Mr:3d
FUERST, Ernst, 40, riding instructor, fr Berlin/Gy, ?Jersey City, NJ, ?NYC - 1913/12/06:2c
FUERST, Jacob, 25, SLP?, NYC-M – 1897/01/31:5a
FUERST, Jg., un. baker, NYC-M - 1919/05/22:6a
FUERST, Johann, 57, popular theater director in Vienna, 1882/11/12:6f
FUERST, Robert, innkeep close to SP Vienna – 1910/03/06:3c
FUERST, Walter, 42, SP, NYC-Bx - 1920/02/14:6a, fam. 19:6a
FUESS, Gottfried, NYC-M – 1903/12/02:4a
FUGMANN, Conrad, NYC-B – 1896/08/12:1a
FUHL, Emil, & daughter Hattie, 6, NYC-Bx – 1906/03/13:1h
FUHLENDORF, Nicolaus, 68, NYC-M - 1916/11/04:6a
FUHLENDORFF, Mathilde, 61, NYC – 1912/10/30:6a
FUHRER % Burger
FUHRMANN, Charles, 80, NYC-Q - 1918/05/12:7a
FUHRMANN, Emilie, b. Schmidt, NYC-Q – 1888/09/08:3b
FUHRMANN, Heinrich, 38, SPD org., Waldenburg/Silesia - 1915/07/18:3c
FUHRMANN, Henry, NYC-Q - 1919/01/04:6a
FUHRMANN, John, 58, engineer, NYC-B – 1906/05/02:4b
FUHRMANN, L.'s wife, NYC-M – 1887/06/28:3c
FUHST % Schwarz
FUHST, Carl, 68, NYC-M – 1912/03/03:7b
FULD, Julius, 5, NYC-M – 1891/03/15:5b
FULLER, Georg W., 45, printer, NYC-B – 1912/10/25:3b
FULLER, Melville W., 77, US Supr Ct Just, obit crit for anti-labor – 1910/07/05:1f, 4a
FULLER, Otto, 50, un. waiter,*Berlin/Gy, NYC-B – 1896/06/15:2e
FULLING, George, innkeep, NYC-B - 1917/02/21:5d
FULLING, Henry, NYC-M – 1912/07/20:6a
FUNDA, William, un. carriagemkr, Bellmore, LI - 1914/10/28:6a
FUNK, Emilie, secy Liberty Frauenchor, 35th birthday in Jersey City, NJ – 1911/02/10:5f
FUNK, Henry, 49, un. carp., NYC-M – 1903/11/21:4a
FUNK, John, NYC-M – 1910/12/15:6a
FUNK, Joseph, machinist, NYC – 1912/12/02:6a
FUNK, Joseph, NYC-M - 1918/11/09:6a

FUNK, Margaretha, NYC-B - 1917/02/24:6a, fam. 4 Mr:7a
FUNK, Michael, 12, NYC-M, +@ Genl Slocum – 1904/06/17:3b
FUNK, Otto, famous library-thief fr Chicago, + Boston, MA – 1885/10/31:1f
FUNK, Wanda, NYC-M – 1906/10/31:6a, 1 Nov:6a
FUNKE, Albert H., pres. Autolyte Co., NYC-Flushing – 1911/02/18:3a-b
FUNKE, Franz, cigarmaker, NYC-M – 1896/04/15:1g
FUNKE, Mathilde, b. Diebeson, NYC-M – 1899/05/16:4a
FUNKE, Sophie, 67, NYC-M - 1915/12/15:6a
FUNSCH, William A., driver, NYC-B – 1905/09/20:1g
FURCH, John, 40, NYC-M – 1904/10/18:4a
FURISCH, Rebecca, 17, @1911 Triangle Shirtwaist Fire, NYC-M – 1911/03/27:1d
FURLONG, Frank, 20, exec. Ossining, NY – 1907/03/04:2c, 5:2b
FURMAN, Charles, Dr., 50, SP, *NYC, NYC-B - 1913/08/15:1d,4c, #16:2c, 17:11c, =18:2c
FURMAN, Lee, 22, Trenton, NJ, exec. Lancaster, PA – 1905/06/30:3g
FURNKAS, Marie, 60, NYC-M? - 1920/06/06:2c
FURTH, Jacob, 53, salesman, NYC, + Selma, AL – 1900/03/02:1e
FUSS, Bernhard, sailor, 21, NYC-B – 1885/09/23:4e
FUSSHOELLER, Gertrud, b. Hollaender, 67, Union Hill, NJ - 1920/04/26:4a
FUSSINGER, Eva, 43, NYC-M - 1916/03/25:6a
FUSSINGER, Victor, 41, SP?, NYC-M - 1915/11/11:6a
FUST % Obmer,
FUXA, Stephan, 60, SP Buffalo, *Moravia, Buffalo, NY – 1901/12/07:3b
GAA, Christine, NYC-M – 1892/06/23:4a
GAA, Ida, 39, SP, NYC-M - 1915/09/12:7a, 11d, 13:6a, fam. 16:6a, =17:2e
GAAB, Friedrich, 3, & Wilhelm, 5, NYC-M – 1887/06/21:3c
GAAL, Josef, NYC-Q - 1917/01/31:6a
GABAL, or Sodak, Michael, fr Hungary, to be exec. In Pittsburgh – 1891/04/09:1e, notes 22 Jy:2a, great protest in NYC 2 Aug:1h
GABEL, John, 34, NYC-B – 1911/12/23:2a
GABELMANN, Jacob, brewery labor organizer, St Louis, MO – 1904/01/19:4c
GABLER, August, 48, baker, Elizabeth, NJ - 1896/03/29:1f
GABLER, Otto, 29, NYC-M – 1890/03/09:5c
GABOR, Charles A., machinist, NYC-Bx - 1913/06/26:6a
GABRIEL, Albert, ~70, SP Newark, NJ, goldsmith, *Ruegen/Gy – 1910/09/24:1d, 25:7a, c, =26:2e, 4c

GABRINOVICS, Nedeljo, one of the Sarajevo murderers, + Theresienstadt jail, - 1916/01/26:2c
GABSCH, Ernst, 75, NYC-B - 1918/06/05:6a
GACHET, Joseph, butcher, Swiss, NYC-M – 1902/02/27:4c
GACKENHEIMER, Anna Julie, NYC-B – 1903/06/08:4a
GACKENHEIMER, Louis, 35, NYC-Q – 1892/09/20:4a
GADE, Grace, 16, NYC-M, + @ Genl Slocum – 1904/06/17:3b
GADE, Henry, 47, NYC-M – 1898/07/29:4a
GADSMAN, Gracie, 61, NYC-M, +@ Genl Slocum – 1904/06/18:3c
GAEBEL, Carl, 76, NYC-M - 1895/03/01:4a
GAEBEL, Dorothea, b. Brickner, NYC-M – 1890/10/30:4a
GAEBELMANN % Fritz
GAEBLER, Charles, NYC-M – 1906/10/12:6a
GAEBLER, Gottlieb Heinrich, 56, un. cigar maker, NYC-M – 1896/12/30:4a
GAEBLER, Richard, barber, NYC-M – 1892/03/18:1f
GAEBLER, Robert, 47, NYC-M - 1916/07/05:6a, 6:3e, 6a, fam. 7:6a
GAEDKE, Frederick, 29, un. baker, SLP, NYC-M – 1891/03/18:4a, =19:1h
GAEHRINGER, Mrs, + 1918, mem. - 1919/05/11:12a
GAENSER, August, NYC-M – 1913/03/03:6a
GAENSER, Rosina, NYC-M - 1919/04/20:2g
GAENTZLER, Friedrich, 34, shoemaker, * 2 Aug. 1844 Hochheim/Hessen, NYC-M - 1878/07/04:4b
GAERTNER, Adam, NYC-M – 1893/11/22:4a
GAERTNER, Albert, 60, cigar manuf. & SPD alderman, Nowaves/Berlin/Gy – 1908/05/03:3d
GAERTNER, Auguste, NYC-M - 1894/01/21:5d
GAERTNER, Emilie, b. Schluckebier, 39, NYC-M – 1908/09/04:6a
GAERTNER, Heinrich, NYC-M – 1900/03/28:4a, 29:4a
GAERTNER, Katherine, b. Ludwig, NYC-B – 1888/11/01:3a
GAERTNER, Martin, 50, brother in Hamburg?, NYC-B – 1883/05/16:3a
GAERTNER, Oskar, 45, un. cigar maker, NYC-M – 1904/12/23:4a, 24:4a
GAERTNER, Phillipine, b. Oberlies, 32, Union Hill, NJ – 1900/02/14:4a
GAERTNER, Rose, NYC-M – 1889/12/12:4a
GAESS, Valentine, 63, un. wood carver & secy Union Hill Arbeiter MC, West Hoboken, NJ - 1920/04/04:12a, 9:6a
GAETJEN, Elise, b. Kaese, 34, NYC-B – 1887/04/29:3d
GAETJEN, Hermann, un. cigarmaker, NYC-M - 1879/04/20:8a
GAETJEN, Hermann's widow, NYC-M - 1879/05/04:5g
GAGE, Conrad, 50, un. cook, NYC-M – 1906/03/19:4a
GAGELMANN, Anna, b. Kromer, 36, NYC-M - 1914/04/14:6a

GAGERN, Heinrich F. W. von, 81, German '48er, + Darmstadt – 1880/05/27:1a
GAGIESCH, John, 17, NYC-SI - 1918/01/25:2d
GAHN, Bertha, 25, fr Bohemia, NYC-M – 1897/11/06:1d
GAHR, Lewis, 51, Newark, NJ – 1913/07/29:2e
GAIFFERT, Christian, NYC-M - 1914/06/25:6a
GAILER, Ferdinand, 50, NYC-B - 1920/06/22:6a
GAILER, Hermann, un. brewer, NYC-M – 1887/06/10:3c
GAINES, Caleb, Negro, lynched Glasgow, KY – 1898/06/17:3f
GAISEN, Hermann, 42, cigarmaker, NYC-M - 1879/04/19:1g
GAISER, Christian, 43, un. butcher, NYC-B – 1912/05/31:6a, 1 June:6a; mem. 1913/05/28:6a, 1914/05/29:6a, 1916/05/29:6a, 1917/05/29:6a, 1918/05/29:6a, 1920/05/29:6a
GAITHERS, Philipp, Negro, lynched Rincon, GA - 1920/06/22:1c
GAJEWSKI % Lang
GALEG, Stephan, 32, fr Hungary, USA 6/1881, NYC-M – 1882/03/01:1e
GALINER, Thomas, 47, NYC-M – 1880/09/08:4d
GALL, Charles, 57, SP, * Pennsylvania, grew up Wuerttemberg/Gy, NYC-Bx - 1914/02/28:3e, 1 Mr:7c, =2:6a
GALL, Edwin B., 23, son of late SP member Charles Gall, NYC-M - 1914/11/07:2a,6a
GALL, Emil, 50, cloth importer, fr France, NYC-M - 1878/03/22:4e
GALL, Flora, 68, NYC-M – 1893/12/31:5c
GALL, Louise, 91, Hoboken, NJ - 1913/11/18:3d
GALL, Vincenta, NYC-Bx – 1906/08/23:6a
GALL, Wilhelmine, NYC-Q - 1916/11/13:6a
GALLAGHER, James J., who tried to kill NYC mayor Gaynor, + Trenton, NJ – 1913/02/04:3f
GALLAGHER, Patrick, NYPD - 1913/06/01:1f
GALLAGHER, Thomas J., 46, NYPD, hero who saved lives, NYC-M – 1907/02/09:3c
GALLAGHER, Veronica, & children Walter, Agnes, NYC-M, + @ Genl Slocum – 1904/06/17:3b
GALLAND, Georg, 43, machinist, NYC-M – 1880/04/28:1f
GALLASCH, Gustav, 38, * Austria, USA 1871, musician & music teacher, NYC-M – 1883/05/09:1d
GALLE, Johann Gottfried, 98, German astronomer, 1910/07/12:2g
GALLEI, Magdalene, NYC-M – 1892/10/01:4a
GALLIENI, Joseph, French war min. - 1916/05/28:1e, 1 June:1f
GALLIFET, Marquis de, French general, repressed 1871 Commune – 1909/07/10:4b-c, 22:4d, 24:4d-e 27:4e
GALM, Franz, un. carp., NYC-M – 1909/03/15:6a

GALMELLOFT, Kate, 32, servant, NYC-M – 1893/10/21:1h
GALZINSKI, Anna, Cresskill, NJ – 1896/04/13:1c
GAMBARDO, Giuseppe, NYC, exec. Ossining, NY – 1910/07/22:5e, 25:2a, done 26:1b
GAMBER, Friedrich, 38, NYC-M - 1879/08/09:3a, = 11:1e
GAMBETTA, Leon, French polit., + Paris, 1883/01/02:1a-b, 2a, 3:1a-b, 5b, 6:1a, 7:1a, & NYC French 8:1d, notes 18:2a
GAMBLE, Henry C., un. typsetter & labor activist, NYC-M, + Chicago, IL – 1893/06/13:1h
GANDER, John, 39?, un. furnit. maker, NYC-M – 1891/11/01:5a
GANGEL, Albert, 15, NYC-Bx - 1913/12/06:6a
GANGHOFER, Ludwig, German writer, - 1920/08/23:4d
GANGOWSKI, Rudolph, NYC – 1901/11/17:1g
GANSS, Jacob, 54, SLP, NYC-B – 1900/04/23:4a, 24:4a, 25:4a, =26:2h, 27:3a
GANTER, Charlie, NYC-M - 1920/01/23:8a
GANTZER, Carl, NYC-M – 1886/10/22:3b
GANZER, Edward, NYC-B – 1906/06/22:1g
GAPON, Pope, exec. by Revolutionaries in Ozersk/Russia – 1906/04/24:1f, 16 June:2c, notes – 1909/03/26:4d
GARDENEIER, Edward, 47, songwriter, NYC-B – 1909/02/18:3b
GARDENER, Simon, un. baker, NYC-M - 1918/11/11:3a
GARDES, Henry A., innkeep, NYC-Glendale - 1913/05/08:2a
GARFALO, Joseph, exec. Ossining, NY – 1913/02/11:1f
GARFIELD, James A., US pres., shot by Charles Guiteau, 1881/07/03:1a-e, 4a-b, 4:1a-e, 5:1a-e, 2a-b, 6:1a-c, 3c, 7:1a-b, 2a-b, 8:1a-b, 2f, better 9:1c-d, 10:5b-c, 11:1d-e, 12:1c, 13:1e, 14:1e, 15:1c, 16:1c, 19:1c, 20:1c, 22:1c-d, 23:1d, fever 24:5c-d, operated 25:1a-b, crit. some European media 24:4a, 25:2f-3a, health worsens 26:1c-d, 27:1c,2a 28:1d, 29:1c, 30:1b, 1 Aug:1c, struggling 6:1d, operated again 9 Aug:1c, 11:1c, 13:1b, 15:1c, 16:1c, 17:1c-d, 2a, 18:1c-d, 19:1c, 20:1b, 22:1d, 23:1a, 24:1c, 25:1d, agony 26 Aug:1c, 27:1c-d, 28:5c, 29:1a-b, 2e, 30:1d, 31:1b, 2c, 2 Sept:1d, 4:5b, 5:1d, 6:1c, 7:1b, 9:1e, 2c, 10:1b, worsens again 12:1c, 13:1e, 15:1b, 16:1d, 17:1d, 18:5e, 19:1b, + 20:1a-d, 3e, 21:1a-g, decent man for a capitalist :2a-b, 4c, 22:1a-f, 2a-b, 23:1a-c, 24:1a-b, 25:5c-d, 26:1a-b, 2a-b, 27:1a-e, 2a-c, 28:1a-b,e, natl mourning 2 Oct:4a-b, 3:4f, Brooklyn G-A soc 16 Oct:7d-e.
GARGOSCH, Emil, NYC-Bx – 1911/11/19:7c
GARIBALDI, Giuseppe, Italian revol., – 1882/06/03:1a, 5:1a, 6:1b, 11:4b, 8a, meeting at NYC Turnhalle 12:4f, 13:1g, French reactions 19:2e-f, obit by Emil Frischauer 25:2b-d, notes 2 Jy:4f, 17 Sept:3d-e. NYC

statue inaug. 1888/06/05:1e. 100th anniv. in NYC – 190706/08:4d, 4
  Jy:4a-b, d-e, 5:1f, 7:6d, 14:19d-e
GARIBALDI, Monotti, 58, son of the revolutionary, + Rome/Italy –
  1903/08/23:1b
GARIBALDI, Theresa, daughter of the revol. – 1903/01/28:2e-g
GARLICK, Esther, NYC-B, + Philadelphia – 1887/04/26:2f
GARLING, Frederick, un. carp., NYC-Bx – 1907/03/17:7c
GARNATZ, Frederick, un. ironworker, SDP, NYC-M – 1903/04/
GARNER, Friedrich, 64, innkeep, USA 1852, NYC-M – 1882/04/08:1e
GARRABRANDT, NYC, note 1900/05/27:5b, trial 2 Oct:3c, 3:3b, 4:1h,
  5:1b, 30 yrs 13:2g
GARRETT, Clarence, 18, Negro, lynched Shelbyville, KY – 1901/10/03:4c
GARRISON, Francis Jackson, 68, son of abol. William Lloyd Garrison, +
  Newtonville, MA - 1916/12/12:2e
GARRY, Elsa, b. Holzhauer, wd Higgins, 32, NYC-Bx – 1909/08/20:6a
GARTELMANN % Bohne
GARTEN, Auguste, 17, NYC-M – 1888/05/19:3a
GARTEN, Katherine, b. Ditton, NYC-M – 1886/11/12:3b
GARTHAUSEN, Friedrich, SLP, USA 1881 fr Altona/Gy, un. basketmaker,
  NYC-M – 1897/04/30:4a, 1 May:1e, 4a, 2:5c, =3:1g, fam. 7:4a
GARY, Joseph, Haymarket judge, scathing obit. – 1906/11/02:1b, 6:4a-b
GARZKE, Anna, NYC-M - 1914/03/26:6a
GASCHKE, Herman, NYC-M - 1916/12/21:6a
GASFELD, Henriette, NYC-M – 1891/04/07:4a
GASLER, Alwine, b. Brandes, NYC-M – 1907/08/21:6a
GASNER, Mrs, Plainfield, NJ – 1902/12/20:2g
GASOLD, Jacob, 60, NYC-B – 1909/06/01:3a-b
GASS, Alwine, 32, NYC-M – 1902/06/07:4a
GASSER % Dessart
GASSER, Conrad, maker of tailor supplies, fr Russia, NYC-M –
  1909/05/17:1f
GASSERT, Charlotte, 15, Harrison, NJ – 1902/03/08:4b
GASSMANN, Michael, Frank, 11, Minnie, 5, NYC-M, +@Genl Slocum –
  1904/06/17:3b, 21:1f, 22:1d
GASSNER, Gosswein, un. carp., NYC-M – 1903/10/18:5a
GASSNER, Leopold, 46, fur dealer, NYC-B - 1918/07/28:1e
GASSRA, John, Czech, cigarmaker, NYC-M - 1879/05/07:1f, 29:4a
GASTEL, Ludwig, 25, NYC-M – 1897/07/07:4a
GASTEL, Mary, child, NYC-M - 1896/01/12:4a
GASTON, Jim, Negro, lynched near Kosciusko, MS – 1902/07/21:1b
GATES, Charles G., 37, NYC millionaire, crit. obit - 1913/11/04:4b-c
GATTELBERG, Anton, NYC-M – 1880/01/11:8a

GATTINGER, Arthur, 62, at US Customs, NYC-M - 1916/01/06:1b
GATZEN, Rudolph, + 17 Apr.,wife 21 May, NYC-? -1879/06/18:4c
GATZENMEIER, William, 34, bartender, NYC-M – 1900/01/17:4a
GATZWILLER, John, 49, NYC-B – 1889/03/08:4a
GAU, Frank H., 68, *Duesseldorf/Gy, USA 1855, NYC-M – 1893/06/27:1g
GAUDIG, G., SPD Leipzig/Gy – 1901/12/17:2c
GAUGGEL, Inocenz, NYC-M – 1897/06/26:4c
GAUL, L., NYC-B – 1913/02/22:6a
GAULAND, Anton, un. baker, NYC-M - 1918/11/15:6a
GAULRAPP, John, un. carp., NYC-M – 1907/06/07:6a
GAUPP, Henry A., 68, NYC-B – 1901/12/20:2g
GAURIEDER, Margarethe, NYC-Bx - 1914/11/10:6a, fam. 11:6a
GAUTIER, Katherina, b. Scherer, 50, NYC-B – 1891/06/28:5c
GAUTSCHI, Gottlieb, NYC-Bx – 1910/05/14:6a
GAUTUMIER, Louis, French soc. MP – 1896/12/10:2f
GAYNOR, John, Dr., nephew of NYC mayor, NYC-M – 1911/02/27:3d
GAYNOR, William Jay, NYC mayor - 1913/09/12:1g, 2a-b, posit. obit 4a-b, 13:1e,4a-b,15:1e,16:1f, 17:1f,2b, 19:1b, 20:1f, 21:1d, =23:1g, Vereinigte Saenger mem. concert 4 Oct:2a
GEBAUER, Sadie, 24, NYC-B – 1909/12/17:1c
GEBERT, Adolph, 43, SLP, un. cornice maker, NYC-M – 1896/12/12:4a, 13:16a, =15:3g, fam. 16:4a
GEBERT, Frederick, 77, NYC-B – 1905/04/08:4a
GEBHARDT, Charles, 35, policeman, Hoboken, NJ – 1898/07/27:1b, 28:1g, 5 Aug.:3c
GEBHARDT, Charles, un. carp., NYC-B – 1911/01/09:6a
GEBHARDT, Emil, 1, NYC-M – 1880/01/29:3a
GEBHARDT, Emil, 47, SPD Gera/Thueringen/Gy – 1908/09/13:3f
GEBHARDT, Emma, Mattamoran, NY or NJ – 1903/11/23:1g
GEBHARDT, Fr., NYC-M – 1911/07/10:6a
GEBHARDT, Frederick, pianomaker, NYC-Q, trial for killing 2nd wife Anna, b. Luther in 1909 – 1910/10/18:2c, 19:1e, 20:1g, 21:1e, etc, 22:1b, to be exec. 25:1f, exec. NYC 9 June 1911:6d, notes 13:3e-f
GEBHARDT, Georg, infant, NYC-B – 1880/08/10:3b
GEBHARDT, Gustav, NYC-B - 1915/11/26:6a
GEBHARDT, Heinrich, 45, furrier, NYC-M – 1893/05/16:1h, 18:2d-e,4a
GEBHARDT, John M., 51, Union Hill, NJ – 1903/07/19:5a
GEBHARDT, John, 45, cigar dealer, Closter, NJ – 1890/11/29:1h
GEBHARDT, John's wife, Union Hill, NJ - 1879/06/18:3a
GEBHARDT, Peter, NYC-B – 1906/06/09:4a
GEBHARDT, William, NYC-M – 1899/06/09:1g
GEBNEY, John, 65, NYC-M – 1883/01/12:1g

GEBRINGER, Martha, 42, NYC-M - 1918/05/13:6a
GECK, Andrew, 52, carp., NYC-B - 1917/05/29:3e
GECK, Karl, 81, SPD Offenburg/Baden - 1915/02/17:4d, =21:3a
GEDDES, Thomas, 23, NYC-B – 1901/11/11:2h
GEDELGE, Augusta, 37, NYC-M – 1881/04/13:1f
GEDICKE, Hermann, 42, NYC-M – 1891/03/09:4a
GEDNEY, George, accountant, & Emma, NYC-M - 1916/12/01:6a
GEERCKE, J. H., un. cigar maker, NYC-M – 1890/02/25:4a
GEESSMAN, Lena, NYC-M, + @Genl Slocum – 1904/06/18:3c
GEHLHARD, F., NYC-M - 1919/02/08:6a
GEHMER, Emma, 26, NYC-M – 1890/07/22:4a
GEHR, Hermann, 38, peddler, USA 1876, NYC-M – 1880/05/24:1e, 26:4a
GEHRIG, Christian, 28, shoe maker, NYC – 1886/06/02:1g
GEHRING, Charles, Jr, brewery owner fr Cleveland, OH, + NYC – 1888/05/30:1e
GEHRING, Ernst, 35, NYC-M – 1893/01/11:4a
GEHRKE, William, 48, un. baker, NYC-Bx - 1916/02/24:6a
GEHRTZ, John, un. carp., NYC-Bx – 1906/10/11:6a
GEHWEILER, Henry, waiter, +@1880 Turnhalle Fire, NYC-M – 1880/01/05:4a, 8:1g, 3a, 9:1e-f
GEIB, August, 35, SPD, MdR Hamburg 1874-76 - 1879/08/08:2a-b; 5th anniv. of + 22 Aug. 1884:2c-d; 25th anniv. 14 Aug. 1904:7f-g
GEIB, Katharina, b. Kilcher, NYC-M – 1889/09/01:4a
GEIB, Lessing J., 59, NYC-Q – 1908/08/01:3a
GEIB, Margarethe, & William, 9, +@1880 Turnhalle Fire, NYC-M – 1880/01/05:4a, 8:1g, 3a, 9:1e-f
GEIB, Peter, 38, innkeep, NYC-M – 1891/07/10:1g
GEIBEL, August, fr Greiz/Vogtland, NYC-B – 1893/04/19:4a
GEIBERT % Weiher
GEID, Henry, (Geib?), 28, un. carp., NYC-M – 1889/07/24:4a
GEID, Katherine, b. Mohr, 28, fr Ostheim/Hessen, NYC-M - 1878/06/22:3b
GEIDEL, see Jackson, William Henry 1911.
GEIER, H., Newark, NJ – 1906/11/30:6a
GEIER, Joseph, 43, SP, NYC-Bx – 1906/01/18:1h
GEIER, Michael, brewer or cooper, NYC-M – 1900/12/05:4a
GEIGER % Schroeder
GEIGER, Charles, 49, draughtsman, NYC-B – 1907/04/12:3a
GEIGER, Frederick, un. carp., NYC-Q – 1907/03/14:6a, 16:6a
GEIGER, Friedrich, 57, un. machinist, Newark, NJ – 1910/10/08:6a
GEIGER, Herman, un. butcher, NYC-B - 1914/01/10:6a
GEIGER, Justin, NYC-M – 1891/08/26:4a
GEIGER, Vinzenz, NYC-B – 1911/12/07:6a

GEIGER, W., NYC-Q – 1913/04/24:6a
GEIGERT, Wilhelm, NYC-M – 1886/11/20:2f
GEIHL, Elizabeth, 55, NYC-B - 1914/01/26:1f
GEIL, Konrad, 29, NYC-B – 1910/12/23:6a
GEILEN, Anthony, NYC-Bx - 1916/11/20:6a
GEILER, Anton, NYC-M – 1904/12/11:5b
GEILFUSS, Reinhold, 62, NYC-M – 1905/06/29:1h,4a
GEIM, Sophie, 42, NYC – 1901/09/21:4c
GEIS, Frank, 34, NYC-B – 1908/09/07:6a, 8:6a
GEIS, Frank, 54, * Deidesheim/Bingen/Gy, NYC-M – 1907/07/23:6a
GEIS, John, 63, NYC-Q - 1878/07/12:3a
GEIS, Julius, 49, brewer, NYC-M – 1896/12/25:1f
GEIS, Louise, NYC-M – 1910/09/07:1c
GEIS, Philip, 15, NYC-B – 1885/05/22:3a
GEIS, Philip, 15, NYC-B – 1885/05/22:3a
GEISDORF, Hermann, *17 Dec 1841 Hohenstein/Sax., SP, Rockville, CT – 1911/12/13:5f
GEISE, William, un. carp., NYC-M – 1908/06/09:6a
GEISELER, Peter, 18, NYC-M, + @ Genl Slocum – 1904/06/17:3b
GEISELMANN, Johannes, 22, mailman fr Jackelhausen/Wuerttemberg, + on SS Bohemia – 1883/03/02:1d
GEISENDOERFER, William, 16, NYC-M - 1913/09/08:6a, fam. 14:7a
GEISER, Adam, 59, Newark, NJ – 1912/04/29:2d
GEISER, Katherina, 25, NYC-M, +@Genl Slocum – 1904/06/22:1d
GEISLER, Christian, NYC-B - 1894/10/15:4a
GEISLER, Frank, Dr., 36, physician, * Bremen, USA 1870, Hoboken, NJ - 1879/10/29:1e, will 12/05:4d
GEISLER, H., NYC-Q – 1914/10/09:6a
GEISLER, Henry, mason, NYC-M – 1897/11/13:1g
GEISLER, Katie, 14, NYC-M – 1892/07/14:4a
GEISS, Eva, 17, (dying) NYC-M - 1879/06/12:1d
GEISSLER, Edith?, 18, NYC-M, +@ Genl Slocum – 1904/06/17:3b
GEISSLER, Eva, b. Kramer, NYC-M – 1891/03/29:5a
GEISSLER, Heinrich, 65, German self-made man, fr worker to manuf. of glassware for chemistry, Bonn/Gy - 1879/03/26:2c
GEISSLER, Louis, NYC-M, +@ Genl Slocum – 1904/06/17:3b
GEIST, Eugen, NYC-B – 1911/01/30:6a
GEIST, Friedrich, 67, NYC-M – 1893/10/04:4a
GEISTINGER, Marie, actress, *1836 Graz, + Klagenfurt – 1903/10/01:1a
GEITNER, Martin, brewery worker,fr Gy, NYC-M - 1895/12/29:1h
GEITZENAUER, John, painter, USA 1862 fr Hessen/Gy, NYC-M – 1887/02/22:1d

GEITZINGER, Paul, 29, NYC-B – 1897/10/23:4b
GELB, Emma, 6, NYC-M - 1878/05/08:3b
GELBHAAR, Max, 43, printer & SPD Chemnitz/Gy – 1908/08/09:3b
GELDER, Rose, 36, SP, NYC, *London of Dutch parents, + Lafayette, IN – 1912/08/26:3a
GELHAAR, Emilie, 47, NYC-B – 1903/12/04:4a
GELHAUS, August, NYC-Woodside - 1918/11/10:12a
GELLAR, Louis, 40, coach driver, NYC-B – 1908/02/11:3a
GELLEHR, A., NYC-B – 1903/12/11:4a
GELLERMANN, Hymie, 25, sign maker, NYC-B - 1918/10/02:2d
GELLERT, Ernest, 22, pacifist, War 2, Ft Hancock, NJ - 1918/04/13:3b
GELLHORN, Walter, Dr. med., Seattle, WA, War 2 in British internment camp - 1916/06/28:2c
GEMEINER, Gulna, NYC-M – 1893/10/30:4a
GEMEINER, William, 6, NYC-M, +@ on Genl Slocum – 1904/06/17:3b
GEMM, Caroline, NYC-M – 1885/09/01:2f
GEMRICH, Carl, NYC-M - 1918/01/07:6a
GENERALOW, Russian patriot, trial & exec. for 13 March attentate on Czar, (with Lenin's brother) – 1887/05/26:5b, 30:2f, 10 June:5b, 17:5e
GENERICH, Lina, NYC-M – 1919/12/26:6a
GENET, Henry W., 64, ex-NYS Senator, NYC – 1889/09/07:2g
GENITZ, Thomas, 61, NYC-M – 1891/07/09:4d
GENNEN, Jakob, NYC-B - 1920/02/14:6a
GENT, Louise, b. Hartwig, 26, Guttenberg, NJ – 1884/08/30:3c
GENTERMANN, Frank, un. carp., NYC-M – 1892/06/16:4a
GENTRY, James B., 55, actor, NYC – 1912/07/26:2b
GENTSCH, Theresa, 58, NYC-M - 1913/12/26:6a
GENTZ, Antoinette, NYC-M – 1890/08/02:4a
GENTZ, August, 47, un. carp., SLP,NYC-M – 1898/04/09:4a,10:1g, =11:1g
GENTZ, Henry, 56, NYC-M – 1904/05/02:3c
GENTZ, Rosa, 2, NYC-M – 1887/06/21:3c
GENTZ, Willy, NYC-M – 1890/10/26:5a
GENTZEN % Martins
GENZ, Paul, 37, fr Prussia, to be exec. – 1896/07/14:3e; appeal rej. 1897/ 03/ 03:4a, 14:1d, exec. Jersey City, NJ 2 Apr:3f, 7:3c, 11:7g, 13:4c-d,14 April:1h, = 15:4c
GENZIUS, John Peter, 59,un. cigarmaker,NYC-M - 1894/02/01:4a
GEORGE, Alfred, 45, foreman, NYC-B – 1911/03/26:7e
GEORGE, Carl, un. cigarmaker, NYC-M - 1895/02/24:5b
GEORGE, Frank, 62, W. Hoboken, NJ – 1888/05/07:3b
GEORGE, Frank, NYC-M – 1903/12/16:4a

GEORGE, Henry, 54, ex-Congressman, son of the Single Taxer, NYC-M, + Washington, DC - 1916/11/15:2a
GEORGE, Henry, US Reformer, NYC-M - 1897/10/30:1a,c,2a-b, 31:1h,4a-c, =1 Nov:1d-e, 2:1c, 17:1c
GEORGE, Louis, SP?, NYC-B - 1918/10/11:6a
GEORGENS, Heinrich, un. carp., NYC-B - 1897/10/11:4a
GEORGER, Joseph Jr., child, NYC-M - 1920/02/01:12a
GEORGES, Charles A., French, USA 1885, NYC-M - 1890/04/22:4d
GEORGIE, Marie, b. Oexlein, Paterson, NJ - 1879/01/30:3a
GERALD, Johann, un. cigarpacker, NYC-M - 1904/03/31:4a
GERARD, Pierre, 70, inventor fr France, NYC-M - 1896/07/14:1d
GERASSIMOW see Philip Sirodzki
GERATZ, Anna, NYC-M - 1901/07/03:1d
GERAU % Rors
GERAU, Franz, Dr., 74, SLP, physician, * Wiesbaden/Hessen, '48er, fdr Brooklyn Labor Lyceum, NYC-B - 1896/02/21:1e-g,2a,22:1d,4a =23:1e,5a,24:1f-g. Noted 21 Dec 1900:1a. Ashes transf. To Fresh Pond Columbarium 1907/05/30:1f
GERAULT-RICHARD, ex-SP,French deputy, crit. Obit - 1911/12/24:13e-g
GERBEL, Frank G., 60, liquor dealer,* Brandenburg, Weehawken, NJ - 1914/05/27:6a, inkl. bottom of column, =29:6a
GERBER % Christen, % Reinhard
GERBER, Charles, 4, NYC-M - 1897/11/01:1f
GERBER, Conroy, 53, NYC-M - 1900/07/20:1e
GERBER, Gottfried, un. carp., West New York, NJ - 1902/11/30:5a
GERBER, Jacob, 47, NYC-M - 1891/07/29:4a
GERBER, John, SP, un. butcher, NYC-B - 1915/01/09:6a, 10:7a
GERBER, John, SP, W. Hoboken, NJ - 1907/10/08:6a
GERBER, Susanna, b. Kuestner, 56, NYC-M or Bx - 1891/06/21:5a
GERBER, Wilhelm, NYC-B - 1918/10/12:6a, 13:11g
GERBHARDT, Theodor, 39, & son, 9, NYC-M - 1882/04/07:1f
GERBICH % Liestmann
GERDEN, Richard, 21, driver, NYC-B - 1900/09/07:1h
GERDES, Ernst, 39, cigar maker, * Hamburg-Altona, NYC-M - 1885/07/08:3b, 4a
GERDES, Margaret, + @Genl Slocum, NYC-B - 1904/06/19:1d
GERDIG, John, 36, SLP?, Paterson, NJ - 1881/11/27:8a
GERDON, Alois, NYC-Q - 1915/10/11:6a
GERE, Carl, ship's engineer,@1900 dock fire, Hoboken, NJ 1900/07/03:1c
GERECKE, Rudolf, 25, pianomaker, War 2,Bergola,NJ - 1914/08/04:3d
GERHARD, Aug. A.F., 81, Winfield, LI - 1914/08/19:6a

GERHARD, August, 48, cigar maker & SPD activist expelled fr Hamburg/Gy, arrived in NYC – 1881/01/19:1g, 20:4c
GERHARD, Catherine, NYC-M - 1895/09/01:5c
GERHARD, Charles, 52, baker, NYC-B – 1898/09/05:3d
GERHARD, Heinrich, un. cigarmaker, NYC-M - 1894/03/20:4a
GERHARD, Katherine, 61, SP, wd of Karl Arnold, *Erfurt/Thuringia, USA 1884, NYC-M - 1914/11/09:6a, 10:2f,6a
GERHARD, Lizzie, b. Obergsoell, 39, NYC-M – 1904/03/04:4a
GERHARDT, Amalie, b. Theile, 56, NYC-M – 1904/04/23:4a
GERHARDT, Benjamin, San Francisco, + NJ on way to Gy – 1885/10/01:3a
GERHARDT, Ernst, un. butcher, NYC-B - 1917/08/02:6a
GERHARDT, Georgiana, 26, cook, fr France, NYC-M – 1891/05/04:1g
GERHARDT, Joseph, *1817 Bonn/Gy, '48er, USA 1850, in Civil War US general, + Washington, DC – 1881/08/20:1d
GERHARDT, Karl, * Hanau/Gy, SLP, Hoboken, NJ – 1897/04/07:4a, =10:4b
GERHARDT, Ludwig, 42, businessman, Elizabeth, NJ – 1909/03/24:3b
GERHARDT, Marie, 53, NYC-B – 1912/01/24:2d
GERHARDT, Minna, Chochocten Ctr, Sullivan Co., NY – 1880/12/10;1c
GERHARDT, Minnie, 26, NYC-Bx – 1900/12/07:1f
GERHERTZ, Dorothy, 68, NYC-Q - 1918/04/09:3f
GERHOLD, August, un. cigarmaker, NYC-M – 1885/02/15:5g
GERHOLD, Dora, NYC-M – 1890/03/01:4a
GERHOLD, Friedrich, 32, NYC–B - 1916/06/12:6a
GERHOLD, Heinrich, NYC-M – 1896/09/11:4a
GERICHTEN, Christina von, infant, NYC-M – 1882/07/29:4c
GERIG, Otto, NYC-Bx – 1910/08/14:7c
GERISCH, Philipp, un. upholsterer, NYC-Bx - 1919/02/20:6a
GERKE, William, 40, grocer, NYC-B – 1900/11/11:1h
GERKE, Wladislaw, un. butcher, NYC-M – 1910/11/10:6a
GERKEN, (Mr.), baker in Hoboken, NJ, & wife, 63, in Elizabeth, NJ – 1903/12/03:3c
GERKEN, John, NYC-M – 1881/01/06:3c
GERKEN, William R., 34, un. cigar packer, Hoboken, NJ – 1885/07/21:3b, =23:3a
GERLACH, Arthur, 40, Union Hill, NJ – 1919/09/01:2b
GERLACH, Charles, Baltimore, MD – 1885/06/17:1b
GERLACH, Frank, 50, NYC-B – 1905/08/03:3c
GERLACH, Georg, laborer, NYC-B – 1882/08/13:5e
GERLACH, George, 46, NYC-B - 1914/02/20:6a
GERLACH, Herman, 59, NYC-B – 1902/01/31:4a

GERLACH, John, 21, NYC-B – 1909/01/11:3a
GERLACH, Katie, 7, NYC-M, @1883 School Fire, NYC-M 1883
GERLACH, Lizzie, 18, NYC-SI – 1889/10/02:4e, 5:4d, 12:1f
GERLACH, Ludwig, 52, un. carp., NYC-M – 1908/06/12:6a, 13:6a, fam. 15:6a. Mem. – 1909/06/10:6a
GERLACH, Max, 31, un. upholsterer, SP, NYC-Q – 1908/03/14:6a, 15:7b, =17:2b, fam. 18:6a
GERLACH, Philip, 43?, NYC-M – 1889/05/28:4a
GERLACH, R., + Tucson, AZ, NYC-B – 1913/02/06:6a
GERLACH, Thomas, 30, painter, NYC-M – 1897/08/19:1c
GERLING, Emilie, 51, NYC-M - 1894/01/10:4a
GERLINGER, Jacob, 53, NYC-B – 1891/06/25:4a
GERLINGER, Louis, 35?, SLP, un. brewer, NYC-M – 1892/03/27:5d
GERMAN, Fredericka, 46, & Frieda, 15, NYC-M, +@Genl Slocum – 1904/06/18:3c, 23:1b
GERMANN, Franz, 50, NYC-M – 1911/08/06:7a
GERMANY, Friedrich III, Emperor, dying – 1888/03/03:1e, 17 Apr:1a, 18:1a, 19:2d, 20:1a, 21:2e, 23:4e, 2 May:1h, 5 June:2c-d, 13:1h, 2c, 14:2a, 15:1a, 16:1a-e, 2a-b, 18:1g, 2a-b, + 19:1a-b, 2b, 21:2f-g
GERMANY, Victoria, Empress of – 1901/08/06:1g, 7:1b, 21:2h
GERMANY, William I, Emperor, dying, 1888/03/08:1a, 9:1a-b, 2a-b, +10:1a-c, 2c, 12:1c, prep. =13:2g, 15:4e, 17:1h, crit. NYC mem. 16:2b-c, in Milwaukee 21:2b, d-e, NYC 22:1a-c, 2a, NYC workers discuss boycott of memorial ceremony 23:4a, 26:2f, 29:2g, & crit. Carl Schurz position 23 Apr:2b & 5 May:2c, 7:1g, 8 June:2c-d, 12:2c, NYC Kriegerbund mem. 3 May:4e,
GERMICH, Charles, 31, NYC-B – 1911/06/15:6a
GERMINER, William's 2 children, NYC-M, + @Genl Slocum – 1904/06/17:1b
GERN, Chr., NYC-M – 1893/08/08:4a
GERNE, Wilhelm, 34, un. stone cutter, Newark, NJ – 1902/06/11:4a
GERNER, Amelia, b. Becker, 22, NYC-B – 1899/12/13:4a
GERNER, Carl L., 74, un. cigarmaker, *10 F 1835 Hamburg, SP, USA 1880, NYC-B – 1909/02/25:2e,6a, 26:6a, 27:6a, =1 Mr:2b, fam. 2:6a
GERNER, Friedericke, NYC-M - 1918/06/09:7a
GERNER, Friedrich, 50, NYC-M – 1891/06/28:5c
GERNER, Mary, b. Kreps, 22, NYC-B - 1916/09/27:6a
GERNER, Selma, wd Wolf, 70, un. cigarmaker, SP, *Leipzig, USA 1881, NYC-M – 1910/03/29:2e-f, 6a, 30:6a, =31:2b
GERONIMO, Apache freedom fighter, + Fort Sill, OK – 1909/02/18:1b
GERSCHOWITZ, Annie, 17, & cousin Tillie, 19, USA 1910, NYC-M – 1911/02/13:1g

GERSCHUNI, Gregory Andrejowitsch, Russian revol., + Zuerich/Switz. – 1908/03/22:7f, 23:1e-f, 25:3d-e, 3 Ap:4e-f, =Paris/Fr. 15 Ap:4e
GERSDORF, Edward, machinist, NYC-M – 1912/01/10:6a
GERSING, Wilhelm, un. cigarmaker, NYC-M – 1881/03/27:8a (bottom)
GERSPACHER, Emil, brewer, NYC-M – 1902/12/28:5b
GERST, Gertrud, NYC-M – 1890/01/10:4a
GERSTEIN, Mollie, 17, @1911 Triangle Shirtwaist Fire, NYC-M – 1911/03/28:1b
GERSTENBERGER, Annie, NYC-M, + @ Genl Slocum – 1904/06/17:3b, 18:3c
GERSTENBERGER, Emil, 39, SPD Berlin, ed. Der Steinarbeiter – 1902/05/17:2c
GERSTENBERGER, Richard,38,NYC-M,+@Genl Slocum– 1904/06/22:1d
GERSTENMEYER, Ludwig, un. carp., NYC-B – 1907/11/08:6a
GERSTER, Elisabeth, 75, NYC-B – 1882/04/28:1g
GERSTER, Etelko, 65, German opera singer, + Bologna/Italy - 1920/09/29:4d
GERSTNER, Florian, 66, SLP, shoemaker, *Baden (city), USA 1857, NYC-M - 1879/10/27:1e
GERSTNER, John, NYC-Q - 1918/10/15:6a
GERSTNER, Margarethe, + 12 Mr 04, mem. 1905/03/13:4a
GERSTNER, Reinhold, un. painter, NYC-M - 1915/07/19:6a
GERTEL, Christian, 10, NYC-M – 1882/03/08:1f
GERTEN, Ferdinand, un. cigarmaker, NYC-M – 1884/10/08:3c
GERTINGER, Frank, 27, electrician, NYC-M – 1907/08/05:1d
GERTZ, P.J. Theodor, 52, NYC-M – 1892/08/09:4a
GERVAISE, Louis, 62, carp., NYC-M – 1907/02/15:5f
GESCHEIDT, Harry M., NYC lawyer, + 12 Jan., his will - 1914/02/03:3a
GESCHEIDT, Katie, b. Eisenbarth, NYC-M – 1898/02/01:4a
GESCHWINDER, Anton, silk weaver, New Jersey – 1905/01/21:3b
GESCHWINDER, Charles, Elizabeth, NJ – 1913/03/01:6a
GESCHWINDNER, Conrad, 74, NYC-M - 1894/01/10:4a
GESECKUS, Edgar, 28, druggist, fr Mecklenburg, USA 1898, NYC-M – 1899/02/18:3b
GESELL, Caroline, NYC-B – 1893/01/14:1f
GESSEN, Samuel, 59, cigarmaker, NYC-M – 1882/12/01:4d
GESSER, Michael, NYC-B – 1892/07/10:5c
GESSERT % Keller
GESSLEIN, Victoria, 50, Paterson, NJ – 1911/11/19:7f
GESSNER % Wolff
GESSNER, Frank, un. glassmaker & ed. Der amerikanische Glassarbeiter and National Glass Budget, SP Alleghany Co., PA – 1906/02/06:3e

GESSNER, George, 63, un. carp., NYC-M – 1906/12/23:7b
GESSNER, Joseph G., 33, NYC-M – 1906/11/14:6a
GESSWEIN, Frederick, jewelry tools maker, NYC-M – 1889/09/14:1d-e, 15:1h, 4b, 16:2g, 18:2b, 19:2g
GETMANN % Thiese
GETSCHLIG, Isaac, 38, un. cigarmaker, NYC-M - 1894/12/21:4a
GETTING, August, Orange, NJ – 1884/12/19:3a
GETTING, Samuel, or Gitten, 20, NYC-Q – 1906/07/16:1b, 2c
GETZNER, Emma, 43, NYC-B – 1897/05/02:5c
GETZNER, Frank, 35, laborer, NYC-SI – 1906/07/15:1e
GETZOW, Morris, SLP, Newark, NJ - 1895/02/22:4a
GEVERS % Warnken
GEWEHR, Wilhelm, 55, SPD Elberfeld, ed. Freie Presse - 1913/10/10:4d, =19:3c
GEX, Xavier, druggist, Tomkinsville, NY? – 1882/09/22:1g
GEYER, Alex, 41, NYC-M – 1892/06/17:4a
GEYER, Andrew, NYC-Bx - 1916/03/11:6a
GEYER, Carl Adolf, sailor on SS Frisia, + Hoboken, NJ – 1880/08/19:4e
GEYER, Charles, NYC-M – 1919/11/16:12a
GEYER, Georg, NYC-M – 1900/01/18:4a
GEYER, Katherina, 69, NYC-M - 1894/01/29:4a
GEYER, Philipp, 65, *Pfaffenhofen/Elsass, close to John Most, Paterson, NJ – 1908/12/04:1d
GEYER, Robert, 31, NYC-M – 1903/07/17:4a
GIAUGUE % Heidel
GIBBONS, Mary & Maggie, NYC-M, +@Genl Slocum – 1904/06/17:3b, 18:3c
GIBIER, Paul, Dr., head of Pasteur Institute, NYC-M – 1900/06/11:1d
GIBLIN, Charles, to be exec. NYC-M for killing Mrs Goelz – 1889/07/24:1h, postponed 20 Aug:4d, 22:1f, Appeals for life sentence 24 Sept:2g, 25:2g, 26:1c, 28:1f, 3 Oct:2g, 4.2f. @Mrs Goelz
GIDALI, Maria, 37, NYC-M - 1919/03/01:6a
GIEBE, Babette, b. Ritter, NYC-M – 1885/08/25:3b
GIEBERT, George H., NYC-M – 1904/10/29:4c
GIEGERICH, Agnes, 39, NYC-M – 1890/08/08:4a
GIEGERICH, Elisa, NYC-M – 1892/07/31:5c
GIEGERICH, R., NYC-M – 1905/06/08:4a
GIEL, Eduard, NYC-M – 1900/07/01:5b
GIEMON, Charlotte G., 41, NYC-M - 1878/05/20:3b
GIERACK, Joseph, coppersmith, Pole, & wife, USA 1910, NYC-Bx - 1913/11/18:1e
GIES, John, 44, un. carp., NYC-M – 1884/07/30:3d

GIESE, Albert, 62, carp., & wife Philomena, 68, NYC-M – 1908/09/20:11a
GIESE, Elsie, NYC-Bx - 1918/11/21:6a
GIESE, Jakob, NYC-M – 1896/04/30:4a
GIESECKE, Charles, salesman, * 18 Oct 1862 Varel/Oldenburg, NYC-M – 1888/09/12:1f
GIESELBACH % Eckert
GIESELBERG, Isabel, NYC-M - 1894/01/28:5d
GIESELER, William, 50, un. painter, NYC-M – 1888/09/18:3a
GIESEN, Dorothea, NYC-M – 1890/10/20:4a
GIESINGER, Valentin, 20, worker at Singer Factory, Elizabeth, NJ – 1900/02/23:4b
GIESLER, Adelia, 61, Newark, NJ – 1901/07/04:3b
GIESSEN, Peter, cigarmaker, NYC-M – 1891/02/19:4a
GIESSEN, William, 50, silkweaver, NYC-M – 1893/09/16:1f
GIETZ % Zuillich
GIETZ, Gerhard, 85, Fairview, NJ – 1912/09/24:6a
GIETZ, Marie, NYC-M – 1886/12/21:3a
GIEZENDONNER, Jacob, un. carp., NYC-M – 1907/01/19:6a
GIFFORD, Malcolm Jr., US army, Hudson, NY, War 1 - 1917/11/20:5e
GIGERICH, Charles, 53, butcher, NYC-M? – 1909/12/30:1d
GILBERT, George Henry's wife, 82, actress, + Chicago – 1904/12/03:2g
GILCHRIST, Emily, 25, Weehawken Heights, NJ – 1904/05/18:3c
GILDEMEISTER, August, 48, doorman, NYC-B - 1913/06/02:1e
GILDERSLEEVE, John, smith, Hoboken, NJ – 1885/11/21:2e
GILIARD, Margarethe, NYC-M – 1892/12/06:4a
GILLAN, George, 12, NYC-M, +@Genl Slocum – 1904/06/17:3b
GILLES, Eileen, US writer,+ Sassari/Sardinia - 1914/01/18:1a
GILLESPIE, Harrison, 16, & James, 13, Negroes, lynched Salisbury, NC – 1902/06/12:2f
GILLETTE, Chester, exec. Auburn, NY – 1908/03/31:1d, note 12 Aug. 1909:2b
GILLETTE, Walter R., Dr., ex-vp Mutual Life Insr. Co – 1908/11/08:1f
GILLIAN, John, un. cigarmaker, NYC-M - 1917/11/05:6a
GILLIAR, Joseph, 51, un. tailor, *Philippsburg/Gy, Jersey City Heights, NJ – 1902/09/05:4a, 6:4a, 7:5b,e , =8:1g, fam. 16:4a
GILLIAR, Marie Louise, b. Volk, 58, SP?, Jersey City, NJ - 1914/10/26:6a
GILLMAN, Nathan A., druggist, NYC-Bx - 1913/05/16:1f
GILLMANN, Minnie, 15?, NYC-M – 1892/06/26:5c
GILLMER, David T., 60, ex-mayor, Paterson, NJ – 1902/08/18:3c
GILMORE, Felix, Negro, lynched Prescott, AK - 1916/05/28:1e
GILSDORF, John, NYC-M – 1903/04/17:4a
GIMPEL, John, 50, painter, *Berlin/Gy, NYC-M – 1880/06/11:1e-f, 12:4b

GINADER, Julius, un. cornice maker, NYC-M – 1889/10/15:4a
GINDERMELLEK, John, SP, New Haven, CT - 1918/01/17:6a
GIPPEL, Morris Loeb, 40, NYC-M - 1894/09/13:3d
GIRARDI, Alexander, actor, + Vienna - 1918/06/05:4f
GIRARDIN, Emile de, 79, French journalist, crit. Obit – 1881/04/28:1a, 2b
GIRGOS, Adolf, un. carp., NYC-Q – 1906/08/26:7a, 27:6a
GIRINA, Anna, 25, NYC-M - 1915/03/09:6a
GIRRBACH, Gottlieb, 55, NYC-M – 1882/06/23:3c
GIRSCHING, Mary, 30, NYC-M – 1902/05/11:5e, =14:3b
GISIN, Lisette, + not advertised, but fam. thanks 1881/04/26:3b
GISSYNG, Emma, b. Schweck, 20, SP, NYC-M - 1914/04/08:6a, 09:6a
GITTINGS, Ms – 1898/11/22:1g
GITTLIN, Celia, 17, @1911 Triangle Shirtwaist Fire, NYC-M – 1911/03/27:1d, =28:1f
GLAAS, Joseph, 51, furnit. maker, NYC-M - 1917/12/05:6a, 6:6a
GLAB % Heiss
GLABAU, Olga, 1, NYC-M - 1878/01/28: 3d
GLACKMEYER, Adolf, fr Montreal, + NYC-M – 1885/05/03:1g
GLADE % Gromann
GLADE, Conrad, un. cigarmaker, NYC-M – 1886/10/26:3b
GLADE, Hermann, & wife Caroline, 40, NYC-B - 1916/09/20:2a
GLADEWITZ, Gustav, SPD Bochum/Gy, un. weaver – 1904/06/04:2d
GLADSTONE, William, British politician, 1898/05/29:1h, 4 June:2c-d
GLADTKE % Salomon
GLAESSNER, Millia, 76, NYC-B – 1908/07/07:2e
GLAETTLI, Rudolf, NYC-M, note on his late father-in-law Hirland Thomann – 1893/10/10:4a
GLAHN, Ernst F. C. Von, 45, innkeep, Asbury Park, NJ – 1900/10/28:5g
GLAHN, Mabel von, 7, Woodridge, NJ - 1913/05/17:2d
GLAHN, Th. S. von, 71, NYC-M - 1894/01/12:4a
GLAHN, William von, 18, NYC-Bx – 1904/01/05:3e
GLANDER % Juergens
GLAS, George, 39, SP, un. butcher, NYC-B - 1919/01/17:6a, 18:6a, fam. 21:6a
GLASBERG, Johann Baptist, NYC-M – 1892/08/05:4a
GLASBRENNER, Jacob, 53, NYC-M – 1892/08/19:4a
GLASENAPP, Georg von, 35, fr Brandenburg area, ex-officer, in USA journalist, NYC-M? - 1879/01/24:1e
GLASER, Adolf, un. metalworker & alderman, SP Bruenn/Moravia – 1909/02/14:3f; mon. unveiled in Bruenn cemetery – 1910/09/11:3b
GLASER, Charles, NYC-M – 1892/09/13:4a
GLASER, Christian, un. brewer, NYC-M – 1891/12/15:4a

GLASER, Helen, 19, NYC-Bx – 1910/09/30:6a
GLASER, Isidor, un. carp., NYC-M – 1901/07/24:4a
GLASER, John, 34, fr Zips?/Slov. NYC-M - 1919/03/08:6a
GLASER, Mary, 8, NYC-M – 1905/04/07:1g
GLASER, Mary, NYC-M – 1908/12/26:6a
GLASER, SPD MdL Wuerttemberg, = Bad Cannstatt – 1896/08/04:3f
GLASER, Stephan, hotel porter, Hoboken, NJ – 1910/07/05:2c
GLASER, W. J., exec. Albany, NY – 1899/12/16:1g
GLASING, Jacob, 65, NYC-M - 1894/01/21:5d
GLASS, Bella, 29, & Henry, 2, & Harry, 6, NYC-B – 1904/10/18:3c, 19:3d, 20:4c
GLASS, Frank, 38, NYC-M - 1914/02/16:6a
GLASS, Georg, NYC-Q,+ 15.01.19, mem. - 1920/01/15:8a
GLASS, Regine, b. Weil, NYC-M – 1892/08/28:5c
GLASSBRENNER, Adolf, German poet & humorist, 100th anniv. Mem. 1910/04/10:3d-g
GLASSHEIM, Samuel, 28, painter, NYC-M – 1893/06/15:1e
GLASSHOFF, John, un. carp., NYC-M – 1893/05/14:5b
GLASSMAN, Otto, dying, NYC – 1912/10/04:1e
GLATTFELDER, Anton, NYC-M - 1920/05/01:2a
GLATZ, Louis, un. typesetter, NYC-B – 1907/03/24:7c, 25:6a
GLATZ, William, 46, NYC-Bx – 1906/03/27:3f, 4a, 28:4a
GLATZMEYER, William, Dr., 42, alderman, Newark, NJ – 1900/03/07:4b
GLAUB, Christian, un. cigarmaker, NYC-M - 1894/06/10:5c
GLAUS, Jacob, NYC-M - 1914/01/08:6a
GLEBE, Jacob, 63, NYC-M – 1900/05/15:4b
GLEISNER, Ernst, un. butcher, NYC-M - 1920/06/07:6a
GLENBOWSKY, Leonhard, barber, NYC-B – 1887/10/22:2c
GLIEME, Alex Guido, 30, NYC-M - 1895/04/27:4a
GLISSMANN, Claus, 39, shoemaker & SPD activist expelled fr Hamburg/Gy, arrived in NYC – 1881/01/19:1g, 20:4c
GLITSCH, Frederick, Newark, NJ – 1905/10/24:4a
GLOCK, Edmund, 53, NYC-M – 1899/10/27:2h
GLOCK, Louise, 21, NYC-M - 1918/02/16:6a
GLOCKE, Alfred, NYC-M – 1903/05/01:4a
GLOECKLEN, Emily, NYC-B - 1919/05/25:12a
GLOECKLER, John, bartender, NYC-M – 1887/10/05:2e, 6:2d
GLOECKNER % Ludwig
GLOECKNER, Charles, NYC-B - 1920/06/06:12a
GLOECKNER, Ernestine, 52, NYC-M - 1896/01/15:4a
GLOECKNER, John, NYC-Bx – 1912/01/27:6a
GLOEDE, Friedericke, b. Zehnke, 78, NYC-M – 1890/06/26:4a

GLOEKNER, Ed., NYC-M – 1898/02/14:4a
GLOONECK, Elizabeth, NYC-M - 1919/07/25:6a
GLORICK, George, cooper, NYC-B – 1900/11/21:2h
GLOSS, Emil, 42, un. tailor, NYC-M – 1912/07/27:2e, 6a
GLOSTETTER, Dominik, NYC-M – 1892/07/02:4a
GLOVER, Ralph, NYC-M – 1905/03/03:4a
GLOY, John, SLP, *Kellinghusen/Holstein, USA 1870s, Chicago, IL – 1899/03/29:2d
GLUCK, August, 28, janitor, & wife, 26, NYC-M – 1908/07/19:1e
GLUCK, Julia, 6, NYC-M – 1896/04/23:1g
GLUCKEN, Frederick, NYC-M – 1899/02/02:4a
GLUECK % Kimmich
GLUECK, John, brewer, Minneapolis brewer, + NYC – 1908/08/20:2b
GLUECK, Louis, 26, NYC-M? - 1913/10/14:1f
GLUECK, Mr., obit by wd Henriette, b. Rosenberg, NYC? - 1878/03/19:3b
GLUECKLICH, Jacob, former manuf. fr Laun/Bohemia, USA 1888, NYC-M – 1889/11/01:1d-e
GLUECKMAN, Herman, Dr., dentist, NYC-B – 1911/08/10:3a
GLUECKMANN, Bernard, NYC-M - 1878/03/23:4a
GLUTSCH, Therese, NYC-M – 1899/08/30:4a
GLUTTING, Franz, Newark, NJ - 1919/08/26:6a
GNEIB, Philomena, b. Kessler, NYC-M – 1897/12/13:4a
GNEITLING, Dorothea, b. Wagler, NYC-M – 1891/03/09:4a
GOBAT, Charles Albert, Dr., Swiss, 1902 Peace Nobel Prize, + Bern - 1914/03/17:6e
GOCK, Mary, NYC-B – 1902/04/24:1g
GODARD, Louis, French balloonist, + Paris – 1885/03/09:2e
GODARD, Paul, French, precious stone expert, NYC-M – 1904/10/19:2h
GODAU, August, 34, locksmith, SPD Koenigsberg/Gy – 1887/07/19:2c, =29:6c. 25th anniv. + – 1912/07/21:3c
GODENOUGH, Ralph, journalist, NYC-M – 1909/11/17:2f
GODKIN, Edward L., 71, ex-chief ed NY Evening Post, crit notes – 1902/05/22:1d
GODLEY, French & Will, Negroes, lynched Pierce City, MO – 1901/08/21:1g, 29:3b
GODLEY, Mont, lynched Pittsburg, KS – 1902/12/28:1a
GODWIN, Parke, 88, reformer, NYC? – 1904/01/09:2a-b
GOEBBELS, Adolf, 21, NYC-M – 1892/01/16:4a
GOEBEL % Kachler
GOEBEL, Anton, 63, NYC-M – 1881/03/30:3a
GOEBEL, Charles, 55, ex-alderman, Fort Lee, NJ - 1920/07/06:2f
GOEBEL, Christian, 18, NYC-B – 1892/10/07:4a

GOEBEL, Conrad, 67, NYC-M - 1878/05/17:3a
GOEBEL, F., 35, NYC-B – 1902/09/10:1e
GOEBEL, Friedrich, 55, NYC-M – 1892/06/25:4a
GOEBEL, Georg, 49, NYC-B – 1909/02/05:6a
GOEBEL, George M., NYC-M – 1892/07/30:4a
GOEBEL, George, 67, NYC-M – 1890/01/14:4a
GOEBEL, John, un. carp., NYC-M – 1882/11/03:3a
GOEBEL, Katharina, b. Hund, 31, fr Ziegenhagen/Hessen area, NYC-M – 1881/08/16:3c
GOEBEL, Rosa, 75, NYC-M – 1888/03/26:1h
GOEBEL, Therese, 27, servant, NYC-B – 1884/10/23:3a
GOEBEL, William, Kentucky gov., 1900/02/02:1e, 3:1c-d, 4:1c-d, 5:1h, =9:1d, 13:1c, 19:1b, 21:1e, 25:5g, 3 Apr:1g, 5:3c, 7:1e, 18:1d,19 Jy:1d, 28:1f-g, 29:5b, 31:1e, 4 Aug:3b, trial, killer got life 19 Aug:1g, 20:2a-b, trial continues 1 Oct:1c, 10:1c, 24:3c. Another of the murderers rec life 1903/05/01:1b. Investigation closed, NYVZ crit 1911/01/16:1d, 4c
GOEBELER, Friedrich, NYC-M - 1913/08/22:6a, 23:6a
GOEBELL, Arthur G., 35, car salesman, NYC-B - 1916/08/05:3e
GOEBELLS, Joseph, West Hoboken, NJ – 1908/05/13:6a
GOEBELSMANN, Dietrich, 67, un. baker, NYC-B - 1918/09/03:6a
GOEBEN, Ferdinand, 31, smith & SPD activist expelled fr Hamburg/Gy, arrived in NYC – 1881/01/19:1g, 20:4c
GOEBEN, Fredi, 4, NYC-M – 1890/07/05:4a, 6:5a
GOEBEN, Wilhelmine, b. Rawald, NYC-M – 1882/05/30:3b
GOEBLER, William, 42, NYC-Q - 1914/09/17:6c, will 21 Nv:2f
GOECHIUS, Max, carp., NYC-B – 1905/05/01:1g
GOECKE, Anna, 50, textile worker, NYC-Bx - 1916/05/11:2c
GOEDE, Gustav, 62, worker, NYC – 1912/02/22:1f
GOEDECKE, Hermann, 72, SP, * Solingen, USA 1872, co-fdr NYVZ, NYC-B - 1917/06/16:6a, = 28:5f
GOEDECKE, Marie, b. Wassig?, NYC-M – 1900/04/12:4a
GOEGG, Amand, about the German '48er in London exile (not +) 1881/12/06:2c. + Renchen/Baden – 1897/07/24:2c
GOEGGEL % Ellmer
GOEHLER, Frank, un. machinist, NYC-M – 1902/07/18:1g, 3f
GOEHLER, Paul, child, NYC-M – 1891/02/20:4a
GOEHMANN, Christian, NYC-M – 1886/05/11:3c
GOEHRING, Henry, 23, NYC-M – 1901/07/03:1d
GOELET, Robert, 67, realtor, NYC-M - 1879/09/24:1g
GOELKE, Barbara, NYC-M – 1892/08/23:4a
GOELKEL, Kaspar, un. carp., NYC-M – 1892/08/14:5c
GOELLE, Konrad, 56, NYC-B – 1912/12/17:6a

GOELLER, Louise, 48, & daughter Elsie, 28, ex-Hackensack, NJ, NYC-M - 1916/08/26:6c
GOELTZE, John, & Panzeter family, NYC – 1899/02/17:3c
GOELZ, Magdalene, NYC-M – 1888/02/17:1f,18:4e,22:2f, 8 Mr:2f, trial of Charles Giblin 21 June:1a, guilty 22:1h
GOEPEL, Walter, 33, piano supplies dealer, NYC-M - 1919/08/21:6a
GOEPFERICH, Jack, un. woodcarver, NYC-M – 1892/08/22:4a, 23:4a
GOEPFERT % Hauck,
GOEPFERT, Frederick's wife, NYC-M – 1883/07/29:8a
GOEPFERT, Julius, NYC-B - 1919/06/18:6c
GOEPPELE, Chr., NYC-B – 1907/10/08:6a
GOEPPER, John, 46, butcher, NYC-B – 1893/10/19:4d-e
GOEPPERT % Kromann, % Methfessel
GOERGEI, Arthur, 98, fr Zips, Hungarian revol. genl - 1916/05/24:4b
GOERING, Amalia, 34, NYC-M - 1915/06/19:6a
GOERING, Hugo, un. brewer, NYC-M – 1909/09/17:6a
GOERLICH, Julius, 66, maker of surgical instruments, NYC-Bx – 1908/11/20:6a
GOERLITZ % Weber
GOERLITZ, Ernst, ca. 40, *Gy, NYC theater magr, + Los Angeles, CA - 1915/12/13:1c
GOERLITZ, Karl, 42, ed. at Hafenarbeiter, SPD Magdeburg/Gy – 1908/08/16:3d
GOERSDORF, Emil, NYC-B 1920/11/23:6a
GOERSEN, A. C. F., Dr., exec. Philadelphia, PA – 1885/03/06:1d
GOERTZ, Ambrose, Dr., 40, * St Petersburg/Russia, USA 1878, NYC-M – 1881/11/07:4b, 9:3b
GOERTZ, Gustav, 38, insurance agent, * Hamburg, USA 1856, NYC-M – 1881/02/23:1e
GOERZ, George, 52, NYC-B – 1891/04/05:5a
GOESCHEL, Max, 31, NYC-M – 1904/03/10:4a
GOESS, Louise, NYC-B, + 22 V 16, note - 1916/06/03:2e
GOETER, John, organist at Flatbush German-Reformed Church, NYC-B - 1879/01/22:4e
GOETHEL, Louisa, 21, NYC-M – 1890/03/30:5b
GOETSCHALK, John B., theater mgr, NYC – 1900/08/18:1c
GOETTEL, Armine, b. Stroe, 28, NYC-M – 1892/05/19:4a
GOETTELMANN, Henry, infant, NYC-M – 1892/10/16:5c
GOETTELMANN, Marie, b. Walter, NYC-M – 1889/03/15:4a
GOETTELMANN, Rosa, 30, NYC-M – 1892/11/14:4a
GOETTLER, Charles, NYC-Q - 1896/03/29:5a, fam. 1 May:4a
GOETTLER, John, 53, NYC-M - 1895/07/11:4a

GOETTLER, Karl F., 56?, NYC-M – 1891/03/24:4a
GOETTLER, Nanette, 71, NYC-M – 1888/02/03:3a
GOETTLER, Peter, un. waiter, NYC-M – 1889/07/25:4a
GOETTSCHE, Maria, NYC-M – 1904/09/15:4a
GOETTSCHE, Peter, 69, Portchester, NY - 1920/12/08:6a
GOETZ % Herriger, % Marquart, % Monatsberger, % Rheinisch
GOETZ, A., NYC-B – 1913/04/08:6a
GOETZ, Conrad, Elizabeth, NJ - 1920/03/23:6a
GOETZ, Elizabeth, 59, NYC-B - 1915/07/13:2d
GOETZ, Friedrich, Irvington, NJ – 1913/01/24:2a
GOETZ, Georg, 58, mgr butcher shop, NYC - 1913/08/04:1b
GOETZ, Georg, un. typesetter, NYC-M – 1903/08/24:4a
GOETZ, Gottlieb, Guttenberg, NJ - 1920/08/19:6a
GOETZ, Henry, 14, NYC-M – 1892/08/22:4a
GOETZ, John G., 19, NYC-B – 1892/06/25:4a
GOETZ, Joseph, Hoboken, NJ – 1896/08/12:3e
GOETZ, Katharina, 23, & kids Albert & Eduard, 5, NYC-M, +@Genl
  Slocum – 1904/06/17:3b, 4a, 18:3c, 25:1d
GOETZ, Kunigunde, 18, NYC-M – 1891/08/15:4a
GOETZ, Leon, NYC-M, + @ Genl Slocum – 1904/06/18:3c
GOETZ, Samuel, shoe manuf., NYC-M – 1897/04/06:4c
GOETZE % Koeller
GOETZE, comrade, 39, SPD Tilsit/East Prussia, War 1 - 1915/11/14:3c
GOETZE, Gottfried's wife, widow of famous G-A painter, 1904/11/16:3d
GOETZE, Gustav A., Jersey City, NJ – 1882/03/22:4e
GOETZE, Henry, NYC-M - 1879/10/06:3a
GOETZE, Josepha, b. Schilling, NYC-M – 1907/01/26:6a
GOETZE, William, innkeep, NYC-M – 1886/02/12:1g, 17:4a
GOETZENBERGER, Julius, NYC-M - 1915/07/02:6a
GOETZENBERGER, Karl, 54, un. mason, SPD Munich/Gy –
  1910/04/17:3a
GOETZMANN, Christian, farmer, Lyons, NY – 1885/07/18:1d
GOHRISCH, Gustav, 24, SLP, Meriden, CT – 1898/01/02:12c
GOHS, Leonard H., NYC-B - 1918/05/29:6a
GOLD, Arthur, 12, West Hoboken, NJ – 1904/08/11:4a
GOLD, Emilie, 32, West Hoboken, NJ – 1896/06/20:4a, fam. 23:4a
GOLD, Franz, 54, weaver, SP, fr Silesia/Gy, West Hoboken, NJ –
  1913/03/22:6a, 23:11b, fam. 1 Ap:6a
GOLD, Johanna H., 57, SP?, West Hoboken, NJ – 1910/02/12:6a
GOLD, Morris, baker, NYC-B – 1909/11/30:6a
GOLDBACH, John, 51, hat-store, NYC-M – 1880/05/27:1f, 28:1g
GOLDBERG, Bella, 107, NYC – 1911/03/02:1f

GOLDBERG, David, shirtmaker, NYC-M – 1898/02/19:3e
GOLDBERG, Dora, 24, fr Russia, NYC-M – 1888/02/15:1h
GOLDBERG, Harry, 23, NYC-B – 1912/12/28:3c
GOLDBERG, Jennie, NYC-M – 1893/11/21:4a
GOLDBERG, John, 21, boxer, NYC-M – 1912/04/12:1c
GOLDBERG, Louis, tailor, NYC-B – 1900/12/24:3b
GOLDBERG, Rosa, 35, servant, NYC-B – 1903/05/01:4a
GOLDBERG, Salomon, 36, tailor fr Poland, NYC-M – 1886/10/08:4c
GOLDBERGER, Ludwig, 45, fr Miskolcz/Hungary, + NYC-Ellis Island – 1903/02/26:3c
GOLDE, Esther, Dr., Socialist, Poland, exec. Warsaw – 1905/11/28:2d
GOLDEN, John, 40, subway driver, NYC-M – 1896/07/11:1e
GOLDENKIRCH, Nikolaus, NYC-B – 1888/03/28:1h, 29:2d, 4 Apr:2d, trial of alleged murderer 4 Dec:2d, 5:2d-e, etc, not guilty 7:2d
GOLDENTHAL, David & Mandel, both 65, NYC-B – 1918/02/17:1f
GOLDFADEN, Abraham, Jiddisch poet, NYC-M – 1908/01/11:2c
GOLDFARB, Max, painter, NYC-M – 1915/12/19:1b
GOLDFARB, Morris, in clothing trade, fr Russia, NYC-M – 1915/12/31:6c
GOLDFARB, Sarah, NYC-M – 1902/06/02:3b
GOLDFUSS, Charles, painter, NYC-M – 1898/04/14:1c
GOLDHAMMER, John B., 40, NYPD, NYC-M – 1909/02/20:2a
GOLDMANN, Barnett, 53, NYC-M – 1895/08/31:1g
GOLDMANN, Carolina, 26, NYC-M – 1891/07/03:4a
GOLDMANN, John H., 52, blouse manuf., NYC-M – 1907/02/15:5f
GOLDMANN, Rosa, NYC-M – 1891/04/11:4a
GOLDMARK, Karl, music composer, * 18 May 1832 Keszthely/Hungary, + Vienna – 1915/01/04:5f
GOLDNAGEL, Henry, painter, NYC-M – 1892/05/29:1e
GOLDRAM, Nathan, 67, court translator, * Poland, Hoboken, NJ - 1920/11/04:1c
GOLDRINGER, Hanna, 50, NYC-M – 1906/08/08:2c
GOLDSCHMIDT, Aron, 45, & family, NYC-M – 1896/12/21:1f, =24:1e, note 26:2e
GOLDSCHMIDT, Henriette, Dr., 95, German feminist, * Krotochin/Posen, + Leipzig - 1920/03/11:4e-f
GOLDSCHMIDT, Hermann, 49, un. cigarmaker, NYC-M – 1882/12/07:3b
GOLDSTEIN, Joseph, 24, tailor, NYC-M – 1893/09/15:1h
GOLDSTEIN, Emily, 66, Newark, NJ - 1917/12/10:1b
GOLDSTEIN, Hermann, SPD MdR, = in Dresden/Sax. – 1909/0704:3c grave in Dresden rec monument – 1911/10/01:3b
GOLDSTEIN, Hyman, 12, NYC-B - 1918/12/14:5f
GOLDSTEIN, Jacob, NYC-M – 1893/04/26:4e

GOLDSTEIN, Jacob,@1911 Triangle Shirtwaist Fire, NYC-M –
  1911/03/27:1d, =28:1c
GOLDSTEIN, Lena, 22, @1911 Triangle Shirtwaist Fire, NYC-M –
  1911/03/27:1d, =28:1c
GOLDSTEIN, Max, Berlin/Gy journalist, *Silesia, worked 1870s for N.Y.
  Handels-Zeitung and as Philadelphia correspondent NYSZ, publ. N.Y.
  Musik-Zeitung, married in Berlin Helene Reuleaux – 1880/05/ 27:1d, 11
  Jy:4c-d, + 35 yrs old 1883/10/26:2e
GOLDSTEIN, Sadie, NYC-M – 1912/05/25:3c
GOLDSTEIN, Yetta, 20, @1911 Triangle Shirtwaist Fire, NYC-M –
  1911/03/28:1b
GOLLEREND, S.S., 36, sailor on interned steamer Vaterland, + Hoboken,
  NJ - 1917/08/03:2g
GOLLERSTEPPER, Augustine, USA 1891, NYC-Bx – 1896/09/13:1h
GOLLHARDT, Mr., NYC-M - 1916/05/09:6a
GOLLI, Michael, Spanish anarchist, exec. Madrid – 1897/08/21:1a
GOLLNICK, Emil, NYC-M – 1910/04/21:6a
GOLLUBER, Louis, NYC-M – 1902/11/23:5b
GOLNICK, L., West Hoboken, NJ - 1916/01/14:6a
GOLTZ % Mueller
GOMER, Charles, machinist, ex-NJ assembly, + Salisbury, NC –
  1907/09/30:3b
GOMER, Elisabeth, 56, NYC-B – 1892/08/14:5c
GOMEZ, Maximo, Cuban revol. General, + Havanna – 1905/06/18:5d,
  19:2b, =21:1g
GOMPRICHT, Herman, Yonkers, NY – 1906/09/07:6a
GONNERMANN, Louise, b. Schramm, 49, Schenectady, NY –
  1893/07/11:4a
GONSER, John, NYC-Q – 1907/10/29:6a
GONZALES, N. S., S. Car. publisher, + by Lt-Gov. Tillman –
  1903/01/16:1g, 20:1b, 21:1e
GOODLAND, Jacob, tailor, USA fr Russia 1886, NYC-M – 1891/02/25:2h
GOODMAN, Aaron, 83, NYC-M - 1894/01/09:4a
GOODMAN, Anna, 43, NYC-B – 1912/03/07:3a
GOODMAN, Isaac, NYC-M – 1891/04/01:4a
GOODMAN, Moses, 58, blouse manuf., NYC-M – 1910/01/31:1e, =1 Fb:1b
GOODWIN, Ed, Negro, lynched in Little River County, GA –
  1899/03/24:1d, 25:1c
GOOS, Charles, merchant, War 2,Danbury, CT - 1917/11/26:1g
GOOSMANN, Rudolph, NYC-M - 1918/11/09:6a
GOOSS, Edith, 6, Jersey City Hgts, NJ – 1919/12/04:6a, fam. 10:6a
  mem 1920/12/03:6a

GORDEJEW, A., Russian patriot, exec. 12 Fb in Wechneudinsk, Russia – 1906/08/04:4e, 7 Oct 1906:6f-g
GORDES, John, NYC-M – 1899/04/30:5h
GORDIN, Jacob, playwright, NYC-M – 1909/06/14:2d
GORDON, British general, prisoner in Khartum/Sudan, comment 1884/11/04:2c, 6 Fb 1885:1a-d, 2b, executed by locals 11 Fb:1a-c, 13:2a-b. S.a. Genl Earle.
GORDON, Jack, Negro, lynched Lincolnton, GA – 1919/10/07:1c, 8:4c
GORDON, Maggie, NYC-M – 1906/11/05:1b, 8:1e-f
GORDON, Samuel, Dr., 35, physician, SP, Newark, NJ – 1906/11/11:1b
GORDY, J. E., NYU history prof., with wife & daughter, NYC-M – 1909/01/01:1e
GORGES, August, 38, un. carp., NYC-M – 1887/04/30:3c
GORGIO, Antonio, exec. Auburn, NY – 1904/09/06:1g
GORI, Pietro, Italian anarchist, lived NYC 1890s – 1911/01/30:4d
GORMAN, Arthur P., US Senator, NY – 1906/06/05:1b
GORTMEYER % Kopf
GORTNER, Philip, cooper, NYC - 1913/11/21:6a
GORZOLOWSKI, Emil, 27, NYC-Bx – 1910/02/16:6a
GORZYCKI, Kasimir, Dr., 46, Polish socialist – 1912/04/25:4e
GOSDA, Ada, 28, silk weaver, NYC-M – 1909/06/01:6a
GOSE, Christian, 66, NYC-M – 1892/06/29:4a
GOSEWISCH, Margarete, b. Kulken, 70, NYC-B - 1919/03/22:6a
GOSMANN, Marie, 59, NYC-M – 1903/03/02:4a
GOSPODINOW, Nikola, leader Bulg. tobacco workers - 1915/09/07:4d-e
GOSS % Bechamp
GOSS, Catharina, 30, NYC-M - 1879/05/05:3a
GOSS, John, (+28 Dec), NYC-M – 1886/01/18:3a
GOSS, Joseph, tailor, NYC-B – 1897/03/23:4b
GOSS, Martin, 6, NYC-B – 1919/08/14:6b
GOSS, Mary, 59, NYC-M, +@Genl Slocum – 1904/06/22:1d
GOSSARD, James, IWW martyr, + Newton, KS, jail – 1919/08/21:2c
GOSSMANN, Alex, baker fr San Francisco, + NYC-M – 1887/07/14:2g
GOSSWEYLER, Johanna, 43, NYC-M – 1891/11/27:4e
GOTHMANN, Bernardina, 16, NYC-B – 1898/01/03:4b-c
GOTTBERG, Werner von, Prussian lieutenant from Stolp/Pomerania, USA ~20 yrs ago, here a laborer, Passaic, NJ – 1880/11/06:1e
GOTTFRIED, ..., >80, in Gy a high court employee, USA 1860s, Paterson, NJ – 1889/06/30:1h
GOTTFRIED, Abram, NYC-M – 1892/07/06:1h
GOTTFRIED, Josef, un. carp., NYC-M – 1903/02/02:4a
GOTTHARD, August, NYC-Bx? – 1911/05/12:6a

GOTTHARD, Nora, 70, NYC-M – 1900/05/15:1e
GOTTHEIMER, George, 50, NYC-M – 1890/03/31:4a
GOTTHOLD, John, exec. Townsonton, MD – 1881/04/30:1d
GOTTLIEB, Dora, 26, Minnie, 20, Tillie, 18, workers, Orange, NJ – 1910/11/28:1c
GOTTLIEB, Dorian, 53, carpenter, NYC-M - 1916/12/02:1f
GOTTLIEB, Edward O., NYC-M - 1917/03/13:6a
GOTTLIEB, William, 3, NYC-M – 1891/06/16:4e
GOTTMANN % Winkel
GOTTSCHALDT, Martin, 21, college student, NYC?, 1911/10/07:1f
GOTTSCHALK, Albert, 5, NYC-B - 1894/10/05:4a
GOTTSCHALK, August, machinist, NYC-M – 1903/01/16:4a
GOTTSCHALK, Charlotte, 23, servant, NYC-M - 1895/11/02: 1g
GOTTSCHALK, Edward, 7, NYC-B – 1881/01/10:3b
GOTTSCHALK, Hermann, 69, engineer, SP, *Hilden/Gy, co-fdr NYVZ, NYC-M – 1908/12/23:1e,6a, 24:6a, =26:1g,4a, fam. 26:4a
GOTTSCHALK, Rudolph, 4, NYC-B - 1879/02/22:1c
GOTTSCHALK, William, 75, silk weaver, *Brandenburg/Gy, SDP, West Hoboken, NJ – 1903/02/28:3d
GOTTSCHALL, Rudolf von, 86, '48er, German poet, + Leipzig/Gy – 1909/03/24:4c
GOTTSEYER, William, 41, NYC-M – 1897/12/26:1d
GOTZEN, John, un. archit. Iron worker, NYC-M – 1900/08/09:4a
GOULD, Jay, US capitalist, crit. obit. – 1892/12/03:1b-d
GOUNOD, Charles F., French composer, – 1893/10/18:1b, = 28:1a
GOVERNALE, Salvatore, exec. Ossining, NY – 1909/02/02:2b
GRAAP, Carl, NYC-M – 1910/08/02:6a
GRAB, Otto, NYC-Q – 1911/11/15:6a, fam. 19:7c
GRABBEL, Friedrich, 55, tailor, NYC-M – 1898/05/13:3e
GRABE, Eduard, un. carp., NYC-M – 1889/12/11:4a
GRABE, Frederick, 76, * Gy, taught German at Nebraska U, then Boys' HS in Brooklyn, + Hempstead, LI - 1916/01/11:6a
GRABLOVIC, Anton, Slovene soc., shoemaker & ed. Delavec, + Laibach/Slovenia – 1904/08/13:2e
GRABUSCH, Katherina, NYC-Q - 1920/11/05:6a
GRACE, Anthony W., exec. Ossining, NY - 1913/08/05:6c
GRACE, William R., 71, ex-mayor of NYC – 1904/03/22:2h
GRAD, P.G., NYC-B – 1891/07/26:4a
GRAEBNER, Louis, un. smith, NYC-Q – 1916/09/04:6a, fam. 9:6a
GRAEF % Hasselmann
GRAEF, Arnold, author, court translator, US consul in Dresden 1854-56, * 1812 Franzburg/Aachen, USA 1846, NYC-B – 1883/09/01:3b

GRAEF, Carl, un. carp., NYC-M – 1912/02/04:7c, =8:2b
GRAEF, William, butcher, NYC-B – 1905/02/16:3c
GRAEFE % Krug
GRAEFE, Albrecht von, Dr., 1828-1870, German eye doctor – 1882/06/11:2d-e
GRAEFER, C., Jersey City, NJ, fam. 1882/08/20:8a
GRAEFF, Carl, tobacco manufacturer in Bingen/Rhein, + Salt Lake City, UT - 1878/07/29:4e,30:4d
GRAEHLING, Carl, 53, NYC-M – 1897/01/30:4a
GRAESER, (comrade), SPD Elberfeld/Gy – 1904/05/04:2d
GRAESS, Charles, carp., NYC – 1911/12/07:1f
GRAEULICH, Johann Heinrich, 55?, NYC-M – 1891/08/11:4a
GRAEWE, J. C. W., Hoboken, NJ – 1889/02/22:4a
GRAEWE, Meta, b. Westervelt, 78, Hoboken, NJ – 1892/09/17:4a
GRAF % Blum/Ufert, % Feldmann, % Pauline
GRAF Sr., Louis, 55, un. cigarmaker, NYC-M - 1918/11/15:2g
GRAF, Alma, 13, & Frank, 10, Jersey City, NJ – 1912/01/01:1e
GRAF, Anna Louisa, b. Bachmann, 62, NYC-Bx – 1911/10/13:6a
GRAF, Barbara, 31, NYC-M - 1920/03/04:6a
GRAF, Charles, 75, carp., NYC-M – 1896/07/28:1e
GRAF, Charlotte, NYC-M, + @Genl Slocum – 1904/06/18:3c
GRAF, Elisabetha, NYC-M - 1895/04/19:4a
GRAF, Georg W., 36, milkman, NYC-B – 1898/11/05:4a
GRAF, Guenther, 64, pianomaker, Union Hill, NJ - 1914/03/14:2c
GRAF, Helena, 23, NYC-M - 1919/02/17:6a
GRAF, Jacob, NYC-Q - 1918/12/13:6a
GRAF, John, NYC-M – 1907/09/07:6a
GRAF, Julie, 12, NYC-Q – 1909/12/20:6a
GRAF, Kaspar, 50, grocer, USA ~1871, NYC-M – 1891/10/22:1h
GRAF, Katie, 52, NYC-M – 1893/11/22:4a
GRAF, Louis, wine dealer, NYC-B – 1909/10/08:2c
GRAF, Magdalena, NYC-M – 1919/11/12:6a
GRAF, Marie, 40, NYC-M - 1896/03/03:1h
GRAF, Marie, 48, NYC-Q - 1918/10/26:6a
GRAF, Michael, NYC-B – 1909/10/27:6a
GRAF, Michael, NYC-Bx – 1907/07/02:6a
GRAF, Oscar, Elizabeth, NJ - 1919/03/09:12a
GRAFERE, Lulu, NYC-M, + @Genl Slocum – 1904/06/17:3b
GRAFF, Anton, 23, German citz, NYC-B – 1916/06/25:11a
GRAFF, Franz, NYC-Q - 1920/08/28:6a
GRAFF, Karl, 29, carp., USA 1881, NYC-M – 1893/09/16:1f

GRAFF, Otto A., conductor of NYC Liederkranz s. 1914, NYC-B - 1917/05/10:2f
GRAFING, Lillie, 28, NYC-M, +@ Genl Slocum – 1904/06/17:3b
GRAFSTEIN, Charles, un. carp., NYC-Bx – 1907/01/27:7c
GRAFT, Jakob, embroidery shop, NYC-M - 1895/10/20: 5d
GRAFULLA, Claudius, conductor 7th Regt NYNG band, *Minorca/Spain, NYC-M – 1880/12/04:1d
GRAHAM, Daniel, NYC-M – 1893/12/02:4a
GRAHAM, Michael, chief NYC fire brigade, NYC-B – 1909/02/16:2a
GRAHAM, Robert Cunningham, Engl. Socialist MP, his life (not +) 1890/12/01:1d-e
GRAHL, Bernhard M., NYC-M – 1888/01/17:3a
GRAHL, Charles William, 4, NYC-M – 1882/11/05:5e
GRAHL, Emil, 51, NYC-M – 1904/02/13:4a
GRAHL, Julius, 42?, NYC-M – 1889/01/05:3c
GRAHL, Oscar, NYC-B – 1904/01/23:4a
GRAHN, Max, 76, ex-NYC?, Tampa, FL – 1919/12/09:8a
GRAHN, Pehr A., 87, NYC-Q - 1920/09/24:6a
GRALOW, Ernestine, NYC-M – 1889/11/07:4a
GRAMFIRE, Lillian, NYC-M, + @Genl Slocum – 1904/06/16:1c, 17:3b
GRAMLICH % Schlee
GRAMLICH, Frank, un. beer driver, NYC-SI – 1901/11/10:5a
GRAMLICH, William G., 29, NYC-M – 1905/07/02:5a
GRAMLICH, William, 32, NYC-M – 1885/05/24:1f, 25:1f, inquest 27:3a, 29:3a, 2 June:3a
GRAMM, John, 50, grocer, & son John, 7, NYC-M – 1898/05/04:1e, 12:4c
GRAMM, Karl, 64, SPD Hamburg, co-fdr Tischler-Zeitung – 1901/10/28:2d
GRAN, Moritz, un. printer, NYC-Bx - 1916/05/07:7b
GRANATA, comrade, Italian Socialist, + Messina earthquake – 1909/02/23:4d
GRANERT, Henriette, NYC-B – 1910/01/07:6a, fam. 10:6a
GRANGER, George, 22, exec. Ossining, NY – 1907/02/25:3e, 5 Mr:2b
GRANT, Julia D., widow of president, her = - 1902/12/22:1d
GRANT, Ulysses, US president, 1885/04/03:1f, 4:1f, 5:5d, 6:1g, etc, dying 30 May:1e-f, 24 Jy:1a-e, 2a-b, 25:1a-b, 2a-b,c, 27:1g, 2b-c, etc, 29:1e-g, 31:1e-f, burial preps 4 Au:1g, 5:1e-f, 6:1e-f, 2c, 7:1e-f, 8:1e-f, =10:1b, collection for monument 22:4a. Crit. notes to inaug. Mausoleum 1897/04/27:2a-b, 28:1h, 29:3b-c, 29:1g
GRANTZ, Louise, b. Fernau, 57, NYC-Spring Valley – 1887/03/03:3d
GRANZ, August, 54, NYC-B – 1910/08/20:6a, 21:7c
GRAPP, Tessie, 38, & her husband, NYC-M – 1910/07/31:7f

GRAS, Francois, innkeep, NYC-M - 1878/08/08:4d
GRASMUCK, Adam, 62, NYC-M - 1892/07/08:4a
GRASS, J., cigarmaker & SPD activist expelled fr Hamburg/Gy, arrived NYC - 1881/06/16:4a
GRASS, Justine, 50,Guttenberg, NJ - 1916/05/24:6a, fam.28:7d
GRASSE, Marie, & daughter Emilie, NYC-M - 1909/12/01:2f
GRASSE, William, 60, un. painter, * Graz/Austria, USA 1887, NYC-? - 1917/08/16:2f,6a, 17:6a, 18:6a, = 19:7e
GRASSL, Nikolaus,21,SP, German-Hungarian, NYC-M -1916/09/06:2d
GRASSMANN, John, NYC-Metropolitan - 1914/01/30:6a
GRASSMEHER, Charles, NYC-M - 1902/07/24:4a, 25:4a, fam. 29:4a
GRATER, Lizzie, 20, servant, NYC-M - 1896/03/18:1h
GRATZ, Henriette, 33, NYC-M - 1887/03/21:3c
GRATZER, Gustav, 67, cutter, NYC-M - 1892/03/11:1g
GRATZER, Meinrath, NYC? - 1886/09/18:3b
GRAU, Georg, NYC-M - 1911/04/18:6a
GRAU, Maurice, ex-mgr NYC Metrop. Opera, + Paris/France - 1907/03/15:2e
GRAU, Robert, music impresario, Mt Vernon, NY - 1916/08/10:2b
GRAU, Samuel, 58, NYC-M - 1891/09/20:5f
GRAU, William, 1, NYC-M - 1889/07/01:4a
GRAUBNER, Albert, NYC-M - 1920/04/06:6a
GRAUBNER, Marie, geb. Schaefer, NYC-Bx - 1919/09/24:6a
GRAUE, Anna, NYC-M - 1917/04/12:6a
GRAUE, August, 31, silk weaver, Hoboken, NJ - 1897/03/02:4c
GRAUER, Oswald, 59, SPD Berlin-Hoppgarten, alderman - 1915/01/03:3d
GRAUL, Charles, NYC-Q - 1920/07/11:12a
GRAVELIUS, Christian, 67, confectioner, * Gruenberg/Hessia, ex-Intl Workers' Assoc., NYC-B - 1894/09/21:4a, = 22: 1h,4a
GRAVENHORST, C. J. H., 75, innovative German beekeeper, +Wilsnak/Altmark - 1898/09/18:12h
GRAVES, Frederick, NYC-M, +@ on Genl Slocum - 1904/06/18:3c
GRAVES, Helen, 26, NYC-B - 1918/12/25:2f
GRAVEUR, Joseph C., 45, pres. Alhambra Garage Co. & social reformer, NYC-B, + Philadelphia - 1916/09/28:2a
GRAY, Elisha, 65, inventor in telegraphic devices, Newtonville, MA - 1901/01/22:2f
GRAY, Emma, b. Muck, 41, NYC-M - 1902/01/30:4a
GRAY, Franklin, Dr. med., Jersey City, NJ - 1916/06/12:5f
GRAY, John, innkeep & local polit., NYC-M - 1893/03/26:1d
GRAYNER, Ernst, 49, fr Holzhausen/Gy, Jersey City, NJ - 1913/11/22:5e

GREAT BRITAIN, Edward VII, King of, 68, very negat obit – 1910/05/07:1e-f, 8:6a-c, 22:6b-c
GREAT BRITAIN, Victoria, Queen, 50th anniv. Of rule, very crit. Edit, esp. that New Yorker rich hail an imperialist monarchy – 1887/06/22:1b-e, 23:1a, 2a-b, 24:1a, 3a, 27:1g. +, crit obit – 1901/01/23:1h, 3b, 2a-b, mourning affected by US Anglophiles crit. 24:1a-b, 2b-c, =26:1b, 27:4a-b, 31:1a, 3 Fb:1a, Michael Davitt sums her up 4 Fb:1b, 2c, 5:1a
GREB, Jacob, un. carp., NYC-Bx – 1910/01/06:6a
GREB, Sophie, b. Rippke, NYC-M – 1893/08/16:4a
GREBNER, John, NYC-M - 1894/10/16:4a
GREEDINGER, John, NYC-B – 1903/03/09:4a
GREELEY, Horace, publ. & reformer, 100th anniv. – 1911/02/03:4a-b
GREEN, Andrew H., ex-NYC Comptroller, co-owner NYSZ, NYC-M – 1903/11/14:1f-g, 15:1c-d, 4b-c, 17:1h, =18:1h
GREEN, George, exec. Greenwood, ARK – 1881/07/23:1e
GREEN, George, Negro, exec. Trenton, NJ - 1915/01/06:2f
GREEN, Katie, 23, NYC-B – 1904/11/11:1f
GREEN, Rosie, 18, NYC-B - 1913/10/08:3b
GREENBAUM, Israel, 30, tailor, NYC-M – 1892/03/11:1g
GREENBAUM, Samuel, NYC-M – 1904/11/21:4a
GREENBERG, 17, North Tarrytown, NY – 1912/10/17:1f
GREENBERG, Chiwa, 55, NYC-M – 1902/05/27:2f
GREENBERG, Dinah, 18, @1911 Triangle Shirtwaist Fire NYC-M, NYC-B – 1911/03/27:1d
GREENBERG, Sadie, 5, NYC-M – 1893/03/02:4b
GREENBERGER, Jacob, 62, NYC-M – 1890/10/16:4a
GREENBURG, Leopold, 33, NYC-B - 1915/01/05:6c
GREENE, Max, hatmaker, mortally wounded during strike, NYC-B - 1913/11/29:2a
GREENFIELD, Nathan O., local polit., exec. Syracuse, NY – 1881/08/06:1c
GREENSTEIN, Molly, 6, NYC-M – 1893/04/23:5c
GREENVELT, Otto,War 2, (dying), Elizabeth,NJ -1918/11/12:2f
GREENWALD, Albert & Richard, 5, NYC-M, + @ Genl Slocum – 1904/06/16:1e, 25:1d
GREENWALD, Jonas, 71, NYC-M – 1893/11/26:5d
GREENWOOD, Gertrude F., 20, teacher, NYC-M - 1879/08/27:1e
GREFF, W., West Hoboken, NJ – 1905/05/30:4a
GREFTES, Andrew, silk weaver, Paterson, NJ – 1896/09/18:1e
GREGOR, Carl G., NYC-M – 1893/06/02:4a
GREGOR, Meta M., NYC-B – 1899/02/02:4a
GREGOROVIUS, Rosa, 70, Hoboken, NJ – 1891/10/14:4a

GREGOROVIUS, Rudolph, G-A journalist, incl. NYVZ, *10 May 1845 Posen/Gy, USA 1859, Hoboken, NJ – 1900/06/22:1d
GREHER, Katie, 11, NYC-M, +@ Genl Slocum – 1904/06/17:3b
GREIE, Emil, 37, SLP, Elizabethport, NJ – 1899/01/23:4a, =25:3e, fam. 25:4a
GREIE, Johanna Cramer-, SP activist & writer, *6 Jan 1864 Dresden/Gy, USA 1877, Elizabeth, NJ, her life 26 Fb 1911:20d; + 23 Aug:1c-d, 24:1f, 4a, 6a, 25:2a, 5f, 6a, =26:1g, 2a, fam. 27:7c, poem by Geo. Biedenkapp 27:8a, note 27:20g, by W. Rosenberg 28:3b-e, by Emma Schien 3 Sept:20c, 10:3a, 20f. Mem. 1912/08/22:6a, 1916/08/20:20a
GREIF, Martin, German poet, 1911/04/02:1a
GREIFELD, Max, 28, bookkeeper, mother-in-law Mrs Horn & servant Ms Dreier, NYC-B - 1879/03/14:1e, = 17:4d
GREIFEN, Friedericke, b. Boehm, 52, NYC-M – 1889/06/08:5b
GREIFENBERG, Antonie, child, NYC-M – 1890/12/11:4a
GREIFENBERG, Karl, * Thorn/West Prussia, SPD, arrived NYC – 1880/12/18:1g, typesetter at NYVZ, + 38 yrs old, NYC-B – 1889/03/29:1h, 4a, 30:4a, =31:5c
GREIFENSTEIN, George, 57, NYC-M – 1892/06/17:4a
GREIFF, Hans, NYC-Bx – 1919/11/18:6a
GREINEISEN, Alfred, 44, un. cook, Union Hill, NJ - 1913/06/05:6a
GREINEISEN, Ernest A., 67, un. silkweaver, Union Hill, NJ – 1912/02/05:6a, fam. 18:7c
GREINER, John, 54, NYC-M – 1910/04/15:6a
GREINER, John, 60, stonecutter, NYC-M – 1909/08/05:6a
GREINER, Karl, NYC-M – 1909/07/25:7a
GREIS, Charles, Newark, NJ – 1907/08/08:6a
GREISEL, Emma, 15, NYC-M, +@Genl Slocum – 1904/06/22:1d
GREISIGER, John, West Newark, NJ – 1912/07/03:6a
GREISS, Clara, 12, NYC-M, +@Genl Slocum – 1904/06/22:1d
GREISS, Gottfried's wife, NYC-M, + Newburgh, NY – 1903/08/27:1g
GREISSLER, ..., 18, NYC-M, + @Genl Slocum – 1904/06/18:3c
GREMM, Georg, 39, NYC-M – 1898/01/27:4a
GRENDEL, Karl Heinrich, 52, NYC-M or Bx – 1892/10/06:4a
GRERE, (Ms), NYC-M – 1891/06/28:5c
GRESCH, Joseph, 40, Hoboken, NJ – 1887/09/07:4e
GRESE, Elizabeth, NYC-Bx - 1916/05/06:6a
GRESKO, Andrew, 106 (!), fr Austria, Clearfield, PA - 1916/08/31:1f
GRESNAG, Marte, 26, NYC-M – 1891/09/20:5f
GRESS, Elisabeth & Walter, NYC-M, +@Genl Slocum – 1904/06/18:3c
GRESS, Eliza, 42, NYC-M, + @Genl Slocum – 1904/06/17:3b
GRESS, Fredericke, 50, NYC-M – 1902/06/05:4a

GRESS, Isidor, 46, un. carp., NYC-M – 1902/09/15:4a
GRESS, Louis, worker, & Jennie, NYC-M - 1895/01/12:1f
GRESS, Otto, 43, Sarah, 12, NYC-M, + @ Genl Slocum – 1904/06/21:1f
GRETEN, Bertha, NYC-M - 1895/10/12: 4a
GRETSCH, Benjamin, un. cigarmaker, natl secy SLP 1889-91, *6 Mr 1860 Kiew/Ukraine, NYC-B 1894/12/12:1g,=13:3e
GRETSCH, Joseph M., New Haven, CT – 1893/07/21:4a
GRETSCH, Louis, painter & burglar, NYC – 1910/05/27:1e
GRETTLER, Caroline, 65, NYC-M, + on Genl Slocum – 1904/06/18:3c
GRETZ, Bertha, NYC-M – 1889/08/06:1h
GRETZ, Joseph, 25, butcher-clerk, NYC-B - 1913/05/21:3b
GRETZNER, Pauline, 17, NYC, married Robert Bowman – 1897/02/26:1e
GREULICH, Hermann, Swiss deputy, SP, Zuerich/Switz., *9 Ap 1842 Breslau/Gy, to visit US, en route to Chicago # – 1904/08/07:4c-g, 20:2a-b, in Yorkville 21:1e, 22:1g, 23:1d-e, Paterson 27:1g, 28:5f, Passaic 29:4a, B'lyn 31:1e, Bronx 3 Sept:1g, 4:5g, Cleveland 9 Oc:12a, farewell by NYC SP 5 Oct:1g. 70th birthday 9 Apr 1912:4c-d, 22:4f, 23:4e
GREULICH, Margarete, 50, Swiss labor artist - 1917/07/08:20d
GREVE, Carl, un. cigarmaker, NYC-M - 1878/10/31:3a
GREVEL, William, 55, co-owner Fleischmann's Vienna Café, NYC-M – 1909/08/19:2c
GREWE, August, un. cigarmaker, NYC-M - 1878/05/30:3b
GREWE, Elise, b. Huesing, 67, NYC-M – 1912/07/21:7a
GREWE, Frieda, 25, NYC-M – 1896/09/12:4a
GREWE, Marie, 17, NYC-M – 1886/06/29:3b
GREWES, Lillian, NYC-M, + @Genl Slocum – 1904/06/21:1f
GREY, Bertha, 25, @1911 Triangle Shirtwaist Fire, NYC-M, NYC-B – 1911/03/27:1d
GRICHS, Georg, un. carp., NYC-M – 1900/02/20:4a
GRICK, William, NYC-B - 1896/04/03:4a
GRIEG, Edward, Norwegian composer – 1907/09/05:1e
GRIEGER, Albert, NYC-Q – 1909/08/15:7c
GRIEGER, Maria, NYC-Q – 1912/10/20:7b
GRIER, Ulrich, 50, tailor, NYC-M – 1883/11/10:4b
GRIESBECK, Albert, 34, NYC-Q – 1912/01/11:6a
GRIESDECK, Joseph, SLP, *Wuerttemberg, shoemaker, then beer dealer, NYC-B – 1899/12/11:3c, 4a, fam. 14:4a
GRIESEL, Sophie, b. Messin, NYC-Q – 1910/05/26:6a
GRIESEMER, Michael, NYC - 1913/05/16:6a
GRIESER, Valentin, 68, SP, un. cigarmaker, New Haven, CT - 1917/06/21:6a, mem. 1918/06/19:6a
GRIESHABER, Anton, cooper, NYC-M – 1913/03/07:6a

GRIESHABER, August, 66, un. baker, NYC-Bx - 1917/02/01:6a
GRIESHABER, Rudolf, NYC-M - 1920/07/30:6a
GRIESHABER, Wilhelmine, b. Maurer, NYC-Q - 1901/07/06:4a
GRIESSER, Jakob, 33, + Boston, MA - 1911/01/07:6a
GRIESSMANN, Paul, NYC-M - 1910/04/30:6a
GRIFFEL, Conrad, tinsmith, 44, NYC-M - 1913/01/18:1b
GRIFFION, Preston, Negro, lynched Monroe, LA - 1914/08/08:2d
GRIGAL, Christopher, 58, Hoboken, NJ - 1920/11/07:12a
GRIGER, Andreas, 58, NYC-M - 1878/12/06:1g
GRIGOROWITSCH, Dimitri, 1822-1900, Russian writer, 1900/07/29:7a-c
GRILL, Andrew, 49, worker, Yonkers, NY - 1912/10/04:1e
GRILLENBERGER, Karl, SPD MdR for Munich/Gy - 1897/10/21:1b,2b, # 4 Nov:2d, =7:7d-f. Grave mon. inaug. In Nuernberg - 1898/11/16:3e
GRILLPARZER, Franz, poet, # 100th anniv. by Julie Romm - 1891/01/11:4d-f
GRIMINGER, Andrew F., 69, NYC-M - 1894/01/28:5d
GRIMLE, William, tailor, NYC-M - 1893/10/12:4b
GRIMM % Dennecke, % Ende, % Mueller
GRIMM, Anna H., 60, NYC-B - 1916/05/10:3d
GRIMM, Elisabeth, 17, NYC-B - 1886/11/16:2c-d
GRIMM, Frederick J., 7, NYC-M - 1891/08/12:4a
GRIMM, Fritz, un. carp., NYC-M - 1902/07/18:4a
GRIMM, John, NYC-B - 1911/07/06:6a
GRIMM, Josephine, NYC-Bx - 1914/07/17:6a
GRIMM, Maria S., 51, NYC-M - 1891/08/08:4a
GRIMM, Max, foreman, W. Hoboken, NJ - 1897/12/25:4b
GRIMM, Sebastian, 52, NYC-M - 1891/03/30:4a
GRIMM, Selma, 34, NYC-M, +@ Genl Slocum - 1904/06/16:1c, 17:3b
GRIMME % Koch
GRIMME, August, Elizabeth, NJ - 1917/02/08:6a
GRIMMEL, Frederick, 77, NYC-B - 1891/07/02:4a
GRIMMER, Oskar, un. painter, NYC-M - 1912/03/12:2c, 13:6a, fam. 14:6a
GRIMMLER, Barbara, 2, NYC-B - 1885/08/19:4c inquest (+19 Jy)
GRIMMLER, Martha, West New York, NJ - 1917/06/02:6a
GRIMPE, comrade Mrs, 59, SPD Elberfeld - 1913/09/07:3d
GRINNELL, Addie, 84, actress, NYC-B - 1913/11/12:6a
GRINNELL, District Attney in Haymarket case, + Chicago - 1898/06/13:2a
GRISSELMANN % Loeb
GRITZINGER, Gottlieb, collector, Jersey City, NJ - 1887/08/04:1f
GROB, George, machinist, SP, NYC-B - 1912/04/25:6a
GROB, Gottlieb, 38, cook, Swiss, NYC-M - 1894/05/04:1h
GROB, Jacob, NYC-M - 1911/05/13:6a

GROB, John, 27, un. carp., NYC-Bx – 1908/08/27:6a
GROB, John, pianomaker, NYC-M – 1907/11/07:2d
GROB, Justus, 63, carp., NYC-B – 1908/09/29:3b
GROB, Lisette, b. Stein, fr Mittelbach/Bavaria, Union Hill, NJ – 1890/01/29:4a
GROB, William, mem. poem – 1900/12/03:4a
GROBATSCHEK, John, mason, NYC-M – 1888/09/18:2f
GROBE, Ernestine, NYC-M – 1913/02/12:6a, 13:6a
GROBE, Heinrich, 72, SP, NYC-M – 1907/04/05:6a, 6:2b,6a, fam. 9:6a
GROBEL, Marie, b. Spieker, 64, Secaucus, NJ - 1917/03/03:6a, fam. 7:6a
GROBEL, Robert, 67, liquor dealer, Swiss?,Secaucus, NJ - 1920/04/20:6a
GROBHOLZ, Michael, 38, Jersey City, NJ - 1914/01/02:3c
GROBLEWSKY, Joseph, NYC, to be exec.for + wife – 1885/11/ 21: 2d, 24:2e, 7 Ja 86:2e, 8:2d, appeal 12:2f, 23 Nov:2c, decl insane 4 Jan 87:2e
GRODE, Christopher, 29, NYC-M – 1891/02/20:4a
GRODE, Margarethe, NYC-M – 1891/03/29:5a
GROEBER, Frank, NYC-M – 1909/05/08:6a
GROEHL, Jack, NYC-B - 1918/03/19:6a
GROEHL, John, 48, NYC-SI - 1919/02/25:6a, 26:6a, fam. 2 Mr:12a
GROEMLING, Adam, 60, NYC-B – 1908/06/19:6a
GROENEBAUM, Leopold, 76, NYC-M – 1891/07/25:4a
GROENEMEYER, Heinrich, un. cigarmaker, NYC-Q – 1910/04/18:6a
GROENEWALD, Theodor, NYC-B, trial – 1887/05/18:2f-3b, 19:2a-b, 20:3a, 21:3a, to be exec. 24 May:2d, 27:2d, 28:2e, 9 June:2e
GROENINGER, Adele, b. Relin, NYC-M – 1890/03/31:4a
GROENINGER, Hans, infant, NYC-B – 1890/07/21:4a
GROENLUND, Lawrence, 53, writer, *Copenhagen/Denmark, NYC-M – 1899/10/17:1f
GROENTHAL, Barbara, 16, servant, NYC-B – 1881/01/04:1e, =7:3a, murderer James Walsh executed 1882/07/21:2g, 22:1g
GROESCHEL % Vogel
GROESCHL, Ferdinand, 50, NYC-B - 1895/02/25:4a
GROETTER, William, 35, mail carrier, NYC? – 1900/08/17:2g
GROFF, I., SP, benefit for, NYC? – 1908/12/11:5f, rev. 14:5d
GROFF, William, NYC-Q - 1920/05/12:6a
GROFSKI, Theodore von, NYC-B – 1905/04/27:3d, 20 May:3d
GROH, John, 39, of Groh's Brewery, NYC-M – 1900/03/02:1e
GROHMAN, Edith, b. Faerber, 22, Newark, NJ - 1913/05/28:1f
GROLKA, Amelia & Olga, NYC-M, + @ Genl Slocum – 1904/06/18:3c
GROLLEMUND, Rudolph,16, (dying)Jersey City, NJ - 1917/08/16:2a
GROLLIMUND, Albert, cooper?, NYC-M – 1893/09/04:4a, 6:4a
GROMANN, August, 75, NYC-M – 1912/10/17:6a

GROMANN, Henriette, b. Glade, 61, NYC-M – 1902/10/29:4a
GROMPE, Alfred, 39, cigarmaker, NYC-M – 1899/02/02:4a
GRONWALDT, May, NYC-B – 1891/08/11:4a
GROPPE, William, 70, shoemaker, NYC-B – 1913/05/14:3a-b
GROSCH, George, 34, NYC-M – 1894/01/10:4a
GROSCH, William, 22, Hoboken, NJ – 1914/01/28:2e, 1 Fb:1d
GROSCHE, Paul, 15, USA 1879, Verona, NJ – 1887/12/30:4c
GROSCHWITZ, John, un. painter, NYC-M – 1918/09/02:6a
GROSS, Albert, NYC-B – 1914/09/13:7a
GROSS, Anna, 16, servant, NYC-B – 1906/07/27:3a
GROSS, August, 56, NYC-M – 1891/08/26:4a
GROSS, Barbara, 60, NYC-M – 1889/09/15:1d
GROSS, Bertha, 26, NYC-B – 1912/07/06:3b
GROSS, Carl, NYC-Q – 1891/07/11:1h
GROSS, Franz, machinist, NYC-M – 1890/06/20:4a
GROSS, Friedrich, 35, iron worker, dying, NYC – 1900/08/08:3c
GROSS, Georg, NYC-M – 1908/05/27:6a, 28:6a
GROSS, Gertrud, 71, NYC-B – 1887/08/24:2e
GROSS, Gottlieb, tailor & SPD Beefelden/Hessia, Gy – 1909/05/16:3b
GROSS, Gustav, NYC-M – 1915/04/15:6a
GROSS, Heinrich, 67, SPD Hamburg – 1914/12/27:3a, 3 Ja 1915:3a-b
GROSS, Helene, 18, servant, NYC-Q – 1915/08/25:2b
GROSS, Henry, sailor on USS Maine, + Havana/Cuba, NYC-M –
    1898/02/18:1b
GROSS, Herman's wife, NYC-M – 1888/08/06:3b
GROSS, Jacob, 32, dyer, NYC-M – 1907/02/26:2b
GROSS, Jacob, NYC-M – 1891/03/16:4a
GROSS, Josephine, 56, NYC-M – 1891/03/14:4a
GROSS, Julia, 16, NYC-M – 1895/04/24:1g, 25:1g
GROSS, Louis F., tugboat captain, Fairview, NJ – 1920/08/07:1g, 15
    Sept:2e
GROSS, Louisa M., Paterson, NJ – 1896/06/05:4b
GROSS, Rosa, 35, d. 7th NYC-M – 1894/08/08:1g
GROSS, Rudolf, Union Hill, NJ – 1893/04/23:5c
GROSS, Theresa, Easton, PA, + at son's in NYC-B – 1888/11/15:3b
GROSS, Wilhelm, un. carpenter, NYC-M – 1895/11/25: 4a
GROSSE, Ludwig, American relief worker, + Berlin/Gy – 1917/01/23:1c
GROSSE, Max, Yonkers, NY – 1918/12/24:6a
GROSSER, Boleslaw, 29, lawyer & Soc., + Warsaw, PL– 1913/01/15:4d
GROSSER, William, NYC-Bx – 1910/02/06:7c
GROSSKOPF % Reisel
GROSSKOPF, Friederike, NYC-M – 1907/07/08:6a

GROSSKOPF, Wilhelm, un. carp., NYC-M – 1903/09/17:4a
GROSSMAN, Rachel, 17, @1911 Triangle Shirtwaist Fire, NYC-M – 1911/03/27:1d
GROSSMANN, Adolph, 35, fr Hungary 1886, & wife Minnie, 32, NYC-M – 1904/03/24:2h
GROSSMANN, Arthur, 10, NYC-M – 1909/06/01:6a
GROSSMANN, Frederick, 27, * Russia, NYC-M - 1894/03/02:1g
GROSSMANN, Ida Katherina, 4, Jersey City Heights, NJ – 1901/07/03:4a
GROSSMANN, Jennie, 22, servant, NYC-M – 1891/06/21:1g
GROSSMANN, John, 50, NYC-M – 1892/04/09:4a
GROSSMANN, Joseph, 22, + during strike, NYC-M – 1906/07/06:1e
GROSSMANN, Karl, NYC-Bx - 1914/07/16:6a
GROSSMANN, Max, 41, SP Hungary, un. printer, chief edit. Budapest Volkstimme, + Budapest - 1913/08/05:4f, = 9:4d
GROSSMANN, Max, NYC-Q - 1918/05/17:6a
GROSSMANN, Moritz, un. cigarmaker, NYC-M – 1900/04/24:4a
GROSSMANN, Sarah, 44, NYC – 1900/08/08:3g
GROSSMANN, Theodor, 50, tortoise-shell polisher, NYC-M – 1888/04/27:4b
GROSSWEILER, Edward, 80, NYC-B - 1920/04/18:2e
GROSZ, Jean, 35, * Hamburg, USA 1881, SLP, un. cigarmaker, NYC-M – 1885/05/11:1f,3a, =12:3d, 4a, 13:1d
GROSZ, Minna, NYC-M – 1885/09/29:3b
GROTE, Ernst, 37, NYC-M – 1897/08/14:4a
GROTE, Henry, NYC-M – 1907/04/07:7b
GROTE, Hermann, NYC-B - 1878/08/06:3a
GROTE, Sophie, b. Kundmueller, 26, NYC-M – 1892/07/10:5c
GROTE, Wilhelmine, NYC-Bx – 1911/01/04:6a
GROTE, William, 50, worker, Hastings, NY, War 2 - 1915/08/17:1d
GROTH, Karl K., 74, Union Hill, NJ, & 7:3c
GROTH, Klaus, 80, Plattdeutsch poet, + Gy – 1899/06/04:1f, 4f-h, 11:4f-h
GROTHE % Kerschowsky
GROTHE, Ida, 50, innkeep, SPD Halle/Saale/Gy – 1908/12/06:3c
GROTHE, Wilhelm, SPD Halle/Gy – 1904/08/13:2e
GROTHE, William, NYC-M – 1891/07/07:4a
GROTIAN, Mildred, NYC-M - 1917/01/15:6a
GROTT, John, 58, farmer, NYC-Q – 1892/09/25:1g
GROTTHUS, Jeannot von, 55, German writer, + Berlin - 1920/09/29:4d
GROTTIAN, Friedrich, 63, NYC-M - 1917/08/03:6a
GROTTKAU, Paul, ~55, SLP militant, a.e. NYC, Chicago & Milwaukee – 1898/06/05:5d
GROUSSARD, Leopold, confectioner, * France, NYC-M - 1894/10/13:2d

GROWALD, Elsie, 10, NYC-M, + @on Genl Slocum – 1904/06/18:3c
GRUB, Jacob, NYC-M - 1915/01/06:6a
GRUBE, Afra, 34, NYC-M – 1880/10/24:5e
GRUBE, Sophie, 23, NYC-M – 1897/07/28:1d
GRUBE, William, 46, NYC-B – 1911/07/12:1f
GRUBENMANN, J., un. cornice maker, NYC-M – 1889/11/14:4a
GRUBER, Emma, 39, & Carrie, 14, Harry, 14, NYC-M, + @ Genl Slocum – 1904/06/17:3b
GRUBER, G., 54, plumber, Jersey City, NJ – 1902/04/26:3c
GRUBER, Joseph, 44, linotypist-machinist, SDP, Jersey City, NJ – 1902/04/26:1e, 4a
GRUBER, Laurenz, * 10 June 1860 Austria, + Chicago, IL - 1914/02/23:6a
GRUEN, Balthasar, German anarchist, + Hanau/Gy – 1882/09/26:2f
GRUEN, Bruno, 54, NYC-Bx - 1914/04/28:6a
GRUEN, Lena, 25, servant, NYC-B 1895/05/11:4a
GRUENBLATT, Anna, 4, NYC-B – 1899/03/25:1c
GRUENDLER, August, 45, NYC-M – 1903/07/17:4a
GRUENDLER, Edward, 68, Hollbrook, LI – 1911/02/07:6a
GRUENDLING, John, Newark, NJ – 1907/02/06:6a
GRUENEBAUM, Fannie, servant, fr Russia, NYC-M – 1900/04/12:1c
GRUENEBAUM, Leopold, NYC-M – 1891/07/16:4a
GRUENENTHAL, John, 50, NYC-B – 1880/12/24:2g
GRUENEWALD, Gustav, NYC-B – 1907/07/24:6a
GRUENEWALD, Marie, b. Sprenger, NYC-M – 1890/02/23:5b
GRUENFELDER, Louis, machinist, NYC-B – 1906/07/24:6a
GRUENINGER % Kalter
GRUENINGER, Frederick, 68, Jersey City Hgts,NJ - 1916/08/16:6a
GRUENINGER, Fritz's wife, Jersey City Heights, NJ – 1896/09/14:4a
GRUENSTEIN, Abraham, 24, NYC-M – 1891/08/26:4a
GRUENWALD, Emilie, 16?, NYC-M – 1891/08/26:4a
GRUENWALD, John, exec. NYC-B – 1889/12/06:1e, 7:1d, 2b
GRUENWALD, Karoline, NYC-B – 1898/04/06:4b
GRUENWALD, Theodor, barber fr Heidelberg/Gy, + on SS Palatia on way to NYC – 1897/12/26:1h
GRUETTER, Edward, 14, NYC-M – 1898/12/03:4a
GRUETTER, Wilhelmine, b. Wilke, NYC-M – 1890/06/26:4a
GRUETZNER, August L., machinist, NYC-M - 1895/05/21:4a
GRUHL, Karl, 49, draughtsman, SPD Nowawes/Berlin – 1911/07/16:3b-c
GRUMEL, Martin, carp., 49, NYC-M – 1901/03/10:1g
GRUND, Josef, un. machinist, NYC-M – 1886/09/14:3c
GRUNDER, Louis, NYC-M - 1920/02/15:12a
GRUNDIG, Julius, 62, NYC-M – 1887/04/02:3c

GRUNDKE, Rudolf, 39, un. painter, *Muensterberg/Silesia, Gy, USA 1904, SP, Hoboken, NJ, + Los Angeles, CA - 1912/10/21:6b
GRUNDLACH, Paulina, b. Bruckner, 25, NYC-M - 1892/07/08:4a
GRUNDLER, Carl, brewer or cooper, NYC, + Lowell, MA - 1905/06/29:4a
GRUNDLER,..., German, exec. Casablanca on 28 Jan. - 1915/03/02:4f
GRUNDMANN, P. H., 77, '48er, SPD veteran Bielefeld/Gy - 1899/01/22:13a
GRUNDT, Paul, 29, NYC-M - 1882/05/21:5f
GRUNER, Friedrich, 28, NYC-M - 1892/05/08:5a
GRUNEWALD, J., West Hoboken, NJ - 1916/01/22:6a
GRUNING, Lena, 29, Charles, 4, Henry, 5, NYC-M, +@Genl Slocum - 1904/06/22:1d, 23:1b, 25:1d
GRUNO, Otto, NYC-M - 1906/07/31:6a
GRUNTZ, Katharina, 74, NYC-M - 1915/01/27:6a
GRUNTZ, Nicholas, 73, un. cigarmaker, NYC-Bx - 1915/08/20:6a
GRUNZIG, Alexandra "Almy," b. Allen, NYC-M - 1895/02/21:4a
GRUNZIG, Julius, chief edit. NYVZ 1890-92, then its theater critic, *31 Mr 1855 Berlin, USA 1883, SDP, #, NYC-M - 1901/10/13:1f-g, 2a-b, 5a, 14:2a-b, 4a, =15:1e, 4a, 16:3b
GRUPP, John, machinist, NYC-M - 1908/02/12:6a
GRUPPE, M., 75, NYC-M - 1893/08/18:4a
GRUSCHKA, Adelheid, b. Feichtiger, 40, NYC-Q - 1901/11/06:4a
GRUSHOW, Adolph, 22, grocer, NYC-M - 1896/10/24:1e
GRUSZKA, Pauline, 24, servant, NYC-M - 1913/01/29:6d
GSCHEIDEN, Louis, 53, NYC-M - 1912/01/22:6a
GSCHEIDLE % Conrad
GSCHWIND, Arthur, 28, Roslyn, LI - 1901/05/14:1f, 18:1d
GSCHWIND, Georg, NYC-M - 1893/09/11:4a
GUBNER, Walter D., horse-rental, NYC-B - 1902/10/14:3c
GUBRICKE, August, 26, NYC-B - 1899/01/23:2h
GUBSER, Anna, NYC-M - 1908/09/14:6a, 15:6a
GUDE, Caesar, machinist, NYC-M - 1900/06/16:1h
GUDMUNDSON, Magnus, Icelander, + NYC on way to Winnipeg, CN - 1887/08/03:1e, =4:4d
GUELTIG, William, 18, NYC-B - 1910/01/18:6a
GUEMBEL % Curschmann
GUENDEL, Charles H. O., NYC-Q - 1906/05/13:5a
GUENDTHARDT % Anderson
GUENKEL, Louis, NYC-Bx - 1911/04/13:6a
GUENSCHT, Louise, b. Huxhagen, 50, NYC-B - 1918/01/16:6a, fam. 19:6a
GUENTHER % Adler, % Huber
GUENTHER, Carl, un. cigarmaker, NYC-M - 1879/10/04:3a

GUENTHER, Carrie von, 65, NYC – 1912/10/10:2e
GUENTHER, Charles, fish. boat capt,Newark, NJ – 1908/08/12:2b, 14:6a
GUENTHER, Charles, NYC-M – 1906/05/21:4a
GUENTHER, Christian P., NYC-Q - 1919/03/21:6a
GUENTHER, Dr. med., fr Russia, War 2, NYC-M - 1915/11/18:1b
GUENTHER, Ernestine, 21, silkweaver, Paterson, NJ – 1906/10/03:3d
GUENTHER, Friedrich, 13, NYC-M – 1905/05/20:6a, 21:6a
GUENTHER, Friedrich, NYC-M - 1916/05/01:6a
GUENTHER, Georg, 57, Harrison, NJ - 1917/03/23:6a
GUENTHER, Georg, NYC-M - 1916/08/02:6a
GUENTHER, Heinrich, 71, NYC-M – 1892/10/07:4a
GUENTHER, Henry A., 52, un. carp., NYC-Q – 1908/09/01:6a
GUENTHER, Henry W., musician, NYC – 1887/03/16:2f
GUENTHER, Johanna, NYC-M - 1895/02/18:4a
GUENTHER, John A., 35, chauffeur, NYC-B – 1909/09/05:1e, 7:3b
GUENTHER, John, NYC-M - 1914/01/19:6a
GUENTHER, Joseph, NYC-B - 1919/02/21:6a
GUENTHER, Laura, Elizabeth, NJ – 1913/03/05:6a
GUENTHER, Lizzie, NYC-M – 1891/03/19:4a
GUENTHER, Louis, NYC-M - 1917/11/23:6a
GUENTHER, Marie, 65, SP, NYC-M – 1910/06/11:6a, 12:7c, =13:2a, fam. 15:6a
GUENTHER, Mathias, 70, SP, un. cigarmkr, *25 Sept 1844 Wuerzburg/ Bav., USA 1881, NYC-M - 1913/11/08:2f,6a, =10:2d, fam. 13:6a
GUENTHER, Michael, NYC-M – 1911/04/15:6a
GUENTHER, Peter, 64, innkeep, NYC-SI - 1916/04/23:11e
GUENTHER, Wilhelm, Elizabeth, NJ - 1915/06/16:6a
GUENTZER, John William, NYC-M – 1890/12/12:4a
GUENZBURG, Jacob, bank clerk, NYC-M - 1894/04/11:3d
GUENZBURG, Sophie, Russian revol., sentenced to death together with Freifeld and Stotlanofsky – 1890/11/18:1a, 2c, NYC workers demand clemency 2 Dec:1h, 3:1f, 2c
GUENZLER, John, un. millwright, NYC-B – 1901/07/21:5a
GUERIN, Marie, servant, NYC-M - 1878/02/04:4d
GUERR, Louise, b. Hansen, 27, NYC-M – 1883/03/01:3c
GUERTEL, Mary, 35, Hoboken, NJ – 1890/07/19:2e
GUETERBOCK, Bernhard, local editor fr NYSZ, NYC-M – 1893/05/28:5e, 29:1g, 30:1c-d, 3 June:2d, 4:1h
GUETH, G., Newark, NJ – 1910/11/10:6a
GUETH, Johann Georg, SLP Newark, NJ, needs help – 1884/07/30:4d
GUETTING, Paulina, 6, NYC-B – 1878/07/22:3b, 24:3c
GUETTINGER, Jules, NYC-Bx – 1913/03/09:7b

GUGEL % Mayer
GUGGENBACH, Henriette, NYC-B - 1920/10/23:6a
GUGGENHEIMER, Randolph, 59, *Lynchburg, PA, NYC polit, + Long Branch, NJ - 1907/09/13:2c
GUHLKA, Max, musician, NYC-M - 1904/10/22:1g
GUILLAUME, Emil, 36, newspaper dealer, * Pforzheim, ex-jewelry maker, NYC-M - 1879/02/14:1d
GUIMHARD, Guilbert, French novel writer, + Paris - 1911/10/07:2d
GUITEAU, Charles, presidential murderer, s.a. Garfield. His wife 1881/07/30:1e, his trial prep. 22 Aug:2d-e, French reactions 1 Aug:2e, 23 Sept:2d, trial preps 29:1c, 30:1b,d, etc 9 Oct:4a-b, 13:1b, 15:2d, 24:2f, 5 Nov:1b, begins tomorrow 13 Nov:1b-c, 15:1c-d, 19:1c-d, 20:5c, 21:1d, etc, 9 Dec:1c, 2c. Guilty 26 Jan. 1882:1e, 2b, 27:1e, 5 Fb:5c-d, hopes for life sentence 12 May:1d, exec.1 Jy:1a-f, 2a-b, 4:2b, his sister 10 May:1g
GULAE, Adolph, 45, & Walter, 18,Sayville, LI - 1916/12/26:1f
GULDEN, Otto von, tailor, NYC-B - 1908/04/11:1f
GULDENSUPPE, William, masseur fr Hessen/Gy, NYC-M - 1897/07/01:1f-g, 2:1h, 3:1h, 4:1f-g, 5:1c, killed by Martin Thorn, 33, barber,*near Posen as Torzenski, & Auguste Nack, 8:1h, 3f, 9:1h, 3f, 10:1h, 11:1h, head found? 14:1h,15:1h, 16:1d, 17:1h, 18:1f,28:1e, 30:3c, 6 Aug:1g, 7:1f, 8:1g, trial 19:1e, 29:1d; 3 Sept:1h,4a, 5:1f, 15:1f, 16:1g, 17:1f,20:1f,21:1h,22:1c, 23:1f, 25:4b; 8 Oct:2c, 12:1f, 13:3f, 14:1g, 15:1g; 7 Nv:1h, 8:1d,9:1a-b,10:1a-c, 11:1a-d, 12:1f,12:1f, 14:1c, 4a-b, 15:1f, 16:1f, 17:1h, 18:1e, 20:1f, 21:1h, 23:1h, 24:1f, 25:4e-, 27:1c-d, 3f, 28:1d,2b, 29:1f, 30:1c-d; 1 Dec:1c-e, 2:1h, 3:1f, =6:1f, Thorn to die 4:1h, 5:1h, post. 1 Jan. 1898:1e, Mrs Nack only 15 yrs 11:1h. Ghost story - 1899/09/04:4c
GULEWSKI, Morris, 3, NYC-M, + @Genl Slocum - 1904/06/18:3c
GULH % Fichte
GULHARDT, Lorenz, 41, baker, USA 1856, NYC-M - 1881/03/29:1f
GULZOW, Frieda, Secaucus, NJ - 1914/10/24:6a
GUMBINGER, K., NYC-Bx - 1914/10/28:6a
GUMLICH, Max, un. brewer, NYC-M - 1903/08/02:5a, 4:4a
GUMPERT, Jacob, NYC-M - 1909/04/14:6a
GUMPRECHT, Wilhelmine, Yonkers, NY - 1905/10/14:4a
GUNDBERG, Carl, NYC-M - 1897/05/12:4a
GUNDELFINGER % Lind
GUNDERSHORK, Fritz, NYC-M - 1889/09/08:5a
GUNDING, James, inventor, Philadelphia, + NYC-M - 1898/07/18:3f
GUNDLACH, August, NYC-M - 1898/08/25:4a
GUNDLACH, Ferdinand, 64, basket weaver fr Saxony, SP, NYC-M - 1911/02/21:2d, 6a, 22:6a, fam. 28:6a
GUNDLACH, Hyronimus, 58, NYC-M - 1910/12/12:6a

GUNDLACH, Joseph, SP, 80th birthday, NYC-M – 1908/11/09:2c
GUNDLACH, Ludwig, un. cornicemaker, NYC-M - 1895/04/21:5a,23:4a
GUNDLACH, Marie, 64, #, SP activist & cigarmaker, *Zeitz/Saxony/Gy, birthday #, NYC-M – 1913/03/12:2d
GUNDLACH, Wilhelm, 84, educator close to SP, *Pyritz/Pomerania/Gy, USA 1868, NYC-M – 1913/03/25:1c-d, 2d, 4a, =26:1e, 6a, mem. Eve 28:2a, 30:1d, rev. 31:2d, lt by Kati Dobronyi 1 Apr:3b-c
GUNDLER, Jacob, un. baker, Atlantic City, NJ - 1919/07/16:6a
GUNDLIEB, Charles, brewery worker, NYC-M - 1894/06/29:5a
GUNKEL, Adolph, 32, fr Bremen/Gy, ex-innkeep, NYC-M – 1907/11/27:1g, 29:6a
GUNKELSTEIN, Sophie, 5, NYC-M – 1891/06/21:5d
GUNNER, John, 67, ret. NYPD captain, NYC-M – 1898/05/20:4a
GUNST, George, 22, NYC-B – 1911/09/22:3a
GUNTERMANN % Schaefer
GUNTHER, Charles G., NYC mayor 1863, NYC-M – 1885/01/24:4a
GUNTHER, Charles, 27, hotel clerk, NYC-B – 1902/07/05:4b
GUNTHER, Felix, 28, NYC-B – 1904/11/05:4b
GUNTHER, Frank, NYC-M - 1917/11/13:6a
GUPFINGER, Peter, un. baker, NYC-M – 1898/12/30:4a (s.a. bottom)
GUPPER, Eugen, 41, NYC-M - 1878/05/03:3b
GURTNER, Christian, 50, tailor, Swede, NYC-M – 1897/02/24:3g
GUSEY % Kohlmann
GUSTAFENSON, John, un. carp., NYC - 1914/04/15:6a
GUSTAFFSON, Algot, Swede, Dem. politician, NYC-B - 1895/06/19: 3e
GUSTAFSON, Frank, Swede, smith, NYC-M – 1904/10/25:1f
GUSZKOWSKY, Michael, tailor, killed during strike, Chicago, IL - 1915/11/25:1f
GUT, Jacob, Newark, NJ – 1910/06/21:6a
GUTBROD, Joseph, 36, Hoboken, NJ –1892/09/22:4a
GUTEKUNST, August, un. carp., NYC-M – 1890/07/01:4a
GUTEKUNST, Charles, cooper, NYC-M – 1913/02/11:6a
GUTEMANN, William, 76, NYC-B – 1890/05/07:4a
GUTENKUNST % Wuestel
GUTERMUTH, Louis W., dealer, NYC-M – 1882/06/12:1f, 13:4d, 14:1e-f, inquest 15:1e-g, 16:1e-f, 17:1f, 20:4c-d,
GUTFLEISCH, ..., worker, NYC-M – 1891/09/22:1f
GUTGESELL, Peter, NYC-M - 1918/10/29:6a
GUTH, Agnes, dressmaker, Swiss, NYC-M? - 1913/05/02:2d
GUTH, Agnes, NYC-M - 1913/12/18:2d
GUTH, Henry, 74, NYC-B – 1911/09/29:3a

GUTH, Joseph, 32, bookkeeper, fr Austria-Hungary, NYC M - 1913/05/02:2c
GUTH, William, 21, coachman, NYC-M – 1912/04/11:2b
GUTHEIM, Louis, 82, NYC-M – 1891/08/18:1g
GUTHERMANN % Schwarz
GUTHINGER, Charles H., 42, theater mangr, NYC-M – 1909/12/07:1b
GUTHNER, Louise, NYC-M – 1907/10/09:1d
GUTHOFF, Dietrich, 33, worker in sugar ref., NYC-B – 1883/10/18:2g-3a
GUTMAN, Charles, NYC-Bx - 1914/10/03:6a
GUTMAN, K., decorator, NYC-M – 1902/06/02:3b
GUTMANN, Emma, NYC-M – 1892/08/19:4a
GUTMANN, Heyman, cigarpacker, NYC-M - 1878/03/16:4e
GUTMANN, Jakob, merchant, South Amboy, NJ – 1880/11/20:4e
GUTSCHE, Anna, 62, NYC-B - 1914/05/07:6a
GUTSMANN, Bruno, 65, *Gleiwitz, Silesia, SP alderman in Basel, Switz. – 1913/04/14:4d, 27:3c
GUTTENDORFER, Georg Leonhard, 33, un. butcher?, NYC-M – 1910/04/12:6a
GUTTENGER, August, innkeep, White Plains, NY - 1916/05/16:2f, 21:1f
GUTTENTAG, Jakob, 50, SPD Munich, brewery empl. - 1914/08/16:3b
GUTTHORST, Hermann, NYC-B – 1907/01/01:3a
GUTTMANN % Schlueter
GUTTMANN, Albert, 14, office messenger, NYC-M – 1886/04/29:1g
GUTWERTH, Carl, 50, tailor, Jersey City, NJ – 1897/11/27:3c
GUTZKOW, Karl Ferdinand, 67, German writer, + Frankfurt - 1878/12/22:3a-b, 1879/01/12:7c-d, 19:7d-e. 30th anniv.+ – 1909/01/10:18b-e
GUYER, Adolf, un. cigar maker, NYC-M – 1892/02/18:4a
GWERSINSKI, George, 30, smith, NYC-M – 1910/06/21:1f
GWINNER, Henry M., 63, president of Hoole Manuf. Co, * Philadelphia, parents fr Elsass, NYC-M – 1883/10/20:1f
HAAF, Carl, Newark, NJ – 1908/08/17:6a
HAAG % Parbs
HAAG, Anna, textile worker, Newark, NJ – 1910/11/30:1g
HAAG, Daniel, shoemaker, NYC-M – 1897/07/01:4c
HAAG, Georg, un. carp., NYC-M - 1919/07/23:6a
HAAG, James J., jeweler, NYC-M - 1918/02/09:1e
HAAG, Johanna, b. Bock, NYC-M – 1891/06/20:4a, fam. 23:4a
HAAG, John, 47, NYC-M - 1894/01/21:5d
HAAG, Joseph, 30, un. painter, NYC-M - 1919/01/28:6a
HAAG, Louis, old, NYC-M - 1878/09/12:1g
HAAG, William, Newark, NJ – 1905/04/13:4a

HAAG, Wilmer, 12, NYC-M, +@Genl Slocum – 1904/06/22:1d
HAAGE, Anna Maria, 32, NYC-M - 1895/07/25: 4a
HAAGE, Gottlieb, 41, un. millwright, NYC-M – 1900/08/03:4a
HAAGER, Maggie, 9, NYC-M – 1882/01/03:3b
HAAGER, Philipp, infant, NYC-M – 1882/03/02:3b
HAAK % Lohmann
HAAKE, Carl's wife, NYC-M – 1889/11/03:5a
HAAR, Charles, un. butcher, NYC-M – 1908/02/28:6a, 29:6a, fam. 12 Mr:6a, mem. 1913/02/26:6a
HAAR, Marie, b. Sichter, 68, NYC-B - 1917/06/30:6a
HAARBAUER, Sophia, b. Andresjohn, 75, NYC-M – 1890/07/06:5a
HAAREN, Maria, b. Rust, 56, NYC-M – 1891/03/14:4a
HAAREN, Walter E., 22, chemist, NYC-B - 1914/11/14:1f
HAAS % Flugrath, % Kneuer, % Schreibels
HAAS, Albert, un. bag maker, NYC-M – 1888/05/02:3a
HAAS, Amalia, b. Wissig, NYC-M – 1885/08/26:3a
HAAS, Andreas, SP, Garfield, NJ – 1912/07/07:7a
HAAS, Anna, b. Eckert, 37, NYC-Q – 1912/11/07:6a
HAAS, Appolonia, b. Schumann, NYC – 1911/10/19:6a
HAAS, Babette, NYC-M – 1901/09/26:4a
HAAS, Barbara, NYC-Bx – 1919/12/16:6a
HAAS, Bertha, NYC-B – 1903/12/19:4e
HAAS, Charles, Jersey City, NJ - 1919/03/04:6a
HAAS, Charles, machinist, NYC-M – 1903/05/19:2h, 4a
HAAS, Constans, un. carp., NYC-M – 1899/08/27:5a
HAAS, Ernst, NYC-B – 1908/09/30:2f, 1 Oct:6a
HAAS, Franz X., 63, NYC-M - 1917/10/03:6a
HAAS, Friedrich, 35, un. painter, fr Schleswig-Holstein, NYC-M - 1895/05/23:4a
HAAS, Georg, Jersey City Heights, NJ – 1901/01/03:4a, 4:5a
HAAS, Gertrude, & Anna & Gertrude, 13, NYC-M, + @Genl Slocum – 1904/06/16:1c, f, 25:1d
HAAS, Henry, 72, Newark, NJ – 1901/07/04:3b
HAAS, Henry, un. carp., NYC-M - 1915/05/23:11f
HAAS, Hertop B., NYC-M – 1879/10/14:4a
HAAS, Jacob, 34, worker at Ehret's Brewery, & 2 sons, 7 & 6, NYC – 1912/09/01:1e
HAAS, John Martin, 102, *Bavaria, turner, USA 1844, Buffalo, NY – 1911/02/13:6c
HAAS, John, 30, NYC-M – 1891/09/24:4a
HAAS, John, brewer, NYC-M – 1901/07/26:4a, 27:4a
HAAS, Joseph, un. painter, NYC-B - 1919/05/04:12a

HAAS, Karl, NYC-M – 1906/04/23:4a
HAAS, Louise, 16, NYC-B – 1897/08/19:1e
HAAS, Margarethe, +10 Mr 98 W. Hoboken, NJ, her will – 1900/12/13:3b
HAAS, Maria, child, NYC-M? – 1891/11/01:5a
HAAS, Phoenix, 17, NYC-M – 1896/08/13:1h
HAAS, Sophie, 17, NYC-M – 1892/09/16:4a
HAAS, Wilhelm, NYC-M – 1892/03/11:4a
HAAS, William, 55, painter, NYC-Bx – 1908/07/03:1e
HAASE % Thiel
HAASE, Friedrich, German actor, plays now in USA – 1881/10/09:4g-5b, 23:2f. +Berlin – 1911/03/18:1b
HAASE, Gustav, SP, 25th Wedding Anniv., NYC-B – 1910/08/20:5f
HAASE, Hugo, 56, German soc., leader USPD, + Berlin # – 1919/11/08:1a-b, 4a-b, 9:4a-e, =15:1b, obit. By Karl Kautsky fr Berlin Freiheit 1 Dez:6a-c, 2:6a-e, 3:3a-e, 4:3a-e, etc., 6 Dec:4e, 23:4a
HAASE, Oscar, bus. agent Structural Bridge & Iron Workers' Union #2, * 24 Sept 1843 Berlin, USA, ~ 1874, SLP, then with John Most, NYC-M – 1904/12/03:1f-g, 4a, 4:5b, =5:1e, 7:3e
HAASS, Chr., tailor & SPD activist expelled from Berlin?/Gy, arrived NYC – 1880/12/18:1g
HABECKER, Dorothea, NYC-B – 1911/07/22:6a, 23:7a
HABECKER, Frank, 39, un. cigar maker, fr Angermuende/Brandenburg, SLP, NYC-M – 1892/02/04:4c, 5:4a, 6:4a, fam. 10:4a
HABEDANK, Albert, 25, NYC-M – 1892/04/09:1d
HABEL, A., Dr., 60, * Austria, USA 1850s?, Freethinker, NYC-M - 1879/01/05:5e
HABEL, Michael, NYC-Q - 1916/08/22:6a
HABELMANN, Theodor, 87, classical singer, fr Gy to USA 1863, + Honesdale, PA - 1920/06/08:2d
HABENICHT, Robert, NYC-M – 1901/01/31:4a
HABER, Auguste, 4, NYC-M - 1878/03/19:3b
HABER, Guenther, 40, photographer, NYC-M – 1892/06/23:1e
HABERER, Andreas, NYC-M – 1905/05/07:5a
HABERKNECHT, May, 7, NYC-M, @+1883 School Fire, NYC-M
HABERKORN, Hermann's wife, NYC-M – 1898/02/15:4a
HABERMANN, John, un. cigarmaker, NYC-M – 1883/08/20:3c
HABERMANN, Michael, 46, cigarmaker, NYC-M – 1897/06/12:4a,b
HABERMANN, Samuel, NYC-M – 1893/02/15:1f
HABERMANN, tailor & SPD Magdeburg/Gy, + 23 Aug. 1886, his life – 1887/05/16:2c-d
HABERSAAT, W., West Hoboken, NJ - 1917/03/12:6a
HABERSTROH, Marie, NYC-M - 1916/03/21:6a

HABICH, Emma, b. Pfeifer, NYC-M – 1898/11/30:4a
HABINAY, Arthur, un. carp., NYC-B – 1910/08/23:6a, 24:6a
HABINAY, Rosine, b. Fischer, NYC-B – 1899/01/02:4a
HACHEMEISTER, Henry, partner at Ringler Brewery, NYC-SI – 1907/07/13:3b
HACK, Benjamin, 70, NYC-M - 1916/07/22:2d
HACK, Felix, un. carp., NYC-B - 1913/12/15:6a
HACK, Franz, 31, pianomaker, NYC-M - 1916/09/15:2e
HACKBARTH % Eberhardt; HACKEL % Douai
HACKENBERG, Marie, 42, SPO Bruenn/Moravia - 1915/01/17:3c
HACKENBROCK, Meta, 65, NYC-M - 1918/07/26:6a
HACKER, Edward, 41, & wife, 30, NYC-M – 1908/08/20:1g
HACKER, Ernst, 37, cigarmaker & SPD activist expelled fr Hamburg/Gy, arrived in NYC – 1881/01/19:1g, 20:4c
HACKER, Henry, 47, NYC-B - 1920/05/26:6a, 30:12a
HACKERT, Adolf, 72, un. cigarmaker, *Leipzig/Gy, NYC-M – 1909/09/11:6a, 12:7c, =13:2f, fam. 19:7a
HACKERT, Adolph, NYC?, ashes at sea – 1911/05/26:3c
HADENKAMP, Margaret, 11, NYC-M, +@ Genl Slocum – 1904/06/17:3b
HADER, Andrew, NYC-M - 1914/06/25:6a
HADERER, Rosa, infant, NYC-M – 1891/09/24:4a
HADESER, Louis, NYC-M – 1891/03/25:4a
HAEBE, Ferdinand, 70, fr Stuttgart/Gy, & wife Selma, 68, NYC-B – 1901/11/17:1b
HAEBERLE, Frank, NYC-Q – 1912/11/03:7b
HAEBERLIN, Louis H., 65, NYC-B – 1890/12/28:1g
HAECKEL, Ernst, Dr., 85, German biologist, + Jena - 1919/08/10:1d
HAECKEL, Ernst, Dr., German scientist, 70th bithday 1904/02/16:2a, 17:1g, 18:2a-b; + 1919/08/10:1d
HAECKER, Friedrich G., SP?, bus. mgr Philadelphia Tageblatt – 1908/09/04:2e
HAEFE, Karl, NYC-Bx - 1917/07/03:6a
HAEFELE, Elisabeth, NYC-SI - 1919/01/03:6a
HAEFELE, Gebhardt, NYC-B – 1907/07/08:6a
HAEFELE, Gottlob, NYC-B – 1913/02/23:7b
HAEFELE, Minnie, NYC-M - 1894/01/28:5d
HAEFELFINGER, Anna Barbara, b. Denger, 77, NYC-M – 1900/01/11:4a
HAEFELFINGER, Mathias, 60, Swiss silkweaver, NYC-M – 1881/05/23:4c
HAEFELI, K. Eusebius, 29, weaver, Paterson, NJ - 1895/08/07:4a
HAEFELINGER, Wilhelm, weaver?, West Hoboken, NJ – 1910/10/26:6a
HAEFFNER, Johanna, SP Vienna, + 11 Apr in Vienna – 1909/05/30:3f
HAEFNER, Hugo, NYC-M – 1892/07/16:4a

HAEFNER, Johanna, NYC-M - 1895/01/31:4a
HAEFNER, John, 14, NYC-M - 1881/09/25:5f, 26:1f
HAEFNER, William, NYC-B - 1908/03/13:6a
HAEGE, Bertha, NYC-B - 1895/08/30: 4a
HAEGE, John, NYC-B - 1914/11/10:6a
HAEHLE, comrade, SPD Chemnitz/Gy - 1910/03/06:3c
HAEHNEL, Auguste, wd Schrader, 69, Jersey City Heights, NJ – 1912/05/17:6a
HAEHNEL, Christina, SLP?, Jersey City Heights, NJ – 1899/11/11:4a
HAEHNEL, Fritz, SP?, Jersey City Heights, NJ - 1914/06/22:6a
HAEHNEL, Hermann, 45, cheese plant mgr, Monroe, NY – 1904/06/14:2f
HAEHNER, Gustav, 30, un. cigarmaker, NYC-M – 1890/03/14:4a
HAEHNERT, Maria, b. Rust, NYC? – 1883/07/28:3b
HAELIG, William, quarry owner, Somerville, NJ – 1905/11/06:3c
HAENELL, Anton, un. carp., NYC-M – 1905/12/14:4a
HAERDTNER, Henry, 20, West New York, NJ – 1912/08/13:6a, 14:6a; mem. - 1913/08/12:6a
HAERING, Heinrich, 4, NYC-M - 1879/04/13:8a
HAERSCHELMANN, E., un. iron worker, NYC-M – 1900/03/04:5a
HAERTEISS, Elise, NYC-M – 1901/09/21:4a
HAERTEL, August, un. cigarmaker, NYC-B - 1918/10/11:6a
HAERTEL, Katherina, 3, NYC-M – 1891/05/24:1h
HAESE, Otto, un. woodworker, NYC-M – 1890/01/17:4a
HAESSIG, O., NYC-Bx - 1915/10/01:6a
HAETSE, Josef, striking worker, Syracuse, NY - 1913/05/07:1b
HAEUER, Kaspar, NYC-B - 1917/02/22:6a
HAEUSLER, Frank, NYC-B – 1919/11/21:6a
HAEUSLER, Katharina, NYC-M – 1912/07/20:6a
HAEUSLER, M., Dr.med., fr Hungary early 1903, NYC-M – 1903/08/05:3b
HAFER, Henry, 54, fr Thueringen?, un. cigarmaker, NYC-M – 1900/07/21:4a
HAFERKORN, Hermann, 42, NYC-M – 1899/11/29:4a
HAFFELEIN, Anna C., b. Hitzel, NYC-M – 1891/04/07:4a
HAFFEN, Matthias, NYC-M or –Bx – 1891/03/12:4a
HAFFNER, Carl, 80, NYC-B – 1897/08/31:4a
HAFFNER, Elisa, b. Douai, NYC-M? – 1887/12/06:3b
HAFFNER, Elisabeth, NYC-M - 1894/01/24:4a
HAFFNER, Frank, 38, spinner at Botany Mills, Passaic, NJ - 1913/08/30:2a
HAFFNER, G., Yonkers, NY – 1907/09/11:6a
HAFFNER, Henry, NYC-M – 1885/05/07:3b, 8:1d, @1885 Manhattan Fire
HAFNER % Lohse
HAFNER, Charles, 40, NYC-B – 1899/12/26:1h, 27:2h

HAFNER, John, 47, NYC-M – 1910/08/19:6a
HAFNER, Peter, 42, NYC-B - 1894/01/21:5d
HAFNER, Stella, 30, NYC-M – 1912/01/06:1c
HAFT, Max, Hoboken, NJ - 1916/05/01:6a
HAGDORN % Krieg
HAGEDORN, Ernst, un. carp., NYC-M – 1887/07/27:3c
HAGEDORN, Rebecca, b. Hein, 28, NYC-B – 1891/03/21:4a
HAGELOCH, Georg, un. carp., NYC? - 1915/04/13:6a
HAGELOCH, Marie, b. Bertche, 46, NYC-M - 1894/11/12:4a
HAGEMEYER, August, 61, NYC-M - 1894/01/10:4a
HAGEN % Ott
HAGEN, Emilie, 60, NYC-M – 1890/02/11:1h, 12:2g
HAGEN, Henry, machinist, NYC-M – 1910/04/11:5f
HAGEN, Marie, b. Reif, fr Oberlangenstadt/Gy, + Oneida, NY NYC-M – 1890/05/02:4a, 3:4a
HAGEN, Mary, 47, NYC-M – 1880/05/11:1d, 13:2f
HAGEN, Peter, brewer, NYC-M – 1908/01/08:1a, 9:2c
HAGENBECK, Carl, 69, German animal importer & circus, + Hamburg – 1913/04/16:2d
HAGENBECKER, Christopher, 50, baker?, NYC-B – 1909/05/17:3a
HAGENBRUCKER, Mary, NYC-M, + @on Genl Slocum – 1904/06/18:3c
HAGENBUCHER, Mrs, 32, NYC-M?, +@ Genl Slocum – 1904/06/17:1b, 18:1c
HAGENBUECHLE, Carl, un. machinist, NYC-M - 1895/08/24:4a
HAGENBUSCH % Heinle
HAGENLOCHER, Hortense, 4, NYC-M - 1878/03/22:3b
HAGENLOCHER, Michael, 32, brewer, NYC-B – 1887/02/19:3b
HAGER, Carl Christian, 64, un. typesetter, NYC-B – 1897/03/13:4a
HAGER, Dietrich, NYC-M – 1909/12/09:6a
HAGER, Gottlieb, 32, butcher, NYC-M – 1889/07/20:1d
HAGER, John, child, NYC-M – 1881/09/24:3b
HAGER, Kunigunde, 51, NYC-M – 1892/09/18:5e
HAGERMAN, Charles, 35, Jamesburg, NJ - 1915/12/28:2d
HAGERMANN, Henry, 35, merchant, NYC-M – 1881/09/08:4b
HAGMAN, Christian, 33, painter, fr Frankfurt/Main USA 1882, NYC – 1896/04/27:1h
HAGMILLER, Michael, un. carp., NYC-B – 1909/05/06:6a
HAGNER, Alex, state judge, NYC-Q – 1880/04/09:4a
HAGNER, Julius, 50, NYC-Bx – 1912/10/28:6a
HAHKOLA, Mary, 25, servant, NYC-M, + Hastings, NY - 1915/05/11:2c
HAHN % Suesse
HAHN, Augustus, 65, pianomaker, NYC-M – 1906/07/22:1g

HAHN, Benjamin F., 73, NYC-M – 1890/10/19:5b
HAHN, Bertram, NYC-Q – 1913/02/02:7b
HAHN, Ernestine, 57, NYC-Q - 1917/11/23:5g
HAHN, Frederick, 48, porter, NYC-M– 1908/08/23:1c
HAHN, Frederick, baker, W. Hoboken, NJ – 1901/07/03:1f
HAHN, Frederick, Kearney, NJ - 1915/12/21:6a
HAHN, Georg, 51, NYC-B – 1908/04/01:6a, 2:6a
HAHN, George, un. carp., NYC-Bx – 1907/03/17:7c
HAHN, Harry, upholsterer, NYC-M – 1903/05/31:1e
HAHN, Heinrich, 67, NYC-M – 1892/06/16:4a
HAHN, Isaac, 76, NYC-M – 1892/12/08:4a
HAHN, Jakob, innkeep, NYC-Q – 1899/05/05:4c
HAHN, Katherine, b. Klausmann, 61, NYC-M – 1891/07/17:4a
HAHN, Marie, 30, Jersey City, NJ – 1898/07/05:4b
HAHN, Martin, furniture maker, 41, NYC-M – 1889/08/25:5e
HAHN, Mathilde, b. Kruse, NYC-M – 1886/07/12:3b, 13:3f
HAHN, Peter, un. carpenter, NYC-M - 1895/10/23:4a
HAHN, Reinhold, + before 1881, & Margarethe, + 1881 Snake Hill, NJ, left 2 sons who now in their 20s, searched by relatives – 1897/04/17:1g
HAHN, Samuel, Dr., * Hungary, USA 1867, Ethical Culture?, NYC-M – 1880/03/10:4a
HAHN, William, 13, NYC-B – 1892/07/28:2d
HAHRMEL, Gustav, 33, & Emma Rothmann, 24, both just fr Bremen, married in NYC-M – 1899/05/19:1e
HAID, John, 69, NYC-B – 1904/11/28:3c
HAIDER % Herzog, MEYER % Herzog
HAIDER, G., NYC-B – 1906/11/10:6a
HAILER, Franz, un. carp., NYC-M – 1898/09/12:4a
HAIMBACH, Simon, deli-owner, NYC-M – 1911/08/27:1f
HAIMER, Caspar, stonecutter, War 2, NYC-Q - 1917/02/21:1c
HAIN % Fink
HAIRE, Robert, Rev., 70, SP, Aberdeen, SD - 1916/04/03:4c
HAIST, Louise, NYC-M – 1898/02/01:4a
HAITZEN, George, 55, artist, NYC-M – 1899/02/15:1h
HAJEK, Appolonia, 76, NYC-M - 1920/05/10:6a
HAJEK, John, 40, NYC-M – 1898/05/07:4a
HALBACH, Max, ex-pres. Butcher's Union #174, NYC-B, + Utica, NY, = NYC - 1919/08/06:6a
HALBE, Fritz, 52, innkeep, SPD Hannover/Gy – 1908/07/05:3c
HALDER, Max, 63, NYC-Bx – 1920/12/08:6a
HALDER, Margaret, un. cigarmkr, NYC-M – 1913/12/20:6a, 21:7c
HALE, Charles, Negro, lynched Lawrenceville, GA – 1911/04/09:1f

HALEVY, Ludovic, French playwright, Paris/Fr – 1908/05/23:4g
HALIDA, Mary, 10, Perth Amboy, NJ – 1912/07/03:1e
HALIX, Anton, NYC-M – 1891/07/17:4a
HALL, A. Oakley, NYC mayor under Boss Tweed – 1898/10/10:3d
HALL, Charles, Negro, lynched Monroe, LA – 1914/08/08:2d
HALL, J. Edward, SLP, * 22 Aug. 1851 Glen Cove, LI, NYC-M – 1889/05/04:1h, 2b, 12:5b, 27:4a
HALL, Theodor, * Denmark, pres. Un. pianomakers, NYC – 1880/07/19:3b, =20:4a
HALLBACH, John, SP?, & wife, NYC-M – 1919/01/22:6a
HALLE, Aaaron, trial – 1900/05/18:1h, 19:3c, 22:3h, 23:3c, guilty 21 June:1g, 26:3b,
HALLE, Aaron, NYC, exec. Ossining, NY – 1902/08/02:3g, done 5:3d
HALLEN, Joseph, 50, fr Duesseldorf/Gy, Guttenberg, NJ - 1879/03/14:1g, 21:4d
HALLENBECK, Darius, machinist, NYC-B – 1901/03/14:4a
HALLENBECK, P., trial of Van Wormer brothers – 1902/04/01:1g, 8:3b, 18:2h, to die 19:1d
HALLER, Andreas, 36, SLP, painter, NYC-B – 1898/05/23:4a, b
HALLER, David, 38, printer, NYC – 1903/04/02:3e
HALLER, Friedrich, un. carp., NYC-M – 1903/07/19:5a
HALLER, Henry, NYC-M - 1914/12/05:6a
HALLER, Joseph, un. baker, NYC-Bx – 1912/03/02:6a
HALLER, Philip, silkweaver, + 12 June, Union Hill, NJ – 1885/06/24:2g
HALLER, William, SLP, Cincinatti, OH – 1881/03/07:2d
HALLINGER, Edward H., exec. Newark?, NJ – 1892/12/23:2c
HALLS, Murray H., ~70, active in Tammany, NYC – 1901/01/20:1h
HALLSTEIN, Lillian, b. Wolf, NYC-M - 1918/10/09:6c
HALLUM, Monroe, Negro, lynched near Kosciusko, MS – 1902/07/21:1b
HALLY, Louis, mason, USA ~1856 fr Gy, NYC-M – 1881/12/27:1f
HALM, Charles, NYC-Bx - 1918/11/02:6a
HALM, Christian, NYC-M – 1892/08/09:4a
HALM, Georg, NYC-M – 1881/08/30:3d
HALM, J., Hoboken, NJ - 1914/09/27:7c
HALM, Otto, alias Hakam, fr Galicia, improvisator, + Frankfurt/Main, Gy – 1885/11/23:6c
HALVES, Frederick, Dr., NYC-M - 1894/12/25:1h
HAMANN % Tewes
HAMANN, August, un. cigarmaker, NYC-M – 1882/11/11:3b
HAMANN, Franz, 40, un. cigarmaker?, NYC-B – 1897/09/07:4a
HAMANN, Friedrich, SP?, New Haven, CT - 1914/12/13:11a
HAMANN, Henry, NYC – 1911/09/02:6a

HAMANN, Karl, 34, NYC-M – 1893/03/28:4a
HAMANN, William, 58, SDP?, + Milwaukee, WI – 1904/03/01:4a, 2:4a
HAMBALEK, Eugen, Orange, NJ - 1914/03/10:6a
HAMBERGER, William, sailor on USS Maine, + Havana/Cuba, Jersey City, NJ – 1898/02/18:1b
HAMBURG, Carl, 56, Jersey City, NJ – 1893/07/06:3d
HAMBURGER, Jacob, 38, Newark, NJ – 1910/02/10:3c
HAMBURGER, John, 46, un. carp., NYC-M – 1887/06/30:4a, 1 Jy:4e
HAMBY, Gordon Pawczek, NYC, exec. Ossining, NY - 1920/01/30:1e
HAMEL, Peter, 19, NYC-B – 1892/08/09:4a
HAMILTON, Angus, 35, war correspondent - 1913/06/15:11a
HAMILTON, Ed, Negro, lynched Shreveport, LA - 1914/05/14:2e
HAMILTON, James J., exec. Ossining, NY, 1893/04/04:1d
HAMILTON, William, Negro, lynched Asotin, WA – 1903/08/06:1f
HAMM, Fritz, Talcott, VT – 1903/05/07:4a
HAMMA, Albert, un. carp., NYC-Bx – 1912/02/12:6a
HAMMARTH, Irene, 3, NYC-Q – 1900/09/24:3b
HAMMEL, Anna Katherina, NYC-M - 1894/01/23:4e
HAMMEL, Bertha, 40, NYC-B – 1897/10/02:4b
HAMMEL, Helene, landlady, NYC-M - 1918/02/15:2c
HAMMEL, Magdalena, 44, NYC-M – 1892/06/16:4a
HAMMER, Anna M., 71, NYC-B – 1892/07/28:4a
HAMMER, Conrad, 71, NYC-B - 1915/08/06:6a
HAMMER, Henry, * Denmark 1827, NYC-B – 1891/10/11:5d
HAMMER, Joseph, un. brewery worker, NYC-B - 1894/02/19:4a
HAMMER, Karl, un. carpenter, NYC-M - 1895/10/05: 4b
HAMMER, Otto, 52, SDP, NYC-B – 1902/03/23:5a, =26:1h
HAMMER, William John, 37, NYC-M – 1910/03/22:3d
HAMMERANDT, Johann, un. carp., NYC-M – 1893/10/22:5a
HAMMERL, Charles, 20, NYC-M – 1880/12/02:3b
HAMMERSTEIN, Oskar, 72, theater manager, * Berlin/Gy, USA1863, NYC-M - 1919/08/02:2f, 3:4b
HAMMERSTEIN, Oskar, impresario, NYC, noted – 1919/08/03:6b
HAMMESFAHR, A.E., un. printer, NYC-B - 1918/01/08:6a
HAMMESFAHR, Carl, worker fr Fremont, OH, + Chicago, IL – 1888/02/11:3b
HAMMESFAHR, Ernst, NYC-B – 1897/05/19:4a
HAMP, Louise, 62, SP, fr Austria, NYC-M - 1915/04/21:6a, 23:2c, fam. 24:6a
HAMP, Robert, 36, NYC-M - 1914/11/14:6a
HAMPARTJEMIAN, Bedros, NYC, exec. Ossining, NY – 1909/12/06:3c, done 7:6a

HAMPE, Adolf, un. cigarmaker, fr Braunschweig?, NYC-M – 1905/08/04:4a, 6:5b
HAMPE, Adolph & Minna, NYC-M, see under DENNECKE
HAMPE, Wilhelm, 35, NYC-M – 1891/04/09:4a
HAMPEL, Kurt, 6, NYC-M – 1903/04/30:4a
HAMPTON, Pete, Negro, lynched Pierce City, MO – 1901/08/21:1g, 29:3b
HANAUER, Louis N., printing business, Arlington, NJ, + NYC – 1907/02/16:5e
HANAUER, Moses G., 45, coffee dealer, * near Frankfurt/Main, NYC-M – 1883/01/09:1g
HANCOCK, Winfield Scott, 67, ex-genl US Army – 1886/02/10:4d, 11:1f
HAND, Nuphines, 70, NYC-B - 1919/01/05:11d
HAND, Otto, NYC-M, +@ on Genl Slocum – 1904/06/16:1e
HANDINGER, Hermann, model-maker, *Switzerland, & wife, Newark, NJ – 1903/07/22:1f
HANDKE, Hermann, Newark, NJ - 1918/03/12:6a
HANDKE, Pauline, b. Frost, 47, NYC-M – 1898/10/03:4a
HANDKE, Reinhold, NYC-M – 1885/05/19:3d
HANDS, Richard, druggist,NYC-M – 1885/06/01:1e, 2:1e, 3:1e, 4:1g, 5:1g, 6:4d
HANEBERGER, John, un. carp., NYC-B – 1891/08/21:4a
HANEL, Frank, NYC-B - 1916/09/14:6a
HANEL, Joseph S., NYC-B, exec. Ossining, NY - 1916/09/02:1a
HANF, Ferdinand, un. carp., NYC-M – 1897/08/12:4a
HANFT, George, 59, Florist, Pearl River, NY – 1886/04/09:3a
HANFT, Joseph M., un. cutter, NYC-M – 1882/05/10:1g, mem. 7 My 83:3b
HANFT, Max, Newark, NJ – 1907/11/03:7d
HANGER, Katherina, 14, NYC-M – 1891/04/05:5a
HANGER, Madeline, 51,& grandson Eduard Armac,7, Paterson, NJ - 1915/08/20:6d
HANIER, Louis, 40, innkeep, French, NYC-M – 1881/12/31:1f, 8 Jan. 1882:5d, murderer McGloin tried, 2 Mr:1g, 3:1f, 4:1f, to be exec. 7:1d,
HANK, Johann, 32, NYC-M – 1891/02/20:4a
HANKE % Vogel, % Ziegast
HANKE, Carl, un. carp., NYC-M – 1897/03/25:4a
HANKE, D., NYC-Q, 1920/06/30:6a
HANKE, Elisabeth, b. Bauder, NYC-Bx – 1912/05/10:6a
HANKE, Olga, 2, NYC-M – 1900/03/21:4a
HANKE, Theresia, 75, NYC-Bx – 1905/12/22:4a
HANNA, Marcus A., US Senator & banker, 1904/02/16:1f, 17:1g, Samuel Gompers praised Hanna, NYVZ disgusted 7 May:1d
HANNEMANN, Bertha, 19, NYC-M – 1898/09/07:4a

HANNEMANN, Georg, 2, NYC-M – 1892/03/22:4a
HANNEMANN, Leonard, hotelier, NYC-Q – 1882/05/27:1g
HANNI, 76, RC Archbishop of Milwaukee, crit. Obit – 1881/06/10:2b
HANNIG, Laurina, NYC-M – 1885/04/17:3c
HANNIG, William, 61, NYC-M – 1906/05/19:4a
HANNIGAN, Lauretta, 20, NYC-M - 1895/03/24:1f
HANNIS, Herman, NYC-M - 1915/06/22:6a
HANNLAY, Edward, 53, NYC-Q – 1885/09/19:3b
HANOLD, Joseph, 54, realtor, NYC-B – 1908/09/04:3b
HANS, Franz, carp., NYC-M – 1883/11/22:4b
HANSCH, John, 60, salesman, NYC-M – 1892/08/21:1h
HANSEL, Mathew, 65, innkeep, NYC-B – 1900/03/13:1e
HANSELE, Lawright, Norwegian, painter, NYC-B - 1918/06/29:6a
HANSELMANN, George M., NYC-B – 1887/08/02:2d
HANSELMANN, Thomas, Rev., NYC-Q – 1911/07/22:3a
HANSEN % Guerr
HANSEN, Andrew, hotelier, Mt Vernon, NY – 1910/12/26:2e
HANSEN, Catherine, NYC-M – 1907/07/08:6a
HANSEN, Christian, 40, NYC-M - 1878/05/07:4d
HANSEN, Christina, 37, NYC-M – 1900/06/28:4a
HANSEN, Hans, 16, dying, War 2, NYC-B - 1914/08/13:6d
HANSEN, Heinrich, un. cigarmaker, NYC-M? – 1912/02/02:6a
HANSEN, Johannes, officer on interned German steamer Kronprinzessin
    Caecilie, + Boston - 1917/02/19:6a
HANSEN, Julius, Prof., NYC-M – 1891/04/09:4a
HANSEN, Marie, b. Petersen, 79, fr Flensburg/Gy, NYC-B – 1900/02/22:4a
HANSEN, Marie, b. Rothfelder, 50, NYC-M – 1907/09/06:6a
HANSEN, Mary, 66, NYC-M - 1894/11/02:4a
HANSEN, Mary, 66?, NYC-M – 1891/03/12:4c
HANSEN, Niels, 38, Danish sailor, + on SS City of Montgomery –
    1912/10/12:2a
HANSEN, Oscar, 30, painter, NYC – 1900/05/20:1g
HANSEN, Otto, NYC-M – 1907/04/01:6a
HANSEN, Thomas, 46, Hoboken, NJ – 1906/03/18:1b
HANSEN, Thomas, 65, un. cigarmaker, NYC-M? – 1911/12/09:6a
HANSEN, Viktor A., 25, dairy mgr, Hoboken, NJ – 1909/02/08:2e
HANSEN, Wilhelm, 50, NYC-M – 1896/08/22:4a, 23:5b
HANSEN, William, 65, watchmaker, freethinker, family in Tonawanda, PA,
    + NYC-B – 1897/12/21:2d
HANSING, Gustav, 49, salesman, Hoboken, NJ – 1904/06/17:4b

HANSLIAN, Anton's wife, of Viennese World traveler, + Sunderland on 1 Jy – 1907/08/14:3e
HANSON, Charles, US anarchist, +NYC - 1914/07/09:1e, 12:1e
HANSON, Louis, tailor fr Denmark, NYC-M – 1885/07/07:1g, 17:1f, widow, too 2 Fb 1886:1f
HANSON, Peter, artist fr Denmark, NYC-B – 1887/02/23:1e, 24:1e
HANSON, Wilhelmine, 40, NYC-B – 1900/07/13:4a
HANSSON, Berndt, NYC-M – 1883/08/11:3c
HANSSON, Friedrich, 54, New Haven, CT – 1912/11/21:6a
HANTKE, Hake, 60, fr Gy, Jersey City, NJ - 1913/05/20:2e
HANUSZEK, John, Hoboken, NJ – 1910/05/15:7c
HANZE, Dietrich A., 65, NYC-M – 1891/01/02:4a
HANZL, Frank, machinist, NYC-M – 1906/03/26:4a
HANZLYK, Jos., Union Hill, NJ - 1915/08/29:7a
HAPPEL, Heinrich, NYC-M – 1883/10/30:3b
HAPPEL, Karl J., NYC-M - 1879/04/20:8a
HAPPENBERG % Doruff
HAQUE, Annie, servant, Paterson, NJ – 1892/07/30:1e
HARAN, Caspar, Rev., Greek-Orthodox Church, W. Hoboken, NJ – 1907/05/27:1a-b
HARANOVITCH, Tony, 24, exec. Trenton, NJ - 1915/12/01:6c
HARBURGER, Rosa, 72, NYC-M – 1892/03/27:5d
HARDE, Henry, Jersey City Heights, NJ – 1910/05/03:6a
HARDENFELDER, Henry, NYC-M – 1892/11/22:4a
HARDENFELDER, Lina, b. Dill, 35, NYC-M - 1879/04/23:3a
HARDENFELS, Maria, NYC-M – 1891/04/14:4a
HARDER, Frank, NYC-Q - 1919/05/28:6a, 29:6a
HARDER, Louis, 47, worker, Jersey City, NJ - 1914/01/20:3c
HARDER, Maria, NYC-B – 1912/03/07:3a
HARDICH, Charles E., 30, typesetter, NYC-M – 1897/10/24:1b
HARDIE, James Keir, 59, Scottish labor leader # - 1915/09/27:1f-g, 2b, 4a-b, 23 Oct:4d-e, 24:20e,f, obit by George Bernhard Shaw 7 No:6c-e
HARDT, George, 60, worker, NYC-M – 1880/05/23:5e
HARDY, Frederick, 21, art student, NYC-B – 1899/11/03:1c-d
HARFF, Katharina, b. Koch, 65, NYC-M – 1880/01/06:3a
HARG, Mrs. M. M., NYC-M, +@ on Genl Slocum – 1904/06/17:3b
HARGART, E., NYC-Bx – 1919/10/06:6a
HARI, Mata (Margarethe Zell), Frisian dancer, French to kill her - 1917/07/27:1d, 29 Sept:1e, 5 Oct:3a-c, shot in Paris 16 Oct:1b
HARIER, Joseph, un. carp., NYC-M – 1888/11/10:3b
HARJES, Marie, baby, NYC-Q - 1914/05/23:6a
HARLAN, John Marshall, 78, US Supr Ct, – 1911/10/15:7e

HARM, Friedrich, 61, SPD MdR for Elberfeld/Gy – 1905/10/25:2d
HARMAN, Moses A., free thinker, +1879 Los Angeles, CA, crit notes 30th anniv. of death – 1910/02/04:4a, 28 Mr:1g, 2a
HARMS % Strohmayer, % Thewes
HARMS, Herman, 18, NYC-M, +@Genl Slocum – 1904/06/22:1d
HARMS, Laura, 20, Elizabethport, NJ – 1886/03/19:2g
HARMSDORF, Eleonor, 73, NYC-B - 1916/01/29:6c
HARMUTH % Finke
HARNECKE, John, ~34, grocer, NYC-M – 1886/01/19:1f
HARNEY, George Julian, 80, British Chartists, + Richmond, GB – 1897/12/11:1b, 2b
HARNINGER, Elizabeth, 26, NYC-M - 1915/02/26:6a
HARNISCHFEGER, Ludwig, NYC-M - 1919/05/20:6a
HARONECK, John, 55, fr Bohemia/Austria, cigarmaker, Riverhead, LI – 1908/06/02:3b
HARRAS, H., NYC-B – 1909/05/20:6a
HARRASS, Charlotte, b. Schneider, Hoboken, NJ – 1891/03/19:4a
HARRIGIEL, Henry, NYC-B – 1880/08/26:1e
HARRIMAN, Edward H., 61, RR magnate, crit obit – 1909/09/10:1e, 11:4a, 13:4d, 16:4b-c
HARRING, Charles, NYC-Bx - 1915/08/20:6a
HARRIS, A. D., actor, Lake George, NY – 1912/07/26:2a
HARRIS, Aron, NYC-M - 1916/07/23:6a
HARRIS, Bob, Negro, lynched Watkinsville, GA – 1905/06/30:1h
HARRIS, Carlysle, exec. Ossining, NY – 1893/05/08:1d, 9:1h, 10:2e,4b
HARRIS, Daniel, 69, un. cigarmaker, * England, pres. NYS branch of AFL, NYC-B - 1915/04/06:7b
HARRIS, Jacob, NYC-M – 1890/03/18:4a
HARRIS, Lewis, Negro, lynched Belair, MD – 1900/03/28:3c
HARRIS, Moses J., 53, US Magistrate, NYC-B – 1913/01/29:3b,4c
HARRIS, Philip, 74, NYC-M – 1891/06/28:5c
HARRISON, Benjamin, US pres., 1901/03/17:4b
HARRISON, Carter, Chicago mayor, – 1893/10/29:1f, 30:1f-g, murderer Prendergast tried 24 Dec:1f, 31:1f
HARRISON, Mary, 45, NYC-B – 1913/01/08:1e
HARRISON, Benjamin's wife, of US pres., NYC-M – 1892/10/25:1b
HARRISON, Richard, 27, NYC?, exec. Ossining, NY - 1920/05/15:2g
HARRISON, S. P., SDP, Florida? – 1902/06/14:1e
HART % Dresser
HART, Ella, 30, employee, NYC-M - 1916/03/29:2c
HART, Heinrich, 51, German writer, 1906/06/25:4g
HART, Henry, 90, ex-pres. 3rd Ave RR, NYC-M – 1901/11/08:1f, 9:2b

HARTE, Bret, US writer, posit obit – 1902/05/07:1a, 8:2b-c
HARTENFELS, Jacob, 38, wood carver, NYC-M – 1880/06/30:1b
HARTENSTEIN, Wilhelm, 45, NYC-B – 1904/11/15:4a
HARTER, Anna, b. Wenz, 29, NYC-M – 1900/03/25:5a
HARTFELD, Walter, 28, Hoboken, NJ - 1915/12/02:2d
HARTFORD, Benjamin, 49, SP, #, NYC-Q – 1910/01/25:1b-e, 4a-b, 26:1d,6a, =27:1c-d, 2d, honored 29:1d, 30:6a-c, 3 Fb:2d
HARTH, Wilhelmine, b. Lutz, 54, SP?, NYC-M - 1919/08/13:6a, 14:6c, =15:6b; mem 1920/08/11:6a
HARTHA Jr., August, Cliffe?, NJ – 1919/06/13:6a
HARTIG, George C., infant, NYC-B – 1890/05/11:5a
HARTJE, John C., 38, NYC-M – 1891/03/14:4a
HARTKORN % Wolf
HARTMAN, Frank, 50, NYC-B – 1898/09/04:1d
HARTMAN, William, 36, bookbinder, NYC-B – 1898/06/08:4a
HARTMAN, William, 84, Philadelphia - 1920/02/28:2e
HARTMANN % Hoch, % Schuessler, % Wunderlich
HARTMANN, Anton, 65, un. tailor, NYC-B – 1892/12/26:4a
HARTMANN, Auguste Luise, 77, mother of O. Telzerost, NYC-B - 1913/11/09:7b
HARTMANN, Bertha, 43, Ocean Grove, NJ – 1919/10/13:1f
HARTMANN, Charles, 32, missing since 17 Oct, body fd, New Brunswick, NJ - 1913/11/12:6b
HARTMANN, Charles, NYC-M - 1917/02/20:6a
HARTMANN, Charlie, NYC-M – 1891/02/20:4a
HARTMANN, comrade, 74, SPD Bremen, alderman 1896-1908, – 1909/01/24:3b
HARTMANN, Elizabeth, 75, NYC-B - 1918/03/09:6a
HARTMANN, Frank, NYC-B – 1909/11/17:6a
HARTMANN, Frank, SLP, un. varnisher, dying, NYC-M – 1884/07/03:1g, 4:2d, 8:2c
HARTMANN, Georg, cabinet maker, fr Dresden/Gy, NYC-M - 1878/09/19:4e
HARTMANN, George, NYC-M – 1890/10/11:4a
HARTMANN, Heinrich, SPD Bremerhaven, printer, War 1 on 25 Sept. - 1915/02/07:3b
HARTMANN, Helene, b. Berlaska, 67, NYC-M – 1891/03/15:5b
HARTMANN, Henry A., 47, New Haven, CT – 1897/10/19:4a
HARTMANN, Isaac, 67, NYC-M – 1891/03/30:4a
HARTMANN, Johann, 33, cook, NYC-M – 1902/06/08:1e
HARTMANN, John, 44, tailer, fr. Magdeburg/Gy, NYC-M - 1878/04/19:4d
HARTMANN, John, 47, porter, NYC-B – 1897/06/27:5d

HARTMANN, Karl, 49, NYC-M – 1893/07/30:5a
HARTMANN, Karl, 59, NYC-M – 1905/01/30:4a
HARTMANN, Karl, SPO Wiesenthal/Austria,War 1 - 1915/05/30:3d
HARTMANN, Leo, Russian revol., arrived in NYC – 1881/07/31:4b-e, 4 Aug:2a-b, 5:1g, 2d, 6:2a-b, etc
HARTMANN, Louis, & wife, ex-NYC-M, + Chicago, IL – 1901/06/12:4c
HARTMANN, Margaret, NYC-M, + @on Genl Slocum – 1904/06/17:3b
HARTMANN, Margarethe, NYC-M - 1920/02/01:12a
HARTMANN, Martin, un. carp., NYC-M – 1902/08/16:4a
HARTMANN, Moritz, liberal member of 1848 German Parliament, + 1872, his life, 1904/04/10:15c-d
HARTMANN, Peter, 78, jeweler, NYC-B – 1912/01/19:3a
HARTMANN, Rosa, 21, NYC-M – 1891/03/27:4a
HARTMANN, Rosa, Jersey City Heights, NJ, fam. 1906/11/16:6a
HARTMANN, Theodor, 46, NYC-M - 1895/05/17:4a
HARTMANN, Wilhelm, NYC-M – 1906/03/02:4a
HARTMEYER, William, NYC-M - 1878/03/20:3a
HARTNAGEL, Frederick, un. cigarmkr, NYC-B - 1914/04/26:7d
HARTSTONE, John, 40, waiter, NYC-M – 1903/11/17:1g
HARTUNG, Elise, Frances, Mildred, Elsie, 6, Nellie, 18, NYC-M, +@ on Genl Slocum – 1904/06/17:3b, 18:3c
HARTUNG, Franz, un. carp., NYC-M - 1913/06/14:6a, fam. 21:6a
HARTUNG, Frederick, 56, butcher, NYC-B - 1915/03/14:1b
HARTUNG, Henry, baker, NYC-B – 1910/04/21:3a
HARTUNG, Laura, 10, Clara, 10, NYC-M, +@Genl Slocum – 1904/06/23:1b
HARTUNG, Louisa, 47, NYC-M, +@Genl Slocum – 1904/06/22:1d
HARTUNG, Mathilde, 50, NYC-B – 1880/04/01:4c
HARTWIG % Gent
HARTWIG, Christian, 47, draftsman, NYC-B, + Rutherford, NJ - 1917/09/05:2d, wife fd guilty 1918/04/17:2e, 1 May:2f
HARTWIG, Ernst, 42, salesman, Hoboken, NJ – 1892/08/05:1g
HARTZ, Tycho C. E., fr Schleswig-Holstein?, NYC – 1883/08/26:8a
HARTZENBUSCH, Juan E., Spanish-German playwright – 1880/09/05:3g
HARVEY, William H., exec. Guelph, Ontario – 1889/11/30:1b
HARWELL, Frank & Cornelius, Negro juveniles, lynched Magnolia, Miss., – 1893/02/11:1d
HARZ, Hugo, 60, SPD Jena, un. painter - 1914/10/25:3d
HARZENBERGER, Hermina, 45, carp., NYC-M – 1906/08/03:6a
HARZENMOSER, Gustav, 49, machinist?, NYC-M – 1906/03/20:4a, 21:4c
HARZER, Reinhold, 51, alderman & SPD Jena/Thueringen, Gy – 1912/10/13:3d

HARZHORN, Georg, 65, NYC-B - 1913/05/14:3b
HASCHE % Schroeder
HASCHE, Dietrich, 57, NYC-M – 1892/01/23:4a, fam. 24:4a
HASELOFF, Gretchen, infant, NYC-M – 1881/07/20:3b
HASELOFF, Paul, NYC-M – 1891/12/17:4a, 18:4a
HASEMANN, Henry, grocer, Bayonne?, NJ – 1893/12/12:2c
HASEMANN, Ludwig, 54, SP, un. brewer, * Kaiserslautern/Gy, Newark, NJ - 1915/03/08:2d,6a, fam. 13:6a, mem. 5 Mr 1916:7a
HASEMANN, Wilhelmine, 60, NYC-Q - 1920/05/20:6a
HASENAUER, Fritz, NYC-M – 1910/05/21:6a
HASENAUER, Wilhelm, Elizabeth, NJ - 1913/08/04:6a
HASENBALG, Wilhelm, Lt. in German army, War 1, sister Mrs Snead in Rockledge, NJ - 1914/11/09:2e-f
HASENCLEVER, Wilhelm, * 19 Apr 1837 Arensberg/Westfalia, MdR SPD, ex-pres. Allgemeiner Dt Arbeiterverein, note 3 Apr 1888:2c, 14 Juni:2a, now in asylum 19 Dec:1c, + 1889/07/06:2c-d, mon. in Stuttgart 1890/09/09:2c, memory – 1904/07/24:9e-f
HASENFRATZ, William, 58, SP, hatmaker, *Donaueschingen/Baden, NYC-Bx – 1910/07/13:6a, =16:6a
HASENFUSS, Marie, servant, War 2, NYC-M - 1916/02/06:11b
HASENKRUG, Wilhelm, 76, SPD activist in Magdeburg/Gy – 1909/09/12:3d
HASENZAHL, Jacob, 35, fr Willesdorf/Hessen, NYC-M - 1878/07/04:3c
HASHAGEN, John F., woolen dealer, NYC-B – 1899/11/21:1e
HASLER, Heinrich, 69, weaver, Swiss, SP, Meriden, CT – 1908/01/06:3d
HASLETT, Samuel E., rich eccentric, NYC-B – 1912/02/18:7c
HASNER % Elsaesser
HASPEL, A., un. cigar maker, NYC-M – 1891/08/12:4a
HASPEL, Antinette, NYC-B – 1902/03/13:4g
HASPEL, Georg, NYC-B – 1912/07/24:6a
HASS, August, Metropolitan, LI – 1912/04/09:6a
HASS, Theodor, 25, NYC-B – 1880/07/06:4a
HASSAN, Emma, 56, NYC-M – 1892/09/16:4a
HASSE, Richard, 41, fr Dresden 1912, barman, NYC – 1912/05/14:1d
HASSEK, Alois, 49, SLP, handbag maker, co-fdr Newark Socialist Gesangverein, *Trebitsch/Moravia, USA 1866, Newark,NJ - 1878/04/03:1f, = 4:1e
HASSEL, Josef, 27, fr Hungary this summer, NYC-B – 1902/11/13:4a
HASSELBACH, Annie, 28, Jersey City, NJ – 1892/03/09:1e
HASSELBACH, Ernst, un. cigar packer, secy. #292, NYC-B – 1897/04/20:4b
HASSELBERGER % Immesberger

HASSELKA, John, coal-miner, see 1897 Hazleton Massacre
HASSELMANN, Agnes, b. Graef, NYC-M – 1890/03/31:4a
HASSELMANN, H., NYC-Q – 1913/01/21:6a
HASSELWANDE % Steinel
HASSENPFLUG, M., 28, NYC-M – 1893/03/28:4a
HASSERBROOK, Conrad, 75, NYC-B – 1893/03/31:4a
HASSINGER, Henry, 54, NYC-M – 1896/12/02:1g
HASSLACH, Alex, NYC-B - 1919/04/03:6a
HASSLER, August, clerk, + 2 Jy, NYC-M – 1887/07/14:1g
HASSLER, John's infant child, fr Gross-Sonnenteich/Holstein on way to Pacific Coast, NYC-M – 1888/05/15:1d
HASTEDT, Henry, 23, NYC-M - 1895/03/09:4a
HASTEDT, Louis, 60, NYC-Q - 1919/04/03:6a
HASTINGS, Hugh J., publ. N.Y. Commercial Advertiser, NYC-M – 1883/09/13:4a, =16:1f,4a
HATAL, Michael, carp. & variete musician, NYC-M – 1899/10/30:1e
HATHAWAY, Belle, Negro, lynched near Hamilton, GA – 1912/01/24:1b
HATTENHORST, Herman, 45, owner Inst. Physical Culture, NYC-B - 1895/11/26: 1f, 28: 4a, 30: 4a
HATYING, Alexander, locksmith, killed during strike in Budapest, Hungary – 1912/06/16:3d-e
HATZEL, Theodor, 53, un. typesetter, NYC-M – 1896/04/14:4a, =16:3f
HATZFELDT, Sophie von, 76, Countess, lover of Ferdinand Lasalle, leader of German socialists, + Wiesbaden/Gy – 1881/02/20:4e-g, 27:5a
HATZLEY, James, merchant, fr Belfast, NYC-M - 1879/02/20:1d
HAU, Charles, NYC-M – 1899/11/15:4a
HAUBER, A., Jersey City Hgts, NJ – 1919/08/15:6a
HAUBER, Carl, 71, un. typesetter, NYC-B – 1897/02/15:4a, 16:4a
HAUBERT, J., NYC-M – 1891/08/11:4a
HAUBOLD, Otto, West Hoboken, NJ – 1912/09/14:6a
HAUCH % Apfel
HAUCK, Barbara, b. Jaeger, 56, NYC-M – 1897/02/26:4a
HAUCK, Charles, sailor on USS Maine, + Havana/Cuba, NYC-B – 1898/02/18:1b
HAUCK, Clara, 9, NYC-B – 1901/03/19:4a
HAUCK, E., NYC-Q - 1914/10/19:6a
HAUCK, Friedrich, 64, un. cigarmaker, NYC-M – 1900/08/24:4a
HAUCK, Henry, 50, NYC-B – 1904/10/21:4b
HAUCK, Jean, SPD Ludwigshafen/Baden/Gy, – 1909/03/28:3a
HAUCK, Joseph, un. carp., Saugerties, NY – 1908/01/14:6a
HAUCK, Katharina F., b. Goepfert, 29, NYC-M – 1881/07/21:3c
HAUCK, M., NYC-Q – 1912/07/27:6a

HAUDELL, Frederick, freight handler, see 1900 dock fire, Hoboken, NJ 1900/07/03:1c
HAUDY, Marie, b. Woelfling, 64, NYC-Bx – 1919/12/30:6a
HAUEL, Bernard, 2, NYC-M – 1880/07/24:3a
HAUENSTEIN, Charles, NYC-M – 1912/12/03:6a
HAUENSTEIN, Conrad, 59, printer, & son Conrad Jr., 21, NYC-M – 1904/05/11:3d
HAUENSTEIN, Johanna, 69, NYC-Bx - 1917/01/07:7a
HAUERSCHMIDT, Louis, married in NYC Lena HEER – 1886/06/22:3a
HAUERT, Charles, NYC-B - 1918/02/09:6a
HAUERT, Phillip, un. silversmith, NYC - 1913/12/14:11a
HAUF, Barthold, NYC-B - 1916/08/10:6a
HAUFELD, Henry, 1, NYC-M – 1893/12/29:4a
HAUFF, Carl, NYC? – 1885/05/11:3a
HAUFF, Wilhelm, German writer, on him – 1902/11/30:14f-h
HAUG, Anna Auguste, b. Heydenreich, NYC-B – 1890/19:5b
HAUG, Charles, 18, tailor, NYC-B – 1898/04/25:4b
HAUG, Wilhelm, 55?, NYC-Q - 1895/02/16:4a
HAUGEN, Jacob, NYC-M – 1889/05/05:5a
HAUGENBUSCH, Louisa, NYC-M, +@ on Genl Slocum – 1904/06/17:3b
HAUGER, Alois, 69, Hoboken, NJ – 1892/05/05:4a
HAUK, W., NYC-M - 1915/06/19:6a
HAULDSCHMIDT, Theodor, gardener, & little son, Long Branch, NJ – 1904/08/31:3c
HAUN, Helene, 66, NYC-M - 1915/10/02:6a, 3:7a
HAUPT, Ernst, 50, liberal co-publ. Zittauer Morgenzeitung, + Leipzig/Gy – 1908/05/03:3d
HAUPT, Maria, b. Schein, fr Eisenach/Thueringia, NYC-M - 1878/06/17:3b
HAUPTMANN, Joseph, 28, NYC-Bx – 1906/03/06:4a
HAURY, John, Elizabeth, NJ – 1893/04/15:3d
HAUS, August, un. carp., NYC-M – 1903/10/07:4a
HAUSAMANN, Babetta, b. Schmidt, 41, NYC-M – 1880/02/26:1g, =27:1f
HAUSCHILD, Robert, 67, SPD Chemnitz, alderman - 1915/10/03:3c
HAUSE, Emma, 2, Jersey City Heights, NJ – 1898/12/25:1e
HAUSELT, Charles, 61, pres. NYC Bavarian Society, USA 1850, NYC-M – 1890/02/09:5b, 15:3d, 17:4e
HAUSER % Renker
HAUSER, Alois, Berlin/Gy art restorer & original – 1919/09/13:4f
HAUSER, Anna Paulina, 20, NYC-M - 1918/11/01:6a
HAUSER, Bella, NYC-M – 1911/03/29:6a
HAUSER, Carl, cartoonist, NYC - 1915/04/16:4c
HAUSER, Conrad, 53, NYC-B – 1899/09/01:4a

HAUSER, Ernst, 41, un. typesetter, NYC-Bx – 1907/05/07:6a
HAUSER, Frederick, 72, NYC-M – 1909/06/09:1d
HAUSER, George, 54, NYC-B – 1890/03/30:5b
HAUSER, Jakob, 43, SP, un. sheet metal worker, USA 1888 fr Wuerttemberg, NYC-B - 1913/08/13:6a, 14::6d,8a, =16:3e
HAUSER, Jakob, glassworker, fr Pittsburgh, PA, + Steubenville, N.Y. - 1878/04/18:3a
HAUSER, John, NYC-M – 1898/09/07:1f
HAUSER, John, SP, co-fdr NYVZ, + Washington, DC – 1908/05/10:7b
HAUSER, Julius, Jersey City, NJ - 1914/02/07:6a
HAUSER, Katharina, 17, USA 1891, NYC-B – 1891/06/10:2f
HAUSER, Max, 38, NYC-M – 1907/02/08:6a
HAUSER, Wilhelm, NYC-Q – 1901/05/07:4a
HAUSEROTH, Annie, 70, NYC-B - 1915/12/09:6b
HAUSIG, Rudolph, un. carp., NYC-M – 1899/02/23:4a
HAUSKNECHT, Carl, un. carp., NYC-M – 1897/01/28:4a
HAUSLE, John, NYC-Metropolitan – 1909/03/31:6a
HAUSLER, Karl, NYC-M - 1920/03/19:6a
HAUSMANN, Heinrich, 31, NYC-M – 1888/01/09:3a
HAUSMANN, Henry, NYC-B – 1911/08/18:6a
HAUSMANN, Louise, b. Mueller, 34, NYC-M – 1904/01/09:4a
HAUSSLER, Julia, 19, NYC-Bx – 1908/11/25:3c
HAUSSMANN % Jonas
HAUSSMANN, Jacob, NYC-M – 1908/05/03:7b
HAUSTEIN, Friedrich Wilhelm, 68, NYC-Bx – 1910/10/08:6a
HAUSTEIN, Helene, 21, NYC-B – 1897/04/03:4a
HAUSTEIN, Henry, un. carp., NYC-M – 1893/07/09:5a
HAUSTEIN, Hermann, 54, locksmith, SPD Dresden/Gy – 1901/01/24:2f
HAUSTETTER, Anton, cabinetmaker, fr Philadelphia, + NYC-M - 1879/05/07:1f
HAUSWIRTH, Johann Ludwig, 66, tailor, NYC-M – 1882/04/19:1e
HAUSWIRTH, Joseph, 72, NYC-M – 1909/01/23:6a
HAVARAK, Eli, 35, & wife, NYC-B - 1920/01/07:1e
HAVEL, Bertha, b. Schubert, 34, NYC-M – 1897/07/04:5g
HAVEL, Joseph, NYC-Q – 1906/11/06:6a
HAVEMEYER % Mayer
HAVEMEYER, Charles, 35, sugar magnate, Roslyn, LI – 1898/05/11:4a
HAVEMEYER, Theodore, NYC sugar baron – 1897/04/27:3f, crit. obit – 1897/05/13:2a-b, 16:4a-b
HAVEMEYER, William F., sugar manuf., + NYC - 1913/09/08:2d
HAVEMEYER, William, 8, NYC-M, +@ on Genl Slocum – 1904/06/18:3c

HAVERKAMP, August, SPD Bremerhaven, * 5 Jy 1864 Oldenburg - 1915/03/14:3a
HAVERSMANN, Justine, NYC-M – 1881/09/03:1f
HAVERSTICK, William H., NYC-M – 1883/03/22:1f, 20:4c, 23:1e, = Carlisle, PA 25:1f, 28:1g
HAVESIEL, B., butcher, married Marie Verner, 20,both fr Guttenburg (Kuttenberg?)/Bohemia, NYC – 1906/03/14:3g
HAWARTH, Joseph, 62, silkweaver, Paterson, NJ - 1913/11/01:3b
HAWKIN, Charles, 18, NYC-B, + @on Genl Slocum – 1904/06/17:3b
HAWKINS, Francis, 23, fr Islip, exec. Riverhead, LI – 1888/12/11:2d, 12:2g, =13:2e
HAWLITSCHECK, Hugo, un. painter, NYC-Bx – 1910/05/22:7b, 23:6a, 24:6a
HAWLITSCHEK, Auguste, SP, NYC-Bx - 1916/07/02:7a, 3:6a
HAX, Ferdinand, Newark, NJ – 1909/02/04:6a
HAX, Theresa, 46, Newark, NJ – 1905/11/18:4a
HAY, John, US Secy of State, crit. Obit – 1905/07/02:1g, 3:2a-b, 3f, =6:2g
HAYDEN, Patrick, innkeep & local politico, Jersey City, NJ – 1886/11/26:3a, 27:2d, =30:2e
HAYES, Patrick, exec. Philadelphia, PA – 1881/01/07:1d
HAYES, Rutherford B., ex-pres. USA – 1893/01/18:1b
HAYMARKET EXECUTIONS see @1886 Haymarket
HAYN, Maria, b. Aumueller, NYC-M - 1894/10/15:4a
HAYO, Elise, 33, NYC-M – 1896/08/12:4a
HAYWOOD, Bill, labor leader, on his courageous wife (not +) – 1907/04/28:20d
HAZELIUS, Arthur, Dr., fdr Nordic Museum, + Stockholm/Sweden – 1901/06/19:3f-g
HAZLETON MASSACRE 1897 see p. 712
HEANEY, William, NYPD - 1913/05/05:2c
HEBBEL, Katherina, 55, NYC-M – 1902/09/11:4a
HEBBELER, Christopher, 54, NYC-B – 1919/09/06:6a
HEBERMANN, Charles, 41, Jersey City, NJ – 1892/01/16:1e
HECHLER, Henry, un. carp., NYC-M – 1902/03/16:5a
HECHMAN, William, 3, NYC-M, +@Genl Slocum – 1904/06/23:1b
HECHT % Jaeger
HECHT, Abraham, 63, NYC-B - 1894/01/12:4a
HECHT, Carl, 53, NYC-M – 1901/11/27:4a
HECHT, Frederick, 28, NYC-M – 1897/04/15:1f
HECHT, John P., Dr., Jersey City, NJ – 1912/02/13:2d
HECHT, Josef, 84, NYC-M - 1894/01/23:4e
HECK % Hutter

HECK, Christian's wife + NYC – 1885/12/04:4a
HECK, F., un. carp., NYC-M – 1888/12/28:3b
HECK, Frank & Sarah, 26, NYC-B - 1920/04/11:3b
HECK, Henry, fr Philadelphia, + Chicago – 1884/08/14:1b
HECK, Justus, 58, NYC-M - 1878/09/06:3a
HECK, Ludgard, 49, NYC-M – 1887/02/14:4d, 15:1b, 16:3a, =17:2e
HECK, Philip, 19, Elizabethport, NJ – 1900/10/20:4a
HECKE, Friedrich, 38, pianomaker, NYC-M – 1881/07/05:3d
HECKEL, George J., NYC-M – 1886/07/07:3b
HECKEL, Sophia (Heckler?), servant, NYC-M – 1907/08/05:3c, 6:2c, 19:2d
HECKER, Friedrich, = Summerfield, MO – 1881/03/31:2e-f, NY Turnverein grieves 4 Apr:1g
HECKER, Henry, un. carp., NYC-M - 1914/11/13:6a
HECKER, Jakob, 30, NYC-M – 1890/11/23:5a
HECKER, Jennie, 26, sales clerk, NYC-B – 1887/07/07:2e
HECKER, John M., 45, un. brewer, NYC-SI – 1904/03/10:4a, fam. 22:4a
HECKER, Joseph P., Hoboken, NJ – 1890/11/09:5b
HECKERMANN, William, 40, carpenter,Jersey City,NJ - 1894/12/12:4c
HECKERT, Julia, infant, NYC-M, + @on Genl Slocum – 1904/06/17:3b
HECKERT, Louis, NYC – 1892/08/19:4f
HECKERT, Rudolph, 30, machinist, NYC-B – 1898/08/16:4c
HECKLER, Charlotte, Arlington, NJ – 1910/11/28:1c
HECKLER, Sarah, 70, NYC–Bx - 1915/12/30:1b
HECKMANN, Barbara, NYC-M – 1906/04/30:4a
HECKMANN, Charles, 59, carp., NYC-M – 1880/11/17:4f
HECKMANN, Elizabeth, NYC-M – 1897/01/21:4a
HECKMANN, George C., un. cigarmaker, NYC-M - 1917/02/12:6a
HECKMANN, Katrina, 24, & Lillian, 5, NYC-M, +@Genl Slocum – 1904/06/25:1d
HECKNER, August, un. woodworker, SPD Breslau/Gy – 1910/04/03:3c
HEDBOWUY, John, machinist, NYC – 1889/10/25:4a
HEDDEN, William H., butcher, Grove, NJ – 1891/02/13:4d
HEDDERICH, John Jacob, Hoboken, NJ – 1888/04/24:2h
HEDDERICK, Robert, NYC-M, + @on Genl Slocum – 1904/06/17:3b
HEDMAN, Osende, 68, agate cutter, fr France, NYC-Q - 1913/08/27:2f
HEEDE, Rosie, infant, NYC-M – 1886/04/03:3a
HEEDE, Thomas, 65, dry goods dealer, NYC-M – 1898/11/17:1d
HEELEIN, Theresia, b. Peters, 57, NYC-Q – 1896/07/15:4a
HEER % Hauerschmidt
HEER, Heinrich, NYC-M – 1890/05/02:4a
HEERLEIN, Harry, 29, SP?, Dunellen, NJ - 1920/06/25:6a

HEERLEIN, Henry Frederick, 6, NYC-M – 1890/12/08:4a
HEERLEIN, Henry, NYC-M – 1884/07/20:5g
HEERLEIN, John, SLP, NYC-M, married Martha Krogmann – 1893/06/05:1f
HEERLEIN, Martha, b. Krogmann, 26, NYC-M – 1902/06/18:4a, 19:4a
HEERLEIN, Martha, infant, NYC-M - 1895/07/22: 4b
HEERN, Charles von, barber, Newark, NJ – 1903/08/18:3c
HEERWART, Eleonore, 77, fdr of German Kindergarten Union, + Eisenach/Gy – 1912/01/14:20e-f
HEES, VAN, Carl, 63, SP?, un. cigarmaker, NYC-M - 1917/01/15:6a, 16:6a, 19:5d, fam. 18:6a
HEES, VAN, Edna, 2, NYC-M – 1907/04/17:6a
HEES, VAN, Otto, 36, NYC-M - 1914/11/02:6a, fam. 6:6a
HEESE, Mary, NYC-M – 1891/03/01:1h
HEFERLE, 48?, fr Switzerland, NYC-M – 1889/02/20:4a
HEFFERMANN, M. J., 50, journalist, NYC-B – 1888/06/23:1f
HEFFNER, Heinrich married Caroline Bellinger, both fr Baden, in Newark, NJ – 1884/09/27:3b
HEFMANN, Jessie, to be exec. St Petersburg/Russia, for part. In killing Alex II, NYC workers protest, – 1881/05/21:1g, 23:1f-g, she had alr been secretly exec 24:2c, 25:2d
HEFT, Joseph, un. butcher, fr Bavaria?,NYC-B - 1918/12/09:6a
HEFT, Valentin, cook at Pabst's in Harlem, NYC-M – 1910/05/10:2f
HEFTER, Antoinette, b. von Koeppel, NYC-M – 1892/06/13:4a
HEGEDORN, Zacharias, 68, gardener, NYC-B – 1911/02/16:3a
HEGEDUS, Charles C., playwright fr Hungary, Yonkers, NY – 1899/12/15:1e
HEGEL, Michael, 9, NYC-M – 1880/08/03:1g
HEGEMAN, Thomas, Dr. med., NYC-B - 1917/12/21:2c
HEGEMANN, Charles, musician, NYC-M – 1882/08/22:4e, 21:4d
HEGENBUCHER, Mary, NYC-M, + @on Genl Slocum – 1904/06/17:3b
HEGER, Emil, 53, painter, NYC-B - 1919/03/01:6c
HEGER, Ernst, Cincinatti, OH, teacher, + Phillipines – 1902/07/24:1g
HEGER, Franz, un. butcher, NYC-B – 1915/08/24:6a
HEGERS % Vogler
HEGERTY, Karl, NYC-M – 1892/05/29:5b
HEGG, Barbara, NYC-M, + @on Genl Slocum – 1904/06/18:3c
HEGHMANN, Henry, West Hoboken, NJ - 1916/06/27:2g
HEGMANN, Friedrich, 15, No. Bergen, NJ – 1908/03/31:6a, fam. 4 Apr:6a
HEHL, Ernst, 56, machinist, NYC-M? - 1913/12/08:6a, 9:6a
HEHL, George, 14, NYC-M, +@ on Genl Slocum – 1904/06/17:3b

HEHNER, Adam, SP?, un. cigarmaker, Jersey City Heights, NJ – 1906/10/31:6a
HEIBNER, Herman, 35, stevedore, Jersey City, NJ – 1898/01/07:3d
HEID, Martin, 45, Paterson, NJ – 1904/04/20:4b
HEIDE, Charles, 49, mason, Hoboken, NJ – 1880/11/30:4c
HEIDE, Charles, painter, NYC-M – 1892/08/02:1h
HEIDECKER, Henry, 58, baker, NYC-Q – 1911/08/15:1f
HEIDEGGER, Louise, 44, Newark, NJ - 1914/04/18:1e
HEIDEL, Ida, b. Giaugue, NYC-M - 1916/05/18:6a
HEIDEL, Wilhelm, SP, NYC-Q – 1911/04/03:6a, 5:2d
HEIDELBACH, Jacob, 47, SP, NYC-M – 1906/02/12:4a, 18:5g
HEIDELBERG, L., NYC-M – 1893/10/10:4a
HEIDEMANN, Frank, 28, *Dortmund/Gy, exec. Trenton, NJ – 1911/05/24:1f
HEIDEMANN, Hermann, SPD Schildesche/Saxony, War 1 - 1914/11/01:3b
HEIDEN, August, 27, NYC-M – 1892/08/08:4f
HEIDENKAMP, John, NYC-M, +@ on Genl Slocum – 1904/06/17:3b
HEIDENREICH, Gottlieb, un. carp., NYC-M – 1907/04/02:6a
HEIDENREICH, Gustav, NYC-M - 1915/06/03:6a
HEIDENREICH, Henriette, NYC-M – 1891/03/24:4a
HEIDENREICH, Jakob, NYC-M – 1891/08/26:4a, 27:1d
HEIDER, Frederick, shoe dealer, NYC-B – 1900/01/05:1e
HEIDER, Henry J., NYC-M - 1916/05/16:6a
HEIDER, Katherina, 22, NYC-M - 1894/02/01:4a
HEIDERICH, Peter Jr., 39, NYC-B – 1912/07/04:6a
HEIDICKER, Otto, 24, NYC-Q – 1906/11/19:3a
HEIDINGER, Christina, un. cigar maker, NYC? – 1887/05/17:3c
HEIDINGSFELDER, Elsa H., teacher at PS 22, NYC-B – 1908/08/04:3a
HEIDT, Elisabeth, 66, NYC-M – 1891/04/06:4a
HEIDT, Michael, 52, NYC – 1912/09/01:7e
HEIDT, William, 63, NYC-B - 1913/12/03:3c
HEIDT, William, NYC-M – 1891/02/20:4a
HEIFER, Henry, 67, NYC-M - 1878/04/10:3b
HEIL, Henry, NYC-M - 1915/10/02:6a
HEIL, John W., NYC-M – 1890/11/14:1e
HEIL, John, 24, NYC-M – 1884/08/22:1g & 24:1g
HEIL, Wilhelm, un. carp., NYC-M – 1882/05/10:3c
HEILBECKER, Karl, SPD Wiesbaden, War 1 - 1914/11/01:3b
HEILE, Peter, 61, innkeep, NYC-M – 1880/07/09:1f
HEILMANN, John, 50, NYC-Q – 1905/07/18:4a
HEILMANN, John, un. carp., NYC-M – 1912/02/10:6a
HEILMANN, Katharina, un. cigar maker, NYC-M – 1885/09/05:3b

HEILMANN, Nicolaus,48,un. cigarmaker,NYC-M - 1894/06/03:5b
HEILNER, Julia, 48, NYC-B - 1915/04/24:1g, 25:11c, 26:1e
HEILPRIN, Michael, 65, writer and '48er, *Petrikau/Russian Poland, Summit, NJ – 1888/05/12:1g
HEILSHORN, Margarethe, 33, & George, 2, NYC-M, +@Genl Slocum – 1904/06/22:1d, 23:1b
HEILWIG, Leo, 43, liquor-dealer, NYC-M – 1919/08/12:6a
HEIM, Albert, NYC-Bx – 1911/06/05:6a
HEIM, Carl, ~50, shoemaker, USA 1887, NYC-M – 1891/05/03:1f
HEIM, Elisa, b. Baumann, 36, NYC-M – 1900/02/01:4a, fam. 4:5b
HEIM, Henry, Swiss?, SLP, NYC-M – 1900/05/22:4a, =24:2f, fam. 24:4a
HEIM, Hermann, NYC-M – 1889/06/08:5b
HEIM, Johann, NYC-M - 1917/05/22:6a
HEIM, Johanna, NYC-M – 1893/12/31:5c
HEIM, John B., NYC-M – 1906/08/16:3b
HEIM, Lottie, 24, NYC-M – 1891/08/27:1d, 4a
HEIM, Louise, b. Nickel, 61, NYC-B – 1891/03/16:4a
HEIM, Margarethe, NYC-M – 1891/04/02:4a
HEIM, Robert, West Hoboken, NJ - 1918/07/14:12a
HEIMANN % Dettmar
HEIMANN, comrade, 46, un. woodworker & SPD Zittau/Sax. - 1914/01/11:3f
HEIMANN, Eva, NYC-Q - 1894/06/20:4a
HEIMANN, Louis, tailor, NYC-M – 1892/08/16:4c
HEIMANN, Louise Paul, 44, NYC-Q - 1916/05/07:7b
HEIMATH, Charles, NYC-M – 1890/08/01:4a
HEIMBERGER, Ferdinand, 55, NYC-B – 1908/04/07:6a, 8:6a
HEIMBERGER, Sebastian, 61, grocer, NYC – 1905/03/19:5h
HEIMCHEN, Ernst, 40, cook, NYC-M – 1907/03/01:1f
HEIMKE, Carsten, 46, NYC-B – 1891/07/15:4a
HEIMKE, John, 42, Jersey City, NJ – 1891/08/27:1d
HEIMS, Christina, 45, grocer, NYC-B - 1879/04/15:4a
HEIMSOTH, Adam, 21, NYC-B - 1915/11/08:2e
HEIMST, George, 70, NYC-M – 1891/08/15:4a
HEIN % Hagedorn
HEIN, Albert, carp., NYC-M – 1899/08/19.3b
HEIN, Ernst, 77, NYC-Bx - 1917/06/24:1f
HEIN, Hugo's wife, NYC-Bx – 1910/11/16:6a
HEIN, Jacob, 49, SP, NYC-B - 1916/01/24:6a,b, 25:6a
HEIN, John, 55, gardener, NYC-M – 1905/05/29:3e
HEIN, William, NYC-B – 1903/03/07:4a
HEINBERGER, Anton, paper hanger, NYC-M – 1891/06/20:4a, 21:5a

HEINBOCKEL, Claus, 60, NYC-B – 1885/05/23:4e, 24:4a
HEINDEL, George, worker at Heller & Merz, Newark, NJ – 1905/04/24:3d
HEINDL, Alex, 84, NYC-B - 1917/09/06:6b
HEINDL, Theodore, un. machinist, NYC-M, + Baltimore, MD – 1910/09/15:6a
HEINE, Carrie, 47, NYC-M – 1888/04/03:1e
HEINE, Charles, 52, mechanic, NYC-M - 1894/02/07:1g, 8:4a
HEINE, Franz, NYC-B – 1899/02/12:5a, 13:4a
HEINE, Heinrich, German poet, his grave in Paris 1880/05/16:3c-d, & 22 Aug:3g. Notes on his mother Elisabeth von Geldern 1 May 1881:2g-3b; Ludwig Fraenkel on Heine's low personal morality 6 Aug. 1893:3; Georg Brandes on Heine 20 Mr 1898:9e-h, grave in Paris 14 Nv 1898:2e; Bronx mon. inaug 9 Jy 1899:1,4, 24:1g; on him 3 Mr 1901:3e-g, Austrian singing soc hon. his grave 1 Jy:2f, his friend Philbert Audebrand in Paris 8 Dec 1901:9c-d. 50th anniv. of +, 1906/02/17:2a-b, 12 Mr:4e, 15:4h
HEINE, Henry, capt Norwegian bark "Mississippi," NYC-M – 1880/05/30:5d
HEINE, John, un. pianomaker, NYC-M – 1892/03/13:5a
HEINE, Karl, 62, woodcutter & SPD Hamburg/Gy, ed. Hamburger Echo – 1908/05/24:3b
HEINE, Mathilde, wd of Heinrich, + Paris – 1883/03/25:4a, 5a, 1 Apr:5a-c
HEINE, P., Union Hill, NJ – 1910/07/12:6a
HEINECKE, Franz, NYC-B – 1893/11/23:4a
HEINECKE, Friedrich, 64, barber, SP, Westfield, NJ – 1907/01/11:3c
HEINECKE, Wilhelm, NYC-M – 1908/07/18:6a
HEINEMANN, John, un. carp., NYC-M – 1902/07/04:4a
HEINEMANN, Louis, carp., NYC-B - 1913/08/15:6a
HEINEN, Dietrich, un. carp., NYC-M – 1904/04/30:4a, 1 May:5b
HEINER, Gottlieb, 26, baker, Red Bank, NJ – 1896/12/27:1g
HEINES, John F., 61, supt in shoe factory, & wife, 55, NYC-Q – 1910/12/16:1e
HEINICKE % Kunath
HEINICKE, Emil, 39, un. carp., NYC-M – 1912/03/12:2c, 13:6a
HEINICKE, Emil, 71, un. wood carver, Bridgeport, CT – 1919/09/24:6a, fam. 27:8a
HEINICKE, Friedrich, 33, un. cigarmaker, NYC-Q – 1885/10/30:3a
HEINICKE, Gustav, 37, Rahway, NJ – 1900/05/17:4a
HEINICKE, Wilhelm, 33, NYC-M - 1917/03/02:6a
HEINKEL, Carolina, & daughter Klara, 3, NYC-Q – 1887/11/29:2d, =2 Dec:4f, 3:2d
HEINLE, Josephine, b. Hagenbusch, 61, NYC-M – 1891/03/30:4a
HEINLEIN, Nicholas, 72, NYC-B – 1897/09/16:4a

HEINRICH % Hufnagel, % Keller
HEINRICH, Amelia, 18, NYC-Bx, +@Genl Slocum – 1904/06/22:1d
HEINRICH, Casper, 36, NYC-B – 1892/06/19:5c
HEINRICH, Christopher, bird dealer, Jersey City, NJ - 1913/07/23:6d
HEINRICH, Frederick. W., 44, silk dealer, NYC-M - 1919/05/26:2g
HEINRICH, George A., NYC-M – 1891/03/29:5a
HEINRICH, H., 81, watchmaker,*Cranz/Gy, Hoboken, NJ – 1903/03/08:5f
HEINRICH, John, 32, oyster dealer, NYC-B – 1890/07/02:2e, 3:2f
HEINRICH, Julia, ex-opera singer, NYC, + Hammond, LA – 1919/09/19:1d
HEINRICH, Leo, Rev., Denver, CO, * 15 Aug 1867 near Koeln –
    1908/02/24:1f, 25:2f, 27:1e, = Paterson, NJ 1 Mr:1d, 2:3e, 3:2d
HEINRICH, Leopold, 57, pianomaker, NYC-M - 1894/09/23:5a
HEINRICH, Sophia, b. Brugger, NYC-M – 1891/07/26:4a
HEINRICHS, Elizabeth, NYC-B – 1906/11/01:3b
HEINRICHS, Emilie, b. Sanders, 53, NYC-M – 1885/12/07:3b
HEINRICHS, John, NYC-M - 1920/01/06:8a, fam. 11:12a
HEINRICHS, Karl, ~35, fr Saxony, + on SS Weser, on way to NYC –
    1880/01/09:4a
HEINRICHS, Louisa, NYC-M – 1892/07/26:4a
HEINRICHSHOFEN, Heinrich von, insurance agent, St Louis, MO,
    German army, War 1 - 1915/06/30:1e
HEINRICK, O., 35, + Newark, NJ – 1902/07/12:4b
HEINS % Ellerhorst
HEINS, August, SLP Syracuse, NY – 1898/01/09:1b
HEINS, Frank, 12, NYC-M, + @on Genl Slocum – 1904/06/17:3b
HEINS, Gottlieb, 27, musician, NYC-M – 1889/08/03:4c
HEINS, Henrietta, 10, NYC-M, + @on Genl Slocum – 1904/06/17:3b
HEINS, Ida, 14, Margaret, 7, NYC-M, +@Genl Slocum – 1904/06/22:1d
HEINS, John, 37, grocer, NYC-B – 1911/10/05:1d
HEINS, Maggie, 15, NYC-M – 1881/09/26:1d, 27:1f
HEINS-HENRYOT, Alphonse G., SP, un. carp. & journalist, USA 1887,
    NYC-B - 1916/01/31:6a, =3 Feb:6c, 4:2e, fam. 6:7a; mem.1917/01/30:6a
HEINSIUS, Peter, 75, SPD Mannheim/Gy – 1897/11/17:2d
HEINSOLT, Hermann, 45, innkeep, NYC-M – 1887/07/29:3a
HEINSTADT, Peter, NYC-M - 1917/02/22:6a
HEINTSCH, August, director Social Printing House, Berlin, =10th -
    1878/03/26:2f, 2 Apr:2e
HEINTZ, Christian, 54, furniture dealer, NYC-B – 1890/11/17:4c, 19:4a
HEINTZ, Louis J., Bronx Street Comm., NYC-Bx – 1893/03/14:4a
HEINTZ, Peter, SLP, NYC-B – 1890/11/13:4a
HEINTZE, Ferdinand, hotelier & ex-sheriff Hudson Co,*17 D 36
    Eisenach/Gy, Jersey City, NJ – 1909/03/13:3c-d

HEINZ, Adam, NYC-Bx - 1914/08/20:6a
HEINZ, Edward, 59, NYC-B - 1915/08/09:6a
HEINZ, Gottlieb, Jersey City, NJ – 1909/07/31:6a, 1 Aug:7b
HEINZ, Hermann, 12, NYC-M – 1905/04/17:4a
HEINZ, Jacob, NYC-M – 1890/03/22:4a
HEINZ, Josef, SPO Saaz/Bohemia, shoemaker, War 1 - 1915/02/21:3b
HEINZ, Otto, 50, NYC-Q - 1915/12/22:2e
HEINZ, Philip, NYC-Q - 1914/12/27:7a
HEINZ, Wilhelm, 70, NYC-M – 1908/09/18:6a
HEINZE, F. Augustus, US copper magnate, (not +), crit – 1903/10/26:1c-d,
  + Saratoga Springs, NY - 1914/11/05:2f, 6:1c
HEINZE, Johann, 42, un. furrier, NYC-M – 1882/10/07:3b, 10:3b
HEINZE, Louis, 61, NYC-M – 1892/12/08:4a
HEINZEL, Clara, NYC-M – 1892/07/28:4a
HEINZEL, Stephan, tailor & SPD Kiel/Gy, city alderman 1899/12/17:18f
HEINZELMANN, John, 40, NYC-B - 1919/08/09:6a
HEINZELMANN, Samuel P., 73, US major-genl, * Pennsylvania, +
  Washington, DC – 1880/05/02:5b
HEINZEN, Carl F., 67, + Roxbury, MA – 1910/08/22:4e-f
HEINZEN, Karl Peter, '48er & publ. of radical G-A NPs in 1850s & 1860s,
  * 22 Fb 1809 Grevenbroich/Gy – 1880/11/14:5c; grave monument inaug.
  Forest Hill Cemetery, Boston – 1886/06/26:5c
HEINZMANN, Joseph, 38, un. carp., NYC-B – 1893/06/01:2e, 2:4a, 3:4a
HEISCHMANN, Franz, 58, NYC-M – 1892/08/08:4a
HEISE, Peter, Homestead, PA, steelworker – 1892/07/08:1a
HEISER, Frank, NYC-M – 1892/02/22:4a
HEISER, George, fr Gy, NYC-B - 1895/09/07: 3b
HEISING, Adolf, 48, SPD Karlsruhe, un. tobacco worker - 1915/03/28:3a
HEISLER, Alfred, SPD Leipzig/Gy activist – 1907/12/29:3e
HEISLER, Anna, NYC-M – 1887/08/18:3f
HEISMANN, Lina, 44, NYC-M - 1878/05/08:4d
HEISS, Gabriel, 46, NYC-M – 1890/06/26:4a
HEISS, Marie, b. Glab, 59, NYC-B – 1905/01/10:4a
HEISSENBUTTEL, Henry, NYC-B – 1890/03/30:5b
HEISSIG, Arthur, NYC-M - 1914/09/30:6a
HEIST, Georg D., Dr., Philadelphia, PA - 1920/08/11:2d
HEISTERMAN % Nekerman; HEISTERMANN % Rohleff
HEITER, August, NYC-Bx – 1912/11/17:7b
HEITER, Friedrich, 52, fr Nuernberg/Gy, un. furnit.mkr, labor activist,
  NYC-M – 1893/05/20:4a, 22:2d
HEITER, Rev., publ. Buffalo Volksfreund, crit obit – 1911/04/17:4d

HEITKAMP, Fritz, SP, miner?, * 20 Dec 1884 Marten/Westfalia, USA 1906, + 8 Nov. Pana, IL = 1913/11/22:2f
HEITLER, William, 35, wire worker, Ridgewood, NJ – 1911/08/05:2a
HEITMANN % Kues
HEITMANN, Claus, 28, innkeep, NYC-M – 1880/02/16:1e
HEITMANN, Gesche Metta, infant, NYC-M – 1889/02/12:4a
HEITMANN, Henry, carpenter, * near Bremen/Gy, USA 1885, NYC-M – 1886/03/27:5e
HEITMANN, Henry, NYC-B - 1919/08/16:6a
HEITMANN, Mary F. L., 54, NYC-B - 1914/01/27:6a
HEITNER, M., NYC-Q - 1913/12/30:6a
HEITTE % Suessmeier
HEITZ, Friedrich Rudolf, 35, NYC-M - 1920/06/01:6a
HEITZ, Joseph, 54, carp., NYC-M – 1904/04/12:2f
HEITZENROEDER, Heinrich, SPD Langendiebach/Frankfurt a. Main, building techn., War 1 - 1914/11/01:3b
HEIZMANN, Louis, Bayonne, NJ – 1909/10/23:6a
HEKTOR, Charlotte, b. Petersen, 78, NYC-B – 1907/07/20:6a
HEKTOR, Heinrich, 62, + Dornum/East Frisia/Gy, bro in NYC? – 1888/03/09:3b
HEKTOR, Jan, 60, un. carp.?, NYC-M – 1890/03/08:4a, =10:2e
HELB, G., Newark, NJ – 1907/05/05:7c
HELBIG, Albert, 5, NYC-M – 1892/02/24:4a
HELBIG, Andreas, NYC-B – 1910/12/02:6a
HELBOCK, Joseph, 48, un. pianomaker, NYC-M – 1898/07/06:4a
HELBOK, Rosa, b. Muench, 20, NYC-M - 1894/06/05:4a
HELBURN, Georg, un. typesetter, NYC-B – 1893/09/17:5a
HELD % Bratsch
HELD, Adolf, Prof. of Economy at Bonn U, Gy – 1880/09/12:4c
HELD, August, 23, Jersey City Heights, NJ – 1891/03/18:4a
HELD, August, Yonkers, NY - 1917/04/05:6a
HELD, George, Yonkers, NY - 1918/08/26:6a
HELD, Henry, NYC-M – 1908/11/17:6a
HELD, John, 57, upholsterer, NYC-M – 1896/11/13:3e
HELD, Michael, NYC-M   1896/12/13:16a
HELD, Robert, Newark, NJ - 1914/04/04:6a
HELD, William, 7, NYC-M – 1880/06/15:1g, 21:1g
HELFENSTEIN, Alfred, newspaper man, Union Hill, NJ - 1916/08/05:2d
HELFER, John, laborer, NYC-M – 1882/01/18:1e
HELFERICH, Rosa, 2, NYC-M – 1880/12/13:3b
HELFRICH, Fritz, NYC-M – 1896/10/13:4a
HELLEIN, Willie, 18, NYC-B – 1906/01/01:4a

HELLEMEYER, Carrie, 41, NYC-M – 1910/12/30:6a
HELLEMEYER, John, NYC-M – 1897/03/22:4a
HELLER, Charles F., 30, NYC-B – 1896/12/24:4c
HELLER, Henry, NYC-M – 1904/06/01:4a
HELLER, Isidor, 32, student, fr Austria, War 2, NYC-M - 1917/04/10:2f
HELLER, Jakob, tailor, Mt Carmel, NJ – 1899/01/11:4c
HELLER, John, 35, sawmill worker, NYC-M – 1890/06/21:1f
HELLER, Otto F., NYC-Bx - 1918/12/31:6a
HELLING, Phillip, 62, NYC-B – 1900/07/22:1g
HELLINGER, John, NYC-M – 1891/11/22:1e
HELLMEISTER, Henry, 38, brewer, + May 1878, body found & sent to Gy – 1879/01/22:1g
HELLMER, Adam, 51, cooper, NYC-M – 1893/06/21:1g
HELLMUTH, Christine, b. Scheller, 52, Jersey City, NJ - 1916/10/03:6a
HELLMUTH, Sabina, 70, NYC-M – 1881/02/21:3b
HELLSTERN % Schreibels
HELLWIG, Leo, 43, liquor dealer, NYC-M - 1919/08/11:6a
HELMAN, Albert, 44, NYC-M – 1882/12/08:1g
HELMECKE, Ludwig, 62, un. tailor, NYC-M – 1892/12/23:4a
HELMERS, Dietrich, un. cigarmaker, NYC-B – 1892/04/14:4a
HELMIG, Bernard, 62, NYC-Q – 1919/09/23:6a
HELMKE, Dietrich, 53, NYC-B – 1902/06/20:4b
HELMKEN, Christopher, 40, NYC-M – 1898/09/05:1d
HELMREICH, Klara, b. Zuck, NYC – 1912/08/21:6a
HELMREICH, Wilhelm, un. cigarmaker, 76, NYC-M - 1916/05/01:6a
HELMSTEDT, William, child, NYC-SI – 1901/07/25:4a, fam. 27:4a
HELPENSTELL, Katie, NYC-B – 1900/11/26:4a
HELT, Herman, NYC-Q – 1901/08/19:1e
HELTRICK, Robert, NYC-M, + @on Genl Slocum – 1904/06/18:3c
HELVIG, Emil, tailor, NYC-M – 1905/07/07:3f
HELWIG, Caspar, 60, Newark, NJ – 1886/07/13:2e
HELWIG, Emma, NYC-M – 1906/08/18:6a
HELWIG, Frank, NYC-Q - 1919/05/13:6a
HELWIG, Fritz, un. carp., NYC-M – 1890/02/06:4a
HELWIG, Kurt, 64, SPD Georgenthal/Thueringen, smith & alderman – 1913/04/20:3c
HELWIG, Richard W., druggist, NYC-M – 1887/12/28:2e
HEMAN, Rudolf, 20, *Graefenberg/Duesseldorf, NYC-M – 1891/01/06:2g
HEMBERG, John, 45, NYC-M – 1899/08/11:4a
HEMENWAY, J., Morristown, NJ – 1907/10/02:6a
HEMER, Gotthardt, 48, un. brewer, NYC-B – 1899/04/30:5h
HEMHASER, Babette, Newark, NJ – 1902/01/29:3b

HEMM, Anna, 19, fr Gy this year, Jersey City, NJ – 1907/08/20:3c
HEMMER, Frank, un. carp., NYC-M – 1901/12/21:3a
HEMMERLE, Therese G., child, NYC-B – 1891/01/12:4a
HEMMERSTAHL, Arnold, 40, NYC-B – 1904/10/30:5h
HEMMING, Dorothy, teacher, NYC-B - 1918/06/02:11g, 3:1d
HEMMING, Emma M., NYC-M – 1901/07/22:4a
HEMMING, Eugene, Negro, lynched near Hamilton, GA – 1912/01/24:1b
HEMMING, Gottlieb, SP, NYC-Q - 1919/01/09:6a
HEMMJE, John, SP, NYC-B, + Edeweck, Oldenburg/Gy – 1910/11/12:2e
HEMMY, John, Swiss?, NYC-M – 1881/12/25:8a
HEMPEL, Charles, 52, coppersmith, NYC-Q – 1912/10/04:3c
HEMPEL, Henry, NYC-B - 1914/05/05:6a
HENCHEN, Philippine, b. Mildenberger, NYC-M – 1908/03/15:7b
HENCKE % Closa
HENCKEL, Auguste, Hoboken, NJ - 1895/01/04:$a
HENCKEN, Charles, 18, NYC-B, + @on Genl Slocum – 1904/06/17:3b, 18:3c
HENCKLER, Barbara, 52, NYC-M – 1883/03/16:3c
HENCKLER, Friedrich, 55, un. tailor, NYC-M – 1883/02/17:3c
HENDEL, Antonie, b. Siebert, NYC – 1901/08/20:4a
HENDEL, Christian, NYC-M – 1904/11/19:4a, 20:5b
HENDEL, Julie, infant, NYC-M – 1885/05/27:3b
HENDEL, Julius, infant, NYC-M – 1884/07/18:3c
HENDENKAMP, Frank, 9, NYC-M, +@Genl Slocum – 1904/06/22:1d
HENDERSON, Anthony, Negro, lynched Unadilla, GA – 1897/01/08:1b
HENDERSON, Barbara, NYC-M, +@ on Genl Slocum – 1904/06/17:3b
HENDERSON, John, Negro, lynched, Corsicana, TX – 1901/03/14:1f
HENDERSON, Leopold, 54, janitor, NYC-M – 1891/01/28:3a
HENDERSON, W.H., journalist San Francisco Chronicle, + San Francisco - 1879/11/07:1e
HENDRICK, Hans, Swede, NYC-M – 1882/08/11:4b
HENDRICKS, David, ship capt, & Henry, 9, NYC-B, + on ship Mystery – 1887/07/12:1c-d, 13:2g, 15:2e, inquest 20:4d, 27:2e
HENDRICKS, Ernst, 42, NYC-Q – 1913/02/05:6a
HENDRICKS, Thomas A., US vice-pres. – 1885/11/26:1c, 27:2c
HENDRICKS, Tillie, 16, NYC-Bx, +@Genl Slocum – 1904/06/22:1d
HENDRIX, James, miner, killed by militia, Kanaaha Co., W.Va – 1913/02/16:1e
HENDRIX, Joseph C., ex-Congressman, NYC-B – 1904/11/10:4a
HENGARTNER, Henry, West New York, NJ - 1920/03/04:6a
HENGSTERBERG, Ida, 29, Union Hill, NJ – 1891/05/22:4a
HENIG, Anton, 40, worker, NYC-M – 1890/06/08:1f

HENING, Edwin R., 62, NYC-B - 1894/02/01:4a
HENJE, Heinrich, 52, NYC-B - 1891/03/27:4a
HENKE, Alfred, peddler, * Angeroeberg(Angerburg?)/East Prussia, NYC-M - 1889/04/11:4a
HENKE, F. Ernst, 50, machinist, SP?, Lindenhurst, LI - 1905/12/13:4a, 14:4a
HENKE, Freddy, 2, Breslau, LI, 1891/05/02:4a
HENKE, Frieda, 14, Orange Valley, NY - 1902/11/14:3c
HENKE, Helene, 8, Lindenhurst, LI - 1903/09/19:4a
HENKE, Otto, Jersey City Heights, NJ - 1887/03/16:3d
HENKEL, Wilhelm, 67, NYC-M - 1879/02/09:8a
HENKEL, Wilhelm, un. carp., NYC-M - 1887/09/24:3a, 4a
HENKEN, Sophia, NYC-B - 1902/05/13:1g
HENKIRCH, John, weaver, Passaic, NJ - 1897/03/01:1e
HENKY, J., NYC-Bx - 1919/07/20:7a
HENL, Willy, child, NYC-B - 1913/08/03:7a
HENLIN, Martin, NYC-M - 1892/06/23:1e
HENN, Albertine, NYC-B - 1916/04/11:6a
HENN, Anna, 80, NYC-M - 1902/01/02:1b
HENN, August, 19, NYC-B - 1902/08/30:2g
HENNE, Antonia, 37, singer, * Cincinatti, OH, + NYC-M - 1887/07/21:2f
HENNE, Friedrich W., 34, fr Thueringia?, NYC-B - 1919/02/15:6a
HENNE, Louis, un. carp., NYC-M - 1900/11/19:4a
HENNE, Michael, 47, NYC-B - 1917/08/28:6a
HENNE, Theodor, 35, varnisher, NYC-M - 1893/01/11:2e
HENNEBERG, Marie, NYC-M - 1905/02/26:5a
HENNEBERGER % Amon
HENNECKE, Wilhelm, NYC-M - 1913/01/15:6a
HENNESSEY, William Murray, innkeep, NYC-M - 1914/10/14:5f, 15:3f
HENNIG, Adolph, un. baker, NYC-Bx - 1917/01/04:6a
HENNIG, Aug. William, 26, NYC-M - 1894/01/15:4a
HENNIG, Auguste M., b. Schmidt, 21, NYC-M - 1909/06/04:6a
HENNIG, Frank, 24, Hoboken, NJ - 1891/03/30:4a
HENNIG, Josephine, 45, SP?, NYC-M - 1908/05/24:7b
HENNIGE, Elizabeth, 41, NYC-B - 1897/05/27:4b
HENNIGER, Ella, NYC-B - 1911/07/11:6a
HENNING, Alfred F., 45, salesman, Hoboken, NJ - 1902/06/17:4b
HENNING, Elisabeth, 47, NYC-M - 1891/03/24:4a
HENNING, Henry, NYC-M - 1889/06/29:4a
HENNINGER, John, 39, worker, NYC-B - 1885/12/25:1g
HENNINGER, L., Newark, NJ - 1912/10/29:6a
HENNS, Barbara, 58, NYC-B - 1887/04/16:2e, 22:2f

HENRET, Eugen, machinist, NYC-B – 1904/08/15:4a
HENRI, Pierre L., French, USA 1876 fr Paris, NYC-M – 1880/02/12:1d
HENRICH % Dietrich
HENRICH, John Wilhelm, 16, NYC-B – 1904/07/22:4a, fam. 26:4a
HENRICHS, Jacob, un. pianomaker, NYC-Q – 1890/09/03:4a
HENRICH-WILHELMI, Hedwig, 76, German Freethinker – 1910/03/21:4d
HENRY, Andrew, 30, Democratic polit., Hoboken, NJ – 1898/05/15:1e, 17:4c, =19:4a, trial of murderer Wm Reid began 19 Jy:4c; Reid exec. Jersey City 24 Fb 1899:3f
HENRY, Colonel, French secret service, suicide in Dreyfus Affair – 1898/09/02:1f
HENRY, Emile, French anarchist, exec. Paris – 1894/05/21:1c
HENRY, Lizzie, 44, NYC-M – 1893/06/16:4a
HENRY, Moritz, 40, Jersey City, NJ – 1896/04/15:4a
HENRY, William, Elizabeth, NJ – 1909/11/24:6a
HENSCHEL % Naumann
HENSCHEL, Anna, 2, NYC-M – 1887/06/17:3c
HENSCHEL, George, 20, painter, NYC-M – 1880/03/19:1g
HENSCHEL, Peter, 28, NYC-B – 1886/01/21:2e, 23:5d
HENSEL, M., un. cigarmaker, NYC-M – 1894/06/16:3g
HENSEL, Paul, SPD militant in Berlin/Gy = 1887/02/14:4e; 25th anniv. of death mem. 1912/02/12:4d
HENSELER, Martha, 37, SDP, Union Hill, NJ – 1904/12/20:4a
HENSELER, Peter, 60, SP, Union Hill, NJ – 1908/11/07:6a, fam. 10:6a, =11:2a
HENSEN, Bob, exec. Trenton, NJ– 1901/12/28:3b
HENSEN, Sophie, 40, servant, fr Sweden, NYC-M – 1881/04/25:1a
HENSER, George, NYC-Bx – 1909/12/28:6a
HENSLE, Charles L., 25, NYPD, NYC-M – 1899/12/09:1e
HENSLER, Friedericke, NYC-B – 1901/09/16:4a
HENSLER, Hermann, bookkeeper, NYC-B – 1883/07/30:3a
HENSLER, Thomas, un. butcher, NYC-M – 1916/03/23:6a
HENSSLER, Sarah F., b. Catlin, 55, NYC-M – 1890/11/24:2e
HENTJES, Carl, NYC-M – 1891/04/12:5a
HENTSCHEL, Emil, 35, NYC-B – 1897/07/26:1c
HENTZE % Peterson
HENTZE, Ernst, SP, NYC-M – 1919/08/30:6a
HENZE, George, un. cigarmkr, NYC-M – 1914/01/01:6a
HENZE, Magdalene, b. Stricker, 40, NYC-B – 1917/02/28:6a
HENZE, Wilhelm, 55, in New Jersey – 1903/06/12:4a
HENZE, William, Jersey City Heights, NJ – 1891/01/14:4a
HENZEL, Christian, NYC-M – 1890/10/18:4a

HEPKE, Amalie, 38, NYC?, husband Konrad Hepke a smith fr Hannover/Gy – 1881/11/06:5e
HEPLER, Gottlieb, 18, NYC-M? – 1911/07/06:1c
HEPP, Elisa, b. Lamy, fr Paris/France, NYC-M – 1883/05/28:3b
HEPP, John G., 70, NYC-M – 1892/06/18:4a
HEPP, Julius, 58, NYC-B – 1893/10/30:4a
HEPP, Martin J., NYC-M – 1891/01/02:4a
HEPPER, Otto, West Hoboken, NJ - 1918/11/03:12a
HEPPLER, Adolph, New Brunswick, NJ – 1897/07/07:4a
HEPTING, Johann, 19, fr Aumund/Bremen, USA Sept. 81, NYC-B – 1881/09/15:3b
HERB, John Martin, 50, NYC-M – 1885/01/29:3d
HERBEN, Gedula, Jersey City Heights, NJ – 1891/04/23:4a
HERBERGER, Karl, un. printer, NYC-B - 1918/09/22:12a
HERBERT, Ernest, NYC – 1912/12/03:6a; mem. 1913/12/02:3a; 1914/12/02:6a; 1915/12/02:6a
HERBERT, James, 37, shoemaker, & wife Mary, NYC-M 1895/05/07:1h
HERBERT, Joseph, NYC – 1880/05/16:5f
HERBERT, Julius, 50, NYC-B – 1911/06/26:6a, 27:6a
HERBERT, Karl, un. painter, NYC-Q - 1914/07/23:6a
HERBERT, Leopold, un. butcher, NYC-B – 1910/05/14:6a
HERBICH, Georg, 53, tailor, NYC-M – 1889/09/05:4e
HERBICH, Marie, NYC-M – 1901/12/14:3d
HERBIG, John & Pauline, Passaic, NJ - 1916/02/28:6c
HERBOLDSHEIMER, Magdalena, b. Schoene, 55, NYC-M – 1892/07/26:4a
HERBST, Elisabeth, 66, NYC-M – 1891/04/06:4a
HERBST, Ferdinand, 75, Hoboken, NJ – 1900/10/23:3b
HERBST, Robert, 16, NYC – 1900/05/11:1e
HERBST, Wilhelm, 31, laborer & SPD activist Frankfurt-Bockenheim – 1908/03/15:3c
HERCE, Joseph, un. waiter, NYC-M – 1901/04/11;4a
HERDE, William, NYC-M - 1918/01/12:6a
HERDEGEN, Caroline, NYC-M – 1890/07/30:4a
HERDEKOPF, Meeker?, 40, NYC-M, + @Genl Slocum – 1904/06/17:3b
HERDEN, Clara, b. Strauch, 32, NYC-Bx - 1918/10/13:11g, fam. 17:6a
HERDER % Holler
HERDER, Adolph, un. cigarmaker, Jersey City, NJ – 1884/11/16:5e
HERDER, Charles, 55, worker, NYC-M 1895/05/12:5b
HERDER, Felix, 43, USA ~ 1886 fr Austria, NYC-M – 1896/08/29:1g
HERDER, Phillipina, b. Derscheidt, 22, NYC-M – 1890/08/16:4a
HERDES, John O., 62, carp., NYC – 1898/02/08:3g

HERDMAN, Hazel, Fairfield, NJ - 1914/02/08:1g
HERDMANN, Ludwig, un. carp., NYC-B - 1913/11/24:6a
HERDS, Frank, 83,watchmaker, Jersey City, NY - 1915/08/12:2d
HERETH, Michael, un. carp., NYC-B - 1909/08/02:6a
HERF, Wilhelm, Dr., German journalist, USA 1914, + Bangor, ME - 1917/08/03:2b
HERFAHRT, George, 34, policeman, NYC-B - 1895/04/08:2c
HERGENHAHN, William, 39, SP, un. autom. worker, NYC-M - 1919/06/26:6a, fam. 1 Jy:6a
HERGENROTHER, Emma, NYC-Bx - 1915/11/25:2b
HERGERT, Helene, child, NYC-M - 1891/10/30:4a
HERGERT, Louise, 2, NYC-M - 1895/01/05:4a
HERGERT, Theodor, 7, NYC-M - 1904/03/15:4a, fam. 17:4a
HERGIST, Carl, (or Hagist), NYC-M - 1898/10/27:4a, fam. 29:4a, 30:5c
HERING % Reinert
HERING, August, NYC-M - 1886/11/04:3c
HERING, Emma, NYC-Q - 1915/04/21:6a
HERING, Henrietta, 32, NYC-B - 1894/01/09:3c
HERINGER, Frederick Charles, 50, NYC-M - 1899/04/21:4a
HERITIER, Louis, Swiss SP, = Geneva/Switz. - 1898/09/02:2e
HERLING, R., 56, clerk at Knauth, Nachod & Kuehne, NYC-M - 1900/03/13:2h
HERMAN, E. H., ~75, Waterbury, CT, + NYC-Q - 1900/06/08:1e
HERMAN, Harry, painter, NYC - 1912/10/04:1e
HERMAN, Joseph, NYC-M - 1888/04/27:4b
HERMAN, Louise, NYC-M, @+ on Genl Slocum - 1904/06/18:3c
HERMAN, Mary, 44, @1911 Triangle Shirtwaist Fire, NYC-M - 1911/03/28:1c
HERMAN, Max, un. butcher, Winfield, LI - 1916/06/02:6a
HERMAN, Walter F., dentist, NYC-B - 1910/12/17:6a
HERMANN, Alexander, 55, fr Poland?, magician artist, successor of original Hermann (who * Hannover 1812), s. 1861 USA, NYC-M - 1896/12/18:3g
HERMANN, Annie see Annie Walters
HERMANN, August, SP, Jersey City Heights, NJ - 1918/09/04:6a,b =6:6a, fam. 12:6a; mem. 1919/09/02:6a, 1920/09/02:6a
HERMANN, Carl G., NYC-SI - 1891/06/26:4a
HERMANN, Charles, 23, barkeeper, * Hamburg, USA 1872, dying, NYC-M - 1878/12/18:4d
HERMANN, Eduard, brother of SP Anton Hermann, fr Alt-Paulsdorf/ Sudetenland, War 1 - 1915/05/01:6f-g
HERMANN, Frederick, 72, un. carp., NYC-B - 1918/01/01:6a, 2:6a;

HERMANN, Frederick, NYC-M - 1918/10/26:2g; Mem. 1919/10/24:6a
HERMANN, Helena, 7, Jersey City, NJ – 1908/10/29:6a
HERMANN, John, 5, NYC-M – 1891/03/11:4a
HERMANN, John, NYC-B – 1908/04/28:6a
HERMANN, Julius, 41, innkeep, Jersey City, NJ – 1909/03/12:1f
HERMANN, Karl, 52, restaurant, fr Gy 1882, NYC-M – 1887/05/10:2f
HERMANN, Karl, SPD Wehrheim/Taunus/Gy, War 1 - 1914/11/01:3b
HERMANN, Kasper, NYC-M = 1888/01/24:4a
HERMANN, Kate, 50, NYC-M, + @on Genl Slocum – 1904/06/17:3b
HERMANN, L., Newark, NJ - 1913/10/09:6a
HERMANN, Louise, b. Klennzen, 79, fr Esslingen/Gy, NYC-M - 1879/03/16:8a
HERMANN, Mary, & kids 3, 1.5, Camden, NJ – 1896/07/28:1g, 29:4b
HERMANN, R., NYC-B – 1905/05/15:6a
HERMANN, Robert E., 32, bartender, NYC-M - 1896/03/18:1h
HERMANN, Wilhelm, NYC-M – 1891/03/25:4a
HERMANOFFSKY, Hirsch, fr Russia to US 1890, NYC-M – 1891/11/15:1h
HERMELY, Edward, 41, NYC-B – 1892/08/01:4a
HERMES, Otto, MdR (Liberals), for Landshut/Silesia + Berlin – 1910/03/22:4c-d
HERMINGHAUS, Hermann, SDP, St Louis, MO – 1903/08/24:2d
HERMIS, Annie, NYC-M, + @on Genl Slocum – 1904/06/18:3c
HERNER, William, Union Hill, NJ – 1912/01/27:6a
HERNIA, Peter, 35, exec. Hackensack, NJ – 1902/09/20:1e, =21:5e
HERNING, Charles, 70, NYC-B – 1881/09/12:4d
HEROLD, Anton, 26, baker, NYC-M – 1892/10/08:1c
HEROLD, Carl, 71, brushmaker, NYC-M – 1893/04/07:1f
HEROLD, Eduard, 46, un. baker, NYC-M - 1917/05/09:6a, 10:6a
HEROLD, Georg, tailor, Hasbrouck Hgts, NJ - 1913/05/07:3d
HEROLD, Ida, b. Roitzsch, 28, NYC-M – 1884/10/14:3e
HEROLD, J., 40, NYC-M – 1893/05/10:4a
HEROLD, Mark, 43, blouse manuf., NYC-M – 1910/06/07:6a
HEROT, Marie, 63, NYC-M, + @on Genl Slocum – 1904/06/17:3b
HERR, Albert, 17, Plainfield, NJ – 1919/10/02:1c
HERR, Catherine, Plainfield, NJ – 1919/10/02:1c
HERR, Edward, Guttenberg, NJ - 1915/08/05:6a
HERR, Maria, 43, NYC-M - 1920/02/11:6a
HERR, Mathias, Elizabeth, NJ - 1916/12/09:6a
HERRA, Lena, 43, NYC-M - 1914/05/24:11g
HERRBRECHT % Kohler
HERRBRECHT, Remy, Jersey City Heights, NJ – 1907/11/04:6a

HERRE % Hessel; HERRICH % Bechter
HERRIGER, Mr., 70, & Mrs, 72, 48ers, West Hoboken, NJ, rev. Golden Wedding – 1893/05/27:3c
HERRIGER-GRAFT, Marie Louise, b. Goetz, 68, West Hoboken, NJ - 1917/04/11:6a
HERRING, Henry, 50, janitor, NYC-M – 1899/10/19:1e
HERRING, Hermann, NYC-M – 1893/05/27:4b
HERRING, John, Populist, murderer Archie Kinsauls exec. 1900/09/29:3f
HERRING, Morris, Jersey City, NJ – 1891/08/27:1d
HERRLEIN, Eduard, NYC – 1903/03/04:4a
HERRLEIN, Maria, b. Wickhorst, NYC-M – 1899/04/24:4a
HERRLICH, Charles, undertaker, NYC-M - 1917/04/01:11g, 2:6a, mem - 1919/03/22:6a
HERRLING, Kate, 38, & son Edgar, 6, NYC-B – 1912/11/21:1d
HERRLINGER, Charles, NYC-M – 1911/11/25:6a, fam. 28:6a
HERRMAN, Karl, Jersey City Heights, NJ – 1901/08/31:4b
HERRMAN, Louis P., exec. Ossining, NY – 1896/04/23:1d, 24:1h
HERRMANN, Adolf, SPD killed 1906 by cops, grave monun. In Hohen-Neudorf – 1909/10/10:3a-b
HERRMANN, Caroline, 39, NYC-Greenpoint - 1896/03/23:4a
HERRMANN, Charles, 27, fr Holland, NYC-M – 1884/09/23:1e
HERRMANN, Christian, un. carp., NYC-M? – 1891/05/15:4a
HERRMANN, Elizabeth, b. Bohr, NYC-Q - 1914/05/29:6a
HERRMANN, Engelbrecht, 21, painter, Jersey City, NJ – 1881/07/07:1g
HERRMANN, Falk, NYC-M - 1894/01/29:4a
HERRMANN, Franziska, b. Seibert, 32, NYC-M – 1894/05/11:4c 14:4a
HERRMANN, Frederick, NYC-M – 1902/03/01:4a
HERRMANN, Gottlieb, 44, NYC-B – 1909/05/04:6a
HERRMANN, Johann, NYC-M - 1878/03/15:4c
HERRMANN, John A., 45, baker, NYC-M – 1888/11/22:4c
HERRMANN, John H., Dr., 70, NYC-M – 1892/10/16:5c
HERRMANN, John, 57, NYC-Q – 1910/12/29:6a
HERRMANN, Karl, 40, basket weaver & SPD activist expelled from Hamburg/Gy, arrived NYC – 1880/11/30:1d-e, 2 Dec:2a-b, 6 1d-e
HERRMANN, Katherine, b. Leonhardt, NYC-M – 1897/08/16:4a
HERRMANN, Paul, 50, electrician, NYC-M? - 1915/12/18:1e
HERRMANNS, Wilhelm, NYC-M – 1893/05/02:4a, fam. 16:4a
HERRNSTADT, Simon, 40, lumber dealer, fr Gy, War 2, NYC-M - 1915/09/08:2d
HERRON, Archie, to be exec. for + Rev. Prickett in Metuchen, NJ – 1908/07/29:3b

HERRON, Carrie Rand, fdr Rand School, NYC, + Florence/Italy - 1914/01/16:2b
HERRSCHAFT, Georg, West Rutky?, NJ – 1911/05/23:6a
HERSCHBEIN, Ida, 66, NYC-B - 1916/02/17:6a
HERSCHEL, Herman, 67, NYC-M - 1918/12/01:7a
HERSCHMANN, Karl, 80, NYC-M – 1891/04/05:5a
HERTEL % Poeschel
HERTEL, Julia, teacher, NYC-B – 1910/05/31:1f
HERTER, Joseph, 75, NYC-Q - 1920/10/27:6a
HERTFELDER, Friedrich, 71, NYC-M – 1893/03/07:4a
HERTH, Louis, 38, NYC-B – 1910/04/25:6a
HERTIG, Swiss labor organizer, + 17 Fb in Winterthur/Switzerland – 1888/02/27:1g
HERTING, Hermann, 2, NYC-M – 1882/01/14:3b
HERTLE, Emma, NYC-M – 1906/01/03:4a
HERTLEIN % Seemar
HERTLEIN, Anna, b. Polle, 32, SLP?, Union Hill, NJ – 1897/12/31:4a
HERTLEIN, Julius, NYC-B - 1920/09/09:6a
HERTLEIN, Kasper, to be exec. tom. Hartford, CT – 1896/12/03:1c
HERTLING, Georg von, 75, German chancellor - 1919/01/06:1b
HERTNER, Jacob, West Hoboken, NJ – 1896/11/03:4a
HERTZ, Fannie, 45, Newark, NJ - 1916/05/22:1b
HERTZ, Gottlob, NYC-Bx – 1912/06/13:6a
HERTZ, Helene, 50, fence, * Koeln/Gy, USA 1857, + NYC-Blackwell's Isl. – 1883/09/18:1f
HERTZ, Moses, NYC-B – 1891/01/12:4a
HERTZBERG, Henry, 40, Chicago, IL, + Hoboken, NJ – 1888/06/28:2d
HERTZOG, Frederick, 45, insurance agent, Hicksville, LI – 1903/09/18:2h
HERVE, Ferdinand, 50, art dealer, fr France, NYC-M – 1897/07/03:3a
HERWEGE, Maria, 59, & son, Hoboken, NJ – 1911/04/27:3a
HERWEGH, Emma, b. Siegmund, widow of German poet Georg Herwegh – 1904/04/24:13g; Notes 1905/06/18:14c-e
HERWEGH, Horace, 58, son of '48er poet, + Paris/Fr., – 1901/05/31:2h
HERY, Jacob, NYC-M - 1916/07/15:6a
HERY, John, 55, un. carp., NYC – 1911/02/12:1c, 7b, 13:6a, fam. 19:7b
HERZ % Prosser/Kramer
HERZ, Cornelius, Dr., 52, German-born main actor in 1893 Panama Scandal in Paris – 1898/07/07:3f
HERZ, Ernst C., NYC-M – 1891/07/07:4a
HERZBERG, Emanuel, Dr. med., 68, USA 1858, NYC-M – 1880/03/28:7b
HERZENBACH, J., NYC-B – 1912/10/22:6a

HERZENBERGER, Henrietta, 45, NYC-M, + @on Genl Slocum – 1904/06/19:1c, 21:1f
HERZENSTEIN, Russian banker & Duma member, killed near St Petersburg – 1906/08/02:1e
HERZIG, Frieda, No. Bergen, NJ - 1917/01/13:6b, 19:2f
HERZL, Theodor, Zionist leader, + Edlach/Reichenau – 1904/07/04:1f
HERZMANN, Joseph, RR fireman, fr Union Hill, NJ?, + Kingston, NY – 1902/11/20:2b
HERZOG % Mayer
HERZOG, Anastasia, b. Meyer, 57, NYC-M - 1895/12/02: 4a
HERZOG, August, cigarmaker, NYC, + Chicago, IL – 1888/02/29:3c, fam. 23 Mr:3b
HERZOG, Catherina, b. Haider, 55, NYC-M – 1903/07/04:4a
HERZOG, Georg, tailor, then innkeep, SLP, NYC-B – 1900/02/27:1d, 4a, 28:4a
HERZOG, Henry, weaver?, Union Hill, NJ - 1914/12/13:11a
HERZOG, Ignaz, 57, un. carp., NYC-M – 1896/06/26:4a
HERZOG, Ignaz, bartender, NYC-M – 1897/07/31:1h
HERZOG, Louis, 61, handkerchief importer, USA 1878 fr Switzerland, Montclair, NJ - 1913/05/01:1f
HERZOG, M., NYC-M - 1917/12/04:6c
HERZOG, Moses, shopkeeper, USA ~1852 fr Worms/Gy, NYC-B – 1882/02/04:1f, inquest 1 Mr:1e
HESING, Anton Caspar, ex-publ. Illinois Staatszeitung, * 06. Ja 1823 Oldenburg/Gy,USA 1840, + Chicago - 1895/04/01:1b
HESKLOTZ, Gus, NYC-Q – 1908/10/27:6a
HESLER, Caroline, 40, servant, NYC-B – 1880/03/29:3a
HESS, A.E., War 2, Ft Collins, CO - 1918/04/13:1a
HESS, Anna, 45, NYC-M, + @on Genl Slocum – 1904/06/18:3c
HESS, Arnold, Overbrook, NJ – 1912/10/23:3d
HESS, August, un. carp., NYC – 1911/10/26:6a
HESS, Catherina, b. Lautenschlaeger, 40, NYC-B – 1885/02/05:3d
HESS, Frederick, 76, *Koblenz/Rhineland, USA 1855, publ. San Francisco Deutscher Demokrat, + there - 1913/05/05:1c
HESS, Gcorg, 55, carpenter., NYC-M – 1901/04/12:4a, 14:5a
HESS, Gcorge, 60, workers, NYC-M – 1892/07/30:1e
HESS, Helene, b. Pauli, 57, NYC-M – 1891/02/27:4a
HESS, Henry, NYC-B - 1913/05/02:6a
HESS, Henry, un. baker, Jersey City Hgts, NJ, =1913/05/13:5f
HESS, Hermann, 45, coppersmith, Orange, NJ – 1899/06/10:4b
HESS, Jacob Van, 32, un. carp., NYC-M – 1887/06/29:3a, 30:3c
HESS, Karl Friedrich, 39, un. carp., NYC-M – 1901/10/07:4a

HESS, Peter, un. butcher, NYC-M - 1915/06/20:7c
HESS, Sophie, NYC-M - 1918/09/02:6a
HESS, Sybille, widow of late German socialist Moses Hess – 1904/02/21:16c-d
HESS, Valentine, barber, Seacliff, LI – 1907/08/18:11e
HESS, William C., principal PS 30, * Gy, NYC-Q – 1907/02/26:2f
HESSE, Henriette, 71, NYC-B – 1907/03/18:3a
HESSE, John, 63, NYC-M – 1890/08/08:4a
HESSE, Minna, Jersey City Heights, NJ – 1891/03/17:4a
HESSE, Otto, 43, NYC-B – 1893/10/23:4a
HESSE, Otto, 44, fr Berlin, & wife Minna, 40, NYC-M – 1889/02/14:4a
HESSE, Sabina, b. Daenner, NYC-M – 1882/05/07:5f
HESSE, William, un. carp., NYC-M – 1906/03/31:4a
HESSEL, Emilie, b. Herre, 44, NYC-M – 1891/03/16:4a
HESSEL, Wilhelmina, 46, NYC-M, + @on Genl Slocum – 1904/06/17:3b
HESSELBACH, Minnie, 21,tobacco worker,NYC-M – 1896/11/25:1c, 26:1
HESSELBARTH, Elisabeth, 25,NYC-M - 1917/01/18:6a, fam. 23:6a
HESSELNBERG, Ewald, un. typesetter, NYC-M – 1901/02/12:4a
HESSELSCHWERT, Johann, un. carp., NYC-M – 1888/12/28:3b
HESSENLEPP, Benjamin, 45, liquor dealer, NYC-M – 1896/08/11:1a
HESSER, John, brewer or cooper, NYC-M – 1901/01/24:4a
HESSER, Philip, 24, carpenter, NYC-M – 1897/03/16:1d
HESSLER, John, 2, NYC-M – 1880/05/09:5b
HESSLER, Philipp, 38, un. carp., NYC-B – 1905/11/15:4a, fam. 18:4a
HESSNER, William, 36, plumber, NYC-Q - 1920/10/25:1e
HESTER, Patrick, Molly Maguire, exec. Bloomsburg, PA - 1878/03/26:1c, 2d, 3 Apr:2g
HESTER, William, un. baker, NYC-M – 1888/02/14:4h
HESTERMANN, Friedrich, un. carp., NYC-M – 1896/11/05:4a
HETORFER, John, 45, un. beerdriver, NYC-M – 1902/06/29:5b
HETTERICK, Lizzie, 30, Adolph, infant, NYC-M, +@Genl Slocum – 1904/06/21:1f, 25:1d
HETTERLING, Leonhard, un. carp., NYC-M – 1892/12/11:5b
HETTICH, Ernest, fam. – 1898/06/18:4a
HETTIG, John, un. carp., NYC-M – 1904/06/18:4a
HETTING, Martina, 65, NYC-M – 1893/12/18:4a
HETTINGER, August, NYC-M - 1914/03/19:6a
HETTINGER, Fritz, 59, SP?, NYC-Q - 1917/06/23:6a
HETTINGER, Louis, NYC-Q – 1911/09/09:6a
HETTINGER, Wilhelm, 40, NYC-Q – 1904/07/07:4a
HETTLER, Jacob, NYC-M - 1916/01/22:6a
HETTRICH, George, NYC-B – 1912/05/31:6a

HETTRICK, G., 25, exec. Trenton, NJ – 1902/04/05:3b
HETZEL, George, engineer, Newark, NJ – 1902/02/13:1e
HETZEL, Math., un. carpenter, NYC-M - 1896/01/01: 4a
HETZEL, Valentin, 46, innkeep, NYC-M – 1897/01/13:1f
HETZENDORF, John's wife,50,NYC-B +Paterson,NJ - 1917/08/02:2d
HETZLER, Jacob, un. baker, NYC-M? - 1919/03/05:6a
HETZLER, John, un. brewer, NYC-M - 1918/04/13:6a
HEUBECK, police comm., killed in Florisdorf/Vienna – 1883/12/18:1c
HEUBEL, Frieda, b. Steffmann, Port Richmond, LI - 1920/01/31:8a
HEUELER, Augusta, NYC-M, + @on Genl Slocum – 1904/06/17:3b
HEUER, Dora, & children Dora & Herman, NYC-M, +@Genl Slocum – 1904/06/17:3b
HEUER, John, SP?, Newark, NJ - 1917/02/04:7a
HEUER, Mathilde, USA 1877 fr Gy, NYC-M – 1885/03/04:1e
HEUERMANN, Angeline, 66, NYC-B - 1915/01/19:6b
HEUERT, Stanley's wife, 36, Yonkers, NY - 1913/06/16:2b
HEUMANN, Leopold, NYC-M – 1892/07/02:4a
HEUNINGER, Alex, SLP, fr Cincinatti?, OH, settled in German Gulch, Montana, killed by cattle barons over water rights – 1885/06/30:2e-f
HEUSCHKE, Clara Bertha, b. Weisseborn, NYC-M – 1904/02/26:4a
HEUSELER, Charles, un. butcher, NYC-M - 1920/03/20:8a
HEUSER, Anna, b. Martling, 47, NYC-B – 1900/07/28:4a
HEUSER, Mary, 17, NYC-M, +@Genl Slocum – 1904/06/22:1d
HEUSER, Theodor, 50, worker, NYC - 1914/08/13:2c
HEUSER, Theodor, electrician, NYC-B – 1904/10/19:4c
HEUSLER % Bendler
HEUSLER, Anton, 60, Hoboken, NJ – 1910/12/28:6a
HEUSLER, August, 31, NYC-M – 1902/02/27:4a, 28:4a
HEUSLER, Stephen, NYC-B – 1909/01/30:6a
HEUTTNER, Mary, 40, NYC-M – 1883/08/15:1c
HEUWETTER, Conrad, un. baker, NYC-M – 1912/03/12:6a
HEWIG, Conrad, un. carp., NYC-M – 1907/06/16:7a
HEWITT, Abram S., ex-NYC mayor – 1903/01/19:1d, 2c
HEWITT, Mr., British suffragist - 1913/06/20:1c
HEWITT, William, NYC-Q – 1907/03/27:6a
HEYBRINK, Henry, machinist, NYC-M – 1913/04/02:3b
HEYD, Henry, 16, NYC-M – 1891/07/06:4c
HEYDE % Schroeder
HEYDE, Charles, 57, SP, ex-secy genl Brotherhood of Metallworkers, * Stettin/Pomerania, USA 1882, NYC-B - 1917/04/26:2b, 27:6a, 28:6a, = 1 May:6f-g
HEYDECKER, Jacobine, NYC-M - 1894/10/16:4a

HEYDEN, Auguste Auf Der, 56?, NYC-M – 1891/03/30:4a
HEYDEN, Emma, b. Pfeil, NYC-Bx - 1920/09/05:8a
HEYDEN, Gustav von der, silkweaver, *11 June 1835 Ronsdorf/Gy, & wife Emilie, b. Hasenclever, also fr Ronsdorf, SP, Golden Wedding, Paterson, NJ – 1908/11/28:9f
HEYDENREICH % Haug
HEYDT, Henry A., 49, treas. of C. Heydt & Co, NYC – 1909/06/06:1c
HEYER % Foernster
HEYER, Julius, un. cigarmaker, vet SPD Hamburg/Gy – 1903/08/22:2d-e
HEYL, Emil, 24, supt in wallpaper factory, NYC-B – 1911/02/09:3b
HEYL, Luise Katie, NYC-M - 1917/03/31:6a
HEYL, Martha, b. Mathies, NYC-Bx – 1911/05/17:6a
HEYLAND, Emma, 22, NYC-M – 1892/01/10:1h
HEYM, August, 45, un. pressman, NYC-M – 1908/02/14:3a
HEYM, Ernst, 28, NYC-B – 1892/06/21:4a
HEYMANN % Schmidt
HEYMANN, Adolph, 38, laborer, NYC-M – 1886/07/08:3b
HEYMANN, Balthasar W., 73, un. carp., NYC-M – 1908/07/29:6a, 30:6a, fam. 1 Aug:6a
HEYMANN, Eugen, un. carp., NYC-SI – 1911/10/06:6a
HEYMANN, Felix, 36, fr Elsass, NYC-M – 1880/12/28:1e
HEYMANN, Heinrich, *Breslau/Gy, New Haven, CT – 1902/04/27:5a
HEYNEMANN, Robert, 21, NYC-M – 1892/06/17:4a
HEYNEN, Carl, un. carp., NYC-M – 1912/12/30:6a
HEYNER, Doris, b. Mathiesen, NYC-M – 1897/02/14:5a
HEYS, Georg, 56?, varnisher, NYC-B – 1887/04/18:3d
HEYSE, Paul, SPD Germany, 70th birthday – 1900/03/18:6f-g; 80th 1910/03/20:6d-f, + 1914/04/03:4a-b, 2 May:4e-f
HEYWENGL, Louise, 66, NYC-SI – 1899/06/07:1e
HIBBARD, A., SP?, Newark, NJ - 1914/09/29:6a
HIBBELER Jr., Christian, un. brewer, NYC-B - 1918/10/05:6a
HICKEL, Karl, new SPD MdR, fr Bischweiler/Elsass, his life (not +) – 1890/03/20:2c-d
HICKEN, Sarah, 47, Philadelphia - 1917/04/19:2b
HICKENBERG, Joseph, 32, stockbroker fr Wiesbaden/Gy, NYC-M - 1894/10/21:3e
HICKLER, Simon, chief edit. Waechter & Anzeiger in Cleveland, OH – 1910/05/18:4d
HICKS, Rosa, 15, NYC-M – 1886/09/02:2g
HICKS, Wesley, Negro, lynched Franklin, KY – 1885/05/27:1c
HIDDESEN, Karl, 59, mason & SPD Bremen/Gy – 1913/04/13:3a
HIEM, John, Newark, NJ – 1907/03/16:6a

HIERGESELL, Lizzie, 14, NYC-Q – 1900/11/07:1g
HIERONIMUS, John, un. carp., NYC-M – 1910/05/22:7b
HIESKE, Wilhelm, 26, USA 1881, NYC-B – 1882/10/10:3a
HIGENUS, William, un. machinist, NYC-M – 1908/01/12:7a
HIGGINS, Frank W., 50, ex-NYS gov., + Olean, NY – 1907/02/13:1f
HIGGINS, James, Negro, lynched Springfield, TN, with 4 others – 1881/02/20:5c
HIGGINSON, Thomas Wentworth, abolitionist & historian – 1911/05/11:4b, =13:2d
HIKL, Ferdinand, un. baker, NYC-M – 1908/07/21:6a
HILBERT, Albert F., gardener, Newark, NJ - 1914/09/27:7e
HILBERT, Hermann, un. carp., NYC-M – 1908/01/27:6a, fam. 1 Fb:6a mem. – 1909/01/25:6a
HILBURGER, Lorenz, NYC-B - 1915/03/10:6a
HILD, Bernhard, un. carp., NYC-M – 1898/05/03:4a
HILD, Lizzie, 15, worker, Newark, NJ – 1893/02/19:5e
HILD, Oscar, clerk at import agency and secy local AKK, & Margaretha Wilke Hild, 30th wedding anniv., NYC-B - 1916/04/26:5d
HILDEBRAND, ., 45, NYC-B – 1902/05/18:5c
HILDEBRAND, Henry, 47, Hoboken, NJ – 1893/09/24:5d
HILDEBRAND, John, infant, NYC-M – 1906/08/08:2c
HILDEBRAND, John, un. carp., NYC-M – 1892/02/20:4a
HILDEBRAND, Julius, merchant, fr Hannover area, cousin H. Hildebrand in Bremen, NYC-M - 1878/09/02:4b
HILDEBRAND, Karoline, NYC-B – 1909/03/25:6a
HILDEBRAND, Peter, infant, NYC-M – 1898/09/03:1f
HILDEBRANDT % Stuettgen
HILDEBRANDT, Elise, b. Schuetzler, NYC-B - 1895/02/07:4a
HILDEBRANDT, Ferdinand, 64, un. cigar maker, NYC-M – 1891/10/21:4a, 22:4a
HILDEBRANDT, George's wife, 24, ex-Mrs Charles Eastmore, Battle Creek, MI, + Bolton, NJ - 1913/10/09:2e
HILDEBRANDT, Johanna, b. Borgas, 63, *Hildesheim/Gy, NYC-B – 1888/04/07:3a
HILDEBRANDT, John H. G., 71, NYC-M – 1891/03/30:4a
HILDEBRANDT, John, ret. tobacco dealer, NYC-M - 1915/08/16:1g
HILDEBRANDT, John, tailor, NYC-M - 1878/03/20:1g
HILDEBRANDT, Joseph, 88, tailor, *4 No 1820 near Hildesheim/Gy, USA 1851, SP, NYC-B – 1909/04/11:1g, 12:6a, 13:6a, =14:2c
HILDEBRANDT, Lina, b. Schmitt, 64, NYC-M – 1891/08/13:4a
HILDEBRANDT, Marie, 29, NYC-B – 1897/09/27:1e
HILDEBRANDT, Paul, 47, editor NJ Freie Presse – 1892/07/08:4f

HILDEBRANDT, Robert, 45, NYC-M – 1897/02/14:5a, 15:4a
HILDREW, George, 60, ret. sailor, NYC-Sailors Snug Harbor - 1916/10/20:2d
HILFERS, Frederick, 82, * 31 Jy 18 in Hannover, USA 1860s,un. cigarmaker, East Orange, NJ - 1916/07/21:2d
HILGENDORFF, Mary, 81, NYC-M - 1919/07/08:1e
HILKE, William, un. waiter, NYC-M - 1917/01/25:1f
HILKEN, Frederick, 10, W. Hoboken, NJ – 1899/06/02:3d
HILKEN, Louis O., 67, ret. importer, active in G-A clubs, NYC-B - 1914/09/11:2e
HILKER, Henry, Jersey City Heights, NJ – 1900/06/03:5a
HILL, Benjamin, US Senator fr Georgia, 1882/08/17:1c
HILL, Carl B., 21, NYC-Bx?, exec. Auburn, NY – 1910/04/19:3e
HILL, David B., 67, ex-NYS Gov., crit obit 1910/10/21:2c, 4a
HILL, Frank, US consul in Frankfurt/Main – 1912/05/24:1b, 11 June:1f
HILL, James J., 79, RR Magnate, + St Paul, MN, crit. obit - 1916/05/30:2f
HILL, Joe, IWW, see Hillstrom
HILL, John, 19, exec. Camden, NJ – 1893/04/15:3e
HILL, Louis, 55, NYC-M - 1917/06/29:6a
HILL, Massy, Negro, lynched Winchester, TN – 1881/11/07:1d
HILL, Pacy, exec. Auburn, NJ – 1909/04/27:5e
HILL, Robert F., 28, exec. Camden, NJ – 1901/02/06:4a
HILLBRECHT, Martin, West New York, NJ - 1920/05/26:6a
HILLEBRAND, John, Union Hill?, NJ – 1892/08/07:1e
HILLEBRECHT, Heinrich, 64, *Marienstein/Hannover, NYC-Bx – 1883/05/04:3c
HILLENBRANDT, P., 48, NYC-B – 1893/10/31:4a
HILLER, Christina, 68, NYC-M, + @on Genl Slocum – 1904/06/17:3b
HILLER, Ferdinand, German composer, + Koeln – 1885/05/12:1b
HILLER, Hanna, NYC-B – 1891/08/15:4a
HILLER, Hugo, SPD Frankfurt, his = 1885/07/28:2f
HILLER, Jakob, 49, varnisher, NYC-M – 1882/09/16:3a
HILLER, Wilhelm, 58, NYC-M – 1892/06/29:4a
HILLERS, M., 70, NYC-M – 1893/12/27:4a
HILLERT, Max, Dr., 64, banker at Knauth, Nachod & Kuehne, then realtor, NYC-B – 1912/07/07:7d
HILLGRUBER, H., 52, NYC-M - 1894/01/15:4a
HILLIG, Ernst, NYC-Bx - 1914/10/30:6a
HILLMANN, Caroline, 55, NYC-B - 1916/03/31:5f
HILLMANN, Christine, 80, NYC-B – 1911/01/02:3a
HILLMANN, Hugo, SLP veteran, NYC-B, benefit for him – 1885/09/10:4d-e, rev. 15:4d

HILLQUIT % Feldman
HILLSTROM, Joseph, IWW, poet (Joe Hill), to be exec. by Utah - 1915/ 09/22:4b, 24:2g, exec. 19 No:1d, #20:1g, 2d, 4a, = in Chicago 26:1e
HILMER, Ernst, smith & SPD activist in Hamburg/Gy - 1909/09/12:3b
HILPERT, John A.,50, stone cutter,USA June 1879, Hoboken, NJ - 1879/07/19:3a
HILS, John, NYC-B - 1902/10/17:4a
HILSCHER, Elisabeth, 40, NYC-Q - 1911/04/20:6a
HILSS, August, NYC-Q - 1906/12/30:7b
HIMMEL, John's wife, NYC-M - 1889/09/22:5b
HIMMELFAHRT, Moritz M., 32, tailor, fr Poland, NYC-M - 1880/06/15:1g
HIMMELMANN, Frederick, NYC-B - 1920/07/03:6a
HIMMELSBACH, Emilie, NYC-M - 1893/08/07:4a
HIMMELSBACH, Robert, un. cigarmaker, NYC-M - 1890/10/26:5a
HIMMER, A., Newark, NJ - 1904/01/19:4a
HIMMLER, Emil, 46, un. painter, NYC-M - 1913/03/22:6a
HIMPEL, Hermann, Hoboken, NJ - 1911/11/30:6a
HINCK, John F., 38, flour dealer, NYC-M - 1881/05/03:4a
HINCK, John, 48, salesman, NYC-B - 1907/01/01:3a
HINDENBERG, Morris's wife & Bessie, 1, NYC-M - 1907/01/03:1d
HINDERER, David, un. cabinetmaker, NYC-M - 1903/02/10:4a, fam. 14:4a
HINDERLANG, Katherina, 23, NYC-M - 1886/10/25:3b
HING, Eng, NYC, member Hip Sing Tong, exec. Ossining, NY - 1914/10/29:2, 1915/02/06:1d
HINGLEBERG, Mrs, NYC-M - 1895/01/20:1g
HINK, Harriet, NYC-M, + Paterson, NJ? - 1880/01/23:1d, 24:1d, 25:1e, 26:1g, 27:1e, 2 Mr:1f
HINKELBEIN, Arthur, NYC-M - 1902/07/09:4a
HINKLE, W. H., contractor, Mt Carmel, NJ - 1899/01/11:4c
HINKLEBEIN, Mrs, 45, & Elvira, 21, Mt Vernon, NY, + Danbury, CT - 1918/07/21:11f
HINRICHS, August, NYC-Q - 1893/02/28:4a, 1 Mr:4a
HINRICHS, Christoph, 53, un. cigarmaker, NYC-M - 1884/10/11:3b
HINRICHS, Georg, West Newark, NJ - 1918/07/26:6a
HINRICHS, Otto, cigarmaker, NYC-M - 1894/05/16:4a
HINRICHS, Wilhelm, NYC-Bx - 1910/07/26:6a
HINSCHING, Nicolas, 42, un. baker, NYC-B - 1909/07/28:6a, 29:6a, fam. 31:6a
HINTERHOLZNER, Heinrich, un. carp., NYC-Bx - 1915/08/03:6a
HINTON, Richard, missionary, active 1886 Henry George campaign, + London - 1901/12/22:1b

HINUEBER, George, coal peddler, NYC-M - 1879/01/25:4b
HINZ, Amanda, 30, NYC-M - 1918/12/21:6a
HINZ, Daniel, 42, pianomaker?, NYC-M - 1881/12/17:3a, 18:5e
HINZ, Hans, NYC-M - 1887/11/04:4f
HINZE, Georg, 47, NYC-B - 1902/11/01:4a
HINZMANN, Charles, 6, NYC-M - 1900/06/13:3g, 14:2g
HIPFL, Henrietta, b. Metz, 31, NYC-M - 1909/08/04:6a
HIPP, Louis, un. cigar maker, NYC-M - 1889/06/06:4a
HIPPEL, Heinrich, 31, un. beer driver, NYC-B - 1887/05/26:3d
HIPPELL % Schmitt
HIPPER, Leo, 5, NYC-M - 1889/04/13:4e, 18:2g, 27:4d, 26:1d
HIPPERLING, Charles, un. machinist, NYC-Q - 1913/05/14:6a
HIPPLE, Wilhelm, barber, Newark, NJ - 1886/08/05:2e
HIRIS, Matthias, NYC-Q - 1912/04/04:6a
HIRSCH % Levy
HIRSCH, Albert, NYC-Q - 1916/05/05:6a
HIRSCH, Andreas, NYC-M - 1892/08/16:4a
HIRSCH, Charles, NYC-B - 1904/12/14:4a
HIRSCH, Ernestine, 78, NYC-M - 1891/06/26:4a
HIRSCH, Frank, engineer, NYC - 1905/03/15:1d
HIRSCH, Harry, 25, NYC-B - 1903/09/15:4a
HIRSCH, Henry, 52, NYC-M - 1892/05/29:5b
HIRSCH, Henry,52, cloth salesman,* Gy, NYC-M - 1894/03/19:1h
HIRSCH, John, 73, NYC-M - 1896/06/18:4a
HIRSCH, Josef, 84,cotton manufacturer, NYC-M - 1916/01/18:1d
HIRSCH, Julius, 57, NYC-M - 1890/05/23:4a
HIRSCH, Julius, 66, un. typesetter, NYC-M - 1903/05/30:4a
HIRSCH, Julius, SP, NYC-M - 1918/10/12:6a, 13:11g
HIRSCH, Max, Dr., 75, writer & Liberal MdR, + Berlin - 1905/06/28:2c
HIRSCH, Meyer, NYC-M - 1892/07/31:5c
HIRSCH, Moritz, 63, Baron, Vienna millionaire & philanthropist, + near
    Pressburg, crit. obit - 1896/04/22:1g, 23:1a, 24:2c
HIRSCH, Moses, 80, NYC-M - 1892/03/21:4a
HIRSCH, Nathan, NYC-M - 1893/01/30:4a
HIRSCH, Otto, 61, Elizabeth, NJ - 1907/12/14:3d, 6a
HIRSCH, Rosalina, 22, NYC-M - 1891/07/24:4a
HIRSCH, Salomon, 62, coffee dealer, NYC-M? - 1913/09/11:6a
HIRSCHBAUM, August, 70, NYC-M - 1894/01/28:5d
HIRSCHBERGER % Peemoller
HIRSCHBERGER, George, laborer, NYC-M - 1891/09/12:1e
HIRSCHBERGER, Johann, NYC-M - 1892/07/20:4a
HIRSCHBIEL, John, 31, un. carp., NYC-Q - 1898/10/01:3d, 4a, 2:5a

HIRSCHBIEL, Martin, un. cigarmaker,NYC-M 1894/01/15:4a,16:4a
HIRSCHHEIDE, Ernst, un. butcher, NYC-Bx – 1907/09/27:6a
HIRSCHHORN, Anton, 50, cigar dealer, NYC-M - 1894/09/06:1b
HIRSCHKIND % Adler
HIRSCHKOWITZ, Ida, 5, NYC-M – 1901/01/04:3d
HIRSCHMANN, Charles, candy maker, NYC-B - 1916/04/08:5f
HIRSCHMANN, Eleonore, 58, NYC-B – 1911/12/25:6a
HIRSCHMANN, Henry, pres. Yale Knitting Co., NYC-B? - 1917/06/30:5e
HIRSCHMANN, Otto, 44, un. typesetter, SDP, NYC-B – 1901/06/27:4a, 28:4a
HIRST, Theodor, machinist, NYC-B – 1901/11/18:4a
HIRTES, Georg, NYC-M - 1913/08/12:6a
HIRTH, Augustus C., Yale U student, NYC-Bx – 1899/12/24:1g
HIRTH, John, un. carpenter, NYC-M - 1895/11/30: 4a
HIRTH, Kate, NYC-B – 1911/02/27:3b
HIRTH, Wilhelmina, b. Schramm, 64, NYC-B – 1908/11/21:6a
HIRZ, Joseph H., 50, chemist, dying, NYC-B - 1915/09/28:6d
HIRZEL, Andreas, 40, fr Switzerland, driver, NYC-M – 1880/03/03:1g
HISSIGER, Johann, NYC-B - 1916/06/23:6a
HISSNER, Joseph, 10, boy scout, War 2, NYC-B - 1917/06/04:6a
HITNER, Margareth, 27, Pottsdown,PA? - 1913/07/22:3e-f
HITZ % Wurm
HITZ, Evelyn, 16 mo., NYC-M - 1920/02/21:6a
HITZ, Pauline, 20, NYC-M - 1917/04/23:6a, fam. 26:6a, mem. 1918/04/22:6a, 1919/04/22:6a, 1920/04/22:6a
HITZEL, Hermann, 32, un. brewer or cooper, NYC-M – 1887/10/20:3c
HITZELBERGER, C., NYC-B – 1911/10/14:6a
HITZELBERGER, John, 42, Hoboken, NJ - 1914/07/04:6a
HITZELBERGER, Joseph, 70, Jersey City, NJ - 1914/02/06:6a
HITZLER, Reinhard, machinist, Mt Vernon, NY – 1909/01/27:6a
HLADIK, Julius, un. carp., NYC-M – 1902/08/19:4a
HLUBOKY, Charles, 22, un. bronce worker, NYC-M - 1920/01/09:6a
HOB, Georg, NYC-B – 1913/04/11:6a
HOBART, Garrett A., US vice-pres., crit. Obit – 1899/11/22:1h, 23:2a, =23:2d, will 28:4b
HOBRECHT, Hermann, officer on SS Imperator of HAPAG, + saving lives in Hoboken, NJ - 1913/08/29:1d
HOBS, Anna Olga Magdalena, 1, NYC-M - 1878/05/14:3c

HOCH, Adolph, Chicago, on trial for killing his 5 successive wives – 1905/02/01:1f, sent. to death 20 May:1e, 21:5c, post 29 Jy:1f
HOCH, Agnes, wd Hartmann, NYC-M – 1899/08/09:4a
HOCH, Johann, *near Bingen/Rhine, stud. Chem. in Berlin, exec. Chicago, IL – 1906/02/24:1c-d, =25:1a
HOCH, Johann, NYC-M – 1904/06/28:4a
HOCH, John, 24, NYC-B – 1892/05/17:2e
HOCH, Julius, 73, *Liechtenstein, + Newark, NJ – 1912/10/12:2d
HOCH, Nicholas, Steinway worker?, NYC-Q – 1884/12/16:3b
HOCHDORF, Harold, lawyer, dying, NYC-M – 1912/01/21:1b
HOCHHALTER, Dorothea, 77, NYC-M – 1890/09/15:4a
HOCHHAUS, William, ex-millionaire, + poor, NYC-M – 1912/05/08:1e
HOCHHEIMER, Emmanuel, Dr. med. 63, NYC-M - 1917/05/31:6a
HOCHLEITNER, Anna, 53, NYC-M - 1878/07/23:4e
HOCHMANN, Charles, un. varnisher, NYC-M – 1893/03/08:4a
HOCHREITER, Henry, NYC-Bx – 1910/08/30:6a
HOCHREITER, Maria, b. Mueller, NYC-M – 1891/04/14:4a
HOCHREUTER, Friedrich, un. cigarmaker, NYC-M – 1889/04/29:4a
HOCHSCHWANDER, Henry, 21, USA 2 weeks ago, * Mannheim, NYC-B – 1882/03/10:1f
HOCHSTATTER, Gottlieb, un. butcher, NYC-M - 1918/10/24:6a
HOCHSTEDTER, M., 45, servant, NYC-M – 1907/02/20:3a
HOCHULI, Jacob, 38, millwright, Swiss?, NYC-M - 1895/03/30:4a, 04/04:4a
HOCK % Klement; HOEFER % Sergel
HOCK, Anna M., NYC-M - 1878/05/20:3b
HOCK, John, exec. Auburn, NY – 1897/01/21:1b
HOCK, Marie, NYC-M - 1896/01/27:4a
HOCK, Mark, un. cigar maker, NYC-M – 1891/04/05:5a
HOCKDER, Mary, 70, NYC-M, +@ on Genl Slocum – 1904/06/17:3b
HOCKEL, Anton, 60, carp., USA 1866, Babylon, LI – 1900/05/11:1d
HOCKER, Adam, CLP (ex-SP), un. cigarmkr, NYC-M – 1919/10/21:6a
HOCKER, John, un. butcher, NYC-M - 1918/10/24:6a
HOCZIAR, Katie, 18, servant, fr Austria, + Yonkers, NY – 1900/08/21:1b
HODEL, John, un. carp., NYC-B - 1916/09/04:6a
HODGEWEDDE, Walter, 8, Jersey City Hgts, + Hoboken, NJ – 1904/07/11:1a, 12:1f
HODGINS, John E., 38, NYPD - 1914/10/08:5e
HOECHBERG, Karl, 31, SPD Frankfurt/Main, Gy – 1885/07/06:1f
HOECKELE, Andreas, 57, un. baker, NYC-B - 1919/01/29:6a
HOECKELE, Louisa K., NYC-B – 1910/05/25:6a
HOEDE, Th.'s wife, NYC-M - 1894/02/20:4a

HOEDEL, Emil, exec. Berlin for attempt on William I - 1878/08/17:1a, 2b, 10/02:2e
HOEDEMAKER, J. E., 20, druggist, NYC-B – 1889/07/03:1f
HOEFER, Augusta, NYC-Q – 1882/06/27:3c
HOEFER, Franz, 59, NYC-B – 1908/09/19:6a, 20:7b, fam. 2 Oct:6a
HOEFER, Henry, 62, NYC-Bx – 1883/01/13:4d
HOEFER, Johanna, 22, NYC-M – 1907/09/20:1e
HOEFER, Selma,65,SP, Jersey City,NJ - 1915/04/30:6a, 3 My:6a
HOEFER, Wilhelmine, *Wohlgefaehrt/Weimar, USA 1848, with husband Sergel or Soergel, searched by sister in Dresden/Gy – 1881/05/12:3b
HOEFERMANN, Charles, Elizabeth, NJ – 1908/11/06:6a
HOEFFNER, Joseph, un. carp., NYC-M – 1904/11/24:4a, 25:4a
HOEFFNER, Valentin, 35, baker, (s.a. Susanna Leuser), NYC-B – 1885/03/10:2g-3a
HOEFLING % Froehlich
HOEFLING, Emma, 52, NYC-B – 1905/12/08:1f
HOEFNER, George, NYC-Q - 1915/11/04:6a
HOEFNER, Henry, 19, machinist, NYC-B, lynched in Forsythe, Montana – 1912/04/26:3a
HOEFT, Henry's wife, 52, NYC-M – 1880/12/04:1f
HOEG, K., 47, NYC-B - 1894/02/03:4a
HOEGER, Karl, 66, SP, un. typsetter, + Vienna - 1913/10/29:4c-d
HOEHL, August, 52, SP, Haledon, NJ - 1917/01/13:6a, fam. 17:6a, =18:6a
HOEHL, Heinrich, 28, NYC-M – 1891/06/25:4a
HOEHL, Joseph, un. baker, NYC-M? - 1919/03/25:6a
HOEHLEIN, Ernst, 26, NYC-B – 1903/11/26:4a
HOEHMANN, Ernst, NYC-M - 1919/06/21:6a
HOEHN, Anna, NYC-B – 1907/11/13:6a
HOEHN, John, NYC-M – 1881/04/04:3d
HOEHN, Theresia, 61,SP, NYC-B –1910/12/30:6a, =1 Ja. 1911:7c, fam. 3:6a
HOEHN, William, Dr. med., 46, NYC-M – 1883/11/19:3a
HOEHN, Willy, 8, NYC-M – 1891/04/05:5a
HOELDERLIN, Maria, NYC-B – 1892/04/11:4a
HOELEMANN, Friedrich, NYC-B – 1909/06/28:6a
HOELKE, Gustav, waiter, NYC-B – 1903/10/05:2h
HOELLANDER % Fusshoeller
HOELLEIN, Amandus, 68, NYC-B - 1915/12/24:6a
HOELLER, Marie, NYC-M – 1898/06/22:4a
HOELSCHER, John, 47, NYC-M – 1891/04/09:4a
HOELZEL, Marie, & daughter Hannah, 7, NYC-M - 1917/09/06:2e
HOELZER, Albert F., 50, NYC-M – 1904/07/13:4a, fam. 31:5b

HOELZER, Edward, NYC-M – 1906/12/26:6a
HOELZER, Theodor, NYC-M – 1890/12/08:4a
HOELZLE, Henry H., 26, NYC-M – 1892/05/12:1g
HOENACK, Hugo H., 52, un. wood carver & manager "Café Cosmopolitan," NYC-M – 1899/04/14:3c
HOENACK, Hugo, 1, NYC? – 1887/08/19:3c
HOENIEL, Charles, 22, Newark, NJ - 1879/02/24:4d, 03/12:4e
HOENIG, William, 50, NYC-M – 1892/05/11:4a
HOENNIKE, August, infant, NYC-M – 1886/12/13:2g
HOEPFNER % Fischer
HOEPFNER, Albert, 39, waiter, NYC-B – 1907/05/09:1a
HOEPFNER, Ernst, un. typesetter, NYC-B – 1890/12/27:4a
HOEPPNER, comrade, 70, baker & SPD alderman in Dresden/Gy – 1913/04/13:3d
HOEPPNER, Ernst, carp., NYC-B – 1899/03/04:4a
HOEPPNER, Henry, Newark, NJ – 1908/09/15:6a
HOERDUM, Christen, Danish SP leader – 1911/06/20:4d-e
HOERETH, Frederick, machinist, NYC-B – 1892/08/01:4a
HOERGER, Charles Louis, 72, un. typesetter, NYC-B – 1903/11/15:5a
HOERIG, August, SPD Hamburg/Gy, + 1884/09/13:2e
HOERING, Charles W., 34, Newark, NJ - 1917/10/30:2c
HOERMAN, John, 48, NYC-M - 1916/01/12:6a
HOERNER, John, un. butcher, NYC-B - 1919/02/24:6a
HOERSCHELMANN, William, 56, SP, un. engineer, NYC-B, note (not +) 1911/07/17:5d
HOERZ, Erich, un. machinist, NYC?, + Konkakee, IL - 1915/04/26:6a
HOERZ, Gottlob, 45, NYC-M – 1898/11/10:4a
HOES % Muench
HOESCHEN, Auguste, b. Tenkert, NYC-M – 1905/05/19:7b
HOETH, Joseph, NYC-B – 1909/08/28:3c
HOETTELBACH, Richard, 80, un. carp., Fort Lee, NJ - 1918/06/05:6a
HOEVELING, Henry von, un. painter, NYC-M – 1900/11/20:4a
HOEVEN, Julius, 50, NYC-M - 1894/01/29:4a
HOF, Daniel, 1, NYC-B – 1901/07/03:1d
HOF, Friedrich, 53, NYC-M – 1883/03/07:3c
HOFACKER, Julius, NYC-B – 1886/07/09:2e
HOFELEIN, Louis, farm laborer, NYC-B – 1881/09/24:3b
HOFER % Nopper
HOFER, Franz, SP, edit. Vienna Vorwaerts, *4 Oct 1866 Bruenn/Moravia – 1912/09/15:3f
HOFER, Gottlieb, 36, un. weaver, 1906 fr Switzerland, SP, Jersey City Heights, NJ – 1912/08/07:3c, 6a

HOFER, John, NYC-M – 1904/06/28:4a
HOFER, Louise, NYC-Q - 1917/12/09:7a
HOFF, A., merchant, NYC-B – 1905/06/22:4a, 24:3e
HOFF, Bernhardina, 36, teacher, *Sweden, NYC-M 1894/05/30:1g
HOFF, Robert, 40, Swiss, NYC-B – 1903/09/16:4a
HOFF, Thomas, 50, killed 7 Jan., West Orange, NJ – 1906/01/17:1d, 18:3d
HOFFACKER, B. J., 64, NYC-M – 1892/04/30:4a
HOFFELLER, Philip, 66, West New York, NJ - 1916/01/04:6a
HOFFENREICH, Friedrich, 31, bank clerk, fr Austria, NYC-M – 1891/05/08:2h
HOFFERBERT, Henry, NYC-M – 1891/03/25:4a
HOFFERBERTH, Louis, 68, NYC-M – 1906/03/04:5b
HOFFERT, Ph., un. cigarmaker, NYC-B – 1910/12/16:6a
HOFFERT, William, Hoboken, NJ – 1909/07/10:6a
HOFFMAN, Chas A., genl-mgr Linde Shim Co., NYC-M - 1913/10/25:1d
HOFFMAN, Edna, 2, Jersey City, NJ, +@Genl Slocum – 1904/06/19:1c
HOFFMAN, Elisabeth, NYC-M, + @on Genl Slocum – 1904/06/16:1c
HOFFMAN, Ella, 14, NYC-M, +@Genl Slocum – 1904/06/22:1d
HOFFMAN, Elsie M., 30, NYC-Q - 1918/10/22:6a
HOFFMAN, Ferdinand B., carp., NYC-M – 1898/09/23:3g
HOFFMAN, Frederick, NYC-M – 1897/04/26:1f
HOFFMAN, Ida, 29, servant, Orange, NJ - 1913/05/08:1e
HOFFMAN, Katherina, 72, newspaper stand, fr Ireland 1848, NYC – 1909/08/08:20b-c
HOFFMAN, Louis, NYC-M – 1896/08/11:1a
HOFFMAN, Louise, NYC-M – 1906/07/19:6a
HOFFMAN, Martha, embroiderer, NYC-M – 1903/03/10:3b
HOFFMAN, Minnie, NYC-M – 1891/11/26:1e
HOFFMAN, Philip, 42, roofer, NYC-B – 1901/08/16:4b
HOFFMAN, Rachel, 16, servant, NYC-B – 1900/05/21:3c
HOFFMAN, Samuel & Max, 8, NYC-B, + Nassau, NY – 1911/07/29:1d
HOFFMAN, Sophia, 74, Newark, NJ– 1912/01/17:6c
HOFFMAN, Sophia, NYC-M, + @on Genl Slocum – 1904/06/16:1c
HOFFMAN, William's wife, 49, Hoboken, NJ – 1897/01/19:1h, 20:1b
HOFFMANN % Landahl, % Rahardt, % Schmeling
HOFFMANN, A., NYC-B 1904/07/20.4a
HOFFMANN, Adam, 33, metal worker & SPD Neckarau/Baden – 1908/09/20:3a
HOFFMANN, Agnes, 59, NYC-Bx - 1915/10/02:6a, 3:7a
HOFFMANN, Amond, 54, NYC-M – 1900/07/17:4a
HOFFMANN, Anton, un. carp., NYC-M – 1899/03/11:4a
HOFFMANN, August, NYC-B – 1884/07/21:3b

HOFFMANN, August, 16, NYC-M – 1893/03/25:4a
HOFFMANN, Bertha, b. Graupner, 51, NYC-M – 1910/05/08:7a, fam. 12:6a
HOFFMANN, Carolina, 73, Yonkers, NY - 1918/12/10:6a
HOFFMANN, Catherina, 72, NYC-M – 1912/05/23:1e
HOFFMANN, Ch., NYC-B – 1907/09/27:6a
HOFFMANN, Charles L., painter & decorator, NYC-M – 1889/12/15:5b
HOFFMANN, Charles, 19, un. baker?, NYC-B - 1916/01/07:6a
HOFFMANN, Charles, beer driver, NYC-M – 1896/08/11:1b
HOFFMANN, Christine, Wakefield, NJ – 1907/02/20:6a
HOFFMANN, Clara, 53, NYC-Bx - 1916/05/16:6a
HOFFMANN, Clara, NYC-B – 1889/02/22:4a
HOFFMANN, Conrad, NYC-Q - 1914/12/31:6a
HOFFMANN, E. N., NYC-M – 1901/01/19:3a
HOFFMANN, Emil, 17, NYC-B - 1917/08/06:6a
HOFFMANN, Ernst, NYC-B – 1880/05/28:1e
HOFFMANN, Florence, 31, NYC-B? – 1913/01/18:6a
HOFFMANN, Frank J., 32, tinsmith, NYC-B – 1908/05/03:1f
HOFFMANN, Franz, machinist, Yonkers, NY – 1901/10/27:5a
HOFFMANN, Frederick, Ossining, NY (dying) – 1897/01/09:3g
HOFFMANN, Friedericke, NYC-M – 1891/04/02:4a
HOFFMANN, Friedrich, un. carp., NYC-B – 1888/04/30:3a, fam. 2 May:3a
HOFFMANN, Friedrich Wilhelm, Union Hill, NJ – 1883/06/10:1f
HOFFMANN, Fritz, Jersey City Hgts, NJ – 1919/09/10:6a
HOFFMANN, Georg, NYC-M – 1906/06/21:6a
HOFFMANN, George, 51, un. tailor, NYC-B – 1889/11/30:4a
HOFFMANN, George, 54, stonecutter, NYC-B - 1894/10/24:4b
HOFFMANN, George, 60, un. carp., NYC-M – 1904/04/26:1e, 28:4a
HOFFMANN, George, Tully/Syracuse, NY - 1878/10/06:5e
HOFFMANN, Hans, SPD Bayreuth/Gy – 1909/03/14:3a
HOFFMANN, Henry, sailor, NYC-B – 1899/08/19:4a
HOFFMANN, Henry, un. baker, NYC-Bx – 1914/10/08:6a
HOFFMANN, Henry, un. beer driver, NYC-B – 1900/05/21:2f
HOFFMANN, Hermann H., 33, NYC-B – 1906/06/24:7d
HOFFMANN, Hyman, 48, & wife Sophie, NYC-M – 1902/07/19:1e
HOFFMANN, Ida, b. Blumentritt-Schnorr, SLP?, NYC-M – 1892/07/27:4a,d
HOFFMANN, Jacob, 48, NYC-M - 1915/12/03:6a
HOFFMANN, Jacob, un. mason, NYC-M – 1889/10/04:4a
HOFFMANN, Jakob, 56, machinery dealer, NYC-M – 1886/03/11:2f
HOFFMANN, Johann F., 47, NYC-M – 1904/02/09:4a
HOFFMANN, Johann, 85, NYC-Bx – 1913/07/22:6a

HOFFMANN, John D., 45, baker, NYC-B – 1907/03/19:3a
HOFFMANN, John T., ex-NYS Gov., – 1888/04/28:4d
HOFFMANN, John, 30, NYC-B – 1892/07/10:5c
HOFFMANN, John, 48, un. cigarmaker, NYC-M – 1896/04/16:4a
HOFFMANN, John, 56, NYC-M – 1889/10/24:4a
HOFFMANN, John, 59, NYC-M – 1888/05/12:3a
HOFFMANN, John, NYC-Bx – 1910/07/10:7c
HOFFMANN, John, un. carp., NYC-M – 1901/05/26:5a
HOFFMANN, Joseph, 1, NYC-B – 1888/05/15:2c
HOFFMANN, Joseph, furrier, NYC-B – 1893/10/15:1g
HOFFMANN, Joseph, NYC-Bx - 1913/07/13:6a
HOFFMANN, Joseph, NYC-Q – 1900/05/25:4a
HOFFMANN, Joseph, or John, 64, cigardealer, SP, NYC-M – 1908/04/15:2d, 6a
HOFFMANN, Joseph, SP?, NYC-M – 1902/05/10:4a
HOFFMANN, Julius, Dr. med., 76, SP, early NYVZ trustee, * Worms/Rhein, NYC-M - 1917/01/26:2b,6a
HOFFMANN, Karl, '48er, chief-edit. Wiener Tageblatt, + Vienna – 1882/06/12:2f
HOFFMANN, L.'s wife, b. Ochs, 72, NYC-M – 1891/03/16:4a
HOFFMANN, Leopold, 50, NYC-M – 1892/08/13:4a
HOFFMANN, Lizzie, 45, NYC-Q – 1906/01/30:4a
HOFFMANN, Lorenz, un. cigarmaker, his wife died NYC-M - 1879/07/17:3a
HOFFMANN, Louis, 75, NYC – 1902/08/02:4d
HOFFMANN, Louis, Elizabeth, NJ – 1906/06/05:4a
HOFFMANN, Louisa, 63, NYC-M - 1913/06/28:6a
HOFFMANN, Louise, NYC-M – 1883/08/03:4c
HOFFMANN, M., 63, NYC-M - 1894/01/10:4a
HOFFMANN, Margaret, & daughter Johanna, 12, NYC-M – 1907/01/16:6c
HOFFMANN, Maria, 55, SLP?, Jersey City Heights, NJ – 1898/11/20:5a, fam. 23:4a
HOFFMANN, Mathias, 42, un. carp., NYC-B – 1891/12/01:4a, 3:4a
HOFFMANN, Minnie, 40, Newark, NJ – 1885/10/15:2g,3a, 20:2g, 22:2g, husband William tried – 1885/11/21:2o, rcc. 10 yrs 20 Oct. 1886:2d
HOFFMANN, Mrs, 33, NYC-M – 1904/06/20:1d
HOFFMANN, Mrs, 48, Newark, NJ – 1887/04/04:2c
HOFFMANN, Petronella, b. Doerr, 42, Newark, NJ– 1901/12/30:4a
HOFFMANN, Rudolf, 45, Hoboken, NJ – 1910/04/08:2c
HOFFMANN, Sylvia, 8 months, NYC-B - 1914/08/22:6d
HOFFMANN, William, 22, & Frederick, 10, Portchester, NY – 1881/06/21:1e

HOFFMANN, William, 31, NYC-B - 1920/05/17:6a
HOFFMANN, William, NYC-B - 1914/08/27:6a
HOFFMANN, William, NYC-M - 1912/05/06:6a, 7:6a
HOFFMANN, William, NYC-M - 1920/02/21:6a
HOFFMEYER, Adolf, NYC-M - 1894/01/12:4a
HOFFNER, George C., 33, NYC-B - 1905/04/16:5a
HOFFRICHTER, Pauline, NYC-Q - 1919/07//04:6a
HOFFRITZ, Paul, 34, NYC-B - 1913/08/07:3c-d
HOFFSTETTEN, ., von, Bavarian officer & friend of Ferdinand Lassalle, SPD - 1887/01/06:2c, =8 Fb:6d
HOFFWEDEL, Anna, NYC-B - 1891/06/22:4a
HOFMAN, Adolf, un. carp., NYC-B - 1915/06/09:6a
HOFMAN, Albert, 40, v-p Union Hill First Natl Bank, Woodcliffe, NJ - 1917/08/10:2f
HOFMAN, L., teacher at Yorkville Free German School, NYC-Bx - 1909/01/09:6a
HOFMANN % Bayersdorfer
HOFMANN, Albert, un. beer driver, NYC-B - 1910/09/30:6a
HOFMANN, Alfred, NYC-B - 1913/02/06:6a
HOFMANN, Anna, b. Boerner, 68, NYC-B - 1914/07/11:6a, fam. 14:6a
HOFMANN, Barbara, NYC-M - 1896/04/16:4a, fam. 19:5a
HOFMANN, Edmond, 8, NYC-M - 1905/05/27:4b
HOFMANN, Edward, un. smith, USA 1870s, SLP, co-fdr Ohio <u>Volks-Zeitung</u>, Cincinatti, OH - 1897/01/13:2e
HOFMANN, Edward, 18, deaf-mute, + NYC 26 Sept, inquest 1884/12/14:1f
HOFMANN, Friedrich Wilhelm, 74, un. cigarmaker & SPD Leipzig - 1910/05/15:3c
HOFMANN, Heinrich, SLP, un. cigarmkr, fr? Hanau/Gy, NYC-M? - 1893/01/09:4a, 10:4a, fam. 15:5c
HOFMANN, Joseph, 44, un. bricklayer, NYC-Q - 1907/12/25:6a
HOFMANN, Louis, 57, SPD Greiz/Gy - 1901/07/29:2f
HOFMANN, Louis, 62, NYC-M - 1915/09/03:6a
HOFMANN, Max, NYC-M - 1912/07/30:6a
HOFMANN, May, 10, NYC-M - 1910/07/31:7c
HOFMEISTER, Charles, 32, stable laborer, NYC-M - 1903/01/21:1e
HOFMEISTER, Henry, SP,ex-officer NYVZ & trustee of Yorkville Free German School, un. carp., NYC-M - 1915/03/26:2d,6a, 27:6a, 28:7c, = 29:6b, fam. 30:6a
HOFPAUER, Max, 70, Munich actor, - 1920/12/30:4g-h
HOFRICHTER, Max, un. bricklayer, NYC-Q - 1907/05/20:6a, 21:6a, fam. 25:6a
HOFSTADT, Kathe, 14, NYC-Q - 1906/11/18:7b

HOFSTADT, Kathy, NYC-Q – 1906/05/19:4a, fam. 22:4a
HOFSTAEDTER, J., Newark, NJ - 1913/06/11:6a
HOFSTAEDTER, Johann, 19, SLP, NYC-B – 1890/02/13:4a, 15:2f
HOGAN, Thomas, shot by Pinkertons, Jersey City, NJ – 1887/01/21:1a-b, 28:1c, Pinkertons freed by jury, bitter edit. 4 June 1887:1b-c
HOGFELDT, Mathilde A., servant, fr Sweden, USA 1881, NYC-B – 1881/04/16:2g, 18:3g
HOHENFELD, Helene, & son Hans, 23, NYC-B - 1916/10/16:2e
HOHENFELS, Stella, 63, actress at Burgtheater in Vienna, wife of Alfred von Berger - 1920/03/30:6f
HOHENHAUSEN, Arthur von, 28, journ. for G-A media, fr Hessen, soc., NYC? – 1887/10/15:1e
HOHENLOHE-SCHILLINGSFUERST, Chlodwig von, ex-German chancellor – 1901/07/07:1b
HOHENSTEIN, Arthur, 10, NYC-M – 1893/08/12:1f
HOHENWALD, Karl, un. cooper, NYC-M – 1900/09/09:5a
HOHER, Gustav, Hoboken, NJ – 1901/07/04:3b
HOHL, Georg, un. carp., NYC-M – 1904/12/18:5b
HOHLMANN, Heinrich, un. cigarmaker, NYC-M – 1881/11/30:3b
HOHLSTEIN, Louis, 13, NYC-B – 1898/11/19:4a
HOHLWEG, Paul, 2, NYC-M – 1880/03/16:1g
HOHMANN, Auguste, b. Wendler, NYC – 1912/08/22:6a
HOHMANN, Benedict, 41, machinist, NYC-M – 1881/07/05:3d
HOHMANN, Charlie, 39, SP, stonecutter & innkeep, NYC-B – 1911/07/11:6a, 13:2c; mem. – 1912/07/10:6a
HOHMANN, G., NYC-M – 1908/12/31:6a
HOHMANN, George, 60, NYC-M – 1880/04/06:1g
HOHMANN, Wilhelm, un. carp., NYC-M – 1901/06/23:5a
HOHN, Jacob, NYC-M - 1915/04/01:6a
HOHN, John O.M., 18, SP, NYC-Bx - 1918/06/08:6a, 9:7a, fam. 22:6a
HOHN, Julia, 20, NYC-B - 1894/08/03:4c
HOHN, Maria, NYC-M – 1907/12/25:6a
HOHWIESNER, Caroline, NYC-B – 1892/07/06:4a
HOK, Rosa, b. Lindner, NYC-Q – 1899/03/04:4a
HOLBACH, Joseph, 55, & Helen, 50, NYC-Q - 1919/01/21:2a
HOLBERG, Frederick, grocery clerk, NYC-Bx – 1910/08/13:5e
HOLBERT, Louis, Negro, & wife, lynched in Meridien, MS, in Febr. – 1903/09/23:1b
HOLD, Annie, NYC-B – 1891/04/02:2f
HOLDE, Emma, NYC-M - - 1918/09/22:11a
HOLDENBACH, Emma, 34, NYC-B – 1898/12/08:2g
HOLDER, Babette, NYC-M - 1896/02/06:4a

HOLDER, Pauline, infant, NYC-M – 1884/10/12:5e
HOLDORF, Hans, musician, SP?, fr Schleswig-Holstein, NYC-M – 1893/01/08:1g
HOLEN, John, NYC-M – 1885/07/21:4a
HOLL, John, 49, NYC-B – 1914/03/24:6a, 25:6a, fam. 27:6a, mem. 1915/03/22:6a, 1916/03/22:6a, 1919/03/22:6a
HOLLAENDER % Fusshoeller
HOLLAENDER, Amalie, b. Wissmann, NYC-Bx – 1913/07/25:6a
HOLLAENDER, Arnold, 57, un. carp., NYC-M – 1897/03/02:4a, 3:4a
HOLLAENDER, Daniel, Greenville, NJ – 1920/03/13:8a
HOLLAENDER, John, 32, Paterson, NJ – 1905/07/30:1e
HOLLAND, Caroline, NYC-Q – 1909/08/11:6a
HOLLAND, Charles G., 60, journalist, NYC-M – 1906/03/27:3d
HOLLAND, Felix, driver, NYC-M – 1890/09/04:1g
HOLLAND, Henry A., lawyer, NYC-M – 1880/01/13:1f
HOLLANDER, Fannie, @1911 Triangle Shirtwaist Fire, NYC-M – 1911/03/27:1d
HOLLE, August, worker, NYC-M – 1892/08/02:2f
HOLLE, Frank, Jersey City Heights, NJ – 1909/05/20:6a
HOLLE, Georg, 35, Newark, NJ – 1915/12/06:2g
HOLLEBEN, Theodor von, 75, German ambassador in USA till 1903 – 1913/02/02:1b
HOLLENBACH % Aegerter
HOLLENBACH, Frederick, Newark, NJ – 1917/12/20:6a
HOLLENDER, George, 55, iron worker, Jersey City, NJ – 1883/06/10:1f
HOLLER, (Mr.), reporter for NYVZ, married Bertha Herder, both NYC-B – 1880/08/23:4d
HOLLER, Barbara, 53, NYC-M, + @ Genl Slocum – 1904/06/16:1c, 17:3b
HOLLERICH, Henry G.,32,& son Frank,4, NYC-Bx – 1918/10/18:6a
HOLLFELDER, Anthony, 40, builder, NYC-Richmond Hill – 1916/07/30:7f
HOLLINGER, H., 22, NYC-B – 1902/04/28:2c
HOLLINS, Frank C., banker, NYC-M – 1909/03/05:3d
HOLLMANN, Frederick, 18, waiter, NYC-B – 1904/04/24:1g
HOLLREISER, Anna Phillipina, b. Satter, 48, NYC-M – 1884/12/09:3c
HOLLREISER, Bernhard, 73, NYC-Bx – 1910/02/28:6a, 1 Mr:6a
HOLLWEDEL, William, 57, beer bottler, NYC-B – 1905/12/30:3c
HOLLWEG, Wilhelm, 47, NYC-M – 1904/02/29:4a
HOLM, Peter, Danish Soc. Deputy, his = – 1898/10/24:2f
HOLMER, Nelson, 45, fr Sweden, NYC-M – 1900/10/07:1e
HOLMES, H. H., exec. Philad., PA – 1896/05/07:1b, # 8:1c-e, = 9:1b, 12:1g
HOLMES, Henry, Negro, lynched Monroe, LA – 1914/08/08:2d

HOLMES, James H., 74, last surv. John Brown's 1856 guerilla in KS, + Red Bank, NJ – 1907/11/23:1d
HOLMES, Morris B., exec. Pittsburg, PA – 1908/03/13:1b
HOLOCH, Robert, 44, un. xylographer, SPD Stuttgart, Gy – 1902/02/24:2c
HOLRICKE, Joseph E., basket weaver, NYC-M – 1902/08/06:2h
HOLST, Margarethe, NYC-B – 1906/09/07:6a
HOLSTEIN, Lina, 3, ?, NYC-M – 1892/01/11:4a
HOLT, Alfred, Negro, lynched Owensboro, KY – 1896/12/27:1b
HOLT, Frank, instructor at Cornell U & pacifist, tried to kill warmonger J.P. Morgan – 1915/07/04:1f, 11b, 5:1g, 2a-b, 4a, 6:1b,4a + Mineola, NY jail 7:1g, identified as fugitive ex-Harvard prof. Erich Muenter 8:1g,2a, 17:1f
HOLTERBRAU, Charles, 69, Jersey City, NJ – 1900/09/10:2g
HOLTHUSEN, William, un. cigarmaker, NYC-M? – 1892/11/10:4a
HOLTIEN, Frederick, un. carp., NYC-B – 1900/08/20:4a
HOLTJE, John, 48, plumber, NYC-M? – 1915/11/15:1f
HOLTKE, Theodor, 23, USA 1881, NYC-M – 1882/10/10:3a
HOLTMANN, Christoph, un. music instrument maker, SPD Hamburg/Gy – 1908/04/19:3a
HOLTON, Wilhelm, 57, NYC-B – 1912/10/25:3a
HOLTZ, G.H., 47, NYC-B – 1891/06/28:5c
HOLTZSCHUH, Henry, Jersey City, NJ – 1907/09/14:6a
HOLY, Michael, un. carp., NYC-M – 1918/05/08:6a
HOLZ, Adolph, 67, banker, * Breslau/Silesia, USA 1898, NYC-M – 1916/04/09:11e
HOLZ, Arno, German labor writer, *Rastenburg/East Prussia, 50th birthday – 1913/04/27:6c-f
HOLZ, Gretchen,19, & Ella, 16, Hoboken, NJ – 1885/09/01:1c, 2:1c-d, =3:2g, inquest 4:1g, 11;1e druggist fd not guilty of murder for mistaking prescription 5 Jan. 1886:1a-d, 6:1e-g
HOLZ, Louis, ~60, Jersey City, NJ – 1910/01/10:3d-e
HOLZ, Mrs, Newark, NJ – 1909/04/18:7b
HOLZAMER, Wilhelm, 38, German poet, + Berlin – 1907/09/16:15f-g
HOLZAPFEL, Isidor, NYC-B – 1907/08/26:3c
HOLZBAUER, K., cigarmaker & SPD activist expelled fr Ottensen/Gy, arrived NYC – 1881/06/16:4a
HOLZE, Gustav, 41, Yonkers, NY – 1919/01/19:12a
HOLZENTHAL % Cordes; HOLZHAUER % Garry
HOLZER, Frederick, sailor on USS Maine, + Havana/Cuba, NYC-B – 1898/02/18:1b
HOLZHAUER, Carl, SP, un. cigarmaker, * Mecklenburg Prov./Gy, USA 1881, co-fdr AKK, NYC-Bx - 1915/04/01:2d,6a,fam. 6:6a
HOLZHAUER, George, 45, drayman, Newark, NJ - 1895/03/05:4c

HOLZHAUER, Kurt, NYC-M – 1919/10/11:8a, fam. 20:6a
HOLZHAUSEN, Otto, NYC-M – 1891/03/14:4a, 15:5b, fam. 19:4a
HOLZKAMP, Lillie, 14, NYC-M – 1890/08/31:1f
HOLZKAMPF, Bernhard, cigarmkr, NYC-Q - 1914/02/28:6a
HOLZMACHER, Gustav, un. machinist, NYC-M - 1915/01/09:6a
HOLZMANN, Carl, 34, tailor, family in Rochester, NY, + Rahway, NJ – 1882/01/30:1f
HOLZMANN, Hedwig, 38, NYC-M – 1893/02/02:4f
HOLZMANN, J., 40, NYC-M – 1891/02/27:4a
HOLZMANN, Johann G., 46, NYC-M – 1891/09/20:5f
HOLZMANN, Johannes, "Senna Hoy," Berlin anarchist, + by police in Warsaw/Poland – 1906/02/11:5b
HOLZMANN, Leopold B., 36, shopkeeper, NYC-B - 1913/11/22:3d-e
HOLZMEISTER, Joseph, 49, un. carp., NYC-B - 1915/04/07:6b
HOLZMILLER, Austin, 35, NYC-Bx - 1917/03/04:11f
HOLZMUELLER, Oscar, 32, NYC-M - 1917/03/06:6a
HOLZSCHUH, (Mr), fam. 1888/02/17:3b
HOLZSCHUH, George, 15, NYC-B – 1906/06/23:6a
HOLZSCHUH, George, NYC-B – 1905/11/08:4a
HOLZSCHUH, Marie, 22, NYC-B – 1906/08/13:6a
HOLZWARTH, August, NYC-M – 1889/01/05:3c
HOLZWARTH, Henry, NYC-M - 1914/06/19:6a
HOLZWASSER, Jonas, 85, tailor, NYC-M – 1907/10/22:1f
HOMANN, John, NYC-M – 1906/03/06:4a, 8:4a
HOMANN, Julia, b. Eppenetter, NYC-M – 1886/10/09:3c
HOMRIGHAUSEN, H., 72, un. cabinetmaker, labor act. Gy & USA, NYC-M - 1894/07/23:1e,4a, = 24:1g
HONECK, Maria A., 79, NYC-M – 1891/09/20:5f
HONEGGER, Henry, 66, watchmaker, fr Interlaken/Switz., NYC-B – 1912/10/30:6c
HONER, A., 63, NYC-B - 1916/06/08:6a
HONIG, Hannchen, b. Berliner, 73, NYC-M – 1891/07/07:4a
HONNECKER, Joseph, NYC-M - 1916/08/29:6a
HONNICKE, Charles, 44, worker, NYC? – 1905/02/14:1g
HONNINGS, Auguste, b. Wilkomm, 30, NYC-M – 1896/08/09:5a
HOOD, Alice, NYC-B – 1908/08/10:1d, 11:1g
HOOD, Bertha, fr Switzerland, NYC-B – 1908/08/10:1d, 11:1g
HOOF, Peter, 55, un. painter, NYC-M - 1920/02/20:6a, 21:6a
HOOG, Susie, 48, NYC-M, +@ on Genl Slocum – 1904/06/17:3b
HOOPS, Titzke?, 65, NYC-M – 1891/04/14:4a
HOOS, Henry, Elizabeth, NJ - 1915/06/27:7a, fam. 1 Jy:6a

HOOVER, ..., killed in Augusta, TX after trying to organize Negro laborers – 1887/06/04:2c
HOPE, Jimmy, famous bank burglar, NYC-M – 1905/06/03:1c
HOPF, August, 43, NYC-M - 1894/11/20:4b
HOPF, August, NYC-M – 1910/01/28:6a
HOPF, Gustav, 30, Hoboken, NJ – 1883/07/06:3c
HOPF, Gustav, NYC-M – 1892/07/29:4b
HOPF, Katherina, 51, NYC-M? – 1911/10/26:6a
HOPF, Nettie, 13, NYC-M – 1907/11/12:6a
HOPFE, Louise, NYC-Bx – 1912/11/01:6a, fam. 7:6a
HOPFE, Marie, 22, NYC-Bx - 1915/06/01:6a
HOPFENSACK, Barbara, NYC-M – 1891/07/03:4a
HOPFER, Carl G., 79, NYC-Q – 1901/02/12:4a
HOPFER, Lena, 47, NYC-M – 1906/05/13:1f
HOPFER, Lina, b. Schroeder, NYC-Q – 1901/11/12:4a
HOPFER, Martha, 28, NYC-Q - 1916/01/23:7a
HOPFGAERTNER, Joseph, Newark, NJ - 1914/08/09:7b
HOPP, Ferdinand, 29, Newark, NJ - 1916/03/02:2f
HOPP, Mary, 8, NYC-M, @ 1883 Manhattan School Fire.
HOPP, Richard, 32, bathhouse attendant, NYC-B – 1903/03/07:1e
HOPPE % Schwarze; HORENBURG % Kues
HOPPE, Alfred, Dr., 25, SPD Koenigsberg/East Prussia, War 1 - 1915/05/02:3b
HOPPE, Anna, b. Volz, 33, NYC-Q – 1898/06/14:4a
HOPPE, Carl Friedrich, 72, NYC-M - 1914/10/21:6a
HOPPE, Carl, un. cigarmaker, NYC-M - 1895/06/11:4a
HOPPE, Chr., NYC? – 1898/08/08:4a
HOPPE, Ella, 11, NYC-B – 1887/11/17:4f
HOPPE, Emilie, 1, NYC-B - 1878/10/27:8b
HOPPE, Fritz, 59, SP, un. cigarmkr, *4 Oc 1847 Rinteln/Gy, USA 1880, NYC-M – 1905/05/18:6a, 21:1e
HOPPE, Gustav's wife, 75, Jersey City Hgts - 1918/03/12:6a
HOPPE, Henry, 56, butcher, NYC-M – 1904/11/27:5g
HOPPE, Henry, un. typesetter, Hoboken, NJ – 1907/02/05:6a
HOPPE, Louise, 1, NYC-M – 1882/07/19:3c
HOPPE, Louise, NYC-M – 1886/04/26:5g
HOPPE, Lydia, NYC-B - 1895/06/03:4a
HOPPE, Mamie, 38, dept store detective, NYC-Bx – 1911/06/03:1d
HOPPE, Marie, 81, SPD Bremen/Gy – 1900/02/10:2e
HOPPE, Moritz, 73, chemist, NYC-M – 1898/10/02:5e
HOPPE, Reinhard, 63, Hoboken, NJ - 1916/03/16:6a

HOPPE, Richard, 62, wife Anna, 60, & granddaughter Louisa Byrnes, NYC-B – 1906/12/10:3a
HOPPE, Robert, Jersey City Heights, NJ – 1907/07/02:6a
HOPPEL, Charles, Dr., NYC-M – 1885/08/13:1g
HOPPEL, Marg., b. Borngesser, 67, NYC-M – 1889/07/19:4a
HOPPENTHALER, Elizabeth, 52, Irvington, NJ – 1910/06/10:3b
HOPPER, Heinrich Wilhelm, 41, NYC-M – 1901/12/19:4a
HOPPNER, Adolf, NYC-M – 1897/04/06:4a
HORACH, Paul, Newark, NJ – 1906/07/03:6a
HORAK, John, 73, un. cigarmkr, NYC-M - 1914/01/02:6a
HORAN, William A., machinist, union-leader & KoL veteran, NYC-B – 1889/11/12:1g, =15:1f, memorial meeting 25:1h, rev. 5 Dec:1a
HORBATH, Carl, 20, SP, NYC-M - 1916/08/29:2e
HORCHLER, Elizabeth, b. Schwabe, 38, NYC-SI - 1916/12/22:6a
HORENBURG, Frieda, child, NYC-M - 1895/07/30: 4a
HORIK, Steven, coal-miner, @ 1897 Hazleton Massacre
HORK, Ida, 40, NYC-B - 1896/01/28:2d
HORM, Ellen, NYC-M – 1880/09/10:4d
HORN % Kemmel, % Winarsky
HORN, Adam, 44, NYC-M - 1896/01/20:4a
HORN, Anton, grocer, NYC-M – 1880/07/01:1f
HORN, August, NYC-M – 1892/07/16:4a
HORN, Augusta, 77, NYC-M - 1916/12/02:1f
HORN, Carl Anton, 67, NYC-M – 1892/07/03:5c
HORN, Carl, 36, SP, baker, fr Frankfurt/Main, NYC-M? - 1913/10/14:1d, 15:2g,6a, 16:6a
HORN, Charles, policeman, NYC-B – 1900/10/09:4a
HORN, Ernst, NYC-B – 1906/04/11:4a
HORN, Felix, NYC? – 1889/01/15:4a
HORN, Georg, 77, ex-MdR for SPD – 1919/09/27:5d-e
HORN, Isaac, NYC-M – 1892/07/29:4a
HORN, John, 45, NYC-M – 1893/05/26:4a
HORN, Louise, 55, NYC-B – 1887/12/30:4a, 31:2d
HORN, Marie, NYC-M – 1897/12/16:4a
HORN, Mrs, 60, & son-in-law Max Greifeld, servant H. Dreier, NYC-M - 1879/02/15:1g, 24:4b, 03/14:1e
HORN, Theodore Von, 38, un. carp., NYC-M – 1897/02/02:1f
HORN, Tom, Western outlaw, exec. Cheyenne, Wyoming – 1903/11/21:1d
HORN, William, 51, un. carp., NYC-Bx – 1908/06/16:1d,6a, 17:6a
HORN, VAN, J., Negro, lynched near Trail Lake, Mississippi – 1904/06/04:3f
HORNBACHER, F., 17, NYC-B – 1902/05/15:4b

HORNBRUCH, Wilhelmine, Elizabeth, NJ - 1915/07/08:6a
HORNECKER, Wilhelm, 58, NYC-M - 1891/03/25:4a
HORNEICKER, Johanna, 58, NYC-B - 1901/07/04:1e
HORNER, A., Yonkers, NY - 1910/09/10:6a
HORNER, Harry, 45, worker at DuPont Powder Works Gibbstown, NJ, Paulsboro, NJ - 1913/12/09:1b
HORNER, Martha, 27, NYC-B - 1915/03/16:6c
HORNICKER, Auguste, 58, NYC-M - 1908/10/02:1e
HORNIKEL, Mrs, Berlin/Gy, + Newark, NJ - 1908/09/06:9f
HORNING, Ada, 37, Paterson, NJ - 1897/03/27:3c
HORNING, Charles, NYC-B - 1920/05/19:2a
HORNUNG, Friedrich, NYC-M - 1918/11/01:6a
HORNUNG, Louise, 8, NYC-M - 1896/01/25:1e
HORNY, John T., Union Hill, NJ - 1916/02/17:6a
HOROWITZ, Harry, exec. Ossining,NY - 1914/04/14:1g,2a-b,4a-b
HOROWITZ, Isidor, 28, USA 1906 fr Lemberg/Galicia, NYC-M - 1906/11/09:2e
HOROWITZ, Pauline, 19, @1911 Triangle Shirtwaist Fire, NYC-B - 1911/03/27:1d
HORR, John, un. cigarmaker, NYC-M - 1882/02/21:3c
HORRMAN, August, partner at Atlantic Brewing Co., NYC-SI - 1900/02/10:1b
HORST, Carl, 55, laundry mgr, NYC-M - 1897/03/23:3f
HORST, Henry, NYC-B - 1913/02/18:6a
HORSTMANN, Albert, 15, NYC - 1912/07/13:6a
HORSTMANN, Anna, NYC-M - 1901/05/12:5a
HORSTMANN, Christian, 47, NYC-B - 1917/02/15:6a
HORSTMANN, Heinrich, NYC-M? - 1894/03/28:4a
HORSTMANN, Henry, 38, NYC-M - 1910/04/25:6a
HORTELMANN, France, 75, NYC-B - 1905/12/31:1f
HORTER, Adam, Newark, NJ - 1917/02/27:6a
HORVAT, Steve, + during strike,McKees Rocks, PA - 1909/08/13:1c
HORVATEK, Albert, 56, SPO, MdL for Marburg/Krain - 1915/02/28:3c
HORVATH, Andreas, 23, carp., killed Budapest/Hungary at voting rights meeting - 1910/01/19:4e
HORVATH, John, un. carp, NYC-M - 1913/04/03:6a
HORVATH, Stephen, company fireman, NYC-M? - 1914/06/02:3d
HORWATH, Marie, 40, Swiss, NYC-M - 1879/07/19:1e
HORWAY, Johanna, 38, Ella, 5, Karl, 1, NYC-M, + @ Genl Slocum - 1904/06/17:3b
HORWITZ, Charles, NYC-M - 1896/04/21:1f
HOSANN, Robert, 61, machinist, NYC-M - 1892/04/16:4a

HOSCHLE, Heinrich, 25, sailor, Hoboken, NJ - 1915/07/26:1c
HOSE, Sam, Negro, lynched Palmetto, GA – 1899/04/25:1b, 2a-b
HOSEAS, Carl, un. cigarmaker, NYC-M - 1879/08/25:3a
HOSMER, Harriet, US sculptress – 1908/04/19:20f-g
HOSSELMEYER, Henry, 24, NYC-M – 1912/05/18:6a
HOSSER, Charles, brewer or cooper, NYC-M – 1900/12/09:5b
HOTTENFELS, John, NYC-M – 1880/06/29:1c
HOTTENRATH, Catherine, NYC-M – 1882/08/23:4d
HOTTER, Bernhard, cooper, 56, NYC-B – 1890/01/01:1g
HOTZ % Engelbrecht, % Kuhn
HOUGHTON, George, stoker, killed during strike, Buffalo, NY – 1909/09/01:2c
HOUPT, Carl, 47, NYC-B – 1908/06/10:6a
HOUSAR, Martin, Elizabeth, NJ – 1910/03/27:7b
HOUSKA, Frank, NYC-B - 1917/01/05:6a
HOUSMANN, Heinrich, Dr., NYC-B – 1892/06/11:4a
HOUSTON, J.J., Irish patriot, exec. Dublin - 1916/05/09:1b
HOVELING, Sophie von, NYC-M – 1901/08/20:4a
HOVEY, Edward, to be exec. NYC-M – 1883/07/19:4d, 23:3a, 9 Oct:4d, 10:1f, 11:4c, 13:1g, 15:1c, 17:1g, 18:3b, 19:1b, done 20:2g-3a
HOVORKA, Joseph, cigarmaker, Czech, NYC-M – 1898/05/27:3f
HOWARD, George, gangster, + 4 June 1878, mother a German fr Strassburg, his life - 1879/03/10:1d-e
HOWARD, John, Rev., Negro,lynched Hawkinsville,GA – 1909/12/03:4a-b
HOWARTH, Joseph, 26, linotype operator, Paterson, NJ – 1911/03/07:3b
HOWE, Julia Ward, US feminist, 88th anniv. 1907/05/26:20a-c, + 1910/10/23:20a-b
HOWELL, David T., judge & politician, Newark, NJ – 1908/10/18:1g
HOWELLS, Henry Dean, 83, US writer - 1920/05/30:4f-g
HOXIE, H. M., v-p of Jay Gould's railroad empire, such as Manhattan Elevated, NYC-M – 1886/11/24:4c
HOXSEY, Thomas D., 66, polit., abolitionist & friend of labor, Haledon, NJ – 1881/06/01:2b
HOYT, Edwin, exec. Bridgeport, CT – 1880/05/14:1b, 17:1d
HRABI, Emilie, 38, cigarmaker, Czech?, NYC-M? – 1912/11/12:3e
HRABOWSKYI, Pawlo, Ukrainian poet, + in a Czarist goal, by M. Kiczura – 1903/12/06:7f-h
HRADECKY, Franz J., un. printer, Jersey City Heights, NJ – 1911/12/21:6a
HRDLICKA, Joseph, NYC-Q – 1917/12/22:6a
HUBACH, Carl Otto, fin. edit. NYSZ, NYC-M - 1915/01/10:1h,7a
HUBACH, Hedwig, 18, Newark, NJ - 1894/06/05:4a
HUBER % Denig, % Scherpf

HUBER, Bertha, 78, NYC-M – 1899/06/09:1g
HUBER, C., NYC-B – 1913/04/29:6a
HUBER, Charles, German explorer, fr Strasburg/Elsass, + in Arabia – 1885/01/18:7e-f
HUBER, Elise, 53, NYC-B – 1893/11/21:4a
HUBER, F. Max, brewer, + 6 Apr, NYC-B - 1917/04/13:3e
HUBER, Frank X., 38, NYC-B – 1912/09/11:6a
HUBER, Franz, un. carp., 52, NYC-M – 1905/10/31:4a
HUBER, Georg, 45, jeweler, NYC-M – 1902/03/01:3c
HUBER, Gottfried, NYC-B – 1899/02/05:1g
HUBER, John J., NYC-B - 1894/08/28:4a
HUBER, Joseph, 68, SP?, hatter,*Bavarian Suebia, Yonkers, NY - 1915/03/25:6a, 31:2e
HUBER, Josephine, NYC-M – 1908/02/18:6a
HUBER, Lukas, brewery worker, + 20 Fb, inquest, NYC-B – 1886/03/12:2d
HUBER, Mary, b. Guenther, NYC-B - 1917/06/08:6d
HUBER, Max, NYC-B - 1918/10/12:6a
HUBER, Minie, NYC-B - 1918/03/18:6a
HUBER, Otto, NYC-B – 1909/01/01:6a
HUBER, Peter, NYC-Bx – 1911/02/27:6a
HUBER, Philip, 48, brewer, NYC-M – 1897/08/15:5a
HUBER, Sabina, 58, Newark, NJ - 1878/03/29:3a
HUBER, Theodor, NYC-M - 1920/02/01:12a
HUBER, Theresa, NYC-M – 1892/08/09:4a
HUBER, William, shoemaker, NYC-M – 1896/12/25:4a
HUBERT, George, 72, NYC-M – 1892/06/30:4a
HUBERT, Leonhard, 61, NYC-M – 1905/05/18:6a
HUBERT, Marie, NYC-M, fam. 1887/04/15:3d
HUBERTUS, Franz, un. carp., NYC-M – 1910/03/22:6a
HUBNER, Joachim, NYC-M – 1881/02/14:3c
HUBOLD, Albert, un. baker, *23 Jan 1856 Proschmuenden/Gy, Madison County, NJ – 1911/10/12:5e
HUCHSHAUSEN, Anna, 20, & baby, USA 1890, NYC-M – 1892/04/18:2f
HUCK, Gertrude, b. Sturm, Jersey City Heights, NJ – 1898/12/30:4a
HUDEC, Josef, SP, Pole, un. typesetter & MdR for Lemberg - 1915/02/21:3c, =5 Mr:4f
HUDLICK, Michael, Slovak RR worker, + Roseville, NJ – 1910/04/15:1a
HUDSON, Cl., Negro, lynched Belgreen, AL – 1891/03/31:1b
HUEBNER, Carl, 46, secy of Germania Theater, USA 1850s fr Vienna, NYC-M – 1880/09/26:5f, 27:3b
HUEBNER, Carl, artist, NYC-M – 1900/08/10:3b

HUEBNER, Frederick, 34, NYC-M - 1918/10/30:6a
HUEBNER, Frederick, mason, NYC-B - 1882/03/01:1f
HUEBNER, Gustav, NYC-M - 1903/09/24:4a
HUEBNER, Johanna, b. Decke, NYC-M - 1899/10/12:4a
HUEBNER, John, NYC-B - 1907/09/27:6a
HUEBNER, Max, 50, lawyer, NYC-SI - 1904/01/11:1d
HUEBNER, Paul, 11, NYC-Q - 1913/12/31:2e, 1 Jan. 1914:6a
HUEBSCH, Adolph, Dr., Rabbi, NYC - 1884/10/14:1f
HUEBSCH, Benjamin, NYC-M - 1891/07/09:1f
HUEFNER, Adam, NYC-M - 1907/03/09:6a
HUEFNER, Georg, 4, NYC-M - 1908/01/20:6a
HUEFNER, George, 25, NYC-M - 1893/04/21:4a
HUEFNER, Margarethe, 49, NYC-Q - 1918/01/05:6a,fam. 11:6a
HUEGEL, Harry, Jersey City Heights, NJ - 1918/10/12:6a
HUEGELMAYER, Frank, Elizabeth, NJ - 1913/04/01:6a
HUEGIN, Ernst, NYC-M - 1896/12/03:4a
HUEGLE, Wendelin, 34, NYC-M - 1880/02/21:4f
HUEGLI, William, enbalmer, NYC-M - 1908/07/18:1f
HUEHNEWINCKELL, Elsa, infant, NYC-M - 1890/07/06:5a
HUELSEBERG, George A., NYC-B - 1899/07/10:4a
HUELSEN, Fritz, 66, un. carp., NYC-M - 1905/01/02:4a, 3:4a
HUELSEN, Henry P., 29, un. painter, NYC-M - 1896/09/24:4a
HUELSENBOESCH, Anna & Maria, infants, NYC-M - 1882/07/29:4c
HUELSEWEDE, Anna, 50, NYC-B - 1904/09/19:4a
HUELZ, Barbara, 70, NYC-M - 1897/01/03:5a
HUEMER, John, 58, NYC-M - 1878/01/28:3d
HUEMMER, George, NYC-Q - 1910/12/30:6a
HUEMMER, Karl, 43, NYC-B - 1908/09/25:6a
HUEPFEL, Adolph G., 73, brewery owner, NYC-Bx - 1917/07/16:1d
HUER, Catherina, 63, NYC-B - 1903/07/30:4b
HUERLEMANN, John, un. carp., NYC-M - 1885/09/21:3a
HUERTA, Victoriano, Mexican general, - 1916/01/14:1d, 15:4d
HUESER, Auguste, NYC-B - 1893/10/15:1g
HUESING % Grewe; HUETHER % Kruekel
HUESING, Carl, NYC-M - 1892/07/29:4a
HUETER, Julius, 31, un. cigarmaker, NYC-Bx - 1903/03/03:6a, fam. 5:7a
HUETHER, Josef, un. carp., NYC-M - 1889/04/06:4a
HUETTEMANN, Ewald, Elizabeth, NJ - 1912/05/18:6a
HUETTENBERGER, Peter, 56, SPD Elberfeld/Gy - 1901/02/07:2e
HUFMANN, Conrad, NYC-M - 1891/04/12:5a
HUFNAGEL, J., NYC-Bx - 1907/06/07:6a
HUFNAGEL, Jacob, North Bergen, NJ - 1917/06/09:6a

HUFNAGEL, Mathilde, b. Heinrich, NYC-B – 1891/06/25:4a
HUFNAGEL, Wilhelm, SP Jersey City Heights, NJ - 1918/09/02:6a, =4:6b, fam. 10:6a; mem. 1919/08/31:7a, 1920/08/31:6a
HUFNER, John H., 25, NYC-Q - 1918/04/26:6a
HUGER, Susan, 6, Clifton, NJ – 1908/10/20:3c
HUGERSHOFF, William, NYC-Q - 1918/07/13:2f, 6a, fam. 17:6a
HUGHES, Clovis, French soc. Poet, journalist & polit., + Paris – 1907/06/13:4d
HUGHES, Jack, lynched Columbia, MO - 1915/11/01:2f
HUGI, Gottlieb, un. carp., NYC-M – 1890/04/21:4a
HUGO, Adele, 85, daughter of Victor, + near Paris - 1915/04/23:6a
HUGO, Victor, French writer & social critic, 80th anniv. – 1881/02/26:2d, 20 Mr:4g-5b, 25 Mr:3d-e, 84th birthday 1885/03/29:3d-e, + Paris 23 May:1a-b, 2b, 24:1a-b, 4a-d, 26:1a-b, =27:1a, 28:1a, =30:2a-b, 1 June:1a, 2:1a-b, 2 June:1a, 11:2c-d, NYC Progressive forces grieves 1 June:4c
HUHN, Charles, un. baker, NYC-M - 1894/07/05:4a
HUHN, Frederick W., (+16 Nov), NYC-B, inquest 1882/11/24:3a
HUHN, Heinrich, 81, '48er, freethinker, Belleville, IL – 1911/11/26:4f-g
HUISBERG, Adelheid C., b. Bollten, 36, NYC-B – 1892/06/28:4a
HULBERG, Hulda, 39, NYC-B - 1895/10/29: 4b
HULLMUND, Alie J., 27, & baby Frederick, NYC-B – 1907/10/16:2c
HULSTEDE, Christine, fr Bremen/Gy, NYC-B – 1902/06/20:4a
HUMANN, Klara, 22, NYC-M – 1899/03/05:5a
HUMANN, Viola, 4, NYC-Bx – 1907/08/03:6a
HUMBSER, Johann, singer, 63,* Fuerth/Gy + Cincinatti, OH – 1887/07/29:6c
HUMEL, Mrs, NYC-M – 1897/11/26:4a
HUMER, Hilda Emma, 3, NYC-Bx - 1920/03/04:6a
HUMMEL % Brandmeier, % Dardenne
HUMMEL, Anna, b. Faultisch, NYC-M – 1892/06/20:4a
HUMMEL, Conrad, 58, NYC-B – 1886/06/08:2c
HUMMEL, George, + 31 May 1886, mem. – 1887/05/31:3d
HUMMEL, Gottlob, ?32, NYC-M – 1891/02/10:4a
HUMMEL, Gottlob, NYC-M – 1891/06/05:4a
HUMMEL, Gustav, 52, carp., NYC-M – 1886/08/03:2d
HUMMEL, James H., 72, ventilator manuf., Mt Vernon, NY – 1913/02/27:2g
HUMMEL, Josiah, exec. Lebanon, PA – 1880/05/14:1b
HUMMEL, Karoline, 74, NYC-B – 1891/12/10:4a
HUMMEL, Leonhardt, baker, NYC-M - 1913/11/10:6a
HUMMEL, William, exec. Williamsport, PA – 1900/06/06:3b
HUMMELL, Clara, 15, NYC-M – 1900/05/11:3c

HUMPF, M., 44, grocery clerk, Jersey City, NJ – 1885/02/27:3c
HUMPHRIES, John E., 63, Seattle, WA judge who jailed 100 soc. in 1913 - 1915/05/31:2d
HUND % Goebel
HUND, Eduard, 63, butcher, Jersey City, NJ – 1885/08/07:2g
HUND, John Otto, 63, pres. League for Personal Freedom, NYC-M – 1888/06/12:3b, 4a, =14:1f
HUNDERTPFUND, Wilhelm, 68, NYC-M – 1906/12/08:6a
HUNDEMANN, Charles, NYC-B – 1891/03/18:4a
HUNDMANN, comrade, SP in London, 70th birthday – 1912/03/25:4c
HUNDT, Emil, 56, NYC-M – 1893/10/30:4a
HUNELMANN, Louis, fresco-painter, missing, pres. +, NYC-M – 1891/03/28:2h
HUNER, Georg, 30, fr Buchholz/Hannover, candystore in Boston, + NYC-B – 1880/11/30:4c
HUNKEN, Catherina, 22, NYC-M – 1891/03/09:4a
HUNOLD, Friedrich, 66, tailor, * Gy, NYC-M - 1894/05/25:1h
HUNSTEIN, Conrad, 20, painter on ship Saale, @1900 dock fire, Hoboken, NJ 1900/07/03:1c, =6:1h
HUNTENBERG, Charles A., 69, NYC-B – 1892/06/07:4a
HUNTER, Benjamin, exec. Camden, NJ - 1879/01/09:1f, 10:4b
HUNTER, Charles, Negro, lynch. Springfield,IL – 1908/08/16:1g,7f, 17:4c
HUNTINGDON, Collis P., 79, RR magnate, crit notes – 1900/08/16:2a-b
HUNYAK, Rudolf, un. carp., Avenel, NJ - 1914/03/29:7c
HUNZER % Friedel, HUPPERT % Lambert
HUPF, Karl Ludwig, 60, NYC-M – 1891/06/24:4a
HUPFER, August, NYC-Q – 1908/10/14:6a
HUPP, Friedrich Christian, 56, NYC-M – 1892/07/30:4a, 31:5c
HUPPELSBERG, Helene, 55, NYC-B - 1878/08/04:3f
HUPPER, or HUPERT, Mr., worker, NYC-M - 1879/02/11:1g
HURD, Minnie M., 60, ret. PS teacher, NYC-B - 1913/08/08:2d
HURLEY, Daniel, leader of local clockmakers, NYC-B – 1882/12/12:1f
HURP, Leopold, 72, NYC-M - 1878/01/28:3d
HURRIER, F., NYC-M – 1903/09/16:4a
HURST, Frederick, Hoboken, NJ – 1904/01/16:4a
HURTIG, Fred, 21, grocery clerk, NYC-M – 1893/05/26:2c-d
HUSEMANN, Hermann, 52, un. metalworker & SPD alderman in Bielefeld/Gy – 1907/07/18:3a
HUSENITZER, Ferdinand, Newark, NJ – 1906/06/03:5b
HUSENITZER, Maria, Newark, NJ – 1911/12/28:6a
HUSER, Adolphg, 38, bartender, Hoboken, NJ – 1898/09/06:1d
HUSI, Joseph, Swiss?, NYC-M - 1879/05/11:8a

HUSK, Bela, un. baker, NYC-M – 1910/11/02:6a
HUSSEY, Jack, police captain, NYC-M – 1887/06/23:2f, 22:3a, 24:4a, 28:2g, 12 Aug:1e, notes on + 8 Oct:4a, 11:4d, 12:2e, 13:1g, 14:4a, 15:1g
HUSTMEYER, John W., 60, ret. NYC hotelier, Hoboken,NJ - 1913/05/26:2a
HUT, Michael, NYC-B – 1901/07/04:4a
HUTCHENREUTER, Alvin, un. carp., NYC-Q - 1917/07/24:6a
HUTCHINSON, William, iron worker in Troy, NY, + during strike – 1883/06/13:1d, 12:1d, =14:1d-f, 2a, 15:1e-f, 16:1c-d, 17:4a-c, 20:1d,14 Jy:1e
HUTH, Emil, 60, SPD Stoetteritz/Saxony, un. printer - 1914/11/01:3b
HUTH, Louis, 52, un. carp., Richmond, VA - 1920/12/24:6a
HUTH, Louise, 48, SP?, NYC-M – 1915/11/04:6a,5:6a, fam.18:6a
HUTH, Michael, un. cigarmaker, SLP, NYC-M – 1882/11/01:1g
HUTH, Rudolph, SPD Bernburg/Thueringen/Gy – 1908/04/05:3d
HUTLER, Jakob, merchant, fr Bremen?/Gy, NYC-M – 1885/06/26:3b
HUTMACHER, Christian, Yonkers, NY – 1904/10/24:4a, fam. 27:4a
HUTMANN, Ernst, NYC-M – 1908/03/31:6a
HUTSON, Tip, Negro, lynched Palmetto, GA – 1899/03/17:2h
HUTTEL-MAIER, M. Pauline, b. Mack, 28, NYC-M – 1892/07/28:4a
HUTTEN, Michael, NYC-M – 1912/07/20:6a
HUTTENMEYER, Augusta, b. Furthmann, 28, Jersey City Heights, NJ – 1912/09/07:6a, fam. 13:6a
HUTTER, Karl, 62, inventor of Portland beer cork, NYC-M - 1913/06/17:2f, his will 27:2e
HUTTER, Luise, b. Heck, NYC-M – 1910/08/29:6a
HUTTER, Thomas, 59, NYC-B – 1919/11/07:8a
HUTTESHEIMER, Valentin, 43, NYC-M – 1893/12/27:4a
HUTTMANN, Hermann, NYC-M – 1898/04/05:4a
HUTTWAGNER, Albert, NYC-M - 1917/05/13:7a
HUX, Anton, NYC-M – 1919/09/13:8a
HUXHAGEN % Guenscht
HUYGENS, Cornelia, Dutch Socialist & writer, + Amsterdam – 1902/11/13:2e
HYBESCH, Josef, Czech SP, MdR for Bruenn/Moravia, 60th birthday – 1910/02/20:3c-d, 70th birthday - 1920/05/11:4b
HYLLA, Franz, un. cigarmaker, NYC-Bx – 1910/03/13:7c
HYMAN, Abraham, 84, NYC-M – 1893/12/31:5c
HYMAN, E. Louis, 55, innkeep, NYC-M – 1903/07/25:2h
HYMANN, Otto, un. butcher, NYC-B - 1918/11/11:3a
IBLER, Josef, Jersey City, NJ - 1915/03/30:6b

IBSEN, Carl, 65, SP,fr Frankfurt/Main,USA 1880s, un. brewer, ed. NYC Brauerzeitung and Baeckerzeitung, labor org. in OH & PA, then NYC, NYC-M - 1915/09/24:1f,2b,4b-c,6a, 26:11d,=27:2e, fam.28:6a
IBSEN, Hendrik, Norwegian poet, 1906/05/24:1a, 3e, 27:4a-b, 27:9b-e, =2 June:1c, 3:11e-f,12a-b, 17:4h, & workers' art 29 Jy 1907:4e-f. & Marxism 20 June 1909:6c-e
IBSEN, Marie, b. Sperling, 52, *Frankfurt/Main, SP, Nanuet, NJ – 1911/03/14:2c, 19:13f-g
IBURG, Charlie, NYC-M – 1890/07/06:5a
ICKE, Elizabeth, 65, NYC-M – 1897/01/16:4a, 17:5c
ICKE, Rosa Elise, 6, NYC-M – 1888/03/29:3b
ICKEN, Israel, un. carp., 54, NYC-B – 1906/07/08:7a
IDE, August, 65, mason, SPD Halberstadt/Gy – 1908/04/26:3d
IDELHEISER, Max, 14, Newark, NJ – 1886/11/19:2f
IDEN, Grace, 10, Henrietta, 9, NYC-M, + @ Genl Slocum – 1904/06/17:3b, 22:1d
IFFLAND, William J., 60, NYC-Bx - 1917/11/16:6a
IGLY, John, West Newark, NJ – 1912/09/21:6a
IGNATIEW, Alexis Pawlowitsch, ex-governor of Kiew, killed by revol. – 1906/12/23:1a, =27:2b
IHM, Daniel, 49, butcher, Newark, NJ – 1886/03/26:2e
IHRER, Emma, SPD Berlin/Gy – 1911/01/21:4e, =29:3b. Mon. inaug. Cem. Friedrichsfeld – 1912/09/22:3a
IHRLICH, Jacob, un. carp., NYC-M - 1913/05/09:6a
ILCHERT, Friedrich, NYC-Bx – 1909/04/02:6a
ILG, Alex, 4, New Haven, CT – 1889/04/26:4a
ILG, Alfred, 62, Swiss, engineer, advisor to king of Ethiopia, + Switzerland – 1916/01/09:1c
ILG, William F., 22, NYC-Bx – 1905/10/30:4a
ILIC, Danilo, exec. Sarajewo 3 Fb for + archduke Franz Ferdinand - 1915/03/02:4d, 18:3d-e
ILL, Viola, 17, Newark, NJ – 1903/02/20:1c, =21:1c
ILLG, Gustav A., 42, NYC-M – 1896/08/15:4a
ILLGE % Boehm
ILLGEN, comrade, 38, un. metallworker & SPD activist in Meissen/Sax. – 1909/07/25:3d
ILLIG, Charles, 34, lithographer, NYC-M - 1894/01/07:1h
ILLIG, G., 65, NYC-M – 1893/08/08:4a
ILLIG, John A., 4, NYC-Bx – 1890/07/11:4a
ILLING, Laura, NYC-Q – 1911/11/29:6a, 30:6a
ILLMENSEE, Matthew, 47, pillow store, NYC-M – 1891/02/17:1f
ILMANSEL, George, 47, janitor, NYC-M – 1885/06/24:1f

ILSE, John, un. cigarmaker, NYC-B – 1887/12/07:2h
ILTGEN, Peter, NYC-M – 1913/03/08:6a, fam. 11:6a
IMAND, Joseph, 44, un. furnit. Maker, NYC-M – 1890/02/22:4a, =25:2f
IMANDT, Balthasar, 42, NYC-M – 1883/01/26:3c
IMBECK, William, un. brewery worker, NYC-M - 1894/07/27:4a
IMBER, Naftali Herz, Jiddisch poet, NYC-M – 1909/10/11:1a
IMBERG % Unsold
IMFELD, Joseph J., 22, jeweler, Newark, NJ, (dying) - 1879/03/22:4d
IMGRUND, Gertrude, 68, Hoboken, NJ – 1910/12/13:6a
IMGRUND, Heinrich, NYC-M – 1889/08/10:4a
IMHAUS, Ida M., NYC-B – 1903/05/20:4a
IMHOF % Rothfus
IMHOF, Lorenz, un. carp., NYC-B – 1887/04/01:3d
IMHOFF, Bernhard, sculptor, NYC-M – 1882/07/18:3g
IMHOFF, Emma, 63, NYC-M – 1882/12/25:1e
IMHOFF, Katherina, NYC-M – 1890/03/31:4a
IMHOFF, Maria, b. Scherger, NYC-B – 1906/07/31:6a
IMLER, Albert, 23, NYC-M – 1892/12/26:1d
IMM, Joseph, NYC-M - 1917/06/08:6a
IMMELMANN, Lt, German air ace, War 1 - 1916/06/25:1b
IMMENHAUSEN, Hermann, pianomaker, dying, NYC-M – 1880/03/26:4a
IMMERGRUEN, Paul Julius, G-A poet & journalist, + Springfield, NJ –
    1900/01/01:4b
IMMESBERGER, Friedrich W., 1, NYC-M – 1886/02/26:3b
IMMESBERGER, Katie, b. Hasselberger, NYC-M – 1890/08/19:4a
IMMHOF, Frank, NYC-B - 1916/06/22:6a
IMMICKE, Friedrich, 63, un. cigarmaker, NYC-M – 1904/01/24:5a
IMPOLUZZO, Antonio, innkeep, NYC-M, exec. Ossining, NY -
    1917/05/18:2a
IMSEN, Carl, NYC-M – 1893/09/17:5a
IMWOLDE, Johann, SPD Bremen, shoemaker, alderman - 1915/08/22:3c-d
INERSCHICK, Mr., fam. 1891/02/17:4a
INGERMAN, Anna, Dr., #, *Russia, active in G-A SP & Eastern Europ.
    Labor, her life (not +), NYC-M – 1911/02/26:19d-e
INGERSOLL, Robert G., the atheist philosopher & reformer, his life
    1880/05/30:4c-d, & 11 Oct:2a-b. Posit Obit 1899/07/22:2h, 23:4a-b,
    will 24:3h, =25.3b, 28:2h
INGRAM, Annie, servant, fr Birmingham/Engl., murdered 24 Mr 87 near
    Rahway, NJ, first thought to be Annie Larsen – 1887/04/17:1d, 22:1f,
    26:3a, 28:2d, 29:2h, 3 May:2e, 13 June:2d,16:1e-f, 17:2g, 29 Sept:4c, 20
    Oct:1b, 21:1g, 25:1g
INSEL % Rieding

INTERBITZEN, D., NYC-Q – 1911/08/05:6a
INTLEKORFER % Maier
IRELAND, John, 80, Archbishop, St Paul, MN - 1918/09/26:1g
IRMSCHER, Wilhelm, 59, NYC-M – 1881/03/21:3c
IRON, Gabriel, NYC-M – 1891/09/02:4a
IRONS, Martin, 68, machinist & union leader, + Bunceville, TX – 1900/11/19:1b
IRONS, Martin, leader 1886 RR strike, + homeless in Texas after blacklisted, obit by Eugene Debs – 1905/01/15:9c-d
IRVING, Fannie, NYC-M?, +@ Genl Slocum – 1904/06/17:1b, 18:1c
ISAACS, Abraham, un. cigarmaker, NYC-B - 1895/06/13:4a
ISBERGER, Louis, 70, NYC-M – 1892/07/31:5c
ISELIN, Charlie, NYC-B – 1891/07/14:4a
ISENBERG, Celia, 17, @1911 Triangle Shirtwaist Fire, NYC-M – 1911/03/28:1c
ISENECKER, Wilhelm, SP, * 1847 Altona/Hamburg, USA 1881, un. cigarmaker, Boston, MA - 1915/08/06:2d
ISING, Gustav, 64, West New York, NJ – 1911/07/28:2d
ISLER, comrade, SLP, worker, * Switzerland, Pittsfield, MA – 1884/08/24:7g
ISLER, Herman, 5, Rose, 2, NYC-B – 1912/02/01:6c
ISRAEL, Henry, 32, un. waiter, NYC-M – 1892/08/14:5f, 15:4a
ISRAELSOHN, Behr, 50, NYC-B – 1892/07/18:2d, 5 Aug:2c
ISSLER, Anna, 44, NYC-B – 1896/05/05:4a
ITALIENER, Benjamin, NYC-M – 1905/12/30:4a
ITALY, Umberto, King – 1900/07/30:1a, 31:1a, 2a-b, 1 Aug:1a-b, 2a-b, 2:1g-h, 2a-c, 3:1a-b, 4:1f-g, 5:1a-b, h, 4a-b, etc, =10:1c. S.a. G. Bresci
ITGESS, Simon, painter, fr Russia, NYC-Brownsville – 1897/07/01:1e
ITTLER, Caroline, b. Wolf, 6X?, NYC-M – 1892/07/25:4a
ITTNER, Walter E., un. painter, NYC-B – 1913/04/12:6a, 13:7a
IUGIGO, Shikok, first Japanese to be exec. In USA, on 3 Fb – 1889/12/17:1h, to be 5 May 22 Mr 1890:1h, 17 Sept::2h, appeal 8 Jan 1891:2f, refused 3 Jy:1g, done 14 Jy:2e, 16:1h
IZONSKY, Adam, 31, dying, shot during strike, Auburn, NY – 1913/04/05:1g
JABANSWKY, Anton, 30, un. carp., NYC-M – 1901/10/25:4a
JACKSON, Charles, NYC, exec. Ossining, NY – 1905/07/18:1e
JACKSON, Kid, Negro, lynched Montgomery, AL - 1915/08/19:2b
JACKSON, Mary, Negro, lynched Marshall, TX – 1912/02/16:1b
JACKSON, Will, Negro, lynched Tunica, MS – 1907/10/13:1b
JACKSON, William Henry, 74, bank cashier, NYC-M – 1911/07/28:1e, 30:1f, 2 Aug:1f, murderer tried 22:1e, 23:2f, 29:1g, 30:1c, jail 2 Sept:1c

JACKSTAEDT, Joseph, un. carpenter, NYC-Bx – 1911/06/30:6a
JACOB, Abraham, NYC-M – 1890/03/18:4a
JACOB, Heinrich, 44, NYC-M – 1892/06/11:4a
JACOB, Heinrich, SP, NYC-Bx - 1914/10/08:6a
JACOB, John, Jersey City Heights, NJ – 1906/10/30:6a
JACOB, Lilie Antonie, 1, NYC-M - 1878/06/20:3b
JACOB, Louis, SPD Leipzig/Gy activist – 1907/12/29:3e
JACOB, Louise, 6, NYC-M - 1878/12/21:3a
JACOB, Mathias, un. baker, NYC-Bx - 1914/01/16:6a
JACOBI, Aaron, ex-NYC, + Frankfurt/Main – 1889/02/14:4a
JACOBI, Abraham, Dr. med., * 6 May 1830 Hartum/Weser, USA 1853, 48'er, co-fdr German Hospital & Mt Sinai Hospital, 70th birthday 4 May 1900:2b; Socialist in his youth, crit note that now an enemy of org. labor 1 Mr 1910:4b-c, 6 Mr 10:13a, 13:13b-c. + Bolton Landing, NY, obit by Dr. Aronson crit. his extreme pro-British stance - 1919/07/12:2g, 13:6a-d
JACOBI, Albert, un. carp., NYC-M – 1904/05/07:4a
JACOBI, Alwin, un. cigarmaker, killed during strike, NYC-M – 1885/03/24:1e-f, 25:1f, 2c
JACOBI, Emilie, 64, NYC-M - 1919/03/22:6a, fam. 26:6a, mem. 1920/03/19:6a
JACOBI, Gustav A., 42, NYC-M - 1917/02/02:6a, 3:6a
JACOBI, Gustav, tobacco expert, fr Leipzig?, NYC-M – 1905/03/13:1g, 16:3d
JACOBI, Herman's wife, War 2, NYC-Q - 1914/09/16:3e
JACOBI, Josef, 78, NYC-M - 1920/05/10:6a
JACOBI, Margarethe, 46, NYC-M – 1887/03/28:1d
JACOBS % Fahl, Preusse, % Riechelmann
JACOBS, Albert, NYC-B – 1901/06/03:4a
JACOBS, Auguste, un. cigar maker, NYC-M – 1886/12/30:3b
JACOBS, Clara, 5, NYC-M – 1881/07/18:3b
JACOBS, Friedericke, 36, NYC-M – 1896/12/04:2f
JACOBS, Friedrich, 48, NYC-M – 1891/07/26:4a
JACOBS, Heinrich's wife, NYC-M – 1898/04/11:4a
JACOBS, Isaac, fr Poland, NYC-M – 1890/02/17:1f-g, 18:1h, 12 Mr:1f-g, 13:1h
JACOBS, Jacob, 45, used clothes dealer, NYC-B – 1880/02/27:2g
JACOBS, John, 63, innkeep, War 2, Hoboken, NJ - 1917/02/09:2e
JACOBS, Julius, driver, NYC-M – 1900/01/02:1d
JACOBS, Marcus J., 43, mgr Columbia Theater, Newark, NJ – 1907/09/27:3c
JACOBS, Pauline, 64, NYC-B - 1915/10/27:6a
JACOBS, William, 56, Jersey City Heights, NJ – 1905/02/18:4a

JACOBSEN % Zeitler
JACOBSEN, Beta Margaretha, 61, NYC-M – 1892/07/06:4a
JACOBSEN, Henry, un. cigarmaker, NYC-M – 1893/03/04:4a
JACOBSEN, Hermann, NYC-M – 1893/10/31:4a
JACOBSEN, J. S. M., ship carpenter from Hamburg, who led 8-hr day movement in Nelson/New Zealand, 82nd birthday of a brave man – 1906/01/02:3h
JACOBSEN, Katherina, NYC-M – 1906/02/20:4a, fam. 25:5a
JACOBSON, Adolph, NYC-M – 1893/12/30:4a
JACOBSON, Charles A., 44, upholsterer, fr Sweden, NYC-M – 1890/06/10:4d
JACOBSON, Christian, 33, watchman, NYC-M – 1897/01/02:1f
JACOBSON, Mary, 60, NYC-M - 1894/01/12:4a
JACOBSON, Sam, 54, un. cigarmaker, SDP, *Grabow/Stettin/Gy, NYC-M – 1903/11/20:2f, 4a, 21:4a, 22:5c, =23:2f, fam. 23:4a
JACOBY, Alphons, 66, NYC-M - 1919/03/01:1g
JACOBY, Hermann, NYC-M – 1905/01/14:1g
JACOBY, Johann, '48er, *1805 Koenigsberg/Gy – 1896/04/12:7a-c, 19:7a-e
JACOBY, Julius, NYC-M – 1891/05/23:4d
JACOBY, Leopold, socialist poet, journalist & contrib. to NYVZ, * Lauenburg/Gy, + Zuerich/CH - 1896/01/07:1c, 2a-b
JACOBY, Martha, NYC-B - 1913/05/02:6a
JACOBY, Max, 28, Hoboken, NJ – 1891/03/02:4a
JACOBY, Max, Dr. med., social reformer, Roosevelt, NJ - 1915/04/11:9g
JACOBY, Oscar, 52, NYC-M – 1902/03/30:5a, 31:4a
JACOBY, Otto, 60, un. baker, NYC-Q - 1914/03/27:1f
JACOBY, Rosalie, 63, NYC-M – 1892/11/13:5b
JADLINOWSKI, Minna, NYC-M – 1891/05/08:4a
JAECK, Robert, un. carp., NYC-B – 1910/09/26:6a
JAECKH, Gustav, SPD Leipzig, * 12 Oc 1866 Salach/Wuertt., – 1907/01/16:4d
JAECKLE, Christian, 54, NYC-B – 1886/04/12:4e
JAECKLE, Hermann, SPD Frankfurt-Ostend, War 1 - 1914/11/01:3b
JAECKSTEDT, Christian, un. carp., NYC-Bx - 1913/08/17:7b
JAEGELER, John, 90, NYC-M – 1891/04/09:4a
JAEGER % Hauck, % Meier, % Wingenfield
JAEGER, Adolph S., 50, fr Koblenz/Gy, businessman, USA 1868, NYC-M – 1893/06/20:1h
JAEGER, Agnes Tanner, 47, NYC-M - 1895/09/28: 4a
JAEGER, Andreas, 80, NYC-M – 1884/07/15:4d
JAEGER, Charles, 38, worker in chair factory, & 3 kids, Binghamton, NY – 1899/08/05:1g
JAEGER, Clara, NYC-M – 1897/08/05:1h,3c

JAEGER, David, 65, NYC-Bx – 1909/11/07:7b
JAEGER, Elise, b. Ladousseur, NYC-B – 1891/03/02:4a
JAEGER, Emma, b. Hecht, 50, NYC-M – 1902/09/07:5b
JAEGER, Emma, NYC-M – 1887/04/18:3d
JAEGER, Franz, 40, SLP, NYC-M – 1880/10/14:3a, =15:1f
JAEGER, Franz, 57, un. typesetter, NYC-M – 1907/07/03:6a, 4:6a
JAEGER, Franz, typesetter, SP Vienna/Austria, lived USA 1880s–1908/06/07:3e
JAEGER, Gotthelf, NYC-B – 1908/11/07:3c
JAEGER, Hermann, 61, un. cigarmaker, NYC-M – 1908/02/10:3b
JAEGER, Jacob, un. baker, NYC-M - 1919/08/11:6a
JAEGER, Josef, Hoboken, NJ – 1889/01/09:3d
JAEGER, Konrad, 65, NYC-B – 1908/08/24:6a, 25:6a, 23:7b
JAEGER, Leonhard, 40, carp., NYC-M – 1881/07/11:1g
JAEGER, Ludwig E., ex-clerk at German Consulate Chicago, +Wintrop, MA with daughters Anita, 4, & Olie, 5 – 1911/11/05:1f
JAEGER, Marie, NYC? – 1880/09/11:3b
JAEGER, Mary, 38, NYC-Q – 1911/08/20:1f
JAEGER, Meta, b. Morken, 49, NYC-B - 1878/05/26:8b
JAEGER, Peter, un. cigarmaker, NYC-M – 1886/11/03:3c
JAEGER, Peter's wife, NYC-Q - 1879/07/11:3a
JAEGER, Wally, b. Saenger, 36, NYC-M - 1895/12/15: 7e
JAEGER, William, 48, NYC-B – 1901/07/03:1d
JAEGER, William, carpenter, NYC-M – 1880/03/29:1c
JAEGERS, Peter, un. cigarmaker, *Duesseldorf/Gy, NYC-M – 1910/11/22:6a, 23:6a, 24:6a
JAEGGI, Adolf, cigarmaker, * Holland, lived London & in Gy, USA 1878, NYC-M – 1881/09/14:4e
JAEHNE, Gustav, 21, un. music sheet engraver, NYC-M – 1888/02/07:3a, 8:3b, fam. 10:3b
JAEHNE, Julius, 59, un. cigarmaker, NYC-M – 1900/11/30:4a, =2 Dec:5b, fam. 4:4a
JAEHNE, Otto, NYC-Bx – 1908/12/27:7b
JAENICKE, Alfred, 25, jeweler, NYC-M – 1887/10/06:4e, 7:2f
JAFFE, Marcus, soc., bus. mgr. Jewish Vorwaerts, NYC-M - 1917/05/23:2f, =24.2f
JAHKE, Frederick's wife, 80, NYC-B – 1912/12/15:1g
JAHN, Albert, SPD Giebichenstein/Prussian Saxony – 1899/11/12:1b
JAHN, Amalia, b. Schreiter, NYC-B – 1910/02/10:6a
JAHN, Amalie, 80, NYC-M – 1893/02/01:1e
JAHN, Bernhardt, Newark, NJ – 1908/08/30:7c
JAHN, Berthold, West Newark, NJ - 1915/06/02:6a

JAHN, Carl, 43, West Hoboken, NJ – 1905/04/16:5a, fam. 19:4a
JAHN, Carl, ironworker, NYC-M – 1911/06/27:1e
JAHN, Ernest A., ex-alderman, NYC-B – 1908/05/28:3b
JAHN, Ernst, Dr., eye doctor, Detroit, MI – 1881/07/16:1c
JAHN, Julius, 18, butcher, NYC-B – 1911/01/02:3a
JAHN, Ludwig, NYC celebr. 100th anniv. First Turntag in Berlin – 1911/06/19:2c-d, 4c
JAHN, Minna, b. Begiebing, Union Hill, NJ – 1886/06/07:3a
JAHN, Wilhelm, estate owner near Danzig & member of Landtag, USA 1850s,worked as veterinarian in Calif. & St Louis, MO, + NYC-M - 1878/05/27:4b-c
JAHNE, Augusta, 63, NYC-M – 1905/06/13:4a
JAHNKE, Ferdinand, 66, un. worker, NYC-Q – 1895/10/27: 5a
JAHNS, Marie L., 43, NYC-M – 1897/04/29:4a, 30:4a, = 1 May:1g
JAHODE, Joseph, 41, cigar maker, NYC-M – 1887/11/24:4a
JAHR, Rudolph, SLP?, NYC-M – 1893/03/10:4a
JAHRLING % Loewenthal
JAHRLING, Anna Matilda, b. Bading, NYC-M - 1919/01/22:6a
JAHRMARKT, Karl, Yonkers, NY – 1905/10/28:1f, 4a
JAKISCH, Hermann, 64, NYC-M – 1892/07/26:4a
JAKLITSCH, Ernst, 22, * Jackson, KS, parents fr Unter-deutschau/ Gottschee, + Ebental/Klagenfurt by Slovene militia - 1920/05/03:3f-g
JAKOB, Johann, NYC-M – 1909/07/05:6a
JAKOB, Magdalena, 46, NYC-B - 1916/09/12:6a
JAKOBIK, Richard, 4, NYC-B - 1918/07/02:6a
JAKOBS % Schneider
JAKOBSKOETTER, Johann, ex-MdR (Cons.), + Erfurt – 1911/02/11:3b
JAKOBY, Elise, ?31, Newark, NJ – 1891/12/12:4a
JAKOFSKY, Ida, 19, @1911 Triangle Shirtwaist Fire, NYC-M – 1911/03/27:1d
JAKOSCHITZ, Maximilian, NYC-M – 1917/10/29:6a
JAKOWSKY, Anna, + 23 Dec 86, trial of murderer – 1887/05/13:3c, 12:3a
JALLOFF, Dr., liberal publisher, murdered in Moscow – 1907/03/28:1a
JAMES, Henry, Negro, lynched near Charlotteville, GA – 1898/07/14:4d
JAMES, Jesse, bandit, + 1882/04/05:1b, =8:2b
JAMESON, Jordan, Negro, lynched Magnolia, Ark. – 1919/11/12:6b
JANAUSCHEK, Andreas, 32, fr Austria, Jersey City?, NJ – 1891/05/26:2e, 27:2f
JANAUSCHEK, Franziska, 75, actress, * 20 Jy 1829 Prague, USA 1867, till 1878 at German theaters, then English, + Amityville, LI – 1904/11/30:3d
JANCONSKY, John, 32, chemist, NYC-B - 1917/10/07:1d
JANDA, V. Jersey City Heights - 1919/04/30:6a

JANICKE, Ferd.,un. metalworker,NYC-M - 1914/02/15:7b, =17:6e
JANN, Caroline, b. Birk, 32, NYC-M – 1886/10/21:3b
JANN, Gottfried, 71, SP, un. typesetter & historian of Typographia Local 7, NYC-Q - 1920/06/17:2a,4c,6a, fam. 22:6a, more 23 Jy:5g
JANN, Katharina, b. Scheffenbuck, fr Muessingen/Wuertt., NYC-M - 1917/03/14:6a
JANNAKA, Ferdinand, 57, NYC-Bx – 1882/07/10:4b
JANOWITSCH, Ludwig, Polish socialist, + in labor camp of Jakutsk, Siberia – 1902/08/12:2e
JANOWITZ, Leopold,32, jeweler, NYC-M - 1894/08/19:5f
JANOWSKY, Jacob, un. carp., NYC-M – 1908/05/30:6a
JANSEN % Petersen
JANSEN, Gerhard, Paterson, NJ – 1911/02/16:2b
JANSEN, Hans, NYC-M, @ Genl Slocum – 1904/06/23:4b
JANSEN, Menno, 28, drygoods dealer, NYC-M – 1880/09/20:1f
JANSON, Mathias, un. carp., NYC-B – 1909/05/12:6a
JANSON, Philip, un. typesetter, Hoboken, NJ – 1885/06/11:3d
JANSON, W., NYC-B - 1919/04/10:6a
JANSS, William, machinist, NYC-B – 1906/04/18:4a
JANSSEN, Henry, 50, un. brass worker, NYC-M – 1904/04/02:4a
JANSSEN, Henry, NYC-B - 1919/04/24:6a
JANSSENS, Peter's wife, NYC-M - 1878/10/16:3a
JANSSON, Lars, NYC-M - 1914/07/22:6a
JANTHEY, Frederick J., 28, NYC-B – 1911/07/16:7b
JANTZ, Diederich, 24, med. Stud. in Germany, USA 1877, NYC-M - 1878/06/20:4f
JANTZEN, Anna, 16, servant, NYC-B – 1906/07/27:3a
JANTZEN, Hans, artist, NYC-Bx – 1897/02/16:3f
JANTZEN, Heinrich, 38, SPD Grohn-Vegesack/Bremen/Gy, War 1 - 1915/11/14:3b
JANUS, Ignaz, un. furrier, SLP, NYC-M – 1889/10/20:5b, = 21:2d
JANUSCH, Felix, un. typesetter, NYC-B – 1898/12/28:4a
JANZ, Engelbert, NYC-B - 1914/04/15:6a
JAPAN, Mutsuhito, Emperor of, negat. Obit – 1912/07/30:1b, 4d, = 1912/09/15:11a
JARENTOWITZ (Jantowitz?), Joseph, un. carp., NYC-Q - 1916/10/13:6a, 14:6a
JARGSDORF, Anna Margarethe, 67, NYC-B - 1915/06/03:6a, fam. 6:11g
JARNO, Georg, 52, German operetta composer, + Breslau - 1920/06/15:4d
JARNOWSKY, Louis, 40, NYC-M – 1892/07/30:1e
JAROSCH, F., 59, un. carp., NYC-Q – 1899/03/23:4a, 24:4a, fam. 27:4a
JAROSCH, Ferdinand, 21, NYC-Q – 1900/08/22:4a

JAROSCH, Wendel, NYC-M – 1901/07/03:1d
JAROSKA, Josephine, NYC-B – 1896/12/13:1h
JARVIES, Henry, un. carp., NYC-M – 1907/11/20:1d, 6a
JASCHKE % Baumgaertner
JASINKA, Catherina, 28, NYC - 1913/12/30:1d
JAUCH % Merkel
JAUCH, Andrew, 60, pianomaker, NYC-M – 1888/03/14:4f
JAUCH, Mary, 59, NYC-M – 1896/08/11:1a
JAUER, John J., NYC-B, + Baltimore, MA – 1910/08/24:1d
JAWORSKA, Alexis C.J., 60, printer, NYC-B - 1895/03/25:2d
JAYNASCHEK, Charles, 40, Pole, upholsterer, NYC-M – 1898/05/04:4a
JAZDZEWSKI, Rev., MdL in Prussia for Polish Catholics s. 1873, + 1911/02/12:3d
JEAURES, Jean, French Soc. & European patriot, killed by French nationalist in Paris - #1914/08/01:1a-b,4a-b, mem. meeting in NYC prep. 12:2a, rev. 15:2a, in Providence, R.I. 13:2f; 1st anniv. of his murder 1915/08/19:4b,30:4d, 3 Sept:4e-f; his life, by Romain Rolland 1916/02/27:6c-e. Life praised – 1919/10/31:4f
JEFFERSON, Alex, exec. NYC-B – 1884/07/30:4a, 31:3a, 1 Aug:2g-3a, done 2:1e
JEHLE, Alois, 62, NYC-M – 1910/01/03:6a
JEHLE, Julius, 60, un. tailor, NYC-M – 1883/09/17:3c
JEHLEN, Barbara, NYC-M – 1905/03/12:5a
JEHLEN, Gustav, NYC-M – 1904/05/28:4a
JELLIG, Daniel, NYC-B – 1887/06/15:3b
JELLINEK, Adalbert, 77, Innsbruck U librarian & friend of SP – 1908/03/29:3e
JENCHEN, Ernst Karl, NYC-Bx – 1906/12/25:6a
JENKINS, Frank, NYC-M – 1891/06/22:4a
JENNE, John, 32, Union Hill, NJ – 1885/07/31:3a, inquest 4 Aug.::4e
JENNER, Fritz, 53, NYC-M – 1891/01/02:4a
JENNERICH, Berthold, NYC-B – 1885/04/18:2f
JENNICKE, Edgar, 40, art teacher, mother in Wittenberg/Gy, NYC-M - 1913/06/01:11b
JENNINGS, Emerson P., 62, SP, typesetter, NYC-Q + Palmerton, PA - 1916/08/26:2b
JENS, Edward, NYC-M - 1914/08/01:6a
JENS, Louise, 41, NYC-M – 1898/08/29:4a, 30:3f
JENSEN, Charles, 67,undertaker, Elizabeth, NJ - 1916/05/22:6b
JENSEN, Hans, NYC-M – 1905/02/22:4a
JENSEN, Karl, 72, merchant, NYC-B – 1907/02/10:7e
JENSEN, Lydia, 18, Jersey City Heights, NJ – 1900/08/17:3c, 18:4a

JENSEN, Marie Christine, b. Thiel, NYC-M – 1912/06/01:6a, fam. 6:6a
JENSEN, Rasmus, 45, carp., NYC-M – 1890/12/05:4d
JESCHKE, Ophelia, geb. Battiste, 29, NYC-B – 1919/08/07:6a
JESINEW, W., 26, alias Boris Smirnow, Russian Socialist, + Butyrki Jail/Moscow – 1912/12/31:4d
JESPER, Rudolf, 40, NYC-M – 1891/03/27:4a
JESSEN, John, 63, worker, NYC-M – 1893/05/02:1g,4a, 3:4a
JESSEN, Theodor, un. cigarmaker, NYC-M – 1898/12/18:4a, 11:14a
JESSICH, Frank, Elizabeth, NJ - 1918/06/05:6a
JETTER, Jakob, NYC-Q - 1914/10/20:6a
JEWELL, William J., US Senator, fr Camden, NJ – 1901/12/28:3b
JINDRA, John, 79, Czech baker, NYC-M – 1899/05/04:3b
JOACHIM, Joseph, 76, Berlin violinist, dying – 1907/08/11:7b
JOACHIMSEN, Johann, cigarmaker, SPD activist expelled fr Berlin?/Gy, arrived NYC – 1880/12/18:1g
JOARGE, Joseph, Hoboken, NJ – 1901/05/07:3d
JOB, Henry, 54, un. cigarmaker, NYC-M - 1915/11/16:6a
JOBST, comrade, SP Karlsbad/Boh., mem. celeb. - 1913/06/29:3a
JOCHEM, Otto, SPD Danzig/Gy, + 21 Jan. – 1908/03/29:3c
JOCHHEIM, Kate, NYC-M – 1897/08/05:1g
JOCHUM, Stephan J., 24, salesman, NYC-M – 1892/01/09:4d
JOCKEL, Ferdinand, 27, fr Berlin? To USA 1886, NYC-SI – 1887/01/18:4d, =19:5f
JOCKERS, Benjamin, NYC-B – 1906/08/06:3a
JOCKISCH, Otto A., NYC-M - 1920/10/18:6a, 19:6a
JOECKEL, Geo. A., NYC-M – 1891/06/28:5c
JOECKLE, William, NYC-Bx – 1906/06/06:4a
JOECKS, Hermann, 52, Jersey City Heights, 52 - 1918/08/23:6a
JOEHRDAN, Peter H., NYC-B – 1906/05/19:4a
JOERG, Katherina, 64, +St Louis, MO – 1911/04/28:6a
JOERG, Kilian, 60, *Iffhenn/Bavaria, NYC?, + St Louis, MO – 1910/12/08:6a
JOERGENSEN, L., 36, cigarmkr, SPD Bremen/Gy – 1892/07/05:1h
JOERGENSEN, Peter, un. carp., NYC-M – 1910/11/29:6a, 30:6a
JOERGER, Joseph, 50, un. carp., NYC-M – 1898/07/04:4a
JOERN, John, un. painter, NYC-M - 1915/10/29:6a
JOERUS, Georg, NYC-B – 1902/04/03:4a
JOERY, Rudolf, un. carp., NYC-M – 1902/06/27:4a
JOGISCHES, Leo, editor Berlin *Rote Fahne* – 1919/03/17:1a
Johann, 5, (no family name given), memorial poem by grandfather J.B., NYC? – 1913/01/29:6a

JOHANNEK, Josef, 19, fr Bohemia, + on SS Wilhelm der Grosse en route to New York - 1913/06/11:2f
JOHANNESSEN, A., NYC-M – 1907/01/10:6a
JOHANNSEN, Wilhelm, 35, fr Hamburg-Altona, Gy, NYC-B – 1886/01/12:3a
JOHANSEN, Henry, 21, NYC-M – 1881/05/24:1f
JOHE, Eugene, NYC-Bx – 1912/08/28:6a
JOHN, Evelyn, child, NYC-Q - 1919/03/01:6a
JOHN, Otto, un. cigar maker, NYC-M – 1892/01/13:4a
JOHNER, Mathaeus, un. carp., NYC-M – 1892/12/22:4a
JOHNS, William, 33, un. cigarmaker, NYC-M - 1919/05/23:6a
JOHNSON, Alexander, Negro, lynched Monticello, AK – 1898/07/16:1h
JOHNSON, Eduard, Negro, lynched in Chattanooga, TN – 1907/11/16:3d
JOHNSON, Emanuel, 27, worker, Dane, NYC-M – 1893/06/15:1g
JOHNSON, exec. In Ossining, NY – 1907/06/25:4a-b
JOHNSON, Franz, 32, un. carp., NYC-B – 1890/08/22:4a
JOHNSON, Frederick, NYC-B – 1908/03/18:6a
JOHNSON, Geo. J., Negro, lynched Boyan, TX – 1896/06/12:1b
JOHNSON, Gustav, 70, NYC-B – 1902/01/01:1c
JOHNSON, Henry, Negro, lynched Echo, Lousiana – 1907/06/02:7f
JOHNSON, Jacob S., exec. Somersetville, NJ – 1897/05/06:1f
JOHNSON, John B., 79, * England, ex-Free Soiler & Abolitionist, SLP, NYC – 1886/12/22:1c, =25:4b
JOHNSON, John, 55, mayor of Paterson, NJ – 1907/09/25:3d, 26:3d
JOHNSON, John, exec. Auburn, NY – 1893/11/14:1c, 15:1b
JOHNSON, John, Negro, lynched Amite City, LA – 1897/01/21:1c
JOHNSON, Leonard, Negro, lynched Rusk, TX – 1910/06/22:1f
JOHNSON, Morris N., 70, inventor, NYC-M - 1916/10/01:11e
JOHNSON, Riley, Negro, lynched Clarksville, TX – 1911/11/08:1f
JOHNSON, Rufus, exec. Mt Holly, NJ – 1906/03/24:3d, done 25:5f
JOHNSON, Sam, Negro, lynched Alexandria, VA – 1912/09/26:2b
JOHNSON, Tom L., Cleveland, OH mayor?, =NYC-B – 1911/04/13:4d, 14:1d
JOHNSON, Victor, Manhattanville, NY – 1903/12/12:4a
JOHNSON, William, Negro, lynched Hemphill, TX – 1908/06/23:1e
JOHNSTON, Charles H., secy Brickmakers' Union, Chicago, (dying) - 1915/07/07:2f
JOHNSTON, Griffin J., exec. Trenton, NJ - 1915/01/06:2f
JOKAI, Stanley, worker at DuPont, Gibbstown, NJ - 1913/12/09:1b
JOLEIFSKY, Kalman, fr Poland?, NYC – 1904/06/06:3d
JOLY % Schaefer
JOLY, Frank, NYC-M - 1918/10/04:6a, 5:6a, fam. 8:6a

JONAS, Alexander, NYVZ chief editor, on 20th anniv. NYVZ – 1898/02/12:5a-b; 70th ann. 1904/03/17:3e, 27:4c, 28:3c. +, *Berlin/Gy, NYC-M – 1912/01/31:#1a-b,g, 2a, 4a-b, 6a, 1 Fb:6a, 2:1g, 2a, 6a, 3:1e, 2b, 5a-f, 6a, =4 Fb:1b, 6a-g, #:7a-c, e, poem by Biedenkapp :13c, obit by Julie Romsch :20a, 1000s at =5:1a-g, 2b-c, 4a-b, 7:2b, 3d-e, 6:3e, 8:2d
JONAS, Emma, b. Haussmann, 20, NYC-Bx - 1920/12/21:6a
JONAS, John, NYC-M – 1890/09/29:4a
JONES, "Mother," on her, by Wm Mailly – 1902/08/10:4f-h, 24:16c-d
JONES, Amos, Negro, lynched Hattieburg, MS – 1903/08/10:1h
JONES, Ben, Negro, lynched in Little River County, GA – 1899/03/24:1d, 25:1c
JONES, Charley, Negro, lynched near Bankston Ferry, MS – 1897/12/11:1c
JONES, Henry T., writer, SP, Milwaukee, WI, + Colville, WA – 1912/08/21:5f
JONES, Jim, Negro, lynched Houston, MS – 1913/02/08:5f, 9:1b
JONES, Joe & Moses, Negroes, lynched Little River Co., GA – 1899/03/24:1d, 25:1c
JONES, Martin, Negro, lynched Skipwith, MS – 1883/07/05:3c
JONES, Paul, Negro, lynched Macon, GA – 1919/11/04:1d
JONES, Robert, Tom & Virgil, Negroes, lynched Russellville, KY – 1908/08/02:11d
JONG, DE % Phillips; JONGHAUS % Felbeck
JONKE, Alois, NYC-B - 1919/06/28:6a
JOOS, August J., un. carp., SP?, secy Greater NY Labor Council, 50th birthday – 1912/08/12:5e
JOOST, Arthur, 33, Hoboken, NJ – 1908/11/23:2e
JOOST, Henry, 38?, NYC-M – 1891/03/23:4a
JOOST, Robert, 43, textile worker, NYC-B – 1910/01/25:6a
JOPP, John Edward, 3, NYC-M – 1880/03/06:4f
JORDAN, Barbara, 75, NYC-M – 1896/07/20:1d
JORDAN, Daisy, 15, servant, NYC-B – 1913/02/10:2f
JORDAN, Dawson, Negro, lynched Ellisville, GA – 1911/04/09:1f
JORDAN, Georg, 39, NYC-M – 1892/09/12:4a
JORDAN, George, machinist, Newark, NJ – 1903/04/19:1f
JORDAN, John, un. carp., NYC-M – 1888/03/15:3a
JORDAN, Kathy, 55, NYC-M – 1883/10/21:5g
JORDAN, Peter, NYC-Q – 1892/08/08:1e
JORDAN, William, Negro, lynched Enland, AK – 1902/05/20:1b
JORDI, Hans, 33, Swiss socialist & publisher - 1920/02/03:6e
JORN, Edward, 37, NYC-M – 1912/03/10:7c
JORNS % Albinger
JOSCHONEK, Ferdinand, 40, Hoboken, NJ - 1914/12/06:11b

JOSE, Peter, NYC-B - 1913/11/12:6a
JOSEFFY, Rafael, pianist, * Hanfalu/Hungary, NYC-M - 1915/06/26:2c
JOSEFIK, John, worker Raritan Copper Works, Perth Amboy, NJ – 1912/12/03:3c
JOSEPH, Albert, SPD activist & un. mason in Berlin/Gy, =1885/04/28:2e-f
JOSEPH, Bertha, Jersey City, NJ – 1891/01/12:4a
JOSEPH, Emma, 50, NYC-M – 1903/10/20:4a
JOSEPH, Frank, 7, NYC-M, + on Genl Slocum – 1904/06/18:3c
JOSEPH, Hermine, 20, cashier, NYC-M – 1903/01/17:1a
JOSEPH, Jacob, Rabbi, 59, fr Wilna, NYC-M – 1902/07/30:1g, =31:1d-e, 4 Aug:2h, 6:1f-g, 7:2a-b, notes on riot at = NYC 1902/08/08:1g, 9:1g, 14:2b, 20:1f, 1 Oct:1h
JOST, Bernhard, SPD Berlin, bookbinder – 1910/11/20:3a
JOSTEN, John A., 54, NYC-M - 1878/06/02:8b
JOUBERT, Piet, 68, general, Boer patriot, + Pretoria – 1900/03/29:1a
JOUSSEN, Mrs, 41, NYC-M - 1878/05/27:3b
JOVANOVIC, Mirko, exec. Sarajewo 3 Fb. for + archduke Franz Ferdinand of Austria - 1915/03/02:4d, 18:3d-e
JOYNER, Archie, Negro, lynched Amite City, LA – 1897/01/21:1c
JOYNES, J.L., English labor poet – 1893/02/02:2b-c
JUCHEM, Alwine, 15, NYC-B – 1907/04/05:6a
JUD, Emily, 29, fr Baden Prov./Gy, worker in jewel factory, War 2, NYC-B - 1918/09/14:5f
JUDD, Margaret, 1, & Joseph, 6, NYC-M, +@ Genl Slocum – 1904/06/29:
JUDIS, Charles, 60, un. painter, NYC-M - 1913/05/03:6a, 4:7c
JUDIS, Lizzie, 26, NYC-Bx – 1907/10/16:6a, fam. 20:7b
JUDIS, Margaretha, b. Koch, NYC-M – 1905/05/04:4a
JUDIS, Otto, 32, NYC-Bx - 1914/06/01:6a, fam. 3:6a
JUDITZ, Emma A., 4, NYC-M – 1882/01/10:3b
JUELICH, Joseph, 54, SP, fr Koeln, USA ca. 1895, fdr of Ferrer Modern Sunday School, NYC-M - 1919/08/25:2f-g, 4c,6a, 26:6a, = 27:3c-e, poem 28:4g, fam. 29:6a, notes 31:4a-b; mem. by H.C.W. Schmidt & by school 9 Ap 1920:5e-g, 24 Ag.:6a
JUELLIG, Jacob, West New York, NJ – 1909/12/29:6a
JUELLNER % Loechner
JUENGERT, Agnes, b. Muck, 26, NYC-M – 1891/11/02:4a
JUENGLING, Frieda, 54, NYC-M – 1909/10/02:6a
JUENGST, Daniel, farmer, Croton Falls, NY – 1906/04/16:1d
JUENGST, Heinrich, 77, ex-NYC?, + Munich/Gy – 1909/01/03:7a
JUERCHER, Karl, weaver, NYC-M - 1918/03/25:6a
JUERGENS, Emil, 52, porter, NYC-B – 1907/11/12:3a
JUERGENS, George, 14, NYC-B – 1905/02/01:4a

JUERGENS, Kaethe, b. Glander, 36, fr Fehrdin/Gy, NYC-Q – 1882/10/24:3b
JUERGENS, Paul, 72, silkweaver, dying, Paterson?, NJ – 1908/11/26:6a
JUERGENS, Paul, SP, Paterson?, NJ – 1909/04/14:2c
JUERGENS, W.B.A., 77, spice shop, NYC-B - 1916/04/12:6b
JUERGENSEN, Chr., Hoboken, NJ – 1891/06/21:5a
JUERGENSON, Anna, 19, SP (Lettonian branch), NYC-B, = Hastings/Hudson - 1915/04/10:6c
JUHAN, James, butcher, fr Hungary, NYC – 1912/03/01:1f
JUHASZ, Imre, un. carp., NYC-M - 1915/04/16:6a
JULIAN brothers, Negroes, lynched near New Orleans, LA – 1893/09/18:4c, 26:1d
JUNCKES, Bernhard, 3, NYC-B – 1899/04/09:5a
JUNCKES, Frieda, b. Runker, NYC-B – 1902/12/06:4c
JUNCKES, Maria, b. Franz, 34, NYC-B – 1898/09/13:4a
JUNG, Anna, 49, NYC-Bx – 1911/09/11:6a, 12:6a
JUNG, Annie, child, NYC-M - 1878/07/28:8b
JUNG, Barbara, 42, fr Saxony?, NYC-B - 1879/03/20:3a
JUNG, Bertha, seamstress, NYC-M – 1880/11/09:1d
JUNG, Christian, 57, NYC - 1913/11/26:6a
JUNG, Gustav, 40, machinist, NYC-M – 1902/08/09:3c, 4a
JUNG, Jacob's wife, NYC-M – 1886/09/22:3b
JUNG, Jakob, NYC-M – 1891/12/13:5c
JUNG, John Ernst, 61, NYC-B – 1903/04/25:4a, 26:5a
JUNG, Joseph, 8, NYC-M – 1913/03/26:6a, fam. 31:6a; mem. 24 Mr 1915:6a
JUNG, Katherina, 100, fr Gy, Clifton Heights, OH – 1888/08/17:4f
JUNG, Louise, 5, NYC-M – 1888/01/07:4f
JUNG, Mathias, 67, NYC-M – 1904/09/19:4a
JUNG, Mathias, NYC-B – 1908/11/14:6a
JUNG, Peter, 46, waiter, NYC-M – 1883/07/07:1f
JUNG, Peter, un. cigarmaker, NYC-M - 1879/01/14:3b
JUNG, Philipp, 48, NYC-M – 1889/09/14:4a
JUNG, Theobald, 47, un. bricklayer, NYC-M – 1907/05/23:6a
JUNG, Tillie, NYC-M – 1886/12/25:2g
JUNG, Wendel, 71, beer manuf., NYC-M – 1887/01/03:1f, 19:2g, 20:3e
JUNGANDREAS, Bernhard, NYC-B – 1909/10/01:6a
JUNGANDREAS, Mary, b. Hofmeister, 68, NYC-B – 1902/09/05:4a
JUNGBLUT % Mahnke
JUNGBLUTH, Ferdinand, NYC-M – 1913/01/26:7a
JUNGBLUTH, Nikolaus, un. cigarmaker, NYC-B – 1909/01/08:6a
JUNGE, Ewald, 35, Congers, NY – 1910/08/26:2a

JUNGE, Franz, SP, ret. dance teacher, & wife, NYC-Bx, Golden Wedding, 2#, fr Berlin 1868 - 1920/05/02:3c
JUNGE, Rudolf, NYC-M - 1915/12/08:6a
JUNGERT, John, 46, un. brewer, NYC-M – 1910/10/22:6a, 23:7a
JUNGERWALD, Johanna, NYC – 1899/09/26:1e
JUNGHAUS, Guenther, 58, NYC-M – 1893/03/08:4a
JUNGSBERGER, John, 30, NYC-B – 1906/11/08:3a
JUNKER, August, beer driver, Newark, NJ – 1892/06/11:2e
JUNKER, George, ex-pres. German Cigarmakers Union, NYC-M? –
 – 1895/05/17: 1g, 4a
JUNKER, Hilda, West New York, NJ - 1916/04/25:6a
JUNKER, Josef, un. carp., NYC-M – 1904/01/18:4a
JURCO, John, Rev., at Slavic Luth. Church in Jessup, PA - 1913/05/26:1c
JUSKIV, Pedro, 44, dying, shot during strike, Auburn, NY – 1913/04/05:1g
JUST, Fritz, NYC-M – 1887/08/08:3c
JUST, Herman F., 63, NYC-B – 1897/01/03:5a, 5:4a
JUST, Leontine, NYC-M, + @ Genl Slocum – 1904/06/18:3c
JUSTA, Alex, 4, & Rudolph, 1, NYC-M – 1881/02/25:3c
JUSTIETZ, Robert, un. butcher, NYC-B - 1913/10/06:6a
JUSTUS, John, 22, NYC-M – 1892/10/07:4a
JYLAND, Fritz, fr Riga/Lettonia, NYC-B - 1913/11/25:6a
KABUSZEWSKI, Adolph, 31, exec. Newark, NJ - 1915/01/27:2f
KACHEL, Ferdinand, un. varnisher, NYC-M – 1880/09/05:8a
KACHEL, Solomon, 53, NYC-Bx - 1913/05/15:1f
KACHLER, Ferdinand, 54, un. cigarmaker, SDP, NYC-M – 1904/07/30:4a
KACHLER, Ida, b. Goebel, 50, NYC-M – 1902/11/29:4a, 30:5a
KACIN, Alois, un. carp., NYC-M - 1915/03/18:6a
KACOUSKY, Charles, 77, carp., fr Bohemia, NYC-M – 1893/06/01:1h
KADAKILL, Oskar, un. cigarmaker, & wife, NYC-M – 1905/07/31:4a
KADEIT, Auguste, 33, metallworker, * Koenigsberg, SPD Breslau/Gy –
 1909/09/05:3b
KADEL, August, NYC-Bx -- 1912/05/09:6a
KADELBACH, Hermann, NYC-M – 1907/07/14:7b
KADEN, Wilhelm Aug., 63, SPD Dresden, un. cigarmkr, MdR -
 1913/06/25:2f
KADISCH, Mrs, NYC-M -- 1901/10/25:1b, 24:1h
KAECHELE, Christian, 47, un. carp., NYC-M – 1908/12/03:6a, 4:6a
KAEDING, August, 73, SP, wallet mkr, USA 1869 fr Gy, Newark, NJ -
 1914/05/11:6d
KAELIN, Joseph, 47, NYC-B – 1891/04/03:1d

KAEMMERER, Alfons, 5, NYC-B – 1906/09/09:7a
KAEMMERER, J.'s wife, NYC-M – 1887/10/29:2g
KAEMMERER, Wilhelmine, 46, NYC-M – 1890/12/06:4a
KAEMMERLE, Christian, butcher, NYC-M – 1890/06/27:4d
KAEMPCHEN, Heinrich, 64, German labor poet, + Linden/Bochum/Gy – 1912/03/31:9e-g
KAEMPF % Roesel
KAEMPF, August, 38, SLP, carpenter, * Gruenstadt/Prussia, SPD 1867, USA 1868, NYC-M - 1879/03/29:1e, 3c, = 30:5e
KAEMPF, Christina, b. Lan, 66, NYC-M – 1891/03/29:5a
KAEMPF, Christopher, Woodridge, NJ - 1916/11/09:6a
KAEMPF, Florenz, NYC-Q – 1907/10/30:6a
KAEMPF, R., NYC-B – 1904/01/30:4a
KAESE % Gaetjen
KAESE, Albert, child, NYC-M – 1889/02/12:4a
KAESE, Phillipina, b. Riechers, 33, NYC-M – 1892/06/17:4a
KAESER, J., Yonkers, NY – 1906/06/13:4a
KAESEWIGER, Christopher, cobbler, NYC-B – 1908/07/09:3b
KAESSEL % Fink
KAESTNER, Christian, 52, NYC-M – 1892/10/28:2f
KAEUFER, August, (misspelled Keufel on 22.), NYC-M – 1904/06/22:4a, 23:4a
KAFF-ESSENTER, Franziska von, 50, educator, *Waldstein Castle/Bohemia, + Berlin – 1899/11/14:3f
KAFFNER, Fritz, 43, NYC – 1912/11/07:6b
KAFFSACK, Hulda, b. Dehnert, 58, NYC-B - 1919/02/12:6a
KAH, (Kuh?) August, NYC-Q – 1917/11/17:6a
KAHL, Caroline, b. Nebel, 77, NYC-M – 1887/03/26:3d
KAHL, Gustav, 23, NYC-M – 1892/05/07:4a
KAHL, Hermann, NYC-Q - 1914/02/27:6a
KAHL, Louis, 60, NYC-B – 1892/07/30:4a, 31:5c
KAHLENBERG, Robert, SP, un. cigarmkr, *4 Aug. 1843 Halberstadt/ Gy, USA 1881, 70th birthday, New Haven, CT - 1913/08/04:6c; + NYC-M - 1918/04/02:3f,6a
KAHLERT, Karl, NYC-M – 1904/09/05.3d, 4a
KAHLERT, Katie, NYC-M – 1903/08/18.4a
KAHLKE, John, NYC-M - 1918/02/27:6a
KAHN, Albert, 18, bartender, Newark, NJ – 1882/06/21:1e
KAHN, August, 33, at firecracker factory, Jersey City, NJ – 1914/10/04:1g
KAHN, Charles, 29, NYC-B - 1920/05/29:6a
KAHN, Emil, un. baker, NYC-M - 1918/01/03:6a
KAHN, Ferdinand, 52, NYC – 1899/04/06:1g

KAHN, Henry, NYC-Q - 1913/10/15:6a
KAHN, Louis F., jeweler, NYC-M – 1885/05/11:4a
KAHN, Louisa, 46, NYC-Q – 1908/02/10:3a
KAHN, Michael, un. painter, NYC-B – 1906/10/09:2e
KAHN, Susanna, 23, NYC-M - 1894/02/01:4a
KAHRES, Marie, 41, NYC-B – 1906/09/17:6a
KAHRS, Charles, 39, NYC-B - 1919/01/10:6a
KAIL, Frank, 52, NYC-M – 1904/03/18:4a
KAILER, Wolf, 28, grocer, NYC-B – 1907/10/21:3a
KAIN % Weindorf
KAINZ, Joseph, 52, actor, *Wieselburg/Hungary, + Vienna –
   1910/09/21:1b, # 2 Oct:8c-f
KAISER % Dettinger, % Eckert, % Lang, % Ottmann
KAISER, A., 63, NYC-M – 1893/10/10:4a
KAISER, Adam J., 56, fr Bavaria?, NYC-M – 1887/03/21:3d
KAISER, Anna Maria, 76, NYC-M - 1878/03/26:3b
KAISER, Annie, 5, NYC-B – 1899/11/27:4a
KAISER, Charlotte, 55, NYC-B - 1894/08/29:4a
KAISER, Christian, NYC-M – 1905/01/31:4a
KAISER, Cl., NYC-B - 1915/11/04:6a
KAISER, Eduard, NYC-M – 1913/03/21:6a
KAISER, Elisa, 1, NYC-M – 1880/05/31:3b
KAISER, Ferdinand & Josefa, fr Steiermark?/Austria, NYC-M -
   1918/10/21:6a
KAISER, Friedrich, NYC-M – 1883/05/16:3c
KAISER, Harry, 15, NYC-Q – 1909/06/01:1b
KAISER, Heinrich, NYC-M? - 1879/03/03:3a
KAISER, Henry, & 2 relatives?, + Wilkesbarre, PA – 1903/01/26:1g
KAISER, Ida, SPD Breslau/Gy – 1911/11/05:3b
KAISER, John, NYC-M – 1890/03/19:4a
KAISER, John's wife, Troy, NY – 1896/04/20:1h
KAISER, Joseph, 18, sheet metal worker, Jersey City, NJ – 1909/05/20:3e
KAISER, Julia, 22, NYC-M - 1894/01/25:4a
KAISER, Julius, NYC-M - 1894/10/15:4a
KAISER, Karl, 50, Hoboken, NJ – 1891/03/30:4a
KAISER, Karoline, 76, Hoboken, NJ – 1906/12/23:1d
KAISER, Konrad, NYC-B – 1909/12/21:6a, 22:6a
KAISER, Leila May, N.Y. Public Library librarian, NYC-B -
   1914/10/21:2e
KAISER, Ludwig, 3, NYC-M - 1878/03/04:4g
KAISER, Moritz, Swiss, tenant farmer, with family in Ivy Landing, IL -
   1878/03/06:2e

KAISER, Walter, waiter, New Brunswick, NJ – 1903/11/19:1g
KAISER, William, 17?, button maker, NYC-B - 1917/09/01:6c
KAISER, William, 67, music teacher, NYC-B – 1913/01/23:2a, 6a
KAISERTREU, Alphons von, 36, Polish noble, bookkeeper, NYC-M – 1891/10/02:4a
KAJAWA, Jacob, 24, quarry worker in Lemont/Joliett, IL, killed during strike – 1885/05/08:2d, 10:1c, 14:2b-c, s.a. Staeber; Polish.
KALAJEW, who killed Grandduke Sergius of Russia, his trial & exec. 1905/04/19:1a, 4 May:2c, 15:2h, 16:2d-e, 10 June:2c
KALAMAIKOWSKY, Josef's wife, NYC-M – 1885/07/21:3b
KALAT, Gottlieb, fr Bohemia, NYC - 1885/08/11:1f, 12:1f, 15:1e
KALB, Conrad, 41, un. piano maker, NYC-M – 1886/10/04:3b
KALB, Frank, NYC-M – 1890/12/05:4a
KALB, Fritz, 28, NYC-M – 1887/07/19:3c
KALB, Gussie, NYC-M, + @ Genl Slocum – 1904/06/18:3c
KALBERSBERG, Gustav, fr Prenzlau/Brandenburg, + St Louis, MO – 1881/07/14:4e-f
KALENBERG, Max, 22, un. baker, NYC-M – 1910/08/13:2a
KALENBORN, Hortensia, wd Fippinger, 46, NYC-B – 1911/04/10:6a
KALIN, Simon, 49, salesman, NYC-M – 1910/02/19:1d
KALINA, Vincent Philipp, 54, NYC-M - 1915/03/30:6a
KALINOFSKY, Louise, b. Bedarf, 69, NYC-M – 1908/11/18:6a
KALLENBERG, Johann Heinrich, NYC-M – 1892/07/25:4a
KALLENBERG, Sophie, NYC-M – 1891/07/28:4a, 29:4a, fam. 31:4a
KALLIWODA, Heinrich, 58, music teacher & writer close to SLP, '48er, NYC-B - 1879/01/20:4d
KALLMAN % Tiefenbacher
KALMBACH, John, NYC-B – 1907/12/12:6a
KALSCH, Johann, 25, NYC-B - 1896/02/03:3a
KALSHOVEN, James M., 50, laundry owner, NYC-M – 1897/12/31:1d
KALTBRENNER, Christian P., rental stable owner, NYC-B - 1895/05/16:4a
KALTENBACH, Henry, musician, NYC-B – 1903/06/17:4b
KALTENBACH, Wilhelm, un. cigarmaker, NYC-B – 1887/12/16:3b
KALTENBOECK, Charles, West N.Y.,NJ - 1914/09/09:6a,fam.11:6a
KALTENMAIER, W., 59, brewery owner, Clifton, NJ – 1892/03/30:4d
KALTER, Caroline, b. Grueninger, 36, NYC-M - 1894/03/11:5b
KALTER, Theresia, 53, NYC-Q - 1919/02/28:6a
KALTERMANN, Charles, 63, NYC-M? – 1912/09/05:6a
KAMBERGER, infant, NYC-M – 1885/10/17:1f
KAMBERGER, Louis, 65, NYC-M - 1920/11/16:6a

KAMM, C., 80, widow of Fritz Kamm (+1867), herself active in SP till 1870s, NYC-M - 1896/01/28:2e
KAMM, Christian, 45,un. carp.,SP,*Graetzingen/Wuertt., Gy, USA 1880 NYC-M – 1912/08/22:6b, 23:3c-d, 24:4a-b, 6a
KAMMERER, Albert, un. typesetter, NYC-M – 1908/01/14:6a
KAMMERER, Anton, 36, NYC-M – 1888/10/06:2h
KAMMERER, Heinrich, 71, NYC-M – 1906/05/25:4a
KAMMERER, Hermann, his + 2 Jy, NYC-M – 1907/09/19:1e
KAMMERER, Stephan, NYC-M – 1905/09/09:4a
KAMMIJAN, Franz, 62, un. cigarmkr, SPD Leipzig/Gy – 1905/09/13:2d
KAMPE, Herman, NYC-B - 1919/06/10:6a
KAMPER, Georg, NYC-B – 1909/09/14:6a
KAMPF, Isabella, 18, silk weaver, NYC-B – 1911/11/27:2e
KAMPFEN, William, 50, worker, NYC-M – 1896/04/15:1g
KAMPFMUELLER, W. H., sportsgoods salesman, NYC-B – 1893/01/12:2e
KAMPMEYER, Jennie, 50, Camden, NJ - 1914/12/04:2d
KAMPS, Bertha, b. Wendt, 43, Jersey City, NJ - 1920/05/19:6a
KAMPS, William, NYC-M - 1920/08/10:6a
KAMSOL, Andreas, 49, NYC-B - 1915/10/18:6a, 19:6a
KANDLER, Mrs, NYC-M – 1898/06/08:4a
KANDLER, Robert, NYC-M - 1918/07/06:6a
KANDZIA % Plischke
KANE, John, NYC-B – 1903/03/02:4a
KANE, Robert, NYC, exec. Sing Sing - 1915/02/27:6b
KANEKO, Kichi, Japan.-Amer. SP, publ. Progressive Woman, Girard, KS, + Japan – 1909/11/27:2d, 5 Dec:20c-e
KANITZ, Hans Count von, 72, German polit., MdR and leader of Bund der Landwirte - 1913/07/01:1f,4c
KANKOWSKI, Martin, exec 6 Jan. – 1882/01/23:4d, his family 8 Dec:1d, Noted (@ Philomena Mueller) – 1887/06/02:1f
KANN, George, on his + a while ago, NYC-B – 1909/02/12:3b
KANN, Samuel, 30, striking tailor fr Austria, killed by scab, NYC-M – 1909/02/06:1g, =9:1g, 10:1g
KANNEGIESSER, William, carp., USA 1889, NYC-M – 1893/05/09:4c
KANT, Immanuel, 100th anniv. of death noted, 1904/02/28:9b-c
KANTE, Franz, 35, West Hoboken, NJ – 1902/11/02:5b
KANTER % Cohn
KANTNER, Mary 15, NYC-M, @Genl Slocum – 1904/06/23:1b
KANTOW, Frank, 65, smith, NYC-B - 1913/12/23:3b, 6a
KANTROWITZ, Jacob, NYC-M – 1891/02/20:4a
KANTROWITZ, Martin, 35, druggist, NYC-M – 1900/03/01:2h

KANZER, Henry, 41, NYC-M, + Hoboken, NJ – 1904/07/11:1a, 12:1f
KANZLER % Rudolph
KANZLER, Emil, Jersey City, NJ - 1918/08/07:6a
KANZLER, Hugo, lace importer, NYC-M – 1911/06/13:5f
KAPELL, Otto, 54, SPD, * Berlin, un. carp., 1896/11/10:2d
KAPFER, Hans, 11, Riverhead, LI – 1909/06/16:1f
KAPFF, Emma, infant, NYC-M - 1878/03/27:3a
KAPLAN, Anna, b. Schoen, NYC-M – 1911/12/06:6a
KAPLOWITZ, Louis Leib, painter, USA 1891, NYC-M – 1897/05/04:3e
KAPP, Ferdinand, 67, NYC-B – 1891/04/12:5a
KAPP, Friedrich, + Gy, letter by NYC German Society – 1884/11/17:1f
KAPP, Katherina, NYC-B – 1892/06/17:4a
KAPPE, Karl, 47, un. ironworker, *Oberkirchen/Gy, USA 1891, SP, NYC-M – 1913/03/03:6a, 4:3f,6a
KAPPE, Maria Elisabeth, NYC-M – 1909/11/29:6a
KAPPELL, Adolph, 79, actor, Chicago, IL - 1916/11/01:2f
KAPPELMAN, Becky, 16, @1911 Triangle Shirtwaist Fire, NYC-M – 1911/03/27:1d
KAPPELMANN, Eduard, SPD, Frankfurt-Niederrad, War 1 - 1914/11/01:3b
KAPPELMEIER, Peter, 42, Jersey City, NJ – 1898/02/03:3c
KAPPENBERG % Vollmer
KAPPENBERG, August, NYC-M - 1915/07/31:6a
KAPPENBERGER, Anton, NYC-B – 1914/02/06:6a
KAPPNER, Josef, SP Arad/Hungary, War 1 - 1915 /01/10:3d
KAPZUCKER, Mollie, 30, NYC-M – 1900/07/24:3f
KARAKOZOFF, gov. Of Odessa, killed by revol. – 1907/08/06:1c
KARAWAJEW, Dr., Russian SP, 2d Duma – 1908/03/20:1e, 4 Ap:4d
KARCH % Ohliger,
KARCHER, Christopher, 56, NYC-M – 1910/12/08:6a
KARCHER, Michael, tailor, NYC-B – 1885/12/25:5d
KARCHER, Pius, 56, NYC-B – 1897/09/06:3c
KARCHER, Tessie, 11, NYC-B – 1909/11/05:6a
KARDEL, Henry, longshoreman, @1900 dock fire, Hoboken, NJ 1900/07/02:1g
KARHAN, Amalia, NYC-B – 1906/11/03:6a
KARIG, Louis, 56, NYC-M – 1890/02/26:4a
KARL, Anton, un. brewery worker, NYC-M - 1894/07/27:4a
KARL, Barbara, 60, NYC-M, @Genl Slocum – 1904/06/22:1d
KARL, Christine, 51, NYC-M – 1899/10/31:4a
KARL, Christoph, 63, NYC-M – 1887/09/09:3b
KARL, Conrad, driver, NYC-Bx – 1880/07/06:4a

KARL, Dora, b. Thorn, 19, Newark, NJ - 1915/09/07:6a
KARL, Franz, NYC-M - 1915/04/25:7b
KARL, John A., NYC-B - 1914/07/25:6a
KARL, Joseph, 63, un. carp., NYC-B – 1907/06/26:6a
KARL, Valentin, un. carp., NYC-B – 1891/05/11:4a
KARLMANN, John, NYC-Q - 1920/03/11:6a
KARLMER, Julius, 40, druggist, NYC – 1904/11/09:4a
KARLSON, Kalia, 23, servant, fr Sweden, NYC-M – 1896/04/13:3a
KARMANN, Johanna, 39, SDP, NYC-B – 1905/04/30:5b, 1 May:4a, 2:4a, fam. 4:4a
KAROLIY, Ottilie, ex-wife of lt-col. Heinrich von Schwarz in Vienna, + NYC-B – 1897/08/25:1e
KAROLUS, Charles, 40, NYC-M – 1897/05/15:4a, 16:5a, fam. 23:5a
KARPE, Julius, 30, musician fr Vienna, dying, NYC-M - 1915/10/21:6c
KARPIES, Heinrich A., NYC-M – 1892/06/19:5c
KARPP, Wilhelm, NYC-M - 1915/04/16:6a
KARR, Henry M., 19, Opera singer, NYC-B – 1911/10/09:5f
KARR, William Frank, 9, NYC-M – 1905/01/23:4a
KARREIS % Kayser
KARRENBERG, August, NYC-M – 1909/10/02:6a
KARSCHNER, Mabel E., Tiffin, OH, + Newark, NJ – 1903/02/20:1c, 21:1c
KARST, August L., engineer, Guttenberg, NJ – 1903/02/14:4a
KARST, Charlotte, b. Roth, 31, NYC-M – 1888/04/18:3a
KARST, Leontine, 10, NYC-M, @on Genl Slocum – 1904/06/17:3b
KARSTENS, Hermann, NYC-M – 1891/08/15:4a
KARSTENS, William, 28, cable worker, Newark, NJ – 1897/07/27:3c
KASCAK, Balint, Elizabeth, NJ – 1907/05/07:6a
KASCH, John, NYC? – 1892/07/18:1g
KASCHAU, Christian J., NYC-M – 1887/07/19:3c, =21:2e; grave monument inaug. 26 May 1888:3a, 28:1h
KASCHAU, Heinrich C. A., NYC-M – 1887/08/05:3c
KASKA, Anna, 1906 fr Tarnopol/Poland, NYC-M – 1906/10/22:1b
KASMIRE, George E., 39,police judge,* NYC of German parents, NYC-M - 1879/09/03:4a
KASOLKE % Norwig
KASPAR, George, NYC-Q – 1910/06/13:6a
KASPER, Gottfried, NYC-M - 1913/07/16:6a
KASPER, P., NYC-M - 1918/12/15:12a
KASPER, St., worker at DuPont in Gibbstown,NJ – 1913/12/09:1b
KASPINER, Jennie, 16, NYC-M – 1891/01/12:4a
KASPRZAK, 46, Soc., exec. Warsaw, PL – 1905/09/22:2d, 27:2d

KASSEBAUM, Louis H., 29?, un. furnit. Maker, NYC-M – 1885/10/21:3a
KASSEBAUM, Valentin, NYC-M – 1889/02/18:4a
KASSEL, Adam, 56, upholsterer, NYC-M – 1898/08/13:4b
KASSENBOEHMER, Franz, 30, USA 1890, NYC-B – 1891/02/19:2e
KASSNER % Maenchen
KASSNER, George, NYC-M - 1917/05/01:6a
KAST, Georg, un. carp., NYC-M - 1915/07/08:6a
KAST, Stephanie, b. Kempf, 69, NYC-B – 1891/06/26:4a
KAST, Theodore, NYC-B – 1904/06/04:4c
KAST, William, 39, gardener, NYC-SI – 1900/06/04:1c
KASTE, Franz, new fr Gy, Philadelphia, PA – 1883/07/07:1c
KASTEN, Gotthelf, Hoboken, NJ - 1915/08/29:7a
KASTEN, Max, 30, hotelier, NYC-M – 1902/06/02:1f
KASTEN, William, 63, NYC-Q – 1907/04/13:6a
KASTEN, William, un. painter, NYC-M – 1910/11/29:6a, 30:6a
KASTENSCHMIDT, Agnes, 16, Jersey City, NJ – 1900/08/11:1c
KASTNER, William, painter, NYC-M – 1912/02/02:6a
KATH, Paul, 41, un. carp., NYC-M – 1903/06/24:4a, 25:1b, fam. 25:4
KATHMAYER, Lueder's infant son, Hoboken, NJ – 1885/08/17:3a
KATHMEIER, Charles H., 45, & wife, NYC-B – 1902/04/12:2e
KATKOW, Russian journalist & German-baiter – 1887/08/02:2c, 9:1a
KATSCH, Karl, 55, NYC-Bx – 1911/09/16:6a
KATSCH, Karl, un. cigarmaker, NYC-Q – 1908/03/03:6a
KATSCH, Karoline, child, NYC-Bx – 1906/05/15:4a
KATSCH, Lizzie, 38, NYC-Q - 1914/05/03:7a
KATSCH, Louis, un. cigarmaker, NYC-Bx - 1913/07/07:6a
KATSCH, Mathilde, 27, NYC-M – 1910/12/09:6a
KATZ, Augusta, NYC-M – 1891/08/15:4a
KATZ, Bela, fr Hungary, NYC-M – 1904/08/03:3d
KATZ, Charles, ice factory engineer, NYC-M – 1903/07/29:1d
KATZ, Gussie, 21, fr Hungary, NYC-M – 1899/02/27:3c
KATZ, Samuel, 39, SP, knitter & SP org. in Hudson Co., NJ - 1914/04/06:6a, 7:2d
KATZENBERG, Michael, 45, worker, NYC-M – 1891/03/01:1h
KATZENSTEIN, Simon, 63, soap manuf., NYC-Bx – 1912/08/27:2a
KATZER, Anna, NYC-M – 1890/03/31:4a
KATZER, Karl, 57, NYC-M – 1900/03/23:4a
KATZER, Wilhelm, 39, un. carp., NYC-M – 1885/05/20:3a
KATZKY, David Salomon, 70, & wife Pauline,68, Golden Wedding at Brooklyn Germania Hall, NYC-B - 1878/03/25:1g
KATZMANN, Annie, 46, worker, + in sweatshop fire, NYC-M – 1893/06/14:1e

KAUBE, Wilhelm, 24, NYC-M – 1885/07/09:3b
KAUER, Jakob, musician, NYC-M - 1879/07/16:1d
KAUFER, Hermes, ret. Builder, Newark, NJ – 1911/09/24:1f
KAUFF, Arthur, 1, NYC-M - 1916/09/19:6a
KAUFFMANN, Gustav, deputy-mayor of Berlin, Gy – 1902/10/03:1b
KAUFFMANN, H., 64, NYC-M – 1891/04/11:4a
KAUFFMANN, Karl, fr Nuernberg, + Elizabeth, NJ – 1903/02/24:2d
KAUFMAN, Charles, 52, milk dealer, Hoboken, NJ – 1896/08/12:3e
KAUFMAN, David, 17, NYC-B – 1919/08/8:6b
KAUFMANN % Ahrens, % Messler
KAUFMANN, August, un. typesetter, NYC-M, + Chicago – 1882/01/10:3b, 12:1e, body in NYC 23 Fb:3c, fam. 27:3b
KAUFMANN, Bernhard, 36, *Handschuhheim/Heildelberg/Gy, SP, NYC-B – 1910/12/15:2a, 6a
KAUFMANN, Bernhard, 36, SP?, NYC-B – 1910/12/16:6a
KAUFMANN, Bertha, 52, NYC-M – 1881/03/23:3c
KAUFMANN, Berthold B., NYC – 1912/10/20:7b
KAUFMANN, C.F., 53, un. cigar maker, NYC-B – 1896/08/19:4a
KAUFMANN, Carl, baker, NYC-M – 1907/06/16:1f
KAUFMANN, Dietrich, merchant, NYC-B – 1890/11/09:5c
KAUFMANN, Franz, NYC-M – 1891/09/19:4a
KAUFMANN, Frederick, landlord, NYC-M – 1898/07/14:1g
KAUFMANN, Frieda, 25, & daughter Frieda, 5, NYC-B – 1912/11/21:1d
KAUFMANN, Friedrich, 50, musician fr Hannover/Gy, USA 1870, NYC-M – 1883/03/06:4b
KAUFMANN, George, St Louis, Mo – 1897/04/14:4a
KAUFMANN, Gustav, 65, SPD org. Zoenitz/Sax., alderman 1887-1912 - 1913/08/17:3d
KAUFMANN, Henry, 54, NYC-B – 1891/03/16:4a
KAUFMANN, Henry, clerk, Jersey City, NJ – 1903/07/10:4b
KAUFMANN, John, 27, Perth Amboy, NJ - 1914/08/10:2g
KAUFMANN, John, 61, un. cigarmaker, NYC-M – 1908/01/28:6a
KAUFMANN, Joseph, 65, painter, NYC-B – 1911/02/25:1f
KAUFMANN, Kate, 41, NYC-B – 1891/04/12:5a
KAUFMANN, Katherina, NYC-M – 1892/07/10:5c
KAUFMANN, Mary Emma, 24, NYC-M – 1904/05/04:1e
KAUFMANN, Mathilde, b. Hitzfeld, '48er, *8/31/1826 Berlin, USA 1850, NYC-M – 1905/12/21:2g
KAUFMANN, Paul, 27, NYC-M – 1891/07/29:4a
KAUFMANN, Peter, NYC-Q - 1917/10/20:6a
KAUFMANN, Sigismund, Swiss?, NYC-M - 1879/05/25:8a
KAUHAUSEN, Andreas, NYC-M – 1902/11/23:5b

KAUL, Anna, 19, NYC-M – 1891/04/04:4a
KAUL, Carl, 80, NYC-B - 1918/04/26:6b
KAUL, Wilhelm, NYC-M – 1907/02/12:6a
KAULBACH, Hermann, genre painter (artist), Munich – 1909/12/10:1b
KAULFUSS, Daniel, 39, SP, Trautenau/Bohemia, ed. Trautenau Echo – 1910/05/05:3b
KAUPP, Georg, 39, *Philipsburg?/Baden, USA 1879, NYC-M - 1879/12/08:1e
KAUSCHKY % Wilke
KAUSCHKY, Christian, ?67, SLP, NYC? – 1890/10/18:4a, 19:5b, fam. 21:4a
KAUSLER, Herman, 33, NYC-B – 1898/08/21:5a
KAUSTER, Gershon, 42, NYC-M – 1911/07/29:7a
KAUTH, Frank, 40, driver, NYC-B – 1909/05/08:2d
KAUTH, Frank, 52, fresco-painter, NYC-B – 1900/09/24:3b
KAUTSKY, Johann, Prague-born Viennese theater painter, 1896/09/17:2e
KAUTSKY, Minna, SP Vienna activist & writer, 70th birthday 1907/06/23:11a-e; + Berlin – 1913/01/06:4d, 12:3a-b
KAUTZMANN, Adam, NYC-Q - 1916/11/04:6a
KAUZ, Anna, NYC-M - 1916/06/10:6a
KAVEN, Herman C., Hoboken, NJ – 1907/06/08:6a
KAWECKY, Franz, NYC-Bx – 1909/10/27:6a
KAYLOR, Michael, 53, Austrian, War 2, NYC-Q - 1918/11/08:5e
KAYMER, Mathilde, 24, NYC-M - 1879/11/27:4g
KAYSER, H., 47, NYC-B – 1891/04/12:5a
KAYSER, Helena, b. Karreis, 54, NYC-M – 1891/09/02:4a
KAYSER, Max, +29 Mr 1888, SPD Breslau/Gy, 20th anniv. of death – 1908/04/19:3a
KAYSER, Max, 28, ex-MdR, * Tarnowitz/Silesia, + Breslau – 1888/03/31:1c, 2d
KAYSER, Rev., Gary, IN, War 2 - 1915/08/27:1f, 28:2e
KAYSER, Wilhelm, un. typesetter, Hoboken, NJ – 1908/10/07:6a
KEARNEY, Dennis, Irish-born Calif. Labor leader – 1907/04/26:1d
KEARNEY, Richard, exec. Freehold, NJ – 1888/07/18:2h, 19:1c-d
KECK, Gustav, 48, Singer Factory worker, Elizabeth, NJ – 1907/02/08:3c
KECK, Johanna C., b. Ruhle, 59, NYC-M – 1891/03/18:4a
KECK, Joseph, 55, un. tailor, NYC-B – 1886/05/11:3c
KECKEISEN, Gottfried, NYC-M – 1908/07/24:6a
KECKLER, Henriette, 76, NYC-B – 1902/08/09:4a
KEDL % Engel
KEEBER, Wilhelm, 34, NYC-M – 1892/07/22:4a
KEEGLER, Frederick, 10, NYC-M, +Genl Slocum – 1904/06/25:1d

KEELY, John E. W., inventor, + Philadelphia, PA – 1898/11/19:1g
KEETENSCH, Lizzie, 30, NYC-M, + on Genl Slocum – 1904/06/21:1f
KEFFLER, Frank, 50, NYC – 1912/10/04:1e
KEGEL, Max, 52, writer & poet, SPD, + Munich/Gy – 1902/08/21:2e, 31:4c, 2 Sept:2c
KEGLER % Marx
KEHLENBECK, Louisa, NYC-M – 1884/08/03:1g
KEHLKE, Johann, fr Klein-Beuster/Magdeburg, long note (not +), NYC? – 1881/08/11:1e
KEHOE, Jack, Molly Maguire, exec. Pottsville, PA - 1878/12/19:1c
KEHR, Rudolf, (real name possibly Krenstetter) porter, NYC-M – 1881/08/15:1g
KEHRBAUM, Marie, b. Foersterling, 50, NYC-M – 1900/06/26:4a, 27:4a
KEHRBAUM, Valentin, 56, SLP, un. tailor, * Koenigsberg/East Prussia, 50, NYC-M – 1892/03/21:4a, =24:2e
KEHRER, Otto, NYC-B – 1892/07/12:4a
KEHRER, Sophia, NYC-M – 1907/08/02:1c, 20:1e
KEIDEL, Charles, 45, mgr at Knabe Piano Co., fr Baltimore, + Atlantic City, NJ - 1913/05/19:2c-d
KEIDEL, Herman F., 52?, Knabe Piano repr. in Baltimore, MD, NYC-M – 1889/02/18:4e, 27:2e
KEIDEL, Karl, shoemaker, '48er, fr Frankenthal/Gy, + Pirmasens/Gy – 1909/04/25:3a
KEIDEL, Louise, 21, NYC-B – 1899/07/10:4a
KEIL, Charles, Newark, NJ - 1917/12/17:2e
KEIL, Ernst, fdr. monthly Gartenlaube, * 6 Dec. 1816 Langensalza/ Saxony, + Leipzig/Saxony - 1878/03/26:1b
KEIL, Friedrich, 32, NYC-M – 1901/05/11:4a
KEIL, Magnus, 69, un. tailor, NYC-M - 1894/09/07:4a
KEIL, Martin, NYC-B – 1905/02/28:3e
KEIL, Mrs, b. Neuschaefer, NYC-M – 1891/01/04:5a
KEIL, Richard, Newark, NJ - 1914/06/12:6a
KEIL, Wilhelm, * 9 Apr 1800 Tromso/Norway, G-A typesetter, + Dayton, OH – 1880/08/16:2e
KEIL, Willy, NYC-M – 1892/06/18:4a
KEILBACH, Paul, 36, Jersey City, NJ - 1916/05/24:6a
KEILBACH, Peter, 70, NYC-M – 1881/05/07:4a
KEIM, August, NYC-Q - 1915/08/14:6a
KEIM, George, furniture maker, NYC-M - 1878/03/07:4f
KEIMER, Hermann, NYC-B – 1899/10/08:5a
KEIMLING, Alfred, SPD, lockmaker, *10 Fb 1878 Dresden, ed. Leipziger Volkszeitung, War 1 - 1915/09/25:4d-e

KEINER, Friedrich, 61, NYC-M – 1892/07/15:4a, 16:4a
KEISER, Rose C., 30, fr Utica, NY, NYC-M – 1883/12/14:4c, 15:3a, inquest 18:4a, 19:2-3a
KEISLER, Edith, Dr. med.,Philadelphia, PA - 1913/10/26:11b
KEITEL, August, machinist & SPD activist, *Berlin/Gy 1845, expelled, arrived NYC – 1880/12/11:1g. SLP, + Cleveland, OH – 1893/01/07:2c
KEKULE, Adam, NYC-M - 1918/04/13:6a
KELBAUER, Annie, NYC-M – 1907/07/08:1g
KELER, Kate, 12, NYC-M, +@Genl Slocum – 1904/06/22:1d
KELLENBERGER, Elise, 33, NYC-M - 1878/09/01:8b
KELLENER, Max, 35, steward on interned German steamer Vaterland, NYC-M - 1917/03/10:1e
KELLER % Spring, % Suehring
KELLER, Adam, 33, Steinway worker, NYC-Q – 1884/12/21:5f
KELLER, Adolph, carp., Elizabeth, NJ – 1905/12/28:3e
KELLER, Alexander, un. carp., NYC – 1912/04/09:6a
KELLER, Andreas, 14, NYC-M – 1893/05/16:1g
KELLER, Anton, 67, Kearney, NJ, + Newark, NJ – 1893/03/23:2d
KELLER, Antonie, b. Pfalmer, Hoboken, NJ – 1888/05/14:3a
KELLER, Charles, 45, laborer, NYC-B – 1881/08/27:3b
KELLER, Charles, 5, NYC-M – 1880/07/20:3b
KELLER, Charles, un. carp., NYC-M – 1899/08/18:4a
KELLER, Christian, NYC-B – 1910/02/27:7c
KELLER, Elizabeth, b. Gessert, 54, NYC-M – 1911/05/08:6a, mem. 5 May 1912:7a
KELLER, Eva, b. Heinrich, NYC-M – 1906/12/04:6a, 5:6a
KELLER, Ferdinand H., 42, NYC-M – 1892/08/05:4a
KELLER, Frank, NYC-M – 1911/12/10:7a
KELLER, Frank, un. iron worker, NYC-M? – 1910/08/30:2d
KELLER, Frederick, NYC-M – 1901/11/04:4a
KELLER, Friedrich Wilhelm, German popular actor – 1885/04/05:5a
KELLER, Georg, machinist, NYC-M – 1898/06/21:4a
KELLER, George, 37, realtor, Newark, NJ - 1913/05/29:6a
KELLER, H., NYC-Bx - 1916/07/22:6a
KELLER, Israel, NYC-M – 1898/02/20:5a
KELLER, Jacob, NYC-M – 1884/11/11:3b
KELLER, John Charles, NYC-M – 1909/07/10:6a
KELLER, John, 69, upholsterer, NYC-M – 1883/07/29:8a
KELLER, Karl, un. carp., NYC-M – 1892/05/28:4a
KELLER, Katherine, 52, NYC-M - 1916/03/29:6a
KELLER, Louis, Elizabeth, NJ - 1916/10/27:6a
KELLER, Louis, NYC-M – 1911/02/22:6a

KELLER, Martin, 60, fr Lorsch/Hessen, NYC-M - 1916/03/30:6a
KELLER, Matthew, tailor, NYC-M – 1887/08/13:3a
KELLER, Michael, butcher, NYC-B – 1907/08/30:3c
KELLER, Peter, NYC-Q – 1905/12/16:4a
KELLER, Peter, Swiss?, West Hoboken, NJ - 1917/10/13:6a
KELLER, Rudolph, NYC-M – 1911/09/18:6a, 19:6a
KELLER, Theresia, NYC-M – 1891/03/14:4a
KELLER, Thomas H., mgr Peters Cartridge Co., NYC-M - 1916/02/02:2e
KELLER, Wilhelmine, b. Obs, 62, NYC-M – 1891/08/23:5d
KELLER, William, 45, carp., Newark, NJ – 1906/08/02:3c
KELLER, William, 68, NYC-M – 1913/04/01:6a
KELLERMANN, Friedrich, 27, NYC-M – 1885/03/07:3c
KELLING, Max, 40, NYC-B – 1893/11/15:3c-d, 16:1h
KELLNER, August, SPD Glauchau/Saxony – 1899/05/28:1d
KELLNER, Georg, 5, NYC-M – 1881/06/30:3a
KELLNER, Henry, NYC-B – 1919/10/03:6a
KELLNER, John Jr., 6, NYC-B – 1896/06/11:4b
KELLNER, Louise, NYC-B – 1912/12/20:6d, fam. 26:6a
KELLNER, Philipp, 35, saddlemaker, NYC-M – 1902/05/16:1b
KELLY, Frank, NYC, exec. Sing Sing - 1920/08/27:2f
KELLY, John, Tammany leader, NYC-M – 1886/06/02:2b, f-g
KELLY, Timothy, Irish patriot, exec. Dublin – 1883/06/10:1a
KELLY, William, Dublin merchant, NYC-M - 1879/01/24:1f, 25:4a
KELM, Rudolph, Jersey City Heights, NJ – 1909/01/19:6a
KELPIN, Georg W., artist, Philadelphia, PA – 1885/12/23:1b
KELSCH, Kate, NYC-M, +@ on Genl Slocum – 1904/06/17:3b
KEMBLE, Peter, decorator, NYC-M – 1900/11/18:5a
KEMMEL, Elisabeth, b. Horn, 56, NYC-M – 1891/09/02:4a
KEMMER, George, 32, worker, NYC-Q - 1914/10/17:6c-d
KEMMERER, John, NYC-Q - 1914/01/29:6a
KEMMLER, Annie, 6, Ludmilla, 4, Amy, 1, daughters of John, * 1831 Wittenberg, medical student, USA 1862, where laborer, all + So. Holyoke, MA - 1879/06/23:1b
KEMMLER, William, exec. Ossining, NY – 1890/08/07:1d-e, 2a
KEMNITZ, Katherine, b. Lukey, Riverdale, LI – 1882/04/02:8a
KEMNITZ, Richard, NYC-M – 1909/03/02:6a
KEMPEL, John, & wife, wd Flaschhaus, NYC-Q – 1881/09/08:1e, 9:1e
KEMPEN, Bernhard, 49, butcher, NYC-B - 1915/12/29:6a,b
KEMPER, Anton, 43, grocer, NYC-M – 1902/05/11:1g
KEMPER, Hermann, 60, NYC-Q – 1908/11/13:3a
KEMPER, Josephine, 63, NYC-M – 1887/11/08:2g

KEMPER, Louis, SP, natl secy United Brewery Workers of Am., +
 Cincinatti - 1914/10/12:1e, = 20:2a
KEMPF % Kast
KEMPF, Bertha, 26, NYC-B – 1910/11/24:3a
KEMPF, Christ., Greenville, NJ - 1915/11/20:6a
KEMPF, E., NYC-M – 1911/02/07:6a
KEMPF, Friedrich, icedealer, * 1809 Meisenheim/Rhein, took part in 1833
 Frankfurt uprising, USA 1834, + Belleville, OH – 1883/01/19:2d
KEMPF, Henrietta, Woodridge, NJ - 1915/06/24:6a
KEMPF, Wilhelm, NYC-B – 1908/06/14:7c
KEMPINGER, Joseph, NYC-B – 1905/01/23:4a
KEMPKE, Fritz, 77, NYC-M - 1918/06/02:7a, fam. 5:6a
KEMPTER, Hermine, Jersey City Hgts, NJ - 1915/06/03:6a
KEMPTER, Karl, Union Hill, NJ - 1919/05/26:6a
KENCHER, Katherine, NYC-M, + on Genl Slocum – 1904/06/18:3c
KENDT, Max, 55, Jersey City, NJ - 1913/10/25:3b
KENHOLZ, Anton, 62, NYC-B – 1897/08/18:4a
KENKENKAMP, Henry, 60, farm laborer, NYC-Q – 1900/08/29:3b
KENNEDY, John, exec. Auburn, NY – 1899/08/03:3e
KENNEDY, John, NYS treas. - 1914/02/16:1a,2b, 17:1f,4c
KENNEL, Philip, 67, NYC-M - 1920/04/30:6a
KENNGOTT, William, un. brewer, NYC-M – 1896/08/14:4a
KENNY, William, 1st Ward Demo. Polit., NYC-M – 1885/06/26:1g
KENT, Edmund, Irish patriot, exec. Dublin - 1916/05/09:1b
KENTZLER, Jacob, 51, stable hand, NYC-M – 1891/12/03:1c
KENTZNEY, Albert, 56, building manager, NYC-M – 1899/02/15:1h
KENZEL, Herman, 32, baker, NYC-Q – 1898/09/04:1d
KEOGH, L., un. carp., *Ireland, but rep of German Carp. Union #309,
 NYC-M – 1903/07/11:4a, 13:3h
KEPLER, Herbert L., NYC-M – 1905/05/19:1g
KEPPE, Hermann, 7, NYC-B – 1891/09/30:4a
KEPPLE, Jessie, 18, @1911 Triangle Shirtwaist Fire, NYC-M –
 1911/03/27:1d
KEPPLER, F. H., 63, NYC-M – 1897/08/12:1e
KEPPLER, Fritz, NYC-M – 1891/04/03:2h
KEPPLER, Irene, 12, NYC-M, + @Genl Slocum – 1904/06/16:1c, 17:3b
KEPPLER, John A., un.carpenter,NYC-M - 1894/11/17:4e
KERBECK, Otto, NYC-M – 1893/07/05:4d
KERBER, (Mr), Boston, MA – 1897/12/05:5a
KERBER, Charles, un. cigarmkr, NYC-B – 1919/10/03:6a, 4:6a
KERBER, Gustav, 55, carp., *Crimmitschau/Sax., SDP, Holyoke, MA –
 1901/05/21:2h

KERBER, Philip, un. wood carver, NYC-B – 1891/01/02:4a
KERFS, Ida, b. Belles, NYC-M - 1914/08/18:6a, 19:6a, fam. 21:6a
KERGEL, Adolf, 55, machinist, SP, *Marienwerder/Danzig, Gy, USA 1886, NYC-Bx – 1912/09/07:6a, 8:7b, 9f, =10:3d
KERKER, Christopher, 55, un. baker, NYC-M – 1908/10/23:6a
KERLING, Mr., fam. 1899/05/26:4a
KERLS, Hermann, NYC-M – 1892/07/21:4a
KERN, Adam, 40, fr Bochingen/Gy, NYC-B – 1898/07/05:4a
KERN, Arthur, 7, NYC-B – 1897/08/09:4a
KERN, Bertha, 21, NYC-M – 1893/01/31:4a
KERN, Casimir, 59, NYC-M – 1892/06/17:4a
KERN, Charles, 43, NYC-M - 1916/09/06:6a
KERN, Charlotte, 36, NYC-M – 1903/02/05:4a
KERN, Friedrich, 31, NYC-B – 1892/01/13:2c
KERN, Friedrich, un. carpenter, NYC-M - 1894/04/17:4a
KERN, George, hotelier, Allentown, PA – 1899/11/11:1f
KERN, Hermann, machinist, NYC-M – 1892/12/16:4a
KERN, Hermann, NYC-Q - 1913/09/28:7b
KERN, J., Newark, NJ – 1909/03/09:2d
KERN, Johann, 74, NYC-B – 1891/04/11:4a
KERN, Josef, NYC-B – 1903/07/07:4a
KERN, Katherina, 45, Newark, NJ – 1906/08/12:7a
KERN, Oscar, 25, NYC-M - 1918/11/09:6a, fam. 12:6a, mem. 1919/11/07:8a, 1920/11/06:6a
KERN, Paul, NYC-M – 1888/10/15:3a
KERN, Richard, 28, SP?, NYC-M - 1920/05/10:6a
KERN, William, NYC-B - 1916/10/08:1a
KERNDL, Eleonore, 14, NYC-Bx? – 1913/04/27:11a
KERNDL, Eleonore, NYC-M - 1914/04/25:6a, mem. 1915/04/25:7b
KERNDTER, Michael Georg,59,SLP, NYC-B - 1896/02/16:5a, 17:2d
KERNICKE, Frieda, 61, NYC-B - 1914/03/24:2e
KERNOFF, Annie, 17, shot during strike, Auburn, NY – 1913/04/05:1g
KERNS, Frank, actor, NYC-M - 1916/10/17:1f
KERRIGAN, Daniel, 37, "sport," NYC-M – 1880/01/29:3a
KERRIGAN, Frank, Interboro RR coach, NYC - 1916/06/10:1f
KERSCHOWSKY, Bertha, b. Grothe, NYC-M – 1901/11/03:5a
KERSTEIN, Ernestine, 32, cook, USA 1880, NYC-M – 1881/01/16:5e
KERSTEN, Charlotte, b. Siebert, 56, NYC-Q – 1907/09/18:6a
KERSTEN, Gustav, NYC-M - 1913/05/07:6a
KERSTEN, Margaretha, NYC-Q – 1901/09/17:4a, fam. 21:4a
KERWIN, Frederick, 19, NYC-B – 1902/07/17:4a
KERZIER, John, 8, Jersey City, NJ – 1901/09/18:3b

KESS, Marie, 75, NYC – 1888/03/08:3a
KESSEL, Annie, 2, NYC-M, + @on Genl Slocum – 1904/06/17:3b
KESSEL, Charles, un. baker, NYC-M – 1891/09/30:4a
KESSEL, Friedrich, 72, NYC-B – 1892/07/26:4a
KESSELBACH, Hermann, 37, NYC-B - 1916/02/01:6c
KESSELBACH, William, NYC-B - 1913/06/25:6a
KESSIE, Frederick, NYC-Bx – 1908/01/12:7a
KESSLER % Bur, % Gneib, % Reichenbacher
KESSLER, Annie, 40, landlady, NYC-M – 1909/11/02:1c
KESSLER, Augusta, NYC-M, + @on Genl Slocum – 1904/06/18:3c
KESSLER, Babette, 45, NYC-M, +@ on Genl Slocum – 1904/06/17:3b
KESSLER, Becky, 19, @1911 Triangle Shirtwaist Fire, NYC-M – 1911/03/27:1d
KESSLER, Conrad, 35, waiter, NYC-M – 1898/06/25:2e
KESSLER, Gustav, 72, SPD Berlin/Gy – 1904/08/13:2e-f
KESSLER, Johann, 50, NYC-M – 1892/06/10:4a
KESSLER, John E., 67, hotelier, dying, NYC-B – 1911/11/11:2c
KESSLER, John, butcher, Hoboken, NJ – 1887/08/10:2
KESSLER, Lipmann, NYC-Q – 1908/05/25:1e
KESSLER, Mrs, NYC-M, +@Genl Slocum – 1904/06/23:1c
KESSLER, Otto, NYC-B – 1912/11/23:6a
KESSLER, Sadie, 35, servant, NYC-B - 1917/09/07:6c
KESSLER, Sophia, NYC-M – 1890/07/12:4a
KESSLER, Waldemar, 62, metal plater, fr. Berlin/Gy, d. 20th NYC-M - 1894/11/25:5a
KESSLING, Philip, 72, NYC-B – 1884/09/01:3b
KESSNER, Friedrich, (Lessner?), 85, German Communist, + London – 1910/02/15:4e-f, 1 Mr:4b-c
KESTLER, George, brewer, NYC-SI – 1897/06/15:4a
KETCHUM, Thomas, "Black Jack," exec. Clayton, NM – 1901/04/26:1e
KETTEL, Michael, 40, NYC-B – 1881/05/13:4a
KETTELER, Baron von, German envoy in China – 1900/06/17:1a, 18:1a, 2 Jy:1h, 3:1g, 25 Aug:1b, 1 Oct:2c, 2 Jan. 1901:1a
KETTELER, Ernst, 38, fr Bavaria, butcher, NYC-M – 1890/12/08:1g
KETTELHARDT, Engeline, infant, NYC-M   1890/08/10:4a
KETTENBEIL, A., Dr., NYC-M – 1903/03/19:4a
KETTERER, John, NYC-B – 1892/07/30:4a
KETTERER, Karoline, NYC-M – 1901/12/21:3a
KETTERER, Wilhelm Hans, 15, NYC-M – 1903/03/14:4a
KETTERER, William, organ maker, SP, *22 May 1860 in the Black Forest, Baden, lived Odessa/Russia till USA 1885, NYC-Bx – 1912/08/27:6a, c, 28:6a, =30:2d

KETTERING, Dorothea, NYC-B - 1917/08/01:6a
KETTERL % Wogatzky
KETTERLE, August, 19, NYC-M - 1891/04/11:4a
KETTERLE, Heinrich, 4, NYC-M - 1891/02/20:4a
KETTLER, Minna, b. Pleis, 45, NYC-M - 1904/08/09:4a
KETZEL, Franz, Hoboken, NJ - 1903/05/03:5a
KETZER, Reinhold, NYC-B - 1908/08/25:6a
KEUFFER, Andreas, 40, carpenter, NYC-M - 1895/01/05:4a
KEUPP, N., NYC-B - 1908/08/04:6a
KEUTEL, William, un. carp., NYC-M - 1910/11/14:6a
KEUTGEN, Theodor, 50, business mgr N.Y. Handels-Zeitung, NYC-M - 1886/12/24:3a
KEYSER, J.C., un. cigarmaker, NYC-M - 1894/02/08:4a
KEYSER, Sarah, infant, NYC-M - 1892/07/16:4a
KEZEL, Bertha, 24, NYC-Bx - 1911/01/29:7b, fam. 1 Fb:6a
KEZEL, Ernst, 54, un. marble cutter, NYC-Q - 1913/10/04:6a, fam. 8:6a
KHUEN-HEDERVARY, Karl, 65, Hungarian prime-minister 1910-11 - 1914/04/26:1e
KIBALTSCHITSCH, exec. for plot to kill @Alex II of Russia
KICK, Gustav, 42, NYC-M - 1882/07/17:3c
KIDDE, Franz Emil, 65, * Dresden, USA 1865, insurance employee, Montclair, NJ - 1909/07/06:3b-c
KIDERLEN-WAECHTER, Alfred von, Dr., 60, German state secretary - 1912/12/31:1d
KIEDARSCH, John, 56, baker, NYC-B - 1912/03/06:3a
KIEF, John, brewer or cooper, NYC-M - 1899/01/12:4a
KIEFER, Alois, 67, SPD Munich, un. printer - 1902/02/26:2c
KIEFER, Carl, ?62, NYC-M - 1892/07/24:5b
KIEFER, Caspar, 50, NYC-Q - 1919/11/18:6b, 19:6a
KIEFER, Dietrich W.,54, un. machinist, NYC-B - 1920/04/24:6a
KIEFER, Franz, 65, NYC-M - 1891/04/04:4a
KIEFER, Fritz, NYC-M - 1907/07/05:6a
KIEFER, George, 4, NYC-M - 1878/01/28:3g
KIEFER, George, NYC-Q - 1915/03/12:6a
KIEFER, John G., NYC-B - 1915/02/13:6a
KIEFER, N., West N.Y., NJ - 1919/11/04:6a
KIEHL, Jacob, ex-NYC-B, + San Francisco, CA 22 Mr, will - 1900/05/18:4b
KIEHL, Louis, trolley driver, Plainfield, NJ - 1908/09/24:3b
KIEHL, William, 9, NYC-B - 1886/07/21:2c
KIEHN, Pauline, 69 & Frederick, 70, pianomaker, dying, NYC-SI - 1917/02/06:2g

KIEL, Dora, 82, Jersey City Heights, 52 - 1918/08/23:6a
KIEL, Henry, 42, butcher, NYC-Q – 1912/11/07:3b
KIEL, Martha, 40, Union Hill, NJ, + Utica, NY - 1920/01/01:8a
KIELE, Otto, 45, un. cigar maker, NYC-M – 1896/12/07:4a, fam. 10:4a
KIELLAND, Alex, Norwegian writer, his life 1897/02/14:9f-g, + 1906/04/22:1d-f
KIEM, Alois, Jersey City, NJ – 1909/10/15:6a
KIENDEL, Valeska, NYC-M – 1897/10/26:4a
KIENE, Wilhelm, 37, NYC-M – 1893/10/25:4a
KIENER, Wenzel, 37, SP, NYC-B - 1915/07/17:6a, fam. 21:6a
KIENESS, Georg, 6, Guttenberg, NJ – 1905/06/24:1d
KIENINGER, Georg, SP Vienna & un. woodworkers' official – 1911/02/26:3d
KIENK, Minnie, 19, NYC-M, + @ Genl Slocum – 1904/06/17:3b
KIENLE % Schlauch
KIENLE, Marie Anna, b. Scheurer, 26, Caldwell,NJ - 1919/02/26:6a
KIENTSCH, Robert, 32, NYC-M – 1904/01/20:4a
KIENTZ, Emma, 22, NYC-M – 1891/03/15:5b
KIENTZ, Jacob, NYC-M - 1918/04/18:6a
KIENZI, Frederick J., 48, Mt Vernon, NY – 1910/05/25:6a
KIENZLE, Emilie, 21, NYC-Q - 1916/10/20:6a
KIENZLE, Franz X., NYC-B – 1903/05/30:4a
KIENZLE, Heinrich, NYC-M – 1909/10/09:6a
KIER, Dorothea, 3, NYC-M – 1893/03/05:5c
KIERSCHNER, Franz, actor at Germania Theater, NYC-M, to celebrate 25th jubilee as actor, first time on stage 1855 in Graz – 1880/11/07:4e
KIESEL, George, 35, innkeep, NYC-M – 1881/06/16:4c
KIESEL, Lillian, 12, NYC-M, + on Genl Slocum – 1904/06/17:3b, 18:3c
KIESEL, Max, un. cigarmkr & SPD Berlin-Reinickendorf - 1913/05/25:3b
KIESELE, Karoline, 42, NYC-M – 1887/06/17:4d
KIESELICK, Klara, 55, Newark, NJ – 1904/11/10:4b
KIESER, Jacob, 21, worker, NYC-B – 1919/09/05:6b
KIESLING, Alex, 63, pianomaker, NYC-M – 1888/11/20:1d
KIFERSTEIN, Friedrich W., ex-paper manuf. Emsleben/Gy, +Oregon City, OR – 1912/02/01:2c
KIGNER, Beatrice, b. Weitzmann, 24, New Brunswick, NJ - 1915/11/28:1g
KIGNER, David, 28, New Brunswick, NJ - 1915/11/28:1g
KIKEL, John, 46, SP, fr Gottschee, in US a.e. labor org. in Alabama, s. 1904 innkeep, NYC-B - 1915/03/21:2f,6a 1 Apr:6a, =3 Apr.:2f
KILCHER % Geib; KILIAN % Weigel
KILIAN, George, 58, NYC? - 1914/02/15:7c

KILIAN, Heinrich, 69, SP, Jersey City, NJ - 1914/12/30:6a, 31:6a, fam. 1 Jan. 15:6a
KILIAN, Josephine Elizabeth, 60, SP, Jersey City, NJ - 1918/11/18:3a
KILIAN, Peter Henry, 42, SP, West Hoboken, NJ - 1913/02/01:6a, 2:7c, fam. 6:6a
KILIAN, Peter, un. carp., NYC-B - 1913/10/01:6a
KILLGUS, Christian, un. carp., NYC-Astoria - 1891/03/21:4a
KILLIAN, H., NYC-B - 1914/01/24:6a
KILLINGER, Wilhelm, 43~, NYC-M - 1890/01/29:4a
KILLSBERGER, Theodor, NYC-B - 1918/02/16:6a
KILSO, Esther, NYC-B - 1906/11/01:3b
KILSPERGER, Emil, 17, NYC-B - 1896/08/25:4a
KIMBALL, C. P., Chicago, IL, ex-US consul in Stuttgart/Gy - 1891/03/20:1f
KIMBLERN, Calvin, Negro, lynched Pueblo, CO - 1900/05/24:1g
KIMMEL, Henry, 54, NYC-B - 1918/07/19:6a
KIMMEL, Henry, NYC-M - 1887/09/26:2g
KIMMEL, Jennie, NYC-M - 1895/05/14:1h
KIMMEL, Ralph, RR employee, NYC-M - 1898/11/17:1d
KIMMELSTIEL, Michael, salesman, NYC-Q - 1913/10/08:3a
KIMMEN, Anna, NYC-M - 1905/11/17:4a
KIMMICH, Dorothea, b. Glueck, NYC-M - 1893/11/21:4a
KIMMICH, Wilhelm, 48, un. carp., SLP, NYC-M - 1898/09/22:4a, 23:4a, =24:3d, fam. 24:4a
KIND, Louis, 60, un. cigarmkr, *Pfaffenwisbach/Gy, SDP, Meriden, CT - 1901/07/27:2h
KIND, Morris, 50, & son Sydney, 14, NYC-B - 1912/01/16:3a
KINDER, Louis, Negro, lynched George's Station, NC - 1880/03/03:1c
KINDERMANN, Julius Jr., NYC-Bx - 1913/10/02:6a
KINDL, Ottilie, NYC-B - 1891/03/14:4a
KINDLER, Carl, 65, smith, NYC-B - 1898/12/28:3b
KING, Adam, Negro, lynched in Little River County, GA - 1899/03/24:1d, 25:1c
KING, Albert, 25, driver, fr Sweden, Mt Vernon, NY - 1903/01/08:1a
KING, Annie, 40, NYC-M - 1910/04/25:2a
KING, Catherine, NYC-M, + @on Genl Slocum - 1904/06/17:3b
KING, Garfield, 18, Negro, lynched Salisbury, MD - 1898/05/27:3g
KING, Lewis, banker, NYC-M - 1880/02/15:5d
KING, Vincent C., 64, NYC-M - 1896/07/02:4a
KINGER, Clara, 37, NYC-M, +@Genl Slocum - 1904/06/22:1d
KINKEL, Adolph, 31, SLP, NYC-B - 1898/04/06:4a, 7:4a
KINKEL, Conrad, un. carpenter, NYC-M - 1895/01/14:4a

KINKEL, Gottfried, German '48er – 1882/11/16:2b-c, 18:2d-e, 3 Dec:3c-d, =10:2a. Memory – 1904/04/17:9-h
KINKEL, Heinrich, 30, NYC-B – 1892/07/15:4a
KINKEL, Johanna, 1st wife of poet Gottfried Kinkel, 40th anniv. of her + – 1898/08/21:10d-e
KINKEL, John Philip, 61, NYC-M – 1890/01/23:4a, 24:1e, trial of murderer 22 May 1890:1g, 21:4d
KINKEL, Karl, 50, NYC-Bx, un. cigarmaker - 1917/03/14:6a
KINKHARDT, Annie M., 52, NYC-M – 1906/12/28:1d
KINSTLER, Harry, 35, NYC-M – 1904/01/24:4a
KINZE, Paul, NYC-B – 1912/06/04:6a
KINZER, Martha, NYC-Q - 1920/09/14:6a
KIPFER, Benedict, 27, Hoboken, NJ - 1895/03/08:4a
KIRALY, Joseph, un. carp., NYC-M - 1918/01/25:6a
KIRCHER % Weiland
KIRCHER, Caroline, b. Maurer, 59, NYC-M – 1899/07/16:5b
KIRCHER, Ella, & Elise, 7, Harold, 5, NYC-B, +@Genl Slocum – 1904/06/23:1b
KIRCHER, Georg, 65, NYC-Q - 1916/04/23:7c
KIRCHER, John F., 57, NYC-B – 1885/02/28:2g
KIRCHER, Joseph, 78, * Fulda/Gy, radical student, USA 1834, + Belleville, IL – 1888/05/14:4f
KIRCHER, Kate, 16, father fr Hanau?, NYC-M – 1891/07/02:4a
KIRCHHERR, Karl Friedrich, un. brewer, NYC-M – 1908/08/10:6a, 11:6a
KIRCHHERR, Philip, NYC-B - 1914/12/05:6a
KIRCHHOEFLER, Christian, 40, restaurant owner, & family, NYC-B – 1904/03/23:3c, =25:3c
KIRCHHOFER, Handrina, NYC-B – 1908/10/12:6a, fam. 14:6a
KIRCHHOFF, Heinrich, 54, NYC-M – 1884/12/02:3c
KIRCHHOFF, John, 37, wool dyer, NYC-M – 1892/06/05:1h
KIRCHHOFF, Laurenz's wife, NYC-Q – 1898/12/22:4a
KIRCHHOFF, William F., 30, NYC-M – 1906/04/21:4a
KIRCHHOFFER, August, NYC-B – 1908/10/11:7c
KIRCHLECHNER, Ignaz's wife, New Haven, CT - 1919/04/01:6a
KIRCHMANN, Julius von, 82, Prussian Democrat, member 1848 Frankfurt parliament – 1884/11/05:2d
KIRCHNER, Adelheid, 53, NYC-M - 1919/06/25:6a
KIRCHNER, Alexander, NYC-B – 1893/06/27:3b
KIRCHNER, Augusta, NYC-M - 1916/05/12:6a
KIRCHNER, Barbara, 65, Richfield, NJ – 1890/03/18:4a

KIRCHNER, Charles H., 24, NYC-B, US Signal Corps pilot, + Everman, TX - 1918/01/22:6b
KIRCHNER, Charles, 30, worker, NYC-B – 1888/02/15:1f, =17:1c
KIRCHNER, E., b. Bauer, ?35, NYC-B – 1892/08/14:5c
KIRCHNER, Fritz, NYC-M – 1892/10/04:4a
KIRCHNER, Georg, 46, Newark, NJ – 1910/05/20:6a
KIRCHNER, Gustav, 40, NYC-M – 1908/12/15:6a
KIRCHNER, John L.,23,music teacher,Newark,NJ - 1914/01/02:3b
KIRCHNER, John, 17, NYC-M – 1889/08/11:5e, 10:1e
KIRCHNER, Justus, 39, Union Hill, NJ – 1904/02/22:4a
KIRCHNER, Lena, NYC-M – 1911/06/01:6a
KIRCHNER, Martha, 44, NYC-Bx - 1918/12/08:12a
KIRCHNER, Minna, b. Tippmann, 48, NYC-M – 1899/01/07:4a, fam. 9:4a
KIRCHNER, Minnie, 22, fr Gy to Chicago, + Hoboken, NJ – 1910/08/20:3b
KIRCHOFF, Henry, 50, secy local Crematorial Burial Soc., NYC-Bx - 1919/06/16:1f
KIRHAHN, Carl, 1, NYC-M – 1886/04/10:3g
KIRNER, Rev., school director fr London, Engl., NYC-M – 1887/10/20:2g, 2 Nov:1c, 17:4d
KIRSCH, Charles, NYC, on ship Minnesota – 1881/05/18:1d
KIRSCH, Ernst, NYC-M – 1908/05/23:6a
KIRSCH, Gustav, un. carp., NYC-M – 1908/07/03:6a
KIRSCH, Henrietta, 38, NYC-M – 1887/11/29:2f
KIRSCH, Katie, 21, NYC-B – 1893/03/30:2e
KIRSCH, Morris, worker, Newark, NJ – 1901/09/27:1h
KIRSCH, Rachel, 7, NYC-M - 1878/01/28:3d
KIRSCHENHOEFER, Louis, >70, NYC-B – 1907/03/23:3b-c
KIRSCHGESSNER, Clara, 48, NYC-M – 1893/05/20:4a
KIRSCHNER, Friedrich, alias Mayer, gold worker, NYC-Bx – 1892/01/12:4a
KIRSCHNER, Lizzie, NYC-M – 1891/04/02:4a
KIRSCHNER, Philip, 7, NYC-M – 1904/09/05:1e, 6:2b
KIRSCHNER, Richard H., ca 40, New York Times employee, + Bridgeport, CT - 1915/06/28:1f
KIRSCHNER, Robert, 35, saddlemaker, N. Adams, MA, + NYC-M – 1898/11/23:4a
KIRSTEN, Edward, NYC-M - 1917/01/16:6a
KIRSTEN, Ernst, un. carp., NYC-M – 1887/12/16:3b
KIRSTEN, Hermann, 73, slipper maker, SPD activist Meissen/Saxony – 1907/12/29:3e

KIRSTEN, Julius, un. shoemaker, SPD Elbing/Westprussia –
1910/05/08:3b
KIRSTEN, Pauline, b. Bohne, NYC-B – 1882/07/28:3d
KISKA, John, un. carp., NYC-M – 1907/02/09:6a
KISLING, John, varnisher, NYC-M – 1880/05/29:3b
KISS, Alexander, fr Hungary, exec. Newton, NJ – 1904/10/28:3d
KISS, John, worker, fr Hungary, USA 1906, Newton, NJ – 1908/07/04:2a
KISSEL, Carl, 54, SP, Bloomfield, NJ – 1910/06/17:6a, 18:6a
KISSEL, Georg, 39, NYC-B - 1894/12/31:4a
KISSEL, Heinrich, NYC-M – 1892/08/09:4a
KISSEL, Karl Theodor, 25, un. brewer, Elizabeth, NJ - 1920/09/04:6a,
fanily thanks 10:6a
KISSEL, Maria A., NYC-B – 1891/03/11:4a
KISSELL, Karolina, b. Platte, NYC-SI – 1899/05/20:4a
KISSELSTEIN, Hermann, 39, NYC-Q – 1908/03/07:1b
KISSEN, Vladimir, 21, dentist, fr Russia, War 2, Hoboken, NJ -
1914/09/10:2f
KISSLING, Hugo, SP, NYC-M - 1915/03/07:7a, 8:2d,6a
KISTENBERGER % Lamotte
KISTENBERGER, Emma, 14, NYC-B - 1914/11/13:6a
KISTENBERGER, John, NYC-Q – 1919/12/21:2g, 22:6a
KITCHENER, Horatio, British general - 1916/06/07:1d
KITMURA, Fr.,Japan. acrobat,+ W. Hoboken,NJ - 1913/05/17:3b
KITTEN, Hermann, NYC-M – 1896/08/13:4a
KITUMEN, Lydia, 18, servant fr Finland, USA Nov. 1904, NYC-M –
1904/12/08:1e
KITZ, Henry, Union Hill, NJ – 1911/09/05:6a
KITZING % Becker
KITZMANN, Henry, 55, butcher, NYC-Q - 1919/05/15:2e
KLAAR, Ernst, 59, German journalist & labor poet, + Klotzsche/Dresden
- 1920/11/09:4d
KLAEHNE, Otto, NYC-M – 1910/06/23:6a, fam. 26:7c
KLAESSIG, Emil, 48, * Lichtenstein/Saxony, SPD, in USA first anarchist
(Most), then 1894-1901 head of NYSZ office in Berlin – 1905/04/06:3b
KLAGER, Henry, 21, NYC-M – 1891/07/29:4a
KLAHRER, Frank, 32, butcher, NYC-M – 1905/04/01:1g
KLAIBER, Andreas, un. carp., NYC-M – 1889/03/19:4a
KLAIBER, Jakob, machinist, SLP, benefit after he was invalidated, NYC
– 1886/08/06:4e
KLAMETH, Alois, NYC-M – 1907/11/27:6a, 28:6a
KLANG, Leopold, 40, cooper, NYC-B – 1880/05/21:4c
KLAPPE, Katharina, NYC-M – 1886/08/30:4d

KLAPPER, August, NYC-B – 1902/05/14:4a
KLAPPER, Carl, 49, waiter, NYC-M – 1880/04/04:5e
KLAPPER,Moses, 67,mgr Huepfel Brewery,NYC-Bx - 1914/03/09:1d
KLASKER, Charles, 35, undertaker, NYC-B – 1897/04/02:4b
KLATBAUR, John, NYC-M, +@ Genl Slocum – 1904/06/18:3c
KLATT, Gustav, NYC-Bx – 1912/02/19:6a
KLATT, Ursula, b. Vosseler, 48, NYC-Bx – 1907/11/12:6a
KLATTHAAR, Katherine, 56, & George, 6, NYC-M, + on Genl Slocum – 1904/06/17:3b
KLATZ, John, 30, fr Poland, NYC-B – 1907/10/21:3a
KLAUKEMEYER, Friedericke, NYC-B – 1911/06/15:6a
KLAUKEMEYER, William, un. printer, NYC-Q – 1913/01/11:6a
KLAUS, Friedrich, NYC-M – 1906/10/08:6a
KLAUSMANN % Hahn
KLAUSNER, Andrew, 48, SDP, * Spramberg/Wuertt., New Haven, CT – 1905/03/31:4a, fam. 2 Apr:5a
KLEBER, Nicolaus, machinist, NYC – 1912/08/27:6a
KLEBS, Alexander, *1827 Koenigsberg/Gy, Calif. 1850, actor German-Am. Theater, + San Francisco – 1880/12/27:2d
KLEE, Adele, NYC – 1903/12/04:3d
KLEE, Walter, 33,SP,bus. agent for Butchers' Union 211,NYC-B - 1916/05/29:2b,6a, 30:6a, = 1 Juni:2b
KLEEMANN, Paul, SPD, Leipzig City Council, in 1890s NYC - 1916/01/23:7e
KLEES % Brandt
KLEH, Charles, 47, employee at Eimer & Amend, NYC-M – 1899/08/09:3c
KLEHR, William, 53, Yonkers, NY - 1919/02/24:6a
KLEIBER, Charles, 30, icedealer, Union Hill, NJ – 1905/08/10:3d
KLEIMANN, Henry C., 35, dockworker, Hoboken, NJ – 1887/11/29:2e
KLEIN % Begley
KLEIN, ..., un. fresco painter, NYC-M – 1889/11/25:4a
KLEIN, A., ship steward, see 1900 dock fire, Hoboken, NJ 1900/07/12:1f
KLEIN, Albert, NYC-B – 1909/01/16:6a
KLEIN, Alfred, un. baker, NYC-M - 1920/01/31:8a
KLEIN, Amelia M., 9, NYC-M, +@Genl Slocum – 1904/06/25:1d
KLEIN, Anna, b. Zaborsky, NYC-Q – 1898/12/22:4a
KLEIN, Anna, fr Hungary, NYC-M – 1903/09/16:1e
KLEIN, Anton, innkeep, NYC-M - 1878/02/12:4e, 19:4e
KLEIN, August, un. cigarmaker, NYC-M – 1880/02/29:5g
KLEIN, Barbara, b. Bicking, NYC? – 1885/01/06:3c
KLEIN, Carolina, b. Lelong, 62, NYC-M – 1890/02/22:4a

KLEIN, Cibilla?, 13, NYC-B – 1880/01/18:5f
KLEIN, Claus, West New York,NJ - 1915/01/03:7d
KLEIN, Edward, 14, 50, NYC-M – 1892/03/15:4a
KLEIN, Elise, 91, Paterson, NJ - 1914/07/15:2c
KLEIN, Elizabeth, NYC-M, + @ Genl Slocum – 1904/06/18:3c
KLEIN, Emma, 25, NYC-M, + @ Genl Slocum – 1904/06/17:3b
KLEIN, Fannie, 30, NYC-M – 1909/12/25:1e
KLEIN, Fritz, potter, SPD Sommerfeld/Brandenburg/Gy – 1909/04/04:3d
KLEIN, Georg, 16, NYC-B – 1884/10/28:3a
KLEIN, George, innkeep, New Rochelle, NY - 1913/12/23:3b
KLEIN, Geza, 50, tailor, NYC-M? - 1913/06/25:3d
KLEIN, Gustav, 40, tailor, NYC-B? – 1913/01/18:6a
KLEIN, Henry, 50, NYC-B – 1884/10/03:2g
KLEIN, Jacob, 23, BYC-Bx, @1911 Triangle Shirtwaist Fire –
  1911/03/28:1c
KLEIN, Jacob, NYC – 1905/09/22:1g
KLEIN, John Fred Sr., 62, NYC-M – 1896/07/10:4a
KLEIN, John, 84, NYC-B – 1889/01/05:2g
KLEIN, Joseph E., SP, lawyer for Tenants' League, NYC-B -
  1918/10/04:2f; mem. Service – 1919/09/27:6f
KLEIN, Karl, 35, NYC-M – 1893/08/13:5a
KLEIN, Karoline, 19, NYC-B - 1878/04/25:3a, 28:8b
KLEIN, Kate, 44, NYC-M, + @ Genl Slocum – 1904/06/17:3b, 18:3c
KLEIN, Lizzie, 21, NYC-M, +@ Genl Slocum – 1904/06/17:3b
KLEIN, Louis, 2, NYC-B – 1898/07/06:4b
KLEIN, Louis, cigar sales clerk, NYC-M? - 1919/06/04:2a
KLEIN, Marie, NYC-M – 1910/05/17:6a
KLEIN, Otto, painter, NYC-M – 1906/04/06:2f
KLEIN, Peter J., policeman, NYC-B - 1895/07/05: 4a
KLEIN, Philip, NYC-M – 1901/07/04:4a, 5:4a
KLEIN, Richard, Newark, NJ - 1914/07/16:6a
KLEIN, Samuel, 38, printer, NYC-B - 1920/12/31:6b
KLEIN, Simon, 30, peddler fr Hungary, USA 1884, NYC-M –
  1888/03/08:1f
KLEIN, Tina, 73, & Tillie, 10, Julius, 6, NYC-M, +@Genl Slocum –
  1904/06/23:1b
KLEIN, Wilhelm, 45, New Brighton, NJ – 1887/01/04:2f
KLEIN, William, 57, painter, NYC-B – 1901/04/29:3c
KLEINBERGER, Siegmund, 56, NYC-M – 1891/03/25:4a
KLEINDANZ, Caroline, NYC-M, + @ Genl Slocum – 1904/06/18:3c
KLEINDICKS, Walter M., 72, lithographer, NYC-M – 1896/07/24:1f
KLEINDIENST, August, un. carp., NYC-M – 1892/10/07:4a, fam. 10:4a

KLEINDIENST, Grover, ammo. worker, Springfield, NJ - 1914/09/19:2e
KLEINDIENST, Max, machinist in Elizabeth, NJ, notes lost 4 brothers in German army - 1914/08/29:2c
KLEINE, Helene, b. Link, d. 22nd NYC-B - 1894/12/25:4a
KLEINE, Oscar C., 78, un. bartender, NYC-B – 1904/03/05:4a
KLEINE, Oskar, 78, SP, NYC-B – 1904/03/08:3c
KLEINER, Elizabeth, Elizabeth, NJ – 1908/03/28:6a
KLEINER, Lorenzo, 59, lathe turner, NYC-M – 1881/07/20:1g
KLEINER, Marie, 68, widow of Cincinatti brewer, NYC-M – 1900/03/27:4a
KLEINFELDT, Charles, 54, NYC-B – 1904/10/28:4a
KLEINHANS, Lewis C., 38, secy of Cooper ChemCo, Newark, NJ – 1913/02/19:6a
KLEINHAPPEL, Mathias, 49, NYC-M - 1917/06/10:7a
KLEINHAUS, Peter see Schroeder, Peter
KLEINHENZ, Barbara, 44, NYC-M, +@Genl Slocum – 1904/06/22:1d
KLEINMAN, Wolf, 51, haberdasher, Newark, NJ - 1914/08/26:2g
KLEINMANN, Harry, secy German Waiters' Union, NYC, NYC-M - =1918/05/09:2c
KLEINMANN, Sigismund, 35, journalist, NYC-M - 1895/06/01:4a
KLEINPETER, A., NYC-B – 1892/07/31:5c
KLEINSCHMIDT, Charles, 40, NYC-M – 1881/08/13:1g
KLEINSCHMIDT, Minnie, 22, NYC-M – 1903/08/11:1e
KLEINSCHMIDT, Valentin, 35, un. beer driver, NYC-M – 1902/04/23:4a
KLEINSEN, Mary A., NYC-B – 1901/07/04:1e
KLEINWAECHTER, John, NYC-B – 1902/11/05:4a, fam. 16:5a
KLEIS, Andreas, Greenville, NJ – 1910/06/22:6a
KLEISSNER, Carl, 58, W. Hoboken, NJ – 1882/07/30:8a
KLEIST, E. Walter von, music teacher fr Koenigsberg/Germany, Newark, NJ – 1881/02/13:5f
KLEIST, Frederick, Jersey City Heights, NJ – 1908/12/28:6a
KLEIST, Heinrich von, 100th anniv. Of death, 1911/12/03:6c-f, 10:18d-g
KLEM, Albert, NYC-M - 1914/11/04:6a
KLEM, Kate, 21, NYC-M, +@Genl Slocum – 1904/06/22:1d
KLEMENT, Anton, NYC-M – 1892/10/12:4a
KLEMENT, Margaretha, b. Hock, 26, NYC-M – 1880/10/27:4f
KLEMENZ, Elisa, b. Neckermann, 32, fr. Offenbach/Gy, NYC-M - 1894/04/07:4a
KLEMM, Charles, NYC-M – 1910/02/14:6a
KLEMM, Charles's wife, NYC-M – 1907/07/10:6a
KLEMM, Ellen J., NYC-M – 1885/05/20:4a
KLEMM, Paul, & wife, Silver Wedding, NYC-M – 1903/12/26:2e

KLEMMER, Marie, NYC-B, +Somerville, NJ – 1906/07/30:1e
KLEMP, Robert, 43, NYC-M - 1913/05/03:6a
KLEMPNER, Philip, 22, RR employee, Trenton, NJ - 1917/10/08:2f
KLENCK, Charles, Bertha, Minnie & William F., 2, NYC-M, +@Genl
   Slocum – 1904/06/17:3b, 18:3c, 21:1f
KLENCK, William, 42, NYC-B – 1911/07/26:3b
KLENEN, Meta, NYC-M, +@ Genl Slocum – 1904/06/17:3b
KLENERT, August, NYC-M – 1890/05/12:4a, 13:4a
KLENGEL, Otto, NYC, 53, un. baker - 1914/02/12:6a
KLENK, John, 32, Union Hill, NJ – 1896/12/08:4b
KLENKE, M., ~55, NYC-M? – 1911/03/06:1g
KLENNER, Ethel, & Meta, NYC-Bx, + @Genl Slocum – 1904/06/18:3c
KLENNZEN % Hermann, KLEPPERT % Fritz
KLEPTINGER, Louis, 55, NYC-M – 1912/07/12:1e
KLESS, Margaretha, NYC-B – 1896/12/24:4a
KLETT, Martin, NYC-Q – 1912/11/13:6a
KLEVENZ, Jacob, 39, sexton RC Trinity, NYC-B – 1908/06/22:1c
KLIEBER, Frank, NYC-M - 1915/09/29:6a
KLIEMANN, Bertha, 30, cook, NYC-M – 1883/11/28:2g
KLIEMANN, Karl, NYC-M - 1918/08/06:6a
KLIMKE, Albert, SP, NYC-M – 1912/04/12:6a, 13:6a, fam. 14:7d
KLINE, Nancy, NYC-M, + @Genl Slocum – 1904/06/18:3c
KLING, M., NYC-M – 1907/09/20:6a
KLINGE % Schwartz
KLINGE, Emilie, Hackensack, NJ – 1908/02/22:3b
KLINGELHOEFFER, Auguste, b. Clever, 34, NYC-M – 1897/10/04:4a
KLINGENSCHMIDT, Charles, trav. Salesman, NYC-M – 1908/06/08:3e
KLINGER, Max, painter & sculptor – 1919/12/20:5d
KLINGER, Paul, Orange, NJ - 1913/05/29:6a
KLINGS, Karl, soc. Pioneer, *3 Mr 1825 Solingen/Gy, fd Der Deutsche
   Arbeiter (Chicago), + Essec, Illinois – 1908/06/30:4d
KLINK, Albert, SPD alderman Tiefwerder/Prussia, War 1 - 1914/12/06:3c
KLINK, Catharina, 15, NYC-M – 1884/10/14:3e
KLINK, Georg, 22, NYC-M - 1894/05/06:5e
KLINK, Henry, Bayonne, NJ - 1920/08/13:6a
KLINK, Joseph, 56, Newark, NJ – 1912/11/22:2e
KLINKEL, F., NYC-M – 1904/05/31:4a
KLINKER, Alfred, artists & illustrator, NYC-M - 1915/10/23:6c
KLINKERFUSS, Wilhelm, 37, un. tailor, NYC-M – 1882/03/13:3a
KLINKHARDT, Walther, importer, NYC-M – 1902/04/16:1g
KLINKO, John, 58, NYC-Bx - 1917/11/02:6a
KLINZ, Heinrich, NYC-M - 1915/02/23:6a

KLIPHAN, Franziska, 19, NYC-M – 1888/07/14:3b
KLIPHAN, Jacob, 46, un. cigarmaker, NYC-M – 1885/04/16:3c
KLIPPERT, Conrad, un. brewer, NYC-M – 1900/06/13:4a
KLITSCH % Rahardt
KLOBE, Adolph, fr Zuerich/Switz. 1899, NYC-B? – 1900/01/03:3d
KLOBUS, Jennie, 15, worker, NYC-B – 1902/01/26:5g
KLOCKNER, Nicholas, 67, un. machinist, Newark, NJ - 1915/06/14:6a,d
KLOCKNER, Wilhelmine, 57, Newark, NJ - 1914/12/27:7a
KLOEBER, Gustav, NYC-M – 1909/03/04:6a, 6:6a
KLOESS, Theodore, 75, NYC-M – 1899/09/03:5a
KLOETTEL, Anton's wife, 19,NYC, + Mauch Chunk,PA – 1881/01/06:1f
KLOETTLE, Richard, 38, un. carpenter, + with 6 members of family in Chicago, IL - 1896/02/06:1h
KLOFANT, Carl, 53, NYC-M – 1891/03/30:4a
KLOH, Frederick, un. painter, NYC-Bx - 1913/08/30:6a
KLOOR, Louis, 72, NYC-Bx – 1905/03/12:5a
KLOPPMANN, Clara, NYC-M – 1905/01/01:5f, 2:1e
KLOPPMANN, J. F., 40, stevedore, NYC-B – 1880/12/01:2f
KLOPSCH, Oscar E., 76, NYC-B – 1891/06/23:4a
KLOS, Alois F., 44, NYC-B – 1911/03/07:6a, 8:6a
KLOS, Fannie, 30, labor leader, + Denver, CO – 1908/05/17:20e
KLOS, William, Kingston, NY, see William H. Wilm
KLOSE, Gottlieb, SPD Berlin, now in USA, note (not +) 1883/08/07:2e
KLOSER, John A., 46, un. carp., fr ?Vorarlberg/Austria, North Bergen, NJ - 1919/07/10:6a. fam. 17:6a
KLOSS, Karl, carp., union leader & SPD alderman in Stuttgart/Gy – 1908/02/25:4e, 8 Mr:3d, grave mon. inaug. 1909/05/02:3d
KLOTH, Christian, 52, potter & SPD fr Berlin/Gy, arr NYC – 1880/11/30:1d-e, 2 Dec:2a-b, 6:1d-e
KLOTZ % Boltz
KLOTZ, Charles, baker, NYC-B – 1890/10/21:2e, 22:3b, fam. 27:4a, trial of his murderer ends with "not guilty" 27 Fb 1891:4a
KLOTZ, John, un. carp., NYC-M – 1908/01/04:6a
KLUBER, Johann, fr Elsass 2 months ago, NYC-M – 1884/09/15:1g
KLUECK, Konrad, 52, NYC-M - 1896/04/06:4a
KLUEGLEIN, Emil, un. carp., NYC-Bx – 1905/05/16:6a
KLUEPFEL, Martin, NYC-Q- 1916/03/27:6a
KLUEPPELBERG, Robert, un. painter, NYC-M - 1915/12/14:6a
KLUG % Wagner
KLUG, Margarethe, 34, NYC-M – 1892/06/07:4a
KLUGE, Christoph, passenger, on SS Bohemia – 1890/02/21:2f
KLUGE, Georg, 40, NYC-B – 1880/10/30:1g

KLUGE, John, NYC, 1906/12/02:7c, fam. 3:6a
KLUGE, Julius, goldworker, * Hanau/Gy, SP, NYC-Glendale –
  1906/11/30:6a, 1 Dc:6a, 19 Dc:2b
KLUGE, Oswald, 63, SP?, NYC-B - 1914/12/21:6a, 22:6a, 23:6a
KLUGE, Sophie, 12, NYC-M – 1887/05/10:3c
KLUGER, Josef, 84, tailor, '48er, + Villach/Austria – 1912/08/04:3e-f
KLUMB, Peter, 38, NYC-B – 1904/08/04:4a
KLUMP, R., 74, NYC-M - 1894/01/10:4a
KLUSKA, Hanslan, un. baker, NYC-M - 1920/07/20:6a
KLUTH, L., music merchant, NYC-B – 1888/03/08:2g
KLUTSCHAK, Henry W., NYC-M – 1890/03/30:5b
KLUTZ, Mrs, NYC-B, + on ship Mystery – 1887/07/12:1c-d, 13:2g
KNAB, Peter, 80, NYC-M – 1891/07/26:4a
KNABE, Helene, Dr., Indianapolis, IN – 1911/10/25:1b
KNABE, Hermann, clerk, NYC-M – 1903/06/16:2g
KNACKE, Wilhelm, 3, NYC-M – 1891/03/09:4a
KNACKFUS % Dausz
KNAEPPLE, Franz, 58, un. typesetter, NYC-Bx – 1903/06/20:4a
KNAPP, A., 40, tea salesclerk, NYC - 1914/02/14:3a
KNAPP, Barbara, NYC-M – 1910/10/14:6a, fam. 18:6a
KNAPP, George, 50, detector of fake banknotes, NYC-M – 1880/11/17:1g
KNAPP, Heinrich, 46, fr Pfungstadt/Gy?, NYC-M – 1893/08/10:4a
KNAPP, Martin, 70, shoemaker, NYC-M – 1880/11/10:1f
KNAPP, Pauline, child, NYC-M – 1911/03/20:6a
KNAPPKE, Amalie, b. Balschun, 28, NYC-M – 1881/07/08:3b
KNAPPKE, Heinrich, German interned at Ft MacPherson - 1918/05/27:3g
KNAPPLE, Charles, 31, NYC-M – 1908/09/19:2b
KNAUB, Franziska, 45, & son John, 15, NYC-M – 1881/11/10:1g, 4b,
  11:1g, 13:1f-g, inquest 23:4b, 1 Dec:1e, 2d
KNAUER, Lorenz, 48, tailor, NYC-M – 1881/08/24:4c
KNAUER, Oscar, ~60, carp., NYC-Astoria – 1886/09/01:2e, 2:3b
KNAUER, Peter, NYC-M – 1897/07/24:1f
KNAUS, Henry, undertaker, NYC-M – 1899/02/26:1f, 3 Mr:1e, 17:1f,
KNAUSS, Charles A., printer, Paterson, NJ – 1904/02/20:3e
KNAUSS, Heinrich, un. printer, NYC-B - 1917/01/29:6a,30:6a
KNAUTH, Pauline, NYC-M – 1891/02/25:4a
KNEBEL, Franz, 41, NYC-M - 1917/11/24:6a
KNECHT, Barbara, 49, Newark, NJ – 1908/08/21:3e
KNECHT, Barbara, 60, Newark, NJ - 1914/04/21:6c
KNECHT, William, 63, Newark, NJ – 1891/07/29:4a
KNEFFEL, Anton, un. carp., NYC-M – 1887/11/15:2g
KNEFLER, John, NYC-M, +@ Genl Slocum – 1904/06/17:3b

KNEIP, Magdalene, NYC-B - 1920/02/21:6a
KNEIPP, Sebastian, Rev., German water cure inventor – 1897/06/18:1a
KNEISCH, Philomena, NYC-M – 1891/07/24:4a
KNEISEL, Joseph, NYC-M – 1881/09/17:1f
KNELL, Henry, secy Philadelphia Steel & Forge Co., & family - 1913/12/28:1e, 29:2e
KNELL, Jacob, 68, NYC-B – 1892/06/25:4a
KNELLER, Christian's wife, NYC-M – 1882/03/22:4c
KNELLER, Ludwig, 70, jeweler, Newark, NJ – 1912/07/29:2d
KNELS, Jacob, 47, un. carp., NYC-M – 1904/10/04:4a, =7:3b
KNEUER, Maria, b. Haas, 36, NYC-M – 1892/02/23:4a
KNEWITZ, Hermann, liquor dealer, NYC-M – 1907/03/19:1g, 20:5b
KNICHEL, Jacob, 55, NYC-M – 1908/07/20:6a
KNICHEL, Joseph, 27, NYC-M – 1905/01/12:4a
KNIE, Karl, 64, SPD, un. printer,+ Stuttgart - 1916/03/19:3c
KNIEBERT, Philipp, ex-policeman, NYC-B – 1899/04/13:2f
KNIEBUSCH, Hermann, NYC-M – 1891/04/02:4a
KNIEP, Wilhelmine, 64, NYC-Bx – 1913/01/08:6a
KNIERIEM, George, 55, NYC-M – 1905/04/22:4a
KNIERIEM, Marie, NYC-B – 1897/04/29:4a
KNIES, Lina, b. Zimmermann, SP?, NYC-Bx – 1908/03/27:6a
KNIES, Nicolaus Carl, 71, SP, NYC-M - 1917/01/10:6a, 11:6a,c-d, =12:2c, fam. 16:6b
KNIESTE, Henry, NYC-B – 1901/07/09:4a
KNIEVEL, Albert, NYC-M - 1916/05/21:7a
KNIEWELL, John, un. carp., NYC-M – 1905/08/07:4a
KNIPSCHILD, Clemens, NYC?, + Hampton, VA – 1888/04/12:2f
KNIRIEM, Mathilda, 53, NYC-M – 1902/09/20:4a
KNITTEL, Fritzie, 27, nurse, fr Austria?, NYC – 1912/02/28:1d
KNITTEL, Samuel, infant, NYC-M – 1892/08/08:4f
KNITTLER, Hermann, tailor, Jersey City Heights, NJ – 1885/05/13:2g
KNITZKOW, Carl, NYC-B – 1892/05/17:2e, 20:2c, 21:2d, 25:2e
KNOBELMANN, Dora, Newark, NJ - 1920/08/07:6a
KNOBLACH, Maria, 51, NYC-B - 1916/12/13:6a
KNOBLAUCH, Anna, b. Flache, NYC-M – 1892/07/20:4a
KNOBLE, Marie, 75, "pencil Mary," NYC-B – 1898/11/09:1h
KNOBLOCH, Adam, 43, NYC-M – 1892/08/20:4a
KNOBLOCH, Adolf, NYC-M – 1881/09/07:3d
KNOBLOCH, John, 45, NYC-B – 1890/03/09:5c
KNOBLOCH, Lizzie, 25, NYC-B - 1896/03/19:4a
KNOBLOCH, Phillipine, 54, NYC-M - 1918/03/18:6a
KNOCH, Andreas, NYC-Bx – 1912/05/08:6a

KNOEBEL, Karl, 35, bartender, NYC-M – 1893/05/22:1h
KNOECHEL, Margaretha, b. Steenbock, NYC-M – 1911/02/14:6a
KNOEDEL, Konrad, 33, carp., NYC-M – 1896/07/14:1c
KNOEDEL, Ludwig, 50, NYC-M – 1904/04/14:4a
KNOEDLER, Jacob, 44, NYC-Bx – 1909/10/27:6a
KNOEDLER, Jacob, 90, NYC-Bx? – 1911/01/04:3c
KNOEFFLER, John, NYC-M, + @Genl Slocum – 1904/06/18:3c
KNOELER, Henry, ~50, machinist, NYC-M – 1893/09/24:5d
KNOELLER, Elmer, 26, coachman, Jersey City, NJ – 1908/02/23:3c
KNOELLER, Katherina, 61, NYC-B – 1908/07/15:3b
KNOEPFLE % Burkard
KNOERINZER, John, Jersey City Hgts - 1916/02/17:6a
KNOERR, Josef, Dr.,40, SP Basel/Switzerland – 1912/11/10:3d
KNOERR, Max, Munich/Bavaria, ATB, War 1 - 1914/11/01:3b
KNOF, Oscar, 29, SLP, NYC-Q – 1887/02/19:3b, =22:2e, fam. 22:3d
KNOLL, Andrew, coachman, NYC-Q – 1907/08/31:1c
KNOLL, Elisabeth, NYC-M – 1888/06/26:1c
KNOLL, Emil, NYC – 1885/08/21:1f
KNOLL, Gustav, 67, un. carp., NYC-Q - 1920/03/26;6a
KNOLL, John, 45, Newark, NJ – 1902/12/20:2g
KNOLL, Otto, 69, SP, on <u>NYVZ</u> bd of trustees, NYC-M - 1920/09/20:6a, 22:6a, wake 23:2a, = 24:2d, fam. 30:6a
KNOOB, Karl, un. cigarmaker, NYC-B – 1908/03/25:6a
KNOOP, Gerhard, un. cigarmaker, Hoboken, NJ – 1886/10/18:3c
KNOOP, Martin, 24, NYC-B – 1892/08/01:4a
KNOP, Otto, 24, *Berlin/Gy, Hoboken, NJ – 1899/07/08:4a
KNOPF, Hannah, 32, & Julius, 4, NYC-M – 1902/08/20:1h
KNOPF, Henry, un. brewer, NYC-M – 1909/08/11:6a
KNOPF, Josef, teacher & SP Vienna/Austria – 1910/01/09:3c
KNOPF, Julius, NYC-M – 1892/06/24:4a
KNOPH, John, SP, NYC-B – 1906/01/26:4a
KNOPP, (Mr.), un. cigarmaker, NYC-M – 1904/12/20:4a
KNOPP, Alfred, 58, insurance agent, NYC-M - 1913/12/26:2c
KNOPP, Henry, 17, worker, West Hoboken,NJ - 1913/12/20:2e
KNOPS, Anna, Elizabeth, NJ – 1902/05/24:4a
KNORR, Carl, West Hoboken, NJ - 1915/06/16:6a
KNOTSER, Emil, Dr., ed. of <u>Puck</u>, NYC-M – 1888/04/30:3a, 9 My:2c
KNOTT, Margarethe, NYC-M – 1891/02/27:4a
KNOWLES, Freeman, 64, ex-Congress (Populist), ed. Soc. <u>Lantern</u>, + Deadwood, SD – 1910/06/02:2c
KNUDSEN, Charles, NYC-B - 1915/12/18:6a

KNUDSEN, Peter, SP mayor Kopenhagen/DK – 1910/11/08:4d, =10:4d
KNUEBEL, Lizzie, 43, NYC-Q – 1916/06/16:6a
KNUEPPEL, Otto, NYC-M – 1906/02/25:5a
KOBBE, Gustav, critic for N.Y. Herold, NYC-M – 1918/07/28:1d, 30:6c
KOBBERGER % Burk
KOBEL, Charles J., NYC-Q – 1914/07/20:6a
KOBEL, J., NYC-B – 1911/06/14:6a
KOBIN, August, NYC-M – 1890/01/09:4a
KOBLER, Henriette, 43, NYC-M – 1895/05/03:1g, 4:1e
KOBLER, Nicholas, NYC-M - 1914/09/26:6a
KOBLOCH, Jacob, un. machinist, NYC-M – 1888/01/25:4g
KOBRE, Max, 58, banker, NYC-M - 1916/06/05:3f-g
KOBURGER, Mrs B., Newark, NJ, + NYC-B – 1883/12/14:2g
KOCH % Bartels, % Engels, % Konop, % Kottnauer, % Mackmann, % Reichert, % Rieth, % Zimmer,% Judis
KOCH, Adolph, 40, at Ruppert's Brewery, NYC-Bx? – 1910/12/20:3e
KOCH, Albert E., NYC-Q – 1897/02/06:4a, 5:4a
KOCH, Albert, NYC-M – 1887/07/23:3a
KOCH, Albin, ATB Heubach/Frankfurt?, War 1 - 1914/11/01:3b
KOCH, Alfons, fresco-painter, fr Breslau/Gy, NYC-M – 1889/02/18:4a
KOCH, Anna, NYC-B – 1901/01/07:4a
KOCH, Arison, brewer?, NYC-M – 1903/07/05:5b
KOCH, Arthur, 54, Coney Island comedian, NYC - 1915/07/08:1c
KOCH, August, NYC-Q - 1917/11/16:6a
KOCH, August, un. carp., NYC-Bx - 1914/06/24:6a
KOCH, August, un. cigarmaker, NYC-B – 1896/04/24:4a
KOCH, Auguste, b. Grimme, 48, NYC-M – 1890/09/24:4a, fam. 30:4a
KOCH, Bertha, 60, NYC-M - 1913/09/07:1b
KOCH, capt., Finnish revol., – 1906/08/18:4c
KOCH, Charles, Hartford, CT, + NYC – 1900/07/01:5e
KOCH, Christian, NYC-B - 1920/05/12:6a
KOCH, Conrad, 48, * Bavaria, baker, NYC-M – 1882/05/26:1e
KOCH, Eduard, 30, NYC-B – 1892/08/28:5c
KOCH, Edward, 66, un. pianomaker, NYC-Bx – 1910/04/06:6a
KOCH, Elisa, b. Neeb, 55, NYC-M – 1919/11/29:8a
KOCH, Elisabeth, 29, NYC-M – 1892/06/17:4a
KOCH, Elizabeth, 26, NYC-B – 1902/02/05:4a
KOCH, Frederick, 26, W. Orange, NJ – 1904/05/06:4a
KOCH, Frederick, 53, & John, 20, NYC-Q – 1912/06/05:1d
KOCH, Georg, un. machinist, NYC-M – 1903/10/03:4a
KOCH, George, 73, NYC-Q – 1883/09/04:3d
KOCH, George, un. brewer, NYC-M – 1906/04/10:4a

KOCH, Gustav, 26, artist, NYC-M – 1890/09/19:1c, 20:2h, 22:2c
KOCH, Gustav, innkeep, + 13th, NYC-M - 1878/03/20:4d
KOCH, Henry August, 59, SP, un. machinist, *5 Mr 1861 Oberkirchen/ Bueckeburg, NYC-Q - 1920/05/21:1b,6a, 23:12a
KOCH, Henry C. F., will of, NYC – 1900/09/25:3b
KOCH, Henry, 27, Hoboken, NJ – 1904/07/11:1a, 12:1f
KOCH, Henry, 59, un. pianomaker, NYC-M – 1890/12/26:4a
KOCH, Henry, 60, Jersey City Heights, NJ – 1912/09/25:6a
KOCH, Henry, 64, NYC-B – 1898/12/24:1b
KOCH, Henry, 72, NYC-M – 1912/11/05:6a
KOCH, Henry, Newark, NJ - 1908/04/09:3c
KOCH, J., NYC-Q - 1913/12/24:6a
KOCH, John Georg, 72, NYC-M – 1891/08/26:4a
KOCH, John, 45, SDP?, fr Bavaria?, NYC-B – 1903/11/21:4a
KOCH, John, 60, NYC-B – 1911/11/10:2f, 11:3a
KOCH, John, NYC-B – 1904/05/06:4a
KOCH, John, un. carp., NYC-M – 1901/02/21:4a
KOCH, Karl, NYC-Bx – 1909/04/26:6a
KOCH, Louis, NYC-B – 1891/07/05:5a
KOCH, Louis, NYC-M - 1914/02/22:11a
KOCH, Mamie, 25, NYC-M – 1892/06/10:4e
KOCH, Maria, wife of ed. N.J. Freie Presse, Jersey City, NJ – 1885/10/05:1e-f, =7:1f, inquest 18 Dec:3a
KOCH, Michael, barber, NYC-M – 1891/10/02:1g
KOCH, Paul, 40, SP, Am. Gas Furnace Co. worker, Elizabeth, NJ – 1906/01/06:3b, 4a, =8:3g, fam. 10:4a
KOCH, Robert, 5, NYC-B – 1900/05/18:4a
KOCH, Susanna, 56, NYC-M – 1891/07/02:4a & 5:5a
KOCH, Theresa, 4, NYC-B - 1914/04/05:7a
KOCH, W., West Hoboken, NJ - 1919/01/08:6a
KOCH, William, innkeep, NYC-M – 1893/05/16:1g
KOCHANOWSKY, B., 52, Polish exile, '48er, Quincy, IL - 1879/01/04:2e
KOCHE, Friedrich, 18, insurance clerk, NYC-M - 1894/04/24:4b
KOCHEN, F., NYC-Bx - 1917/12/22:6a
KOCHENDORFER, Frank, saddler & SLP activist, praised (not +) NYC-M – 1892/10/20:1f
KOCHER, Andreas, NYC-M – 1903/12/29:4a
KOCHER, Mary, 35, NYC-M – 1911/09/23:1d
KOCHER, Stephan, NYC-M – 1901/10/14:4a
KOCHMANN, John, NYC-M? – 1889/03/10:5d
KOCHORST, H., fr Rotterdam/NL, USA 1893, NYC-M – 1893/10/19:1h
KODELLI, exec. Lancaster, PA – 1907/10/04:1e

KOEB, Magdalene, 72, NYC-M, + @Genl Slocum – 1904/06/17:3b
KOEBEL, Henry, Westchester, NY - 1918/07/12:6a
KOEBELER, G., US Navy, + Havana/Cuba, NYC-B – 1898/02/18:1b
KOEBER, Adolf, 1, NYC-B – 1910/04/21:3b-c
KOECHER, Mary, 7, and smaller siblings, NYC-B – 1902/03/28:4a
KOEGEL, Christian, un. laborer, NYC-M – 1891/04/21:4a
KOEGLER, William, 52, machinist, NYC-B – 1910/10/16:1b
KOEHL, Georg S., 19, NYC-M – 1891/03/14:4a
KOEHL, Margarethe, b. Doll, NYC-M – 1891/08/11:4a
KOEHLER % Scholl, % Warnken
KOEHLER, Adolf (+1918) see Kohler
KOEHLER, Christian, 14, NYC-M – 1904/10/01:1d
KOEHLER, Christian, 45, SP, Lawrence, MA - 1915/11/30:2d
KOEHLER, Frederick, NYC-M – 1896/08/11:1b
KOEHLER, George, NYC-M – 1892/06/22:4a
KOEHLER, Harry A., 40, realtor, NYC-M, + @on Genl Slocum –
  1904/06/16:1c, 17:3b
KOEHLER, Henry, 45, musician, NYC-M – 1890/07/01:1g, 2:1h
KOEHLER, Henry, liquor dealer, NYC-M – 1880/05/13:1f
KOEHLER, Henry, NYC-B – 1901/07/04:1c
KOEHLER, Jacob, NYC-B – 1906/11/01:3c
KOEHLER, John, 45, innkeep, NYC-M – 1881/06/01:1g
KOEHLER, Louis, 37, un. cornice-maker, NYC-M – 1899/05/17:4a, 18:4a
KOEHLER, Margaretha E., 10, NYC-B – 1909/12/03:6a
KOEHLER, Max, NYC-M – 1880/05/09:5d
KOEHLER, Mrs, midwife, fr Tharau/Saxony, USA 1880, NYC-B –
  1891/05/09:2f
KOEHLER, Otto, 5, & sister Tilly, NYC-M – 1881/08/02:3d
KOEHLER, Otto, 64, SP?, Jersey City Hgts - 1916/03/09:6a
KOEHLER, Paul, 2, NYC-M – 1904/12/26:4a
KOEHLER, Philip, un. carp., NYC-M - 1915/05/29:6a
KOEHLER, Philipp, MdR (Antisem.) negat obit – 1911/01/13:4d
KOEHLER, Robert, 45, NYC-B – 1891/04/12:5a
KOEHLER, Robert, 78, bookbinder & Sudeten German SP, +
  Reichenberg/Bohemia – 1919/09/13:5c-d
KOEHLER, Sebastian, NYC-M – 1905/10/19:4a
KOEHLER, Theresia, NYC-Q – 1888/08/24:3c
KOEHLER, Tilly, 6, NYC-M – 1881/06/27:3a
KOEHLER, William J., 44, deli-owner, NYC-M – 1900/06/16:1g
KOEHLER, William, NYC-M – 1911/07/04:6a
KOEHLIN, Henry, 40, varnisher, NYC-M – 1892/06/21:1h
KOEHM, Bernhard, pianomaker, NYC-M – 1889/04/20:1e

KOEHN, Charles, 58, iron caster, NYC-M – 1896/08/30:1h
KOEHN, Minnie Johanna, 52, NYC-B - 1920/10/27:6a
KOEHN, Wilhelmine, b. Schoenfeld, NYC-M – 1883/09/02:8a
KOEHNE, August, brewer or cooper, NYC-M – 1900/09/07:4a
KOEHNKEN, Louis, NYC-B – 1891/09/19:4a
KOELCH, Otto, NYC-M – 1890/11/25:4a
KOELLER, Anna Katherina, b. Goetze, 44, NYC-Q – 1903/09/19:4a
KOELLER, John, NYC-Q – 1912/12/22:7a
KOELLER, Joseph, un. carp., NYC-M – 1912/10/20:7b
KOELLHOFER, H., clothes dealer, Newark, NJ – 1902/01/18:2h
KOELLING % Bruns
KOELLMAYR, Ludwig, 23, sailor, USA 1910, NYC-Bx - 1915/08/26:6a, =27:2d, fam. 28:6a
KOELLN, Julius, 28, cigarmaker & SPD fr Wandsbek/Gy, arr NYC – 1880/11/30:1d-e, 2 De:2a-b, 6:1d-e
KOELSCH, Adam, NYC-M - 1918/05/16:6a
KOELSCH, Carolina, NYC-M – 1891/04/12:5a
KOELTZE, August, 80, fdr of Koltztown, MO, USA 1856, not +, but tragic fate 1896/05/01:2d
KOEMPEL, Robert A., Dr. med. 60, NYC-Bx - 1917/02/15:1e
KOENECKE, Wilhelm, friend of John Most, NYC-M – 1898/02/08:4d, 9:4a
KOENEN, Helene Dorothea, 57, SP, NYC-B – 1913/03/07:6a, 9:7b, =10:2a, fam. 12:6a
KOENIG % Kraemer
KOENIG % Schlueter, % Wesenack
KOENIG, Adolph, butcher, NYC-M – 1904/05/04:1e
KOENIG, Anton, 51, carp., NYC-M – 1898/01/05:1g
KOENIG, August, 34, SLP, un. typesetter, * Koenigsberg/East Prussia, NYC-M – 1885/04/18:1e, 3b, 19:8a, =20:1c, fam. 20:3b
KOENIG, August Ferdinand, infant, NYC-M – 1884/09/30:3b
KOENIG, B., 28, NYC-M – 1893/08/08:4a
KOENIG, Babetta, NYC-Astoria – 1886/10/08:3a
KOENIG, Carl, 10, sole survivor in NYC of a family that + of cholera on SS Scandia, to be adopted in Chicago – 1892/10/09:1g, 16:5b
KOENIG, Eduard, infant, NYC-B – 1898/01/17:4a
KOENIG, Eduard, SP, NYC-B - 1918/02/11:6a, fam. 15:6a, mem. 1920/02/09:6a, mem. 1919/02/09:12a
KOENIG, F. H., SP, * 6 Sept 1839 Kehdingbruch/Hannover, USA 1867, NYC-B, 70th birthday – 1909/09/06:2f, 10:5f, 80th birthday – 1919/09/06:1g,2a, 11:1e, + 22 Nov:2a,4d,6a, 23:12a, =24:2d
KOENIG, Franz, un. carp., NYC-B – 1904/05/27:4a
KOENIG, Frederick, 24, NYC-M – 1907/12/24:2c

KOENIG, Frederick, Newark, NJ – 1908/12/12:6a
KOENIG, Friedrich, NYC-Bx – 1909/08/10:6a
KOENIG, Friedrich, NYC-M – 1908/06/14:7c
KOENIG, Georg, 14, Newark, NJ - 1914/04/21:6c
KOENIG, George, 64, NYC-B – 1891/03/09:4a
KOENIG, Gottfried, fr Austria?, NYC-B - 1918/10/26:2g
KOENIG, Henry, 4, NYC-M – 1881/04/16:4e
KOENIG, Johann, NYC-M – 1886/04/15:5c
KOENIG, Karl, 18,circus acrobat fr Baden city,+ Mt Vernon, NY - 1915/03/06:1d, 7:11b
KOENIG, Lenchen, 5, NYC-M – 1886/05/01:7b
KOENIG, Lottchen, 6, NYC-M – 1881/04/12:3c
KOENIG, Margarethe M., SP, 76, NYC-B - 1918/08/27:6a, 28:2g,6a
KOENIG, Marie, 54, SP Haida/Bohemia – 1913/02/13:4d
KOENIG, Mathias, 52, NYC-Q – 1912/04/27:6a
KOENIG, Moses, merchant, NYC-M – 1901/02/07:4b
KOENIG, Mr & Mrs, SP NYC-B, 25th wedding anniv. 1916/04/11:2c
KOENIG, Paul, NYC-B - 1918/05/06:6a
KOENIG, Pauline, West Newark, NJ - 1914/02/16:6a
KOENIG, Peter, 46, un. printer, ex-NYC, Colorado Springs, CO – 1919/08/03:7a
KOENIG, Reinhold, NYC - 1915/04/21:6a
KOENIG, William, NYC-B – 1903/07/16:4a
KOENIGSBERG, Hirsch, 70, NYC-M – 1912/07/11:1d
KOENIGSREUTER, John, Elizabeth, NJ - 1914/06/21:7c
KOENIGSROETHER, John, 70, stonecutter, NYC-B – 1900/05/26:1e
KOENIGSTEDT, Franz, 49, SPD Magdeburg/Gy, innkeep & alderman – 1908/04/12:3c-d
KOENMANN, Louis, driver, NYC-M – 1907/07/28:1e
KOENNECKE, Wilhelm, un. printer & SPD expelled fr Berlin/Gy,arrived NYC – 1880/11/20:1e, 7 De:2e
KOENNINGER, Albert, NYC-M – 1910/01/01:6a
KOEPF % Rist
KOEPKE, Catherine, 40, Passaic, NJ - 1913/06/10:2d
KOEPKE, Franz, 26, un. butcher, USA 1906, SP, Hoboken, NJ – 1908/09/16:6d
KOEPL % Rist
KOEPNICKER, John, carpenter, NYC-B - 1894/04/18:4e
KOEPPE, Arnold, 7, NYC-B – 1907/08/11:1d
KOEPPE, Frank, 8, NYC-M – 1919/12/14:3a; mem. 1920/12/13:6a
KOEPPEL, Frederick, NYC-Bx - 1915/02/25:6a
KOEPPEL, VON % Hefter

KOEPPER, Lillie, 16, NYC-M, +@Genl Slocum – 1904/06/25:1d
KOEPPING, Albert, 22, Port Jervis?, exec. Ossining, NY – 1904/06/14:4d,
    Note 4 Jy 1904:3b
KOERBER, Ernst von, Dr. 69, Austrian Prime Minister 1900-1905, +26 Fb
    Vienna, laud. obit - 1919/04/17:4c
KOERIGE, Charles, 56, NYC-M – 1902/06/18:4b, 17:4b
KOERNER, Christine, 53, & Kate, 28, & Annette, child, NYC-M –
    1885/05/04:1b, 5:1g, =6:1f, see 1885 Manhattan Fire
KOERNER, George, 43, stevedore, Hoboken, NJ – 1912/12/23:2c, 24:6a
KOERNER, Henry, NYC-M – 1880/09/14:4d
KOERNER, Margarethe, 69, NYC-M – 1892/06/07:4a
KOERNER, Ottilie, b. Zing, NYC-B - 1913/12/02:3a
KOERNER, Reinhold, 30, un. cigarmaker, NYC-M - 1878/06/05:3b
KOERNER, Theodor, NYC-M - 1894/01/11:4a
KOERNIG, Wilhelm, 65, un. bricklayer, SP, NYC-Bx – 1905/05/21:1e,
    22:6a, 23:6a, =24:3e
KOERPER, Frederick, NYC-M – 1903/04/26:5a
KOERSTER, Karl, un. carp., NYC-M – 1882/12/17:8b
KOERWIN, Otto, 51, un. basketweaver, NYC-B – 1907/06/12:6a, 13:6a,
    fam. 15:6a
KOERY, Charles, 32, pianomaker, NYC-M - 1879/03/12:1d
KOESSLER (?), Wilhelm, un. cigarmaker, NYC – 1882/03/26:8a
KOESTER, Edward, NYC-M – 1897/01/21:4a
KOESTER, Louis, NYC-? - 1878/08/11:8b
KOESTER, Richard, 35, painter, Hoboken, NJ – 1883/06/07:3b
KOESTER, Robert, un. carpenter, NYC-M - 1894/09/10:4a
KOESTLER, Sophie, b. Tanz, NYC-M – 1908/04/25:6a
KOESTNER, Nicolaus, NYC-Metropolitan - 1916/04/26:6a
KOETTER, E., un. cigar maker, NYC-M – 1897/03/04:4a
KOETTLER, Irene & Lillian, NYC-M, +@ Genl Slocum – 1904/06/18:3c
KOETZLER, Emilie, b. Dimler, 37, NYC-M – 1891/04/04:4a
KOETZNER, Gracie, 11, NYC-M, @ 1883 School Fire, NYC-M
KOFLER, Leo, ~70, church organist & musician, New Vernon, NJ –
    1908/11/28:2d
KOHL, Fritz, NYC-M – 1908/02/29:6a
KOHL, Jakob, NYC-Q - 1916/05/16:6a
KOHL, John H., 32, NYC-M – 1891/03/09:4a
KOHL, Max A., fam. (no obit) - 1913/08/02:6a
KOHL, Philip, 50, tailor, NYC-Bay Ridge – 1884/07/20:1g
KOHLBERGER, Hermann, butcher, Philadelphia, + NYC – 1911/04/13:1e
KOHLENBECK, Albert, 11, NYC-M – 1891/06/26:4a
KOHLER % Neukamb, % Streit

KOHLER, Adolf, NYC-M - 1918/02/06:6a, mem. 1919/02/02:6a
KOHLER, Alois, SP, Civil War vet, NYC-M, 50th wedding anniv. - 1916/06/01:5f
KOHLER, Charles, 37, NYC-B - 1900/07/20:4a
KOHLER, Charles, 80, ret. candy store owner, NYC-B - 1918/04/10:6b
KOHLER, Edward, carp., Alpine, NJ - 1911/08/01:3c-d
KOHLER, Harry, NYC-M, +@Genl Slocum - 1904/06/17:3b
KOHLER, Henry A., insurance agent, & infant son, +@ Genl Slocum, NYC-M - 1904/06/20:1b
KOHLER, Mary, b. Herrbrecht, Secaucus, NJ - 1914/03/10:6a
KOHLER, Mary, NYC-M, +@Genl Slocum - 1904/06/22:1d
KOHLMANN, Hermann, 26, 6/1903 fr Hungary, NYC-M - 1903/06/16:2g
KOHLMANN, John, 50, NYC-B - 1916/01/16:11b
KOHLMANN, Louise, b. Gusey, 29, Jersey City Heights, NJ - 1878/06/04:3b
KOHLRIESER, Johanna, 25, NYC-B - 1905/09/29:3c
KOHN % Fink
KOHN, August, lawyer, NYC-M - 1895/04/04:1e
KOHN, Edward, 32, NYC-M - 1891/04/01:4a
KOHN, Gustav, 44, NYC-M - 1890/10/18:4a
KOHN, Heinrich, Dr., SPO Bruenn/Moravia, War 1 - 1915/01/10:3b, = 2 May:3d
KOHN, Lottie & Marcellus, NYC-M - 1889/02/04:4a, 6:4a
KOHN, Louis, 7, Meyer, 2, & Sarah, infant, NYC-M - 1904/01/29:4b
KOHN, Nathan, 40, NYC-M - 1895/05/08:3f
KOHN, O., 57, NYC-M - 1892/06/19:5c
KOHN, Rosetta, 16, Newark, NJ - 1903/02/20:1c, =23:1b
KOHNA, Rosa, 19, fr Bohemia, USA 1891, NYC-M - 1892/01/07:1g
KOHUT brothers, sentenced to life - 1886/01/29:1f, 30:4d, 4 Feb:4a, appeal 31 Aug:2f, 1 Sept:2a-b, 4f, 4:1b, 4e, 6:2c, 9:2a, 22:2c, 27:5g
KOHUT, Jakob, machinist, NYC-M - 1891/02/18:4a
KOKO, Anna, 21, servant, Finnish, NYC-B - 1916/03/29:5f
KOKOSKY, Samuel, ed. SPD mag Neue Welt (Berlin) - 1899/05/25:2d
KOLB, Ferdinand, 51, SP, sculptor, lived London/GB, deported 1914, War 2 in Newark, NJ - 1915/05/17:3e
KOLB, George A., secy Marine Engineers Union, NYC-M - 1903/07/08:1g
KOLB, Jacob, 83, * Gernsheim/Hessen, NYC-M - 1894/11/17:4a
KOLB, John G., 64, NYC-B - 1899/11/27:1d
KOLB, John Jacob, 72, butcher, NYC-M - 1907/02/26:2b
KOLB, John, 38, * Gruenstadt/Bav., note in Philadelphia - 1883/12/06:1c
KOLB, Lorenz, 45, weaver?, NYC-M - 1880/08/09:3a
KOLB, Ludwig, Elizabeth, NJ - 1907/12/22:7c

KOLB, Magdalena, 72, NYC-M, + @Genl Slocum – 1904/06/17:3b
KOLB, Mrs, Newark, NJ, inquest 1880/05/06:4a
KOLB, Nathan, 76, civil war vet, fr Koblenz, NYC-M - 1916/02/07:1c
KOLB, Sophie, b. Seibert, NYC-B – 1891/06/22:4a
KOLB, Valentine, NYC-Bx – 1910/07/12:6a
KOLB, Wilhelm, 47, SPD, + Karlsruhe - 1918/05/30:4d
KOLBE, John J., 47, NYC-Q - 1920/02/04:6a, 3:8c
KOLBEL, Andreas, 32, un. machinist, NYC-M – 1887/04/12:1f
KOLBERT, Rebecca, 28, servant, NYC-B – 1912/03/20:2b
KOLDITZ, Emma, NYC-B – 1904/07/18:4a
KOLISH, Leo, SPD, editor at Mannheimer Volkstimme, * Bohemia, War 1 - 1915/07/31:4d
KOLITZKI, John, 67, cooper?, fr Budislaw/Russian-Poland, NYC-M – 1893/10/10:3d
KOLKE, Louis, Newark, NJ – 1900/06/19:3b, 20:4b
KOLKSCHNEIDER, Elisabeth, b. Fromme, NYC-M – 1890/09/21:5a
KOLKSCHNEIDER, Heinrich, un. carp., NYC-M – 1911/03/31:6a
KOLLENBAUM, E., NYC-Q – 1910/11/29:6a
KOLLER, John, un. carp., NYC – 1912/02/21:6a
KOLLER, Michael, Rahway, NJ – 1904/04/16:4a
KOLLHOFER, A., Newark, NJ – 1909/02/18:6a
KOLLIGS, Charles, 40, shipping clerk, *Wittlich/Rhine, Hoboken, NJ – 1897/11/01:4a
KOLLMANN, Wilhelm, NYC-B – 1912/10/01:6a
KOLLMEYER, Katharina, (Kallmeier?) NYC-M – 1885/02/23:1f, 24:1e, inquest 13 Mr:1g
KOLLOFF % Forman
KOLM, Anna, b. Seuserling, 41, Jersey City Heights, NJ – 1905/01/03:4a
KOLMER, Carl, 59, NYC-B – 1908/07/15:3b
KOLP, Ludwig, un. cigarmaker, NYC-B - 1916/02/01:6a
KOLTER % Staats
KOLTSCHAK, adm., exec. 1920/04/23:3a-c
KOLTZER, Henry, 12, NYC-M, + @on Genl Slocum – 1904/06/18:3c
KOMISUK, Fanny, 27, servant, Passaic, NJ – 1909/12/15:2c
KOMP, Albert, soc. since 1850s, 80th birthday, NYC – 1911/07/30:13c
KOMPASS, Wanda H., NYC-Bx - 1911/06/15:6a
KOMPOVIC, Andrew, 62, exec. Trenton, NJ – 1912/11/05:2d
KONEBERG, Charles, 8, Hoboken, NJ – 1886/07/21:2d
KONFELD, Meyer, infant, NYC-M – 1906/08/08:2c
KONJETZKE, Gottlieb, fireman, NYC-M – 1901/08/12:4a
KONNING, Gerth, sailor, fr Holstein, NYC? – 1882/04/07:4c

KONOGENEWA, Zenaide, Russian patriot, exec. St Petersburg –
 1906/09/09:1a, 10:1a, done 13:1a
KONOP, Louise, (Knop?), b. Koch, 67, NYC-B – 1891/04/14:4a
KONOPKANNIKOWA, Sinoida, Russian patriot, exec. Moscow –
 1906/11/27:4f; mem. 1913/03/16:5a
KONOVITZ, Ida, 20, @1911 Triangle Shirtwaist Fire, NYC-M –
 1911/03/27:1d
KONOW, Franziska, 3, NYC-M – 1882/07/27:3d
KONOWITH, Anton, cloakmaker, wife Annie, & 2 sons, NYC-M –
 1904/09/14:1d, 15:2c
KONRAD, John, jeweler, 35, NYC-M - 1920/06/09:2e
KONRAD, Joseph, NYC-M – 1912/09/05:6a
KONRAD, Ludwig, Orange, NJ - 1918/11/27:6a
KONTAK, Emil, un. baker, NYC-M - 1915/12/01:6a
KONTES, Barbara, NYC-M – 1891/04/14:4a
KONZ, Mary, 49, NYC-M – 1905/12/09:4a
KONZELMANN, Anna Maria, 85, NYC-B - 1920/01/16:6a
KOOP, Catherina, 41, NYC-M - 1894/01/10:4a
KOORMSKY, Bertha, 19, fr Russia, NYC-B – 1908/01/27:3a
KOOTBOTH % Wendisch
KOPANKIEWITZ, Joseph, NYC-M – 1885/05/06:1e-f
KOPER, Maria, NYC-M - 1918/10/28:6a
KOPF, Friedrich, butcher, NYC-M – 1884/09/01:4c, inquest 2:4c, 3:4a,
 4:4a, 7:1g, 10:1g, 24:1f
KOPF, Marcus's wife, Frances, 8, Ella, 2, NYC-M, +@ Genl Slocum –
 1904/06/17:3b
KOPF, Rebecka, b. Gortmeyer, 32, NYC-B – 1892/09/22:4a
KOPF, Theodor, 5, NYC-M, +@Genl Slocum – 1904/06/22:1d
KOPI, A., Weehawken, NJ - 1914/10/13:6a
KOPKA, Moritz, 45, butcher, NYC-M – 1898/03/09:3e
KOPKE, Tewes, NYC-M - 1894/01/24:4a
KOPP, August M., 36, lineman, NYC-M – 1890/09/16:1f, =17:1g, notes
 20:2h, 1 Oct:4d
KOPP, Herman O., 28, bank clerk, NYC-M - 1917/03/25:11g
KOPP, John, 14, Orange, NJ - 1913/11/17:6a
KOPP, John, Yonkers, NY – 1907/09/19:6a
KOPP, Joseph, 52, un. cigarmaker, NYC-M – 1901/07/26:4a, 27:4a
KOPP, L., Yonkers, NY – 1910/08/23:6a
KOPP, Mathaeus, 57, un. cigarmaker, NYC-M – 1904/05/03:4a
KOPP, Sebastian, un. carp., NYC-M – 1888/11/24:3c
KOPP, Sophie, NYC-M - 1918/01/10:6a
KOPP, Theodor, 63, un. cigarmaker, NYC-M – 1905/01/14:4a

KOPPE, Emma, 26, NYC-B - 1906/07/25:6a, fam. 28:6a
KOPPE, Fritz, 60, Newark, NJ, lathe turner, USA 1873, Newark, NJ - 1890/02/04:1e
KOPPE, Richard, un. engineer, NYC-B - 1914/04/23:6a, 24:6a, =27:2b, fam. 27:6a
KOPPE, S., & wife Matilde, on SS Bourgogne, NYC-M - 1898/07/09:4a
KOPPELMANN, Hattie, 2, NYC-M - 1908/05/08:1c
KOPPINGER, John, carver, Hoboken, NJ - 1882/03/27:4d, 28:1e, 30:3b, 6 Apr:3b
KOPPISCH, Helene, Elizabeth, NJ - 1906/01/04:4a
KOPPLEMAN, William, 26, tramway conductor, NYC-M? - 1906/05/16:2h
KOPPLER, Irene, 19, NYC-M, + @ Genl Slocum - 1904/06/18:3c
KOPPMIER, Mrs, b. Oberlies, NYC-M - 1890/09/30:4a
KOPS, John, sailor, NYC-B - 1912/05/06:2d
KORB, Arno, accountant, NYC-M - 1896/01/06:1c
KORBELIK, Joseph, 41, NYC-M - 1919/11/15:6a
KORBER, Arthur, NYC-M - 1909/01/03:1f
KORCZEWSKI, Stanislav, un. carp., NYC-M - 1914/05/07:6a
KORFF, Max, 62, insurance agent, NYC-M - 1915/05/25:1f
KORINEK, Karl, 50, Czech metallworker & SP Vienna/Austria - 1908/07/12:3e
KORMANN, J., Newark, NJ - 1905/12/28:4a
KORMINSKI, Joseph, RR worker, + Jersey City, NJ - 1898/11/19:1f
KORMINSKY, Abraham, 85, NYC-M - 1891/03/17:4a
KORN, Charles, NYC-M - 1911/04/23:7a
KORN, Eduard, NYC-M - 1903/02/22:5a
KORN, Elizabeth, 37, NYC-M - 1907/12/26:6a
KORN, Frederick, 49, butcher, NYC-M - 1902/02/28:3c
KORN, Gustav, 30, cigarmaker, NYC-M - 1899/06/17:4b-c
KORN, Herman, NYC actor, 40th anniv. on stage, - 1920/01/08:5d
KORN, Julius, restaurant owner, Keansburg, NJ - 1915/12/03:2e
KORN, Sebastian, NYC-M - 1903/03/12:4a
KORNAHRENS, Maria, 67, NYC-B - 1891/06/28:5c
KORNBERG, Henry, 54, janitor at Jewish Theol. Sem., NYC-M - 1893/12/05:4d
KORNELZ, William, carp., NYC-B - 1892/02/26:1c
KOROSKENY, Julius, fr Hungary, Chambersburg, NJ - 1886/08/04:2f
KOROSKY, Richard, 16, NYC-M - 1915/02/18:6a
KORST, Ludwig, NYC-B - 1895/06/20:4a
KORTE, Lizzie, NYC - 1912/03/18:6a
KORTE, Marie, SP?, NYC-B - 1917/01/23:6a, 24:6a
KORTEN, Anna, b. Moger, 59, West Hoboken, NJ - 1915/03/20:6a

KORTJE, Walter, un. metal worker, NYC-M - 1917/02/08:6a
KORTSTEGER, Albert, 30, un. typesetter, NYC-M - 1880/12/31:3a
KORYSINSKI, Orton, 35, Swedish sailor, NYC-M - 1907/08/09:1f
KORZ, Friedrich, NYC-M - 1906/01/05:4a
KOSAK, John, NYC-M - 1905/08/14:4a
KOSCHNICK, Helmuth, un. machinist, NYC-Bx - 1919/12/20:8a, 21:7a
KOSECK, William, 78, musician, Pole, NYC-M - 1898/06/03:3e
KOSER, Michael, 50, un. carp., NYC-B - 1913/05/26:6a, 27:6a
KOSINSKY, Theodor, 50, butcher, NYC-B - 1917/10/03:6c
KOSS, Friedrich, un. cigarmaker, Hoboken, NJ - 1889/05/14:4a
KOSS, John, un. cigarmaker, NYC-M - 1906/11/13:6a
KOSS, Karl, fr Duesseldorf/Gy, + 26 June on SS Pennland - 1892/07/06:1h
KOSSMANN, Julius, NYC-Q - 1918/05/18:6a
KOSSMANN, Max, musician, NYC-M - 1878/08/28:4d, 09/05:1f
KOSSUTH, Franz, 73, Hungarian politician - 1914/05/26:1b
KOSSUTH, Ludwig, Hungarian revol., his life 1893/05/24:2b-c; +
   Turin/Italy 1894/03/21:1b, 22:1a, NYC parade 26:1g, rev. 5 Apr./5d
KOSSWIG, Gustav, SP, New Britain, CT - 1917/01/03:2e
KOSTEN, William, 35, barber, NYC-M - 1887/12/09:1g
KOSTER % Ried
KOSTER, Margarethe, 46, NYC-M, +@ Genl Slocum - 1904/06/21:1f
KOSTER, Minnie, + near Paterson, NJ - 1908/03/04:3c
KOSTKA, Anton, un. baker, NYC-Bx - 1916/01/05:6a
KOSTOMAROFF, Nikolai, Russian historian, + 1885/05/10:3g
KOTEK, Josef, Czech journalist, fr Prossnitz/Moravia, exec. for treason on
   23 Dec - 1915/01/28:1f
KOTHE, Antonie, 69, NYC-Bx - 1917/02/22:6a
KOTHUBER, John, un. baker, NYC-M - 1912/01/29:6a
KOTOCEK, Martha, 33, NYC-Q - 1913/01/01:3b
KOTOKU, Chiyo, #, Japanese socialist, her current life - 1909/02/28:20e
KOTOKU, Denjiro, Dr., Japanese scientist & socialist, tried with wife
   Chiyo & 24 others for sedition, NYC protests 1910/12/11:1a, 13:2e,
   Kotoku, Ms Kanno Sugako, T. Numura, T. Okamoto, U. Morichika, K.
   Takeda exec. Tokyo 25 Jan. 1911::1a, 4d, 26:4b, # of the martyrs 3 Fb:1c-
   e, NYC reactions 12:6c-e, 19:13a-b, 20b. Notes on the martyrs 1911/
   04/04:4e-f, 5:4e-f, Kotoku's last words to the people 25 May 1911:4e-f
KOTOWA, Tatiana, Russian revol., + as fugitive - 1909/02/15:2e
KOTOWSKY, Michael, 23, exec. St Louis, MO - 1882/01/07:1f, 27:2e
KOTTNAUER, Wilhelmine A., b. Koch, wd Petersen, 54, NYC-M -
   1893/03/18:4a
KOTTWITS, Paul, Teicha/Rietschen/Gy, War 1 - 1914/11/01:3b
KOTZLAN, Josef, un. cabinet maker, NYC-M - 1893/11/22:4a

KOUDOS, Abraham, 14, newspaper boy, NYC-M – 1905/02/15:3d
KOVACS, John, NYC-M – 1910/05/19:6a
KOWALEWSKI, Sofia, Russian Socialist & Mathematician –
  1891/03/05:2c
KOWALEWSKY, Otto, un. carp., NYC – 1912/09/12:6a
KOWALSKY, Frank, 29, worker, fr Austria, Elizabethport, NJ –
  1900/07/08:1e
KOWALSKY, un. cigar maker & SPD activist, Berlin/Gy – 1886/08/30:2e
KOZIG, Mrs, fam. 1907/07/31:6a
KOZLOWSKY, anton, un. carp., NYC-B – 1911/12/15:6a
KOZLY, George, 29, killed during Pittsburgh, PA strike – 1913/01/29:2b
KRABATZ, Cole, 21, gold worker, fr Poland, NYC-M – 1896/05/07:1d
KRABITZ, Louis, NYC-M – 1892/10/08:2h
KRACHT, Ferdinand, 69, un. cigarmaker, NYC-Q - 1918/05/25:6a
KRACKELER % Lehnhoff
KRAECKER, Julius, saddler & MdR for SPD, * Breslau, 1888/10/03:1a,
  =22:2d, note 7 Nov:2f
KRAEMER, Frederick, NYC-M – 1885/01/19:3b
KRAEMER, Adam, un. painter, NYC-M – 1897/02/28:5a
KRAEMER, Carl, machinist, NYC-B – 1903/04/18:4a
KRAEMER, Friedrich, 55, silkweaver, Paterson, NJ – 1900/07/27:1b
KRAEMER, Joseph, un. mason, NYC-M – 1900/03/09:4a
KRAEMER, Lorenz Theodor, NYC-B – 1911/08/27:7c
KRAEMER, Louis, 65, furrier fr Russia, & wife, 60, NYC-B –
  1910/10/08:2b
KRAEMER, Michael, 25, NYC-Q - 1896/03/2:1b
KRAEMER, Peter, artist, incl. G-A press, * 24 Jy 1823 Zweibruecken/Pfalz,
  NYC-M – 1907/08/02:6a
KRAEMER, Robert Justus, SLP, NYC-M – 1886/11/02:3c, =4:1g
KRAEMER, Salomea, b. Koenig, 50, NYC-M – 1899/11/27:4a
KRAEMER, Sophie, b. Fleischmann, 62, NYC-M – 1892/0615:4a
KRAEUTER, Ernst, 60, SPD, ex-alderman Freiburg/Breisgau -
  1915/07/04:3a
KRAEUTER, William, 70, machinist, Newark, NJ – 1890/10/21:2f
KRAFFT, Aldan von, 52, un. machinist, NYC-M – 1892/01/07:4a
KRAFFT, Leonhard, 54, un. carp. & mgr Stuttgart Labor House, + there -
  1915/01/24:3d
KRAFFT, Louisa, 30, NYC-M, + @ Genl Slocum – 1904/06/17:3b
KRAFT, Andrew, cook, NYC-M – 1905/03/07:4a
KRAFT, Babetta, 7, NYC-M – 1882/10/31:3a
KRAFT, Frederick, 48, Portchester, NY - 1913/10/13:3b
KRAFT, Heinrich's wife, NYC-M – 1886/09/14:3c

KRAFT, Hermann, 45, NYC-B – 1887/07/07:2e
KRAFT, Hugo, 38, tin-caster & SPD from Berlin/Gy, arrived NYC – 1880/11/30:1d-e, 2 Dec:2a-b, 6:1d-e
KRAFT, Johanna, 45, servant, NYC-Q - 1915/01/18:2e
KRAFT, John, 24, watchmaker, fr Wuerttemberg/Gy, New Brunswick, NJ – 1881/06/18:1f
KRAFT, Joseph, NYC-M – 1909/05/29:6a
KRAFT, Louis, 20, bookkeeper, anarchist fr Russia, 1894 USA, NYC-M – 1897/01/21:1f
KRAFT, Louisa, NYC-M, + @ Genl Slocum – 1904/06/18:3c
KRAFT, Peter, 19, woodcarver, NYC-B – 1884/10/08:3b
KRAHMER, Moritz, alias Krauss, 34, clerk, * Brehna/Saxony, USA 1876, NYC-Ward's Island - 1879/04/30:1g
KRAIL, H., NYC-Q - 1915/01/09:6a
KRAKECECK, Frank, 80, NYC-Q - 1913/09/09:6c
KRAKER, Josef, & Rosie Deutschmann, both Gottscheer, NYC?, married – 1912/05/10:6d
KRALL, Franz, 40, un. baker, NYC-M - 1913/06/27:6a, 28:6a, fam. 3 Jy:6a
KRAMER % Frank, % Geissler, % Vordach
KRAMER, Amadeus, SP, & wife Maria, Newark, NJ, Golden Wedding - 1920/10/11:5e
KRAMER, Anna Schmitt, 47, NYC-B - 1918/05/12:7a
KRAMER, Anna, 39, NYC-B – 1905/08/02:4a, 4:4a
KRAMER, August, un. carp., SP, Newark, NJ – 1913/02/09:7a, 13:6a
KRAMER, Barbara, NYC-M, +@ on Genl Slocum – 1904/06/18:3c
KRAMER, Christian, NYC-M – 1885/05/08:3e
KRAMER, G. W., 50, tailor, NYC-B – 1912/07/06:3b
KRAMER, Gertrud, b. Herz, wd Prosser, 35, NYC-M – 1904/07/21:1h
KRAMER, Gustav, un. butcher, NYC-B - 1913/10/03:6a
KRAMER, Herman, 50, grocer, E. Rutherford,NJ - 1913/05/16:2e
KRAMER, Herman, miner, + Blockton, AL – 1897/10/02:1d, 3:4b
KRAMER, Johanna, b. Greie see Greie-Cramer, Johanna
KRAMER, John, NYC-B – 1885/05/26:2f
KRAMER, John, NYC-B – 1903/11/14:4b
KRAMER, Marie, common-law wife of NYSZ correspondent P. Wolff, + Washington, DC – 1891/09/24:1h
KRAMER, Max, 50?, music teacher, at Stevens Inst. Technol., USA 1880s, NYC-M - 1920/04/05:2d
KRAMER, Otto, Jersey City, NJ - 1918/02/02:6a
KRAMER, Peter, Berlin "water poet," + 1850s, his life – 1886/10/14:6c
KRAMER, Theodor, 25, NYC-B - 1919/02/09:12a
KRAMER, W., NYC-M - 1918/02/09:6a

KRAMER, Wilhelmina, NYC-B – 1910/06/11:6a
KRAMER, William, on late owner Atlantic Garden concert hall, NYC – 1900/08/23:3b
KRAMMER, Hermann, 20, fr Russia, painter, NYC – 1901/06/30:5b
KRAMPF, Morris, 9, NYC – 1903/07/11:3g
KRANDEP, Hermann, 38, bartender, NYC-M – 1893/03/23:4e
KRANENBERGER, Philip, jeweler, NYC-M – 1888/04/27:4b
KRANICH, Wilhelm, stoker on SS Knickerbocker – 1881/07/23:2e-f, 24:5f, 27:1d, 28:1b
KRANIK, Frank, miner, Port Hope, NJ – 1909/11/19:2b, 20:3c
KRANK, Michael, un. carp., NYC-Q – 1912/11/23:6a, 24:7a
KRANTZ, Bernhard Heinrich, 31, un. furrier, NYC-M – 1889/02/06:2g, 4a
KRANTZ, un. painter, NYC – 1899/11/11:1b
KRANTZER, Michael, NYC? – 1896/09/03:4a
KRANZ, Carl, un. cigarmaker, NYC-M - 1895/07/05:4a
KRAPF, Georg, 83, Newark, NJ – 1901/07/04:3b
KRAPKA, Joseph, 46, fr Prossnitz/Bohemia, SP, ed. for Hlas Lidu – 1909/05/02:3e
KRAPKA, SP in Prossnitz/Moravia, monument inaug. 1910/07/24:3d
KRAPP, George F., cashier, NYC-M – 1905/10/05:1e
KRASA-NOWAK, Minna, 37, textile worker & SP Vienna/Austria – 1911/06/11:20e, 18:20c-e
KRASENSKY, Wilhelm, 47, printer & SP Vienna/Austria – 1908/01/05:3e
KRASNOBRODSKI, J., Russian revol., exec. near St Petersburg – 1908/07/18:4e
KRATOCHWIL, Ernst, 66, NYC-B - 1917/02/12:6a
KRATOCHWIL, Frank, 61, un. ironworker, NYC-M – 1905/01/21:4a
KRATSCHLIK % Armbruster
KRATZ, Philipp, NYC - 1913/12/02:6a
KRATZENSTEIN % Loewenstein
KRATZENSTEIN, Philip, 40, un. waiter, NYC-M – 1892/06/28:4e
KRAUKE, Max, 24, worker, NYC-M – 1906/09/15:6c, 16:7c
KRAUPA, Wenzel, Bohemia, LI – 1890/12/29:1f, =30:1g
KRAUS, Anton, SP?, glovemaker, Sudeten German, NYC-M - 1920/05/15:6a, 16:2g, =20:6c
KRAUS, Anton, un. carp., NYC-M – 1897/03/31:4a
KRAUS, Bernhard, 57, NYC-M – 1891/07/24:4a
KRAUS, David, Jersey City Hgths, NJ - 1916/01/21:6a, 22:6a
KRAUS, Frank, 58, cigarmkr, NYC-Q - 1913/11/06:3c
KRAUS, Fritz, Newark, NJ - 1916/04/25:6a
KRAUS, Herman, 5, NYC-M – 1910/04/24:1d
KRAUS, Imanuel, NYC-M – 1891/10/02:4a

KRAUS, Jacob, un. cigar maker, NYC-M – 1882/10/25:3b
KRAUS, John, 55, tobacco dealer, Trenton, NJ – 1901/11/29:1b
KRAUS, John, un. carp., Jersey City, NJ – 1886/01/06:2d
KRAUS, John, un. cigar maker, NYC-M – 1881/02/28:3c
KRAUS, Joseph A., NYC-M - 1917/08/01:6a
KRAUS, Joseph, NYC-M – 1903/07/08:4a
KRAUS, Leopold, innkeep, NYC-M - 1878/04/30:4a
KRAUS, Martin, >70, War 2, NYC-B - 1914/08/20:6c, 22:6a
KRAUSE, ..., restaurant owner & SPD activist in Gera/Thueringia, = 1886/07/07:2d
KRAUSE, Adolf, NYC-M – 1908/04/01:6a
KRAUSE, Adolf, un. painter, NYC-M - 1915/12/17:6a
KRAUSE, August, 64, SP?, NYC-M - 1915/03/08:6a, 9:6a, 10:6a, =11:6e, fam. 14:11a; mem. 1916/03/07:6a
KRAUSE, Auguste, NYC-M - 1920/12/22:6a
KRAUSE, B., NYC-B – 1907/06/01:6a
KRAUSE, Clara, 68, NYC-M - 1918/12/06:6a
KRAUSE, Daniel, 23, SLP, bookbinder, NYC-M – 1883/02/07:4d, 8:3b
KRAUSE, David, 21, Russian Socialist, exec. Lodz on 8/19 – 1905/10/05:2c
KRAUSE, Edward, 22,SLP, *Ciska/Bohemia, USA 1869, wood carver, NYC-M - 1879/06/11:1f,3a, 12:1g, = 13:4b
KRAUSE, Edward, baker, NYC-B – 1887/06/09:2e
KRAUSE, Frank J., exec. Allentown, PA – 1900/05/24:1g
KRAUSE, Frederick, NYC-M – 1909/08/19:2d
KRAUSE, Friedrich, 79, NYC-M – 1911/02/01:6a
KRAUSE, Heinrich, 28, NYC-M – 1900/02/10:4a, fam. 16:4a
KRAUSE, John, West New York, NJ - 1920/03/15:6a
KRAUSE, Kate, 35, NYC-B – 1900/07/07:2g
KRAUSE, Marie, 77, NYC – 1906/07/29:7a
KRAUSE, Ottmar, SP, locksmith, Dover, NJ - 1914/08/13:6a,c, =#15:3d
KRAUSE, Paul Gerhard, NYC-M – 1891/07/07:4a
KRAUSE, Theodor, 32, electrotypist, NYC-B – 1897/07/04:5b
KRAUSE, Theodore Frederick, 63, Elizabeth, NJ – 1919/11/16:6a
KRAUSE, William, 38, Jersey City, NJ - 1915/07/18:11b
KRAUSE, William, 38, worker, NYC-M – 1883/12/26:3e, 27:1g, inquest 29:3a, 31:1f
KRAUSER, Karl A., 13, NYC-M – 1891/03/18:4a
KRAUSHAAR, Charles W., 61,art dealer, NYC-M - 1917/01/07:11c
KRAUSS, Charlotte, b. Frey, 53, NYC-M – 1898/07/29:4a
KRAUSS, comrade, 40, French deputy for Lyons, SP – 1904/10/18:2d
KRAUSS, Henry, NYC-B – 1900/03/23:4a
KRAUSS, John, Newark, – 1901/12/29:5a

KRAUSS, Wilhelm, un. machinist, NYC-M - 1914/06/27:6a
KRAUSSEN, August H., 8, NYC-M - 1881/11/21:3a
KRAUT, Christian, NYC-B - 1915/10/05:6a
KRAUTWURST, Annie, NYC-M, +@ Genl Slocum - 1904/06/17:3b
KRAUTZ, Robert, 33, brush maker, NYC-M - 1896/09/10:1g
KRAVITZ, Mary, 30, NYC-B - 1916/06/03:5e
KRAWITSCHKY, Olga, 22, NYC-B - 1892/04/05:4b
KREBS, Antoinette, 7, NYC-M - 1887/08/13:3c
KREBS, Barbara, NYC-B - 1885/01/04:5f
KREBS, Carl August, German composer, Dresden/Gy - 1880/05/24:1b
KREBS, Christina, b. Schultze, 27, NYC-Bx - 1916/02/27:7a
KREBS, Georg, infant, NYC - 1886/01/12:3a
KREBS, Peter, SLP, un. cigarmaker, * 8 Aug. 1838 Oggersheim/Pfalz/Gy,
  NYC-M - 1889/05/19:5d, f, 20:4a, 21:4a, =22:1h, 23:4a
KRECH, Adalbert, 54, capt. Of SS Waldersee, + Hoboken, NJ -
  1907/05/11:2b, 12:1c
KRECHT, Anna, NYC-B - 1912/10/20:11f
KREECK, Max, NYC-M - 1904/03/23:4a
KREET, Heinrich, SPD & labor org. in Hamburg, * 1837
  Adensen/Nordstemmen, + Hamburg - 1916/03/19:3a
KREFFT, August, 67, un. printer, NYC-Bx - 1910/12/30:6a
KREFT, Ernst, 42, SP, typesetter, Philadelphia, PA - 1905/11/21:3f
KREH, George, 65, Jersey City, NJ - 1891/07/09:4a
KREHBIEL, John D., 60, NYC-M - 1891/03/14:4a
KREHER, August, 47, NYC-M - 1880/05/28:3a
KREHER, Hermann, shoe dealer, Hoboken, NJ - 1903/11/15:1d
KREIDLER, Joseph, 54, hotelier, Tarrytown, NY - 1910/08/20:1c
KREILE, Mary, NYC-Q - 1907/05/01:1e
KREIN, Joseph, ship's steward, @ 1900 dock fire, Hoboken, NJ -
  1900/07/03:1c
KREISCH, Joseph, 53, tailor, NYC-Bx - 1912/02/24:6a
KREISCHER, Edward, 36, brick factory owner, NYC-SI - 1894/06/09:3e
KREISEL, Abraham's wife, fr Polodosh/Russia, + on sea on way to
  husband in NYC, but 3 children arrived safely - 1899/10/31:3b
KREITIEL, Thomas, 50, Newark, NJ 1900/04/05:4a
KREITZMACHER, Louis, 56, cloakmaker, NYC-M - 1894/08/10:1g
KREJSA, Carl, 18, NYC-M - 1901/04/09:4a
KREKACA, Martin, NYC-M - 1900/08/30:2h
KRELLIG, Rudolf, un. carp., NYC-M - 1912/12/30:6a, 31:6a, 1 Jan
  1913:6a
KREMER, Auguste, NYC-M - 1898/06/19:5a
KREMER, Charles, 21, NYC-Q - 1912/04/07:7a

KREMER, Stephanie, b. Blaettler, 29, NYC-Q – 1910/05/19:6a
KREMMLER, John, NYC-M – 1881/07/18:3b
KREMPEL, Michael, 44, NYC-M – 1891/04/01:4a
KREMPLER, Moritz, NYC-Q - 1918/11/10:12a
KREMSER % Theus
KREMSER, Gretchen, 42, NYC-M – 1902/05/30:4a
KRENNSTETTER, Rudolf see Kehr, Rudolf
KREPS % Gerner
KREPS, Clara, 54, NYC-B – 1919/11/18:6a
KRESS, Adolf, Elberfeld/Gy, ATB? War 1 - 1914/11/01:3b
KRESS, Elizabeth, 21, NYC-M – 1881/11/02:1g
KRESS, Ludwig, 37, NYC-B - 1895/03/18:2c
KRESSE, Frieda, b. Friedrichs, 28, NYC-M – 1882/04/11:4b
KRESSMAN, Ida, (Kressmar?), + 1915, mem. 1916/08/27:7a, 1917/08/27:6a, 1918/08/27:6a
KRESSMANN, Jakob, NYC-M - 1917/01/24:6a
KRESTAN, Vincens, un. carp., NYC-M - 1914/08/29:6a
KRETSCHMANN, Edmund, 42, USA 1883 fr Vienna, carp., innkeep of "Zum groben Michel," 5th Ave. G-A anarchist watering hole, NYC-M – 1896/05/19:4a, 20:1g
KRETSCHMAR, Frank, landlord, NYC-M – 1891/05/04:1h, 5:1g, 9:2f, note 21 Oct:2g, 23:1g
KRETSCHMAR, G. A., Dr., NYC-M – 1887/12/07:2h
KRETSCHMAR, Hedwig, SDP, fr Leipzig?, NYC-Q – 1905/02/06:4a, 7:4a
KRETSCHMER, Anton, 55, NYC-M – 1904/09/29:4a
KRETSCHMER, Hugo, Newark, NJ - 1915/04/27:2g, 28:6a
KRETZ, Rosine, 50, NYC-M – 1883/11/07:3b
KRETZER, Heinrich, NYC-B - 1916/01/28:6a
KRETZER, Jacob, innkeep, NYC-Q – 1908/08/13:2g
KRETZSCHMAR % Victorica
KRETZSCHMAR, Dr., 44, Brooklyn polit., USA fr Gy as child, NYC-B – 1891/04/29:2e
KRETZSCHMAR, family 1885/05/19:3d
KRETZSCHMAR, Minna, 23, & Richard, 11, Alfred, 10, Maria, child, NYC-M – 1885/05/04:1b, 5:1g, 6:1f, 7:1d, fam. 19:3d, @Manhattan Fire May 1885
KREUSCHAUF, West Hoboken, NJ - 1918/01/30:6a
KREUTZ, Hans, un. cigarmaker, SPD expelled fr Ottensen/Gy, here SLP, NYC-M – 1884/08/23:3d, =24:5g, 8a, rev. 25:1g
KREUTZER, Conradin, German composer, 100th anniv. Of birth celebrated by NYC-M Kreutzer Club - 1880/11/24:4b
KREUTZER, Katherina, 54, NYC-Bx – 1893/07/29:1h (East 153rd)

KREUTZER, Valentin, 19, NYC-M – 1882/08/10:4c, 11:1f, 18:1f
KREUTZKAMP, Henry, NYC-M – 1905/08/18:4a
KREY, John, cooper, Newark, NJ – 1888/06/22:1e-f
KREY, Otto, NYC-M – 1909/04/15:6a
KREZ, Elizabeth, NYC-B - 1916/11/21:6c
KRICHEL, Gertrude, NYC-Bx – 1914/09/08:6a
KRIEBE, Karl F., carpenter & SPD activist expelled fr Hamburg/Gy, arrived NYC – 1880/12/11:1g
KRIEG % Ulbricht
KRIEG, Benedict, 81, NYC-M - 1920/02/21:6a
KRIEG, Christine, b. Ratzel, 40, NYC-M – 1887/07/06:3b, 8:2g
KRIEG, Frank, NYC-B – 1908/06/18:6a
KRIEG, Louisa, b. Hagdorn, 57, NYC-M – 1910/01/09:7c
KRIEGER, Frank, SLP?, Guttenberg, NJ – 1893/07/05:4a,d, 14:4a
KRIEGER, Frederick, 25, NYC-M – 1903/08/26:4a
KRIEGER, Friedrich, 64, NYC-Bx - 1915/11/19:6a
KRIEGER, Fritz, 26, brewery worker, NYC-M – 1900/03/07:1d
KRIEGER, John A., 43, v-p Boston Molasses Co., ex-NYC, + Boston, MA – 1914/10/18:11b
KRIEGER, John, SP?, Hoboken, NJ - 1914 /06/24:6a
KRIEGER, M., West Hoboken, NJ - 1916/03/17:6a
KRIEGER, Paul, 38, painter, NYC-M - 1895/06/22:1g
KRIEGER, Rose, 21, NYC-Bx – 1913/04/01:6a
KRIEHMIG, Frank, 47, un. furrier, NYC-B – 1904/12/01:4a
KRIEHN, Anthony, 30, cooper, NYC-B - 1916/04/22:5d
KRIELE, Julius, sales agent, NYC-M – 1892/12/03:4b
KRIEMEYER, Henry, 54, NYC-B - 1914/02/03:3b
KRIETE, John, 37, NYC-B – 1911/03/07:3a
KRIETE, Lena, 32, NYC-M – 1893/08/12:1g
KRIETE, William, 45, waiter, NYC-B – 1900/12/06:4b
KRIETZ, Joseph, 51, mechanic, NYC-B – 1908/11/05:3b
KRIMMELBEIN % Lutz
KRING, George, NYC-B, + on ship Mystery – 1887/07/12:1c-d, 13:2g
KRINGER, Eva, Hoboken, NJ, +@Genl Slocum – 1904/06/16:1c, 17:3b
KRINKE % Schirmer
KRIOFSKY, Georg, NYC-D – 1912/05/08:3a
KRISCH, John, un. carp., NYC-Q - 1919/05/14:6a
KRIST, Frederick, exec. Auburn, NY – 1901/11/21:3c
KRISTOF, Andreas, un. carp., NYC-B – 1904/05/04:4a
KRITZ, Frank, 24, woodcarver, USA 1904, NYC-M – 1908/06/22:1b
KRITZMANN, John, 80, scissor-sharpener, NYC-M - 1920/12/15:1e
KRIZAN, Juraj, & wife, 1902 fr Hungary, Paterson, NJ – 1902/06/21:1e

KROECK, Daniel, NYC – 1881/06/14:3c
KROECKER, Catherine, 69, Union Hill, NJ - 1914/12/27:7a
KROECKER, Franz, 59, Union Hill, NJ – 1911/11/18:6a
KROEDLER, Wilhelm, SLP, mechanic, * Russia, NYC-M - 1894/04/09:4a, =10:1g, 12:4a
KROEGER, Ludwig, Barmbeck, ATB, War 1 - 1914/11/01:3b
KROENCKE, Henry August, 17, NYC-M – 1904/12/24:4a
KROENKE, H., NYC-Bx - 1917/03/24:6a
KROENKE, Heinrich M., 42, NYC-M – 1891/07/07:4a
KROENKE, Maria, b. Lemmermann, 43, NYC-M – 1887/05/21:3c
KROESEL, Chr., un. cigarmaker, NYC-M – 1897/09/29:4a
KROETZ, William, un. cigarmaker, NYC-M – 1881/02/22:3b
KROFT, Wilhelm, un. cigarmaker, Hoboken, NJ – 1891/06/18:4a
KROGBIEN, William, NYC-M – 1900/09/11:4a
KROGEL, William, un. carp., NYC-M – 1904/01/31:5a
KROGER, George, NYC-M - 1918/09/08:6a
KROGER, Getje, 53, NYC-M - 1914/05/21:6a
KROGER, Henry, 30, NYC - 1914/03/21:6a
KROGER, Hermann, 45, grocer, NYC-M – 1882/04/05:4c
KROGMANN % Heerlein
KROGMANN, Bernhardine, 69, NYC-M - 1915/04/10:6a
KROHN, August, painter & SPD Konstanz/Gy – 1912/04/28:3a
KROHN, William Charles, un. painter, NYC-M - 1919/08/19:6a
KROHNE, Margarethe, b. Ansa....?, 77, NYC-M – 1892/07/21:4a
KROHNE, William, 67, NYC-B – 1910/09/17:3a
KROHNEY, Henry, 39, NYC-M – 1900/07/20:1e
KROIT, Rosie, 54, NYC-M – 1906/03/02:4a
KROLL, Anton, 63, NYC-M - 1913/10/11:6a, 12:7b
KROLL, Elizabeth, b. Baule, NYC-M – 1907/05/08:6a
KROMANN, Anna F., b. Goeppert, NYC-B – 1886/03/22:5e, 23:3d
KROMANN, Karoline, NYC-M - 1894/04/19:4a
KROMER % Gagelmann; KRONAUER % Dinninger
KROMM, Mathilde, NYC-M – 1903/10/23:4a
KRONAWETTER, Ferdinand, Dr., 75, Viennese liberal polit., 1913/02/05:4c-d, 14:4e
KRONEMEYER, Andreas, 23, un. driver, NYC-SI – 1902/10/16:4a, 18:4a
KRONENBERGER, Franz, fr Herfeld/Bavaria, USA 1902, NYC-M – 1908/10/20:2d
KRONENBETTER, George, 46, un. cook, NYC-B - 1920/01/08:6a
KRONENBITTER, Kordula, 83, NYC-M – 1909/10/21:6a
KRONENBITTER, Matthias, 47, un. carp., NYC-M – 1904/05/10:4b
KRONENGOLD, Arnold, 58, NYC-M – 1898/09/29:3h

KRONIMUS, Moritz, 62, SP, * Pfalz Prov.,NYC-M - 1917/01/02:6a, 4:6a, =5:6c, fam. 9:6a, mem. 1918/01/01:6a, 1919/01/02:6a
KRONKE, Joseph, butcher & local politician, Polish?, Detroit, MI – 1900/09/06:1g
KRONMANN, Annie, NYC-M – 1899/08/11:3e, 13:5a, 18:1f-g, 19:1h; trial of killer 22 Dec:1e, 28:1e, guilty 30:1f; 1 Jan. 00:2b
KRONZ, Michael, 52, NYC-B - 1916/05/25:6b
KROOS, John, 42, pres. Central Dairy, NYC-Bx - 1913/05/27:2e
KROPKE, August, un. carp., NYC-M – 1912/01/28:7a
KROPP % Niemann
KROPP, Frederick, 81, un. printer, NYC-B - 1915/05/26:6a
KROPP, Magdelene, NYC-M – 1907/11/16:6a
KROTH % Schmitt
KROTZ, Anton, 48, un. cigarmaker, fr Schwaben?, NYC-B – 1901/11/01:4a, 2:4a
KROTZ, Anton, un. cigarmaker, SDP, NYC-B? – 1901/11/13:4a
KROTZ, Henry, NYC-M – 1908/11/23:6a
KROUPA, Joseph, NYC-B – 1911/01/28:6a
KROUSBEIN, Peter's wife, NYC-B - 1879/05/06:4e
KROUSBORN, Peter, un. cigarmkr, NYC-B – 1892/11/27:5d
KROUTH, John, 63, NYC-M – 1901/02/25:4a
KROUTWURST, Edward, 34, un. carp., SLP, NYC-M – 1899/08/10:1g, 4a
KRUCHEN, Charles, owner of Helvetia Hall, Paterson, NJ – 1908/10/10:3b
KRUCK, Michael, 10, NYC-M – 1902/12/12:1f
KRUECK, Luise, b. Feltmeth, NYC-M – 1892/07/04:4a
KRUEGER % Bidlingmaier, % Umbach
KRUEGER, ..., 21, NYC-M – 1909/02/10:1b
KRUEGER, Albert, un. typesetter, NYC-M – 1891/12/18:4a
KRUEGER, August, NYC-B – 1892/01/03:5e
KRUEGER, Barbara, NYC-M – 1891/11/22:1c
KRUEGER, Bertha, 56, NYC-Q - 1914/01/19:6a
KRUEGER, Charles W., fire chief, NYC-M – 1908/02/17:1e
KRUEGER, Edmund, NYC-M – 1891/03/27:4a
KRUEGER, Elizabeth, b. Luebler, NYC-Q – 1907/09/13:6a
KRUEGER, Else, NYC?, rev. of her socialist" baptism"– 1892/03/14:1e
KRUEGER, Friedrich, 37, NYC-M - 1879/02/09:8a
KRUEGER, Fritz W., 57, NYC-B – 1912/05/31:6a
KRUEGER, George, 70, NYC-M - 1918/11/21:6a
KRUEGER, Gustav, 46, West New York, NJ – 1912/10/16:3d
KRUEGER, Henry, watchmaker, 55, NYC-M – 1899/03/04:1c
KRUEGER, Hermann, NYC-Q – 1908/11/14:6a

KRUEGER, Julius, un. cigarmaker, ex-pres. NYC German Cigarworkers' Union, NYC-M – 1889/08/03:4a
KRUEGER, Leopold, un. baker, NYC-B – 1904/02/25:4a
KRUEGER, Marie, & infant, NYC-M – 1907/11/19:2b
KRUEGER, Mathilde, 59, NYC-M – 1896/04/23:1e
KRUEGER, Oscar A., 56, NYC-Bx – 1909/06/14:6a
KRUEGER, Paul, "Ohm," ex-president of Transvaal, + Glarus/Switz. – 1904/07/15:1g, =16:1b, 17:1b
KRUEGER, Paul, Hoboken, NJ – 1910/11/07:6a
KRUEGER, R., un. carp., Jersey City, NJ – 1901/01/10:4a
KRUEGER, Wilhelm G., 43, inventor of patented balloon-type aircraft, USA 1850s fr Graudenz/Westprussia, NYC-M – 1882/05/02:4d
KRUEGER, Wilhelm, 58, carp., NYC-M – 1881/10/08:3b
KRUEGER, William, & wife, Newark, NJ – 1907/02/22:3c
KRUEKEL, Franz, NYC-B – 1909/03/29:6a
KRUG, Elisabeth, b. Huether, NYC-M – 1907/03/31:7c, 1 Apr:6a
KRUG, Ferdinand, 50, un. carp., NYC-Bx – 1913/03/22:6a
KRUG, Franz, NYC-B - 1917/11/24:6a
KRUG, Georg, NYC-M - 1917/01/17:6a
KRUG, John, 87, & Barbara, 86, NYC-M - 1917/01/06:2d
KRUG, Karl, Newark, NJ – 1906/12/30:7b
KRUG, Maria, b. Graefe, 67, Newark, NJ – 1904/02/24:4a
KRUG, R. L., NYC-M – 1910/02/06:7c, 8:6a
KRUG, Theresa, 72, Newark, NJ – 1912/06/18:1b
KRUGGE, Otto von, guard, East Rutherford, NJ - 1914/01/09:2e
KRUMFUSS, Fritz, 44, SP?, NYC-B – 1910/04/10:7c
KRUMM, Daniel, Hoboken, NJ – 1910/07/24:7c
KRUMM, Emil, 46, NYC-M - 1913/12/22:6a
KRUMM, Friedrich, Groetzingen, ATB, War 1 - 1914/11/01:3b
KRUMM, Louis, 40, baker, NYC-B – 1908/10/19:3a
KRUMMACHER, John, NYC-B – 1891/04/11:4a
KRUNNOW, Ernest, 44, bookkeeper, NYC-M – 1905/04/01:1g
KRUPP, Alfred, German manufacturer, crit. Obit – 1887/07/15:1b
KRUPP, Friedrich Alfred, German industrialist – 1902/11/23:1a, 24:2a-b, 25:1b, 26:1h, 27:1a, 2d-e, 28:2b, 29:2a-b, etc. 8 Dec:2e-f, 15:2d, 17:2c-d, 19:2c, 23:2d, 31:2h. More on his + 1903/01/19:1h, 2a, 27:2f-g, 11 June:2c
KRUSA, Clara, b. Bobertz, Elizabeth, NJ – 1902/05/04:5a
KRUSE % Hahn
KRUSE, Carolina, 71, NYC-M – 1899/04/16:5a
KRUSE, Charly, 28, SLP, NYC-Q – 1888/12/20:3c
KRUSE, D., 57, NYC-Q – 1898/05/21:4a
KRUSE, Friedrich, 30, NYC-Q – 1912/04/18:6a

KRUSE, Hugo, sailor on USS Maine, + Havana/Cuba, NYC-Q – 1898/02/18:1b
KRUSE, Karl, 75, NYC-M – 1884/08/05:3c
KRUSE, Louise, 52, NYC-M – 1887/08/20:3a
KRUSINSKY, Anthony, 38, Hyde Park, NY - 1915/12/27:2d
KRUSKOPF, Fritz, un. cigarmaker, NYC-M - 1894/04/25:4a
KRUSPE, Adolph, NYC-M – 1913/02/06:6a
KRUST, Jean, NYC-M – 1906/10/20:6a
KRYGEER, Jakob, un. typesetter, NYC-M – 1896/09/20:5a
KRZYZANOWSKY, Vladimir, Polish patriot, * 1824 Roznova/Posen, NYC-M – 1887/02/02:6c
KUBALLE, Charles, machinist, NYC-Q – 1910/01/26:6a
KUBANECK, Franz, NYC-M - 1914/10/18:7b
KUBANECK, Franziska, 64, NYC-M - 1918/05/04:6a
KUBIN, Dr., physician on SS Prinz Eitel Friedrich, + Hoboken?, NJ – 1907/06/13:2e
KUCH, Alois, un. carp., NYC-M – 1907/08/06:6a
KUCHER, Margaret, NYC-B, + on@ Genl Slocum – 1904/06/18:3c
KUCK, Louise, 40, NYC-B – 1892/02/28:1h
KUCKELHORN, Emil, 45, engineer, NYC-M or Bx – 1892/12/4e, 13:1f, 14:1d,4a. Trial of his killer 18 Ap 1893:1f, 19:1h, to be exec 25:1d,
KUCKS, Henry, 57, War 2, NYC-B - 1915/10/18:2d
KUDECKE, Heinrich, 42, NYC-M – 1890/10/15:4a
KUDERA, August, NYC-M, + @on Genl Slocum – 1904/06/18:3c
KUDERER, Josef, 56, NYC-M - 1913/12/13:6a
KUDLICH Feier in NYC 1903/12/06:4c-e, 13:9c
KUDLICH, Hans, Dr., '48er, liberator of Austrian peasantry, USA 1854, 80th birthday cel. in NYC – 1903/09/13:5e; + Hoboken, Dr., NJ - 1917/11/11:6f-g, 11a-b
KUEBLER, Franz, 16, NYC-M – 1888/08/23:1g
KUEBLER, Henrietta, Paterson, NJ – 1898/05/23:3d
KUEBLER, Julia, 34, singer, * Karlsruhe/Baden, NYC-M - 1917/12/28:5e
KUEBLER, Monica M., NYC-M - 1913/05/15:6a
KUECHENMEISTER, Louis, NYC – 1911/11/12:1d
KUECHENMEISTER, Louis's wife, NYC-M – 1911/06/20:2c
KUECHLER, Emil, anarchist, exec. Halle/Gy, 1885/02/08:1d, 9:1a, 23:2f-g
KUECHMANN, George W., 25, bookkeeper, NYC-B – 1902/06/16:4a
KUECHMANN, John, 43, SLP, NYC-M – 1888/12/22:3c, =24:2f, 25:3a
KUECHMANN, Mary, b. Feunel, NYC-B – 1906/02/28:4a
KUEHL, Fritz Th., fr Schleswig?, NYC-M – 1881/08/03:3c
KUEHL, Johanna, 44, NYC-M – 1899/09/11:4a
KUEHL, Margarethe, NYC-M – 1891/06/23:4a

KUEHL, Otto, Newton Heights, LI – 1910/03/08:6a, fam. 11:6a
KUEHLKE, Henry, 32, un. cigar packer, NYC-M – 1887/04/07:3e
KUEHLMANN, Frederick, NYC-B – 1909/01/14:6a
KUEHLWEIN, Mrs, 61, Middletown, NY - 1915/07/22:1e
KUEHN % Schladitz
KUEHN, ..., member Deutscher Kriegerbund, NYC-M – 1890/01/11:4a
KUEHN, August, 70, SPD, MdR, *Altenlohm/Silesia, + Langenbielau/ Silesia - 1916/04/18:4d
KUEHN, Gertrud, NYC-M – 1892/10/12:4a
KUEHNE % Schreck
KUEHNE, Dominick, NYC-M – 1901/03/28:4a
KUEHNE, Dorothea, b. Hovekamp, 47, NYC-M – 1891/06/04:4a
KUEHNE, Gerhard, SP?, Leonia, NJ - 1914/01/18:7a, 19:6a
KUEHNE, son of August, 1, NYC-M - 1879/07/21:3a
KUEHNE, Werner, un. Butcher, NYC-M – 1911/06/19:6a
KUEHNER, Otto, Hoboken, NJ - 1915/04/05:6a
KUEHNHOLD, Jacob, NYC-Bx – 1908/12/04:6a
KUEHNKE, Luise, NYC – 1912/08/01:6a
KUEHNLE, Friedrich, NYC-M – 1888/11/08:3b
KUEHNY, Maria, b. Schumacher, NYC-M – 1890/05/26:4a
KUEHST, Wilhelm, barber & SPD activist expelled fr Berlin/Gy, arrived NYC – 1880/12/11:1g
KUEHWEIDNER, Alois, 42, NYC-M – 1902/05/10:4a
KUEL % Schaper
KUELL, Emil, 39, Jersey City Heights, NJ – 1907/07/11:6a
KUELL, Karl, 53, Elizabeth, NJ - 1914 /02/05:6a, fam. 10:6a
KUELLER, D., Newark, NJ – 1913/04/12:6a
KUEMMEL, Ernst, fr Breslau/Gy, NYC-M – 1908/02/07:6a
KUEMMEL, Fredi, child, NYC-M – 1896/06/22:4a
KUEMMEL, Friedrich, 62, lathe turner, fr South Germany ~ 30 yrs ago,NYC-M – 1882/03/25:1g
KUENECKE, Joseph K., 30, janitor, wife Mary & child Elsie, infant, 1906 fr Hannover, Newark, NJ – 1907/06/04:2d
KUENEMUND, Wilhelm, 43, NYC-Bx - 1915/08/02:6a
KUENNE, Karl, tobacco worker, SPD Halberstadt, Gy – 1909/05/30:3d
KUENNEMUND, Ernst, NYC-M – 1891/03/24:4a
KUENSTING, Heinrich, 65, NYC-M - 1915/07/06:6a
KUENSTLER, ?, 45, NYC-M - 1920/10/20:6a
KUENSTLER, ..., 1, son of Rudolph, NYC-M – 1880/07/19:3b
KUENSTLER, Frieda, 8, Hoboken, NJ – 1882/02/27:3b
KUENSTLER, Hugo, Dr., 37, physician, NYC-M – 1882/11/28:4b
KUENSTNER, Joseph, 31, Hastings, NY – 1919/09/03:6a

KUENTZEL % Oerther
KUENTZLER, Jacob, NYC-M - 1917/03/16:6a
KUENZEL, Ernst, SPD Leipzig/Gy - 1904/07/24:9e-f
KUENZERT, Karl Gustav, US Sold., NYC?, + 5 Nov 1918 French front,
  mem. - 1919/11/04:6a
KUENZLE, Karl, 47, SP?, un. butcher,NYC - 1915/03/30:6a, fam. 3 Apr:6a
KUENZLE, Marie, Newark, NJ - 1900/07/10:4b
KUENZLI, Jacob, 80, Jersey City Heights, NJ - 1901/07/04:3b
KUEPFER, Elise, Jersey City, NJ - 1893/08/11:4a
KUEPFERLE, Anton, NYC-B, * 11 Jne 1884 Sollingen/Baden, USA 1906,
  War 2 in London/GB - 1915/05/21:1c
KUERBS, John, NYC-Q - 1900/12/29:4a, 30:5a
KUERSCHNER, 48, Prof., writer, close to SPD - 1902/08/27:2c
KUERSCHNER, Karl, *1846 Anhalt-Dessau, shoemaker & SPD activist
  expelled from Altona/Gy, arrived NYC - 1880/11/30:1d-e, 2 Dec:2a-b,
  6:1d-e. + SP, NYC-M - 1903/12/26:1d, 4a, 27:5a, =28:1g, fam. 28:4a
KUERZDOERFER, Adam, Greenville, NJ - 1902/12/02:4a
KUES, Auguste, b. Horenburg, NYC-M - 1905/03/17:4a, fam. 20:4a
KUES, Heinrich, 60, NYC-Bx - 1907/01/29:6a, 30:6a
KUES, Johanne, b. Fricke, *Braunschweig/Gy,NYC-M - 1894/02/17:4a
KUES, Minnie, b. Heitmann, 26, NYC-M - 1903/07/05:5b
KUESTER, Henry, 20, NYC-M - 1878/04/03:3g
KUESTER, John, (Kuesser?), NYC-M - 1889/03/04:4a
KUESTERS, Pauline, NYC-M - 1898/09/03:4a
KUESTNER % Gerber
KUESTNER, John Sr., 80, un. printer, NYC-Bx - 1918/08/08:6a
KUFNER, Charles, 39, beerdriver, Newark, NJ - 1898/01/03:1g
KUGEL, John, tinsmith, Winfield, LI - 1893/09/16:1g
KUGELMAN, Hattie, 20, dying, Newark, NJ - 1914/01/20:2f
KUGELN % Walder; KUGLER % Boescher
KUHL, Jakob, 38, shoe dealer, Jersey City, NJ - 1883/03/25:1d
KUHL, Johann, 42, NYC-M - 1882/12/08:1g
KUHL, Ludwig, 41, mason & SPD activist expelled fr Hamburg/Gy, arrived
  in NYC - 1881/01/19:1g, 20:4c
KUHL, Philipp, 52, un. cigarmkr, NYC-B - 1913/08/08.6a
KUHLER, Bertha, 20, @1911 Triangle Shirtwaist Fire, NYC-M -
  1911/03/27:1d
KUHLES, Margarethe, b. Seitz, NYC-B - 1898/03/06:5b
KUHLKE, Edward C., un. cigarpacker, NYC-M - 1914/11/24:6a
KUHLMANN, Frederick, mailman, Elizabethport, NJ - 1893/02/15:3d
KUHLMANN, John, 26, Jersey City, NJ - 1914/09/29:6c
KUHLWILM, Louise Babette, b. Seebach, 36, NYC-M - 1899/09/16:4a

KUHLWISSER % Meyer
KUHN, Charles, NYC-M - 1915/12/27:6a
KUHN, Christian, 38, NYC-B – 1896/08/12:3e
KUHN, David, 44, NYPD, NYC-B - 1916/03/23:6b
KUHN, Elise, NYC-Bx – 1887/05/06:3d
KUHN, F., NYC-Bx - 1917/02/03:6a
KUHN, Friedrich, 36, baker, USA 1891, NYC-M – 1909/01/14:1f
KUHN, Fritz, 36, baker, USA 1891, NYC-M – 1909/01/14:1f
KUHN, Jacob, exec. Auburn, NY – 1912/06/19:1e
KUHN, John, NYC-Bx - 1914/02/03:6a
KUHN, John, un. baker, NYC-M – 1904/05/09:1g, body fd 27 May:4a
KUHN, Joseph Adam, 68, un. cigarmaker, NYC-B - 1917/11/26:6a
KUHN, Joseph Jr., 30, SP, US Army, War 1, NYC-B - 1918/10/30:6a, 2 Nov.:5d
KUHN, Joseph Rudolph, 57, SP, NYC-B - 1919/01/28:2g,6a
KUHN, Karl, 61, NYC-M - 1913/11/10:6a, 11:6a
KUHN, Louise, 42, NYC-Bx – 1906/07/04:2e
KUHN, Ludwig, Newark, NJ – 1908/09/15:6a
KUHN, Margarethe, b. Hotz, 22, NYC-M – 1892/06/14:4a
KUHN, Margarethe, b. Schnessler, NYC-M – 1904/02/20:4a
KUHN, Marie, 30?, NYC-M – 1891/07/07:2e
KUHN, Michael, 62, NYC-Q – 1902/01/23:4a
KUHN, Nettie, fr New Orleans, + NYC-M – 1898/09/17:3d
KUHN, Philipp, fr Karlshafen/Gy, NYC-M – 1909/01/08:6a
KUHN, Robert, West Hoboken, NJ – 1912/12/03:6a
KUHN, Valentin, NYC-M – 1912/11/02:6a
KUHN, William, innkeep, Hoboken, NJ – 1901/02/15:4a
KUHN, William, ruined wealthy man, Perth Amboy, NJ – 1911/02/17:2d
KUHNE, Hermann, Jersey City, NJ – 1901/05/30:3b
KUHNIK, Marie, NYC-M – 1882/10/31:3a
KUHS, Karolina, NYC-B - 1916/03/08:6a
KUKUCK, Johann Christopher, 47, NYC-M - 1918/04/28:7b
KULAKOW, Anton, Russian undercover agent in nihilist movement, in 1875-78 active in USA as Anton Charles Robertson, + 1880/12/13:1a-b
KULIK, George, coal-miner, @ 1897 Hazleton Massacre
KULKEN % Gosewisch
KULKMANN, Carl, 71, SP, carpenter, * 28 June 1843 Glaz/Silesia, USA 1882, 70th birthday, NYC-Q - 1913/06/28:5e; + 1915/06/15:6a,d, 16:6a, =17:2d, fam. 20:7c; mem. 1916/06/14:6a
KULKMANN, Emily Dorothy, b. Miller, 20, NYC-B – 1912/10/29:6a
KULKMANN, Henry, 26, SP?, NYC-Q - 1914/05/18:6a, fam.23:6a; mem. 1915/05/16:7c

KULKMANN, Martha, 2, NYC-B – 1887/12/15:3a
KULL, Jacob, 53, laborer, Slausens Point, NY – 1896/06/26:1f
KULL, John, NYC-Metropolitan - 1919/07/29:6a
KULL, Wilhelm, Hoboken, NJ – 1899/03/24:4a
KULSKO, Jakob, coal-miner, @see 1897 Hazleton Massacre
KUMERFORD, John, NYC-M – 1905/06/10:4a
KUMM, Wilhelm, 33, un. cigarmaker, Hoboken, NJ – 1887/03/24:3d
KUMMER, Heinrich's wife, NYC-M – 1885/11/06:3a
KUMMER, Rudolf, 40, NYC-M – 1909/06/09:6a
KUMMER, Ruth, Hoboken, NJ - 1917/03/20:6a
KUMP, Joseph, NYC-B – 1907/10/02:6a
KUMPF, Andreas, machinist, NYC-M – 1890/07/10:4a
KUMPF, Sophie, NYC-B – 1887/05/18:3b
KUMROW, Charles, 20, Utica?, exec. Ossining, NY - 1916/12/18:1b, 20:1f,
KUNATH, Anna, b. Heinicke, NYC-B - 1894/02/08:4a
KUNDERMANN, Charles, NYC-M – 1911/03/18:6a
KUNDMUELLER % Grote
KUNEMANN, Henry, 45, carp., NYC-M – 1882/03/26:8a
KUNERT % Schwabe; KUNITZ % May
KUNERT, William, cigarmaker, Austrian, NYC-M 1878/02/08:4a
KUNKEL, Adam, NYC-B – 1908/05/19:6a
KUNKEL, Andreas, SLP, Newark, NJ - 1879/03/01:3a, 4e
KUNKEL, Andrew, 2, NYC-M – 1887/09/26:2g
KUNKEL, Frank K., 60, laborer, killed during strike in Milwaukee, WI – 1886/05/06:1d
KUNKEL, Frank, NYC-B - 1915/06/02:6a
KUNKEL, Otto's wife, NYC-Q – 1898/06/05:5a
KUNKEL, Robert, 58, printer & SPD Duisberg/Gy – 1912/06/23:3b
KUNKEL, Sebastian, un. cigarmaker, NYC-M – 1905/10/14:4a
KUNLEY, George, worker, NYC-M - 1895/06/27:3g
KUNNIANTZ, Bogdan, alias Ruben and Radin, Russian SP, + Baku jail – 1911/06/21:4d
KUNST, Friederika, b. Baumann, 59, NYC-M – 1892/07/22:4a
KUNST, Louis, 50, NYC merchant fr Debreczin/Hungary, note (not +) – 1881/11/03:4c
KUNTNER, Margaretha, 30, NYC-B - 1917/05/05:6a
KUNTZ % Ochs,
KUNTZ, Anna, NYC-Bx - 1919/01/26:6a
KUNTZ, Auguste, NYC-Bx – 1903/07/02:4a
KUNTZ, Georg, un. carp., NYC-M – 1888/09/22:4h
KUNTZ, Heinrich, un. cigarmaker, NYC-M - 1879/02/28:3a

KUNTZ, Jacob, 62, farmer, 1840s fr Bavaria, Homestead Station,NJ –
 1880/07/08:1d-e,=9:1f, 10:4g, 13:4c
KUNTZ, Johann, 40, NYC-M – 1902/11/03:4a
KUNTZ, John, 53, NYC-B – 1882/11/30:3a
KUNTZ, Joseph, 41, innkeep, + 2 May, his will, NYC-M – 1880/06/19:4a
KUNTZ, Joseph, 45, owner Kuntz Brewery, NYC-Bx – 1890/05/13:4f
KUNTZKOBELD, comrade, SPD activist, Frankfurt-Hoechst, Gy –
 1906/11/20:4d
KUNTZLER, Elsie, actress "Elsie Orr," 21, NYC-B, + Metuchen, NJ -
 1918/06/19:6a
KUNZ, Adolph, 48, chemist, wife & 3 children, 23, 16, 10, NYC-B –
 1910/10/15:1c, 18:3a
KUNZ, Albert, un. carp., NYC-M – 1905/06/24:4a
KUNZ, E., un. cigarmaker, NYC-M – 1885/03/22:8a
KUNZ, Frank, 48, NYC-Q - 1919/06/09:5f
KUNZ, Gussie, NYC-B, + @Genl Slocum – 1904/06/18:3c
KUNZ, Jacob, 29, & daughters Karoline,6, Barbara, 1, Newark, NJ –
 1907/02/04:3c
KUNZ, John, NYC-Q - 1920/03/27:8a
KUNZ, Margareth, b. Bender, 70, NYC-Q, 1917/12/29:6a
KUNZ, Richard, NYC-B - 1919/03/19:6a
KUNZ, Rose, NYC-B - 1914/12/30:6a
KUNZE, August, NYC-M – 1892/06/16:4a
KUNZE, Carl, 47, restaurant owner, Newark, NJ - 1917/11/21:2d
KUNZE, Dietrich, 68, NYC-Q – 1909/03/28:7e
KUNZE, Heinrich, 68, Hoboken, NJ – 1891/06/26:4a
KUNZE, Jacob, 70, NYC-M - 1916/03/29:6a
KUNZE, John G., 73, SLP, NYC-M – 1893/12/06:4a, 7:4a
KUNZE, Otto, 53, un printer, NYC-M - 1895/02/10:5b
KUNZELMANN, Bertha, NYC-M – 1896/06/13:1d
KUNZELMANN, Frederick A., pianomaker, Port Jervis, NY –
 1909/12/15:2c
KUNZELMANN, John, un. carp., NYC-M – 1893/06/19:4a
KUNZEMAN, Jacob, innkeep, ex-assembly & alderman, NYC-M –
 1902/08/23:2g
KUNZER, Charles, 51, butcher, NYC-B – 1910/11/01:3b
KUNZMANN, Marie, NYC-M – 1904/02/23:1g
KUPFER, Julia, 23, NYC-B - 1919/06/07:6a
KUPFER, Samuel, Slovak RR worker, + Roseville, NJ – 1910/04/15:1a
KUPFERLE, Anna, exec. 29 May 1915 by French as alleged German spy,
 noted - 1920/04/10:4?
KUPFERSCHMIDT, Mrs, NYC-M – 1900/02/11:5a

KUPFERSMITH, Tillie, 16, @1911 Triangle Shirtwaist Fire, NYC-M – 1911/03/27:1d
KUPFFER, Anton, 50, meat dealer, NYC-M – 1897/05/21:4b
KUPKA, Joseph, 46, Steinway worker?, NYC-M – 1881/03/09:3c
KUPKE, Karl, tailor, SLP, *Kestenburg near Breslau/Gy, Philadelphia, PA – 1887/07/06:5e-f
KUPPER, Paul, 4, West Hoboken, NJ - 1919/03/06:6a
KUPPERMANN, Jermaine, peddler, Port Jervis, NY – 1909/01/10:1f
KUPPLER, Charles, 42, machinist, NYC-B – 1908/07/18:3b
KUPPLER, Jacob, fr Moessingen/Wuertt./Gy, NYC-B – 1889/02/20:4a
KUPPLER, John Georg, 1, NYC-B – 1888/07/13:3c
KURITZ, Benny, 19, @1911 Triangle Shirtwaist Fire, NYC-M – 1911/03/27:1d
KURKEL, Michael, 27, NYC - 1915/11/05:2d
KURNOTOWSKY, Victor, 45, Russian socialist, + Paris/France – 1912/10/15:4d
KURTH, Gerhard, NYC-M – 1889/05/17:4a
KURTH, H., un. carp., NYC-M – 1896/08/14:4a
KURTH, William, 23, un. cigarmaker, NYC-B – 1907/09/10:6a
KURTZ, Benedikt, 62, NYC-M – 1904/03/24:4a
KURTZ, Emilie, 75, Jersey City, NJ - 1916/03/17:6c, 18:6c
KURTZ, Ferdinand, 50, NYC-B – 1893/05/10:2e
KURTZ, Stephan, un. butcher, NYC-B - 1919/04/26:6a
KURTZ, Thomas Wood, 2, NYC-B - 1878/07/17:3c
KURTZ, William, 19, printer, NYC-M – 1888/03/06:1d
KURTZER, Augusta, NYC-Bx – 1907/12/04:1b
KURZ, Adam, USA 1886, worker, NYC-B – 1886/07/09:2d
KURZ, August, NYC-M – 1891/10/14:4a
KURZ, Christian, Hoboken, NJ - 1918/03/23:6a, fam. 27:6a
KURZ, John, 16, worker, NYC-B – 1907/11/11:2d
KURZ, John, un. butcher, NYC-M – 1907/04/18:6a
KURZ, Sarah, 19, NYC-M – 1904/09/05:1e, 6:2b
KURZMANN, Ferdinand, 74, lawyer, NYC-M - 1917/12/25:1d
KURZMANN, John, 40, coal-peddler, NYC-M – 1904/03/02:1d
KUSK, Harry, 39, NYC-B – 1893/11/24:4a
KUSKE, Friedrich, NYC-M – 1887/04/23:1e
KUSKENEN, Felix, 29, Hoboken, NJ, married Rosa Takkaren, 22, NYC – 1898/11/25:3c
KUSS, Gustav, 59, leather worker, NYC-Q - 1917/04/15:11c
KUSS, William, 29, un. carp., NYC-B – 1906/04/18:4a
KUSSMAUL, Adolf, Prof. Dr., Heidelberg U & medical researcher – 1902/05/29:1b

KUSSNOW, Paul, 17, NYC-B – 1890/02/21:4a
KUSSRON, Martin, NYC-M – 1900/03/05:4a
KUSSROW, Fritz, 3, NYC-M – 1889/08/26:4a
KUSSROW, Hermine, child, NYC-M – 1889/05/19:5d
KUSTER % Roschitz
KUSTERER, Christian, un. carp., NYC-M – 1884/10/03:3d
KUTSCHE, Karl, 37, SP, beer driver, Newark, NJ - 1918/10/14:6a
KUTSCHE, Marie, 45, ex-NYC, SP?, + Munich, Gy – 1905/12/24:5b
KUTSCHER, Franz, 47, SP?, mayor of Lichtowitz/Bohemia & MdR – 1912/03/31:3e
KUTSCHER, Hugo, NYC-M – 1896/08/29:4a
KUTTLER, Edward, 27, US Army, Park Ridge, NJ - 1918/09/27:2e
KUTZELMANN, Daniel, NYC – 1897/08/30:4a
KUTZNER, Paul, NYC-M? – 1911/11/14:6a
KUTZSCHER, Adolf, 75, un. cigarmaker, NYC-M - 1919/08/22:6a, 23:6a, =27:2d
KUTZSCHER, Clara, 73, NYC-M - 1917/12/03:6a
KUTZSCHER, Emilie Richter, 60, NYC-M - 1895/10/10: 4a
KUTZSCHER, Georg, NYC-M – 1900/03/05:4a
KUVEKE, Henry, 57, un. carp., NYC-M – 1910/11/23:6a
KUZNY, Dominick, 87, French army vet, NYC-M - 1914/01/25:1d
KWASNIEWSKI, Gustav, 69, teacher & SPD Berlin/Gy – 1902/07/29:2d
KWIATEK, Josef, 30, lawyer, SP Austria—Polish branch, *Plotzk/Russian Poland – 1910/02/13:3c-d
KWIATKOWSKI, Joseph, exec. Trenton, NJ – 1913/01/15:2a
KWIATKOWSKI, Russian-Polish Nihilist, exec. St Petersburg – 1880/12/02:2d
KWINSCHINSKY, Frances, wd Hall, 68, Cornwall, NY, + NYC-M – 1907/11/21:2c
KYLE, Henry, Negro, lynched Spring Creek, GA – 1883/10/17:1b
LA FONTAINE, Frederick, 60, travelling salesman, & wife Ermine, 40, NYC-B– 1895/07/07:5b
LA VINE, Anna, NYC-M - 1920/01/14:6a
LAAS, Theodor, 55, NYC-M – 1882/07/17:3c
LAASCHE, Emma, 20, NYC-B – 1900/09/30:1d
LABASOWITZ, Sarah, 17, @1911 Triangle Shirtwaist Fire, NYC-M – 1911/03/28:1c
LABEE, Tunis, exec. Paterson, NJ – 1889/06/28:2f
LABER, Friedrich, 40, un. carp., NYC-M – 1907/06/02:7b, 3:6a
LABER, Katherina, 30, NYC-M – 1890/01/31:4a

LABON, Frederick, ship's steward, @1900 dock fire, Hoboken, NJ 1900/07/03:1c
LABRIOLA, Antonio, Prof. & Italian soc. Polit. – 1904/02/23:2c-d
LABRIOLA, Joseph, exec. May's Landing, NJ – 1907/09/21:3b
LABRO, Albert, 39, NYC-Bx – 1892/10/25:4a
LABRO, Mary, fr Prussia 1881, NYC-M – 1882/02/17:1g, 20:4d
LACH, Julius, 53, conductor of worker glee clubs, * Hamburg, #, Jersey City Heights, NJ – 1912/03/29:2e
LACH, Marie, fr Hamburg/Gy – 1902/08/19:4a
LACHINGER, Charles, 60, musician, NYC-B - 1920/01/02:6a
LACHMAN, Louis, 64, married Mrs Cohen, NYC-B – 1899/05/20:2g
LACHMANN, Joseph, innkeep, NYC-M – 1900/11/27:1g
LACHMANN, Otto, worker & SPD militant in Berlin/Gy = 1887/02/14:4e, 25th anniv. of + 1912/02/12:4d
LACHNER, Auguste, NYC-M - 1915/02/20:6a
LACHNER, Gertrud, 19, NYC-M – 1899/08/05:4a
LACHNER, Reinhard, 73,un. upholsterer, NYC-M - 1919/04/06:12a
LACHS, Eleonore, Guttenberg, NJ - 1915/11/20:6a, fam. 22:6a
LACKENBACHER, Robert, 22, SPO Vienna, student, War 1 - 1914/12/20:3d
LACOMBE, Albert T., SP, Newark, NJ – 1913/03/07:1c
LACOMBE, French anarchist, + in Paris jail – 1913/04/06:1b
LACOWITZ, Theodor, NYC-B – 1902/12/08:4a
LADEHOFF, Hans, 46, Hoboken, N.J. - 1878/09/25:3c
LADEWIG, Albert, 23, West Hoboken, NJ - 1914/01/14:6a
LADEWIG, Hermann, 52, Union Hill, NJ – 1912/05/15:6a
LADEWIG, William, musician, * Battenberg/Hessen, USA 1876, NYC-B – 1891/10/27:2e
LADOUSSEUR % Jaeger
LADRO, Peter Franz, 65, NYC-M – 1891/03/27:4a
LAECHNER, G. Peter, un. cigar maker, NYC-M – 1891/11/26:4a
LAEGLER, Louis, un. butcher, NYC-M - 1914/11/07:6a
LAEMCHEN % Wolkenstein; LAEMMCHEN % Uhl
LAEMEG, M., @ 1900 dock fire, Hoboken, NJ 1900/07/03:1c
LAEMLER, Henriette, NYC-M – 1891/04/11:4a
LAEMMLE, Lucie, b. Sierck, 50, NYC-B – 1908/09/29:6a
LAENGER, Adolph, 79, NYC-Bx – 1891/07/26:4a
LAER, William VAN, 52, NYC-M – 1905/01/03:4a
LAFARGUE, Paul, & wife Laura, b. Marx, Soc. Leaders, + Paris – 1911/11/27:2e, 28:4a-b, 29:4d, 3 Dec:20d, 9:4e-f, 13:4d-f, =15:4e-f,
LAFF, Abraham, bookbinder, NYC-B – 1906/12/22:1g
LAFOND, Parisian unionized waiter, murdered by police – 1903/12/12:2d-e

LAGEMANN, August, SLP?, un. bricklayer, * Altmark district/Brandenburg, NYC-M – 1892/05/11:4a, 12:4a, 13:4a, =16:4e, fam. 16:4a
LAGER, Theo., Secaucus, NJ - 1918/01/10:6a
LAGGIO, Angelo, + Ossining, NY - 1916/01/14:1f,4d
LAHMANN, Theodor, engraver fr Chicago, IL, + NYC-M – 1912/05/02:2d
LAHN, Clara, 20, NYC-Bx, +@Genl Slocum – 1904/06/19:1c
LAHN, Dora, NYC-B, + @ Genl Slocum – 1904/06/17:3b
LAHN, Robert, 71, NYC-B - 1913/11/06:3c, 7:6a
LAHN, Theodor von, 43?, un. cigar maker, NYC-M – 1891/04/06:4a
LAHR, John, 19, elevator boy, NYC-M – 1891/02/07:1c
LAHR, Peter, 69, un. bricklayer, NYC-M - 1894/07/15:5a
LAHRES, Ernestina, 1, NYC-M - 1895/02/24:5b
LAHRHELM, Regina, NYC-M – 1905/02/09:4a
LAIBLE, Anna, NYC-B – 1896/07/15:4a
LAIBLE, Paul, 68, NYC-B – 1897/04/11:5a
LAIBLE, Philip, NYC-B, + Saranac Lake, NY – 1911/07/21:6a
LAIBLE, T., NYC-M – 1893/10/19:4a
LAIBLER % Barth
LAIBLER, Otto, NYC-B - 1895/06/10:4d
LAIDLAW, William, ex-secy of Russell Sage, crippled when saving his boss' life, and then dismissed, + poor as symbol of US capitalism – 1911/08/09:4d. @ Sage, Russell
LAINBACH, George, 50, brewery worker, Paterson, NJ - 1914/09/25:2b
LAINE, Henry, un. cigarmaker, * Belgium, SP, New Haven, CT – 1907/01/16:6a, =27:7f
LALEWEC, Margaretha, b. Mohr, NYC-M – 1903/06/07:5a
LAMBECK, Albert, 3, NYC-M, +@Genl Slocum – 1904/06/23:1b
LAMBECK, Dora, 70, NYC-Q - 1913/07/22:2c
LAMBECK, Henry, NYC-M, + @Genl Slocum – 1904/06/17:3b, 18:3c
LAMBERT, Anna, 56, NYC-M - 1916/02/22:6a
LAMBERT, Friedrich, 25, Newark, NJ – 1908/11/20:3c
LAMBERT, John J., NYC-M – 1891/03/23:4a
LAMBERT, Lina, b. Huppert, ?34, NYC-B – 1893/01/16:4a
LAMBERT, Theodore, 23, exec. Camden, NJ - 1895/12/20: 3d
LAMBRECHT % Doelger
LAMBRECHT, Albert, 3, & Ernestine, 9, NYC-M, +@Genl Slocum – 1904/06/23:1c
LAMBRECHT, Johanna, Union Hill, NJ? - 1920/07/13:6a
LAMBRECHT, William, NYC-M – 1907/05/24:6a
LAMELA, Spanish peasant soc., exec. Xerez de la Frontera – 1892/02/11:1a-b, 12:1a, NYC prot. 19:1g

LAMM, Amelia, 40, Frank, 18, Lillie, NYC-M, +@ Genl Slocum – 1904/06/16:1c, 17:3b, 25:1d
LAMM, Lina, & son Henry, NYC-M - 1916/08/12:6a
LAMMENS, Frank, see John Meierhoefer
LAMMERS % Langbein
LAMOTTE, John, 5, NYC-B – 1900/12/21:4a
LAMOTTE, Margarethe, b. Kistenberger, NYC-B – 1892/11/09:4a
LAMPE % Thieke
LAMPE, Adolph, NYC-M - 1894/10/16:4a
LAMPERT, Leopold, 49, SPD Heidingsfeld/Wuerzburg/Gy, alderman - 1915/11/07:3a, 14:3a
LAMPRECHT, Karl, Dr., German historian - 1915/05/12:1b
LAMY % Hepp
LAMY, Josef, Elizabeth, NJ - 1917/02/14:6a
LANDAHL, Johann Christoph, 61, * Gaderbusch/Mecklemburg, NYC-M – 1889/08/24:4a
LANDAHL, Meta, b. Hoffmann, Jersey City Heights, NJ – 1900/09/08:4a, fam. 10:4a
LANDAU, Ferdinand, 56, salesman, ex-Heidelberg student, Scranton, PA, + NYC-M – 1906/01/02:4b
LANDAU, Hugo, Union Hill, NJ - 1919/02/11:2e
LANDAUER, Ernst, 45, NYC-M – 1880/10/11:4f
LANDAUER, Gustav, German polit., + Munich - 1919/05/11:9c-e, notes 1919/08/16:4f
LANDAUER, John, 25, cigarmaker, NYC-M – 1899/08/24:1f-g
LANDECK, Julius, SP, fr Elberfeld/Gy, & wife, NYC-B, had Silver Wedding – 1907/09/30:5
LANDECK, Richard, 66, SP?, un. printer, *Elberfeld, Jersey City, NJ - 1915/02/03:6a, =6:2f
LANDEN, Frederick, 35, painter, NYC-M – 1892/04/30:2g
LANDER, Louis, 6, NYC-M, +@ on Genl Slocum – 1904/06/17:3b
LANDER, Thomas, 54, telegrapher, NYC-B – 1898/07/15:1g
LANDER, Wilhelm A., 31, NYC-B – 1892/06/11:4a
LANDERT, Lorenz, un. carp., NYC-M – 1886/05/31:3b
LANDGRAF % Richter
LANDGRAFF, Emil, 85?, NYC-B – 1892/08/14:5c
LANDIERS, Angelo, exec. Ossining, NY – 1908/07/21:1f
LANDRIN, Emile, French Socialist, + Paris - 1914/02/23:4c
LANDSBERG, Aurelia, 50, NYC-M - 1914/10/23:2c
LANDSBERG, Henry, NYC-M – 1908/09/17:6a
LANDWEHR, Friedrich, Jersey City Heights, NJ – 1912/12/09:6a
LANDWEHR, Heinrich, cigarmaker, Babylon, LI – 1881/02/26:1g

LANDWEHR, Herman, deli-owner, SLP, Hoboken, NJ – 1898/09/05:4a, =7:4b-c, fam. 7:4a
LANE, Charles, SP, NYC-M – 1908/10/30:1f
LANG % Richter
LANG, Alexander, machinist, NYC-Bx? – 1905/12/07:4a
LANG, Amelia, 15, NYC-M, +@Genl Slocum – 1904/06/22:1d
LANG, Anna, 26, servant, NYC-Q - 1918/03/14:2e
LANG, Anton, NYC-M – 1919/09/02:6a
LANG, August, 66, NYC-B - 1920/03/11:6b
LANG, Auguste, b. Kolbe, NYC-B – 1909/09/26:7b
LANG, Carl, 55, Steinway employee?, NYC-M – 1880/03/07:8d
LANG, Carl, SLP, NYC – 1887/02/05:3c, =7:2g
LANG, Dorothea, NYC-M - 1917/05/23:6a
LANG, Emma, 12, servant, Jersey City, NJ - 1879/01/13:4f
LANG, Ernestine, b. Kaiser, 60,NYC-B - 1920/06/09:6a,fam. 12:6a
LANG, Frederick, exec. New Brunswick, NJ – 1909/03/24:3b
LANG, Heinrich, NYC-B – 1896/08/27:4a
LANG, Henry, 14, Hollis, LI – 1909/06/11:6a
LANG, Henry, NYC-B – 1910/06/04:6a
LANG, Jacob, 51, un. brewer, NYC-M - 1918/06/11:6a
LANG, Jacob, NYC-B - 1920/02/15:12a
LANG, John, NYC-M - 1915/11/24:6a
LANG, Joseph, NYC-B – 1907/06/09:7c
LANG, Louis, 45, carp., Jersey City, NJ - 1914/06/06:2e
LANG, Pauline, tailor, ~50, NYC-M – 1888/09/05:3b
LANG, Philipp, NYC-M – 1911/06/24:6a
LANG, Rosa, 25, servant, @1880 Turnhalle Fire, NYC-M – 1880/01/05:4a, 8:1g, 3a, 9:1e-f
LANG, Theofila, b. Gajewska, 51, NYC-M - 1915/02/24:6a
LANG, William, 56, carp., NYC-Q – 1896/10/05:4e, 6:4c
LANG, William, carp., (dying) NYC-M – 1883/03/27:4c
LANGBEIN, Caroline, b. Lammers, 57, NYC-B – 1896/04/23:4a
LANGBEIN, Henry Wilhelm, 54, NYC-M – 1902/01/23:4a
LANGBEIN, Mary, 40, NYC-M – 1885/12/22:1b
LANGBEIN, William, 40, NYC-B – 1896/08/10:1a
LANGE % Cantius
LANGE, Alwine, NYC-M – 1886/12/11:3a
LANGE, Amalia, ?, – 1903/07/23:4a
LANGE, Anna E., 84, NYC-B – 1891/07/02:4a
LANGE, Anton, pharmacist & Turner, Milwaukee - 1878/06/29:2f

LANGE, August, 39, cigar maker & SPD activist expelled fr Hamburg/Gy, arrived NYC – 1881/01/19:1g, 20:4c. NYVZ staff, NYC-M - 1918/03/13:2g,6a, 16:6a, =17:11d
LANGE, Ernst, 63, un. carp., NYC-M - 1913/05/12:6a
LANGE, Ferdinand Emil, goldleaf beater, NYC-M – 1899/03/30:4a
LANGE, Franz, NYC-M – 1883/02/09:3c
LANGE, Friedrich Albert, German philosopher + 1875, mem. 1892/01/10:3b-e; his work 1905/12/10:16e-f
LANGE, Gottlieb August, 70, Newark, NJ – 1897/07/24:1f
LANGE, Gustav, un. cigarmaker, NYC-M – 1902/11/15:4a, 16:5a, fam. 19:4a
LANGE, Henriette, NYC-M – 1913/10/21:6a
LANGE, Henry, 69, NYC-B - 1919/01/10:6a
LANGE, Henry, carp., NYC-M – 1880/06/26:4b
LANGE, Hulda, 3, NYC-M – 1890/11/29:4a
LANGE, John D., 74, pres. em. Ethical Culture Society, ex-NYC, + Berlin/Gy - 1916/04/21:2a
LANGE, L. A., merchant in Hamburg-Altona, vet '48er – 1911/02/03:4d-e
LANGE, Leo, silkweaver, NYC-M - 1878/03/06:4f
LANGE, O.'s wife, NYC-M – 1902/04/11:4a
LANGE, Paul, 37, NYC-M - 1894/11/26:4a
LANGE, Paul, store clerk, ex–curassier in Koenigsberg/Gy, NYC-M – 1908/09/26:2c
LANGE, Wilhelm, 34, NYC-B – 1902/01/16:4a
LANGE, Wilhelm, 86, SPD Barmen/Gy – 1919/11/05:4e
LANGEMANN, Adolph, 35, grocer, Newark, NJ – 1899/06/03:3d
LANGEN, Anna, b. Bauer, 54, NYC-M – 1906/07/07:6a
LANGEN, August, 52, West Hoboken, NJ - 1919/01/21:6a
LANGENAU, Martin, 81, shoemaker, NYC-SI - 1914/01/11:11b
LANGENBACH, Charles, NYC-M – 1912/02/20:6a
LANGENBERG, Charles, 50, Newark, NJ – 1908/09/13:7e
LANGENBERG, Ferdinand, NYC-B - 1879/06/25:4d
LANGENBERG, Friedemann A., 54, NYC-B – 1886/06/07:3a
LANGENHAGEN, Elise, 43, NYC-M – 1892/09/03:4a
LANGER, Lina, NYC-B – 1892/06/09:4a
LANGER, Peppie, 20, fr Hungary, NYC-M - 1893/05/29:1h
LANGERMANN, Adolf, un. carp., Ravenswood, LI – 1906/01/05:4a
LANGES, George, 23, laborer fr Silesia/Gy, USA 1877, NYC-M – 1880/06/18:1d-e
LANGFANG, Rosa, NYC-B – 1902/12/13:4a
LANGFELD, Wilhelm, 40, carp., SPD Berlin/Gy – 1908/12/13:3b

LANGFELDER, Rosie, 25, washer, NYC-M – 1904/03/24:2h
LANGGUTT, Adam, 32, NYC-M – 1901/04/23:4a, 24:4a
LANGHAMMER, Heinrich, Newark, NJ - 1919/01/15:6a
LANGHANS, John, NYC-Q - 1918/06/12:6a
LANGMAN, Bertha, 18, telephonist, NYC-B – 1908/09/12:1f
LANGNER, Hugo, 53, un. cigarmaker, NYC-M – 1903/12/05:4a
LANGNER, William Jr., 31, NYC-Bx - 1918/04/18:6a
LANGRAFF, Henry, exec. St Louis, MO – 1888/08/11:1c
LANGREDER, Anna, b. Wehmann, NYC-B – 1891/04/07:4a
LANGREUTER, H., 54, capt SS "Berlin," family in Oldenburg, + NYC – 1911/05/05:6a
LANGROCK, Emma, 6 mo., NYC-M - 1878/07/23:3c
LANGROCK, Minna, 1, NYC-M – 1880/07/23:3b
LANJENSEE, Albert, 62, NYC-Bx - 1920/04/17:6a
LANKOTA, J., 61, NYC-M – 1883/11/28:3b
LANKOW, Ferdinand, Greenville, NJ - 1919/07/22:6a
LANNERMANN, Hugo, NYC-M, +@Genl Slocum – 1904/06/17:3b
LANSNER, Fannie, 21, foreman, @1911 Triangle Shirtwaist Fire, NYC-M – 1911/03/27:1d
LANTZ, Johanna, infant, NYC-M – 1899/08/09:4a, fam. 11:4a
LANZ, Georg, 41, NYC-M – 1891/04/11:4a
LANZ, Hermann, 65, waiter, NYC-M - 1913/05/23:1c
LANZ, John, un. brewer, NYC-M – 1908/04/22:6a
LAPP, George, NYC-B, +Somerville, NJ – 1906/07/30:1e, 2 Aug:3a
LAPPE, Otto, un. carp., NYC-M – 1904/01/25:4a
LARKIN, Irish patriot, exec., mass-meeting in NYC protests 1883/11/24:2g
LAROQUE, Louis, lawyer, former partner of Joseph H. Choate, Jefferson, LI - 1913/08/07:1b
L'ARRONGE, Adolf, 70, comedy writer, + Berlin/Gy – 1908/05/27:2b
LARSEN % Feuerstein
LARSEN, Ch., un. carp., NYC-M – 1902/01/29:4a
LARSEN, Jennie, 20, fr Kopenhagen 9/1902, NYC-M – 1902/10/02:1h
LARSEN, Joergen, 49, SLP, New Haven, CT – 1900/04/20:4a, fam. 24:4a
LARSEN, Selma, governess, fr Sweden, Staatsburg, NY – 1897/07/21:1f, 22:1c, 23:1e
LARSEN, Therese, NYC-Bx – 1912/09/16:6a
LARSON, August, NYC-M – 1902/05/05:4a
LARSSON, John, un. cigarmaker, NYC-B - 1918/10/28:6a
LASALLE, Wilhelm, 37, NYC-M - 1919/03/03:6a
LASCH, Barbara, NYC-M – 1892/02/26:4a
LASCH, John D., NYC-M – 1892/07/21:4a
LASCH, Joseph, NYC-M - 1917/04/04:6a

LASKI, Max J., 31, bookbinder, NYC-M – 1890/12/11:4c
LASKOWITZ, David, 50, fr Russia, landlord & realtor, Newark, NJ 1911/10/11:2b
LASLOG?, Louis, 43, NYC-M – 1892/08/28:4c
LASRANINA, Joseph, 26, actor, War 2, NYC-B - 1917/11/26:2b
LASALLE, Ferdinand, German soc. leader, memorial cerem. in NYC 1880/08/31:2a,d, 1 Sept:1f; in NYC 1881/08/25:3d, 3 Sept:3b, 4:5f, rev. 5:1g; rev. fest NYC 1882/04/10:1e-f, Brooklyn 16 Sept:3a, 18:1b; in Brooklyn 1883/04/23:4c, NYC 1883/09/02:1f, rev 3:1e-f, note 22 Oct:1d; in NYC-M & Hoboken, NJ 1884/08/31:5d, rev. 8 Sept:3a; 20th anniv. of + comm.. in NYC & Hoboken 6 Apr 1885:4d, rev Hoboken 7:2g, NYC 12:5d, 31 Aug.:1e-f, 1 Sept:1b, in Newark, NJ 15 Sept:3a, Buenos Aires 6 Oct:4d; Celebr. in NYC 30 Aug. 1886:1e, in Gy 11 Sept.:4d, 13:1f, 15:4e, in Brooklyn 18:4d, rev 20:4a. In NYC, rev. 1888/04/17:2f. 25th + day, in NYC 1889/08/31:1h, 2a-c, rev. 2 Sept:2c; His life 1896/07/ 19:4c-e. NYC comm.. 8 June 1903:2c-d. 50th anniv. of + - 1914/08/30:6b-d, 31:4a-c
LASSE, Karl, NYC-Q – 1919/10/05:12a
LASSEN, P.J., 60, & wife, NYC-Q - 1919/02/03:2b
LASSER % Roth
LASTE, William, un. carp., NYC-M – 1911/03/26:7b
LASTER, Arthur, exec. Paterson, NJ – 1905/04/10:1b, 14:4b, done 15:1b
LATH, Engelberth, 45-50 yrs, fr Austria, Newark, NJ – 1909/12/20:3b
LATREMOUILLE, Hilaire, exec. Albany, NY - 1879/08/21:1c
LAU, Georg, stonecutter, SPD Dresden/Gy– 1901/12/17:2c
LAU, George, NYC-M, +@ on Genl Slocum – 1904/06/18:3c
LAU, Paul, NYC-M - 1918/11/09:6a
LAU, Therese, b. von Aex, 62?, NYC-M – 1891/01/21:4a
LAUB, Julius, NYC-M - 1915/09/01:6a
LAUBACH, Henry, Union Hill, NJ – 1905/12/27:3e
LAUBE, Adolph, 36,SP?,iron worker, NYC-M - 1920/11/15:6a, fam. 25:6c
LAUBE, Arnold, silk dyer, Paterson, NJ – 1912/06/29:1d
LAUBE, Gustav, NYC-M – 1907/07/09:6a
LAUBE, Heinrich, Dr., Viennese theater regisseur, on his +, by Helene von Radovicka – 1884/08/10:4e-g, 24:7c-d
LAUBE, Johann Samuel, 72, un. tailor, SLP, *Polnisch-Lissa/Prussia, USA 1857, NYC-B – 1890/04/06:5a, =7:1g, fam. 8:4a; Mem. 1917/08/18:2e
LAUBENBERGER, Johann, NYC-B - 1891/07/18:4a
LAUBENHEIMER, Melchior, 56, NYC-M – 1887/04/16:3d
LAUBER, Fritz, 75, SPD Heidelberg - 1913/10/05:3a
LAUBER, Johann, worker, USA three weeks ago, NYC-B - 1879/10/24:4c
LAUBMEIER, John, 31, SP, un. machinist, NYC-Q – 1917/10/12:6a, 13:6a
LAUCKEN, Gottfried, un. waiter, NYC-M - 1917/06/03:7a

LAUCKHARDT, Hermann, 60,un. typesetter,NYC-M - 1914/07/21:6a
LAUDENSCHLAGER, James K., 60, spice dealer, Phila – 1919/09/24:2e
LAUDERMAN, John's, White Plains, NY, + @on Genl Slocum – 1904/06/17:3b
LAUDERSCHLAEGER, Max, 18, dying, NYC-B - 1914/08/23:11d
LAUE, Emma Bartel, NYC-M - 1918/12/22:7a
LAUENROTH, Lillian, 28, NYC-B - 1915/08/22:1e
LAUENSTEIN, William, NYC-B – 1901/01/12:4a
LAUER, Edward, 20, NYC-M – 1891/11/04:4a
LAUER, Franz, NYC-M - 1916/01/10:6a
LAUER, Georg, un. woodworker, NYC-M – 1897/01/31:5a, 1 Fb:4a
LAUER, Julius Caesar, Dr., NYC-Q - 1914/04/23:1d
LAUER, Konrad, un. carp., NYC-M – 1903/11/11:4a
LAUER, Marie Anna, NYC-M – 1905/02/25:4a
LAUER, William, 51, Harrison, NJ - 1916/10/20:6a
LAUER, William, 60, cigarmaker, Newark, NJ – 1909/09/07:3c
LAUERMANN, Jakob, barber, NYC-M – 1881/11/22:1f
LAUFELT, Marie, 17, NYC-B – 1904/10/19:3d
LAUK, Gustav, un. carp., NYC-M – 1889/07/26:4a
LAUN, Amelia, 40, NYC-M, + @on Genl Slocum – 1904/06/16:1c
LAUNER, Gustave, 32, NYC-M - 1918/09/02:1f
LAURENY, Henry, 45, fr Austria, bricklayer, NYC-M – 1906/04/29:1g
LAURINGER, Frank, 39, Jersey City, NJ – 1903/07/11:1f
LAUROESCH, Christian, butcher, NYC-M – 1897/11/26:1g
LAUS, Michael, 72, NYC-B – 1880/03/02:1f
LAUSMANN, Emil, SPO Karlsbad/Bohemia, War 1 - 1915/01/31:3d
LAUSTER, Lena, NYC-Bx – 1909/11/16:6a
LAUT, Jacob, 36, NYC-M - 1894/01/12:4a
LAUTENSCHLAEGER, Frank, 60, NYC-M – 1892/07/20:4a
LAUTENSCHLAEGER, Jacob, Yonkers, NY - 1917/02/22:6a
LAUTENSCHLAGER % Hess
LAUTENSCHLAGER, P., Newark, NJ – 1904/12/10:4a
LAUTERBACH, August, tobacco plant owner, NYC-M – 1888/01/03:2h
LAUTERBACH, Edward, 60, stoker, Newark, NJ - 1920/07/04:2d
LAUTERBACH, John W., 58, importer, NYC-M – 1893/02/05:1h
LAUTERWASSER, Theodor, 4, NYC-M – 1888/02/15:3a
LAUTH, Eva, 22, NYC-M – 1892/10/27:4a
LAUTNER, Mary, b. Stengel, & Bertha, NYC-B - 1895/08/28: 4a,d
LAUWEH, Albert, NYC-B – 1912/03/28:6a
LAUWERISS, Joseph, NYC-M – 1881/07/17:5g
LAUX, Adolph, 28, NYC-Q – 1883/10/23:3a, fam. 28:5f
LAUX, Albert, un. upholsterer, Jersey City, NJ – 1897/09/23:4a

LAUX, Christina, b. Roth, 68, Jersey City, NJ – 1890/02/05:4a
LAUXMANN, Jacob, un. pianomaker, NYC-Bx - 1918/10/20:12a
LAWRENCE, John, Negro, lynched Girard, KS – 1885/07/08:1b
LAWRENZ, Otto, machinist, NYC-M – 1904/07/08:3d
LAWROFF, Peter L., Russian soc., his life – 1892/06/19:4f-g, 5a-b, + Paris # – 1900/02/12:1c-d, 2c, =5 Mr:2d; grave mon. 1902/07/09:2c
LAWSON, Lizzie Mary, b. Siebenkaes, 25, NYC-M – 1907/06/03:6a
LAX, Eugen, un. typesetter, NYC-M – 1889/02/01:4a
LAZARUS, S., 62, NYC-M – 1891/03/15:5b
LAZARWICH, Wasa, 42, NYC-M - 1917/03/15:6a
LE COMPTE, Edward, brewery engineer, NYC - 1914/12/27:11e
LE CONTE, Cincinatus, president of Haiti – 1912/08/09:1c, 10a
LE FRANCAIS, G., vet Paris Commune, + Paris/F. – 1901/06/05:2e
LE MOULT, Adolph, flower store, NYC-Bx – 1912/07/23:1b
LE NOIR, William F.,26,un.bricklayer, NYC-Bx - 1914/06/13:6a
LEAHM, Marie, 40, * Gy, alleged German agent, + Wilkes-Barre, PA - 1916/01/20:2f
LEARNED, Marion D., Dr., 60, Prof. of German at Pennsyl. U, * Dover, DE, + Philadelphia - 1917/08/03:2e
LEAWELL, Frank, Negro, lynched Ekton, KY – 1905/10/13:2f
LEBA, Annie, 12, killed during Pittsburgh, PA strike – 1913/01/29:2b
LEBAUDY, Jacques, 45, French, excentric, "King of the Sahara," Westbury, LI - 1919/01/12:1f, 13:2c, 14:2f, 15:2e, 16:2d, 17:2d, 20:1g, 22:1f
LEBEL, Johann, Austrian Lt-Col., connected to Redl spying scandal, + Vienna - 1913/06/25:1b
LEBENSKY, John, un. carp., NYC-Q - 1914/12/05:6a
LEBERFING, Karoline Anna, NYC-B – 1891/08/14:4a
LEBERLE, Alvine, 51, NYC-B – 1911/10/26:6a, fam. 28:6a
LEBERSANG, Jean, cook fr France, NYC-M – 1886/02/19:2e-f
LEBKUECHER, Julius A., 67, mayor of Newark 1894-96, * Baden Prov., USA 1848 - 1913/05/14:3c
LEBKUECHNER, Antony, 9, & Charles, 4, NYC, killed by mother Wilhelmina, who * 26 May 1852 Worms/Rhein, USA 1871, NYC – 1888/03/26:2e, 27:2g, 4 Apr:1a-b, trial 30 May:4d
LEBKUECHNER, Wilhelmina, NYC-M – 1890/01/10:4e
LEBNOW, Anna Christina, 3, NYC-M, 1 @ Genl Slocum – 1904/06/18:3c
LEBOFSKY, Philipp, tailor, NYC-B? - 1913/10/28:3b
LEBSANFT, Albert Otto, 3, NYC-M – 1897/09/25:4a
LEBSANFT, Anna, 4, NYC-M – 1892/06/21:4a
LEBSANFT, J., NYC? Ashes at sea – 1911/05/26:3c
LEBSANFT, William, 40, SP?, NYC-Bx – 1906/04/14:4c, 15:5b, fam. 17:4a

LECHLEITNER, John, un. butcher, NYC-M – 1909/04/03:6a
LECHNER, Adolf, 28, brewer, NYC-M – 1886/10/21:3b
LECHNER, Georg, un. machinist, NYC-M – 1890/07/04:4a
LECHNER, George, NYC-M – 1892/03/12:4a
LECLAIRE, Marie, 39, boardinghouse owner,NYC-M 1895/03/03:1d
LEDECKY, Antonie, 67, & Fanny, 35, fr Prag/Bohemia, NYC-M – 1893/11/23:1f
LEDER, Gussie, 15, War 2, NYC-M - 1914/12/30:1f
LEDERBERGER, Jacob, 24, painter, NYC-M – 1891/08/16:1f
LEDERER % Maschler
LEDERER, Caroline, NYC-M? – 1911/01/29:1b
LEDERER, Emanuel, theater mgr, * 1842 Budapest/Hungary, USA 1860, NYC-M - 1917/08/22:2b
LEDERER, Josephine, sales clerk, NYC-B – 1901/12/08:1d
LEDERER, Louis, NYC-M - 1914/12/08:6a
LEDERLE, Rufus, 63, un. printer at New Yorker Morgen-Journal, NYC-B - 1915/07/03:6a
LEDERMANN, Jennie, 20, @1911 Triangle Shirtwaist Fire, NYC-M – 1911/03/27:1d
LEDIGER, Geo. Henry, 23, NYC-M – 1891/07/05:5a
LEDOGAR, Gertrude, 22, NYC-Bx – 1912/06/13:6a, fam. 16:7d
LEE, Abbie S., teacher at NYC Workingman's School of Soc. Ethical Culture, NYC, = Hannover, CT - 1896/05/04:3f
LEE, Florence, SP, NYC-M – 1906/05/18:1d
LEE, William, exec. Crisfield, MD – 1906/07/27:1d
LEEBOLD, Harry E., Repl. Ward polit., NYC-B – 1908/04/14:3b
LEFFER, Charles, tailor, NYC-B – 1904/07/27:3c
LEFFLER, Louisa, 9, NYC-M, +@ on Genl Slocum – 1904/06/17:3b
LEFKOWITZ, Karl, 19, tailor, NYC-M – 1909/07/27:6d
LEFLORE, Joe, Negro, lynched near Canton, MS – 1899/10/21:1c
LEGIEN, Carl R., German trade unionist & MdR (SPD), crit. obit. - 1920/12/28:1a, 4a-d
LEGLER, Carl, NYC-M – 1881/02/22:3b
LEGNER, Anton, 51, un. carp., SP Vienna/Austria – 1908/07/12:3e
LEGRAVE % Lichtenstein
LEHANE, Cornelius, Irish soc.,NYC 1914,NYC-M - 1919/01/03:3f
LEHANE, Edmund, NYPD, NYC - 1914 12/16/2f
LEHECKA, Joseph, 37, NYC-M – 1909/12/20:6a, 21:6a
LEHECKA, Joseph, un. carp., NYC-M – 1912/03/24:6a, 25:6a
LEHECKA, Maria, NYC-M – 1909/01/30:6a
LEHLBACH, Martha, 25, Jersey City, NJ – 1880/11/26:4e, 27:4a
LEHLE, John, fr Geisslingen/Wuertt., NYC-M - 1879/07/19:1e

LEHMAN, Henry, infant, NYC-M - 1895/01/03:1h
LEHMAN, Jane, 2, NYC-M – 1891/09/29:4d
LEHMAN, Lena, 24, NYC-M - 1895/01/03:1h
LEHMAN, Margaret, 39, NYC-B - 1878/03/04:4f
LEHMAN, Max, 3, NYC-M – 1896/07/15:1c
LEHMAN, Sarah, 2, NYC-M - 1895/01/03:1h
LEHMANN % Spiel
LEHMANN, Adolph C., un. typesetter, NYC-M – 1888/11/09:3c
LEHMANN, Alex, NYC-M – 1884/09/13:1g
LEHMANN, Andreas, 45, un. tailor, NYC-M – 1890/07/19:4a, 20:5a
LEHMANN, August, 77, SPD Toenisheide/Elberfeld/Gy - 1915/11/07:3a
LEHMANN, B., NYC-M – 1893/09/02:4a
LEHMANN, Carl, 64, baker, * Lahr/Baden, USA 1853, NYC-M -
    1878/08/22:4d, 25:4c, 30:4b
LEHMANN, Charles, 72, guard, & wife Elisabeth, 70, NYC-M –
    1885/05/11:1d
LEHMANN, Charles, 72, watchman, & his wife, NYC-M – 1885/05/11:1d
LEHMANN, Charles, NYC-Q - 1917/08/01:6a
LEHMANN, Daniel, SPD militant, = in Pforzheim/Baden – 1883/09/19:2e;
    Mem. meeting in NYC – 1908/09/06:3a
LEHMANN, Eduard, NYC-Q – 1904/01/12:4a
LEHMANN, Ernst, 22, Elisabethport, NJ – 1891/09/26:1h, 27:5d
LEHMANN, Franz August, 53, SLP, un. cigarmaker, * 5 Mr 1842
    Eilenburg/Saxony, USA ca. 1875, NYC-Q - 1895/05/06:4a, =9:1e
LEHMANN, Frederick L., 58, janitor, NYC-M – 1891/05/01:2e
LEHMANN, Friedrich, 25, waiter, Swiss, NYC-M – 1892/10/08:1h
LEHMANN, Fritz, 31, NYC-M – 1898/09/05:1d
LEHMANN, Herman, 58, liquor dealer, fr Thueringia?, NYC-M –
    1911/04/18:6a
LEHMANN, Kate, NYC-M – 1886/07/10:2g, 18 Nov:1e, 25:1g, 30:2f
LEHMANN, Leopold, 64, un. cigarmaker, NYC-M – 1902/02/25:3b
LEHMANN, Margareta, 47, NYC-B - 1917/11/06:6d
LEHMANN, Max's wife, NYC-M – 1886/06/09:3a,
LEHMANN, Minna, 41, NYC-M – 1893/10/04:4a
LEHMANN, Oskar, un. printer, NYC-B - 1919/01/25:6a
LEHMANN, Otto, 62, NYC-Bx – 1913/01/03:6a
LEHMANN, Paul, 26, un. typesetter, NYC-M – 1884/10/30:3b
LEHMANN, Richard, NYC-B – 1919/09/17:6a, fam. 18:6a
LEHMANN, Rosie, NYC-B - 1915/11/12:1f
LEHMANN, Wilhelm, 51, NYC-M – 1908/07/01:6a
LEHMANN, William, NYC-M – 1897/08/29:5a
LEHMKUGEL, H., un. cigar maker, NYC-M – 1888/07/19:3b

LEHMS, Therese, b. John, 51, NYC-M – 1901/05/10:4a, fam. 12:5a
LEHN, Edward von, 58, Newark, NJ – 1909/12/24:6a
LEHN, Matthias, un. brewer, NYC?, fam. 1906/02/20:4a
LEHN, Robert, Jersey City Hgts - 1913/11/22:6a
LEHNER, Frank J., 28, NYC-M – 1893/11/02:4c
LEHNER, Gustav, un. baker, NYC-M - 1914/12/10:6a
LEHNER, John, 59, cigarmaker, NYC-B – 1881/07/02:1e
LEHNERT, Anna, NYC-B – 1892/06/29:4a
LEHNERT, George, 16, NYC-M – 1889/10/09:2g
LEHNERT, John, NYC-M – 1887/06/17:3c
LEHNERT, P., NYC-Q - 1914/01/30:6a
LEHNHOFF, Elizabeth, b. Krackeler, 74, ex-SP, NYC-Bx – 1912/06/03:6a, =6:3d
LEHNHOFF, Georg August Wilhelm, 80, SP, * 11 June 1836, un. cigarmaker, NYC-Corona - 1917/01/07:7a, =9:2b
LEHNHOFF, Theodor H., NYC-B – 1912/07/07:7a, 9:6a
LEHNHOFF, Wilhelm, 53, un. cigarmaker, NYC-Q - 1918/10/12:6a
LEHNHOFF, Wilhelm, un. cigarmaker, SP, 70th birthday, NYC-M – 1906/06/11:3f
LEHNIGER, Alfred, 8, NYC-M – 1883/02/25:8a
LEHNIGER, Emilie Pauline, NYC-M – 1887/06/21:2c, fam. 23:3c
LEHNING, John, 32, butcher, NYC-B – 1892/08/15:2d
LEHNSTUHL, Ernestine, 57, NYC-Bx - 1917/09/03:6a
LEHNSTUHL, Moritz, un. cigarmkr - 1913/07/24:6a
LEHOCKY, Joseph, un. carp., NYC-M – 1912/06/08:6a
LEHR, Elisabeth, 18 months, NYC-B – 1882/07/20:3d
LEHR, Friedrich, NYC-M – 1888/03/02:3b
LEHR, Georg, barber, NYC-M – 1881/09/23:4a
LEHR, Henry, 23, driver, NYC – 1886/05/21:3a
LEHR, Jacob, carp., NYC-M – 1881/10/18:3c
LEHR, Jakob, 54, barber, NYC-B – 1890/05/24:2d
LEHREN, Madeline, 51, NYC-B – 1901/03/23:2h
LEHRER, Max, 22, & Sam, 19, @1911 Triangle Shirtwaist Fire, NYC-M – 1911/03/27:1d
LEHRITTER, Charles, 53, NYC-M – 1893/11/02:4c
LEIB, Franz, 73, un. cigarmaker, SP, ex-pres. Soc Coop. Publ. Co. (NYVZ), * 11 Oct 1831 Bernkastel/Mosel, USA 1872, NYC-Bx – 1904/02/12:2h, 4a, 13:4a, 14:5d
LEIB, Magdalena, 66, SLP?, NYC-M – 1898/07/25:4a
LEIBEL, Marie, NYC-M – 1893/12/29:4a
LEIBKOWITZ, Clara, fr Russia, NYC-M – 1907/03/12:2f

LEIBOLD, Friedrich J., 67, music band leader, *Nuernberg, USA 1850, NYC-M - 1897/10/16:2f
LEIBOLD, Heinrich, 27, carpenter, NYC-B - 1878/04/22:4e,24:1f
LEIBOLD, John, 90, leather shop, NYC-M - 1916/09/22:2d
LEIBRAND, Otto, 37, NYC-M - 1890/02/25:1g
LEICHT, Andreas, 43, un. brewer, fr Lower Franconia?, NYC-Bx - 1910/11/07:6a
LEICHT, Louis, 19, NYC-M - 1887/05/07:4c, fam. 12:3d
LEICHTFUS, Henry, NYC-Q - 1899/04/05:4b
LEICHTMANN, Adolf, 39, butcher, NYC-M - 1891/04/04:1h
LEIDGEB % Roth
LEIDIG, John, 55, Newark, NJ - 1905/04/14:4b
LEIDIG, Max, 17, NYC-Q - 1915/06/09:6a
LEIDNER, Christian, NYC-B - 1911/05/01:6a
LEIDRICH, John, 30, NYC-M - 1896/08/11:1b
LEIDY, Henry, Negro, lynched Newton, LA - 1908/11/12:2c
LEIENDECKER, August, 70, NYC-B - 1916/06/10:6b
LEIFERT, Margarete, 37, NYC-B - 1900/01/10:4a
LEIFHEIT, Henry, 66, un. carp., NYC-M - 1913/04/15:6a
LEIGHTON, Augustus D., NYC-M, exec., 1882/03/15:1g, 20 Ap:1f, done 19 May:4a, 20:1e
LEINER, Jakob, 41, un. carp., NYC-Bx - 1913/03/11:6a
LEININGER, Joseph, NYC-M - 1907/04/29:6a
LEINWEBER, August, un. baker, NYC-M - 1887/05/14:3c
LEIPHOLD % Spina
LEIPOLD, Katherine, 64, Secaucus, NJ - 1912/02/24:6a
LEIPOLD, William, 48, NYC-M - 1891/03/30:4a
LEIPZIGER, Henry, Dr., 63, educator, * England, USA 1865, NYC-M - 1917/12/02:11b
LEIPZIGER, Ida, Union Hill, NJ - 1917/06/28:6a
LEISCHMANN, Walter, 35, & Arthur, 32, sales clerks just fr Canada, NYC-M - 1907/11/19:2b
LEISE, Ellen, NYC-B - 1899/03/21:4a
LEISE, Katherina, b. Stenger, NYC-M - 1886/07/22:3c
LEISER, Gustav, 52, employee Columbia Photo Engraving Co., * Woldenberg/Neumark, NYC-M - 1916/04/18.2b
LEISER, Henry, 27, machinist, Elizabeth, NJ - 1895/03/19:2e
LEISLER, Wilhelm, chair German Furriers' Union, + Hamburg/Gy - 1915/03/14:3a
LEISMAN, Herman, janitor, NYC-M - 1909/06/08:1e
LEISS, Emil, NYC-Q - 1917/09/02:7a
LEIST, Adolph, 63, NYC-M - 1914/11/23:6a, 24:6a

LEIST, Elise, b. Weidmann, NYC-M – 1887/03/22:3e
LEIST, Gustav F., 66, Carlstadt, NJ - 1920/11/15:6a, 16:6a
LEIST, Otto, 63, Newark, NJ - 1917/07/09:2c, 11:6a
LEIST, William, 17, NYC-M – 1903/03/15:5a
LEISTNER, Philipp, SLP?, un. machinist, NYC-M – 1893/05/24:4a
LEITMAN, Leah, tailor, SDP?, fr Hartford, CT – 1905/06/10:1g
LEITNER, Joseph, un. carp., NYC-M – 1882/02/05:3a
LEITROCK, George, NYC-Wakefield, 1916/09/02:6a
LEITSCH, Charles, 60, lathe turner, NYC-M – 1891/06/09:4a
LEIZ, Henry, un. printer, NYC-M - 1894/04/01:5b
LELONG % Klein
LEMBERG, William, 63, worker in frame factory, NYC-B – 1900/11/25:1h
LEMKE, G. Gustav, un. weaver, NYC-Bx – 1910/05/03:6a
LEMKE, W., NYC-M – 1905/08/21:4a
LEMKEN, Martin, butcher, NYC-B – 1893/10/23:2d, 24:2d
LEMKOHL, Frieda, NYC-M – 1898/09/06:1c
LEMLEIN, Florence, NYC-B – 1906/12/30:7b
LEMMEL, Anna, fam. 1920/10/19:6a
LEMMERMAN, Maria, 75, NYC-B – 1913/04/15:6a
LEMMERMANN % Kroenke; LEMP % Wright
LEMPERLE, Rudolph, brewer or cooper, NYC-SI – 1901/03/04:4a
LENAU, Nikolaus, 1802-1850, German poet, 50th anniv. of death +
   1899/05/21:14c-e; His work 1900/09/02:4c-d
LENCKNER, Theodore, 21, fr Gy, War 2, NYC-M – 1915/06/17:1c
LENDHOLT, Friedrich, SPD activist, Hamburg/Gy – 1906/11/20:4d
LENDZIMMER, John de, 81, Pole, ex-Prussian officer, + Summer 1881,
   will 1882/03/25:1g
LENG, Peter's wife, NYC-M – 1885/07/21:3b
LENGER, George, 36, NYC-M – 1893/05/20:4a
LENGHEIM, August, 54, un. waiter, NYC-M – 1910/05/07:6a
LENHARDT, Georg, NYC-B – 1909/03/11:6a, 12:6a
LENHART, George, barber, NYC-B – 1907/02/24:1d
LENIKER, Arthur, 22, un. mason, New Haven, CT - 1915/04/06:1e
LENKEL % Lindkloster
LENKOHL, Agnes, 50, NYC-M, + Hoboken, NJ – 1904/07/11:1a, 12:1f
LENNARTZ, Albert, conductor?, NYC-Q – 1901/07/16:4a
LENNARZ, Henry, *Duesseldorf/Gy, un. cigarmaker, SLP, New Haven, CT
   – 1900/01/14:1c, 5a, =16:1g, Fam. 19:4a
LENOIR, Pierre, European patriot, exec. Paris for having worked (Caillaux
   affair) for European peace of understanding – 1919/09/20:1b, 25 Oct:1b
LENSCH % Meyer

LENSCH, Heinrich, 31, cigar maker & SPD activist expelled from Altona/Gy, arrived NYC – 1880/11/30:1d-e, 2 Dec:2a-b, 6:1d-e
LENTHE, John, NYC-M – 1907/09/28:6a
LENTZ, Edward, 21, Union Hill, NJ - 1915/03/08:6a
LENTZ, Friedrich N., 58, tin smith, NYC-M – 1892/01/28:1g
LENTZ, Lillian, 26, NYC-Q - 1916/10/23:6a, fam. 1 Nov:6a; mem. 1917/10/22:6a, 1918/10/22:6a, 1919/10/22:6a
LENTZ, William, 37, NYC-Bx – 1912/05/23:1e
LENZ, (Mrs), 46, NYC-M – 1891/07/11:4d, 12:5c
LENZ, Albert, married Caroline Spahn, NYC-B – 1902/10/14:3b
LENZ, Carrie, 25, NYC-M – 1890/09/12:4d, 13:2g
LENZ, Charles A. Jr, 23, US Army, Newark, NJ, War 1 - 1918/06/27:2e
LENZ, Charles, cashier, NYC-B – 1891/07/18:2e
LENZ, Elisabeth, 48, NYC-B – 1898/12/24:1b
LENZ, Henry, NYC-B – 1907/04/02:6a
LENZ, Jacob, NYPD, inquest, NYC-B – 1885/02/27:3a-b
LENZ, Oscar, un. waiter, NYC-M – 1902/06/04:3h
LENZ, Otto, 12, NYC-M – 1888/05/30:3a
LENZ, Peter, un. cigarmaker, NYC-M – 1898/03/29:4a
LENZ, Reinhard, 38, NYC-B – 1892/04/05:4b
LENZ, Valentin, 28, cigarmaker, NYC-B – 1893/09/29:3c, 30:2d
LEON, Daniel De see De Leon
LEONARD, Annie, 65, NYC-B – 1904/03/21:3c
LEONHARD, Friedrich, 50, NYC-M - 1913/12/29:6a
LEONHARDT % Herrmann
LEONHARDT, George, NYC-M – 1909/08/16:6a
LEONHARDT, Hermann, SPD Bremerhaven/Gy – 1908/08/23:3b
LEONHARDT, Hermann, un. cigarmaker, NYC-M – 1886/12/08:2g
LEONHARDT, Robert, NYC-M – 1900/03/16:4a, 17:4a
LEONON, Samuel, secy Longshoremen's Union, + Erie, PA - 1915/04/22:1f
LEOPOLD % Bosseir
LEOPOLD, Matthew, 60, shoemaker, NYC-B – 1900/06/25:3c
LEOPOLD, Michael, 58, NYC-B – 1912/07/12:1e
LEOPOLD, Walter, 28, SPD Zeitz/Thueringen, ed. at Halle Volksblatt – 1913/04/20:3c
LEPP, Adolf, German labor poet & SPD activist, + Zwickau/Sax. – 1907/02/17:3e-g
LEPPERT, Jacob, NYC-Q – 1910/01/29:6a
LEPPIG, Adam, NYC-B – 1905/08/06:5b
LEPPIG, John, ex-pres. Bayerischer VFV, NYC? – 1907/05/01:3c
LERCH % Zimmer
LERCH, Anton, NYC-M - 1896/03/13:4a

LERMACK, Rosie, 19, @1911 Triangle Shirtwaist Fire, NYC-M – 1911/03/27:1d
LERNER, Max, SP, NYC-M - 1920/09/05:2a
LERNIT, August, NYC-M – 1890/01/14:4a
LESLIE, Frank, publisher, + a few months ago, comment on trial over will – 1880/04/15:4b, 16:2b, 21:1g, 22:4a, 24:2g, trial 13 Jy:4c, 2 Dec:4b
LESSING, Christian, 69, NYC-B – 1908/11/18:1e
LESSING, G. E., German writer, 100th anniv. Of death, 1881/03/02:2a-b
LESSING, Jonathan F., NJ State Senator, + Cape May, NJ – 1907/04/26:3b
LESSMANN, Hermann, NYC-M – 1885/05/12:1e, 19:3b, 20:4a, 21:3a, notes 19 May:3b, 20:4a, 21:3a, 16 Oct:1g, 17:1g
LESSNER, Friedrich, among oldest SPD vets, 82 years (not dead), lives in London – 1907/06/09:11a
LESSURE, Rufus, Negro, lynched Thomasson, AL – 1904/08/19:1d
LETSCH, Theodor, 61, un. pianomaker, NYC-M – 1898/06/26:5a
LETTENBERGER, C., NYC-B - 1916/01/04:6a
LETZINGER, Adam's infant child, NYC-M – 1886/08/20:3b
LEUCKERT, Ida, b. Sonnenschein, NYC-B – 1900/05/07:4a
LEUE, Henriette, SP, USA 1880 via London, NYC-M – 1910/11/22:2c, 6a
LEUE, William, 43, *Brandenburg/Gy, un. cigarmaker?, mgr local Labor Lyceum, SP, Union Hill, NJ – 1911/09/16:6a, 19:1e, =19:3f, fam. 23:6a
LEUPOLD, Gustav, sailor on USS Maine, + Havana/Cuba, Newark, NJ – 1898/02/18:1b
LEUSCHUETZ, Regine, 13, NYC-M – 1881/07/29:1g
LEUSER, Susanna, dying, NYC-B – 1885/03/10:2g-3a
LEUTE, Johann, 57, NYC – 1882/03/11:3b
LEUTE, Nicolaus, 49, Swiss?, NYC-M - 1878/03/28:3a
LEUTEL, Heinrich, SP, NYC-M, remigr. to Berlin (not +) – 1911/08/09:3a
LEUTENEGGER % Schuchmann
LEUTERITZ, Hermann, NYC-B – 1911/07/11:6a
LEUTHART, Theodor, infant, NYC-M – 1882/07/29:4c
LEUTHAUSER, George, electrician, NYC-M – 1897/08/19:1c
LEUTHOLD, Heinrich, Swiss poet, + 1879 Zuerich, review of his work 1882/05/28:4g-5b
LEUTIGER, Reinhold, NYC-M – 1901/07/03:4a
LEUTNER, Marie, 45, NYC-Bx - 1919/04/17:P6a, 18:6a
LEVANDOVSKI, Michael, & wife, NYC-B - 1915/11/03:1e
LEVANDOWSKY, Frank, 40, worker, NYC-B – 1902/05/09:4a
LEVANOFSKY, France, servant, NYC-B - 1916/05/22:1f, 23:6a
LEVARIE, Frank, exec. Trenton, NJ – 1919/08/20:2e
LEVENDUSKY, Anna, Bayonne, NJ - 1917/07/18:2d
LEVENTHAL, Hyman, 84, NYC - 1914/01/14:6d

LEVENTIN, Louis, 18, gold leaf beater, NYC-M – 1901/05/23:4b
LEVERENZ, Frederick, stoker fr Hamburg/Gy, +on SS Polynesia – 1892/07/31:5d
LEVERS, Friedrich, 67, NYC-M – 1893/12/31:5c
LEVI, Anna, NYC-M, + @Genl Slocum – 1904/06/17:3b
LEVIN, Babetta, ~50, NYC-M – 1880/05/07:1d
LEVIN, Morris, infant, NYC-M – 1899/06/09:1g
LEVINE, David, 48, peddler, NYC - 1913/11/30:1f, 12/01:1f
LEVINE, Joseph, 60, clothes shop, NYC-Walker St - 1913/06/17:2d
LEVINE, Max & Pauline, NYC-B, @ 1911 Triangle Shirtwaist Fire, NYC-M – 1911/03/27:1d
LEVINE-NIELSEN, Eugen, German soc., on his + # – 1919/11/09:4a-e
LEVINO, Jonathan, ca. 20, NYC-M - 1878/03/22:1f
LEVINSON, Benjamin, NYC-M - 1915/11/25:6a
LEVKOWSKY, Nume, Polish noble & vet 1830 uprising, NYC-M – 1887/06/01:1c
LEVY, A., 76, NYC-M – 1893/03/26:5a
LEVY, Benjamin, clerk to Immigration Commission, * Altona/Hamburg, NYC-M - 1878/03/20:4e
LEVY, Bernhard, un. furrier, NYC-M – 1886/03/23:3d
LEVY, Caroline, 51, NYC-M – 1892/05/11:4a
LEVY, Caroline, b. Hirsch, 72, NYC-M – 1891/04/21:4a
LEVY, Cecilia, 30, NYC-M – 1903/07/02:1f
LEVY, Charles, un. baker, NYC-M - 1920/11/21:12a
LEVY, Gustav, 64, NYC-M – 1890/07/06:5a
LEVY, Hannah, b. Maas, NYC-M – 1890/09/16:4a
LEVY, Isaac, 56, clothing manuf., NYC-B - 1913/10/22:3b, 23:3d, 24:3a, 26:1b, 28:3a
LEVY, Joseph, druggist, Paterson, NJ – 1885/06/13:3a
LEVY, Leopold S., salesman, NYC-M – 1899/05/22:1e
LEVY, Leopold, 43, butcher, NYC-M – 1905/03/14:4b
LEVY, Leopold, 66, accountant, NYC-M - 1895/11/30: 1f
LEVY, Louis, 54, realtor, NYC-M – 1904/07/01:3g
LEVY, Louis, Rabbi, NYC-M – 1912/12/04:1d
LEVY, Lucien, 38, fr France, NYC-M - 1878/06/12:4e
LEVY, Robert, NYC-M – 1893/04/05:4a
LEVY, Walter B., 27, NYC-M – 1919/09/15:6a
LEVY-DAVID, Cerf, 90, Parisian theater manager – 1883/12/30:5e
LEWENSTEIN, Louis, 35, baker, fr NYC or New Haven, CT – 1892/04/10:1b
LEWES, G.H., English Goethe scholar - 1878/12/29:7a
LEWIN, Lesser, 60, NYC-M – 1892/02/20:4a

LEWIN, Susanna, 70, * SchubinPosen, NYC-M - 1878/02/24:8b
LEWIN-DORSCH, Hannah, SPD activist & student Zuerich U, + there – 1911/09/10:20d
LEWINSKI, Joseph, 72, Viennese actor at Burgtheater – 1907/02/28:2d
LEWINSKY, Hannah, 32, NYC-M – 1890/06/15:5a
LEWIS, Charles, Negro, lynched near Jackson, MS – 1897/12/13:1d
LEWIS, Claude, 19, Negro, striker in Indianapolis, IN, killed by company goons - 1913/12/03:1d
LEWIS, Isaac, Negro leader in 8th ward, NYC-M – 1880/02/09:1d
LEWIS, John, exec. NYC-M – 1889/07/24:1h, done 23 Aug:4e, 24:2e
LEWIS, Rosa, 60, NYC-M – 1900/10/18:1h
LEWIS, Samuel, 25, druggist, NYC-M – 1899/04/14:4a
LEWIS, Sarah, 50, NYC-B – 1903/01/03:1g
LEWIS, Susan, 21, teacher at PS 21, NYC-Bx - 1915/01/07:1d
LEWIS, Toby, Negro, lynched Shreveport, LA - 1914/12/04:1d
LEWISOHN, Leonard, director Montefiore Home, NYC – 1902/03/16:5a
LEWITH, Louis, NYC-M – 1900/05/25:3c
LEXOW, Emil, art painter, Turner, Milwaukee - 1878/06/29:2f
LEY, Emma, 48, NYC-Q – 1918/08/27:6a
LEY, John, 65, Jersey City, NJ – 1907/01/17:6a; mem. – 1909/01/15:6a
LEYDEN, Ernst, Dr., 78, German scientist, * Danzig, + Berlin – 1910/10/06:1e
LEYEN, Jennie, 19, @1911 Triangle Shirtwaist Fire, NYC-M – 1911/04/01:1f
LEYENDECKER, Philipp, 71, NYC-M – 1893/05/30:4a
LEYER, L., un. brewer, NYC-M - 1917/01/08:6a
LEYH, George F., manufacturer, NYC-B – 1902/12/06:1e, 10:1g, 11:1b, 12:3c, 17:4a, 19:2h,
LEYH, Wilhelm F., 46, NYC-M – 1906/08/06:6a
LIBAS, Lena, 28, NYC-M – 1905/08/01:4a
LICHEY, William, NYC-M - 1918/11/11:3a
LICHNER, Michael, 62, driver, Ravenswood, LI – 1909/02/12:1a
LICHT, Henry, NYC-B - 1918/03/08:6a
LICHT, Rebecca, NYC-B - 1920/03/04:6c
LICHTENBERG, Georg Christoph, German scientist & aphorist, 100th ann. + – 1902/03/16:14f-h
LICHTENBUR, Charles, 57, Jersey City, NJ – 1905/09/17:5f
LICHTENSTEIN, D., 50, fr Russia, NYC-M – 1887/08/02:1c
LICHTENSTEIN, Moses, cigar manufacturer,NYC-M - 1879/11/18:4b
LICHTENSTEIN, Sadie, b. Legrave, NYC, + Johnstown, NY – 1905/04/22:1e, 23:1g
LICHTENSTEIN, Sarah, 19, North Tarrytown, NY – 1912/10/17:1f

LICHTMAN, Jacob, grocer, USA 1899, NYC-B – 1902/12/31:2h
LICK % Berger
LIEBECK, George, 21, NYC-B – 1907/02/25:3a
LIEBENGUTH, Joseph, 70, NYC-M – 1902/03/22:1g
LIEBENOW, Gustav, 54, mason, SPD Weissensee/Gy – 1908/06/21:3d
LIEBENOW, Martha, 29, NYC-M, +@Genl Slocum – 1904/06/25:1d
LIEBER, Georg S., 50, travelling salesman, NYC-M – 1898/11/03:4a
LIEBER, George, sailor on USS Maine, + Havana/Cuba, NYC-M – 1898/02/18:1b
LIEBERMANN % Ohrbach
LIEBERMANN, Antoinette, NYC-Bx – 1908/04/14:1b
LIEBERMANN, Arthur, Nihilist fr Russia, in exile worked for a London Jewish NP and freelance for NYVZ, + Syracuse, NY – 1880/11/23:1c, 2c
LIEBERMANN, Joseph,40, worker,*Russia, NYC-M - 1894/10/ :1c
LIEBERMANN, Leon, tailor, Hoboken, NJ – 1891/01/29:2d
LIEBERMANN, Morris's wife, NYC – 1912/09/07:1c
LIEBERNOW, Hannah, NYC-M, +@ Genl Slocum – 1904/06/18:1b
LIEBERT, John A., carp., NYC-M – 1886/10/16:3b
LIEBERTZ, Peter, 64, NYC-M – 1891/07/29:4a
LIEBETREU, Carl Ferd., 71, * Berlin, USA 1886, journalist a.e. for Belletristisches Journal and NYVZ, NYC-M – 1904/04/22:3b
LIEBFRIED, Christian, 56, NYC-B – 1904/10/19:3d
LIEBHABER, Charles, 55, NYC-M – 1896/07/20:1c
LIEBIG, Edward, NYC-M – 1897/11/13:1g
LIEBIG, Frederick, L. E. A., 53, NYC-B – 1911/01/28:6a, 29:7b
LIEBIG, Justus von, German chemist, 100th anniv. Birth – 1903/05/12:2b-c
LIEBIG, Otto, infant, NYC-M – 1888/07/27:3c
LIEBIG, Paul, 14, NYC-M – 1887/07/22:3c
LIEBIG, William, NYC-M – 1898/05/05:4a
LIEBISCH, Theodor, tanner, NYC-M – 1898/06/03:3e
LIEBKNECHT, Karl, USPD leader, + with Rosa Luxemburg in Berlin, - 1919/01/12:1a-b, 18:1a-b, 4a-b, = 27:1a-b, NYC mem. meet 28:2e, 3 Feb.:1f,2e, Newark mem. meet 17 Fb:2d, memory, by Clara Zetkin,15 Jan. 1920:3a-f,5a-e, 6a-e, 16:3a, by Ludwig Rosenberger 1 Aug. II:1-2, genl 5 Sp:9d-e. On his + # – 1919/11/09:4a-e
LIEBKNECHT, Natalie, 70, writer & widow of SPD leader, Berlin/Gy – 1909/02/04:4d, 16:4e-f
LIEBKNECHT, Wilhelm, SPD MdR & a father of German socialism, 60th birthday 1886/04/15:5c, 70th birthday - 1896/03/29:3a-d, 30:1a; + 1900/08/08:1a-b,2a,4b-d, 9:2b-c, 10:2b-c, =12:1h, 13:1a, his life 18:2c-e, NYC soc. meet 10:1c, 13:3b, 15:1c-e, Brooklyn soc. 16:1h, Newark, NJ 17:3d, Jersey City Heights, NJ 17:4b, 18:3b, his = 23 Aug:2c-e, 24:2c-e,

27:2c-e, life 25:4f-g, 25:2c-f, bourgeois reactions 5 Sept:2f-g, A. Bebel on 9:7a-h. Mon. in Berlin 4 Fb 1901:2f, progress 8 Aug:2e, 12 Sept:2d, mem. 20 Aug:2c-d, 21:2c-d
LIEBLANG, Joseph, Yonkers, NY – 1906/01/04:4a
LIEBLER, Charles, NYC-B – 1904/06/10:4a
LIEBLER, Paul H., 46, NYC, mgr Liebler Co. in Jersey City, + Hollis, NJ - 1914/02/04:3d
LIEBLICH, Louis, NYC-M – 1881/09/07:1f
LIEBMAN, Harry, 25, carp., NYC-M – 1911/08/24:1b
LIEBOWITZ, Hannah, 13, Emilie, 11, & John, 6, NYC-M – 1900/04/26:3b
LIEBOWITZ, Julius, 5, & Moses, 3, NYC-M – 1902/08/20:1h
LIEBROCK, Frederick, 53, NYC Road Dept employee, dying, NYC-B - 1914/12/11:6c
LIEBSCH, Johann, SPO, Zeidler/Bohemia, War 1 - 1915/02/21:3b
LIED, Lisette, 75, NYC-M – 1882/02/17:3c
LIEDCHEN, Theodor, 34, waiter, West Hoboken, NJ – 1911/07/24:2d
LIEDE, Rudolph, worker, NYC – 1911/04/07:3e
LIEDER, Adolph, NYC-B - 1878/02/18:3b
LIEDLER, George M., NYC-M – 1891/08/11:4a
LIEDTKE, Berthold, NYC-M – 1888/05/30:3a
LIEFHOLD, Karl, SP, un. baker,Jersey City, NJ - 1918/09/27:6a
LIEGANSER, Jakob Heinrich, 20, USA 1880 fr Gy, Jersey City, NJ – 1880/10/30:1g
LIEHR, Bernhard, NYC-B – 1910/06/17:6a
LIER, Hermann, 48, tailor & SPD activist Leipzig – 1908/03/15:3e
LIESEGANG, Heinrich, 73, un. tailor, NYC-M 1894/07/21:4a
LIESENHEIM, Emilie, NYC-M – 1892/06/13:4a
LIESKE % Boirke;
LIESKE, Hermann, 28, NYC-M – 1890/01/09:4a
LIESKE, Julius, German anarchist, trial in Frankfurt/Main – 1885/07/11:1e-f, 13:1e-g, 2a-g, 16:2c-d, 20:2f, 24:2d, appeal lost 8 Sept:2c, 30:2c, exec. 18 Nov:1b, 2b, 23:2d-e, 30:5a-b, 1 Dec:2b-c, 7:2e-f, 14:4d
LIESS, Louis, 28, NYC-M – 1891/07/29:4a
LIESTMANN, Friedericka, b. Gerbich, NYC-M – 1899/07/31:4a
LIET, Oscar, NYC-M – 1881/05/13:3c
LIETH % Freimuth
LIETH, August Von Der, 84, & wife Katherine, 85, NYC-B – 1900/02/24:1g
LIETKE, Robert,28, pianomaker, NYC-Mt Vernon - 1917/01/30:1f
LIEVRE, Eugene, NYC – 1885/12/04:4a
LIFFLAND, Annie, 1, NYC-M – 1907/02/15:5f

LILIENCRON, Detlev von, German writer, posit. obit of a decent man – 1909/07/23:1b,4d, 25:6c-e, 13b-e; his = 8 Aug.:6c-d, mem. in NYC 1909/12/29:5e. 1st anniv. Of death 1910/08/21:8a-b
LILIENTHAL, Friedrich W., Dr., co-fdr NYVZ, *9 Mr 1833 Steinheim/ Westfalia, NYC-M, + near Hunter, NY – 1910/07/29:1f-g, 6a
LILIENTHAL, Henrietta, 42, NYC-M - 1916/05/30:2a
LILIENTHAL, John, un. bartender, NYC-B – 1903/07/07:4a
LILIENTHAL, Louis, 59, realtor, NYC-M – 1908/12/18:2b
LILIENTHAL, Minnie, NYC-B – 1891/07/26:4a
LILIENTHAL, Samuel, 60, NYC-M – 1890/06/26:4a
LILLY, Bernard, 32, alderman, Bayonne, NJ – 1903/11/11:3c
LIMBACH, Sebastian, NYC-M – 1910/11/19:6a
LIMBACHER, Anna M., NYC-B – 1892/06/18:4a
LIMBACHER, Christine, 42, shoe worker, NYC-B – 1907/07/30:3a
LIMBERG, Carl, car racer, + NYC - 1916/05/14:11d
LIMBERGER, Martin, 48, NYC-Q – 1913/04/22:6c
LINCK, Dora, 20, NYC-B – 1900/03/08:4b
LINCK, Francis P., NYC-M – 1907/12/14:6a
LINCK, Francis P., un. typesetter, NYC-B – 1891/01/05:4a
LINCK, Rudolf F., 53, SP, un. brewer, NYC-M - 1920/08/05:6a, fam. 9:6a
LINCOLN DAY, comments – 1885/04/17:3a; 1897/02/16:2a; 1899/02/ 14:2a; 1900/02/12:2a; 1905/02/13:2a-b; 100th anniv. 1909/02/07:20a-b, 12:1c-e, 2b, 2d, 4a-b, 13:2b, 14:6a-b, 15c-g
LINCOLN, Mary Todd, widow of the president, – 1882/07/21:2e, 22:2c-d
LIND, Jenny, the Swedish Nightingale, + London – 1887/11/03:4e
LIND, Wilhelmine, b. Gundelfinger, Meriden, CT – 1899/01/06:4a, 10:4a
LINDAU, Gustav, un. cigar maker, Jersey City Heights, NJ – 1886/06/23:3b
LINDAU, Paul, 80, German writer - 1919/02/03:2b
LINDAUER, Xavier, painter, fr Bavaria, NYC-M – 1880/08/04:1f, 10:4b, trial of killer 16 Nov:1f, 17:1e, rec. life 18 Nov:1d-e
LINDBLAD, August, 42, Swiss, watchmaker, & wife Lena, 40, Jersey City, NJ – 1907/03/25:1f
LINDE, Henry E., Rutherford, NJ – 1908/03/01:11a
LINDE, Victor, mason, & wife Hulda, NYC-M – 1907/08/07:1d, 8:1f
LINDEMANN % Schirmer
LINDEMANN, A., NYC-Bx - 1918/01/11:6a
LINDEMANN, Carl, Dr., portrait painter & Turner, * Braunschweig, USA 1866, Philadelphia - 1878/03/19:2f
LINDEMANN, Charles, 59, * Hannover/Gy, NYC-M – 1889/02/10:5b
LINDEMANN, Charles, 60, deputy sheriff, NYC-M – 1891/02/17:4e
LINDEMANN, John, 38, NYC-B – 1885/12/10:2f
LINDEMANN, Wilhelm, fr Schleswig?, NYC-M? – 1881/08/05:3d, 6:3c

LINDEMAYER, Minnie, 42, NYC – 1887/09/22:1e
LINDEN, Anna, NYC-M – 1891/04/12:5a
LINDENBAUM, Anna, NYC-M, +@ on Genl Slocum – 1904/06/18:3c
LINDENFELDER, Lena, 26, NYC-B – 1897/07/11:1c
LINDENKOHL, Gustav, 60, crematorium employee, Linden, NJ –
    1908/06/15:6a, =16:1f
LINDER, Robert, 45, cigarmaker, Hoboken, NJ – 1907/08/26:3b
LINDER, Sophie, NYC-M – 1882/03/04:3b
LINDER, Valentin, un. carp., NYC-M – 1908/08/26:6a, 27:6a
LINDERMEIER, Frederick, 42, NYC-B – 1907/11/25:1e
LINDES % Wahl
LINDHART, Frank, NYC-M – 1908/10/17:6a, 18:7c
LINDHEIM, Georg W., Dr., 27, NYC-M – 1898/09/17:1c
LINDHEIM, L., 81, NYC-M – 1892/08/26:4a
LINDHORN, Carl Eduard, 64, SDP?, un. cigarmaker?, Oneida, NY –
    1901/01/04:5a, fam. 10:4a
LINDKLOSTER, Phillipine, b. Lenkel, 45, NYC-M – 1905/05/20:4a
LINDLAU, Caroline, b. Seidenberg, 55, NYC-M – 1888/08/28:3b
LINDNER % Hok
LINDNER, Anton, un. butcher, NYC-B – 1913/01/26:7e
LINDNER, Emil, 51, NYC-Q – 1906/01/05:4a
LINDNER, Emil, NYC-Q - 1917/06/01:6a
LINDNER, Emilie, b. Streech, NYC-Q – 1905/05/16:6a
LINDNER, Ernst, 69, SP, * Silesia, USA 1883, Bevier, MO - 1914/03/24:2f
LINDNER, George, ?38, NYC-B – 1890/10/08:4a
LINDNER, George's wife, NYC-M – 1886/03/25:3d
LINDNER, Hermann, 58, un. typesetter, *Burgstaedt/Sax., SP, NYC-B –
    1911/10/10:1f, 6a, fam 17:6a
LINDNER, John, Hoboken, NJ - 1915/12/14:6a
LINDNER, Lizzie, NYC-Q – 1909/03/30:6a, 31:6a, fam. 2 Apr:6a
LINDNER, Rosa Paula, 15, NYC-B – 1909/07/10:6a, fam. 13:6a
LINDNER, Theodor, 61, NYC-B – 1901/07/03:1d
LINDSBERG, Annie, NYC-M? Bellevue Hospital - 1914/08/19:2f
LINGENAU, Ferdinand, East Prussian official, exiled to USA, + St Louis?,
    left $7,000 to German SPD, causes polit. problems as SPD is banned -
    1878/06/07:2f, 08/03:2e, 09/11:2e; will voided by family 1880/07/23:2e;
    German court awarded $ to kin 1882/01/20:2f, 26 Apr:1d-e
LINGG, Hermann, German poet, 70th birthday – 1890/02/09:7c-d
LINGLEY, William, exec. Ossining, NY - 1913/05/06:2c & 9:2e
LINGSWEILER, E., 71, NYC-M – 1893/08/18:4a
LINK % Kleine, % Nuber, % Ritting
LINK, Emil, 18, NYC-M – 1882/01/31:3c

LINK, Gustav, NYC-M – 1901/07/08:4a
LINK, John, barber, NYC-B - 1915/04/03:6a
LINK, Joseph, 43, & Katharina, 39, NYC-M – 1907/07/31:1c
LINK, Karl, NYC-B – 1904/05/04:4a
LINK, Lorenz, NYC-M - 1919/01/26:6a
LINK, Lottie & Eddie, NYC-M, + @on Genl Slocum – 1904/06/17:3b
LINK, Robert, NYC – 1883/01/29:3c
LINKE, Franziska, 57, NYC-M – 1896/04/19:5a
LINKE, Gustav, SP, weaver fr Glauchau/Sax., Yonkers, NY - 1920/02/17:8a,18:2f,6a,20:6a
LINKE, Joseph, NYC-B – 1907/11/11:6a
LINKE, Natalie, 16, NYC-Bx - 1918/08/08:6a
LINKE, Robert, 59, un. brewer, New Haven, CT – 1908/05/19:6a
LINKE, Selma, 35, Jersey City Heights, NJ – 1901/04/11:4a
LINKER, B., un. baker, NYC-M - 1916/01/16:7b
LINKOFF, Karl, 30, NYC-B - 1913/10/01:3b
LINKS, Joseph, un. brewer, NYC-M – 1890/12/19:1f, 20:4a
LINN % Petri
LINN, Anna, b. Wolf, 42, NYC-M – 1905/05/20:4a
LINNEBACH, Carl, 45, NYC-M - 1914/04/21:6a,22:6a, fam. 24:6a
LINSTROW, John & son Frank, 19, NYC-M – 1906/07/02:3e
LINTZ, Samuel, 30, mason, NYC-B – 1898/03/06:5c
LINZE % Muenster
LINZMAYER, Elizabeth Rumpf, 64, NYC-Glendale - 1916/08/07:6a
LINZMEIER, John, *Verden/Hannover, USA late 1860s, SDP, un. cigarmaker, NYC-M – 1904/07/02:4a, 3:5a,f
LIPP, Frank, 63, * Passau//Bavaria/Gy, shoemaker & singer, USA 1882, + Cocva, FL – 1908/05/17:7c
LIPP, Frank, Cocoa, FL – 1888/07/07:4e
LIPPE, Louise von der, 69, NYC-M - 1917/10/05:6a
LIPPE-DETMOLD, Prince of, died in insane asylum in Gy, comment on aristocrats 1905/01/17:2c-d
LIPPELT, William, 59, SLP, un. tailor, * Oschersleben/Saxony, USA mid-1870s, co-fdr Rochester Labor Lyceum, + Palmyra, NY - 1917/12/05:2d
LIPPERT % Rosch
LIPPERT, Charles, 61, NYC-D – 1912/09/28:3b
LIPPIATT, Gerald, org. for United Mine Workers, + by company goons in Trinidad, CO - 1913/08/26:4b
LIPPMANN, Adolf, NYC – 1890/08/19:4a
LIPPMANN, Martin, NYC, + Port Trela, Honduras – 1903/08/12:4c
LIPPMANN, Roman Iwanowitsch, alias "Count Zuboff," NYC-M – 1896/07/31:3d

LIPPMANN, Samuel, NYC-B – 1911/07/12:1f
LIPPOLD, Eduard, NYC-M - 1920/07/16:6a
LIPPOLD, Karl H., 35, NYC-M – 1889/09/21:2g
LIPPOLT, Jacob, NYC-B – 1913/03/19:6a
LIPPS % Baader
LIPPSTADT, Mary, NYC-M - 1918/02/13:6a
LIPTOK, Loslo, painter, fr Bohemia, NYC-M – 1892/06/17:1g
LIS, Anna, 79, NYC-B – 1892/07/10:5c
LISIESKI, Franz, NYC-Bx – 1908/09/28:6a
LISKA, Paul, his mother-in-law Maria Cecilia +, NYC-M – 1901/03/09:4a
LISKA, Paul, un. carp., NYC-M - 1914/11/07:6a
LISKA, Theresa, NYC-M – 1903/06/02:4a
LISS, John, NYC-M – 1904/10/20:1g
LISSAGARAY, Olivier, 68, French journalist & historian of 1871 Commune – 1901/02/09:2d
LISSKE, Max, NYC-Q - 1920/05/10:6a, 11:6a
LISSNER, Hermann, un. carp. & SPD Chemnitz/Sax. - 1913/05/04:3e
LIST, Albert, 69, NYC-Bx – 1913/02/11:6a
LISTMANN, Peter, NYC-M – 1900/11/20:4a
LITCHMAN, Charles H., 58, KoL activist 1880s, Marblehead, MA – 1902/06/22:1h
LITHAUER, Henry, NYC-M - 1918/12/24:6a
LITT, John, 63, cigarmaker, NYC-M – 1901/11/11:2g
LITTAUER, Morris, 51, realtor, NYC-B – 1908/12/19:3a
LITTLE, Frank, IWW leader, lynched Butte,MO - 1917/08/02:1g,2b, 3:4a-b, 4:1c-d, 11a, = 6:1f,8:1b
LITTLEFIELD, Charles, ex-Congressman for Maine - 1915/05/03:2e
LITTMANN, Karl, NYC-M – 1896/08/09:5a
LITZ, Ferdinand, 41, NYC-M - 1894/04/04:4a
LITZ, Julius, 3, NYC-B – 1888/09/18:4g
LITZKE, Ida, 6, NYC-B – 1903/02/13:4a
LIVINGSTON, Frank, Negro, lynched Eldorado, AK - 1919/05/23:3f
LIVINGSTON, Louisa, 42, NYC-M – 1891/04/11:4a
LLOYD, George K., 61, metal worker, ex-KoL 1880s, Yonkers, NY – 1909/05/14:2c
LOACH, Edward, 41, machinist, fr Birmingham/Engl., NYC-B - 1913/05/25:1d
LOBEJAEGER, Albert, NYC-M – 1919/08/22:6a, 24:12a
LOBEJAGER, Fritz, 51, painter, NYC-M – 1898/02/26:4a
LOBENGULA, King of the Matabeles, victim of British imperialism — 1893/11/02:1a, 3:1a, 4:1b, 6 Dec:2a-b, 9:1b
LOCH, Tillie, 19, Chicago, + NYC at sister's home – 1896/05/21:1e

LOCHAU, Viktor von der, 51, * Potsdam, ex-Prussian officer, USA ~1865, public notary, Chicago, IL – 1880/04/15:1d
LOCHHAUS, Johanna, b. Drautz, NYC-M – 1888/11/08:3b
LOCHMANN, Frederick, mail carrier, NYC-M – 1888/06/23:4a
LOCHMUELLER, William, 70, laborer, NYC-M – 1898/07/30:1g
LOCHNER, Waldo, clerk, NYC-M – 1911/08/20:1d
LOCHOR, Louis, SLP?, un. beerdriver, Czech?, Guttenberg, NJ – 1893/05/05:4a, fam. 11:4a
LOCHOW, M. von, 70, NYC-B – 1892/11/22:4a
LODEGAST, G., West Hoboken, NJ – 1911/03/18:6a
LODERMANN, Josephine, 32, NYC-M - 1916/06/13:6a
LODY, Carl Hans, German patriot, exec. London - 1914/11/11:2b
LOEB, Catherine, b. Grisselmann, NYC-M – 1890/09/29:4a
LOEB, Hugo, 17, 1906 fr Hamburg/Gy, NYC-M – 1907/07/19:2a
LOEB, Jacob, mazzes baker, NYC-M – 1897/07/29:3h
LOEB, Lena, NYC-M – 1909/01/30:1b
LOEB, Max, baker, NYC-M – 1882/03/13:1e
LOEB, Ms, 72, servant, NYC-M - 1913/07/01:1f
LOEBL, Simon, 47, Newark, NJ – 1908/01/28:3c
LOEBLICH, Max, chair music engravers' union s. 1887, + Leipzig - 1914/08/15:4d
LOECHNER, Rosie, b. Juellner, +1911 Coatsville, PA, mem. 1912/01/14:7b
LOECKEL, Franz, 50, NYC-M – 1886/12/21:3a
LOEFFEL, Marguerite, 29, NYC-M, +@ Genl Slocum – 1904/06/28:1c
LOEFFER, Andrew, 70, artisan, NYC-B - 1914/07/03:6a
LOEFFLER % Weidenmueller
LOEFFLER, Anna, 22, NYC-Q – 1914/04/08:6a
LOEFFLER, August, 65, security guard, fr Gy, NYC-M - 1894/04/19:1f
LOEFFLER, Frederick, NYC – 1903/10/30:1g
LOEFFLER, Friedrich, NYC-M? – 1892/10/19:4a
LOEFFLER, Friedrich, Prof. Dr., German scientist, discoverer of dyphteria bacteria, * 24 June 1852 Frankfurt/Oder, + Berlin - 1915/04/10:2a
LOEFFLER, Hermann, SP Newark, NJ – 1904/08/11:4a
LOEFFLER, Jakob, un. carp., NYC-M – 1893/04/14:4a
LOEFFLER, John, fr NYC-B, US army, + Manila/Philippines – 1900/11/02:4a
LOEFFLER, John, NYC-Q – 1882/01/06:1g, 21:3a, note 10 Mr:3a
LOEFFLER, Katherina, b. Zingler, NYC-B – 1891/04/05:5a
LOEFFLER, Paul, 38, watchman, NYC-M – 1887/12/31:1g, 2 Jan. 1888:2f
LOEFFLER, Richard, 56, SP, un. cigarmkr, * Leipzig, USA 1880, Boston, then NYC-M – 1907/03/30:2d, 6a, 31:6a-b, 7c, 1 Apr:6a
LOEFFSTEDT, Charles, New Haven, CT – 1910/06/30:6a

LOEGLER, Charles, 27, un. bartender, NYC-B – 1910/01/12:6a, mem. 10 Jan. 1911:6a
LOEHE, Auguste, 50, Paterson, NJ – 1913/08/20:6a
LOEHLEIN, Barbara Ostertag, 69, NYC-B - 1920/11/26:6a
LOEHLEIN, Kasper, 52, NYC-B – 1897/06/29:4a
LOEHMANN % Wendt
LOEHNSBERG, Alma, 14, Newark, NJ – 1903/02/20:1c, =21:1c
LOEHR, Frank, 50, driver, NYC – 1902/11/22:2h
LOEHR, Joseph, 52, NYC-M – 1900/10/27:4a, 28:5a
LOEHR, Mary, 64, NYC-Bx – 1909/12/14:6a
LOERZER, Paul, un. pianomaker, NYC?, fam. 1880/07/19:3b, benefit for family 18 Oct:4e
LOESCH % Frey
LOESCH, Philipp, NYC? – 1888/12/27:3c
LOESCHBORN, George, 47, un. carp., NYC-Q – 1904/12/10:4a
LOESCH-KRAMER, Ms., midwife, NYC-B? – 1893/03/10:4e
LOESCHNER, Emma, 12, NYC-M – 1899/11/30:4a, fam. 4 Dec:4a
LOESCHNER, Wilhelm, 44, NYC-M – 1889/12/20:4a
LOESCHNER, Wilhelmine, 40, SP?, NYC-M – 1907/04/21:7c, 22:6a, fam. 25:6a
LOESER, George, Guttenberg, NJ – 1911/11/22:6a
LOESER, Paul, 67, *Ludwigsburg/Gy, at NYSZ 1859, 1864-1900, + chief-ed., NYC-M – 1900/11/14:3d
LOESSLER, Louis, 9, NYC-M, + @ Genl Slocum – 1904/06/17:3b
LOESSMANN % Michel
LOETTERLE, Christian, tailor, NYC-M – 1886/09/09:3a
LOEV, Friedrich Ernst, 2, NYC-B - 1878/07/29:3a
LOEW, Gustav Adolf, NYC-M – 1892/01/21:4a
LOEW, Joseph, laborer fr Prussia, NYC-B – 1886/06/24:2c
LOEWE, Emil, NYC-B – 1911/04/24:6a, 25:6a
LOEWE, Henriette, b. Thamm, NYC-B - 1896/01/27:4a
LOEWE, Wilhelm, '48er, NYC 1853-61, then returned & became MdR, + – 1886/11/04:4d
LOEWENBERG, Phil, 7, Henry, 9, Deborah,12,NYC-B,+ on ship Mystery – 1887/07/12:1c-d, 13:2g,15:2e
LOEWENHERZ, Samuel, wealthy art dealer, + Dec. 1886 NYC, on lover Mrs Diss Debar (scandal), 1888/04/17:2e, 19:2e, 21:4c, 25:4c, 27:4c, 30:4c, 1 May:1f-g, 2:1g-h, 4:2e
LOEWENSTEIN, Simon, fr Bueckeburg/Gy, & Sophie, b. Kratzenstein, both SP, Silver Wedding celebr., NYC-B - 1914/12/08:5c-d
LOEWENSTEIN, Daniel, 38, butcher, Newark, NJ – 1912/12/17:2e

LOEWENSTEIN, Gabriel, weaver, MdL (SPD), Nuernberg/Gy – 1911/02/03:4d
LOEWENSTEIN, Lilli, 22, NYC-Q – 1901/09/18:3b
LOEWENSTEIN, Marie A., 72, NYC-B – 1892/07/24:5b
LOEWENSTEIN, Sigmund, SPD activist in Barmen/Gy – 1908/03/01:3a
LOEWENTHAL % Zumpe
LOEWENTHAL, August, Dr., Hoboken, NJ – 1886/12/09:2d
LOEWENTHAL, Charlotte, 80, Hoboken, NJ – 1903/06/28:1d
LOEWENTHAL, Helena, b. Jahrling, 58, NYC-B - 1917/11/24:6a
LOEWENTHAL, Max, 50, peddler fr Russia, & son Benjamin, 18, NYC-M – 1887/03/14:4b, 15:3c
LOEWENTHAL, Moses, 60, dying, NYC-B – 1880/06/17:1g
LOEWENTHAL, Simon, NYC-M – 1892/09/25:5b
LOEWER, Henry G., 48, un. brewer, NYC-M - 1914/12/01:6a
LOEWINGER, Kate, 36, NYC-M – 1896/05/25:3g
LOEWY, Benno, lawyer & chair Star Opera Company, a local German theater, NYC-M - 1919/08/21:5e, 6a-b
LOEWY, Caroline, NYC-M – 1891/03/11:4a
LOEWY, Max, journalist for G-A newspapers, NYC-B – 1908/01/05:7c
LOFF, Henry Ray, Dr., oriental scholar at Princeton U - 1878/11/18:1e
LOFFLER, Robert, NYC-Bx - 1917/08/29:6a
LOFGREN, John E., ship stoker, married Emma Anderson, both Swedes, NYC-M – 1880/02/26:4d
LOFINK, John, NYC-Bx - 1918/07/24:6a
LOFTUS, Ella, 22, Hoboken, NJ - 1915/01/30:6b
LOGAN, John A., US Senator fr Illinois, 1886/12/27:1g
LOH, Henry, un. carp., NYC-M – 1897/06/13:5a
LOHMAN, Adolph, 36, fr Bremen ~1882, ex-NYC innkeep, oil dealer, Bogota, NJ – 1907/11/27:1g
LOHMANN, Albert F., 53, theater magr, NYC-M - 1915/12/11:2e
LOHMANN, Ann, b. Trow, 66, "Madame Restell," abortionist,* Paineswick/England, NYC-M - 1878/04/02:4c-d, = 3:4d
LOHMANN, August, 17 mo., NYC-M – 1880/07/17:3a
LOHMANN, Charles F., 5, NYC-B – 1889/02/18:4a
LOHMANN, Dora, b. Haak, NYC-M – 1885/03/23:3b
LOHMANN, Emmy, 29, NYC-Bx - 1917/07/05.6b
LOHMANN, Friedrich, 55, NYC-B – 1893/12/29:4a
LOHMANN, Gustav, 43, NYC-M – 1889/12/31:4a
LOHMANN, Henry, SLP, Newark, NJ – 1886/02/23:2g, 4d, =25:2e
LOHMANN, Louise, 4, & sister Anna, 2, NYC-M - 1878/06/11:3b
LOHMANN, Michael, 46, NYC-M – 1889/10/07:4a
LOHMILLER, John, carpenter, NYC-M – 1884/07/15:4d

LOHMUELLER, Charles, worker at Ft Lafayette Arsenal, NYC (dying), NYC-B – 1903/02/20:1f
LOHMUELLER, Joseph, 45, carp., NYC – 1910/03/29:1f
LOHR, Valentin, NYC-B - 1917/06/28:6a
LOHRINGER, Gustav W., 25, USA 1883, grocer, NYC-M – 1893/05/10:1c
LOHRMANN, Daniel, 66, cabinetmaker, * Geisslingen/Wuertt., USA 1849, NYC-M - 1879/08/09:1f, = 11:1g
LOHSE, Christine, b. Hafner, NYC-B – 1890/02/05:4a
LOHSE, Oscar, 32, NYC-M - 1895/01/19:4a
LOHSE, Paul, un. machinist, NYC – 1912/06/18:6a
LOHSE, Wilhelm, un. carp., NYC-M – 1904/05/02:4a, 3:4a
LOHSE, Wilhelmine, b. Mitznmaier, NYC-M - 1878/05/24:3b
LOLIES, Gustav, NYC-M - 1915/04/16:6a
LOLL, Hulda, 49, NYC-Q – 1909/04/16:6a, 17:6a
LOMBERG, Philip & Freddy, NYC-B, + on ship Mystery – 1887/07/12:1c-d, 13:2g
LOMBROSO, Cesare, Italian scientist 1909/10/20:2d
LOMBROSO, Italian socialist – 1909/11/06:4e-f
LOMMEL, Anna, 50, NYC-B - 1920/10/13:6a
LOMTATIDSE, W. J., Russian socialist - 1915/12/29:4d
LONDON, Jack, US writer, ex-SP, + Santa Rosa, CA - 1916/11/23:1d
LONG, Frederick, SP, typesetter, +Philadelphia, PA – 1911/02/06:1f, 7:4e, =10:2c
LONG, Marie G., 52, SP, NYC-M - 1914/05/02:6a, =4:2a
LONG, Richard, NYC-M? - 1913/11/28:2e
LONGARD, Franz, 49, NYC-M – 1908/12/16:6a, 17:6a
LONGBART, Nathan, 45, tailor, fr Russia, NYC-M – 1903/06/07:1e
LONGENECKER, David R., Dr., 64, dentist, Roadville Ctr, LI – 1912/07/29:2c
LONGEVIN, Pierre, vet 1870 Commune, + Paris - 1913/06/17:4e
LONGFELLOW, Henry Wadsworth, US poet, long obit by S. Schewitsch – 1882/03/26:4b-d
LONGO, Rafaele, exec. Trenton, NJ - 1914/05/27:2e
LONGUET, Charles, 64, vet Paris Commune, + Paris/F – 1903/08/20:2d-e
LONGUET-MARX, Jenny see MARX
LOOF, Bruno, 25, SPD, journalist for <u>Chemitzer Freie Presse</u>, + Langensalza/Saxony - 1878/04/10:2d-2
LOOS, Christina, b. Eberhardt, 54, NYC-M – 1890/04/08:4a
LOOS, Frederick, NYC-M – 1909/04/14:6a
LOOS, Georg, NYC-M – 1908/01/03:6a
LOOS, Johann C., NYC-M – 1900/03/06:4a
LOOS, John, 38, beer driver, NYC-B – 1896/08/11:1c

LOOSE % Borrs
LOOSE, Henry, 69, tailor, NYC-M – 1889/07/14:1g
LOOSE, Meta, 16, trial of dad Carl, NYC-M – 1909/02/12:1a, exec. Ossining, NY – 1910/07/22:5e, 25:2a, done 26:1b
LOPEZZI, Anni, worker, shot by police in Lawrence, MA, trial 1912/02/21:2b
LOPPE, William, gardener, 27, NYC-B – 1882/01/03:4e
LOPPINGER, Viola, 19, NYC-SI – 1905/08/29:3h
LORBER, Janusz, tailor, Newark, NJ – 1911/07/24:3d-e
LORCH, Anton, un. typesetter, NYC-M – 1891/08/23:5d
LORCH, Wilhelm, NYC-M – 1888/05/19:3a
LORENTZ, John, cigar store, ex-New Orleans & Cape Town, RSA, NYC-M – 1887/10/19:1g
LORENZ, Dominick, 60, cook, NYC-B – 1888/05/15:2c
LORENZ, John, NYC-M – 1890/08/30:4a
LORENZE, August, 53, NYC-B – 1904/03/01:4a
LORENZEN, J., fr Flensburg/Gy, NYC-M – 1888/02/16:3c
LORENZEN, John, NYC-Q – 1896/08/11:4a
LOREY, Frank, NYC-B – 1913/02/13:6a
LORICH, Ida, 25, shot during strike, Buffalo, NY – 1913/04/10:1d
LORINO, Dr., NYC-M – 1888/02/23:1c
LORINSER, Joseph, 46, NYC-M - 1917/05/16:6a
LORM, Hieronymus, 80th birthday, Austrian poet – 1901/08/25:11g-h, 12a
LORUENSER, Karl, 41, NYC-M - 1878/07/06:3c
LOSCH, Anna Maria, b. Schmitt, 50, NYC-B – 1891/04/02:4a
LOSEL, W., Yonkers, NY – 1906/11/13:6a
LOSS, Theodor, NYC-M – 1904/09/29:4a
LOSSMANN, Gesche, 73, NYC-M – 1892/06/20:4a
LOTH, C. Max, 74, NYSZ journalist, NYC-M - 1916/05/31:2f
LOTH, Kornell, fr Hungary, exec. Dannemora, NY – 1893/01/17:1f
LOTHER, August, landlord, Newark, NJ – 1880/05/27:1f
LOTT % Ferger
LOTT, August, 58, un. millwright, NYC-B – 1908/04/25:6a
LOTT, Christine, 68, NYC-B - 1917/11/20:6a
LOTT, Karl, NYC-Bx - 1917/04/03:6a
LOTT, Wilhelm, 47, un. painter, *Achern/Baden, New Rochelle, NY – 1910/07/29:6a, 30:2b, 6a
LOTTENBURGER, Karl, SPD Dresden/Gy – 1901/03/29:2d
LOTTERHOFER, John, un. carp., NYC-M – 1893/07/27:4a
LOTTI, W., NYC-B – 1891/04/04:4a
LOTZ, George, 30, student, NYC-M – 1893/07/29:1h
LOUB, Charles M., Dr., 47, NYC-M – 1911/03/25:7b
LOUIZHARLONER, Richard, 35, NYC-M – 1900/08/10:3a

LOUSDALE, William, 40, un. typesetter, NYC-M – 1897/01/21:1e
LOVECRAFT, Frederick. A., 32, theater director, NYC-M – 1893/10/27:2e
LOVELACE, Jerry, Negro, lynched Manchester, GA – 1911/10/20:2e
LOVENTHAL, Mary, @1911 Triangle Shirtwaist Fire, NYC-B – 1911/03/30:1a
LOVETT, Robert, Negro, lynched Morgan, GA - 1913/08/16:2b
LOW, Henry L., State Senator for Middletown, NY– 1888/12/04:4d
LOW, Seth, ex-mayor of NYC & enemy of labor - 1916/09/18:2f
LOWITZ, Martha, b. Braun, 20, NYC-M – 1890/12/23:1h, inquest 27 Jan 91:2g, trial 19 Fb:4d, life 21:1f
LOY, Franz, SP, NYC-M – 1908/04/24:6a
LOZIER, Dr., feminist, NYC-M – 1888/04/30:1b
LUBANDE, Stanislaus, NYC-M – 1908/08/28:6a
LUBBEN, Henry, electrotypist & his wife, NYC-M – 1899/11/17:2h
LUBBERGER, Henry, un. carp., NYC-M – 1886/09/11:3c
LUBBERT, Charles, NYC-M, + @on Genl Slocum – 1904/06/18:3c
LUBERMANN, Johanna, White Plains, NY, +@Genl Slocum – 1904/06/25:1c
LUBLINGER, Francis, 21, NYC-M – 1896/06/12:2e
LUCA, Christian M., 45, grocer, fr Peterkaese/Hannover/Gy, NYC-B – 1889/08/23:1e-f, =24:2d, note 25:1c, 28:1c, 18 Sp:2c, trial of murderers 17 Oct:1e-f, 18:4e, etc, guilty 24:2f
LUCAS, Adam, 35, NYC-M – 1891/03/14:4a
LUCAS, Robert, 32, NYC-M, +@Genl Slocum – 1904/06/23:1c
LUCCHENI, who killed empress @Elizabeth of Austria, + in jail – 1910/11/01:4f
LUCE, James C., merchant marine capt & hero, New Rochelle, NY - 1879/07/11:4a
LUCHS, G. B., * Bredstedt/Gy, Hoboken, NJ – 1888/09/03:3a
LUCHS, Harry, 20, Hoboken, NJ – 1912/10/21:2a
LUCHT, Johann, 58, NYC-Hoboken, NJ – 1898/05/09:4a
LUCHT, Max, un. butcher, NYC-B - 1918/02/12:6a
LUCIANO, Antonio, 29, exec. Trenton, NJ – 1912/01/17:2f
LUCKE, Emanuel, 18, fr Baden to USA 1882, dying, NYC-M – 1884/12/08:1f
LUCKENBURG, Henry W., 72, piano dealer, NYC – 1900/08/31:4a
LUCKHARDT, Henry, 9, NYC-Bx – 1912/03/25:1d, 4c
LUCKMEYER, Henry, carpenter, Newark, NJ - 1894/08/10:4a
LUDERMANN, Johanna, White Plains, NY, +@ Genl Slocum, her will – 1904/06/25:1c
LUDKENS, Anna, 35, NYC-M – 1900/11/24:1d
LUDLONG, Sam, 45, grocer, Austrian, War 2, NYC - 1918/11/09:1d

LUDMEYER, Morris, tailor, NYC-M - 1914/12/16:1e
LUDWIG % Gaertner
LUDWIG, Albert, 57, un. cigarmaker, SP, NYC-M – 1906/06/04:4a
LUDWIG, Alexander, 53, NYC-B – 1903/03/19:4a, 20:4a
LUDWIG, Amalie, NYC-M – 1905/01/14:4a, 15:5b, fam. 17:4a
LUDWIG, Anton, 68, NYC-B - 1913/08/09:6a
LUDWIG, August, 15, NYC-B – 1893/07/12:3b
LUDWIG, August, 71, NYC-M – 1909/03/18:2a
LUDWIG, August, un. printer, NYC-B - 1915/05/11:6a
LUDWIG, Emma, NYC-M – 1901/07/04:1d
LUDWIG, Erdmann, NYC-M – 1890/12/16:4a
LUDWIG, Franz, 64, NYC-Bx – 1908/03/14:6a
LUDWIG, George, 15, NYC-M, + @on Genl Slocum – 1904/06/17:3b
LUDWIG, John H., 59, SP, piano manuf., NYC-Bx - 1917/03/29:2d, 6 Apr:6b
LUDWIG, Karl, un. painter, Newark, NJ – 1911/01/09:6a
LUDWIG, L., NYC-Bx - 1913/07/25:6a
LUDWIG, Lillie, NYC-M, +@ on Genl Slocum – 1904/06/18:3c
LUDWIG, Lorenz, 36, NYC-B – 1889/02/06:4a
LUDWIG, Margaret, 60, NYC-B - 1917/10/03:6c
LUDWIG, Marie, b. Gloeckner, NYC-Woodside – 1890/09/26:4a
LUDWIG, Martina, b. Oechsle, 54, Swiss?, NYC-M – 1906/03/05:4a
LUDWIG, Otto, NYC-M – 1887/12/01:3b
LUDWIG, Paul, un. smith, 35, NYC-M? – 1912/03/14:2a
LUDWIG, Reinhard, No. Bergen, NJ - 1913/08/29:6a
LUDWIG, Sophie, b. Bockholdt, NYC-M – 1889/07/24:4a
LUDY, Anna, b. Mauch, 48, NYC-M – 1899/08/22:4a
LUEBBE, Friedericka, b. Michaelsen, 73, NYC-M – 1891/03/14:4a
LUEBBEN, Eduard, 23, NYC-M - 1878/11/29:3a
LUEBKART, Fritz, 16, NYC-M - 1920/03/09:6a
LUEBKEMANN, H., un. cigarmaker, NYC-M – 1898/06/18:4a
LUEBKING, John F., ~40, hotelier, NYC-SI – 1886/03/31:1g, 7 Apr:4e
LUEBLER % Krueger
LUECK, Theodor, Hoboken, NJ – 1888/10/08:3a
LUECKEL, Wilhelm, 47, NYC-M – 1909/09/13:6a, 14:6a, fam. 17:6a
LUEDEKE, Adolph, 52, Express Co., employee, Newark, NJ – 1909/02/08:3b
LUEDEMANN, 72, NYC-B – 1899/02/02:4a, 3:4b
LUEDEMANN, Friedrich, 32, NYC-M – 1888/10/11:2h
LUEDEMANN, Henry, 30, NYC-M – 1897/01/21:1g
LUEDEMANN, Wilhelm, 32, SLP, Hoboken, NJ - 1896/01/24:4a
LUEDER, Friedrich August, 72, NYC-B – 1888/01/05:3a

LUEDER, Friedrich, NYC-M – 1898/05/03:4a
LUEDER, William, NYC-Bx - 1920/08/07:6a
LUEDERITZ, Friedrich, NYC – 1912/12/31:6a
LUEDERS, Elizabeth, 37, NYC-M - 1915/04/21:6a
LUEDERS, Sophie, 59, NYC-B – 1905/05/13:6a
LUEDOLFF, J. W., NYC-M – 1900/07/18:4a
LUEDTKE, Julius, 47, carpenter, NYC-M - 1895/05/15:4a
LUEGER, Karl, Dr., Vienna mayor, crit obit – 1910/03/11:4d
LUEHRING, Gustav, 36, grocery clerk, NYC-M – 1911/04/04:1f
LUEHRS, Charles, 13, Hoboken, NJ – 1880/07/01:1g
LUENEBERG % Finke
LUENING, Dr., physician, German soc, + Zuerich/CH – 1896/07/04:2b
LUERS, Henry, 65, clothes dealer, NYC-B – 1906/07/03:1f
LUESCHER, Ulrich, Swiss, NYC – 1883/04/28:3a
LUETGERT, Adolph K., Chicago sausage manuf., + Joliet, IL – 1899/07/28:1b, 29:3e
LUETH, Otto, Cleveland, OH, exec. Columbus, OH – 1890/08/30:1d
LUETJEN, Henry, 40, elevator man, NYC-B – 1908/06/04:3a
LUETJENS, A., 58, SPD Kiel, reporter for Schleswig-Holsteinische Volkszeitung - 1915/07/04:3b-c
LUETTGE % Pahlek
LUETTICH, Richard, 49, NYC-B – 1900/07/27:1b
LUETTINGER, George, SDP, Syracuse, NY – 1904/12/15:1d
LUETTMANN, Johann, 62, carp., fr Schleswig-Holstein?, NYC-M – 1885/05/14:3d, 4b, 15:3c
LUETZNER, Friedrich, NYC – 1908/09/11:6a
LUGEMANN, Friedrich G., baker, NYC-M – 1882/03/01:1e
LUGER, Remigius, un. woodcarver, NYC-M - 1896/01/16:4a
LUICK, Gottlob F., un. brewer, NYC-M – 1907/01/20:7c
LUIHN, Louis, W. Newark, NJ - 1913/12/10:6a
LUKAS, John, un. driver, NYC-M – 1901/11/08:4a
LUKASCHICK, Rose, Jersey City, NJ – 1910/07/15:2b
LUKEY % Kemnitz
LUKOSKI, Frank, RR worker, + Jersey City, NJ – 1898/11/19:1f
LULLMANN, Carrie, 24, NYC-M, +@Genl Slocum – 1904/06/22:1d
LUM, Dyer L., 51, US anarchist, NYC-M – 1893/04/09:1f
LUMPP, Margarethe, 45, NYC-M – 1880/12/22:1g
LUND, Charles, 68, Swede, Red Bank, NJ – 1911/08/19:2e
LUND, William, 50, cigarmaker, Newark? - 1913/10/30:2e
LUNDEL, Charles, NYC-M, + @on Genl Slocum – 1904/06/18:3c
LUNDIN, Charley, 7, NYC-M – 1899/11/08:3f
LUNDSTROM, Victor, NYC-M - 1919/01/07:6a

LUNGER, Ida, 23, NYC-B – 1898/07/30:1g, 31:1b
LUNING, Maria, NYC-B – 1891/04/06:4a
LUNKEL, (Mrs), NYC-Bx – 1908/06/10:6a
LUNOW, Frank, 64,build. mgr,& wife Agnes,NYC – 1914/03/27:1f
LUNTZ, Moritz, 53, artist, NYC-B – 1903/11/21:2f
LUNZ, Sidonie, 1, NYC-M – 1887/11/01:2g
LURTON, Horace, US Supreme Court Justice – 1914/07/13:1f
LUSTAK, Frank, Passaic, NJ – 1915/12/28:2d
LUSTGARTEN, May, 22 months, NYC-M – 1902/02/14:3f
LUSTGARTEN, William, director Tax Lien Co., NYC-M – 1917/08/30:2c
LUSTIG, Max, Newark, NJ – 1908/05/02:6a
LUSTIG, Philip, painter, NYC-M – 1892/07/30:4d
LUSTIG, Rhoda, + 29 Oct 1909, hubby Maurice on trial 5 Jan. 1910:6b, sentenced to + – 1910/05/16:1c, 1 Jy:1b
LUTACUS, Katie, 46, NYC-B, + on Genl Slocum – 1904/06/17:3b
LUTHER, Alice, 30, Jersey City, NJ – 1903/08/14:3d
LUTHER, Christine, b. Adler, 52, NYC-B – 1910/10/04:6a, fam. 10:6a
LUTHER, Martin, German Reformator, crit. Look at 400th birth anniv. celebr. In Berlin & NYC 1883/11/10:2a-b, 11:1a-b, 12:1f
LUTHER, William, NYC-B – 1911/07/04:6a
LUTHIE, Emil, Swiss?, W. Hoboken, NJ – 1913/09/09:6d
LUTHIN, Joseph, 60, paper dealer, Hoboken, NJ – 1900/01/16:4b
LUTHJE, August, 45, SP, un. painter, USA 1905 fr Gy, NYC-M – 1915/03/03:6a, 4:2a,6a, =5:2d, fam. 7:7a
LUTJE, Nicholas, 41, furrier, NYC-B – 1898/07/13:4b
LUTTER, Charlotte, 67, Newark, NJ – 1908/08/21:3e
LUTTER, Ida, NYC-M – 1915/03/14:11a
LUTTMANN, F., W. Hoboken, NJ – 1909/10/16:6a
LUTTRINGHAUSEN, George, 66, NYC-B – 1894/01/09:4a
LUTZ % Harth
LUTZ family, of American Watch Co., suffering – 1899/05/28:5f, 30:3d
LUTZ, Albert, un. carp., NYC-M – 1916/03/18:6a, 19:6a
LUTZ, Andreas, NYC-M – 1892/10/27:4a
LUTZ, Andrew, 64, NYC-B – 1897/11/20:4a
LUTZ, Anna, 5, NYC-M – 1892/05/03:4a
LUTZ, Anton, un. carp., NYC-M – 1905/04/07:4a
LUTZ, Babette, b. Schneider, 41, NYC-B – 1906/12/01:6a
LUTZ, Balthasar, 44, SLP, tailor, fr Basel/Switz., NYC-M – 1899/11/24:1d, 4a, =26:1d, 27:4a, fam. 2 Dec:4a?
LUTZ, Charles, un. carp., NYC-Bx – 1911/02/11:6a
LUTZ, Dora, b. Krimmelbein, 46, NYC-M? – 1893/09/06:4a
LUTZ, Elisabeth L., 90, NYC-M – 1907/03/19:1f

LUTZ, Elisabeth, b. Bernins, 25, NYC-M – 1891/04/09:4a
LUTZ, Friedericke, Guttenberg, NJ – 1912/12/01:7a
LUTZ, Georg, NYC-B – 1904/01/25:3b
LUTZ, Hermann, 18, NYC-M – 1903/05/19:4a
LUTZ, John, 20, NYC-M - 1894/08/13:3a, 14:1b
LUTZ, John, 50, fr Hungary, NYC-M – 1890/07/05:2g
LUTZ, John, 62, un. master-brewer, NYC-B - 1920/08/09:6a
LUTZ, John, exec. Wilkesbarre, PA – 1902/01/22:1e
LUTZ, John, un. varnisher, married Elisabeth Klahr, both NYC-B – 1881/08/30:3c
LUTZ, Marie, NYC-M – 1892/05/11:4a
LUTZ, Mary, 60, NYC-M – 1906/07/27:1f
LUTZ, Philip C., businessman, Westfield, NJ - 1917/08/21:2g
LUTZ, Theodor, 56, NYC-M – 1899/08/05:4a
LUTZ, Theodor, 66, SPD Baden-Baden, druggist, MdL (1903) & alderman fr Neuenburg/Wuertt. - 1913/05/11:3a
LUTZ, Wilhelm, chair Williamsburg Manuf, NYC -1914/05/12:1e
LUTZE, H., NYC-B - 1917/08/29:6a, fam. 31:6a
LUTZELBERGER, William, 27, NYC-B – 1905/08/28:3d
LUX, Gottlieb, 54, tailor, NYC-M – 1883/07/25:4a
LUX, Robert, machinist, NYC-Bx - 1913/08/15:6a
LUX, Robert, NYC-M – 1904/08/20:4a, fam. 28:5a
LUXEMBURG, Rosa, #, German Socialist, her life – 1909/02/ 28:19e; murdered with Karl Liebknecht in Berlin, - 1919/01/12:1a-b, 18:1a-b, 4a-b, 21:4d, 27:1a-b, NYC meeting 28:2e, 3 Feb.:1f, 2e, Newark meeting 17 Feb:2d, more on her = 13 June:1c-d, 4a-b, 16:1b, 15 July:4e-f; mem. by Clara Zetkin 1920/01/15:3a-f, 5a-e, 6a-e, 16:3a, poem by Bruno Schoenlank, 31 May:4g, more 23 June:4b, 27 June, II:1-2, 9 Jy:3a-c, edit by Otto Jenssen 18 Jy:7d-e; on her + # – 1919/11/09:4a-e
LUXEN % Paffen
LUXENBURG, Arthur, 32, NYC-Q - 1916/01/18:6a
LUXENBURG, Benjamin, S?, NYC? – 1896/11/07:4a
LUXENBURG, Martha, b. Rapp, NYC-Q - 1919/04/09:6a, mem. 1920/04/08:6a
LUZ, Rosine, b. Bruckmann, 71, fr Freudenstadt/Wuertt., NYC-M – 1882/05/30:3b
LWAASENSKI, Frank, RR worker, + Jersey City, NJ – 1898/11/19:1f
LYCANDER, Peter, NYC-Bx - 1919/02/17:6a
LYDING, George, 50, NYC-B - 1894/01/24:4a
LYNCH, Dan, Newark, NJ - 1915/10/12:6a
LYON, Minnie, 5, NYC-M – 1897/07/19:4a

LYONS, Dan, exec. NYC-M – 1888/08/20:1e, 21:1h, 22:1e
LYONS, Daniel, boss of Whyo Gang, NYC – 1887/08/17:4c, 15:2e, 27 Sept:1e, 1 Oct:4
LYONS, John, exec. Paterson, NJ – 1904/08/05:3e
LYONS, Thomas J., un. printer, NYC-B – 1897/11/15:1d, 16:1f, 17:4a, 18:1e
LYSER, Gustav, 63, ex-soc. Journalist, USA 1874, = Milwaukee, WI – 1909/10/15:4d
MAAG, Henry, 65, un. typesetter, NYC-B – 1905/08/09:4a
MAAGS, John P., 51, manufacturer, NYC-M – 1900/07/11:3b
MAAK, Heinrich, 59, un. carp., NYC-B, + Becket, MA - 1918/01/13:11g, 16:6a, 17:6a, mem. 1919/01/12:12a
MAAR, Charles, +1908, NYC-B, mem. – 1909/02/26:6a
MAAR, John, 49, un. beer bottler, NYC-B - 1918/11/04:6a
MAAS % Levy
MAAS, Anna, b. Portugall, 32, NYC-B – 1884/08/05:3c
MAAS, Barbara, 37, NYC-M - 1894/01/08:4a
MAAS, Barbara, NYC-M – 1892/06/09:2e
MAAS, Carl F., *1850, typesetter & SPD activist exp. fr Hamburg/ Gy, arrived NYC – 1880/11/30:1d-e, 2 Dec:2a-b, 6:1d-e; typesetter at NYVZ, NYC-B - 1914/01/26:2a,6a, 27:6a, =28:3d, fam. 29:6a; note 15 My:6a, 25 Jy:6a, mem. 1915/01/25:6a, 1916/01/25:6a, 1917/01/25:6a-b
MAAS, Elise, 38, NYC-B – 1897/10/17:5a
MAAS, Henry, 15, Jersey City, NJ – 1900/05/07:1h, 8:2g, =11:4b-c
MAAS, Henry, 35, NYC-B – 1908/08/15:3b
MAAS, Peter, un. cigarmaker, NYC-M – 1904/04/14:4a
MAAS, Philipp, NYC-M - 1915/02/05:6a
MAASS, Albrecht, 19, NYC-M – 1898/01/10:4a
MAASS, Heinrich, un. typesetter, NYC-SI - 1914/03/31:6a
MAASSEN, Julius, 83, judge & liberal democrat, Koeln/Gy - 1915/08/22:3e
MAAZ, Bertha, 59, Glenbrook, CT – 1912/10/04:6a
MABEL, Christina, b. Miller, 43, NYC-B – 1891/01/18:5a, fam. 20:4a
S.a. Mc
MacCARTNEY, Frederick O., 38, SDP, MA Assemblyman for SDP, *2 Nov 1864 Prairie du Chien, WI,+ Haverhill, MA – 1903/05/27:1a-b, 2a-b, =#31:1h, 2 June:4b; grave mon. inaug. Rockland, MA – 1908/08/16:1d
MacDONALD, Frank, SP, ex-chief ed. Call, *20/09/1874 Stoneham, MA, NYC-Bx - 1918/05/30:3e,6a
MacDONALD, Michael, exec. Ossining, NY – 1899/08/01:3e
MacDONALD, Mrs Ramsay, b. Gladstone, 41, wife of British labor leader, 1911/09/23:4e-f
MACEWICZ, Oscar, 50, un. typesetter?, NYC-M – 1888/04/20:3a

MACH, Ernst, Sudeten German physicist, + Vaterstaetten/Munich - 1916/04/02:6d-e, 9:6c-e
MACHA, Alois, 31, SPO Baden/Vienna, War 1 - 1914/11/29:3c
MACHACEK, Maria, 80, NYC-M - 1907/06/20:2d
MACHENBACH, Hermann, NYC-M - 1891/08/04:4a
MACHMANN, Louis, 24, barber, NYC-B - 1881/10/22:3b
MACHNOW, Edwin, 4, NYC-M - 1885/10/14:3c
MACHOW, ... von, +Feb. 1894 NYC, note - 1900/12/13:1g
MACK % Huttel-Maier
MACK, Annie, NYC-M, + @Genl Slocum - 1904/06/16:1d,
MACK, Elise, NYC-M - 1913/01/15:6a
MACKAY, John W., California silver magnate, *1831 Dublin, + London, crit obit - 1902/07/21:1f; his will 1902/08/22:2c,g
MACKE, Julius, 45, un. brewer, NYC-M - 1912/07/26:6a
MACKEY, John, ex-Assist. D.A., Hackensack, NJ - 1911/03/10:3d
MACKIN, John, appeal rej. 1897/03/03:4a, 14:1d, exec. In NJ?, 2 Apr:3f, 7:3c, 11:7g, 13:4c, done 14:1h
MACKIN, Sam, Negro, lynched Augusta, GA - 1898/10/27:3c
MACKMANN, Elizabeth, b. Koch, 88, NYC-M - 1917/03/15:6a
MADDEN, Owen, mobster, head of Gopher Gang, dying, NYC-M - 1912/11/07:6c
MADEA, J., un. carpenter, NYC-M - 1895/06/03:4a
MADEHEIM, Hermann, NYC-B - 1892/06/26:5c
MADENWIRTH, Daniel, un. carp., NYC-M - 1896/12/27:5d
MADER, Thomas, 2, NYC-M - 1905/07/11:1f
MADERO, Francisco J., Mexican president - 1913/02/24:1a-c, 2d, 4a-b, 25:1a,2c,4b, 2 Mr:11d
MADES, Emil, Greenville, NJ - 1907/03/23:6a
MADISON, William, prof. thief, alias Ira McPherson, NYC-M - 1906/12/19:1g
MADONNA, Vincente, striking worker, Paterson, NJ = 1913/07/06:1g
MADSEN, Waldemar, 38, un. pianomker, NYC-M - 1893/04/04:4a
MAECKEL, Henry, un. painter, NYC-M - 1914/07/15:6a
MAEDER, Friedrich, SP, un. cigarmker, * Saxony, USA 1904, Newark, NJ - 1915/11/19:6a,20:6a, 21:11d, =22:2b,fam. 25:6a
MAEDER, Julius, NYC-B - 1914/07/23:6a
MAEDICHE, E.O., NYC-B - 1919/01/16:6a
MAEGDE, Hermann, NYC-M - 1892/06/30:4a
MAEHR, Frederick, SP, Hoboken, NJ - 1916/02/26:6a
MAELSCHKE, Friedrich, 60, Elisabethport, NJ - 1889/08/25:5e
MAENCHEN, Katherine, b. Kassner, Bridgeport, CT - 1889/03/27:4a
MAENNICKE, Herman, NYC-M - 1916/11/28:6a

MAERKLE, Jeanette, NYC-B – 1888/07/07:3b
MAERZ, Louise, 42, NYC-M – 1900/05/06:1d
MAESEL, Arthur, 41?, NYC-M – 1891/03/29:5a
MAEVERS, Charles, 82, NYC-M – 1909/08/29:1d
MAGATSCH, Richard, barber, fr Austria, War 2, North Beach, NJ - 1915/02/05:6d, 6:1g
MAGEE, Edward, Negro, lynched near Navasota, TX – 1899/07/16:1h
MAGER, Martin, 34, NYC-B - 1913/08/20:6a
MAGERLE, Henry, machinist, NYC-B – 1902/08/29:4a
MAGERSUPPE % Schuppert
MAGIN, Louise, 56, NYC – 1912/04/09:6a
MAGLER, Catherine, 71, NYC-M – 1888/09/19:1e
MAGNUS, Clementine, NYC-M – 1907/01/10:6a
MAGNUS, Susanna, Hoboken, NJ – 1911/08/16:6a, 17:6a
MAGNUSON, Otto, un. painter, NYC-M - 1918/11/29:6a
MAGRATH, Georg F., 20, bookkeeper, NYC-M – 1891/03/30:4a
MAGSAMEN, Max, NYC-Bx - 1915/05/25:6a
MAHAN, Alfred T., US Navy admiral & author - 1914/12/02:1c
MAHAN, John, striker, killed in Uniontown, PA – 1891/05/05:1c
MAHDI, Sudanese patriot – 1885/08/18:2e, =7 Sept:2d
MAHEDI, Francis, firefighter, NYC-M – 1886/03/13:4d, =15:4e
MAHER, Robert, NYC-Bx – 1905/05/18:6a
MAHILER, Israel, butcher, fr Rumania, NYC-M – 1904/08/27:1d,
MAHLER, Elise, b. Reichhelm, 35, SLP?, NYC-M – 1883/11/05:4e, 8:2d
MAHLER, Mrs, NYC-M – 1897/08/03:1h
MAHLING, Charles, 4, NYC-M – 1881/10/19:3b
MAHN % Rohweder
MAHN, Emilie, 62, SPD Magdeburg/Gy – 1908/06/07:3d
MAHN, Max J., NYC-M - 1914/01/10:6a
MAHNCKE, Henry, 53, un. cigarmaker, NYC-M – 1910/02/18:6a, fam. 22:6a
MAHNKE, Katie, b. Jungblut, 41, NYC-M – 1891/10/05:4a
MAHNKEN, Carsten, 6, NYC-M – 1893/03/12:5a
MAHNKEN, Louise, b. Behrens, + 26 Aug. in Scharmbeck/Osterholz/ Hannover - 1878/09/14:3c
MAHRING, Katherine, 57, NYC-M – 1893/11/14:1c
MAI, Philipp, 60, alderman in Mannheim/Gy, USA 1880s, innkeep, SP, NYC-M – 1906/11/08:3b
MAIBAUER, Ernst, Newark, NJ - 1917/08/02:6a
MAIER, Albert, NYC-M? – 1911/12/13:6a
MAIER, Alois, un. butcher, NYC-M – 1913/02/05:6a
MAIER, Anna, NYC-B – 1905/04/23:5b, fam. 26:4a

MAIER, C., NYC-M - 1915/09/11:6a
MAIER, Carl, NYC-M – 1912/06/11:6a
MAIER, Ch., NYC-M – 1907/02/23:6a
MAIER, Charles, un. brewer, NYC-M – 1891/10/18:5b
MAIER, Christian, NYC-M - 1917/01/23:6a
MAIER, Conrad, 46, un. furnit. Maker, SLP?, NYC-B – 1891/04/28:4a
MAIER, Eliza, 74, NYC-Q – 1910/06/24:2c
MAIER, Frank, infant, NYC-M? - 1878/07/21:8b
MAIER, Frank, NYC-M - 1917/04/26:6a
MAIER, Franz, NYC-Q - 1918/11/28:6a
MAIER, Fritz, secy Arbeiter Harmonie GV, NYC-B - 1918/01/17:6a, 18:6a
MAIER, Georg, 54, NYC-Bx – 1907/01/12:6a
MAIER, George's wife, NYC-M – 1900/11/17:4a
MAIER, George, Yonkers, NY – 1904/11/06:5b
MAIER, Hugo, inkeep, SLP, note (not +), NYC-M – 1880/06/25:1g
MAIER, Jacob, cigar maker, NYC-B – 1886/11/19:3b, fam. 23:3a
MAIER, Johann Jakob, 1, NYC-M – 1882/06/11:8a
MAIER, Joseph, NYC-M – 1886/08/23:3c
MAIER, Lina, Jersey City Heights, NJ – 1911/04/11:6a
MAIER, Louise, b. Intlekorfer, 54, NYC-M - 1914/08/28:6a
MAIER, Maria, Hoboken, NJ – 1885/07/03:3c
MAIER, Mary M., NYC-B – 1911/10/04:3a
MAIER, Robert, un. brewer?, NYC-M – 1911/07/19:6a, fam. 21:6a
MAIER, Robert, un. carp., NYC-M – 1898/09/05:4a
MAIER, William, 6, NYC-M – 1881/05/01:5f
MAILLY, William, 41, SP natl secy 1903-04, NYC-M – 1912/09/05:1g,2a, #, wake 7:1d, =8:1e,7b, 9:1a-b,2c, mem 1913/09/04:4c
MAIN, Georg, silk manuf., Paterson, NJ - 1916/07/29:2f
MAIR, Johannes, NYC-Q – 1914/07/28:6a
MAIRE, Bruno, NYC-B – 1911/02/28:2f, 6a
MAISCH, Georg, Jersey City Heights, NJ – 1907/08/08:6a
MAISCH, Gottlieb, 40, NYC-M – 1900/06/29:4b
MAISCH, Marie, NYC-M – 1896/05/28:4a
MAISCHNER, William, 32, brewer, NYC-M – 1896/05/14:1e
MAIWALD, Henry, machinist, NYC-B – 1910/02/05:6a
MAIYO, Michael,65, Hungarian, +Hastings, NY - 1917/11/04:11e
MAJBACH, Werna, 25, fr Austria, Bloomfield?, NJ – 1912/02/13:2e
MAJE, Dick, NYC-M – 1911/09/09:6a
MAJONE, Pasquale, 24, exec. NYC-M – 1883/03/10:1e-f
MAJOR, Louis, 38, Bayonne, NJ – 1907/01/08:6a
MAJORS, Hank, Negro, lynched Waco, TX – 1905/08/09:1e
MAKAMUL Emil, 19, NYC-M – 1919/11/25:6a

MAKART, Hans, art painter, + Wien/Austria – 1884/10/04:1c, 15 Mr:4g-5a
MAKOWSKI, L., NYC-B - 1919/01/16:6a
MALAPERT, Hugo von, fr Frankfurt/Main, son of aide to Kaiser Wilhelm I, + Chicago, IL – 1881/06/16:1b
MALBURGA, Albert, carp. Fr Sweden, NYC-M – 1910/01/04:2b
MALEMPRE, Jean, 50, weaver & SP Verviers/Belgium – 1909/02/26:4f
MALEY, Anna, US socialist, her current life – 1909/02/28:20a-b
MALICOT, Eva, 9, Yonkers?, NY, + @Genl Slocum – 1904/06/21:1f
MALINAK, Andreas, exec. Newark, NJ – 1898/06/10:4c
MALLABAR, Henry R., clerk, fr England, @Genl Slocum hero, NYC – 1907/12/08:9f
MALLERY, Lock, Negro, lynched Springfield, TN, with 4 others – 1881/02/20:5c
MALLON, Michael, Irish patriot, exec. Dublin - 1916/05/09:1b
MALLSCHATZ, Franz, watchman, NYC-M – 1890/09/03:2h
MALMO, Max, + 12 July Lobenstein/Gy, family in NYC? - 1878/08/21:3c
MALON, Benoit, 1871 Commune in Paris vet – 1893/09/16:2b-c
MALSCH, Friedrich W., 48, NYC-M – 1887/04/21:3e
MALSCH, Sophie, NYC-B – 1906/08/24:6a
MALTER, Eduard, 33, NYC-M – 1887/08/26:3b
MAMAJEWA, Anastasia, Russian student & patriot, exec. 30 Oct – 1906/11/03:1a, 3 Dc:4d
MAMMEN, Frieda, infant, NYC-B – 1883/08/03:3c
MAMROTH, Ernst S., 33, wood sculptor, fr Berlin/Gy, USA 1880, NYC-M – 1881/03/16:1e
MAMZELL, Anna, 60, NYC-SI - 1918/01/04:6a
MANCHESTER, Samuel, un. painter, NYC-M – 1892/03/25:4a
MANDEL, Henry, 62, NYC-M – 1891/09/20:5f
MANDEL, Joseph, Jersey City Heights, NJ – 1901/03/16:4a
MANDEL, Joseph, un. cigarmaker, Jersey City, NJ - 1920/09/13:6a
MANDEL, Marie, Jersey City Heights, NJ – 1905/05/05:7c, 6:6a
MANDELBAUM, Baruch, 51, NYC-M – 1890/08/01:4a
MANDELBAUM, Friederike, + Hamilton, Ontario - 1894/02/27:2d
MANDELBAUM, William, 16, NYC-M – 1880/08/31:1f
MANDERBACH, Karl, 42, NYC-M – 1890/03/11:4a
MANGEL, Franz, NYC-Q – 1912/06/09.6a
MANGELSDORFF, Gustav, NYC-Q – 1913/04/28:6a
MANGLER, Jacob, 55, NYC-B – 1899/04/13:4a
MANGOLD, Chr., un. typesetter, NYC-M – 1901/03/12:4a
MANGOLD, Ernst Arago, 48, NYC-B – 1896/12/05:4a, fam. 13:16a
MANGOLD, Josephine Karl, 49, NYC-M - 1878/06/03:3b
MANGOLD, W., NYC-B – 1906/01/09:4a

MANHARD, Frank, un. baker, NYC-M - 1917/01/31:6a
MANHEIMER, Mamie, 36, NYC-M, +@ Genl Slocum - 1904/06/17:3b, 18:3c
MANKE, Carl, see also WANKE, Carl
MANKE, Wilhelmine, b. Mittmeier, NYC-M - 1886/01/01:3c
MANKER, Rudolph, butcher, NYC-Bx - 1896/07/17:1g
MANKOFSKY, Rose, 22, @1911 Triangle Shirtwaist Fire, NYC-M - 1911/03/27:1d
MANKOWSKI, Anton, 63, Polish socialist & bookbinder, + Vienna - 1899/11/28:2d
MANN, Carrie, NYC-B - 1891/02/27:4a
MANN, Christian, 56, NYC-Bx - 1908/12/10:6a
MANN, Fritz W., 28, Union Hill, NJ - 1893/07/27:4a
MANN, Georg, carpenter, NYC - 1900/08/31:4a
MANN, George J., 19, fr NYC, exec. Canton, OH - 1880/06/26:1c
MANN, Ignatz, infant, Bayonne, NJ - 1908/07/08:1e
MANN, Johanna, textile worker, NYC-M - 1889/10/04:1e
MANN, Rose, 17, Plainfield, NJ - 1912/09/07:1c
MANNBERGER, Friedrich Wilhelm, NYC-Bx - 1908/03/30:6a
MANNBERGER, Lydia, 72, Verona, NJ - 1918/12/15:12a
MANNER, Ferdinand, 55, NYC-M - 1880/07/27:1g
MANNES, Wilhelm, un. carp., NYC-M - 1897/10/24:5a
MANNEWITZ, Auguste, Socialist Ladies' Soc.,NYC-M 1895/04/15:4a
MANNEWITZ, William, SP, treasurer Free German School of Stapleton, NYC-SI - 1906/01/
MANNHEIMER, A., NYC-B - 1903/04/06:4a
MANNING, Daniel, Albany, NY, politico - 1887/12/28:1a
MANNINGER, Minnie, 18, NYC-B - 1904/09/25:5h
MANNOW, Julius, exec. Chicago, IL - 1896/10/31:1f
MANNSBERGER, Bertha, 38, NYC-Bx - 1918/01/28:6a
MANOLESCU, George, 38, famous Italian mobster, + Milan/It. - 1908/01/24:4e
MANOWITSCH, Abraham, 40, musician, NYC-M - 1892/08/16:4c
MANSFELD, Max, *30 Jan 1848 Altona/Gy, fdr <u>Plattdeutsche Post</u>, NYC-M - 1909/08/19:1c
MANSFIELD, Richard, US actor - 1907/08/31:1e
MANTEL, Joseph, NYC-M - 1907/04/12:6a
MANTEL, Rosie, infant, NYC-M - 1892/08/08:4f
MANTELL, John, NYC-B - 1906/01/23:4a
MANTELL, Joseph, un. mason, NYC-M - 1904/02/18:4a
MANTESANA, John, exec. Trenton, NJ - 1909/01/12:3b
MANTEUFFEL, Julius VON, 23, USA 1878,+ Chicago - 1879/07/24:1d

MANTHEY, Charles, carriage factory foreman, NYC-M – 1900/05/31:3b
MANTZ, Conrad, (or Mautz), un. typesetter, NYC-M – 1902/03/12:4a
MANTZ, Julius, musician, & cousin Amalia Mantz, + Syracuse, NY – 1880/02/15:5b
MANUEL, William, Negro, lynched Hemphill, TX – 1908/06/23:1e
MANZ, August, Newark, NJ - 1914/09/15:6a
MANZ, Jacob, carp., + Dec. 1892, note on reburial, NYC-B – 1893/09/30:3e
MANZ, Jacob, NYC-M – 1892/06/21:4a
MANZ, Joseph, 35, un. upholsterer, NYC-M – 1893/08/18:4a
MANZEL, Emil, 60, NYC-M - 1917/02/09:6a
MAPERUS, Michael A., fr Luxemburg, hotelier, NYC-Q – 1891/09/16:2g
MARALIUS, John, 71, civil war vet, NYC-B – 1900/12/08:1f
MARBACH, Rudolf von, NYC-M – 1913/04/22:6a
MARCHESCHI, Lena, 33, servant, NYC-M - 1918/04/23:1f
MARCK, William, un. carp., NYC-B – 1890/07/01:4a
MARCKHOFF, Lillie, 4, NYC-B – 1883/03/29:3d
MARCKHOFF, Theodor, NYC-B – 1880/07/24:3a
MARCUS, J. P. W., 86, SPD Hamburg, 1909/12/26:3a
MARCUS, Jacob, 18, tailor, NYC-B - 1915/12/22:3e
MARCUSE, Rudolf, NYC-B - 1920/01/10:6a
MARECK, Frank S., 59, * Zebrau/Bohemia, USA 1872, Baltimore, MD – 1906/11/26:2e
MARENDI, Giuseppe, NYC, exec. Ossining, NY - 1916/02/05:2e
MARENMILLER, Joseph, brewer, NYC-B – 1892/05/13:2f
MARESCH, Anton, un. carp., NYC-M – 1909/05/31:6a
MARESCH, Franziska, 39, SLP?, NYC-M – 1886/01/26:2g
MARGER, Joseph, un. mason, NYC-Q – 1904/02/18:4a
MARGOLIN, Abraham, veteran soc. & labor movement, Philadelphia, PA - 1917/01/31:2c
MARGREITER, Samuel, * Fuegen/Tyrol, NYC-B – 1890/11/30:5c
MARGULES, Max, Dr., 65, meteorlogist, Vienna - 1920/11/26:4e
MARHOFER, Margarethe, NYC-M – 1881/05/12:3b
MARIA, Czarina of Russia, 1880/06/04:1b, =8:1a
MARIEN, Adrian, 63, worker, East Pittsburgh, PA - 1913/07/26:2e
MARIETTON, Jean-Jules, French Soc. deputy for Lyon - 1914/06/09:4d
MARINZEL, John, NYC-B - 1915/02/03:6a
MARK, Carlos, NYC-B – 1905/03/30:4a
MARK, Celia, NYC-M - 1916/08/21:2c
MARK, Franz, NYC-Q - 1915/10/11:6a
MARK, Tillie, 16, NYC-M – 1892/08/19:4a
MARK, Wilhelmina, b. Busch, NYC-M – 1892/07/06:4a

MARKARDT, Martin, road repair worker, NYC-B – 1881/05/14:1e
MARKERT, Henry W., 72, candy manuf., NYC-M – 1898/02/07:1b
MARKERT, Peter,27, tailor, War 2,Jersey City,NJ -1917/06/13:1f
MARKMANN, Franz Joseph, NYC-M - 1920/05/06:6a
MARKMANN, Friedericke, b. Roos, NYC-Q – 1900/12/06:4a
MARKMANN, Lina, NYC-M – 1905/01/11:4a, fam. 14:4a
MARKMANN, Wilhelm, 58, liquor dealer?, NYC-Q – 1909/04/29:6a
MARKOFF, Ruben, 65, NYC-M – 1908/02/12:6d
MARKOWITZ, Bertha, 22, fr Kowno/Russia, NYC-M – 1898/09/13:1g
MARKOWSKY, Eugene von, * Bromberg/Gy, USA 1887, NYC-M – 1888/02/29:1c, 1 Mr:1g, 9:4f
MARKOWSKY, Jules, Homestead, PA, steelworker killed by Pinkertons – 1892/07/08:1a
MARKS, Zephaniah, peddler fr Pol., NYC-M – 1883/02/03:1f, 5:1g, 6:1g
MARKUS, Anton, un. brewer, West Hoboken, NJ - 1917/05/02:6a
MARKWAHN, Albert, un. pianomaker, NYC-M – 1888/02/23:3a
MARKWALD, Erna, NYC-B - 1920/10/29:6a
MARMO, Joseph, to be exec. Newark – 1905/04/11:3d, post.? 13:3d
MARNET, Barbara, b. Streubert, 58, NYC-Bx – 1913/09/04:6a
MARON, George, killed during strike in NJ, trial 1900/05/29:4a, 31:4b
MARON, Hermann, Dr., 63, German journalist, + Berlin, 1883/01/13:2e-f
MARQUARD, Anna M., 57, NYC-B – 1892/04/01:4a
MARQUARD, Karl, 66, NYC-M – 1893/03/26:5a
MARQUARDT, Annie, 33, NYC-M – 1900/07/19:1e
MARQUARDT, Charles, clerk, NYC-Q - 1914/01/05:2f
MARQUARDT, Christian Karl, 69, NYC-M - 1915/10/21:6a
MARQUARDT, Elizabeth, 78, Guttenberg, NJ - 1914/01/18:7c
MARQUARDT, Ernst, un. cigarmaker, NYC-B – 1889/07/14:5a
MARQUARDT, Louise, b. Cornelius, NYC-M – 1890/11/02:5a
MARQUARDT, Ludwig, exec. Ossining, NY - 1915/12/18:1d
MARQUARDT, Martin, 44, NYC-M – 1912/03/31:7a, fam. 7 Apr:7a
MARQUART, Elisabeth, b. Goetz, 47, NYC-B – 1892/05/18:4a
MARQUER, Adolf, NYC-Bx – 1905/10/07:4a, 8:5b
MARSCH, Anton, 70, jeweler, NYC-B – 1910/01/19:3a-b
MARSCHALL, Bernhard, 76, NYC-B – 1890/10/31:4a
MARSCHALL, Caroline, 78, NYC-M – 1891/09/06:5a
MARSCHALL, David, 14, NYC-M, +@Genl Slocum – 1904/06/25:1d
MARSCHALL, Emil, 48, NYC-B – 1899/03/11:4a
MARSCHALL, Franz, stonecutter, SP Vienna/Austria– 1908/06/07:3e
MARSHALL, A., ed. Albany *Times Union* - 1914/12/03:1d
MARSHALL, Cornelius A., pres. Liberal League of Newark, NJ, and "good man" – 1887/07/18:2e, 25:2d

MARSHALL, Daniel, NYC-M, +@ Genl Slocum – 1904/06/17:3b, 18:3c
MARSHALL, Eugene, Negro, lynched Shelbyville, KY – 1911/01/16:1d
MARSHALL, Harry, grocer, killed during longshoremen strike, Hoboken, NJ – 1907/05/18:1g-2a, =21:1c
MARSHALL, Wendelin, 52, un. carp., NYC-M - 1915/02/24:2a, 25:6a, 26:6a, 27:6a, fam. 2 Mr:6a, mem. 1916/02/23:6a
MARSHANG, Sebastian, un. carp., NYC-M – 1887/12/10:4e
MARSILY, Adolph, 58,merchant, *Belgium,NYC-M - 1894/09/15:1h
MARSTELLER, L.H., millionaire, NYC-M – 1893/12/24:5f
MARTELS, Alvina, 67, W. Hoboken, NJ – 1912/03/23:6a, fam. 30:6a
MARTENS, Carl, 46, NYC-M – 1890/01/15:4a
MARTENS, Carl, SP?, New Haven, CT - 1915/07/22:6a
MARTENS, Carl, un. cigarmaker, Jersey City Heights, NJ – 1891/03/06:4a
MARTENS, Ida, 18, Yonkers, NY – 1910/08/15:2b
MARTENS, Johanna, NYC-M – 1890/05/04:5a
MARTENS, Louise, SP?, New Haven, CT - 1914/11/02:6a
MARTENS, Mathilde, b. Starke, 27, NYC-B – 1892/06/26:5c
MARTENSEN, Niels P., Dane, NYC-M – 1910/03/02:1e
MARTH, Anna, NYC-M, + @on Genl Slocum – 1904/06/18:3c
MARTH, William C., 48, ironmonger, NYC-B – 1895/07/04: 4c
MARTIN, Andreas, un. carp., NYC-M – 1908/12/11:6a
MARTIN, August, 43, NYC-B – 1897/01/25:4a
MARTIN, August, Jersey City, NJ, exec. Trenton, NJ - 1915/02/03:2c
MARTIN, August, NYC-B – 1907/12/22:7c
MARTIN, B. G., 29, NYC-M – 1891/03/25:4a
MARTIN, Camille, 27, Swiss,Newark, exec. Trenton, NJ - 1920/09/15:2e
MARTIN, Catharina, 72, NYC-M – 1913/03/15:6a
MARTIN, Edmund, 49, un. brewer, * Franconia/Gy, USA 1884, SP, NYC-B – 1907/03/31:7c,e, 1 Ap:6a
MARTIN, Frank, 22, NYC-M – 1890/01/23:1h
MARTIN, Frederick, West Hoboken, NJ – 1912/06/30:7b
MARTIN, I.B., ex-hotel owner, NYC-M - 1918/06/21:1e
MARTIN, Jacob, 68, un. carp., NYC-M – 1909/02/06:6a
MARTIN, Joe, Negro, lynched Laramie, WY – 1904/08/30:1g
MARTIN, Joh. Aug., 75, un. bricklayer, NYC-M - 1917/04/23:6a
MARTIN, John, 21, NYC-M – 1899/09/20:4a, fam. 22:4a
MARTIN, John, un. carp., NYC-M – 1899/11/29:4a
MARTIN, Joseph, 64, un. carp., ex-SP, USA 1860s, NYC-M – 1907/08/06:6a, 5:1f, 7:2a
MARTIN, Lewis J., Congressman, Newton, NJ - 1913/05/06:1c
MARTIN, Marie, NYC-M – 1891/06/22:4a

MARTIN, P. Ross, 38, *Prince Edward Isl., CN, SLP, San Francisco, CA – 1899/09/19:3c
MARTIN, Reinhardt, SLP, Jersey City Heights, NJ – 1887/12/03:3b
MARTIN, Richard, 27, butcher, Unionville, NY – 1900/04/06:2h
MARTIN, Walther, 4, NYC-M - 1920/05/18:6a
MARTINE, hon. Randolph B., state judge, NYC - 1895/03/31:1e
MARTINEZ, Juan Hernandez, * Matanzas/Cuba, commission agent, wife b. Houghton, NYC-M - 1878/02/06:4b, 7:4a,c
MARTINS, Charlotte, b. Gentzen, NYC-M – 1901/01/21:4a
MARTINS, Susie, 11, + 8th NYC-M - 1894/03/21:1f
MARTLING % Heuser
MARTTING, Frederick, NYC-B - 1919/03/10:6a
MARTZ, Conrad, 57, policeman, Elisabeth, NJ- 1894/01/26:3c
MARUCCHI, Pietro, IWW member, - 1919/03/28:6c
MARUP, Adolph, 68, un. cook, *Copenhagen/DK, NYC-M – 1906/03/22:3b
MARUSZEWSKI, John, exec. Auburn, NY – 1912/08/15:1a
MARX % Aveling; Longuet
Marx, August, 16, NYC-M – 1893/01/06:4a
MARX, August, 65, NYC-M – 1890/10/30:4a
MARX, Catharina Henriette (+Fb 1884), NYC, her will 1885/06/12:4a, probate 10 Nov:2g, 24 Mr 1886:1f
MARX, Christoph, NYC-Q – 1905/10/19:4a
MARX, Dorothe, 17, NYC-M - 1916/05/16:6a
MARX, Emma, b. Nickel, NYC-M – 1909/12/21:6a
MARX, Ethel, 9, Camden, NJ – 1907/10/09:1d
MARX, Ferdinand, NYC-M - 1896/01/13:4a
MARX, Gaston, exec. Wethersfield, CT – 1905/05/19:1c
MARX, Gustav, Chicago gangster, exec. Chicago, IL – 1904/04/23:1g
MARX, Irving, 22, hardware store, NYC-B – 1909/10/03:2a
MARX, Jenny, b. von Westfalen, wd of Karl, repr. Of obit. By Friedrich Engels – 1881/12/24:2d
MARX, Josephine, 7, NYC-M, + @1883 School Fire, NYC-M
MARX, Karl, German Communist, + London – 15 Mr 1883:1a-c, 2a-b, 17:1g-2a, 18:1f, 4a-g, 8a, NYC reactions 19:1e-g, 4e, 20:1c-e, 2a, 21:2b, 22:2b-f, 4a, 27:2b, 30:1d, 3 Apr:2d, 5:2c-e, article by J. Dietzgen 18 May:2a-b, worldwide reactions 1 June:2d-e; rev. NYC memorial 1889/03/04:2f; poem by Leopold Jacoby 1891/03/15:4d-e; 10th aniv. + 1893/03/14:2a; by Dr. Paul Ernst – 1897/11/28:2c-e; Marx the journalist, by Dr. F. Krieger in Die Zukunft 1901/02/03:4c-e. Crit. recent insults by Carl Schurz and Abraham Jacobi – 1906/02/07:2a-b. 25th + ann. – 1908/03/14:4a-b, 15:1c-d,7e, 16:6b-c, #15a-d, 23:6c-d, 13a-b, 30:6d-f,

Marx on trade unions 29 Mr:6d-f, on Darwinism 5 Apr:6a. Memorial meet
  in NYC, rev 1909/03/15:1c-d, 2d
MARX, Louisa, b. Schimenz, NYC-Q – 1907/10/08:6a, fam. 12:6a
MARX, Maria Anna, b. Kegler, 49, NYC-M – 1892/07/31:5c
MARX, Philipp, un. wheelwright, NYC-M – 1889/07/27:4a
MARX, Siefer, peddler killed in Portchester, NY = 1883/06/09:1d
MARX, Simon, 45, NYC-M – 1893/02/27:4a
MARX-LONGUET, Jenny, + Paris – 1883/02/05:2d
MAS, Louis, Spanish anarchist, exec. Montjuich jail – 1897/05/22:2d
MASBACH, E., 68, NYC-M - 1894/01/29:4a
MASCHIN, Albert, 67, NYC-B – 1891/01/02:4a
MASCHLER, Carolina, b. Lederer, 56, NYC-M – 1891/03/15:5d
MASER, Georg, NYC-M – 1907/12/29:7c
MASER, Helen, b. Stengel, 31, NYC-B - 1917/05/05:6a
MASER, S. G., Swiss?, NYC-M – 1881/03/20:5g
MASKE, Fritz, 22, SPD Berlin – 1910/08/07:3f
MASKE, William, NYC-B - 1913/09/11:3a
MASQUERIER, Louis, NYC communist, +1889, his will 1891/02/14:2e
MASSATSCH, Karl, 46, natl secy German Metallworkers' Union,
  *Hernals/Vienna, + Stuttgart 15 De - 1915/01/13:4e
MASSENA, Andre Edmond, Count of, grandson of Napoleon's general, +
  in poorhouse in Salem, OR – 1880/03/07:7a-b
MASSER, Louis, NYC-M – 1891/09/29:4a
MASSET, Louise, French nanny, exec. London, England – 1900/01/10:2h
MASSITIER, John, NYC-B – 1900/01/01:2g
MASSOW, John, Newark, NJ – 1908/05/08:6d
MASTERSON, Peter B., 30, NYC alderman – 1886/12/27:4c, 29:3a
MASUR, Karl, NYC-M - 1917/06/14:6a
MASURI brothers, Russian patriots, 3 alr .exec – 1906/11/14:2a
MATCHETT, Charles, H., socialist, *1843 Needham, MA, 1896 SLP pres.
  Candid., + Allston, MA – 1919/10/26:1d
MATEJOVIC, Mathias, NYC-M – 1907/03/15:6a
MATESKY, W., NYC-Q - 1918/08/21:6a
MATHE, H., cigarmaker & SPD activist expelled fr Ottensen/Gy, arrived
  NYC – 1881/06/16:4a
MATHERN, S., NYC-?, - 1920/02/07:8a
MATHES, Henry B., barber, NYC-SI – 1892/07/2f
MATHESIUS, Heinrich, 54, NYC-B – 1878/07/05:3c
MATHIAS, Benjamin, 72, weaver, SPD Reichenbach/Silesia –
  1908/02/16:3c
MATHIES % Heyl ; MATHIESEN % Heyner
MATHIES, Alois,, 45, No. Bergen, NJ – 1909/08/11:6a

MATI, Hilda, 28, servant fr Finnland, Belvidere, NJ - 1913/05/24:2d
MATIJOWIC, Magdalene, NYC-M – 1909/03/21:7a
MATT, Charlotte, NYC-M - 1894/01/28:5d
MATTACHEN, Fritz, 56, bookkeeper, NYC-M – 1882/03/04:1f
MATTER, Theophile G., fr Reissweiler/Elsass, USA 1878, NYC-M - 1878/08/30:4b, 31:4b
MATTERN, Auguste, NYC-M – 1890/05/21:4a
MATTERN, Charlotte, 22, NYC-M - 1878/07/31:3d
MATTERSON, Charles A., 46, employee North German Lloyd, Hoboken, NJ – 1902/02/22:3c
MATTES, Adolph, NYC-M – 1885/05/07:3b, 8:1b.@Manhattan Fire 1885
MATTES, Martin, un. carp., NYC-M – 1907/06/20:6a
MATTES, Mary, 58, NYC-M, +@Genl Slocum – 1904/06/25:1d
MATTES, Sebastian, un. carp., NYC-M – 1884/08/08:3c
MATTHAES, Heinrich, 53, comedian at NYC German Theater, NYC-M - 1916/02/13:11b
MATTHEIS, Charles, NYC-M – 1887/09/09:3b
MATTHES, Elisabeth, NYC-M, + @ Genl Slocum – 1904/06/18:3c
MATTHES, Karl, 52, NYC-M – 1908/12/31:6a, fam. 4 Jan. 09:6a
MATTHEWS, Warren, Negro, lynched Ocean Springs, MS – 1901/02/04:1e
MATTHIAS, John, 38, NYC-B – 1898/09/05:1d
MATTKE, Friedrich, un. machinist, NYC-M – 1905/02/08:4a
MATTLER, Elsie, 15, NYC-M, +@Genl Slocum – 1904/06/23:1c
MATTMUELLER, Christian, NYC-M – 1909/09/27:6a
MATTY, Karl, NYC-M – 1893/05/03:4a
MATZ, Dr., SPD Stettin/Gy – 1911/02/12:3d
MATZ, Gustav, un. cigarmaker, NYC-M – 1884/11/04:3a
MATZDORF, Anna, b. Sahs, NYC-M – 1892/06/24:4a, fam. 29:4a
MATZDORF, Charles, un. tailor, NYC-M – 1891/12/24:4a
MATZDORF, Julie, NYC-M – 1886/01/27:3b
MATZDORF, Marie, NYC-M - 1920/10/21:6a, fam. 23:6a
MATZDORFF, Lilly, infant, NYC-M – 1882/07/29:4c
MATZKE, Caroline, 72, NYC-B – 1903/01/03:3g
MATZNER, Johann, carp. & SP activist in Vienna – 1908/03/01:3e
MAUCH % Ludy
MAUCH, John, Newark, NJ - 1920/06/11:6a
MAUCH, Joseph, NYC-M – 1893/05/31:1f
MAUCH, Paul, NYC-Bx – 1908/08/20:6a
MAUDSCHKE, Alfred, 52, SP, NYC-M – 1919/01/23:6a, 24:6a, =25:2e
MAUE, Frederick, 40, clerk, NYC-M – 1906/08/04:2d
MAUER, Gottlieb, 80, War 2, MYC-M - 1917/04/23:2d
MAUER, Michael, 42, un. carp., NYC-M – 1889/12/26:4a

MAUER, William, wine dealer, NYC-B – 1911/11/16:3a-b
MAUERER, Katharina, b. Barth, 45, NYC-M - 1878/03/08:3c
MAUL, Georg, un. carp., NYC-Q - 1895/05/21:4a
MAULBECK, J. F., 32, in New Jersey – 1903/01/12:3c
MAUPAL, Ferdinand P., 57, * Kuhardt/Bavaria, large silk dyer in Weehawken, NJ, + on trip to Cuba, - 1920/03/01:2a
MAURER % Grieshaber, % Kircher, % Ulrich
MAURER, Anna, b. Merz, Jersey City, NJ – 1903/05/22:4a
MAURER, Catherine, NYC-M, + @ Genl Slocum – 1904/06/18:3c
MAURER, Christian, 24, NYC-M – 1882/11/11:3b
MAURER, Conrad, 55, baker, NYC-M - 1895/05/08:3e
MAURER, Conrad, SPD activist expelled fr Berlin/Gy, his life (not +) 1884/11/05:2d
MAURER, George, un. machinist, NYC-M – 1890/05/23:4a
MAURER, Joseph, 57, NYC-B – 1900/10/06:2h
MAURER, Kate, 13, NYC-M, +@Genl Slocum – 1904/06/22:1d
MAURER, Otto, 53, shop for artist supplies, NYC-M – 1900/05/18:1e
MAURER, Tillie, 14, NYC-M, + @on Genl Slocum – 1904/06/18:3c
MAUS % Rossmeisl
MAUS, Charles, 60, un. cigarmaker, NYC-M - 1917/03/31:6a
MAUS, Frances, NYC-B – 1912/06/15:3a
MAUS, John, 65, NYC-B – 1908/10/27:3b
MAUS, John, driver, exec. Somerset, PA - 1913/10/24:6e
MAUSCHWITZ, VON % Wagner
MAUSER, Peter V., 76, German rifle inventor - 1914/05/30:1d
MAUSS, Henry, 60, Hoboken, NJ - 1914/10/08:2b
MAUSSMANN, Peter, NYC-M – 1911/12/29:6a
MAUTZ, Conrad, (or Mantz) un. typesetter, NYC-M – 1902/03/12:4a
MAWSDEY, James, Lancashire cotton spinner & Tory Party member – 1902/02/27:2e
MAX, Gabriel see Von Max
MAX, Gabriel von, German artist, * 1840 Prag, + Munich - 1915/12/21:4f
MAXIM, Sir Hiram, 76, weapons manuf. - 1916/11/25:2d
MAXIMOFFSKY, Russian general, killed by revol. – 1907/10/29:2a, 30:1e
MAX-MUELLER, Friedrich, Dr., 73, German scientist, spec. for India at Oxford, GB – 1900/10/29:1d
MAXWELL, Charles M., pres. Typographia #6, NYC-B - 1913/08/30:1d
MAXWELL, William Henry, 68, ret. Brooklyn School Superinten., * Ireland, USA 1874, NYC-B - 1920/05/04:6b
MAY % Burkhardt
MAY, Ada, 9, NYC-B – 1891/02/20:4a
MAY, Amelia, 21, NYC-M – 1891/04/12:5a

MAY, Charles, SLP, NYC-B – 1886/02/17:3d
MAY, Charlotte, 51, NYC-M, + @on Genl Slocum – 1904/06/17:3b
MAY, Christine, b. Henings, 33, NYC-M – 1887/04/21:2f, 22:3d
MAY, Frank, cigarmaker, NYC-M - 1895/11/10: 5c
MAY, Franz, NYC-B – 1898/01/04:4a
MAY, Gustav, 36, anarchist, NYC-M – 1885/01/20:3b
MAY, Gustave, veteran Paris Commune, cigarette paper importer, ex-SLP, NYC – 1896/04/30:4d
MAY, Henry C., 23, NYC-M – 1899/09/03:5a
MAY, Johann, 69, un. furnit mkr, NYC-M – 1904/02/23:4a
MAY, John, San Francisco brewery union leader – 1891/02/12:1d, 5 Mr:1c
MAY, Karl, German writer, 1912/04/03:4a-b
MAY, M., 60, NYC-M – 1893/11/02:4c
MAY, Margaret, b. Kunitz, 52, NYC-M – 1901/12/27:4a
MAY, Minna, 31, NYC-M – 1886/03/20:3b
MAY, Nathan, 59, travelling salesman, NYC – 1901/01/20:1h
MAY, Wilhelm, shoemaker, SPD Elberfeld/Gy – 1886/07/07:2d
MAYBERGER, Henry, un. carp., NYC-M – 1898/08/27:4a
MAYER % Schott
MAYER, Mary, b. Spitzer, 40, fr Schriesheim/Baden, Elizabethport, NJ – 1887/04/21:3e
MAYER, Adolf, 66, SP?, Yonkers, NY - 1918/05/30:6a, mem. 1919/05/28:6a
MAYER, Adolph, NYC-B – 1892/07/24:5b
MAYER, Albert, +@ Genl Slocum, NYC-M – 1904/06/19:5a
MAYER, Benedikt, NYC-B - 1894/03/15:4a
MAYER, Caroline, b. Turkowsky, 71, mother of Christian Bardorf, NYC-B – 1912/10/18:6a
MAYER, Catherine, 34, nurse, NYC-B - 1916/02/08:6b
MAYER, Charles & Anton, Orange, NJ – 1902/11/06:4b
MAYER, Charles, 45, un. cigarmaker, NYC-B - 1920/08/28:6a
MAYER, Charles, NYC-M – 1891/04/07:4a
MAYER, Clara, NYC-B - 1916/07/18:6a
MAYER, Clara, Westchester, NY – 1909/08/14:6a, 15:7c
MAYER, Cornelius, 50, glass manuf., NYC-B – 1880/06/28:1g, 10 Jy:1g
MAYER, Elise, NYC-M – 1891/03/17:4a
MAYER, Frances, 42, Bayonne, NJ, + @on Genl Slocum – 1904/06/18:3c
MAYER, Frederick. F., NYC-M - 1915 /02/25:6a
MAYER, Georg, un. carp., NYC-M – 1886/05/15:3a
MAYER, Gustav, 35, musician fr Denver, CO, + Hoboken, NJ - 1913/10/14:2b
MAYER, Henry, un. baker, NYC-M - 1920/02/01:12a

MAYER, Hermann, 35, NYC-Bx - 1918/10/11:6a
MAYER, John M., Ft Lee, NJ - 1911/12/13:6a
MAYER, Joseph, NYC-Q - 1911/04/14:6a, 15:6a
MAYER, Julius A., Dr., 27, dentist, NYC-M - 1902/12/09:1g
MAYER, Karl, liberal publisher & polit., MdR, + Stuttgart/Gy - 1889/05/28:4a, 17 Oct:2b
MAYER, Katherina, b. Schueler, 46, fr Mainz/Gy, NYC-M - 1910/03/08:6a
MAYER, Laura, 24, NYC-B - 1903/04/29:4b
MAYER, Louisa, NYC-M, +@ on Genl Slocum - 1904/06/16:1c, 17:3b
MAYER, M., NYC-Q - 1918/10/11:6a
MAYER, Marcus, 75, theater director, NYC-M - 1918/01/02:2f
MAYER, Marie, 63, NYC-Bx - 1920/01/21:6a
MAYER, Martin, 58, realtor, NYC-B - 1900/04/06:2g
MAYER, Michael, Lyndhurst, NJ - 1908/02/08:6a
MAYER, Minna, b. Herzog, NYC-M - 1892/10/08:4a
MAYER, Natalie, b. Havemeyer, Rahway, NJ - 1900/07/16:1e, 17:1h
MAYER, Nathan, 35, merchant, NYC-M, + Hoboken, NJ - 1879/08/25:4d,26:1g, = 27:1g, 09/26:1e
MAYER, Robert J. von, 64, German scientist - 1878/04/09:2c, 14:3d-g
MAYER, Robert, 55, NYC-Bx - 1906/07/20:6a
MAYER, Rosa, NYC-Q - 1915/01/23:6a
MAYER, Rudolph Adalbert, 63, musician & inventor, * Munich, USA 1856, + Opelousa, LA - 1903/12/14:1b
MAYER, Therese Buckenmaier, 84, fr Hechingen/Hohenzollern, Woodstock, L.I. - 1916/01/15:6a
MAYER, Wilhelmina, b. Gugel, NYC-M - 1900/08/14:4a
MAYER, William F., NYC-M - 1905/08/14:4a
Mayer, William, bartender, NYC-M - 1892/11/18:4d
MAYER, William, Colonel, 72, *Vienna, USA 1855, publ. N.Y. Herold, + Berlin/Gy - 1906/04/18:1g
MAYFIELD, A., Negro, lynched Trail Lake, MS - 1904/06/04:3f
MAYHEW, Arthur, exec. Ossining, NY - 1897/03/13:1h
MAYR, Andreas, 26, NYC-M - 1906/07/13:6a
MAYR, Katherina, ?57, NYC-M - 1890/01/04:4a, 5:5b
MAYSCHACK, John, 29, chemist, fr Gy, War 2, Detroit, MI - 1917/07/30:1b
MAYWOON, Paul, 28, exec. Trenton, NJ - 1917/08/15:2d
MAZEY, Alexander, un. baker, NYC-M - 1918/05/15:6a
McAULIFFE, James, witness in Glennon trial, + 15 Fb, inquest, NYC? - 1902/02/28:1f-g, 11 Mr:1e, 15:3c, 16:5c, 26 Jy:1h, 2b-c, 8 Ap:1g, 12:2g,
McAULIFFE, John, mine workers' leader, + Denver, CO, rev. of memorial meeting in Chicago - 1882/07/27:2f-g

McBRIDE, John, 61, ex-pres. AFL, + Globe, AZ - 1917/10/11:6d
McBRIDE, Sean, Irish patriot, exec. Dublin - 1916/05/07:1b
McCABE, Peter, mobster, leader of "Gopher Gang," NYC-SI - 1913/07/11:5f
McCALL, John A., ex-pres NY Life Insur. Co., crit. obit - 1906/02/19:1d
McCANN, Evelyn, 23, teacher, NYC-B - 1914/01/05:1e
McCARREN, Patrick Henry, Tammany man, NYC-M – 1909/10/25:4a-b
McCLELLAN, George B., US genl, + Orange, NJ – 1885/10/30:1g, 31:2a-b
McCLENNON, Walter, Negro, lynched Huntingdon, TN – 1901/10/05:1e
McCOY, Garfield, Negro, lynched Newton, GA – 1903/06/27:1a
McCULLOUGH, John H., NYPD Captain, NYC-M – 1893/03/07:1g
McDANIELS, Hiram, Negro, lynched Clarksdale, MS – 1909/09/07:3e
McDERMOTT, John, NYC inspector, * Troy, NY, NYC-M – 1880/04/20:4h, =23:2g, note 7 Jy:1g
McDIARMAD, John, Irish patriot,exec.Dublin - 1916/05/13:1c,2c
McDONAGH, Thomas, Irish patriot, exec. Dublin - 1916/05/04:1a-b, 4d
McDONALD, Alexander, 58, British coal-miner & MP – 1881/11/22:2d
McDONELL, Calvin, Negro, lynched Shelby County, TN – 1892/03/10:1b
McDONNACK, Hugh, un. carp., NYC-M – 1888/05/07:3b
McDONNELL, Joseph P., 1870s ed. of Socialist and Labor Standard, Haledon, NJ – 1906/01/17:3f
McDONNELL, Molly Maguire, ex. Mauch Chunk, PA - 1879/01/15:1c, 2e
McFARLANE, Charles F., NYPD?, NYC-M – 1903/06/16:1g
McGLOIN, Michael, exec. NYC-M – 1883/03/10:1e-f
McGLYNN, Edward, Rev. Dr., social reformer, Newburgh, NY – 1900/01/08:1d, =9:1e, 2b
McGOWAN, Frank A., ex-mayor Trenton, NJ, + Hoboken, NJ - 1915/06/28:2d
McGOWAN, James, NYC railroad, killed during strike, NYC – 1889/02/06:1f, 9:2f, 10:1e, note 16 May:1f
McGOWEN, Frank B., ex-pres. Reading RR, + Washington, DC – 1889/12/15:1c, 17:2e
McGRANN, Michael, steward, NYC-M, +@ on Genl Slocum – 1904/06/16:1c, 17:3b
McGREGOR, Hugh, ex-AFL leader, + Washington, DC – 1911/03/01:1d
McGUIRE, Frederick, exec. Sing Sing – 1892/12/20:1b
McGUIRE, John, 60, NYC-M – 1882/03/19:8a
McGUIRE, Peter J., ex-natl secy Brotherhood Carp. & Joiners, + Camden, NJ – 1906/02/21:2c
McHUGH, Patrick, Molly Maguire, exec. in Bloomsburg, PA - 1878/03/26:1c, 2d, 3 Apr:2g
McINTOSH, Samuel, Negro, lynched Tampa, FL – 1910/07/10:1e

McKANE, John Y., Irish-born NYC Democrat, NYC-B – 1899/09/06:1f
McKANN, Felix, exec. Norwich, N.Y. - 1879/06/07:1c
McKEGNEY, John, carpenter, killed by a Tammany ward heeler, NYC –
 1886/10/27:1a, 28:1a, =30:2e, trial 21 Jan. 1887:4a, 22:4d
McKENNA, Anna J., b. Loehr, NYC-M – 1890/10/16:4a
McKENNA, James, ex-v.p. Typo. Union #6, NYC-M – 1897/01/15:1f
McKEON, John, District Attorney & Tammany heeler, NYC-M –
 1883/11/23:4c
McKINLEY, William, (s.a. Leo Czolgosz), US pres., shot in Buffalo, NY –
 1901/09/07:1a-c, 2a-b, 8:1a-b, f,g, 4a-c, 9:1a-c, 1f,h, 2a-b, 10:1a-c, f-h, 2a,
 3b, 11:1a-e, 2a-b, 12:1a-d, g, 2a-b, 13:1a-d, 2a-b, 4c, +14:1a-e, 2a-b,
 15:1a-e, h, 4a-c, many socialists & anarchists arrested w/o reason 16:1f-g,
 2a-b, 3d, 4a, 17:1a-d, f, h, 2a-c, g-h, 3d, 4b, =18:1a-b, 2a, 20:1b-c, f-g,
 2a-c, German press 20:2c-d
McKINLEY, Ida, b. Saxton, widow of ex-pres. – 1907/05/27:1f
McKINNEY, George, Negro, lynched Newton, GA – 1903/06/27:1a
McKINNEY, Henry, Negro, 17, lynched Columbia, FL? – 1910/07/05:2e
McKNIGHT, Kane, Negro,lynched Shreveport,LA - 1914/12/04:1d
McLAUGHLIN, Frank, 12, NYC-M, + @on Genl Slocum – 1904/06/17:3c
McLEAN, John, publ. Washington Post - 1916/06/11:1a
McLEAN, Negro, lynched Nashville, TN – 1883/08/25:1d
McLOUGHLIN, John, 27, un. steamfitter, killed by scabs during strike,
 NYC-M – 1910/03/30:2d
McLOUGHLIN, Mrs, philanthropist, NYC-B - 1913/07/03:3a-b
McMACKIN, John, ex-NYS Secy of Labor, crit obit – 1906/08/15:4c-d
McMAHON, Marie Edme de, French genl & polit. - 1893/10/18:1b, 20:1b,
McMAHON, Thomas, 40, NYC-B – 1911/08/31:6a
McMANUS, Jack, mobster, NYC-M – 1905/05/27:1h, 3 June:1e
McMANUS, Peter, Molly Maguire, ex. Pittsburgh, PA - 1879/10/10:1d, 2d
McNALLY, James, 45, longshoreman, killed during strike, NYC-B –
 1886/04/29:1g
McNEIL, George E., 69, AFL leader, Boston, MA – 1906/05/20:1b
McQUEEN, William, *Leeds/Scotland, US anarchist, +Leeds –
 1908/11/25:2a
McSWEENEY, Terence, mayor of Cork, Ireland, with 10 others -
 1920/10/26:1a-b, 4a, 29:1e, 30:1a, = 1 No:1a
MEADOWS, John, Negro, lynched Griffin, GA – 1898/08/09:1d
MEADRACH % Deitz
MEAKER, Lucie E., exec. Windsor, VT – 1883/03/31:1b
MEBOLD, David, 75, NYC-M – 1890/08/02:4a, 3:5b
MECHLER, Angelus, NYC-M – 1891/06/23:4a
MECHMANN, Gertrud, 67, SLP?, NYC-M – 1898/01/31:4a, fam. 4 Fb:4a

MECHMANN, Wilhelm H., 80, SDP, NYC-M – 1903/07/09:4a
MECKE, Hermann, 72, SP?, NYC-M - 1916/02/16:6a
MECKENROTH, Julius, waiter, NYC-M – 1899/06/20:1g
MECKER, Georg, Dr., 60, physician, Newark, NJ – 1899/09/17:1g
MECKLENBURG, F., 75, *16 F 1834 Elbing/Gy, SP, NYC, +Medical Lake, WA – 1909/05/29:2b
Mecklenburg, Johann, 10, Hoboken, NJ – 1892/09/13:4a
MEDEM, Edgar von, 58, journalist for G-A media, *Kurland Prov., USA 1880s, NYC-Bx - 1916/03/17:2f
MEDER, Daisy, 11, NYC-M, +@ on Genl Slocum – 1904/06/17:3c
MEDER, Emil, NYC-M - 1918/11/09:6a
MEDER, Martin, 36, carp., *Metzenseifen/Upper Hungary, Hoboken, NJ – 1898/05/16:4a, 17:4a
MEDERLE, Xavier, 62, shoemaker, NYC-M – 1887/08/24:3a
MEDPATH, James, journalist & Irish patriot, NYC-M – 1891/02/11:1h, 12:1h, =13:4d, 16:4d
MEDWITZ, Mary, NYC – 1910/07/06:2e
MEERBOTT, L., NYC-Q – 1907/08/08:6a
MEFFLER, David, 55, worker, Jersey City, NJ - 1916/07/30:1a
MEGGENHOEFER, Matthew, brewery employee, NYC-M – 1898/11/13:1h, 14:4a
MEHLEM, Franz, NYC-B - 1895/06/24: 4a
MEHLHAFT, Friedrich, SPD Hamburg/Gy – 1911/12/03:3b
MEHLHORN, William, 65, Paterson, NJ – 1910/05/14:6a
MEHLING, Joseph, NYC-B - 1914/02/21:6a
MEHLINGER, Camille, NYC-B – 1912/09/24:6a
MEHMEL, Julius, 60, NYC-M - 1895/10/02: 4a
MEHNKEN, Frederick, mineral water dealer, NYC-SI – 1896/07/10:4b
MEHRBACH, Moses, 56, NYC-M – 1892/03/27:5d
MEHRER, Philipp, un. typesetter, NYC-M – 1893/05/03:4a
MEHRING, Franz, SPD, German labor historian, 70th anniv. - 1916/03/19:6c-e, died 1919/02/02:4b-e
MEICHUR, Lizzie, 12, NYC-M, + @ Genl Slocum – 1904/06/17:3c
MEIER % Wegener
MEIER, Adolph, 40, formerly Germania, NJ, + in Florida - 1920/08/15:2a
MEIER, Andrew, NYC-B – 1885/05/24:1f
MEIER, Carl, West New York, NJ - 1920/02/29:12a
MEIER, Conrad, 31, NYC-M – 1882/01/05:3b
MEIER, David, 69, un. tailor, SLP, * Moeglingen/Wuertt., NYC-M – 1888/11/27:3b, 28:3b, 29:3b, =30:1d, fam. 30:3c
MEIER, Frederick, 78, dying, NYC-B – 1910/09/03:3a

MEIER, George, NYC-M – 1885/02/04:3b
MEIER, Henry, un. painter, NYC-M – 1910/12/07:6a
MEIER, Hermann H., 80, German shipping magnate, + Bremen – 1898/11/19:1b
MEIER, Jacob, 68, Hoboken, NJ – 1913/09/24:6a
MEIER, Johann, NYC-B – 1889/04/02:4a
MEIER, John, Harrison, NJ – 1919/01/19:12a
MEIER, Joseph, NYC-M – 1900/03/16:4a, 17:4a
MEIER, Meta, b. Jaeger, NYC-M – 1902/02/05:4a
MEIERHOEFER, John, 55,farmer,West Orange, NJ – 1879/10/11:1e, trial of his killers, (wife & her lover Lammens)1880/03/16:1d, 15 Oct:1e, 16:1f, 19:4d, 21:4c, 22:1g, 23:4e, both sent. to death 8 Nov:4d, 14 Dec:4f, 15:4c, 16:4d, Lammer's wife found 28 Dec:4d, 30:4d, 4 Jan. 1881:4c, 5:4e, 6:1f, both exec. in Newark, NJ 7 Jan 1881:1c-d, 2c-d
MEIERHOEFER, Matthias, un. carp., NYC-M – 1890/04/19:4a
MEIGEL, Leo, NYC-B - 1918/04/01:6a
MEINCKE, Wilhelmine, 56, NYC-B - 1916/01/11:6b
MEINE, August, NYC-M – 1903/03/28:4a
MEINECKE, Henry, Hawthorne, NJ – 1909/10/19:6a
MEINECKE, Robert, NYC-M – 1891/07/16:4a
MEINECKE, Thomas, 17, & William, 12, Jersey City, NJ – 1907/01/26:1d
MEINELL, Henry C., 50, brewery collector, NYC-M – 1891/07/12:5d
MEINER, Heinrich, 53, NYC-B – 1913/03/20:6a
MEINHARDT, August, 36, SLP, W. Hoboken, NJ – 1898/09/07:4a, 8:4a, fam. 10:4a, =10:4c
MEINHARDT, Hedwig, b. Deutschert?, NYC-B - 1916/01/19:6a, 20:6a, = 22:2a
MEINHARDT, John, Rudolph, 15, & Walter, NYC-M, +@ Genl Slocum – 1904/06/18:3c, 23:1b
MEININGER, Harry, 1, NYC-Bx, +@Genl Slocum – 1904/06/22:1d
MEININGHAUS, Charles, Yonkers, NY – 1911/12/30:6a
MEINITZ, Albert E., 20, NYC, + Providence, RI – 1912/02/09:2c
MEINS, Carl, 40, NYC-B – 1893/10/18:4a, fam. 19:4a
MEINS, John, 14, NYC-B – 1881/12/27:3a, 28:3a
MEIS, Konrad, NYC-B, will of, 1883/01/27:3a
MEISE, Fritz, Elizabeth, NJ - 1914/11/06:6a
MEISE, Fritz, un. cigar maker, NYC-M – 1887/02/22:3d
MEISENHELDER, Gottlieb, NYC-M – 1881/04/20:3b
MEISER, Henry, NYC-M – 1911/07/26:6a
MEISINGER, Henry, driver, NYC-M – 1904/07/03:1g
MEISLEIN, George, un. brewer, NYC-M - 1916/12/26:6a
MEISLOHN, John, 37, NYPD, NYC-M – 1910/05/03:1c

MEISNER, Carl, un. cigar maker, SLP, NYC, married Marie PFAL, SLP – 1897/02/23:1g
MEISNER, Ernst, NYC-Q - 1917/06/15:6a
MEISNER, Klara, NYC-B – 1907/11/23:6a
MEISSE, August, 45, West Hoboken, NJ - 1917/12/03:1c, 5:6a
MEISSNER, Alfred, writer, * Teplitz/Bohemia, + Vienna – 1885/06/02:1b, 2:2d
MEISSNER, August, un. carp., NYC-M – 1883/05/18:3c
MEISSNER, Charles, 41,machinist, NYC-B - 1895/06/25:1h,27:4a
MEISSNER, Frederick. A. C., 30, painter, NYC-M – 1896/12/22:3f
MEISSNER, Friedrich Ludwig, 85, NYC-Q - 1917/11/05:6a
MEISSNER, Georg, 36, NYC-B – 1901/02/01:4a
MEISSNER, Henry, Westchester?, NY – 1913/03/26:6a
MEISSNER, Hugo, machinist, NYC-Q - 1913/07/18:3b, 19:3a
MEISSNER, Lucinde, NYC-Bx - 1920/09/09:6a, 10:6a
MEISSNER, Otto, 62, coffee dealer, & wife Marie, 52, NYC-B – 1912/01/14:1d
MEISSNER, Theresa, b. Schuetz, 67, NYC-Q - 1917/05/15:6a
MEISSNER, Wilhelm, 75, tanner, * Oppeln/Silesia, USA 1879, Jersey City Heights, NJ - 1919/03/13:6a, =16:2f, mem. 1920/03/07:12a
MEIST, Karl, SPD activist & MdR 1893-1907 for Remscheid, + Koeln/Gy – 1908/03/04:4d, 15:3c
MEISTER, (Mr), 50, Union Hill, NJ – 1889/02/24:5b
MEISTER, August, silkweaver & SPD Brandenburg/Gy – 1887/01/26:5e
MEISTER, Eduard, un. cigarmaker, NYC-M – 1901/12/15:5a
MEISTER, Georg, 60, security guard, NYC-Q - 1917/05/08:1b
MEISTER, Heinrich, 64, SPD MdR for Hannover – 1906/04/18:2e-f
MEISTER, Herm., 3, NYC – 1880/02/24:4c
MEISTER, John H., 45, baker fr Bavaria, & wife, USA 1868?, NYC-B – 1893/08/10:1e
MEISTER, Willie, 12, NYC-M – 1892/02/21:1h
MEITZEL, Georg, NYC-M – 1905/03/12:5a
MEIXNER, Anna, NYC-Q – 1906/10/01:6a
MELBOURNE, William, NYC-M, +@ Genl Slocum – 1904/06/17:3b
MELCHING, George, 35, shoemaker, Hoboken, NJ – 1897/06/13:5h
MELCHING, Louisa, b. Stern, NYC-M – 1892/08/04:4a
MELCHING, Margarethe, 57, NYC-B – 1905/05/22:6a
MELENJ, Theophil, 36, Ukrainian Soc., member Ukrainian Legion, War 1 - 1915/09/11:4d
MELIN, John, Pocantico Hill, NY, ruined by John D. Rockefeller, son alr +, wife + 10 Apr - 1913/05/23:2f
MELINSE, Marguerite, servant, NYC-B – 1902/08/09:4a

MELIUS, Emma, NYC-M – 1887/05/11:2g
MELLENBECK, Robert K., 18, Hoboken, NJ – 1900/06/11:1e
MELLENBURG, Frederick, & wife, Paterson, NJ – 1892/09/29:1g
MELLER, Eva Katherina, NYC-Bx – 1911/04/07:6a
MELLER, Henry, un. Carp., NYC-M – 1911/07/13:6a
MELLER, Katherine, 40, NYC-M – 1892/11/06:5c
MELLINGER, Vernon, 34, mgr tobacco bus., Phila – 1919/08/26:2d
MELLOHN, Frederick, innkeep, NYC-B – 1887/10/15:2c
MELTZER, Gottfried, 46, brewery owner, NYC-B – 1881/07/21:3c
MELTZNER, Samuel, 22, driver, NYC-M – 1910/08/23:1f
MELVILLE, Hermann, 72, NYC-M – 1891/10/02:4a
MELZER, Alice, worker, Newark, NJ – 1910/11/27:1a
MEMECKE, Emil, 25, photographer, NYC-M - 1879/09/23:4b
MENCHEN, Frank, 40, iron wares shop, Rockville Ctr, L.I. - 1917/12/02:11d
MENCK, Fritz, un. carp., NYC-M – 1891/04/30:4a
MENDE, Alvin, 74,shoemkr, W. Hoboken, NJ - 1915/09/11:2e,12:7a
MENDEL, Arthur, NYC-M, + @ Genl Slocum – 1904/06/18:3c
MENDEL, Louis, 55, ex-innkeep in Newark, NJ, iron monger in NYC – 1903/02/09:1g
MENDEL, Melville, lawyer, & daughter Lillian, 12, NYC-Q – 1912/12/08:1f
MENDELL, Albert, paperhanger, NYC-M – 1891/05/01:2e
MENDELS, C. S., 60, banker, Newark, NJ – 1880/06/25:4b
MENDELSOHN, Isaac, 48, silk dealer, NYC-M - 1920/10/11:2a
MENDELSOHN, Joseph, 26, worker, + in sweatshop fire, NYC-M – 1893/06/14:1e
MENDELSOHN, Robert von, 60, German banker, + Berlin - 1917/08/23:2c
MENDELSTAM, Helen, Russian revol., USA 1908, Newark, NJ – 1909/04/05:3b
MENDER, Henry Carl, 32, waiter, NYC-M – 1911/03/29:1f
MENDLER, Gottlieb, NYC-B – 1911/07/08:6a
MENG, J., NYC-B – 1909/12/06:6a
MENGE, Charlie, infant, NYC-M – 1881/04/30:3a
MENGE, Elisabeth, 19, NYC-M – 1898/02/14:4a
MENGE, Wilhelm, 14, NYC-M – 1891/06/07:5a
MENGER, Georg, 70, Newark, NJ – 1909/07/12:3c
MENGES, Peter, 67, NYC-M - 1917/10/03:6a
MENK % Brueckel
MENKE, George, 22, machinist, Newark, NJ – 1910/04/05:3c
MENKEN, Friedrich, innkeep, NYC-M – 1892/06/21:4c
MENNE, Adam, West Newark, NJ - 1914/09/16:6a

MENNELL, Anton, 73, NYC-M – 1885/09/25:4b
MENNICKE, Alma, NYC-B – 1892/07/22:4a
MENNINGER % Wehle
MENNINGER, Henry, 39, cooper, USA ~1874, NYC-M – 1884/07/20:1g
MENNINGER, John, 74, NYC-M – 1881/10/29:3b
MENNINGER, Lottie, 7, NYC-M – 1909/12/03:1c, 4:3c
MENSCH, George, un. carp., NYC-Bx - 1913/07/01:6a
MENSCHING, Maria, b. Pister, NYC-B - 1878/06/21:3a
MENSEL, A., NYC-M - 1914/04/20:6a
MENSING, Henry, 32, Paterson, NJ - 1920/05/25:2e, = 28:2b
MENSING, Henry, 80, shoemaker, NYC-M - 1916/05/24:5d
MENSING, Sophie, 74, NYC-B – 1910/06/22:1d
MENTH, Joseph, Paterson, NJ - 1915/08/27:6a
MENZEL, Adolf von, painter, + Berlin – 1905/02/10:1e
MENZEL, Eduard, 63, NYC-M - 1915/11/16:6a
MENZEL, Hermann, 47, NYC-B – 1893/06/29:4a
MENZEL, Robert, 17, NYC-M – 1903/09/09:4a
MENZEL, William, 31, NYC-B - 1914/09/10:6a
MENZEL, William, 56, un. iron moulder, NYC-B – 1910/12/17:6a
MENZEN, Marie, 7, (+25 Mr), NYC-M, inquest 1882/04/08:1f-g
MERG, Anna, b. Sulzmann, 49, NYC-SI - 1914/11/07:6a
MERGARDT, Gustav, 33, NYC-M – 1883/04/16:3b
MERGENTHALER % Spannknebel
MERGENTHALER, John, un. brewer, NYC-M – 1909/02/23:6a
MERGER, Tim, NYC-B – 1899/12/29:1f
MERINGER, Alfons, Newark, NJ - 1916/04/07:6a
MERINGER, Philipp, 47, NYC-M – 1892/09/17:4a
MERK, August, fr Swiss Labor Confed., + Zuerich/Switz. 1907/01/21:4d
MERKEL, Christine, b. Jauch, 63, SDP?, NYC-M – 1905/03/26:5a
MERKEL, Elizabeth, 43, NYC-M – 1909/12/20:6a
MERKEL, George, un. machinist, NYC - 1914/03/27:6a
MERKEL, Jacques, 44, un. printer, SLP, *Gernsbach/Baden, NYC-M –
    1891/01/17:1b,4a, 18:5a, =19:1d
MERKEL, John, 44, machinist, Newark, NJ – 1902/12/19:4a
MERKEL, Joseph, un. carpenter, NYC-M - 1894/06/09:4a
MERKEL, Karl, 71, NYC-B - 1917/11/22:6a
MERKEL, William H., 23, printer, Mt Carmel, NJ – 1899/01/11:4c
MERKERK % Scherer
MERKL, George, 26, barman, NYC-B – 1897/03/30:1g
MERKLE, A., NYC-B - 1917/09/21:6a
MERKLE, Abraham, un. carp., NYC-M – 1890/01/13:4a
MERKLE, August, un. typestter, NYC-B – 1909/12/31:6a

MERKLE, Katharina, b. Mueller, 58, NYC-B – 1909/02/15:6a
MERKLE, Louis, 19, NYC-Bx – 1910/07/20:6a
MERKLI, Heinrich, un. carp., NYC-M – 1904/06/22:4a
MERKT, Franz, NYC-M? – 1912/09/11:6a
MERRIFIELD, Samantha H., 47, SP, + Roxbury, MA – 1911/12/27:2a
MERRY, Martin, Homestead, PA, steelworker – 1892/07/07:1b,2a
MERSCH, Alois, toy dealer, NYC-M – 1883/01/07:1f
MERSELES, Matilda, NYC-B, + @ Genl Slocum – 1904/06/17:3c
MERSH, John, 20, driver, killed in Milwaukee, WI strike – 1886/05/06:1d
MERTEN, Susanna, SLP, NYC-M – 1886/12/25:2g
MERTEN, Wilhelm, 58, un. typesetter, *Sehla/Brandenburg, USA via London, friend of John Most, NYC-B – 1910/05/21:2e,6a, 22:7b, 23:2a, =24:2b, fam. 28:6a
MERTEN, Willie, 5, NYC-M – 1886/01/28:2g
MERTENS % Arndt
MERTENS, Th., SLP?, NYC-M – 1883/08/22:3c
MERTENS, William, 35, SP?, Newark, NJ - 1914/09/29:6a
MERTGES, Kate, 20, servant, NYC-M – 1897/11/02:1g
MERTIN, Rudolph, 77, NYC-B - 1915/11/17:6a
MERTZ, Frederick, 53, NYC-B – 1901/03/23:4a
MERTZ, Frederick, police detective, Bloomfield, NJ - 1915/12/19:1d, 20:2b
MERTZ, Fritz, 40, nurse, NYC-M – 1892/07/04:1e
MERTZ, Valentin, un. carp., NYC-Bx – 1903/12/31:1h
MERTZINEG, Joseph, 22, driver, Polish patriot, NYC-B – 1906/01/04:4a
MERTZINGER, Maria, 20, servant, Metuchen, NJ – 1899/01/19:4c
MERWITZ, Gustav, 45, NYC-M – 1886/07/08:3b
MERXNER, Valentin G., infant, NYC-M – 1905/12/01:5b
MERZ % Anger, % Oelschlaeger, % Maurer
MERZ, Albert, 56, NYC-B – 1912/05/24:6a
MERZ, Charles, 27, NYC-M – 1893/10/10:4a
MERZ, Conrad, NYC-Q - 1917/11/23:6a
MERZ, Eduard, roofer & SP Zug/Switzerland – 1888/07/31:2c-d
MERZ, Elise, NYC-M - 1894/05/02:4a
MERZ, F., 64, NYC-M – 1893/08/31:4a
MERZ, Frank, NYC-B – 1911/01/15:7c
MERZ, Frederick, 18, NYC-M – 1904/10/01:1d
MERZ, Irene E., 24, NYC-M - 1917/05/09:6a
MERZ, John, sailor on USS Maine, + Havana/Cuba, NYC-B – 1898/02/18:1b
MERZ, Maragarethe, b. Neitz, 38, Ft Lee, NJ – 1912/05/18:6a
MERZ, Peter, musician, 58, NYC-M – 1912/07/31:2a
MERZ, Reinhold, Newark, NJ – 1911/01/30:3c

MERZ, Rudolph, 32, NYC-Q – 1912/09/21:6c
MERZ, Walter, 14, NYC-M – 1891/02/10:4a
MERZ, William, NYC? – 1890/08/06:4a
MERZBACHER, Benedikt H., salesman, NYC-M – 1896/07/11:1g
MERZBACHER, Pauline, 55, NYC-Q – 1911/10/20:2e
MERZWEILER, Max, NYC-Bx – 1909/04/08:6a
MESERAU, John C., salesman, NYC-B – 1901/05/09:4a
MESKE, Carl's wife, & Anna, 16, NYC-M, + @ Genl Slocum – 1904/06/17:3b
MESLE, Anna, 26, (dying), NYC-B - 1917/08/03:5e
MESOW, Elise, 15, Jersey City, NJ – 1902/11/17:1a
MESSERSCHMIDT, Andreas, NYC-M – 1906/07/28:6a
MESSERSCHMIDT, Friedrich, un. cigarmaker, NYC-M – 1881/05/26:3a
MESSERSCHMIDT, Gustav, 54, NYC-Bx – 1912/12/21:6a
MESSERSCHMIDT, John, NYC-M – 1887/05/16:3c
MESSIN % Griesel
MESSING, Jacob, button hole maker, fr Russia, NYC-M – 1908/10/10:1f
MESSINGER, Charles, sales clerk, NYC-B – 1900/02/06:1e
MESSINGER, David, un. brewer, NYC-M – 1907/01/16:6a
MESSINGER, William, NYC-M – 1906/02/26:4a
MESSLER, Joseph, 60, brass worker, fr Austria, NYC-B - 1920/04/15:4a, 16:4a
MESSLER, Katherine, b. Kaufmann, 43, NYC-M – 1903/07/10:4a, 11:4a
MESSMER, Jacob, un. butcher, NYC-M - 1916/03/03:6a
MESSNER, Jacob, 55, engineer, NYC-M – 1897/11/17:1d
METH, Elisabeth, b. Braun, NYC-B – 1888/04/06:3b, fam. 9:3a
METHE, Heinrich, 54, NYC-M – 1897/08/19:4a
METHE, Henriette, 50, NYC-Bx – 1906/09/16:7c
METHE, Max, 57, cigar dealer, Bogota,NJ - 1913/06/04:6c
METHFESSEL Anna, b. Goeppert, 51, NYC-Q - 1913/12/10:6a
METHFESSEL, Anna, b. Stier, NYC-B – 1902/04/08:4a
METIEN, Evelyn, 22, NYC-Q – 1907/08/21:3a, 6 Aug:3a
METJE, Carl, NYC-M - 1918/10/24:6a, =31:5e
METSCH % Zerweck
METT, Hulda, 62, Jersey City, NJ – 1909/01/12:6a, fam. 15:6a
METT, Reinhold C., SP?, Jersey City Heights, NJ – 1903/12/21:4a, fam. 23:4a
METTLER, Albert, 12, NYC-M, +@Genl Slocum – 1904/06/19:1c
METZ % Hipfl
METZ, Alfred, 2, NYC-M - 1879/03/04:3a
METZ, August, un. carp., NYC-M – 1888/03/21:3c
METZ, Heinrich, 32, NYC-M - 1894/01/22:4a

METZ, Michael, 31, cigarmanuf., fr Lorsch/Hessen?, NYC-M – 1897/05/02:1g
METZ, Michael, 55, NYC-M - 1895/01/03:4a
METZ, Sophie, 17, NYC-B – 1910/10/29:3c
METZ, William, weaver?, NYC-B – 1910/08/22:6a
METZE, Fritz, driver, NYC-M – 1908/08/24:1f
METZENDORF, Elisabeth, 5, Newark, NJ – 1891/06/22:4a
METZENDORF, Wilhelm, 84, & wife, Golden Wedding, Newark, NJ – 1885/07/29:3b
METZER, Franz, SLP, NYC-B - 1894/12/02:5a
METZGER, Adam, 44, machinist, NYC-M - 1895/12/04: 4a
METZGER, Adolph, 32, RR worker, Elizabeth, NJ – 1897/01/08:4a
METZGER, Alfred, 40, glass manuf., Newark, NJ – 1900/12/19:1g
METZGER, Anton, * 6 Jan. 1871 Gross-Ostein/Bavaria, + Elisabeth, NJ – 1887/10/31.2c, = 3 Nov:2c
METZGER, August, NYC-M – 1909/04/21:6a
METZGER, Christian, NYC-M - 1916/04/04:6a
METZGER, Christian, cabinetmaker,NYC-M - 1878/06/23:2e, 28:4e
METZGER, Eugen, NYC-M - 1894/08/13:4a
METZGER, F., NYC-B – 1912/07/18:6a
METZGER, Friedrich, 35, beer driver, NYC-M – 1898/09/06:1c
METZGER, Helen, 3, NYC-B – 1907/08/26:3a
METZGER, Helene, b. Daenzer, 30, NYC-B – 1908/03/19:3a, 20:3b, 21:3c
METZGER, Jacob, 55, elevator man at Labor Temple, NYC-M - 1915/02/13:6c
METZGER, Jacob, NYC-M – 1888/06/22:1d
METZGER, Johann J., 47, NYC-M – 1891/06/22:4a
METZGER, Johann M., 42, tailor, NYC-M – 1880/05/28:1e
METZGER, John, un. butcher, NYC-M – 1908/01/05:7c
METZGER, Joseph, 30, NYC-M – 1882/02/04:1g
METZGER, L., Dr.med., NYC-B – 1898/12/05:1h
METZGER, Peter, 39, RR driver, Jersey City, NJ – 1905/01/30:3b
METZGER, Simon, 27, cigarpacker, NYC-B – 1888/01/13:2d
METZGER, Wilhelm, SPD Hamburg/Gy, MdR, 60th birthday – 1908/05/24:3b; + 1914/12/03:4d
METZKI, Louise, 14, servant, NYC-M – 1893/08/10:1f
METZLER, Ignaz, NYC-M - 1916/10/01:7a
METZLER, Jakob, 62, NYC-M – 1891/04/01:4a
METZLER, Margarethe, b. Molke, wd Jargosch, NYC-M – 1905/06/20:4a
METZNER % Abel
METZNER, Adolph, NYC-M – 1892/08/15:4a
METZNER, Theodore, 72, shoemaker, SPD Berlin/Gy – 1902/09/03:2c

MEUNIER, Constantin, French progressive sculptor – 1905/04/30:4f-h, 14 May:12g-h, 10 Sept:4c-e
MEUTER, Anna, 55, NYC-M – 1907/04/07:7c
MEWES, Henry, 56, silkweaver, NYC-M – 1889/07/19:1h
MEYER Engels, Freise, Muth, Nusbaum, Swaenson, Worms,
MEYER, Abraham, 34, innkeep, NYC-M – 1904/12/26:1g, 24:1e
MEYER, Adelheid, NYC-B – 1891/07/31:4a
MEYER, Adolph, NYC-M – 1895/03/29:2d
MEYER, Albert, 16, NYC-M, +@ Genl Slocum – 1904/06/17:3c
MEYER, Alexander, Dr., 76, MdR, + Halle?/Gy – 1908/07/12:3b
MEYER, Alfred, 15, NYC-M – 1900/07/23:1c
MEYER, Alfred, Muehlhausen/Elsass, exec. for treason – 1915/10/10:3a
MEYER, Andreas, 23, Swiss, NYC-M – 1882/06/16:1g
MEYER, Andreas, un. butcher, NYC-M – 1906/07/12:6a
MEYER, Annie, b. Rabe, NYC-M – 1887/02/02:2g
MEYER, August, 67, NYC-M – 1917/05/12:6a
MEYER, August, NYC-B – 1907/12/06:6a
MEYER, Auguste, b. Delius, No. Bergen, NJ – 1906/11/03:6a
MEYER, Carl E., champagne importer NYC, then San Francisco, on ship Carmania – 1906/01/09:3f
MEYER, Carl L., un. cigar maker, NYC-M – 1896/10/29:4a
MEYER, Carl, 40, salesman fr Davenport, IA, + NYC-M – 1882/08/20:5d
MEYER, Carl, un. cigarmaker, NYC-M – 1903/03/07:4a, fam. 12:4a
MEYER, Charles A., 35, merchant in Gy, here bookmaker, NYC-M – 1886/04/05:4d
MEYER, Charles, 55, Hoboken, NJ – 1915/08/11:6c
MEYER, Charles, 7, NYC-M – 1905/10/26:4a, 27:4a
MEYER, Charles, Union Hill, NJ – 1916/01/17:6a
MEYER, Christoph, un. carp., Jersey City Heights, NJ – 1885/02/04:3b
MEYER, Christoph, un. cigarmaker, NYC-M – 1880/04/11:5f
MEYER, Clara, 64, NYC-M – 1920/03/04:6a
MEYER, Diedrich, NYC-B – 1892/07/21:4a
MEYER, Dora, 19, NYC-B – 1897/08/04:4c
MEYER, E., 25, NYC-M – 1894/01/29:4a
MEYER, Eduard, 24, NYC – 1885/08/12:3b
MEYER, Edward, SP, bookkeeper, married Christine Baumert, SP, NYC-M – 1909/10/01:3a-b
MEYER, Elisabeth, 40, NYC-M, + @ Genl Slocum – 1904/06/17:3b
MEYER, Elisabeth, b. Braeutigam, 69, NYC-M – 1899/07/16:5b
MEYER, Elise, b. Kuhlwisser, 31, NYC-M – 1892/03/28:4a
MEYER, Ella, child, Newark, NJ – 1893/06/20:4f
MEYER, Emma, 70, NYC-M – 1906/07/15:7a

MEYER, Ernst, 28, bottler, NYC-M – 1897/11/02:1g
MEYER, Felix, insurance agent, NYC-M – 1898/04/27:3h
MEYER, Franz, 34, NYC-B – 1906/08/08:2c
MEYER, Frederick W., 85, clerk at Austrian-Hungarian Cons. Genl, * Elberfeld/Gy, USA 1853, NYC-M – 1888/02/14:1h
MEYER, Frederick Hermann, SP, NYC-B - 1915/03/22:6a, =24:2d
MEYER, Frederick, 28, machinist, NYC-B – 1903/08/08:3c
MEYER, Frederick, NYC-M – 1903/08/27:4a, 28:4a
MEYER, Friedrich, 38, Jersey City, NJ – 1886/01/27:2g
MEYER, Friedrich, 66, NYC-M - 1917/04/16:6a
MEYER, Fritz, exec. Ossining, NY – 1900/05/20:1f, 21:3h, done 22:2h
MEYER, Georg, St Louis, MO – 1882/05/05:3f
MEYER, George, 53, worker,NYC-Q - 1913/12/02:3a,3:3e
MEYER, George, 68, street musician, NYC-B - 1916/04/29:5b
MEYER, Georgine, 3, Paterson, NJ – 1898/05/27:4a
MEYER, Gottlieb, 39, taylor, fr Kuessnacht/Switz., USA 1886, NYC-B - 1895/05/08: 4b
MEYER, Gustav Theophilus, 66, portrait painter, NYC-M – 1882/05/22:1e
MEYER, Hans, 17, NYC-M – 1900/09/21:4a
MEYER, Heinrich, NYC-B – 1892/10/08:4a
MEYER, Heinrich, SPD Frankfurt-Eschborn,War 1 - 1914/11/01:3b
MEYER, Henry Daniel, 49, un. cigarmaker, Hoboken, NJ – 1899/08/14:4a, fam. 17:4a
MEYER, Henry, 21, salesman, NYC-M – 1880/06/24:1e
MEYER, Henry, 25, machinist, NYC-B - 1916/06/16:6b
MEYER, Henry, 27, NYC-M - 1894/12/19:4a
MEYER, Henry, 32, Freeport, LI, War 2, + Ossining, NY - 1918/11/19:2f
MEYER, Henry, 37, lithographer, Swiss, NYC-B – 1902/05/01:4a
MEYER, Henry, 45, NYC-B – 1909/06/25:3b
MEYER, Henry, 73, NYC-M – 1909/09/11:6a
MEYER, Henry, Dr., his trial, 1893/12/05:1h,6:1f-g, 7:1f,8:1f-g,9:1f-g, 10:5f, 12:1h, 13:1f-, 14:1f-g, 16:1f-g, etc
MEYER, Henry, un. baker, NYC-M - 1918/11/13:6a
MEYER, Henry's wife, NYC-B – 1884/10/29:3b
MEYER, Henry R., 26, US Army, War 1 in France, NYC-Cedar Manor, LI - 1918/10/22:5g
MEYER, Hermann, 51, NYC-B – 1892/06/14:4a
MEYER, Jacob, NYC-B – 1913/02/24:6a
MEYER, Jakob, silk weaver, Paterson, NJ – 1885/09/25:4d
MEYER, John B., *11 June 1839 Koeln/Gy, SDP, silk weaver, NYC-M – 1902/11/12:4a, 13:4a, fam. 14:4g, =16:1g
MEYER, John D., 55, restaurant owner, NYC-B - 1916/03/11:6c

MEYER, John M., 62, NYC-M - 1894/01/08:4f
MEYER, John, 17, fr Bremen?, on ship Salier – 1881/09/02:1g
MEYER, John, 25, casketmaker, NYC-M – 1901/04/14:1g
MEYER, John, 60, NYC-M – 1906/08/17:6a
MEYER, John, 60, NYC-M – 1912/03/28:1d
MEYER, John, 67, NYC-M – 1891/07/16:4a
MEYER, John, NYC? – 1899/08/25:3c
MEYER, John, NYC-M – 1902/07/03:4a
MEYER, John, un. brewer, NYC-M – 1893/08/02:4a
MEYER, John, un. carp., NYC-Bx – 1912/01/24:6a
MEYER, Joseph H., jeweler, NYC-B – 1903/01/17:3b, 18:1d
MEYER, Joseph, & wife, Paterson, NJ – 1908/02/25:3b
MEYER, Joseph, 55, NYC-M – 1898/08/23:4a, 28:5e
MEYER, Joseph, un. butcher, NYC-M – 1904/09/08:4a
MEYER, Josephine, 62, Irvington, NJ - 1919/06/28:2d
MEYER, Karoline, NYC-M – 1910/03/25:6a
MEYER, Kate, 38, NYC-B - 1894/07/30:4a
MEYER, Kate, NYC-M, +@ Genl Slocum – 1904/06/18:3c
MEYER, Katherina, NYC-M – 1908/02/18:6a
MEYER, Katherine E., 63?, NYC-B – 1890/05/05:4a
MEYER, Konrad E., German poet, 1825-1898, mem. 1908/12/20:3f-g
MEYER, Konrad Ferdinand, Swiss poet – 1898/12/25:16c-f, his will 31:2d
MEYER, Leonhard, SDP?, un. brewer, + Seattle, WA – 1900/12/10:2h
MEYER, Leopold, 19, Jersey City, NJ, + as "George Wilson" in Sioux City, IA - 1879/03/30:5d
MEYER, Leopold, 32, worker, USA 1882?, NYC-B – 1886/03/02:2e
MEYER, Lizzie, 60, near Hackensack, NJ – 1904/08/18:3f
MEYER, Lottie, 11, & Edith, 3, Bayonne, NJ – 1905/01/14:3b
MEYER, Louis H., 34, NYC-M - 1917/10/05:6a
MEYER, Louis, 35, butcher, Winfield, NJ – 1884/08/22:3b
MEYER, Louis, machinist, Newark, NJ – 1887/01/17:2d
MEYER, Louise, b. Lensch, 50, NYC-B – 1901/08/11:5a
MEYER, Marie S., NYC-B – 1891/07/17:4a
MEYER, Marie, 46, NYC-M – 1911/11/04:6a
MEYER, Marie, NYC-M – 1897/06/03:4a
MEYER, Martha, NYC-B – 1905/03/16:4a
MEYER, Martin P., Hoboken, NJ – 1883/05/29:4e
MEYER, Max L., lawyer, NYC-M - 1878/04/18:4a, 27:4d
MEYER, Melchior, 60, NYC-M – 1899/08/29:4a, 30:4a, 3 Sept:4a-b
MEYER, Meta, 59, NYC-M, + @Genl Slocum – 1904/06/21:1f
MEYER, Otto, innkeep, Paterson, NJ – 1898/01/19:3d
MEYER, Philip L., realtor, NYC-B – 1891/11/12:2f

MEYER, Raimund, brewer?, NYC-M – 1892/09/02:4a
MEYER, Rebecca, b. Ehlers, ?34, NYC-M – 1892/09/20:4a
MEYER, Reinhard, carpenter & SPD activist expelled from Berlin/Gy, arrived NYC – 1880/12/11:1g
MEYER, Richard D., NYC-Q - 1916/03/13:6a
MEYER, Richard, 79, businessman, NYC-B – 1909/01/15:3a
MEYER, Richard, NYC-Q - 1915/12/06:6a
MEYER, Rudolf, German liberal politician – 1899/01/18:2b, 31:2e-g
MEYER, Siegfried P., old SP activist fr Berlin, USA 1867, + Pittsburgh, PA 7/1872, memory, with notes by W. Liebknecht – 1900/05/20:7d
MEYER, Sigmund, married Theresa Vogt, NYC-M – 1898/02/01:1e
MEYER, Simon, 68, NYC-M – 1892/06/09:4a
MEYER, Sophie, 84, West Hoboken, NJ – 1901/07/04:3b
MEYER, Sophie, b. Brand, NYC-M – 1910/10/21:6a
MEYER, Theodor, 6, NYC-M – 1886/03/08:3c
MEYER, Theodore Leo, Dr., 70, NYC-Bx – 1910/11/26:6a
MEYER, Tillie, b. Press, 55, NYC-Bx - 1917/11/19:6a
MEYER, Victor, Dr., 45, physician, NYC-M – 1909/03/03:1f
MEYER, W., NYC-Q – 1914/12/04:6a
MEYER, Wilhelm C., 36, NYC-B – 1891/07/18:4a
MEYER, Wilhelm, 26, restaurant worker, fr Stuttgart/Gy, NYC-M – 1885/12/24:2g
MEYER, William, manuf., Middleton, NY – 1907/05/15:2d
MEYER, William, NYC-B - 1918/12/17:6a
MEYER, William, NYC-M – 1908/08/20:6a
MEYER, William, NYC-M? – 1911/11/15:6a
MEYER, William, NYC-Q – 1908/07/20:3a
MEYER, William, worker, Harrison, NJ, + Newark, NJ – 1901/09/27:1h
MEYER, Wolf, 106, tailor, fr Gy ~ 1858, vet Napoleonic wars, + Newark, NJ – 1883/09/02:5e
MEYERBACH, Sophie, 65, NYC-B – 1911/06/20:3b
MEYERHAUCK, Mary, 37, & husband, Hoboken, NJ – 1900/07/18:1d, 19:1h, 23:1d
MEYERHEIM, Eduard, 76, German genre painter, - 1879/02/10:2g
MEYERHOFF, Augustus, diamond worker, NYC-M – 1890/05/08:4e
MEYERHOFF, Christian, 62, un. tailor, NYC-M – 1893/11/20:4a
MEYERHOFF, Johann H., fr Westfalia?, NYC-M – 1912/02/29:6a
MEYERHOFF, Johann H., NYC-M – 1912/03/01:6a
MEYERHOFF, John, NYC-B – 1892/06/07:4a
MEYERHOFFER, Friedericke, 54, NYC-M – 1908/08/21:3e
MEYERS, Alfred, 28, art-painter, NYC-M – 1892/09/03:4c
MEYERS, Bernard, waiter, NYC-M – 1906/04/01:1g

MEYERS, Charles W., 55, druggist, NYC-B - 1914/12/26:2e
MEYERS, Elizabeth, NYC-M, + @ Genl Slocum - 1904/06/18:3c
MEYERS, Frederick, 35, driver, NYC-M - 1900/05/22:3g
MEYERS, John, painter, NYC - 1912/05/26:1c
MEYERS, Lena, 24, fr Russia, NYC-M - 1896/06/24:1e
MEYERS, Nathan, 28, cigarpacker, NYC-M - 1896/03/24:4d
MEYERS, Robert, cloth dealer, Bloomfield, NJ - 1912/09/27:2c
MEYERS, Rose, 54, NYC-M - 1916/04/29:5c
MEYERS, Samuel, 8, NYC-M - 1900/07/19:1e
MEYERS, William, 26, NYC-M - 1880/06/29:1c
MEYERS, William, infant, NYC-M - 1880/06/29:1c
MEYERSTRASS, Catherine, 33, servant, NYC-B - 1882/04/13:4c, 15:2g
MEYN, Henry P., NYC - 1903/02/14:3b
MEYNE, William, child, NYC-M - 1899/03/24:4a
MEYSENBURG, Malwina von, German writer & reformer, '48er, + Rome/Italy - 1903/05/17:7b-e
MEYTROFF, Charles, tailor, NYC-M - 1895/10/09: 1d
MEZER, Gustav, Newark, NJ - 1908/08/12:2b
MEZGER, Maria, 46, NYC-Bx - 1915/01/26:6a
MICHAEL, Carrie, NYC-M, +@ Genl Slocum - 1904/06/17:3c
MICHAEL, Fried., 24, NYC-M - 1889/05/12:5b
MICHAEL, Heinrich, 55, NYC-M - 1891/03/27:4a
MICHAEL, Oskar, wholesaler, Orange, NJ - 1916/06/12:5e
MICHAEL, William, 17, NYC-M, + @Genl Slocum - 1904/06/17:3c
MICHAELIS, Betty, NYC-M - 1892/05/11:4a
MICHAELIS, Carl, 47, NYC-M - 1891/10/14:4a
MICHAELIS, Emma, NYC-M? - 1916/11/11:2e
MICHAELIS, Frederick, 40, carp., NYC-M - 1887/11/09:2f
MICHAELIS, Hermann, Hoboken, NJ - 1891/03/16:4a
MICHAELIS, M., un. typesetter, NYC-M - 1906/10/02:6a
MICHAELIS, Otto, NYC-Q - 1909/04/30:6a
MICHAELIS, Walter R., publ. Illinois Staats-Zeitung, Chicago,+ Deposit, NY - 1910/08/08:2d
MICHAELS, Margaret, NYC-M, + @ Genl Slocum - 1904/06/18:3c
MICHAELS, William, 14, NYC-M, +@ Genl Slocum - 1904/06/17:3b
MICHAELSEN % Luebbe
MICHAILITSCHENKO, comrade, Russian soc., exec. Kronstadt - 1906/08/17:4e-f
MICHAILOW, exec. for plot to kill Alex II of Russia, see Alex II
MICHAILOWSKI, Nikolai, progressive Russian writer, + St Petersburg - 1904/03/07:2d
MICHALEK, John, un. carp., NYC-M? - 1913/10/29:6a

MICHALOCHOSS, Paul, cigarmaker *Austria,NYC-M - 1894/11/19:1d
MICHEL, Anna Magdalena, 2, NYC-M - 1881/07/18:3b
MICHEL, Anna, 62, NYC-M - 1891/04/01:4a
MICHEL, Conrad, 75, Steinway worker?, NYC-M - 1881/01/17:3c
MICHEL, Emma, 44, NYC-B - 1911/11/09:6a
MICHEL, Friedericke, b. Loessmann, 57, Newark, NJ - 1910/12/03:6a
MICHEL, Johanna, NYC-M - 1905/07/21:4a
MICHEL, John, 46, SP, & wife Salome, b. Adam, 47, both fr Brumath/Elsass 1892, silver wedding, NYC-B - 1906/12/30:9c-d
MICHEL, John, 69, tailor, *near Butzbach/Gy, SP, NYC-B - 1909/03/13:6a, 14:7e
MICHEL, Louise, French revol., *1839, her life - 1881/02/13:4b-5b, 11 May:2e-f; her life, 1893/04/16:5c-d, 23:5a-b; 1895/04/07:5d; on her + 10 Jan. 1905:1f-g, NYC workers grieve 15:1c, rev. 16:1a-b, notes by Anna Nill 22:9a-b, on her = 7 Fb:2d-e, 24 Mr:1h, 4b-c, 5 Apr:2d, 13:3e, by Otto Crola 1 May:14a-c, 8:7a-c, 15:14a-c; her life 1907/06/16:16a-d
MICHEL, Margaretha, b. Ehlenberger, 71, NYC-B - 1910/12/30:6a
MICHEL, Oscar R. J., 43, SP, NYC-Q - 1909/06/02:6a, =4:2d
MICHEL, Sigmund, Elizabeth, NJ - 1904/07/16:4a
MICHELBACHER, Joshua J., 36, NYC-M - 1891/09/20:5f
MICHELL, Gottfried, 23, worker, USA 1888, NYC-M - 1891/12/15:2f
MICHELS, Friedrich, 56, NYC-M - 1882/02/25:3b
MICHELS, Henry, un. baker, NYC-M - 1887/01/24:3c
MICK, Franz, un. cigarmaker, SDP?, NYC-M - 1904/03/24:4a
MIDAS, Philip, 51, publ. of Die Lanterne, NYC-B - 1886/02/03:6d
MIDNET, Friedrich, NYC-M - 1910/08/02:6a
MIEDL, Victor, un. carp., NYC-M - 1912/06/24:2f, 25:6a, 26:6a, =28:1f
MIEDREICH, Jacob, NYC-B - 1909/10/06:6a
MIELENHAUSEN, Jennie, NYC-M - 1911/04/17:6a, fam. 20:6a
MIELENZ, Charles, Chicago, IL - 1900/08/18:1b
MIELICH, Aloysius A., NYC-B - 1911/11/03:6a
MIER, Ferdinand, 46, fr Elsass, NYC-B - 1881/05/01:5d
MIEROSLAWSKY, Ludwig, 64, Polish general, + Paris/France, - 1878/12/10:2d
MIERSCH, Johannes, musician & prof. at Cincinatti College of Music - 1916/09/10:11a
MIERZINSKY, Katherina, b. Fels, NYC-M - 1914/05/10:7a, 11:6a
MIESCKOWSKI, Alfons, 28, fr Russia, NYC-M - 1891/07/14:1g, 22:2e
MIESNER, John, Greenville, NJ - 1905/02/04:4a
MIETHKE, Minna, 19, servant, NYC-M - 1909/07/14:1f
MIGDAL, Henry, miller, fr Russia, NYC-M - 1898/09/13:1e
MIGNARY, Marie, 21, fr Paris/F, NYC-M - 1900/05/02:3g

MIHI, Ottilie, 74, NYC-Union Course, LI - 1916/07/22:2d
MILDENBERGER % Henchen
MILDENBERGER, Louis Christoph, infant, NYC-M – 1889/03/19:4a
MILDENBERGER, Michael, un. carp., NYC-B – 1892/05/10:4a
MILDENHAIN, Annie, 4, NYC-M – 1891/07/11:4a
MILES, Thomas, Negro, lynched Shreveport, LA – 1912/04/10:3b, 11:4c
MILETIC, Svetozar, Dr., 74, member Hungarian Parl. – 1901/02/26:2e
MILEWSKI, Eduard, SP, Lithuanian writer, + Lemberg/Galicia - 1915/06/20:3d
MILHAUPT, John, 40, driver, & wife Luisa, NYC-B – 1909/08/28:1b
MILHAZER, George, 26, striker,+ McKees Rocks, PA – 1909/08/13:1c
MILHOLLAND-BOISSERIN, Inez, 30, ex-SP, lawyer & feminist, + Los Angeles, CA - 1916/11/27:2e
MILKE, Friedrich, 57, un. typesetter, SDP, NYC-B – 1902/01/17:4a, 18:3c, 19:5a, =20:3b, fam. 23:4a
MILKENBECHER, Karl, waiter, NYC-M – 1907/03/05:1f
MILL, Johanna, NYC-B - 1914/02/09:2d
MILLAR, Richard, "count," (pseudonym), alleged German spy, + Denver, CO - 1915/08/10:5f
MILLATZ, Otto, 40, umbrella mkr, NYC-M – 1899/02/17:3d, 18:4a, fam. 21:4a
MILLBERGER, Adam, NYC-M – 1891/03/23:4a
MILLER % Burkhardt; MILLER % Mabel
MILLER, ..., 61, city councilman, Hoboken, NJ – 1888/12/07:3c
MILLER, Adam, 44, NYC-M – 1892/05/28:4a
MILLER, Andreas, NYC-Q – 1919/08/26:6a
MILLER, Anna, child, NYC-M – 1884/12/01:3b
MILLER, Anne Marie, b. Kropac, & son Karl-Heinrich, Union Hill, NJ – 1881/05/20:3c, 21 Jy:3c
MILLER, Annie, 16, @1911 Triangle Shirtwaist Fire, NYC-M – 1911/04/08:1c
MILLER, Aron, 60, tailor, NYC-M – 1912/07/11:1d
MILLER, Arthur, Indianapolis, IN - 1895/06/19: 4a
MILLER, August, 52 stone cutter, dying, NYC-B – 1912/01/24:2d
MILLER, Bernard's wife, & children, NYC-M, + @ Genl Slocum – 1904/06/16:1d
MILLER, Charles A., NYC-M – 1906/12/15:6a, 16:9e
MILLER, Charles W., 1, NYC-M – 1882/06/06:3b
MILLER, Charlie, 16, exec. Cheyenne, WY – 1892/04/23:1b
MILLER, David, 65, wife in Winnipeg/CN, + NYC-M – 1882/09/25:4e
MILLER, Edward, NYC-M, + @ Genl Slocum – 1904/06/18:3c
MILLER, Elizabeth, & George, 3, Edgar, 1, Elizabeth,NJ - 1915/01/31:11g

MILLER, Elsie, NYC-B - 1917/03/23:6a
MILLER, Emma, 43, NYC-B – 1913/01/24:6a
MILLER, Ernest, un. cigarpacker, NYC-Bx - 1919/03/09:12a
MILLER, Flora, NYC-M, +@ Genl Slocum – 1904/06/17:3b
MILLER, Frederick, 40, carp., & wife Amelia, 36, NYC-M – 1909/11/03:2f
MILLER, Frederick, 67, NYC-M – 1888/09/12:1f
MILLER, Frederick, NYC-M – 1901/11/28:1f, 11 Dec:3c
MILLER, Friedrich, infant, NYC-M – 1881/09/24:3b
MILLER, George, 22, bartender, NYC-M – 1887/04/22:4a
MILLER, George, un. carp., NYC-M - 1916/05/08:6a
MILLER, H., 40, NYC-M, + @Genl Slocum – 1904/06/17:3b
MILLER, H.A., NYC-? - 1919/03/08:6a
MILLER, Heinrich, 76, SP?, un. carp., NYC-M - 1919/03/12:6a, fam. 18:6a
MILLER, Heinrich, un. cigar maker, NYC-M – 1891/12/12:4a
MILLER, Henry, 50, NYC-B – 1885/05/07:2g
MILLER, Henry, 50, painter, NYC-M – 1897/08/13:1e
MILLER, Henry, 55, NYC-B – 1900/07/27:4a
MILLER, Henry, 89, San Francisco millionaire, *Brockenheim/ Wuerttemberg, USA 1847 - 1917/01/13:4d, 15:4f
MILLER, Henry, Newark, NJ – 1910/06/25:6a
MILLER, Henry, worker, Newark, NJ – 1901/09/27:1h
MILLER, Herman & Helen, NYC-M, +@ Genl Slocum – 1904/06/18:3c
MILLER, John, 17, SLP?, NYC-M – 1884/07/24:3d
MILLER, John, 22, NYC-M – 1892/06/28:4a
MILLER, John, 31, bookkeeper, NYC-M – 1896/08/14:1f
MILLER, John, 65, un. cigarmaker, NYC-M – 1909/11/02:6a
MILLER, John, un. carp., NYC-M – 1911/03/17:6a
MILLER, Joseph, 32, un. carp., Newark, NJ – 1905/02/13:4a
MILLER, Joseph, exec. Paterson, NJ – 1905/04/14:4b, done 15:1b
MILLER, Julia, 18, Jersey City, NJ – 1887/05/16:2d
MILLER, Julius, NYC-M – 1903/05/09:4a
MILLER, Katharina, 55, NYC-M – 1903/07/11:1f
MILLER, Konrad, 57, mason, NYC-M – 1885/06/02:1g
MILLER, Louis P., 26, NYC-B – 1902/09/12:4a
MILLER, Louis, 25, NYC-B – 1910/07/21:3a
MILLER, Louis, 55, Jersey City, NJ – 1884/08/14:3a
MILLER, Mannie, 90, NYC-B - 1915/12/27:2d
MILLER, Martha, b. Baltz, 75, NYC-B – 1905/09/11:4a
MILLER, Minna, b. Dobbert, NYC-Q – 1897/10/27:4a
MILLER, Moses, & family, Butler, NJ - 1917/12/04:2e
MILLER, Nicholas, worker, Newark, NJ – 1901/09/27:1h
MILLER, Oscar, 54, tailor, NYC-M – 1893/11/14:1e

MILLER, Otto, 70, shoedealer, NYC-M – 1913/03/11:3a
MILLER, Owen, 68, secy Am. Fed. of Musicians, + St Louis, MO - 1919/03/05:5f
MILLER, Rosalie, 56, Swiss?, NYC-M – 1904/12/22:4a
MILLER, Stephan, NYC-M – 1891/01/02:4a
MILLER, Stephan, NYC-M – 1901/07/09:4a
MILLER, Theodore, NYC-Bx – 1909/02/09:6a
MILLER, Theresia, 5, NYC-M – 1882/01/26:3c
MILLER, Wallace, Negro, lynched Cadiz, KY – 1909/08/11:1d
MILLER, William L., 40, trav. salesman, NYC-B – 1895/05/06:3d
MILLER, Yetta, 35, & Yetta, 7, Sarah, 9, Joseph, 14, Isaac, 12, NYC-M – 1904/09/05:1e, 6:2b
MILLHAUSER, Leo, 21, NYC-M – 1910/02/15:5e
MILLINKOVITZ, Ida, NYC-M - 1920/12/17:6a
MILLOECKER, Karl, composer, + Vienna/Austria – 1900/01/01:1b
MILLS, Geo. C., NYC-B, to be exec. 1885/02/21:1g, 1 Apr:2g, done 11:1e-f
MILLSTEIN, Stanley J., 19, exec. Sing Sing - 1916/12/20:1f
MILMIRE, Miles L., 63, Swede, carpenter, NYC-B – 1897/08/27:4b
MILNER, Bernard, SP, former worker for N.Y. Call, student at Syracuse U, + Syracuse, NY - 1917/01/31:2b
MILZ, George Joseph, 49, un. cabinet maker, Jersey City Heights, NJ – 1905/11/02:4a, 3:4a
MINESCHENK, Paula, 3, NYC-Q – 1910/02/17:6a
MINGO, JACK, Negro, lynched Eatonville, NJ – 1886/03/09:4c, 13 Apr:2d, 21:2d; notes 5 June 1888:1f
MINITELLO, Filipo, artist & printer at Messager Franco-Americain, NYC-M - 1879/06/18:1f
MINITZKI, Isaac, 109, born in Moscow, NYC-M – 1903/12/01:2f
MINK, Anna P., 19, NYC-M – 1910/08/22:6a, fam. 27:6a; 1910, mem. 1911/08/21:6a
MINK, Edward L., 49, Newark, NJ – 1911/07/11:1e
MINKE, Anton, baker, NYC-M - 1878/02/11:4b, 21:4e
MINKE, H., NYC-Bx – 1912/01/21:7b
MINKE, John, un. carp., NYC-M – 1903/02/28:4a
MINKNER, Ferdinand, NYC-B – 1910/08/03:6a
MINKUS, Caroline, NYC-M – 1912/03/14:6a
MINNER, Catherine, 56, NYC-B – 1885/05/30:2g
MINSKI, Hannah, NYC-Bx, + @ Genl Slocum – 1904/06/18:3c
MINTEN, George, 66, NYC-B – 1906/02/17:4a
MINTKE, Paul, grocery clerk, NYC-M – 1899/04/25:3g
MINTZ, J. J., Dr., 47, *Witebsk/Russia, USA 1891, SP, NYC-Bx – 1912/06/15:6d

MINZESHEIMER, L., 74, NYC-M – 1893/10/25:4a
MIQUEL, Johannes von, Dr., Prussian Finance Min. – 1901/09/09:1g, 20:2d-e, 24:2c
MIRECKI, Josef, Polish patriot, exec. Warsaw – 1908/11/03:4d
MIRON, J., captain of SS Saale, see 1900 dock fire, Hoboken, NJ 1900/07/02:1g
MIRTHES, William, NYC-M – 1905/05/20:4a, fam. 27:4b
MISKINSKI, Julia, servant, Woodcliffe, NJ - 1920/05/26:2b
MISKOVITZ, John, NYC-B - 1913/12/01:6a
MISPEL, Wilhelm, un. carp., NYC-M – 1904/05/11:4a
MISSBACH, Max, 52, NYC-M - 1919/08/04:6a
MISTERFELD, Gustav, Greenville, NJ - 1917/06/20:6a
MITCHELL, Charles, Negro, lynched Urbana, OH – 1897/06/05:1c, 7:2a-b, 10:1h
MITCHELL, James, silk manuf., Paterson,NJ - 1913/05/05:1f
MITCHELL, John P., NYC mayor - 1918/07/07:1e, 8:1f, 9:3f, 10:1f, 11:1d
MITCHELL, John, pres. Un. Mine Workers – 1919/09/10:1c, 11:4b,13:1e
MITSCH, Joseph, 72, at NYC farm in New Springville, NY - 1913/05/10:1e
MITSCHALK, Oswald, 60, SP, gold leaf beater, * Dresden/Saxony, East New York, NJ - 1917/01/02:6a, 07:7d
MITSCHERLING, Barbara, NYC-M – 1886/07/30:4d, 13 Aug:3a
MITSCHLE, Ernst, 23, baker, NYC-B – 1896/10/15:1e
MITTELBERG, Anna, NYC-M – 1890/08/22:4a
MITTELDORF, Friedrich, 59, locksmith, NYC-B – 1906/12/04:3c
MITTELSDORF, Mary, 75, NYC-B – 1911/08/24:3b
MITTELSTAEDT, Leopold, Dr., NYC-M – 1880/03/31:3a
MITTELSTAEDT, Paul, 56, carp., NYC-Bx - 1918/05/21:6a, = 23:3f, fam. 23:6a, mem. (Mittelstadt) 1919/05/18:12a
MITTELSTAEDT, Rudolph, NYC-M - 1895/11/09: 4a
MITTELSTEDT % Wetz
MITTENDORF, David, 12, NYC-B - 1918/07/24:6b
MITTENDORF, George, NYC-B – 1905/05/31:4c
MITTENDORF, Mollie, 40, NYC-B - 1920/06/01:5e
MITTENZWEIG, E., Jersey City Heights - 1919/04/08:6a
MITTERMAIER, Xaver, un brewer, NYC-M - 1918/09/10:6a
MITTERMUTH, Frances, 12, NYC-M, @1883 School Fire, NYC-M
MITTMEIER % Manke
MITZENHEIM, August, un. carp., NYC-M – 1882/07/24:3c
MIX, Albert, un. baker, NYC-M - 1920/11/27:8a
MLADEK, Joseph, 32, un. carp., NYC-M – 1896/10/04:5a
MLADEK, Theresa, NYC-M – 1901/08/25:5a
MOCK % Barrett

MOCKER, Xaver, NYC-Q - 1913/09/02:6a
MODER, Thomas, NYC-M - 1913/07/31:6a
MODJEWSKA, Helene, Polish actress, + Bay City, CA – 1909/04/09:2a
MODUSSKY, Anna, 30, fr Russia, NYC-B – 1900/10/11:3b
MOEBS, George, 59, painter, NYC-M – 1899/11/15:3b
MOEBUS, Adam, NYC-Bx – 1890/05/26:4a
MOECKEL, Adolphine, NYC-B – 1905/06/20:4a
MOECKEL, Hermann, NYC-B – 1909/10/17:7a, 19:6a
MOECKEL, Katherina, NYC-Bx – 1912/02/15:6a
MOECKEL, Lizzie, 17, NYC-B – 1900/07/24:4a
MOEGLING, Theodor's widow, + Wimpfen/Gy – 1903/04/09:2e
MOEHLE, William, 28, SLP?, NYC-M – 1892/10/04:4a
MOEHLIN, John, NYC-B – 1907/02/11:6a
MOEHLSTEIN, Anna, NYC-M - 1917/09/29:6a
MOEHN, George, un. typesetter, 42, NYC-M – 1890/05/04:5a, fam. 6:4a
MOEHRLE % Thern
MOELL, Edwin Emil, child, NYC-Bx – 1912/02/09:6a
MOELLENBROCK, Johann, un. cigar maker, NYC-M – 1883/03/13:3c
MOELLER % Fentsch
MOELLER, A. E., 66, Danish SP activist, lawyer – 1911/11/01:4d-e
MOELLER, Amenia, 44, Jersey City Heights, NJ – 1904/12/29:4a, 30:4a, fam. 5 Jan. 1905:4a, 6:4a
MOELLER, August, 50, NYC-B – 1908/01/30:3a
MOELLER, Elisabeth, 57, NYC-B – 1891/03/30:4a
MOELLER, Emil, 5, NYC-B – 1899/01/02:4a
MOELLER, Frieda, NYC – 1912/07/27:6a
MOELLER, Fritz, machinist, NYC-Q – 1906/06/11:4a
MOELLER, Heinrich, fr Schleswig-Holstein?, NYC-M – 1880/02/28:4f
MOELLER, Louise, 56, Jersey City, NJ - 1920/04/24:6a, fam. 28:6a
MOELLER, Martha, 35, NYC-M, + @Genl Slocum – 1904/06/18:3c
MOELLER, Minnie, 53, NYC-M - 1917/06/05:6a
MOELLER, Otto, 35, bookbinder,USA 1895,NYC-B - 1895/12/18:2d
MOELLER, Peter, 54, SP, goldsmith, fr Hanau, USA 1880s, Providence, RI - 1917/04/28:2b
MOELLER, Richard, NYC-M – 1891/04/06:4a
MOELLER, Theodor, 52, SLP, Springfield, MA – 1888/04/11:3b
MOELLER, Theodor, SP, Jersey City Heights, NJ, silver wedding – 1910/11/02:5e
MOELLER, William, Greenville, NJ – 1904/07/02:4a
MOENCH, Marie, b. Kaiser,Albany,+ Jersey City,NJ - 1879/04/26:4g
MOENKE, William, Bloomfield, NJ - 1915/05/03:6a

MOERIKE, Eduard, German poet, 100th anniv. Of birth NYC-M – 1904/09/25:12g-h
MOERSCHEN, August, un. cigarmaker, NYC-M – 1881/07/13:3c
MOERSHEIMER, Louis, 24, pharmacy clerk, fr Alzey/Rhine, USA 1875, NYC-M - 1879/02/08:4b
MOESCHLER, Emil, 49, jeweler, NYC-M – 1908/08/15:1f
MOESLEIN, John/Hans, NYC-M - 1914/09/09:6a, 10:6a
MOESLEIN, Katherina, 58, NYC-M – 1890/10/11:4a
MOESSLINGER % Strangfeld
MOETT, Henry, fr Tagkanic, NY, note – 1880/02/05:1b
MOETTES, Sebastian, un. carp., NYC-M – 1886/03/29:3b
MOGENHEIMER, William, NYC-Q - 1917/08/02:6a
MOGER % Korten
MOGER, William Henry, 58, merchant, NYC-B – 1900/12/26:2g-h
MOGK % Weigel
MOHLAM, Sophia, NYC-M – 1891/04/12:5a
MOHLE, Andrew, 45, barman, Union Hill, NJ – 1898/02/02:3d
MOHLLENHOFF, Johann A., 47, china store, * Bedehorn/Hannover, active G-A, co-fdr local Zoo, Cincinnati, OH – 1881/07/16:1c
MOHN, Franz, tailor, NYC-M – 1880/06/19:1e
MOHNHAUPT, Franz, 29, NYC-M – 1891/08/23:4a
MOHNKORN, Therese, b. Dummbach, 52, NYC-M – 1892/08/19:4a
MOHOJEWICH, Lazar, alias George Morris, innkeep & local politico, * Turkish Empire, exec. New Orleans – 1907/08/10:1d
MOHR % Lalewec
MOHR, (Mr), NYC-M – 1885/11/18:4c
MOHR, ..., homeless man, ~60, NYC-M – 1905/01/05:1f
MOHR, Annie, NYC-B – 1900/08/02:4a
MOHR, August, 1, NYC-M – 1891/07/05:5a
MOHR, Catherina, 22, servant, NYC-M – 1890/07/15:3a
MOHR, Catherina, 37, NYC-M – 1881/06/01:1g
MOHR, Charles, 56, NYC-B – 1886/01/06:5e
MOHR, Frank Dr., C., NYC & Providence, RI - 1915/09/02:1g, 3:2a, 5:1f, 6:1f, 30:6c
MOHR, Friedrich, 72, Prof. Dr., Bonn/Gy University - 1879/10/17:2e
MOHR, George, 50, janitor, NYC-B – 1901/12/10:4b
MOHR, Henry, NYC-B – 1896/05/21:4a
MOHR, Lorenz, brewer or cooper, NYC-M – 1902/11/13:4a
MOHR, Paul, saddle maker, NYC-B – 1908/06/10:3a
MOHR, Richard, 20, un. cigarmaker, NYC-M – 1882/08/09:3d
MOHRBACH, John G., 42, NYPD, NYC-B? – 1909/02/10:6a
MOHRBUTTER, Elsie E. Stoll, 23, Newark, NJ - 1915/09/15:6a

MOHRENBERG, Emil, 62, un. cigarmaker, NYC-M – 1906/06/12:4a
MOHRMANN, Frederica, 23, NYC – 1889/03/01:1c
MOJE, Otto, 30, stoker on steamer Cafagny, NYC-B - 1913/05/14:3b
MOLAS, Spanish anarchist, exec. Montjuich jail – 1897/05/22:2d
MOLDENSCHANDT, Max, un. cigarmkr, & wife, NYC-B – 1919/09/17:2b
MOLDT, H., Newark, NJ – 1910/08/27:6a
MOLETON, Elisabeth B., 18, servant, 11/1884 fr Gy, Hoboken, NJ – 1885/01/04:5d
MOLITAN, Margaret, Bronx Brewing Co, Mt Vernon, NY, + @on Genl Slocum – 1904/06/18:3c
MOLITOR % Engesser
MOLITOR, Eva, 8, NYC-B, + @on Genl Slocum – 1904/06/21:1f
MOLITOR, Marie, 34, librarian at Astor Library, Mt Vernon, NY, +@ Genl Slocum – 1904/06/17:1b, 18:1f, 3c
MOLKE % Jargosch/Metzler
MOLKE, Elise, 19, NYC-M, + @Genl Slocum – 1904/06/22:4a
MOLKE, Elizabeth, 30, NYC-M, +@Genl Slocum – 1904/06/22:1d
MOLKENBUER, Hermann., cigarmaker & SPD activist expelled fr Ottensen/Gy, NYC 1881/06/16:4a. USA 1881-93, + Germany – 1896/07/31:1e
MOLL % Wehmeyer
MOLLACK, Frank, un. baker, NYC-M – 1903/05/29:4a, 30:4a
MOLLAN, George, infant, NYC-B – 1890/07/02:4a
MOLLENHAUER, John, 56, shoemaker, NYC-B – 1898/04/03:1c
MOLLER, Catherine, 30, Edward & Edwin, 5, NYC-M, +@Genl Slocum – 1904/06/24:1d, 25:1d
MOLLER, Elise, NYC-Q – 1911/06/27:6a
MOLLER, Emma, 64, NYC-Q - 1919/01/30:6a
MOLLER, Jost, 87, NYC-B - 1894/01/23:4e
MOLLER, William, 56, treasurer Ferd. Muench brewery, Mt Vernon, NY - 1915/12/15:6b
MOLLINISS, Carl, 62, NYC-M - 1917/10/31:6a
MOLOSKY, Anna, servant, NYC-M – 1886/07/20:1e
MOLOSKY, John, 18, striking Standard Oil worker, Bayonne, NJ - 1915/07/22:1f, 23:4a
MOLOWSKY, Pavel, 50, mgr Sons of Israel Synaguoge, family in Slonim/Grodno, War 2, NYC-M - 1916/03/30:1a
MOLTEN, Frank H., travelling salesman, NYC-M – 1898/07/09:1g
MOLTKE, Helmut Graf von, + Berlin, crit. edit – 1891/04/25:1c
MOLTMANN, Catherine, b. Brendeke, 77,Yonkers, NY - 1920/09/07:6a
MOLZ, Philip, 32, un. carp., fr Hunsrueck? area/Gy, NYC-M – 1897/02/27:4a, fam. 6 Mr:4a
MONACH, Louis, 35, watchmaker, fr Paris, NYC-M – 1904/06/23:1g

MONARCH, Otto, NYPD, NYC-B – 1900/05/04:3b
MONATSBERGER, Fritz, innkeep, NYC-M – 1912/12/23:2e
MONATSBERGER, Katherina, b. Goetz, 48, NYC-M – 1907/11/15:6a
MONE, Mary, NYC-M – 1897/07/20:4a, 21:4a
MONE, Wilhelm, 50, un. carp., NYC-M – 1900/06/14:4a, 15:4a
MONECKER, Katherina, fr Gibsheim/Frankfurt, USA 1891, NYC – 1891/04/19:1d
MONGK, Catherina, b. Wohlfeil, NYC-B – 1891/04/14:4a
MONICH, Samuel, fr Feressen, Hungary, exec. Morristown, NJ – 1906/08/8:03d, 11:3c
MONOWITZ, David, 58, & wife, Paterson, NJ - 1918/01/13:11g
MONSCH, Emil, tailor, 28, NYC-M – 1891/06/16:4e
MONSEES, K., NYC-M – 1893/07/30:5a
MONSEES, Minnie, 39, NYC-M – 1890/07/10:4a
MONSEUR, Eugene, Prof., 52, Belgian Liberal – 1912/12/27:4f
MONTANUS, Peter, 38, tailor, NYC-B – 1887/08/25:2e
MONTEFIORE, Moses, Sir, Jewish philanthropist, 99th birthday – 1883/10/24:1d
MONTEMARTINI, Giovanni, Prof., Italian Socialist – 1913/07/23:4f
MONTEZ, Lola, born Eliza Gilbert, grave in NYC-B – 1902/02/03:3b
MONTWID, Bernar, barber & publ.Lithuanian NP, exec. Hartford, CT - 1915/08/07:2e
MOODY, Dwight L., Rev., 72, evangelist – 1899/12/23:1b, 26:2a
MOOK, Hannah, b. Worms, NYC-M – 1892/07/14:4a
MOONELIS, Emma, NYC-M – 1891/02/20:4a
MOORE, John, Negro, lynched near Hamilton, GA – 1912/01/24:1b
MORALES, Manuel, Spanish anarchist who tried to kill the king – 1906/06/04:1a,2a-b,=5:1b
MORAWSKI, Franz, SPD Kattowitz/Gy – 1906/07/10:4d, =13:4d
MOREN, Adam, SLP Activist, NYC? – 1910/02/08:5f
MORENZ, Bernhard, 60, NYC-M – 1903/09/26:4a
MORGAN, Charles, Negro, lynched Bluefields, W.Va – 1893/04/06:1g
MORGAN, Dudley, Negro, lynched Hallville, TX – 1902/05/23:1g
MORGAN, Edwin D., millionaire, posit. obit – 1883/02/15:2c
MORGAN, J. Pierpoint, 76, US capitalist, crit. obit – 1913/04/01:1c, 2a,4a, 3:6a, =15:2c
MORGAN, Thomas J., 65, machinist, then lawyer, SP, Chicago, IL – 1912/12/14c-d
MORGENROTH, Mattie, NYC-M – 1891/03/23:4a
MORGENSTEIN, Jacob, 50, NYC-M? - 1913/10/25:6d
MORGENSTERN, Blume, 25, NYC-M – 1901/04/03:3b

MORGENSTERN, Carl, 60, laborer, NYC-M - 1915/12/27:1f
MORGENSTERN, Dr., rightwing writer in Vienna – 1887/04/23:6b
MORGENSTERN, Israel, NYC-M – 1891/02/27:4a
MORGNER, Max, un. music engraver, NYC-M – 1898/07/24:5h
MORHART, Johann, co-fdr Greenville Free German School, SP, Jersey City, NJ – 1908/12/29:2d,6a
MORHENN, Karl, NYC-B – 1911/12/25:6a
MORIAN, Carl, 62, engineer, NYC-Q – 1902/02/16:5a, 17:4a, fam. 20:4a
MORIAN, Charles A., 21, soc.?, NYC-B – 1891/11/25:4a, 26:4a
MORIAN, Margarethe, b. Bernwelly, 80, NYC-B – 1885/07/29:3b
MORIAN, Rosa, b. Engel, 63, NYC-B – 1905/05/28:5a, 30:4a
MORIARTY, Daniel, ship captain, NYC-M – 1908/09/13:1e
MORIO, Mary, 14, NYC-M, +@Genl Slocum – 1904/06/22:1d
MORISSE, Swantzie, 74, NYC-M - 1920/01/20:8a
MORISSE, William, 71, NYC-M - 1919/06/27:6a
MORITZ % Wagner
MORITZ, Alexander, 39, SP Rochester, NY, *Hungary – 1913/01/25:5c
MORITZ, Charles, West Hoboken, NJ - 1918/02/02:6a
MORITZ, Francis, NYC-Bx – 1911/08/21:6a
MORITZ, George, 17, & Walter, 14, NYC-Bx – 1910/03/14:1e, 2e
MORITZ, Jacob, 45, NYC-B - 1894/01/31:4a
MORITZ, Karl, 62, un. cigarmaker, NYC-M - 1920/01/09:6a
MORKEN % Jaeger
MORNHINBERG, Joseph, NYC-M – 1900/09/12:4a
MORRATH, Elisa, NYC-M – 1882/09/25:3c
MORRIS, Catherine, NYC-M, + @on Genl Slocum – 1904/06/18:3c
MORRIS, Clara, Lady of the Night, NYC-M - 1879/01/03:4b
MORRIS, Edward Lyman, 43, curator Brooklyn Museum of Natural Science - 1913/09/15:1c
MORRIS, Estelle, 45, NYC-Q – 1912/05/30:5f
MORRIS, Frank, 18, exec. Uniontown, PA – 1896/09/02:1b
MORRIS, John E., 26, Homestead, PA, steelworker – 1892/07/08:1a
MORRIS, Sarah, 35, NYC – 1912/05/26:7d
MORRIS, Tom, Negro, lynched Redwood, LA – 1903/05/04:1b
MORRIS, William, English poet & socialist, #, + London – 1896/10/04:1a-c, 8 Nov:4c-e,7c-e
MORRISON, George C., banker, Baltimore, MD – 1912/09/18:3c-d
MORRISON, Robert, celluloid manuf., NYC-B – 1909/11/17:1d
MORRISSEY, John, NYS Senator, ex- prizefighter & congressman, + Troy, NY, sarc. obit - 1878/05/03:2b,4a, 5:2a-c. Will 1880/11/29:1e
MORRISSEY, Patrick Henry, ex-union leader who turned - 1916/11/30:4c
MORS, Eva, NYC-M – 1901/09/07:4a

MORS, Gustav, 57, SP, un. carp., NYC-Bx – 1906/09/13:6a, =14:6a
MORSBACH, Hermann, 61, SPD Solingen/Gy – 1910/05/08:3c
MORSE, Nathan S., 59, mgr Daily News, NYC-M – 1883/04/05:1d
MORSE, William, exec. Ossining, NY – 1910/01/04:1b
MORSECK, Joseph, fr Bohemia, painter, NYC-M – 1891/08/23:1f
MORTAN, Anna, NYC-Q – 1902/12/22:4a, 23:4a
MORTENSEN, Elsie, Jersey City Heights, NJ – 1905/10/19:4a
MORTIMER, John J., 34, SP, labor leader in Winnipeg/CN, + Pembina, Minnesota – 1908/12/27:20e
MORTON, James R., exec. Camden, NJ – 1892/08/27:2e
MORWITZ, Dr., publ. Philadelphia Demokrat, crit. Notes to his 70th birthday – 1885/06/12:2e
MOSBACH, Fr. J., NYC-M - 1916/06/30:6a
MOSBACH, H., NYC-M – 1881/07/17:5g
MOSBACHER, Meyer, 63, NYC-M – 1893/05/10:4a
MOSCHELES, Felix, 85, artist, + Turnbridge Wells, GB - 1917/12/25:1e
MOSE, Paul, 27, Austrian, NYC- SI– 1917/09/18:1d
MOSEBAUER, John, 64, NYC-B – 1891/07/07:4a
MOSECKER, Carl, un. carp., NYC-M – 1898/08/27:4a
MOSECKER, Charles, 27, NYC-B –– 1915/03/22:6a
MOSELEY, Judge, Negro, lynched Lockhardt, MS – 1911/11/08:1f
MOSER, Anna E., b. Freygang, 55, NYC-M – 1907/12/28:6a
MOSER, Anna Marie, 86, NYC-Richmond Hill - 1917/05/05:1e
MOSER, Carl, machinist, NYC-B – 1906/02/02:4a
MOSER, Edward, 55, NYC-M - 1917/05/05:1e
MOSER, Frederick C., 38, deputy sheriff, Newark, NJ - 1913/05/05:2d, 6:3d
MOSER, John, 70, '48er fr Suebia (Schwaben), Elgin, IL – 1890/11/05:4c
MOSER, Pauline, b. Schumacher, 57, NYC-B – 1891/04/01:4a
MOSER, William, 56, un. baker, NYC-B - 1917/01/30:6a, 31:6a
MOSES, Charles, innkeep, dying, NYC-M - 1914/04/03:2c
MOSES, Pauline, 43, NYC-M – 1893/07/20:1e
MOSKELEISEN, Solomon, 35, Jewish labor org. fr Minsk/Russia, NYC-M – 1903/02/11:1e
MOSKOWITZ, Morris, 27, musician at Empire State Theater, NYC-B – 1912/05/22:2a, 23:3c
MOSKOWITZ, Yetta, 25, & son Nathan, 1, NYC-M – 1908/10/22:2b
MOSLEY, Elmore, Negro, lynched Dispuntana, VA – 1904/01/16:1b
MOSS, comrade, 25th Wedding anniv., NYC-Q – 1911/11/12:9g
MOSS, Gerhard, sailor on USS Maine, + Havana/Cuba, NYC-B – 1898/02/18:1b
MOSS, H.C., Dr., Venice, IL - 1878/02/25:3b
MOSS, Tom, Negro, lynched Shelby County, TN – 1892/03/10:1b

MOSSBACH, P., un. mason, NYC-M – 1884/11/02:8a
MOST, Albert, 64, NYC-B – 1899/04/09:5b
MOST, Conrad, 54, NYC-B – 1892/08/30:4a
MOST, Johann, G-A anarchist, NYC, + Cincinatti, OH – 1906/03/18:1c-d, 19:1e, 2, 4a-b, funeral plans 21:1g, review 2 Apr:1c, 9:1b
MOSTLER, Gustav, 53, journalist for G-A newspapers in the MidWest, s. 1906 chief ed. Brauer Zeitung, * Aschersleben/Saxony, USA 1890, + Cincinatti, OH - 1917/04/12:2e
MOTT, Lucretia, 88, US abolitionist + Philadelphia – 1880/11/13:2c
MOTTELER, Julius, 69, SPD militant, MdR 1903-07, + Gy – 1907/10/10:4e-f
MOTTL, Felix, 55, ex-conductor NY Philharm., + Munich/Gy – 1911/07/03:2f, 6 Aug:3a
MOTTOLA, Italian Socialist, + Messina earthquake – 1909/02/23:4d
MOTZ, John, machinist, Newark, NJ – 1881/01/08:1d, 11:4d
MOTZ, Julius, un. carp., NYC-M – 1912/02/28:6a
MOTZ, Therese, & daughter Johanna, 18, dying, NYC-M – 1885/12/25:1f
MOTZEN, Elisa, NYC-M – 1891/04/09:4a
MOTZER, Marie, 73, NYC-B - 1915/03/30:6b
MOURAINE, Eugene, 3, NYC-M – 1887/07/18:3a
MUCK % Gray, % Juengert
MUCK, Friedrich, *07/18/1863 Schmalkalden/Gy, brassworker, SP, NYC-B – 1911/05/22:6a, 26:3a, fam. 26:6a
MUDD, Samuel A., Dr., the physician who treated John Wilkes Booth, + Bryantown, MD – 1883/01/19:2f
MUDE, Catherine, NYC-M, + @ Genl Slocum – 1904/06/17:3c
MUEGGE, J. H., NYC-M – 1885/03/28:3a
MUEHL % Petry
MUEHL, Christian, un. carp., NYC-B - 1914/06/10:2f
MUEHL, Karl, typesetter, SPD Berlin/Gy – 1908/07/26:3a
MUEHLBACH, Annie, 4, NYC-M – 1888/12/25:3a
MUEHLBACH, Karl, 46, enamel worker, NYC-M – 1904/03/06:1d
MUEHLBAUR, Franz, Jersey City, NJ – 1904/06/18:1c
MUEHLBERGER, Jacob, 47, NYC-M – 1880/05/28:1e
MUEHLE, F. W., 32, NYC-B – 1891/01/02:4a
MUEHLECK, Barbara, 33, SDP?, NYC-M – 1904/12/30:4a
MUEHLEISEN, Christian, 40, NYC-M – 1889/02/10:5b
MUEHLEMANN, R., NYC-B – 1911/07/28:6a
MUEHLENBRUCH, Meta, 42, NYC-M – 1893/12/29:4a
MUEHLFEITH, Franz, SDP?, NYC-M – 1904/12/22:4a
MUEHLFEITH, Herman, 57, NYC-M - 1915/01/22:6a, 23:6a, 24:7a, mem. 1916/01/20:6a

MUEHLFELD, Heinrich, Dr., 35, NYC-M – 1890/01/18:4a
MUEHLHAEUSER, Jean, NYC-M – 1907/04/22:6a
MUEHLHAUSER, Henriette, NYC-M – 1886/11/05:1e
MUEHLHAUSER, Susanne, 64, NYC-M – 1891/03/23:4a
MUEHLHEINRICH, Henry, un. cigarmaker, NYC-B – 1907/01/15:6a
MUEHLHEISER, C. Joseph, 78, NYC-M – 1892/08/21:5b
MUEHLING, Therese, NYC-Bx - 1918/11/03:12a
MUEHLRAD, Albert, 28, NYC-B – 1888/01/30:2h
MUEHSAM, Adolph, 55, sales agent, NYC-M – 1899/08/30:3e
MUELL, Auguste, 62, NYC-M - 1919/01/02:6a, 03:6a
MUELLENBACH, Andrew, West Hoboken, NJ - 1916/06/16:6a
MUELLENDER, Jakob, 48, NYC-M – 1893/07/03:4a
MUELLER % Bocke, % Bollin, % Eigner, % Hausmann, % Reiher, % Richter, % Schauble, % Schultz, % Storck
MUELLER, Adalbert, Jersey City, NJ - 1918/06/05:6a
MUELLER, Adam, 68, NYC-B – 1888/03/07:3c
MUELLER, Adele, 4, NYC-M – 1890/04/30:4a
MUELLER, Albert, 33, silk weaver, NYC-B – 1893/08/22:3b
MUELLER, Alexander, 77, surveyor, SPD Weimar/Thueringen – 1911/08/07:4d
MUELLER, Alfons, Dr., NYC-M – 1907/01/10:6a
MUELLER, Alwine, textile worker & SP Lodz/PL, exec. 1907, mem. by Clara Zetkin – 1910/06/26:20d-e
MUELLER, Amalie, b. Schoppe, NYC-B – 1891/10/18:5b
MUELLER, And., NYC-B – 1902/03/22:4a
MUELLER, Andreas, NYC-M – 1888/03/03:3a
MUELLER, Anna, b. Luther, fr Weida/Thueringen, NYC-Q, + Islip, NY – 1909/10/23:1e, 25:1e, hubby admits 26:1e-f, 27:2e, 28:1g, 30:1f;
MUELLER, Anna, b. Hein, NYC-B – 1899/11/06:4a
MUELLER, Anna, b. Stahl, NYC-Bx – 1907/03/02:6a
MUELLER, Anna, NYC-M – 1911/03/15:6a
MUELLER, Annie, NYC-M – 1899/09/26:1c, 27:3e
MUELLER, Arnold, NYC-M – 1912/07/05:6a, fam. 9:6a
MUELLER, Arthur, 54, NYC-B – 1903/07/30:4a
MUELLER, August Richard, un. carp., Union Hill, NJ - 1913/11/29:6a
MUELLER, August, 45, NYC-M – 1886/08/13:3b
MUELLER, August, 66, Haledon, NJ - 1912/10/19:6a
MUELLER, Auguste, Newark, NJ - 1915/12/07:6a
MUELLER, Bernhard, NYC-Q – 1910/10/24:6a, 25:6a
MUELLER, Bertha, b. Schoenholz, NYC-B - 1920/10/03:2a
MUELLER, Carl A., 50, superintendent Natl Sulphur Co., Bayonne, NJ - 1919/07/19:2d

MUELLER, Carl, 30, NYC-B – 1907/07/25:6a
MUELLER, Carl, 31, un. electrical worker, NYC-B – 1904/02/15:4a
MUELLER, Carl, 32, NYC-B – 1882/07/28:4d
MUELLER, Carl, 42, carp., Newark, NJ – 1912/11/12:3c
MUELLER, Carl, 49, un. carp., NYC-B – 1908/08/16:7a, 17:6a, fam. 20:6a
MUELLER, Carl, brewer/cooper, NYC-M – 1905/03/23:4a
MUELLER, Caroline, 55, NYC-SI – 1899/06/07:1e
MUELLER, Catharina, b. Goltz,71,Jersey City Heights, NJ - 1895/08/25: 5a
MUELLER, Ch. P., NYC-M - 1894/01/22:4a
MUELLER, Chr., NYC-B – 1900/01/06:4a
MUELLER, Christ, NYC-M – 1899/07/24:4a, 25:4a
MUELLER, Christian, 60, furrier, NYC-M – 1892/08/20:1h
MUELLER, Christian, 75, Homestead, NJ - 1916/10/07:6a
MUELLER, Christian, 80, Secaucus, NJ – 1890/04/12:2f
MUELLER, Christian, un. machinist, NYC-B – 1887/03/07:3c
MUELLER, Clara V., 29, NYC-B – 1912/11/21:6a
MUELLER, Clementine, 60, NYC-M - 1916/07/10:6a
MUELLER, Daniel, 64, fr Eisenach/Thueringen, NYC-Q – 1898/09/01:4a
MUELLER, Daniel's wife, 54, NYC-Q – 1887/11/14:3a
MUELLER, David, 82, Jersey City, NJ – 1891/06/29:4a
MUELLER, Dietrich, 52, NYC-M – 1907/11/27:6a
MUELLER, Dr., Vienna physician, =1898/11/05:2d
MUELLER, Eduard, 22, worker, Newark, NJ – 1888/02/06:2d
MUELLER, Eduard, 84, SPD Hamburg/Gy – 1910/02/24:4d
MUELLER, Edward, 42, NYC-Bx – 1908/09/06:7c
MUELLER, Edward, un. carp., NYC-M – 1890/05/18:5a
MUELLER, Elisa, 53, NYC-M – 1883/03/07:3c
MUELLER, Elisabeth, b. Ock, 23, NYC-M – 1892/04/02:4a
MUELLER, Elise, 59, NYC-M – 1892/06/28:4a
MUELLER, Elsie, 1.5, NYC-B – 1909/01/13:6a
MUELLER, Emil, 26, NYC-B – 1908/05/24:7b
MUELLER, Emil, un. machinist?, NYC-Q – 1906/01/09:4a
MUELLER, Emma A., NYC-M - 1916/06/16:6a
MUELLER, Emma, 1, NYC-Q – 1901/06/07:4a
MUELLER, Erhard, machinist, NYC-B – 1908/10/11:7c
MUELLER, Ernestine, 15, Newark, NJ – 1903/02/20:1c, =21:1c, 22:1d, 4b
MUELLER, Ernst, 10, NYC-Q – 1904/07/30:4a
MUELLER, Ernst, NYC-Q – 1912/01/20:6a
MUELLER, Eva, 45, fr Gamelsburg/Bavaria, NYC-M – 1889/02/12:4a
MUELLER, F.A., exec. by British as German agent in London - 1915/06/22:1f, 7 Jy:1d
MUELLER, Fidelis, 27, NYC-M – 1891/07/29:4a

MUELLER, Franz A., Dr., 45, NYC-M – 1888/05/17:3a
MUELLER, Franz, 57, New Haven, CT – 1912/08/23:6a, 25:6c, =25:7c
MUELLER, Franz, 72, Hoboken, NJ – 1898/09/15:3c, will 25:1e
MUELLER, Franz, NYC – 1912/11/14:6a
MUELLER, Franz,, 57, cigarmaker, SP,* Stettin/Gy, New Haven,CT – 1912/08/23:3c, 6a, 24:6a, =25:7c
MUELLER, Frederick, 17, NYC-B – 1904/01/22:4a
MUELLER, Frederick, NYC-M? – 1888/02/17:3b
MUELLER, Frederick, NYC-Q – 1904/06/04:4c
MUELLER, Friedrich D., 81, NYC-M - 1920/06/06:12a
MUELLER, Friedrich J., 32, NYC-M - 1919/04/18:6a
MUELLER, Friedrich, 12, NYC-M? – 1883/01/05:4c
MUELLER, Friedrich, 35, NYC-B – 1890/11/09:5b
MUELLER, Friedrich, 47, nickel-plater, NYC-M – 1881/03/26:1g
MUELLER, Friedrich, NYC-M – 1902/04/23:4a
MUELLER, Friedrich's wife, NYC-M – 1897/12/09:4a
MUELLER, G., NYC-M – 1907/07/09:6a
MUELLER, Geo., silk weaver, Paterson, NJ – 1893/02/14:4f
MUELLER, Georg William, 46, NYC-Bx - 1919/01/06:6a
MUELLER, Georg, SP, un. carp., NYC-B - 1915/03/29:6a,b,c, 30:6a, 31:6a, = 1 Apr:2d, fam. 4:11a; mem 1916/03/28:6a
MUELLER, Georg, SPD, Bockenheim/Frankfurt - 1879/11/10:2d
MUELLER, Georg, un. carp., NYC-M – 1908/11/27:6a
MUELLER, George, ~55, fr Elsass, USA 1857, Hoboken, NJ – 1880/05/15:4c
MUELLER, Gertrud, child, NYC-M – 1912/01/30:6a
MUELLER, Gottfried, 56, cigar maker, NYC-M – 1891/07/07:1f, 4a
MUELLER, Gottfried, NYC-M – 1902/07/07:4a
MUELLER, Gustav E., un. baker, NYC-Bx – 1913/01/04:6a
MUELLER, Gustav, 29, stevedore?, Hoboken, NJ – 1909/02/07:7e
MUELLER, Gustav, un. carp., NYC-M – 1902/07/17:4a
MUELLER, H.H., fr Schleswig?, Hoboken, NJ - 1879/08/07:3a
MUELLER, Heinrich, 35, NYC-M – 1888/06/07:3b
MUELLER, Heinrich, 37, un. carp., NYC-B – 1893/02/22:4a
MUELLER, Heinrich, 74, SP, * Saxony, in Gy at Chemnitz Freie Presse, Chicago, IL - 1914/04/17:2b
MUELLER, Heinrich, SPD Auerbach/Saxony, alderman, 70th birthday – 1912/07/30:4d
MUELLER, Heinrich, un. carp., NYC-M – 1906/06/11:4a
MUELLER, Heinrich, un. cigarmkr, fr Braunschweig?, NYC-M – 1901/10/07:4a, fam. 9:4a

MUELLER, Helen, 37, & daughter Helen, 7, NYC-M, +@ Genl Slocum – 1904/06/17:3b
MUELLER, Helene, b. Does, 76, NYC-M – 1904/03/29:4a
MUELLER, Henriette, b. Lueneburg, 43, NYC-M – 1899/06/22:4a
MUELLER, Henry A., 40, NYC-B – 1900/07/10:4a
MUELLER, Henry, 24, fr Muenchweiler/Gy, NYC-M – 1888/04/28:2h
MUELLER, Henry, 26, NYC-M – 1880/06/24:4e
MUELLER, Hermann A., NYC – 1896/10/19:4a, fam. 30:4a
MUELLER, Hermann, 67, merchant, & wife, 55, Garfield, NJ – 1913/03/25:2b
MUELLER, Hugo, Dr., 51, German actor, * Posen – 1881/08/07:4e
MUELLER, Ida, b. Werner, NYC-M – 1907/02/28:6a
MUELLER, Jacob, ?34, NYC-M – 1892/07/21:4a
MUELLER, Jacob, NYC-M – 1907/08/09:6a
MUELLER, Jacob, un. brewer, NYC-Bx – 1908/04/17:6a
MUELLER, Jacob, un. carp., NYC-Bx - 1916/04/23:7a
MUELLER, James, 35, machinist, Guttenberg, NJ – 1896/08/13:1h
MUELLER, Jean, NYC-M - 1916/11/26:11g
MUELLER, Johann, 38, SP Temesvar/Hung., carp. & mgr local Arbeiterheim, War 1 - 1915/06/13:3d-e
MUELLER, Johann Hermann, un. carp., NYC-M – 1892/03/19:4a
MUELLER, Johann, NYC-M - 1878/09/15:8b
MUELLER, Johanna, NYC-M – 1891/07/03:4a
MUELLER, John C., innkeep, NYC-M – 1891/02/14:2f
MUELLER, John C., NYC-M – 1892/03/03:1e
MUELLER, John Emil, un. carp., NYC-M – 1897/05/01:4a
MUELLER, John G.H. NYC-M - 1894/10/16:4a
MUELLER, John H., 78,cigarmaker, War 2,NYC-B - 1917/04/14:1c
MUELLER, John Melchior, carp., NYC-M – 1901/02/27:1b
MUELLER, John O., 60, Newark, NJ – 1911/11/11:2e
MUELLER, John, 2, NYC-M – 1889/09/28:4a
MUELLER, John, 22, bartender, NYC-B – 1889/01/19:1h
MUELLER, John, 36, un. baker, SDP, NYC-Bx – 1905/08/27:5b
MUELLER, John, 56, NYC-Q – 1906/01/20:4a
MUELLER, John, 68, un. typesetter, NYC-B – 1908/01/31:6a
MUELLER, John, Jersey City Heights, NJ - 1913/10/04:6a
MUELLER, John, machinist, NYC-M – 1902/01/04:4a
MUELLER, John, un. cigarmaker, NYC-Q - 1917/10/26:6a
MUELLER, Joseph, grocer, NYC-B – 1897/10/12:4f
MUELLER, Joseph, NYC-Q – 1918/02/27:6a
MUELLER, Julius, un. cigarmaker, NYC-M – 1907/03/08:6a
MUELLER, Julius,63, barge capt, Philadelphia,PA -1916/04/22:2b

MUELLER, Katherina Henr., child, NYC-M – 1888/05/10:3a
MUELLER, Lina, Newark, NJ - 1878/04/13:1f
MUELLER, Lina, NYC-M – 1890/07/13:5b, 14:4a, fam. 18:4a
MUELLER, Lizzie, 17, servant, NYC-SI – 1902/06/24:3b
MUELLER, Louis, un. carp., NYC-M – 1909/04/28:6a
MUELLER, Ludwig, 35, NYC-M – 1891/07/17:4a
MUELLER, M.B., NYC-M - 1894/01/10:4a
MUELLER, Magdalena, NYC-B – 1903/06/02:4a
MUELLER, Magdalene, 40, NYC-M – 1898/01/07:4a
MUELLER, Margaret Elsa, 9, Jersey City, NJ - 1913/11/04:6a
MUELLER, Margarethe, b. Rauh, 36, NYC-Bx – 1883/04/20:3c
MUELLER, Maria, 21, New Haven, CT – 1906/12/18:6a
MUELLER, Maria, b. Brandt, 64, NYC-M – 1892/10/28:4a
MUELLER, Marte? Marie?, NYC-M – 1892/06/10:4a
MUELLER, Martha, 22, NYC-M – 1899/11/25:4a
MUELLER, Mary, 32, NYC-B – 1902/05/18:5f
MUELLER, Matthias, 54, NYC-M – 1891/04/11:4a
MUELLER, Max E. O., NYC-B – 1907/04/20:6a
MUELLER, Max, 78, tailor & Zeppelin pioneer, +Vienna - 1920/06/17:4d
MUELLER, Max, ed. Paterson, NJ, Volksfreund – 1902/09/27:2f
MUELLER, Max, Orange, NJ - 1918/12/11:6a
MUELLER, Max's wife, East Haven, CT - 1916/06/25:7a
MUELLER, Meta, b. Grimm, NYC-Q - 1895/01/25:4a, 29:4a
MUELLER, Michael, 44, Civil War vet., NYC-B - 1878/11/14:4d
MUELLER, Michael, 90, turner, SPD Aschaffenburg/Bav., – 1899/11/15:2f
MUELLER, Michael, infant, NYC-M – 1882/07/29:4c
MUELLER, Michael, un. carp., NYC-B – 1892/12/27:4a
MUELLER, Oscar, machinist, NYC-M – 1892/05/08:5a
MUELLER, Oskar, un. silk embr.?, Swiss?, NYC-B – 1912/09/06:6a, 7:6a
MUELLER, Otto H., infant, NYC-M – 1892/08/08:4f
MUELLER, Otto, 44, NYC-B – 1909/07/01:6a, 4a, 2:6a, =5:2c, fam. 9:6a
MUELLER, Otto, NYC-M, SP, married Bertha Schmidt – 1912/12/08:9e
MUELLER, Paul, NYC-M – 1892/03/27:5d
MUELLER, Pauline, 72, NYC-B – 1919/12/02:8a
MUELLER, Peter, un. baker, NYC-M - 1895/12/11: 3a
MUELLER, Philip, ice dealer, War 2, NYC-M - 1917/07/13:2a
MUELLER, Phillipine, b. Braun, NYC-B – 1891/09/20:5f
MUELLER, Philomena "Minna," b. Schmidt, 34, *Katenheim/Gy,
  Hoboken, NJ, + by Martin Kankowsky – 1881/05/19:1e-f, 20:1e-f,
  21:1d-e, 23:1g, 24:4a, 25:1e, 26:4c, 27:4c, 2 Jy:1e, her will 30:4a, 31:5f;
  trial 5 Oct:4c, 6:1d-g, 7:1e-g,

MUELLER, Philomena 8:1e-g, 11:4a-d, 12:1d-e, 13:1e-f, 14:1g, 4a-c,
  15:1g, 4a-c, 18:1g, 4a-d, 19:1f-g, 20:4a-b, guilty 22:1g, 23:5c, 25:4d,
  ,26:1f, to + 6 Nov:5c, appeal 13:5f, 21:1e, 29:4d, 8 Dec:4d, 10:2g-3a,
  22:4c, 29:4c; 1 Jan. 1882:5d, 2:1e, 4:4c, 5:1f, 6:1f, Kankowsky exec.
  Hudson County Jail, NJ 7:1e-f, =12:3b, note 23:4d
MUELLER, Rebecca, 76, husb. + Apr 1917, NYC-B - 1918/01/08:3e
MUELLER, Richard Gustav, 3, NYC-M - 1900/10/09:4a
MUELLER, Robert, 58, weaver, alderman for SPD in Reichenbach/Saxony
  - 1901/11/28:2c
MUELLER, Robert, baker, NYC-B - 1890/07/25:4a, 26:4a
MUELLER, Rosa, 50, NYC-M - 1913/09/18:6a
MUELLER, Rosie, nanny, NYC-M - 1898/08/20:3e
MUELLER, Rudolf, fr Breslau/Gy, station. shop, NYC-M - 1879/08/27:1f
MUELLER, Samuel, 52, USA 1887, SP, NYC-M - 1907/01/30:2b
MUELLER, Sebastian, NYC-M - 1920/10/01:6a
MUELLER, Sophie, 63, NYC-B - 1912/10/17:6a
MUELLER, Theodor, 73, un. machinist, NYC-M - 1915/08/24:6a
MUELLER, Theodor, NYC-Q - 1904/12/11:5b
MUELLER, Thomas, 31, worker, NYC-B - 1882/04/02:5d
MUELLER, Thomas, NYC-M - 1892/07/10:5c
MUELLER, Valentin, 43, NYC-M - 1891/06/03:4a
MUELLER, Valesca, 29, NYC-M, +@ on Genl Slocum - 1904/06/17:3b
MUELLER, W. Max, Dr., prof. of Egyptology at U of Pennsylvania, *15
  May 1862 Gleissenberg/Gy, USA 1888, Philadelphia, PA -
  1919/07/14:2g, his will 19:2d
MUELLER, Wilhelm "Willie", child, NYC-M - 1896/03/01:5a
MUELLER, Wilhelm, 60, NYC-M - 1891/07/17:4a
MUELLER, Wilhelm, 72, NYC-Bx - 1911/03/03:6a
MUELLER, Wilhelm, child?, Jersey City Heights, NJ - 1904/06/12:5b
MUELLER, Wilhelm, un. woodworker, NYC-M - 1895/02/16:4a
MUELLER, Wilhelmine, NYC-Q - 1891/01/18:5a
MUELLER, William, 70, fr Rheinpfalz, cavalry officer in Gy, tailor here,
  NYC-M - 1905/03/07:4a
MUELLER, William, machinist, NYC-B - 1907/07/25:6a
MUELLER, William, un. pianomkr, NYC-M - 1892/11/07:4a, 8:4a
MUELLER, Barbara, NYC-M - 1894/03/26:1e, 10 Apr./3e
MUELLER-JAHNKE, Klara, poet & SPD, *5 Fb 1861 Belgard/Pommern, +
  Berlin - 1905/11/13:2e; mem. 1908/04/26:11a-b
MUELLNER, Johann, 67, SP activist in Vienna - 1908/02/09:3d-e
MUENCH % Helbok
MUENCH, Albert, NYC-M - 1915/01/09:6a

MUENCH, Ferdinand, 56, * near Heidelberg, brewery owner, NYC-M – 1890/06/03:4e
MUENCH, Frank, innkeep, NYC-M – 1883/12/20:1e
MUENCH, Friedrich, German liberal, USA 1834, + Herrmann, MO – 1881/12/18:4g
MUENCH, Katherina, b. Hoes, 37, NYC-B – 1909/01/16:6a
MUENCH, W., NYC-M – 1910/04/04:6a
MUENCHLER, Charles, 48, NYC-B – 1911/02/19:1a
MUENDEL, Philip, Guttenberg, NJ – 1891/11/28:4g
MUENKEL, Ludwig, NYC-B - 1914/11/07:6a
MUENKER, Henry H., machinist, SLP, *24 May 1834 Ferndorf/Siegen/Gy, USA 1859, NYC, + Comfort, TX – 1882/04/20:1g, =25:2d
MUENS, Friedericke, b. Reichboldt, NYC-M – 1887/06/25:3a
MUENSTER, Annie, b. Linze, 25, NYC-B – 1899/03/11:4a
MUENSTERBERG, A., Newark, NJ – 1905/10/20:4a
MUENSTERBERG, Hugo, Dr., Prof. Harvard U, *1 Jn 1863 Danzig/Gy, USA 1892, + Cambridge, MA. NYVZ lauds that though for one side (Germany) in capitalist civil war, promoted postwar reconciliation, which few bourgeois patriots on either side do – 1916/12/17:1e, 18:4d
MUENTER, Erich, Harvard prof., see his pseudonym Frank Holt
MUENTER, Leona, wife prof. Erich Muenter – 1906/04/28:1g, 1 May:1g,3:4a, 6:1d
MUENZER, Alma B., child, NYC? - 1917/10/02:6a, mem. 1918/09/29:6a
MUENZER, Hermann, 2, NYC-M – 1902/02/16:5a
MUENZING, John, NYC-M – 1892/07/03:5c
MUESSIG, Oscar, 51, un. carp., NYC-M – 1911/07/22:6a
MUESSLE, Edward, 73, NYC-Q – 1919/08/05:6a, 6:6a
MUESSLE, Sophie, 49, NYC-Q – 1903/11/08:5b
MUFFEL, Karl Jacob, 15, NYC-M - 1878/09/03:3a
MUHRING, Henry, 58, cigarmaker, NYC-M – 1898/09/15:1g
MULL, A's wife, NYC-M - 1919/01/02:6a
MULL, Hermann, 44, NYC-M - 1913/11/13:6a
MULLEN, Herbert, Paulboro, NJ, worker at Dupont Powder Works in Gibbstown, NJ - 1913/12/09:1b
MULLER, Edward, 10, NYC-M, +@Genl Slocum – 1904/06/22:1d
MULLER, Florence, NYC-M, + @ Genl Slocum – 1904/06/18:3c
MULLER, Fritz, un. baker, NYC-M - 1918/11/03:12a
MULLER, Irene, 5, NYC-M, + @ Genl Slocum – 1904/06/18:3c
MULLER, Jacob, 4, NYC-M, +@Genl Slocum – 1904/06/25:1d
MULLER, Martha, 35, NYC-M, +@ on Genl Slocum – 1904/06/17:3b
MULLER, Wilhelm, 49, Newtown, LI – 1902/08/08:4a
MULLERLEIB, Chr., baker, NYC-M - 1878/07/02:1f

MULLET, A. B., federal architect, notes on death 1890/10/23:2b
MULLIN, Joseph, NYC-M, exec. Ossining, NY – 1900/07/21:3b, 23:3c, 24:4c
MUMM, George, 60, NYC-M – 1891/03/25:4a
MUNCH, John M., 47, un. machinist, NYC - 1914/04/03:6a
MUND, August, SDP, Cherry Hill, NJ – 1903/05/23:4a, 24:1g, 5b, =25:3c
MUNDER, Ernst Heinrich, NYC-M – 1891/03/29:5a
MUNDHARDT, August, 5, NYC-M – 1880/01/12:1f
MUNDORF, Bernhard, un. tailor, NYC-M – 1890/03/30:5b
MUNDORFF, Friedrich Wilhelm, 21, NYC-M – 1906/07/27:2e
MUNDSCHENK, Friedrich Peter, 57, un. tailor, NYC-B – 1885/02/26:3d
MUNDT, Charles, machinist, NYC-M – 1892/12/18:5a
MUNDT, Emilie, 26, fr Gy, NYC-M - 1895/05/01:2d
MUNDT, Konrad, 17, NYC-B – 1890/04/16:4a
MUNDT, Martin, 28, businessman, NYC-M – 1892/06/27:4e, 28:1h, inquest 8 Jy:1f, note 11 Jan 1893:1e
MUNKEL, Valentin, 20, dying, NYC-M – 1887/08/11:1e
MUNSCHAUER, Felix, exec. Frederick, MD – 1881/11/12:1c
MUNTERBERG, Amalia, 50, War 2, NYC-B - 1917/08/03:5e
MUNTERICH, Johannes, NYC-M – 1904/02/10:4a
MUNZ, Albert, 30, & wife Bertha, NYC-B – 1898/08/16:1g
MUNZ, Gottfried, 40, butcher, Jersey City, NJ – 1910/12/13:2b
MUNZ, Rudolph, 59, secy investment co., Newark, NJ – 1909/06/17:3c
MURAT, Katharina, countess, 86, *Wiesbaden/Gy, +Palmer Lake, CO – 1910/04/16:4e-f
MURBACH, Adam, 33, un. tailor, NYC-M – 1883/08/30:3c
MURBACH, Henry, 65, NYC-M – 1897/06/26:1c
MURDACO, Nic, exec. Jersey City, NJ – 1906/01/26:3e, 27:3c, =30:3d
MURMANN, John, NYC-M – 1905/10/17:4a
MURPHY, Frank, 13, killed during strike, Buffalo, NY – 1913/04/10:1d
MURPHY, Franklin, 74, ret. NJ governor - 1920/02/25:2f
MURPHY, Joe, + during hunger strike for Irish freedom, (see McSweeney, Terence), - 1920/10/26:1a
MURPHY, Michael C., Tammany leader, NYC-M – 1903/03/05:3a, =9:1b
MURRAY, Martin, 26, Homestead, PA, steelworker – 1892/07/07:1b,2a
MURRY, Therese, b. Schiebl, NYC – 1912/10/01:6a
MURSKA, Elias, 29, painter, NYC-M – 1880/09/07:1g
MUSCHENHEIM, Christian, NYC-M – 1893/11/02:4c
MUSKAT, Jean, photographer & SPD Nuernberg/Gy – 1909/02/14:3a
MUSKOPF % Bauer
MUSS, Friedrich, Union Hill, NJ – 1883/02/10:3b
MUSSLO, William, un. carp., NYC-Q – 1909/01/24:7b

MUST, Charles, NYC-M – 1911/07/29:6a
MUSTAFA, Maestra, 83, conductor at Vatican & last Papal castrati – 1912/04/12:4f
MUTER, John, 68, silk weaver, Paterson, NJ – 1912/09/28:3d
MUTH, Adam, 49, un. cigarmaker, NYC-M – 1890/05/23:4a
MUTH, Annie Elizabeth, 62, NYC-M, + @ Genl Slocum – 1904/06/17:3c
MUTH, August, NYC-Q – 1908/07/26:7c
MUTH, Bertha, + 1909, mem. – 1910/09/15:6a
MUTH, Grace, 47, Jersey City, NJ - 1918/12/02:1e
MUTH, John, 59, NYC-B - 1913/12/11:6a, 12:6a
MUTH, Josephine,b. Meyer, 18, fr Aargau/Switz., NYC-M – 1887/03/22:2g
MUTH, Karoline, b. Stern, NYC-M – 1910/11/23:3a, 24:6a
MUTH, Lizzie, 11, Lena,8,NYC-M, @ Genl Slocum – 1904/06/21:1f, 22:1d
MUTH, Michael, 38, NYC-B - 1908/11/05:6a, fam. 9:6a, mem. 1909/11/02:6a
MUTH, Otto, NYC-Q – 1912/04/13:6a
MUTH, Philipp, NYC-Bx – 1910/06/28:6a
MUTKE, Hugo, un. baker, NYC-M – 1907/10/25:6a
MUTT, George, un. carp., NYC-Bx – 1912/06/04:6a
MUTT, Pauline, 26, chorus singer, NYC-M – 1905/07/14:4b
MUTTER, Leopold, 49, un. carp., NYC-B – 1902/05/04:5a
MUTZ, Franz, *Solingen/Gy, SLP Syracuse, NY, + Jersey City Heights, NJ – 1899/07/10:3d, 14:3d
MUTZ, William, West Hoboken, NJ – 1903/02/13:3b
MUZICK, Prokop, 22?, Czech, brass caster in Europe, cigar-maker here, NYC-M - 1878/12/05:1g, 6:1f
MUZZARELLI, Antoine Jules, French educ., NYC-M – 1908/10/16:1b
MYER, Albert J., US genl & chief signal officer, + Buffalo – 1880/08/25:1c
MYERS, Emma, 25, White mulatto, NYC-M – 1899/11/21:1h
MYERS, Yetta, 19, @1911 Triangle Shirtwaist Fire, NYC-M – 1911/03/30:1a
MYLORD, Anna, b. Harre, 54, Hoboken, NJ – 1908/08/31:6a, 1 Sep:6a
MYLORD, Ernest, 65, un. cigarm., W. Hoboken, NJ - 1917/12/27:2g,6a
NABOTTONY, Louis, NYC-M, +@ Genl Slocum – 1904/06/18:3c
NACHTIGAL, Gustav, Dr., German Africa explorer – 1885/05/06:1b
NACHTMANN, Martin, 50, realtor, NYS Assembly 1869-72, 1877, & president Bavarian VFV, NYC-M – 1886/12/09:4c
NACK, Auguste, NYC, see William Guldensuppe
NACO, Joseph, exec. Auburn, NY – 1911/06/09:6d, 13:3e-f
NADELSTONE, Alice, 13, worker, + in sweatshop fire, NYC-M – 1893/06/14:1e

NADER, Max, 26, machinist, Hoboken, NJ - 1916/02/17:2b
NAEF, George, Paterson, NJ – 1898/12/27:3c
NAEF, Walter, Orange, NJ - 1916/12/02:6a
NAEFNER % Feisel
NAEGELI, Albert, photographer, NYC-M – 1901/01/18:1e
NAEGELI, Henry, co-fdr Swiss Benevolent Soc., NYC-M – 1881/05/27:3b
NAEHER, Charles, 76, pres. German Sav. Bank, NYC-B – 1909/09/14:2a
NAGEL, August, East New York, NJ - 1920/11/23:6a
NAGEL, Charles, 44, NYNG unit manager, NYC-M – 1882/01/21:1f
NAGEL, Charles, 44, NYC-M – 1892/08/26:4a
NAGEL, Ellen, Irish, husband Henry fr Holzminden/Saxony, NYC-M - 1878/10/8:4b, 9:4c, 16:4b, 11/22:1g
NAGEL, Franz, brewer, Waterbury, CT – 1892/08/11:4a
NAGEL, Goetz's wife, 25, NYC-B - 1920/12/16:2d
NAGEL, Hermann, un. carp., NYC-M - 1917/01/16:6b
NAGEL, John, 73, SP,grocer, ex-pres. Soc. Coop. Publ. Co., * Riendorf/ Hannover, USA 1870, - 1918/03/28:1g,4a,6a, 29:6a, 30:6a, 31:1f,6a, = 1 Apr.:1g, fam. 2:6a, mem. 1919/03/27:6a, 1920/03/27:8a
NAGEL, John, un. carp., Yonkers, NY – 1912/08/10:6a
NAGEL, Josephine, 9, NYC-B – 1912/08/15:1d
NAGEL, Nettie, b. Nirmaier, 30, NYC-M - 1895/08/24: 4a
NAGELSCHMIDT, Simon, NYC-M – 1885/05/08:3e
NAGELSCHMIDT, Tilly, 25, NYC-B - 1917/07/21:5e
NAGLE, Mary, 80, NYC-M – 1893/09/07:1h
NAGLER, Adolf, 38, NYC-B – 1893/11/22:4a
NAGY, Damonkas, un. carp., NYC-M - 1916/01/29:6a
NAGY, Ladislaus, Elizabeth, NJ – 1907/01/27:7c
NAGY, Odon, un. carp., NYC-M - 1915/04/19:6a
NAGY, Stephan, 53?, *Pest/Hungary, NYC-M – 1891/06/17:4a
NAHL, Charles, German-born genre painter (Western life) and Turner, San Francisco, CA - 1878/03/19:2e
NALBACH, Emma, b. Caslow, 27, fr NYC-B, + Columbus, OH - 1916/02/24:6a
NALBACH, Malvine, 42, NYC-B – 1911/04/02:7b
NANNIG, Hermann, NYC-B – 1911/01/16:6a
NANSEN, Peter, writer, Swede, + notes on life 1918/10/13:9d
NAPHTAL, Joseph, 31, bicycle racer, NYC-Lexington Ave - 1916/05/22:1f
NAPOLEON, Louis, son of Napoleon III - 1879/06/20:1a, 2d, 21:1a, 2c-e
NAROVSKY, Gustav, NYC-M – 1903/01/30:4a
NASKO, Louis, NYC-M - 1919/02/02:6a
NASS, Fanny, 60, NYC-M – 1893/11/21:1d
NAST, Julia, 35, nurse, NYC-M – 1899/04/30:5b

NAST, Thomas, G-A cartoonist, + Ecuador, body to be brought to USA 1906/01/15:2c-d
NASTY, Adolph, un. carp., NYC-Bx – 1907/11/30:6a, fam. 8 Dec:7d, mem. 1908/11/28:7b
NATAJEWSKI % Schulz
NATANSON-BEBROF, Mark, Russian soc.,+ Bern/CH - 1919/08/21:4e
NATHAN % Saloneck
NATHAN, Alexander, 23, SP, NYC-Bx - 1917/05/28:1f
NATHAN, M., NYC-M – 1912/07/02:6a
NATHANSON, Morris, cantor, NYC-M – 1897/11/03:1h
NATZ, Hermann, wood carver, NYC-M – 1899/09/06:4c
NAUEN, Robert, worker & SPD militant in Berlin/Gy = 1887/02/14:4e; 25th anniv. of + 1912/02/12:4d
NAUL, Joseph, 51, NYC-B – 1897/07/10:4b
NAUMANN, Albert, NYC-Bx - 1917/12/04:6c
NAUMANN, Andreas, 75, un. carp., NYC-M – 1909/04/12:6a, 13:6a
NAUMANN, Emma Louise, b. Henschel, 37, SP, NYC-B – 1910/10/18:2b, 6a, =20:2b
NAUMANN, Friedrich, German liberal polit. – 1919/08/27:4d
NAUMANN, Fritz, SLP, NYC-M – 1890/11/27:4a
NAUMANN, Joseph Friedrich, liberal MdR - 1919/08/27:6b
NAUMANN, Margarethe, NYC-M – 1904/12/23:4a
NAUMANN, Robert, un. sheet metal worker, NYC-M, + Boston, MA – 1899/12/05:4a
NAUMER, John, city magistrate, NYC-B - 1917/12/06:2d
NAUMOW, Russian revol., exec. St Petersburg – 1907/09/28:4d-e
NAUSOLD, William, USA 1884 fr Gy, NYC-B – 1887/11/30:4d
NAVALZEK, John, 12, killed during strike in Milwaukee, WI – 1886/05/06:1d
NAVRETZKA, Anton, un. carp., NYC-B – 1893/03/17:4a
NEALIS, Elizabeth, NYC-M, +@ on Genl Slocum – 1904/06/18:3c
NEANDER, August A., druggist, NYC-M – 1904/07/10:1b
NEBEL % Kahl
NEBEL, Louis, 37, NYC-M - 1894/01/30:4c
NECKE, Daisy, 11, NYC-M, + @on Genl Slocum – 1904/06/17:3c
NECKERMANN % Klemenz
NECKERMANN, William, NYC-M – 1901/04/26:4a
NEEB % Koch
NEEBE, Oskar's wife, Chicago, = 1887/03/14:1g, 16 Apr:1b
NEEBE, Oskar, 66, only of 1886 Haymarket eight to be pardoned, after release labor org., * NYC, + Chicago - 1916/04/23:1b
NEEF, Julius, 61, NYC-B–1920/08/02:6a

NEEF, Margarethe, NYC-M – 1898/01/20:1d
NEES, Christian Gottfried, 1776-18??, early Socialist, member '48 Prussian diet – 1903/09/13:13g-h, 14a, 20:12c-e
NEES, John, brewer, NYC-M – 1905/11/08:4a
NEFF, Dina, b. Schipper, 33, wife of mgr of Workingmen's Benefit Fund camp, Fosterdale,NY - 1918/12/29:11b, 12a, = 4 Jan. 1919:5g,6a,
NEFF, Emma, NYC-M – 1902/11/06:4a, 7:4a, fam. 9:5a
NEGENDANK, August, 59, *Berlin/Gy, un. cigarmaker, SDP?, NYC-M – 1903/11/15:5a,f, =16:3b
NEGER, John, 38, NYC-B – 1893/04/02:5a
NEGLER, Gottfried, innkeep, NYC-M – 1888/09/19:1e
NEHER, William, NYC-B - 1914/12/12:6a
NEHRWEIN, Catherina, 52, teacher, Jersey City Heights, NJ, + Mt Holly, NJ – 1887/08/11:2f
NEIBERT, Friedrich W.K., 74, glass manuf., NYC-B–1916/10/13:3f
NEIDHARDT, Oscar, 56, druggist, NYC-B – 1910/05/31:3a
NEIDLAND, John, 40, baker, Long Branch, NJ – 1893/12/02:3b
NEIDLINGER, Frederick, 26, brewer, NYC-B – 1896/08/06:4b
NEIDT, Franz, *Memel/East Prussia, Gy, SPD Ilmenau/Thueringia & MdL – 1909/01/24:3e
NEIGHER, Handy, Negro, lynched Gaston, SC – 1893/08/01:1e
NEILSSON, Lilian Adelaide, English actress, 1880/08/22:4d
NEISNER, August, tailor, NYC – 1904/06/07:2f
NEISSER, Max, 68, ex-SPD, ed. Hamburg Fremdenblatt – 1913/01/09:4d
NEITZ % Merz
NEKERMAN, Julia, b. Heisterman, NYC-B – 1911/04/24:6a
NEKERMANN, Leonard, NYC-B– 1915/04/10:6a
NEKRASSOW, Nikolaj A., Russian poet – 1878/02/05:3g
NELIUS, Karl, West Newark, NJ– 1913/10/27:6a
NELLE, August, 4, NYC-M – 1893/02/17:4a
NELLE, August, 61, un. carp., NYC-Bx - 1915/02/09:6a, 10:6a
NELLE, Gottlieb, 58, NYC-Bx – 1909/11/06:6a
NELLE, Wilhelm, 6, NYC-M – 1893/02/10:4a
NELSON % Pulitzer
NELSON, Mary, & her 16 yr old son, Negroes, lynched Okenah, OK – 1911/05/26:2f
NELSON, Waldemar, NYC-M – 1891/10/14:4a
NELSON, William, NYC-M, exec. Ossining, NY – 1907/07/29:3d, 30:6c
NEMBACH, Bertha, NYC-M – 1911/04/25:6a
NEMECEK, Joseph, Newark, NJ - 1913/09/13:6a
NEMETT, Joseph, 65, veterinarian, 1848-49 Colonel in Hungarian army, 1861-65 adjutant of general Franz Sigel, + Chicago, IL – 1881/01/29:1c

NEMMER, Betty, b. Sons, Jersey City Heights, NJ – 1913/04/01:6a
NENKE, ..., nailsmith & SPD org. in Zittau/Saxony – 1885/12/24:6c
NENTSCHEL, Edward, NYC-M – 1881/06/18:4a
NEP, Albert, NYC-Q - 1913/09/19:6a
NEPPEL, Emil, 54, SP, * near Strassburg/Elsass, USA < 1885, Yonkers, NY – 1917/08/19:7a, 17d, =20:2b, fam. 26:6a, mem. 24 Sept:3e
NERBERER, Rebecca, 19, @1911 Triangle Shirtwaist Fire, NYC-M – 1911/03/27:1d
NERF, Barbara Graf, NYC-M - 1913/09/09:6a, 13:6a
NERTLINGER, Max, 63, Newark, NJ – 1906/08/01:2e
NES, Conrad, NYC-M – 1911/06/15:6a
NESKUS, Daniel, 56, sexton Luth. St Paul, NYC-M – 1898/02/28:1h
NESPOR, Louis, Czech?, tailor, NYC-M – 1896/05/12:1g
NESS, Christine, 50, NYC-M - 1916/04/13:2g
NESS, Julia, 42, NYC-B - 1913/12/18:3a
NESSLER, Philipp, un. carp., NYC-Bx – 1893/09/02:4a
NETHERLANDS, Frederick, King of – 1890/11/24:1h, 2c
NETTE % Tietz
NETTE, Heinrich, 59, NYC-M - 1895/08/16: 4a
NETTLER, Albert & Fred, NYC-M, +@ Genl Slocum – 1904/06/18:3c
NETZEL, Carl, 65, NYC-M – 1896/08/13:4a
NETZER, Josephine, NYC-M – 1887/02/19:3d
NEU, John, 60, NYC-M - 1920/03/04:6a
NEU, Margarethe, b. Benedum, NYC-B – 1888/06/09:3b
NEU, Nicholas, 55, un. driver, NYC-M – 1905/04/30:5a
NEUBAUER, Carl, 82, NYC-Q – 1900/08/18:2h
NEUBAUER, Gustav, bartender, NYC-B – 1900/08/05:1e
NEUBAUER, Joseph, 64, un. carp., USA 1878, SP, NYC-Bx – 1906/12/08:6a, 9:9c
NEUBER, Marie, 43, NYC-B – 1902/12/14:5a
NEUBERGER, Bertha, 50, NYC? – 1912/09/15:7e
NEUBERGER, Karl S., dry goods importer, NYC-M – 1897/08/10:1h
NEUBERN, Ottomar, artist & SPD Hamburg/Gy – 1908/03/29:3a
NEUBERT, F., 37, NYC-B – 1894/01/08:4a
NEUBERT, Hermann, 38, NYC-M – 1907/10/18:6a, fam. 20:7b
NEUBERT, Hermann, 67, NYC-Q – 1909/01/29:6a, fam. 3 May:6a
NEUBERT, Hermann, un. printer, NYC-B – 1918/11/07:6a, 28:6a
NEUBERT, Marie, 65, Dutch Kills, NY – 1908/12/01:6a
NEUBURG, Albert, 61, cooper, NYC-B – 1883/09/20:3a
NEUBURGER, Adolph, NYC-M – 1913/04/16:6a
NEUDERMANN, Morris, 30, student fr Rumania, NYC-M – 1904/05/19:2h
NEUDOERFER, Valentin, 42, un. cigarmaker, NYC-M – 1900/07/02:4a

NEUENDORFF, Adolph, composer & conductor, *13 June 1843 Hamburg/Gy, NYC-M – 1897/12/05:1f
NEUENSTEIN, Louise, 17, NYC-M – 1894/02/03:4a
NEUER, Babette, NYC-M – 1889/03/21:4a
NEUFELD, William, exec. Ossining, NY – 1901/01/15:2h
NEUFFER, Edmund, 52, SLP?, NYC-M - 1896/04/06:4a
NEUGASS, Solomon, 23, chemist, NYC-M – 1905/09/12:4a
NEUGEBAUER, John "Hans," un. carp., NYC-M - 1913/11/09:7b, =10:2d, fam. 12:6a
NEUGEBAUER, Rudolph, 44, + Topeka, KS – 1912/07/07:7a
NEUHAEUSER, Emil, Elis., NJ - 1920/04/13:6a
NEUHAUER, Mary, 30, Jersey City, NJ – 1896/08/12:3e
NEUHELLER, Albert, machinist, NYC-B – 1909/12/08:6a
NEUKAMB, Margaretha, b. Kohler, 64, fr Stapenbach/Bavaria, NYC-M - 1878/05/29:3b
NEULAND, Leopold, * 1827 Krakau/Poland, USA 1862, NYC-M – 1889/10/01:4d
NEUMAIER, John, NYC-M – 1906/10/27:6a
NEUMAN, Gustav, machinist, NYC-M – 1901/01/03:4a
NEUMANN % Ortland
NEUMANN, Adam, 52, German labor leader, + Hamburg - 1920/02/26:4f
NEUMANN, August, 23, NYC-M – 1884/07/06:5e
NEUMANN, August, NYC-Q – 1908/08/27:6a
NEUMANN, August, pianomaker, USA 1876, NYC-M - 1878/02/14:4d
NEUMANN, Carl F., 65, NYC-M – 1891/06/26:4a
NEUMANN, Carl, Union Hill, NJ - 1917/04/26:6a
NEUMANN, Catherine, 72, NYC-B – 1892/07/07:4a
NEUMANN, Eduard, 26, baker, fr Philadelphia, NYC-M - 1878/02/04:4d
NEUMANN, Franz, Newark, NJ – 1919/09/05:6a
NEUMANN, Friedrich, 81, & wife Justine, 76, Jersey City Heights, NJ – 1906/11/27:3d
NEUMANN, Gabriel, 25, tailor, USA Jan. 1880?, dying, NYC-M – 1880/03/26:4a
NEUMANN, H.J., innkeep, NYC-M – 1892/12/14:1g
NEUMANN, Henry, 50, innkeep, Hoboken, NJ – 1904/07/08:3d
NEUMANN, Henry, 65, un. woodcarver, NYC-M - 1895/03/21:4a
NEUMANN, Hermann, Jersey City, NJ - 1914/01/14:6a
NEUMANN, Jacob, 70, NYC-B – 1911/10/24:3a
NEUMANN, Julius, NYC-B - 1917/02/09:6a
NEUMANN, Karl, pianomaker & SP, ex-NYC, his new life in San Francisco, CA – 1911/09/04:1g
NEUMANN, Lena, 67, NYC-M - 1916/07/03:6a

NEUMANN, Louis, 45, b. Bavaria, ed. At NYSZ, then N.Y. Tagesnachrichten – 1892/12/06:1c
NEUMANN, Max Paul, 30, NYC-B - 1918/10/16:6a
NEUMANN, Otto, worker, Newark, NJ – 1901/09/27:1h
NEUMANN, P.F.H., 54, NYC-M - 1894/01/13:4a
NEUMANN, Siegfried, Dr., veterinarian,Newark,NJ - 1879/03/01:4e
NEUMANN, William, NYC-Q - 1914 /11/28:6a
NEUMAYER, Caroline, NYC - 1914/04/21:2f
NEUMAYER, Jeanette, 38, NYC-M – 1906/08/14:3e
NEUMEISTER, Friedericke, NYC-M - 1896/02/08:4a
NEUMUELLER, Theodor, NYC-M – 1885/05/06:1e-f
NEUNER, Anton, 27, NYC-B – 1887/05/24:3c
NEUNER, Ludwig, un. tailor, NYC-M – 1905/03/16:4a
NEUPERT, John G. "Hans",48, un. butcher,NYC-M - 1919/05/06:6a
NEURATH % Fuchs; NEUSCHAEFER % Keil
NEURESEK, Joseph, 66, innkeep, Newark, NJ - 1913/09/12:2f
NEUSCH, Charles, 30, innkeep, NYC-Q – 1910/12/18:11a
NEUSCH, Ignatz, un. brewer, NYC-B – 1909/04/11:7b
NEUSCH, Victor, un. carp., NYC-B – 1912/04/20:6a
NEUSCHAFFER, Henry, 50+, candymaker, NYC-M – 1903/06/03:2f
NEUSCHBONDER, Adam, woodcarver, NYC-B – 1891/07/29:4d
NEUSTADT, Samuel A., insurance agent, NYC-M – 1906/08/17:3d
NEUWIRTH, Anton, un. silkweaver, NYC-M – 1893/01/15:5c
NEUZUCKER, Nathan, 63, NYC-M – 1880/01/14:4d
NEVE, Johann Christian, German anarchist, became mad in jail 1890/11/04:2b, + in jail – 1896/12/30:1h,3e, Mem. in NYC 6 Jan 1897:3d, 9:2d
NEVEN, Amalie, b. Biehler, 55, NYC-B /03/20:6a
NEVEN, Eduard, NYC-B - 1914/04/04:6a
NEWALD, Eugen, 48, journalist for G-A media, * Wiener-Neustadt/Austria – 1913/02/04:2a
NEWBRAND, Isidor, Yonkers, NY – 1907/04/23:6a
NEWMAN, George D., diamond cutter at Tiffany's, & wife, New Rochelle - 1913/11/18:1f
NEWMAN, Ignatz, NYC-M – 1892/06/21:4a
NEWMAN, Mary, 34, NYC-B – 1896/04/15:4b
NEWMAN, Moses, Jersey City, NJ – 1886/11/30.2e
NEWMAN, Otto, SLP, NYC-B - 1894/02/14:4a
NEWMAN, Robert Layton, artist, NYC-M – 1912/04/01:2e
NEWMANN, Malke, 32, NYC-M – 1892/08/14:5c
NEWMEISTER, Henry, 56, watchman, NYC-M - 1895/02/01:3d
NEWTON, Ella, 1892/12/09:1d, 7:4c, 11:5c

NEWTON, R. B., counsel of "Boss" McKane, of Coney Island, NYC-B – 1902/05/15:4b
NEYLON, Margaret, 24, servant, NYC-SI - 1918/08/17:2a
NICELAY, Richard F., 50, West New York, NJ - 1913/10/27:6a
NICHOLAS, Charles, 70, NYC-B – 1905/03/24:4a
NICHOLAS, Czar of Russia, - 1919/03/08:4e-f
NICHOLS, Alfred Bull, prof. of German at Simmonds College, missing 9/9, body fd - 1913/11/29:1b
NICHOLSON % Zimmermann; NICKEL % Heim, % Marx
NICKEL, Christian, 47, NYC-M – 1882/10/20:3c
NICKEL, Gottlieb, NYC-M - 1918/12/07:6a
NICKEL, Louis, 51, un. machinist, NYC-M – 1901/08/13:4a, 14:4a fam. 18:5a
NICKELWEIT, John, un.cabinet maker, SLP,NYC-M - 1894/09/13:4a
NICKENDAI, Franz, un. baker, Jersey City,NJ - 1917/10/10:6a,
NICKL, Joseph, NYC-Q – 1908/11/28:7b
NICKSON, Gustav, ~30, cigarmaker, NYC-M – 1887/01/24:3b
NICLAUS, Veronica, 74, NYC-B - 1916/11/06:6a
NICOLAI % Andres
NICOLAI, Henry, 65, un. polisher & buffer, Elizabeth, NJ - 1916/08/07:6a
NICOLAI, Katherine, 78, Hoboken, NJ – 1910/12/19:6a
NICOLASEN, Hermann, 43, NYC-Elmhurst - 1917/10/10:6a
NICOLAUS, Jan, shoe cobbler, NYC-M – 1905/04/18:4c
NICOLAY, Peter, 49, un. carpenter, NYC-M - 1894/08/18:4a
NIEBERG, Friedrich, 73, NYC-B – 1891/09/06:5a
NIED, E., SP Newark, NJ, 25th wedding anniv. 1910/10/02:9e-f
NIEDERLAENDER, John, Yonkers, NY – 1911/06/21:6a
NIEDERMANN, August, un. carp., NYC-M – 1903/08/20:4a
NIEDERMANN, Mrs, Hoboken, NJ – 1890/07/05:2e
NIEDERMAYER, Georg, or Niedermeyer?, NYC – 1912/01/24:6a
NIEDERMEYER, Peter, Chicago gangster, exec. Chicago, IL – 1904/04/23:1g
NIEDERSTEIN, Apolonia, b. Bauer, 64, NYC-Q – 1904/10/14:4a, 15:4a, fam. 19:4a
NIEDERSTEIN, John, Sr., 69, * Bonn/Gy, USA 1866, NYC-Q – 1905/01/31:4a, 1 Feb:3e,4a
NIEDORF, A., Newark, NJ – 1908/10/09:6a
NIEHAUS % Flanagan
NIEHAUS, August, contractor, Ridgefield Park, NJ? – 1911/07/26:3b, 29:2c?
NIEHUS, Joseph, un. carp., NYC-M - 1917/01/17:6a
NIEKE, August, NYC-M – 1908/04/22:6a

NIELE, Ferdinand, 65, NYC – 1913/01/08:6a
NIELSCH, E. O., Hoboken, NJ – 1912/08/30:6a
NIELSEN, H., fr Schleswig?, NYC-M – 1885/01/11:5f
NIELSEN, Lars Peter, Winfield, LI – 1908/10/15:6a
NIELSEN, Olivia, Danish SP, + Aarhus/DK – 1910/07/28:4d
NIEMANN, Carl, NYC-B – 1898/12/18:4a
NIEMANN, Dora, b. Kropp, NYC-M – 1889/11/12:4a
NIEMANN, Elisabeth, b. Velte, NYC-M – 1892/08/11:4a
NIEMANN, Hedwig, b. Raabe, 60, German actress, + Berlin – 1905/04/23:5a
NIEMANN, Heinrich, 64, SPD Hamburg/Gy – 1899/10/04:2e, 22:12d
NIEMANN, Louis, 39, NYC-M – 1900/02/24:4a, 26:4
NIEMANN, Wilhelm, un. cigarmaker, NYC – 1903/09/26:4a, 27:5a
NIEMEIER, Minnie, 29, NYC-M – 1895/09/04: 4a
NIEMEYER, Friedrich, un. carp., NYC-M – 1904/03/13:5d
NIEMEYER, Fritz, NYC-M – 1897/07/17:4a
NIENDORF, Robert, 63, carp., NYC-M – 1898/02/02:1g
NIENSTEDT, Minna, 49, & nephew Francis, infant, NYC-B – 1906/12/05:3a
NIEPER, Kate, 26, NYC-B – 1887/07/02:3a, =4:2d
NIER, John T., NYC-M – 1905/12/13:4a
NIES % Armbruster
NIETZEL, John, 41, mgr Crocker-Wheeler Co, East Orange, NJ – 1908/07/10:3c
NIETZSCHE, Friedrich, German philosopher, notes by A. Wildmann, St Louis – 1899/12/10:4c-d, + 1900/08/26:1f, 27:2b-c, 30:4c-e
NIEWENHUS, Ferdinand Domela, Dutch soc. – 1919/12/10:4e-f
NIGHTINGALE, Florence, 92, British humanitarian – 1910/09/04:20c-d
NIGLUTSCH, John, ex-NYS Assembly, NYC? – 1887/11/08:1g, 10:2d, 4e
NIKISOROW, Wladimir, 22, Russian patriot, + Tagansk Prison in Moscow – 1903/12/12:2d
NIKITENKO, Russian revol., exec. St Petersburg – 1907/09/28:4d-e
NIKLAS, Joseph, 19, NYC-B – 1907/06/16:7a
NIKOLAUS, Johann, 39, brewer?, NYC-B – 1888/07/13:3c
NIKON, Cardinal, Orthodox Cardinal of Georgia/Russia, killed by revl. – 1908/06/11:1a
NIKONOROWNA, Marina, Russia revol., + Paris, her = 1898/11/28:2d
NILES, Kossuth, 65, US admiral - 1913/12/07:1c
NILL, John, un. bricklayer, NYC-Q – 1901/03/29:4a, 30:4a
NIMPSCH, Helene, NYC-B – 1906/12/06:6a, fam. 10:6a
NIPPERT, Wilhelmine, b. Thiel, 64?, Valhalla, NY – 1907/06/17:6a, 18:6a
NIRMAIER % Nagel

NISHKOSKI, Andrew, coal-miner, see 1897 Hazleton Massacre
NISS, William, Newark, NJ – 1881/04/13:1f
NISSEN, John, 57, NYC-B – 1912/10/03:6a
NISSEN, Oskar, Dr., 68, SP Norway – 1911/01/25:4e
NITSCHE, Eduard, Newark, NJ - 1918/01/24:6a
NITSCHKE, E's wife, 63, NYC-Bx - 1914/05/14:6a
NITSCHKE, Ferdinand, 70, night guard, NYC-M – 1898/05/28:1g
NITTINGER, Benjamin, tech. drawer, Newark, NJ – 1909/07/27:2e, 28:3c
NITZEL, John, un. carp., NYC-M – 1898/03/06:5d
NITZSCHE, Friedrich Ferdinand, machinist, NYC-B – 1892/03/12:4a
NITZSCHE, Oswald, NYC-B – 1899/09/14:4a, 15:4a
NOBILING, Karl, Dr., exec. Berlin for attempt on William I - 1878/ 09/11: 1a, 13:1a; nephew persec. 8 Oct 1899:12g, sister + 24 My 1903:1b
NOCHTRIEB, Charles, un. baker, NYC-M – 1919/11/04:6a
NODDENBAUM, Herman, 53, West Hoboken, NJ – 1912/01/17:6a
NOE, Giovanni, Italian Socialist, + Messina earthquake – 1909/02/23:4d
NOEHRING, William, 35, bird dealer, NYC-B – 1904/07/11:1h
NOELDECHEN, A., NYC-B - 1915/12/11:6a
NOELLE, Caroline, NYC-M – 1892/07/12:4a
NOELTE, Charles, Newark, NJ, + Trenton, NJ– 1901/12/31:3b
NOERKEL, Alex, 22, butcher, NYC-M – 1890/02/15:1c
NOGUES, Spanish anarchist, exec. Montjuich jail – 1897/05/22:2d
NOLAN, James, exec. NYC-M – 1889/07/24:1h, done 23 Aug:4e, 24:2e
NOLAN, James, IWW martyr, + Sacramento, CA, jail – 1919/08/21:2b-c
NOLL, Andreas, NYC-Bx - 1915/10/22:6a
NOLL, G., NYC-M – 1911/08/08:6a
NOLL, Katie, 40, NYC-M, +@Genl Slocum – 1904/06/17:3c, 22:1d
NOLLE, Julius, 28, pianomaker, NYC-Q – 1891/01/23:2e
NOLTE, Georg, SP?, Newark, NJ - 1914/04/21:6a
NOLTE, William, Newark, NJ – 1883/08/25:3a
NOLTEN, Marianne, b. Bayer, NYC-B - 1878/08/28:1e, 29:3a
NOLTING, Charles, 43, NYC-B – 1906/07/20:3a
NONNE, Elizabeth, 47, NYC-M - 1917/07/29:7a
NONNENBACHER, Bertha, 68, NYC-M – 1912/07/11:1d
NONNENMACHER, Ferdinand, un. carp., NYC-Q – 1916/06/18:7a
NOPPER, Elise, b. Hofer, 43, NYC-B – 1892/04/17:5c
NORCROSS, Henry L., tried to kill @Russell Sage – 1892/03/12:4d
NORDBRUCH, E. M., b. Boettcher, NYC-M – 1890/04/06:5a, 7:4a
NORDBRUCH, Ludwig, 59, Lyndhurst, NJ - 1919/03/20:6a
NORDEN, Leon, 52, wine dealer, NYC – 1912/10/15:2a
NORMANN, Julius, 43, NYC-M – 1892/07/13:2f, 14:4a
NORMILE, Dennis, 35, NYC-M – 1886/07/01:4c

NORWIG, Louise, b. Kasolke, NYC-M – 1893/06/09:4a
NOSSER, Louis, 40, Tenderloin "sport," NYC-M – 1906/03/16:1g
NOTH, August, NYC-Bx – 1912/03/16:6a
NOTH, Frank, Newark, NJ – 1912/03/16:6a
NOTHDURFT, Gottlieb, 52, NYC-B - 1917/06/19:6a
NOTHSCHAFT, George, 30, painter, NYC-Corona – 1904/06/26:5g
NOTLING, Hermann, 45, tailor, NYC-M - 1918/07/25:1b
NOTTENBERG, Esther, 45, NYC – 1903/10/13:1d
NOTZ, Eldridge, 22, musician, NYC-SI – 1904/05/06:2h
NOTZINGER, Lucien, exec. Gainesville, TX – 1880/05/03:1c
NOVAK, Johann, Slovak, USA 1882, + Jersey City, NJ – 1882/11/08:3a
NOVAK, Mathias, un. carp., NYC-M – 1908/08/13:6a
NOVAKOVSKI, Leon, Bayonne, NJ – 1910/10/07:6a
NOVESKY, Franziska, 26, NYC-M - 1918/10/20:12a
NOVISKI, Joseph, un. carp., NYC-Bx – 1905/05/14:6a
NOVOTNY, Alex, un. painter, NYC? - 1915/05/13:6a
NOVOTNY, Hermann, un. butcher, NYC-M - 1913/12/31:6a
NOWARRA % Stehr
NOWOTNY, Franz, 39, NYC-M – 1885/05/27:3b
NOWOTNY, Kate, 51, NYC-M - 1914/09/08:6a
NOZER, Carl, 59, Newark, NJ – 1904/01/19:4a
NUBER, Caroline, b. Link, 43, West Hoboken, NJ - 1919/01/13:6a
NUCHESS, Edward, salesman, NYC-B - 1916/07/20:5f
NUCHLITZ, John, 52, laborer, NYC-B – 1906/12/05:3a
NUERNBURG, Mary, candy store, NYC-B - 1896/01/05:1h
NUESKE, Dora, b. Becker, NYC-B – 1909/06/24:6a
NUESSLEIN, Bernhard, NYC-M – 1910/11/26:6a
NUGENT, Michael J., NYPD - 1914/10/17:6c, 21:2e
NUNAMANN, Louis, 4, NYC-SI – 1912/08/23:1d
NUNCIC, Anton, NYC-M – 1911/05/01:6a
NUNCLE, Arthur, NYC-M, + @ Genl Slocum – 1904/06/17:3c
NUNEMANN, Charles, 32, liquor salesman, NYC-M – 1896/06/14:1h
NUNGESSER, August, NYC-M – 1889/03/11:4a
NUNGESSER, B., NYC-B – 1902/10/29:4a
NUNGESSER, Emma, b. Sennerwald, NYC-M – 1889/05/24:4a
NUSBAUM, Katharina, b. Meyer, NYC-M – 1902/02/13:4a, fam. 17:4a
NUSBAUM, Mathias, 70, NYC-M - 1920/02/14:6a
NUSBAUM, Mathilda E., NYC-Bx – 1908/06/13:6a
NUSBAUM, Rosa, 45, NYC-M – 1892/06/24:4a
NUSBAUM, Wilhelm, un. carp., NYC-M – 1903/12/18:4a
NUSS, John, un. carp., NYC-Q – 1910/12/18:7a
NUSS, Leonard, Jersey City Heights, NJ – 1906/05/05:4a

NUSSBAUM, Constantin, weaver?, Irvington, NJ - 1913/09/11:6a
NUSSBAUM, Franz, NYC-M – 1909/02/06:6a
NUSSBAUM, George, un. carp., NYC-Bx – 1910/11/17:6a
NUSSBAUM, Heinrich, NYC-M – 1891/07/16:4a
NUSSBAUM, Sadie, 18,@1911 Triangle Shirtwaist Fire, NYC-M – 1911/03/27:1d
NUSSBICKEL, Wilhelm, 54, NYC-M – 1893/07/13:4a
NYSTROM, Carl H., 57, Swede, machinist, Yonkers, NY-1913/06/30:1f
O'BRIEN, James, 25, fr Baltimore, exec. Lancaster, PA – 1905/06/30:3g
O'BRIEN, Joseph, writer & IWW member, NYC-M - 1915/10/29:2e
O'BRIEN, Larry, sport & local politician, NYC-M – 1887/02/03:2e
O'BRIEN, Michael, innkeep & Tammany Hall, NYC-M – 1906/05/07:1d
O'CONNELL, W. M., Victor, CO, marshall, was fair to strikers – 1904/08/08:1c
O'DONNELL, Patrick, Irish patriot, to be exec. London, mass-meeting in NYC protests 1883/11/24:2g, 1 Dec:1a, 2:1a, 5:1f, 10:1a, 15:2a, 17:1a, exec. done 18:1a-b, edit. "Wie Helden sterben" How heroes die 18:2a
O'DONOVAN, William, Irish patriot, NYC-M – 1886/05/05:2a
O'HANRAHAN, Michael, Irish patriot, exec. Dublin - 1916/05/06:1c
O'NEILL, Tom, Negro, lynched Meridien, MS – 1910/04/14:3b
O'SULLIVAN, Thomas, NYC judge, – 1913/07/30:2c
OAKLEY, Patrick Napoleon, 42, alderman, NYC-M – 1891/03/26:4c
OBACH, George, 39, butcher, NYC-Q – 1908/10/29:2d
OBENHAUSER, Frederick, pocketbook maker, NYC-B – 1906/12/26:3a
OBER, Frederick A., archaeologist, 65, Hackensack,NJ - 1913/06/02:3a-b
OBERBAUER, Gabriele, 29, USA 1863?, NYC-M – 1890/01/02:1g
OBERDORF % Weidner
OBERDORFER, Albert, NYC-Bx – 1905/12/27:4a
OBERDORFF, Josiah, 59, musician, York, PA – 1911/01/09:2d
OBERENDER, Wilhelm, NYC-M – 1891/04/05:5a
OBERGSELL, Johann, NYC-M – 1891/03/11:4a
OBERGSOELL % Gerhardt
OBERHOFER, John, NYC-M – 1909/04/22:6a
OBERKRIESER, Beatrice, b. Bavra, NYC-M – 1892/09/03:4a
OBERKRIESER, Milada, 3, NYC-M – 1887/06/14:3d
OBERLE, Andrew, 50, NYC-B – 1887/08/04:1f
OBERLE, Mathias, NYC-M - 1917/09/03:6a
OBERLE, Nicolaus, NYC-M – 1892/10/12:4a
OBERLE, Valentin, 56, Newark, NJ – 1911/04/21:2e
OBERLIES % Gaertner, % Koppmier
OBERLIES, (widow), b. Becker, Union Hill, NJ – 1888/04/04:3b
OBERLIES, Carl, 25, Union Hill, NJ - 1896/01/11:4a

OBERLIES, Carl, un. cigarmaker, NYC-M – 1890/07/11:4a, 13:5b
OBERLIES, Eva, 5, Union Hill,? NJ – 1888/04/05:3a
OBERLIES, Jacob, 79, SP, un. cigarmaker, fr Rheinpfalz, USA 1860s, Union Hill, NJ - 1917/05/27:7a, 11g, 28:6a, = 29:2f
OBERLIES, Ludwig, 22, Union Hill, NJ – 1890/10/31:4a
OBERLIES, Ludwig, 30, un. cigarmaker, NYC-M - 1879/03/22:3a
OBERLIES, Wendel P., child, NYC-M – 1889/07/01:4a
OBERLIND, Richard, 27, NYC-M – 1903/03/02:3b
OBERLY, William, ~50, NYC-M – 1883/10/10:1d
OBERMAIER, Christian, NYC-Q - 1916/02/06:7a
OBERMANN, George, + Newark, NJ – 1881/01/08:1d, 11:4d
OBERMEYER, Egedin, Hoboken, NJ - 1914/08/12:6a
OBERMEYER, John, barber, ca. 70, USA 1868, & wife Margarethe, NYC-M – 1892/08/30:1g
OBERMEYER, Joseph, 55, NYC-M – 1880/07/11:5f
OBERMUELLER, Friedrich, NYC-M – 1900/05/13:1e
OBERNIER, Louise, 37, Frank, 7, Lizzie, 5, Charlie, 2, NYC-B, + on ship Mystery – 1887/07/12:1c-d, 13:2g
OBERREUTER, John, 19, NYC-M – 1906/08/17:6a
OBERST, Aug., 44, NYC-M - 1914/12/12:2f
OBERST, Christopher, 52, brew. eng., NYC-M – 1912/06/29:1c, 30:1f
OBERT, Joseph & Marie, b. Schreiber, fr Baden, 25th Wedding Anniv., NYC-B – 1911/06/24:5d-e
OBERT, Joseph, NYC-B – 1919/08/16:6a, 17:6a
OBMANN, Matthew, 65, & Anna, 62, NYC-Q - 1914/12/27:1e
OBMER, Johanna, b. Fust, NYC-M – 1890/05/01:4a
OBOM, Frithjof, 44, un. typesetter, NYC-B – 1897/01/15:4a
OBREGON, Genl, Mexican revol. - 1915/06/13:14c
OBS % Keller
OBSTFELDER, Richard, 35, NYC-M – 1886/11/22:3b
OCH, Felix, Elisabeth, NJ – 1912/07/17:6a
OCH, Georg, un. brewer, NYC-M – 1891/04/19:5a, 20:5a
OCHNER, Elise, 39, NYC-B – 1893/06/13:4a
OCHNER, F., 50, SP?, Newark, NJ - 1914/04/14:6a
OCHS % Edwards
OCHS, Adolf, NYC-B – 1909/11/21:1e, 22:3a, 23:3b
OCHS, Adolph, 25, NYC-M – 1886/07/08:2e
OCHS, Carrie, NYC-M, + @ Genl Slocum – 1904/06/16:1c, 17:3c
OCHS, Conrad, NYC-M – 1910/04/20:6a
OCHS, Franziska, b. Kuntz, 59, NYC-M – 1892/03/27:5d
OCHS, Heinrich, 30, NYC-M - 1917/05/22:6a, fam. 25:6a, mem. 1918/05/20:6a

OCHSENREITER, Ph., 38, NYC-M – 1891/06/28:5c
OCK % Mueller
ODELL, Marietta, 19, silk weaver, Wanakee, NJ – 1902/04/21:3c, 25:3b, 4 May:1d
ODENDAHL, Anton, NYC-B - 1914/06/01:6a
ODENDAHL, Otto, NYC-M?, - 1895/10/16:3f, 17:1d
ODENTHAL, Franz, NYC-M – 1901/02/08:4a
ODENTHAL, John, 44, un. furn. maker, NYC-M – 1890/07/12:4a, 13:5b
ODERSTEIN, Julie, 19, @ 1911 Triangle Shirtwaist Fire, NYC-M – 1911/03/27:1d
ODERWALD, Theresia, 59, NYC-M – 1891/09/20:5f
ODEY, J., Negro, lynched near Clayton, MS – 1902/07/18:1f, 19:2b
OEBERG, Friedrich N., 59, iron caster, NYC-B – 1896/10/16:4c, 18:5a
OECHLER, Christian, 32, Union Hill, NJ – 1897/02/04:4c
OECHSLE % Ludwig
OED, Paul, 47, SP, candy maker, NYC-Bx – 1910/09/23:6a, =26:1b, fam. 27:6a
OEHLECKER, Cecilie, b. Bauer, NYC-B – 1899/04/18:4a, fam. 21:4a
OEHLECKER, Wilhelm, SLP, NYC-Q – 1897/10/13:4a, 16:1e
OEHLER, Alfred, Dr., co-fdr NYC German Press Club, + June 4 in Goettingen/Gy - 1913/06/20:6a
OEHLER, Charles, 41, stenographer, NYC-Bx - 1917/12/01:6b
OEHLER, Edward, 23, NYC-M – 1899/10/06:4a
OEHLER, Lena, 22, NYC-B – 1913/03/30:7b, 31:6a
OEHLER, Lorenz, 50, un. brewer, fr Suebia?, NYC-B - 1914/10/20:6a
OEHLER, Rita, NYC-M, + @ Genl Slocum – 1904/06/17:3c
OEHLMANN, Auguste, b. Rubrecht, 72, NYC-M - 1920/11/22:6a, 23:6a, fam. 4 Dez.:8a
OEHLMANN, George, un. cigar packer, NYC-M – 1908/12/12:6a, fam. 17:6a
OEHLMANN, Otto, child, NYC-M - 1894/12/25:4a
OEHME, Arthur, NYC-M – 1898/11/29:4a
OEHME, Heinrich, un. glove maker, SPD Nuernberg/Gy, ed. Fraenkische Post – 1905/05/03:2d
OEHRLEIN, August, NYC-M – 1909/03/10:6a
OELSCHLAEGER, Bernhard, 40, NYC-M – 1900/12/14:1e
OELSCHLAEGER, Henriette, b. Merz, 29, NYC-M – 1885/12/10:3b
OELSCHLAEGER, Lizzie, 22, NYC? – 1888/04/14:2f
OELWIG, Ida, 27, on SS Trave, husband in Green Bay, WI – 1890/12/15:2g
OERDING % Steinberg
OERSCHLER, Jacob, brewer/cooper, NYC-M – 1900/08/17:4a
OERTEL, Anton, 66, SPD Einsiedel/Saxony – 1899/05/28:1d

OERTEL, Ernst G., Dr., chief ed. Cons. Berlin Deutsche Tageszeitung, crit. obit. - 1916/07/25:2e, 26:4c
OERTEL, Frederick William, NYC-M - 1880/03/21:8a
OERTEL, Karl, SPD, MdR for Nuernberg/Gy - 1900/04/05:2c, =23:2d, notes 27:2d
OERTER, Anna, NYC-M - 1901/02/16:4a
OERTER, Oscar, 18 months, NYC-M - 1904/04/12:4a
OERTHEL % Wirth
OERTHER, Eva, b. Kuentzel, 37, NYC-B - 1896/07/14:4a
OERTY, Jacob Ulrich, 40, fr Teufen/Appenzell/Switzerland, + on ship Labrador on way to NYC - 1881/01/28:1e
OESEN, J.F. von, 37, NYC-M - 1893/12/10:5a
OESSWEIN % Ritter
OESTERLE, Christine, 76, NYC-M - 1903/09/24:2h
OESTERLING, Charles, 76, NYC-M - 1885/05/06:3a
OESTERREICHER % Allmendinger,
OESTMANN, Wilhelm, 37, Steinway worker?, NYC-M - 1881/06/17:3a
OESTREICH, Anna, 68, NYC-B - 1904/03/29:4a
OESTREICH, Georg, 1, NYC-M - 1880/10/11:4f
OESTREICH, John, un. printer, NYC-M - 1894/04/04:4a
OESTREICH, Katie, 4, NYC-M - 1886/12/09:2g
OESTREICHER, Anna, 18, servant, NYC-M - 1895/05/12:1h
OESTREICHER, Theresia, 77, NYC-B - 1890/05/02:4a
OETERS % Tienkens
OETINGER, Otto, druggist, 40, NYC-B - 1913/01/08:1e
OETTGEN, William, NYC - 1914/07/30:6a
OETTINGER, Charles, & daughter, & son?, NYC-M, +@Genl Slocum - 1904/06/17:3c
OETTINGER, Dominicus, NYC-Q - 1910/02/25:6a
OETTINGER, Friedrich, NYC-Q - 1907/01/21:6a
OETTINGER, Fritz, 54, SDP, NYC-M - 1901/02/25:4a, 26:4a
OETTINGER, John, un. printer, NYC-B - 1917/01/06:6a
OEXLE, Gottlieb, 65, NYC-B - 1891/04/01:4a
OEXLEIN % Georgie
OFENBRAUN, Albert, 2, NYC-M - 1880/06/29:1c
OFFENBACH, Jacques, Koeln/Gy-born composer in France, praise - 1880/05/30:4c, + in Paris 6 Oct:1b
OFFER, Adam, 84, furnit. Manuf., NYC-B - 1906/12/20:3a
OFFERMANN, Hermann, 34, NYC-M - 1897/08/23:4a
OFFINGER, Christian, NYC-M - 1886/07/02:3a
OGINSKA, Helene, 18, Lithuanian noble & revol., + Sibirian jail - 1890/08/29:1a

OHEROGGE, Henry, 23, grocer, NYC-M – 1900/03/06:3b
OHL, Carl, NYC-M, +@Genl Slocum – 1904/06/17:3c
OHL, George, 40, barber, NYC-B – 1900/10/23:4a
OHLANDT, Mary, NYC – 1902/02/14:3a
OHLENDORF, William, 72, butcher, NYC-B – 1905/06/28:3c
OHLENSCHLAEGER, Cornelius, 35, NYC-B – 1893/02/18:3d
OHLENSCHLAGER, Charles, 26, un. bartender, NYC-B – 1905/03/09:4a
OHLENSCHLAGER, Henry, 63, NYC-Q – 1913/07/13:6a, 14:6a
OHLENSCHLAGER, Maria, 44, NYC-B – 1901/04/16:4a
OHLHAUS, John W., 27, NYC-M – 1891/06/23:4a
OHLIGER, Eva, b. Karch, NYC-M – 1892/10/16:5c
OHLINGER, Friedrich, 28, NYC-B – 1893/10/31:4a
OHLMANN, Leopold, 49, Jersey City Heights, NJ – 1908/03/28:6a
OHLRAU, Minnie, 29, NYC-M – 1889/05/30:4a
OHLROGGE, Carl, 52, NYC-SI – 1906/03/08:4a
OHLSEN, Edward, SP, un. cigarmkr, * Norway, Hamburg 1870s, USA 1881, NYC-Bx - 1913/06/20:2e,6a, 21:6a, =23:6c, 24:3f,4a, fam. 23:6a
OHLSEN, Henry D., grand juror, NYC-B – 1898/04/16:2f
OHLSEN, Mathilde, NYC-B – 1892/06/13:4a
OHLTERS, Henry J., grocer, 55, NYC-M – 1905/10/26:4c
OHM, Dora, un. cigarmaker, SDP, Bridgeport, CT – 1902/04/23:4c
OHMER, Lorenz, NYC-Bx - 1918/03/26:6a
OHNECKE, Philip, fr Gibsheim/Gy, USA 1891, NYC – 1891/04/19:1d
OHNESORGE % Schnull
OHNEWALD, John C., 29, NYC-B – 1907/01/09:3b
OHR, Gustav A., 19, fr Gy, exec. Canton, OH – 1880/06/26:1c
OHRBACH, Augusta, b. Liebermann, NYC-M - 1918/10/14:6a
OHRY, Anna Maria, b. Schaefer, 65, NYC-M – 1892/07/06:4a
OHSE, Rudolf, 46, un. cigarmaker, NYC-M - 1917/11/24:6a
OHSE, Theodor, NYC-M - 1917/11/24:6a
OHSE, W., NYC-M – 1913/03/04:6a
O'KEEFE, John M., NYPD, + 3 Nov 1898, trial now, NYC-M – 1899/05/21:1f, 19:1h, 3c
OKELMANN, Johannes, 39, cigarmaker & SPD activist expelled from Hamburg/Gy, arrived NYC – 1880/11/30:1d-e, 2 Dec:2a-b, 6:1d-e
OKOLSI, Henry, 60, mason, NYC-M – 1884/07/20:1g
OKRZEJA, Stefan, 19,Polish patriot,exec. Warsaw - 1905/08/04:2d, 9:2c-d
OLAH, Mare, servant fr Hungary, NYC-M – 1904/12/22:3a
OLASHAK, Helene, 36, & daughter, NYC - 1914 /01/20:1f
OLDENBURG, Henry, 42, sales agent, NYC-B – 1886/12/25:2d
OLDENDORF, Wilhelmina, b. Ricking, NYC-B – 1891/05/22:4a
OLDENWALDER, Jacob, 40, painter, Bayonne, NJ – 1909/04/13:3c

OLDTMANN, Carl, SP, fr Altona/Hamburg, un. cigarmaker, New Haven, CT - 1916/04/12:2d
OLDTMANN, Mathilde, NYC-M – 1893/04/25:4a
OLINSKY, Isaac, 70, NYC-M - 1918/08/15:1f
OLIVIER, A., peddler, Swiss, NYC-M – 1893/09/13:1b
OLLIVIER, Emile, French polit. & historian – 1913/08/21:1f
OLLMANN % Baer
OLMO, Juan, NYC-M – 1907/11/15:6a
OLMS, Ernst, Yonkers, NY - 1917/07/10:6a
OLMSTEDT, John, machinist, NYC-B – 1909/11/30:3b
OLOWSKY, Albert, 44, locksmith, NYC-M – 1889/07/09:1h
OLPP, Elisabeth Margarethe, b. Schmidt, NYC-M – 1892/06/13:4a
OLSEN, August, 40, steel worker, Newark, NJ – 1912/06/29:3b
OLSEN, August, 50, cigarmaker, NYC-M - 1895/04/05:1f
OLSEN, August, NYC-M - 1915/12/20:6a
OLSEN, Christian, Rev., 55, Norwegian Luth. Church, NYC-B – 1911/12/17:7d
OLSEN, Otto, ironworker, NYC-M – 1910/07/22:1f
OLSEN-HOEPKE, Rudolph, sailor on SS Prinz Joachim, * Lehe/Bremerhaven, + Kingston, Jamaica - 1913/05/09:3d,6a
OLT, Margarethe, 11, NYC-M - 1878/03/16:3c
OLTNER, Frederick, 51, shoemaker, USA 1864, NYC-M – 1890/07/06:4g
OMLIN, David, 27, innkeep & SP Zug/Switz. – 1908/02/16:3e
OMMER, Joseph, NYC-M – 1905/11/02:4a
ONDRACEK, John, 48, SP?, Czech, co-fdr Ferrer Modern Sunday School, NYC-M - 1919/04/06:12a, 16:6a
O'NEIL, Marjorie, 15, daughter of SP member M.C. O'Neill, NYC-B - 1916/04/23:11b
ONYSKINO, Mikotsky, striking worker, Bayonne, NJ - 1915/07/24:2d
OPDYKE, George, 75, mayor NYC – 1880/06/13:5d, =16:4a, will 2 Jy:4c
OPEL, Anna, NYC-Q - 1915/08/21:6a
OPETZ, Vincent, fr Austria, NYC, + New Brunswick, NJ – 1898/07/14:1e, 15:1g
OPIFICIUS, Louis, 60, mgr & SPD Frankfurt/Main – 1910/05/01:3a
OPITZ, Charles F., 78, NYC-B – 1898/08/09.4a
OPITZ, Emilie E., 71, NYC-B – 1885/07/06:3c
OPPEL, Andrew, laborer at Piel's Brewery, NYC-B – 1907/09/17:3b
OPPELT, Louis, 30, US Army, Jersey City, NJ - 1917/10/22:1e
OPPENHEIMER, B., 42, NYC-M – 1893/03/12:5a
OPPENHEIMER, B., bill collector, NYC-M – 1900/08/25:2h
OPPENHEIMER, Emil, 45, butcher, NYC-M - 1916/12/04:2a
OPPENHEIMER, George's wife, 29, NYC-M? – 1913/10/21:1b

OPPENHEIMER, Heinrich, 73, NYC-M – 1893/10/26:4a
OPPENHEIMER, Karoline, NYC-M – 1891/04/11:4a
OPPENHEIMER, Max, 52, shoemaker, NYC-M – 1883/05/20:1e
OPPENHEIMER, R., 73, NYC-M – 1893/08/31:4a
OPPENHEIMER, Solomon, 50, Newark, NJ - 1878/04/25:4e
OPPENHYM, Anna, b. Cohen, 34, NYC-M – 1889/02/12:4a
OPPER, Frederick, body fd, NYC-B – 1901/08/16:4a
OPPERMANN, August, 69, NYC-M – 1892/06/11:4a
OPPERMANN, Robert, 67, butcher, NYC-M – 1910/08/01:1a
OPPMANN, Charles, Elizabeth, NJ - 1914/03/28:6a
OPRAVIL, Johann, un. metal worker, SP Vienna/Austria – 1910/09/04:5b
ORB, Johann, 58, MdL & SPD Offenbach/Hessen, 1911/12/03:3b
ORBACH, Moritz, 50, journalist, fr Berlin/Gy, USA 1884, NYC-M – 1885/11/27:1g
ORBEL, Eduard, 89, Newport, NJ – 1904/02/28:5a
ORBEL, Friedrich Wilhelm, SLP, Waterbury, CT - 1894/09/22:4a, 26:4a, = 27:1f
ORBEL, Theodor Bernhard, NYC-M – 1892/06/16:4a
ORDEMANN, W., NYC-Q - 1915/06/02:6a
ORDHOEFER, Henry, un. carp., NYC-M – 1889/01/24:4a
ORF, Hermann, 33, NYC-B - 1920/07/04:2e
ORGEL, Fritz, NYC-M – 1892/08/16:4e
ORGENIUS, Walter, painter, NYC-B - 1915/07/10:1d
ORGONIK, Mina, SP, 42nd birthday, Jersey City, NJ – 1911/03/21:5e
ORIOLA, Waldermar, Count, MdR (Natl-Libs), crit obit – 1910/04/19:4d
ORLAMUNDER, Charles A., 65, musician & his wife, NYC-M, + N. Bergen, NJ – 1909/09/05:1c
ORLEMANN, Louis H., Pompton, NJ – 1905/08/18:3g
ORLOPP % Wood
ORME, Joseph A., 32, SP, NYC - 1916/06/12:5f
ORNTH, Hieronymus, 51, SPD Leipzig, un. mason & alderman, * Kohlenthal/Silesia - 1915/11/07:3b
OROSS, Joseph, fr Hungary, exec. Pittsburgh, PA – 1896/09/02:1b
ORR, Elsie, actress, + 1918, see Elsie Kuntzler
ORT, Daniel, 32, fr Netherlands, NYC-M – 1884/10/04:1f
ORT, John, NYC-M – 1909/03/05:6a
ORTH % Dunst
ORTH, Adolf, 15, NYC-M - 1917/01/15:6a
ORTH, Franciska, 59, NYC-B - 1917/01/07:7a, 8:6b
ORTH, Fritz, 48, engineer at NYVZ, *Gleissweiler/Gy NYC-B – 1903/06/10:3d,4a, 11:4a, =14:5d
ORTH, John, 38, laborer, NYC-B – 1880/03/28:3c

ORTH, Konrad, 60, NYC-B – 1909/05/03:6a
ORTH, Otto, 21, NYC-Q – 1911/10/02:6a
ORTHABER, Anton, 45, NYC-M – 1905/11/07:4a
ORTLAND, Georg, 27, NYC-Bx - 1918/10/18:6a
ORTLAND, Heinrich, SP, NYC-M married Martha Reimer, NYC-Q – 1906/10/08:3c
ORTLAND, Henry's daughter +, NYC-M – 1903/04/11:4a
ORTLAND, Ida, b. Neumann, SDP, * 25 May 1865 Magdeburg/Gy, NYC-M – 1905/01/19:4a, 20:4a, 21:2f,4a, =22:5b, fam. 23:4a
ORTLAND, William H., 23, SP, NYC-M - 1915/03/29:6a,c, 30:6a, =31:3f-g, fam. 2 Ap:6a; mem. 1916/03/27:6a
ORTMANN, Albert, NYC-Bx - 1918/12/09:6a
ORTMANN, Carl, SPD Stettin/Gy– 1908/06/07:3d
ORTUNG, Eugen, 53, un.pianomaker, NYC-M - 1894/10/30:4a
OSBORNE, Fanny, 13, NYC-M, + Genl Slocum – 1904/06/26:1c
OSBORNE, William H., actor, *Engl., USA 1825, NYC-M - 1879/01/16:1g
OSER, Franz Joseph A., 3, NYC-M – 1892/05/09:4a
OSER, Louis, 52, un. brewer, NYC-M – 1892/06/21:4a
OSKLAND, Herman, 56, carp., Jersey City, NJ - 1915/11/02:2c
OSMERS, Mildred, 5, NYC-M, + @on Genl Slocum – 1904/06/21:1f
OSMOND, John L., worker, NYC-M, exec. Ossining, NY – 1893/06/13:1d
OSSENKOPF, August, 53, worker at Singer Co., War 2, Elizabeth, NJ - 1915/12/18:2e
OSSIPANOW, Russian patriot, trial & exec. for 13 March attentate on Czar, (with Lenin's brother) – 1887/05/26:5b, 30:2f, 10 June:5b, 17:5e
OSTEN, Charles von, 27, waiter, NYC-M – 1880/09/20:1f
OSTEN, Otto, 30, electrician, NYC – 1912/11/09:1d, 10:1d, 11:3f
OSTENDORF, Robert W., electrician, Jersey City, NJ – 1887/07/07:2f
OSTER, Annie, NYC-M – 1898/04/23:1h
OSTER, Elisabeth, b. Vigelius, NYC-B – 1891/06/21:5a
OSTER, Emma, 27, NYC-M - 1894/01/31:4a
OSTER, Franz, 49, NYC-M – 1892/08/03:4a
OSTER, Jakob, (dying), NYC-M – 1891/06/18:1g
OSTERHAUS, Peter, Union general, * Duisburg/Gy, =Koblenz/Gy - 1917/01/06:1d
OSTERHELD, George, 47, Yonkers, NY 1878/06/15:3b
OSTERMANN, comrade, 52, SPD & alderman in Rixdorf/Gy – 1909/09/05:3c
OSTERMANN, Franz N., 25, SP, fr Hungary?, NYC-M - 1919/07/22:6a; mem. 1920/07/21:6a
OSTERMANN, Henry, ret. restaurant owner, NYC-B, + Berlin/Gy where ret. since 1907 - 1916/02/15:6b

OSTERMANN, Jacob, NYC-M - 1920/03/27:8a
OSTERMANN, Paul, innkeep, NYC-B, + Germany - 1912/08/23:3a
OSTERMEIER, Caroline, 52, NYC-B - 1880/03/20:4b, 22:2g, inquest 3 Apr:1g, husband John tried 7 Oct:1g, rec. life 3 Nov:1g
OSTERNDORF % Brooks
OSTLER, Anton, 40, un. wood carver, Jersey City, NJ - 1898/07/04:4a
OSTLER, August, 49, Newark, NJ - 1904/01/05:3d
OSTRAND, Otto, bartender, fr Sweden, NYC-B - 1901/06/26:4a
OSTRONSKA, Josephine, 13, servant, Hackensack, NJ - 1906/10/04:3c
OSTROWSKY, Becky, 20, @1911 Triangle Shirtwaist Fire, NYC-M - 1911/03/27:1d
OSWALD, Anna, b. Emriger, 41, NYC-M - 1880/06/05:3b
OSWALD, Daniel, NYC-M - 1909/01/09:6a
OSWALD, Ellie, 24, fr Washington, Dc, + NYC-M - 1911/06/19:2e
OSWALD, John, un. pianomaker?, NYC-M - 1884/08/29:3d
OSWALD, Julius F., NYC-Ridgewood - 1916/01/23:7a
OSWALD, Konrad, tailor, NYC-M - 1883/11/06:3a
OSWALD, Louis's wife, NYC-M - 1887/01/07:3c
OSWALD, Louise, NYC-M - 1903/06/02:4a
OSWALD, Mary, & daughter Euphemia, Camden, NJ - 1899/04/26:4c
OSWALD, Minnie, NYC-M - 1889/02/26:1h, 27:4a
OSWALD, Mrs, SLP, Newark, NJ - 1879/08/27:4e
OSWALD, Wilhelm, brewer or cooper, NYC-M - 1890/11/09:5b
OSWALD, William, 74, SP, un. pianomaker, NYC-M - 1911/09/03:7a, 4:2d, 6a
OTERO-GONZALES, Francesco, 20, exec. Madrid for shooting on King Alfonso - 1880/04/15:1b
OTIS, Harrison Gray, owner of Los Angeles Times, + Los Angeles - 1917/07/31:3e
OTT, Alois, 48, NYC-M - 1916/11/23:6a
OTT, Arthur, 25, un. painter, NYC-M - 1917/03/31:6a
OTT, Charles, NYC-B - 1881/01/24:5a, 28:3a
OTT, Elizabeth, b. Senning, 59, NYC-B - 1919/12/03:6a
OTT, F., NYC-B - 1910/02/12:6a
OTT, Frederick, 50, deli-owner, NYC-M - 1892/09/13:4d
OTT, Georg, un. brewer, Guttenberg, NJ - 1892/06/05:5d, fam. 8:4a
OTT, Johannes, 2, NYC-M - 1890/05/23:4a
OTT, John, 48, musician, NYC-M - 1908/09/20:1f
OTT, John, 78, NYC-Bx - 1919/07/15:6a
OTT, Margareth, 70, NYC - 1914/04/16:6a, 17:6a
OTT, Maria, b. Hagen, NYC-M - 1909/12/04:6a
OTT, Mrs,, NYC, fam. 1898/06/10:4a

OTT, Philipp, 77, & wife, 81, NYC-B – 1893/04/19:2d
OTT, Volkmar, *Dochsdorf/Vogtland/Saxony, NYC-M – 1890/07/19:4a
OTT, William, NYC-B – 1897/12/08:4a
OTTE, Charles, NYC-M – 1907/11/12:6a
OTTEN, Alma M., NYC-M – 1891/07/02:4a
OTTEN, Joseph, 19, NYC-B – 1897/06/14:3d
OTTENBACHER, Gottlieb, un. carp., NYC-M – 1903/01/13:4a
OTTENBACHER, Gottlob, 36?, un. upholsterer, NYC-M – 1890/01/12:5a
OTTENBACHER, Pauline, 27, NYC-M – 1886/09/10:3c
OTTENDORF, Philipp, 76, NYC-B – 1890/01/22:4a
OTTENDORFER, Oswald, *26 Fb 1824 Zwittau/Moravia, USA 1850, publ. NYSZ, NYC-M – 1900/12/16:1g, 5a, 17:4a, will 25:3b,25 Jy 1902:2c
OTTENS % Weber
OTTER, (Mr.), NYC-B – 1886/11/20:2f
OTTERBECK, Maria, NYC-B – 1892/08/13:4a
OTTERSEN, Louis, 36, innkeep, NYC-M – 1881/08/07:5e
OTTERSTEDT, Charles, 23, un. baker, NYC-B - 1915/08/31:6a, mem. 1916/08/29:6a
OTTERSTEDT, Henry, 38, birch beer maker, Hoboken, NJ – 1904/07/11:1a, 12:1f
OTTERSTEDT, Martha, 19, NYC-B – 1913/02/15:3a, 6a
OTTINGER, Andrew, 7, Emma, Kittie, & Charles, 16, NYC-M?, @Genl Slocum – 1904/06/17:1a
OTTMANN, August, 56, NYC-M – 1892/06/10:4a
OTTMANN, Carl, NYC-B - 1915/01/30:6a
OTTMANN, Henry, 45, NYC-M – 1891/03/23:2e
OTTMANN, Henry, 53, fr Winnweiler/Bav., USA bef. 1852, NYC-M – 1882/06/21:1e
OTTMANN, Jakob, un. baker, NYC-M – 1910/07/22:6a
OTTMANN, Louise, b. Kaiser, 44, *Stuttgart-Heslach/Gy, NYC-M – 1902/07/09:4a
OTTMANN, Thomas, NYC-M – 1908/12/21:6a, 22:6a
OTTO % Schanne
OTTO, Adolph, 7, NYC-M – 1885/05/28:3d
OTTO, Albin, 37, baker, NYC-Bx - 1915/01/22:2d, 24:7a
OTTO, Anna, 15, NYC-Bx – 1917/02/10:6a
OTTO, August, 62, SP, un. cigarmaker, * Saxony, USA 1880s, Weehawken Hghts, NJ - 1916/01/18:2d,6a, =19:6a, 6d
OTTO, August, 66, NYC-B – 1893/01/17:4a
OTTO, Augusta, NYC-M – 1900/09/08:4a
OTTO, Carl, 64, NYC-B – 1893/09/02:4a
OTTO, Christian, 56, NYC-M – 1912/04/16:6a

OTTO, Elisabeth, 70, NYC-SI – 1912/08/08:1d
OTTO, Elizabeth, 56, dying, NYC-SI – 1911/06/22:2f
OTTO, Fr., NYC-M – 1906/04/08:5a
OTTO, Fred, 21, painter, NYC-B – 1904/06/14:3c
OTTO, Henry R., 35, druggist?, Union Hill, NJ – 1904/01/28:3d
OTTO, Henry, brewer, Newark, NJ – 1919/11/11:8a
OTTO, John M., Dr., 52, NYC-M – 1903/12/30:2h
OTTO, John, baker, NYC-B – 1881/08/06:1f
OTTO, Julius, NYC-M – 1906/03/13:4a
OTTO, Lillian, 48, Jersey City, NJ - 1914/11/25:2f
OTTO, Martha, NYC-M – 1890/06/04:4a
OTTO, Mathilde, 22, worker, Belleville, NJ – 1910/11/27:1a
OTTO, Richard, un. painter, NYC-M – 1892/10/13:4a
OTTO, Robert, 50, SP, *Saxony, Westfield, NJ – 1912/11/05:3f, 6a
OTTO, Rudolf, un. furrier, NYC-M – 1891/07/09:4a
OTTUSCH, Anna Maria, NYC-B - 1917/02/09:6a
OTTUSCH, John, NYC-B - 1920/08/18:6a
OVEL, Clemens, un. cigarmaker, NYC-M – 1889/07/12:4a
OVER, John, 35, smith, USA 1892, NYC-M – 1893/07/11:4e
OVEREND, Elizabeth, servant, NYC-M – 1906/03/19:1d
OVERLANDER, John, 40, Passaic, NJ – 1912/05/08:3c
OVERMEYER, Frank, 30, Jersey City, NJ – 1912/04/29:2d
OVERMEYER, Henry O., 60, pres. US Sugar Trust, + Commack, LI – 1907/12/05:3f
OVERSON % Bosch
OWEN, Robert, the Welsh reformer, his life – 1896/04/26:3a-e, 1902/02/23:7g-h, 50th anniv. Of death – 1908/12/06:16f-g
OYWIK, Peter, un. carp., NYC-B – 1890/11/27:4a
OZIONI, Ernst, 51, NYC-M – 1891/06/26:4a
PAAR, John, & his wife, Silver Wedding, NYC? – 1907/03/19:5e
PAASCHE, Hans, Cpt., pro-Communist son of the German National Liberal leader - 1920/05/27:4c-d, 6 June, II:1-3, 3 Jy:3d, 18:4d
PABST % Enz
PABST, Friedrich, brewer, Milwaukee, WI – 1904/01/02:1e
PABST, Georg, NYC-M - 1920/06/13:12a
PABST, Hans, servant, fr Gy, NYC-B - 1914/03/28:3e
PABST, John, 40, NYC-M – 1908/01/16:3b
PABST, Karolina, b. Schwendemann, 52, NYC-M – 1885/03/28:3a
PABST, Richard, NYC-M – 1909/10/22:6a
PACES, Josef, Czech SP, USA 1902, + Mitchell, NE – 1909/08/16:4d-e
PACH, Joseph, 21, NYC-M – 1892/08/22:4c
PACHTMANN, Fred W., 74, NYC-M – 1888/10/27:4f

PACK, Annie, @1911 Triangle Shirtwaist Fire, NYC-M – 1911/03/27:1d
PACKENHAM, Patrick, exec. NYC-M – 1889/08/23:4e, 24:2e
PADLEWSKY, Stanilaus, Polish patriot who shot 18 Nov 1890 a Russian
   police general in Paris, murdered San Antonio, TX # 1892/01/29:1a-e,
   30:1b, 31:1a-b, Mem. In NYC 6 Fb:1d, 9:1d, 10:1g, 21:5c, Rev. 29
   Fb:2d, 1 Mr:1a-b. Notes 1893/01/04:2c
PADLEWSKY, Theodor, un. carp., NYC-B – 1912/09/11:6a
PAECHTER, Anna, 15, NYC-B - 1914/09/29:6c, 7 Oc:6c
PAEPERER, Otto, Westchester, NY - 1918/03/30:6a
PAESLER, Emil, knife-sharpener, USA 1872, NYC-M – 1888/01/27:4a
PAETOW, Chris, NYC-B – 1901/12/19:4a
PAETZOLD, Heinrich, baker, + 9 Apr 1892 New Haven, CT, heirs searched
   by notary in Kosten/Posen - 1915/03/07:7g
PAFFEN, Kathe Luxen, fr Mayen/Gy?, NYC-Flatbush - 1919/07/13:2d
PAHL, John, 49, laborer, NYC-M - 1895/10/18: 1c
PAHLE, Theodor, NYC-M – 1910/01/07:6a
PAHLEK, Maria, b. Luettge, North Bergen, NJ – 1907/04/28:7b
PAHLOW, Arnold, SP?, NYC-M - 1913/12/20:6a
PAHLOW, G., 66, un. painter, NYC-Bx – 1903/01/08:3c
PAIN, Oliver, French journalist & advisor to the Mahdi , + Sudan –
   1885/07/15:4d, 20 Aug:2b, 25:1a
PAINE, Thomas, birthday celebr in New Haven, CT – 1882/01/30:1c,
   100th anniv. + in New Rochelle, NY – 1909/06/03:2c-d, #6:1d-f
PALACKY, Franz, Czech historian, memory—NYVZ lauds was in favor of
   dividing Bohemia into German & Czech part — 1898/07/11:2d-e
PALDA, Leo, SP, Czech, chief ed. Delnicke Listy, USA 1866 fr Bohemia, +
   Cedar Rapids, IA - 1913/06/23:2c
PALEY, Henry,25,SP,clerk, NYC-Bx - 1915/08/16:6c,19:5f,=21:2b
PALKOWITSCH, Ferdinand, 45, fr Hungary, smith, & wife, Orange, NJ,
   1892/05/21:1f
PALLAS, John J., un. patternmaker & Tammany politico, NYC-M –
   1905/10/17:1d
PALLAVICINI, Johanna, b. Regelin, NYC-M – 1899/06/18:5b
PALLISTER, Thomas, Sing Sing escapee – 1893/05/11:1f-g, 17:1f, 19:1g
PALLOS, Spanish anarchist, exec. – 1893/10/01:1f, 4:1b, 5:1a, 7:1a
PALLWITZ, Carl,20,SP,fr Libau/Kurland, NYC-Bx - 1916/05/31:5e
PALM, Carl, un. cigarmaker, NYC-M - 1919/03/01:6a
PALM, Meta, 19, NYC-M – 1893/10/25:4a
PALMA, Michael De, exec. Trenton, NJ – 1919/08/20:2e
PALMAY, Albert, 58, NYC-B – 1892/06/25:4a
PALME, Joseph, SP, publ. Nordboehm. Volksbote in Bodenbach/Bohemia,
   +23 Fb, body fd 1911/08/07:4d

PALMER, Anton, 64, un. mason, SLP?, NYC-M – 1899/01/18:4a
PALMER, Courtland, millionaire, yet friendly to workers, NYC-M – 1888/07/24:4e, 25:2c, 26:2h, 27:1a-b, will 8 Aug:1d
PALMERI, Careno, exec. Trenton, NJ – 1919/08/20:2e
PALMIERA, Jose, Spanish ship stoker, + during strike, NYC – 1912/06/09:1d
PALTE % Berger
PAME, Peter, 34, butcher, NYC-M – 1891/04/17:4d
PANCK, Jerome, waiter, NYC-M – 1882/04/01:4b
PANCRITIUS, Paul, Dr., 35,fr Gy,USA 1891,NYC-M - 1896/02/06:4a
PANELS, J., NYC-B – 1912/11/20:6a
PANKOPF, Carl, SP, & wife, Newark, NJ – 1908/08/18:1f, 6a
PANNASCH, Amalie, 70, NYC-M – 1912/12/06:6a
PANNASCH, Heinrich, 2, NYC-M – 1892/03/27:5d
PANNICKE, Julie, Jersey City Heights, NJ – 1900/08/28:4a
PANTER, Albert, NYC-M – 1919/10/04:6a
PANTZNER, Clarence, 25, NYSNG,NYC-Q - 1914/04/03:2e
PANUSCHKA, Frank, un. carp., NYC-M – 1905/12/29:4a
PANZE, Dietrich, 56, NYC-M – 1891/09/20:5f
PANZENBECK, Anna, NYC-M – 1912/12/19:6a, 21:6a
PANZENBECK, Caecilie, 8, NYC-M – 1887/09/22:2g
PANZENBECK, John, NYC-M - 1914/12/30:6a
PANZER, Emma, 19, NYC-M? – 1893/05/27:3d
PANZER, Maria, b. Hurdes, NYC-M – 1891/04/09:4a
PANZETER, Fanny, & children, & boarder John Goeltze, NYC – 1899/02/17:3c, husband rec 25 yrs – 1899/06/25:5a
PAP, John, 26, fr Hungary, New Brunswick,NJ - 1914/09/24:3f
PAPE, E., NYC-M – 1891/06/04:4a
PAPE, Heinrich, NYC-M - 1915/01/09:6a
PAPE, Henry, un. cigarmaker, NYC-B - 1894/04/20:4a
PAPE, Johann G., 62, NYC-B – 1892/06/20:4a
PAPE, Louis, un. carp., NYC-M - 1914/10/22:6a
PAPP, Nicholas, worker, Bridgeport, CT - 1916/05/12:1e
PAPPENBERGER, John, NYC-M - 1920/01/02:6a
PAPSDORF, Oswald, NYC-B - 1894/10/15:4a
PAPST, Elisabeth, b. Scheer, 67, NYC-B – 1891/08/11:4a
PAPST, Ferdinand, varnisher, NYC-M – 1893/11/06:4a
PARBS, G., NYC-Bx – 1906/04/28:4a
PARBS, Laura, b. Haag, 43, NYC-M – 1900/12/14:4a
PARCHALL, Anton, grocery clerk, Little Ferry, NJ – 1912/05/06:1e
PARISETTE, Chr., 47, NYC-M – 1892/08/23:4a
PARISETTE, Henry, NYC-M – 1890/05/23:4a

PARISETTI, Albert, NYC-M – 1891/01/04:5a
PARIZOT, Gustav F., 43, manager, *Bremen, Gy, Bloomfield, NJ – 1912/04/29:2d
PARKS, Sam, ex-business agent Housesmiths & Bridgemen's Union #2, NYC, + Ossining, NY – 1904/05/05:1g, =7:1c, 8:5f
PARNELL, Fanny, 28, sister of Irish leader, + Bordentown, NJ – 1882/07/25:2d-e
PARR, Edward, exec. Philadelphia - 1879/06/11:1c, 14:2b
PARRY, David MacLean, 65, pres. Natl Assoc of Manuf, + Indianapolis - 1915/05/14:2f
PARSONS, Eli, Negro, lynched Memphis, TN - 1917/05/23:3e-f
PARSONS, H., v-p of General Electric, Schenectady, NY – 1912/04/29:2f
PARSONS, Henry H., 30, lawyer, + Purchase, NY - 1920/06/19:1d
PARSONS, Lucy see 1886 Haymarket
PARTENHEIMER, Albrecht, 63, Yonkers, NY - 1920/05/23:12a
PARUSCHEK, Joseph, NYC? – 1890/03/23:5b
PASBURG, Oskar, NYC-M – 1889/05/27:4a
PASCALE, Domenico Di, exec. Auburn, NY – 1912/03/19:3f
PASCH, Carrie, 14, Jersey City Heights, NJ – 1907/09/22:7b
PASCH, Fritz, 38, musician, 10/1904 fr Koeln/Gy, NYC-M – 1905/01/22:5d
PASCHBURG, Robert, NYC-M - 1915/12/25:6a
PASCHECK, Emil, 21, Hackensack, NJ – 1903/02/02:4b
PASSBURG, Georg, 70, SLP, un. cigarmaker, USA 1880 fr Gy, NYC-M - 1917/12/30:11f-g,31:6a, 1918/01/01:2f,6a =01/03:3f, fam. 16:6a; mem 1918/12/27:6a
PASSELEI, Friedrich, un. cigar maker, NYC-M – 1889/04/20:4a
PASSOW, Hugo, 53, un. cigarmaker, NYC-M – 1903/06/02:4a
PASTEUR, Louis, Dr., scientist, + Paris, - 1895/09/29: 1b, = 10/06: 1b
PASTLER, Henry, NYC-M – 1893/04/26:4d
PATALAS, Joseph, 35, un. cigarmaker, NYC-M – 1902/11/15:4a, fam. 18:4a
PATERMANN, Wilhelm, NYC-B – 1904/12/25:5a
PATERSON, Selma, 19, textile worker, Chicago, IL – 1913/09/21:1b, 23:4a-b
PATNEY, Alfred E., 30, shoemaker, killed during strike, Cincinatti, OH – 1912/07/14:1c
PATSCHKE, Gustav, 55, un. tailor, * Aschersleben/Gy, USA 1857, NYC-B – 1890/04/07:4a
PATSCHKE, Pauline, NYC-M – 1885/10/05:3a

PATTBERG, Christian, un. machinist, SP, * 28 Nov 1852 Nuernberg/Gy, USA 1872, NYC-B – 1907/03/28:1f, 6a, 29:6a, 30:6a, 31:6a-b, =31:7e, fam. 1 Apr:6a
PATTBERG, Maria, 67, NYC-B - 1920/04/08:6a
PATTENBAUM, Elizabeth, NYC-M, + @Genl Slocum – 1904/06/18:3c
PATTIS, Adelina baroness Lederstroem, 76, great actress –1919/11/16:9e-g
PATTY, Carman, striking worker at Armour & Co., fertilizer, Roosevelt, NJ - 1915/01/20:1a, =24:1g
PAUCKNER, John, worker, Bavarian, Cincinatti, OH - 1878/03/25: 1d-e
PAUL, Anna, 24, NYC-B - 1917/08/23:6a
PAUL, Anna, 50, NYC-Astoria – 1904/06/27:4a
PAUL, Conrad, 78, NYC-M – 1893/03/27:4e
PAUL, Florian, 81, SP, weaver, fr Silesia, member of 1864 deleg. Silesian weavers to King of Prussia, USA 1880s, NYC-B, 75th birthday - 1908/08/26:3d-e, + 1914/03/16:2b, 17:4c-d, 6a, 18:3c, fam. 28:6a
PAUL, Friedrich, 22, NYC-M – 1883/01/04:1f
PAUL, Friedrich, NYC-M – 1893/10/15:1g
PAUL, Henry, 78, worker at Singer Sewing Machine Co., Elizabeth, NJ – 1908/07/14:3c
PAUL, Hermann, 50, un. typesetter, NYC-B – 1903/03/06:1d, 4a, 7:1e, 4a, =9:3c, fam. 13:4a
PAUL, Jacob, NYC-Q - 1915/08/14:6a, 15:7a
PAUL, Peter, 56, un. carp., SP?, NYC-M – 1907/02/04:6a, 5:6a
PAUL, Wilhelm, 48,carpenter & innkeep, NYC-B - 1878/03/27:1e
PAULI % Hess
PAULI, Elsie, 18, & Katie, NYC-M, +@ Genl Slocum – 1904/06/17:3c
PAULI, Jean, 57, NYC-M - 1917/04/10:6a
PAULI, John, 79, + Boston – 1889/02/10:5b
PAULI, N. , fireman, NYC-B – 1908/08/07:6a
PAULOW, Wladimir, Russian prosec., killed by revol. – 1907/01/10:1a-b
PAULSEN, Andreas, Dane, building worker, 28, NYC-M – 1890/11/29:4c
PAULSEN, Ernst, 57, un. painter, NYC-Bx, +FL – 1911/03/07:3f, 6a, 9:6a, 12:7b, =13:2d, fam. 13:6a; mem. 1912/03/05:6a
PAULSEN, Frank G., 55, carp., fr Saxony/Gy, NYC-M – 1892/09/30:1f, 1 Oct:1g, 13 Dec:1g, 14:4d,16:1d, killer Roehl fd guilty 17:1f, 24:1g
PAULY, Mathilde, 44, NYC-Q – 1908/08/06:2a
PAULZ, Heinrich, un. baker, NYC-M - 1914/08/30:7a
PAURT, E., Yonkers, NY – 1906/11/14:6a
PAUSEWANG, Leopold, Sayville, LI – 1905/06/19:1e
PAUTSCH, Gustav, un. butcher, NYC-M - 1903/09/23:4a, fam. 29:4a
PAUVIS, John, bricklayer, NYC-M - 1894/11/10:1e
PAVLIK, John, Polish musician, NYC-M - 1892/03/31:1c

PAYNE, Henry C., US Postm.-Genl, + Washington, DC – 1904/10/05:1e
PAYNE, Joe, Negro, lynched Jellico, TN – 1893/02/28:1b
PAYNES, John Howard, author of "Home Sweet Home," = 1883/03/23:1g
PAZAUREK, Prokop, 87, NYC-M – 1892/12/08:4a
PEACOCK, Abbott, 79, Irish freethinker, NYC-M – 1886/02/13:4b
PEARSE, Patrick, Irish patriot, exec. Dublin - 1916/05/04:1a-b, 4b
PEARSE, William, Irish patriot, exec. Dublin - 1916/05/06:1c
PEARSON, Henry George, NYC Postmaster – 1889/04/21:1f
PEARSON, Hilma, 22, servant, Swedish, NYC-M - 1895/04/02:4a
PEARY, Robert E., 64, Polar explorer - 1920/02/21:1b
PECH, Frank, Elizabeth, NJ - 1916/04/27:6a
PECH, Hedwig, 53, NYC-Bx - 1920/09/23:6a, fam. 28:6a
PEEMOLLER, Elisabeth, b. Hirschberger, 47,NYC-Bx - 1918/01/13:7a
PEEMOLLER, Henry, NYC-M - 1917/02/26:6a
PEGENKOPF, Mrs, b. Weissgerber, NYC-M – 1903/09/29:4a
PEISER, Heinrich, NYC-M – 1892/06/23:4a
PEISKER, Edmund, NYC-M - 1878/08/08:3a
PELIUSCH, Olga, 11, NYC-M, +@ on Genl Slocum – 1904/06/18:3c
PELLATH, Michael, Newark, NJ – 1909/02/12:6a
PELLNITZ, Fr., NYC-M – 1888/03/03:3a
PELTZER, William, 55, actor in G-A theater, + Chicago, IL – 1887/05/06:1f
PELTZMEYER, John, 46, carp., NYC-B – 1899/07/11:4a
PELZ, Charles, 51, weaver, Paterson, NJ – 1897/01/03:5d
PELZ, Katharina, 38, NYC-B - 1917/11/05:3e
PELZ, Siegfried, 58, SPD Munich, sales clerk, fr Silesia - 1913/06/22:3b
PENIG, Rudolph, 36, waiter, NYC-B – 1912/02/10:1f
PENNER, Jacob, 45, fr Russia, baker, active in Jewish orgs, NYC-B – 1912/01/10:2c
PENNY, Virginia, labor organizer 1860s-1870s, NYC, benefit planned – 1893/01/29:1f-g
PENRHIN, Lord, quarry-owner in Wales, obit "End of a Tyrant" 1907/05/07:4f
PENTECOST, Hugh Owen, 59, ex-minister & lawyer, SP, NYC-M – 1907/02/04:1f, 15:2c
PENTZ, Ernst von, 40, NYC-B – 1887/11/07:1g
PENZINATO, Paul, 62, Elizabeth, NJ - 1918/12/27:6a
PEPLIES, Otto, SPD Braunschweig, tailor & ex-alderman, *1842 Gumbinnen/East Prussia - 1915/10/03:3a
PEPPLER, William J., 28, clerk, NYC-M – 1903/03/31:1h
PEREBOOM, Anna, NYC-M – 1891/03/24:4a
PEREGRIN, William, SP, War 2, Akely, MN - 1918/03/14:1d

PERINKE, Julius, stonecutter, NYC-M – 1899/03/06:4a, 7:4a
PERKINS, George W., capitalist - 1920/06/19:4c
PERLE % Sleight
PERLE, August, 73, NYC-M – 1907/01/12:6a
PERLITZ, Karoline, Elizabeth, NJ – 1913/03/07:6a
PERLL, Wilhelmine, 71, NYC-Bx – 1907/10/21:6a
PERLMAN, Louis, 34,silk manuf., Paterson, NJ - 1916/07/31:3g
PERLMUTTER, Max, un. capmaker, NYC-M – 1891/06/06:1h
PERMITT, Heinrich, 45, SPD Sande/Schleswig/Gy – 1909/04/04:3b
PERNOD, Christian, NYC-M – 1889/01/24:4a
PEROE, Peter, fr Finland, silversmith, NYC-M – 1892/04/05:4b
PEROWSKAJA, Sophia, exec. April 1881 St Petersburg/Russia, her heroic life – 1882/11/05:4c-e
PERSAU, Jean, NYC-Bx – 1911/04/12:6a
PERSAU, Leopold, 42, NYC-M – 1891/03/23:4a
PERSIA, Muzaffar-Ed-Din Mirza, Shah of Persia – 1907/01/09:1a
PERSIA, Nasr-Ed-Din, Shah of - 1896/05/02:1f, 5:1d
PERSINA, Karl, NYC-M – 1904/01/16:4a
PERSKY, Joseph, 21, cloakmaker, NYC-M – 1896/12/03:3e
PERSON, Karl's wife, + on SS Oskar II on way home to New Haven, CT – 1908/11/20:3c
PERTHOLD, Andreas, NYC-Bx - 1920/09/26:12a
PESCHL % Rudert
PESKOWA, Lydia, 28, Russian Marxist journalist, + Oct. in Bern/CH - 1916/11/16:4d
PETAR, John, NYC-M – 1900/06/14:4a
PETELER % Freyseng
PETER, Albert, NYC-M, + 28 Mr, fam. 1882/05/17:3d
PETER, Anna, 40, NYC-M - 1919/03/16:12a
PETER, Carl, 67, un. carp., Jersey City,NJ - 1913/06/18:6a
PETER, Conrad, un. metal worker, NYC-M – 1904/03/22:4a
PETER, Emil, New Haven, CT – 1909/02/20:2d
PETER, George, NYC-M – 1891/07/02:4a
PETER, Katharina, 50, NYC-M – 1883/03/13:3c
PETER, Leopold, un. carp., Lynnbrook, LI – 1912/04/12:6a
PETER, Ottilie, NYC-M – 1891/03/19:4a
PETER, Stefan, 48, NYC-B – 1892/08/05:4a
PETER, William, NYC-M – 1893/09/24:5c
PETERHANSL, Anna, NYC-B – 1907/01/26:6a, fam. 30:6a
PETERHANSL, Frank, 62, SP, un. machinist, NYC-B - 1917/02/14:6a, fam. 19:6a
PETERMANN, Dr., 56, Gotha/Thueringen - 1878/10/15:2d

PETERMANN, Emil, SPD Apolda/Sax. - 1914/04/21:4d
PETERMANN, Frederick, NYC-Metropolitan - 1908/12/23:6a
PETERMANN, John Karl, SP, NYC-B - 1908/10/29:6a, 30:6a
PETERS % Heelein
PETERS, Auguste, 34, Guttenberg, NJ - 1916/07/11:6a
PETERS, C.F.A., 34, NYC-M - 1892/07/08:4a
PETERS, Caroline, b. Schliher, NYC-B - 1886/11/27:3b
PETERS, Franz W. O., 67, pianomaker, NYC-M - 1889/02/27:4a
PETERS, Franziska, b. Zugschwert, 54, NYC-M - 1896/03/08:5a
PETERS, Gerhardt, NYC-Bx - 1909/05/25:6a
PETERS, H., NYC-B - 1908/03/05:6a
PETERS, Helen, 27, NYC-M, + @ Genl Slocum - 1904/06/18:3c
PETERS, Jessie, 30, NYC-M - 1904/11/04:3e
PETERS, Johannes, un. cigarmaker, * 1855 Hamburg/Gy, USA 1881, SPD in Gy, un. cigarmaker, NYC-M - 1882/01/08:5e, =9:1g
PETERS, John C., 22, + during boxing match, Hoboken, NJ - 1904/10/03:1d
PETERS, Lilian, 18, NYC-M, + @Genl Slocum - 1904/06/29:1c
PETERS, Mary Adelaide, NYC - 1912/06/17:6a
PETERS, Rudolph, 28, elevator worker, NYC-B - 1907/09/22:9f
PETERS, Simon, innkeep, fr Hungary?, NYC-M - 1912/01/16:6c, =18:5f
PETERS, Wilhelmina, 61, Jersey City, NJ - 1912/12/05:6a
PETERS, William, SP, shoemaker, deli-owner & a co-fdr NYVZ, * Holstein Prov., Nyack, NY - 1915/07/11:7a, 11b
PETERSCHACK, John, fr Kaschau/Upper Hungary, Note - 1892/07/09:2e
PETERSEN % Hansen, % Hektor
PETERSEN, Anna Sophia, b. Jansen, 57, NYC-M - 1908/03/21:6a
PETERSEN, Charles, 23?, + St Louis, MO, fr NYC-M - 1890/04/10:4a
PETERSEN, Charles, 29, laborer, Swede, NYC-M - 1896/05/25:3g
PETERSEN, Charlotte, 65, Jersey City, NJ - 1902/08/01:4a
PETERSEN, Gustav, NYC-M - 1892/07/27:4a
PETERSEN, Hans Christian, 67, SP, tailor, * Ottense/DK, USA 1881, NYC-M - 1916/02/13:7a,9g
PETERSEN, Henry, carp., NYC-M - 1890/07/10:4a
PETERSEN, Louis, 49, waiter, NYC-M 1885/05/15:4a
PETERSEN, Maria, Elizabeth, NJ - 1907/09/13:6a
PETERSEN, Marie, 41, Jersey City Heights, NJ - 1907/07/20:6a
PETERSEN, Niels Lorenz, 81, furrier and SP, + Copenhague/Denmark - 1894/07/29:7g
PETERSEN, P. J., SLP, NYC-M - 1888/04/04:3b
PETERSEN, Peter, 69, NYC-M - 1894/10/18:4a
PETERSEN, Waldemar, 53, NYC-M - 1919/01/07:6a

PETERSON, Emil, un. carp., NYC-B - 1917/01/15:6a
PETERSON, Gottfried, baker, 50, NYC-B - 1909/06/04:2e
PETERSON, Henry, 66, deli-owner, NYC-M - 1906/01/18:4b
PETERSON, Peter, 45, driver, Swede, NYC-B - 1905/02/09:3b
PETERSON, Peter, laborer, NYC-B - 1886/07/09:2e
PETERSON, Peter, married Gussie Hentze, both Little Ferry, NJ - 1899/12/13:5b
PETERSON, Wade, Negro, lynched Shelbyville, KY - 1911/01/16:1d
PETERSON, William, NYC-B - 1915/04/13:6a
PETMEKY, Franz Josef, exec. Auburn, NY - 1885/08/22:1c
PETRI % Fischer
PETRI, Christina J.M. Schmidt, 49, NYC-B - 1879/05/04:5g
PETRI, Heinrich Carl, 21, NYC-M - 1891/07/16:4a
PETRI, Jacob, *Maarburg/E./Gy, NYC-M - 1897/11/01:4a
PETRI, John, fr Frankfurt?/Gy, NYC-B - 1892/07/29:4a
PETRI, John, owner Kaisergarten rest. on Coney Isl., + Passaic, NJ - 1914/08/12:2f
PETRI, Margarethe, b. Linn, NYC-M - 1882/11/12:8a
PETRI, Philip, 67, un. cigarmaker, NYC-M - 1901/03/28:4a
PETRICH, Julius, 46, NYC-M - 1917/04/07:6a
PETRICK, Frederick, 26, un. metallworker, NYC-M - 1909/03/20:6a, fam. 23:6a
PETRICZEK, Franz, 38, un. sugarbaker, *Vienna, SDP, NYC-B - 1902/05/30:3c, 4a, 31:4a, 1 June 1902:5a, =3:3b
PETRIE, James, 60, co-frd Enterprise, East Rutherford, NJ - 1915/09/07:6c
PETRIK, Anna, 43, NYC-M - 1899/11/08:4a, fam. 10:4a
PETRIKOFFSKY, Marie, 19, fr Russia, NYC-M - 1890/01/23:1g
PETRINA, Nicolo, Italian Socialist, + Messina earthquake - 1909/02/23:4d
PETROLL, Agnes, 5, NYC-Bx - 1907/09/15:7b
PETROLL, Gustav, 46, NYC-Bx - 1915/07/13:6a
PETROSINO case 1909/05/19:2
PETROSINO, Joseph, NYPD Lieutenant, +Palermo/Italy - 1909/03/14:1b, 15:1e, 16:1e, 17:1d, 10 Ap:1d, 11:1c, =13:2f
PETRY, Anna, b. Muehl, NYC-M - 1885/06/11:3d
PETRY, Katherina, NYC-M - 1894/10/16:4a
PETRY, Ludwig, NYC-B - 1919/08/20:6a
PETSCHAUER, Josef, 24, NYC-B - 1896/02/08:4a
PETSCHNIG, Florian, SP, un. machinist, married Ms Fichte, NYC-B - 1907/11/28:5e
PETTEK, Joseph, un. carp., NYC-B - 1909/01/15:6a
PETTER, Rudolf, un. carp., NYC-M - 1916/06/02:6a
PETTINGER, Maria, NYC-M - 1902/05/28:4a

PETTO, Martha, 27, servant, USA 12/1904, NYC-B – 1905/02/26:5a
PETTY, Sam, Negro, lynched Leland, Miss. - 1914/02/25:2b
PETZEL, Anton, 37, NYC-Metropolitan – 1905/10/29:5b
PETZKE, Frank, Marion, NJ – 1910/01/26:6a
PETZOLD % Eichenrodt
PETZOLD, Max, 46, SP, Newark, NJ – 1912/01/10:6a, 11:2b, 6a
PETZOLD, Reinhold, 35, baker, fr NYC or New Haven, CT –
    1892/04/10:1b
PETZOLD, un. structural iron worker, NYC-M – 1903/06/26:4a
PEUKERT, Oskar, 72, SPD, fr Leipzig, + Munich/Gy – 1913/02/16:3a
PEZOLD, Charles, NYC-Bx – 1900/07/08:1e
PEZZI, Louisa, 58, Italian SP, + Florence – 1911/04/05:4d
PFAFF, August Robert, 4, NYC-M – 1885/02/15:5g
PFAFF, Carl Heinrich, child, NYC-M - 1879/07/24:3a
PFAFF, Catherina, 1, NYC-M – 1885/08/12:3b
PFAFF, Felicitas, exec. Marseilles as alleged German spy - 1916/08/23:1d
PFAFF, Henry, SP, porcelain worker, NYC-M - 1920/10/06:1b,6a, = 12:2b
PFALZ, Henry G., 47, conductor for New York Arbeitersaengerbund,*
    Dresden/Sax., USA 1889, NYC - 1914/04/23:2e, 24:6a, 25:3e, 26:7c,
    fam. 26:7d; mem. 1915/04/22:6a,1916/04/22:6a
PFALZ, Henry G., NYC-M – 1903/07/16:4a
PFANNKUCH, Wilhelm, SPD Berlin, 70th birthday, note by Karl Kautsky –
    1911/12/10:3a-b
PFANNSTIEHL % Faber; PFANNSTIEL % Busch
PFARR, Christoph, 46, NYC-M - 1919/02/10:6a
PFARR, Joseph, un. cigarmaker, NYC-B – 1902/01/15:4a
PFAU, J., NYC-M – 1893/10/10:4a
PFAU, Ludwig, 73, German literary critic and liberal politician, + Stuttgart -
    1894/04/15:4c; inaug. of monument 1896/12/04:2e
PFEFFER, Fred, NYC-B – 1897/05/08:2e
PFEFFER, Louis, 61, NYC-M – 1902/04/22:4a
PFEFFER, William, 62, NYC-B - 1917/12/28:2d
PFEHLER, F., 45, shoemaker, Red Bank, NJ – 1912/12/03:3c
PFEIFELMANN, August, NYC-Bx – 1919/09/20:6a
PFEIFENBERGER, Julius, NYC-B – 1913/08/12:6c
PFEIFER % Eichhorn, % Eimer, % Habich
PFEIFER, Anton, NYC-M - 1915/02/09:6a
PFEIFER, Carl, West New York, NJ - 1918/08/19:6a
PFEIFER, Ernst, ATB Kraftsdorf/Thuer., War 1- 1914/11/01:3b
PFEIFER, Frederick, 54, Guttenberg, NJ - 1915/05/29:6a
PFEIFER, George, baker, NYC-B – 1910/07/21:3a
PFEIFER, Gussie, 22, embroiderer, NYC-Bx – 1905/09/18:1c

PFEIFER, Jacob, policeman, Newark, NJ - 1878/03/26:1e
PFEIFF, Olga, 24, NYC-M - 1886/03/17:3a
PFEIFFER, Christopher, Jersey City, NJ - 1914/10/04:1g
PFEIFFER, Eliza, b. Steiger, 36, SP, NYC-B - 1906/12/02:7c, 3:6a
PFEIFFER, Elizabeth, 43, NYC-B - 1916/01/09:11d
PFEIFFER, Emma, SP, NYC-Q - 1909/08/04:6a, =5:1f, fam. 9:6a
PFEIFFER, Gustave G., NYC-M - 1917/07/08:7a
PFEIFFER, J's wife, + during East St Louis, MO strike - 1886/04/10:1b, =12:1a, inquest 13:1e-f etc.
PFEIFFER, Karl, NYC-Bx - 1907/02/10:7a
PFEIFFER, Leopold, NYC-Q - 1900/06/17:5a
PFEIFFER, Lillian, NYC-M, + @ Genl Slocum - 1904/06/18:3c
PFEIFFER, Loretta A., 19, NYC-M - 1905/08/06:1h, 7:3e
PFEIFFER, Richard, NYC-B - 1914/10/25:7b
PFEIFFER, Robert, Jersey City Hgts, NJ - 1915/05/14:6a
PFEIFFER, Rudolph, 19, NYC-Q - 1914/01/12:6a, 11:7d, fam. 17:6a
PFEIFFER, Sophia, 79, & son Charles, 36, NYC-B - 1901/03/23:2g
PFEIFFER, Theodor, 32, smith at Singer in NJ, USA 1866 - 1879/01/18:1f
PFEIFFER, Wilhelm, un. cigarmaker, NYC-M - 1894/12/23:4a
PFEIFFER, William, 14, Newark, NJ - 1905/04/24:3d
PFEIL, Emanuel, un. pianomaker, NYC-B - 1889/04/21:5c
PFEIL, Emma, b. Baalmann, 48, NYC-M - 1904/05/16:4a, fam. 19:4a
PFEIL, Heinrich, German composer & Liberal politician - 1899/05/14:12b
PFEIL, John, & wife Edith, ca 50, NYC-M - 1920/05/23:3b
PFEILER, William, SLP, NYC-M - 1897/02/21:5a, 22:4a
PFENNIG, Adolph, 29, grocer, NYC - 1885/09/25:4b
PFENNIG, Dora, 45, NYC-M, +@Genl Slocum - 1904/06/18:3c
PFENNIG, John, 68, NYC-Q - 1900/08/08:4a
PFENNIG, Martha, 52, Hoboken, NJ - 1901/10/02:4a
PFENNIG, Wolfgang, West New York, NJ - 1908/02/24:6a
PFENNING, John, ~20, worker, Jersey City Heights, NJ - 1891/09/11:4d
PFEUFFER, Wilhelm, 27, bartender, NYC-Bx - 1912/01/04:6a, 5:1d
PFINDER, George, 40, carp., NYC-M - 1897/04/14:2e
PFINGSTEN, Johanna, NYC-Bx - 1917/12/04:6c
PFINGSTHORN, Albert, 40, realtor, Mt Vernon, NY - 1913/05/27:2c
PFIRSCHING, Emma, NYC-B - 1918/06/11:6a S.a. Firsching
PFISTER, A., NYC-M - 1914/07/02:6a
PFISTER, Eugene, NYC-M - 1886/09/07:3d
PFISTER, Fred, NYC-B - 1886/07/28:2c, 5 Aug:4c, 6:2c, 7:2c, 10:2c, 11:2d, 14:2d, 17:1a-c, 21:2c, 28:2e, 23 Sept:3c
PFISTER, Georg, NYC-Q - 1901/07/25:4a
PFISTER, Jacob, NYC-M - 1898/09/07:1f

PFISTER, John B., baker, NYC-M - 1879/03/20:4a, 21:1f
PFISTER, John, 79, ex-sexton at St Leonard's, NYC-B - 1909/02/24:3b
PFISTER, Raimund, 62, NYC-M - 1892/07/15:4a
PFITZNER, Frederick, Newark, NJ - 1920/05/13:6a
PFIZER, Ferdinand, brewer, NYC-M - 1888/10/20:1g
PFIZER, Katie, 25, NYC-M - 1892/05/27:4a
PFLAESTERER, Anna K., 59, NYC-M - 1912/04/14:7d, 16:6a, fam. 17:6a
PFLANZ, Karl, 37, Newark, NJ - 1883/05/28:3a
PFLAUMER, Max, NYC-M - 1900/05/05:4a
PFLIMPFL, Josef, 44, SP & manager for AKK, Vienna - 1909/09/26:3d
PFLUEGER, Gottlieb, 49, pianomaker, NYC-M - 1887/05/10:2f,3c, 11:3c
PFLUG, ..., Steinway worker, fam. 1882/05/06:3c
PFLUMM, Amanda, 52, NYC-M - 1908/12/30:6a
PFODENHAUER, Anna Margarethe, 54, NYC-M - 1898/01/20:4a
PFODENHAUER, Theodor, 70, un. carp., SP, *15 Se 1839 Rudolstadt/Gy, NYC-M - 1909/05/30:7b,c
PFOERTNER, August, NYC-M - 1905/10/15:5a
PFOHL, J., Newark, NJ - 1910/03/29:6a
PFORTNER, George J., 22, NYC-B - 1896/12/24:4c
PFORTNER, Joseph P., 50, butcher, NYC - 1905/03/01:3b
PFRANG, August, 54, SP, brewer, USA 1882, Syracuse, NY - 1913/01/27:6a
PFUND, Theodor von, ship's steward, @ 1900 dock fire, Hoboken, NJ 1900/07/03:1c, 4:1c
PFUNDT, Amandus, un. typesetter, NYC-B - 1910/11/01:6a
PHAIR, John P., exec. Windsor, VT - 1879/04/11:1c
PHELINGER, Gottlieb, 49, innkeep, NYC-M - 1887/05/10:2f
PHELPS, Silas M., exec. Boston, MA - 1912/01/27:1f
PHIFER, Miles, Negro, lynched near Montgomery, AL - 1919/10/01:1e,4a
PHILIPP, Theo., 50, NYC-Q - 1919/03/05:6a
PHILIPP, Theodor, 27, fr Doebern/Saxony, USA 1880, SLP?, un. carp., NYC - 1887/12/27:1h, 4e
PHILIPP, Theresia, NYC-M - 1891/07/03:4a
PHILIPPE % Becker
PHILIPPI, Alfred, edit. Sunday edition NYSZ, *17 Jy 1849 Berlin, USA 1876, NYC-M - 1906/02/07:3g
PHILLIPS, David G., NYC writer, shot by F. Goldsborough - 1911/01/24:2d, 25:1e, 4b
PHILLIPS, Edward, Rev. Dr., Hazleton, PA - 1901/05/18:1e-g, 23:4c, 1 June:1c
PHILLIPS, Gertrude, b. De Jong, NYC-M - 1920/02/11:6a
PHILLIPS, Rose, SP, NYC-M - 1917/06/03:7a, = 5:1e

PHILLIPS, Wendell, 100th anniv. US reformer & abol. – 1911/11/29:4a-b
PIATE % Bredehorst
PICARD, Jean, NYC-M – 1912/03/22:6a
PICK, Henry, 7, NYC-M – 1910/04/14:6a
PICKARD, Alexander, 63, un. painter, NYC-Bx – 1908/11/24:6a, 25:6a
PICKARD, Benjamin, British leader of miners – 1904/02/05:2d
PICKARD, Henriette, b. Wolff, NYC-Bx – 1906/11/03:6a; mem. – 1911/11/02:6a
PICKART, Richard, Elizabeth, NJ – 1911/12/12:6a
PICKEL, Peter, 63, merchant, NYC-M – 1882/03/03:1g
PICKETT, Charles, Negro, lynched Ellisville, GA – 1911/04/09:1f
PICKETT, Richard, Negro, lynched Laurens, NC – 1913/08/13:3f
PICKNER, Henry, un. machinist, NYC-B – 1907/11/21:6a
PICKRUHL, Karl, NYC-B – 1891/06/24:4a
PIEK, Henry, + as child, mem. – 1911/04/12:6a
PIENEMANN, Fred, ship stewart, Hoboken, NJ – 1896/08/11:1d
PIEPER, F. B., NYC-M – 1891/04/11:4a
PIEPER, Julius, 41, un. carp., NYC-Q – 1898/08/14:5e
PIERCE, Sarah Tahknawata, 30, Mohawk from Caughnawagha/Montreal, + NYC, = Montreal - 1894/09/29:3g
PIERNEY % Stocker
PIERZCHALLY, Wilhelm, un. carp., NYC-M – 1903/03/10:4a
PIESCHEL, Alfred, infant, NYC-M – 1888/09/01:3b
PIESCHEL, Herda, infant, NYC-M – 1891/10/21:4a
PIESCHEL, Karl, SP, USA 1880 fr Leipzig, Maywood, NJ - 1920/05/06:6a, = 12:3e
PIESCHEL, Marie, NYC-M, + Narrowsburg, NY – 1897/07/10:4a, 11:5a, fam. 13:4a
PIETJAN, Paul, machinist, NYC – 1906/09/07:6d
PIETSCH % Caspar
PIETSCH, Gustave, will, NYC – 1902/05/17:3b
PIETZ, Carl, 45, fr Darmstadt/Gy, NYC-M – 1893/12/02:4a
PIETZ, George, SLP,un. cab.maker,NYC-M - 1894/02/11:5c,13:4a
PIETZKER, Ernst, 28, architect, NYC-M – 1885/08/06:1g
PIETZSCH, Charles, 47, NYC-Q – 1905/06/30:4a
PIEZER, Michael, Elizabeth, NJ - 1915/05/09:7a
PIGER, John, Greenville, NJ – 1903/07/01:4a
PIGOT, Lillie, 25, fr Elsass to USA 1890, NYC-Q – 1891/01/27:4e
PIKART, Cornelius, carp., Paterson, NY – 1904/10/30:5d
PILATI, Hubert F., Hoboken, NJ - 1917/05/03:6a
PILGER, Louis, un. machinist, NYC-B – 1901/08/16:4a
PILLING, Ernst Ferd., laborer, * Saxony, NYC-M 1894/11/21:3a

PIMM, Henrietta & George, NYC-M, + @ Genl Slocum – 1904/06/17:3c,
PINES, James, 39, un. trolley driver, leader 1895 strike, NYC-B –
   1900/07/02:3h
PINGREE, Hazen S., ex-gov of Michigan – 1901/06/19:1b
PINKERTON, Allan, fdr of Pinkertons, + Chicago – 1884/07/02:1c
PINKERTON, Robert A., 59, head Pinkerton agency, very crit. obit –
   1907/08/18:1f
PIO, Gus, NYC-M - 1916/03/19:7a
PIPER, Frank, Negro, lynched Alexandria, LA – 1904/05/11:1c
PIPP, Henry, 38, innkeep, Westchester, NY – 1901/04/15:1h
PIRANKY, Maria, NYC-M – 1891/03/15:5b
PIRCHER, Louis, German soc. in Paris/Fr. s. 1879, * Steiermark/Austria,
   shoemaker – 1909/07/11:3b-c
PIRINGER, Anna, SDP?, NYC-M – 1904/08/22:4a
PISCH, Albert, Jersey City Heights, NJ – 1901/01/23:4a
PISCHKER, Gustav, 64, Jersey City, NJ - 1917/11/13:6a
PISTER % Mensching
PISTER, Hubert, NYC-M - 1915/03/28:7c
PISTOR, Karl, SPD Frankfurt-Oberrad, War 1 - 1914/11/01:3b
PITSCHKE, William F., judge, NYC-M – 1890/02/17:4f
PITTEL, Joseph, 65, NYC-M – 1903/11/23:4a
PITTINGER, John, 80, Oxford, NJ – 1912/10/23:3c
PITTROFF, Karl, ATB Reichenbach/Vogtland, War 1 - 1914/11/01:3b
PITZER, William, un. typesetter, NYC-M – 1900/05/11:4a
PIUS, Joseph, 2, NYC-B – 1890/12/20:4a
PIVA, Vittorio, 32, Italian socialist, + Rome – 1907/08/26:4d
PLACE, Martha, to be exec. Ossining, NY – 1898/07/13:4a, 15:4b,
   1899/03/17:1h, 19:1f, 2b, 20:3c, done 21:1f
PLAETZ, Georg, un. cigarmaker., NYC-B – 1893/08/14:4a
PLANTENBERG, Louis, 28, Newton Village, LI – 1883/07/14:3c
PLANTIKO, Hermann, Dr., 36, lawyer fr Berlin, NYC-M – 1887/06/29:1g
PLAPPER, Carl, 34, NYC-M – 1900/07/22:5a
PLAPPER, Henry, NYC-M – 1903/10/28:4a
PLASCHKE, Elisabeth, 12, Jersey City Heights, NJ – 1888/02/22:3b
PLASSMANN, Caroline, 17, NYC-M – 1892/05/03:4a
PLASSMANN, Friedrich, 50, un. cigarmaker, SLP?, NYC-B –
   1898/01/18:4a, 19:1f,4a
PLATE, Bernhard E., un. carp., NYC-Bx – 1913/04/28:6a, 29:6a
PLATE, Conrad, 54, un. carp., NYC-M – 1887/02/05:3c
PLATE, Fritz, 50, NYC-B – 1910/07/06:6a
PLATE, John, 52, NYC-B - 1894/01/21:5d

PLATE, Ludwig, 65,SP, un. machinist,*Apr. 1848 Braunschweig, USA 1885, NYC-B - 1913/12/06:6a, 7:7a,d, =8:3f, fam. 10:6a
PLATE, M. D., 68, NYC-M – 1899/02/12:5a
PLATE, Marie, SLP, NYC-B - 1896/01/08:4a
PLATT, Anton, un. carp., NYC-M – 1912/06/01:6a
PLATT, Thomas, 76, US Senator, NYC-M, on his defeat 1906/06/20:3g, + noted 1910/03/07:2c, 8:2e,4a-b
PLATTE % Kissell
PLATTE, Friedrich, 71, NYC-B – 1905/04/14:4a
PLATZ, Anna, NYC-B - 1915/04/02:5e
PLATZ, Hannchen, 89, NYC-M – 1891/04/09:4a
PLATZ, Otto, un. carp., NYC-Bx – 1910/06/04:6a, 5:7b
PLATZBLATT, Moritz, 1, NYC-B – 1896/09/16:2d
PLECHANOW, Georg, Russian marxist - 1918/06/06:4c, 21 Jy:6c-d
PLEHWE, Russian Interior Min., + by revol. – 1904/07/29:1a, 29:2a-b, 3d-f, 30:1h, 2c, 3e-f, 31:1b, 9a-f, 2 Aug:1c, local Jews on Plehwe 15:2f, notes 18:2d, 19:2e-f
PLEIS % Kettler
PLENGE, Rosine, 32, NYC-Bx – 1910/08/06:6a
PLENNIS, John, NYC-B – 1907/08/01:6a
PLESS, August A., 25, NYC-M – 1900/05/17:1e
PLETSCHER, Heinrich, 49, un. carp., Swiss?, NYC-Bx – 1906/02/18:5b
PLETSCHER, Regina, 67, NYC-M – 1908/09/23:6a
PLEWE, Hermann, NYC-B - 1893/10/12:4b, 15:5b
PLISCHKE, Martha, b. Kandzia, 34, Newark, NJ - 1919/06/03:6a
PLOCEK, Joseph, NYC-Q - 1915/09/12:7a
PLOEGER, Gustav, 46, un. cigarmaker, NYC-M - 1895/10/17: 4a
PLOEGER, Jacob, 60, pianomaker?, NYC-M – 1883/05/31:3b
PLOEGER, Louis, NYC-Bx – 1912/04/03:2c
PLOETZ, Anna, b. Rodehan, NYC-M - 1915/04/02:6a
PLOTKIN, Rebecca, 70, & granddaughter Rebecca Mesnickoff, NYC-B – 1901/12/05:4a
PLUECKEBAUM, Pauline, 42, NYC-M - 1915/02/06:6a
PLUENNECKE, John, Rev., German Methodist Church, War 2, Seguin, TX - 1919/01/01:2f
PLUMEYER, Hermann, 56, un. printer at NYSZ, * Braunschweig/Gy,USA 1881,NYC-B - 1914/02/19:3b,6a, 20:6a
PLUNDECKE, Julie, NYC-M – 1883/07/24:3d
PLUNKETT, Jerold, 12, NYC-M, + @on Genl Slocum – 1904/06/21:1f
PLUNKETT, Joseph, Irish patriot, exec. Dublin - 1916/05/06:1c
POBJEDONOSZEW, head of Holy Synod in Russia, harsh obit – 1907/04/17:4f-g

PODRATZKY, Franz, machinist, NYC-B – 1910/11/30:6a
POE, Edgard Allan, 50th anniv. Of death – 1899/10/08:13e-f
POEHLAND, Gretchen, 4, NYC-B – 1892/05/18:4a
POEHLAND, Marie, b. Weidenbaum, 38, NYC-B – 1905/09/22:4a
POEHN, Eliza, 61, NYC-M - 1914/05/10:6a, 11:6a
POEHN, Oscar, NYC-M - 1916/03/07:6a
POELLOT, Leonard, 53, NYC-Bx - 1914/05/07:6a
POELLOT, Louis, 29, NYC-M – 1892/11/05:4a, 6:5c, fam. 8:4a; Mem. 1893/11/03:4c
POELLOT, Marie, W. New York, NJ – 1907/02/19:6a
POESCHEL, Rosalie, b. Hertel, 52, Union Hill, NJ – 1888/05/19:2g
POESENECKER, Theo. Conrad, 38, fr Nassau/Gy?, NYC-M – 1893/12/14:4a
POESL, John, Guttenberg, NJ - 1915/01/23:6a
POESSING % Does
POETER, Albert, NYC-M – 1886/01/14:3a
POETHIG, Richard, 28, NYC-M - 1919/08/27:6a, 28:6a, mem. 1920/08/25:6a
POETSCHKE, William, 28, NYC-Q – 1910/12/20:1a
POETTGEN, William, 36, SP?, NYC-M - 1914/01/23:6a
POETZSCH, Elizabeth, NYC-M - 1918/11/10:12a
POGANY, George, 47, varnisher, fr Hungary, SP, NYC-B – 1908/01/15:1c
POHL, Meta, 13, NYC – 1892/12/22:4a
POHLE, Reinhard, 49, NYC-M – 1892/03/18:4a
POHLIG, Mrs, 28, Paterson, NJ - 1920/06/17:2d
POHLMANN % Prelle, ZIEGLER % Precht
POHLMANN, Diedrich, 49, hotelier, Jersey City Heights, NJ – 1888/04/12:2f
POHLMANN, John, un. butcher, NYC-M - 1920/08/04:6a
POKORNY, comrade, 42, glasscutter, SP Bruenn/Moravia – 1910/06/05:3b
POKORNY, Wenzel, 64, SLP, un. weaver, Union Hill, NJ – 1898/12/25:5a, 26:1g, 4a, =27:1g
POLACK, Christine, b. Bush, NYC-B – 1892/05/11:4a
POLAK, Max, his infant son +, NYC-M – 1909/10/01:6a
POLANSKY % Selig
POLB, Theodore, Prof., 38, Reading, PA   1900/05/23:1b
POLER, Albert, 40, machinist, Newark, NJ - 1914/09/04:6d
POLHEMUS, Charles's wife, 20, Point Pleasant, NJ - 1913/05/08:2b
POLIS, Albert, 53, manager Hamburg-Amerika Linie, * Hamburg, USA 1914, Hoboken, NJ - 1915/02/28:11e
POLISH, John, (a) striking quarry worker Lemont/Joliett, IL, killed by militia – 1885/05/08:2d, 10:1c, 14:2b-c, s.a. Staeber; Kajowa

POLIWANOFF, Peter, Russian revol., + Lorient/F – 1903/09/02:2e
POLL, Hedwig, NYC-Q – 1906/11/25:7c
POLLACK, John, un. painter, NYC-Bx - 1916/11/29:6a
POLLAK, Adolph, NYC-M – 1907/01/17:1f
POLLE % Hertlein
POLLINGER, Anton, 26, un. butcher, NYC – 1912/08/25:7a, c
POLLIS, Dom., un. carp., NYC-M – 1905/01/19:4a
POLLITZ, Hugo, 45, fur dealer, NYC-M – 1889/08/08:4e
POLLWITZ, Mrs, NYC-B, + on ship Mystery – 1887/07/12:1c-d, 13:2g
POLNICK, Julius, 73, NYC-M - 1915/04/30:6a
POLONSKY, Marina, Russian revol., + Paris/France – 1898/10/28:2e
POLSTER, Dominik, un. painter, Hoboken, NJ - 1918/11/05:6a
POLTER, Georg, 63, NYC-B – 1901/10/10:4a
POMERANTZ, Michael, butcher, Philadelphia, PA – 1896/04/25:3f
POMMER, Charles W., un. brewer, secy Brewer Union #1, *18 Oct 1852
  Thueringia, USA 1860, NYC- Bx – 1913/06/09:3d,6a, 10:6a, =11:3c
POMMER, Henry's wife, Newark, NJ – 1912/12/30:6a
PONGRATZ, Anna, 59, Union Course, LI - 1917/02/15:6a
PONTY % Zukschwert
POOK, Hermann G., un. carp., NYC-M – 1903/10/08:4a
POOLE, Joseph, Irish patriot, exec. in Dublin – 1883/12/19:1a
POPART, Marie, b. Skalizky, 31, NYC-M – 1891/11/09:4a
POPE LEO XIII, + Rome – 1903/07/21:1b, 2b, 22:1d,2c, 23:2c,3c, 24:1h,
  =25:1b, 26:1c, 29:1b, 30:1h, 2b-c, 31:1h, 4 Aug:2, 2 Sept:2c-d
POPE PIUS IX, + Rome – 1878/02/08:2f-g
POPE PIUS X, + Rome - 1914/08/20:1e,4a-c, 22:1e
POPE, Amalia, 77, NYC-B – 1907/01/14:6a
POPOVICH, Svetozar, NYC-Q, + Harrisburg, PA – 1917/11/08:6a
POPP, Bernhard, NYC-M - 1920/11/16:6a
POPP, Caspar, 32, NYC-B – 1907/08/27:3a
POPP, Charles, 27, NYC-M - 1916/12/17:11e
POPP, Conrad J., NYC-M – 1896/10/12:4a, 13:4a
POPP, Ernest A.,52,un.cigarmkr,NYC-B - 1914/08/19:6a,c,20:6a
POPP, Friedrich, un. baker, NYC-M – 1887/01/06:3c
POPP, Josephine, 65, NYC-Bx - 1918/02/18:6a
POPP, machinist, NYC-M?, fam. 1897/02/07:5b
POPPE, Alois, 67, SLP, NYC-B – 1886/05/21:3b
POPPE, Carl Christoph, 19, NYC-B - 1894/01/25:4a
POPPE, Charles, 38, restaurant, NYC-M – 1882/07/20:4e
POPPE, Franz, 81, German poet, * 24 Mr 1824 Rastede, + Oldenburg -
  1915/10/28:4g
POPPE, Philipp Wilhelm, un. carp., NYC-M – 1901/06/16:5b

POPPE, Robert, NYC-M – 1919/09/18:6a
POPPENHUSEN, Conrad, 65, ex-pres. L.I. RR, fdr of an educational instit. For poor, good obit., NYC-B – 1883/12/22:1f
POPPER, ..., 65, NYC-M – 1905/04/11:3c
POPPINGER, August, NYPD, NYC-B - 1915/10/26:6b
PORGES, Julius, teacher at Jewish Free School #3, fr Budapest/Hung., NYC-M – 1882/06/16:1g
PORITZ, Elizabeth, actress, NYC-B, + Philadelphia, PA - 1913/11/27:1b
PORK, Henry, NYC-M, +@ on Genl Slocum – 1904/06/18:3c
PORRET, Friedrich, 60, tailor, NYC-M – 1899/08/24:1g
PORS, Hans, 53, un. cigarmaker, NYC-Bx – 1905/12/03:5b
PORSUS, Emilie, b. Stohloch, 26, NYC-B – 1890/06/20:4a
PORTEN, VAN DER, Charles F., SP, cigarmaker, NYC-B - 1916/09/02:2a, = 5:4d
PORTER, David Dixon US admiral – 1891/02/14:1c, =18:1e
PORTER, Preston, Negro, lynched Limon, CO – 1900/11/17:1c, 19:1c
PORTH, Auguste, b. Wichmann, NYC-M – 1885/11/21:4a
PORTH, Georg, 54, teacher, waiter & SP org., *Kamien/Galicia, + Budapest/Hungary – 1912/05/19:3f
PORTH, Julius, 41, NYC-M – 1889/11/23:5a
PORTUGAL, Carlos, King of, killed by anarchist – 1908/02/02:1a-b, 3:1a-b,4a-b, 17:1b
PORTUGALL % Maas
POSAUTZ, Mary, NYC-M – 1918/12/23:6a
POSPISIK, Joseph, pianomaker, NYC-M – 1911/07/14:1f
POSSEHL, Franz, 57, locksmith & SPD Rostock/Gy – 1912/08/18:3b
POST, Anna, 50, NYC-M, +@ on Genl Slocum – 1904/06/17:3c
POST, Charles W., 60, US industrialist, pres. of Postum Cereal Co. in Battle Creek, MI, crit. obit - 1914/05/10:1d
POST, Henry, 50, salesman, NYC-B – 1904/03/22:3c
POST, Philippine, b. Bongardt, 49, NYC-B – 1912/11/04:6a
POSTLER, comrade, 48, secy of Leatherworkers' Union, + Vienna/Austria – 1909/08/15:3e
POTOKI, Andreas, Count, gov. of Galicia, + by Ruthenian patriot – 1908/04/13:2a, 14:1d, 15:1a, 29:4e-f
POTOSKY, Amalia, 79, NYC-M – 1891/04/12:5a
POTSCHIEMBA, Louise, b. Waldmann, NYC-M – 1882/03/17:3b
POTTER, Bill, Negro, lynched Livermore, KY – 1911/04/22:1c
POTTER, Daniel, Dr., 64, NYC-M - 1916/08/19:1d
POTTIER, Eugene, French labor poet, + 1888, his life – 1896/11/15:3a
POTTLEBAUM, Herman, 50, NYC-M, +@ Genl Slocum – 1904/06/17:3c
POTTS, Gustav, painter, & his wife, NYC-Bx – 1892/07/10:5d

POTTS, Helen, 19, + 1 Fb, inquest, NYC-M – 1891/03/22:1g, 24:2f, etc
POUNCEFOOTE, Lord, 74, ex-amb. in US – 1902/05/25:1h
POWELL, Samuel, 64, former mayor, NYC-B - 1879/02/07:4e
POYDIES, Solomon, Negro, lynched Lacassine Mill, LA – 1901/12/09:1b
PRAAST, Rudolf, 58, shoemaker, SLP, NYC-B – 1898/07/14:1d, 4a
PRACHT, Adolf, 67, un. cigarmaker, NYC-B – 1899/02/06:4a
PRACHT, Frank, SP, un. cigarmaker, NYC-M - 1917/09/21:6a
PRACHT, Martin, un. cigarmaker, NYC-B – 1893/09/12:4a, 13:4a
PRACHT, Regina, 70, NYC-M – 1907/09/16:6a
PRAEGER, Dietrich, 6, Jersey City, NJ – 1885/11/26:1e, =27:3a
PRAETORIUS, Edward L., 49, publ. St Louis Times - 1915/11/02:2b
PRAGER, Robert P., lynched Collinsville, IL - 1918/04/06:1g, 8:1c, 12:1f, 16:2a, = St Louis 24:6b, trial of murderers 14 May:1d, 30:1f, 31:1e, freed 2 June:1d, 5:2e
PRAGER, Sigmund, 54, insurance agent, NYC – 1897/01/14:1d
PRAHM, Otto, 21, son of SP member Rainer Prahm, Secaucus,NJ, - 1920/09/16:6a, 17:6a, 18:2f, fam. 24:6a
PRANDEL, Hans, 38, un. butcher, NYC-M - 1916/02/08:6a
PRANG, Louis, former German radical, lithographer, * Breslau, USA 1850, + Los Angeles —1909/06/16:1f, 17:4c
PRAUNIER, Georges, 28, French soldier, NYC-M - 1917/11/05:2e
PRAUSE, Auguste, NYC-Q – 1900/03/03:4a
PRAVICA, Rosa, NYC-M - 1916/12/11:6a
PRAWDZWESKI, Annie, 15, NYC-M, +@Genl Slocum – 1904/06/18:3c
PRAWITZKI, Henrietta, 14, NYC-M, + @ Genl Slocum – 1904/06/17:3c
PRCHAL, Prokop, 43, un. tailor, NYC-M – 1883/07/23:3c
PRECHT, Sophie, b. Ziegler, 67, NYC-M – 1909/10/09:6a
PRECHT, William, un. cigarmaker, NYC-M – 1905/06/12:4a, 13:4a
PRECHTEL, John, un. butcher, NYC-Bx - 1917/12/06:6a
PREDE, Albert, 37, NYC-M – 1890/07/21:4a
PREIBE, Theodore, 34, stone mason & dem. Pol., NYC-M – 1894/11/02:3d
PREIGER, Adolf, SPD Friedrichsdorf/Taunus, War 1 - 1914/11/01:3b
PREININGER, Maria, 48, NYC-Bx – 1905/12/26:4a, =27:4a, fam. 28:4a
PREITSCHAT, Rudolph, Newark, NJ – 1904/07/14:3c
PRELLE, Gertrude, b. Pohlmann, NYC-M - 1878/05/28:3b
PRESCH, August, 56, cigar packer, NYC-M - 1894/10/06:4a
PRESCHEL, Gustav, 61, fr Glauchau/Silesia, Union Hill, NJ – 1887/04/21:3e
PRESCHING, Therese, 24, Hoboken, NJ – 1905/01/02:1a, 13:3c
PRESS % Meyer
PRESSEL, George, 33, NYC-M - 1894/01/12:4a
PRESSERT, Gottwald, 57, NYC-Bx – 1908/04/21:2b

PRESSLER, Hermann, West Newark, NJ - 1917/02/18:7a
PRESTIN, Paul, NYC-M - 1904/09/27:4a
PRESTON, Tom, Negro, lynched Gaston, SC - 1893/08/01:1e
PRETSCHER, Valentin, un. machinist, NYC-B - 1907/12/30:6a
PREUSE, Marie, b. Evers, 32, NYC-M - 1892/07/31:5c
PREUSS, August, NYC-B - 1918/11/09:6a
PREUSS, Caroline, NYC-B - 1918/11/12:6a
PREUSS, Ernestine, 45, NYC-M - 1911/05/15:6a
PREUSS, Frank, 38, iron worker, NYC-B - 1915/06/17:6c
PREUSS, Minna, b. Gross, NYC-B - 1889/04/20:4a
PREUSSCHOFF % Wickert
PREUSSE, Adolf B., 22, electrician, NYC-B - 1907/09/14:3b
PREUSSEN, Karl Friedrich, nephew of William I, + Berlin - 1885/06/16:1a
PREVISO, Eduard, ~63, Sudeten German adventurer, '48er, + in Mexico - 1883/03/21:2e
PREY, Eduard, un. carp. & SPD Hamburg/Gy - 1900/01/03:2e
PRICE, Sandy, Negro, lynched Watkinsville, GA - 1905/06/30:1h
PRICE, Vincent, Dr., US industrialist, inventor of baking powder, * Troy, NY, + Chicago - 1914/07/17:2f
PRICKETT, F. D. B., Rev., Metuchen, NJ, killed by Archie Herron - 1908/07/16:1g, 17:3c, 28:1e
PRIEBE, John, un. mason, NYC-M - 1900/11/20:4a, 21:4a
PRIEBE, Valentin, NYC-M - 1904/10/07:4a, 8:4a, 9:5a
PRIEBST, Gustav, 45, NYC-M - 1902/01/01:1c
PRIESTER, Fritz, un. baker, NYC-M - 1910/12/02:6a
PRIETH, Louis, bus. magr Freie Zeitung, Newark, NJ - 1878/10/18:4d, =21:4d
PRIGGAN, Heinrich, 15, NYC-B - 1892/07/22:4a
PRIGGE, George, 34, NYC-B - 1894/01/31:4a
PRILL, Ernst, un. upholsterer, NYC-M - 1894/01/10:4a
PRINCE, Albert, un. carp., NYC-M - 1898/02/05:4a, 6:5a
PRINCE, Samuel, Tammany politician - 1914/08/12:4c
PRINCIP, Gavrilo, murderer of Franz Ferdinand of Austria in Sarajevo, + in jail near Prague - 1918/05/02:1d
PRINSKY, Hugo, 34, NYC-M - 1890/03/30:5b
PRINZ, Benjamin, 26, balloon pilot, Newark, NJ, + Asbury Park, NJ - 1910/08/13:1e
PRINZ, Heinrich, 65, SPD alderman in Frankfurt/Main - 1909/07/10:4e
PRIORI, Lorenzo, exec. Ossining, NY - 1901/02/07:3d
PRISCO, Anielo, 32, "Zopo the Gimp," mobster, NYC-M - 1912/12/17:1f
PRISJASCHNUK, Matrona, Russian school teacher & revol., + in Kiew Jail - 1910/03/29:4e-f

PRISSGRAFF, Henry, 26, porter, NYC-M – 1891/11/21:1h
PRITZER, Alfons, 40, NYC-M - 1915/08/23:6a
PRITZL, Wolfgang, un. brewer, NYC-M – 1909/12/30:6a
PROBANSKA, Marie, 16, fr Posen/Gy, USA 1884, NYC-M – 1885/02/12:1f
PROBANSKI, Joseph, un. brewer, NYC-M - 1916/11/04:6a
PROBBER, Louis, 19, grocer, NYC-Bx – 1909/05/03:1e, 4:2c, 8:2d, 30 June:6a
PROBST, Emil, 44, NYC-M – 1890/05/12:4a
PROBST, Jacob, 53, NYC-B – 1905/12/16:4a
PROBST, John, driver, NYC-M – 1893/05/04:1g
PROBST, Joseph, NYC-Bx - 1916/12/29:6a
PROBST, Kate, 26, NYC-M, +@ Genl Slocum – 1904/06/17:3c, 18:3c
PROBST, M., NYC-B – 1906/10/05:6a
PROCHASKA, Marie, 14, Jersey City, NJ – 1886/02/01:2e
PROCHNOW, Bertha, NYC-B – 1896/08/26:4a
PROCHNOW, Fritz, un. cigarmaker, SP, *Arch/Pomer./Gy, NYC-M – 1911/03/28:6a, 29:2c, 6a, =31 March:2c, ashes at sea 26 May:3c
PROCHNOW, Theresa, 55, NYC-M – 1902/02/25:4a
PROEBSTER, Frank, worker in chemical factory, NYC-B – 1903/06/11:4b
PROEFRIEDT, William, 63?, NYC-M – 1891/04/04:4a
PROEHL, John, 45, un. cigarmaker, NYC-M – 1903/03/16:4a, 17:4a
PROESCHER, Charles, 40, butcher, NYC-M - 1878/11/19:4b,28:1g
PROESSLER, Bernhard, 40, un. baker, Hoboken, NJ - 1914/12/31:6a
PROESTLER, Sebastian, SLP, fr Unterduerrbach/Wuerzburg, NYC-M – 1892/06/07:4a, 22 Dec:4f
PROETZENBERGER, Otto, Viennese worker killed by police – 1911/10/03:4e, 15:19b-c
PROKATZ, Hugo, 62, NYC-Q - 1920/09/17:6a
PROLETZ, Charles, un. carp., NYC-M – 1902/02/07:4a
PRONK, Heinrich J., ~40, artist fr Koeln, USA 1889, NYC-M – 1891/10/07:1h
PROPANSKI, John, 60, cooper, NYC-M – 1909/07/01:6b, =2:6a
PROPHET, Margarethe, b. Wagner, NYC-M – 1891/06/23:4a
PROPPE, William, SP?, 64, NYC-Bx - 1917/05/20:7a, 22:6a
PROSCH, Joseph, 72, NYC-M – 1902/02/22:4b
PROSCHWETZ, Max, machinist, NYC-M – 1904/12/24:4a
PROSI, Fritz, un. carp., NYC-M – 1911/05/11:6a
PROSS, Eduard, 1, NYC-M - 1878/07/07:3a
PROSSER % Kramer; PROTZ % Thierfeldt, % Winterstein
PROTZ, Berta, NYC-M - 1916/09/19:6a
PROTZ, Paul, Elizabeth, NJ – 1913/01/14:2g

PROTZKY, Mary, b. Boehme, 49, Ravenswood, LI – 1903/10/04:5a, fam. 6:4a
PROTZMANN, Louis, 41, NYC-B - 1894/01/12:4a
PROTZNER, Charles, 33, NYC-M - 1916/11/19:7a
PROVO, Charles, 53, un. cigarmaker, SLP, New Haven, CT – 1896/04/18:1d,4a, fam. 22:4a
PROVO, John, 45, un. cigarmaker, New Haven, CT – 1898/02/16:4a, =17:1g
PRUEBENAU, Robert, mechanic, NYC-M - 1894/08/04:4a,
PRUEFER, Gottlieb, un. carp., NYC-M – 1887/06/24:3b
PRUSCHEN, Diedrich, un. fireman, NYC-M – 1896/08/14:4a
PRUSSE, Gotthold, 41, German naval engineer, builder of trade submarine Deutschland, USA 1916, War 2, Baltimore,MD - 1917/09/19:1e
PRUTZ, Robert, German poet – 1901/02/24:12c-e, 3 Mr:15a-e, 10:15b-e
PRUTZ, Robert, Progressive German poet, *1816, his life – 1900/06/24:13b-d
PRUZINSKI, Vincent, SP, fr Hungary?, NYC-B – 1908/10/09:6a
PTOMEY, Ed & Will, Negroes, lynched Allentown, AL – 1905/03/16:1c
PUCHTA, Karl E., 70, NYC-M – 1891/07/03:4a
PUCK, Louis, 54, dock security guard, War 2, Hoboken, NJ - 1917/04/11:2c
PUCKELWALDT, Antoinette, 22, NYC-B – 1903/01/14:4a
PUDOR, John, striker at Standard Coke Works, Morewood near Mt Pleasant, PA – 1891/04/03:1b, =4:1a-b, 5:1f,4a.
PUEHLHORN, Kati, b. Schaettler, NYC-M – 1913/08/27:6a
PUELLE, William, NYC-M – 1905/02/24:4a
PUERNER, Henry, 37, NYC-M - 1894/01/10:4a
PUETZ, John, un. cigarmaker, NYC-M – 1898/05/29:5f, 30:4a
PUFAHL, Emil, NYC-B – 1903/08/29:4a, 30:4a
PUGH, Benjamin, NYC, exec. Ossining, NY – 1901/08/05:4c, 6:3b
PUILS, Peter, NYC-M - 1916/02/03:6a
PULHAM, Charles H., NYT reporter, NYC-M - 1879/05/14:4c
PULITZER, Anna, b. Nelson, 28, fr Denmark, NYC-M – 1902/09/20:1a, 19:1f, 21:1f-g, 24:1h, 25:1f-g
PULITZER, Joseph, NYC publ. NY World – 1911/10/30:2e-f, 31:3b
PULITZER, Mrs, murderer W. Hooper – 1903/01/22:2h
PULLER, Gustav, superintendent Widmann's Silk Dyeing Co., Paterson, NJ, + War 2 - 1920/10/29:2c
PULLERSON, Louis, exec. Ossining, NY – 1899/08/01:3e
PULLICH, Otto, 48, realtor, & wife, NYC-M – 1901/10/03:1g
PULLMANN, William H., treas. Of Sunday School, NYC-M, + @Genl Slocum – 1904/06/17:1b, 3c
PULT % Albrecht

PULVERMACHER, Louis, 50, realtor, NYC-M – 1909/07/21:1f
PURCELL, archbishop of Cincinatti – 1883/07/06:1c
PURCHA, Emil, cigarmaker, NYC – 1882/10/04:3c, 3:4d
PURSCHT, John, ex-Jersey City, NYC-M – 1884/12/06:1f
PURY-HERVE, Alexander VON, baron, ex-NYSZ journalist, +
 Washington, DC – 1908/08/12:6a
PUSHINSKY, Louisa, 13, fr Kishinew 1905, NYC-M – 1907/06/22:1d
PUSHNIK, Casper, 41, un. baker, NYC-M - 1916/12/08:6a
PUSTALKA, Anna, widow Schoeplein, fr Dortmund/Gy, NYC-M -
 1895/08/29: 1g, 30: 1d
PUSTALKA, Charles, NYC, exec. Ossining, NY – 1896/04/23:1d, 24:1h
PUSTKUCHER, Lina, Hoboken, NJ – 1898/02/03:3c
PUTNEY, Edith, teacher at Newton HS, Elmhurst, LI - 1917/07/01:11e
PUTSCHEL, Louis, 33, SP, Trenton, NJ - 1918/03/08:6a
PUTT, Adelaide, b. Traumueller, 20, NYC-B – 1910/09/02:6a
PUTTKAMER, Rosa von, baroness, NYC-B – 1898/07/29:1g
PUTTKE, Georg, NYC-B - 1918/10/11:6a
PUTTRICH, Ludwig, 84, lawyer & SPD Leipzig/Gy, MdL 1879-84 –
 1908/08/23:3d
PUTZ, Adolf, NYC-M – 1886/12/21:3a, fam. 5 Jan. 1887:3b
PUTZAR, Carl, NYC-Q - 1920/07/27:6a
QUACKENBUSCH, Charles S., son of ex-mayor of Albany, NY, + NYC-M
 – 1892/01/09:4e, 10:1g
QUADE, Sara, b. Schreier, 48, Bayonne, NJ - 1917/10/28:7a
QUANZ, Anna Maria, b. Radermacher, 54, NYC-M – 1890/03/11:4a
QUAY, Matthew, US Senator fr PA – 1904/05/29:1h
QUELCH, Harry, Engl. Soc., + London – 1913/09/30:4e
QUELL, John, NYC-B – 1896/07/09:4a
QUENSEL, Caroline, 74, West Hoboken, NJ – 1912/06/22:6a
QUENZER, Joseph A., 57, cooper, NYC-M – 1910/11/28:6a, 29:6a
QUERLING, John, cigar dealer, & wife Bernardine, NYC-M –
 1890/06/14:1h, 15:5a
QUICK % Vogel
QUICK, Peter, 61, NYC-M – 1890/10/16:4a
QUIMBY, Harriet, US aviator, + Boston, MA – 1912/07/02:2b
QUINN, James, KoL leader 1880s, NYC-B – 1901/04/24:2h
QUINN, John, 43, un. cigarmaker, NYC-M - 1919/05/23:6a
QUINTUS, J., Newark, NJ – 1902/12/23:4a
QUIRR, Martin, un. cigarmaker, NYC-M – 1906/12/06:6a
QUIST, Charles, ship stoker, fr Sweden, NYC-B – 1902/12/17:4b
QUITTNER, Bertha, b. Rosenthal, Schenectady, NY, + NYC-M –
 1903/07/28:3b-c

RAAB, Carl Philip, G-A journalist, Cleveland, OH – 1900/06/01:1b
RAAB, Daniel, 54, NYC-M – 1891/12/13:5c, fam. 22:4a
RAAB, Edmund (Edward?), 35, painter, NYC-Q – 1910/06/09:2a, 10:6a
RAAB, Ignaz, 29, SP Vienna/Austria – 1912/11/20:4d
RAAB, Jacob, publisher, NYC-B – 1897/07/11:1f
RAAB, Jacob, un. brewer?, NYC-M – 1905/10/23:4a
RAAB, Johanna, 83, NYC-M – 1891/07/25:4a
RAAB, Lilly Meta, b. Bornheck, 29, NYC-B – 1891/06/26:4a
RAABE % Niemann
RAABE, Wilhelm, German writer, + 1910, mem. 1911/09/24:20d
RABA, Mathias, NYC-M - 1914/06/15:6a
RABACH, F., German carpenter, New Orleans - 1878/10/12:2e
RABE % Meyer
RABE, Gustav, NYC-M - 1919/06/21:6a
RABELIN, Charles, 57, coachman, NYC-B - 1915/01/27:2a
RABENKLAU, Gustav, 41, butcher, NYC-B – 1911/04/13:2c
RABOLD, Carrie, 53, War 2, Paterson, NJ - 1914/11/21:2e
RABUSCH, Hermann, 38, Hoboken, NJ – 1901/11/16:4a
RABUSE, George, NYC-B - 1919/03/16:12a
RACHEL, Georg Wilhelm, Dr.med., SLP, *2 Aug. 1845 Dresden, USA
   1866, NYC, 1893- San Francisco, CA – 1898/12/09:4c
RACK % Senf
RACKELMANN, Conrad, 54, Jersey City Heights, NJ – 1912/06/03:6a
RACKL, Joseph, 71, SPD Landshut/Bavaria – 1909/05/02:3b
RACKOW, Henry, SPD activist in Berlin 1870s, + 1 March 1916 in
   London/GB - 1916/04/06:4e-f
RADATT, Joseph, NYC-Bx – 1912/01/20:6a
RADDATZ, Lena, 44, NYC-M - 1920/01/20:8a
RADECKE, John, NYC-M – 1906/11/11:7b
RADEMACHER % Quanz
RADEMACHER, Carl, 61, Guttenberg, NJ - 1913/12/16:2a
RADEMACHER, Henry, Hoboken, NJ - 1918/06/26:6b
RADEMACHER, Mrs, & children Ida & Albert, NYC-B – 1908/09/02:3b
RADESTOCK, Max, SPD Langebrueck/Dresden/Gy – 1913/02/09:3f
RADINSKI, Frank, RR worker, + Jersey City, NJ – 1898/11/19:1f
RADLICH, Franz, NYC-Bx - 1917/02/18:7a
RADO, Peter, 92?, un. cigarmkr, NYC-B – 1892/07/20:4a, 21:4a
RADUSCHKY, G., un. carpenter, NYC-M - 1895/10/15: 4a
RADZIUS, Felix, exec. Pottsville, PA – 1908/05/27:2d
RAELING, G., 60, NYC-B – 1902/05/21:1b
RAETH, Adam, NYC-M - 1878/06/14:4a
RAETHER, Otto, un. metall worker, SPD Stuttgart, 1908/10/18:3e

RAETSCH, Arthur, 30, glassworker fr Berlin, SP, NYC-Bx – 1911/10/10:1d, 12:6a
RAETSCH, Arthur, SP, benefit for ailing comrade, NYC – 1911/02/18:3a-b
RAETZE, Robert A., 37, architect, & wife , b. Coles, NYC-M – 1913/01/06:1h
RAFALSKY, Albert, SP, NYC-SI - 1915/07/10:6a, =21:2c
RAFFA, Albert, 20, NYC-B, + Rhinebeck, Iowa – 1903/06/10:4a
RAFFA, Anna, b. Wichmann, 46, NYC-Q – 1902/06/23:4a, 24:4a, =27:4b, fam. 29:5b, mem. 1910/06/22:6a
RAFFA, Bruno, 26, Craig Colony, NY - 1917/01/28:7b
RAFFA, Martha, 4, NYC-B – 1889/03/23:4a
RAFFA, Theodor, 65, SP, un. carp., * Muehlbach/Hessen, USA 1882, NYC-B - 1917/05/02:2e,6a, 3:6a, 4:6a, =6:11b, fam. 7:6a; mem. 1918/05/01:6a
RAGOZIMISKOWA, Ms, Russian patriot, exec. St Petersburg – 1907/10/29:2a, 30:1e
RAGUSE, Emanuel, un. carp., NYC-M – 1888/04/27:3b
RAHARDT, Katharina, 77, NYC-B – 1887/12/08:4f
RAHARDT, Lena, b. Klitsch, 52, NYC-B – 1912/10/20:7b, fam. 26:6a
RAHARDT, Marie, b. Hoffmann, 39, NYC-B – 1888/07/23:3c
RAHN, Elsie, 23, servant, NYC-M – 1909/11/30:5e
RAHN, Hermann, 43, NYC-B – 1906/01/11:4a
RAHN, Marie, 20, servant, USA 1885, NYC-M – 1886/05/25:4d
RAICHLEN, Katharina, b. Schwartz, 42, NYC-M – 1883/09/21:3d
RAINAN, Barbara, NYC-B – 1912/01/01:1c, 3:6b
RAISCH, Fritz, NYC-B – 1906/05/19:4a
RAISER, Rosie, 5, NYC-M – 1882/01/27:3c
RAISINGER, Frank, farmer, exec. Bridgeton, NJ – 1905/02/15:3c, 16:4a
RAKEBRAND % Reise
RAKUTT, Wilhelm, union off. & SPD Koenigsberg/Gy – 1911/02/19:3c
RAMAGE, Adam, 63, un. papermaker, SLP, * Scotland, USA 1856, Springfield, MA - 1895/05/22:1d
RAMDEL % Rathgeber
RAMGE, Margarethe, NYC-M – 1891/03/24:4a
RAMI, Joana, 18, fr Syria, textile worker, + Lawrence, MA strike – 1912/01/31:2f
RAMM % Fiorelli
RAMM, Auguste, b. Stahl, 44, SP, * Reinfeld/Luebeck, NYC-M – 1907/11/25:6a, 26:2b,6a, fam. 28:6a
RAMM, Carrie, child, NYC-M – 1896/08/29:4a
RAMM, Dorothea, b. Thies, 86, NYC-Q – 1905/06/08:4a

RAMM, Ernest, SP, NYC, his son married Ms Lilian Welz, NYC-Bx - 1913/06/16:2a
RAMM, Georg, 10, NYC-M - 1896/10/27:4a
RAMM, Henry, SP, NYC-M - 1917/08/12:7a, fam. 16:6a; mem. 1918/08/11:12a
RAMM, Willie, child, NYC-M? - 1885/07/09:3b
RAMMELKAMP, Lizzie, 44, NYC-M, +@Genl Slocum - 1904/06/25:1d
RAMMELKAMP, Stella, NYC-M, + @ Genl Slocum - 1904/06/18:3c
RAMMENSTEIN, Carrie, 4, NYC-Q - 1907/09/22:7b
RAMMENSTEIN, Margarethe, b. Ziegler, NYC - 1901/05/22:4a
RAMMLER, August, NYC? - 1886/03/11:3a
RAMRATH, Heinrich, 51, un. cabinetmaker, NYC-B - 1895/06/04:4a, =6:1g, 13:4a
RAMSAIER, Charles, mailcarrier, NYC-M Ave - 1913/11/26:1d
RAMSAY, William, Dr., 63, British chemist, 1904 Nobel Prize, obit crit. wartime German–baiting - 1916/08/26:4g
RAMSPERGER, Gustav, 88, druggist, NYC-M - 1912/05/06:6d
RAMUS, Elisa, 47, NYC-M - 1891/01/02:4a
RAMUS, Frederick, 60?, NYC-M, +@Genl Slocum - 1904/06/23:1b
RANDAUP, Carl, 75, realtor, NYC-Bx - 1913/05/21:1d
RANDELOW, Louisa, 29, NYC-M, + @ Genl Slocum - 1904/06/21:1f
RANDIG, Emil A., engineer, NYC-B - 1910/08/26:6a
RANDOLPH, John F., secy of Thomas Alvah Edison, West Orange, NJ - 1908/02/18:1g
RANDOLPH, Sydney, Negro, lynch.Gaithersburg,MD, 1896/07/05:1g, 7:1h
RANK, Friederike, 21, NYC-B - 1908/06/12:3a
RANZWEILER, John, 26, NYC-B - 1884/07/28:3c
RAPALLO, Charles A., judge, NYC - 1887/12/29:2e
RAPE, F.'s wife, Waterbury, CT - 1890/05/14:4a
RAPHAELI, Martin, 63, worker at Singer Factory, SP, Elizabeth, NJ - 1905/10/31:4a, 5 Nov:5g
RAPP % Luxenburg
RAPP, Barbara, 63, NYC-M - 1919/06/30:6a
RAPP, C. J., 45, ex-alderman (Republican), NYC-M - 1890/01/15:1h
RAPP, F., West Hoboken, NJ - 1918/03/17:7a
RAPP, Henriette, NYC-M 1891/03/27:4a
RAPP, Ignaz's wife, NYC-M - 1896/10/01:2e, 4:4b
RAPP, J., NYC-Q - 1912/02/06:6a
RAPP, Joseph, fr Breslau, Gy, NYC-Q - 1899/06/17:4a
RAPP, Mrs, b. Schulz, 20, NYC-M - 1883/01/03:3c
RAPP, W., NYC-M - 1910/12/06:6a

RAPP, William, 54, machinist, NYC-M – 1909/03/14:1g
RAPPAPORT, Philip, 70, USA 1866 fr Gy, Socialist & Turner, =16 Jan. Indianapolis, IN - 1914/01/25:19c
RAPPOLD, Hugo, 38, cigarmaker, NYC-B - 1879/10/21:4c
RAPPOLD, Jakob, his 2 yr old son +, NYC-B – 1903/08/22:3c
RAPSECK, Mathias, Newark, NJ – 1906/06/23:6a
RARICK, Alfred, Kenville, NJ – 1898/04/29:3f
RASCHER, Louis, SP, Elizabeth, NJ – 1911/12/29:6a, 30:6a
RASCHER, Oscar, NYC-M – 1890/01/13:4a, 14:4a
RASMUSSEN, Sophus, Danish anarchist, chief ed. Skorpionen, 1907/12/03:4e
RASPAIL, Francois Vincent, 84, French socialist & deputy, + Paris, 1878/01/29:2f-g, = 26 Feb.:2e
RASPUTIN, Russian monk - 1916/05/12:1d, 13:4c
RASSMAN, Martha, NYC-M – 1897/01/01:4a
RASSMANN, August, 29, SLP, un. cornice maker, *Benshausen/Thueringen, NYC-M - 1895/12/05:4a, = 7: 1e, 8:1e
RASSMANN, Harry, 24, machinist, Monmouth Junction, NJ - 1917/08/27:2d
RASTAETTER, Franz, un. cornicemaker, NYC-M – 1898/01/05:4a
RASTER, Hermann, edit. Illinois Staats-Zeitung, 1891/07/28c, 2 Aug.:4a-b, memorial 12:1h
RATHER, Gustave, Greenville, NJ – 1899/07/19:4a
RATHFORM, Alexander, 64, NYC-B – 1908/07/15:3b
RATHGEBER, Christian, NYC-M - 1919/03/18:6a
RATHGEBER, Ursula, b. Ramdel, NYC-M – 1891/03/16:4a
RATHJE, Louise Behrends,27,SP,NYC-M - 1919/06/06:6a,fam.8:6a
RATHMANN, Carl, brewer, St Louis, MO, at sea on steamer Kaiser Wilhelm – 1912/07/17:1b
RATHMANN, Henry, NYC-M – 1907/06/24:6a
RATHNER, Augustine, 57, NYC-M - 1917/03/15:6a
RATJEH, Henry, NYC-M - 1895/02/14:4a
RATS, Charles, NYC-B - 1919/02/14:6a
RATZ, Gustav's, un. cigarmaker, NYC-M – 1884/08/23:3d
RATZ, H., NYC-Q - 1914/11/13:6a
RATZ, Henry, 27, carpenter, NYC-M - 1894/02/21:4h
RATZ, Henry, un. carpenter, NYC-M - 1895/04/06:4a
RATZEL % Krieg
RATZLAFF, ..., NYC?, fam. Thanks 1882/07/28:3d
RAU, Adolph, 37, lithographer, NYC-B – 1897/07/10:4b
RAU, Emil, NYC-M – 1898/06/09:1b
RAU, Eva, 14, Newark, NJ – 1913/03/07:6a

RAU, Francis, NYC-M – 1892/12/07:4a
RAU, J., 60, shoemaker, SPD Philippsburg/Baden – 1911/02/12:3a
RAU, Stephan, 45, NYC-B – 1892/10/30:5d
RAU, Willi, 3, NYC-M – 1893/03/19:5a
RAUB, Gussie, (dying), Newark, NJ – 1909/07/12:3b
RAUBITSCHEK, K., 38, realtor, NYC – 1882/05/06:3a-b
RAUCH, Adolph, un. waiter, NYC-M – 1890/01/13:4a
RAUCH, Barbara, NYC-B - 1915/05/11:6a
RAUCH, Bertha, b. Spess, NYC-B – 1896/06/14:5b
RAUCH, Elizabeth, b. Freitag, 72, NYC-M - 1917/01/22:6a
RAUCH, Joseph, NYC-Q – 1908/10/13:6a
RAUCHER, August, 63, butcher, Jersey City, NJ – 1907/02/20:2b
RAUFEISEN, Constantin,un. carpenter, NYC-M - 1894/08/20:4g
RAUHERZ, Michael, 53, SP, un. carp., USA 1880s, NYC-B - 1919/03/24:6a, 25:6a, =27:2d, fam. 28:6a
RAUN, Ida M., 61, NYC-M - 1920/09/18:6a
RAUSCH % Wilson
RAUSCH, Barbara, NYC-M – 1890/02/24:4a
RAUSCH, Charles, Newark, NJ - 1915/07/28:6d
RAUSCH, Christina, b. Dunst, NYC-B – 1892/07/15:4a
RAUSCH, Edward, 20, plumber, NYC-M – 1893/06/01:1h
RAUSCH, Elizabeth, NYC-M - 1895/08/07: 4a
RAUSCH, Emma, 9, NYC-B – 1903/03/02:3b
RAUSCH, Henry, 48, Jersey City, NJ – 1904/09/04:1e
RAUSCH, John, NYC-M - 1894/10/15:4a
RAUSCH, Mrs see also Hofmann, Albert
RAUSCH, Tilly, 6, NYC-M - 1895/04/26:3d
RAUSCHENBERG, Henry, NYC-M – 1885/03/11:3c
RAUSCHER, Christian, SPD Hanau/Gy – 1910/07/10:3c
RAUSCHER, Helene, b. Bohn, 66, NYC-B - 1918/01/13:1f
RAUSCHER, Jakob, 52, NYC-M – 1900/05/13:1e
RAUTENBACH, Wilhelmine, 73, NYC-M - 1920/11/29:6a
RAUTENKRANZ, Joseph, 64, NYC-M - 1913/06/11:6a
RAUTH, John, NYC-B - 1920/04/28:6a
RAUTTER, Hermann, un. machinist, NYC-M – 1911/01/11:6a
RAVACHOL trial in Paris 1892/04/26:1a d, 23 June:1a,
RAVACHOL, exec. in Montbrison/Paris – 1892/07/06:1b, done 12:4b
RAVE, Robert, 55, machinist, fr Saxony, USA 1868, NYC-B – 1896/05/06:4c
RAVENSKY, Josef, machinist, NYC-M – 1897/11/27:4a
RAVINIUS, Robert's wife, 40, & Laura, 15, Wm, 13, Albert, 10, Liz, 3, West Point, NY – 1897/10/02:1f

RAVSKI, Constantin, West Orange, NJ – 1911/12/27:6a
RAWALD % Goeben
RAWN, Ira C., v-p Illinois Central RR, + Chicago – 1910/07/21:1c
RAYLAN, Nicolai de, clerk at Russian consulate in Chicago, spied on socialist meetings, + Phoenix, AZ – 1906/12/23:1g, 20:1d, 24:2c, 25:1f
RAYLOR, Edward, director Bridgeport Projectile Co., Bridgeport, CT - 1916/04/13:2c
RAYMANN, Peter, NYC-M – 1901/07/03:1d
RAYSER, Christian, fr Markgroeningen/Gy, NYC-B – 1884/09/05:3c
REBACCI, Pietro, 19, exec. Ossining, NY - 1914/06/23:1e
REBE, Mary, 35, NYC-B – 1900/07/18:3d, 19:1e
REBENTISCH, Elizabeth, Jersey City Hgts,NJ - 1916/10/10:6a
REBER, Emma, NYC-M - 1915/12/31:2f
REBER, Henry, NYC-M – 1887/10/25:2e
REBER, Marie, b. Brand, 37, NYC-M - 1918/12/18:6a
REBHAN, John, Jersey City Hgts - 1914/01/17:6a
REBISCHING, August, machinist, NYC-B – 1905/12/27:4a
REBMANN, L., NYC-Q - 1915/10/09:6a
REBSAMEN, Ida, b. Degen, NYC-M – 1891/03/02:4a
REBSTOCK, George, Metropolitan, LI – 1908/02/09:7a
RECHHOLTZ, Phillipine, 34, NYC-M - 1896/01/04:4a
RECHNER, Martin, 43, un. carp., NYC-B – 1911/10/10:6a
RECHODOM, E., Dr., 48, * Prague/Bohemia, - 1878/04/23:3b
RECHSTEINER, Balthasar, NYC-M – 1902/12/06:5b
RECHTER, Jacob, 60, NYC-M – 1892/06/20:4a
RECHTMANN, Joseph, un. cigarmaker, SDP, NYC-M – 1904/03/02:4a
RECKLEIN, Frank, 34, un. driver, NYC-SI – 1902/09/10:4a
RECLUS, Jean Jacques, 75, Prof. Of Geography & Socialist, * France, + Brussels – 1905/07/05:1e
REDD, Jim, Negro, lynched Monticello, AK – 1898/07/16:1h
REDDERSON, Carl, 74, Paterson, NJ – 1911/06/28:6a
REDDICK, Jim, Negro, lynched Boyan, TX – 1896/06/12:1b
REDDING, George, New Haven, CT, exec. Wethersfield, CT – 1912/11/02:2d
REDDY, James, head of "Gopher Gang," NYC-M – 1912/01/22:2f
REDEL, Otto E., 29, stoker on steamer "St Louis," Lyndhurst, NJ - 1914/11/28:5e
REDEPENNIG, Herman, 66, un. painter, NYC-M - 1918/11/25:6a
REDER, Gustav, un. carp., NYC-Bx – 1913/09/28:7b
REDL, Alfred, Austrian colonel & Russian spy, + Vienna - 1913/06/05:1a, 10:4d-e, 13:4e, 16:4e-f, 3 Jy:4c, 31 Aug:3a
REDLICH, Abraham, 62, NYC-M – 1891/07/03:4a

REDLING, Rose, 26, NYC-M - 1895/06/19:3c
REDMOND, John E., Irish autonomist - 1918/03/07:2d
REDOKOWITZ, Emil, un. butcher, NYC-M - 1919/03/13:6a
REE, Anton, Dr., 76, Hamburg/Gy, Liberal MdR 1881-1884, 1891/01/27:2d
REED, Gottlob, 48, Yonkers, N.Y.?, - 1878/05/16:3a
REED, John, US soc., + Russia - 1920/10/19:1d,4c, NYC soc. meet 22:2b, 24:1d, 25:1d, 26:2a-b, obit by Lincoln Steffens 7 Nov.:9f-g, edit 10:4c, meeting prep 22:2f
REENTS, Adele, NYC-M – 1911/06/16:6a
REES, Rosetta, b. Strauss, 52, NYC-M – 1891/04/04:4a
REESE, Barbara, b. Schmidt, NYC-M - 1878/05/21:3b
REESE, Charles, un. painter, NYC-M - 1916/03/23:6a
REESE, John, Negro, lynched Henderson, TX – 1905/11/13:1d
REESE, Metha, NYC-M - 1894/10/15:4a
REESE, Michel, San Francisco, - 1878/08/20:2c
REESE, Negro, lynched near Mississipi City, LO – 1900/06/11:1c
REEVELL, Rita, NYC-M, +@ on Genl Slocum – 1904/06/17:3c
REGAL, Ida, b. Sabian, 75, NYC-Bx - 1919/04/22:6a
REGELE, Friedrich, NYC-M – 1909/08/28:6a
REGELMANN, Babetta, 34, NYC-M – 1892/09/04:5b
REGELMANN, Frederick, 54, un. carp., NYC-M – 1909/06/03:6a, fam. 5:6a; mem. – 1910/06/01:6a
REGENAULT, Karl, 42, NYC-M – 1892/07/14:4a
REGER, Conrad, NYC-Bx – 1908/02/27:6a, 28:6a, 3 Mr:2b, fam. 3:6a
REGER, John, ~40, brewer, NYC-B – 1901/03/27:2g
REGER, Max, 43, German conductor, + Leipzig - 1916/06/12:4f
REGITZ, Charles, 62, NYC-B - 1906/07/20:3b
REGNER, Caroline, Greenville, NJ - 1915/12/07:6a
REGNERI, Bartholomaeus, un. typesetter, NYC-M – 1896/10/03:3a
REH, Anton, 65, Newark, NJ – 1901/07/04:3b
REHAEUSER, George, un. carp., NYC-M – 1902/11/27:4a
REHAN, Fritz, 33, SP, NYC-M - 1919/01/06:6a, fam. 9:6a
REHBACH, M., NYC-Q – 1912/06/27:6a
REHBACH, Paul, 24, NYC-B – 1892/06/12:4a
REHBACK, August, NYC-M – 1891/08/15:4a
REHBEIN, Heinrich, 66, SP, NYC-B - 1918/07/03:6a, 4:6a
REHBERG, Johanna, 17, sales clerk, 1905 fr Hannover, NYC-B – 1907/10/08:3b
REHBERGER, Christian, NYC-B – 1889/07/19:4a
REHBERGER, Heinrich, child, NYC? – 1883/04/26:3a
REHDER, Edward, NYC-B – 1910/03/06:7c
REHDER, Minnie, NYC-B – 1913/07/10:6a

REHFELD, Katharina, b. Eberle, 75, NYC-M - 1917/12/16:11a
REHFELD, L., 60, un. painter, NYC-M - 1918/01/23:6a
REHFELDT, Otto, ret. Rest. owner, *20 No 1860 Muenster/Westf., NYC-M
 - 1907/11/09:5e,6a
REHFUSS, Wilhelm, un. butcher, NYC-B - 1914/09/29:6a
REHKOPP, Charles, un. engineer, NYC-B - 1894/04/27:4a
REHLE, Georg, 27, NYC-M - 1892/04/10:5b
REHM, ..., bricklayer, NYC-B, fam. 1888/11/17:3c
REHM, Wilhelm, SLP, NYC-M - 1894/09/17:4a, 23:5a
REHMANN, John Gottlieb, un. carp., Hoboken, NJ, fam. 1887/05/09:3c
REHMANN, Mary E., 1, NYC-M - 1878/03/06:4f
REHMER, John, 22, bank messenger, NYC-B - 1903/06/18:4a
REHN, Katie, 17, NYC-M - 1904/12/10:2h
REHSE, Anna Margarethe, b. Strueven, 75, NYC-B - 1899/12/08:4a
REHWAGEN, Otto, NYC-Bx - 1917/01/19:6a
REIBER, Carl, Hoboken, NJ - 1918/11/11:3a
REIBER, Charlotte, NYC-M - 1917/01/05:6a
REIBRECHT, Paulina, NYC-M - 1920/03/13:8a
REICH, Adolph, insurance agent, pres. TV, & wife Emma, kids Tilly 23,
 Edith 15, Albert 13, Gustav 8, (2 others survived), Jersey City, NJ -
 1898/01/03:1f-g, 4:3d
REICH, Amelia, NYC-M - 1895/07/02: 1e
REICH, Anna, b. Steuer, 44, NYC-B - 1911/10/11:6a
REICH, Bertha, NYC-B - 1906/12/28:6a
REICH, E., NYC-Bx - 1919/06/03:6a
REICH, Ernst, 46, un. furrier, NYC-M - 1884/12/16:3b
REICH, George, Newark, NJ - 1908/07/19:7b
REICH, Gustav, 28, NYC-B - 1891/08/27:1d
REICH, Gustav, 50, NYC-Bx - 1910/04/22:6a
REICH, Jacob, NYC-M - 1916/06/13:6a
REICH, Lena, NYC-M - 1887/04/21:1g, 22:4a, 26:1, trial of husband
 Adolph 2 June:1d, 3:3a, 4:1d, 7:1g, 8:2f-g, sent. to death 9:4d, 10:3b,
 postponed 1 yr 30 Jy:2g to be exec. 30 Nov 11 Oct 1888:11:1h, 20
 Nov:1f, 23:3d, postponed again 28 Nov:2h
REICH, Morris, mobster, NYC - 1913/07/11:1f
REICH, Richard, 36, engineer, NYC-SI - 1903/11/06:1g
REICHART, Max, 33, NYC-M - 1918/03/18:6a
REICHBOLDT % Muenker
REICHEL, Louis, un. carp., NYC-M - 1905/05/15:6a
REICHELT, Arthur, NYC-M - 1918/01/11:6a
REICHENBACH, Ernst, NYC-M - 1907/11/09:6a
REICHENBACH, Heinrich G., NYC-B - 1918/11/10:12a

REICHENBACHER, Sophie, b. Kessler, 39, Jersey City, NJ – 1908/03/05:6a
REICHER, Robert, 61, fr Solingen/Gy, Troy, NY – 1885/05/10:8a
REICHERT, August, 68, Newark, NJ - 1913/06/12:6c
REICHERT, Ernestine, b. Koch, 42, NYC-M - 1895/12/02: 4a
REICHERT, Eugen, Newark, NJ – 1908/03/19:6a
REICHERT, Frieda, 22, USA 1909, NYC-B – 1910/03/11:3b
REICHERT, Hermann, cook, fr Bavaria, NYC-M – 1891/07/10:1f
REICHERT, Ludwig, un. wood carver, NYC-M – 1891/12/25:4a, 26:4a
REICHERT, Otto, NYC-M - 1915/12/25:6a
REICHERT, Paul, painter on ship Saale, @1900 dock fire, Hoboken, NJ 1900/07/03:1c
REICHERT, Peter, NYC-Bx - 1917/08/24:6a
REICHERT, Robert, NYC-B – 1910/10/20:6a
REICHFELD, 70, restaurant owner, NYC-M - 1915/07/15:2b
REICHHARDT, Charles, NYC-M(Ward's Isl.) +6th - 1878/07/23:4a
REICHHELM % Mahler
REICHLE, Albert, un. machinist, NYC-B - 1913/05/21:6a
REICHLE, Charles, NYC-B – 1908/05/06:3d
REICHLIN, Agathe, Lorain, PA, – 1903/05/05:4c, 3 May:1h, 15:1g
REICHLING, Herman, butcher, NYC-Q - 1913/05/17:3b
REICHMAN, Arthur, realtor, NYC-Bx – 1913/09/11:1b
REICHMANN, Albert, 66, businessman, NYC-M – 1897/11/24:1e
REICHMANN, Frederick, 40, carp., NYC-B – 1909/01/11:3b
REICHMANN, Jacon, brewer, NYC-M - 1878/01/31:4e, 6 Feb.:4c
REICHMANN, M., striker in East St Louis, MO – 1886/04/10:1b, =12:1a, inquest 13:1e-f etc
REICHRATH, John, NYC-B – 1910/01/24:6a
REICHSTEINER, Mrs, 24, NYC-M - 1894/05/10:2d
REICKS, John, Tobyhanna, PA, + Wilkesbarre, PA – 1903/01/26:1g
REID, Negro, lynched Statesboro, GA – 1904/08/17:1d, 18:1f, 2c, 19:1d
REID, Whitelaw, 75, US writer & ambassador in England – 1912/12/16:1b, = 1913/01/05:1e
REID, William, exec. Jersey City, NJ – 1899/02/24:3f
REIDENHARDY, Viktor, artist (portrait painter), NYC-M – 1908/09/13:1d
REIF % Hagen
REIFENBACH, comrade, 85, SPD vet living in Zuerich/Switz., '48er – 1902/01/07:2c
REIFSCHNEIDER, Julius, 56, stenographer, NYC-B – 1908/11/12:3b
REIGENDANZ, Clara, NYC-M – 1886/04/01:4a
REIGER, Regina, 84, Newark, NJ – 1913/09/07:1e
REIHER, Adolf J., 35, NYC-M – 1905/11/23:4a

REIHER, Sophie, b. Mueller, 74, NYC - 1914 /03/08:7b
REIHL, August, Atlantic City, NJ – 1900/11/26:3h
REIL, Henry, NYC-M? - 1913/11/28:6a
REIL, Willie, NYC-M – 1904/06/28:4a
REILLY, "Scar," mobster, NYC-M – 1908/02/29:1f
REILLY, Gertrude, 2, daughter of SP James Reilly, Jersey City, NJ – 1910/09/20:6a
REIMANN, Adolf, 50, sales agent, Jersey City, NJ - 1915/05/24:6d
REIMANN, Albert, 60, silk weaver, NYC? – 1911/09/09:3e (s.a. Ernst)
REIMANN, Emil, SP Reichenberg/Bohemia, un. woodworker - 1915/05/02:3d
REIMANN, Erich, druggist, USA 1890, NYC-M – 1893/09/08:1g
REIMANN, Ernst, *1852 Forst/Lausitz/Gy, SP, Union Hill, NJ – 1911/09/10:7b, =12:1f
REIMANN, Quires, 82, NYC-B - 1917/09/29:6c
REIMBOLD, Gertrude, 24, NYC-M - 1915/02/17:6a
REIMER, Christopher, 64, NYC-M – 1892/10/14:4a
REIMER, Martha, NYC-Q married Heinrich Ortland, SP NYC-M – 1906/10/08:3c
REIMER, Otto Georg, 48, ex-MdR (SPD), NYC 1880-1890 as cigar maker, + Celle/Hannover – 1892/03/03:1a, 2b-c
REIMER, Otto, SP?, Hoboken, NJ - 1914/04/07:6a, fam. 10:6a
REIMER, Peter, 27, construction worker, Hoboken, NJ - 1915/01/22:2e
REIMER, Sophie, b. Schuldt, 46, ex-NYC?, + Hamburg/Gy – 1891/10/27:4a
REIMER, William, NYC-M – 1911/10/27:1c
REIMERS, Henry, realtor, NYC-B – 1909/03/16:3b
REIMERS, Jacob, 60, farmer fr Gy,+ on ship "Pres. Grant"way to daughter in Chicago – 1911/06/02:2f
REIMERS, P. W., NYC-B – 1891/06/28:5c
REIMHERR, George, 65, furnit. Dealer, NYC-B – 1900/10/15:3b
REIN, Lorenz, un. cigarmaker, Greenville, NJ - 1894/02/17:4a
REIN, Otto, 61, *Eisenach/Thueringia, civil war vet, White Plains, NJ – 1900/03/10:1b
REINACHER, Henry, 42, un. typesetter, NYC-M – 1897/02/11:4a
REINACKER, John, 65, un. typesetter, NYC-M – 1899/04/13:4a
REINAU, Franz, theater mgr & actor, + Atlanta, GA – 1909/01/03:1f
REINBLAD, Albert, 70, Swede, NYC-Greenpoint – 1912/07/19:2g
REINBOLD, Joseph, 39, pres. Reinbold Co., Belleville, NJ – 1913/10/16:6c
REINCH, Bertha, 51, NYC-Q - 1918/01/02:6b
REINCKE, Fritz, 40, USA a short time ago, NYC-M – 1911/02/18:3a

REINCKE, Peter Adolph, Dr., SPD MdR for Lennep-Mettmann/Gy, * 7 Apr 1818 Koenigsberg, + Berlin – 1886/12/24:5b
REINDERS, Klaas Peter, carpenter & MdR (SPD) for Breslau/Gy - 1879/05/26:2d. Memorial 1909/06/06:3c-d
REINECK % Boebert
REINECK, Frank, 16, Mt Holly, NJ – 1904/06/15:3d
REINECKE, August, NYC-M – 1897/07/06:4a
REINECKE, Franz, 59, worker,, East Rutherford, NJ - 1916/04/18:2f, 19:6a
REINECKE, Herman, un. cigarmaker, NYC-M – 1901/08/15:4a
REINECKE, Lina, NYC-Q – 1902/12/11:4a
REINER, Georg, 75, NYC-B – 1882/07/29:3a
REINER, Hannah, 28, shirtmaker, NYC-M – 1911/07/23:7e
REINER, Jacob, painter, NYC-B - 1879/09/15:1f
REINER, Rose, 45, NYC-M – 1903/12/26:1d
REINERS, Becky, 19, @1911 Triangle Shirtwaist Fire, NYC-M – 1911/03/27:1d
REINERS, Richard, weaver, NYC-M - 1913/05/21:6a
REINERT, Frieda, b. Hering, NYC-B – 1892/06/09:4a
REINFARTH, Anton, NYC-M – 1906/05/07:4a
REINHARD, Charles S., 28, cigar dealer, NYC-M – 1898/11/06:5e
REINHARD, Dorothea, b. Gerber, fr Unterbissenbach/Gy, NYC-B – 1892/05/09:4a
REINHARD, Frank, New Haven, CT – 1910/05/07:6a
REINHARD, John, NYC-M – 1892/07/04:4a
REINHARD, Leo, un. carp., NYC-B – 1883/10/30:3b
REINHARDT % Desel
REINHARDT, August, mason, *Durlach/Baden, NYC-M – 1888/04/12:2f
REINHARDT, Charles, 59, SP, un. lockmaker, * Gross-Bottwar/Wuert., USA 1880, Yonkers, NY - 1917/01/17:6a, 18:3e-f, 6a, =21:11e
REINHARDT, Charles, 74, scale manuf., NYC-B – 1912/09/05:2c
REINHARDT, Chris, 45, guard, NYC-B – 1911/06/02:7f
REINHARDT, Fritz, 61, NYC-M – 1909/01/06:6a
REINHARDT, Gustav, diamond cutter (not +), note, NYC-B – 1891/03/18:2e
REINHARDT, John, innkeep, Paterson, NJ – 1898/10/21:4b
REINHARDT, John, Newark, NJ - 1914/08/15:6a
REINHARDT, Louis, 19, US Soldier, NYC-M, = Apuillac/France - 1917/07/26:2f, 29.2b
REINHARDT, Mary Ann, NYC-SI, + July by husband Edward - 1878/10/09:1e-f, 10:1c-e; Edward to be exec. 11 Jy – 1879/05/24:1d-g, 4a
REINHART, Martin, 38, NYC-B – 1893/08/01:4d

REINHART, William J., 21, Cornell U student fr Paterson, NJ – 1903/02/24:2d
REINHOLD, John C., state ranger, Hackensack, NJ – 1913/10/25:6e
REINHOLD, Mathias, plasterer, Newark, NJ – 1897/09/22:3c
REINHOLD, Milda, 15, servant, Passaic, NJ – 1909/12/15:2c
REINICKE % Scherer
REINICKER, Charles, 38, brewer, & wife, 28, NYC-M – 1906/03/27:1a
REINIG, August, Newark, NJ – 1906/04/24:4a
REININGER, Eva, 3, NYC-M – 1912/09/06:6a
REINITZ, Bernhard, 50, janitor, NYC-Bx – 1912/12/09:6b
REINKE, E.A., business agent, Tarrytown, * Gy, missing s. 30 De, body found, War 2 - 1915/03/29:6a
REINMANN, Reinhardt, Hoboken, NJ - 1916/08/29:6a
REINMUTH, Ludwig, NYC-M – 1911/08/29:6a
REINSCH, Ernst, 28, German soldier on leave, ?Schleswig area, + NYC-B - 1879/02/10:4d
REINSDORF, Bruno, un. painter, Clifton, NJ - 1918/03/24:7a
REINSDORF, Friedrich August, anarchist, exec. Halle/Gy, 1885/02/08:1d, 9:1a, 23:2f-g, his last letter 3 Mr:2d
REINSTAEDTER, Fritz, 78, SPD Wermelskirchen/Gy – 1910/05/08:3c
REINSTETTEL, Josef, 36, un. carp., NYC-M – 1892/11/18:4a
REINTHALER, Charles, child, NYC-B – 1913/02/15:6a
REIS, Charles, machinist, NYC-M – 1885/04/11:3b
REIS, Henry, infant, NYC-B? – 1896/04/16:4c
REIS, Jacob, NYC-Q - 1915/01/16:6a
REIS, Kilian, NYC-M – 1893/12/30:4a
REIS, Michael, 45, un. typesetter, NYC-M – 1902/10/11:4a
REIS, P. A., NYC-B – 1906/07/12:6a
REISBINK, 72, NYC-SI – 1904/01/02:1e
REISCHEL, John, NYC-M - 1916/06/09:6a
REISE, Wilhelmine, b. Rakebrand, NYC-B – 1890/05/29:4a
REISEL, Frieda, b. Grosskopf, NYC-Bx - 1918/02/18:6a
REISELEITER, Louise, 59, NYC-B - 1914/01/04:11c
REISER, Adam, un. carp., NYC-M – 1906/11/29:6a
REISER, Christine, 76, NYC-M – 1893/12/29:4a
REISER, John, No. Bergen, NJ - 1918/12/27:6a
REISLING, Emma, 24, NYC-M, +@ Genl Slocum – 1904/06/17:3c
REISMANN, Leopold, un. butcher, NYC-M – 1908/05/27:6a
REISS, Ethel, NYC-B – 1897/05/12:1f, 11:1f, 16:4b
REISS, Frederick, 85, NYC-B – 1910/08/16:2a
REISS, Johanna, 40, NYC-M – 1897/12/26:1d, 27:4a
REISS, John, painter, Elizabeth, NJ – 1904/01/05:3d

REISS, Katie, 25, & Lizzie, NYC-M, +@Genl Slocum – 1904/06/18:3c, 25:1d
REISS, Michael, un. carpenter, NYC-Q - 1918/02/02:6a
REISS, Valentin, un. carp., NYC-M – 1889/12/27:4a
REISSMANN, Katharina, NYC-Bx - 1918/08/10:6a
REISSNER, Jos., 12, NYC-Bx - 1914/03/15:7c
REISZ, George, 45, insurance collector, NYC-M – 1909/11/01:2c
REIT, Georg, NYC-M – 1906/08/07:1e
REITEMEYER, Peter, un. machinist, NYC-M - 1895/05/07:4a
REITER, Charles, un. carp., NYC-B – 1912/09/01:7a
REITER, Wilhelm, 58, Highwood, NJ – 1893/08/02:1g
REITH, Carl, 54, NYC-M – 1899/08/11:4a, fam. 14:4a
REITHMANN, Christian, 60, NYC-B - 1915/04/05:2d
REITKOWSKY, Simon, laborer, Elisabeth, NJ - 1894/02/03:2c
REITZ, John, 51, un. cigarmaker, NYC-Bx – 1906/01/06:4a
REITZEL, Robert, 56, *Schopfheim/Baden, Freethinker, +Detroit, MI – 1898/04/01:1f, mem. in NYC 24 Apr:1g. 15th anniv. of death, by August Lott – 1913/03/30:8e-f
REIZ, Tessie, NYC-M, +@ on Genl Slocum – 1904/06/17:3c
REIZBERGER, John, Newark, NJ – 1909/06/07:6a
RELIN % Groeninger
REMELIUS, Josef, 39, NYC-M – 1895/12/24: 4a
REMENYI, Eduard, violonist fr Hungary, +San Remo/It, mem. meeting NYC – 1898/05/30:1e
REMI, Maurice, businessman, fr Hungary, & wife, fr Vienna, NYC-Bx – 1907/09/24:1g
REMLING, Christopher, NYC-B - 1917/08/31:6a
REMLINGER, Eugen, NYC-M – 1888/09/14:3b
REMMELE, Carl, machinist, NYC-Q – 1898/07/23:4a
REMMER, Henrietta, 16, NYC-M – 1898/04/14:1c
REMMER, Herman's wife, 75, Poughkeepsie?, NY – 1904/09/09:1d
REMMKE, Johann, 22, NYC-M - 1896/01/13:4a
REMPLE, E., NYC-M – 1887/10/19:1g
REMSTEDT, Ferdinand, 63, un. cigarmaker, NYC-M - 1918/03/08:6a, 9:6a
RENARD, Carl, 50, ex-city editor Rochester Abendblatt, + Newark, NJ – 1908/02/17:3c
RENARD, Victor, French Soc., + 11 Oct near Lille - 1915/06/26:4d
RENAUDIN, Aurien Charles, 22, French sailor, + NYC-M – 1882/05/19:4d
RENFER, Harry, 4, NYC-B – 1897/11/13:4a
RENK, John, NYC – 1912/12/08:7a
RENKER, Susanna, b. Hauser, 41, NYC-Q - 1894/11/10:4a
RENKL, George, NYC-B – 1906/07/10:6a

RENLER, John, 50, shoemaker, NYC-M – 1892/03/15:1f
RENNAIER, Gustav, machinist, W. Hoboken, NJ - 1913/12/02:2c
RENNER, Carl Louis, NYC-M - 1920/01/22:6a
RENNER, Emma, NYC-Q - 1917/11/14:6a
RENNER, Franz, 48, un. carp., NYC-B – 1890/06/16:4a
RENNER, Friedrich, NYC-M – 1882/03/07:3c
RENNER, George, un. typesetter, NYC-B – 1896/11/11:4a
RENNER, Michael, 70, NYC-M - 1918/03/18:6a
RENNER, Robert, 11, Philadelphia, PA - 1919/06/07:6a
RENNHAUSER, Minnie, 17, NYC-M – 1891/10/31:4f
RENNINGER, Wilhelm, 39, SLP, Union Hill, NJ – 1899/07/22:4a & column bottom, 23:5a, fam. 25:4a
RENSCH, Albert, NYC-B – 1905/05/30:3c
RENSCH, Julius, 34, carp., NYC-B – 1885/01/03:3b, 4:5e, 17:2e
RENSLY, Emma, NYC-M, + @Genl Slocum – 1904/06/18:3c
RENTMEISTER, John, 47, silk weaver, Paterson, NJ – 1896/08/25:4c
RENTSCHLER, Daniel John, 1, Kearney, NJ – 1907/02/17:7b
RENTSCHLER, Mr., NYC-M - 1878/04/25:3a
RENZ, Franz, SP, painter, Central Islip, LI – 1913/09/26:1c
RENZ, Gustav, Dr., *1837 Austria, Cleveland, OH, + NYC-B during trip – 1883/04/26:2e-f
RENZ, Henry, Newark, NJ - 1919/01/16:6a
RENZ, John, 45?, NYC-B – 1891/06/29:4a
RENZ, William, NYC-M, + Hoboken, NJ – 1904/07/11:1a, 12:1f
RENZ, Wladislaus, 30, Newark, NJ – 1908/08/08:1f
REPFICH, Emma, 23, servant, Arverne, LI - 1915/08/26:2f
REPP, Dominick, NYC-Q – 1912/02/17:6a, 18:7c
REPP, Louise, b. Schott, NYC-M – 1892/07/12:4a
REPP, Mary, 40, NYC-M – 1906/03/24:4a
REPPEL, Emil s.a. Neppel, Emil
REPPLER, Michael, 45, NYC-M – 1891/01/02:4c
RESCH, Elisabeth, 76, NYC-B – 1891/04/01:4a
RESCH, Joseph, Bayonne, NJ – 1919/12/07:3a
RESCHAK, Louise, 24, NYC-M – 1913/02/22:6a
RESER, Conrad, 64, tailor, NYC-M – 1905/02/03:3c
RESKOWICH, Stephen, Russian, War 2, Newark?, NJ - 1914/09/02:2f
RESLAGE, Amalia C., 3, NYC-M - 1878/04/16:3b
RESS, Carl, 63, un. tailor, SDP, * Ibind/Bavaria, USA 1860, NYC-B – 1904/05/07:4a, 8:1f, 5b, 9:4a, =10:3c, fam. 10:4b
RESS, Dorothea M., NYC-B – 1907/01/20:7c
RESS, Urban, brewer or cooper, NYC-M – 1890/10/26:5a
RESTL, Helene, NYC-M - 1917/01/06:6a

RETELL, Peter, NYC-M – 1883/04/23:1e, 26:4a
RETTBERG, Ludwig, 37, un. ironmolder, NYC-M   1894/05/27:5a
RETTGER, William, 19, shot by scabs during quarry worker strike, Cleveland, OH – 1896/07/03:1d, 4:1c, =5:4b
RETTIG, Harry, 26, milkman, NYC-M – 1907/06/11:3e
RETTIG, Joseph, un. cooper, NYC-M - 1895/11/19: 4a
RETTIG, Karl, 50, shoemaker, * Gastein/Mainz, USA ca. 1850, search by his brother in Germany, lived in NYC-B - 1879/04/19:1f
RETTNER, Andrew, miner, Port Hope, NJ – 1909/11/19:2b, 20:3c
RETZER, Anton, 32, un. carpenter, NYC-B - 1894/01/08:4a
RETZLAFF, C., 80, NYC-B – 1893/09/30:4a
REUBER, Karl, carp. & labor poet, SDP, Pittsburgh, PA – 1902/12/05:2f
REUBOLD, David, Manhattanville, NY - 1913/05/19:6a
REUGERS, Amanda, 17, NYC-B – 1905/01/31:3c
REULEAUX % Goldstein
REULING, Gertrude, 22, NYC-M, +@Genl Slocum – 1904/06/25:1d
REUSCH, Ernst, SPD Kiel/Gy– 1901/12/17:2c
REUSS, John, 55, tailor, NYC-M – 1887/12/28:2g
REUSS, Peter Gustav, un. baker, NYC, fam. – 1906/07/14:6a; mem. – 1907/07/09:6a
REUTER, ..., NYC, fam. 1889/11/17:5a
REUTER, August, carp., SPD Magdeburg/Gy – 1898/09/24:2c,
REUTER, C.'s daughter, 5, Montclair, NJ – 1900/01/05:4a
REUTER, Edward, 32, dishwasher, NYC-M – 1898/09/04:1c
REUTER, Emil, 54, flour dealer, & wife Ida, 49, NYC-B – 1899/01/28:4b
REUTER, Fritz, German writer, 100th anniv. Celebr in NYC 1910/07/26:5a, # 13 Nov:5a-e, his work, by F. Mehring 20 Nov:3e-g
REUTER, Fritz, un. bartender, NYC-B – 1893/04/09:5a
REUTER, Henrietta, 34, & Marion, 10, NYC-M – 1907/07/17:2c
REUTER, Lina, NYC-M – 1892/06/09:4a
REUTER, Martin, 59, servant, fr Bavaria, USA 1883, NYC-M – 1884/12/26:1f
REUTER, Wilhelm, Elizabeth, NJ – 1912/11/08:6a
REUTER, William, NYC-Q – 1908/02/22:6a
REUTLINGER, Mrs, & infant child, NYC-M – 1885/09/15:1f
REUTTER, John, 61, butcher, NYC-M – 1911/03/31:3b
REUTZELMANN, Mr., ice cream dealer, NYC-B – 1898/09/07:1g
REWALD, Justus Henry, 67, NYC-M – 1903/05/23:4a
REWICK, Gustav, 60, NYC-M – 1892/07/04:4a
REXHAEUSER, Ludwig, Bavarian labor leader - 1914/01/26:4d, 18 Mr:4d
REYHER % Baumgarth
REYMANN, Solomon, Rabbi, NYC – 1883/05/09:3a

REYMERS, H., NYC-Bx – 1919/09/05:6a
REYNER, Toby, 8, NYC-B – 1907/08/30:3b
REYNOLD, Lizzie, Yonkers, NY – 1910/11/22:6a
REYNOLDS, Jessie Diane, 28, actress, NYC-M – 1890/01/25:2g
RHEIL, Henry, 42, & wife Mary, 40, Deans, NJ - 1914/11/05:2e
RHEIN % Rook
RHEIN, Marie, NYC-B - 1917/04/24:6a
RHEIN, Victoria, NYC-B - 1918/10/20:12a, fam. 29:6a
RHEINBOLDT, William, NYC-M – 1888/01/11:3a
RHEINFRANK, John, coal-dealer, & wife, NYC-M, +@ Genl Slocum – 1904/06/26:1c
RHEINHEIMER, Peter, un. upholsterer, NYC-M – 1892/10/09:5b
RHEINISCH, Anna Sabina, b. Goetz, 67, NYC-M – 1902/01/10:4a
RHEINISCH, Frank, un. carp., NYC-M – 1904/11/08:4a
RHEINISCH, Heinrich, 24, un. pianomaker, NYC-M – 1882/08/11:3d
RHEINTHALER, Rose, 15, NYC-Q - 1917/02/03:6a
RHODES, Cecil, English imperialist, very negat – 1902/03/27:1e, 2a-b, =28:1e, 5 Ap:1a, 7 May:2f
RHONER, Frank, 68, lumber dealer, & wife Frieda, 54, NYC-B – 1898/11/28:1g
RIBER, Bessie, actress fr Sandusky, OH, + 10 Mr in Rutherford, NJ – 1885/05/07:1g, 9:1g
RICE, Oscar E., exec. Auburn, NY – 1899/08/03:3e
RICHARD, Ernst, Dr., 55, prof. Columbia U, fdr German-Amer. Peace Society, * Bonn/Gy, USA 1883, NYC-M - 1914/11/21:1d
RICHARDSON, Addie, 35, NYC-B - 1916/03/18:6b
RICHARDSON, Charles, Negro, lynched Marion, Ark. – 1910/03/19:1d
RICHARDSON, E., Negro, lynched Gadsden, AL – 1906/02/12:1e
RICHARDSON, Henry C., 53, NYC-B - 1878/08/12:3a
RICHARDT, M., NYC-B – 1905/11/17:4a
RICHESON, Clarence, Rev., exec. Boston, MA – 1912/05/22:1d, 4d, 5c-d
RICHMONSKY, Victoria, 21, fr. Neu-Czasnitz/Bohemia,USA 1875, servant, NYC-M - 1878/03/12:4a
RICHSTEIN, Auguste, NYC-M - 1914/01/09:6a, 10:6a, fam. 13:6a
RICHTER % Dette
RICHTER, ..., boy, 2, NYC-B – 1883/04/19:3c
RICHTER, Amelia, NYC-M, + @ Genl Slocum – 1904/06/17:3c
RICHTER, Anna Maria, b. Landgraf, NYC-B – 1887/12/24:3a
RICHTER, Anna, 35, Union Hill, NJ - 1920/07/13:2d
RICHTER, Anna, b. Walther, 43, NYC-M – 1900/02/12:4a, fam. 14:4a

RICHTER, Wilhelm, & wife, & Cathy, 3, Lillian, 4, NYC-B, +@ Genl Slocum – 1904/06/18:1b, 3c,d, =21:1e
RICHTER, August, decorator, NYC-M – 1902/02/28:1h
RICHTER, August, Jersey City, NJ - 1915/11/18:6a
RICHTER, August, un. cigar maker, NYC-M – 1885/09/25:3b
RICHTER, Carl, 35, tailor, Swiss, NYC-M – 1892/09/04:5e
RICHTER, Catherine, 40, NYC-B – 1910/05/24:1f
RICHTER, Charles, 32, brewery worker, NYC-M – 1885/06/02:1g
RICHTER, Christina, 9, Lydia, 10, NYC-M, +@Genl Slocum – 1904/06/19:1d, 22:1d
RICHTER, Christine, 86, NYC-Q - 1917/10/04:6a
RICHTER, Christine, NYC-M – 1893/03/22:4a
RICHTER, Elizabeth, b. Lang, NYC-B – 1907/01/02:6a
RICHTER, Emil, 59, cigarmaker, NYC-Q - 1914/12/16:2f
RICHTER, Erna C., NYC-M – 1891/04/11:4a
RICHTER, Ernst, 76, NYC-M - 1914/05/03:7a
RICHTER, Eugen, German liberal pol., MdR – 1906/03/11:1d, 12:4b, 15:4c
RICHTER, Frederick, NYC-B – 1902/04/24:1g
RICHTER, Fritz, 62, NYC-Bx – 1909/05/19:6a
RICHTER, Hans, German cond. & Wagner specialist, * 4 Apr. 1843 Raab (Gyor)/Hungary - 1916/12/08:1b
RICHTER, Heinrich F., Schleswig?, NYC-M – 1882/12/18:3a
RICHTER, John, Elizabeth, NJ - 1920/02/26:6a
RICHTER, John, un. carp., NYC-M – 1905/01/10:4a
RICHTER, Joseph, NYC-M - 1894/08/27:1c
RICHTER, Julius, music-teacher, USA 1891, NYC-M – 1893/07/13:1g
RICHTER, Louise, b. Mueller, 77, NYC-M – 1913/02/13:6a
RICHTER, Marie, servant, USA 1885, NYC – 1886/01/15:2e
RICHTER, Otto, 65, potter & SPD Pieschen/Saxony – 1911/06/18:3e
RICHTER, Ottomar's wife, ex-NYC, Philadelphia, NY – 1888/11/14:3b
RICHTER, Sophie, 66, NYC-M – 1911/09/04:6a
RICHTER, Wenzel, SPO Warnsdorf/Bohemia, War 1 - 1915/05/30:3d
RICHTER, Wilhelm, 57, un. typesetter, NYC-B – 1900/01/17:4a
RICHTMEYER, Annie, 60, NYC-M – 1906/02/27:1a
RICK, Arnold, 60, NYC-B – 1903/08/10:3b
RICK, Henry, NYC-M - 1914/09/24:6a
RICKEL, Katherina, NYC-M – 1896/06/23:1e
RICKER, Emma, NYC-M – 1891/03/19:4a
RICKERMANN, Otto, 54, machinist, Swiss?, NYC-M – 1910/11/14:6a
RICKERT, Ella, 29, NYC-B – 1909/11/30:6a
RICKING % Oldendorf
RICKS, Moses, 25, Negro, lynched Clarendon, AK – 1898/06/16:3f

RIDDER, Herman, 64, publ. NYSZ, * NYC, NYC-M - 1915/11/02:4c,6a, 3:2f, =5:2d
RIDDER, Max, 48, druggist, NYC-Q - 1912/04/25:3a-b
RIEBE, Mary, NYC-M - 1892/08/27:1g
RIEBLING, Johanna, b. Stueck, NYC-M - 1915/04/05:6a
RIEBLINSKY, Reinhold, NYC-Q - 1916/03/16:6a
RIECHELMANN, Christina, b. Jacobs, NYC-B - 1891/03/15:5b
RIECHERS % Kaese
RIECHERT, Max, NYC-B - 1913/04/26:6a
RIECHMANN, William, NYC-B - 1911/01/10:6a
RIECKEN, Christoph, 69, SP, un. cigarmk., NYC-Bx - 1917/01/16:6a, 17:6a, =19:2d,6a, fam. 19:6a
RIECKER, Frederick., ca. 50, clockmaker, NYC-B - 1893/05/02:2e
RIED, Anna, b. Koster, 24, NYC-B - 1896/07/19:5a
RIED, Heinrich, NYC-M - 1892/12/27:1g
RIED, John, 51, SP, un. carriage maker, * March 1867 Frankfurt/Main, USA 1883, NYC-B - 1918/12/23:3g, 24:6a, 25:2f, =29:11d, fam. 31:6a, mem. - 1919/12/21:7a
RIEDE, Adolf, 45, un. typesetter, NYC-B - 1910/04/04:6a
RIEDEL, Adolph, un. ironworker, NYC-M - 1918/02/11:6a
RIEDEL, C. H., exec. Newcastle, DE - 1888/08/11:1c-d
RIEDEL, Emil, un. fireman, NYC-M - 1911/01/17:6a
RIEDEL, Emma, 45, NYC-B - 1900/03/14:4a-b
RIEDEL, Frances, b. Brunner, 87, NYC-M - 1891/07/05:5a
RIEDEL, John, 51, butcher, NYC-B - 1917/09/04:6a
RIEDEL, Julius, 41, pres. Plastics' Assoc., NYC-M - 1890/01/27:4a
RIEDEL, Minna, 66, NYC-M - 1897/03/22:3g
RIEDEL, Wilhelm, NYC-B - 1918/02/02:6a, mem. 1919/02/02:6a
RIEDER, John, 63, & wife Gertrude, NYC-B - 1900/09/08:1h
RIEDIG, Ernst, 43, un. brewer, NYC-M? - 1913/05/15:6a
RIEDING, Emilie, b. Insel, 49, NYC-M - 1891/02/26:4a
RIEDSCHLE, Emil, NYC-Q - 1909/12/10:6a
RIEF % Siebert
RIEG, Barbara, NYC-B - 1908/07/27:4d, 31:4a, 22 Aug:1f
RIEG, Gottlieb, 58, NYC-M - 1891/10/14:4a
RIEGEL, Frederick, 66, NYC-M - 1920/02/15:12a, 17:8a
RIEGEL, Helene, 61, NYC-M - 1920/10/16:6a
RIEGER, ..., comrade, carp., SPD Koeln/Gy - 1912/09/15:3e
RIEGER, Conrad A., brewer or cooper, NYC-M - 1901/04/13:4a
RIEGER, Eduard, 48, un. piano maker, NYC-M - 1886/04/24:3b
RIEGER, Emma E., b. Fritz, 56, NYC-M - 1892/06/12:4a
RIEGER, F., 41, NYC-M - 1893/09/30:4a

RIEGER, Herman, 40, worker, NYC-M - 1915/12/15:2c
RIEGER, Jakob, 66, shoemaker, NYC-M - 1887/03/07:3a
RIEGER, Karl, brewer, NYC-Q - 1898/04/24:5a
RIEGER, Mary, 60, NYC-Q - 1918/08/04:12a
RIEHL % Siemer
RIEHL, Wilhelm, NYC-M - 1891/04/09:4a
RIEHL, William, Dr., NYC-M - 1888/01/16:3a
RIEK, Paul, Elizabeth, NJ - 1911/02/01:6a
RIEKER, Robert, NYC-B - 1920/08/5:6a, 6:6a
RIEL, Louis, Metis patriot, exec. Battleford/CAN with 8 other POWs - 1885/11/23:1b, 2b, 28:1b, notes 16 Nov:1b, 3 Dec:1b, =12:1d
RIEL, Phillip, Jersey City, NJ - 1913/01/06:6a
RIEM, comrade, SPD Dresden/Saxony =1914/01/11:3d-e
RIEMANN, Adolph, NYC, + Florida, NY - 1912/12/25:6a
RIEMANN, Friedrich W., 62, NYC-B - 1919/12/16:8a
RIEMANN, Heinrich, NYC-M - 1890/06/12:4a
RIEMENSCHNEIDER, Heinrich, 76, NYC-M - 1891/04/06:4a
RIEMER, Louise, b. Finkenberg, 33, NYC-M - 1890/07/06:5a
RIEMER, Paul, SP, + 21 Oct 1920, Boston,MA? - 1920/11/26:5d
RIENKENS, Hermann, NYC-M - 1910/01/01:6a
RIEPE, Theresa, 26, Mt Vernon, NY, + Charleston, SC - 1917/12/07:2e
RIEPERT, Angelina, NYC-B - 1887/12/06:2c
RIERL, Georg, 65, tailor, b. in Nuernberg/Bav., NYC-B - 1892/12/23:4a
RIERL, Sibilla Margaretha, 75, NYC-B - 1906/12/06:6a
RIES, Conrad, NYC-M - 1891/04/02:4a
RIES, Karl, NYC-M - 1903/07/20:4a
RIES, Oskar, 38, lithographer, SPD Nuernberg - 1910/10/17:4d
RIESACHER, August, machinist, NYC-B - 1903/01/19:4a
RIESE, Arnold, SP, MdR, Vienna/Austria - 1912/02/11:3f; mem. 1913/08/10:3a
RIESE, John, 64, pres. Consumers' Brewery, NYC - 1910/03/29:3b
RIESENBERGER, Nicholas, innkeep, No. Bergen, NJ - 1919/11/13:2c
RIESER, Fannie, NYC-M - 1901/03/12:3d
RIESOHN, Ch. J., NYC-M - 1912/05/21:6a
RIESS, Catherine, NYC-B, + @Genl Slocum - 1904/06/18:3c
RIETH, Lina, NYC-M - 1889/07/16:4a
RIETH, Susanne, b. Koch, NYC-M - 1885/04/15:3d
RIETHE % Conrad
RIETZEL, Hermann, pianist, NYC-M - 1882/05/28:5d, 15 June:1b
RIETZL, C., NYC-M - 1905/03/03:4a
RIFFEL, R's wife, Elizabeth, NJ - 1916/01/22:6a
RIGA, Maria, 68, NYC-M - 1893/04/20:4a

RIGA, Reinhard, 64, NYC-M – 1896/07/26:5a
RIGMANN, Walter, NYC-M – 1910/09/30:6a
RIHA, Max, 18, NYC-M – 1885/07/04:3c
RIHA, Wilhelm, 72, tailor, NYC-M – 1893/12/02:1g, 2:4a
RIHLE, Wilhelmine, NYC-Q – 1901/07/02:4a
RIHM, Georg Sr., un. painter, NYC-SI - 1917/05/05:6a
RIHM, Sybilla, 53, NYC-M – 1912/08/28:6a, 29:6a
RIIS, Jacob, 65, Danish-born social reformer, + Barre, MA - 1914/05/27:6a
RIKER, Thomas, 50, laborer, NYC-M – 1893/05/04:4e
RILEY, Joe, Negro, lynched Russellville, KY – 1908/08/02:11d
RILL, Matheis, NYC-B – 1910/01/02:7c
RILLING, Jacob, NYC-M – 1907/04/28:7b
RINDERER, J., Newark, NJ – 1909/02/20:6a
RINDT, Hugo, bookprinter & SPD journalist, + Berlin – 1909/08/08:3b
RINGELMANN, Joseph, music teacher at Free German School, NYC-Bx - 1915/05/15:5f, 16:7c, 17:6b
RINGER, Alfred, 11, NYC-M, +@Genl Slocum – 1904/06/23:1c
RINGLE, Ludwig, 64, NYC-M – 1893/12/15:4a
RINGLER, Alfred, 9, NYC-M, + @Genl Slocum – 1904/06/29:1c
RINGLER, Ettie, 3, NYC-Q - 1914/03/14:6d
RINGLER, Eva, NYC-M, + @on Genl Slocum – 1904/06/17:3c
RINGLER, George, 49, NYC-M – 1889/06/06:4a, 5:4a
RINGLER, Louis, 30, NYC-M – 1885/04/13:1e
RINGWALD, Ch., NYC-M - 1917/03/07:6a
RINK, William, 52, fr Austria, painter, NYC-M – 1889/07/20:1d
RINKEL, Frieda Antoinette, (or KINKEL) 2, NYC-B – 1889/09/29:5b
RINNBLAD, Johann Gustav, fr Holmstrad/Swed., hosp. mgr,USA 1897,NYC-M – 1897/03/09:1f, 10:3e
RINNINSLAND, Charles, NYC-M – 1909/05/13:6a
RINO, Frederick, striking RR car driver, St Louis, MO – 1900/06/11:1f
RINS, Theodore, 59, lace importer, War 2, NYC-SI - 1917/03/05:1c
RINZINGER, Moritz, 50, NYC-M – 1887/01/24:3b
RIPKE, Carl, 41, un. painter, NYC-M - 1894/03/12:4a
RIPLEY, Sidney Dillon, NYC-M – 1905/02/25:4a
RIPP, Anton, un. carp., NYC-M – 1890/04/21:4a
RIPP, George, un. mason, NYC-M – 1904/02/18:4a
RIPPE, William, teacher Yorkville Free German School, NYC-M – 1899/03/03:4a, fam. 12:5b
RIPPEL, Adam, NYC-M – 1911/04/05:6a, fam. 8:6a
RIPPERT, John, West New York, NJ - 1918/03/22:6a
RIPPKE % Greb; RIPPSTEIN % Claussen
RIPPSTEIN, Joseph, 23, NYC-B – 1902/02/27:4a, 28:4a

RIST, Antonio, worker at Standard Coke, Morewood, PA – 1891/04/03:1b,
=4:1a-b, 5:1f,4a (see Morewood, PA)
RIST, Gustave, 24, engineer, Bloomfield, NYC, + Peru – 1910/07/21:3b
RIST, Katherina, b. Koepl, 52, NYC-B – 1910/04/18:6a; mem. –
1911/04/17:6a
RISTTOV, Nikolaus, mason, during strike in Budapest, Hungary –
1912/06/16:3d-e
RITKY, Josef, 48, un. metal worker, SP Vienna/Austria – 1910/10/09:3b
RITT, Robert's wife & stepdaughter, 13, NYC-B - 1913/07/01:3a
RITTEL, Jos., 57, NYC-M - 1894/01/12:4a
RITTENBECK, Martin, 30, Hackensack, NJ – 1912/11/13:2e, 14:3b, 15:3b
RITTENBERG, Max, Chicago, IL – 1885/11/13:1c
RITTER % Giebe
RITTER, Franz, 52, undertaker, NYC-Bx – 1908/05/09:2e
RITTER, John, un. carp. & labor org., SLP, * 1850 Mattersheim/Pfalz/Gy,
ex-NYC, + Philadelphia – 1888/12/05:1g
RITTER, Julius, Jersey City Heights, NJ – 1907/11/16:6a
RITTER, Katharina, 49, NYC - 1914/03/16:6a, 17:6a
RITTER, Leopoldine, NYC-B – 1887/03/07:3c
RITTER, Marie, b. Oesswein, 42, NYC-M – 1885/12/10:3b
RITTER, Max Josef, un. brewer, SP, Detroit, MI – 1912/07/17:6a, 22:3a-b
RITTER, Pauline, NYC-Bx - 1917/02/13:6a
RITTER, William, 28, NYC-B – 1893/07/27:4a, 30:5a
RITTERBUSCH, Fr., 36, NYC-M – 1892/07/18:1f
RITTIG, Johann, ed. Sunday ed. NYSZ. *26 Mr 1829 Prag/ Bohemia, '48er,
USA 1850?, at Staats 1857-61, 1873-85, NYC-M + trip in Europe –
1885/06/19:4a
RITTING, Charlotte, b. Link, NYC-M – 1886/04/16:3b
RITTKE, Anton, NYC-M – 1882/01/05:3b
RITTLER, Georg, Hoboken, NJ – 1907/07/10:6a
RITTLER, Joseph, 20, worker, Hoboken, NJ – 1892/12/21:1f
RITTMANN, Christian, 63, Harrison, NJ - 1917/03/04:7a
RITTMANN, Frederick, 18, NYC-Bx – 1911/12/13:6a
RITTWIEGEL, Gottfried, Newark, NJ – 1892/06/13:1c
RITZ, Jennie, 4, Newark, NJ – 1896/11/10:4c
RITZ, John, 50, NYC-B – 1887/12/07:2e
RITZ, Michael, 12, NYC-M – 1893/06/19:4c
RITZ,..., boy, NYC-M, + @ Genl Slocum – 1904/06/18:3c
RITZEL, Andreas, NYC-M? – 1912/01/24:6a, mem. 22 Jan. 1913:6a
RIVENSKY, Anton, 59, cigarmaker, NYC-M – 1882/04/12:1g
RIX, Gustav, 53, NYC-M – 1902/01/11:4a

RIZAL, Jose, Phillipino patriot – 1896/12/31:1a
ROACH, John J., 41, reporter for The Citizen, NYC – 1891/04/02:2e
ROACH, John, ship builder & local politico, NYC-M – 1886/07/16:4c, note 11 Jan. 1887:3b
ROACH, Red, Negro, lynched Roxboro, NC – 1920/07/08:1b
ROBER, Laura, paper store, widow of "Beefsteak John" Rober, restaurant owner, NYC-B – 1917/09/14:6d
ROBERSON, Douglas, Negro, lynched Mobile, AL – 1909/01/24:1b
ROBERT, Cornelius, Irish patriot,exec.Dublin – 1916/05/09:1b
ROBERT, Gustav, German member French Foreign Legion, exec. – 1892/07/12:4b
ROBERTS, Alice, actress, NYC-M – 1890/02/10:4e
ROBERTS, Blanche, 13, NYC-B, +@Genl Slocum – 1904/06/25:1d
ROBERTS, Charles, 26, Jersey City Heights, NJ – 1896/01/26:5a
ROBERTS, Clara, NYC-M, + @on Genl Slocum – 1904/06/18:3c
ROBERTS, Lord, British polit. – 1914/11/15:1b
ROBERTS, William H., NYC-B – 1912/12/09:6a
ROBERTSON, Hannah, 20, Hewlitt, LI – 1891/08/05:4d, 4:1h, 6:1e, =10:1f
ROBERTSON, Lewis, Negro, lynched Watkinsville, GA – 1905/06/30:1h
ROBESCH, John, 77, NYC-B – 1892/06/16:4a
ROBIN, Paul, 75, French socialist, + Paris – 1912/09/17:4f-g
ROBINSON, George, Negro, lynched Tunica, MS – 1907/10/13:1b
ROBINSON, Harry W., 45, SLP, lawyer, *Boston, active in Irish-Am. orgs – 1895/02/10:1e
ROBINSON, Hermann, ex-secy Central Fed. Union, NYC-Bx - 1918/05/11:1f
ROBINSON, Richard, Negro, lynched Watkinsville, GA – 1905/06/30:1h
ROBLOSKY, Valeryi Stanislaus, striking worker, NYC-M – 1910/07/29:1a-b, 4a, =31:1d
ROBRECHT, Carrie, 22, worker, Newark, NJ – 1910/11/27:1a
ROBST % Bauer
ROCHEFORT, Marquis de, negativ. Obit? – 1897/11/14:4c-d CHECK
ROCHEFORT-LUCAY, Henri comte de, 83,French anarchist polit. & writer, + Aix-les-bains - 1913/07/02:1d,2f,4c, 6:6c-d,
ROCHOW, Elisabeth, NYC-SI – 1904/07/01:4a, 2:4a
ROCHOW, Georg, 54, NYC-SI – 1912/01/04:6a
ROCK, Helen, 20, NYC-M, + @ Genl Slocum – 1904/06/17:3c
ROCKE, Herman, 52, NYC-M – 1883/04/18:3b
ROCKEFELLER, John D., millionaire, on him – 1905/09/17:4c-e
ROCKEFELLER, Stephan J., 40, innkeep, NYC-M – 1892/03/31:4c-d, trial of his murderer 18 May:4c, 19:1g

ROCKER, Greta, 7, NYC-M – 1891/07/18:4a
ROCKIN, Andreas J., 50, druggist, NYC-M – 1884/09/14:1e, 27:1e
ROCKWELL, Charles's wife, War 2, Paterson, NJ - 1917/02/05:2f
RODBERTUS, Karl, German reformer (utopian) in 1840s, +1875, 100th anniv. – 1905/08/27:4c-e
RODDENBAUM, Herman, 53, West Hoboken, NJ – 1912/01/17:6a
RODE, August, NYC-Bx – 1906/08/06:6a
RODE, Elizabeth, Jersey City, NJ – 1909/04/04:7c
RODE, Hermann, 30, coachman, NYC-B – 1908/05/29:3a
RODE, Joseph, NYC-B – 1901/12/15:5a
RODEHAN % Ploetz
RODEHAN, Bertha M., NYC-M - 1894/06/26:4a
RODEHAN, Isabella, 4, NYC-M - 1894/02/18:5c
RODEMAIER, Heinrich, Jersey City Heights, NJ – 1906/06/08:4a
RODEMEYER % Freise
RODEMEYER, Agnes, NYC-Q – 1904/09/10:4a
RODEMEYER, Auguste, 48, NYC-Q – 1909/01/06:6a, 7:6a
RODEN, Daniel, 61, un. cigarmaker, + Toronto, CAN – 1897/10/29:4a
RODEN, Johanna, 72, NYC-M – 1901/11/25:4a
RODEN, Martha Hahn, 49, NYC-B - 1915/01/15:6a
RODENBERG, William, 61, NYC-M - 1894/01/10:4a
RODER, Hermann, 53, druggist, * Pforzheim, USA 1887, Jersey City, NJ - 1917/08/07:2f
RODERSCHATT, Peter, 55, hatmaker, NYC-B – 1910/08/04:3a-b
RODIN, Auguste, 77, French sculptor, + Paris - 1917/12/26:4e
RODRIGUEZ, Andrew, stoker,during strike, NYC-M – 1912/07/09:1d
RODRIGUEZ, Antonio, lynched Rock Springs, TX – 1910/11/14:1a, 12:2b, 11:4c-d, 15:4v
ROEBSAM, Henry, NYC-M - 1915/01/19:6a
ROECK, Oscar, NYC-Q – 1911/11/15:6a
ROEDE, Alexander, NYC-B - 1915/01/31:7d
ROEDEL, Hermann, un. upholsterer, NYC-M - 1916/07/07:6a
ROEDER, Adam, 54, NYC-B – 1893/12/29:4a
ROEDER, Andrew, 32, barber, NYC-B – 1888/01/31:2c
ROEDER, August, 37, brushmaker, NYC-B – 1888/07/14:3b
ROEDER, Bertha, fr Berlin, USA 1867, NYC-M – 1882/01/31:1g
ROEDER, Charles, un. carp., NYC-B – 1905/12/26:4a
ROEDER, Ewald, NYC-M – 1913/02/05:6a
ROEDER, Frederick, 65, Jersey City, NJ – 1907/04/27:1f
ROEDER, Gustav, NYC-B - 1916/05/28:7d
ROEDER, Gustav, realtor, NYC-M – 1900/08/22:1e
ROEDER, H., West Hoboken, NJ – 1903/01/30:4a

ROEDER, Heinrich, un. carp., NYC-Bx – 1910/05/01:7a
ROEDER, Henry, un. carp., NYC-M – 1907/01/20:7c
ROEDER, Michael, 36, NYC-B – 1892/10/27:4a
ROEDER, Michael, NYC-B - 1919/08/04:6a
ROEDER, Ph. NYC-M – 1908/03/31:6a
ROEDIG, William, 45, NYC-M – 1907/06/18:6a
ROEDIGER, Hugo, Hoboken, NJ – 1919/12/06:6a
ROEDLER, Emily, 10, NYC-M - 1914/02/17:6a
ROEDNER, Louis, 71, NYC-Q – 1907/05/01:1e
ROEGNER, Chr., 31, NYC-B – 1887/11/14:3a
ROEHL, Frank W., Sing Sing escapee – 1893/05/11:1f-g, 17:1f, 19:1g
ROEHL, Mrs, b. Endress, NYC-B – 1891/04/27:4a
ROEHLIG, George, plant director Botany Worsted Mills, Passaic, NJ - 1918/10/31:2e
ROEHLING, John G., NYC-B – 1913/01/18:6a
ROEHM, Friedrich, NYC-M – 1903/05/04:4a
ROEHM, Gottlieb, 44, carp., NYC-B – 1899/02/18:2h
ROEHM, Gustave, 64, un. carp. Yonkers, NY - 1920/12/04:6a
ROEHM, Stephan, 45, Union Hill, NJ – 1904/04/17:5b
ROEHM, Tesi, 5, NYC-M – 1898/04/11:4a
ROEHR, Charles A., 54, un. mason, NYC-B – 1907/10/10:6a, fam. 12:6a
ROEHR, Henry Edward, 61, colonel, NYC-B – 1901/03/09:3c
ROEHR, Margarethe, 1, NYC-B – 1888/08/06:3b
ROEHR, Mrs, Pleasantville, NJ – 1906/12/29:3c
ROEHRICHT, Paul, 45, jeweler, No. Plainsfield, NJ – 1899/09/13:1h, trial of Mrs Fingerhut 28:3f; 19 Dec:1g, 20:1g, 21:1d, 23 Dec 99:1c; rec 6 months – 1900/03/17:4a
ROEHRIG % Freese
ROEHRIG, Franz, machinist, West Hoboken, NJ – 1897/02/24:4a
ROEHRIG, Franz, un. brewer, NYC-M – 1892/05/03:4a
ROEHSIG, Louis, 39, NYC-B – 1903/11/23:4a
ROEL, Thomas A., 3, Newark, NJ - 1878/04/05:4d
ROELL, John, 63, NYC-M – 1906/08/06:6a
ROELLIG, Robert, un. baker, *Saxony, USA 1901, IWW, NYC-M – 1912/05/19:7a, =22:5d
ROEMER, Charles, 35, NYC-B – 1893/12/31:5c
ROEMER, John, NYC-M – 1885/06/20:3c
ROEMER, K., un. carp., NYC-M - 1917/07/26:6a
ROEMER, Louis H., beer manuf., NYC-M – 1887/11/02:1c
ROEMER, Marie, b. Weissenborn, 51, SP?, NYC-M – 1896/12/29:4a, =31:1f
ROEMER, Otto, 46, NYC-M - 1894/10/12:4a

ROEMER, Richard, SP, fr Saxony, co-fdr Yorkville Free German School, + Roxbury, MA - 1919/03/02:2e, 12a, 4:6a
ROEMISCH, William, 54, laborer, NYC-M – 1897/12/12:1d
ROEMMDE, K., 32, NYC-B – 1893/10/23:4a
ROENTGEN, Albert, 65, Newark, NJ - 1916/09/17:7a
ROEPER, Henry G., 34, NYC-B – 1910/01/22:6a
ROEPER, Karoline, W. Hoboken, NJ – 1897/07/07:4a
ROEPER, Wilhelm, 34, NYC-M - 1894/01/13:4a
ROEPPEL, Ferdinand, 46, bookkeeper, NYC-M – 1886/01/13:4d
ROESCH, Anton, 54, NYC-B – 1891/06/20:4a
ROESCH, Charles, NYC-B - 1915/03/07:7a
ROESCH, comrade, Jersey City Heights, NJ – 1899/05/23:4c
ROESCH, Ede, NYC-B – 1919/11/18:6a
ROESCH, F. Wilhelm, Jersey City, NJ – 1889/05/13:4a
ROESCH, Jacob, NYC-M – 1901/07/02:4a, 3:4a
ROESCH, Ludwig, 64, Yonkers, NY - 1920/07/29:6a
ROESCHLAU, Emil Otto, 40, Hoboken, NJ - 1914/05/16:6a
ROESEL, John, & wife Kitty, NYC-M – 1902/02/14:1g
ROESEL, John, NYC-B – 1911/01/05:6a
ROESEL, Louis, 22, stonecutter, exec. Elizabeth, NJ – 1899/03/11:3c
ROESEL, Margaretha, b. Kaemp, & infant son, NYC-M – 1882/10/20:3c
ROESEL, Reinhard, child, NYC-M – 1885/12/12:3d
ROESICKE, Richard, MdR for Dessau/Gy, (Liberal) – 1903/07/24:2c, =20 Aug.:2d
ROESKE, Albert, 53, SPD Hamburg, alderman, *Noerenberg/Pommern – 1910/10/10:4f, =23:3a-b
ROESLER, Emma, NYC-M - 1895/12/14: 4d
ROESLER, Robert, 64, un. cigarmaker, NYC-M - 1919/04/30:6a
ROESNER, Leonard, 56, *Baden/Baden Prov., '48er, barber, then innkeep & insurance agent, USA ~ 1853, NYC-B – 1883/11/24:2f
ROESSEL, Emil, 3, NYC-M – 1886/07/31:3a
ROESSELE, Fr. Anatole, Dr., 24, NYC-M – 1887/01/01:2f
ROESSLE, Henry, NYC-B – 1884/08/25:3a
ROESSLE, Lisette, (ex-NYC), Guttenberg, NJ – 1882/08/23:4d
ROESSLER, Rudolf, 48, NYC-Bx - 1917/05/27:7a
ROESSNER, Teresa, 11, NYC-M, see 1883 School Fire, NYC-M
ROESTOW, Christiane F., 72, NYC-M – 1892/06/14:4a
ROETH, Elise, b. Scheuermann, 51, NYC-B – 1910/05/17:6a
ROETH, Helene, 20, NYC-M, @Genl Slocum – 1904/06/23:1b
ROETH, John, 74, un. painter, NYC-M - 1919/08/14:6a
ROETH, Mrs, NYC-M – 1893/12/06:4a
ROETHER, Andreas, 47, un. cigarmaker, NYC-M – 1904/06/03:4a

ROETHER, John, 57, un. bricklayer, ex-SLP, fr Hamburg 1881, NYC-M – 1900/11/01:4a, =4:5c
ROETHING, Julius, 72, tailor,SPD Leipzig – 1911/09/27:4f, = 8 Oct:3b-c
ROETHLISBERGER, Elise, b. Moser, 29, Swiss, Cincinatti, + NYC visiting her sister – 1882/04/26:1g
ROETTOFS, John, + 31 VII 19 mem 1920/07/31:6a
ROGEARD, Auguste, opponent of Napoleon III, + Paris – 1896/12/23:2d
ROGER, Jean, Guttenberg, NJ - 1917/10/13:6a
ROGERS, Charles H., exec. Ossining, NY – 1908/07/21:1f
ROGERS, Henry H., v-p Standard Oil, negat obit, NYC-M – 1909/05/20:1f
ROGERS, M. Thomas, 31, * Devonshire/England, NYC-M - 1878/03/16:4e
ROGERS, Mary Mabel, exec. Windsor, VT – 1905/12/09:1c
ROGGENBAUCH, Charles, un. machinist, NYC-M – 1906/11/15:6a
ROGGENSTEIN, John, NYC-Bx - 1917/03/03:6a
ROGH, Joseph, 26, cigarmaker, NYC-M – 1899/05/18:3g, fam. 21:5a
ROGIER, Charles, 85, Belgian polit. – 1885/05/28:1a
ROGOWSKI, Albert, 28, chair maker, NYC-M? - 1913/12/30:1d
ROGOZINSKY, Hermann, fr Poland, NYC-M – 1890/02/17:1f-g, 18:1h, 12 Mr:1f-, 13:1h
ROHDE, John F., 42, NYC-B – 1882/01/07:3b
ROHDE, William, 40, NYC-B – 1911/08/17:6a
ROHE, Isidor, brewery worker, NYC-M - 1894/09/17:4a
ROHEIMER, Johann, carp., NYC-M - 1917/09/10:6a, 11:6a
ROHLAND, Oscar, 59, Boonton, NJ - 1917/11/17:6a
ROHLEFF, Wilhelmine, b. Heistermann, Harrison, NJ – 1905/11/23:4a
ROHLING, Catherine, b. Conrad, NYC-B – 1890/02/20:4a
ROHLING, Frederick, 2, NYC-M – 1891/03/30:4a
ROHLLING, Henry, 51, driver, Hoboken, NJ – 1904/07/11:1a, 12:1f
ROHLS, Alfred, 45, NYC-SI - 1918/04/23:6a
ROHMANN, F., un. cigar maker, NYC-M – 1883/05/16:3c
ROHMELT, Martha, 64, NYC-M - 1916/09/04:6a
ROHMELT, Traugott, 59, un. carp., NYC-M - 1917/01/18:6a
ROHN, Gustav, NYC-B – 1899/09/12:4a
ROHNE, William, 58, NYC-B – 1903/07/10:1f
ROHNER, Emilie, b. Zuckert, New Haven, CT – 1891/05/31:5b
ROHR, Annie, 12, NYC-M – 1905/02/21:4a
ROHR, August, 42, NYC-M – 1891/04/11:4a
ROHR, August, 71, un. cigarmaker, Jersey City, NJ – 1913/10/25:6a
ROHR, Frank, 64, gardener, Hoboken, NJ - 1914/12/04:2d
ROHR, Max, NYC-B – 1911/03/27:6a
ROHRBACH, John, 31, clerk, NYC-B – 1908/08/24:3a
ROHRBACH, Kurt – 1919/12/22:6a

ROHRBACH, Margareta, NYC-B - 1916/09/27:6a
ROHRECKER, John, NYC-M - 1915/10/05:6a
ROHRSCHEID, Henry M., innkeep, NYC-M - 1883/02/09:4d
ROHRSEN, Friedrich, 38, USA ~ 1881, NYC-M - 1896/06/23:1e
ROHRSSEN, Christ., NYC-M - 1904/09/15:4a
ROHUT, Emil, 19, French, NYC-M - 1893/02/28:4e
ROHWEDER, Minnie, b. Mahn, 36, NYC-M - 1891/04/04:4a
ROHWELT % Brandes; ROITZSCH % Herold
ROKAHR, E., NYC-M - 1918/05/04:6a
ROKITANSKY, Carl, Dr., 74, Sudetengerman scientist & liberal politician, *Koeniggraetz/Bohemia, + Vienna - 1878/08/04:2d-e
ROKOFSKY, Sam, 46, NYC-B - 1918/07/25:6b
ROLD, M., 76, NYC-M - 1893/05/30:4a
ROLF, Wilhelm, 32, SLP, NYC-M - 1885/01/04:8a, =5:4c, 6:4d
ROLL, Charles, NYC-M ,+ 17 June, inquest - 1882/06/29:1g, 30:1f
ROLL, Henry, 48, NYC-M - 1898/09/05:1d
ROLL, Joseph, 52, un. cigarmkr, NYC-M - 1914/11/05:6a
ROLL, Maria, b. Vetter, 74, NYC-M - 1891/03/30:4a
ROLLE, Anton, SP?, Jersey City Heights, NJ - 1918/12/21:6a
ROLLER, Albert, 45, NYC-Q - 1908/01/11:3b
ROLLETT, Hermann, 84, poet, '48er, + Vienna - 1904/06/01:2c
ROLLINGER, Michael Emil, butcher, exec. Chicago, IL - 1899/11/18:1d
ROLLMANN, Charles, un. carp., NYC - 1913/05/04:7c
ROLLOFF, John, NYC-Bx, SP? - 1919/08/01:6a, 2:6a
ROLLOFF, John, SP, un. carp., NYC-Bx - 1919/08/02:6a
ROLLOFF, Tobina, 67, NYC-M - 1909/06/20:1b
ROLLWAGEN, George D., 26, NYC-M - 1878/08/27:3b
ROLLWAGEN, Hans, SPD Augsburg/Bavaria, MdL & alderman - 1912/10/12:4d
ROLPH, J. D., Newark, NJ - 1908/08/31:6a
ROLSER, Conrad, NYC-M - 1914/01/15:6a
ROMANIA, Carol I, King of, crit. obit. - 1914/10/12:4c
ROMANSKI, Kasimir, Polish artist, NYC-M - 1895/06/29:1g
ROMANSKY, Joseph, 54, worker at Singer's?, SP, Elizabeth, NJ - 1906/01/25:4a, =2Fb:3d, fam. ? Fb:4a
ROMEIS, Emil, driver, + 5 May, NYC-M 1886/09/16:1g, 17:1g
ROMEZZO, Antonio, exec. Lancaster, PA - 1912/05/24:1b
ROMM, Julie, b. Zadek, SP, writer & editor of NYVZ's womens' page, active soc. in Gy, Russia, USA early 1890s, NYC-M - 1916/01/08:1d, 9:6a-c, 7a, =10:2c, fam. 15:6a
ROMMEL, Anna F., 60, NYC-M - 1898/05/05:1g
ROMMEL, David Thomas, NYC-M - 1915/12/09:6a

ROMMERY, Frederick, 45, beer driver, NYC-B – 1897/12/25:4d,
ROMOSER, Fritz, NYC-M - 1914/11/10:6a
RONDHOLZ, Emma, 16, Hoboken, NJ - 1914/01/05:3c
RONGE % Engelkerr
RONGE, Johannes, Rev., 74, fdr of German-Catholic Church, exc. 1844, + 1887/10/28:1g
ROO, Gertrud, b. Wolf, NYC-M – 1891/12/10:4a
ROOK, Carl Friedrich, 50, un. pattern maker, NYC-B – 1905/09/13:4a
ROOK, Johanna, 70, NYC-M - 1920/03/23:6a
ROOK, Maria, b. Rhein, ex-NYC?, Koeln-Kalk/Gy, + Antwerpen/Belg. – 1909/07/27:6a
ROOKE, F. S., telephonist & woman hero, Folsom, CO – 1908/09/13:20b
ROOS % Markmann
ROOS, Abraham, 61, NYC-M – 1891/09/03:4a
ROOS, Florentine, NYC-M – 1892/06/13:4a
ROOS, John, 58, NYC? – 1912/05/22:1b
ROOS, Leonard F., art dealer, NYC-M – 1902/11/30:1g, will 3 Dec:1g
ROOSEVELT, Theodore, US pres.,crit. obit. - 1919/01/07:1g, 4a-b, =9:1e
ROPPELT, Charles G., 16, NYC-M – 1908/07/23:6a, fam. 27:6a
RORS, Sarah, wd of Dr. Franz Gerau, NYC-B – 1901/04/14:5a
ROSA, Nicolaus, NYC-M – 1909/05/09:7a
ROSBERG, John, 67, un. carp., NYC-B – 1893/11/02:4c
ROSBITZKI, R. von, SPD Wandsbeck, alderman & journ. Hamburger Echo – 1911/11/19:3c
ROSCH, Elisabeth, b. Lippert, 25, NYC-Q – 1910/03/23:6a
ROSCHE, Victor, 52, machinist, NYC-M – 1903/01/30:1e
ROSCHITZ, Margaretha, b. Kuster, 27, NYC-B – 1889/09/09:4a
ROSCHKE, Clara, NYC-B – 1904/07/10:5a
ROSE, Addie, NYC-B, + @on Genl Slocum – 1904/06/18:3c
ROSE, Amelia, 19, Annie, NYC-M, @Genl Slocum – 1904/06/17:3c, 22:1d
ROSE, Benjamin R., 55, salesman, NYC-M – 1909/09/07:1e, 10:1d
ROSE, Bertha, NYC – 1900/01/07:1f
ROSE, Heinrich, un. cigarmkr, NYC-M - 1914/08/16:7d
ROSE, Heinrich's wife, NYC-M – 1889/02/13:4a
ROSE, Isabella, + 26 Sept 1902 NYC, hubby rec 19 yrs – 1903/11/20:2h
ROSE, Joseph W., NYC – 1912/11/29:6a
ROSE, Louis, 50, painter, NYC-Q – 1885/05/31:5c
ROSE, Mary, 12, NYC-@, not +, note on birth mother Lena Falkenmeyer – 1906/12/15:3a
ROSE, Michael, 41, guard, dying, NYC-M – 1910/12/26:2f
ROSEGGER, Peter, Austrian writer, 60th birthday – 1903/08/16:3f-g, 4e; 70th birthday, # – 1913/08/17:13a-d; mem. 1918/08/26:4f

ROSELAND, Eva, poet, 23, NYC-B – 1897/02/21:1d
ROSEMANN, Benjamin, 15, Charles, 17, Emmerich, 3, & little sister, NYC-Q – 1919/08/26:2f
ROSEN, Eva, fr Romania, NYC-M – 1895/05/14:1h
ROSEN, Julie, fr Austria 1907, @1911 Triangle Shirtwaist Fire, NYC-M – 1911/03/28:1b, 1f
ROSEN, Max, un. cigar maker, NYC-M – 1892/02/28:5e
ROSEN, Pauline, 17, seamstress, NYC-M - 1913/06/15:1e
ROSENAGEL, Annie, NYC-M, + @ Genl Slocum – 1904/06/17:3c
ROSENBAUM, Martha, b. Wolfstein, 31, NYC-M – 1892/07/04:4a
ROSENBAUM, William, butcher, NYC-M – 1890/09/12:4d, 13:2g
ROSENBAUM, Yetta, 25, @ 1911 Triangle Shirtwaist Fire, NYC-M – 1911/03/28:1b, 1f
ROSENBERG % Glueck
ROSENBERG, Bernard, 50, un. cigarmaker, NYC-B – 1897/08/31:4d
ROSENBERG, Berthold, *29 Oc 1860 Hamburg/Gy, missing in USA s. 1883, needed by Hamburg civil court – 1908/07/02:6a
ROSENBERG, Daniel D., 23, medical student, NYC-M – 1902/05/01:4c
ROSENBERG, David, 40, NYC-B – 1906/11/17:2b
ROSENBERG, Friederike, 78, NYC-M - 1878/09/18:3c
ROSENBERG, Helen, NYC-M - 1894/01/10:4a
ROSENBERG, Henry, NYC – 1885/09/15:3a
ROSENBERG, Hyman D., ex-rabbi Beth Jacob, NYC-B – 1893/04/19:2d
ROSENBERG, Jennie, 21,@ 1911 Triangle Shirtwaist Fire, NYC-M – 1911/03/27:1d
ROSENBERG, Julia, NYC-B – 1912/10/14:2c
ROSENBERG, Louis, exec. Ossining, NY - 1914/04/14:1g,2a,4a
ROSENBERG, Maria, 28, Newark, NJ – 1891/02/06:1c
ROSENBERG, Minnie, 23, NYC-B – 1912/02/29:2e
ROSENBERG, Morris, builder, NYC-M – 1902/01/01:1c
ROSENBERG, Moses, 62, sock dealer, NYC-M – 1896/04/12:14e
ROSENBERG, Philipp, 86, ret. butcher, NYC-M? - 1913/12/16:2f
ROSENBERG, Rebecca, 47, NYC-B - 1878/08/03:4c
ROSENBERG, Samuel, tailor, NYC-M – 1908/04/14:1b
ROSENBERG, Siegfried, cutter, NYC-M – 1896/10/06:1g
ROSENBERGER, Elisabeth Bauer, NYC-M – 1918/07/20:6a
ROSENBERGER, Frank William, 1, NYC-M – 1899/12/07:4a
ROSENBERGER, Mary, 41, NYC-M, @ Genl Slocum – 1904/06/17:3c, 18:3c
ROSENBERGER, Rosa, NYC-M – 1904/11/17:2h, c
ROSENBERGER, Solomon, carpet pattern maker, NYC-M – 1891/02/18:1g
ROSENBLATT, Anna, 80, NYC-Q – 1912/12/12:6c

ROSENBURG, Barbara, 68, NYC-M – 1898/04/08:1g
ROSENBURG, David, roofer, NYC-M – 1906/08/08:3b
ROSENBUSCH, Eliza, Yonkers, NY – 1897/09/19:11c
ROSENCRANZ, Ernest, druggist, NYC-M – 1887/12/10:4d
ROSENER, Leo, NYC-B – 1903/07/07:4a
ROSENFELD, Alexander, 27, NYC-B – 1909/01/11:3a
ROSENFELD, Lawrence, 32, subway car driver, NYC-M – 1907/03/16:5e
ROSENFELD, Louis, 30, NYC-M – 1891/08/27:1d
ROSENFELD, Max, 35, leader of Poale Zion party, * Drohobycz/Galicia, + Vienna, = 1919/04/20:3g
ROSENFELD, Sophie, NYC-M - 1895/10/28: 1c
ROSENFELDER, Christian, SLP, un. engineer, NYC-M – 1893/07/22:4a, 23:1e,5c, fam. 24:4a
ROSENGARTEN, Nathan, 19, painter, SLP, NYC-M – 1898/08/22:1g
ROSENHEIM, Hermann, innkeep, NYC – 1907/09/13:1d
ROSENHEIMER, Falk, 50, NYC – 1912/06/21:2f
ROSENHEIMER, Julius T., manuf., + 14 June 07 Pelham Bay, note – 1908/04/14:1g
ROSENKAMPF, Emil, 47, un. cigarmaker, NYC-M – 1896/07/25:4a
ROSENKRANTZ, Ida, 26, NYC-Q – 1911/10/03:3b
ROSENOW, Emil, 33, MdR for SPD, writer, + Berlin – 1904/02/10:2b; mem. 1912/05/19:11a, 29 Jy:2e
ROSENSTEIN, William, commission dealer, NYC-B – 1893/05/18:2d
ROSENSTOCK, James, 56, NYC-M – 1891/04/04:4a
ROSENTHAL % Quittner
ROSENTHAL, Abraham, 18, NYC-B – 1897/09/08:1d, =9:3f
ROSENTHAL, Charles, 45, treas. Internatl Plating Co, NYC-M – 1908/03/20:1f
ROSENTHAL, Hermann, gambler, killed by policemen (connected to Lt Charles Becker trial), NYC-M – 1912/07/17:1d, 4a, 18:1g, 4a, 20:4a, etc
ROSENTHAL, James, NYC-M – 1891/10/03:4a
ROSENTHAL, Joseph, NYC-M – 1890/10/26:5a
ROSENTHAL, Leopold, un. typesetter, NYC-M – 1906/12/18:6a
ROSENTHAL, Morris, grocer, & wife Bessie, NYC-B – 1913/10/01:3a
ROSENTHAL, Robert, exec. by British as alleged German agent - 1915/07/16:2f
ROSENTHAL, Siegfried, un. cigarmaker, NYC-M – 1904/04/18:4a
ROSENTHALWEG, Michael, NYC-M - 1894/01/13:4a
ROSENZWEIG, Cecilie, servant, NYC-M – 1909/03/31:2f
ROSENZWEIG, S., NYC-M – 1906/05/30:4a
ROSENZWEIG, Sam, 11, NYC-Bx - 1918/06/28:2f
ROSENZWEIG, Saul's wife, NYC-Q – 1905/10/09:4a

ROSHKE, Theo., NYC-Bx - 1915/10/09:6a
ROSNACK, Michael, miner, Port Hope, NJ - 1909/11/19:2b, 20:3c
ROSS, Arthur, exec. Trenton, NJ - 1910/08/17:2g
ROSS, Eva, b. Appel, NYC-M - 1892/07/12:4a
ROSS, Henry, innkeep, NYC-M - 1915/05/11:2c
ROSS, John, NYC-M - 1915/01/09:6a
ROSS, Joseph, 42, bricklayer, NYC-M - 1894/07/21:1g
ROSS, William, 42, fireman, NYC-M - 1917/01/03:1d
ROSSA, Jeremiah O'Donovan, Irish patriot, +NYC-SI - 1915/06/30:5f, =2 Aug.:2d
ROSSBACH, Anna, 43, NYC-M - 1919/07/05:6a, fam. 10:6a
ROSSBACH, Ernst, 50, butler, NYC-M - 1903/10/01:2h
ROSSE, Emil, NYC-B - 1907/08/26:3c
ROSSE, Louise, 32, NYC-Q - 1909/02/13:6a
ROSSI, Emilie, 19, actress, NYC-M - 1890/09/19:1c, 20:2h, 22:2c
ROSSINGER, Justine L., 18, fr Sweden, NYC-M - 1885/10/06:2e
ROSSKOPF, Anna A., b. Dick, 59, NYC-B - 1891/04/06:4a
ROSSMAESSLER, Emil Adolf, 1806-1867, German botanist, memory 1906/03/18:3f-g
ROSSMANN, Friedrich, 75,un. carp., USA 1854 fr Mecklemburg-Schwerin,NYC-M - 1905/31:4a,d
ROSSMEISL, Elizabeth, b. Maus, Newark, NJ - 1918/10/25:6a
ROSSNAGEL, Valentin, un. mason, NYC-M - 1885/01/04:8a
ROSSNER, Anton, NYC-M - 1905/05/08:4a
ROSSNER, Mary, 26, servant, USA 1895, NYC-SI - 1899/04/26:1d
ROST, Alfred, 32, Linden, NJ - 1914/08/07:6a
ROST, Robert, un. carp., NYC-M - 1914/08/23:7c
ROSTA, Julius, 14, sweeper, during strike in Budapest, Hungary - 1912/06/16:3d-e
ROTENBURG, William, innkeep, NYC-B - 1917/04/16:2c
ROTH % Breyer, % Laux
ROTH, Abraham, tailor, & wife, NYC - 1910/07/29:1e
ROTH, Adam, NYC-B - 1917/09/08:6a
ROTH, Adam, NYC-M - 1907/11/03:7d, fam. 5:6a
ROTH, Adolph, NYC-M - 1910/06/09:6a
ROTH, Anna, b. Lasser, 38, NYC-M - 1899/01/01:5b
ROTH, Anna, geb. Leidgeb, NYC-B - 1919/10/19:12a
ROTH, Barbara, 60, servant, NYC-B - 1916/05/04:3e
ROTH, Bertha, child, NYC-M - 1883/10/26:2e
ROTH, Carl, child?, NYC-M - 1901/09/15:5a
ROTH, Charles, 41, lawyer, NYC-M - 1897/05/15:1e
ROTH, Charles, NYC-M - 1898/09/06:1c

ROTH, Emil E., 45, fr Elsass, USA 1873, NYC-B – 1888/03/06:1c-d
ROTH, Ferdinand, NYC-B – 1903/01/23:4a, 24:4a
ROTH, France, 18, stenographer, NYC-M – 1898/01/06:1e
ROTH, George, Chicago, striking worker – 1885/04/10:1g, 11:1b
ROTH, Heinrich, SP, NYC-M - 1917/02/08:6a
ROTH, Helen, 20, NYC-M, + @on Genl Slocum – 1904/06/17:3c
ROTH, Jacob, NYC-B – 1907/08/25:7c
ROTH, John, 65, NYC-M – 1900/04/16:4a
ROTH, Joseph, NYC-M – 1887/05/02:3c
ROTH, Joseph, un. carp., 69, NYC-B – 1906/07/08:7a
ROTH, Josephine, 42, NYC-M, + @on Genl Slocum – 1904/06/17:3c
ROTH, Louise, b. Buerkle, 38, NYC-M – 1910/07/09:6a
ROTH, Martin J., 42, NYC-B – 1896/08/10:1a
ROTH, Michael, inquest, NYC-M – 1886/01/09:1f
ROTH, Michael, NYC-B – 1892/04/05:4b
ROTH, Philip A., & family, ex-Arizona, + Willsayville, NY - 1918/08/19:1f
ROTH, Philip, 53, NYC-M - 1915/08/14:6a
ROTH, Philipp, 45, un. carp., NYC-B – 1890/08/11:4a
ROTH, Philipp, 48, un. cigarmaker, NYC-M – 1893/07/08:4a
ROTH, R. Arthur, NYC-Q – 1919/09/27:8a
ROTH, Rosa, NYC-M? - 1919/03/07:6a
ROTH, Samuel, 46, shoemaker, + 22 June Ward's Island, NYC-M (s.a.
  Farrish, Froehlich) – 1887/06/30:1e, 6 July:1g, 16:3a-b,
ROTH, Susanne, b. Schnellbacher, NYC-M – 1891/07/17:4a
ROTH, Valentin, 60, NYC-B – 1903/12/28:4b
ROTH, William, NYC – 1912/12/07:6a
ROTH, William, un. butcher, NYC-B – 1907/10/08:3a
ROTH, William, Yonkers, NY - 1913/12/03:6a
ROTH, Willie, 6, dying, NYC-M – 1897/11/01:1f
ROTHACKER, Carl Victor Hugo, Dr., ex-Heidelberg U, NYC, +
  Rochester, MN - 1914/02/19:2b
ROTHAERMEL, William, 28, roofer, NYC-B – 1890/01/01:1g
ROTHAUG, Michael, 62, innkeep, NYC-B – 1897/03/08:3c
ROTHBAUER, Franz, 44, SP?, Newark, NJ – 1913/08/03:7a
ROTHBURST, Heinrich, 67, NYC-M – 1899/03/28:3g
ROTHE, Ernst, NYC-M – 1907/04/30:6a
ROTHE, John, 51, SDP, NYC-B – 1905/03/14:4a
ROTHEN, Frederick, 68, Weehawken, NJ - 1920/06/04:6a
ROTHEN, Wilhelmina, b. Stelte, Weehawken, NJ – 1919/12/04:6a
ROTHENBACH, Charles, 42, sawmill-owner, NYC-B – 1913/09/09:6c
ROTHENBERGER, Charles, 70, NYC-B - 1919/01/19:11c
ROTHENBERGER, W., NYC – 1888/03/13:3a

ROTHENBURG, Harris, Rabbi, 68, NYC-B - 1920/02/02:2d
ROTHENGATLER, Max, 51, baker, NYC-M - 1895/11/30: 1f
ROTHENHAEUSLER, Friedrich, Dr., NYC-M – 1885/09/11:1d
ROTHER, Franz, 60, liquor dealer, NYC-Q – 1908/05/
ROTHERMEL, Frieda, NYC-B – 1910/03/10:3a
ROTHERMEL, G., NYC-M – 1893/06/13:4a
ROTHERMUND, Friedrich, 35, gardener, White Plains, NY – 1901/04/27:1g
ROTHFELDER % Hansen
ROTHFISCHER, Ludwig, 30, un. butcher, NYC-M - 1914/10/25:7b,11g
ROTHFUS, Hildegard, b. Imhof, NYC-M – 1889/06/16:5b
ROTHFUSS, Adolph, 48, un. baker, West Hoboken, NJ - 1917/03/25:7a
ROTHHAR, Jacob, brewer or cooper, NYC-M – 1890/12/17:4a
ROTHHAUB, Caroline, NYC-M – 1897/11/18:4a, 20:4a
ROTHKOPF, Henry, 35, merchant, NYC-M - 1895/09/01: 5e
ROTHKUGEL, Pauline, b. Schiff, NYC-M – 1891/07/26:4a
ROTHMAN, Emily, NYC-M, + @ Genl Slocum – 1904/06/17:3c
ROTHMAN, William C., 5, NYC-M, +@Genl Slocum – 1904/06/22:1d
ROTHMANN, Julius, 26, barber, NYC-M - 1894/04/04:4d
ROTHMERHUSEN, Christ., NYC-M – 1905/06/13:4a
ROTHPELZ, Fannie, Salvation Army, 35, NYC-B – 1906/01/12:3c
ROTHSCHILD, Alphonse, Baron de, banker, + Paris – 1905/05/27:1d, =30:1g
ROTHSCHILD, David, NYC banker, + Ossining, NY – 1908/11/19:6b
ROTHSCHILD, Hirsch, 81, NYC-M – 1892/09/20:4a
ROTHSCHILD, Max, NYC-M – 1899/10/11:4a
ROTHSCHILD, Samuel, 42, NYC-M – 1892/07/25:4a
ROTHSCHILD, William, NYC-B - 1914/07/27:6a
ROTHSTEIL, Henry, shop owner, NYC-M – 1908/06/19:1h
ROTHSTEIN, Harris, 84, NYC-M – 1903/04/04:2g-h
ROTHWEILER, Franz, 51, NYC-M – 1901/02/11:4a, 12:4a
ROTHWEILER, Friedrich, NYC-Bx – 1909/07/08:6a
ROTHWERLE, August, 41, NYC-M - 1919/01/07:6a
ROTSTEIN, Emma, 22, @1911 Triangle Shirtwaist Fire, NYC-M – 1911/04/01:1f
ROTTECK, Florentine, NYC-M – 1898/03/23:4a
ROTTERMANN, Hanna, NYC-M, + @ Genl Slocum – 1904/06/18:3c
ROTTINGER, Ernest, NYC-M, + @ Genl Slocum – 1904/06/18:3c
ROTTMANNER, Emil, SPD Munich, now St Gallen/Switz., his life (not +) – 1910/02/20:3a
ROTTNER, Theo, 22, @1911 Triangle Shirtwaist Fire, NYC-M – 1911/03/27:1d

ROUSS, Charles B., 62, millionaire, NYC, crit – 1902/03/05:2a-b
ROUVEL, comrade, SPD Breslau/Gy – 1909/03/28:3c
ROVENSKY, Karl, SPO? Granesau/Austria, War 1 – 1915/05/30:3d
ROWALD, August Carl, 46, NYC-B - 1894/01/08:4a
ROWAN, Catherine, NYC-M – 1909/05/22:6a
ROWE, Max, Dr., 28, NYC-B - 1920/10/21:1d
ROWENSKY, John, 61, NYC-B – 1907/10/24:6a
ROYER, Carl, NYC-M - 1917/12/07:6a
RUBELMANN, Emma, 36, servant, NYC-B - 1895/04/03:4c
RUBENSTEIN, Harold, 22, US Navy, NYC-B, War 1 – 1918/06/24:2f
RUBENSTEIN, Ms, 25, teacher, NYC-B – 1911/08/10:3a
RUBIN, Hermann, un. waiter, SDP, NYC – 1901/03/27:1d
RUBIN, Ruth, Dr., 24, dentist, NYC-M - 1920/10/21:1d
RUBRECHT % Oehlmann,
RUCH, Jacob, NYC? – 1900/08/28:3b, 27:1g
RUCHSER, Rosa, 27, NYC-B - 1918/10/29:6a
RUCKER, Mary, 17, Little Ferry, NJ – 1912/05/06:1e
RUCKGABERLE, Charles J.F.,un. butcher, NYC-M - 1918/05/29:6a, mem. 1919/05/27:6a
RUCKTERSTUHL, Emma, 52, NYC-B – 1912/11/24:1f
RUDA, William, NYC-Bx – 1911/05/26:6a
RUDERMANN, Louis, typesetter, NYC-M – 1909/01/17:1d
RUDERT, Thekla, b. Peschl, NYC-M – 1903/09/02:4a
RUDLOFF, John, 50, NYC-M – 1905/12/03:5b
RUDNIG, Karoline, NYC-M - 1914/05/10:7a, 11:6a
RUDOLF, Ida Marie, NYC-M - 1920/03/10:6a
RUDOLPH, August, NYC-B – 1910/11/16:6a
RUDOLPH, Elsie, NYC-M - 1920/01/08:2f
RUDOLPH, Hermann, 60, painter, NYC-Q – 1912/10/28:3b
RUDOLPH, Max, SP, un. butcher, NYC-B - 1918/10/28:6a, fam. 1 Nov.:6a
RUDOLPH, Sophie, b. Kanzler, 50, NYC-M - 1894/05/25:4a
RUDOLPH, William, "The Missouri Kid," mobster, exec. Union, MO – 1905/05/09:3f
RUEBIN, Julius, Greenville, NJ – 1904/10/19:4a
RUEBSAM, Charles C., 38, merchant, & wife, NYC-Bx – 1902/08/17:1f, 19:4a, =20:2g
RUEBSAMEN % Stadt
RUECHER, Peter, NYC-M - 1917/11/03:6a
RUECKEL, Bartholomaeus, un. carp., NYC-M – 1890/09/14:5a
RUECKERT, Felix, 40, janitor, * Berlin/Gy, NYC-B - 1920/07/19:5f

RUECKERT, Friedrich, vice-pres. White Metal Co., USA 1914, Hoboken, NJ - 1920/05/11:2b, 12:2e, = 13:1d, 17:2e, 20:2d, will 16 June:2e
RUECKWALDT, Gottlieb S., innkeep, Paterson, NJ - 1890/06/15:5d
RUED, Jacques, Swiss?, un. painter, NYC-M - 1893/01/16:4a, fam. 18:4a
RUEDIGER, Arthur, 32, un. baker, NYC-M - 1918/12/21:6a
RUEDT, Gottlieb, un. carp., NYC-M - 1903/03/18:4a
RUEFER, Sebastian, 35, NYC-M - 1892/06/17:4a
RUEFFEL, William, 67, NYC-M - 1915/06/28:1b
RUEGE, Alexander, un. clothing cutter, NYC-M - 1882/03/15:3b
RUEGEN, Julia, 23, NYC-M - 1894/02/01:4a
RUEGER, Albert, 25, un. upholsterer, NYC-B - 1890/03/28:4a
RUEGER, Frederick, West New York, NJ, + Greeley, PA - 1917/08/17:6a
RUEGG, Marie, NYC-B - 1914/07/28:6a
RUEHE, Emilie, NYC-M - 1908/11/09:6a
RUEHE, Wilhelm, barber, SP, USA 1879? fr Berlin, NYC-M - 1908/11/17:2d,6a, 18:6a, =19:2b
RUEHL % Huebner
RUEHL, Heinrich, 70, NYC-B - 1890/02/20:4a
RUEHL, Katharina, b. Schutter, 20, NYC-M - 1883/05/19:3c
RUEHL, Paul, 71, NYC-B - 1907/10/22:6a
RUEHL, Therese, wife SLP member Paul, NYC? - 1879/01/02:3a
RUEHLE, Kurt, NYC-M - 1908/01/01:6a
RUEHLE, Minna, b. Schallentraeger, 54, NYC-Q - 1901/07/03:1d
RUEHLER, Harry, NYC-M, + @ Genl Slocum - 1904/06/17:3c
RUEMELIN, mayor of Stuttgart/Gy, & friend of SPD - 1899/04/16:12h
RUENTZLER, Emma, NYC-M - 1893/09/17:5a
RUESS, Friedrich, 41, NYC-M - 1920/12/17:6a
RUETER, John Henry, 1, NYC-M - 1882/03/29:3c
RUETHE, Hermann Friedrich, SLP, un. waiter, candid. NYS assembly 1893, * Pomerania, NYC-M 1895/04/21:5a, =23:3e
RUETTINGER, Emmanuel, lace merchant fr Dresden/Gy, father living in Stuttgart, NYC-SI - 1891/03/14:1c, inquest 15:1h, 16:1h, 18:1e, 20:1f, 21:2h, 24:2f, 1 Apr 1891:1h, 3:2h, 16 Fb 1892:1e
RUF, Adam, NYC-M - 1911/05/18:6a
RUF, Elisabeth, b. Frey, NYC-B - 1903/11/25:4a, fam. 29:5c
RUFF, Emma, 13, NYC-M - 1889/02/10:5b
RUFF, Frederick, Newark, NJ - 1912/09/17:3c
RUFF, Frederick, NYC-B - 1908/07/08:6a
RUFF, Kathe, 1, NYC-M - 1887/06/08:3b
RUGE, Arnold, 60, civil engineer, NYC - 1912/04/09:2d, 6a
RUGE, Dietrich, NYC-M - 1916/02/27:6a
RUGE?, Johanna Alwine, see BUGE?, Johanna

RUGEN, Heinrich, 44, NYC-B – 1892/07/02:4a
RUGG, Charles A., 27, NYC-Q, exec. NYC-Q – 1885/05/16:1e, 29:3a-b
RUGGABER % Schroeder
RUGGIARI, Stefano, 17, exec. Trenton, NJ - 1914/12/23:2c
RUH, Teudpert, 43, NYC-M – 1900/08/23:4a
RUHE, Anton, un. cooper, NYC – 1911/10/26:6a
RUHE, Christian, 21, NYC-Bx – 1890/07/01:1g
RUHL % Zinsmeister
RUHL, Bertha, 52, NYC-M – 1907/12/07:6a
RUHL, Martin, 20, NYC-M – 1893/02/21:4a
RUHL, Viktor, 50, NYC-M – 1883/08/23:4d
RUHLE % Keck
RUHLE, Albert, NYC-M – 1891/07/19:5b
RUHLE, comrade, SPD Scheinfeld/Bavaria – 1912/03/03:3a
RUHLING, Herman, NYC-B – 1904/06/09:3c
RUHN, Emelina, b. Baldach, 46, NYC-M - 1878/05/09:3b
RUJKTER, P. C. De, 34, Dutch labor poet, + Amsterdam – 1889/06/19:2c
RULL, Juan, Spanish anarchist, exec. Barcelona – 1908/08/09:1b
RULLE, August, NYC-Q - 1916/09/14:6a
RULLMANN, Friedrich W., 66, mgr Academy of Music, NYC-M – 1887/07/22:2f
RULOF, Friederika, 37, NYC-M – 1899/06/14:1e
RUMMELE, Rudolph, 35, weaver, Garfield, NJ – 1910/08/13:2a
RUMP, C.A.L., NYC-M – 1908/02/12:6a
RUMPF, W. L., NYC-Bx – 1911/12/11:6a
RUMPFF, Louis, 64, shadowy undercover agent accused of entrapment, + Frankfurt by "nemesis" Julius Lieske 1885/01/15:1c-e, 2a, 16:2a-c, 17:1a, 2c-d, lt by a victim 19:4d, notes 21:2e-f, 28:1d, 4 Fb:2d, 6:2d-e, 10:2c-e, 13:2e, =14:2e, 18:2d, 31 Mr:2d-e
RUMPS, Frederick, NYC? - 1915/04/06:1e
RUNAPAR, Louis, USA 1896, NYC-B? – 1896/08/10:1b
RUNDH, Stephan, Slovak RR worker, + Roseville, NJ – 1910/04/15:1a
RUNDSPADEN, Auguste, 16, NYC-M – 1886/03/23:3d
RUNDSPADEN, Friedrich Carl, 79, un. carp., NYC-M – 1911/05/01:6a
RUNDUSCH, Charles, NYC-M – 1891/06/26:4a
RUNGE, Franz, machinist, NYC-M – 1892/11/08:4a
RUNGE, Margaret, NYC-Bx - 1916/09/28:2b, 29:2d
RUNGE, Philipp, 47, innkeep, NYC-B - 1879/03/04:4c
RUNGE, William H., NYC-M – 1891/03/30:4a
RUNTZEL, Frederick, & wife, both ca. 50, NYC-B - 1920/02/18:6a
RUOFF, Marie, 20, servant, NYC-SI – 1899/05/24:3d
RUOSS, Christian, NYC-M – 1892/09/26:4a, 27:4a

RUPLER, Henry, 35, NYC-Q – 1898/09/05:1d
RUPP % Eberenz
RUPP, Charles, 35, undertaker, NYC-B – 1902/05/14:1e
RUPP, Christopher & Caroline, Jersey City, NJ (ex-farmers in Sullivan Co., NJ) 1913/10/02:2d
RUPP, Kathe, 17, Rome, N.Y., killed in Jersey City, NJ - 1894/05/17:1h
RUPP, William, NYC-M – 1891/02/20:4a
RUPPE, Heinrich, un. beerdriver, NYC-M - 1917/04/02:6a
RUPPE, Reinhold, un. butcher, NYC-M – 1913/10/24:6a
RUPPENHEIM, Otto, 7, NYC-B – 1905/07/06:4a
RUPPERT, August, Metuchen, NJ - 1920/05/18:6a
RUPPERT, Christian, cook, NYC-Bx – 1907/02/03:7d
RUPPERT, Georg, 32, barman, * Gy, NYC-M - 1895/02/13:4a
RUPPERT, John J., 46, NYC-M – 1890/08/01:4a
RUPPERT, Philip, 37, fr Albesheim/Pfalz/Gy, NYC-M – 1887/07/27:3c
RUPPERT, Regina Friedericka, b. Tufft, 40, SLP?, NYC-M – 1892/09/23:4a
RUPPERT, Valentin (+1867), will 1890/09/17:2g
RUPPRECHT, Barbara, b. Hengel, 73, NYC-B – 1890/02/15:4a
RUPPRECHT, Geo., 61,SP,un. cigarmaker, NYC-M - 1919/08/07:6a
RUPPRECHT, George, 26, carriage maker, fr Bavaria, Elizabeth?, NJ - 1896/03/04:3d
RUPPRECHT, George, 61, un. cigarmkr, SP, NYC-M – 1919/08/07:6a
RUPPRECHT, John, 53, worker, NYC-M –1891/02/04:1f
RUPPRECHT, John, un. brewer, NYC-M – 1896/08/14:4a
RUPPRECHT, Lorenz, un. carp., NYC-M – 1896/10/31:4a
RUSCHITZKA, Georg, 43, SPD Dortmund, brewer - 1914/09/27:3c
RUSIC, Steve, exec. Pittsburgh, PA – 1911/03/22:1d
RUSKIN, John, English writer & close to Labor, 1900/02/11:7b-d
RUSNOK, George, Slovak, striker in Braddock, PA, sent. to + for killing scab – 1891/02/10:1c, 11:2a, NYC workers protest 23 March:1g, 24:2b, 25:1h, 9 Apr:1e, 22 Jy:2a
RUSS, Charles, 40, sculptor, NYC – 1885/02/08:1e, 13:3a, inquest 20:3b, 5 Mr:2g, 26:2g
RUSS, Claus, 60, interned German sailor fr SS Pennsylvania, *Hamburg, +Hoboken, NJ - 1916/02/10:6b
RUSS, Karl, Dr., ornithologist, 1899/10/22:12a
RUSSELL, Henry, Negro, lynched Montgomery, AL – 1915/08/19:2b
RUSSELMANN, Christian, fr Delmenhorst/Oldenburg/Gy, NYC-M – 1889/02/12:4a
RUSSIA, Alexander II, Czar of Russia, killed by revol., 1881/03/14:4b-d, 2a, 15:1a-b, 2a-b, rd lt 16:4e, Mass-meeting 17:1g, 18:1e-f, Johann Most

20:4e-f, 27:4b-d, protest vs US condol. 21:1g,2c, =28:1a, 2a-b, by Sergius Schewitsch 3 Ap:4b-c, Kansas Mennonites on his + 9:2f, labor edits praise the deed 10:4b-c, 4g,5b, 12:2e-f, debate on his + among US soc. 24:4e,g, in Europe 24:7a-b, his killers exec. 8 May:4f-g, comment by Leo Hartmann, Russian revol. Just arrived in NYC 31 Jy:4b-e, 1 Aug:1g, NYC anarchists celeb. 10th anniv. of his + 14 Mr 1891:1h
RUSSIA, Alexander III, Czar of - 1894/11/02:2a
RUSSIA, Sergius, Grandduke of, uncle of Czar, + by revol. 1905/02/18:1a-b, 2b, NYC reactions 24 Fb:4b; 15 Mr:2d-e; 7 Ap:2d. S.a. Kalajew
RUST % Haaren, % Haehnert
RUST, Frederick, un. cigarmaker, NYC-M – 1909/05/11:6a
RUST, Josephine, 50, NYC-B – 1907/01/21:3a
RUTHENBERG, J., un. cigarpacker, NYC-M – 1883/10/28:5f
RUTHER, Moritz, SLP, un. cigarmkr, 1899 SLP alderman in Holyoke, Crimmitzschau/Sax., + Holyoke, MA – 1914/12/03:5f
RUTKOWSKI, Otto, 67, SP, bookbinder, active in Free German School, fr West Prussia Pr., NYC-B - 1920/07/02:6a, =3:2f,6a
RUTTER, William, 54, laborer, Ridgefield Park, NJ – 1907/11/21:1d
RUTTINGER, Meta, 39, NYC-M, +@ Genl Slocum – 1904/06/17:3c
RUTZ, Charles H., 60, NYC-Q - 1914/09/08:6a
RUTZ, Jacob, West Hoboken, NJ - 1914/10/31:6a
RUTZEL, Valentin, 41, musician, NYC-M – 1885/04/13:1e
RUZICKO, Anna, 47, NYC-M – 1888/10/29:3a, fam. 2 Nov:3b
RYBAK, Stanislaus, Ochrana undercover agent in Polish SP, killed in Cracow 3 wks ago – 1910/08/25:2e
RYDEN, Ernst, Yonkers, NY - 1918/04/06:6a
RYLKE, Karl, 67, un. fur presser, NYC-M - 1917/11/02:6a
SAAL, Lorenz, un. cigarmaker, NYC-M – 1904/07/27:4a
SAALBACH, A. Otto, 21, NYC-M – 1903/05/09:4a, 10:5a
SAAM, Anna Martha, 18, NYC-M – 1886/08/16:3b
SAAR, Barbara, 48, NYC-B – 1885/02/11:3a
SAAR, Ferdinand von, Austrian poet, 70th birthday – 1902/10/19:14g-h; + Vienna – 1906/08/12:3b-c
SABIAN % Regal
SABO, Mrs, 38, Perth Amboy, NJ - 1913/12/20:2e
SABOL, Michael, fr Hungary, striker in Braddock, PA, sent. to + for killing scab – 1891/02/10:1c, 11:2a
SABOR, Adolf, 65, SPD MdR for Frankfurt/Main – 1907/03/12:4d
SABOT, Michael, 17, coal-miner & hero, = Johnstown, PA – 1902/07/16:2b-c

SABROE, Peter, Danish SP deputy, 1913/08/12:4d-e
SACHER, M., Newark, NJ – 1904/08/03:4a
SACHS, Albert, smith, NYC-M – 1904/09/01:3a
SACHS, Franz, 70, Yonkers, NY - 1918/01/18:6a
SACHS, Gussie, 15, dying, NYC-M – 1900/04/23:1d
SACHS, Hannah, NYC-M – 1906/12/19:6a
SACHS, Louis, NYC-M – 1893/02/06:4a
SACHS, Mary, Jersey City, NJ – 1919/08/20:2e
SACHS, Samuel, NYC-M – 1908/05/08:1c
SACHS, Theodor W., Dr. med., Chicago, IL - 1916/04/03:1b
SACHSEN-WEIMAR, Sophia von, (German society scandal) 1913/09/19:1c, 24:2g,4c,25:1b, 5 Oct:11a
SACHTLEBEN, Carl Wilhelm, 42, NYC-M – 1891/01/17:4a
SACK, Eduard, German liberal educator – 1908/06/09:4f-g
SACKERSDORF, Otto von, engineer, ex-Prussian officer, '48er, ex-pres. Liederkranz, NYC-M - 1879/02/18:1e
SACKHEIM, Jean, stenographer, NYC – 1912/02/24:3a
SACKMAN, Margaret, 34, Hermann, 7, NYC-M, @ Genl Slocum – 1904/06/18:3c, 22:1d
SACKMANN, Max, painter, wife Celia & daughter Rosie, 14, NYC-M – 1908/02/05:1g
SACKMANN, Wilhelmine, 67, Ossining, NY – 1890/01/22:4a
SADDLER, Josie, 23, fr Albany, NY, NYC-M – 1900/12/05:1d
SADLER, Mary, 1, NYC-B – 1908/07/07:2e
SAEHR, Ellen, 28, NYC-Q – 1912/08/20:3a
SAELZER, Henry, 64, NYC-M - 1920/10/01:6a
SAEMNER, Heinrich, un. wood worker, NYC-M – 1880/06/29:3b
SAENGER % Jaeger; Schellenberger
SAENGER, Andreas, 35, brewery worker, NYC-M – 1883/08/25:4c
SAENGER, Peter, 40, NYC-B – 1887/10/01:2d
SAENGER, William, 61, night-guard, Newark, NJ – 1893/03/28:2d
SAEVECKE, Emilie, b. Fuchs, NYC-M – 1892/05/19:4a
SAEVECKE, Gustav, 32, bookbinder & SPD activist expelled from Chemnitz/Gy, arrived NYC – 1880/11/30:1d-e, 2 Dec:2a-b, 6:1d-e. SLP, + NYC-B – 1899/01/19:1e, 20:4a, =21:2h
SAFFE, Ernst A., NYPD, NYC M – 1898/05/20:4d-e, 21:1g
SAFFER, John, un. carp., NYC-B – 1883/02/13:3b
SAFTMEIER, Christina, 58, Jersey City, NJ - 1914/03/12:6d
SAGE, Russell, millionaire, anarchist attentate (@Laidlaw) – 1891/12/05:1a-d, 6:1a-d, 5a-b, etc. 88th birthday, sharply crit 1903/08/07:2c, 5 Aug:3f. Sharply crit 1904/06/04:2c. +, scathing obit – 1906/07/24:4c-d,

28:6a, 29:6b. 1st anniv. death, biting comments – 1907/03/17:6b-c. More crit comments – 1909/08/18:4d
SAGER, William, NYC-Q – 1912/06/22:6a
SAGINSKY, Esther, 15, dying, NYC-B – 1886/01/23:1g
SAHM, Carl, 63, musician, composer, * Grumbach/Rhein, NYC-M – 25th jubilee – 1882/03/19:5d & 10 Apr:1e-f. + 1883/02/09:1g, 3c, 10:3b, 11:4a-b, 8a, =12:1e-f, fam. 18:8a, poem 25 Feb:8a. Collection for widow 1884/12/14:5e, monument 27 Apr 1885:4c, monument 12 May 1885:4c, 25:4b, 1 June:4e, inaug. in Lutheran Cem. Middle Village, LI 5 May:4c, 12:4c, 25:4b, 1 June:4d, 6 June:4e, 8:1c-e, 4e
SAHM, Carl, 56, lithographer, NYC-B – 1912/04/13:2c
SAHM, John C., 55, upholsterer, NYC-Great Neck - 1916/04/19:6a
SAHM, Peter, 44, butcher, & wife Sophie, 40, & daughter Sophie, 16, NYC-M – 1909/04/21:1g, 24:1d
SAHMSMUELLER, Charles, 50, painter, NYC-M - 1894/05/17:1e
SAHMSMUELLER, Lena, 85, NYC-M - 1894/05/17:1e
SAHR, Wilhelm, un. carp., NYC-M – 1890/11/20:4a
SAHS % Matzdorf
SAIDEL, Valentin, see Seidel, Valentin
SAILER, Lukas, NYC-M - 1920/04/27:8a
SALADIN, Anna Maria, 53, NYC-M – 1889/06/07:4a
SALADIN, Joseph, 48, NYC-M – 1883/04/11:3d
SALADIN, Simon, Paterson, NJ – 1904/04/08:4a
SALBACH, Otto, +Providence, NJ, = NYC-M – 1909/03/25:6a
SALBACH, Robert, NYC-B - 1918/10/29:6a, fam. 3 Nov.:12a; mem. – 1919/10/28:6a
SALCH, William, NYC-M – 1906/04/13:4a
SALDERN, Freiherr von, German naval off. interned in Japan, & wife - 1917/03/05:1d
SALGMANNS % Weser
SALIG, Frederick, 52, NYC-M – 1883/02/20:3c
SALINGER, Henriette, 31, NYC-M – 1886/03/20:3b
SALINGRE, Hermann, German comedy writer, - 1879/02/28:1e
SALISBURY, Lord, ex-Prime Minister of Great Britain – 1903/08/23:1d
SALLER, Wenzel, NYC-B – 1908/06/05:6a
SALOMON, Felix, secy Carl Sahm Club, NYC-Wards' Isl. – 1908/08/11:7f
SALOMON, Henry, NYC-M - 1879/10/23:1d
SALOMON, Johann Baptist, 72, NYC-B – 1892/05/19:4a
SALOMON, Johann, SPO Warnsdorf/Bohemia,War 1 - 1915/05/30:3d
SALOMON, Rosa, b. Bartfelt, 47, SP, *Erfurt/Thueringen, USA 1887, NYC-M – 1912/03/08:6a
SALOMON, Tina, b. Gladtke, 40, NYC-M – 1904/01/09:4a

SALONECK, Johanna, b. Nathan, NYC-M – 1890/05/23:4a
SALOVSKY, comrade, SP Bruenn/Moravia – 1898/11/25:2e
SALSEDO, Andrae (+1920) see Toni Tazio
SALUZ, Swiss labor leader, killed in St Gallen on 2 Nov. – 1887/12/08:2c
SALVER, David, 55, worker, NYC-M - 1895/02/03:1d
SALVER, William, 27, worker, NYC-M - 1895/02/03:1d
SALZBERG, Abraham, 40, furrier, NYC-B – 1910/02/22:3a
SALZBERG, Edward, 34, bookkeeper, NYC-B – 1912/02/18:1c
SALZER, Jacob, machinist, NYC-M – 1902/09/24:4a
SALZER, Theodor, 61, NYC-B - 1919/01/28:6a
SALZMAN, Julius, 65, carp., NYC - 1913/11/10:2e, 11:1b
SALZMANN, Anna, 15, NYC-M – 1891/07/02:4a
SALZMANN, Katherina, 79, NYC-M – 1892/06/24:4a
SALZMANN, Oskar, 39, NYC-M – 1900/11/06:4a, 8:4a
SAMELE, Erna, NYC-M - 1920/10/02:6a
SAMLER, Anton, 35, carp., Guttenberg, NJ – 1893/07/17:2d
SAMPSON, W. T., 61, US admiral & war hawk, crit. Comment – 1902/05/07:3c, 8:2b
SAMUELS, Joseph, fr Austria 1898, cigarmaker, NYC-M – 1900/03/22:3b
SAND, Martin, NYC-M – 1912/04/25:6a
SAND, William, West New York, NJ - 1916/02/03:6a
SANDER, Fritz, NYC-M – 1909/04/14:6a
SANDER, Heinrich, engraver, *21 Nov 1867 Deutz/Gy, +Bridgeport, RI? – 1911/07/16:7b
SANDER, Hermann, 24, sailor, see 1900 dock fire, Hoboken, NJ 1900/07/03:1c
SANDER, Rudolph, Jersey City Heights, NJ – 1903/07/26:5a
SANDER, Rudolph, Jersey city, NJ – 1907/10/02:6a, 3:6a
SANDERMANN, Louis, un. painter, NYC-M - 1915/05/09:7a, 10:5d, =13:5f, fam. 13:6a
SANDERS % Heinrichs
SANDERS, Georg, 40, cigarmaker, NYC-M – 1882/11/24:1g, his killer got 4 yrs – 1883/01/10:3b
SANDERS, George, Negro, lynched Marshall, TX – 1912/02/16:1b
SANDERS, Helen, NYC-M, +@ on Genl Slocum – 1904/06/18:3c
SANDMANN, Rudolph, 65, un. carp., SLP, NYC-M – 1898/07/30:1g, 1 Aug:4a, –2:3f
SANDMEIER, Jacob, Newark, NJ – 1910/09/28:6a
SANDNER, Anton, 56, baker, NYC-M – 1896/11/03:1g
SANDOHL, Viktor, machinist, NYC-B - 1920/03/01:2a
SANDOS, Anton, 66, beltmaker & inventor, NYC-B – 1912/03/21:6c
SANDQUIST, Fritz, 4, NYC-B – 1892/05/15:5b

SANDSTROEM, J., Yonkers, NY - 1914/08/05:6a
SANDVOS, Fritz, + 7 June 1919, mem 1920/06/07:6a
SANDVOSS, Hermann, NYC-M - 1892/11/27:5d
SANDVOSS, Hermann's wife, NYC-M - 1890/06/14:4a
SANGER, Hermann's wife, NYC-M - 1910/06/04:6a
SANGER, Reinhard, stoker, trial of his killer 8 July 1890:2g, 9:4d
SANGERSTOCK, Adam, NYC-M - 1885/12/24:2e
SANIAL, Lucien, SP NYC, 78th birthday - 1912/09/15:1f
SANIE, Martha, 32, NYC-M - 1892/07/25:4a
SANNT, Henry, 64, Jersey City, NJ - 1900/04/25:1e
SANTING % Spahn
SANWALD, S., NYC-B - 1913/02/18:6a
SARABIA, Manuel, Mexican revol., + Boston - 1915/07/05:4c
SARCEY, Francisque, 71, French journalist, + Paris -1899/06/01:2d
SARDOU, Victor, French poet - 1908/11/09:2d
SARGENT, Frank P., 54, un. fireman, AFL org., immigr. Comm. Under Roosevelt - 1908/09/05:2c
SARTORIUS, Otto, ex-MdR (Liberal), +Mussbach/Bavaria - 1911/02/12:3a
SARZANO, Michael, exec. Auburn, NY - 1914/12/10:6d
SASKE, Frank, silkweaver, Jersey City Heights, NJ - 1891/01/21:2e
SASONOW, Igor, who in 1904 killed Russian Interior Minister Plehwe, trial 1905/04/26:2c, escaped 4 May:2d. + Zarantui Jail - 1910/12/14:1c, 11 Jan 1911:4f, 20 Mr:4e
SASS, Henry, 26, un. painter, * Breitenberg/Holstein, USA 1885, NYC-B - 1895/12/12: 3f,4a, = 14: 1e, 17:4a
SASS, Peter, un. furniture maker, NYC-M - 1890/10/01:4a, fam. 3:4a
SASSULITSCH, Vera Ivanovna, Russian socialist, her current life - 1909/02/28:20c. + 1919/06/27:4d
SATINK, Hermann, 49, shoemaker & SPD activist in Oldenburg/Gy - 1909/08/29:3a
SATTELBERG?, Anton see Gattelberg?
SATTER % Hollreiser
SATTLER, Albert, * Gaetingen/Wuertt., USA 1854, remigrated several times, NYC-M - 1879/05/03:1d
SATTLER, Fritz, 68, shoe maker, NYC-M - 1891/05/23:2g
SATTLER, Georg, un. carp., NYC-M - 1904/08/12:4a
SATTLER, Helene, 5, NYC-M - 1905/01/22:1f
SATTLER, Otto, 34, NYC-M - 1898/09/16:3d
SATZ, Henry, 39, NYC-B - 1889/12/31:4a
SATZNER, Adam, 75, Central NY bandleader s. 1860s, + Lyons, NY - 1911/08/07:2g
SAUER, Beda, NYC-M - 1910/07/13:6a

SAUER, Carl Heinrich, NYC-B - 1917/06/17:7a
SAUER, Eduard,43, NYC-Q – 1912/06/29:6a
SAUER, Fanny, 18, fr Osthofen/Hessen to USA, note on (not +) –
    1885/11/28:2f
SAUER, Franz, NYC-M - 1917/08/01:6a
SAUER, Heinrich, NYC-M - 1915/03/19:6a
SAUER, Hermann, 45, *Muenniswil/Switzerland, Union Hill, NJ –
    1907/11/12:6a
SAUER, John, worker, NYC-B – 1903/09/10:4a
SAUER, Joseph, 57, SLP, NYC-B - 1894/01/20:4a
SAUER, Joseph, un. carp., NYC-B – 1887/10/19:3b
SAUER, Karl, NYC-M – 1910/12/13:6a
SAUER, Martin, Jersey City Heights, NJ - 1920/12/28:6a
SAUER, Michael, 66, Newark, NJ – 1901/07/04:3b
SAUER, Sophie, 34, NYC-B – 1891/10/17:4a
SAUER, Sophie, 40, nurse, NYC-M - 1916/07/11:1d
SAUER, William F., ex-alderman (1875), *10 Mr 1846 Bavaria, NYC-M –
    1883/04/15:1e, 18:2c, =24:4c
SAUERBORN, August, machinist, NYC-M – 1904/12/29:4a, 30:4a
SAUERBORN-BENDER, Regina, NYC-M – 1911/06/06:6a
SAUERBREI, John, grocer, Newark, NJ – 1897/05/22:1c
SAUERBRUNN, Henry, NYC-M - 1915/04/01:6a
SAUERLAENDER, William, 52, NYC-M – 1897/01/02:1d
SAUKE, John, un. cigarmaker, NYC-M – 1888/12/28:3b
SAUL, Charles A., 36, NYC-M – 1891/06/28:5c
SAUL, Mannie, 51, NYC-B – 1890/11/30:1f
SAUL, Rudolf, Hoboken, NJ – 1904/09/21:4a
SAUL, Wilhelm, 74, NYC-M – 1893/10/31:4a
SAUPE, Paul, at Internatl News Co., NYC-M – 1893/09/24:5c
SAUPE, Selma, NYC-B - 1916/01/17:6a
SAURER, John, 53, un. brewer, NYC-M – 1888/05/02:3a
SAUSTMANN, Max, traveling salesman, NYC – 1903/10/22:2h
SAUTER, Ferdinand, 100th anniv. Viennese poet – 1904/05/29:11f-h
SAUTER, Heinrich, NYC-M – 1891/04/05:5a
SAUTER, Jacob, brewer or cooper, NYC-M – 1903/08/09:5a
SAUTER, Jakob, SPD Fiankfurt-Sachsenhausen, War 1 - 1914/11/01:3b
SAUTHOFF, Anna, b. Spaeth, NYC-M – 1883/01/11:3c
SAUTHOFF, Chr., 57, un. carp., NYC-M – 1886/03/22:5e
SAUTHOSS, Carrie, NYC-B – 1910/02/18:6a
SAVAGE, Edward, Jersey City, NJ, exec. Trenton, NJ – 1910/08/31:1b
SAVIAK, John, 28, exec. Wethersfield, CT – 1910/02/10:2d

SAWARIAN, Simon, 47, Armenian Socialist, * Tiflis, + Konstantinopel - 1913/12/08:4d-e
SAWIN, Lillian, +25 Jy, body found Mt Vernon, NY – 1911/08/03:2e
SAX, Jakob, shoemaker, 56, NYC-B – 1883/02/02:3c
SAX, Sadie, 23, dressmaker, fr Providence, RI, NYC-M – 1898/01/06:1e
SAXONY, Albert, King of, + Dresden/Gy – 1902/06/20:1e, 22:4a
SAYLER, Anton, 70, NYC-M – 1891/04/09:4a
SCALES, Negro, lynched near Florence, KY – 1885/09/12:1b
SCENIN, John, 63, NYC-M – 1909/11/03:2f
SCHAACK, police capt who helped frame the Haymarket Martyrs, + Chicago – 1898/06/13:2a
SCHAAD, Alfred, 28, NYC-B – 1901/06/30:5a, mem. 10 Jy 1901:4a
SCHAAD, Phil., un. carp., NYC-Bx – 1907/03/06:6a
SCHAADE, Robert, NYC-B – 1905/01/25:4a
SCHAAF % Bartholdi
SCHAAF, Carl Edward, 56, NYC-M – 1901/12/26:4a
SCHAAF, Carl, 37, NYC-M – 1893/04/03:4a
SCHAAF, George, 73, un. carp., NYC-M - 1917/11/23:6a
SCHAAF, Ida, 46, NYC-M - 1895/09/18: 4a
SCHAAL, John, 46, SP, *21 No 1869 Rohlen/Austria, USA 1891, Hartford, CT - 1915/11/11:6a, 15:6a, fam. 19:6a
SCHABERG, Ernst, 48, NYC-M – 1911/08/31:6a
SCHACHME, Joseph, Rabbi, NYC-M – 1898/12/29:1f
SCHACHNER, Lorenz, NYC-B - 1917/01/19:6a
SCHACHT, Albert Martin, NYC-M – 1885/08/11:3b
SCHACHT, Daniel, 22, NYC-M – 1892/08/15:4a
SCHACKERMANN, Frederick, SP, NYC-B - 1917/06/16:6a
SCHAD, Anna, child, NYC-M – 1905/08/05:4a
SCHADBOLT, Frederick, 30, hat store magr, Newark, NJ - 1915/12/28:2b
SCHADE, August, 41, NYC-B – 1892/09/28:2e
SCHADE, August, un. cigarmaker, NYC-M – 1881/09/17:8a
SCHADE, Charles, Jersey City Hgts, NJ – 1905/03/27:4a
SCHADE, F., 72, SP, Wilkesbarre, PA – 1909/06/09:5f
SCHADE, Frederick, SDP Wilkesbarre, PA, his life (not +) – 1900/11/03:3d
SCHADE, Fritz, SLP, Chicago, = 1879/10/01:2e
SCHADE, Henry, ferry empl., NYC-M – 1892/07/10:5e
SCHADE, Lidia, 1, NYC-M – 1888/03/01:3a
SCHADE, Robert, NYC-B - 1912/05/28:6a
SCHADE, Wilhelm, un. cigarmaker, NYC-M – 1884/07/13:5f
SCHADER, Ernestine, b. Seltenreich, NYC-M – 1887/07/29:3d
SCHADER, George A., NYC-M – 1893/05/27:4a
SCHADER, Joseph, 87, NYC-Bx – 1907/06/21:6a

SCHADEWITZ, Charles, un. engineer, NYC-M – 1904/10/18:4a, 19:4a, fam. 23:5c
SCHADRACK % Zimmermann
SCHADT, Henry, un. baker, NYC-M - 1919/05/15:6a
SCHAECHTELE, Frederick William, 34, un. brewer, NYC-M – 1899/06/29:1c, 4a, 30:4a
SCHAEDLE, Johann, shoemaker, NYC-M – 1888/06/15:1g
SCHAEDLER, Georg, un. carp., NYC-B – 1889/05/13:4a
SCHAEDLER, Jacob, un. painter, NYC-M – 1910/03/13:7c, 14:6a
SCHAEDLER, MdR for Catholic Zentrum Party for Bamberg/Gy, crit. obit – 1913/02/18:4d
SCHAEDLER, Sienda, 33, NYC-SI – 1899/06/10:1e
SCHAEDLICH, Gustave, 62, NYC-B - 1920/10/30:8a
SCHAEFBAUER, Rupert, electrician, Jersey City, NJ – 1901/01/16:1e
SCHAEFER % Berndt, % Graubner, % Ohry, % Sinniger
SCHAEFER, Adolph, 25, baker, NYC-M – 1881/11/02:1g
SCHAEFER, Anna, b. Chitel, NYC-Q – 1912/01/08:6a, 9:6a
SCHAEFER, Anna, NYC-M – 1887/01/15:3c
SCHAEFER, Anna, NYC-M - 1916/02/28:6a
SCHAEFER, Annie L., Newark, NJ - 1919/04/07:6a
SCHAEFER, Annie, 24, NYC-B – 1882/07/25:4c
SCHAEFER, August, un. carp., NYC-M – 1883/10/19:3b
SCHAEFER, Barbara, 49, NYC-B – 1892/07/03:5c
SCHAEFER, Charles, fr Gy, NYC-M - 1895/11/18: 1g
SCHAEFER, Christian, NYC-M – 1910/05/17:6a
SCHAEFER, comrade, 45, SPD Mannheim/Gy – 1909/03/28:3a
SCHAEFER, Conrad, un. carp., NYC-M – 1898/06/17:4a
SCHAEFER, Damian, 51, un. cigar maker, NYC-Q – 1905/04/29:4a
SCHAEFER, Fannie, b. Blohm?, NYC-M – 1891/03/31:4a
SCHAEFER, Frederick C., brewer, NYC, his will 1899/12/18:3d
SCHAEFER, Frederick, 42, innkeep, NYC-M – 1880/07/15:1g, 16:1g, 21:1e
SCHAEFER, Friedrich, 40, NYC-M - 1916/12/08:6a
SCHAEFER, Friedrich, 80, NYC-M – 1897/05/21:4a
SCHAEFER, Friedrich, art potter, 66, NYC-B – 1913/09/30:3d
SCHAEFER, Fritz, SDP, un. cigarmaker, NYC-M – 1902/05/16:3b, 18:5a
SCHAEFER, G., NYC-Q – 1910/01/21:6a
SCHAEFER, Georg, pianomaker, NYC-Q – 1900/12/14:1c, note 22 Fb 1901:1g
SCHAEFER, Gustav, 36, un. cigarmaker, SLP, NYC-M – 1892/04/03:5a,d, =4:1g, mem. 17 May:2f
SCHAEFER, Helene, 35, NYC-M – 1888/01/09:3a

SCHAEFER, Henry, 24, druggist, NYC-M – 1900/07/11:3b
SCHAEFER, Henry, baker, NYC-M – 1892/07/29:4a
SCHAEFER, Ida, b. Maier, NYC-M – 1892/06/10:4a
SCHAEFER, J., 59, NYC-M – 1893/08/27:5a
SCHAEFER, Jakob, music teacher, conductor Hudson City Liedertafel.*1822 Wuerttemberg, USA 1850s, Hudson City, NJ – 1882/02/25:4b
SCHAEFER, John, 67, un. cigarmaker & NYVZ reporter, *Lorsch/Hessen, NYC-M – 1899/02/02:1d-e, #3:4a, 4:4a, =6:1f-g
SCHAEFER, John, Elizabeth, NJ - 1919/05/15:6a
SCHAEFER, John, un. carp., NYC-M – 1889/03/05:4a
SCHAEFER, John, Wakefield, NJ - 1918/07/27:6a
SCHAEFER, Josef, 67, turner & SP Vienna – 1908/11/08:3e
SCHAEFER, Joseph, NYC-B – 1891/07/17:4a
SCHAEFER, Josephine, 35, NYC-M – 1897/12/23:1f
SCHAEFER, Julius, SP, +26 June, body fd, NYC-Q – 1910/07/13:2c, 6a
SCHAEFER, Karl F., 81, weaver & other work, *Meerane/Saxony, SP, Meriden, CT – 1904/06/21:4d
SCHAEFER, Lena, 36, and her newborn child, NYC-M – 1881/07/09:4c
SCHAEFER, Margarethe, NYC-M - 1919/08/26:6a
SCHAEFER, Maria, b. Fries, NYC-B – 1891/04/12:5a
SCHAEFER, Marie, b. Joly, 55, NYC-M - 1895/05/10:4a
SCHAEFER, Martha, NYC-M - 1895/04/01:1e
SCHAEFER, Martin, 64, NYC-M – 1892/06/24:4a
SCHAEFER, Mary E., NYC-SI – 1908/07/23:2b
SCHAEFER, Mary, 23, servant, Boonton, NJ - 1894/07/26:4b
SCHAEFER, Mary, b. Guntermann, 52, NYC-M – 1908/03/14:6a
SCHAEFER, Max, 80, brewery owner, * 23 June 1819 Wetzlar/Gy, USA 1839, NYC-M – 1904/03/25:3e, will 1 April 1904:3b
SCHAEFER, Nathan, 10, NYC-B – 1908/07/09:3a
SCHAEFER, Nicolaus, tailor, + Dec 1884, will NYC-M – 1886/01/14b
SCHAEFER, Philip, 45, brewery employee, Atlantic City, NJ – 1904/09/30:3e
SCHAEFER, Robert, NYC-M - 1914/07/12:11a
SCHAEFER, Robert, un. baker, NYC-M? – 1910/12/16:6a
SCHAEFER, Salomon, Rabbi, & 4 children, NYC-M – 1913/10/09:1e
SCHAEFER, W., 45, NYC-M – 1893/08/18:4a
SCHAEFER, William & Sophie, NYC-B – 1903/03/09:3b
SCHAEFER, William, un. painter, NYC-Bx – 1909/05/01:6a
SCHAEFFER, Anna, NYC-M – 1897/07/30:4a
SCHAEFFER, Annie, NYC-M, + on Genl Slocum – 1904/06/18:3c
SCHAEFFER, Charles Ashford, 103 (!), *Springvale, NJ, + Newton, NJ - 1916/01/18:2b

SCHAEFFER, Christina, NYC-M – 1901/07/03:1d
SCHAEFFER, Cyrach, 46, NYC-B – 1911/06/09:6a
SCHAEFFER, Frank, 45, fireman, NYC-M - 1917/01/03:1d
SCHAEFFER, Frank, fam. – 1912/03/15:6a
SCHAEFFER, Frederick, 37, ret. fireman, with daughter Anna, 11, and mother-in-law Anna Dray, 53, NYC-Q - 1915/12/16:1g
SCHAEFFER, George L., 72, NYC-Q - 1914/11/02:6a
SCHAEFFER, Hermann, pres. Dr Jaeger's Sanitary Woolen Co., NYC-B – 1900/06/21:2h
SCHAEFFER, Louise, 38, NYC – 1896/07/20:4b
SCHAEFFER, Louise, 40, NYC-B – 1910/08/11:3a
SCHAEFFER, Margarethe, NYC-M – 1919/08/26:6a
SCHAEFFER, Maria, 52, NYC-M – 1898/12/25:5a, fam. 27:4a, b
SCHAEFFER, Marie, 69, NYC-M - 1918/03/06:6a
SCHAEFFER, Mary, 70, NYC-B – 1902/11/22:3b
SCHAEFFER, Mary, lady of the night, NYC-M – 1898/04/03:1g, 5:4f
SCHAEFFER, Nikolaus, NYC-M – 1910/02/03:6a
SCHAEFFER, Sarah, Newark, NJ – 1896/05/26:2e
SCHAEFFER, William H. A., alderman & brewery business agent, Newark, NJ – 1907/07/19:3d
SCHAEFFER, William, 38, baker, NYC-M – 1896/10/05:1e
SCHAEFFER, William, NYC-M, + @Genl Slocum – 1904/06/18:3c
SCHAEFFLE, Albert, Dr., 73, Liberal polit., + Stuttgart – 1903/12/29:1a, 2b, 21 Ja. 1904:2e
SCHAEFFLER, John, West New York, NJ - 1916/04/29:6a
SCHAEFFLER, Wilhelm, 54, pianomaker & SPD MdL Heilbronn/Gy – 1910/12/11:3d
SCHAEREN, John, 50, NYC-B – 1898/05/26:4a
SCHAERER, A., Yonkers, NY – 1909/09/28:6a
SCHAERR, Emil, un. printer, NYC-B - 1915/01/09:6a
SCHAETTER, Michael, un. carp., NYC-B - 1914 /01/30:6a, 31:6a
SCHAETTGEN, Jakob, 4, NYC-M – 1882/04/04:3b
SCHAETTLER % Puehlhorn
SCHAETZLE, A., NYC-B - 1913/06/04:6a
SCHAETZLE, Anton, NYC-M – 1885/06/29:3b
SCHAETZLE, Charles, 54?, NYC-M – 1891/03/29:5a
SCHAF, Th., 33, NYC-B - 1894/01/10:4a
SCHAFAROWIC, Karl, alias SCHAEFER, un. carp., NYC-M – 1906/11/13:6a, 14:6a
SCHAFER, John, NYC-M – 1892/09/03:4a
SCHAFF, Louise M. Schaible, 34, NYC-B - 1920/08/17:6a
SCHAFFEL, Theodor, 45, restaurant owner, Bayonne, NJ - 1920/05/21:1b

SCHAFFER, Charles, 45, bottle salesman, NYC-M – 1909/12/08:5b
SCHAFFNER % Doedele
SCHAFFNER, Friedrich, 48, NYC-M – 1891/05/31:5b
SCHAFFNER, Louisa, 71, NYC-B - 1913/06/02:6a
SCHAFFNER, Wilhelm, 32, NYC-M – 1885/02/27:3c
SCHAIBEL, Walpurga, NYC-B - 1918/07/30:6a
SCHAIBLE % Schaff
SCHAIBLE, Anna Margarethe, b. Crov, 43, NYC-B – 1911/05/19:6a
SCHAIBLE, Carl, 54, un. carp., NYC-B – 1908/04/11:6a, fam. 14:6a
SCHAIBLE, John, 53, un. liquor dealer, NYC-B, + Monroe, NY - 1914/08/09:7b, 10:6a, 11:6a
SCHAICH, Morris, tailor, NYC-M – 1892/07/06:4d
SCHAIRE, Julia, 6, NYC-M, +@ Genl Slocum – 1904/06/21:1f
SCHALEK, Edward, 1, NYC-M – 1890/05/24:4a
SCHALK, Charles, un. millwright, NYC-B - 1895/02/10:5b
SCHALK, Martin, 60, fr Elsass?, Jersey City, NJ – 1898/05/21:4a
SCHALL, Amadeus, printer, New Rochelle,NY =1913/11/26:1f
SCHALL, Emil, 35, un. carp., Jersey City, NJ – 1898/09/06:4a
SCHALLENTRAEGER % Ruehle
SCHALLER, Charles Hermann, 63, SP, un. typesetter, NYC-B - 1916/01/19:2a, 6a, 20:2b, 6a
SCHALLER, Pauline, NYC-B – 1908/08/16:7a
SCHALMATZ, Otto, interned sailor fr SS Kronprinzessin Caecilie, fr Berlin, War 2, NYC-Bx - 1917/10/29:6b
SCHAMANN, Franz, SP?, Vienna-Gersthof – 1909/09/26:3d
SCHAMBACHER, George, realtor, NYC-M – 1907/04/15:1c
SCHAMBACHER, Theodore, 65, un. painter, NYC-M – 1919/12/17:6a
SCHANDER, Carl, Elizabeth, NJ - 1917/01/30:6a
SCHANDLIN, Emil, brewery owner, Milwaukee, WI, his will 1905/10/30:2d
SCHANK, Emma, dying, NYC-M – 1899/03/15:3c
SCHANKE, Sadie, NYC-M – 1899/03/05:5f
SCHANKMEYER, George, 43, carp., NYC-M – 1893/07/29:1h
SCHANNE, Elizabeth, b. Otto, NYC-M – 1881/10/31:3b
SCHANNO, August, un. carp., NYC-M – 1886/03/12:2g, 4c, 13:3b
SCHANZ, Charles T., 41, Poughkeepsie, NY – 1910/08/08:2a
SCHANZ, Georg, 35, NYC-B – 1910/03/23:3a
SCHANZENBACH, Maria, b. Balz, NYC-M – 1892/07/19:4a
SCHAPER, Wilhelmina, b. Kuel, NYC-Q – 1902/04/09:4a
SCHAPPERT, William, NYC-M - 1918/07/12:6a
SCHARF, Josephine, b. Wolfsholl, NYC-M – 1888/10/23:3c
SCHARFF % Bamberger

SCHARFF, Mrs, NYC-M – 1881/05/11:3b
SCHARLIBBE, August, 56, un. cigarmaker, SPD Fuerstenwalde/Gy – 1904/04/30:2c
SCHARMAN, Herman B., 82, brewer, * Giessen/Gy, USA 1843, NYC-B - 1920/08/04:5f
SCHARMAN, Julius, 46, partner at brewery, NYC-B - 1914/12/04:1g
SCHARMER, Nellie, 33, NYC-B – 1903/01/03:1g
SCHARN, Katherina, 22, NYC-M – 1900/08/20:1b, 21:1h, 22:1c, 23:1h, 25:1h, 26:1h; 10 Oct:1e, 12:1g
SCHARNHORST, Henry G., 30, NYC-M – 1890/10/15:4a
SCHASS, Abraham, diner owner, War 2, NYC-B - 1915/02/05:2d
SCHASSNER, Adam, NYC-Q – 1920/02/13:6a
SCHATZ, John, 59, worker, NYC-Q - 1916/10/22:11g
SCHATZ, Theresia, NYC-M – 1891/03/25:4a
SCHAU, Emil, teacher, + Dec. 1885, collection for grave monument – 1887/05/10:4c, 20 Dec:1c
SCHAU, Friedrich, Jena/Thuer. ATB, War 1 - 1914/11/01:3b
SCHAU, George W., on his death, 1900/02/08:2h
SCHAU, George, 57, court employee, NYC-M – 1899/11/14:1h
SCHAUB, Albert, East Rahway, NJ – 1891/04/08:4e
SCHAUB, Georg Ludwig, 71, un. tailor, SDP, NYC-M – 1901/04/10:4a, =12:3a
SCHAUB, Mary, b. Guenther, 30, & infant child, Newark, NJ – 1901/06/12:3b, husband Henry on trial 25 June:3c; to be exec. Newark, NJ – 1902/04/15:4b, 19:4a, 25:3b, done 26:1h
SCHAUBLE, Anna Barbara, b. Mueller, 72, Jersey City, NJ – 1907/10/30:6a
SCHAUBLE, Mary, 45, NYC-Q – 1907/02/11:6a, 12:6a, fam. 17:7b
SCHAUBLIN, John Jakob, 40, Jersey City, NJ – 1884/10/27:1g, 28:4d
SCHAUER, Adalbert, NYC-B – 1907/10/03:6a
SCHAUER, Gustav, NYC-Q – 1908/06/30:6a
SCHAUER, Lulu, 12, NYC-B – 1887/06/11:3b
SCHAUERTE, Henry, NYC-Q - 1919/05/10:6a
SCHAUFFERT, Helene, 80, Breslau, Ll – 1887/10/11:2e, 12:2b
SCHAUFLER, Friedrich, NYC-Q - 1916/01/01:6a
SCHAUM, Peter, NYC-M – 1902/12/19:1e
SCHAUMEL, John, pianomaker, NYC-M – 1901/08/22:1h
SCHAUMLOEFFEL, Elise, 51, NYC-M – 1885/12/07:3b
SCHAUP, Charles, 28, Newark, NJ – 1904/01/02:1f
SCHAUP, Ernst - 1915/05/03:6a
SCHAUREN, Mrs, NYC-M – 1891/05/05:4a
SCHAURER, Johanette, b. Lauer, NYC-M – 1883/04/30:3c

SCHAUWECKER, Lorenz, NYC-M – 1886/07/14:3b
SCHAUZER, Virgil "Marat," Russian SP, + Moscow/Russia – 1911/03/15:4d
SCHEBE, Elizabeth, 53, NYC-M – 1919/10/07:8a
SCHEBLER, John, 27, NYC-B – 1907/04/27:3a
SCHECH, George, 68, NYC-B - 1917/05/23:5f
SCHECKENBACH, Valentin, 62, NYC-B – 1904/06/04:4c
SCHEDEL, Georg von, 63,fr ~Stade/Gy, + San Francisco,CA - 1878/08/20:2c
SCHEDEL, M's wife, Philadelphia, PA – 1909/07/24:6a
SCHEDLITSKI, Caroline, 20, servant, NYC-B – 1909/11/03:3a
SCHEEL, Henry, un. butcher, NYC-M - 1914/02/26:6a
SCHEEL, Herman, 46, Jersey City, NJ – 1909/03/16:6a
SCHEEL, William, NYC-M - 1919/06/01:12a
SCHEELE, Anna, 15, +@ Genl Slocum, NYC-M – 1904/06/19:1c
SCHEELE, Clara, 7, NYC-M, +@Genl Slocum – 1904/06/22:1d
SCHEELE, George, 35, plumber, NYC-M - 1895/10/14: 1b
SCHEEPERS, Boer general – 1902/04/01:1a
SCHEER % Papst
SCHEER, Anton, 42, un. tailor, NYC-B – 1902/09/12:4a, 14:5a
SCHEER, Conrad, NYC-B - 1915/03/22:6a
SCHEER, David, Succasunna, NJ, + expl. dynamite plant in Kenville, NJ – 1898/04/29:3f
SCHEER, Elise, 20, NYC-B – 1891/03/15:5b
SCHEER, George, 25, Hoboken, NJ – 1904/07/11:1a, 12:1f
SCHEER, Konstantin, baker & newsp. carrier fr Elberfeld/Gy, SDP, Newark, NJ – 1904/10/13:1e
SCHEER, Peter, 56, un. machinist, NYC-B – 1908/08/14:6a
SCHEERBARTH, Irma, b. Fink, 25, NYC-Bx - 1919/05/08:6a
SCHEERER, Christian, NYC-M – 1890/03/12:4a
SCHEERER, William F., NYC – 1912/11/17:7b
SCHEFER, William, NYC-M – 1891/04/12:5a
SCHEFFENAU, William, NYC-M – 1904/05/02:3c
SCHEFFLE, Elsie, infant, NYC-M, +@Genl Slocum – 1904/06/23:1b
SCHEFFLER, Michael, un. carp., NYC-B – 1911/09/16:6a, 18:6a
SCHEFFLER, William von, ex-ofc. German army, riding instructor at Vassar College & driver, Haslington, NJ – 1900/12/21:1e
SCHEFFMEYER, Frederick, canal inspector, NYC-B – 1908/11/21:1a
SCHEIBE, Carl, NYC-B - 1915/03/30:6a
SCHEIBE, Charles, Jersey City, married Mary Wilhelmine Kronk, NYC – 1905/06/09:1g, 10:2g
SCHEIBEL, Georg, 47, musician & band leader, NYC-M – 1880/08/29:5g

SCHEIBENSTOCK, Franz, NYC-Bx - 1916/03/16:6a
SCHEIBLE, Christian, NYC-Q - 1916/01/29:6a
SCHEIBLE, Ernest, 29, electrician, NYC-M - 1905/09/12:4a
SCHEIBLE, Walter, 18, NYC-B - 1914/08/25:6a; mem. 1915/08/23:6a, 1916/08/23:6a, 1917/08/23:6a, 1918/08/23:6a, 1919/08/23:6a, 1920/08/23:6a
SCHEIBLER, Albert, NYC-M - 1908/02/05:6a
SCHEIBLER, Helene, NYC? - 1899/12/26:4a
SCHEID, Gerhard, driver, NYC-M - 1902/10/18:4a
SCHEIDECKER, M., NYC - 1915/03/27:6a
SCHEIDEL % Brand
SCHEIDERMANN, Joseph, 30, barber, NYC-M - 1886/10/08:4c
SCHEIDING, Gustav, NYC-M - 1880/12/16:1g, 17:1f
SCHEIDWEILER, Philip, 78, & wife, Breslau, LI (now Babylon, LI) - 1887/02/04:1e-f, 5:3a, 7:2f, 8:1f, 9:3a, 11:1f, 22:2f
SCHEIER, Philipp, painter, NYC-M - 1892/03/18:1f
SCHEIKE, Karl, SPD Wehlau/East Prussia/Gy - 1915/10/24:3c
SCHEIN % Haupt
SCHEINER, Joseph, 46, NYC-M - 1878/07/06:3c
SCHEITEMANTEL, Albert's wife, NYC-B - 1895/01/20:4a
SCHEITLER, A., un. Baker, NYC-M - 1911/08/11:6a
SCHELL, Albert, NYC-Bx - 1909/01/07:6a
SCHELL, Barbara, ~ 30, NYC-B - 1893/08/16:1g
SCHELL, C., NYC-B - 1911/09/15:6a
SCHELL, John, NYC-B - 1908/06/17:6a
SCHELL, Katherine, 27, NYC-M - 1905/08/17:3c
SCHELL, Margarethe, NYC-Q - 1885/08/27:2g
SCHELL, William, Hoboken, NJ - 1894/02/04:5c
SCHELL, William, NYC-M - 1891/08/27:1d
SCHELLENBERG, August, NYC-M - 1880/12/02:3b
SCHELLENBERGER, Dorothea, b. Saenger, NYC-M - 1892/06/30:4a
SCHELLENBERGER, Otto, West Hoboken, NJ - 1911/08/31:6a, 1 Sept:6a, fam. 3:7a
SCHELLER % Hellmuth
SCHELLER, Gerhard, *Duesseldorf/Gy, + Greenville, NJ - 1902/07/23:4a
SCHELLER, Peter, Jersey City, NJ - 1915/05/21:6a
SCHELLHAS, 57, barber, NYC-M - 1888/06/06:1h
SCHELLHORN, Karl, 92, photographer close to SP, + Vienna - 1909/08/22:3f
SCHELLING, B., un. carp., NYC - 1912/08/13:6a
SCHELLMANN, Alois, NYC-M - 1891/07/02:4a

SCHEM, Alex, asst-superint. city schools & publ. of a G-A dictionary, *Wiedenbrueck/Westfalia, USA 1851, Jersey City, NJ – 1881/05/24:2e
SCHEM, Alexander J., lawyer, West Hoboken, NJ – 1911/07/26:3a
SCHEMBER, Joseph von, 40, building worker, NYC-B – 1908/01/10:3a
SCHEMITZ, Joseph, 47, NYC-B – 1896/09/03:4a
SCHENCK, Charles T., 47, secy local SP, Philadelphia, PA - 1920/11/13:2a
SCHENCK, Margarethe, 10, NYC-SI – 1886/11/29:3c
SCHENCK, Valentin, 24, NYC-B – 1891/07/29:4a
SCHENDORF, August, NYC-B – 1904/09/11:5a
SCHENK, Carl, NYC-M – 1902/06/26:4a, fam. 29:5b
SCHENK, Charles, 49, un. cigarmaker, SP, NYC-M – 1908/06/01:2d, 6a
SCHENK, John, un. brewer, NYC-Bx - 1918/12/18:6a
SCHENK, Leopold, chief editor of Puck, NYC, * Heidelberg, + South Carolina, a good employer – 1886/04/14:1g
SCHENK, Lorenz, un. brewer, Guttenberg, NJ – 1892/05/31:4a, 1 June:4a, fam. 4:4a
SCHENK, Wilhelm, un. cigarmaker, NYC-M – 1880/08/21:3b
SCHENKER, Jean B., Swiss?, NYC-M – 1881/11/17:3c
SCHEPERS, Thomas, 40, NYC-M? - 1918/07/07:1d
SCHEPP, Andreas, un. carp., NYC-M – 1902/12/27:4a, 28:5b
SCHEPPLER, Joseph, 50, peddler, NYC-M – 1890/06/07:2f
SCHEPPLER, Philipp, NYC-M – 1912/08/05:6a
SCHERB, Gustav Adolph, 46, NYC-M – 1910/10/14:6a
SCHEREMETIEW, police inspector in Bialystok who org. a pogrom, killed by revol. — 1906/12/06:1a
SCHERER % Birnbach; SCHERER % Gautier
SCHERER, Andrew, 8, Paterson, NJ – 1908/11/28:3c
SCHERER, Catherine, b. Reinicke, 59, SLP, *Halberstadt/Gy, fr Berlin to Newark, NJ – 1892/05/05:1h,4a
SCHERER, Frank, 30, Central Valley, NYC – 1909/10/25:1f
SCHERER, Georg, 43, un. butcher, * Bingen/Rhein, NYC-B - 1914/10/17:6a,c
SCHERER, George, 47, NYC-Bx – 1913/02/02:7b, 3:6a, 4:6a
SCHERER, Gottlieb, ~50, Swiss, butcher, NYC-B – 1905/12/13:1f
SCHERER, Johanna, b. Merkerk, + 22 Nov 19, mem - 1920/11/22:6a
SCHERER, John, painter, 65, NYC-M – 1892/06/23:2e
SCHERER, John, Union Hill, NJ, inquest 1891/08/28:4a
SCHERER, Kaspar, 49, NYC-M – 1893/03/28:4a
SCHERER, Magdalene, b. Foerster, NYC-B – 1892/07/25:4a
SCHERER, William, Elizabeth, NJ – 1907/11/10:2a
SCHERF, Mary, NYC-M, +@ on Genl Slocum – 1904/06/18:3c

SCHERFF, Heinrich, 45, NYC – 1887/10/22:3a
SCHERGER % Imhoff
SCHERGER, Alwin, NYC-M – 1914/03/28:6a
SCHERL, Marian, 40, Sparkill, NY – 1917/10/28:11d
SCHERM, Ph., NYC-B – 1903/02/26:4a
SCHERMANN, Frederick, NYC-Bx – 1911/06/24:6a, fam. 29:6a
SCHERMEYER, Albert, NYC-B – 1918/11/13:6a
SCHERNEG, William, 53, SLP, un. cigarmaker & innkeep, * Hagen/ Westfalia, USA 1871, co-fdr NYVZ, NYC-Bx – 1895/12/16: 4a, = 17: 1e
SCHERPF, Fritz's wife, 43?, NYC-M – 1891/11/07:4a
SCHERPF, Lisette, b. Huber, NYC-M – 1895/11/10: 5a
SCHERPICH, Hugo, 28, machinist, NYC-B – 1879/08/26:3a, 4d
SCHERPICH, Hugo, 28, un. machinist, NYC-B – 1879/08/26:3a, 27:4d
SCHERRER, Georg, NYC-B – 1915/11/27:6a
SCHERRER, Heinrich, 72, Swiss SP – 1919/12/23:5a-b
SCHERRER, Philipp, NYC – 1912/04/06:6a, 7:6a, fam. 10:6a
SCHERTEL, Frederick, Union Hill, NJ – 1901/01/26:4a
SCHERTZINGER, Ralph Waldo, publ. Peekskill, NY Evening News - 1915/01/29:2e
SCHERZER, Gustav, un. cigarmkr,40, SDP,1892 fr Saxony, NYC-SI – 1900/08/28:2h, fam. 2 Sp:5a
SCHERZER, Mary, 35, Newark, NJ – 1900/07/07:4b
SCHERZER, Willy, mem. poem – 1917/02/05:6a
SCHESKA, John, butcher, NYC-M – 1890/03/19:2e
SCHESLAU, August, un. cigarmaker, NYC-M – 1887/06/24:3b
SCHESSLAU, August's wife, NYC-M – 1880/07/28:3b
SCHETT, Bernhard R., 35, custom office employee, Rutherford, NJ – 1904/02/06:3e
SCHETZ, Stephan, NYC-Bx – 1912/09/12:6a
SCHEU, Friedrich, 32, SLP, un. carp., NYC-M – 1881/12/30:3b, 31:3a
SCHEU, Joseph, Elizabeth, NJ – 1914/06/21:7c
SCHEU, Joseph, musician, SP Vienna, composer of "Lied der Arbeit" – 1904/10/26:2d; inaug. monument in Vienna – 1907/04/21:8d, 16f-g
SCHEU, Ludwig, 74, German liberal polit., 1899/03/12:12f
SCHEUBER, Elizabeth, 68, Jersey City, NJ – 1908/07/24:6a
SCHEUBLEIN, Wilhelmine, b. Schmidt, NYC-M – 1885/04/09:3d
SCHEUER, Friedrich, 43, fr Hessen-Darmstadt to USA 1870, driver, NYC-M – 1893/11/03:4e
SCHEUERING, G., NYC-Q – 1913/10/29:6a
SCHEUERMANN % Roeth
SCHEUERMANN, Albert, 6, NYC-M, +@Genl Slocum – 1904/06/25:1d
SCHEUERMANN, Louisa, 18, NYC-M – 1891/07/26:4a

SCHEUERMANN, Peter, 63, NYC-M – 1892/06/30:4a
SCHEUING, Adam, 30, butcher, NYC-M – 1906/07/17:1d
SCHEUNER, August, un. baker, NYC-M - 1914/08/21:6a
SCHEUPLEIN, Charles, NYC-M – 1887/01/11:3d
SCHEURER % Kienle
SCHEURER, Jacob, NYC-M - 1879/07/31:4b
SCHEURICH, Charles, un. carp., NYC-M – 1909/03/22:6a
SCHEURING, Adam, NYC-B – 1909/09/17:6a
SCHEURING, Peter, NYC-M – 1892/06/28:4a
SCHEUTERMANN, Albert, 47, liquor dealer, NYC-M – 1913/03/02:7f
SCHEVEN, Emma, 48, SP?, W. Hoboken, NJ - 1916/03/26:7a, fam. 31:6a
SCHEWITSCH, Helene, b. von Doenniges, 65, wife of Sergius Schewitsch, ex-NYVZ ed., ex-lover of Ferdinand Lassalle 1860s, NYC 1877-1900, + Munich – 1911/10/04:3c-d, =17:4f
SCHEWITSCH, Sergius, on his resignation as chief editor of NYVZ – 13 June 1890:2a; #, & 20th anniv. NYVZ, by Alex Jonas 13 Fb 1898:20a-d, his life at NYVZ 30 Nv 1905:2b. + 61 yrs old in Munich, long edit NYVZ, # – 1911/10/08:1d-e, 7c, 9:1d, 15:1d
SCHEYE, Charles G.A., 39, NYC-M - 1917/01/04:6a
SCHEYE, Hermann, 62, NYC-M – 1909/12/04:6a, fam. 11:6a
SCHIBLAWSKI, Frank & Oswald, exec. Chicago, IL – 1912/02/16:1b, done 17:1c
SCHICH, Franz, SP? Schoenfeld/Austria, War 1 - 1915/05/30:3d
SCHICHEL, Otto, SLP, un. baker, NYC-M - 1894/09/03:4a
SCHICK, Christina J., b. Spindler, 60, NYC-SI – 1890/06/16:4a
SCHICK, Henry, 43, NYC-M - 1919/06/27:6a
SCHICK, Jacob, 61, NYC-M - 1883/04/09:3c
SCHICK, John, 65, ret. merchant, NYC-B - 1916/02/17:6a
SCHICK, Joseph, Coesskill, NJ – 1909/01/08:6a
SCHICK, Lena, 20, worker, Newark, NJ – 1911/05/05:1e
SCHICK, Marie, NYC-M – 1891/04/07:4a
SCHICK, Minnie, NYC-M, @ on Genl Slocum – 1904/06/17:3c, 18:3c
SCHICK, Philipp, un. carp., NYC-M – 1893/08/13:5a
SCHICKEDANZ, Hugo, NYC-Bx – 1906/12/23:7b mem. - 1916/12/21:6a
SCHICKERING, George, 24, cooper?, NYC-M – 1898/01/25:1e
SCHICKERT, Paul, SP, NYC-M - 1919/05/03:6a, fam. 7:6a
SCHICKLER, Catherine, 84, NYC-M – 1892/09/22:4a
SCHIEB, Herman, 68, driver, NYC-M – 1897/01/23:1g
SCHIEBL, Maria, NYC-M – 1903/05/23:4a, 24:5b
SCHIEFENBUSCH, Nikolaus, SPD Ehrenfeld/Koeln/Gy – 1904/04/04:3b
SCHIEFFELIN, Edward S., 50, drug importer, NYC - 1916/11/08:2c, 10:3f
SCHIEFFLIN, John, NYC-M – 1901/07/03:1d

SCHIEFNER, William, SP, Paterson, NJ - 1914/08/12:6a, 13:6a
SCHIEK, Frederick. A., NYC-M - 1894/02/03:4a
SCHIEKE, Friedrich, 31, typesetter & SPD activist expelled from
  Berlin/Gy, arrived NYC – 1880/11/30:1d-e, 2 Dec:2a-b, 6:1d-e
SCHIEL, Wilhelm, Union Hill, NJ – 1897/03/02:4a
SCHIELLER, Charles, 54, salesman, NYC-B – 1912/08/27:2d
SCHIEMIGER, Gottlieb, + @Genl Slocum, NYC-M – 1904/06/20:1b
SCHIER, Julia, NYC-M, + @ Genl Slocum – 1904/06/18:3c
SCHIEREN, Charles A., ex-mayor of Brooklyn - 1915/03/11:6b
SCHIERENBECK, Anna, 74, NYC-M – 1890/07/26:4a
SCHIERER, Charles, 50, machinist, NYC-M – 1893/03/27:4e
SCHIERK, John, worker, Jersey City, NJ – 1896/07/14:3e
SCHIESEL, George, 42, Secaucus, NJ - 1916/06/09:6a, 10:6a
SCHIESS, Eduard, * Herisau/Appenzell, Switz., Chicago, IL, + NYC-M –
  1882/05/30:1f
SCHIEWECK, Ferdinand, NYC-Q – 1907/03/27:6a
SCHIFF % Rothkugel
SCHIFF, Adam G., foreman at City Sanitation Dept., NYC-Q -
  1920/02/17:3d
SCHIFF, Gustav, 55, NYC-M – 1883/05/05:1g
SCHIFF, Jacob, NYC banker - 1920/09/28:4c
SCHIFF, Philip, tailor, NYC - 1913/05/25:11f
SCHIFFER, A.'s, NYC-M – 1888/03/30:3b
SCHIFFER, Marion, 10, & Ruth, 14, NYC-M, + NYC-B – 1907/06/01:2a
SCHIFFERDECKER, Wilhelm, German libeal polit. – 1899/05/14:12h
SCHIFFLIN, Dorothea, 63, NYC-M – 1891/04/04:4a
SCHIFFMANN, Gussie, 18, @ 1911 Triangle Shirtwaist Fire, NYC-M –
  1911/03/27:1d
SCHILDBACH, Emilie, 39, NYC-B – 1909/07/01:6a, fam. 3:6a
SCHILDBACH, Ernst, un. cabinetmaker, Rochester, NY – 1902/08/31:5a
SCHILDBERGER, Johann, SP, employee of Austrian AKK, and org. of
  Serbian laborers – 1912/09/08:3d
SCHILDE, Paul, un. butcher, NYC-B – 1901/10/02:4a
SCHILDMUELLER, Dorothy, 19, NYC-B – 1909/06/21:6a
SCHILL, Elise, 4, NYC-M – 1881/10/18:3c
SCHILLER, Elise, b. Fotthauer,26, (dying), NYC-B - 1915/04/08:6b
SCHILLER, Frederick. G., 59, NYC-M - 1894/02/01:4a
SCHILLER, Friedrich, 100th anniv. of death, incl. Columbia U
  1905/04/06:3e, 09:14e-g, 16:4c-e, 23 Ap:5g, 9b-c, NYC various Fests 6
  May:3f, 8:1a-c, Buffalo 14:12b, in Strassburg/Elsass 29 May:2e-f, the
  man, by Franz Mehring, Otto Falke etc 7 May:2g-h, 4a-e, 12c-e, 13g-h,

the man 14d-h, 16a, 14:14a-d, 16a-e, 21:16a, 28:3c-d, 4 June:16a; 150th
anniv. of birth celeb. In NYC-Bx – 1907/11/10:4a-b, f
SCHILLER, Josef, weaver & G-A labor poet, *29 June 1846 Reichenberg/
Bohemia, + 16 Au. 1897 Germania, PA, 10th anniv. of death
1907/10/27:3a-d, 3 Nov:3a-d
SCHILLER, Lorenz, NYC-Q – 1911/03/07:6a
SCHILLER, Michael, exec. Columbus, OH – 1904/06/18:2h
SCHILLING % Goetze
SCHILLING, Andrew, 53, plumber, NYC-B - 1917/01/08:6a,9:6a
SCHILLING, Frank George, 1, NYC-M – 1899/03/09:4a
SCHILLING, Gustav, un. brewer, NYC-M? - 1913/06/08:7a, 9:6a
SCHILLING, Henry, 76, NYC-Bx - 1918/05/24:6a
SCHILLING, Herman, 49, innkeep, NYC-B – 1911/06/30:3a
SCHILLING, Jakob, NYC-M – 1882/12/18:3a
SCHILLING, Julius, NYC-M – 1899/06/06:4a
SCHILLING, Lewis C., 81, only survivor of 1836 Alamo battle, + Reno,
NV – 1913/03/24:1b
SCHILLING, Martin, Hoboken, NJ - 1917/05/09:6a
SCHILLING, Mary, NYC-M – 1888/03/16:1g, 6 Mr:4a, husband Fred on
trial 25 Sept:1h, 26:1h, 27:1c, 28:1h, rec. 12 yrs 30:1h, 1 Nov:3a
SCHILLING, Mina, 75, NYC-Bx - 1919/03/04:6a
SCHILLING, Peter, Elizabeth, NJ - 1913/06/02:6a
SCHILLINGER, A., Newark, NJ – 1908/06/02:6a
SCHILLINGER, Emil, butcher, NYC-M – 1901/10/24:1h, 25:1b
SCHILLINGER, Ernst, cigar maker, NYC-M – 1886/03/30:4a
SCHILLINGER, Fred, worker at Standard Chem Works, Elizabethport, NJ
– 1890/02/25:1g
SCHILLINGER, George, 48, NYC-M – 1899/04/25:4a,b
SCHILLINGS, Theodore, janitor, NYC-M – 1899/09/22:1g
SCHIMENZ % Marx
SCHIMKOWITZ, Theresa, 4, NYC? – 1883/09/18:3d
SCHIMMEL, George, innkeep, NYC-M – 1886/11/30:4d, 1 Dec:1g, 3:2g
SCHIMMEL, Gustav, fr Berlin, magr German Life Ins., NYC-B –
1909/09/04:3a-b, 8:3a
SCHIMMELPFENNIG, William, brewer/cooper?, NYC? – 1881/06/11:3b
SCHIMMER, Lorenz, NYC-M – 1905/09/08:4a
SCHIMPF, Frederick, hotelier, Egg Harbor, NJ - 1918/08/12:1c
SCHIMPF, Leonhardt, 37, brewer?, Passaic, NJ – 1913/01/23:6a; mem.
1914/01/22:6a, 1915/01/22:6a, 1916/01/23:7a, 1917/01/22:6a,
1918/01/22:6a
SCHINABECK, Ferdinand, un. butcher, NYC-M – 1905/06/19:4a
SCHINDELMANN, Anton, 60, NYC-M – 1892/07/30:1e

SCHINDEWOLF, F., NYC-Bx - 1916/04/29:6a
SCHINDLER, Adolph, 31, Elizabeth, NJ – 1905/04/04:4a, fam. 7:4a
SCHINDLER, Benedikt, fr Illinois, on way to Germany + Hoboken, N.J. - 1878/09/13:4d
SCHINDLER, Charles, 38, builder, NYC-M – 1893/07/20:1e
SCHINDLER, Frank, 67, NYC-B – 1911/03/04:3b
SCHINDLER, Joseph, NYC-Q - 1917/11/08:6a
SCHINDLER, Marie, Elizabeth, NJ – 1911/10/29:7c, fam. 2 Nov:6a
SCHINDLER, Max, 55, NYC-Q - 1915/07/01:6a
SCHINDLER, Mrs, NYC-B - 1878/07/09:1c
SCHINDLER, Philip, 70, NYC-M – 1892/08/08:4a
SCHINKEL, Otto, fr Schleswig-Holstein?, NYC – 1885/08/15:3d
SCHINKOETH, Wilhelm, un. carp., NYC-M - 1916/03/10:6a
SCHINTZEL, Alexander, 39, un. architec. Iron worker, NYC-M – 1893/10/29:5c, 30:4a, fam. 2 Nov:4c
SCHIPPER % Neef
SCHIRE, Max, 29, barber, NYC-M – 1892/07/18:2d
SCHIRLING, Georg, un. painter, NYC-Q - 1916/07/27:6a, 28:6a
SCHIRM, Friedrich Otto, 4, NYC-M - 1917/05/08:6a
SCHIRMEIER, Galva Koehler, NYC-M - 1919/07/01:6a, mem. 1920/06/29:6a
SCHIRMEIER, Hermann, NYC-M - 1920/02/22:3a
SCHIRMEISTER, Oscar, NYC-B - 1913/12/03:6a
SCHIRMER, Anna, NYC-M, + @Genl Slocum – 1904/06/24:1c
SCHIRMER, Betty, 26, servant, fr Bremen/Gy, Jersey City, NJ – 1900/04/14:3a
SCHIRMER, Conrad, note, NYC-M – 1906/10/23:5e
SCHIRMER, Elsie, b. Lindemann, 56, NYC-B – 1911/04/05:6a
SCHIRMER, Franz, un. brewer, fr Rheinpfalz, NYC-M - 1878/08/28:3a
SCHIRMER, Karoline, b. Krinke, NYC-Q – 1900/05/02:4a
SCHIRRMACHER, Max, 62, bookkeeper at Standard Oil, NYC-M - 1916/05/12:1f
SCHISCHKO, Leonid E., Russian revol., + Paris – 1910/02/10:4e-f
SCHITT, Gustav, window cleaner, NYC-M – 1905/10/29:1c
SCHITTIG, Caspar, NYC-B – 1883/10/18:2g, 15:2g
SCHIWANTZ, John, un. butcher, NYC-B - 1920/10/09:6a
SCHLADITZ, Anna, b. Kuehn, NYC-M – 1891/03/18:4a
SCHLADROWSKI, comrade, 42, Dockworker's Union & SPD Hamburg/Gy – 1907/11/07:3a
SCHLAEFER, Doris, NYC-M - 1894/01/28:5d
SCHLAEGER, Max, NYC-M – 1889/03/01:4a
SCHLAG, Hugo, un. typesetter, SLP, NYC? – 1886/04/12:1g

SCHLAG, John, 40, NYC-M - 1878/04/02:4e
SCHLAG, Robert, 70, case maker, NYC-B – 1911/03/06:6a
SCHLAGETER, Fredericka, NYC-M – 1891/03/31:4a
SCHLAGINTWEIT-SAKUNLINSKI, Hermann von, German explorer, 1882/02/12:3a-b
SCHLAMP, F., 51, baker, NYC-M – 1881/04/11:1e
SCHLAMP, Louis, 45, NYC-M – 1890/06/30:4a
SCHLATHER, Emil, Newark, NJ - 1919/08/05:6a
SCHLATHER, Emil, Newark, NJ – 1919/08/05:6a
SCHLATTER, Gustav Adolph, 45, NYC-B – 1893/12/31:5c
SCHLATTER, Henry, Elizabeth,NJ - 1913/05/13:6a
SCHLATTMAN, Henry, 6, & mother, NYC-M – 1900/08/17:2g
SCHLAUCH, Barbara, 58, NYC-B – 1903/07/11:4g
SCHLAUCH, Georg, 34, NYC-M – 1902/08/29:4a
SCHLAUCH, Regina, b. Kienle, Newark, NJ – 1907/06/26:6a
SCHLAUCHER, Lena, NYC-M - 1894/06/29:4a
SCHLEAPFER, Eleanor, ca 50, NYC-M - 1917/01/17:1f
SCHLECH, N., NYC-B – 1887/04/09:3d
SCHLECHT, Karl, NYC-M – 1892/06/14:4a
SCHLEDORN, Julia, b. Boissier, NYC-M – 1891/04/02:4a
SCHLEE, John, Newark, NJ – 1881/01/08:1d, 11:4d
SCHLEE, Margarethe, b. Gramlich, NYC-B? – 1893/02/26:5a
SCHLEENBECKER, Frank, 7, NYC-B - 1915/01/31:11f
SCHLEGEL, Arnold, NYC-B – 1903/08/10:3b
SCHLEGEL, Bernhard, NYC-Q - 1915/07/19:6a
SCHLEGEL, Caroline, 40, grocer, NYC-M – 1897/11/10:1f
SCHLEGEL, Charles Frederick., 60, SP, Jersey City, NJ - 1917/11/03:6a, fam. 10:6a
SCHLEGEL, John, vinegar manuf., NYC-B – 1911/01/12:6a
SCHLEGEL, Julius, SPD Stenn/Saxony – 1908/12/06:3c
SCHLEGEL, Karl Friedrich, infant, Jersey City Heights, NJ – 1885/05/26:3c,d
SCHLEGEL, Louisa, 72, NYC-M – 1908/07/22:6a, 24:6a, 25:6a
SCHLEGEL, Peter, un. cornice maker, NYC-M – 1888/01/07:4f
SCHLEGEL, Wilhelm, 65, un. carp., NYC-M – 1902/01/18:4a, 19:5a
SCHLEGEL, Wilhelm, NYC-M? – 1893/07/24:4e, fam. 27:4a
SCHLEGLE, Minnie, 20, NYC-B – 1903/01/27:3c
SCHLEHNER, Gottlob, Union Hill, NJ – 1912/08/08:6a
SCHLEICH, Jacob, 64, carp., NYC-B – 1908/08/29:3b
SCHLEICH, Johann, NYC-M – 1901/06/09:5e
SCHLEICH, Vincenz, 52, Hoboken, NJ – 1913/09/02:6a, 3:6a

SCHLEICHER, Barbara, 24, NYC-M – 1891/03/30:4a
SCHLEICHER, Gustav, 56, * Darmstadt/Hessen, USA 1847 (Texas), Congressman, + Washington, DC - 1879/01/11:1b
SCHLEICHER, John, Newark, NJ – 1906/03/31:4a
SCHLEICHER, Max, un. butcher, NYC-M - 1920/10/26:6a, 27:6a
SCHLEIDEN, Matthias Jakob, German scientist & writer, notes on his + – 1881/07/17:3f-g
SCHLEIDEN, Rudolph, 80, MdR (Reichspartei) - 1895/02/28:1a
SCHLEIDER, Lina, 32, NYC-B – 1898/12/24:1b
SCHLEIERMANN, Georg, NYC-M – 1888/03/16:3b
SCHLEIF, Franz, NYC-M – 1892/06/08:4a
SCHLEIFF, Josef, 31, NYC-M - 1894/01/12:4a
SCHLEIPPMANN, Peter, un. brewer or cooper, 48, NYC-M – 1892/05/12:4a
SCHLEISS, John, un. machinist, NYC-M - 1896/02/27:4a
SCHLEISSER, Adolph, butcher, NYC-M – 1907/04/15:3a
SCHLEITER, Frank, Roselle, NJ - 1917/05/29:6a
SCHLEMMER, Louise, b. Mann, 15, Jersey City, NJ – 1887/08/02:1g, 10:1f, husband Joseph tried, 22, 30 Sept:2f, sent. to + 18 Nov:2f
SCHLEMMER, Peter, 65, Harrison, NJ – 1906/06/20:6a
SCHLENGER, John, just arrived fr Gy, + Newark, NJ – 1883/09/13:3b
SCHLENKER, Anna, NYC-M – 1891/06/28:5c
SCHLENKER, George, Elizabeth, NJ - 1915/11/27:6a
SCHLENKER, Katherina, NYC-M – 1890/05/31:4a, fam. 4 June:4a
SCHLENKERMANN, Robert, 32, NYC-M – 1893/01/15:5c
SCHLENNECK, Charles, bartender, NYC-M – 1897/08/18:1e
SCHLENSKY, Mary, 11, Jersey City, NJ – 1885/11/26:1e, =27:3a
SCHLENTZ, Henry, 53, shoemaker, NYC-B - 1917/05/02:2e
SCHLERENACHER, Gustav, 70, innkeep & civil war vet, NYC – 1911/12/04:1f
SCHLERETH, Ad., NYC-M - 1917/06/05:6a
SCHLERETH, John, 51, night guard, NYC-Q - 1917/05/16:5f
SCHLERF, Jacob B., Elizabeth, NJ – 1912/01/04:6a, fam. 9:6a
SCHLERF, Mr., memory 1913/01/02:6a
SCHLERF, son of Jakob, 18, NYC-M – 1907/07/06:6a
SCHLERPH, Otto, NYC-B – 1909/05/22:6a
SCHLESINGER % Frey
SCHLESINGER, F., un. upholsterer, NYC-M – 1890/10/10:4a
SCHLESINGER, Fanny, NYC - 1914/03/27:2d
SCHLESINGER, Johanna, 58, midwife, NYC-M – 1888/06/04.1d
SCHLESINGER, Joseph, 36, *14 Fb 1861 Mobile, AL, NYC-M – 1897/08/29:5g

SCHLESINGER, Julius, Yonkers, NY – 1906/04/05:4a
SCHLESINGER, Sebastian, 79, composer, * Hamburg, USA 1850, ex-German consul in Chicago, +Nizza/France - 1917/01/10:1f
SCHLESSINGER, Max, 45, wine dealer, fr Austria, War 2, NYC-M - 1914/09/13:7d
SCHLETH, Henry's wife, b. Arnold, wife of Queens Co. jail warden – 1913/10/10:3a
SCHLETTER, Camille, 55, un. cigarmaker, NYC-B – 1911/07/19:3a, 20:6a
SCHLETTINGER, Dora, 18, NYC-M, +@Genl Slocum – 1904/06/23:1b
SCHLEY, Fritz, un. carpenter, NYC-M - 1894/02/22:4a
SCHLEY, Winfield Scott, 72, US Admiral – 1911/10/03:3e-f
SCHLEYBACH, Charles, 47, SP, NYC-M - 1915/04/30:6a
SCHLEYER, Gottlieb, 40, Newark, NJ – 1913/10/04:3e
SCHLICHER, Elizabeth, 29, NYC-B – 1891/10/09:4a
SCHLICHTE, Amalie H., b. Tiemann, 72, NYC-M – 1898/12/24:4a
SCHLICHTE, Carl, 52, un. typesetter, SP?, NYC-M – 1909/08/31:6a, 1 Se:6a, =2:2c, fam. 3:6a
SCHLICHTE, Edward, NYC, + New Orleans, - 1878/10/10:4e,11:3a
SCHLICHTE, Gottfried, 21, NYC-M – 1885/03/04:3c
SCHLICHTE, H. W., 72, NYC-M – 1898/02/15:4a
SCHLICHTENMAIER, Margarethe, 40, NYC - 1914/02/03:6a
SCHLICKER, Max see Schleicher, Max
SCHLIE, W., NYC-B – 1912/12/03:6a
SCHLIECKER % Schmidhaeusler
SCHLIEMANN, Frederick Frank?, to be exec – 1909/10/03:1e, 6:1g, 7:1e, 9:1g, exec. Ossining, NY – 1910/03/15:1f
SCHLIER, Martha, NYC-Q - 1915/07/03:6a
SCHLIES, George, sculptor, NYC-B – 1903/06/03:1g
SCHLIESMANN, William, NYC-Bx – 1905/09/14:4a
SCHLIESSMANN, Anton, 49, NYC-Q – 1906/06/07:4a
SCHLIHER % Peters
SCHLIMM, Ottilie, 22, 1906 fr Gy to Jersey City, NJ – 1906/09/15:3c
SCHLIMME, Ernst, 52, East Meadows, L.I. - 1879/03/28:3c
SCHLIMMER, Friedrich, 70, carp., '48er & SPD Kaiserslautern/Gy – 1899/03/19:12g
SCHLIND, Nicholas, >70, gravedigger, Huntingdon, NY - 1916/04/25:2d
SCHLINGER, 42, SP MdR for Krems, Austria – 1912/10/31:4d
SCHLINK % Fiedler
SCHLINTZ, Frieda, NYC-M – 1897/12/23:1g
SCHLITZ, Henry, 32, NYC-B – 1901/07/04:1e
SCHLOBOHM, Adelheid, b. Schnackenberg, NYC-M – 1892/09/02:4a
SCHLOBOHM, Wilhelm, Yonkers, NY – 1906/12/29:6a

SCHLOER, Charles, NYC-B – 1907/07/16:6a
SCHLOESSER, Charles, 50, NYC-B – 1912/03/20:6a
SCHLOOF, Henry, 17, messenger, * Gy, NYC-B - 1895/08/27: 4a
SCHLOOS, (Schlang?, Schlantz?, Microfilm unreadable), Karoline, b. Schmidt, NYC-M – 1889/03/07:4a, 8:4a, fam. 10:5d
SCHLOSS STEIN, Karl F., 59, NYC-B – 1891/04/11:4a
SCHLOSS, Adolph, 30, NYC – 1911/05/25:5f
SCHLOSS, Carl, 23, SP, * USA, NYC-Bx - 1916/08/05:5e-f
SCHLOSSARECK, Th's wife, Yonkers, NY – 1912/05/13:6a
SCHLOSSER, Henry, 65, West New York, NJ – 1911/09/09:6a
SCHLOSSER, John, un. mason, NYC-M – 1901/06/16:5b
SCHLOSSER, Julius, carp., NYC-M – 1909/04/03:1d
SCHLOTH, Cornelius, brewer or cooper, NYC-M – 1903/07/18:4a
SCHLOTTER, Augusta, NYC-B – 1912/12/27:6a
SCHLOTTER, Kilian, NYC-B – 1905/05/2:4a, 3:4a
SCHLOTTERER, Jacob, 55, NYC – 1883/12/24:1e
SCHLOTTHAUSER, Christian, NYC-M – 1893/11/22:4a
SCHLOTTMANN, Heinrich, 39, form maker & SPD exp. fr Ottensen/Gy, arrived NYC – 1880/11/30:1d-e, 2 Dec:2a-b, 6:1d-e; SLP, NYC-B – 1891/08/15:4a
SCHLOTZHAUER, George, un. cigarmaker, NYC-M – 1899/08/19:4a
SCHLUCHTNER, F., 43, iron monger, NYC-B – 1902/05/15:4b
SCHLUCKEBIER, Marie, NYC-Q - 1913/05/23:6a
SCHLUCKEBIER, Wilhelm, 82, un. carp., NYC-Q - 1920/01/06:8a, 7:6a
SCHLUDE, Frank, un. carpenter, NYC-B - 1894/04/30:4a
SCHLUEB, Eugene, NYC-B - 1918/08/11:12a
SCHLUENTZ, William, NYC-Q - 1918/10/09:6a
SCHLUENZEN, Henry, 52, NYC-M – 1893/08/15:4a
SCHLUEPFER, Jakob & John, Union Hill, NJ – 1889/09/06:1h
SCHLUETER % Bading
SCHLUETER, Anton's wife, b. Guttmann, 54, NYC-M – 1899/01/04:4a
SCHLUETER, Bertha, 16, NYC-M – 1897/04/27:1g
SCHLUETER, Elsie & Emma, 7, NYC? – 1905/06/29:1h
SCHLUETER, Frederick, 28, liquor salesman, NYC-M – 1886/01/08:1g
SCHLUETER, Friedericke, b. Koenig,59, Hoboken, NJ - 1878/04/20:3a
SCHLUETER, Gustav, cigar dealer, NYC-B - 1883/10/30:3a, will 1 Dec:2f
SCHLUETER, Hans Ingo, 9, NYC-M? – 1883/03/28:3d
SCHLUETER, Heinrich, 17, NYC-M – 1893/05/14:5b
SCHLUETER, Herman, fr Holstein Prov.,USA 1870s & again 1888, NYC-M, 25th anniv. working f. NYVZ 1914/07/27:4c-d, 25th anniv. chief editor NYVZ 1917/04/29:1f, 2a, + 1919/01/27:1f-g,2b, 4a-c, 6a, 28:1f,4f,6a, 29:1e,2b, 30:1g,2e, = 31:1g,2b-c, 1 Fb:1g, 2 Feb.:4a-b, 6:2b,

early life, by Carl Speyer 8:4e, 10:6a, his will 1 April:1d; memory 1920/01/26:4c
SCHLUETER, Johann Emil, Schleswig?, NYC-M – 1884/07/13:5f
SCHLUETER, Otto, 44, un. painter, NYC-M – 1912/11/22:6a, 23:6a
SCHLUETER, Peter,65,SP?,un. cigarmaker,NYC-B - 1920/09/10:6a
SCHLUETER, Robert, NYC-B – 1907/01/08:6a
SCHLUMANN, Wilhelm, NYC-M – 1891/03/17:4a
SCHLUMBERGER, Emanuel, 26, carp., USA 1880, NYC-M – 1881/04/22:1g
SCHLUMP, John, 21, Bridgeport, CT – 1889/11/12:4a
SCHLUMPF, Reinhard, 37, NYC-M – 1893/10/30:4a
SCHLUND, Fidel, 78, Bavarian member of 1848 German parliament, Newark, NJ – 1882/04/03:1d
SCHLUSKA, Peter, fr Hungary, Newark, NJ – 1901/12/23:1h
SCHLUSS, Alfred, 28, NYC-M – 1896/12/15:1f
SCHLUTER, Hans, 7, NYC-M? - 1878/09/10:3b
SCHMADT, Martha, NYC-M, +@ on Genl Slocum – 1904/06/17:3c
SCHMAGER, Theodor, 82, NYC-M – 1891/07/09:4a
SCHMAHL, George, 37, NYC-B – 1907/06/19:6a, 20:6a
SCHMALFUSS, Louis, 57, innkeep, NYC-M - 1913/06/13:1b
SCHMALZ, Josef, NYC-M - 1919/08/27:6a
SCHMANDER, George, 71, NYC-M – 1891/03/14:4a
SCHMECK, Pauline, 5, NYC-B - 1918/01/08:2e
SCHMEDLING, Emily, NYC-M, +@ Genl Slocum – 1904/06/18:3c
SCHMEIER, Alexander, NYC-M – 1904/09/18:5b
SCHMEITLING, Otto, NYC-Q – 1913/02/27:6a
SCHMELING % Spiegelhalter
SCHMELING, Auguste, b. Hoffmann, NYC-B – 1896/10/17:4a
SCHMELZE, Friedrich, 39, un. carp., NYC-M – 1886/06/14:2g
SCHMERBACHER, Magdalena, NYC-M - 1920/12/14:6a
SCHMERDA, Anna, + 1916, mem. - 1920/09/12:12a
SCHMETTING, Mrs., NYC-B – 1898/10/25:4a
SCHMID % Eckert, % Uebel
SCHMID, Anna, 5, NYC-M – 1906/01/15:4a
SCHMID, Emma, NYC-Bx – 1915/08/14:6a, 15:7a
SCHMID, Franz, un. carp., NYC-M – 1893/01/20:4a, 21:4a, fam. 24:4a
SCHMID, Friedericka, birthday, East Orange?, NY – 1908/11/19:5e
SCHMID, Jacob, NYC-B – 1911/02/19:7b
SCHMID, John, 32, Elizabeth, NJ – 1892/06/24:1h
SCHMID, Marie, Jersey City Heights, NJ - 1920/02/02:6a
SCHMID, Martha, 17, NYC-M - 1919/03/01:6a
SCHMID, Rupert, sculptor, missing, thought +, NYC-M – 1887/06/28:1g

SCHMID, Wilhelm, NYC-Bx - 1914/08/04:6a
SCHMIDHAEUSLER, Martha, b. Schliecker, 34, NYC-B – 1900/02/16:4a
SCHMIDHAUSER, Rudolf, 49, Jersey City Heights, NJ – 1891/03/15:5b
SCHMIDHEINI, P., NYC-Bx - 1914/08/04:6a
SCHMIDL, Joseph, Jersey City Heights, NJ – 1907/04/09:6a
SCHMIDLE, Martin, NYC-M - 1914/12/22:6a
SCHMIDT % Bechstaedt, Brandt, Bussmann, Cornehl, Fuhrmann; Hausamann, Hennig, Hildebrandt, Mueller; Olpp, Reese, Scheublein, Schulz, Sonnemann, Weber
SCHMIDT, A.'s wife, & Elisa, 16, NYC-B – 1881/07/30:3b, 6 Aug:3c
SCHMIDT, Ada, 46, & granddaugther Ada Smith, 4, NYC-M? – 1912/02/14:6a
SCHMIDT, Adam, un. carp., NYC-M – 1906/11/10:6a
SCHMIDT, Adele, b. Eskilden, Elizabeth, NJ - 1918/07/24:6a
SCHMIDT, Adolf, '48er, USA 1849-1856, + Mannheim/Gy – 1899/02/26:13a
SCHMIDT, Adolf, NYC-M – 1910/10/31:6a
SCHMIDT, Adolph Heinrich, 44, NYC-M – 1886/05/25:3b
SCHMIDT, Adolph, NYC-Q – 1910/06/09:6a
SCHMIDT, Albert, 46, MdR (SPD), + Bielefeld/Gy – 1904/10/29:2d-e, 3 Nov:2d
SCHMIDT, Albert, carriage maker, NYC-M – 1910/08/17:3c
SCHMIDT, Albert, NYC-M – 1910/12/28:6a
SCHMIDT, Albert, weaver, SPD Sonnenburg/Thueringen – 1910/02/06:3b
SCHMIDT, Albert,54,machinist,Jersey City, NJ - 1918/04/05:2d
SCHMIDT, Alfred, bank employee, Hoboken, NJ – 1899/05/13:3b
SCHMIDT, Alma, 50, Terre Haute, IN, brought home to Gy bodies of her father, mother, brother & sister, who + betw. 1882 & Spring 1910 – 1910/12/23:2c
SCHMIDT, Anna E., 17, NYC-M – 1897/07/21:4a, 22:4a
SCHMIDT, Anna, 1, NYC-B – 1886/07/03:2e
SCHMIDT, Anna, NYC-M, + @Genl Slocum – 1904/06/17:3c
SCHMIDT, Anna, SP?, NYC-B – 1906/02/13:4a
SCHMIDT, Antonie, 52, NYC-B - 1920/06/01:6a
SCHMIDT, Apolonia, b. Braun, 35, Newark, NJ – 1897/04/10:4a
SCHMIDT, August, 55, West N.Y., NJ - 1915/01/23:6a, 24:7b
SCHMIDT, August, engraver, NYC-M – 1900/10/31:1e
SCHMIDT, August, Newark, NJ – 1906/12/18:6a
SCHMIDT, August, NYC-B, + @ Genl Slocum – 1904/06/21:1f
SCHMIDT, August, un. upholsterer, fr Breslau/Gy, NYC-M – 1883/01/31:3d
SCHMIDT, B., 58, NYC-M - 1894/01/11:4a

SCHMIDT, Bertha, infant, NYC-M – 1892/08/08:4a
SCHMIDT, Bertha, NYC-B, +Somerville, NJ – 1906/07/30:1e
SCHMIDT, Carl Friedrich & George, 35, & Phillipine, 19, NYC-M – 1890/11/29:4a
SCHMIDT, Carl Gustav, ~35, goldsmith, USA ~1887, NYC-M – 1907/12/07:6a,c
SCHMIDT, Carl von, 52, NYC-M - 1915/04/24:6a
SCHMIDT, Carl W., 76,un.cigarmkr, NYC-Bx - 1916/11/01:6a,2:2e
SCHMIDT, Carl, 48, NYC-M – 1902/05/27:2f
SCHMIDT, Carl, 63, engineer, & wife, Emma, b. Heymann, 56, NYC-Astoria – 1887/05/02:3c, 3:3e, =4:2e
SCHMIDT, Carl, fr Barmen/Gy, + on trip to USA – 1888/12/04:1e
SCHMIDT, Carlos, G-A journalist, a.e. for NYSZ, * 1816 Nuernberg/Gy, USA 1850, NYC-B – 1890/05/06:2h
SCHMIDT, Charles John, 51, SLP, Jersey City, NJ - 1895/09/29: 5b
SCHMIDT, Charles, 13, NYC-M – 1900/11/17:2h
SCHMIDT, Charles, 38, baker, NYC-B - 1915/01/13:6c
SCHMIDT, Charles, 50, Carlstadt, NJ - 1917/07/19:6c
SCHMIDT, Charles, 53, SP, NYC-Q - 1915/02/26:6a
SCHMIDT, Charles, 60, shoemaker, NYC-B – 1884/08/11:2g
SCHMIDT, Charles, fam. NYC-M – 1902/08/12:4a
SCHMIDT, Charles, NYC-M – 1889/04/24:4a
SCHMIDT, Charles, NYC-M – 1897/03/06:4a
SCHMIDT, Charles, NYC-M – 1908/02/06:6a
SCHMIDT, Charles, policeman, Carlstadt, NJ – 1910/04/30:2c, =3 May:2e
SCHMIDT, Charles's wife, b. Stern,& son, 8, NYC-M - 1915/10/06:1f
SCHMIDT, Charles's mother, brother & 2 sisters, NYC-M?, + @Genl Slocum – 1904/06/17:1a
SCHMIDT, Christian, 56, NYC-Q - 1915/05/08:6a
SCHMIDT, Christian, tramway employee, NYC-B – 1892/02/28:1h
SCHMIDT, Christian's wife, NYC-B – 1880/12/13:3b
SCHMIDT, Conrad, 37, NYC-M – 1891/08/27:1d
SCHMIDT, David, NYC-M – 1897/10/24:5a
SCHMIDT, Eduard Sr.,51, weaver, Paterson, NJ - 1917/12/07:6a
SCHMIDT, Eduard, NYC-M – 1902/08/08:4a
SCHMIDT, Eduard, NYC-Q – 1910/01/28:6a
SCHMIDT, Eleonore, 56, NYC-M - 1917/05/14:6a
SCHMIDT, Elsa, infant, NYC-M – 1892/06/28:4a
SCHMIDT, Elsa, NYC-M – 1892/07/12:4a
SCHMIDT, Emil, realtor, Hoboken, NJ - 1914/07/07:6c
SCHMIDT, Emilie, 60, seamstress, NYC-M - 1892/01/26:1e
SCHMIDT, Emma, NYC-M, +@Genl Slocum – 1904/06/22:1d

SCHMIDT, Erich, Prof., 60, ex-Rector Berlin U - 1913/05/01:2a
SCHMIDT, Ernestine, 30, garment worker,NYC-B - 1914/10/01:6c
SCHMIDT, Ernst, 52, un. carp., Carlstadt, NJ - 1900/08/17:2g
SCHMIDT, Ernst, Dr. med., Chicago SDP, *2 March 1830 Ebern/Gy, USA 1856, # - 1900/08/27:1c-f, 3b
SCHMIDT, Ernst, Dr., SLP Chicago, 70th birthday - 1899/03/16:2c
SCHMIDT, Ernst, NYC-M - 1903/02/07:4a
SCHMIDT, Eva, NYC-M, + @on Genl Slocum - 1904/06/17:3c
SCHMIDT, Ferdinand, 21, Cornell U student, NYC-M - 1918/10/10:6a, fam. 13:11g, 15:6a
SCHMIDT, Frank, 28, SP, un. baker, Elizabeth, NJ - 1919/01/20:6a
SCHMIDT, Frank, 34,SP, un. pianomaker,NYC-Bx - 1919/08/02:2a
SCHMIDT, Frank, un. typesetter, NYC-M - 1907/09/11:6a
SCHMIDT, Franz, un. carp., NYC-M - 1903/06/02:4a
SCHMIDT, Frederick, 28, NYC-Q - 1912/12/16:2c
SCHMIDT, Frieda, War 2, Newark, NJ - 1918/10/28:2g
SCHMIDT, Friederike, 36, NYC-M - 1892/07/12:4a
SCHMIDT, Friedrich J., 75, un. cigarmaker, fr Koeln/Gy, NYC-M - 1907/03/12:6a
SCHMIDT, Friedrich, 64, ex-carp., innkeep of Union Hall, NYC-M - 1907/08/30:1d
SCHMIDT, Friedrich, smith, NYC-M - 1893/03/09:1h
SCHMIDT, Georg, 53, NYC-B? - 1879/02/06:4d
SCHMIDT, Georg, 58, brewery worker, NYC-M - 1895/04/04:1e
SCHMIDT, George F., weaver, NYC-Bx - 1912/12/11:6a
SCHMIDT, George, 17, NYC-M - 1900/12/25:1e
SCHMIDT, George, 43, NYC-M - 1892/08/09:4a
SCHMIDT, George, 68, NYC-M - 1889/11/16:4a
SCHMIDT, George, carp., NYC-B - 1904/09/06:3c
SCHMIDT, George, Secaucus, NJ - 1915/05/06:6a
SCHMIDT, George, un. carp., NYC-M - 1896/08/24:4a
SCHMIDT, Gladys, 20, NYC - 1909/02/28:7e
SCHMIDT, Gustav, West Hoboken, NJ - 1920/02/03:8a
SCHMIDT, H., NYC-B - 1911/09/05:6a
SCHMIDT, Hans, Rev., trial for + Anna Aumueller 1913/09/15:1g, 16:1f, 17:1f,2a, 4a-b, 18:2a,4a-b, 21:1f, 23:1d, 24:1c, bio 30:3a-b 25 Oct:1f, 19 Nov:1e, 20:1b, 9 Dec:1b; appeal lost 1915/11/27:2a,4d, exec., NY 1916/02/19:1c
SCHMIDT, Hans, 4/1903 fr Gy, NYC-M - 1903/06/21:5b
SCHMIDT, Hans, 46, Jersey City, NJ - 1911/02/21:6a
SCHMIDT, Hans, 48, barge captain, NYC-B - 1881/11/01:4c
SCHMIDT, Harry, 19, Jersey City Heights, NJ - 1890/05/18:5a

SCHMIDT, Heinrich E., 82, prof. Columbia U, NYC-M – 1889/02/14:4a
SCHMIDT, Heinrich, 58, NYC-M – 1898/08/28:5e
SCHMIDT, Heinrich,70,un. cigar packer, NYC-M - 1916/12/24:5a
SCHMIDT, Henry, 31, NYC-Q – 1896/08/16:5c
SCHMIDT, Henry, engraver, NYC-B – 1898/10/30:4h
SCHMIDT, Henry, NYC-M – 1893/09/07:1h
SCHMIDT, Herman, innkeep fr Milwaukee, + Buffalo, NY – 1880/11/20:1b
SCHMIDT, Hermann, 29, * Limburg/Hessen, USA 1878, NYC-M - 1878/12/16:1e, 20:4d
SCHMIDT, Hermann, 47, NYC-Bx - 1918/07/08:2e
SCHMIDT, Hermann, 75, un. typesetter, NYC-B – 1908/06/24:6a
SCHMIDT, Hermann, NYC-M – 1907/03/18:6a
SCHMIDT, Hugo C., 60, * Gy, USA ca. 1890, teacher, Tarrytown, NY - 1920/10/29:2e, 1 Nov:6b
SCHMIDT, Hugo, Frankenberg/Gy ATB, War 1 - 1914/11/01:3b
SCHMIDT, Hugo, SP, grave monument in Jaegerndorf/Austrian Silesia – 1909/06/27:3c
SCHMIDT, Ida, 20, worker, Bayonne?, NJ – 1913/10/23:2e
SCHMIDT, J., 74, & wife, 72, NYC-B - 1915/11/04:6b
SCHMIDT, Jacob's wife, NYC-M – 1898/01/25:1d
SCHMIDT, James A., ex-treas. Carp. Union #387, NYC-M – 1903/11/14:1d
SCHMIDT, James, engineer, NYC-M – 1888/01/11:1c
SCHMIDT, Johann Rudolf, * Basel/CH, NYC-M - 1894/04/15:9f
SCHMIDT, Johanna, 27, NYC-M - 1917/04/07:6a
SCHMIDT, John J., artist (painter), NYC-B – 1907/02/02:3a
SCHMIDT, John, 50, fr Hanau?, SP, NYC-M – 1909/11/27:6a, 29:6a?, fam. 5 De:7b
SCHMIDT, John, 50, NYC-M – 1907/05/18:3c, 19:7b
SCHMIDT, John, 56, jeweler, NYC-M – 1898/01/09:1e
SCHMIDT, John, Ghent, NY, to be exec. – 1899/06/02:1b
SCHMIDT, John, un. brewer, NYC-M – 1896/05/01:4a
SCHMIDT, John, who killed wife, + in Newark, NJ jail – 1886/10/06:2g
SCHMIDT, Josef, smith, NYC-M – 1891/04/16:2g
SCHMIDT, Joseph W., 18, NYC-B, US sailor on ship "North Dakota" – 1910/09/16:2e
SCHMIDT, Joseph, 20, NYC-B - 1913/12/19:2d
SCHMIDT, Joseph, 31, Yonkers, NY - 1920/02/03:8a
SCHMIDT, Joseph, NYC-M – 1909/06/10:6a
SCHMIDT, Joseph, un. baker, NYC-M – 1892/04/24:5a
SCHMIDT, Josephine, NYC-M, +@ Genl Slocum – 1904/06/18:3c
SCHMIDT, Julia, NYC-M – 1893/10/23:4a
SCHMIDT, Karl Paul, 28, waiter, NYC-M – 1904/09/24:1g, 25:5h

SCHMIDT, Karl, 47, model maker, USA 1859, NYC-M – 1891/06/09:2g
SCHMIDT, Karl, 76, un. cigarmaker, NYC-Bx - 1917/01/30:6a
SCHMIDT, Karl, un. carp., NYC-B – 1889/04/07:5c
SCHMIDT, Karl, un. cigarmaker, SLP, NYC-B – 1888/02/28:3b, 29:3b
SCHMIDT, Kath. Marg., 31, NYC-M – 1892/09/10:4a
SCHMIDT, Katherine, 25, NYC-M – 1893/06/22:4a
SCHMIDT, Katherine, 67, NYC-M, + @ Genl Slocum – 1904/06/17:3c
SCHMIDT, Katie, 40, NYC-M, + o@Genl Slocum – 1904/06/18:3c
SCHMIDT, Katie, infant, NYC-M – 1882/01/02:3b
SCHMIDT, Leonhard, NYC-M – 1906/05/10:4a
SCHMIDT, Lizzie, b. Volkmann, 28, NYC-M – 1883/02/17:3c
SCHMIDT, Lorenz, 47, NYC-M - 1878/05/20:4d
SCHMIDT, Louis, farmer, USA 1879, Amityville, LI – 1880/07/03:1g & 22 Aug:5c, 23:1g, 24:1e, 26:3b
SCHMIDT, Louisa, 69, NYC-B – 1910/02/28:2f
SCHMIDT, Louisa, b. Treiber?, NYC-B – 1891/04/06:4a
SCHMIDT, Lt, leader Sebastopol revolt of Russian Navy – 1905/12/14:2e, exec. 19 Mr 1906:1a, 21 Mr 1906:1a, life 22:2c,e-f, 29:1b; 12 Apr:2d, adm. Schuknin, who had him exec., killed by revol. 14 Jy 06:1c
SCHMIDT, Ludwig, 55, NYC-Q – 1885/02/19:3a
SCHMIDT, Margaretha, 50, Bavaria?, NYC-M - 1917/06/14:6a
SCHMIDT, Maria Hadje, NYC-M – 1899/09/26:4a
SCHMIDT, Marie, NYC-B – 1897/07/01:4c
SCHMIDT, Martha, NYC-M, + @ Genl Slocum – 1904/06/18:3c
SCHMIDT, Mathilde, 20, servant, NYC-M – 1887/04/07:1f
SCHMIDT, Max, NYC-M – 1904/12/18:5b
SCHMIDT, Max, NYC-M – 1911/01/29:7b
SCHMIDT, Max, un. painter, NYC-M - 1914/06/08:6a
SCHMIDT, Moritz, SP, 50th birthday, Greenville, NJ – 1913/03/02:9e
SCHMIDT, Nichlas, innkeep, Hoboken, NJ – 1899/12/26:4a
SCHMIDT, Nicholas, NYC-B, + on ship Mystery (see Hendricks) – 1887/07/12:1c-d, 13:2g
SCHMIDT, NYC-B – 1902/04/01:4a
SCHMIDT, Otto, NYC-Bx - 1914/07/28:6a
SCHMIDT, Peter Von Der, 58, un. carp., * Gross-Bieberach/Hessia/Gy, USA 1883, NYC-M – 1919/12/01:8a, 2:2b,6a, 9:8a, fam. 10:6a
SCHMIDT, Ph., NYC-M - 1894/01/11:4a
SCHMIDT, Philipp, fr Kaiserslautern/Pfalz, '48er, MdL, + there, local '48ers fr Pfalz meet - 1878/10/08:4d
SCHMIDT, Robert, Hoboken, NJ - 1918/12/28:6a
SCHMIDT, Robert, un. carp., NYC – 1912/10/27:7a
SCHMIDT, Rudolph, 70, un. tailor, NYC-M – 1905/08/08:4a

SCHMIDT, S. P., NYC-M – 1887/01/28:3c
SCHMIDT, Samuel, 70, NYC-Q – 1899/11/11:4a
SCHMIDT, Siegfried, 3, NYC-M – 1892/05/21:4a
SCHMIDT, Simon, 47, painter, NYC-M – 1903/09/15:1e, 16:4a
SCHMIDT, Sophia, NYC-M, + @ Genl Slocum – 1904/06/17:3c
SCHMIDT, Sophie, 30, NYC-M – 1910/10/16:7c
SCHMIDT, Theodore, Elizabeth,NJ - 1915/04/24:6a
SCHMIDT, Theresa, 32, @1911 Triangle Shirtwaist Fire, NYC-M – 1911/03/27:1d
SCHMIDT, Troster, un. carp., NYC-M – 1905/07/21:4a
SCHMIDT, VON DER % Velte
SCHMIDT, W., fam. 1890/05/11:5a
SCHMIDT, Wilhelm A., 38, SP, un. typesetter, NYC-B - 1913/05/11:7b
SCHMIDT, Wilhelm, 18, NYC-M – 1893/11/06:3b
SCHMIDT, Wilhelm, brewer or cooper, NYC-M – 1890/10/05:5c
SCHMIDT, Wilhelm, Jersey City Hgts, NJ - 1915/04/25:7b
SCHMIDT, Wilhelm, SPD MdR, mon. on grave inaug. Frankfurt 1909/12/19:3a
SCHMIDT, Wilhelm, un. butcher, NYC-B – 1905/08/15:4a
SCHMIDT, Wilhelm, un. carp., NYC-M – 1890/04/06:5a; mem. 1891/04/06:4a
SCHMIDT, William C., 47, realtor, NYC-B – 1912/03/29:3a
SCHMIDT, William, 40, grocer, NYC-SI - 1915/04/24:2b
SCHMIDT, William, 50, NYC-B – 1896/08/11:1c
SCHMIDT, William, 50, SP, un. butcher, NYC-B - 1914/04/13:3b,6a, 12:7b, 14:6a, =15:2b
SCHMIDT, William, 60, cutter, NYC-M – 1896/09/12:1e
SCHMIDT, William, machinist, NYC - 1914/03/30:6a
SCHMIDT, Xavier, NYC-M - 1894/08/16:4a
SCHMIDTELL, Caroline, USA 1890, NYC-SI – 1890/05/14:3a
SCHMIDTMANN, Mrs, Elizabethport, NJ – 1896/04/17:2e
SCHMIEDE, William, NYC-M, + @ Genl Slocum – 1904/06/18:3c
SCHMIEDEL, Wilhelm, 54, NYC-M – 1891/03/18:4a
SCHMIEDEN, William, 28, sailor, NYC-M - 1915/12/19:1e
SCHMIEDER, Bernhard, un. brewery worker, NYC-M 1894/07/27:4a
SCHMIEDERER, B., 65, NYC-M – 1893/09/02:4a
SCHMIEDLE, John, NYC-M – 1906/12/23:7b
SCHMIEDLER, Siegmund,36, mining engineer, fr Kattowitz/Upper Silesia, labor org., USA ca. 1885, Sault St Marie, then NYC, 1895/06/3:1f
SCHMIEDT, Georg, SP?, Jersey City Heights, NJ – 1906/03/01:4a
SCHMIEG, Laura, NYC-B – 1887/08/23:2e
SCHMIELACE, Claus A., NYC-B – 1891/05/31:5b

SCHMIERER, John, un. carp., NYC-M – 1888/03/27:4g
SCHMIERER, Joseph, NYC-B - 1915/07/22:6a
SCHMILLEL, Josefa, 56, NYC-B – 1889/05/20:4a
SCHMINKE, Meta, b. Utermehte, NYC-M - 1918/07/02:6a
SCHMITDKUNZ, Susanne, NYC-M – 1892/07/29:4a
SCHMITT % Losch
SCHMITT, Andreas, NYC-M - 1917/04/29:6a, fam. 3 May:6a
SCHMITT, Arthur, NYC-M – 1908/09/30:6a
SCHMITT, Christian, 58, worker, NYC-M – 1882/08/23:4d
SCHMITT, Christian, locksmith, fr Kees?/Rgeinpfalz, NYC-M – 1889/12/15:5a
SCHMITT, Conrad, NYC-B – 1903/01/12:3b
SCHMITT, Eleonore, b. Hippell,49,NYC-B - 1917/02/16:6a,fam.20:6a
SCHMITT, Emil Joseph, 17, NYC-M – 1885/02/23:3c, fam. 8 Mr:8a
SCHMITT, Emilie, 64, NYC-Bx – 1912/12/25:6a
SCHMITT, Ferdinand, machinist, NYC-B – 1904/11/01:4a
SCHMITT, Franz, NYC-B – 1891/04/04:4a
SCHMITT, Jacob, 48, un. cigarmaker, NYC-M – 1887/07/19:3c
SCHMITT, John, painter, SLP, * Galicia, NYC-M – 1883/09/24:3c, 4b, 22:4a, = with laudatio by John Most 26:1f
SCHMITT, John Joseph, 21, un. cigarmaker?, NYC-Q – 1906/11/20:6a
SCHMITT, John Paul, un. baker, NYC-M – 1902/04/22:4a
SCHMITT, Julius, cabinet maker?, NYC-M – 1889/02/10:5b
SCHMITT, Leonard J., pianomaker, NYC-Bx – 1908/10/01:6b
SCHMITT, Leopold P., 26, NYC-M – 1899/05/25:4a
SCHMITT, Louis, 42, * Tauberbischofsheim/Baden, NYC-B – 1885/06/13:3c
SCHMITT, Louis, cook,@Turnhalle Fire, NYC-M – 1880/01/05:4a, 8:1g, 3a, 9:1e-f
SCHMITT, Louis, un. wood carver, NYC-M – 1890/12/10:4a
SCHMITT, Margarethe, 55, NYC-B – 1880/07/10:4b
SCHMITT, Maria Anna, b. Kroth, * 28 Sept 1804 Grosswaldstadt/Bavaria, NYC-M – 1886/04/05:3a
SCHMITT, Maria, NYC-M – 1890/01/05:5b
SCHMITT, Peter, 72, tailor?, NYC-B – 1891/03/16:4a
SCHMITT, Philip Karl, 10, NYC-B – 1886/06/09:3a
SCHMITT, Raymond, un. carp., NYC-Bx – 1912/12/18:6a
SCHMITT, Robert, 60, night guard, War 2, NYC-B - 1917/09/25:6c
SCHMITT, Sophia, NYC-M, + @ Genl Slocum – 1904/06/18:3c
SCHMITT, wife & 2 kids of John, 33, painter, NYC-M – 1888/12/13:1h
SCHMITT, William, un. book binder, NYC-M – 1891/12/06:5c

SCHMITTBERGER, Max F., 66, police officer, crit. obit., NYC-M? - 1917/11/04:6a-b
SCHMITTHAUSER, Adolph, 52, mineral water dealer, Jersey City, NJ - 1903/02/24:2d
SCHMITTMANN, Augustus W., 70, flour dealer, NYC-B - 1897/06/04:1e
SCHMITZ, Anna, b. Wendisch, NYC-M - 1883/11/27:3b
SCHMITZ, Hettie, 17, Cincinatti, OH - 1915/12/23:1d
SCHMITZ, J., Yonkers, NY - 1910/07/27:6a
SCHMITZ, Max, * 21 Jy 1887 Le Havre/France, Swiss, cotton merchant, War 2, NYC-M - 1915/10/01:2g
SCHMITZ, Theo, 60, NYC-B - 1897/05/14:1d
SCHMITZ, Wilhelm, 83, Berlin/Gy wood worker & Soc. Activist - 1913/09/28:3b
SCHMITZE, Albert, USA 1896? fr Gy, NYC-B - 1897/03/14:1f
SCHMITZLEIN, innkeep, NYC-M - 1898/04/09:1e
SCHMOCK, Jacob, bricklayer, NYC-M - 1895/06/22: 1g
SCHMOGER, August, 74, un. furrier, NYC - 1889/01/11:4a
SCHMOLINSKA, Louise, b. Dobsau, NYC-M - 1882/05/10:3c
SCHMOLL, Eugen K., beer driver, Atlantic City, NJ, + Dec. 1914, noted - 1916/05/25:2b
SCHMOLLINGER, A., NYC-M - 1912/01/02:6a
SCHMOLZ, Helena, NYC-M - 1918/02/03:7a, fam. 6:6a
SCHMOOCK, George, NYC-M - 1918/08/21:6a
SCHMOTT, Conrad, NYC-B - 1913/07/17:6a
SCHMUSI, Joseph, Paulsboro, NJ,worker, + DuPont Powder plant, Gibbstown, NJ - 1913/12/09:1b
SCHMUDE, Mildred, 18, NYC-B, + on Genl Slocum - 1904/06/21:1f
SCHMUHL, Charles, 51, NYC-B - 1912/10/14:2e, 16:6a
SCHMUHL, Heinrich, NYC-M - 1892/06/15:4a
SCHNABEL, Emma, 17, NYC-B - 1917/10/11:6c
SCHNABEL, J., NYC-Q - 1914/01/03:6a
SCHNADELN, Kaete, 20, Glenshaw, PA - 1916/08/12:2e
SCHNAIDT, Herman, 38,un. stonecutter, NYC-M - 1895/11/16: 4a
SCHNABEL, Johann Julius, un. piano maker, NYC-Q - 1910/02/03:6a
SCHNACKENBERG % Schlobohm
SCHNAIBLE, Jack, NYC - 1912/08/10:6a
SCHNAIR, Samuel, NYC-B - 1904/11/23:4a
SCHNALKE, Johanna, b. Freimann, 47, NYC-B - 1899/04/11:4a
SCHNALLKE, Paul, 70, NYC-M - 1919/01/11:6a
SCHNAPP, John, 40, innkeep, Newark, NJ - 1905/05/04:3d
SCHNAPP, William, NYC-M - 1901/03/03:5a
SCHNAUBELT, Chicago martyr, letter 1887/04/23:2c

SCHNAUFER, Adam, 45, Newark, NJ – 1890/11/01:2d
SCHNAUFER, Catherine, b. Dellinger, 29, fr Elchesheim/Baden, NYC-M – 1892/02/01:4f
SCHNEBBE, Carrie, 15, NYC-M, @Genl Slocum – 1904/06/24:1c
SCHNECK, Albertine, * Stuttgart, NYC-M - 1895/12/11: 3a
SCHNECK, Theodor, 48, NYC-M – 1912/01/08:6a, 9:6a
SCHNECKENBURGER, Gottlieb, NYC-M – 1891/08/15:4a
SCHNECKENBURGER, Jacob, 64, un. carp., NYC-Q – 1905/01/17:4a, 18:4a
SCHNEELOCH, Wilhelm, Jersey City Hghts, NJ - 1916/08/12:6a
SCHNEER, Betty, 59, NYC-M – 1898/03/17:1f
SCHNEFEL, Paul, NYC-M - 1895/09/22: 5a
SCHNEID, Rose, NYC-B - 1917/06/12:3e
SCHNEIDER % Harrass, % Lutz
SCHNEIDER, A., & wife, NYC, Silver Wedding – 1913/10/16:5f
SCHNEIDER, Adolph, 37, NYC-B – 1900/01/07:5a
SCHNEIDER, Albert, worker, Jersey City, NJ, + Newark, NJ – 1901/09/27:1h
SCHNEIDER, Amalia, 6, NYC-B, + @Genl Slocum – 1904/06/20:4a
SCHNEIDER, Annie, b. Jakobs, Elizabeth, NJ – 1892/01/16:4a
SCHNEIDER, Anton S., un. painter, NYC-M - 1896/02/19:4a
SCHNEIDER, August, body of wife & missing child fd, NYC-M, + @Genl Slocum – 1904/06/29:4a
SCHNEIDER, Balthasar, NYC-B – 1912/02/06:6a
SCHNEIDER, Bertha, 29, Newark, NJ – 1909/03/30:3e, 29:3b
SCHNEIDER, Bertha, b. Horn, 27, SLP?, NYC-M – 1888/07/20:4g
SCHNEIDER, Carl, 46, NYC-M – 1888/01/31:3a
SCHNEIDER, Carl, 5, NYC-M – 1888/03/01:3a
SCHNEIDER, Caroline Wilhelmina, 4, NYC-M – 1881/04/19:3c
SCHNEIDER, Caspar, NYC-Q - 1919/06/17:6a
SCHNEIDER, Christian, fr Schleswig-Holstein?, NYC-M – 1885/11/04:3a
SCHNEIDER, Conrad, worker, NYC-M – 1880/07/12:4a, 13:1c
SCHNEIDER, Dora, NYC-B – 1890/10/21:2e
SCHNEIDER, Dora, NYC-B, +@Genl Slocum – 1904/06/25:1d
SCHNEIDER, E., NYC-M – 1904/09/15:4a
SCHNEIDER, Edna, 22, NYC-B – 1912/06/15:3a
SCHNEIDER, Elizabeth, Philadelphia, PA - 1919/08/04:2d
SCHNEIDER, Elsi, NYC-B - 1916/04/27:6a
SCHNEIDER, Emma, NYC-M – 1891/07/16:4a
SCHNEIDER, Ernst, Secaucus, NJ – 1910/07/09:1e
SCHNEIDER, Ethel, 20, @Triangle Shirtwaist Fire, NYC-M – 1911/03/27:1d

SCHNEIDER, Eva NYC-M, + @ Genl Slocum – 1904/06/17:3c
SCHNEIDER, Florian,m 51, NYC-M – 1903/07/12:5a
SCHNEIDER, Franz, 62, NYC-M - 1894/01/25:4a
SCHNEIDER, Franz, weaver, SPD Kiel/Gy – 1899/04/23:13b
SCHNEIDER, Frederick, 36, driver, NYC-B – 1899/09/06:2g
SCHNEIDER, Frederick, 51, un. carp., NYC-B - 1914/07/08:6a
SCHNEIDER, Frederick, janitor, NYC-M - 1894/07/31:1e
SCHNEIDER, Friedrich, 58, NYC-M - 1895/02/16:4a
SCHNEIDER, Friedrich, 68, weaver, SPD Elberfeld/Gy – 1912/08/25:3c
SCHNEIDER, Friedrich, shoemaker, NYC-M – 1893/07/19:1g
SCHNEIDER, Georg, 12, Newark, NJ – 1888/04/07:2e
SCHNEIDER, George A., 27, NYC-Bx – 1890/07/13:5d
SCHNEIDER, George, 60, silk worker, Union Hill, NJ – 1907/08/21:2c
SCHNEIDER, George, un. baker, NYC-Bx – 1910/02/12:6a
SCHNEIDER, George, un. baker, NYC-M – 1893/02/25:4a
SCHNEIDER, Gustav, 20, smith, fr Hungary, Newark, NJ – 1883/12/24:1f, 2g-3a
SCHNEIDER, H., 56, NYC-B – 1893/03/31:4a
SCHNEIDER, Heinrich, 32, typesetter & SP Temesvar, War 1 - 1915/02/21:3e
SCHNEIDER, Heinrich, NYC-M – 1892/07/28:4a
SCHNEIDER, Heinrich, Union Hill, NJ – 1891/05/17:5a
SCHNEIDER, Henry, 70, NYC-M – 1892/12/11:5b
SCHNEIDER, Henry, NYC-B - 1919/04/12:6a
SCHNEIDER, Hermann, musician, NYC-M – 1906/07/04:1f
SCHNEIDER, Hermann, NYC-M – 1892/06/19:5d
SCHNEIDER, Hilda, NYC-B - 1916/02/15:6c
SCHNEIDER, Hortense, French actress, + Versailles, - 1920/06/01:4g
SCHNEIDER, Howard J., exec. Washington, DC – 1893/03/18:1c
SCHNEIDER, Israel, 60, NYC-M – 1891/07/29:4a
SCHNEIDER, Jacob, NYC-M – 1891/07/16:4a
SCHNEIDER, James, watchman, 48, NYC-M – 1887/08/04:1f
SCHNEIDER, Jeremiah, 42, NYC-M – 1893/01/06:4a
SCHNEIDER, Johann, plumber, NYC-M? - 1916/01/18:2b
SCHNEIDER, Johann, 3, NYC-M – 1892/06/25:4a
SCHNEIDER, Johann, un. carp., NYC-M – 1903/12/26:4a, 27:5a, fam. 29:4a
SCHNEIDER, John W., NYC-M – 1892/10/14:4a
SCHNEIDER, John, 31, NYC-Bx?, + Camp Meade, Baltimore, MD - 1918/10/10:6a
SCHNEIDER, John, 73, Floral Park, LI – 1912/10/18:6c
SCHNEIDER, John, NYC-Bx – 1913/01/30:6a

SCHNEIDER, John, un. carp., NYC-M – 1889/11/17:5a
SCHNEIDER, Joseph, 28, barrel washer, NYC-M – 1880/05/21:4b
SCHNEIDER, Joseph, 41, builder, NYC-M – 1904/06/22:1e
SCHNEIDER, Joseph, NYC-M – 1909/03/26:6a
SCHNEIDER, Josephine, 49, NYC-B – 1904/02/23:1g
SCHNEIDER, Julius, 65, un. cigar maker, NYC-M – 1892/02/01:4f
SCHNEIDER, Karl, 48, NYC-M – 1892/07/19:4a
SCHNEIDER, Kate, 8, NYC-M, + @Genl Slocum – 1904/06/24:1d
SCHNEIDER, L., NYC-B – 1902/07/23:4a
SCHNEIDER, Lena, 25, Elizabeth, NJ – 1899/10/15:9g
SCHNEIDER, Lilly, NYC-M - 1919/01/21:6a, fam. 25:6a
SCHNEIDER, Lina, servant, NYC-Bx - 1913/12/23:1d
SCHNEIDER, Lizzie, 17, NYC-M – 1897/11/04:1g
SCHNEIDER, Louise, NYC-M, + @ Genl Slocum – 1904/06/18:3c
SCHNEIDER, Ludwig, 65, shoemaker, SPD Frankfurt/Main – 1902/02/08:2c
SCHNEIDER, Max, 54, druggist, NYC-B – 1910/09/16:2e
SCHNEIDER, Michael, 70, Newark, NJ - 1896/03/24:4a
SCHNEIDER, Michael, NYC – 1907/07/26:6a, fam. 3 Aug.:6a
SCHNEIDER, Michael, West New York, NJ - 1920/12/06:6a
SCHNEIDER, Nicholaus, 73, un. typesetter, NYC-M – 1898/05/22:5c
SCHNEIDER, Nikolaus, un. carp., NYC-B - 1919/05/25:12a
SCHNEIDER, Oscar, SLP, un.carp.,Union Hill,NJ – 1895/02/16:2d
SCHNEIDER, Pauline, 59, NYC-B - 1916/01/12:6c
SCHNEIDER, Pius, NYC-M - 1919/01/08:6a
SCHNEIDER, Reinhardt, 40, NYC-B – 1912/01/15:2d
SCHNEIDER, Reinhold, cigarmaker & SPD Goldberg/Silesia, Gy – 1901/12/11:2d
SCHNEIDER, Richard, NYC-M – 1890/05/29:4a
SCHNEIDER, Rosa, b. Basel, NYC-M – 1888/03/12:4d, 17:4a, murderer rec. life 27 Apr:4c
SCHNEIDER, Rosie, 34, NYC-B - 1902/11/14:3b
SCHNEIDER, Rudolf, NYC – 1912/10/12:6a
SCHNEIDER, S., un. printer, NYC-B - 1895/06/19: 4a
SCHNEIDER, Samuel, pres. Hebrew Actors' Club, NYC-M - 1915/11/14:1e
SCHNEIDER, Stefan, un. Baker, NYC-B – 1919/10/19:12a
SCHNEIDER, Thekla, b. Wisch, 25, NYC-B – 1889/01/25:4a
SCHNEIDER, Theresa, 44, NYC-M - 1894/01/22:4a
SCHNEIDER, Wilhelm, 40, waiter, NYC-M – 1891/09/03:4c, 4:4a
SCHNEIDER, Wilhelm, Union Hill, NJ - 1914/01/12:6a
SCHNEIDER, Wilhelmine, Newark, NJ – 1912/05/22:6a
SCHNEIDER, William G., artist, NYC – 1912/11/06:1f

SCHNEIDER, William, 13, NYC-B - 1914/03/15:7e
SCHNEIDER, William, 38, janitor, NYC-M - 1909/12/08:5b
SCHNEIDLING, George, NYC-M, + @ Genl Slocum - 1904/06/17:3c
SCHNEIER, John, NYC? - 1883/03/27:3c
SCHNEIRING, Frederick, servant, Lyndhurst, NY - 1913/07/15:1d
SCHNELL, Henry, 61, un. cigarmaker, NYC-Q - 1919/04/27:12a
SCHNELLBACH, Joseph, Scarsdale, N.Y., + NYC-M 1894/05/12:1e
SCHNELER, Georg, NYC-M - 1906/12/27:6a
SCHNELL, Charles, 2, NYC-M - 1889/01/22:4a
SCHNELL, Christopher, tailor, NYC-M - 1890/12/31:2g
SCHNELL, Elise, fam. - 1912/03/30:6a
SCHNELL, Herman, Newark, NJ - 1919/09/17:6a
SCHNELL, Wilhelm, coal-dealer, SPD Elberfeld/Gy - 1886/05/11:6c
SCHNELL, William, 30, un. baker, NYC-M - 1905/01/13:4a
SCHNELLBACHER % Roth
SCHNELLBACHER, John, * Oct. 1828 Hoechst/Frankfurt, USA 1853, supporter of local G-A school, Newark, NJ - 1878/04/16:4e, = 17:1g
SCHNELLBECHER, Henry, innkeep, & wife Annie, 35, Jersey City, NJ - 1907/01/13:1g
SCHNELLE, August, Hoboken, NJ - 1912/08/17:2d
SCHNELLE, August, NYC-B - 1916/06/07:6a
SCHNELLE, Max, NYC-M - 1881/02/28:3c
SCHNEPEL, Hermann, SP, un. bricklayer, NYC-M - 1915/02/20:6a, 21:7e, =24:2e, fam. 25:6a
SCHNEPF, Engelbert, 59, '48er & civil war vet, NYC-B - 1880/03/27:2g-3a, =29:2g
SCHNEPP, Ignatz, SP?, un. machinist, NYC-Bx - 1917/12/23:7a
SCHNEPP, Leo, Dr., fr Austria, note (not +), NYC-M - 1886/07/17:1e; More notes - 1887/07/22:4d, 23:1e, 27:3a, 24 Sept:4c
SCHNEPPE, Anna, 32, NYC-M - 1893/04/30:5a
SCHNEPPE, Carl, 42, *29/01/1859 Pritzerbe/Brandenburg, ed. at NYVZ, SLP, NYC-M - 1900/05/02:1e, 4a, 3:4a, 4:4f, =5:2f
SCHNEPPE, Carl, 63, NYC-M - 1893/01/16:4a
SCHNEPPE, Charlotte, NYC SP, fr Mannheim?, her life (not +), # - 1911/02/26:19d-e
SCHNEPPE, Minna, 80, NYC-M - 1913/04/
SCHNEPPER, Heinrich, 67, SP, un. carp., NYC-Bx - 1918/02/19:2g, 20:6a, 21:6a, 22:6a, = 23:2d, fam. 26:6a, mem. 1919/02/18:6a
SCHNEPPER, Margarethe, NYC-M - 1896/02/16:5a, =17:2d
SCHNERRING, Friedrich, un. machnist, NYC-M - 1895/07/27:4a
SCHNETZER, John, butcher, NYC-M - 1879/02/24:1f, 12:1d

SCHNEYDER, Konrad, surg. Instr. maker, Philadelphia, PA – 1913/02/26:1e
SCHNIERINGER, Wendelin,34, un. brewer, NYC-M - 1915//09/21:6a
SCHNITGER, August, NYC-Bx - 1914/02/23:6a
SCHNITTINGER, Freda, 16, NYC-M, + @Genl Slocum – 1904/06/18:3c
SCHNITZER, Ludvick, NYC-Bx - 1918/10/12:6a
SCHNITZER, Mary, 36, Swede, NYC-M - 1895/04/28:9e
SCHNITZER, S., 52, Barren Island, NY – 1902/05/16:3a
SCHNITZERLING, Eliza, 36, NYC-M, + @Genl Slocum – 1904/06/17:3c
SCHNITZLER, Christian, NYC-Bx - 1916/04/10:6a
SCHNITZLER, Christina, 26, NYC-Bx, + @ Genl Slocum – 1904/06/17:3c
SCHNITZLER, Helen, 12, NYC-Bx - 1918/06/27:2d
SCHNITZLER, Henry, 28, NYC-Q – 1906/07/30:2a
SCHNITZLER, Henry, 9, NYC-M – 1900/08/09:1e
SCHNITZLER, Kate, NYC-M, + @Genl Slocum – 1904/06/17:3c
SCHNITZLER, William, West Newark, NJ - 1914/09/24:6a
SCHNOHR, Anna, 82, NYC-B – 1910/07/08:6a, =9:2b
SCHNOHR, Carl Ludwig, SLP, un. cigarmaker, NYC-B - 1895/09/27: 4a
SCHNOPER, Martin, un. carp., NYC-Bx – 1909/04/14:6a
SCHNORR % Schiebakoff
SCHNORR, Adam, 47, ex- physician, now wine salesman, fr. Hessia-Darmstadt, NYC-M - 1894/11/16:3g
SCHNORR, Frank, 43, un. varnisher, NYC-M – 1892/09/13:4a
SCHNORR, Friedrich, NYC-M – 1881/10/12:3b
SCHNORR, Louis, 46, cigar maker & SPD activist expelled fr Hamburg/Gy, arrived NYC – 1881/01/19:1g, 20:4c
SCHNUERLE, Jacob, NYC-B - 1915/10/30:6a
SCHNULL, Ernestine, b. Ohnesorge, NYC-Q - 1917/04/19:6a
SCHNUPE, H. T., NYC-M, + @ Genl Slocum – 1904/06/17:3c
SCHNUR, Henry, Steinway worker?, NYC-Bx - 1920/10/13:6a
SCHNURR, Anton, NYC-M – 1901/04/19:4a
SCHNURR, Bernhard, 81, ret. brewery manager, NYC-B - 1917/03/07:2f
SCHNURR, Carl, NYC-M – 1887/08/05:3c
SCHNURR, Sophia, 51, NYC-B - 1894/01/10:4a
SCHOBER, Charles, janitor, NYC-M - 1916/07/29:1d, 30:7e
SCHOBER, Christian, ~50, shoe maker, NYC-M – 1880/11/19:1f
SCHOBER, Elsie, b. Egle, 49, NYC-B - 1920/10/25:6a
SCHOBER, George S., wholesale butcher, Jersey City, NJ – 1911/10/03:2c
SCHOBOHM, Henry, 32, NYC-M - 1894/01/29:4c
SCHOCH, Carl, mason, SPD Magdeburg/Gy – 1902/04/29:2d
SCHOCHELS, Violet, 21, @ 1911 Triangle Shirtwaist Fire, NYC-M – 1911/03/27:1d

SCHOECK, Martha, NYC-M – 1905/11/01:4a
SCHOEFER, Philip L., NYC-M – 1892/06/25:4a
SCHOEFFLIN, Melchior, un. cigarmaker, NYC-M – 1892/04/16:4a
SCHOEFFLING, Maria, 35, NYC-M, +@ Genl Slocum – 1904/06/17:3c, 18:3c
SCHOEFFLING, Wilhelm, NYC-B – 1905/01/25:4a
SCHOELCHER, Victor, 88, Alsatian abolitionist, 1893/12/27:1b
SCHOELL, ..., brewer/cooper?, NYC, fam. 1881/06/13:3b
SCHOELLER, Fr., un. cigar maker, NYC-B – 1896/10/11:5a
SCHOELLER, Frederick, 70, NYC-B – 1881/11/29:4a
SCHOELLER, John, NYC-B – 1911/05/13:6a
SCHOELLIG, Ferdinand, un. carp., NYC-B – 1912/05/13:6a
SCHOELLIG, Joseph, 2, NYC-B - 1879/02/15:3a
SCHOEMANN, Mrs, NYC-M, + @ Genl Slocum – 1904/06/18:3c
SCHOEN % Kaplan
SCHOEN, Alexander, Union Hill, NJ - 1915/03/29:6a
SCHOEN, Frederick, Rockville Centre, L.I. – 1913/09/12:2f
SCHOEN, Jacob, 65, great-secy Indep. Order Brith Abraham, cloakmaker, SLP, member NYVZ coop., USA 1880, NYC-M - 1913/06/28:5e,6a, 20,000 at =30:3f
SCHOEN, John, Republ. Ward polit., NYC-M – 1888/01/31:3a
SCHOEN, Otto C. von, Jersey City, NJ - 1918/03/27:6a
SCHOEN, Paul, machinist, NYC, + Troy, NY - 1914/02/01:7a
SCHOENBERGER, Ida, NYC-M – 1905/12/24:5b
SCHOENBERGER, Mary, 77, NYC-B – 1904/04/08:4b
SCHOENBERGER, Rosa, NYC-Bx - 1915/05/14:6a
SCHOENBORN, Charlotte, 67, NYC-M - 1914/12/04:6a; mem. – 1919/12/02:8a
SCHOENBRUNN, Emanuel, chauffeur, NYC-B – 1913/08/05:1f
SCHOENDORFF, Rudolph, Jersey City, NJ – 1898/09/09:1d
SCHOENE % Herboldsheimer
SCHOENE, August, 58, tailor, NYC-M – 1887/11/07:2h
SCHOENE, Paul, 45, un. carp., NYC-M – 1912/10/25:6a, 26:6a, fam. 29:6a
SCHOENE, William, SP Haledon, NJ, fam. 1911/05/26:6a
SCHOENEBERGER, Jacob, carp., NYC-M – 1893/09/22:4b
SCHOENECK, Frederick, 8, NYC-B – 1912/03/17:7c
SCHOENEMANN, Charles, 36, innkeep, NYC-B – 1904/03/26:4b
SCHOENEMANN, Elisa, 16, NYC-M, +@Genl Slocum – 1904/06/22:1d
SCHOENEMANN, Erich, 28, NYC-B – 1913/08/21:6a
SCHOENEMANN, John, NYC-M, + @ Genl Slocum – 1904/06/17:3c, 18:3c
SCHOENENBERGER, Nic., un. carp., NYC-M - 1915/06/20:7a

SCHOENER, Josef Oswald, 16, NYC-B - 1914/04/27:6a
SCHOENER, Paul, un. carp., NYC-M - 1918/11/21:6a
SCHOENERT, Johanna or Susanna, 30, NYC-M - 1896/04/08:4a
SCHOENFELD % Koehn
SCHOENFELD, August, 60, un. cigarmkr, NYC-Q - 1914/04/13:a, fam. 18:6a, mem. 1915/04/11:7c, 1916/04/14:6a, 1917/04/14:6a
SCHOENFELD, Sarina, NYC-M - 1893/01/10:4a
SCHOENFELDT, Emil, 53, un. typesetter, Hoboken, NJ - 1888/09/01:3b
SCHOENFELDT, Emil, un. printer, NYC-B - 1917/08/18:6a
SCHOENHARDT, Friedrich, NYC-M - 1891/03/16:4a
SCHOENHAUS % Weissenborn
SCHOENHERR, Dorothea, 76, NYC-B - 1905/10/17:4a
SCHOENHERR, Luise Auguste, 1, NYC-M - 1881/07/09:3b
SCHOENHOFF, George H., grocer, NYC-Q - 1913/08/17:11c
SCHOENHOLZ % Mueller
SCHOENIG, Elizabeth, NYC-Q - 1900/08/24:4a
SCHOENIG, Heinrich see Schoernig
SCHOENING, Anna & brother Joseph, 12, Union Hill, NJ - 1900/08/29:4a, 28:3b, 27:1g
SCHOENING, Gustav, pie-baker, NYC-B - 1879/01/06:4c, 02/22:4c
SCHOENING, H., NYC-B - 1905/07/07:4a
SCHOENING, Ottilie, 18, NYC-M - 1882/07/25:3d
SCHOENINGER, Mrs, 54, Newark, NJ - 1920/01/24:2f
SCHOENINGER, Mrs, NYC-M, +@ on Genl Slocum - 1904/06/18:3c
SCHOENLANK, Bruno, Dr., SPD MdR for Breslau/Gy, # - 1901/10/31:1e, 2c-d
SCHOENLANK, Helmut, 22, SPD Cottbus/Gy - 1915/07/11:3d
SCHOENMANN, Caroline, W. Hoboken, NJ - 1907/06/26:6a
SCHOENROCK, Ferdinand, 50, NYC-M - 1890/07/06:5a
SCHOENTAG, John, 11, NYC-Bx - 1916/09/12:6a
SCHOENWANDT, Christ., NYC-Bx - 1919/02/01:6a
SCHOENWECK, John, 62, shoemaker, NYC-B - 1904/05/21:4d
SCHOENWETTER, Henry, 24, tailor, NYC-M - 1898/04/23:2e
SCHOEPFLIN, Charles F., civil engineer, Gardenville, NY - 1912/04/06:1e
SCHOEPFLIN, Martin, un. carp., NYC-B - 1889/03/30:4a
SCHOEPP, Adelheid, NYC-M - 1887/05/26:3a
SCHOEPPELREY, August, NYC? - 1888/02/10:3b
SCHOERLEIN, Friedrich, 29, NYC-M - 1880/10/13:3b, fam. 18 Nov:3b
SCHOERNIG, Heinrich, (Schoenig?) 26, un. carp., NYC-B - 1893/01/28:4a, 29:5c, fam. 2 Fb:4a,
SCHOERNING, Gustav, butcher, NYC-M - 1885/04/30:1f
SCHOETT, Anna, NYC-M - 1899/08/04:4a

SCHOETT, Carrie & Helena, NYC-M, @Genl Slocum – 1904/06/17:3c, 18:3c
SCHOETTGE, Hermann, typesetter & SPD activist – 1908/03/08:3d
SCHOETTL, Charles, 26, NYC-B - 1918/10/11:6a
SCHOETTLING, Else, 3, NYC-M, +@ Genl Slocum – 1904/06/28:1c
SCHOFFERWITZ, Henry, tailor, Hoboken, NJ – 1880/08/19:4e
SCHOLBER, Fritz, 35, un. carp., NYC-Bx – 1910/01/27:2b, 6a, 29:6a
SCHOLDSTROM, John, 70, Swede, cigar maker, NYC-B 1895/04/27:4d
SCHOLER, F., 69, NYC-M – 1893/08/08:4a
SCHOLER, Jakob, NYC – 1885/07/21:3b
SCHOLKES-HELWIG, Henry, 60, ofc. Prussian army, mercenary in Latin Am., + Hammond, IN – 1907/02/10:1b
SCHOLL, Charles, + Cincinatti, OH – 1912/07/08:2c
SCHOLL, Dora, 81, NYC-M – 1908/06/27:1d
SCHOLL, Henry, cigar maker, NYC-M – 1880/09/27:1e, 28:1e-f, 3 Oct:4a-b, the 2 killers sentenced to jail 19 Fb 1881:1e
SCHOLL, Jacob, un. butcher, NYC-M - 1920/02/12:6a
SCHOLL, John, beer driver, NYC-M – 1880/02/16:1g
SCHOLL, Karl, religious reformer, + Munich – 1907/04/21:8b
SCHOLL, Katherine, b. Koehler, 63, NYC-M – 1892/06/23:4a
SCHOLL, Michael, NYC-B – 1912/12/17:6a
SCHOLL, Praiur, 64, paper hanger, NYC-M – 1899/07/11:2h
SCHOLL, Wilhelm, NYC-M - 1915/09/20:6a
SCHOLLE, Wendell, 23, cigarmaker fr Bohemia, NYC-M – 1891/02/28:4d
SCHOLTER, Hermann O., NYC-M – 1905/11/10:4a
SCHOLTT, John, 61, NYC-B – 1912/03/10:7c
SCHOLTZ, Joseph, 48, fr Hungary?, Harrison, NJ – 1907/08/05:6a
SCHOLTZ, Julie, Newark, NJ – 1909/09/07:6a
SCHOLZ, John Reinhardt, 79, NYC-Q – 1912/02/06:2e
SCHOLZ, Marie, 17, NYC-M – 1889/01/05:3c
SCHOMBER, Henry, NYC-M – 1901/05/04:4a, 5:5a
SCHOMBERG, Johanna, 21, NYC-M – 1897/08/28:1g
SCHOMONITZKI, John, striking coal miner, Shenandoah, PA – 1900/09/23:1a
SCHOMS, Anton, * 10 July 1859 Steinen/Switz., USA 1879, NYC-? - 1879/08/29:1g
SCHOPF, John, un. cigarmaker, NYC-M – 1881/08/02:3d
SCHOPF, Rose, 19, 1901 fr Russia, NYC-B – 1902/03/26:4a
SCHOPPE, E.R., druggist, NYC-M – 1891/08/05:1h
SCHOPPEL, E.'s, NYC-M – 1888/05/01:3a
SCHOPS, Carl, 43, accountant, Hoboken, NJ – 1913/09/04:2d, 5:1f
SCHORER % Feldmann

SCHORFELDER, Gregor, 81, dying, NYC-Bx – 1912/10/24:1f
SCHORR, Agnes, 54, SP, Newark, NJ - 1917/06/14:6a
SCHORR, Hermann, 57, So. Newark, NJ - 1914/02/05:6a
SCHORZ, Rosa, 17, NYC-B – 1901/04/01:1g
SCHOTOFF, Julius, cond. Knickerbocker Hotel Band, NYC – 1913/01/31:2d
SCHOTT % Fink, % Repp
SCHOTT, 16, NYC-M, + @Genl Slocum – 1904/06/18:1a
SCHOTT, Anton, 72, Wagnerian singer, NYC 1883-1902, +Stuttgart/Germany – 1913/01/10:2c
SCHOTT, Carrie, NYC-M, + @ Genl Slocum – 1904/06/18:3c
SCHOTT, Edward, 36, architect, NYC-M – 1882/05/02:4d, 3:4d
SCHOTT, Emil, un. baker, NYC-M - 1895/11/07: 4a
SCHOTT, Jacob, 60, NYC-SI - 1916/02/26:1d
SCHOTT, John, NYC-Q – 1913/09/06:6a
SCHOTT, Robert, 71, un. cigarmaker, NYC-M - 1917/10/18:6a
SCHOTT, Veronika, b. Mayer, 50, NYC-M – 1904/04/25:4a
SCHOTT, Wilhelm, NYC-B – 1891/07/09:4a
SCHOTTHOEFER, Konrad, Rev., of RC St Theresa, Summit, NJ - 1916/11/28:2c
SCHOTTLER, Katherina, b. Hellstern, 60, NYC-M – 1892/08/04:4a
SCHOVERING, August, 54, NYC-M – 1891/04/02:4a
SCHRADE, John, 60, Newark, NJ – 1898/11/29:3b
SCHRADER % Haehnel
SCHRADER, Ada, + Cincinatti, OH – 1912/07/08:2c
SCHRADER, Franz, 8, NYC-Hunter's Point – 1887/10/15:4e
SCHRADER, George H., metal manuf. & philantropist, left a.e. $2 mio to "Caroline's Nest" in Hartsdale, a camp for poor children, NYC-B - 1916/03/13:1b, will 19 Sept:2b, 20:1e, 4 Oct:2d
SCHRADER, Gustav, SDP, Jersey City Heights, NJ – 1900/11/23:4a, 24:4a, fam. 28:4a
SCHRADER, Johanna, 58, New Haven, CT – 1907/10/25:6a
SCHRADER, John, un. waiter, NYC-M – 1892/05/17:4a
SCHRADER, Julius, Jersey City, NJ - 1915/12/11:2b
SCHRADER, Karl, liberal MdR, + Berlin - 1913/05/08:4d
SCHRADER, M., NYC-Hunter's Pt – 1885/12/19:3b
SCHRADER, Theodor, 50, builder, SLP, ex-Hamburg-Wandsbek NYC-M - 1895/05/03:1g, =4:4c, 6:1c
SCHRAER, H., Union Hill, NJ – 1905/06/04:5b
SCHRAMM % Gonnermann, % Hirth
SCHRAMM, Adolf A., 13, NYC-Q - 1896/03/17:4a

SCHRAMM, Anna, 76, German actress, *Reichenberg/Moravia, + Berlin - 1916/06/04:1d
SCHRAMM, C. A., ex-soc., writer, + Zuerich/Switz. – 1905/04/05:2d
SCHRAMM, Carl, 30, fr Vienna, USA 1876, NYC-M – 1880/03/05:1g
SCHRAMM, Charles, un. furrier, NYC-M – 1891/01/23:4a, 22:4a
SCHRAMM, Friedrich, NYC-M – 1913/02/25:6a, 26:6a
SCHRAMM, George, 61, ex-barkeeper, NYC-B - 1920/11/23:6b
SCHRAMM, Mary, b. Costello, 21, fr Buffalo, NY, + NYC-M – 1904/08/14:5e
SCHRAMM, William, un. sheet metal worker & SP, & wife Margarethe. Both fr Schleswig-Holstein, married in Flensburg, USA 1881, in Troy, NY, then ~1890 to NYC-B, silver wedding – 1906/12/31:5e
SCHRAMMEIS, Josef, 60, Liberal polit. fr Gersdorf/Steiermark – 1908/11/01:3e; trial of his murd. 1908/12/17:4a-b
SCHRAMMER, Eduard, 45, lawyer, SPD Koeln – 1912/08/12:4e
SCHRANK, Genofeva, b. Frueh, 65, NYC-M – 1897/08/05:4a
SCHRAPNER, Adam, 67, NYC-M – 1899/09/19:3f
SCHRAPPL, Eduard, un. carp., NYC? – 1883/06/12:3a
SCHRATT, Katharina, actress & lover of Emperor Franz Josef, + Vienna, - 1918/01/13:1f
SCHRATWEISER, Jacob, 40, concrete manufacturer, NYC-B – 1908/04/22:3c
SCHRAUB, John, 65, cigar packer, NYC-M – 1896/05/12:1h
SCHRAUER, John, 40, hotelier, Swiss, NYC-M -1895/08/07:3d, 13:4a
SCHRAUER, Pauline, 40, NYC-M – 1889/07/30:4e
SCHRAUMANN, Mathilde, 36, Jersey City Heights, NJ – 1891/03/15:5b
SCHRECK, Adam, 60, carp., Hoboken, NJ – 1909/09/18:2e
SCHRECK, Bertha, b. Kuehne, 37, Hoboken, NJ – 1907/05/12:7b
SCHRECK, Harry, 51, SP, * France, Dover, NJ - 1916/02/24:6a,c, =27:11b
SCHRECK, Victor, 46, Arlington, NJ - 1918/11/30:6a
SCHRECKGAST, Wilhelm, 54, Jersey City, NJ – 1905/04/21:3d
SCHREIB, Lilian, b. Glover, feminist writer, NYC-M – 1911/05/31:2e, 1 June:1e, 2:1e, 3:1f, 5:1f, 7:1c, 8:1e
SCHREIBELS, Catherina, b. Haas, 72, NYC-M – 1892/09/22:4a
SCHREIBER % Obert,
SCHREIBER, Albert, upholsterer, High Bridge, NJ – 1913/01/26:11a
SCHREIBER, Caroline, b. Bovegel, NYC-M – 1891/06/23:4a
SCHREIBER, Charles, 22, Newark, NJ – 1899/05/22:3b
SCHREIBER, Conrad, worker, Newark, NJ – 1880/07/11:5f
SCHREIBER, David, 55, Rabbi at Bushwick Ave Syn., NYC-B – 1902/04/25:1b

SCHREIBER, Eduard, 31, shoemaker & SPD activist expelled fr Hamburg/Gy, arrived NYC – 1881/01/19:1g, 20:4c; SP, +Newark, NJ - 1917/05/09:2f
SCHREIBER, Felix, Dr., 37, music conductor, War 1 - 1914/10/11:1c
SCHREIBER, Frederick, 30, cigar store, Jersey City, NJ – 1909/07/03:3b
SCHREIBER, Friedrich, machinist, NYC-M – 1887/06/21:3c
SCHREIBER, Helene, NYC-M – 1911/10/17:6a, fam. 19:6a
SCHREIBER, Henry, barrel maker, NYC-M - 1894/09/16:5c
SCHREIBER, Hermann, un. carp., NYC-M – 1910/02/09:6a
SCHREIBER, John C., editor Utica Deutsche Zeitung, + Utica, NY – 1907/11/10:1d
SCHREIBER, John, 56, mason, NYC-B – 1906/06/02:1g
SCHREIBER, John, NYC anarchist, note (not +) – 1910/04/03:1d, 7e-f
SCHREIBER, John, NYC-B – 1908/09/25:6a
SCHREIBER, Joseph F., NYC-M – 1896/07/23:4a
SCHREIBER, Louis, 73, *Geyer/Saxony, NYC-Q – 1905/11/29:4a
SCHREIBER, Max, 24, fishmarket worker, NYC-M – 1892/07/14:1h
SCHREIBER, Walter, 3, NYC-Q – 1906/03/02:4a
SCHREIBER, William, Elizabeth, NJ - 1914/02/07:6a
SCHREIER % Quade
SCHREIFER, Leo, 29, silkweaver, Paterson, NJ – 1897/06/17:1e, 18:1e
SCHREIGERT, Carl, 48, technical drawer, NYC-B – 1900/05/24:3b
SCHREINER, Bernhardt, NYC-M – 1911/04/21:6a
SCHREINER, Joseph, 41, builder, NYC-M – 1904/06/22:1e
SCHREINER, Joseph, NYC-B – 1890/01/20:4a
SCHREINER, Mamie, NYC-B – 1904/07/07:4a
SCHREINER, Thomas Ernst, 52, Jersey City, NJ – 1889/04/07:5c
SCHREINERT, John G., 35, chemist, ex-Chicago, Jersey City, NJ – 1907/02/23:3b
SCHREITER % Jahn
SCHREITER, Oskar, tailor, SLP, fr Saxony, USA ~1882, NYC-M – 1888/06/18:1f, 2g, 3b, 19:3b, =20:2g, fam. 21:3b
SCHRELL, Anton, 41, NYC-M - 1914/01/13:6a
SCHREMP, John, 60, security guard, NYC-B – 1909/11/23:6a
SCHRENK, Egidius Richard, un. carp.,NYC-Q - 1915/10/02:6a,3:7a
SCHRENZ % Binder
SCHREY, Sarah, 45, NYC-M – 1908/03/21:1d
SCHREYER, Benjamin, 56, NYC-M – 1892/08/08:4a
SCHREYER, John F., 29, realtor, NYC-M – 1912/02/03:6c
SCHRIEBER, J.F., un. cigarmaker, NYC-M - 1879/02/02:4a
SCHRIEBLE, Elizabeth, 20, fr Gy on SS Weimar, + NYC-M – 1893/01/07:1h

SCHRIEFER, John, NYC-M – 1906/03/24:4a
SCHRIEVER, Johann F., 65, un. cigarmaker, NYC-M – 1899/04/06:4a
SCHRIFFER, William, 24, bartender, Newark, NJ – 1897/08/14:3f
SCHRIMPF, Paulina Beck, 58, NYC-B - 1918/10/14:6a
SCHRING, Frank, 1, NYC-M – 1897/07/24:1e
SCHROBSDORF, Franz, NYC-M – 1911/02/14:6a
SCHROEDER % Brennecke, % Faatz, % Hopfer
SCHROEDER, Adolph, NYC-B – 1901/07/09:4a
SCHROEDER, Alma, Hoboken, NJ – 1890/05/07:4a
SCHROEDER, Anna, 50, NYC-Bx – 1910/09/03:6a
SCHROEDER, August, 32, SLP, NYC-B – 1882/07/29:3c, 30:8a, =31:1f, fam. 9 Aug:3d
SCHROEDER, August, 41, NYC-M - 1914/10/21:6a
SCHROEDER, August, infant, NYC-B – 1882/05/11:3c
SCHROEDER, Auguste, 29, NYC-B – 1901/04/03:4b
SCHROEDER, Carl, un. cigarmaker, NYC-M - 1895/08/08: 4a
SCHROEDER, Charles F., NYC-M – 1912/06/09:11d
SCHROEDER, Christian, 63, NYC-M – 1880/07/27:1g
SCHROEDER, Christian, 73?, NYC-B – 1889/03/22:4a
SCHROEDER, Dr., SP Buffalo, NY, + Neapel/Italy – 1912/03/26:2d
SCHROEDER, Elizabeth, Trenton, NJ - 1915/12/09:2f
SCHROEDER, Emil F., 20, NYC-M – 1886/01/27:3b
SCHROEDER, Emma, b. Heyde, NYC-M – 1899/07/15:4a
SCHROEDER, Ernst, 25, mason, dying, NYC-Q – 1911/07/28:2a
SCHROEDER, Ernst, 55, un. tailor, NYC-B – 1899/11/27:4a
SCHROEDER, Eva, 60, NYC-M – 1882/11/05:5d
SCHROEDER, Frederick A., cigarmaker, 1875 mayor of Brooklyn, *Trier/Gy – 1899/12/02:2h
SCHROEDER, Frederick, NYC-M – 1907/11/07:6a
SCHROEDER, Frederick., 52, *Krefeld/Gy, former US consul in Koeln/Gy, War 2 New Orleans, LO - 1917/05/24:1d
SCHROEDER, Friedrich, 72, painter, SP, *Laasphe/Westfalia, Gy, NYC-B – 1912/05/02:6a, 4:6a, =8:5e-f
SCHROEDER, Friedrich, 59, NYC-M – 1890/03/16:5b
SCHROEDER, Friedrich, 62, un. tailor, NYC-B – 1890/03/29:4a, 30:4a
SCHROEDER, Geraldine, 42, May, 8, Hy, 10, NYC-B – 1911/05/23:3a-b
SCHROEDER, Gustav, 42, tailor, NYC-M – 1896/12/17:1e
SCHROEDER, Heinrich, un. cigarmaker, NYC-M – 1887/06/01:3c
SCHROEDER, Henry L., un. cigarmkr, *15/10/42 Malchow/Gy, SDP, Holyoke, MA – 1901/05/10:1g
SCHROEDER, Henry, Hoboken, NJ - 1918/11/03:12a
SCHROEDER, Henry, NYC-B – 1903/02/02:4a

SCHROEDER, Henry, plumber, Jersey City, NJ - 1915/08/20:1e
SCHROEDER, Henry, un. carp., NYC-M - 1898/03/23:4a
SCHROEDER, Hugo, 33, Jersey City Heights, NJ - 1910/01/30:3c
SCHROEDER, Jennie, 16, NYC-M - 1879/01/07:1g
SCHROEDER, John F., 49, NYC-M - 1891/04/06:4a
SCHROEDER, John William, 34, NYC-M - 1880/01/31:1f
SCHROEDER, John, NYC-M - 1905/04/28:4a
SCHROEDER, John, un. carp., NYC-M - 1904/09/10:4a
SCHROEDER, Josef, NYC-M - 1918/06/23:7a
SCHROEDER, Josephine, b. Geiger, NYC-M - 1918/10/07:6a
SCHROEDER, Lena, un. cigarmaker, NYC-M - 1893/12/17:5d
SCHROEDER, Louise, 2, NYC-B - 1879/05/08:3a
SCHROEDER, Magdalena, b. Ruggaber, 60, fr Nordstetten/Wuertt., NYC-B - 1883/01/13:3a
SCHROEDER, Magdalena, NYC-B - 1906/06/21:6a
SCHROEDER, Magnus, NYC-M - 1891/03/17:4a
SCHROEDER, Margareth, 64, NYC-M - 1882/07/29:4c
SCHROEDER, Margarethe, b. Hasche, 71, NYC-M - 1891/03/16:4a
SCHROEDER, Minna, b. Bergmann, NYC-M - 1896/06/13:4a
SCHROEDER, Mrs, NYC-M - 1884/09/10:3b
SCHROEDER, Nicholas, Jersey City, NJ - 1882/04/07:3a
SCHROEDER, Oskar, Swede, Southampton, LI - 1908/09/17:3a-b
SCHROEDER, Paul, un. machinist, NYC-M - 1907/08/14:6a
SCHROEDER, Peter (born Kleinhaus), to marry, NYC-B - 1900/12/06:4b
SCHROEDER, Peter, 35, Jersey City, NJ - 1898/12/27:3c
SCHROEDER, Peter, produce wholesaler, NYC-B - 1899/12/29:1f
SCHROEDER, Robert, 38, NYC - 1900/08/20:1e, 4a
SCHROEDER, Sarah, 37, wife of Rabbi Schroeder, NYC - 1899/07/29:2h
SCHROEDER, Theodor, mason & SPD activist expelled fr Wandsbek/Gy, arrived NYC - 1881/06/16:4a
SCHROEDER, Wilhelm, 27, nail smith, SPD activist expelled fr Hamburg/Gy, arrived in NYC - 1881/01/19:1g, 20:4c
SCHROEDER, Wilhelm, 36?, un. cigar maker, NYC-M - 1891/09/26:4a
SCHROEDER, Wilhelm, SP, *near Berlin 1860s, USA 1889, NYC-M - 1914/08/31:6a, 1 Se:5f,6a
SCHROEDER, Wilhelm, SPD Berlin-Wilmersdorf, un. cigar sorter & alderman - 1913/11/19:4d, =Hamburg 30:3a
SCHROEDER, William, 14, NYC-B - 1909/07/16:3a
SCHROEDER, William, Elizabeth,NJ - 1915/04/24:6a
SCHROEDER, William, un. baker, NYC-B - 1904/04/30:4b
SCHROEDER-DEVRIENT, Wilhelmine, 1804-1860, German actress, 100th anniv. - 1904/12/25:4c-d

SCHROEDLE, Joseph, NYC-Bx - 1917/04/11:6a
SCHROEFFEL, Mrs, + 29.I.16, NYC-M - 1916/02/17:1d
SCHROER, Frederick., Newark, NJ - 1918/11/05:6a
SCHROER, Henry, waiter, NYC-M – 1910/10/27:6a
SCHROETER, Eduard, 77, fr Hildesheim area to USA 1850, + Sauk City, IA – 1888/04/28:2c
SCHROETER, Louis, NYC-M – 1912/08/29:6a
SCHROETWIESER, S., 66, NYC-B – 1893/10/25:4a
SCHROFF, Josef, SPD Bierstadt/Frankfurt, War 1 - 1914/11/01:3b
SCHROLL, Lena, NYC-M – 1880/03/26:4a
SCHRONK, John, 59, un. tailor, NYC-M – 1886/03/10:3c
SCHROTH, John, 16, & Bertha, 6, Newark, NJ – 1887/11/24:3a
SCHROTZ, Heinrich, un. carp., NYC-B – 1884/10/02:3c
SCHROTZ, Theodor, 37, un. carp., NYC-M – 1910/07/12:6a, 13:6a
SCHROTZ, Thespold, un. carp., NYC-Q – 1913/10/14:6a, 15:6a
SCHRUL, Paul, Wakefield, NY - 1916/02/24:6a
SCHRUM, Maria, b. Flohr, NYC-M 1895/05/18:4a
SCHRUMM, Ida, 58, NYC-M - 1878/02/06:4e
SCHRUMPF, John & William, NYC-M, + @ Genl Slocum – 1904/06/17:3c, 18:3c
SCHUBACH, Henry, NYC-M – 1891/07/05:5a
SCHUBACH, retired tailor, NYC-M – 1888/03/06:1c
SCHUBERT % Havel
SCHUBERT, Adam, 59, un. carp., NYC-M – 1897/09/22:4a
SCHUBERT, Barbara, 54, NYC-B - 1919/05/25:12a
SCHUBERT, Friedrich, SP?, member Brooklyn Labor Lyceum, + Sellersville, PA - 1918/10/22:6a
SCHUBERT, George, NYC-M – 1907/04/18:6a
SCHUBERT, Hans, 40, ship's baker, see 1900 dock fire, Hoboken, NJ 1900/07/03:1c
SCHUBERT, Hermann, un. carp., NYC-M - 1914/05/29:6a
SCHUBERT, John Vollmar, Dr., 46, SP, teacher at HS 46, NYC-Bx - 1916/08/09:2c
SCHUBERT, Karl, un. bricklayer, NYC-Q - 1915/12/04:6a
SCHUBERT, Max, NYC-M – 1909/03/08:6a
SCHUBERT, Nicolaus, Jersey City, NJ – 1890/10/21:2f
SCHUBERT, Stephan, un. painter, NYC – 1913/09/15:6a, 16:6a
SCHUBERT, Susan Hermann, 43, NYC-M - 1920/09/20:6a
SCHUBERT, Theodor, 51, un. woodcarver, NYC-M – 1911/03/04:6a
SCHUCH, Jacob, un. carpenter,NYC-M - 1895/06/23:4a, 07/01: 4a
SCHUCH, Karl, 66, NYC - 1913/11/21:6a
SCHUCH, Philipp, NYC-M - 1914/10/03:6a

SCHUCHMANN, Florence A., infant, NYC-B – 1891/06/21:5a
SCHUCHMANN, Sophie, b. Leutenegger, 48, NYC-B - 1916/02/25:6a
SCHUCHMANN, William, NYC-M – 1891/05/04:4a
SCHUCK, Christina, 66, NYC-B – 1882/04/24:3b
SCHUCKMANN, Philip Valentin, 35, ex-teacher fr Alzey/Hessen, USA 1891, NYC-M – 1896/06/03:3f
SCHUEFFLER, Emma, Hoboken, NJ – 1898/08/25:4c
SCHUEFFLER, Sophie, 63, NYC-M, +Genl Slocum – 1904/06/25:1c
SCHUEFFNER, Emil, Dr., lawyer, * Saxony, '48er, USA 1850, Newark, NJ - 1878/07/24:1f
SCHUELE, Joseph, 43, NYC-M – 1908/01/01:6a, 2:6a
SCHUELEIN, Fritz's, NYC-M – 1888/07/19:3b
SCHUELER % Mayer
SCHUELER, Adam, 29, NYC-M – 1881/08/06:4a
SCHUELER, Caspar's child, NYC-M – 1880/06/30:1b
SCHUELER, Charlotte, b. Vollbracht, NYC-M - 1878/04/24:3b
SCHUELER, Herman, 64, un. carp., SDP, NYC-M – 1901/12/21:3a, 22:1b, 5a, fam. 29:5a
SCHUELER, John, un. carp., NYC-B – 1902/10/13:4a
SCHUENEMANN, ..., little son of W., NYC-M – 1881/04/07:3a
SCHUENEMANN, Wilhelm, 64, un. cigarmaker, SP, *6 Ap 1844 Olenrode/Hannover, USA 1882, Manchester, NH – 1908/02/19:6a
SCHUENEMANN, Wilhelm, NYC-M – 1892/06/15:4a
SCHUENHOFF, Eduard, miner, SPD Borne/Saxony/Gy– 1908/04/26:3d
SCHUENZEL, Louis, NYC-B - 1915/05/26:6a
SCHUERER, Carl Eduard, 93, SP?, NYC-M - 1917/08/19:7a, fam. 21:6a
SCHUERMANN, Lizzie, Hoboken, NJ – 1897/08/04:1f
SCHUERSTAEDT, Lisette, 5, NYC-M - 1895/03/18:4a
SCHUERSTEDT, Anna, 5, NYC-M – 1880/06/16:3a
SCHUERSTEDT, John Hermann, 48, SPL, un. cigarmaker, NYC-M – 1898/03/19:1c, 4a,20:5c,=21:1g
SCHUESSLER, Louis, 34, Jersey City, NJ – 1889/05/15:4a
SCHUESSLER, Max, 60, leather worker, NYC-M – 1902/08/22:3h
SCHUESSLER, Therese, b. Hartman, 59, SDP?, NYC-M – 1903/09/06:5a
SCHUETTE % Weiss
SCHUETTE, Richard, NYC-M? – 1913/03/07·6a
SCHUETTGEN, Christian, 26, NYC-M – 1898/01/02:5e
SCHUETTIG, NYC-M - 1917/06/27:6a
SCHUETTLER, Georg, fr Frankfurt/Main, USA 1881, NYC-M – 1883/06/02:1g
SCHUETZ % Meissner
SCHUETZ, Adolf, NYC-B - 1914/03/27:6a

SCHUETZ, Charles, 42, sales mgr for American Book Co., NYC-Q - 1920/08/06:1f
SCHUETZ, Fritz, *1834 Apolda/Gy, publ. Rundschau, New Ulm, MN - 1888/04/28:2c
SCHUETZ, Heinrich, 50, peddler, NYC-B - 1893/09/14:3c
SCHUETZ, John, un. bricklayer, NYC-M - 1893/02/28:4a
SCHUETZ, Louis, Newark, NJ - 1902/12/21:5c
SCHUETZ, Paul, West Newark, NJ - 1914/03/18:6a
SCHUETZE, Karl, 43, NYC-B - 1903/01/23:4a
SCHUETZINGER, Adam A., * 24 Dec 1826 Muenchen/Gy, NYC-M - 1885/09/04:3a
SCHUETZLER % Hildebrandt
SCHUETZLER, Emil, NYC-M - 1911/11/18:6a
SCHUFFLAY, Joseph, 46, & wife Aranka, b. Boldoghy, NYC-Bx - 1914/01/10:6a, 12:6d, 13:6c
SCHUG, Henry, NYC-Bx - 1914/02/17:6a
SCHUHBAUER, Josef, Edgewater, NJ - 1917/01/15:6a, mem. 1918/01/14:6a; 1920/01/14:6a
SCHUHMACHER, John Francis, US Army, War 1 Mexico, NYC-B - 1914/05/13:2d
SCHUHMANN, John, NYC-Bx - 1913/03/09:7b
SCHUHMANN, Michael, Union Hill, NJ - 1901/07/03:1f
SCHUHMEIER, Franz, SP militant in Vienna, murdered, NYC workers outraged 1913/02/13:2c, 4a, 14:4d, =16:4a, more on the case 23:1c, 26:4d-f, 27:4d-f, 28:4e-f, workers in NYC & Philadelphia grieve 20:2f, 21:2d, his grave 3 Mr:4d, 8:4d, trial 23:1b, 3 June:4e-f, 25 Sept:4c, 26:4d, murderer Paul Kunschak pardonned to 20 yrs instead of death 1 Nov:4e; 4:4e-f, 5:4f-g,6:4d-f,8:3b, monument on his grave inaug. 1914/03/08:3a-b,
SCHUKELER, Moika, NYC-M - 1897/06/17:4a
SCHUKOSKY, Jakob, Pole, striker at Standard Coke Works, Morewood near Mt Pleasant, PA - 1891/04/03:1b, =4:1a-b, 5:1f, 4a
SCHULBERG, Nathan, 40, cigarmaker, NYC-M - 1902/01/01:2g
SCHULD, Anna, 51, Newark, NJ - 1910/04/04:3b
SCHULDNER, Abraham, 35, glazier, NYC-B - 1913/04/05:3a
SCHULDT % Reimer
SCHULDT, August, 42, un. carp., NYC-B - 1913/11/24:6a
SCHULENBURG, Anna, 41, Hoboken, NJ - 1878/05/23:3b
SCHULENBURG, Anni, b. Bruemmer, NYC-M - 1903/03/21:5b
SCHULENBURG, Georg von der, Prussian caval. Off., USA 1896, NYC-M - 1908/09/30:1f
SCHULENBURG, Philipp, 27, NYC-B - 1904/05/09:4a
SCHULER, Andreas, NYC-M - 1914/08/15:6a

SCHULER, Charles & Frederick, NYC-M, +@ Genl Slocum – 1904/06/17:3c, 18:3c
SCHULER, Louise, 41, Yonkers, NY - 1917/03/13:6a
SCHULER, William, NYC-M – 1905/03/20:4a
SCHULHOF, A., Newark, NJ – 1913/01/31:6a
SCHULHOFF, Anton, 50, NYC-M – 1890/08/10:4a
SCHULHOFF, Marie, 52, NYC-M – 1890/09/03:4a
SCHULKNECHT, Heinrich, un. typesetter, NYC-M – 1904/04/13:4a, 14:4a
SCHULKNECHT, Marie, 83, NYC-B – 1896/07/21:4a
SCHULLER, Elsie, Newark, NJ - 1920/02/08:12a
SCHULLER, John, 65, Newark, NJ - 1918/07/06:6a, fam. 14:12a, mem. 1919/07/04:6a
SCHULLMEYER, Paul, 41, carp., NYC – 1904/09/06:2f
SCHULMAN, Levi, 75, NYC-B – 1893/04/02:5a
SCHULMERICH, William, 40, cigar dealer, NYC – 1902/12/06:3c
SCHULT, J. A., 50, Newark, NJ – 1892/09/22:4e
SCHULTE, Gerhard, 44, sailor on SS Bremen, + Hoboken, NJ – 1880/02/26:4e
SCHULTE, Johann Heinrich, estate owner fr Baroy/Dortmund/Gy, murdered Norwalk, CT - 1879/01/02:1e, 7:1g, 13:1f-g, 02/11: 1e-g, 24:1d, 27:1e, new trial of murderer 1880/02/19:1f, 2c, 20:4c, 21:1g, etc,
SCHULTE, Mary, 18, NYC-M – 1904/01/19:4a fam. 24:5a
SCHULTE, Paul, 57, un. cigarmaker, NYC-B - 1916/09/25:6a, 26:6a, fam. 29:6a
SCHULTE, Wilhelm, 55, un. cigarmaker, NYC-M – 1912/01/12:6a
SCHULTEN, Lizzie, 22, NYC-B – 1879/05/16:4e, 17:4e
SCHULTHEISS, Adolf, 54, NYC-M – 1894/01/31:4a
SCHULTHEISS, John Leonhardt, 52, NYC-B - 1913/07/05:6a
SCHULTHEISS, Marie, SP?, NYC-B - 1920/08/07:6a, fam. 11:6a
SCHULTHEISS, Ph., Newark, NJ - 1914/03/09:7b
SCHULTHEISS, Reinhard, 2, NYC-M – 1907/02/22:6a
SCHULTHEISS, Thilmenia, NYC-Q – 1904/01/25:3b
SCHULTHEISS, William, NYC-M – 1913/04/29:6a
SCHULTS, Rudolph, 62, innkeep, NYC-B – 1881/05/26:1e
SCHULTZ, A.B., ex-cartoonist for Puck - 1913/11/19:2c
SCHULTZ, Albert D., policeman, NYC-B – 1900/05/23:2g
SCHULTZ, Albin, 58, insurance agent, USA 1890, War 2, NYC-B - 1915/10/20:6d
SCHULTZ, Alex, NYC-Q – 1904/06/04:4c
SCHULTZ, Bernard, tobacco dealer, & wife, Jersey City, NJ – 1897/12/18:2e

SCHULTZ, Bertha, widow of local SP member, Syracuse, NY – 1913/03/06:2a
SCHULTZ, Blanche, b. Friar, NYC-Bx - 1920/08/27:1e, 28:2b, 29:2d, 30 Sept:1e
SCHULTZ, Carl, ca. 40, NYC-B? – 1893/03/20:1f
SCHULTZ, Carl, tailor & mayor of Little Ferry, NJ – 1912/02/18:1a, 23:2c
SCHULTZ, Charles A., 55, contractor, Union Hill, NJ – 1898/01/07:3d
SCHULTZ, Christian S., 80, NYC-B – 1908/06/12:3a
SCHULTZ, Christina, 81, NYC-Q – 1909/06/25:3b
SCHULTZ, Clara, Jersey City Heights, NJ - 1919/02/21:6a
SCHULTZ, Dona, 7, NYC-M, @enl Slocum – 1904/06/25:1d
SCHULTZ, Eduard, 40, NYC-B – 1908/07/08:1e
SCHULTZ, Emma, & Rudolph, Henry & a little girl, NYC-M, + @ Genl Slocum – 1904/06/18:3c
SCHULTZ, Emma, 10, NYC-M, + @on Genl Slocum – 1904/06/17:3c
SCHULTZ, Ethel, stenographer, NYC-B - 1916/03/29:1d
SCHULTZ, Eva, 35, Elizabeth, NJ – 1913/01/22:2b
SCHULTZ, F. W., artist fr Chicago, + Alexandria, VA – 1909/03/19:1c
SCHULTZ, Franz, 28, Hoboken, NJ – 1900/02/21:4a
SCHULTZ, Frederick Leopold, 68, NYC-M - 1917/08/02:6a, 3:6a, mem. 1918/08/01:6a
SCHULTZ, Frederick, 40, NYC-B – 1908/05/06:3b
SCHULTZ, Frederick, 42, Hoboken, NJ – 1900/05/22:1e
SCHULTZ, Georg, NYC-M – 1880/11/26:3a
SCHULTZ, George, 45, NYC-B – 1908/04/29:6a
SCHULTZ, Gustav, 24, Newark, NJ – 1882/07/28:1f
SCHULTZ, Gustav, 35, un. pianomaker, NYC-Bx – 1890/11/07:4a
SCHULTZ, H., NYC-M – 1907/12/17:6a
SCHULTZ, Heinrich, 9, NYC-B – 1891/04/06:4a
SCHULTZ, Herman Paul, exec. Milford, PA – 1897/12/08:1h
SCHULTZ, Hermann, 48,coal & ice-dealer,NYC-B - 1916/11/17:6b
SCHULTZ, Jacob, 47, NYC-M – 1891/04/12:5a
SCHULTZ, Jacob, 75, carp., NYC-SI - 1916/05/10:3g
SCHULTZ, Joseph, ret. hat manuf., NYC-M – 1913/07/29:2b
SCHULTZ, Julius, Newark, NJ - 1919/06/28:6a
SCHULTZ, K's wife, 39, NYC-Q – 1902/12/06:5b
SCHULTZ, Katherine, NYC-B - 1914/10/05:2e
SCHULTZ, Kilian, 47, cigar dealer, NYC-M – 1886/09/04:3a
SCHULTZ, Lieschen, 2, NYC-M – 1889/04/26:4a
SCHULTZ, Lizzie, NYC, + Shohola, PA – 1896/10/01:1f
SCHULTZ, Louis F., 40, * Buffalo, fdr Detroit Philharmonic Club, + Detroit, MI – 1896/12/17:1a

SCHULTZ, Louis, 19, New Brighton, NJ – 1892/07/07:4c, 9:4b
SCHULTZ, Louisa, NYC-M – 1901/12/10:4b
SCHULTZ, Louise, b. Mueller, 47, NYC-M – 1891/05/29:4a
SCHULTZ, Marie, NYC-Bx – 1909/11/23:6a
SCHULTZ, Mary, 38, NYC-M - 1916/02/02:5e
SCHULTZ, Max, 43, un. cigarmaker, then innkeep, SP, * Breslau/Gy, NYC-M – 1908/11/11:2a, 6a, fam. 16:6a, =18:2b
SCHULTZ, Max, USA 1895 fr Gy, NYC-B – 1896/05/01:4d
SCHULTZ, Otto, 27, collector, NYC-M – 1893/05/10:4d
SCHULTZ, Paul, electro-technician, Kearney, NJ – 1905/05/29:3e
SCHULTZ, Peter, 28, iron monger, NYC-B – 1898/07/24:1g
SCHULTZ, Peter, 65, NYC-M – 1897/08/29:11c
SCHULTZ, Robert, 37, businessman, NYC-B – 1907/08/30:3a
SCHULTZ, Thomas, exec. Chicago, IL – 1912/02/16:1b, done 17:1c
SCHULTZ, William, 54, waiter, NYC-M – 1890/07/01:2g,4a
SCHULTZ, William, 69, NYC-B – 1913/09/02:6a
SCHULTZ, William, baker, NYC-B – 1910/04/20:3b
SCHULTZE % Krebs
SCHULTZE, Albert C., 62, ex-pres. Turnverein, Union Hill, NJ - 1918/01/05:2d,6a
SCHULTZE, Frederick, clothes dealer, NYC-M – 1911/06/03:1d
SCHULTZE, Friedrich, un. carp., NYC-M – 1900/05/26:4a, 27:5a
SCHULTZE, Fritz, 2, NYC-M – 1891/05/07:4a
SCHULTZE, Fritz, SLP, NYC-M - 1894/01/08:4a
SCHULTZE, Gustav, 17, Southhampton, LI – 1912/02/07:3a
SCHULTZE, Henry, 69, janitor,& Annie, 60, NYC-M - 1918/02/24:11c
SCHULTZE, Karl Friedrich Wilhelm, SPD MdR for Koenigsberg, * Sternau/Oder, locksmith, – 1897/03/18:2c, 4 Apr:1b, = 18 Apr:9d-e
SCHULZ % Rapp
SCHULZ, Adam, NYC-M – 1892/06/19:5c
SCHULZ, Agnes, b. Natajewski, NYC-B - 1913/12/16:6a, fam. 19:6a
SCHULZ, Alma, child, NYC-M – 1901/05/17:4a
SCHULZ, Annie, NYC-M – 1902/10/18:4a
SCHULZ, August, 71, SP, un. cigarmaker, NYC-Bx - 1918/03/05:6a, 6:6a, fam. 12:6a
SCHULZ, Auguste, b. Schmidt, NYC-M – 1890/07/26:4a
SCHULZ, Carl, un. typesetter, NYC-M – 1896/11/18:4a
SCHULZ, Charles, NYC-B – 1904/11/17:4a
SCHULZ, Eduard, un. butcher, NYC-B - 1916/04/09:7a
SCHULZ, Emil, NYC-Q – 1914/05/21:6a
SCHULZ, Ferd., 63, un. cigarmaker, NYC-M – 1904/05/02:4a
SCHULZ, Fritz, NYC-M – 1909/05/04:6a

SCHULZ, Gustav, Dr., NYC-B - 1919/02/15:6a
SCHULZ, Henry, 40, un. watchmaker, NYC-B - 1916/06/26:6a,b, 27:6a
SCHULZ, Henry, Hoboken, NJ - 1917/04/27:6a
SCHULZ, Hermann, Hoboken, NJ - 1917/09/16:7a
SCHULZ, J., NYC-M – 1910/11/16:6a
SCHULZ, Jacob, 46, NYC-B – 1891/07/09:4a
SCHULZ, Jacob, un. carp., NYC-M – 1907/03/04:6a
SCHULZ, Jenny, NYC-M – 1892/06/11:4a
SCHULZ, John, Elizabeth, NJ - 1916/05/13:6a
SCHULZ, Karl, un. waiter, NYC-M - 1894/03/13:4a
SCHULZ, Kathrine, NYC-B - 1913/06/01:7b
SCHULZ, L., 67, NYC-M – 1893/06/13:4a
SCHULZ, Lena, 42, fr Pirmasens/Gy, NYC-M – 1905/01/15:5b
SCHULZ, Marie, 30, Jersey City, NJ – 1904/03/23:4a, 24:3c
SCHULZ, Markus, 60, NYC-M – 1900/03/22:4a, 24:3e
SCHULZ, NYC, trial in Milford, PA cont – 1897/06/11:1d
SCHULZ, Paul, NYC-Q – 1919/10/30:6a
SCHULZ, Paul's wife, SP, 43rd birthday, NYC-Q – 1911/09/27:5e
SCHULZ, Sophie, b. Frank, 55, NYC-Bx – 1913/10/17:6a
SCHULZ, Wilhelmine, 49, NYC-Bx – 1907/05/31:6a
SCHULZ, William, 58, wallet maker, NYC-B – 1909/07/09:3b
SCHULZE, August, NYC-M - 1916/06/26:6a
SCHULZE, August, un. bricklayer, NYC-Q - 1916/12/22:6a, 23:6a, mem. 1917/12/20:6a
SCHULZE, Elisa, NYC-M – 1889/05/03:4a
SCHULZE, Emil's son, 17, NYC, Yale student, + New Haven, CT – 1880/01/21:1g
SCHULZE, Franz, child, NYC-M - 1895/03/13:4c
SCHULZE, Gustav, NYC-Q - 1914/04/20:6a
SCHULZE, Hermann, 36, NYC-B – 1893/05/14:5b
SCHULZE, Hermann, NYC-B – 1888/10/16:3a
SCHULZE, R., NYC-M – 1891/04/06:1d
SCHULZE, Wilhelm Ludwig, 49, druggist, NYC-B – 1908/07/03:5b,6a
SCHULZE, Wilhelm,63, un. metal worker, NYC-Bx - 1915/07/25:7a
SCHULZE-DELITZSCH, Hermann, liberal polit.,MdR, negat. obit – 1883/04/30:1c, 6 May:4c-d, 13:4c-e, = 21 May:4e; 100th anniv., – 1908/08/31:4c-d
SCHUM, Lena, 29, NYC-B – 1907/08/23:3a, 27:3a
SCHUMACHER, Anna, 17, Rochester, NY – 1909/08/10:1e
SCHUMACHER, Catherine Louise, 14, NYC-M, +@ Genl Slocum – 1904/06/18:3c
SCHUMACHER, Charles, 24, NYC-B – 1893/05/14:5b

SCHUMACHER, Charles, Hoboken, NJ, see 1900 North German Lloyd Fire 1900/07/01:1c
SCHUMACHER, comrade, SPD activist, + Duennwald/Rhineland – 1906/09/17:4c-d
SCHUMACHER, Edward, 61, NYC-Bx – 1908/02/19:6a
SCHUMACHER, Frederick, 60, Newark, NJ – 1910/12/07:1d
SCHUMACHER, Friedrich, 43, NYC-B - 1915/07/20:6a, 21:6a
SCHUMACHER, Fritz, NYC-M – 1893/12/27:4a
SCHUMACHER, Fritz, NYC-M - 1916/01/27:6a
SCHUMACHER, Harry, 64, SDP, NYC-M – 1904/05/17:4a, 18:4a
SCHUMACHER, Lena, 19, Saugerties, NY, + NYC-M – 1909/06/08:1f
SCHUMACHER, Lizzie, NYC? – 1903/11/23:1g
SCHUMACHER, Lottie, 22, NYC-M – 1896/05/01:1e
SCHUMACHER, Louise, b. Feldmann, 28, NYC-M – 1893/04/07:4a
SCHUMACHER, Ludwig, brewer or cooper, NYC-M – 1905/09/21:4a
SCHUMACHER, Rose, 13, NYC-B – 1905/11/03:3c
SCHUMACHER, Sarah, 53, NYC-M - 1894/01/24:4a
SCHUMACHER, Sebastian, un. carp., NYC-B - 1914/10/26:6a
SCHUMADZI, Julia, 35, landlady, Jersey City, NJ – 1904/04/26:1e
SCHUMANN % Albrecht, Haas
SCHUMANN, Adolf, Naugatuck, CT, + Mt Vernon, NY – 1901/06/28:1e
SCHUMANN, Alfred, 7, NYC-M, +@Genl Slocum – 1904/06/22:1d
SCHUMANN, Annie, 24, NYC-B – 1913/01/03:3a
SCHUMANN, Bruno, ex-alderman, SPD Bielefeld/Gy – 1909/06/06:3c
SCHUMANN, Caroline T., NYC-B – 1880/03/26:4d
SCHUMANN, Emma, 19, Swiss, NYC-M – 1897/01/18:1e
SCHUMANN, Erika, NYC-Bx - 1916/03/28:6a, fam. 4 Apr:6a
SCHUMANN, Frank, NYC-Q – 1897/12/13:4a
SCHUMANN, Frederick, butcher & grocer, NYC-M – 1903/10/03:3f, =5:1g
SCHUMANN, Gottlieb von, SPD Stuttgart, tailor - 1914/08/16:3c
SCHUMANN, Heinrich, 12, NYC-M – 1901/02/16:4a
SCHUMANN, John, 38, carp., NYC-B - 1913/06/17:6c
SCHUMANN, Klara, pianist,wd of Robert, + Frankfurt, 1896/05/22:1a
SCHUMANN, Sophie, 36, NYC-M – 1882/03/04:1f
SCHUMANN, Sophie, NYC? – 1888/07/31:3b
SCHUMANN HEINK, August, German Navy - 1919/02/11:2e
SCHUMANN HEINK, Hans, 28, + San Diego, CA – 1916/01/06:2g
SCHUMFLETH, Margarethe, Jersey City Hgts, NJ – 1892/06/30:4a
SCHUMM, Michael, NYC-M – 1906/08/22:6a, 23:6a, fam. 25:6a; mem. 1907/08/21:6a
SCHUMP, Lizzie, NYC-M, + @ Genl Slocum – 1904/06/17:3c
SCHUNK, Carl, NYC-M – 1891/03/25:4a

SCHUNK, Margarethe, b. Stier, NYC-M – 1910/09/18:7c
SCHUPP, Martin, 67, SP, Newark, NJ – 1908/08/20:1b,6a, =22:2d
SCHUPPE, Carl, Jersey City, NJ – 1909/09/13:6a, fam. 16:6a
SCHUPPERT, Edward, Bayonne, NJ – 1913/02/05:6a
SCHUPPERT, Wilhelmine, 49, NYC-Q – 1912/04/27:6a
SCHUPPERT, Wilhelmine, b. Magersuppe, 28, NYC-M – 1886/10/23:3a
SCHURER, Friedrich, 28, un. silkweaver & SLP, fr Irfersgruenden/ Leipzig/Gy, NYC – 1889/08/28:4a
SCHURR, David M., drug smuggler, NYC-B – 1912/08/28:3a
SCHURR, David, NYC-M - 1920/02/20:6a
SCHURR, Johannes, innkeep, SPD? Wasseralfingen/Gy – 1899/01/29:12h
SCHURR, John, 37, *Hattenhofen/Wuerttemberg, Gy, Hoboken, NJ – 1897/10/18:4a
SCHURR, John, un. carp., NYC-Bx - 1916/05/17:6a
SCHURZ, Carl, G-A leader, NYC-M, sarcastic comments on his praise of William I, 15 Nov:2c, 11 Dec 1888:4e; Crit. Notes to his 70th birthday 2 Mr 1899:2a-b, 5:4a-b, 9:1g, 16:2c; + 15 May 1906:1f-g, 16:4d, 17:1c, =18:2h, 26:1e, 31:h, 1 June:2h, rev. memorial 7:4b, mon. planned 18:2e. NYVZ on his life 18 Apr 1909:6c-e, 25:6c-e, 2 May:6c-e. Monument inaug. Morningside Drive & 116th St 15 Mr 1913:1d, 11 May:11d-e
SCHURZ, George, un. carp., NYC-M – 1898/09/15:4a
SCHUSKY, Betsy, 22, servant, New Jersey – 1888/05/08:2f
SCHUSSEL, Alex, 59, sales agent, NYC-M – 1890/11/30:1h
SCHUSTACZECK, textile worker & SP Vienna/Austria– 1908/06/07:33d-e
SCHUSTER, Adolf, SPD Crimmitschau/Sax., mgr local Konsumverein - 1915/03/21:3c
SCHUSTER, Henry, un. cigarmaker, NYC-M 1895/12/09: 1d,4a
SCHUSTER, Ludwig, brewer, USA 1860s, NYC-M – 1897/01/08:4e
SCHUSTER, Peter, cigarmaker, NYC-B – 1891/03/01:5c
SCHUSTER, Philipp, NYC-M – 1912/03/01:6a
SCHUTHES, Felix, 32, waiter, NYC-B – 1900/09/12:2f
SCHUTT, Edward A., NYC-M – 1891/04/12:5a
SCHUTT, Frank, motorman, NYC-B – 1919/10/11:8b
SCHUTT, Minna, Secaucus, NJ - 1919/01/18:6a
SCHUTT, Peter S., NYC-M – 1912/11/23:6a
SCHUTTE, John C., + 30 Apr 1904, NYC-B, will 1906/12/08:2a
SCHUTTE, William, ~40, NYC-M – 1897/04/30:1e
SCHUTTER % Ruehl
SCHUTTER, C., 74, worker, NYC-M – 1890/12/27:2f
SCHUTZ, Emilie, NYC-M – 1889/09/17:2h, 18:2g, 21:4f
SCHUTZ, John, NYC-M – 1899/11/02:4a
SCHUYLER, John E., NYC, to be exec. 1907/05/15:2e

SCHWAB % Bruederlein
SCHWAB, Albert, butcher, NYC-B - 1914/04/21:6c
SCHWAB, Alwin, Dr. med., 52, NYC-B - 1920/05/16:2d
SCHWAB, Amelia, fr Dresden/Gy, NYC-M - 1895/03/18:1h
SCHWAB, Babette, NYC-B - 1896/08/01:4a
SCHWAB, Benjamin W., 35, North German Lloyd, NYC-M - 1899/09/22:1f
SCHWAB, C. Albert, 58, Irvington, NJ - 1912/12/28:6a, 29:7a, fam. 4 Jan. 1913:6a
SCHWAB, Conrad, 34, un. carp., NYC-M - 1881/08/31:4c
SCHWAB, Elizabeth, 59, NYC-B - 1906/12/07:6a
SCHWAB, Emil, partner at Burr Brewing Co, NYC-M - 1891/02/17:1f
SCHWAB, Franz M., 80, NYC-B - 1919/09/08:3f
SCHWAB, Franz M., NYC, who killed 18 Fb. wife & grandson, trial 1896/04/14:2e, 16:4b, rec. life 17:3c
SCHWAB, Friedrich, 48, NYC-M - 1892/06/25:4a
SCHWAB, Georg, NYC-M - 1903/01/13:4a
SCHWAB, George,55,& wife Matilde,NYC-B - 1914/10/23:2d,1 No:1f
SCHWAB, Gottlieb, 47, engineer,*near Stuttgart, Gy, NYC-Bx - 1912/11/23:6a, 24:7a, 26:6c-d
SCHWAB, Gustav H., 61, head of Oelrichs & Co., + Litchfield, CT - 1912/11/13:2c
SCHWAB, Helen, 23, NYC-M - 1907/11/09:1d
SCHWAB, Henry, 3, NYC-M - 1901/05/04:4a
SCHWAB, Jakob Friedrich, + Frankfurt/Main, father of Julius Schwab, NYC - 1889/04/08:4a
SCHWAB, Jakob, 54, lace dealer, NYC-M - 1887/11/22:4a
SCHWAB, John, NYC-Bx - 1907/04/25:6a
SCHWAB, Justus, innkeep & local anarchist (John Most) leader, *Frankfurt, NYC-M - 1900/12/18:1f-g, 2b, 4a, 20:4a, =21:2h
SCHWAB, Karl, NYC-M - 1912/03/18:6a
SCHWAB, Katharina, 53, NYC-M - 1896/02/19:1h, =22:4b
SCHWAB, Kilian, NYC-M - 1918/01/26:6a
SCHWAB, Leonhardt, 61, machinist, NYC-B - 1910/01/15:6a, fam. 19:6a
SCHWAB, Michael, one of the pardonned @1886Haymarket victims, + Chicago - 1898/07/03:4a, =4:1f; mem. in Chicago 1898/07/10:12a-b
SCHWAB, Nannette, NYC-M - 1891/04/02:4a
SCHWABACH, Lilly, 20, NYC-M - 1887/07/15:4b
SCHWABBAUER, Emil, 54, metal worker, SPD Breslau/Gy - 1910/01/30:3c
SCHWABE % Horchler
SCHWABE, Eduard J., 55, painter, NYC-M - 1898/12/22:2g
SCHWABE, Ernst, carp., NYC-M - 1898/01/25:1b

SCHWABE, Henriette, b. Kunert, 72, NYC-SI - 1916/11/27:6a
SCHWABE, Hermann, 61, un. cigarmaker, NYC-M - 1905/10/09:4a
SCHWABLE, Esther, 22, nurse, Hawthorne,NY - 1917/04/12:2d
SCHWACHA, Gottfried, Newark, NJ - 1918/04/21:7a
SCHWACHA, Maria, b. Bartnik, 62, Newark, NJ - 1912/02/19:6a
SCHWADRON, Sarah, 19, servant, fr Austria, NYC-M - 1909/02/09:1c
SCHWAGER, Fritz, un. carp., NYC-M - 1891/11/27:4a
SCHWAGER, Gottlieb, 50, stonecutter, NYC-Bx - 1911/04/19:1d
SCHWAISE, Clare, b. Dorschel, NYC-M - 1888/10/11:2h
SCHWAKAL, John, 68, un. cigarmaker, NYC-B - 1916/06/08:5e
SCHWAL, Morris,44, peddler, War 2(dying),NYC-B - 1915/06/11:6c
SCHWALB, Wilhelm, 70, NYC? - 1885/04/14:3c
SCHWALB, Wilhelm, 70, un. typesetter, NYC-M? - 1891/08/05:4a
SCHWALBACH, ..., 40, Jersey City Heights, NJ - 1891/08/27:1d
SCHWALBE, Emil, 46, NYC-M - 1892/10/27:4a
SCHWALBE, Friedrich, 70, SPD activist & alderman in Callberg/Chemnitz
  - 1909/06/20:3g
SCHWALKE, Paul, NYC-M - 1897/09/16:4a, fam. 19:5a
SCHWALME, Jacob, 32, tailor, NYC-M - 1892/06/05:1h
SCHWAMB, Michael, 19, NYC-M - 1911/08/11:2d
SCHWANENFLUEGEL, Albert von, 56, NYC-M - 1919/06/25:6a
SCHWANER, John, 73, un. carp., SP, & wife Katharina, USA 1849 fr
  Frankenberg/Hessen,, Golden Wedding, NYC-M - 1906/10/28:7d
SCHWANGT, Wilhelm, 77, SP, * Danzig, US civil war vet, un. metal
  worker, NYC-B - 1916/04/03:2b,6a
SCHWANKE, Ernest, security guard, Newark, NJ - 1900/05/17:1b
SCHWANN, Benedikt, 72, Newark, NJ - 1910/01/03:1c, 4:3c
SCHWANWEDEL, Henry, 59, NYC-B - 1905/10/22:1e
SCHWARK, Ludwig, Greenville, NJ - 1907/12/15:4a
SCHWARM, John, NYC-B - 1891/03/21:4a
SCHWARTZ % Raichlen
SCHWARTZ, Adolph, 53, of Schwartz & Steiner, NYC-Bx - 1915/12/17:1f
SCHWARTZ, Amelia, NYC-M - 1897/01/10:1b
SCHWARTZ, Benjamin, 25, NYC-M - 1895/03/02:1g
SCHWARTZ, Bertha, NYC-M - 1897/12/18:3d
SCHWARTZ, Bruno, watchmaker, fr Chemnitz/Gy, NYC-M -
  1898/09/30:1h
SCHWARTZ, Daniel, 79, NYC-M - 1891/08/15:4a
SCHWARTZ, Emil L., 52, beer driver, Highlands, NJ - 1910/08/07:7f
SCHWARTZ, Ernest, NYC-Q - 1911/11/23:2e
SCHWARTZ, George C., NYC-Bx - 1890/07/13:5d
SCHWARTZ, Henrietta, diamond dealer, NYC-M - 1904/02/18:1h

SCHWARTZ, Henry H., NYPD, NYC-M, dying - 1916/05/30:2b
SCHWARTZ, Henry, 48, NYC-M - 1901/07/02:1e
SCHWARTZ, Irving, NYC-B - 1913/08/05:3a
SCHWARTZ, John, 19, NYC-M - 1907/03/03:9f
SCHWARTZ, Joseph, 23, NYC-B - 1903/06/16:4b
SCHWARTZ, Karl, German in French Foreign Legion, exec. - 1892/07/12:4b
SCHWARTZ, Lena, NYC-M, + @Genl Slocum - 1904/06/17:3c
SCHWARTZ, Louis, 60, shopkeeper, NYC-M - 1878/09/04:1g
SCHWARTZ, Louisa, NYC-M, + @ Genl Slocum - 1904/06/16:1c, 17:3c
SCHWARTZ, Mary, 42, NYC-B - 1901/11/12:2h
SCHWARTZ, Max, 39, tailor fr Russia, NYC-M - 1905/05/20:3g
SCHWARTZ, Max, 50th birthday of famous SP innkeep, NYC-M - 1910/05/02:3d
SCHWARTZ, May, 2, NYC-B - 1906/11/01:3b
SCHWARTZ, Meyer, 17, married? Bessie Klinge, 18, NYC-M - 1907/01/25:1g
SCHWARTZ, Nathan, who killed Julia Connors, - 1912/07/19:1d, =20:1f
SCHWARTZ, Paul, 49, SP, NYC-M - 1919/01/10:6a
SCHWARTZ, Paul, machinist, NYC-B - 1913/08/05:3b
SCHWARTZ, Peter William., fr Bremerlehe, USA 1861, NYC-M - 1879/03/27:1g
SCHWARTZ, Rebecca, NYC-M - 1906/11/26:1c
SCHWARTZ, Rosa, 29, NYC-Bx - 1913/07/12:2c
SCHWARTZ, Rudolph, machinist, NYC-M - 1902/05/08:1g
SCHWARTZ, Sophia, 80, NYC-M - 1901/02/08:2h
SCHWARTZ, Theodor's wife, 79, SPD Luebeck/Gy, wife of MdR - 1912/10/27:3b
SCHWARTZENBERG, Hugo, NYC-Bx - 1914/04/11:6a
SCHWARTZKOPF, Morris, jeweler, NYC-M - 1912/07/30:1g
SCHWARZ % Bescher, % Bonekamp, % Vollmer
SCHWARZ, Adolph, mirror dealer, NYC-M - 1886/03/04:2e
SCHWARZ, Alice, 24, War 2, NYC-B - 1917/11/20:6c
SCHWARZ, Andreas, 44, SLP, un. cabinet maker & ed. NYC Moebelarbeiterjournal, *8 Sp 1850 near Nuremberg/Gy, NYC 1878, + NYC-B - 1895/02/03:1g,5c; =04:3d
SCHWARZ, Anna, NYC-M - 1890/01/08:4a
SCHWARZ, Anton, 57, NYC-M - 1895/09/26: 4a
SCHWARZ, Arthur, druggist, Trenton, NJ - 1916/04/14:2f
SCHWARZ, Augusta, 48, NYC-B - 1896/02/03:2c
SCHWARZ, Barbara, NYC-M - 1891/04/05:5a
SCHWARZ, Carl, NYC-Bx - 1915/02/02:6a

SCHWARZ, Emil, Jersey City Hgts, NJ - 1920/09/16:6a
SCHWARZ, Franz, 36, musician, Hoboken, NJ – 1886/01/19:1f
SCHWARZ, Frederick J., NYC-B – 1912/02/24:6a
SCHWARZ, Frederick, 50, NYC-Bx - 1914/01/12:6a
SCHWARZ, George, 80, NYC-M - 1917/01/25:6a
SCHWARZ, H.G., NYC-M - 1920/06/13:12a
SCHWARZ, Henry, 24, NYC-M – 1898/06/14:4a
SCHWARZ, Hulda, b, Fuhst, 52, NYC-M – 1901/02/20:4a
SCHWARZ, Jette, 68, NYC-M - 1894/01/21:5d
SCHWARZ, John, SLP, cornice-maker, NYC - 1894/05/16:4a, =17:1b, 19:4a
SCHWARZ, Joseph, *29 Jan. 1854 Strassburg/Elsass, NYC-Bx – 1913/01/30:6a, 31:6a
SCHWARZ, Karl, 46, NYC-M - 1920/03/02:6a
SCHWARZ, Magdalene, b. Guthermann, 75, NYC-B - 1914/07/07:6a
SCHWARZ, Martha, b. Wischer, fr Otterndorf/Hannover/Gy, Hoboken, NJ – 1912/05/25:6a
SCHWARZ, Max, Jersey City, NJ - 1916/01/23:7a
SCHWARZ, Michael, Newark, NJ – 1909/01/12:6a
SCHWARZ, Paul, 50, SLP?, NYC-M – 1893/05/10:4a
SCHWARZ, Robert, 60, un. cigarmaker, NYC-M – 1905/06/07:4a
SCHWARZ, Theresa, NYC-B - 1916/12/13:6a
SCHWARZ, William's wife, NYC-B – 1893/12/29:4a
SCHWARZE, Luise, b. Hoppe, 84, NYC-M – 1911/05/12:6a
SCHWARZE, Paul, 53, Hoboken, NJ – 1910/03/15:6a, 16:6a
SCHWARZER, Wilhelmine, b. Froehlich, 36, NYC-M – 1887/06/03:3d
SCHWARZFAERBER, Georg, 31, lithographer fr Bavaria, NYC-M – 1882/01/13:1e
SCHWARZKOPF, Anna, NYC-M – 1890/11/21:4a
SCHWARZLE, Baptist, 35, waiter, NYC-M - 1895/07/24: 1g
SCHWARZWALD, Edward L., ~35, NYC-M – 1900/09/24:1e
SCHWECHTEN, Amalia, 71, Montclair, NJ – 1911/07/13:2d
SCHWECK % Gissyng
SCHWEDLER, Michael L., *4 Ap 1841 Werbig/Gerlow, & brother Peter Carl Fr. W., USA, searched for inheritance in Germany – 1880/01/18:5f
SCHWEDT, Minnie, 18, NYC-M – 1892/06/24:4a
SCHWEERS, Wilhelm, 46, carp., NYC-M – 1888/04/12:1d
SCHWEFEL, Josephine Kaiser, NYC-M - 1918/10/08:6a
SCHWEG, Louis, candy peddler, NYC-M – 1893/07/07:1f
SCHWEGINNIS, Robert, 62, Hoboken, NJ - 1915/11/28:11g
SCHWEGLER, Julius, NYC-Bx – 1890/09/03:4a
SCHWEICHEL, Elise, SPD, 80th birthday – 1911/10/08:20d

SCHWEICHEL, Robert, 86, SPD activist & writer, + Berlin – 1907/05/07:4e, =15:4g, 16:4e
SCHWEICHERT, August, fr Steinweiler/Gy, un. brewer, NYC-M – 1902/02/23:5a
SCHWEIDLER, John, 53, peddler fr Bohemia, NYC-M – 1889/07/26:1h
SCHWEIGER, Charles, 49, smith, Hempstead, NY - 1916/02/09:2e
SCHWEIGER, Joseph, 34, worker at Singer's, Elizabethport, NJ – 1909/05/28:3b
SCHWEIGERT % Windeling
SCHWEIKERT, Catherine, NYC-M, +@Genl Slocum – 1904/06/23:1c
SCHWEIKERT, comrade, SPD Aalen/Wuertt., 1899/01/29:12h
SCHWEIKERT, Ludwig, 61, un. brewer, NYC-B - 1919/05/23:6a
SCHWEINFURTH, Frederick, New Brunswick, NJ – 1900/05/19:3b
SCHWEINKER, Jacob, 78, NYC-M – 1891/03/27:4a
SCHWEINSKOPF, Charles, NYC-M - 1913/12/11:6a
SCHWEISSGUTH, William, un. wood carver, NYC-Bx – 1912/05/25:6a
SCHWEITHART, Matthias, un. carp., NYC-M – 1882/04/04:3b
SCHWEITZER, Ella, NYC-B – 1908/04/15:3a
SCHWEITZER, Frank, 40, & wife, Hoboken, NJ (dying) - 1917/11/20:2f
SCHWEITZER, Franz, un. carp., NYC-M – 1886/06/05:3g
SCHWEITZER, Friedrich, Steinway worker?, NYC-M – 1883/04/14:3d
SCHWEITZER, Henry, 42, insurance employee, NYC-M – 1913/02/08:2c
SCHWEITZER, Herman, 32, dyer, NYC-M – 1897/01/11:1g
SCHWEITZER, Jakob, Union Hill, NJ, will probated 1885/05/11:2g
SCHWEITZER, John, NYC-B – 1883/02/02:3c
SCHWEIZER, Barbara, b. Neu, 67, NYC-M - 1915/06/10:6a
SCHWEIZER, Christian, NYC-Bx - 1915/11/19:6a
SCHWEIZER, Fritz, 38, un. carp., NYC-M – 1904/07/17:5b
SCHWEIZER, George, NYC-M – 1880/06/23:3b
SCHWEIZER, Samuel, 37, NYC-M – 1893/05/14:5b
SCHWELM, Friedrich, 40, un. printer, NYC-M - 1894/04/07:4a
SCHWEMMER, William H., fr Bavaria, + 27 Aug. on ship New Amsterdam, Newark, NJ - 1915/09/04:3e
SCHWEN, Katherine, 78, Newark, NJ - 1917/12/04:2e
SCHWENCK, Christian, 34, NYC-B – 1907/11/20:6a
SCHWENCK, Margaretha Susanna, 72, NYC-B 1902/08/15:4a
SCHWENCKE, August, 60, NYC-B - 1915/10/22:6b
SCHWEND, Friedrich J., 21, NYC-M – 1883/04/25:3b
SCHWEND, Joseph, 41, NYC-Q - 1916/03/28:6a
SCHWENDEMANN % Pabst
SCHWENDEMANN, Friederika, 47, NYC-M – 1904/06/03:4a
SCHWENK, Adam, 11, NYC-M – 1903/03/17:4a, fam. 23:4a

SCHWENK, John Fr., carriage maker, SP, fr Bockenheim/Gy, NYC-M – 1908/10/24:2d,6a, fam. 28:6a
SCHWENK, Karl, 44, NYC-M – 1887/01/05:3b
SCHWENK,Friedrich, 59, SLP, NYC-B - 1894/07/04:4a, =06:4a
SCHWENZER, Jacob, pres. Auto Repair Co., Woodbridge, NJ – 1911/08/17:2d
SCHWEPPENDICK, Louise, 49, NYC-B – 1891/07/19:5b
SCHWEPPENDICK, Wilhelm, 71, *Lippe/Gy, carp., SP, + Windsor, CT – 1909/12/22:3d, 6a, 23:6a?
SCHWERDT, Caroline A., Jersey City, NJ – 1909/05/25:3d-e
SCHWERDTFEGER, August, 74, NYC-B - 1918/01/08:2g
SCHWERDTFEGER, Carl, SP, un. cigarmaker, NYC-B - 1916/10/09:6a, will 9 Dec:1d
SCHWERE, Carl,73, glass worker, War 2,Boston,MA -1917/02/03:2d
SCHWERMER, Esther, NYC-M – 1909/08/14:2c
SCHWERT, Heinrich, 64, NYC-Q – 1910/12/26:6a, 27:6a
SCHWERTEL, Andreas, 57, brewer, NYC-M – 1897/04/05:1g
SCHWERTL, Catharina, NYC-M - 1896/02/03:3a
SCHWERTNER, Gustav, NYC-M – 1919/11/26:6a
SCHWETZENDIEK, Wilhelm,44, carpenter & SPD activist expelled from Berlin/Gy, arrived NYC – 1880/11/30:1d-e, 2 Dec:2a-b, 6:1d-e
SCHWEYGER, Fritz, NYC-B - 1919/01/04:6a
SCHWEZERLE, Jacob, 50, driver, NYC-B – 1901/02/07:4a
SCHWICH % Dreyer
SCHWIEBERT, Henry, NYC-M – 1913/03/17:6a
SCHWIEBERT, William, 13, NYC-M – 1902/05/14:4a
SCHWILLE, Georg, 48, NYC-B – 1892/07/20:4a
SCHWIND, Alfons, 30, worker, NYC-B – 1887/04/16:2d-e
SCHWIND, Anton, NYC-B – 1911/01/28:6a
SCHWIND, Michael, blind musician, on ship "Mystery," NYC-B – 1887/07/12:1c-e, 13:2g
SCHWINDE, Rosa, 67, NYC-Q – 1913/10/23:2e
SCHWING, Anna Marie, 3, NYC-M – 1884/11/20:3c
SCHWING, Frederick., un. cigarmaker, NYC-M – 1887/01/01:3a
SCHWING, William, NYC-M – 1887/03/16:3d
SCHWINK, Albert, accountant, NYC-B - 1915/07/06:6c
SCHWINKEL, Elise, NYC-M – 1881/09/06:3b
SCHWOERER, Josephine, NYC-B – 1892/06/18:4a
SCHWOERER, Katherina, b. Vetter, 64, Jersey City, NJ – 1890/10/18:3a, 20:4a, =21:2f
SCHWURST, William, NYC-Q – 1900/08/22:4a
SCODEL, August, Elizabeth, NJ – 1909/07/31:6a

SCOFF, Albin's wife, NYC-M, +@ Genl Slocum – 1904/06/17:3c
SCORALICK, Philipp, 30, un. painter, NYC-B – 1901/01/09:4a
SCOTT, congressman fr Erie, PA. Very negat. Obit – 1891/09/24:2c-d
SCOTT, Alexander, boxer, NYC-M – 1898/08/27:4d, note 7 Sept:1g
SCOTT, Howard A., exec. Ossining, NY – 1897/06/15:4a
SCOTT, Robert F., British Polar explorer & his crew – 1913/02/11:1a
SCOTT, Thomas A., Railroad millionaire, obit. sharply crit his role in 1877 Pittsburgh massacre of striking workers – 1881/05/23:2d
SCOTT, Walter W., 50, druggist, NYC-B – 1900/05/31:4b
SCOTT, William, 23, exec. Auburn, NY – 1909/06/15:2d
SCRECHER, Elise, 9, NYC-M, + Genl Slocum – 1904/06/18:1b
SCRIMSHAW, Frederick, 55, journalist, SLP, *England, NYC-B – 1900/03/07:3d, 8:1, =9:3b; grave mon. Arlington, NJ – 1902/05/28:4b
SCUDERI, C., Prof., Italian Socialist, + Messina earthquake – 1909/02/23:4d
SCULLY, John McCarthy, 47, Irish patriot, + NYC – 1883/12/31:4d
SCURTI, Sebastiano Camereri, 60, Italian socialist – 1912/08/31:4d
SDABEZYNSKI, Joseph, NYC-M – 1902/04/12:4b
SEAMAN, Georg, NYC-M - 1915/12/17:6a
SEARS, Barnas, US educator – 1880/07/08:2e
SEARS, John, exec. Trenton, NJ – 1911/03/16:1c
SEBALD, Katie, 3, NYC-M – 1885/04/29:3a
SEBASCHUS, Mathilde, Hoboken, NJ – 1911/07/16:7b
SEBASTIAN, Alex, fr Hungary, Ithaca, NY - 1913/05/01:1b
SEBASTIAN, Heinrich, 23, NYC-SI – 1900/05/06:5f
SEBASTIAN, Willy, child, NYC-M – 1888/06/27:3b
SEBOLD, Margaret, 17, Bloomfield, NJ – 1904/09/25:5d
SEBURG, Hermann, 59, foreman & SPD activist in Leipzig/Gy – 1908/03/22:3c
SECCHI, Pietro A., S.J.,60, Ital. astronomer, - 1878/03/01:2f
SECKER, Gottlieb, un. baker, NYC-Bx - 1917/12/06:6a, 7:6a
SEDDON, Richard, PM of New Zealand, crit obit – 1906/06/28:4e-f
SEDELMEYER, Margarethe, dying, Jersey City, NJ – 1912/07/20:2c
SEDGWICK, Arthur George, banker,+ Pittsfield, MA - 1915/07/15:2d
SEDLACK, Anna, NYC-B – 1907/03/13:6a
SEDLMAYER, Marie, 72, NYC-B – 1910/01/27:6a
SEDLMEIER, Vitus, un. carp., NYC-M – 1900/06/20:4a
SEE, Friedrich, tailor, NYC-M – 1901/07/07:1f
SEE, Lorenz, 83, NYC-Bx – 1905/11/19:4a
SEE, Louisa, b. Ahrend, NYC-M – 1900/02/08:4a
SEEBACH % Kuhlwilm
SEEBACH, Franz, NYC-M – 1883/11/15:3b

SEEBACH, Louise, b. Berger, 79, fr Bergzabern/Rheinpfalz, NYC-M – 1910/07/11:6a
SEEBACK, Barbara, NYC-M – 1901/06/12:4a, fam. 15:4a
SEEBER, Lorenz, NYC-M – 1901/03/25:4a
SEEBERGER, Lorenz, NYC-B – 1881/07/20:3b
SEEBERGER, Rosalie, Jersey City Heights, NJ – 1904/01/20:4a
SEEBURGER, Catharina, un. cigar maker, NYC-M – 1896/12/20:7a
SEEDORF % Boe
SEEDORF, H. N., 32, NYC-M – 1893/10/25:4a
SEEFELDT, Friedrich, New Brooklyn - 1920/02/28:8a
SEEGER, August, 55, NYC-M – 1892/04/05:4b
SEEGER, Frederick, 34, deli-owner, NYC-M – 1905/11/07:2f
SEEGERS, Emil, 60, fr Bremen?, NYC-B - 1919/03/31:6a, fam. 3 Apr:6a
SEEHOLZER, Annie, b. Faust, 24, NYC-B – 1883/10/16:3a
SEELHOF, Wilhelm, Kamen/Thuer. ATB, War 1 - 1914/11/01:3b
SEELICKE, Carl, 54, NYC-M - 1894/01/28:5d
SEELIG, Helene, NYC-M – 1892/07/25:4a
SEELING, Julius, 40, (dying) boxmaker, & wife Helene, (dead), 38, NYC-M – 1887/06/18:1f
SEELINGER, Katherina, 48, NYC-Bx – 1906/04/17:4a
SEELINGER, M., NYC-M – 1912/03/27:6a
SEEMAN, Meta, NYC-M, + @ Genl Slocum – 1904/06/17:3c
SEEMANN, Bruno Ch., 49, un. waiter, NYC-M – 1910/02/28:6a, 1 Mr:6a
SEEMANN, Christian, innkeep, NYC-SI – 1908/05/20:2c
SEEMANN, Fritz, Hoboken, NJ – 1906/10/17:6a
SEEMAR, Margarethe, b. Hertlein, fr Aschenroth/Bav., NYC-B – 1887/05/09:3c
SEEMEYER, Ernest C., 57, grocer, NYC-B - 1915/11/21:11d
SEEWAGEN, George, NYC-B? - 1913/06/28:6a
SEEWAGEN, Jacob, 21, brewer, Jersey City, NJ – 1898/01/20:3c
SEEWAGEN, Margaretha, NYC-M – 1906/11/09:6a
SEEWIG, Albert, 37, ex-ship stewart, Freehold, NJ – 1919/11/28:2e
SEFF, J., NYC-M – 1884/09/01:4b
SEFFEL, John, 60, NYC-B - 1918/07/31:3e
SEGALKE, Wilhelmina, 23, NYC-B - 1878/07/23:1d, 24:1e
SEGALL, Wolfgang, NYC-M – 1904/02/15:4a
SEGEL, Michael, 50, un. carp., NYC-B – 1908/09/08:6a
SEGELBACHER, Georg, un. carp., NYC-Q – 1911/01/12:6a
SEGELKEN, William, 52, baker, Jersey City, NJ – 1898/03/26:4c
SEGELKEN, William, NYC-B – 1906/10/23:6a
SEGENDORF, Nathan's little son, 1, NYC-M – 1904/08/02:4a
SEGGERN, Henry von, 60, NYC-B - 1914/06/28:7c

SEGIFFER, Ferdinand, un. baker, NYC-M – 1907/10/30:6a
SEHER, William, NYC-M – 1918/03/19:6a
SEIB, Selma, NYC-Q, her will – 1917/11/14:1f
SEIBEL, Friedrich, SPD Frankfurt/Main – 1899/02/19:12e
SEIBERT % Herrmann, % Kolb
SEIBERT, Catherina, NYC-M – 1902/05/27:3h
SEIBERT, Franz, un. cigarmkr, *27/03/1849 Wuerzburg/Bav., SDP, #, NYC-M – 1901/04/02:1f-g, 4a, 3:2c, 4a, =4:2h, fam. 4:4a
SEIBOLD, Katherine, b. Knauer, 60, NYC-M – 1892/08/26:4a
SEIBOLD, Paul, 39, SP, NYC-M - 1915/12/19:11a
SEICKEL, Adolf, NYC-M – 1901/06/22:4a
SEIDEL, August, 64, SP, un. tailor, NYC-Q - 1915/06/19:6a, =21:2e
SEIDEL, August, un. carp., NYC-M – 1890/07/18:1g, 4a, 19:4a
SEIDEL, Carl, 59, Hoboken, NJ – 1913/01/11:6a
SEIDEL, Franz, 35, German fr Poland, foreman, NYC-M - 1896/02/05:1h
SEIDEL, Georg, 75, un. carp., NYC-Q – 1908/09/11:6a
SEIDEL, Georg, NYC-M – 1911/08/09:6a
SEIDEL, Gottlieb, 68, Newark, NJ – 1904/10/30:5d
SEIDEL, Johanna, b. Martens, 58, NYC-Q – 1898/05/15:5c
SEIDEL, John, restaurant, fr Bohemia ~1882, Portchester, NY – 1900/10/19:1e
SEIDEL, Marie, b. Bodde, NYC-B – 1909/09/10:6a, fam. 16:6a
SEIDEL, Valentin, (Saidel?) NYC-M – 1896/07/14:4a, fam. 9 Aug:5a
SEIDEL, Walter, 6, NYC? – 1888/02/17:3b
SEIDEN % Berger
SEIDENBERG % Lindlau
SEIDENBERG, Mary, 34, NYC-M – 1891/08/12:4a
SEIDENFADEN, W., NYC-Q - 1915/06/16:6a
SEIDENSCHNER, Frank, exec. Ossining, NY - 1914/04/14:1g,2a,4a
SEIDENWAND, Henry, 18, NYC-M, +@ Genl Slocum – 1904/06/17:3c, 18:3c
SEIDL, Anton, conductor, *7 May 1850 Pest/Hungary, NYC-M – 1898/03/29:1g, 30:1d, =31 March:1e, 1 Apr:1e, notes 2:1g, will 3:5d, 6:1h, 21 May:4c; mem. 25 Fb 1899:3c, benefit widow 6 Mr:1f, book 27:4a,
SEIDL, Fritz, German Revol., on his exec. in Munich – 1919/09/22:4d
SEIDLER % Braun
SEIDLER, August, NYC-M – 1881/05/17:3c
SEIDLER, Ignatz, 65, carp., Newark, NJ – 1887/11/01:2d
SEIDT, Richard, baker, NYC-M – 1880/12/03:1f
SEIF, W., NYC-B - 1915/03/16:6a
SEIFERD, Marie, NYC-M – 1886/09/02:3c
SEIFERLING, Friedrich, 46, NYC-M – 1907/07/13:6a

SEIFERT, Adolf, 30, clerk, SP activist in Gablonz/Bohemia –
 1908/03/08:3d
SEIFERT, Albert, 48, * Mainz/Gy, brewery agent, NYC-M – 1896/12/17:4c
SEIFERT, Emil, musician, ex-NYC, Buffalo, NY – 1880/11/11:1c
SEIFERT, Joseph, 20, NYC-M, see Falkenstein, Louis von,
SEIFERT, Julius, 61, ex-MdR, + Zwickau/Gy – 1909/04/18:3b, =25:3b
SEIFERT, William, NYC-B – 1888/02/06:2c
SEIFERTH, Friedericka, 62, NYC-Bx - 1915/08/22:7a
SEIFFERT, John P., organist German Luth. Ch., NYC-Bx – 1904/05/11:4c
SEIFFERT, John's wife, Riverside, NJ – 1902/12/03:3b
SEIFRIED, Pauline, 13, NYC-B - 1913/12/10:6a
SEIGE, Karoline, 58, SPD Poessneck in Sachsen-Altenburg –
 1913/10/26:3b
SEIGEL, Helen, infant, NYC-B – 1906/08/08:2c
SEIGOLD, Louis, 38, bartender, NYC-Bx – 1919/10/05:2g
SEIKOWSKY, Frank, NYC-M - 1917/10/04:6a
SEILER, George Robert, NYC-Bx - 1914/12/29:6a
SEILER, George, 32, baker, NYC-M – 1882/10/30:1d
SEILER, Joseph, 55, barber, NYC-B - 1915/02/09:2e
SEIMER, Emma, NYC - 1914/03/04:6a
SEIMS, George, ship's musician, @1900 dock fire, Hoboken, NJ
 1900/07/03:1c
SEINECKE, Ferdinand, 58, NYC-B - 1914/04/21:6a
SEINS, Esther, NYC-B - 1879/09/16:4c
SEIPELT, Henry, NYC-M – 1913/09/28:7b
SEIPP, Johann H., NYC-M – 1892/07/08:4a
SEIPP, William, 61, brewery owner & ex-treas. Cook County, Chicago, IL –
 1912/03/19:6a
SEIPT, Wilhelm O., un. furrier, NYC-M – 1886/03/04:3a
SEISCHAB, Michael, co-fdr SPD Nuernberg – 1887/10/20:2c
SEISSENSCHMIDT, Wilhelm, 65, NYC-Bx – 1909/04/21:6a
SEITER % Witterer
SEITER, Georg, NYC-M - 1920/06/09:6a
SEITER, George's wife, 30, NYC-B – 1914/02/02:2e
SEITER, Karl, 58, TV Vorwaerts, NYC-B – 1920/01/16:6a
SEITHER, Raphael, tailor, Newark, NJ – 1899/03/10:4a
SEITMAN, Nathan, paperhanger, NYC-B – 1900/10/11:3b
SEITZ % Kuhles
SEITZ % Thompson
SEITZ, Adam, NYC-B - 1916/12/25:6a
SEITZ, Christoph, un. typesetter, NYC-B – 1901/02/09:4a
SEITZ, Ernest, stoker, fr Switzerland, 24, NYC-M – 1908/08/10:1d, 11:1g

SEITZ, Franz, 71, NYC-M – 1892/06/20:4a
SEITZ, Heinrich, NYC-B - 1917/11/13:6a
SEITZ, Joseph, NYC-B – 1906/01/08:4a
SEITZ, Katherine, NYC-B – 1882/01/25:3c
SEITZ, Lina, 18, NYC-B – 1898/12/18:1g
SEITZ, Roxana, 19, Hackensack, NJ – 1902/09/25:3c, 26:3d, 27:3c
SEITZ, Samuel A., leather manuf., Philadelphia, PA – 1912/11/04:2f
SEITZ, Wilhelmine, 35, dying, NYC-B – 1906/01/31:3c
SEIWERT, John, 23, NYC-M - 1894/01/11:4a
SEIZ, Georg, 20, NYC-M – 1890/06/28:4a
SELAUBLE, Lina, 22, NYC-M – 1893/12/08:4f
SELBACH, John, un. engineer, NYC-M – 1905/02/21:4a
SELBY, Eugenie, b. Debs, 51, + Terre Haute, IN – 1909/06/01:1d
SELDIS, Peter, 48, furrier, NYC-M – 1888/06/15:4d
SELIG, Bertha, b. Polansky, 41, NYC-M – 1891/04/04:4a
SELIG, Frederick's wife, 27, Dundee Lake, NJ,@ Genl Slocum, her = 1904/06/25:1c-d
SELIG, Minnie, 18, NYC-M – 1896/11/30:1e, 1 Dec:2f
SELIGMAN, Alfred B., banker, NYC – 1912/06/25:1f
SELIGMAN, Jesse, 26, treas. Gloversville Leather Co., & wife Mary, Gloversville, NY - 1915/12/17:1e
SELIGMAN, Joseph, 61, banker, USA 1838, NYC, + New Orleans – 1880/04/27:4a
SELIGMANN, Edward, 35, worker, NYC – 1902/11/23:1h
SELIGMANN, Rosa, 22, NYC-M – 1893/05/14:5b
SELIN, Christian, 23, tailor, Hoboken, NJ - 1917/04/01:1g
SELJE, Henry, NYC-M – 1902/05/09:3d
SELLECK, Maggie, NYC-B – 1886/08/07:2e
SELLICK, Al, NYPD, his = 1907/04/20:5b
SELLINS, Fannie, org. for United Mine Workers of Am., murdered Pittsburgh, PA - 1919/08/30:2b-c
SELLINS, Fannie, United Mining Workers org., murdered in Pittsburgh, PA – 1919/08/30:2b-c
SELTENREICH % Schader
SELTZ, Karl A. D., 59, NYC-B – 1907/09/16:6a
SELTZER, Joseph, baker, NYC-Bx - 1918/09/24:1f
SELZER, Jacob, 28, @1911 Triangle Shirt. Fire, NYC-M – 1911/03/27:1d
SEMEL, Julia, 35, NYC-M – 1891/03/09:4a
SEMFT, Lena, 26, War 2, NYC-M - 1916/02/09:2e
SEMLE, Jacob, un. brewer, NYC-M – 1910/12/05:6a
SEMM, William, machinist fr Detroit, + Ossining, NY – 1908/12/08:2e

SEMMERDINGER, Roland, 58, SP, un. carp., Fort Lee, NJ - 1919/01/02:6a
SEMMLER, Valentin, 72, NYC-M - 1891/03/29:5a
SEMPER, Gottfried, 76, German architect, + Rome/Italy - 1879/05/31:2c
SENDELBACH, C., NYC-B - 1915/12/21:6a
SENDZIMIR, Joseph de, 78, Pole,fought w. Kossuth 1848, farmer in Amityville, LI - 1881/08/12:1f, 15:1g
SENEKOVITCH, Alois, fr Steiermark?, West New York, NJ - 1918/01/30:6a
SENF, Hugo, 70, weaver & SPD Gera/Thueringen - 1912/05/19:3d
SENGELMANN, Henry, * Hamburg, NYC-M - 1914/04/26:7a
SENGER, Frances, NYC-M - 1885/05/26:3c,d
SENGER, Margarethe, b. Fragesser, NYC-M - 1892/06/08:4a
SENGER, Pauline, 70, NYC-M - 1906/03/25:5a
SENGSTACK, Henry, NYC-M - 1914/11/28:6a
SENK, Katherina, b. Rack, 67, NYC-B - 1913/03/01:6a
SENNER, Joseph Henry, Dr., 62, *Austria, journalist at NYSZ 1881-82, 85-93, immigr. Comm. under Cleveland, NYC-M - 1908/09/29:5e
SENNEWALD, Wilhelm, SLP, NYC-Q - 1898/02/26:4a, 27:5c, = & fam. 1:4d,e
SENNEWALT, Karl, 28, NYC-Q - 1907/12/26:6a
SENNING % Ott,
SENNWALDT, Michel, brewer, Union Hill, NJ - 1900/08/21:4b
SENS, William, un. carp., NYC-B - 1908/05/15:6a
SENSBACH, Philip, 37, NYC-M - 1892/10/12:4a
SENTS, John, un. cigarmaker, NYC-M - 1916/06/28:6a
SERBIA, Alexander, King of, murdered in Belgrad - 1903/06/12:1a-c, 2a-b, 3c, 13:1a-c, 14:4a, etc
SERES, Alexander, fr Hungary 1908, SP, NYC-B - 1911/12/11:2f
SERGEL, Wilhelmine, (Soergel?), b. Hoefer, see Hoefer
SERGER, A. Edward, NYC-M - 1910/04/19:6a
SERTH, Carl Oscar, 48, G-A journalist, * Darmstadt/Hessen, + Cincinatti,- OH 1878/07/30:2e
SESSLER, Anton, Newark, NJ - 1906/12/29:3b
SESSLER, August, un. painter, NYC-M - 1904/12/17:4a
SESSLER, Maria, NYC-Q - 1911/07/07:6a
SESTAUBER, Annie, 14, worker, NYC-M - 1883/12/23:1g, inquest 30:1f
SETTELE, Henry, NYC-Q - 1920/07/15:6a
SETTLER, Louis, 52, NYC-M - 1919/03/01:6a
SETZER, Charles, machinist, NYC-Bx - 1910/07/12:6a
SETZER, Charles, un. machinist, NYC-Bx - 1914/01/23:6a
SETZFAND, Charles, No. Bergen, NJ - 1918/10/01:6a

SEUBERT, Adam, NYC-Bx - 1909/07/17:6a
SEUBERT, Christine, NYC-M - 1915/03/30:6a
SEUBERT, Joseph, NYC-Bx - 1913/03/10:6a
SEUBERT, Mary, b. Wey, SLP?, NYC-B - 1898/02/07:4a, =9:4c, fam. 9:4a
SEUBERT, Wilhelm, 64, un. cigarmaker, SP, *12 Mr 1845 Wuerzburg/Gy, NYC-M - 1909/05/11:1g, 2a, 6a, 12:6a, =13:2c, fam. 14:6a, note 16:13a
SEUFERT, August, NYC-M - 1901/09/07:4a
SEULING, Lorenz, 26, butcher, NYC-M - 1909/05/20:2c
SEUSERLING % Kolm
SEVECKE, Carl, 62, un. carp., NYC-Q - 1906/11/06:6a, 8:6a
SEYDE, Ernst, un. waiter, NYC-M - 1894/06/20:4a
SEYDEN, Annie, 3, NYC-M - 1893/07/26:1b
SEYFFARTH, Gustav, Prof., egyptologist, Columbus, OH? - 1886/03/09:1f
SEYFRIED, Gordon, 12, So. Orange, NJ - 1918/12/02:2c
SEYLER, Jean, NYC-M - 1901/06/02:5a
SEYM, Richard F., 67, SP, un. carp, * Thueringen, SPD Mannheim 1870s, USA 1881, NYC-M - 1917/05/19:6a, 20:6a, = 22:6b, 23:6d
SEYMOUR, Frank, NYC-B - 1911/08/01:6a
SEYMOUR, Horatio, ex-gov. NYS - 1886/02/13:1b
SHAFFER, Hezekiah, exec. Chambersburg, PA - 1879/04/18:1c
SHAKE, August, un. cigarmaker, NYC-M - 1888/03/23:3b
SHANNON, Patrick, 40, alderman 5th Ward (Democrat), * Ireland, NYC-M - 1878/03/28:1f, = 30:1a
SHAPIRO, Harry, SP, USA 1904 fr Russia, NYC-M - 1906/11/30:2d
SHAPIRO, Rosie, 17, @1911 Triangle Shirtwaist Fire, NYC-M - 1911/03/27:1d
SHARP, Charles, Molly Maguire, exec. Mauch Chunk, PA - 1879/01/15:1c
SHARP, Jacob, millionaire, negat. obit, NYC-M - 1888/04/06:4e
SHARP, Mathilda, NYC-M - 1891/03/16:4a
SHARP, Nelson, Rochester, exec. Auburn, NY - 1913/12/11:1b
SHARP, Patrick, ldr of coal-miners, Lansford, PA - 1902/08/ 19:1c, a hero's grave 22:1c-d, 2b; grave mon. Tamaqua, PA - 1903/08/19:1c
SHERIDAN, John J., 47, NYPD detective, NYC-Q - 1902/07/17:1h
SHUMANN, Louis, NYC-M - 1896/08/11:1a
SHAW, Anna Howard, US feminist, posit. obit - 1919/07/04:4d
SHAW, Cornelius, exec. Montrose, PA - 1900/01/10:2h
SHAW, George B., Engl. writer & soc., #, his life (not +) 1910/08/21:3c-e, 28:3b-d
SHAW, Leander, Negro, lynched Pensacola, FL - 1908/07/31:1b
SHEEHAN, Eugene S., NYPD, NYC-B - 1907/10/23:1g
SHEEHAN, William F., ex-Lt Gov. of New York - 1917/03/15:1e

SHEFTET PASHA, Mahmud, Turkish Prime-Minister - 1913/06/12:1b, =13:1e, comment 5 Jy:4e-f
SHELJABOW, exec. for plot to kill Alex II of Russia, see Alex II
SHELLEY, Thomas J., realtor & local democratic ward pol., & children, NYC-M - 1918/06/23:1f
SHEPARD, Elliott F., publ. N.Y. Mail & Express, NYC-M – 1893/03/25:1h, 26:4a-b
SHEPARD, Wish, Negro, lynched Denton, MD - 1915/08/28:2e
SHEPPARD, Otto, NYC-B - 1894/02/03:4a
SHERIDAN, P., US genl, long obit – 1888/08/07:1e, =10:1f
SHERMAN, James S., US vice-pres. – 1912/10/31:1b
SHERMAN, William Tecumseh, US genl, 1891/02/14:1d, 15:1c, 17:4e, 18:1e, =20:1f-g
SHES, Adam, un. cigarmaker, NYC-M – 1888/06/14:3d
SHI KAI, Yuan, Chinese pres., & his eldest son - 1916/06/07:1d, 8:1d
SHIEBAKOFF, Rosalie, b. Schnorr, 28, NYC-M – 1881/04/30:3a
SHIELDS, J.A., US Immigration Commissioner, posit. obit. - 1914/07/09:4c
SHIELDS, William, deputy-sheriff under Boss Tweed, + Mt Vernon, NY – 1901/01/16:1g
SHINGLETON, Burgo, Negro, lynched Hemphill, TX – 1908/06/23:1e
SHIREY, Peter, Bavarian, ad to the heirs, - 1878/10/06:8c
SHONTS, Jim, Negro, lynched Tunica, MS – 1907/10/13:1b
SHONTS, Theodore P., pres. Interboro RR, NYC-M – 1919/11/08:2b, his will 13:1d, 14:2c
SICHEL, Joseph M., NYC-M - 1878/09/27:3a
SICHLER, George J., 77, NYC-Q - 1916/02/01:6a
SICK, Elizabeth, 74, NYC-B – 1893/12/30:4a
SICK, Peter, un. cigarmaker, NYC-M – 1887/10/19:3b
SICKINGER, Joseph, NYC-Q - 1918/03/04:6a
SICKINGER, Josephine, teenager, servant, USA 1891 fr Mainz/Gy, NYC-M – 1891/07/26:1h
SICURO, Prof., Italian Socialist, + Messina earthquake – 1909/02/23:4d
SIDLO, Joseph, 34, Czech stone cutter, NYC-M – 1904/11/13:1d
SIEBEL, Friedrich G., 6?, NYC-M – 1890/10/19:5b
SIEBEL, Henry, un. carp., NYC-Bx - 1916/04/17:6a
SIEBENEICHEN, Anna, & her Frohwein cousins, NYC-M – 1898/08/05:1g, 6:4c
SIEBENKAES % Lawson
SIEBER, Bernhard, un. carp., NYC-M – 1890/01/28:4a
SIEBER, Ernst, SDP, NYC-B – 1900/08/17:4a

SIEBERT % Hendel, % Kersten
SIEBERT, Dietrich, Yonkers, NY – 1912/06/05:6a;, mem. 1913/06/03:6a; 1914/06/03:6a; 1916/06/03:6a
SIEBERT, Fr., 54, boxmaker, NYC-M – 1880/11/04:4b
SIEBERT, Georg, 8, NYC-B – 1892/08/15:4e
SIEBERT, Georg, baker, NYC-M - 1916/04/10:1f
SIEBERT, H. W., 83, tailor, 1st treasurer US SLP in 1874, NYC-M – 1907/03/12:2d, 6a, 13:6a, =14:2e
SIEBERT, Henry, 25, typesetter, SLP, NYC-M – 1882/06/13:3b, =14:1g
SIEBERT, Karl, 12, NYC-M - 1878/03/10:8a
SIEBERT, Louise, (also Stiebinsky), 20, NYC-M – 1882/06/01:1e-f, =2:4c, inquest 10:1f, husband Charles rec 20 yrs 7 Dec:1f, 12:4b
SIEBERT, Mrs, NYC-M – 1890/09/15:4a
SIEBERT, Walburga, b. Rief, 50, fr Weissenborn/Bavaria, NYC-M - 1878/05/05:8b
SIEBURG, Georg, member Queens Labor Lyceum, NYC-B - 1920/01/08:6a
SIEDENTOPF, Heinrich, builder, SPD Quedlinburg/Gy– 1908/04/26:3d
SIEDHOFF, Carl, 91, Heidelberg U student, here private school manager, & wife, 93, Union Hill, NJ – 1887/06/02:3b, =3:2e
SIEDLER, Albert, NYC – 1913/01/07:6a
SIEDOW, Emil, NYC-M - 1917/05/06:7a
SIEFEN, Peter, 39, NYC-B – 1899/01/10:4a
SIEFERT, Henry, NYC?, +@ Genl Slocum – 1904/06/18:3c
SIEFERT, Katherine, b. Schaffner, 45, NYC-B – 1892/07/04:4a
SIEFKE, Henry, grocer, NYC-M, will – 1884/10/21:1g
SIEGEL, Anna, NYC-Bx – 1909/10/21:6a
SIEGEL, Edward, 54, innkeep, SLP, W. Hoboken, NJ – 1898/12/21:3b, 4a, 22:4a
SIEGEL, Emmanuel & Charles, NYC – 1906/09/04:6c, 3:2d
SIEGEL, Harry, hatstore mgr, NYC-B - 1913/12/18:2f
SIEGEL, John, 45, NYC-M – 1906/11/13:2b
SIEGEL, Louis, NYC-B – 1887/06/09:2e
SIEGEL, Sophie, 30, NYC-M, +@Genl Slocum – 1904/06/16:1e, 22:1d
SIEGELACK, Fr., NYC-Bx – 1907/01/20:7c
SIEGELE, Gottlieb, 45, cook, NYC-B – 1910/09/22:6a
SIEGEMUND, Friedrich R., 39, un. waiter, Jersey City, NJ - 1918/03/05:6a
SIEGENTHALER, John, Greenville, NJ – 1912/03/04:6a
SIEGERIST, Otto, >60, SPD Berlin-Charlottenburg – 1902/07/25:2d-e
SIEGERSON, Mary, 30, NYC-M – 1880/11/11:1e, 12:1e, =13:1f, note 17:1g, 18:9a, 20:1g, murderer found 4 Dec:1d, 5:5d, 7:1f
SIEGERT, Gustav, NYC-B – 1900/04/12:4a
SIEGERT, Leonhardt, 69, Jersey City Heights, NJ – 1889/06/13:4a
SIEGERT, Louis, 70, NYC-M – 1896/08/12:1a

SIEGERT, Victor, NYC-M – 1881/11/13:3b
SIEGFRIED, Ernst, SPD activist expelled from Wandsbek/Gy, arrived NYC – 1880/11/30:1d-e, 2 Dec:2a-b, 6:1d-e
SIEGFRIED, Philip, NYC-B - 1918/07/31:6a
SIEGHART, Emilie, 48, NYC-M - 1894/01/12:4a
SIEGLER, Margarethe, 63, NYC-M - 1878/01/28:3d
SIEGMANN, Henry, treasurer Order of St John, NYC-B – 1910/12/21:3a
SIEGMANN, Magdalena, 69, NYC - 1914/03/27:6a
SIEGMOND, Annie & a little boy, NYC-M, + @ Genl Slocum – 1904/06/18:3c
SIEGMUND % Herwegh
SIEGMUND, Johann, NYC-M – 1897/04/25:5d
SIEGOLD, John, West Hoboken, NJ – 1910/08/06:6a
SIEGOLD, Mrs, NYC-M – 1912/11/03:7b
SIEGRIST, Adolph, 38, NYC-M - 1895/02/01:4a
SIEGRIST, Heinrich, un. carpenter, NYC-M - 1894/05/03:4a
SIEGWART, Katherina, b. Held, 56, NYC-M – 1891/03/30:4a
SIELING, Karl Gustav, 66, NYC-B – 1919/10/11:6a
SIEMAN, Otto, 2, NYC-M – 1902/07/12:2g
SIEMANN, Heinrich Karl, 21, NYC-M – 1891/03/23:4a
SIEMENS, Wilhelm, 63, German inventor, + England – 1883/11/21:1a, 2c
SIEMER, Anna, b. Riehl, 40, NYC-B – 1891/03/14:4a, 16:4a
SIEMER, Richard, Hoboken, NJ – 1900/07/19:4a
SIEMERS, Christoph, NYC-Q - 1914/04/28:6a
SIEMS, Helene, 52, Hoboken, NJ - 1895/03/02:4a
SIEPGEN, John, machinist, Paterson, NJ – 1897/02/04:4c
SIERCK % Laemmle
SIERICHS, Lottie, 38, NYC-M, + @Genl Slocum – 1904/06/17:3c, 18:3c
SIES, John, Elizabeth, NJ – 1909/07/11:7c
SIESECKE, Anna, 3, Newark, NJ – 1891/08/26:4a
SIESS, Wilhelm, NYC-M – 1904/03/14:4a
SIESSERWALD, Carl, NYC-M – 1909/09/29:6a
SIETZ, John, 35?, NYC-M – 1889/09/15:5b
SIEVER, Fritz, 70, NYC-Bx – 1910/01/02:1e
SIEVER, Henry, 27, grocery clerk, NYC-M – 1882/10/21:3c
SIEVERS, Emil, NYC-M – 1887/04/02:3c
SIEVERS, Emma, b. Braitling, 29, Springfield, MA – 1886/04/19:5f
SIEVERS, Ernst, 1, Springfield, MA – 1885/11/06:3a
SIEVERS, Juergen, fr Schleswig-Holstein?, NYC-B – 1883/04/10:3d
SIEVERS, Martha, 60, NYC-B - 1914/09/02:3d
SIEVERT, Eugen, 25, SP (Lettonian branch), USA 1907, + NYC-SI – 1913/07/21:3e-f

SIEWERT, Caroline, b. Wolf, NYC-M - 1920/07/06:6a
WOLF % Siewert
SIEVERT, Wilhelm, 47, NYC-M - 1919/11/24:6e
SIEWART, Phoebe, NYC-M, + @ Genl Slocum - 1904/06/18:3c
SIEWER, John E., 58?, NYC-B - 1891/03/21:4a
SIGEL, Elsie, 23, granddaughter of genl Franz Sigel, NYC-Bx - 1909/06/20:1c, 21:3c, 22:1g, 23:1e, 24:2c, 25:1a,2b, 27:6a-b, 29:1e, 6 Jy:2e, 11:6b, 15:1d, 5 Aug:2c; murderer fd 25 Sept:1d, etc
SIGEL, Franz, 77, G-A general '48 revol. & US Civil War, NYC-Bx - 1902/08/22:2c, g, =25:3e, NY Turnverein mem. meeting 14 Sept:5c, grave mon. 23:3b, 24 Oct:3b; Wilhelm Blos' biography of him 28 Sept:4c-f, statue at Riverside Drive & 106th St, 1907/10/13:1f, 18:4a-b, 19:1f, 20:1g;
SIGISMUND, Fuld, 65, NYC-M - 1894/01/25:4a
SIGNAROWITZ, Georg, NYC-B - 1914/11/05:6a
SIMMONS, Edith, 35, movie actress now as Edith Creighton, + New Brunswick, NJ - 1917/07/18:2d
SIGMUND, Frederick, SP & ex-pres Baker Union #3, married Carrie Abel, NYC-Q - 1907/09/08:7e
SIKOROWSKY % Zoelly
SILBERBLATT, Samuel, fr Russia 1904, NYC-M - 1904/05/03:2h
SILBERER, Franz, SP, un. baker & MdR Austria - 1912/02/03:4d, 11:3f, 24 Mr:3c, #17 Ap:1e, 6a, 11 Aug:3e,f
SILBERNAGEL, John D., 54, craftsman, NYC-M - 1896/07/09:1d
SILBERZAHN, Ch., NYC-B - 1907/12/26:6a
SILEMAN, Ludwig, carriage maker, NYC-M - 1903/12/04:1e
SILER, Kate, 69, NYC-M, +@ Genl Slocum - 1904/06/17:3c
SILKE, Conrad, 35, ship stoker, USA 1904, NYC-B - 1912/10/30:6a
SILLBERG, Theodor, un. cigarmkr, NYC-B - 1893/03/19:5a
SILVARIO, Pietro, exec. Trenton, NJ - 1910/08/10:2f
SILVERMAN, Bernard, engineer, NYC-B - 1899/01/13:3c
SILVERMAN, Louis, 30, hatter, NYC-B - 1887/02/16:2e
SILVERMAN, Marcel, jeweler, SDP, NYC-Bx, - 1901/02/07:3f, 3 Mr:1d
SILVERMAN, Marcel's wife, NYC-M - 1902/02/28:1e
SILVERMANN, Simcha, 104, fr Russia 1853, NYC-B - 1911/02/27:3c
SILVERSTEIN, Rudolph, engineer, NYC-Bx 1919/08/11:3e
SILVERSTEIN, Selig, tailor & SP?, NYC-M 1908/04/29:1e
SILVERY, Nicodemus, 62, NYC-B - 1892/06/29:4a
SIMANSKY, William, 49, tailor, USA ~ 1862, NYC-M - 1882/04/01:4b
SIMON % Buechler
SIMON, Ada, 47, music teacher, Boonton, NJ - 1911/03/28:3c
SIMON, Alex, NYC-B - 1904/11/11:4a
SIMON, Arthur, 45, Greenville, NJ - 1901/02/03:5b

SIMON, Auguste, servant, St Louis, IL - 1878/10/14:2e
SIMON, Benjamin, 14, SLP?, NYC-M - 1897/07/26:1d
SIMON, Charlotte, b. Gold, 42, NYC-M - 1892/09/30:4a
SIMON, Clara, NYC-M - 1920/02/03:8a
SIMON, Dora, NYC-M - 1880/03/20:1f
SIMON, Ernst S., 40, silk manuf. Fr Lyons/France, + NYC-M - 1907/07/26:1d
SIMON, Ferdinand, Dr., German scientist & son-in-law of August Bebel - 1912/01/07:1f, 16:4d-e
SIMON, Friedrich, 23, NYC-M - 1890/07/04:4a
SIMON, Gustav, NYC clothes manuf., Anicia de Massy on trial 19 Nv - 1907/04/25:1c, 26:1e, 27:1e, 30:1e, 1 May:2b, 2:1g, guilty 3:1d, 6:5e
SIMON, Gustav, 26, druggist, NYC-Bx - 1917/10/21:11e
SIMON, Hermanda E., 5, NYC-M - 1890/08/11:4a
SIMON, Hermann, silk manuf., Union Hill, NJ, + 27 Sept., caustic note on his will - 1913/10/06:1b, 7:4c
SIMON, John P. L., Dr., 45, Wards' Island, NY - 1889/11/08:1f, 4a, 7:1f
SIMON, John, Dr., 65, NYC-M - 1894/01/29:4c
SIMON, Jules, Republ. Polit. In France, crit. obit - 1896/06/09:2c
SIMON, Michael, un. brewer, NYC-M - 1907/11/09:6a, fam. 25:6a
SIMON, Theodore, Dr., 47, NYC-M - 1892/09/12:4a
SIMON, Wendel, 42, NYC-M - 1891/09/20:5f
SIMONS, August, 54, painter, NYC-M - 1910/09/06:5b
SIMONS, Gustav, blouse manuf., NYC-M - 1906/11/20:1a, 21:6d
SIMONS, Salomon, NYC-M - 1891/03/17:4a
SIMONSOHN, Albert, un. cigarmaker, NYC-M - 1894/03/19:4a
SIMONSOHN, Ellen, nurse, 30, NYC-M - 1893/05/07:5c
SIMONSON, Philip, washer, NYC-M - 1902/07/25:1f
SIMROCK, Karl, 1802-??, Prof. Bonn U & poet - 1902/09/14:9b-d
SIMS, David, Negro, lynched Coahoma, MS - 1905/11/23:4a
SIMSROTT, William A., ex-fin. Secy Switchmen's Mutual Union, + Chicago, IL - 1896/05/13:1b
SINDER, John, 39, NYC-M - 1892/05/06:4a
SINDRAM, William, trial for killing Mrs Crave, NYC - 1881/12/06:1e, 8:4b-c, 9:1e, guilty 11:5d, 13:1g, 20:1g; exec. postponed 9 Fb 1882:1g, appeal lost 1 Mr:1f, 7:1d-e, 8:1g, exec postponed 9:1g, notes 18 Apr:1g, 19:1f, 21:1f, done 22:1e-f, note 22:2a
SINEY, John, ex-pres. US Miners' Assoc., St Clair, PA - 1880/04/19:5c
SINGE, Fritz, Newark, NJ, SP? - 1913/09/30:6a
SINGER, Anton, coachman, NYC-M - 1906/08/07:1e
SINGER, Bernard, ~45, milkman, NYC-B - 1886/08/30:2g, inquest 1 Sept:2e, 2:2d, 11:2a, wife on trial 10 Dec:2d, 20:2c

SINGER, Charles, SLP, NYC-Bx - 1878/09/29:8b
SINGER, Hermann, 68, Jersey City, NJ – 1903/08/21:4c
SINGER, Joseph, 55, NYC-B - 1914/05/08:6a
SINGER, Martin, 48, Union Hill, NJ - 1878/04/22:3b
SINGER, Paul, 67, SPD leader, MdR, NYC mourns, too – 1911/02/01:1a-c, 4a, 5:4a-b, =6:1a-b, NYC mem. 6:1g, 2a, poem by Biedenkapp 12:20g, 13:4e, #18:1b-d, 4e-f, 22:4e, by August Bebel 20 Fb:4d-f, 21:4e-f, 27:4d, 4 Mr:4d; will 1911/07/26:4d; grave monument 1913/03/02:3b
SINGER, will of the fdr of Sewing Machine Co – 1907/03/28:4a
SINJAWSKI, alias Purkin, Russian revol., exec. St Petersburg – 1907/09/28:4d-e
SINKER, Jacob, 55, shoemaker, NYC-M – 1900/08/27:4b
SINN, Jacob, 64, un. cigarmaker, SP, NYC-Bx – 1911/02/16:2a, 6a
SINNIGER Jr., John J. US Army, War 1 in France, NYC-M - 1918/12/01:12a
SINNIGER, Emma, b. Schaefer, 22, NYC-M – 1891/12/12:4a
SINNIGER, Mrs, b. Ziesat, NYC-M – 1890/12/12:4a
SINNOFF, James P., 42, marine court judge, NYC-M – 1880/09/21:4a
SINRAM, Frida, 18, NYC-Q – 1890/12/06:4a
SINSHEIMER, Adolph, NYC-M - 1894/10/15:4a
SIPILA, Charles, NYC-M – 1912/09/04:6a
SIPJAGIN, Russian Interior Minister, killed by revol. 1902/04/16:1h, 18:1d, 24:1e, Balscheneff exec. 13 May:1h, 26:2c, 30:2c,
SIPP, Mrs, and George, 7, dying, NYC-M – 1888/04/04:1g
SIPPEL, Gustav, un. carp., Bayonne, NJ - 1920/06/21:6a, fam. 25:6a
SIRKA, Isidor, fr Austria, mill employee, + Belmont, NJ – 1899/07/25:4b
SIRODZKI, Philipp, "Gerassimow," Russian Socialist, + Lezin/Switz. - 1913/12/10:4d
SIRY, Bertha, NYC-M - 1917/01/06:6a
SISCO, Sanford, exec. Bergen County Jail, NJ – 1885/06/06:3b
SISTARE, George K., 50, banker, NYC-M – 1892/07/29:1g
SITTENHELM, Chr., NYC-B – 1909/01/28:6a
SITTIG, Dorette, un. cigar maker, NYC-M – 1889/03/01:4a
SITTIG, Georg, un. cigar maker, ex-pres. German Cigar Makers' Union, NYC-M – 1885/09/03:3a
SITTING BULL, First Nation freedom fighter, murdered, 1890/12/16:1d, 17:1c, 27:2a-b, 30:2a-b
SKADISKIE, Lizzie, 6, NYC-M, +@1883 School Fire, NYC-M
SKALA, Emanuel, 62, SP, locksmith, * Vienna, silver wedding 9 Jy 1903:3e-f, + NYC-B – 1913/08/24:7c, = 25:2d
SKALA, Leopoldine, 56, cook at Labor Lyceum, NYC-B – 1910/01/02:7c, =3:5d, fam. 10:6a

SKALAK, Frank, 36, un. cornice maker, NYC-M - 1895/12/18:3a
SKALIL, Rudolf, liquor dealer?, Hudson Co., NJ?, fam. 1909/01/10:7a
SKALIZKY % Popart
SKALIZKY, Ferdinand, NYC-M, + Buffalo, NY – 1893/09/13:1b
SKAMENE, Leo, waiter, NYC-B – 1912/05/08:3a-b
SKEFFINGTON, F. Sheehy, Irish patriot & Soc.,exec. Dublin, NYC SP mem. meeting – 1916/05/27:2b, noted 1917/01/10:4b
SKERSETH, Agathe, 15, Audubon, NJ - 1913/06/09:2a
SKIBER, Joseph, *18 March 1879 in Austria?, NYC-B – 1909/03/22:6a
SKLADANY, Johann, 62, textile worker & SP Bruenn/Moravia - 1915/01/24:3e
SKLAVER, Berel, 25, @1911 Triangle Shirtwaist Fire, NYC-M – 1911/03/27:1d
SKORJANZ, Andreas, NYC-M - 1915/11/11:6a
SKOWERLY, Nicholas, 45, NYC-M – 1889/11/20:1e
SKWARSKI, Stanislaus, 55, Newark, NJ – 1905/12/27:3f
SLABERG, Carl, Swede, inventor, NYC-B – 1904/06/09:3c
SLAWEK, John, 20, + on SS Lapland - 1913/05/27:2c
SLEIGHT, Minna, b. Perle, 33, NYC-M - 1894/10/18:4a
SLEIK, Philip, un. tailor, SP?, NYC-M – 1919/11/01:6a
SLEZAK, John, un. carp., NYC-M – 1907/03/04:6a, 5:6a
SLICK, Frank, 42, un. painter & clerk, SP, *Philad., + Chicago, =Quackertown, PA – 1909/03/24:2b
SLIVA, Hans, un. butcher, NYC-B - 1915/06/16:2g
SLOCUM, James, exec. Ossining, NY – 1891/07/03:1g, rev. 14:2e, 16:1h
SLORY, Charles, NYC-Bx - 1920/02/27:6a
SLOUP, Adolf, 50, NYC-M – 1899/06/09:4a
SLOVENICK, Andrew, coal-miner, @ 1897 Hazleton Massacre
SLOWAK, Josepha, Trenton, NJ – 1909/07/28:3c
SLYDNEW, Peter A., Russian socialist, + Siberia - 1914/01/30:4d-e
SMALL, Allen, Negro, lynched Lynchburg, TN - 1903/09/26:1b
SMALL, George, exec. Mt Holly, NJ – 1906/03/24:3d, done 25:5f
SMARCH, John, NYC-M - 1915/07/01:6a
SMETANA, August, 50th anniv. Death of Czech Socialist in Prague – 1901/02/16c-d
SMILER, Harris, exec. Ossining, NY – 1891/07/03:1g, rev. 14:2e, 16:1h
SMITH, Alex, 26, butcher, fr Holland, NYC-M – 1889/02/10:5b
SMITH, Anthony J., NYC-Bx - 1917/10/04:6a
SMITH, Ben, Rev., Negro, lynched Swainsboro, GA – 1911/05/22:1b
SMITH, Bertha, 10, NYC-M, +@Genl Slocum – 1904/06/22:1d
SMITH, C. Sprague, 57, US Reformer, laudat. Obit – 1910/03/31:4b
SMITH, Charles & Davis, Negroes, lynched Clayton, NC – 1884/12/29:1f

SMITH, Ed, Negro, lynched Wetumpka, AL - 1915/01/05:6a
SMITH, Ely, 85, ex-NYC mayor, + Livingston, NY – 1911/07/02:7g
SMITH, Eugene, engineer, 1880s active KoL, Hoboken, NJ – 1913/01/01:1c
SMITH, F.W., NYC-B – 1913/09/25:6a
SMITH, Fannie, NYC-M, +@ on Genl Slocum – 1904/06/18:3c
SMITH, Gant, 42, Negro, lynched Maysville, KY - 1920/03/31:5e
SMITH, Henry, Negro, lynched Desark, AK – 1881/07/13:1c
SMITH, Henry, Negro, lynched, Paris, TX –1893/02/01:1c, 3:1c,2b-c
SMITH, J. Frank, SP, Wilmington, DE – 1911/05/31:6a
SMITH, James H., 65, treas. Theatrical Mechan. Union, NYC-B - 1913/12/18:3c
SMITH, James, exec. Upper Marlboro, MD – 1896/12/19:3f
SMITH, Jean C., Dr., physician on HAPAG steamer Westerwald, + Kingston, Jamaica – 1912/05/13:2e
SMITH, John, Cincinatti, exec. Columbus, OH – 1890/08/30:1d
SMITH, Josef, NYC-Q – 1901/02/23:4a
SMITH, Josephine, 22, NYC-M – 1896/12/24:4a, 25:4a
SMITH, Maggie, 8, Jersey City, NJ – 1885/11/26:1e, =27:3a
SMITH, Mamie, NYC-M, +@ Genl Slocum – 1904/06/18:3c
SMITH, Margaret, 15, NYC-M, +@Genl Slocum – 1904/06/23:1b
SMITH, Mary, 10, Asbury Park, NJ – 1910/11/14:1c, 15:1d
SMITH, Mary, NYC – 1900/05/04:1d
SMITH, Mary, NYC-M, +@ Genl Slocum – 1904/06/16:1c, 17:3c
SMITH, Mildred, 3, NYC-M, +@ Genl Slocum – 1904/06/17:3c
SMITH, Peter J., labor org., officer Intern. Structural Iron Workers' Union, jailed for role in McNamara case, + after pardon Cleveland, OH - 1916/07/30:1c
SMITH, Peter, exec. NYC-M – 1887/04/29:3a, 3:2f, 4:2g, 5:4b, +6:2g
SMITH, Rev. George E., 45, minister African Zion Church, NYC-M - 1894/03/29:1e
SMITH, Robert, Negro, lynched Roanoke, VA – 1893/09/21:4b, 22:1h,2a, 26:1d, 28:1g
SMITH, Sarah Ellen, "temperance fanatic" fr Philadelphia, crit. Obit – 1885/01/22:2e-f
SMITH, Tillie, + Hackelstown, NJ, murderer sent. to jail - 1887/05/18:2e
SMITH, Utes, Negro, lynched Winnsboro, SC - 1915/06/15.1f
SMITH, Will, lynched Wetumpka, AL - 1915/01/05:6a
SMITH, Wright, Negro, lynched Annapolis, MD – 1898/10/06:1b
SMOLENSKI, John, un. furniture maker, NYC-M – 1893/04/25:4a
SMOLKE, Paul, ship's steward, @1900 Dock Fire, Hoboken, NJ – 1900/07/03:1c

SNEAD, Rockledge's wife, NJ, her brother Wilhelm Hasenbalg + War 1, Germany - 1914/11/09:2e-f
SNIZEK, Anton, 42, cigarmaker, Czech, NYC-M - 1901/05/29:4b
SNODOWSKY, Max, NYC-M - 1912/10/29:1d
SOBBE, Dietrich, 53, NYC-M - 1899/03/03:2h
SOBEL, Simon, 34, waiter, NYC-M - 1900/11/20:1g
SOBEL, Sophia, 24, NYC-M - 1904/05/19:3e
SOBOLESKI, Peter, 38, Newark, NJ - 1912/11/11:3c
SOBOTKER, Laurentius, 72, NYC-B - 1879/01/21:4e
SODEN, Mary E., 61, & children Edwin, 37, & Ella, 32, NYC-M - 1908/09/27:1e
SOEBER, Martin, 70, NYC-B - 1914/03/04:5e
SOEHLKE, Charles F., 40, un. printer, NYC-B - 1918/02/04:6a
SOEHNEL, Constantin, un. carp., NYC-B - 1908/01/02:6a
SOEHNLE, Fritz, un. butcher, NYC-B - 1914/02/19:6a, 20:6a
SOELLER, Alfred, NYC-M - 1891/04/01:4a
SOELLER, Oswald, NYC-B - 1891/06/17:4a
SOELLER, William, infant, NYC-M - 1888/05/21:3a
SOELLNER, August, 59, silk weaver, SLP, * Dresden/Gy, USA 1874, NYC-M - 1897/01/04:4a, 3:4a, 5:4a, =6:3g
SOELLNER, Pauline, NYC-M - 1897/02/22:4a
SOFER, Max, exec. Philadelphia, PA - 1908/04/08:5f
SOFKA, Valeska, NYC-Bx - 1918/12/18:6a
SOHL, Henry, lithographer, NYC-M - 1893/07/04:4e
SOHLER, Alois, 37, NYC-M - 1891/07/07:4a
SOHLER, August, un. butcher, NYC - 1913/03/15:6a
SOHLER, Marquard, 54, un. carp., SP?, NYC-Bx - 1906/01/11:4a
SOHLKE, Georg, NYC-M - 1885/05/03:1g
SOHMER, Isidor, waiter, NYC-M - 1918/08/14:1d
SOHNER, Philip, NYC-B - 1918/11/02:6a, 3:12a
SOHR, August, 29, un. bricklayer, NYC-M - 1903/04/12:5a, 13:4a, fam. 15:4a
SOLDAU, Robert, NYC-B - 1906/01/23:4a
SOLDNER, Charles, NYC-Bx - 1909/09/23:6a
SOLGER, Kate, NYC-M - 1906/06/13:4a
SOLKE, Dora, NYC-M, +@ Genl Slocum - 1904/06/17:3c
SOLLE, Kaspar, 12, NYC-Bx - 1913/11/16:7f
SOLLMANN, John, un. carp., NYC-B - 1884/10/20:3b
SOLMAN, Otto, baker, fr Hanza/Finland, NYC-B - 1907/08/27:3b-c
SOLOMAN, Gottlieb, un. carp., NYC-M - 1891/06/14:5b
SOLOMON, Joseph, 45, tailor, NYC-M - 1888/12/31:1h
SOLOMON, Moses, infant, NYC-M - 1903/07/10:1f

SOLOVIEW, Lt., Russian nihilist, exec. - 1879/06/30:2d
SOLTAU, Ernst & Robert, NYC-M? - 1892/07/29:1h
SOLTES, Alex, 64, NYC-M - 1892/07/02:4a
SOLZMANN, Jack, Bayonne, NJ - 1918/10/09:6a
SOMBORN, Jakob, NYC-M - 1892/01/31:1d
SOMLO, Salomon, SP, *16 Mr 184? Olaliszka/Tokay, Hungary, + Zuerich/Switz. - 1912/03/31:3e-f
SOMMER, Adam, Jersey City Heights, NJ - 1897/05/30:5a
SOMMER, Charlie, child, NYC-M - 1889/12/07:4a
SOMMER, Frederick, Jersey City Heights, NJ - 1905/05/05:7c
SOMMER, Friedrich, 40, NYC-M - 1888/09/05:3b
SOMMER, Georg, 60, cigarmaker, NYC-B - 1900/07/03:2h
SOMMER, John, un. fireman, NYC-M - 1900/07/14:4a, 15:5a
SOMMER, Wilhelm, un. fireman, NYC-M - 1900/06/10:5a, 11:4a
SOMMERDIENER, F., NYC - 1913/03/15:6a
SOMMERFELD, Julius, un. tailor, NYC-M - 1893/09/15:4a
SOMMERKALB, Mr., 85, & Mrs, 78, NYC-M - 1886/06/14:1f
SOMMERLING, Philip, exec. Chicago, IL - 1912/02/16:1b, done 17:1c
SOMMERS, Adolph, 47, butcher, NYC - 1915/06/28:2f
SOMMERS, Carl, 40, upholsterer, Jersey City, NJ ? - 1907/03/09:3c-d
SOMMERS, Frank, 38, un. driver, Jersey City, NJ - 1911/09/22:1d
SOMSACK, Irma, b. Bahery, 43, fr Bozenau?, NYC-M - 1905/05/19:7b
SONACK, Catherine, 17, servant fr Hungary 1899, NYC-M - 1899/08/27:1d
SONDERMANN % Wills
SONDERMANN, Hermann, 76, machinist, NYC-B - 1918/02/26:6a
SONNE, Peter, NYC-M - 1915/09/04:6a
SONNEMANN, Henry C., 35, salesman, NYC - 1880/05/24:1e
SONNEMANN, Leopold, publ. Frankfurter Zeitung, crit. obit - 1909/11/02:4c
SONNEMANN, Louise, b. Schmidt, 71, NYC-M - 1891/01/04:5a
SONNENBERG, Amelia, 57, NYC-M? - 1914/01/31:6a, 1 Fb:7a
SONNENBERG, Barbara, 74, NYC-M - 1889/05/29:4a
SONNENSCHEIN % Leuckert
SONNENSCHEIN, David, 27, clothes manuf., Bayonne, NJ - 1914/10/15:2e
SONNENTHAL, Adolph, one of greatest German actors, * 31 Dec 1834 Pest/Hungary of Jewish Parents, to play 14 days at NYC G-A theaters, his life 1885/03/03:2e-f, also 1:2e-f?, 8:4f-g, in NYC 9 Mr:4d, 10:4d, 11:4a, 15:4c-e, 18:4a, etc, review 25:4c, 29:4e
SONNEWALD, Carl, 76, Dutch Kills, NY - 1893/07/27:4a, fam. 29:4a
SONTAG, Carl, 72, German actor, + Dresden/Gy - 1900/06/25:2d

SORENSEN, Annie, 1, NYC-B - 1913/06/10:3b, 11:3a
SORG, John, NYC-M – 1882/10/11:1f
SORGAN, Otto, NYC-M - 1920/10/05:6a
SORGE, Adolph, music teacher, SP, * 9 Nv 1827 Tschonewitz/Thueringia,
 '48er, USA 1852, Hoboken, NJ – 1906/10/27:1g, 2a-b, 4a-b, 6a, =29:3c
SORGE, Katharina, 77, Hoboken, NJ - 1914/12/26:6a, = 29:2d
SORKIN, Rosie, 18, NYC-B, @1911 Triangle Shirtwaist Fire, NYC-M –
 1911/03/27:1d, =28:1f
SOROKO, Konstantin, 50, Newark, NJ – 1910/11/30:6a
SOSCH, Vincent, 45, un. cigarmaker, NYC-M – 1903/12/10:4a
SOSNA, comrade, 24, plasterer, SPD Kattowitz, Gy – 1910/01/30:7c
SOSNA, Lena, 22, Hoboken, NJ - 1904/05/25:4a
SOSNOWSKI, Jeannette, 70, NYC-M - 1892/09/22:4a
SOSSAU, John, 62, painter, NYC-M – 1907/02/26:2b
SOTTER, A., NYC-M – 1907/09/14:6a
SOTTER, Antony, NYC-M - 1914/05/21:6a
SOUDERS, Sylvan, exec. Trenton, NJ - 1913/06/19:2c
SOUTHERN, Charles, 55, SDP, ed. Iron Age, NYC-M – 1902/06/29:5e
SOUTHWICK, Nellie, NYC-M – 1887/12/21:1d
SOWEA, Victor, weaver fr Bohemia, West Hoboken, NJ – 1880/02/07:1g
SPACK, Franz, NYC-M - 1912/09/26:6a
SPAEHNE, Wilhelm, fr Luxemburg, + Chicago, IL – 1892/04/19:1b
SPAETH % Sauthoff
SPAETH, Eugene Charles, 19, NYC-Q - 1915/04/06:6a
SPAETH, Fritz, un. baker, NYC-Bx - 1915/08/18:6a
SPAETH, Gottlieb, 44, NYC-Q - 1915/04/13:6a, 14:6a
SPAETH, Friedrich, dying, wife, 30, cook, alr +, Newark, NJ –
 1887/01/03:1g, 5 Jan.:2f, 7:2f
SPAHN % Lenz
SPAHN, Anna, b. Betz, Jersey City Heights, NJ – 1888/03/15:3a
SPAHN, Jantina, b. Santing, 52, SP, NYC-B - 1915/12/22:6a
SPAHR, Heinrich, NYC-Bx - 1918/12/17:6a
SPAIN, Alfonso, King – 1885/11/26:1a, 28:1a
SPALDING, Franklin S., 49, Episcopalian bishop of Utah & friend of labor
 - 1914/09/27:11f
SPALIN, Rudolph, NYC-B – 1906/04/03:4a
SPANFELDER, Ed., NYC-M - 1918/04/16:6a
SPANGENBERG, Henry, un. cigarmaker, NYC-M – 1883/09/14:3c
SPANGLER, Lizzie, 59, NYC-B - 1898/07/07:4a
SPANKNEBEL, Henry, 26, NYC-M - 1895/02/18:4a
SPANKNEBEL, John, 1, NYC-M – 1887/11/12:3a
SPANKNEBEL, John, 63, un. liquordealer?, NYC-M – 1902/12/29:4a

SPANN, Frederick, NYC-B – 1911/10/14:6a
SPANN, Louis, Newark, NJ – 1902/10/07:4b
SPANN, Sophie, SP, Newark, NJ - 1916/08/14:6a, fam. 20:7a
SPANNAGEL, Julius, NYC-M? – 1893/03/31:4a
SPANNER, John, NYC-M – 1903/05/15:4a
SPANNKNEBEL, Anna Maria, b. Mergenthaler, 50, NYC-M – 1898/08/06:4a
SPANNKNEBEL, Conrad, 69, NYC-B – 1900/01/20:5c
SPARBERT, Wilhelm, un. furrier, NYC-M – 1883/12/10:3a
SPARKS, Richard, 17, exec. Trenton, NJ - 1915/01/06:2f
SPARMANN, Arnold P., Hoboken, NJ - 1915/10/27:6a
SPATH, Nikolaus, NYC-M – 1885/08/12:3b
SPATZ, George, innkeep, dying, NYC-B – 1906/05/07:1d
SPEARMAN, Dave, Negro, lynched near Prosperity, SC – 1881/01/22:1b
SPECHST, August, Dr., 64, Free-thinker, ex-edit. weekly Menschenthum – 1909/07/11:3a
SPECHT, August, 7, NYC-M – 1884/09/25:3d
SPECHT, Frederick J., 27, coachman, Newark, NJ – 1912/11/18:1d
SPECK, Adolf, Prof., 54, NYC-M - 1894/01/25:4a
SPECK, Ed., Elizabeth, NJ – 1909/03/02:6a
SPECK, John, 35, NYC-M – 1892/06/21:4a
SPECK, Minnie, NYC-M, + @ Genl Slocum – 1904/06/17:3c
SPEH, Dietrich, 68, fr Kreuznach/Nahe, NYC-M – 1912/03/08:6a
SPEICHER, Francis, 18, NYC-M - 1920/07/11:12a
SPEICHER, John, NYC-M - 1918/10/13:11g
SPEIDEL, Gregor, engineer, NYC-M – 1906/06/03:5b
SPEIGEL, Hirsch, 45, NYC-M – 1908/07/08:1e
SPEIGHT, William S., worker, NYC-M - 1878/02/06:4e
SPEISBAUCH, Herman, 54,un.carp.,NYC-B - 1913/11/17:6a, 18:6a
SPELLMAN, John, jockey, NYC-M – 1887/11/24:1f
SPELLMAN, Moses, Negro, lynched Hemphill, TX – 1908/06/23:1e
SPELTOW, Emil L., 16, NYC-M – 1886/11/19:1d
SPENCER, Herbert, English social scientist, his dog-eat-dog philosophy crit. sharply 1903/12/09:1e, 10:2b-c, 13:4a-c
SPENCER, William, Negro, lynched Graceton, TX - 1916/10/06.1c
SPENGER, Rose, NYC-M, + @ Genl Slocum – 1904/06/17:3c
SPENGERMANN, Louis, waiter, NYC-M – 1886/02/02:1c
SPENGLER, Andreas, NYC-M – 1903/11/04:4a
SPENGLER, Carl H., 68, fr Ronneburg/Thuringia, NYC-Q – 1889/05/09:4a
SPENGLER, Elisabeth, 61, NYC-M – 1906/03/02:4a
SPENGLER, Lizzie, 23, NYC-B – 1885/05/28:2g
SPENNER, Friedrich, Union Hill, NJ – 1907/04/15:6a

SPERB % Fink
SPERBER, Karl Leopold, 37, NYC-M – 1891/04/17:4a
SPERBER, Konrad A., typesetter, ex-NYVZ, NYC-M – 1911/07/11:2d, 6a
SPERLING % Ibsen
SPERLING, (Mr), NYC-M – 1887/05/30:3c
SPERLING, Helena, 40, Hoboken, NJ - 1895/02/19:1g
SPERLING, Helene, 17, NYC-M – 1891/05/29:4a
SPERLING, Michael, 48, NYC-B – 1888/02/06:2c
SPERNER, Adolf, Hoboken, NJ - 1915//09/22:6a
SPETH, Anton, un. carp., NYC-B – 1913/03/28:6a
SPETHAN, Mike, un. carp., NYC-M – 1902/07/04:4a
SPEYER, Friedrich, 52, NYC-Q – 1896/09/03:4a, 4:4a
SPEYER, Margarethe, NYC-Q - 1915/01/30:6a
SPEYER, Sophie, 62, NYC-M - 1917/11/11:7a
SPIEGEL, Adelaide, b. Borg, NYC-M – 1911/09/20:6a
SPIEGEL, Agnes, 10, NYC-M - 1916/01/03:2f
SPIEGEL, Anton, un. carp., NYC-M – 1886/08/03:3c
SPIEGEL, Charles, Jr., 40, cartoonist for Puck, Passaic, NJ – 1905/01/30:3b
SPIEGEL, Friedrich, 11, NYC-M – 1892/07/29:1h
SPIEGEL, Jacobus D., 26, NYC-M - 1878/05/22:3b
SPIEGEL, Valentin, 43, NYC-M - 1916/06/03:6a
SPIEGELHALTER, Wielandine, b. Schmeling, NYC, + Torrington, CT – 1913/02/16:7c
SPIEHL, Rosa, infant, NYC-B – 1880/09/25:3a
SPIEKER % Grobel
SPIEL, Friedericke, b. Lehmann, 75, NYC-Bx - 1914/01/26:6a
SPIELER, Heymann, 45, peddler, NYC-M – 1902/04/17:2h
SPIELHAGEN, Friedrich, 81, writer, + Berlin – 1911/02/26:1g, 4c-e, 11b
SPIELKAMP, Heinrich, NYC-M – 1910/04/20:6a
SPIELMANN, Max, un. typesetter, NYC-Bx – 1919/11/18:6a, 19:6a
SPIER, Abraham, painter, fr Russia, NYC? - 1913/02/07:3c
SPIER, Charles L., 40, pres. Staten Isl. RR, NYC-SI – 1906/05/08:1h, 10:1b, 24:1e
SPIER, Julius, 30, jeweler, NYC-M – 1891/11/14:4f
SPIES, Joseph, NYC-M – 1910/06/08:6a
SPIESBAUCH, Henry, 20, NYC-B – 1912/08/27:6a
SPIESS, Alexander, NYC-B – 1905/10/23:4a
SPIESS, August, @Haymarket martyr – 1887/02/05:1f
SPIESS, John George, un. brewer, NYC-M – 1897/03/02:4a
SPILLNER, Fritz, SP, 62, un. cigarmaker, NYC-M - 1915/04/09:1c, 6a, 10:6a, = 12:3f
SPILUT, Valentin, 40, NYC-M – 1897/07/17:4a

SPINA, Marie, b. Leiphold, fr Schluechtern/Gy, Weehauken?, NJ – 1896/06/08:4a
SPINDLER % Schick
SPINDLER, Albin, 65, East Orange, NJ – 1910/02/19:6a, fam. 24:6a
SPINDLER, Gustav, 64, SDP, USA ~1880 fr Dresden/Gy, Bloomfield, NJ – 1905/05/11:4a, 15:4c
SPINDLER, Henry, NYC-B - 1918/03/28:6a
SPINDLER, Selma, 47, SPD Doebeln/Saxony - 1915/10/10:3a
SPINK, E., NYC-M – 1912/12/10:6a
SPINK, William S., 30, butcher, NYC-B - 1917/06/17:1f
SPINNER, John, upholsterer, Jersey City, NJ – 1911/03/27:3d
SPINNLER, Karolina, b. Bechter, 46, NYC-Bx – 1911/05/23:6a
SPINNLER, Valentin, NYC-M - 1920/07/10:6a
SPISAK, Martin, un. carp., NYC-Q – 1912/09/17:6a
SPITZ, Frank, 53, brewery collector, Newark, NJ – 1886/06/11:2g
SPITZER, Julius, 57, carp., NYC-M – 1886/02/26:3
SPITZER, Margaretha, NYC-M – 1881/01/25:1d
SPITZFADEN, Clara, NYC-M – 1906/11/04:7b
SPITZKA, Edwin C., Dr., 62, neurologist, *NYC, NYC-M - 1914/01/14:3e-f
SPITZNAGEL, Catharina, 68, NYC-B - 1878/01/28:3g
SPOERER, Emma, Jersey City Heights, NJ – 1909/12/26:7b
SPOERER, William, NYC-B - 1914/10/24:6a
SPOERL, Georg, un. carp., NYC-M – 1888/11/29:3b, 30:3c
SPOERRI, Albert, 58, NYC-Q – 1903/09/29:4a, fam. 1 Oct:4a
SPOHN, Christine, SP, NYC – 1908/08/26:2b
SPOHN, John, un. typesetter, NYC-M – 1893/03/20:4a
SPOHN, William, un. brewer, NYC-M - 1919/01/29:6a
SPONAR, Alois, 60, Paterson, NJ - 1918/01/16:6a
SPONBERG % Berbesky
SPONHEIMER, Elizabeth, b. Bleichert, NYC-Bx – 1913/03/01:6a
SPORKERT, comrade, printer, SPD Hagen/Westprussia, Gy – 1898/10/09:12d
SPRANGER, Eduard, 66, NYC-M - 1915/08/15:7a
SPRATTE, Gustav, 67, un. carp., NYC-M - 1920/12/30:6a
SPRECHTER, Elsie, 9, NYC-M, +@ Genl Slocum – 1904/06/18:3c
SPRECKELS, Claus, 80, *Lamsted/Hannover, USA 1846, sugar king, + San Francisco, CA, crit. obit – 1908/12/27:1g, 28:4a-b
SPRECKELS, Ferdinand, innkeep, NYC-Bx – 1906/03/31:1h; murderer got 7 yrs 1906/10/24:6d
SPREEN, William, 48, brewer, NYC-B – 1909/09/08:3b
SPREITZER, J., NYC-B - 1917/05/03:6a

SPRENGER % Gruenewald
SPREUER, Johann, 33, Denver, CO – 1910/10/20:6a
SPRIESTERBACH, Jacob, 60, hotelier, & wife Augusta, 44, NYC-B – 1908/01/02:3a
SPRING, Auguste, 46, NYC-M, +@ Genl Slocum – 1904/06/17:3c
SPRING, Charles, 46, NYC-M - 1894/01/26:4a
SPRING, G., NYC-B – 1907/03/13:6a
SPRING, Minna, b. Keller, NYC-B – 1892/07/20:4a
SPRINGER, Katherina, NYC-Bx – 1911/10/22:7a
SPRINGER, Minna, 60, NYC-B – 1891/02/17:4a
SPRINGER, Moses, 56, NYC-B – 1888/05/12:3a
SPRINGER, Otto, NYC-B - 1920/07/21:6a
SPRINSTEIN, William, 12, NYC-B – 1902/03/05:4a
SPROTTE, Hermann, 23, Liberty, NY – 1912/04/15:6a
SPROTTE, Sophie, NYC-M – 1903/08/21:4a
SPRUNG, Hirsch, fr Russia, + on SS Lapland - 1913/05/27:2c
SPRUNGMANN, Henry, NYC-M - 1895/06/12:4a
SPURGE, Edward C., 37, engineer at Ozone Vanillin Co., Niagara Falls, NY – 1912/11/08:2b
SREMATZ, Milana, 1, NYC-M – 1887/07/18:3a
SREMATZ, Philipp, 1, NYC-M – 1898/09/06:4a
SROSCYNSKI, John, un. typesetter, NYC-B – 1910/11/03:6a
STAAR, Lilly, NYC-B – 1899/02/02:4a
STAATS, Christine, b. Kolter, 74, NYC-B – 1891/02/26:4a
STABER, Sophie, NYC-B – 1909/07/09:1e,2d, 10:1e-f, 11:c-d,6b, 13:2c, murderers sent. to +. 3 Oct 1909:1e.
STABLER, Julius, 65, NYC-B – 1911/05/17:6a, 16:3a
STACHOW, Emil, 56, NYC-Manhattanville – 1913/07/20:7a
STACHOW, Klara, 20, NYC-M - 1895/02/22:4a
STADEL, Helene, Harrison, NJ - 1914/05/20:6a
STADEL, Gustav, 58, Harrison, NJ - 1914/07/25:6a
STADGENA, Joseph, 53, NYC-M - 1918/05/09:6a
STACK, Emma, 40, Cherry Hill, NJ – 1901/02/08:3b
STACKER, Catherine, 55, NYC-B – 1893/11/21:4a
STADE, Christiane, b. Steiling, 56, NYC-M – 1882/10/16:3b
STADELBERG, Mary, 56, NYC-B – 1898/12/09:4b
STADELHOFER, Richard, NYC-M? – 1911/10/27:6a
STADEN, Jacob von, glass blower, NYC-B – 1891/07/28:2e
STADLER, John, NYC-M - 1914/01/12:6a
STADLER, Thomas, NYC-M – 1901/06/23:5a
STADT, Marie, b. Ruebsamen, Carlstadt, NJ – 1888/01/03:3a
STADTMILLER % Treffert

STADTMUELLER, Peter, 76, alderman & SPD Offenbach/Gy – 1911/06/11:3a
STAEBER, Andrew, 21, quarry worker in Lemont/Joliett, IL, + during strike – 1885/05/08:2d, 10:1c, 14:2b-c, s.a. Polish; Kajowa.
STAEDINGER, Minna, waitress, (dying), NYC-M – 1891/07/02:4d, 3:1f, 4:4c
STAEGEMEIER, Joseph, 45, wife, 48, ex-Newark, NJ, + Philadelphia 1883/07/21:4c
STAER, Charles, un. carp., Union Hill, NJ – 1905/01/22:5b
STAER, Selena, b. Deyn (Dehn?), Union Hill, NJ – 1893/03/17:4a
STAFFELDT, Amalia, 15, NYC-Q – 1907/05/23:1e, murderer fd 27:1d, 28:2a, 30:1c, 31:1c-d
STAHL, Addie, 1, NYC-M – 1891/01/27:4a
STAHL, Andrew, NYC-M – 1906/05/27:5a
STAHL, Anna, straw hat weaver, *1854 Tating/Schleswig, SP, #, her life (not +) NYC – 1911/02/26:20f
STAHL, Carl, 55, NYC-B – 1891/03/30:4a
STAHL, Christian, 42, un. typesetter, NYC-B – 1902/11/18:4a, 19:4a
STAHL, Christian, 46, NYC – 1911/03/02:1f
STAHL, Christian, 63, un. carp., SPD Stuttgart/Gy – 1910/03/13:3b
STAHL, Christian, watchmaker, + 11 Oct., NYC-M, inquest 12 Dec1888:1f
STAHL, Edward, 9, NYC-M – 1896/05/15:4a, =18:1h, fam. 19:4a
STAHL, Emma, 24, NYC-B – 1907/02/28:3a
STAHL, Emmanuel, NYC-M, + @Genl Slocum – 1904/06/18:3c
STAHL, Fritz, Columbia Univ. student, NYC-M – 1913/01/10:3b
STAHL, Henry, 1, NYC? – 1885/06/30:3c
STAHL, Jacob, cigar manuf., NYC-Bx – 1913/01/21:2a
STAHL, Karl, *1842 Darmstadt, 50th anniv. as gym teacher, TV Vorwaerts, Yorkville Free German School, etc NYC-M – 1910/07:26:5a, 1 Aug:2d-e; + NYC-Q - 1916/07/27:6a,c
STAHL, R., 60, Arlington, NJ - 1917/04/13:6a
STAHL, William, 54, hairdresser, War 2, Paterson, NJ - 1914/11/15:11e
STAHL, William, 70, NYC-M - 1879/03/12:1d
STAHLBERG, John, Silver Creek, NY - 1915/12/27:1f
STAHLHUT, Friedrich, un. carp., NYC-M – 1905/10/16:4a
STAHLHUT, Heinrich, 29, un. guard, NYC-Bx – 1908/02/18.5e,6a
STAHLKE, Elisabeth, NYC-B – 1903/06/18:4a
STAHR, Paul, 43, un. brewer, NYC-M – 1903/01/23:4a
STAIBER, Joseph, 51, SP?, NYC-M – 1907/07/12:6a, 13:6a, fam. 16:6a
STALB, Robert, 23, NYC-Bx – 1892/12/03:4a
STALLMANN, John, 26, brewer, NYC-B – 1898/06/30:4b
STALZER, Mathias, NYC-Q – 1909/08/08:7b

STAMM, Charles, NYC-Q - 1915/05/06:6a
STAMM, Karl, un. butcher, NYC-Bx - 1920/09/14:6a
STAMM, Lebrecht, 50, teacher at various G-A socialist schools, * Solingen/ Gy, USA 1883, SDP, NYC-B - 1904/11/30:1f-g, 4a, 1 Dec:1e, 4a, =2:1g-h, 3:1g, note 4:4b
STAMM, Marie, 29, NYC-B - 1920/02/15:2f
STAMM, Pauline, 55, SP, NYC-B - 1913/03/21:6a, =22:2e
STAMM, Robert, 33, *Solingen?/Gy, + Fremont, OH - 1893/09/24:5c
STAMM, Rudolf, SP, NYC, married Anna Wehle - 1909/09/13:5e
STAMMINGER, William, clerk, NYC-M - 1883/10/01:1e, 2:1e
STAMPER, Jos., un. cigar maker, NYC-M - 1892/02/28:5e
STAMPF, Georgine, 35, NYC-B - 1906/05/05:3d
STAMPFL, Joseph, NYC-B - 1918/11/25:5g
STAMPFLI, John, NYC-B - 1907/07/25:6a, fam. 30:6a
STANCHICK, Carl, NYC-M - 1914/09/28:6a
STANCLERT, Camille, 64, Belgian soc., mgr Maison du Peuple, Brussels - 1903/04/04:2c
STANDER, Carl, un. cigarmaker, NYC-M - 1887/11/04:4f
STANFORD, Leland, capitalist, + Hawaii, 1905/03/02:1f, 3:1d, 6:1d
STANG, Anton, SPD, city council Koenigsberg/East Prussia, War 1 - 1916/04/02:3b
STANG, John, un. stonecutter, NYC-Q - 1902/11/08:4a, fam. 14:4a
STANG, Michael, pocketbook maker, NYC-M - 1885/12/18:1g
STANGE, Paul, un. painter, NYC-M - 1910/05/19:6a, 20:6a, 23:2a
STANGE, Rudolf, un. machinist, SLP, * Braunschweig/Gy, NYC-B - 1889/08/17:4a, f, 18:5c, =19:1d
STANGER, Carl, un. carp., NYC-M - 1902/01/12:5a
STANISKA, John, coal-miner, @ 1897 Hazleton Massacre
STANLEY, Henry M., 62, English jounalist & Africa explorer, crit. notes on + - 1904/05/12:2a
STANLEY, William, Negro, lynched Temple, TX - 1915/08/01:1e
STANNE, Rayna, 24, Norwegian, NYC-B - 1905/08/31:3f
STAPF, Lina, 32, NYC-M - 1895/07/21: 4a
STAPF, Otto, innkeep, missing, NYC-M - 1897/07/01:1d
STAPF, Theodor, 83, merchant, USA 1880s fr Munich/Gy, East Orange, NJ - 1908/08/07:3c
STAPPERT, Rudolph, un. cigarmaker, NYC-B - 1895/02/24:5b
STAPPS, Gustav, NYC-M - 1896/11/26:1g
STARCK, Gottlieb, 35, un. beerdriver, NYC-B - 1910/12/26:6a, 27:6a
STARCKE, Alfons, 10, NYC-Bx - 1881/12/08:3a
STARK, Franz, NYC-Q - 1889/03/10:5d
STARK, Iwan, 4, NYC-B - 1889/02/04:4a

STARK, Joseph, NYC-Bx – 1906/03/27:4a
STARK, Karl, 68, SPD Reutlingen/Wuertt., – 1911/04/09:3b
STARK, Peter, 26, NYC-M – 1893/12/27:4a
STARK, Sophie, 78, NYC-M - 1878/04/17:3b
STARK, Valentin, NYC-Q – 1907/02/12:6a
STARKE % Martens
STARKE, Adolf, un. miner, SLP, Braddock, PA – 1898/06/26:12a
STARKE, Otto, un. machinist, NYC-M - 1914/08/21:6a
STARKE, Rudolph, 57, SLP?, NYC-Bx – 1893/01/06:4a
STARKE, Theresia, 54, NYC-B – 1880/03/03:2g
STAROSSON, Franz, SPD leader fr Mecklemburg, 1919 National Assembly – 1919/09/13:5c
STAROST, Amalia, NYC-M – 1893/03/12:5a
STAROST, Julius, 69, un. carp., * 10 Oc 1844 Rotenberg/Oder, USA 1885, NYC-M - 1914/08/21:6a, 22:6a, =23:11b, fam. 25:6a
STARR, John, 23, driver, NYC-M – 1905/07/06:3g
STASKA, John, un. carp., NYC-M – 1913/02/27:6a
STAUB, Adolph, 42, chemo-technician, * Canton Glarus/Switz., USA 1890, NYC-M - 1895/06/11:4c
STAUB, Emil J., NYC-M - 1916/02/06:7a
STAUB, Joseph, 69, machinist, NYC-M – 1905/06/08:2f
STAUB, Karl, Guttenberg, NJ - 1919/04/29:6a
STAUBES, Lebrecht, fam. 1910/06/04:6a
STAUBLI, Louis, Swiss, un. brewer, SP?, Davenport, OH, + Denver, CO – 1909/11/03:6b
STAUDENBAUER, Robert, NYC-M – 1890/02/02:5b, 3:4a
STAUDENMAIER, Catherina, 56, NYC-M – 1890/07/31:4a
STAUDENMEIER, Anton, 52, NYC-M - 1919/03/07:6a
STAUDER, John, clothes dealer, NYC-B – 1885/02/24:3a-b
STAUDERMANN, Philipp, 57, *Wendelsheim/Alzey/Gy, NYC-M – 1903/10/30:4a
STAUDINGER, Robert, 59, NYC-B – 1892/06/08:4a
STAUDT, Elizabeth, b. Ramm, 51, NYC-B – 1900/01/13:4a
STAUF, Philip, NYC-B - 1917/11/08:6a
STAUFER, Georg, 32, SPD Nuernberg/Gy – 1912/09/22:3a
STAUFFENBERG, William, 25, clerk, NYC-M – 1892/06/05:1h
STAUS, Georg, NYC-M – 1881/04/27:3a
STAUS, Kathie, 2, NYC-M – 1880/04/15:4f
STAVERN, VAN, S., exec. Camden, NJ, for + wife – 1902/04/09:4a
STAYER, Anton, un. carp., NYC-M – 1892/05/08:5a, fam. 9:4a
STEAD, William Thomas, Engl. journalist & pacifist, d. on Titanic – 1912/04/17:2b

STEBBINS, Frederick S., 50, SDP, Rochester, NY – 1903/04/04:1g
STECHER % Wegener
STECHHOLZ, Rudolph, un. typesetter, NYC-M – 1891/05/30:4a
STECHROCK, Henry, 32, grocer, NYC – 1892/12/06:4c
STECKEL, Louise, 17, servant, NYC-M – 1890/12/07:1f
STECKER, Carl H., NYC-Bx – 1911/04/12:6a
STECKER, Florian, lace manuf.,Carlstadt, NJ - 1915/06/13:11e
STECKER, Kathie, 41, NYC-M – 1906/05/26:4a
STECKERMAN, Augusta, 15, NYC-M, + @Genl Slocum – 1904/06/21:1f
STECKLE, Joseph, silk weaver, NYC-Q – 1892/04/24:1f
STECKLER, Alfred's wife, + Englewood, NJ – 1907/11/19:1d
STECKLER, Frank, 49, NYC-B – 1910/07/06:2f
STECKLER, Malche, 64, NYC-M – 1892/07/27:4a
STECKMAN, William H., 51, coal-dealer, NYC-B – 1907/06/05:3a
STEEGER, Johann Peter, 73, fr Bayreuth/Bavaria, un. printer at NYSZ,
    NYC-M – 1880/02/28:4f
STEEN, Henriette, b. Boderberg, NYC-B – 1892/11/13:5b
STEEN, William, 22, NYC-Bx – 1909/01/16:6a
STEENBOCK % Knoechel
STEENBOCK, Elizabeth, b. Amman, 55, NYC-M – 1911/01/28:6a
STEFANSKY, Charles, un. butcher, NYC-M - 1914/04/03:6a
STEFEK, Karl, Elizabeth, NJ – 1911/05/12:6a
STEFEK, Wenzel, SP?, Elizabeth, NJ – 1908/01/09:6a, fam. 16:6a
STEFFELE, Arthur, 9, NYC-B - 1920/02/06:6a
STEFFEN, W., NYC-B – 1905/11/10:4a
STEFFEN, William, shoemaker, NYC? – 1885/04/07:4c
STEFFENS, Christopher A., 55, NYC-B – 1909/07/30:6a
STEFFENS, Dietrich, 35, NYC-M – 1883/04/18:1g
STEFFENS, Herman, 62, un. tailor, NYC-M - 1918/08/16:6a
STEFFENS, John, 18, NYC-M – 1892/08/14:5c
STEFFENS, Otto, cook fr Philadelphia, + NYC-M – 1897/12/25:1e
STEFFMANN % Heubel
STEFFMANN, Anna, b. Kuhlemann, NYC-M - 1920/12/15:6a
STEFFMANN, Henry,un. cigarmaker,NYC-M - 1918/03/27:6a, 28:6a
STEFGER, Louis J., 43, NYC-B - 1918/04/26:6b
STEGEMANN, Edward, 81, builder, & wife Dorothy, 71, NYC-B –
    1905/01/15:5e
STEGEMANN, Rudolf, 45, restaurant owner, NYC-M – 1880/07/14:1d
STEGERT, Ernst, SP,un. metal worker, NYC-Bx - 1918/02/10:7a
STEGHERR, Anna, b. Volck, 45, NYC-B – 1887/01/03:3a
STEGMANN, Fritz, SPD Erfurt/Gy, + recently – 1912/08/04:3e
STEHL, George, 14, NYC-M, + @ Genl Slocum – 1904/06/17:3c

STEHLE, Carl, NYC-M – 1902/03/20:4a
STEHLE, Martin, NYC-M – 1890/01/03:4a
STEHLICK, Anna, West New York, NJ - 1918/02/26:6a
STEHLIN, Achaz, 76, NYC-B – 1885/04/25:3b
STEHLIN, Joseph, 38, brewer, NYC-B – 1896/08/12:3e
STEHR, Franziska, b. Nowarra, 40, NYC-M – 1899/08/26:4a
STEIDLE, Therese, NYC-M – 1892/03/08:4a
STEIERT, Frederick, 25, dying, Hoboken, NJ – 1910/12/20:3b
STEIGER % Pfeiffer
STEIGER, Louise's child, Louise, 22, fr Stuttgart/Gy, + Hoboken, NJ – 1885/11/25:2f, 24:2f, note 12 Jan. 1886:2f
STEIGER, Eduard, NYC-B – 1904/02/17:4a
STEIGER, Edward, NYC-Q - 1917/01/28:7b
STEIGER, Hermann, painter, Newark, NJ - 1914/09/29:6c
STEIGER, Isaac, 38, boss baker, NYC-B - 1915/05/02:11g
STEIGER, Jacob, 56, NYC-Q - 1917/02/11:7a, mem. - 1918/02/08:2g
STEIGER, L. W., 56, NYC-Bx – 1908/08/25:1d
STEIGER, L., 32, NYC-B - 1920/05/04:6a
STEIGERT, Hermann, 38, baker, NYC-M – 1907/12/04:1f
STEIGERWALD, Bertha, NYC-M – 1888/09/22:3a
STEIGERWALD, Joseph, NYC-M – 1912/04/28:7a
STEIGERWALD, Moses, 84, NYC-M – 1891/03/23:4a
STEIGLEDER, John, 37, NYC-M – 1911/04/18:6a
STEIHL, Lillian, 16, NYC-M, +@Genl Slocum – 1904/06/25:1d
STEIHL, William, 52, bartender, NYC – 1912/02/13:1a
STEIKOWSKY, Johanna, 47, NYC-M – 1880/05/29:4a
STEIL, Adelaide, 15, NYC-Bx, +@Genl Slocum – 1904/06/23:1c
STEILING % Stade
STEIMLE, Gottlieb, 58, NYC-M - 1920/10/31:12a
STEIN % Grob
STEIN, Adolph, 47, engraver, NYC-Q – 1897/11/05:1d
STEIN, Bertha, 10, NYC-B – 1881/07/02:3a
STEIN, Carrie, 20, servant, NYC-M – 1887/07/28:1c, 29:1d
STEIN, Carrie, 9, NYC-M, + Q Genl Slocum – 1904/06/18:3c
STEIN, Caspar, 28, SLP, NYC-M – 1884/12/17:1g, 3d
STEIN, Christian, NYC? – 1898/01/09:5b
STEIN, David, 34, cigar manuf., NYC-M – 1900/07/18:3c
STEIN, Dorothea, NYC-M – 1891/06/25:4a
STEIN, Ferdinand, salesman, Hoboken, NJ – 1908/12/27:7d
STEIN, Friedrich A., 64, un. pianomaker?, NYC-M – 1889/02/11:4a
STEIN, Friedrich Adam, 23, NYC-M – 1881/01/18:3c
STEIN, Friedrich, journalist for California Demokrat – 1881/11/01:1e

STEIN, George, NYC-M - 1920/01/12:6a
STEIN, George's wife, NYC-M - 1888/01/14:3a
STEIN, Gottlieb, 44, Hoboken, NJ - 1900/03/03:4a
STEIN, Gregor, 32, * Gy, US Airforce, War 1 - 1918/06/15:6c
STEIN, Gustav, 51, * Breslau/Gy, USA 1860, journalist at NYSZ, NYC-M - 1891/10/20:4a, 21:4a, =22:2f
STEIN, Henry, clothes presser, NYC-B - 1898/07/25:4b
STEIN, Henry, Dr. med., NYC - 1916/04/26:1d
STEIN, Isaac, NYC-M - 1900/08/09:1f
STEIN, Jennie, @1911 Triangle Shirtwaist Fire, NYC-M - 1911/03/27:1d
STEIN, John, 61, NYC-M - 1888/05/05:1h
STEIN, John, brewer, NYC-M - 1897/05/28:4a
STEIN, Joseph J., 36, lawyer, ex-NYS assembly, NYC - 1880/06/30:1b
STEIN, Mary, 22, NYC-B - 1880/05/11:1e
STEIN, Paul, 40, un. cement & asphalt worker, NYC-M - 1904/12/16:4a
STEIN, Peter, 57, NYC-M - 1909/06/23:1e
STEIN, Theodor, varnisher, NYC-B - 1882/10/02:3b
STEIN, Tony, 60, NYC-Q - 1913/01/02:6c
STEIN, Wilhelm Ludwig, 82, SPD Offenbach/Gy - 1908/08/23:3b
STEINACHER, Friedrich, 33, carp., NYC-M - 1893/05/09:4c
STEINBACH, Antonia, b. Fiebach, 52, NYC-M - 1899/06/21:4a, c, fam. 24:4a
STEINBACH, Christine, 57, Elizabeth, NJ - 1913/04/14:6a
STEINBACH, Emil, 52, SP, * Lichtenstein/Saxony, Weehawken, NJ - 1906/09/18:6a, fam. 18:6a, =21:5e
STEINBACH, Gustav, 69, un. cigarmaker, NYC-M - 1912/02/24:6a
STEINBACH, Heinrich, NYC-M - 1889/06/03:4g
STEINBACH, Maria, 15, NYC-M - 1895/03/09:4a, 13:4a
STEINBACHER, Joseph, 55, NYC-B - 1903/07/07:3b
STEINBACHER, Katherine, b. Fuchs, NYC-M - 1891/04/12:5a
STEINBERG, Adeline, NYC-M - 1912/02/03:6a, mem. 1917/02/02:6a
STEINBERG, F., NYC-Q - 1913/03/14:6a
STEINBERG, Frank, 53, ex-secy Irving Place (German) Theater, then cashier at Luechow's German Restaurant, NYC-M - 1913/09/16:1d
STEINBERG, Frank, 16, NYC-B - 1909/06/16:3b
STEINBERG, Maria, b. Oerding, 52, NYC-B - 1891/03/30:4a
STEINBERG, NYC-M - 1913/02/07:6a
STEINBERG, Sidney, 13, NYC-M - 1913/07/25:6a
STEINBERGER, Hannah, NYC-M - 1895/02/13:3f
STEINE, Bertha Louise,54,laundry work.,NYC-M - 1918/08/06:6b
STEINBRENNER, Ernst, un. butcher, NYC-B - 1906/01/05:4a
STEINBRENNER, P., NYC-M - 1893/09/30:4a

STEINBRENNER, William H., local pol., Hudson Co., NJ – 1885/06/06:3b
STEINBURG, Adolf von, 25, dying, NYC-M – 1892/07/07:4c
STEINDECKER, NYC-M – 1911/04/23:7a
STEINDEL, Joseph, 38, carriage maker, NYC-B – 1897/07/30:3f
STEINECKER, John, NYC-M – 1891/08/12:4a
STEINEGGER, A., un. typesetter, NYC-B – 1887/11/09:3a
STEINEL, Carlies, West Hoboken, NJ - 1894/04/09:4a
STEINEL, Elizabeth, b. Hasselwande, 70, W. Hoboken, NJ – 1899/06/10:4a
STEINEL, J., NYC-M – 1904/04/09:4a
STEINEL, W., West Hoboken, NJ – 1900/01/28:5a
STEINEMANN, Henry, NYC-M – 1910/07/26:6a
STEINEMANN, Minnie, 39, NYC-B – 1911/01/06:3a
STEINEN, Alwine von den, 67, Newark, NJ – 1905/09/17:5b
STEINEN, Anna Von Den, b. Cantius, Irvington, NJ - 1918/09/20:6a,fam. 24:6a
STEINEN, Anna Von Den, b. Willms, 38, SP?, Saranac Lake, NY – 1906/01/29:4a
STEINEN, Ernst Von Den, child, Newark, NJ – 1900/04/06:4a
STEINEN, Fritz Von Den, 41, * Solingen/Gy, USA ~ 1891, SP, Newark, NJ – 1907/09/11:6a, 12:2b
STEINEN, Hugo Von Den, Newark, NJ - 1913/08/13:6a
STEINEN, Julius Von Den, 66, Newark, NJ – 1905/02/08:4a
STEINER, E's wife, of Chicago, daughter Josephine Bauer + at grandfather Boehm's home in NYC-B - 1915/03/18:6a
STEINER, Anton, West Hoboken, NJ - 1919/06/22:12a, mem. 1920/06/18:6a
STEINER, comrade, SP Rochester, NY – 1911/04/20:2e
STEINER, Gustav, 26, NYC-M – 1891/08/27:1d
STEINER, Karl, 71, SP, fr Vienna/Austria, So. Norwalk, CT – 1907/12/17:6a, 1908/01/06:3d
STEINER, Louis, 44, engineer, fr Gy, NYC-B - 1894/05/08:4d
STEINER, Rosalie, NYC-M – 1906/12/31:1b
STEINER, Samuel, 53, NYC-M – 1899/03/20:1b
STEINER, Virginia, 19, NYC-Bx – 1912/11/03:7d, 4:2b
STEINERT, Henry, judge, NYC-SI – 1913/02/04:1f
STEINERT, John, 45, Elizabeth, NJ – 1892/04/29:2e
STEINFATT, Fritz, 53, SPD Hamburg/Gy, journalist Hamburger Echo – 1911/01/08:3a
STEINFELDER, John, NYC-M – 1911/07/05:1
STEINFUEHRER, Gustav, Dr., 39?, NYC-M – 1890/07/04:4a
STEINGRUBER, Henry, Jersey City, NJ – 1908/08/15:3c-d
STEINHARDT, Max, Philadelphia - 1920/02/11:6a

STEINHART, Benjamin, lawyer, NYC-M – 1907/06/18:2b, 19:3d-e
STEINHAUSER, Frederick, 58, ironworker, Harrison, NJ – 1911/08/05:2a
STEINHEIMER, Georg, 60, SP, un. brewer, chair Brewer Union #69, USA 1878, NYC-B - 1915/08/30:6a,d, 31:6a,=2 Sept:3f
STEINHERZ, Helene Lazarus, NYC-M - 1917/06/10:7a
STEINHEUSER, Frederick, NYC-M – 1911/02/11:6a
STEINHILDER, John, NYC-M – 1910/05/19:6a
STEININGER, Regina, 28, NYC-M - 1894/01/25:4a
STEINITZ, Wilhelm, chess master, *18 May 1837 Prag/Bohemia, NYC-M – 1900/08/14:3b
STEINKEN, Charles, 39, upholsterer, NYC-M - 1879/06/16:4a
STEINKEN, Theophile A., artist & socialist, + Paris – 1904/01/17:3g-h
STEINLE, Franz B., 47, Winfield, LI – 1902/08/01:4a
STEINLEIN, Levi, NYC-M – 1891/04/06:4a
STEINLEIN, Louis, 66, NYC-B – 1891/07/16:4a
STEINMANN, Paul, NYC-B - 1913/06/29:1f
STEINMANN, Peter,machinist,* 20 Nov.1850 Niederurnen/CH, USA 1877, NYC-M - 1878/06/01:4d
STEINMETZ, Dr., Free Thinker, Metuchen, NJ - 1878/07/01:3a
STEINMETZ, Georg, NYC-B – 1891/06/21:5a
STEINMETZ, Leonard, baker, NYC-M – 1892/08/01:4a
STEINMETZ, Paul, 64, NYC-M – 1891/08/12:4a
STEINMETZ, Peter, 30, carpenter, NYC-M – 1892/08/06:1e
STEINMETZ, Ph., West Hoboken, NJ – 1907/02/21:6a
STEINMETZ, William J., NYC-M – 1900/05/15:1e
STEINMEYER, Wilhelm, 26, member Amt Leher Club, NYC-B - 1878/04/08:3b
STEINMUELLER, Frederick, 15, NYC-M - 1917/06/02:6b
STEINS, Oscar, NYC-M – 1891/09/02:4a
STEINWAY, Charles, + Pianomanuf., – 1919/11/26:6c
STEINWAY, William, 60, piano manuf., *5 Mr 1836 Seesen, NYC 1850, NYC-M – 1896/12/01:2a, 3e, 4a, =3:2f, crit 6:4a-c, note 9:3e, 10:2g, 6d, will 11:3d, 20 May 1898:4d, 18 Fb 1900:5d
STEIP, John, 55, NYC-M – 1901/07/03:1d
STEISSINGER, Daniel, 57, NYC-M – 1889/05/23:4a
STEITZ, Wilhelm, NYC-B - 1894/04/19:4a
STELLENWERT, John B., 36, smith, NYC-SI – 1902/12/10:1a
STELLING, Heinrich, NYC-M – 1893/04/16:5e
STELLMACHER, Hermann, Austrian anarchist, exec. Vienna for killing undercover cop, NYC anarchists grieve – 1884/08/04:4c, 8:1a, exec. done 9:1b, NYC G-A soc. crit. Stellmacher 11:2b-c, rev. of memorial 12:4c-e, notes 22:2f-3a, 30:2c, 17 Sept:2f,

STELLWAGEN, Elizabeth, b. Talmon, 50, NYC-Bx – 1906/06/03:5b
STELSBERG, Josephine, NYC-B – 1893/08/18:4a
STELTE % Rothen
STELTER, Louis, NYC-B – 1892/06/15:4a
STELTER, Susanna, NYC-B – 1891/06/29:4a
STELTZ, Bessie, NYC-B, @ Genl Slocum – 1904/06/17:3c
STELZ, George, sexton RC Trinity, Montrose Av, NYC-B – 1897/08/31:1f, 1 Sept:1h, =2:1h, 5:1f
STELZNER, Carl, machinist, & wife Alma, fr Gy 1906, NYC-M – 1909/05/07:2d
STENDEL, Georg, 38, NYC-B – 1900/06/08:4b
STENDTS, Franz, 55, Buffalo, NY – 1909/11/27:1c
STENGEL % Beck, % Lautner, % Maser
STENGEL, Friedrich, 30, beer manuf., NYC-M – 1880/06/24:1e
STENGEL, John, NYC-B – 1905/08/24:4a
STENGER % Leise
STENGER, Francis's wife, 35, NYC-M, + on Genl Slocum – 1904/06/21:1f
STENGER, Jacob, NYC-M - 1918/01/16:6a
STENGER, Nicholas, 60, Winfield, LI – 1905/08/02:3d
STENGLEIN, John, NYC-M – 1908/06/28:7a
STENGLER, George, NYC-Bx - 1918/09/11:6a
STENZ, Mrs, NYC-M – 1886/02/18:2f
STEPHAN, Anna, 24, NYC-Glendale - 1919/01/02:6a
STEPHAN, Anton, un. carp., NYC-B – 1887/01/15:3c
STEPHAN, Daniel, un. carp., NYC-M – 1911/06/09:6a
STEPHAN, Henry, 22, NYC-B – 1891/07/15:4a
STEPHAN, Louis D., 28, NYC-M – 1906/02/04:5a
STEPHANY, Eduard, 29, NYC-M – 1881/10/14:3c
STEPHENS, Alexander H., vice-pres. CSA, + – 1883/03/05:1b, 2c
STEPHENS, Sam, Negro, lynched Toccoa, GA - 1915/06/15:1f
STEPIEL, Henry, 28, driver, NYC-M - 1894/10/19:4a
STEPNIAK, Sergius M.D. (Krawtschinsky), Russian revol. - 1895/12/24: 1d, hon. in NYC 27: 1c, life 29: 4c-d, 1896/01/03:1d, 5:1c, 10:1e,h, 11:1e
STERCKER, Bernhard, NYC-B – 1891/04/07:4a
STERGER, ..., family thanks 1908/12/28:6a
STERN % Melching, % Muth, % Schmidt
STERN, Adolph, NYC-M – 1911/07/24:7c
STERN, August, 45, salesman, NYC-M - 1917/02/17:2b
STERN, Bernhard, 40, cigarstore, NYC-M - 1879/02/15:1d
STERN, Eduard, *1824 in the Baltics, speculator, crit. notes on his +, NYC-M – 1883/01/07:4b
STERN, Elizabeth, 42, widow, NYC-B - 1895/04/04:4b

STERN, Heinrich, 68, un. carp., NYC-M - 1920/03/30:8a
STERN, Jacob, NYC-B - 1892/07/15:4a
STERN, Jakob, 80, ex-Rabbi, journalist, SPD Stuttgart/Gy - 1911/04/18:4d
STERN, Joseph, NYC-M - 1891/04/12:5a
STERN, Leopold, un. painter, NYC-M - 1915/06/24:6a
STERN, Max, 42, Amalg. Ladies' Garment Cutters Union org., * Gy, NYC-M - 1916/02/06:11e
STERN, Rachel, 26, NYC-M - 1888/03/08:1f
STERN, Yetta, 26, NYC-M - 1896/11/13:3e
STERNACK, Carl, NYC-M - 1901/07/24:4a
STERNBERG, Henry J., 45, grocer, NYC-M - 1900/01/03:1g
STERNBERGER, L., Richard von, 26, druggist, NYC-M, * Bonn, USA 1882 - 1883/12/26:4d, =27:1g
STERNBURG, baron Speck von, ex-German ambassador in USA, + Heidelberg - 1908/08/25:2b
STERNE, Theodor, cigar manuf., NYC-M - 1911/06/06:6c
STERNFELS, Morris, NYC-M - 1900/09/25:1e
STERNHAUS, Stella, NYC-M - 1904/08/01:3d
STERNHEIMER, Franz, Elizabeth, NJ - 1907/12/06:6a
STERNNICKEL, Fritz, SP, Newark, NJ - 1914/02/18:6a, 19:6a
STERRY, George, 72, pres. Weaver & Sterry Drugstores, & son, 40, NYC-M- 1908/05/20:1a-b, 21:3e
STERZEL, Friedrich, 37, un. cigarmaker, SLP, * Doebeln/Saxony, NYC-M - 1881/01/22:1g, 3e, 23:8a, =24:1g, fam. 20 Mr:5g
STETTENHEIM, Julius, 84, German cartoonist, * Hamburg, + Berlin - 1916/11/22:6a
STETTLER, Frank, cigarmaker, NYC-B - 1887/03/29:2g
STEUBINGER, August, un. upholsterer, NYC-M - 1892/10/14:4a
STEUCHER, Frederick, 32, butcher, NYC-B - 1904/01/05:3c
STEUDE, Charles, NYC-Q - 1911/01/27:6a
STEUDE, Oskar J., NYC-M - 1911/06/02:6a
STEUER % Reich
STEUER, Henry, 80, NYC-B - 1913/12/03:3d
STEUER, Isaac, cloakmaker, NYC-M - 1897/10/12:1g
STEUERNAGEL, William, un. baker, NYC-Q - 1920/04/14:6a
STEUERWALD, E., NYC-M - 1909/05/29:6a
STEUERWALD, Wilhelm, 54, NYC-M - 1883/06/25:3b
STEUGER, Rose, NYC-M, @ Genl Slocum - 1904/06/18:3c
STEUHL, Peter, NYC-M - 1918/08/11:12a
STEUNENBERG, Frank, ex-gov. of Idaho and "blood hound" of mine owners, killed by bomb - 1906/01/01:1f, 2:4c, 3:1b, attempt to frame IWW 23 Fb:2f, 28:2a-b, etc, 10 Mr:2a

STEURER, Katherine, 64, NYC-M – 1892/07/15:4a
STEURINGER, Ch. G., 41, NYC-Evergreen – 1911/05/30:6a
STEVENS, Alzina Parsons, social worker at Hull House, Chicago – 1900/06/06:3c
STEVENS, John G., president United New Jersey E.B. & Canal Co., – 1886/01/08:2f
STEVERSDORF, Joe, ship's steward, see 1900 dock fire, Hoboken, NJ 1900/07/03:1c
STEWART, George, 22, exec. Trenton, NJ – 1908/02/05:3b
STEYER, Eduard, 52, brewery worker, NYC-M – 1885/01/05:1g
STEYER, Elise, 51, NYC-M – 1904/04/02:4a
STEYER, Fannie, servant, fr Bohemia, NYC-M – 1893/11/25:1h
STIASTNY, L. J., wholesale dealer, NYC-M – 1881/05/31:1d
STICH, George, un. carp., NYC-M - 1915/01/07:6a
STICH, Louis J., 47, hat salesman, NYC-B – 1903/08/01:2h
STICHLER, Friedrich, 26, un. carp., NYC-B – 1911/04/26:6a
STICHT, Anna, NYC-B - 1894/01/21:5d
STICKELBERGER, John, Warren Point, NJ – 1913/02/10:6a
STICKER, Josephine, NYC-M – 1906/04/02:1d
STIEBELING, Friedericke, NYC-M – 1886/06/02:3b
STIEBELING, Georg Christian, Dr., SLP, physician, * 6 Nov. 1830 Gedern/Hessen, USA 1850s, NYC-M, obit by Alex Jonas 1895/06/04:1c-d, 4a, 5:4a, =6:1g, 9:4c. Crit. his son John, who became a Republ. Politico & asst Federal marshall in NYC – 1910/03/31:4b
STIEBLER, Paul, technical drawer, & wife Margot, b. Kuhn, NYC-M – 1900/09/15:2h, 4b, 14:1e, 13:1c
STIECKER, Josef, 65, gardener, NYC? - 1914/10/22:2e-f
STIEF, Caroline, NYC-? - 1879/08/12:4e
STIEFEL, Anna, NYC-M – 1892/06/29:4a
STIEFEL, Christian, un. carp., NYC-M – 1906/06/29:6a
STIEFEL, John, baker, NYC-B – 1896/12/14:3c
STIEFEL, Joseph, un. typesetter, NYC-B – 1887/09/09:3b
STIEFELEIN, J., NYC-B – 1909/06/01:6a
STIEGLITZ, Wilhelm, 64, NYC-B – 1891/04/07:4a
STIEH, Rene B., plumber, NYC-M – 1904/08/16:3b
STIEHL, George, child, NYC-Q – 1908/10/18:7a
STIEMER, Carl, NYC-M – 1909/06/03:6a
STIER % Methfessel, % Schunk
STIER, Paul, builder, local democratic pol. & Queens County Sheriff, fr Gy, NYC-Q - 1916/10/24:1g, will 29:11a
STIERHEIM, Julius, 46, translator for Hungarian at Ellis Isl., & family, NYC-Bx - 1914/01/22:1c

STIEVEL, Dora, 31, NYC-B – 1907/11/10:1g
STIFEL, Otto F., ex-brewery owner & Republ. cand. for Congress, St Louis, MO - 1920/08/20:2f
STIGLITZ, Jennie, @1911 Triangle Shirtwaist Fire, NYC-M – 1911/03/29:1c
STILES, Georg M., merchant & local polit., Elizabeth, NJ – 1888/03/22:2d
STILGENBAUR, John, tailor, Mt Vernon, NY – 1886/11/27:1g
STILLER, Carl, 33, NYC-M - 1894/04/16:4a, 18:4a
STIMPFEL, John, NYC-B – 1904/02/25:4a
STINER, Joseph, 63, municipal court judge, NYC – 1902/09/21:1e
STIRGER, Charles, waiter, NYC-M – 1880/12/06:1g
STIRNER, Max, 1806-1856, German philosopher, on his life & work 1898/11/13:4c-e; 100th anniv. of birth – 1906/07/15:6d-e, 22:6d-f
STITZ % Ebel
STITZ, Charlotte, 15, West New York, NJ – 1913/08/13:3b
STOCK, Adelaide, 38, d. 6th NYC-M - 1894/08/08:1g,3f
STOCK, Carl, 49, NYC-M - 1894/05/01:4a
STOCK, Henry, 44, grocer, NYC-B – 1904/12/22:4a
STOCK, Henry, 64, druggist, NYC-M – 1893/11/22:2e
STOCKBURGER, Mathias, 54, NYC-M – 1911/04/18:6a
STOCKER, Katie, b. Pierney, on her + in Jersey City, NJ – 1892/02/02:1f, 6:1d, husband rec 10 yrs 17 June:1f, 26 June:5d
STOCKERT, Hermann C., 36, un. printer, NYC-M 1895/02/09:4a
STOCKFISCH, Dietrich, 58, NYC-B – 1896/08/12:3e
STOCKFISCH, Marie, 28, servant, New Brighton, NY – 1893/03/21:1d
STOCKFIST, Lena, NYC-B – 1912/03/07:3a
STOCKLEY, Charles, 23, exec. Batavia, NY – 1881/08/19:1f, 20:1d
STOCKMANN % Wendel
STOCKMANN, Gerhard, int. German sailor fr SS Friedrich der Grosse, War 2, Hoboken, NJ - 1915/12/15:2c
STOCKMANN, Henry, 57, NYC-M – 1893/12/30:4a
STOCKMANN, Hulda, 17, NYC-M, +@ Genl Slocum – 1904/06/21:1f
STOCKMANN, Jacob, NYC-M – 1910/10/18:6a
STOCKMANN, Nicholas, Westchester, NY - 1914/05/12:6a
STOCKMAYER, William, notary & insurance agent, NYC-M – 1880/01/06:4a, 7:4c
STOCZ, Johannes, innkeep, NYC-M - 1878/03/29:4a
STOECKEL, Wilhelm, 48, Yonkers, NY - 1917/07/21:6a
STOECKER, Adolf, Rev., anti-semite, crit. obit – 1909/02/10:4b-c
STOEFFEL, Ferdinand, NYC-M – 1891/03/31:4a
STOEGER, Mathias, 41, Cincinatti, + Hoboken, NJ on way to Gy – 1907/07/17:3c

STOEHR, Henry, 6, NYC-M, +@Genl Slocum – 1904/06/23:1c
STOEHR, John, 47, butcher, NYC-M – 1908/06/17:2d
STOEHR, Karl, 43, NYC-M – 1902/09/10:4a
STOEHR, L., NYC-M, + @ Genl Slocum – 1904/06/17:3c
STOEHR, Max, machinist & SPD fr Ottensen/Gy, * Chemnitz/Sax., arr NYC – 1880/11/30:1d-e, 2 Dec:2a-b, 6:1d-e; labor leader in St Louis, then edit. St Louis Tageblatt, 1889-97, Westliche Post till 1912, + 66 yrs old – 1915/02/07:1e
STOEHR, Otto, Reichenbach/Vogtland Arbeiterturnerbund, War 1 - 1914/11/01:3b
STOELTNER, Christopher, Elizabeth, NJ – 1900/07/22:1e
STOERKEL, Katherine G., 54, NYC-B - 1915/06/07:6a
STOESSER, A., NYC-B – 1907/03/21:6a
STOEVER, Frederick, 46, butcher, Hoboken, NJ - 1913/06/06:2b
STOFFERS, William, 38, SLP, Newark, NJ – 1893/04/12:4a
STOFT, Jacob, 64, un. cigarmaker, SLP, NYC-B – 1897/07/20:4a,c, 21:4a, 22:4a, =23:4b
STOFT, Mrs, SLP, NYC-B – 1885/04/13:3c
STOHLOCH % Porsus
STOHRER, John A., NYC-M – 1897/10/18:4a
STOIBER, Bertha, NYC – 1901/03/18:4a
STOLECHNIKOFF, Wladimir R., alias Stark, 61, Russian soc., + Mobile, AL – 1908/02/16:9f
STOLKE, Abraham, shoemaker, fr Poland, NYC-M – 1901/08/20:3c
STOLL, Adolph, 40, NYC-M – 1891/05/19:1g
STOLL, Albrecht, un. brewer, NYC-M – 1907/08/14:6a
STOLL, J., NYC-M – 1907/11/08:6a
STOLL, Magdalen,18, servant,*NYC,NYC-M - 1879/02/05:1g, 11:4c
STOLLE, Frederick J., 54, machinist, NYC-M – 1910/05/14:6a
STOLLE, Wilhelm, SPD MdR for Glauchau/Saxony, 70th birthday – 1913/01/05:3b
STOLP, Oscar, helmsman on ship "Catherine W.", Communipaw, NJ – 1911/02/02:1a
STOLPE, Hermann, 53, carp., & alderman, SPD Goerlitz/Gy – 1911/12/10:3b
STOLPE, Sophia, NYC-M – 1884/07/04:1e
STOLTE, Adelina Bertha, 2, NYC-M – 1889/02/01:4a
STOLYPIN, P., Russian prime-minister, killed by revol. Bogroff – 1911/09/17:1a, 4a-c, 19:1a, 4a, Bogroff exec. 26:1f; 20 Oct:4d-f
STOLZ, Bessie, NYC-M, @ Genl Slocum – 1904/06/17:3c, 18:3c
STOLZ, Carl, un. carp., NYC-M – 1910/08/11:6a
STOLZ, George, 71, Hoboken, NJ – 1890/03/09:2f

STOLZE, Gustav, 60, NYC-M - 1915/08/08:11a, 9:6a
STOLZENBERGER, Ambros, 68, undertaker, ex-pres. Badischer VFV – 1909/09/09:2d
STOLZENBERGER, William, cloth cutter, NYC-M – 1880/07/31:4b
STOLZENBURG, Paul, NYC-M – 1897/04/28:3h
STONE, Minnie, NYC-M, +@ Genl Slocum – 1904/06/18:3c
STONITSCH, Agnes, NYC-B – 1909/04/07:6a
STONITSCH, Peter, Jr., fr Gottschee?/Slov., NYC-B, + Catskill, Ulster Co. – 1906/10/28:7b
STOOTHOFF, Gustav, 57, night watchman, NYC-B – 1907/09/19:3a
STORCH, Despina Davidovitch, reported + NYC-Ellis Island jail - 1918/03/31:11g, =2 Apr:3e, note 1920/08/14:1c
STORCH, Eugen, NYC-M - 1914/08/31:6a
STORCH, Georg, infant, NYC-M – 1883/07/14:3c
STORCH, Reginald, 40, pianist at Crescent Th., NYC-B - 1914/01/23:3a
STORCK, Katherine, b. Mueller, NYC-M – 1892/06/25:4a
STORCK, Stephen O., Dr., dentist, NYC-M - 1913/06/06:2d
STORER, Eugen, 49, printshop owner, NYC-B - 1915/11/08:2e
STOREY, Lawrence C., un. carp., union official, NYC-Bx – 1911/02/26:7c
STORGER, Frederick, Jersey City, NJ – 1909/12/04:3b
STORIL, Friedrich Theo., NYC-B – 1910/12/23:6a
STORJOHANN, Maria, 40, NYC-M – 1887/03/11:3d
STORK, Charles, NYC-B - 1915/06/08:6a
STORK, John, un. cigarmaker, NYC-M - 1896/01/08:4a
STORM, George, tobacco dealer, NYC – 1904/01/19:1e
STORNDORF, Charles, 63,machinist, Hoboken, NJ – 1899/12/21:4b, 22:4a
STORTZ % Uterstaedt
STOTT, Charles M., 44, NYC-M – 1892/06/22:2f
STOTTDREGER, Charles, NYC-M – 1896/08/12:1a
STOTZ, Julius, (Stoltz), 34, un. Kuefer, NYC-M - 1895/09/19: 4a, 3 Oct: 4a
STOTZKY, Carl, NYC-M – 1887/07/21:3c
STOVER, John F., boss-painter, NYC-M – 1902/03/ 15:1f-g, 28 June:3c
STOWITSCH, Wilhelm, SP?, Gottscheer?, NYC-B - 1915/05/20:6a
STRACK, Julius, un. printer, NYC-B - 1917/02/22:6a
STRADEN, Joseph, 63, un. cigarmaker, * near Koblenz/Gy, USA 1882, SP, NYC-B – 1907/01/02:1f,6a,3:6a, =4:3b
STRADINGER, Harriet M., NYC-Bx – 1913/03/06:6a
STRAEFLING, Wilhelm, SLP, un. tailor, NYC-M – 1882/11/13:3b
STRAEHLE, Carl, 29, un. carp., NYC-B – 1891/05/24:5c
STRAEHLE, George, tailor, Lyndhurst, NJ – 1909/05/17:1e, 18:3c, 28:1f
STRAETER % Bauer
STRAHL, A., & wife Augusta, Philadelphia, PA – 1912/11/10:1b

STRAHLAN, Lottie, + 26 Sept in NYC-B – 1881/11/11:4b, 28:1e
STRAILE, Friedrich, 41, NYC-B – 1893/10/31:4a
STRAKOSCH, Charles, 52, insurance agent, NYC-B – 1908/11/23:3a
STRALBE, Frederick, 22, USA 1900, NYC – 1900/10/16:2h
STRANAHAN, James S., ward politico, NYC-B – 1898/09/08:4b-c
STRANCK, John, 19, striker, Bayonne, NJ - 1915/07/24:2d
STRANGFELD, Christina A., b. Moesslinger, 62, NYC-Bx - 1920/05/02:12a
STRANGFELD, Ernst, malter, NYC-M – 1886/03/29:1g, 3b, 30:3d
STRASSER, Catharina, 25, NYC-B – 1910/09/10:6a
STRASSER, Fritz, NYC-Q - 1915/04/25:7b
STRASSER, Jacob, un. shoemaker, fr Suebia?, NYC-B - 1918/11/06:6a
STRASSER, Katherine, NYC-M – 1913/11/03:6a
STRATHMANN, Lina, 20, b. Kessler, NYC-M – 1897/09/18:4a
STRATHMANN, Robert, Elizabeth, NJ – 1906/10/14:7a
STRATMANN, Antonia, NYC-M - 1894/04/28:4a
STRATMANN, Max, 53, NYC-M – 1912/03/21:6a
STRAUB, Annie, worker, Philadelphia, PA – 1881/10/16:4b-c
STRAUB, Charles, 50, NYC-B - 1915/04/29:6b
STRAUB, Elizabeth, boarding-house owner, NYC-Bx – 1913/10/19:1f
STRAUB, Frank, ex-policeman, NYC-M – 1890/11/04:4c
STRAUB, Katherine, 66, NYC-M – 1891/09/02:4a
STRAUB, Lena, 20, worker, NYC-M – 1889/01/16:1f, 17:4a, 23:1h
STRAUB, Louise, NYC-Q – 1913/07/28:2c
STRAUB, Paul, NYC-M – 1880/07/16:1g
STRAUB, R., 40, plumber, NYC-M – 1897/05/14:1d
STRAUB, Wilhelm, 72, fr Paterson, NJ, + NYC-B – 1896/12/26:4a
STRAUBE, Charles, 73, NYC-M - 1916/02/22:6a
STRAUBENMUELLER, Johann, director NYC Free German School, *11 May 1814 Gmuend/Wuertt., '48er, abolitionist, NYC-M – 1897/11/14:1g, =16:1b, poem 21:2c
STRAUBENMUELLER, Paula, NYC-M – 1890/07/10:4a
STRAUBER, Karl, NYC-M – 1908/10/16:6a
STRAUCH % Herden; STRAUSS % Rees
STRAUCH, Gussie, 2, NYC-M – 1891/12/15:2e
STRAUS, Louis, stockbroker, NYC-M – 1907/11/26:1d
STRAUSS, Adolph, 32, NYC-M – 1896/08/11:1a
STRAUSS, Alex, 27, NYC-B – 1884/07/29:3a
STRAUSS, Bernhard, 45, merchant, NYC-M – 1881/08/13:1g
STRAUSS, Charles, insurance agent, NYC-M - 1914/06/06:1f
STRAUSS, Dan, 72, ex-NYPD, *Elsass, USA 1861, NYC – 1906/03/28:4c
STRAUSS, David, NYC-M – 1913/07/10:6a

STRAUSS, Esther, 17, NYC-M – 1888/03/29:4a
STRAUSS, Henriette, 16, NYC-M – 1885/05/07:3b
STRAUSS, Hugo, un. cigarmaker, NYC-M – 1909/09/17:6a
STRAUSS, Jacob, ("son of Theo. Fischbach"), NYC-M – 1919/03/26:6a, fam. 28:6
STRAUSS, Karoline, NYC-M – 1878/04/30:3b
STRAUSS, Martin, 31, iron worker, NYC-B – 1915/07/06:6c
STRAUSS, Max, 40, silver plater, Newark, NJ – 1915/12/28:2b
STRAUSS, Joseph, 59, un. cabinetmaker, co-fdr NYVZ, NYC-Q – 1910/12/21:2d, 6a
STRAUSS, Louis, 27, NYC-M – 1891/11/17:1g
STRAUSS, Maria, 47, NYC-M – 1901/10/05:4a, fam. 8:4a
STRAUSS, Mendel, photographer, & son Samuel, 22, NYC-M – 1900/10/18:1h
STRAUSS, Moses, 60, Rabbi fr Cincinatti, + NYC-M – 1888/10/17:1e
STRAUSS, Nathan F., 54, cigar manuf., NYC-M – 1911/12/20:1b
STRAUSS, Nettie, 16, NYC-M – 1906/12/31:1b
STRAUSS, Regina, NYC-M – 1891/01/12:4a
STRAUSS, Sigmund, cigarmaker, NYC-M – 1898/09/22:2e
STREBE, Caroline, New Haven, CT – 1909/04/06:6a
STREBEL, (Mr.), NYC-Q – 1916/08/21:6a
STREBEL, Marie, 23, NYC-B – 1908/07/29:6b
STREBEL, Nicolaus, un. carp., NYC-M – 1901/07/19:4a
STREBINGER, Louis, 64, NYC-M – 1910/07/05:5f
STRECKER, Emma, b. Benkard, + 18th, NYC-M – 1879/02/28:1e; her will – 1880/02/27:1f
STRECKER, Robert, machinist, NYC-M – 1901/11/01:4a
STRECKFUSS, Sophie, un. cigarmaker?, NYC-B – 1897/09/14:4a
STREECH % Lindner; STREHL % Collins
STREET, William, Negro, lynched Doyline, LA – 1898/06/05:5d
STREHL, Herman, 43, un. patternmkr, NYC-B – 1903/05/09:4a, fam. 24:5b
STREIBLE, John, 57, jeweler, NYC-Q – 1915/01/24:9g
STREICHHAU, Karl, un. carp., NYC-B – 1884/10/21:3a
STREISGUTH, Adolph, 61, Newark, NJ – 1888/04/14:2f
STREIT, Louise, b. Kohler, 36, NYC-Bx – 1911/05/04:6a
STRELITZ, B.H., NYC-M – 1918/01/09:3g
STRELLER, Jenny, 42, Paterson, NJ – 1920/04/10:8a
STRELLER, Lucy, 30, Paterson, NJ – 1910/10/25:6a
STREMPEL, Carl, un. furnit. Maker, SLP, * near Asschaffenburg/Bav., NYC-M – 1891/04/17:4a, 18:4a, 19:5a, c
STRENZ, Wilhelm, fr Glueckstadt/Holstein, NYC-B – 1887/10/01:3a
STREUBEL, Vincent, 9, NYC-M – 1900/07/25:1f

STREUBERT % Marnet
STREUGOTTON, Mary, 16, servant, NYC-B – 1891/07/03:2e
STREUNE, comrade, 80, SPD Lunzenau/Sax. – 1913/05/04:3e
STRIBEL, Philip, 63, Newark, NJ – 1904/09/29:1g, 30:3d
STRICH, Dorothy, NYC-M - 1894/02/01:4a
STRICH, Johanna, + 5 Jy, fr Breslau/Gy, NYC-M, = at sea – 1913/09/03:1f
STRICKER % Henze
STRICKER, Frank, un. carpenter, NYC-M - 1895/02/24:5b
STRICKER, Robert, draftsman, 40, NYC-M – 1891/06/11:1h
STRICKLAND, L., Rev.,Negro, lynch. Palmetto,GA – 1899/04/25:1b, 2a-b
STRICKLER, Johann, Dr., 74, Swiss SP activist, + Bern/Switz. – 1910/10/29:4d
STRICKRODT, Anne, Herman, 14, Louis, 5, NYC-M, @on Genl Slocum – 1904/06/18:3c, 23:1d, 25:1d
STRICKRODT, Charles's wife, 67, NYC-B – 1912/11/01:2d
STRIEBE, A., NYC-Bx – 1905/09/14:4a
STRIEGEL, Henry, 18, Homestead, PA, steelworker, killed during strike – 1892/07/07:1b,2a
STRIEHLE, Christian, NYC-B – 1901/05/02:4a
STRINDBERG, August, 63, Swedish author, his life, by Georg Brandes 1891/03/22:3d-f, + 1912/05/15:2f, =23:1a, 24:4c, & SP 2 Jne:6d-e, 9:16c
STRINGER, Charles, 63, carp., NYC-B - 1916/06/04:1f
STRINGER, John, Elevated RR worker, NYC-M – 1891/02/13:2h
STRIPPEL, Georg, NYC-B - 1915/01/05:6a
STRITTMETTER, William, NYC-Q - 1915/01/12:6a
STRITZKY, Michael, NYC-M – 1910/05/03:6a
STROBEL, Carl William, 56, NYC-M – 1899/01/08:5b
STROBEL, Charles, NYC-Bx - 1918/03/05:6a
STROBEL, Conrad, NYC-Q – 1909/12/17:6a
STROBEL, John, 37, NYC-B – 1908/06/16:2c
STROBEL, Katherine, NYC-M, +@Genl Slocum – 1904/06/16:1c
STROBEL, M., un. cigarmaker, NYC-M - 1894/09/27:4a
STROBEL, Martin, NYC-M – 1908/04/07:6a
STRODTHOFF, Bernhard H., NYC-M – 1890/11/30:5c
STROE % Goettel
STROEBEL, Charles, cook, NYC-M – 1883/04/21:1b, 22:1d
STROEBEL, J. M., malt & hops importer, NYC-M – 1904/05/03:2h
STROEBELE, Amanda, 15, Jersey City Heights, NJ – 1888/12/17:2h, 18:2f, 21:2f
STROEBER, August, worker at DuPont, Philadelphia – 1916/07/22:5e
STROEH, Elisabeth, NYC-M – 1891/06/25:4a
STROEHLA, Lorenz, SP, Weehawken, NJ – 1908/12/06:7c, fam. 8:6a
STROFFBAUCH, Fritz, 59, NYC-Q – 1910/05/02:2b

STROH, Henry, SDP, NYC-B – 1900/12/21:3c, 4a
STROH, Louis H., 53, plumber, NYC-Bx – 1908/06/14:1f
STROH, Michael, NYC-M – 1892/01/19:4f
STROH, Otto, Jersey City Heights, NJ – 1906/07/01:7a
STROHL, Henry, infant, NYC-M – 1882/07/29:4c
STROHM, Emma, 44, NYC-B - 1913/06/15:1b
STROHMAYER, Julia, b. Harms, 52, NYC-Bx – 1912/08/11:7b; Mem. 1913/08/09:6a
STROHMER, Angelica, 50, NYC-M - 1879/08/22:1e
STROHMER, Minnie, dressmaker, NYC-M – 1905/06/18:1g
STROHSCHEIN, August, NYC-M - 1918/11/09:6a
STROM, J., worker at Singer, Elizabeth, NJ, labor activist – 1892/09/14:2d
STROM, W. F., 12, NYC-M – 1893/10/30:4a
STROMBACH % Zander
STROMBERG, Harry, 37, NYC-M – 1911/04/16:1f
STRONG, William L., ex-mayor NYC – 1900/11/03:3d, 15:1h, 16:4b
STROTHOFF, Christopher, 78, NYC-M – 1901/03/31:5c, 1 Apr:4a
STROWER, Lewis, 69, brush manuf., & mother & wife Annie, NYC-B - 1916/10/26:6a, 28:3d
STRUBER, Frederick, 23, brewery worker, NYC-M – 1890/03/04:4e
STRUCHMANN, Karl, 54, SPD Bochum/Ruhr, at Bochumer Volksblatt - 1914/09/06:3b, 13:3c
STRUEBE, Konrad,49,un. cabinetmaker, NYC-M - 1894/06/03:5b
STRUEBEL, Katherine, NYC-M, + @ Genl Slocum – 1904/06/17:3c
STRUEBING, Carl, 35, NYC-M – 1888/04/30:3a
STRUENSEE, Conrad, 45, slipper maker, USA 1868, NYC-M – 1889/10/20:1h
STRUEVEN % Rehse
STRUM, Gottlieb, passenger on SS Weimar – 1897/04/26:1g
STRUPEL, Adam, 50, lamp lighter, NYC-M – 1893/07/05:1g, 2 Aug:4c
STRUPEL, John, 59, cigar dealer, NYC-M – 1882/01/09:1e
STRUPPE, Adam, see Strupel
STRUPPEL, Hermann's wife, NYC – 1880/03/27:3b
STRYKER, Edgar DeNott, Dr., NYC physician, + Holkoi/Korea - 1914/03/31:1f
STUART, Will, Negro, lynched Shelby County, TN – 1892/03/10:1b
STUBERT, Ludwig, un. carp., NYC-M – 1901/09/24:4a
STUBNER, Fridolin, SPD, Glashuette/Pirna, Saxony – 1912/09/29:3b
STUCKENSCHMIDT, Dietrich, 38, NYC-M – 1890/11/30:5c
STUDER, Otto, 45, baker, Paterson, NJ – 1909/07/14:3c
STUDT, Henry, millwright, *Hamburg, SP, NYC-B – 1911/02/22:2c, 6a, 23:6a, =24:2c, fam. 26:7c; mem. 1912/02/21:6a

STUDT, Otto, 1, NYC-B – 1890/10/27:4a
STUECK % Riebling
STUECK, Arthur, 35, NYC-Q – 1910/10/27:6a
STUECK, Hermann, family fr Wiesbaden/Gy, 20, NYC-M – 1887/06/29:3a
STUECK, John Charles, 74, SP,un. carp., fr Wiesbaden/Gy, NYC-M - 1917/04/10:6a,d, 11:6a, fam. 15:7a
STUECKEMAND, F. M., 29, NYC-M – 1891/03/27:4a
STUEHLER, Max, Newark, NJ - 1917/11/16:6a
STUERGHK, Count Karl, Austrian prime minister, killed by Ludwig Adler - 1916/10/22:1a, 24:1c,4b, 26:3e, 27:5d-f
STUETTGEN, Hulda, b. Hildebrandt, 73, Irvington,NJ - 1919/07/19:6a
STUHLMUELLER, Elise, NYC-M – 1901/11/13:4a
STUHLMUELLER, Emily, 12, NYC-M – 1909/06/04:6a
STUHR, Ed, tailor, *Weissenfels/Gy, SP, NYC-Q – 1906/11/12:6a, =15:2b
STULZ, Alexander, 70, butcher, NYC-B – 1910/12/30:3a
STUMPF, Amelia, 31, Hoboken, NJ – 1911/07/08:3d-e
STUMPF, Frederick, 40, innkeep, Hoboken, NJ – 1886/05/06:2d
STUMPF, Jakob, 40, *Switzerland, SP, Alleghany, PA – 1911/01/13:1b
STUMPF, Louis, un. carp., NYC-M – 1888/12/07:3d
STUMPF, Marie, NYC-Q - 1918/01/05:6a
STUMPF, Paul, 85, '48er, SPD Mainz/Gy – 1912/04/01:4d-e
STUMPF, Peter, 55, Newark, NJ – 1905/04/03:4a, 4:4a
STUMPF, William, Kenville, NJ – 1898/04/29:3f
STUNDE, Julius, German NP publ., 60th birthday – 1901/09/08:16e-f
STUNZ, Ernst, 48, SPD Frankfurt/Main – 1909/05/30:3d
STUNZ, Martin, (Sturtz?) 47, smith?, NYC-M – 1880/05/28:1e, 29:4a
STURM % Collins, Huck
STURM, August, NYC-M – 1891/10/03:4a
STURM, Charles, un. furrier, NYC-M – 1890/09/02:4a, 3:4a
STURM, Emma, 7, NYC-M – 1881/11/23:3b
STURM, Frederick, 62, * Strehlen/Silesia/Gy, NYC-B – 1904/03/12:4a
STURM, Julius, 74, *Munich, USA 1846, musician, +Cincinatti, OH – 1898/07/18:1h
STURM, Louise, NYC-M – 1912/04/27:6a
STURM, Max, 70, Paterson, NJ – 1909/02/07:7d
STURM, Michael, 67, NYC-M – 1896/12/17:1e
STURM, Philip, 33, bookkeeper, NYC-M – 1897/01/01:1d
STURM, Wendelin, 74, Jersey City Heights, NJ NYC-M – 1911/03/31:6a
STURM, Wilhelm, un. butcher, NYC-M – 1905/09/26:4a
STURMER % Weileder
STURTZEBECKER, Adolf, NYC-Q - 1920/08/04:6a

STURZENEGGER, George, 33, undertaker, *Switzerland, Jersey City, NJ – 1899/06/10:4a
STUTTER, Sebastian, 76, innkeep, USA 1851, NYC-B – 1911/02/19:1g
STUTZ, August, 68, worker, NYC-M - 1917/10/19:1f
STUTZ, Georg, un. printer, NYC-B - 1917/02/18:7a, 19:6a
STUTZBACH, Minnie, NYC-B – 1889/07/21:1h
STUTZMANN, Louis, NYC-B – 1903/12/01:2f
SUBERVILLE, Louis, 35, bank clerk, fr Orty/Pyrenees/France, NYC-M - 1879/05/08:1f
SUCHMINSKY, Helen, 12, NYC-M – 1907/01/27:7c
SUCK, Julius, Newark, NJ – 1909/12/17:6a
SUCKER, Ernst, NYC-M – 1901/05/27:4a
SUDAN, Khalifa of the – 1899/11/26:1h
SUDEN, Margaret & child Herman, NYC-M, + on Genl Slocum – 1904/06/18:3c
SUDERHOF, Gottfried, Newark, NJ – 1888/04/04:2e
SUDHEIMER, Henry, 64, machinist, Jersey City Heights, NJ – 1910/05/10:6a
SUDHEIMER, Jakobina, b. Bock, 65, NYC-B – 1910/04/15:6a
SUDMANN, Henrietta, 23, NYC-M, +@ Genl Slocum – 1904/06/21:1f
SUDMIKOWICZ, Ignatz, striker, South River, NJ - 1917/06/12:1g
SUE, Leon, 30, French, tanner, NYC-B – 1884/09/01:3b
SUEHRING, Emilie, b. Keller, 25, NYC-M – 1900/08/27:4a, 28:4a
SUELKE, Josef, NYC-M – 1904/06/11:4a
SUENDERHAFT, Johann, 67, un. carp., NYC-M - 1917/01/04:6a, fam. 8:6a
SUERSTEDT, Hermann, machinist, SLP, NYC-B – 1892/06/16:4a, 17:4a
SUERTH, Sophie, infant, Union Hill, NJ - 1895/06/24:4a
SUESSE, Emilie, b. Hahn, 64, NYC-B – 1911/05/25:6a
SUESSE, Ernst, 66, un. carp., NYC-B – 1912/06/09:7c
SUESSENS, Friedrich, NYC-M – 1891/04/06:4a
SUESSHOLZ, Alexander, SP, fr Hungary 1905, NYC-M – 1911/08/11:2d, =14:2a
SUESSKIND, comrade, 54, SPD MdR for Mannheim - 1915/02/28:3a
SUESSMEIER, Clemence, 61, un. painter, fr Palatinate?, NYC-M - 1917/05/09:6a
SUESSMEIER, Magdalene, b. Heitte, NYC-M – 1904/01/20:4a
SUESSMEYER, Baptist, NYC-M – 1910/05/10:6a, 12:6a, fam. 14:6a
SUESSMEYER, Joseph, SP, * Bavaria 11 Dec 1856, + 11.12.1919 NYC, mem., a.e. by Carl Schlossberg - 1920/12/20:5f,6a
SUESSMEYER, Madeline, NYC-M – 1911/04/13:6a
SUETTERLIN, Barbara, West New York, NJ - 1918/07/03:6a

SUGDEN, Sadie M., 34, NYC-B - 1916/07/20:5f
SUHLING, Albert, NYC-M - 1889/06/01:4a
SUHLING, John Max, 28, Roselle Park, NJ - 1904/02/15:4a
SUHR, Anna, 32, NYC-M - 1903/05/03:5a
SUHR, Carl, NYC-M - 1892/07/19:4a
SUHR, Charles, 63, NYC-M - 1917/06/01:6a
SUHR, John, 60, NYC-M - 1891/04/09:4a
SULLIVAN % Wolff
SULLIVAN, Jim, "Little," 39, Tammany politico, NYC-M - 1909/12/23:1d, =25:3d
SULLIVAN, Jim, Irish-American boxer, + NYC - 1895/10/13: 1f
SULLIVAN, Jim, "Big," Tammany pol., NYC-M - 1915/08/17:2f
SULLIVAN, Luther, Negro, lynched Augusta, GA - 1898/10/27:3c
SULLIVAN, Timothy, "Big Tim," Tammany polit. - 1913/09/15:1d, 16:6c, will 18:2d
SULTAIRE, Joseph, 37, SP alderman Milwaukee, WI - 1911/01/16:1c
SULZBACHER, Frederick, cigar dealer, NYC-M - 1911/07/11:2e
SULZBACHER, James, 35, NYC-M - 1908/05/05:1d
SULZER, Hermann, am. park & alderman, NYC-M - 1901/03/17:1d, =20:1e, will 21:3c, 5 Ap:1d, will contested 17:1b
SULZMANN % Merg
SUMMERKATT, Friedrich,58, tassel-maker?, NYC-M - 1878/07/06:4d
SUMNER, William Graham, 70, US pol. Sc., New Haven, CT - 1909/12/28:1f
SUNDERLAND, Peter N., 57, SP, un. cigarmaker fr Hamburg, Jersey City, NJ - 1910/10/07:6a, =12:5e
SUNDERMEHER, Wilhelmine, NYC-M - 1896/03/08:5a
SUNDERMEYER, Heinrich, un. cigarmaker, NYC-M - 1886/05/22:3a
SUNKEL, Fritz, brewer/cooper?, NYC-M - 1892/05/30:4a
SUPE, Giovanni, 35, exec. Ossining, NY - 1916/06/03:1e
SUPPAN, Gottfried, 68, mech. turner, NYC-M - 1887/10/26:4d
SUPPE, Richard, NYC-Q - 1912/01/12:6a
SUPPER, Anna Marie, NYC-B - 1915/01/11:6a
SUPPER, Joseph, steelworker, Homestead, PA - 1892/07/08:1a
SURADA, Anton, un. carp., NYC-M - 1906/08/14:6a
SURAN, Elizabeth, 45, NYC-M -1920/04/12:6a
SURLANLY, Frank, NYC-M - 1914/02/11:6a
SURLAWY, Mary, NYC-M - 1917/05/27:7a
SUSEN, Henry, Newark, NJ - 1920/03/14:12a
SUSMANN, Jacob, NYC-M - 1892/12/11:5b
SUSNOWSKY, Vincent, striker, South River, NJ - 1917/06/12:1g
SUSSDORF, ..., 21, son of Charles F., NYC-M - 1880/07/15:1g

SUSSER, Charles, War 2, Philadelphia, PA - 1917/02/09:2e
SUSSMANN, Felix, cloak maker, NYC-M – 1891/12/13:1f
SUSSMEYER, Joseph, 63, shoemaker, NYC-M – 1919/12/13:8a, 14:3a
SUSTERMANN, Conrad, NYC-M - 1894/01/26:4a
SUTHERLAND, Hadley A., exec. Ossining, NY – 1898/01/10:1e
SUTRO, Adolph, 68, *Aachen/Gy, USA 1850, ex-mayor San Francisco, CA – 1898/08/09:3e
SUTTER, August, NYC-M - 1919/06/26:6a
SUTTER, Charles, 25, RR worker, NYC-B – 1900/07/13:1e
SUTTER, Charles, 56, NYC-M – 1891/08/12:4a
SUTTER, Johann, fdr of US California – 1880/06/22:2d-e, =24:4a
SUTTER, Julius, NYC-M - 1920/03/13:8a
SUTTER, Ludwig, NYC-M - 1918/03/10:7a
SUTTERMANN, Ch., NYC-M – 1900/12/20:4a
SUTTLACH, Herman, 60, cigarmaker, NYC-M – 1880/11/09:1d-e
SUTTNER, Bertha von, Austrian feminist, + Vienna - 1914/06/22:2b, 23:4a-b
SUTTON, Emma R., fd guilty of murder, Dover, NJ – 1900/03/30:3b
SUZZANI, Giovanni, 35, Italian SP & chief ed. RR Workers' Journal – 1910/08/05:4d
SVERAK, Emil, machinist, NYC-M – 1901/09/01:5b
SVOBODA, Mamie, 8, NYC-M, +@Genl Slocum – 1904/06/22:1d
SWAENSON, Olga, b. Meyer, *Copenhagen/DK, NYC-M – 1900/04/16:4a
SWANSON, Olaf, NYC-B – 1904/06/04:4c
SWANSON, Virgil, Negro, lynched near Granville, GA – 1913/08/28:1b
SWEDEN, Oskar, King of – 1907/12/09:1f
SWEETLAND, George A., 50, SLP, Hartford, CT - 1916/12/19:1b
SWENTAMIN, Emil, 30, Alsatian, Freehold, NJ, sent. To + 1916/05/10:3f, exec. Trenton, NJ 6 Jy:2d
SWIENTY, Wilhelm, 29, SPD ed. Hallesches Volksblatt/Gy – 1902/07/21:2d-e
SWINTON, Charles, exec. Ossining, NY – 1912/02/01:2a, 5:6a, 6:1e
SWINTON, John, Scottish-born labor reformer, honored NYC-M – 1890/10/11:1h, 4a, 19:4a-b. + 1901/12/16:1e, =19:3c, 3 Jan. 02:2h, monument planned – 1905/12/11:1g
SYCZEK, Leonard, Rev., Pole, NYC-M - 1896/01/26:1e
SYDE, Richard von, 65, newspaper dealer, nephew of Bismarck's wife, USA 1862, Chicago, IL – 1897/02/25:1f
SYDEKUM, Henry, un. surgical instrument maker, NYC-B – 1910/01/16:7c
SYDOW, Frederick. Bernhard, journalist, NYC-M, War 2 - 1915/06/04:2c

SYLVESTER, Benjamin, 65, typesetter, NYC-M – 1900/03/31:4b
SYVERTSON, Carl, Norwegian sailor, NYC-M – 1891/06/06:2g, 7:1f
SZABO, George, NYC-M - 1917/05/03:6a, 4:6a
SZABO, Joseph's wife, NYC-M – 1909/12/07:2b
SZABO, Karl, un. carp., NYC-M - 1917/12/25:6a
SZABO, Martha, 18, servant, Hackensack, NJ – 1906/10/04:3c
SZAMSKA, Romalda, 22, NYC-B - 1915/02/12:3e
SZEBLEWSKY, Anton, un. carp., NYC-M - 1918/04/18:6a
SZIMMATH, Heinrich, 52, shoemaker, SDP, * Northern East Prussia, USA 1883, Newark, NJ – 1904/05/16:1b, 4a, =18:3e, fam. 19:4a
SZUKALSKI, K., SPD Berlin, + in Posen jail – 1887/08/29:2d
TAAKE, Antoinette, b. Bangert, Elizabeth, NJ – 1900/07/04:4a
TAAKE, Frederick, Roselle Park, NJ – 1908/05/09:6a
TAAKE, Fritz, 64, SP, un. cigarmaker, Roselle Park, NJ - 1917/01/07:7a, 8:6a, =10:6c
TABARIE, Jean A., wine salesman, French, NYC-M – 1880/01/07:4c
TABICK, Sam, @ 1911 Triangle Shirtwaist Fire, NYC-M – 1911/03/27:1d
TABOR, Frederick, druggist, NYC-B – 1896/08/11:1c
TAEGE, Hugo, NYC-Q – 1906/08/09:6a
TAEHLI, Paul, 42, Hoboken, NJ – 1906/09/08:6a
TAENZER, Max, 61, SP, fr Austria 1894, engraver?, NYC-M - 1917/06/05:2g,5f,6a, =8:3e-f, fam. 9:6a
TAFEL, Leonard, Rev. Dr., 81, * Wuerttemberg, USA 1854, biblical scholar, NYC? – 1880/04/05:3a
TALBOT, Albert & Charles, exec. Mayville, MD – 1881/07/23:1e
TALLGESSEN, Thomas, 32, machinist, NYC – 1910/07/29:1e
TALLICH, Catherina, + Cincinatti, OH – 1912/07/08:2c
TALMON % Stellwagen
TAMMEN, John, West Hoboken, NJ - 1918/10/03:6a
TAMSEL, August, NYC-Bx - 1914/05/26:6a
TAMSEN, Eduard J. H., *Hamburg, businessman & NYC polit., NYC-M – 1907/07/25:3e
TAMSEN, Theodor, Atlantic City, NJ – 1900/11/26:3h
TANK, Christian, SDP, * 19 Ap 1831 in ??, + Syracuse, NY – 1905/07/29:4a
TANK, Johanna, 56, Syracuse, NY – 1888/07/11:3c
TANK, Marie, b. Brandt, 47, NYC-B – 1905/05/05:4a
TANNENBAUM, Mayer, NYC-B – 1890/05/11:5a
TANNENBERG, Ernst, 60, NYC-B – 1892/08/15:4a
TANNER % Jaeger
TANNER, Arnold, 54, SP, un. brewer, Swiss, USA ca. 1882, Union Hill, NJ - 1918/09/10:6a

TANNER, Arnold, Guttenberg, NJ – 1898/07/21:4a
TANNER, Josephine, Grantwood, NJ – 1909/05/27:6a
TANNLER, Friedrich, 47, NYC-Q - 1913/09/04:2e
TANNLER, Jenny, NYC-M - 1914/12/16:6a
TANZ % Koestler
TANZER, Jacob, bookbinder, NYC-M – 1908/09/28:6a
TANZMANN, Abraham, Jiddisch actor, NYC-M – 1906/11/15:3d-e
TAPKIND, George, 26, USA 1887, * Scharmbeck/Hannover, NYC-B – 1889/07/19:4a
TAPLEY, Edward J., exec. Jersey City, NJ – 1905/12/22:1e, done 23:2e
TAPPAN, Abraham A., 73, judge, ex-NYS Assembly, 1896/06/02:3f
TAPPEN, Max, NYC-M – 1911/09/13:6a, fam. 15:6a
TASCHNER, August, 53, un. cigarmaker, NYC-M – 1902/08/24:5a
TASSNER, Harry, 36, NYC-Q – 1910/09/29:2c
TATTER, Auguste, 60, NYC-Central Valley – 1910/02/22:6a
TAUB, Annie, NYC-B – 1908/10/13:3b
TAUB, Becky, 18, NYC-M – 1901/09/15:1g
TAUB, Feiga, infant, NYC-M – 1892/06/22:1e
TAUB, Philip, peddler, fr Galizia, Newark, NJ – 1887/11/14:4e
TAUBENBERGER, Philipp, 44, NYC-M – 1889/03/06:4a, 9:4a
TAUBER, Henry, fr Silesia, 58th birthday, NYC – 1912/02/16:3b-c
TAUBER, Josephine, 19, NYC-M – 1905/06/01:2h
TAUBERT, Ch., 58, un. cigarmkr, NYC-M – 1893/02/06:4a, 7:4a
TAUBERT, Julius, NYC-M – 1901/03/28:1e
TAUER, John, 52, NYC-M - 1920/05/29:6a
TAUSCHER, Bernhard, 76, SPD Stuttgart, printer & alderman - 1915/01/13:4d, =16:4c
TAUSCHER, Leonhard, SPD Stuttgart/Gy, 70th birthday – 1910/07/03:3c-d
TAUSCHINSKY, Hyppolyt, Dr., active German labor mov. 1860s-1870s, + Vienna – 1905/03/16:2e-f
TAUSIG, Fritz, NYC-Bx - 1915/02/10:6a, 11:6a
TAUSIG, Jacob, 62, pianomaker, fr Gy, NYC-M - 1895/07/24:1g
TAUTPHOE, Eleonore von, 70, NYC-M – 1892/09/17:4a
TAVERNIER, Jakob, SPD Mainz/Gy – 1899/05/14:13a
TAXIS, Friedrich, 55, machinist, NYC-B – 1909/02/22:6a, 23:6a
TAYLOR, Bayard, U.S. ambassador to Berlin, - 1878/12/20:2c; NYC German singing soc. to sing when corpse arrives 1879/03/03:4c, 10:4b, 11:1e, 12:1e, done 14:4g, 15:1g
TAYLOR, Jerry, Negro, lynched Franklin, Ky – 1885/05/27:1c
TAYLOR, John, 78, pres. Mormon Church – 1887/07/28:1c
TAYLOR, Love, US Senator fr Tennessee – 1912/03/01:2f
TAYLOR, William C., exec. Auburn, NY – 1893/07/28:1a

TAYLOR, William, negro, lynched Sandusky, OH - 1878/09/11:2g
TAZIO, Toni, 30, arrested as anarchist, real name Andre Salsedo, + in jail NYC-M - 1920/05/04:1e, 4a-b, 6:4a-d
TEBER, Marie, 41, NYC-B - 1914/08/10:6a
TEBER, Max, machinist at Ruppert's Brewery, NYC-M – 1912/06/29:1c, 30:7b, fam. 3 Jy:6a
TEGEL, John, un. butcher, NYC-M - 1915/05/16:7c
TEGENER, Fritz, survived murder of 51 G-A Unionists by Confederates 10 Aug 1862 near Rio Grande, + near Austin, TX – 1902/08/17:9g-h
TEICHER, Adolf, un. machinist, NYC-B – 1909/12/30:6a, 1 Dez:6a
TEICHERT, Otto, 44, merchant, Passaic, NJ - 1915/02/06:2b
TEIPER, Charles's wife, 67, & son Frederick, 36, Buffalo, NY - 1916/02/01:1e, 8:1f
TEITELBAUM, Harry, 37, textile dealer, Hoboken, NJ - 1916/02/04:2b
TEITELBAUM, Jacob, 22, SP, copyboy at The Call, fr Russia 1910, NYC-B - 1913/12/23:2c
TELK, John, 45, worker, NYC-M – 1903/10/28:3d
TELLIER, Charles, 90, French pioneer of refrigerator technology, + Paris - 1913/11/10:4f-g
TELLMANN, August, 40, accountant, NYC-M – 1913/01/28:1f
TELZEROST, O. s.a. Auguste Hartmann
TEMBERG, Friedrich, Jersey City, NJ – 1897/07/24:4a
TEMPEL, Georg, NYC-M – 1905/01/30:4a, 1 Fb:4a
TEMPLE, John, Negro, lynched Montgomery, AL – 1919/10/01:1e
TEMPS, Gustav, NYC-B – 1908/02/12:6a
TENKERT % Hoeschen
TENSER, Johanna, NYC-M – 1893/04/14:1f
TEPPERWEIN, Georg, 72, un. baker, * Gy, USA 1882 fr Kopenhagen where labor org. 1865-1882, NYC-M, + Notch, PA - 1916/03/13:5e
TERMULLIGER, Katherine, 18, Ramsey, NJ – 1904/01/05:3b
TERSTEGGE, Albert, Jersey City Heights, NJ – 1887/11/11:3b
TERTSCHEK, Helena, 37, NYC-M - 1916/07/21:6a
TESAREK, Josef, SPO Karlsbad/Bohemia, War 1 - 1915/02/21:3b
TESCHINGER, Oswald, NYC-M – 1893/07/01:4e
TESCHNER, Nettie, 74, NYC-M – 1893/05/14:5b
TESSEWITZ, August, NYC-M – 1912/12/03:6a
TESSIE DU MORTAY, C., 63, French chemist, NYC-M – 1880/06/10:3a
TESSMANN, Louise, NYC-M – 1912/08/16:6a
TETAMOORE, Sophie C., sister-in-law of Rev. Haas, NYC-B, +@Genl Slocum – 1904/06/19:1c
TETSCH, William, New Britain, CT – 1911/03/25:6a
TETZNER, Martha, NYC-B – 1910/02/22:6a

TEUFEL, John, NYC-M – 1905/04/26:4a
TEUSCHERT, Victor, 49, NYC-B – 1910/02/11:6a
TEWEL, Paula, Jersey City, NJ - 1913/06/05:6a
TEWES, Doris, b. Hamann, Jersey City, NJ – 1882/12/19:3a
TEWES, William, 40, USA 1875 fr Zuerich/Switz., banker there, laborer here, NYC-M – 1880/03/31:4c
TEWICH, John, innkeep, NYC-M – 1904/10/16:5h
TEXEL, Wilhelmine, 31, West Hoboken, NJ – 1908/01/03:6a
TEXTOR, Anna, NYC-M – 1900/01/17:4a
THADEN, Peter von, 50, Jersey City Heights, NJ – 1890/01/18:4a
THADEWALD, Lizzie, NYC-M – 1891/07/29:4a
THAIRGEN, Richard, NYC-B – 1912/01/07:7b
THAL, William, baker, NYC-B – 1899/06/10:2h
THALER, Adolf, Newark, NJ – 1913/03/16:7a
THALER, Frances, b. Bumb, 37, NYC-B – 1903/04/30:4a, fam. 9 May:4a
THALER, Joseph, 32, machinist, NYC-B – 1903/08/09:1e
THALER, Julius, un. carp., NYC-B - 1915/12/13:6a, mem 9 De 1916:6a
THALL, Bertha, NYC-M – 1899/07/22:3c
THALMAN, Patrick J., 50, NYC-M – 1898/09/06:1c
THATE, Emil, 38, stone cutter, SPD Leipzig – 1899/03/29:2d
THAU, Henry, un. carp., Yonkers, NY - 1916/05/25:6a, 26:6a
THAULE, Maria C., NYC-M – 1891/02/25:4a
THAYER, Dewitt, + 11 Feb. 1916?, NYC-B - 1916/04/09:7a
THEBES, Henry, 49, NYC-M – 1891/02/20:4a
THEDFORT, Frank, French sculptor, NYC-M – 1883/07/17:1g
THEIL, Anna, 40, cook, NYC-B – 1916/08/22:1f
THEIL, Henry, un. carpenter, NYC-M - 1895/01/04:4a
THEILE % Gerhardt
THEIN, Michael, un. cabinetmaker, * Wuerzburg/Bav., USA 1884, NYC-M 1895/05/11:1g, 4a
THEIS, Ernst, 43, NYC-B - 1915/10/20:6d, 21:6a
THEIS, Henry, NYC-M – 1908/09/27:7c
THEISINGER, Wilhelm, NYC-M – 1905/10/04:4a
THEISS, Friedrich, SPD Dortmund/Gy, ed at local SPD paper – 1898/12/17:2c, 25:13b
THEISS, George J., owner of Alhambra Court & prominent Henry George supporter, NYC-Q – 1889/07/16:2g, will 20:4d
THEISS, George, 32, music hall owner, NYC-M – 1898/01/25:1d
THEISS, Helena Elizabeth, 18, Homestead, NJ – 1908/03/25:6a, fam. 1 Ap:6a
THEISS, Paul, 36, Newark, NJ – 1901/08/11:5a
THELPAP, Annie, 32, NYC-M – 1892/05/30:1e

THERN, Caroline, b. Moehrle, 32, NYC-M - 1895/12/29: 5a
THERN, Elisa, NYC-M - 1892/04/17:5c
THERN, Emmy, 3, NYC-M - 1896/04/04:4a
THERUS, Martha see Theus
THEURER, Christian, 54, SP, un. carp., *Allersteig/Wuertt., USA 1890, NYC-B - 1916/03/31:6a, 1 Apr:6a, fam. 3:6a, = 5:5e
THEURER, John, un. carp., NYC-Bx - 1907/11/08:6a
THEUS, Martha, b. Kremser, (Therus?) NYC-Bx - 1909/02/15:6a
THEWES, Dorothea, b. Harms, 75, NYC-B - 1892/11/06:5c
THEYSKENS, ..., NYC-B - 1919/08/28:6a
THEYSKENS, comrade, SP, NYC-B - 1919/08/28:6a
THIARD DE LA FOREST, Franz, Count, 83, Hungarian noble, USA 1860, + poor NYC-M - 1882/01/17:1g
THIEKE, Louise, b. Lampe, NYC-M - 1886/12/21:3a
THIEL % Jensen, % Nippert
THIEL, August, Arb.turnerbund Leipzig/Sax. - 1914/11/01:3b
THIEL, Benjamin, 64, NYC-B - 1913/05/14:3b
THIEL, Cl., NYC-M - 1905/11/28:4a
THIEL, Frederick, 42, carp., NYC-M - 1904/04/15:2f, 16:4a
THIEL, Gustav, locksmith, alderman & Stuttgart SPD - 1910/04/05:4e
THIEL, Herman, 78, un. cigarmkr, NYC - 1913/11/21:6a
THIEL, Louise, b. Haase, NYC-M - 1908/08/27:6a; fam. 1908/09/01:6a
THIEL, Margaret, 69, NYC-M - 1908/09/23:6d
THIEL, Marie, geb. Baumann, 65, NYC-B - 1919/10/22:6a
THIEL, Mr., 48, member sev. G-A soc., NYC-M - 1878/03/22:3b
THIEL, Philip, 51, NYC-Q - 1909/11/23:6a
THIEL, Valentine, un. painter, NYC-M - 1919/02/07:6a
THIEL, William, ~50, builder, NYC-M - 1891/08/09:1d
THIELE, Auguste, NYC-M - 1894/07/10:4a
THIELE, Bruno, 44, stenographer, NYC-M - 1898/06/26:5e
THIELE, comrade, SPD Mainz/Gy - 1909/05/23:3a
THIELE, E., officer on SS Deutschland, + at sea on way to NYC - 1900/08/07:3b
THIELE, Fritz, 65, SPD Leipzig, 1899/02/04:2d
THIELE, Katharina E., b. Toepper, 40, NYC-B - 1898/03/13:5a
THIELE, Mathilda, Hoboken, NJ - 1900/03/17:4a, 20:4b
THIELEMANN, Elsie, 8, NYC-B - 1912/03/28:6a
THIELMANN, George, worker, NYC-M - 1909/05/18:2c
THIEMAN, Hugo, NYC-B - 1910/05/21:6a
THIEMANN, August, 1, NYC-M - 1888/01/16:3a
THIEME, August, 54, journalist, fdr Waechter am Erie, * Hirschberg/Reuss, USA 1850, + Cleveland - 1879/12/17:2d

THIEME, Katherina, 32, Newark?, NJ – 1908/08/13:3c
THIEMER, John, NYC-M – 1908/03/19:6a
THIERAUF, Conrad, NYC-B – 1884/10/31:3a
THIERFELDER, Albrecht Otto, machinist, *1847 Crimmitzschau/Sax., US 1882, Albany, NY, then New Rochelle, NY - 1915/12/16:2d
THIERFELDT, Josephine, b. Protz, 57, No. Bergen, NJ - 1918/01/26:6a
THIERGARDT, Minnie, NYC-B - 1913/09/23:6a
THIERY, Theodore, pocketbookmaker, French, NYC-M - 1896/02/23:5c
THIES % Ramm
THIES, Ferdinand, 62, SP Burgdorf/Switz., *Gollnow/Pomerania – 1911/09/24:3e
THIES, Henry, 7, NYC – 1902/02/14:3a, 18:1h, 22 May:1e, 23:2c
THIESE, Katherina, b. Getmann, 74, NYC-M – 1886/10/21:3b
THIETZ, Karl, un. brewery worker, NYC-M - 1894/07/10:4a
THIMME, Charles, 6, NYC-M - 1894/10/02:4a
THISSEN, Elisa, NYC-M – 1887/04/21:3e
THITSCHE, Henry, un. cigarmaker, NYC-M – 1899/05/28:5a
THODE, Frieda, Hoboken, NJ – 1909/09/14:6a
THOENE, Henry, un. baker, NYC-M – 1893/07/29:4a
THOLEN, Gustav, painter, NYC - 1913/06/04:3c
THOMA, Henry, NYC-M, +@ on Genl Slocum – 1904/06/18:3c, 18:3d
THOMA, John, cutter, NYC-M – 1883/12/26:2g
THOMA, Nicolaus, German Press Club, NYC-M - 1894/11/06:4a
THOMANN, Hirlande, + Jestetten/Baden/Gy in May 1893, ad by son-in-law Rudolf Glaettli, NYC-M – 1893/10/10:4a
THOMANN, Michael, NYC-M – 1901/01/27:5b
THOMAS, Abraham, 82, peddler fr Gy, NYC-M – 1880/01/26:4d
THOMAS, Anton, 19, NYC-B – 1886/07/12:3b, =13:2e, fam. 14:3b
THOMAS, Anton, Secaucus, NJ - 1916/07/22:6a
THOMAS, Auguste, 19, + on SS Russia of Cholera, on way to NYC – 1893/10/10:4a, 11:1h
THOMAS, C. F., striking RR car driver, St Louis, MO – 1900/06/11:1f
THOMAS, Carl, un. carp., NYC-B – 1911/10/29:7c
THOMAS, Charles F., NYC-M - 1917/04/07:6a
THOMAS, Conrad, 63, NYC-B - 1914/01/21:6a
THOMAS, Elisabeth, b. Kaemmerer, NYC-B - 1896/02/16:5a
THOMAS, Georg, 36, waiter, NYC-M – 1910/04/11:5f
THOMAS, Gottfried, 72, NYC-M – 1892/10/14:4a
THOMAS, Gustav, un. cornice-maker, NYC-M - 1895/07/03: 4a
THOMAS, Henry, Negro, lynched Hemphill, TX – 1908/06/23:1e
THOMAS, Henry, SLP, un. machinist, NYC-M – 1893/04/03:4a
THOMAS, Louise, b. Baumgart, 68, NYC-Glendale – 1908/06/13:6a

THOMAS, Peter, 53, SLP, un. furniture maker, NYC-B - 1894/03/21:4a, = 23:1h, 4a
THOMAS, Washington, school district employee, NYC-M - 1878/11/07:4c
THOMASON, Arthur, 50, violin maker, NYC-B - 1912/03/23:2d
THOMASSCHUETZ, John, German fr Hungary, exec. St Louis, MO - 1898/06/23:3c
THOMMEN, Adolph, jewelry worker, Newark, NJ 1894/01/23:3b
THOMPSON, Hubert O., 42, ex-Comm. Public Works, head of Manhattan Democrats, NYC-M - 1886/07/27:1f, =30:2g
THOMPSON, Jacob H., journalist for N.Y. Times - 1905/09/10:1e, 11:1f
THOMPSON, Jacob, ex-Interior Secy, negat - 1885/03/26:2a-b
THOMPSON, Joseph, 60, waiter, NYC-M - 1909/01/30:1f
THOMPSON, Momme, 64, professor, fr Gy, Greenwich, CT - 1913/08/01:2c
THOMPSON, Phillipine, b. Seitz, 32, NYC-B - 1887/07/28:3c
THOMPSON, Will, 16, Negro, lynched Gaston, SC - 1893/08/01:1e
THOMSEN, Peter, NYC-M - 1883/06/08:3d
THON, Christian, NYC-M - 1891/03/31:4a
THON, Richard, ship steward, War 2, NYC-B - 1915/03/27:1c
THORIN, Annie, 20, servant, Swiss, + Somerville, NJ - 1896/05/12:1g
THORMANN, John, 48, laborer, fr Bohemia,USA 1873,+ Chambersburg, NJ with his wife - 1879/09/04:1g
THORN % Karl
THORN, Emma, NYC-B - 1892/07/09:2c
THORN, Jakob, Elizabeth, NJ - 1918/09/19:6a
THORN, Martin, barber,@William Guldensuppe. Exec. prep. 1898/06/24:1g, note 17 Jy:5c, 1 Aug:1b, done 2:1f, =3:3d
THORNE, Andreas, cafetier, NYC-M - 1899/01/04:1e
THORNE, Thomas W., police inspector, NYC-M - 1885/03/21:4a
THORNHILL, Asa, Negro, lynched Paducah, KY - 1916/10/17:1d
THORNTON, Joseph E., 56, NYC-M - 1892/04/30:2g
THORSCHMIDT, Wilhelm Heinrich, NYC-B - 1898/09/14:4a
THORSEN, Gabriel, NYC-Q - 1918/10/01:6a
THORSMARK, Laurents C., carp., Chicago SLP, co-fdr Vorbote - 1899/09/20:2c-d
THORWALD, Egidius, son of Danish consul in Amsterdam, NYC-M 1889/04/13:4d
THORWART, Leonhart, 49, SPD Stuttgart, clerk - 1909/02/28:3e
THRAM, Gustav, West New York, NJ - 1916/03/11:6a
THRIST, Amelia, 14, NYC-M, + @ Genl Slocum - 1904/06/17:3c
THUEMMLER, Helmut, NYC-B - 1917/01/05:6a
THUENENKOETTER, Amalia Limon, 63, Newport, CT - 1915/06/23:6a

TIEWS, Anna, b. Miller, 51, Jamaica Plains MA – 1909/01/19:6a
TIGHE, James, 66, NYC Police Court Judge, NYC-M – 1911/05/22:1d
TILBACH, Alois, NYC-M – 1891/12/22:4a
TILDEN, Samuel J., ex-NYS governor – 1886/08/05:2g, will 10:1g
TILLETT, Benjamin, 30, portrait of the leader of the current British docker strike – 1889/11/10:4c-d
TILLICH, Irma, SP Graz, Austria – 1912/05/26:3d
TILLMANN, Anna, 44, NYC-B – 1891/02/27:4a
TILLMANN, Johanna, 70, NYC-M - 1919/01/03:6a
TILLY, Egmont von, ex-Prussian officer fr Elbing/West Prussia, teacher, NYC-M – 1887/05/24:1f
TILTON, Theodore, 72, abolitionist, *NYC, s. 1880s Paris/France – 1907/05/26:11d
TIMKEN, Henry, 55, hotelier & treas. local German/Austrian Relief Fund, Hoboken, NJ - 1914/12/15:2a
TIMM, Mary, 26, George, Hedwig & Henrietta, NYC-M, +@ Genl Slocum – 1904/06/18:3c, 23:1c
TIMME, Anna Flora, child, NYC-M – 1882/07/10:3c
TIMME, Anna, 2, NYC-B – 1880/01/28:3b, fam. 29:3a (lower)
TIMME, Emilie Auguste Zimmermann, NYC-M - 1878/02/16:3c
TIMME, Friedrich Wilhelm, her husband, NYC-B - 1878/06/16:8b
TIMME, Robert, un. carp., *27/08/38 Dresden/Gy, NYC-B – 1902/01/24:4a, 25:1f, 4a, 26:5a, fam. 29:4a
TIMMERMANN, Arthur, 20, NYC-M – 1900/12/07:4a
TIMMERMANN, Frank, Dr., dentist, Chicago, IL - 1916/05/08:1c
TIMMERSCHEIDT, Richard Adam, 45, manager of Deutsch- Ostasiatische Bank agency in Hong-Kong, + NYC-M - 1917/07/06:1d
TIMMS, Mary, 34, fr Switzerland, NYC-M – 1880/10/01:1g
TINGERT, John, un. butcher, NYC-M - 1919/02/05:6a
TINS, Wilhelm, NYC-Bx – 1911/04/01:6a
TINSDAHL, Henry, cabinet maker, * Hamburg, USA 1867, NYC-M - 1878/09/23:5e
TIPFEL, Joseph, 45, NYC-M – 1903/11/25:4a
TIPPER, Robert, un. typesetter, NYC-Glendale – 1910/03/14:6a
TIPPMANN % Kirchner
TIPPMANN, John, SP?, un. cigarmkr, NYC-M - 1915/11/05:6a
TIPPOLT, Edward, carp., Paterson, NJ – 1896/05/01:2e
TIRKOT, John, un. cigarmaker, NYC-M - 1919/07/08:6a
TISCHER, Alfred, NYC-Bx - 1916/11/26:11g
TISCHLER, Anna, 8, NYC-M, + @ Genl Slocum – 1904/06/21:1f
TISCHLER, David, 57, dry goods store, NYC-B – 1900/07/26:2g
TISCHLER, Rose, 35, artist, NYC-M - 1917/12/05:1d

THUM, Jeannie, 6, Harrison, NJ – 1898/09/04:1e
THUN, Henry, NYC-M – 1901/07/03:1d
THURGART, Mary, 28, NYC-M – 1880/11/22:3a
THURMAHLEN,…., 32, NYC-M, + @ Genl Slocum – 1904/06/18:3c
THWEAT, Lunn and Robert, Negroes, lynched Springfield, TN, with 3 others – 1881/02/20:5c
TIALKA, Maria, & Emile, 6, Rosa, 7, NYC-M – 1885/11/24:1g, 25:1e, 1 Dec:1e-f
TICE, Joseph M., exec. Auburn, NY – 1892/05/18:1c, 19:1b
TIECK, George, NYC-B, + Yonkers, NY – 1909/06/04:3a
TIEDE, Charles, 47, un. driver, NYC-B - 1917/09/17:6a,18:6a
TIEDEMAN, Charles, NYC-B - 1917/01/20:6a
TIEDEMANN, Carl, 47, un. carp., NYC-M – 1905/04/19:4a, 20:4a
TIEDEMANN, Herbert F., NYC-M – 1911/03/21:6a
TIEDT, Helena, NYC – 1911/10/06:6a
TIEFENBACHER, Barbara, NYC-M – 1903/12/02:4a
TIEFENBACHER, Etelka B., b. Kallman, NYC-M – 1910/12/20:6a
TIEFENBACHER, K., NYC-M - 1919/04/03:6a
TIEFENTHALER % Ellison
TIEFENTHALER, Charles, un. typesetter, NYC-M – 1897/11/10:4a, 11:4a
TIEFLER, William, NYC-Bx - 1918/10/07:6a
TIELY, Mary, 16, Philadelphia, + Jersey City, NJ – 1880/05/31:4d
TIEMANN % Schlichte
TIEMANN, August, NYC-M – 1891/08/19:4a
TIENKEN, Herman, 36, sailor, NYC-M, @1900 dock fire, Hoboken, NJ 1900/07/03:1c
TIENKENS, Harry, collector for Pabst Brewing Co., West New York, NJ – 1908/11/19:1b
TIENKENS, Kath. M., b. Oeters, NYC-B – 1891/06/24:4a
TIERSMANN, Fritz, 45, un. cigarmaker, NYC-M – 1901/12/13:4a, fam. 23:4a
TIERSMANN, Oswald, 4, NYC-M – 1902/06/07:4a
TIETGEN, Charlie, 19, NYC-M – 1889/02/24:5b
TIETGEN, Hermann, + 7 Jy, body fd, NYC-B – 1900/09/24:3b
TIETJEN, August, 12, NYC-B – 1898/11/09:4a
TIETJEN, August, Hoboken, NJ – 1896/08/11:1d
TIETJEN, John, NYC-M – 1906/07/25:1e
TIETJEN, John, waiter, NYC-B – 1900/08/24:1e
TIETZ, Gottfried, 26, sailor on ship "Otto", NYC-M – 1897/10/13:3f
TIETZ, Minnie, b. Nette, NYC-M – 1892/12/08:4a
TIETZE, Leo, 27, butcher, NYC-B – 1907/01/24:3b
TIETZE, Max, 19, NYC-M - 1916/07/06:6a

TISHKOWITZ, Sadie, 5, Newark, NJ – 1910/02/10:1c
TISMAR, Edwin, infant, NYC-M – 1889/07/23:4a
TISZA, Stephan Count,Hungarian politician, murdered, obit "End of a Criminal" – 1918/11/05:4c
TITTEL, Hermann, NYC-Bx - 1916/04/23:7c
TITTMANN, Frank, 37, SP,un.carp.,NYC-B - 1915/11/30:6a,1 De:6a
TITTMANN, John, 67, SP, * 16 May 1845 Gottschee, NYC-B – 1913/01/18:2b,6a
TITTOR, Mrs, NYC-M - 1894/04/26:4a
TJARKS, Caroline, 73, fr Gy in 1913, NYC-M - 1916/08/27:11d
TLASKAL, Wenzel, 34, fr Bohemia, NYC-M – 1891/06/07:1h
TLUSTY, Anna, 65, NYC-M - 1917/01/17:6a, fam. 23:6a
TLUSTY, Frank, 73, un. carp., NYC-M – 1919/11/11:8a, fam. 23:2e
TOBIAS, Philip, 53, jewelry dealer, NYC-M – 1885/11/12:1g
TOBIN, Thomas, NYC, exec. Ossining, NY – 1904/03/15:1h
TODT, Andrew, fr Hungary, striker in Braddock, PA, sent. to + for killing scab – 1891/02/10:1c, 11:2a, 9 Apr:1e, 22 Jy:2a
TOEMAN, Henry, 18, NYC-B - 1914/08/30:11d
TOENSMANN, Franz, 70, NYC-M - 1918/10/17:6a,fam.22:6a,=31:5e
TOEPFER, Johanna, NYC-M – 1912/10/21:6a, fam. 27:6a
TOEWS, Walter, 15, Guttenberg, NJ - 1918/10/14:6a, fam.17:6a
TOLAIN, Henry Louis, former French Socialist, + Paris – 1897/05/06:2d
TOLLE, G. F., a pioneer of New Braunfels, TX – 1881/06/11:2c
TOLLMER, Joseph, NYC-M, + @ Genl Slocum – 1904/06/18:3c
TOLPAGIN, Russian Revol., exec. Moscow – 1907/10/02:6a
TOLRICO, Joseph, exec.Philadelphia, PA – 1908/04/08:5f
TOLSTOI, Leo, Count, 1910/11/17:1a, 21:1c, 4a; obit by Rosa Luxemburg, & mem. meeting in NYC 4 Dec:6c-d; mem. 1911/09/24:20d
TOMAYN, Margaretha, un. cigar maker, NYC-M – 1886/11/29:3c
TOMBO, Rudolph, 38, prof. Columbia U German Dept, NYC-M - 1914/05/23:6a
TOMMANY, Paul, un. Painter?, NYC-M – 1905/05/05:4a
TOMPKINS, George, 14, War 2, Paterson, NJ - 1917/04/04:6c
TONDER, Caecilie, NYC-M – 1892/03/27:5d
TONDRA, Andreas, Yonkers, NY – 1912/03/29:6a
TONJES, Henry, 60, salesman, NYC-M – 1913/04/26:1d
TONJES, Hermann, NYC-M - 1914/07/09:6a
TONN, Elizabeth, 46, NYC-M – 1912/04/19:6a
TONNDORF, Franz, infant, NYC-M - 1878/09/21:3a
TOOLEY, Worthy, Athen, NY, exec. - 1915/12/18:1d
TOPORCZER, Andreas, NYC-M - 1913/08/28:6a
TOPORCZER, Anna Marie, NYC-M - 1920/07/15:6a

TOPP, Emil, 30?, NYC-B – 1891/07/21:1d
TOPPEL, Lizzie, 5, NYC-B – 1893/08/07:1h
TORBURG, Neumann, 61, German sculptor, + Elberfeld/Gy - 1918/01/26:2f
TORNIPORT, Francis, Frieda & Charlotte, NYC-B, +@Genl Slocum – 1904/06/18:3c, 23:1b
TOROK, Lopas, fr Hungary, worked West VA., + NYC on way home – 1908/02/13:1d
TORZENSKY, Martin, NYC, barber, *1864 near Posen/Gy, USA 1880, see Martin Thorm under William Guldensuppe
TOTH, Ferencz, fr Hungary, worked West VA., + NYC on way home – 1908/02/13:1d
TOTH, Gugale, fr Greece, exec. Trenton, NJ – 1911/01/04:3b
TOTH, J., fr Austria, exec. Trenton, NJ - 1914/11/03:2e
TOTH, Laszlo, 48, Harrison, NJ - 1915/11/22:6a
TOTZAUER, John, un. carp., NYC-M - 1915/12/31:6a
TOUSEY, Sinclair, publisher, Yonkers, NY - 1915/07/30:1f
TOUSSENEL, Alfonse, 82, French writer – 1885/06/06:2e
TOUZIL, Therese, Czech Socialist, + Prague/Bohemia – 1910/01/23:3d
TOWNSEND, Winfield, Negro, lynched Montgomery, AL – 1900/10/03:1d
TOWNSEND, Wisner R., Dr. med., NYC-M - 1916/03/13:1d
TOWSKI, Vanda, 10, NYC-M, + on Genl Slocum – 1904/06/17:3c
TRABER, Emil, NYC-M - 1915/12/15:6a
TRABINGER, Charles, 46, Jersey City Heights, NJ – 1892/03/04:2e, 5:4a:4a
TRABOLD, Charles, NYC-Bx – 1905/05/16:6a
TRACHTENBERG, Nathan, 32, peddler fr Russia, NYC-M – 1906/09/18:6a
TRACY, Henry, famous Western outlaw, killed Creston, WA – 1902/08/07:1h
TRAEGER, C. S. Albert, 82, MdR, old liberal, posit. Obit – 1912/02/27:1b,4d; his = in Berlin, Gy – 1912/04/14:3b
TRAEGER, Carl, ex-conductor NYC Beethoven MC, on SS Colima – 1881/10/18:1f
TRAEGER, Oskar, 30, machinist, family in Europe, Hoboken, NJ - 1915/12/02:2d
TRAHMER, C., Newark, NJ – 1910/11/26:6a
TRAIN, George Francis, US reformer, NYC-M – 1904/01/20:2b, 4a
TRAMPLER, Johanna, Newark, NJ - 1914/07/22:6a
TRAMPOSCH, Alois, 32, fr Gottschee?, NYC-Bx - 1913/07/25:6a
TRAMPOSCH, Frank, fr Gottschee?/Austria, NYC-B – 1912/09/04:6a

TRAMPUSCH, Albert, Dr., 82, member 1848 German Parliament, = Vienna – 1898/03/26:2g
TRANTZ, Charles, 56, Jersey City, NJ – 1903/12/26:4c
TRAPHAGEN, Gerard, 9, Jersey City, NJ, + Snake Hill Orphanage – 1882/10/28:1e, 29:4f-g, 5 Dec:2a-b
TRAPP, Benedict, 50, NYC-M – 1893/10/23:4a
TRAUB % Bolten
TRAUB, George, Elizabeth, NJ - 1917/08/24:6a
TRAUB, Gustav, silkweaver, + 25 Apr., body found, NYC-M – 1887/05/16:2e
TRAUB, Ural S., Dr., 40, dentist, NYC-B - 1917/11/14:3e
TRAUBEL, Horatio, US-born Canadian labor poet, + Bon Echo, Ont. – 1919/09/10:2b
TRAUMUELLER % Putt
TRAUTE, Charles, 32, NYC-M – 1892/04/05:4a
TRAUTH, Karoline, b. Dorsh, 58, NYC-B - 1920/07/20:6a
TRAUTMANN, Charles, 62, 20 years in Africa, famous sharp-shooter, Elizabeth, NJ – 1897/08/10:3d
TRAUTMANN, Lewis, 80, Phila – 1892/08/02:2e
TRAUTMANN, Lizzie, 45, West New York, NJ – 1911/06/01:6a
TRAUTNER, Margaret, 78, NYC - 1913/12/06:1e
TRAUTWEIN, Magdalena, Hoboken, NJ – 1893/04/18:4a
TRAVIS, Frank, IWW, murdered Sacramento, CA jail – 1919/08/21:2b-c
TREBER, Conrad, Newark, NJ – 1882/03/03:1g
TREBER, Elisabeth, b. Braun, 69, fr Neustadt a.d. Haardt/Gy, NYC-M - 1878/11/14:3c
TREBRA, Edward, NYC-B – 1919/10/21:6a
TRECKMANN, Johann Friedrich, NYC-M - 1878/05/10:3b
TREFFERT, John, NYC-M – 1909/06/21:6a
TREFFERT, Katherine, b. Stadtmiller, 37, NYC-M – 1901/06/13:4a
TREFZGAR, Lina, 19, NYC-B? – 1893/05/03:4c
TREIBER % Schmidt
TREIBER, William, un. baker, NYC-Bx - 1920/12/12:12a
TREITSCHKE, Heinrich von, 62, German historian, crit. obit – 1896/04/29:1b, 30:2c
TREMEL, Maria, NYC-B – 1919/09/12:6a, fam. 16:6a
TRENKE, Richard, + Auguste Zimm in Phila, to be exec. 1884/11/07:1g
TRENKLE, Joseph, NYC-Bx? – 1912/11/25:6a
TREPING, Minnie, 7, NYC-M, +Genl Slocum – 1904/06/22:1d
TREPOW, Dmitri, Russian general & polit., 1906/09/16:1c, 15:1g, 18:1a, =20:1c, 1 Oct:4e
TRESCHER, Theodor, un. tinsmith, NYC-M – 1886/05/17:4e

TRESCHMANN, Bernard, 22, butcher on SS Pennsylvania, Hoboken, NJ – 1897/05/29:1e
TRESS, George, 32, NYC-M – 1890/07/10:4a
TRETAU, John, 59, SP?, NYC-Bx – 1906/04/15:5a
TRETOW, Dorothea A., Jersey City Heights, NJ – 1905/09/07:4a
TRETOW, Friedrich, 72, Jersey City, NJ – 1898/08/08:4a, fam. 14:5e
TRETOW, Hans Heinrich, 59, Mt Vernon, NY – 1885/02/23:3c
TRETOW, Martha W., Jersey City Heights, NJ – 1896/08/09:5a
TRETOW, Otto, Jersey City Heights, NJ – 1891/09/09:4a, fam. 12:4a
TREUE, Georg, 47, textile worker, alderman & SPD activist in Berlin-Lichtenberg – 1908/02/02:3b
TREUTERN, Henry, 43, Jersey City?, NJ – 1898/09/05:1e
TREUTLEIN, George, brewer, NYC-M – 1897/08/27:4a
TREUTLEIN, John, NYC-B – 1911/05/20:6a
TREVELLICK, Richard, 65, *England, pres. Natl Labor Union 1871-73,+Detroit,MI 1895/02/16:1b
TREYLOWN, James, 25, exec. Morristown, NJ – 1883/04/19:4d
TRIEFSCH, Adam, Jr., 7, NYC-M – 1906/07/08:7a
TRIER, Seligman, 71, NYC-M – 1894/02/01:4a
TRIEST, Felix, German Press Club, NYC-M 1895/04/10:4a
TRIFFIERER, Wilhelm, 63, un. cigarmaker, NYC-M – 1903/04/18:4a
TRILLHOSE, Carl, mason, SPD organizer 1870s, missing s. 1883, declared dead – 1908/04/24:4f
TRILSE, Hermann, 47, union org. in Elbing/Westprussia, tailor, *Falkenberg/Silesia – 1914/02/01:3b
TRIMMEL, Ferdinand, woodcutter & SP Vienna – 1908/02/16:3e
TRIPOLO, C., Jersey City Hgts, NJ – 1920/06/21:6a
TRIPP, Amelia, 85, NYC-M – 1895/04/24:1g
TRISCHE, John, 61, NYC-Q – 1913/08/26:6a
TRITSCHLER, Catherine, 8, NYC-M – 1907/08/02:1g, 3:1g
TRODUDT, Joseph, 42, Czech tailor fr Bohemia, NYC-M – 1891/10/19:4e
TROEBER, William H., 45, movie operator, West Orange, NJ – 1914/12/11:2d
TROEGER, Jakob, un. metal worker, NYC-M – 1886/01/27:3b
TROEGER, Philip Heinrich, 66, NYC-M – 1887/02/02:3c
TROESCHER, Charles, + 18 Nov. 1878, memory – 1879/11/18:4d
TROGNITZ, Wilhelm, SPD Zwickau/Saxony, ex-chief ed. Reussische Volkszeitung – 1910/10/01:4d
TROJAR, Nikolas, 67, un. carp., NYC-M – 1919/07/20:6a
TROLL, Albert, NYC-M, + @on Genl Slocum – 1904/06/17:3c
TROLL, Simon, un. carp., NYC-M – 1913/02/10:6a

TROLLOPE, Anthony, Engl. Writer, on his +, by H. Zimmern, – 1883/01/14:7a-c, 21:5d
TROMERHAUSEN % Braaz
TROMMER, Eduard, 37, Amt Ottener Club, NYC-M - 1918/06/14:6a
TROMMER, John, 26, co-owner brewery, NYC-M – 1907/09/13:1b, 14:1f
TROMP, William, un. carp., NYC-M – 1904/02/21:5b
TROMPETER, (Mrs), SPD Frankfurt/Main – 1897/03/08:2f
TROMPETER, G., physician, Dr., Portchester, NY – 1882/05/06:3a
TRONNER, Wilhelm, SLP, Troy, NY – 1883/10/14:7e
TROOST, Ernst, 61, locksmith fr Iserlohn, SPD org. in Dortmund/Gy - 1913/08/17:3c
TROPIN, George, SP,treasurer Home of the Masses, Detroit, MI, + fr mistreatment in jail - 1920/08/20:2e
TROST, Christian, 42, NYC-M – 1891/03/19:4a
TROST, Franz, un. carp., NYC-M – 1889/11/16:4a
TROST, Gideon, 82, a Quaker, Greenvale, NY – 1880/03/03:3a
TROSTLER, Joseph, SLP, druggist, NYC-M - 1895/06/24:4a
TROTHA, W. von, reporter for Wiener Freie Presse, (dying), NYC-B – 1883/02/01:3a
TROXLER, Josef, un. carp., NYC-M – 1902/08/02:4a
TROYER, Gustav, 31, NYC-M – 1906/04/03:4a
TRUAX, George & wife, Oceanic, NJ – 1910/02/15:3a-b
TRUBERG, A., fr Neustadt/Gy, NYC-M – 1888/03/09:3b
TRUCKENBROT, F., NYC-Bx – 1907/04/28:7b
TRUDEAU, Edward, Dr., US TB res., + Saranac Lake, NY - 1915/11/19:1g
TRUEB, Catharine, NYC-M - 1919/06/27:6a
TRUHE, Minnie, 10, NYC-M, +@1883 School Fire, NYC-M
TRUNK, Antoinette, b. Weichand, * Langenkandel/Gy, NYC-M – 1889/09/07:4a
TRUNK, Gustav, un. carp., NYC-M – 1901/11/09:4a
TRUSCH, Viktor, 67, & wife, NYC-B – 1908/09/15:1f
TRUSCHEL, Philip, 18, worker, USA 1880, NYC-Q – 1881/03/03:1e
TRUSHEIM, Julius, un. baker, NYC-M – 1902/12/29:4a
TRUTZEL, Heinrich, un. cigarmaker, NYC-M – 1900/03/23:4a
TSCHAMBER, Emma, 21, NYC – 1886/10/28:2e
TSCHECH, Elizabeth , 72, daughter of Heinrich Tschech, mayor of Storkow/Prussia, exec. for 1844 murder attempt on the king, NYC-B - 1896/01/28:1f, =17:2d; Note – 1909/07/03:4f
TSCHECHOW, Russian writer, + 1904/08/16:2c-d, 19:2d
TSCHERNE, Joseph, NYC-B – 1905/06/02:4a
TSCHERNYSCHEWSKY, Nicholas Gaw., 59, Russian revol., freed after 25 years jail 1889/09/22:7e-f, +, NYC 4 Nov:1e, 7:1h, 8:1h, rev. 9:1a-d

TSCHIEDEL, Anton, NYC-Q - 1917/07/16:6a
TSCHINKEL, Georg, Newark, NJ - 1907/11/06:6a
TSCHRENIAK, Jakob, 28, Russian revol., + Antwerpen - 1907/03/05:4d-e, 6:4e-f
TSCHUDIN, Heinrich, 69, weaver?, NYC-M - 1910/02/12:6a
TUCH, Isaac, 89, clothes dealer, NYC-M - 1900/09/15:4a
TUCHEL, Gustav A., 60, landlord, NYC-M - 1890/09/14:5e
TUCHT, Anna, 17, + in jail in Essen/Gy, scandal - 1898/09/18:12h
TUCKERMAN, L. B., Dr., 54, SDP, + Cleveland, OH - 1902/03/09:5b
TUENZER, M., Union Hill, NJ - 1918/01/10:6a
TUFT % Ruppert
TULLESKY, Stanislaus, NYC-B - 1903/08/27:4a
TULLY, Patrick, Molly Maguire, exec. Bloomsburg, PA - 1878/03/26:1c, 2d, 3 Apr:2g
TUMBRINCK, August, SP?, NYC-M - 1917/05/02:6a
TURCIK, Cyril, SP Tischau/Bohemia, War 1 - 1914/10/11:3d
TURGENEW, , Russian writer, his mother 1884/07/06:7a, grave 25:2e
TURGENEW, Ivan, Russian writer, 1883/09/05:2e, 9:4c-e, 16:4c-d, =12 Oct:2c, 22 Oct 83:1d, 10 Nov:2d,
TURKOWSKI, Anton, fr Poland, NYC-B, exec. Ossining, NY - 1903/08/04:3f
TURKOWSKY % Mayer
TURNER, Richard, 50, beer bottler, NYC-B - 1909/05/23:7e
TURNER, Sam, Negro, lynched near Kingston, GA - 1897/12/30:1d
TURTOWSKY, Fr.'s wife, fam. 1887/04/25:4c
TUTSCHER Sr., Frank, 67, Arlington, NJ - 1916/11/03:6a
TWAIN, Mark (Sam L. Clemens), US writer, 1910/04/22:1e-f, 23:4a-b, 24:4a-b
TWEED, William,"Boss" - 1878/04/13:2c,4c-e, 14:4a-d, 15:2b-c; his widow = in Suffolk County, 1880/03/11:4b; his son George W., + Middleton, CT - 1905/08/03:1e
TWEELE, Otto, 62, un. carp., NYC-Bx - 1917/06/28:6a
TWITE, Theodor, 65, NYC-B - 1908/08/24:3a
TYBUS, Batavia?, NY, exec. Ossining, NY - 1916/09/02:1a
TYNDALL, John, Prof., English scientist - 1893/12/24:7f-g
TYSON, John, NYC-M, + @ Genl Slocum - 1904/06/18:3c
UBER, Valentin, 52, NYC-B - 1904/03/10:4a
UBRIJANI, Spanish peasant & anarchist, exec. Jerez de la Frontera - 1892/02/11:1a-b, 12:1a, 19:1g
UDERITZ, Christoph Justus, 70, SP?, NYC-B - 1906/06/15:4a
UDVARHELY, Frank, 50, Newark, NJ - 1911/07/14:3c
UEBEL, Rosina, b. Schmid, 63?, NYC-M - 1891/03/27:4a

UEBERICK, Paul, 50, NYC-Bx – 1906/02/13:4a
UECKER, Anna, NYC-M - 1918/09/03:6a
UECKER, Wilhelm, 73, un. carp., SP?, NYC-M – 1911/05/18:6a, 19:6a, 20:6a, fam. 23:6a
UECKERMANN, F., un. carp., NYC-M – 1904/12/20:4a
UEHLEIN, Minnie, (or Uhlein), 41, NYC-M + @SS Genl Slocum – 1904/06/17:3c, 18:3d
UEHLICH, Alvin, NYC-Q – 1901/03/11:4a
UEKER, Julius, machinist, NYC-M - 1895/05/21:4a
UELING, John August, Passaic, NJ – 1897/11/27:3c
UELZEN, William, NYC-B - 1915/01/15:6a
UETTERLING, Josephine, 38, Hoboken, NJ – 1910/12/16:6a
UFERT, Charles, W. Hoboken, NJ, SP, ed. Socialist Review, married Jenny Steiger of Union Hill, NJ – 1907/03/22:3b-c
UFERT, Harry Charles, Weehauken Heights, NJ – 1909/01/25:6a
UFERT, Josephine, b. Boehlau, fr Leipzig, SLP, Union Hill, NJ – 1888/04/17:2h, fam. 19:3a, =20:2d
UFERT, Pauline, b. Graf, wd Blum, 60, West Hoboken, NJ – 1912/01/10:6a
UHL % Bender
UHL, Anton, NYC-M – 1908/07/12:7b
UHL, August, 60, NYC-M – 1891/02/27:4a
UHL, Edward, 65, NYC-M – 1906/08/03:6a
UHL, Elisabeth (Lizzie), 1, NYC-M – 1901/08/03:4a, fam. 5:4a
UHL, Elisabeth (Lizzie), 15, NYC-Q – 1909/11/16:6a
UHL, Elisabeth (Lizzie), b. Lammchen, 23, NYC-M – 1892/06/25:4a
UHL, Franziska, 48, NYC-M – 1891/10/09:4a
UHL, Frederick, NYC-B - 1913/05/09:6a
UHL, Fritz, 42, un. pianomkr, NYC-Q - 1914/05/25:6a, 26:6a
UHL, Helene, 20, NYC-M – 1907/11/14:6a
UHL, Henry, 35, Elizabeth, NJ – 1901/07/04:3b
UHL, Hermann, *1842 NYC, son of ex-publ. NYSZ, its bus. Mgr 1863-1880, & General in NYNG, NYC-M – 1881/02/14:1b, 15:3c
UHL, Jerome, 74, artist, Cincinatti, OH - 1916/04/13:1d
UHL, John, 35, NYC-M – 1891/07/19:5b
UHL, John, un. carp., NYC-M – 1902/06/21:4a,b, 22:5a
UHL, Karl, NYC-B – 1911/08/21:6a
UHL, Kate, 28, NYC-M – 1896/08/11:1a
UHL, L., 20, NYC-M – 1893/08/27:5a
UHL, Lizzie, NYC-Q - 1918/04/07:7a
UHL, P., 73, NYC-B – 1893/05/30:4a
UHL, Russell, tobacco magnate, Wilkesbarre, PA - 1914/04/05:7c
UHLBACH, Mrs – 1880/11/29:4d

UHLE, William, SDP?, NYC-B – 1902/03/18:4a
UHLENDORF, Hermann, NYC-M – 1891/03/24:4a
UHLENDORFF, Louisa, NYC-M, +@SS Genl Slocum – 1904/06/18:3d
UHLIG, Anna, Danellen, NJ – 1887/12/01:3b
UHLIG, Oswald, 54, un. cigar maker, NYC-Bx – 1912/10/28:6a
UHLINGER, Anton, 77, businessman, NYC-B – 1911/06/06:3a
UHLMANN, August, Union Hill, NJ - 1914/08/27:6a
UHLMANN, Louise, 56, West Hoboken, NJ - 1914/03/21:6a
UHLMANN, Margarethe, 72, NYC-B - 1895/04/06:4b
UHLRICH, Hugo O., 50, NYC-Q – 1911/07/14:3b
ULBRICH, Josef, 63, weaver, SP Reichenberg/Bohemia – 1910/03/20:3d
ULBRICHT, Richard, 67, SLP?, NYC-B – 1892/03/21:4a, fam. 23:4a
ULBRICHT, Rosie, b. Krieg, 28, NYC-B – 1897/05/25:4a
ULJANOW, Alexander, 21, exec. for March 13 attentate on Czar – 1887/05/26:5b, 30:2f, + 10 June:5e, 17:5e
ULLAND, Eugenie, b. Adrian, NYC-M – 1893/12/07:4a, 8:4a
ULLHERR, Georg, 23, NYC-M – 1880/10/24:8b
ULLMAN, John L., 76, NYC-M – 1898/09/06:1c
ULLMAN, Louis H., upholsterer, NYC-M – 1893/02/12:1g
ULLMANN, Eduard, NYC-M – 1891/11/13:4a
ULLMANN, Edward, & Lena, & Edward Jr., NYC-M, +@ SS Genl Slocum – 1904/06/17:3c
ULLMANN, Rudolph, Chicago, IL,inventor, & children Julia & Rudolph Jr – 1912/07/16:1b
ULLNER, Charles, un. cornice maker, NYC-M – 1891/12/12:4a
ULLRICH, (misspelled Ullrech) Joseph, Paterson, NJ – 1905/11/22:4a
ULLRICH, Elsie, b. Folgner, 26, NYC-M – 1912/02/19:6a, 20:2e
ULLRICH, Jacob, 42, NYC-B - 1919/04/19:6a
ULLRICH, Julia, 15, NYC-M, + @ SS Genl Slocum – 1904/06/25:1d
ULLRICH, Ludwig, NYC-Bx – 1913/03/27:6a
ULLRICH, Wilhelm, forest laborer, SPD Munich/Gy - 1918/06/05:4e
ULMER, Christina, NYC-B – 1906/11/07:6a
ULMER, Fred, 40, NYC-M – 1891/07/31:4a
ULRICH, Albert, 34, Hoboken, NJ – 1909/06/11:3b
ULRICH, August, 59, fr Chemnitz/Gy, NYC-M – 1886/01/28:2f
ULRICH, Caspar, NYC-B – 1905/02/02:4a
ULRICH, Edward, 50, NYC-M - 1878/03/22:4e
ULRICH, Elizabeth (Lizzie), 1, NYC-B – 1901/07/04:1e
ULRICH, Emma, 28, NYC-M – 1891/01/25:5a
ULRICH, Franz, un. typesetter, NYC-B – 1891/06/13:4a
ULRICH, Georg, 24, NYC-M – 1892/03/27:5d
ULRICH, Gustav, 60, SPD Stuttgart-Degerloch – 1910/09/11:3b

ULRICH, Julia, 15, + @ SS Genl Slocum, NYC-M – 1904/06/27:1h
ULRICH, Julia, 8, NYC-SI – 1911/09/22:2a
ULRICH, Magdalena, NYC-Q - 1918/11/13:6a
ULRICH, Margaretha, b. Maurer, 56, NYC-M - 1895/09/28: 4a
ULRICH, Michael, NYC-B – 1880/10/19:2g
ULRICH, Morris, 46, barber fr Hungary, Hoboken, NJ – 1908/09/02:3e
ULRICH, Nicolas, 40, engineer, NYC-M – 1900/10/27:4c
ULRICH, Otto, 23, un. typesetter?, NYC-Q – 1907/05/18:6a
ULRICH, Peter, SPD Leipzig/Gy – 1910/06/07:4d
ULRICH, Stephan, 51, bar-owner, NYC-B - 1895/04/04:4c
ULRICH, Wendelin, West Hoboken, NJ - 1913/07/22:6a
ULRICH, William, 16, NYC-Q – 1904/04/03:5f
ULSHOEFER, Josephine, 57, NYC-B – 1909/12/05:1b
ULSTEIN, Leopold, Berlin/Gy publ. – 1899/12/31:12a
ULTZEN, Mary, 60, & son William, 40, NYC-B – 1912/12/12:2e
UMBACH, Amalie, 18, NYC-B – 1906/08/16:6a, 17:6a
UMBACH, Bertha, b. Krueger, NYC-M – 1890/02/22:4a
UMBACH, John, 23, NYC-B – 1908/08/29:6a, fam. 4 Sept:6a
UMBACH, Peter, 57, NYC-B – 1911/09/29:6a
UMLAUF, Mrs, East Rutherford, NJ - 1918/09/04:2g
UMLAUF, William, 37, painter, SP, * Vienna, USA 1902, NYC-B –
    1910/03/23:1f, 24:6a, =29:2a
UMLAUFT, Heinrich F., 76, NYC-B - 1894/01/30:4c
UMMELMANN, Heinrich, 59, un. cigarmaker, NYC-M 1895/07/15:4a
UMMERLE, Bertha, Newark, NJ - 1894/07/21:1h; 22:1f
UMSCHEIDT, Hyronimus, stone cutter, NYC-Q – 1880/03/11:4a
UNGEMACH, Georg Karl, NYC-M - 1914/04/25:6a
UNGEMACH, Seifert, 78, NYC-M – 1891/04/12:5a
UNGER, Adam, NYC-M - 1913/12/30:6a
UNGER, Alfred, 29, clerk, NYC-M – 1885/10/20:4a
UNGER, Carl, 38, NYC-Q - 1913/08/30:6a
UNGER, Franz A., 57, NYC-M – 1891/07/18:4a
UNGER, Jakob, NYC-M – 1912/01/23:6a
UNGER, Johanna, NYC-B – 1904/07/04:4a
UNGER, Joseph, 85, pres. German Imperial Supreme Court 1881-1913,
    obit. lauds his tolerance of labor unions - 1913/05/18:3a-b
UNGER, Katherina, 48, +@SS Genl Slocum, NYC-M – 1904/06/16:1c,
    17:3c
UNGER, L., NYC-M – 1904/10/05:4a
UNGER, Leo, NYC-M - 1915/09/23:6a
UNGER, Ludwig, 69, SPO Vienna, chair jewelers' union - 1915/02/21:3d
UNGER, Philip, 63, un. cigarmaker, NYC-B - 1895/10/24:4a

UNGER, Rosa, 20, NYC-M – 1890/01/25:1g
UNGEWISS, Otto, 56, SP, un. cigar maker, * Saxony, USA 1884, NYC 1884-92, then New Haven, CT – 1907/01/31:6a, = 8 Feb:2d, fam. 6:6a
UNGLAUBE, Karoline, NYC-Q – 1913/09/15:6a, fam. 19:6a
UNKEL, Franziska, 80, NYC-B – 1891/03/12:4c
UNKELBACH, Peter, tailor, Newark, NJ – 1903/09/21:3c
UNRATH, Ida, NYC-M – 1920/05/17:6a
UNSOLD, Karoline, b. Imberg, 65?, NYC-M – 1891/03/29:5a
UNTERDORFER, Isaac, tobacco dealer, NYC-M – 1878/07/30:4d
UNTEREINER, Felix, un. painter, SP Temesvar – 1914/11/08:3d
UNTERHALT, Franz, SPD Danzig/Gy, War 1 – 1915/09/19:3a-b
UNTERNEHRER, August,un. painter,Dunellen, NJ – 1920/04/01:6a
URBAN % Folgner
URBAN, Gustav, 62, un. carp., NYC-Q – 1911/11/17:6a
URBAN, Henriette, 81, NYC-Q – 1903/07/11:4a
URBAN, Jacob, NYC-B – 1907/06/08:6a
URBAN, John, 38, NYC-B – 1905/03/27:3e
URBAN, Minnie, 2, & Camilla, child, NYC-M – 1886/11/20:2f
URBAN, Pauline, Jersey City Heights, NJ – 1888/05/19:3a
URBAN, William, 57, SP, *28 Apr 1858 Karlsbad/Boehmen, bus. mgr Chicago Arbeiterzeitung 1915/07/02:1a, 7:4d
URBANSKY, William, un. butcher, NYC-B – 1916/04/23:7c
URFF, Doris, b. Wegener, 33, NYC-Bx – 1911/03/01:6a, fam. 6:6a
URFF, Friedrich, un. typesetter, NYC-M – 1904/11/26:4a
URIANEK, Bretislaw, 23, cigar maker, fr Bohemia, NYC – 1887/02/21:1b
URIATE, Hippolito de, ret. Spanish diplomat, & wife Marie-Louise, NYC-M – 1913/08/30:2a
URIG, Lottie, 23, NYC-Bx – 1910/03/29:1f
URISCH, William, 14, NYC-M – 1903/02/17:3c
URISON, Abe, SLP, Cincinatti, OH, cloth cutter, USA 1890,+ NYC-M – 1896/07/31:1e,4a, = 1 Aug.:1g
URSCHEL, Mrs, Newark, NJ – 1901/12/12:4b
URSPRUNG, John, NYC-Bx – 1919/01/22:6a
URSPRUNG, Valentin, 46, Paterson, NJ – 1894/10/18:4a
URY, Jonas, NYC-B – 1898/08/24:4d
USSER, William, & wife, NYC-M – 1889/09/29:1f
USTER, Lena, 18, NYC-B – 1880/06/02:1g
UTAL, Meyer, 23, machinist, +@ Triangle Shirtwaist Co. fire, NYC-M – 1911/03/27:1d
UTE, August, 56, un. butcher, NYC-M – 1920/06/25:6a
UTERMANN, Charles, 27, NYC-M – 1906/09/05:5e
UTERMEHTE % Schminke

UTERMOHLEN, L., NYC-M – 1893/10/25:4a
UTERSTAEDT, Barbara, b. Stortz, NYC-M – 1891/08/12:4a
UTHMANN, Gustav Adolf, 60, labor song composer, + Barmen/Gy
 – 1920/07/02:1e, 12 Aug.:3d-e, NYC tribute prep. 13 Sept :5d, 28:5e,27 Oct:5d, today 31 Oct.:2a, rev. 1 Nov:1f, 23:5e, 2 Dec:1g
UTHOF, Christoph, NYC-M – 1891/03/30:4a
UTZ, Jakob, 77, NYC-M – 1898/09/22:4a
UTZ, Josephine, b. Bodei, 77, NYC-M – 1897/05/10:4c
VAETH, William, 9, NYC-M, +@Genl Slocum – 1904/06/22:1d
VAHLTEICH, Julius, SP, writer and Turner, * 30 Dec 1839 Gy, + Chicago – 1915/02/27:2d, >1000 at =1 Mr:1a-b, his life, by A. Dreyfuss 7 Mr:6c-d, by R. Roemer 31 Mr:18a-b, by Wilhelm Blos 18 Apr:3c-d
VAILLANT, Auguste, French anarchist, exec. in Paris – 1894/02/05:1f, 6:1a-b
VAILLANT, Eduard, French Soc., 79th birthday – 1911/02/05:19e-g; + – 1915/12/20:1c,2f,4a-b, 1916/01/19:4d
VALBERT, August, NYC – 1912/12/03:6a
VALENTA, Emil, NYC-M – 1910/10/07:6a
VALENTINE, Charles, 56, NYC-M – 1902/01/18:4a, 19:5a
VALENTINE, John, 71, un. machinist, NYC-B - 1920/10/16:6a
VALENTINE, Thomas, 61, director P.S. 19, NYC-B 1879/04/07:4d
VALENTINO, Blastino, striking worker, Paterson, NJ – 1913/04/21:1g
VALLES, Jules, journalist at Le Cri du Peuple, + Paris 1885/02/17:1c, at =, local German Soc.attacked by nat. mob 18:1c, 19:1d, 2a-b, 21:1c, 3 Mr:2d
VAN See under main part of Surname, e.g. Van Beveren, see Beveren, Van, save if part of Surname like Vanderbilt
VANDENDORPE, Desire, Belgian Socialist & alderman Brussels – 1910/02/25:4d-e
VANDERBILT, Cornelius, Jr., 55, millionaire, NYC-M – 1899/09/13:1h
VANDERBILT, Cornelius, US capitalist, NYC – 1882/04/03:1d, 7:4d, will 30 May:1f
VANDERBILT, William H., neg. notes on + – 1885/12/09:2a,4b, =11:4a
VANDERPLOEG, Minnie, 15, silkworker, Fairlawn, NJ - 1914/02/10:2d
VANETTA, Jacob,ex Attney-Genl of New Jersey, - 1879/05/01:4e
VANGEHR, Wilhelm O., technical drawer, *1839 Schneidemuehl/East Prussia, USA 1872, NYC-M - 1878/10/31:1g
VANIMAN, Melvin, US aviator, + Atlantic City, NJ – 1912/07/03:1f
VASOLD, NYC-Q – 1913/04/22:6a
VASSAR, Matthew, 50, brewery owner, nephew of fdr Vassar College, + Poughkeepsie, NY – 1881/08/11:1b
VAUBEL, John, NYC - 1913/11/12:6a

VAUPEL, Annie, NYC-B - 1916/12/30:6a
VAUPEL, Conrad, un. baker, NYC-M - 1911/02/07:6a
VAUPEL, Frederick, NYC-M - 1891/06/25:4a
VECZERA, Ludwig von, father-in-law of Crown-prince Rudolf of Austria,
    + Denver, CO - 1909/11/04:2c
VEDDER, Frank, 70, candy store, NYC-B - 1916/08/02:5e, 3:6a
VEEK, Anna, 53, NYC-SI - 1911/08/22:6a
VEEK, Wm, NYC-SI - 1920/11/02:6a
VEGEL, Ernst, 53, NYC-B - 1914/03/26:6a
VEHLOW, Bernhard, brewer, NYC-B - 1901/04/10:4a
VEIDT, Bertha, 43, Newark, NJ - 1898/10/22:1g
VEIGEL, John, NYC-M - 1917/09/13:6a
VEIT, Julius, NYC-M - 1916/06/10:6a
VEIT, Lena, 26, NYC-Q, +@Genl Slocum - 1904/06/22:1d
VEIT, Peter A., Yonkers, NY - 1919/10/17:6a
VEIT, Rosa, 1, NYC-M, +@Genl Slocum - 1904/06/23:1c
VEITINGER, Herman, innkeep, Jersey City, NJ - 1913/09/13:6c
VELDE, VAN DE, Emile, Belgian soc. deputy, in NYC - 1903/08/31:2b-c,
    1 Sept:1h, 4:4b; crit for praising US capitalism - 1904/09/28:2d
VELTE % Niemann
VELTE, Christian, 57, NYC-B - 1910/04/30:6a
VELTE, Elisabeth, b. Von der Schmidt, 62, NYC-M - 1892/08/07:5a
VELTE, Engelina, NYC-Q - 1913/02/10:6a
VELTE, Henry C., NYC - 1913/11/30:7a
VELTE, Karl, SPD Wehrheim/Frankfurt, War 1 - 1914/11/01:3b
VELTE, Marie, NYC-Bx - 1912/05/09:6a
VELTE, Philip, 29, SLP?, NYC-M - 1897/11/12:4a, 13:4a
VELTEN, Carrie, NYC-M - 1917/08/31:6a
VELTEN, Ottilie, b. Allgeier, NYC-M - 1890/05/16:4a
VELTEN, Philip, West New York, NJ - 1911/06/12:6a
VENYIGER, Bertha, NYC-M - 1920/06/26:6a
VENZEL, Adolph, NYC-B - 1912/05/31:6a
VENZEL, John, 47, NYC-B - 1917/09/10:6a
VERBA, William, 28, SP, NYC-M - 1914/09/01:5f
VERDERBER, George, NYC-B - 1912/04/27:6a
VERDERBER, Gertrude, NYC-B - 1908/04/22:6a
VERDERBER, Joseph, 48, baker, dying, NYC-B - 1911/07/25:3a
VERDERBER, Ludmilla, NYC-B - 1911/07/13:6a, 14:6a
VERDI, Guiseppe, Italian composer - 1901/01/26:1b
VERGANT, Ernst, 67, publ. Vienna Deutsches Volksblatt, crit. -
    1915/03/28:3d

VERHAS, H., NYC-Bx? – 1912/11/17:7b
VERHAS, Ida, 84, NYC-M – 1908/04/24:6a
VERHEYDEN, Leon, Belgian socialist, his = Brussels – 1892/03/23:2c
VERMAETEN, Anton, 83, NYC-M - 1917/08/07:6a
VERMAETEN, Osmar & Edith, NYC-B - 1918/10/30:6a
VERMONDE, Mrs A.@, 102, *Germany, married a French soldier (+1837), USA 1857, NYC-M – 1902/12/15:2h
VERNE, Jules, 76, French writer, + Paris – 1905/03/25:1b, 9 Ap:4c-e
VERON, Kath., 40, NYC-Bx – 1907/02/04:6a
VERSACCIA, Giuseppe, exec. Auburn, NY – 1904/09/06:1g
VERVENKA, Vincent, *Prague, NYC-M? - 1917/06/23:1g
VES, George, 32, fr Hungary, Perth Amboy, NJ, exec. Trenton, NJ – 1909/06/09:3c, 23 Jy:2c, done 26 Jan 1910:2e
VESCHE, Joseph, 65, sugar raffinery worker, NYC-B – 1910/04/30:3a
VESS, George's wife, Perth Amboy, NJ – 1909/05/19:3b-c, 20:2d
VETTER % Roll, % Schwoerer
VETTER, Adolf, 66, Irvington, NJ - 1917/10/09:6a
VETTER, Alwin, 3, NYC-B – 1902/03/18:4a, 19:4a
VETTER, Andreas F., 69, un. brewer, NYC-B - 1916/04/06:6a
VETTER, Anna, NYC-B – 1904/01/29:4a
VETTER, Anton, 1849 Hungarian War Minister, + 1882/08/15:2f
VETTER, August, un. sheet metal worker, NYC-M – 1901/06/02:5a
VETTER, Eugene, NYC-M - 1917/01/26:6a
VETTER, Franz Adam, 20, NYC-M – 1891/04/01:4a
VETTER, Frederika & Margaret, Mamie, 18, NYC-M, + @ Genl Slocum – 1904/06/18:3c, 25:1d
VETTER, Gustav, un. cigarmaker, NYC-M - 1896/03/03:1g, 3a
VETTER, J., NYC-Bx – 1909/10/10:7b
VETTER, Joseph, brewer, NYC-M – 1896/06/19:4a
VETTER, Timothaeus, 39, NYC-M - 1895/10/27: 5a
VICKERY, Tom W., lynched Fort Worth, TX - 1920/12/24:5e
VICTOR, Bernhard, 71, NYC-M - 1894/01/24:4a
VICTOR, Henry, 34, NYC-M - 1878/04/29:3b
VICTOR, Jacob, 23, tinsmith, NYC-B – 1907/12/11:1f
VICTORIAN, Frank, un. carp., NYC-M – 1911/11/21:6a
VICTORICA, Maria Kretzschmar de, + NYC-M - 1920/08/14:1e
VIDIG, Henry, un. baker, NYC-M – 1882/01/11:3b
VIELE, Edward V., clerk, 41, NYC-M – 1880/06/09:1g
VIENOT, Charles, un. machinist, NYC-B – 1910/08/18:6a
VIENOT, Emil, machinist, NYC-M – 1902/10/06:4a, 7:4a
VIERING, George, 54, NYC-M – 1892/06/22:4a
VIERLING, Gustav, SPD Stoetteritz/Leipzig, Gy – 1901/12/11:2d

VIESER, August, 39, un. machinist, NYC-M – 1886/06/28:1e
VIESS, Victoria, 60, NYC-B – 1888/06/27:3b
VIGELIUS % Oster
VIGELIUS, Anton, Jr, NYC-B – 1891/03/18:4a
VIGELIUS, Maria Elisabeth, 58, NYC-B - 1894/01/08:4a
VILAIN, Charles L., 37, NYC-M – 1910/09/15:6a
VILLARD, Henry, German-born banker, crit. obit – 1900/11/13:3b, 14:2a-b will, $70,000 legacies to G-A & German philan. 30 Dec:1g
VILLARET, Albert, 27, NYC-M – 1903/11/27:4a
VILLEBOIS-MAREUIL, de, Boer general, War 1 – 1900/04/07:1a
VILLWOCK, Frederick, NYC-B – 1907/11/17:7b
VILMAR, general, = 1880/06/11:4a
VINAZZA, Luigi, Italian miner, Wilkesbarre, PA – 1902/07/02:1c, 3:2b
VINCENT, Henry, French journalist & supporter of Genl Boulanger, NYC-M – 1893/11/10:2f
VINCENT, Michael, merchant, New Brunswick, NJ - 1879/05/03:4c
VINCENT, Peter, NYC-M – 1891/02/27:4a
VIRCHOW, Rudolf, 81, German scientist, + Berlin, # – 1902/09/06:1f-g, 2g-h, = 1902/09/28:9f
VIRGIN, Conrad see Urgin, Conrad
VISCHER, Friedrich Theodor, 80, German liberal, birthday – 1887/07/01:5c
VITORIT, John, 56, NYC-Bx – 1886/08/07:1c
VITTORIO, head of Mescalero Apaches – 1880/10/26:1d
VIVANTE, Angelo, 46, SP & chief editor Triest Lavoratore - 1915/08/04:4d
VIVANTI, Annie, Italian poet – 1899/06/25:11f-h, 2 Jy:11f-g
VIX, Michael, 56, weaver, NYC-M – 1896/08/05:1b
VOCASEK, Barbara, NYC-M - 1913/09/17:6a
VOCH, Anna, 26, NYC-B - 1920/04/19:4a
VOCLIK, Anton, 50, un. cigarmaker, NYC-M – 1893/09/11:3d
VODEL, Ernst, NYC-M – 1897/05/13:4a
VOEGELE, Christian, SPD activist in Mannheim/Baden – 1907/12/22:8e
VOEGELE, Gottlieb, 84, realtor?, fr Wuerttemberg - 1917/12/04:3d
VOEGELE, Michael, 55, NYC-M – 1901/07/03:4a
VOEGELI, Siegfried, silkweaver fr Lentgen/Switz., NYC-M – 1897/12/25:4a
VOEGELIN, Solomon, Prof., 52, Swiss socialist, + Zuerich – 1888/11/07:2c
VOEGLE, Ferdinand, SP, NYC-B - 1914/06/26:6a, 27:6a,
VOEGTLE, Josephine, 75, NYC-B - 1918/12/14:5g
VOELKE % Winkel; VOELKER % Bielas
VOELKEL, Karl, 60, NYC-M - 1917/08/03:6a, 4:6a
VOELKER, Andreas, 26, NYC-Bx - 1918/11/06:6a

VOELKER, Charles, editor N.J. Deutsche Zeitung Newark, NJ – 1886/07/14:2g
VOELKER, Philipp, 57, NYC-M – 1881/04/04:3d
VOELKL, Michael, SPD Munich/Gy – 1908/04/12:3a
VOEPEL, Katherina, b. Bauer, ~40, newspaper dealer, NYC-M – 1902/02/15:1f-g, =18:1b, 13 Mr:1g, 21:3c, 27:3e, 28:3b, 1 Ap:3b, 4 June:4c
VOETEL, J., NYC-B – 1906/01/24:4a
VOGEL, A., West Hoboken, NJ – 1905/12/04:4a
VOGEL, Agnes Maria, b. Boeckle, 50, NYC-B – 1892/05/13:4a
VOGEL, Albertine, b. Vogelsang, NYC-M – 1883/03/03:3c, fam. 8 Apr:8a
VOGEL, Andreas, un. barrel maker, NYC-M - 1894/05/18:4a
VOGEL, Apollonia, 75, NYC-M – 1892/08/25:2f
VOGEL, Bertha, b. Groeschel, 53, NYC-M – 1903/08/13:4a
VOGEL, Charles C., un. painter, NYC-M - 1916/03/02:6a
VOGEL, comrade, 38, SLP, Buffalo, NY – 1898/03/15:1f
VOGEL, F. J., bookkeeper, NYC-M – 1880/10/27:1e
VOGEL, Frank, 39, NYC-Q – 1908/07/14:3a
VOGEL, Frieda, infant, NYC-M – 1882/07/29:4c
VOGEL, Friedrich, 41, weaver, Paterson, NJ – 1893/10/12:2d
VOGEL, Friedrich, 67, carp., NYC – 1910/03/17:1d
VOGEL, Gustav, weaver?, Paterson, NJ – 1912/09/27:6a
VOGEL, Hedwig, German poet, NYC & San Rafael, CA, wrote for NYVZ, +Berlin – 1898/06/18:1c, 2 Oct:4c-e
VOGEL, Helena, NYC-M – 1893/10/10:4a
VOGEL, Herman, 40, hotelier, Bd Brock, NJ – 1899/10/21:1f, will 23:4a
VOGEL, Hugo, 41, NYC-M – 1894/07/05:4a
VOGEL, Isaac, 50, jeweler, NYC-Bx – 1911/12/07:1d
VOGEL, Jacob, banker, & wife, Fruitvale/Oakland, CA - 1915/02/13:1d
VOGEL, Jakob, Newark, NJ – 1905/08/01:4a
VOGEL, John, NYC-B - 1896/03/05:4a
VOGEL, John, SP, secy AKK #32, Buffalo, NY - 1915/05/08:2f
VOGEL, Julius, 67, NYC-Q – 1918/08/13:6a
VOGEL, Karl, 28, bartender, NYC-M – 1885/03/29:1e
VOGEL, Louise, b. Hanke, 60, NYC-M – 1885/05/12:3d
VOGEL, Maria, b. Quick, 52, NYC-M – 1901/04/13:4a
VOGEL, Peter, 60, goldworker, & wife Minnie, 45, NYC-B – 1907/12/02:2a
VOGEL, Wilhelm, 59, un. cigarmaker, NYC-Q – 1912/06/04:6a, 5:6a
VOGEL, Wilhelm, 72, un. tailor, NYC-M – 1893/04/04:4a
VOGEL, William H.,32, haberdasher, NYC-M - 1894/08/19:1g

VOGEL, William, 64, rich clothes dealer, NYC-M – 1905/03/22:4a
VOGEL,Jakob, Newark, NJ – 1905/08/01:4a
VOGELER, Hermann, 23, NYC-M – 1899/05/26:4a
VOGELEY, Hermann J., NYC-M – 1891/07/16:4a
VOGELMANN, August, carriage maker, NYC? – 1896/11/25:2f
VOGELMANN, Ernst, NYC-Bx – 1911/03/12:7b
VOGELSANG % Vogel
VOGELSANG, Isaac W., 53, Newark, NJ – 1883/03/27:4c
VOGELSANG, Max, 59, NYC-M – 1898/04/09:1e
VOGENBERGER, W., NYC-Bx - 1915/07/24:6a
VOGES, Julius, un. cigarmaker, NYC-M - 1894/01/10:4a
VOGL, Rupert, 31, un. butcher, NYC-M - 1917/08/03:6a, 5:7a
VOGLER, Ernst, 34, machinist, USA Oct. 92, NYC-M – 1892/12/08:4d
VOGLER, John, 78, ret. paint store, Hempstead, LI - 1915/01/31:11f
VOGLER, Magdalena, b. Hegers, Hoboken, NJ – 1900/05/25:4a, 26:4a
VOGLER, Peter, merchant, NYC-M - 1915/12/24:1e
VOGLER, Therese, 58, NYC-M - 1913/12/22:6a, 24:6a
VOGT % Meyer
VOGT, Anna, b. Drescher,43, NYC-M – 1902/02/27:4a,28:4a,fam. 4 Mr:4a
VOGT, August, shoemaker & SP activist fr Koeln/Gy, NYC 1867, +1883, anniv. of + w. notes by W. Liebknecht – 1900/05/20:7d
VOGT, Chr., 14, Jersey City, NJ – 1902/05/17:1e
VOGT, Edmund, 19, NYC-M – 1893/06/09:4b, 12:4f
VOGT, Edward, 46, Union Hill, NJ – 1902/02/11:4a
VOGT, Frederick, 58, gardener, NYC-B – 1898/06/16:4b
VOGT, Friedrich, 50, baker, NYC-M – 1910/03/13:1f, 15:6a
VOGT, Georg Philip, *12 Oct 1852 Offenbach/Gy, NYC-M – 1906/02/26:4a
VOGT, John, 35, smith, NYC-B – 1901/04/13:3b
VOGT, Joseph, 56, NYC-M - 1917/05/05:6a
VOGT, Karl, German scientist, 70th birthday, '48er, in exile in Geneva/Switz. – 1887/07/21:5e
VOGT, Klara, NYC-B - 1894/03/08:4a, 10:4a
VOGT, Margaret, 51, NYC-Bx – 1911/02/18:6a
VOGT, Mary L., 30, NYC-B – 1903/07/10:1f
VOGT, Oscar, NYC, exec. Sing Sing - 1915/02/27:6b
VOGT, Otto, ATB Reichenbach/Gy,War I - 1914/11/01:3b
VOGT, Pauline, 51, NYC-B – 1899/01/24:4a
VOGT, Siegmund, 52, NYC – 1912/10/28:6a
VOGT, Theodor, un. weaver, NYC-M - 1918/03/30:6a
VOIGHT, Martin, coal-stoker, NYC-B – 1919/12/06:6b

VOIGT, Amalie, Jersey City, NJ – 1897/06/24:4d
VOIGT, Charles, 40, coal peddler, NYC-M - 1878/08/17:4a
VOIGT, Charles, West New York, NJ – 1907/04/08:6a
VOIGT, comrade, SPD Stettin/Gy – 1908/03/29:3d
VOIGT, Frederick, 40, wife Frieda, 38,USA 1904,NYC-M – 1909/02/02:1d
VOIGT, Lizzie, 6, West Hoboken, NJ – 1890/09/07:5a
VOIGT, M., NYC-M – 1893/03/29:4a
VOIGT, Max, cement worker, NYC-B - 1913/05/20:3c
VOIGT, Paul, 63, No. Bergen,NJ - 1918/06/29:6a, mem. 1919/06/27:6a, 1920/06/27:12a
VOJACEK, Vengl, & family, Newark, NJ – 1893/09/07:2d
VOLBARTH, Adolph, NYC-B – 1905/03/26:5a
VOLCK % Stegherr
VOLDERS, Jean, Belgian Soc. – 1896/05/13:2b-c, 28:2d, =1 June:2c, # 16 Aug:4c-e; grave monument inaug. In Evere – 1908/11/30:4f
VOLGE, Ernst, 46, janitor, fr Hannover 1904, NYC-B – 1905/04/09:1g
VOLGEN, Charles W., 44, NYC-M – 1891/07/29:4a
VOLINSKY, Anna, collector Montefiore Inst., +NYC-Ward Isl. – 1911/01/03:2d
VOLK % Gilliar
VOLK, Charles G., NYC-M – 1889/11/09:4a, 10:5a
VOLK, Friedericke, b. Metz, 24, NYC-M – 1890/05/29:4a
VOLK, John, NYC-M – 1883/10/31:3b
VOLK, John, NYC-M – 1890/05/01:4a
VOLK, John, un. carp., NYC-M – 1883/01/18:3c
VOLKER, Martin, un. carp., NYC-M – 1891/09/21:4a
VOLKERS, Charles, NYC-B – 1905/01/11:4a
VOLKMANN % Schmidt
VOLKMANN, ..., 40, salesman, NYC-M – 1881/07/27:1e
VOLKMAR, Martha, b. Beermann, 55, NYC-M - 1920/11/27:8a
VOLL, John, NYC-B - 1919/03/18:6a
VOLLBRACHT % Schueler
VOLLBRACHT, Jacob, NYC-Q – 1907/07/13:6a
VOLLBRECHT, August, 71, * Harz area, USA 1867, carpenter, NYC-M – 1904/02/11:4a,c, 12:4a
VOLLKENNER, John, clerk for HAPAG, Hoboken, NJ - 1913/06/27:3c
VOLLMAR, Helena, (or Vollmer) NYC-M – 1891/11/17:4a
VOLLMAR, Josephine, 52, & niece Mary Miller, 12, NYC-Bx – 1902/08/27:1e
VOLLMER, Carl, 80, SP, un. cigarmaker, * 1 Sept. 1840 Stralsund/Gy, USA 1869. First resident to die in new SAH in Cottekill, NY - 1920/11/15:2b, #16:2c-d, 17:2f,6a,=19:2a

VOLLMER, Charles, NYC-Bx - 1916/02/22:6a
VOLLMER, Charlotte, b. Kappenberg, SDP, NYC-M - 1905/04/22:4a, =26:3f
VOLLMER, Georg, craftsman, NYC-B - 1904/09/23:3c
VOLLMER, Joseph, NYC-M, + @ Genl Slocum - 1904/06/16:1c
VOLLMER, Magdalene, 7, NYC-M, +@ Genl Slocum - 1904/06/21:1f
VOLLMER, Marie, b. Schwarz, 29, NYC-M - 1896/06/18:4a
VOLLMER, Mary, 35, NYC-M, + @ Genl Slocum - 1904/06/16:1c, 17:3c
VOLLMER, Monica, 48, NYC-Bx - 1919/07/04:6a
VOLLMER, Paul, 5, Jersey City, NJ - 1882/01/04:3b
VOLLMER, Phebe, NYC-B - 1892/02/22:4a
VOLT, Friedrich, NYC-Q - 1912/11/03:7b
VOLZ, Carl, 24, * Mannheim/Gy, NYC-M - 1878/12/04:4b
VOLZ, Carrie, 18, NYC-M - 1897/05/06:1g
VOLZERINO, a German, NYC-M - 1887/11/19:1e
VONGEHR, Bernhard, 39, NYC-B - 1903/04/04:4a
VOORHIS, Charles H., ex-congressman, lawyer, NYC-M - 1896/04/16:1d
VORBRINGER, H., West Hoboken, NJ - 1916/07/01:6a
VORDACH, Katie M., b. Kramer, 31, NYC-B - 1892/07/10:5c
VORHAUER, Flora, NYC-M - 1919/07/09:6a, fam. 15:6a, 22:6a
VORHAUER, Heinrich, 56, & Adele, 49, Silver Wedding, NYC-B - 1909/05/24:5d
VORHAUER, Henry, un. carp., NYC-M - 1914/11/17:6a
VORHAUER, Walburga, 24, NYC-M - 1912/04/26:6a
VORTMEYER, Frederick, 35, Newark, NJ - 1903/01/06:3b
VOSBRINK % Wehrenberg
VOSBURG, Bill, NYC mobster, = 1904/04/30:1g
VOSS, Carl, Syracuse, NY - 1912/07/24:6a
VOSS, Heinrich, 89, SPD Bremen/Gy - 1912/02/25:3a
VOSS, Johann Heinrich, 1751-1828, his life - 1901/03/03:3e
VOSS, John G., NYC-M - 1906/02/26:4a
VOSS, Tillie, NYC-B - 1912/01/10:2c-d
VOSSDRINCK, Marie, 7, NYC-M - 1889/02/10:5b
VOSSELER % Klatt
VOSSELER, Andreas, 60, fr Thalheim/Wuertt., NYC-M - 1898/09/23:4a
VOSSMER, Hannah, 11, NYC-M, +@Genl Slocum - 1904/06/22:1d
VOTOZIL, Louis, 50, cigarmaker, NYC-M - 1890/01/29:1g
VOWINKEL, Carl, 60, SP, fr Baden Prov., USA 1880s, plumber, NYC - 1914/01/27:6a, 28:3e, 6a, fam. 11 Fb:6a
VROOMAN, Walter, labor organizer, esp. 1880s, + Baltimore, MD - 1904/05/23:1c

WAAG, Felix, Newark, NJ - 1915/11/05:6a
WAAS, Auguste M., 61, SP, * Ziegenberg/Hessen, USA 1880, NYC-M - 1914/01/12:6a, 13:3f,6a, fam. 17:6a
WAAS, Jacob, musician, NYC-M – 1891/02/12:1f
WABNITZ, Agnes, 52, German cloakmaker and labor org., + Berlin 1894/08/30:1a, =09/16:12b
WABNITZ, Hermann, 34, barber & SPD activist expelled from Hamburg/Gy, arrived NYC – 1880/11/30:1d-e, 2 Dec:2a-b, 6:1d-e
WACH, Carl, machinist, NYC-M – 1912/07/09:6a
WACH, Sophie, NYC-M – 1903/04/14:4a
WACHENDORFER, Michael, NYC-M - 1894/05/14:4a
WACHSMUTH, Anna, b. Fritze, 42, NYC-M – 1882/01/24:3c
WACHTEL, John, 50, cigarmaker, NYC-B – 1898/09/07:4b
WACHTER, Andrew A., NYC-M - 1919/01/09:6a
WACHTER, Johann, 49, NYC-B - 1879/02/19:4d
WACHTER, Nicolaus, NYC-Q - 1918/07/26:6a
WACHTLER, Andrew, 43, un. pipe maker, *Fuerth/Bavaria, SDP, NYC-M – 1903/04/11:4f, =13:2f, fam. 14:4a
WACHTLER, Sophie, 39, NYC-M - 1895/06/14:4a
WACK, Peter, NYC-M – 1908/01/22:6a
WACKENHEIM, Eugen, 49, musician, NYC-M - 1915/05/21:1f
WACKER, Frieda, 17, NYC-Bx – 1909/10/17:7a
WACKER, Friedrich, un. cigarmaker, NYC-M – 1883/10/18:3c
WACKER, Henry, NYC-B – 1903/11/20:4a
WACKER, Joseph, 33, carp., Newark,NJ - 1913/12/12:2e
WACKER, Kathrina, NYC-M - 1919/01/25:6a
WACKER, Ludwig F., 58, un. carp., NYC-M – 1903/05/15:4a
WACKERHAGEN, Frederick, 81, Fort Lee, NJ - 1914/08/31:2c
WACKERMANN, William, 27, NYC-B – 1891/06/17:1e
WACKERNAGEL, Dorothea, NYC-M - 1894/01/09:4a
WACKERNAGEL, Ferdinand, 67, NYC-M – 1891/04/14:4a
WADE, Burton, Negro, lynched Shelby, LA – 1904/07/05:1b
WADEWITZ, E., 67, NYC-M - 1917/08/04:6a
WADLER, Jakob A., 19, fur dealer, NYC-M – 1907/03/13:5b
WADMAN, Herbert, bartender who + 5 Mr NYC-Ward's Isl. Hospital – 1901/07/02:1f
WAEGELE, Jacob, 67, NYC-M – 1892/07/14:4a
WAEGELE, Marta, NYC-M – 1892/07/01:4a
WAELDER, Chr., NYC-Bx – 1919/08/21:6a
WAETZEL, W., un. carp., NYC-M – 1901/11/23:4b
WAFROCK, Anna May, 26, (her married name not given, nor city), 1909/11/23:6a

WAFROCK, Anna, 51, NYC-M – 1904/09/07:4a
WAFROCK, Paul, NYC-M – 1899/08/03:4a
WAGECK, Anton, un. carpenter, NYC-M - 1894/03/11:5b
WAGELER % Alsleben
WAGENBLAST, Franz, NYC-M – 1898/06/30:4a
WAGENFUND, Charles, 47, carp., NYC-M – 1890/03/03:2f
WAGENHOEFER, Anna, landlady, NYC-M - 1919/02/12:2b
WAGLER % Gneitling; WAGNER % Prophet
WAGNER, Adam, 50, carp., NYC-B - 1920/06/09:2e
WAGNER, Adam, engineer, NYC-M – 1892/08/06:4a
WAGNER, Adolf, Newark, NJ – 1911/05/17:6a
WAGNER, Adolf, Prof., 82, + Berlin/Gy, - 1917/11/10:1f
WAGNER, Albert, 69, un. pianomaker, NYC-Bx – 1907/12/02:6a
WAGNER, Anna, b. Klug, NYC-M – 1893/01/05:4a
WAGNER, Anna, b. Moritz, NYC-M – 1906/08/13:6a
WAGNER, Anton, machinist, NYC-B – 1883/10/30:3b
WAGNER, Arthur, 14, NYC-M – 1889/05/17:4a
WAGNER, August C., 75, USA fr Gy 1842, Galveston, TX, then Passaic, NJ, civil war vet - 1915/08/09:6c
WAGNER, Barbara, 49, NYC-M – 1892/09/26:4a
WAGNER, Bernard, mail carrier, Eilzabeth, NJ – 1910/09/05:3b
WAGNER, Carl, NYC-M – 1898/01/19:4a
WAGNER, Christian, pres. Wagner Trading Co, a purchasing agent for Entente, NYC-M - 1916/12/10:1f
WAGNER, Conrad, NYC-M – 1898/02/27:5c
WAGNER, Conrad, un. cigarmaker, NYC-M - 1894/04/15:5c
WAGNER, Daniel, 52, NYC-Q - 1894/05/19:4a
WAGNER, Daniel, street sweeper, NYC-M – 1898/04/01:1f
WAGNER, Eddy, 6, Jersey City Heights, NJ - 1894/09/20:4a
WAGNER, Eduard, NYC-M – 1891/05/09:1h
WAGNER, Edward, & wife, Nanuet, NY – 1908/08/25:2d, 13 Sept:2d
WAGNER, Elisabeth, NYC-M - 1894/01/22:4a
WAGNER, Ernst B., G-A journalist, NYC-M – 1892/03/16:1d
WAGNER, F., NYC-M – 1889/06/15:4a
WAGNER, Frank, 40, worker, South Amboy, NJ - 1917/11/11:1e
WAGNER, Frank, 58, NYC-B – 1909/08/09:3b
WAGNER, Frederick, 28, bookkeeper, NYC-M - 1894/09/12:1c
WAGNER, Frederick, Newark, NJ - 1917/02/21:6a
WAGNER, Friedrich, 29, cigarmaker, NYC-M – 1880/05/24:2a
WAGNER, Friedrich, clerk, NYC-M – 1882/08/23:4d
WAGNER, George J., 1, NYC-M – 1905/07/11:1f
WAGNER, George, brewery partner, Bridgeport, CT – 1904/06/14:3e

WAGNER, Gus, 75, SP?, NYC-Bx – 1915/09/16:6a
WAGNER, Gustav, NYC-Bx – 1909/09/20:6a
WAGNER, Heinrich, Hoboken, NJ – 1912/18:6a
WAGNER, Heinrich, NYC-M – 1890/12/14:5a
WAGNER, Henry, 33, carp., NYC-B – 1905/06/09:4b
WAGNER, Henry, NYC-B – 1904/12/21:4a
WAGNER, Herman A., 61, NYC-B – 1899/01/28:4b
WAGNER, Herman, ~60, & wife Pauline, Passaic, NJ – 1896/08/12:3g
WAGNER, Jacob, 32, NYC-M – 1881/09/02:3d
WAGNER, Jacob, un. brewer, NYC-M – 1897/03/02:4a
WAGNER, John M., 67, NYC-B – 1894/01/23:4e
WAGNER, John, 48, plasterer, NYC-B – 1907/05/04:3a
WAGNER, John, 68, NYC-B – 1916/05/18:3e
WAGNER, John, Irvington, NJ – 1901/07/04:3b
WAGNER, Karl, NYC-M – 1914/04/22:6a
WAGNER, Katie, Guttenberg, NJ – 1917/06/01:6a
WAGNER, L., SLP, Newark, NJ – 1895/02/05:4a
WAGNER, Leon, 9, NYC-M – 1885/04/25:1f
WAGNER, Louise, 44, NYC-M – 1893/11/21:4a
WAGNER, Margarethe, b. Dieter, 33, NYC-M – 1898/03/26:4a
WAGNER, Margarethe, Jersey City Hgts, NJ – 1920/02/12:6a
WAGNER, Maria, b. von Mauschwitz, * 25 Nov 1843 Berlin/Gy, USA 1881 – 1883/05/30:1e-f
WAGNER, Mary A., old, Newark, NJ – 1914/10/22:2f
WAGNER, Nicholas, 75, NYC-M – 1889/03/01:1g
WAGNER, Peter, 30, stonecutter, NYC-M – 1892/10/16:1g
WAGNER, Peter, un. carp., NYC-M – 1891/04/26:5a
WAGNER, Richard, German composer, negat. Obit – 1883/02/18:5a-d, 7c-e, notes 1 Apr:3d-f
WAGNER, Robert, Austrian socialist, – 1879/09/15:1b
WAGNER, Thomas, Hoboken, NJ – 1916/04/02:7a
WAGNER, Valentin, exec. Columbus, OH – 1885/08/01:1b
WAGNER, Wilhelm, 64, NYC-M – 1892/08/08:4a
WAGNER, Wilhelm, NYC-B – 1897/12/27:4a, fam. 28:4a
WAGNER, William F., 80, car maker, Orange, NJ – 1910/05/31:3b
WAGNER, William, 43, fr Wuerttemberg/Gy, USA 1879, cooper, NYC-M – 1897/08/13:1g
WAGNER, William, 44, un. carp., NYC-B – 1904/11/06:5b
WAGNER, William, 57, NYC-M – 1890/11/09:5b; mem. 1891/11/08:5c
WAGNER, William, infant, NYC-SI – 1901/07/04:1e
WAGNER, William, NYC-Q – 1920/10/21:6a
WAHL, Christian, un. carp., + Philad., PA – 1913/08/17:7b

WAHL, Eva von, 59, NYC-Q - 1914/11/30:6a
WAHL, Frank, Union Hill, NJ - 1920/08/21:6a
WAHL, Fritz., un. carp., NYC-M - 1889/02/26:4a
WAHL, Joseph, un. carp., NYC-M - 1907/04/19:6a
WAHL, Louise, b. Lindes, 63, fr Otterberg/Gy, NYC-Bx - 1913/05/02:6a
WAHL, Matthew, 75, cigarmaker, NYC-B - 1904/06/25:3c
WAHL, Michael, un. carp., NYC-B - 1888/08/13:3a
WAHL, Theodor, Weehawken, NJ - 1916/03/20:6a
WAHLBURG, Anna M., 6, Hoboken, NJ - 1889/02/15:4a
WAHLE, Johann, infant, NYC-B - 1878/07/10:3c
WAHLE, William, 65, un. carp., NYC-M -- 1908/09/03:5d, 5:6a
WAHLEN, Heinrich, Norristown, PA - 1878/02/25:1b, 26:2f, 20 June:2f
WAHLERS, Frederick, 24, NYC-B - 1892/07/25:4a
WAHLSTAB, William, SLP, un. painter, USA 1858, NYC-M - 1879/04/10:3e, 11:4b
WAHNER, Emil, un. carp., NYC-M - 1913/02/15:6a
WAHRENHOFF, Eddie, 2, NYC-M - 1902/02/14:3f
WAIBEL, Jacob, NYC-M - 1895/03/27:4b
WAICZ, Ludwig, NYC-B - 1916/04/13:6a
WAIGAND, Lucas, NYC-M - 1915/10/14:6a
WAIGAND, Reinmund, un. carp. NYC-M - 1917/01/18:6a
WAITE, Arthur, Dr., exec. Ossining, NY - 1917/05/25:2c
WAITZ, Hermann, 17, NYC-M - 1887/10/15:4e
WAITZ, John, 52, un. cigar maker, NYC-M - 1892/02/21:5c
WAITZ, Valentin, NYC-M - 1885/11/12:3a
WAITZFELDER, Alex, alias "Sheeny Dan," gambler, NYC-M - 1897/01/06:3g
WALCHSHOFER, Peter, 30, NYC-M - 1887/08/08:3c
WALD, Wilhelm, 25, un. carp., NYC-B - 1903/05/29:4a, fam. 3 June:4a
WALDECK, Edmund, 21, NYC-M - 1891/03/16:4a
WALDER, August Robert, Paterson, NJ - 1919/05/03:6a
WALDER, Marie, b. Kugeln, 49, NYC-M - 1893/08/31:4a
WALDERSEE, Alfred von, German politician, 1904/03/06:1c
WALDHAUER, Joseph, brewer, NYC-B - 1901/11/24:1f
WALDHAUSER, Charles, NYC-M - 1908/02/17:6a
WALDHERR, Apollo, 80, leather shop, dying, West N. Y., NJ - 1914/11/19:2d
WALDINGER, Charles, 72, SLP, Paterson, NJ - 1883/08/24:3c, 27:3b
WALDINGER, Charley, 60, weaver?, NYC-M - 1902/07/11:4a
WALDMAN, John, un. carpenter, NYC-M - 1894/08/16:4a
WALDMANN % Potschiemba
WALDMANN, Maud, 16, Newark, NJ - 1903/02/20:1c, =21:1c

WALDNER, Frederick, NYC-M - 1913/05/17:6a
WALDNER, Mathilde, 54, NYC-B – 1904/04/04:3b
WALDSCHMITT, Michael, NYC-M, + Port Jervis, NY – 1908/02/12:1b
WALDSTEIN, Otto von, Austrian noble, murdered Willows, CA – 1907/01/04:1d
WALDVOGEL, Franz, 27, NYC-M - 1894/02/06:4a
WALDVOGEL, George,29, fishmonger, NYC-M – 1899/06/21:3d, 23:1e, trial of murderer 15 Nov:1g,
WALECKA, Leo, 58, SPO, locksmith & secy AKK, + Vienna - 1915/01/10:3c-d
WALENTA, Julius, 21, SPO Saaz/Bohemia, War 1 - 1915/01/31:3d
WALES, James A., cartoonist, NYC-M – 1886/12/07:1f
WALGERING, Heinrich, NYC-M – 1892/10/01:4a
WALHEINLE, Alfred, NYC-M – 1890/05/04:5a
WALINSKY, Stephen, 6, Jersey City, NJ – 1885/11/26:1e, =27:3a
WALKER, Ben. R., NYC-M – 1906/12/05:6a
WALKER, Emma France, b. Diedrich, NYC-M – 1891/03/06:2h
WALKER, Jonathan, abolitionist, + Detroit - 1878/05/04:1d
WALKER, Negro, lynched Coatsville, PA – 1911/10/26:4c
WALKER, Zachary, Negro, on his lynching 13 Aug 1911 Westchester, PA – 1912/05/04:1d
WALKHUTTER,, Anton, 18, NYC-M – 1885/05/02:1g
WALL, William von der, 65, NYC-M – 1913/01/21:6a
WALLACE, Rose, NYC-M, +@Genl Slocum – 1904/06/22:1d
WALLACE, Russell, 91, British scientist - 1913/11/09:6c-d, 7e, 10:4b-c, 28:4d
WALLACH, Eduard, NYC-B – 1902/08/19:4a
WALLACH, John, 45, un. miner fr Seatonville, IL, + NYC-M – 1899/03/29:3d
WALLACH, Moses, 76, NYC-M – 1891/01/04:5a
WALLACH, Willy, 63, *Kassel/Gy, USA 1849?, book & stationary dealer, active G-A, NYC-M – 1882/02/13:3b, 4c
WALLE, Gustave, carp., NYC-B – 1908/11/21:1a
WALLENDORF, Amalia, 56, NYC-M – 1904/09/07:4a
WALLERMANN, Adolph H., 60, NYC-Far Rockaway, - 1918/01/09:6a
WALLEWARD % Brueggemann
WALLHUTTER, Anton, 18, fr Austria, NYC Sept 1884, NYC-M – 1885/05/02:1g
WALLING, Joseph, un. carp., NYC-B – 1911/11/22:6a
WALLSTROM, Marie, b. Buszkowska, NYC-M – 1899/06/27:4a, 28:4c
WALLUHN, Eugene, druggist, fr Berlin, USA 1890, NYC-M – 1900/06/10:5b

WALMANN, Sabine, 70, NYC-Q - 1916/04/19:2a
WALSCH % Wisler
WALSH, James F., exec. NYC-B - 1882/07/21:2g, done 22:1g
WALSH, Kate Opry, 25, NYC-B - 1916/01/05:2e
WALSH, Thomas W., NYPD capt. - 1913/06/22:1f
WALSH, William J., NY Fire Battalion Chief, NYC - 1912/01/14:1f,17:2f
WALTER % Goettelmann
WALTER, A., NYC-B - 1904/02/18:4a
WALTER, Anna, Hoboken, NJ - 1891/09/06:5a
WALTER, Anton, NYC?, fam. 1897/11/14:5a
WALTER, Caroline, 42, NYC-M - 1891/03/17:4a
WALTER, Catharina, un. cigarmaker?, NYC-M - 1893/08/17:4a
WALTER, Charles, 75, tailor, & daughter Emma, 40, NYC-Bx - 1908/11/23:2d
WALTER, comrade, metalworker & SPD Dresden/Gy - 1908/03/29:3a
WALTER, Dora, b. Ziegler, 26, NYC-Bx - 1909/09/06:6a
WALTER, Elizabeth, 67, NYC-M, + on Genl Slocum - 1904/06/17:3c
WALTER, Georg, un. carp., NYC-M - 1905/01/19:4a
WALTER, Heinrich, 57, NYC-M - 1890/08/11:4a
WALTER, J., 34, NYC-M - 1893/11/24:4a
WALTER, Jacob F., pianomaker, NYC-M - 1881/12/11:5a
WALTER, Jakob, NYC-M - 1905/08/10:4a
WALTER, John, NYC-M - 1908/03/12:6a
WALTER, Joseph, 44, SPD Mainz/Gy, mgr Mainzer Volkszeitung - 1915/09/19:3a
WALTER, Karl, un. printer, NYC-M - 1894/02/11:5c
WALTER, Lina, b. Stuerzel, NYC-M - 1892/07/07:4a
WALTER, Louis, un. carp., NYC-B - 1906/01/22:4a
WALTER, Louis, un. carp., NYC-M - 1911/11/20:6a, 21:6a
WALTER, M., 56, NYC-B - 1914/02/05:6a
WALTER, Marie, NYC-M - 1891/03/27:4a
WALTER, Nikolaus, NYC-Q - 1914/03/09:6a, 10:6a
WALTER, Philip G., ca 60, sexton of St Paul, NYC-SI? - 1916/04/07:3f
WALTER, Robert C. T., NYC-Bx - 1918/02/23:6a
WALTER, Robert, 40, NYC-B - 1907/03/30:6a, 31:7c
WALTER, Theodor, 50, grocer, Winfield, LI - 1881/09/02:1g
WALTERS, Alexander, 52, barber, NYC-M - 1903/03/15:1g
WALTERS, Annie [Herrmann], NYC-M - 1882/04/20:4d, 21:1d
WALTERS, Hermann, 50, NYC-M - 1890/06/10:3a
WALTERSPIEL, Helene, 66, NYC-M - 1891/04/05:5a
WALTERT, Balthasar, 52, painter, NYC-M - 1903/09/05:1f, 18:4b-c
WALTGENBACH, Josef, NYC-B - 1900/03/07:4a

WALTHER, Fritz, 70, carpenter, NYC-M - 1920/11/01:1e
WALTHER, George, 22, NYC-M - 1916/06/02:6a
WALTHER, Henriette, b. Wedekind, NYC-Bx – 1892/08/23:4a, 25:1g, 26:4e-f
WALTHER, Jos., NYC-M – 1908/01/28:6a
WALTHER, Joseph, 46, NYC-B - 1895/06/04:4a
WALTHER, Therese, infant, NYC-B – 1882/01/27:3c
WALTON, Joseph, Negro, lynched Lawrenceville, VA – 1901/07/02:3b
WALTZ, Jacob, un. cigarmaker, NYC-M – 1883/10/27:3c
WALWITZ, Joseph, mechanic, exec. Trenton, NJ - 1894/07/21:1e
WALZ, Alois, NYC-M – 1911/07/29:7a
WALZ, Wilhelm, NYC-M – 1912/01/19:6a
WAMBACH, Karl, 36, SP, Prague German, USA 1912, journalist, active in Banat German soc., Philadelphia - 1920/04/21:2a
WAMBOLD, Peter, 40, cook, NYC-B – 1909/01/27:3c
WAMBSER, John, 50, machinist, fr Baden?, NYC-M – 1897/04/08:4a
WAMHOFF, 65, MdR, Nation. Lib. Party, + Sangershausen - 1915/11/14:3c
WAND, Charles, NYC-Q - 1915/04/18:7b
WANDELL, John, 70, machinist, NYC-M – 1905/04/13:1b
WANDER, Ludwig, 64, tailor, NYC-B – 1898/07/30:5f
WANDER, Wilhelm, 76, Freethinking teacher, * Fischbach/Silesia, + Quirl/Silesia, - 1879/06/25:2e
WANDERER, Rudolph, Jersey City Hgts - 1915/09/21:6a
WANDERS, Karl Fr. W., educator fr Hirschberg/Silesia, 100th anniv. comm. – 1904/01/10:13c-d
WANFLUG % Bergmann
WANGENSTEIN, John, 34, NYC-Q – 1889/01/12:4a
WANGUS, Bertha, @ 1911 Triangle Shirtwaist Fire, NYC-M – 1911/03/27:1d
WANKE, Charles, farmer fr Elmira, exec. Buffalo, NY – 1880/02/22:5d, done 5/15:1c
WANKE, Paul, un. cigarmaker, NYC-M – 1882/12/12:3b
WANNEMACHER, C. M., b. Bitt?, 47, NYC-M – 1892/07/10:5c
WANNEMACHER, Charles, NYC-M – 1891/07/16:4a
WANNENMACHER, Josef, NYC-M – 1911/11/15:6a
WANNER, Amelie J., 62, NYC-B – 1890/10/19:5b
WANNER, August, 35, furrier, NYC-M – 1893/05/16:1h
WANNER, Barbara Schilbert, 44, NYC-M - 1915/02/09:6a
WANNER, William, NYC-M - 1917/12/27:6a
WANNINGER, Charles, 43, barman, NYC – 1896/07/19:5c
WANSER, Jacob, innkeep, NYC-M – 1907/02/03:7d
WANZEL, William, NYC-M – 1880/07/27:1g

WANZER, Peter, riverboat captain,(dying),NYC-M- 1917/07/23:2e
WARD, Anton, un. carp., NYC-M – 1889/05/15:4a
WARD, C. Osborne, ~70, un. typesetter & writer, SLP vet, + Yuma, AZ – 1902/03/23:1d
WARD, Edmund F., 51, on exec. co. Internatl Brewery Workers' Union, *Ireland, + Boston, MA - 1915/03/08:2c
WARD, George, Negro, lynched Terre Haute, IN – 1901/02/27:3b
WARDELL, Thomas, coal-mine owner in Summit, MO, killed by starving strikers on Oct 12, review 29 Oct 1888:2c
WARKENTIN, Bernard, pres. Kansas State Bank, killed in Turkey – 1908/05/01:1d
WARLICH, Louis, 50, waiter, Philadelphia - 1913/08/04:2b
WARMBOLD, Ernestine, child, NYC-M – 1881/09/02:3c
WARMBRUNN, Manfred, 43, NYC-M – 1919/11/14:6a
WARMUTH, Elisabeth, 6, NYC-M – 1886/07/27:3b
WARMUTH, George, NYC-M - 1894/10/20:4a
WARNBOCK, Mary, 1, NYC-M – 1882/07/29:4c
WARNECKE % Wunderlich
WARNECKE, Friedrich, 60, NYC-M – 1892/06/20:4a
WARNECKE, Johanna, 79, NYC-Q - 1915/01/30:6b
WARNEKE, August, Elizabeth, NJ - 1919/03/21:6a
WARNICH, Rosanna, 63, NYC-Q – 1900/08/27:4c
WARNKE, Amalia, 67, Newark, NJ – 1901/02/20:4b
WARNKE, Fritz, NYC? – 1884/07/03:3c
WARNKEN % Cordes
WARNKEN, Friedrich, un. cigarmaker, NYC-M - 1895/08/28: 4a
WARNKEN, Heinrich, 45, un. cigarmaker, NYC-M – 1911/11/18:6a
WARNKEN, Henrietta, b. Gevers, NYC-M - 1920/01/31:8a
WARNKEN, Katie, b. Koehler, 47, NYC-M – 1905/12/29:4a
WARRO, John, fr Hungary this summer, NYC-B – 1902/11/13:4a
WARSCHAUER, Louis, 27, un. cigar maker, NYC-M – 1886/03/27:2g
WART, VAN, Isaac, 65, NYC-M - 1919/03/16:12a
WARTENBURGER, John, 33, innkeep, NYC-B – 1908/11/05:3a
WARTERGHEN, VAN, Julia, exec. by Belgium as alleged spy on 18 Aug. 1914, death noted - 1915/12/03:2c
WARTH, John F., 73, NYC-B – 1891/04/02:4a
WASBACHER, Lena, 8, NYC-M – 1881/09/12:4c, 13:4c, 14:4c
WASBUTZKY, Mathilda, 45, NYC-M - 1920/01/20:8a
WASBUTZKY, Theresa, 75, NYC-M - 1920/12/31:6a
WASCHITSCHEK, Johann, 66, un. metal worker, SP Vienna/Austria – 1908/10/18:3f

WASCO, William, fr Hungary, exec. Pittsburgh, PA – 1900/01/10:2h
WASHINGTON, Booker T., Negro leader - 1915/11/15:1f
WASHINGTON, George, DAY by NYC SLP 1885/02/24:4a; 1897/02/21:4a; Comments, NYC-M 1899/02/14:2a, 100th anniv. Death 1899/12/17:2ab WASHINGTON DAY & workers 1900/02/23:2a
WASHINGTON, Jesse, Negro, lynched Waco, TX - 1916/05/16:2b
WASHINGTON, William, Negro, lynched near Talbert, LA – 1903/08/17:1e
WASKO, John, un. carp., NYC-M – 1907/12/10:6a
WASMER, Joseph, un. butcher, NYC-B - 1916/11/21:6a
WASMUTH, William, un. printer, NYC-B - 1920/06/10:6a
WASNER, Otto, 62, Wuerttemberg MdL (SPD), * 8 May 1857 Breslau/Silesia, + Stuttgart. - 1920/01/15:4c
WASSER, Fritz, 52, NYC-M – 1891/09/03:4a
WASSERMANN, Ernst, un. carp., NYC-M – 1909/07/30:6a
WASSERSCHEID % Zimmermann; WASSIG % Goedecke
WASSNER, Gustav, 57, worker, & wife, NYC-M – 1907/08/16:1c-d
WATJEN, Henry Herman Carl, 7, NYC-M - 1878/01/28:3d
WATJEN, Herman, West Hoboken, NJ – 1909/05/09:1d
WATJEN, Mrs, West Hoboken, NJ – 1909/03/12:1d
WATKINS, William, Prof., SLP, + Dayton, OH – 1898/12/31:1h
WATRIN, Prof., German prof. at Istanbul Pharmacological School – 1886/11/19:5d
WATSON, Beulah, 34, movie star, Fort Lee, NJ - 1917/05/28:2d
WATSON, James C., Prof., 43, US astronomer, + Madison, WI – 1880/11/25:2b
WATSON, Joseph, 16, exec. Wethersfield, CT – 1904/11/18:1d
WATSON, Thomas, & wife, ??, fr England 1912, NYC-Q - 1913/07/07:2d
WATT, James, 1736-1819, British inventor, notes to 100th anniv. Death – 1919/10/07:6c-e
WATZ, Robert, NYC-M – 1904/06/05:1g
WATZMANN, Sophia, NYC-M – 1910/09/30:1b
WAUSCHENSKY, Franz, fr Strassburg/Elsass?, + near Wilkes-Barre, PA – 1885/08/18:1b
WAVRA, Emil, infant, father fr Bohemia, NYC-M – 1896/11/27:1d
WAYLAND, Julius A., 58, SP, *Marseilles, IN, ed. Appeal to Reason, + Girard, KS – 1912/11/12:1c, 13:4d, 14:4d; mem. - 1913/10/25:1b
WAYMAN, John T., alderman, Trenton, NJ – 1910/11/12:1b
WAYMANN, John, NYC-B - 1920/12/22:6a
WAYNE, Thomas, 25, steelworker Homestead, PA – 1892/07/08:1a
WEBENBAUER, Alois, 70, NYC-B – 1909/08/02:6a
WEBENBAUER, Margarethe, b. Ziegler, 49, NYC-B – 1888/04/09:3b

WEBER, Thekla, 30, NYC-M – 1893/11/02:4c
WEBER, Albert, pianomaker, NYC-M - 1879/06/28:4a, 07/09:1e
WEBER, Albertine, NYC-M – 1906/03/26:4a, fam. 30:4a
WEBER, Alice M., NYC-M – 1891/04/05:5a
WEBER, Amalia, 7, NYC-Bx – 1911/03/18:6a
WEBER, Anna Martha, b. Goerlitz, 44, NYC-B - 1918/07/25:6a
WEBER, Anthony, 7, NYC-M – 1897/03/24:1b
WEBER, Anton, 54, un. cook & SP, fr Hungary 1906, NYC-M – 1911/01/27:2c, 6a
WEBER, Antonie, NYC-M - 1914/07/01:1c
WEBER, August, un. carp., NYC-M – 1888/05/10:3a
WEBER, Bertha, NYC?, fam. 1885/01/14:3b
WEBER, Caroline, b. Wessel, NYC-Q – 1890/08/10:4a
WEBER, Caroline, NYC-M – 1908/01/27:1f
WEBER, Charles L, horse dealer fr FT Wayne, IN, + NYC – 1897/02/19:1g
WEBER, Charles, 15, NYC-M – 1882/01/27:1g
WEBER, Charles, Newark, NJ – 1908/08/12:2b
WEBER, Charles, NYC-M - 1916/06/18:7a
WEBER, Charles, NYC-M - 1916/12/14:6a
WEBER, Christian, NYC-M – 1880/10/19:3c
WEBER, Christian, un. carp., NYC-M – 1896/06/09:4a
WEBER, Conrad, un. cigarmaker, NYC-B – 1909/12/27:6a
WEBER, Elisabeth, NYC-B – 1891/03/11:4a
WEBER, Elisabeth, NYC-M – 1908/03/07:6a
WEBER, Emil, 40, NYC-B – 1889/02/12:4a
WEBER, Frank, 49, NYC-Bx - 1916/01/23:7a
WEBER, Frank, NYC-M, + @Genl Slocum – 1904/06/29:1c
WEBER, Franz, 29, NYC-M – 1893/12/29:4a
WEBER, Friedrich, 40, musician, NYC-M – 1898/12/29:1g
WEBER, Friedrich, 68, architect, NYC-B – 1893/03/22:2d
WEBER, Georg, ~35, waiter, NYC-M – 1904/12/30:1g
WEBER, Georg, 45, driver, Jersey City, NJ - 1913/09/01:2d
WEBER, Gottlieb, laborer, + Granton, NJ – 1882/05/21:5f
WEBER, Gustav, 32, NYC-M – 1899/01/26:4a
WEBER, Gustav, Jersey City Heights, NJ – 1912/02/18:7c
WEBER, Gustav, NYC-B – 1913/01/24:6a
WEBER, H., NYC-M – 1911/02/23:6a
WEBER, Hans Jakob, 44, USA 1862 fr Duernten/Zuerich/Switz., searched in order to probate a will – 1882/05/22:4e, 8 June:3b
WEBER, Henry, NYC-M – 1907/07/20:6a
WEBER, Hermann, machinist, NYC-M – 1904/03/24:4a
WEBER, Hermann, un. bricklayer, NYC-B – 1911/10/01:7b, 3:6a

WEBER, Isidor, 32, peddler, NYC-M – 1897/04/27:1d
WEBER, Isidor, brewer or cooper, NYC-M – 1905/07/15:4a
WEBER, Jacob, 27, NYC-M – 1893/11/16:1h
WEBER, Jacob, 64, NYC-M – 1910/05/20:6a
WEBER, John, 29, un. painter, NYC-M – 1916/07/09:7a, 10:6a
WEBER, John, 31, striking weaver, NYC-B – 1902/04/22:1h, =24:1g, 25:1h, 14 May:1f, 11 June:1h
WEBER, John, 43, un. carp., NYC-M – 1899/06/15:4a
WEBER, John, 54, NYC-M – 1890/03/30:5b
WEBER, John, 81, un. cabinet maker, NYC-B – 1919/01/20:6a
WEBER, John, NYC-M – 1904/08/12:4a
WEBER, Julius, 78, NYC-B – 1891/04/12:5a
WEBER, Louis, driver, NYC-M – 1903/09/23:2h, 24:4a
WEBER, Louis, un. butcher, NYC-M – 1907/05/01:6a
WEBER, Louis, un. carp., NYC-M – 1898/12/20:4a
WEBER, Louisa, b. Klein, NYC-B – 1892/08/13:4a
WEBER, Louise, b. Schmidt, 36, fr Leipzig, NYC-M – 1889/02/10:5b
WEBER, Margaret, 4, NYC-B – 1918/07/09:6b
WEBER, Margaret, 69, NYC-B – 1907/02/24:1d
WEBER, Margarethe, 59, NYC-B – 1901/06/15:4a
WEBER, Maria, b. Ottens, NYC-M – 1893/01/29:5c, 30:4a
WEBER, Martin, 50, locksmith, Paterson, NJ – 1898/10/22:4c
WEBER, Mary, 75, NYC-B – 1911/03/15:3b
WEBER, Michael, NYC-B – 1906/11/01:6a
WEBER, Michael, NYC-M – 1908/01/05:7c
WEBER, Oswald, coffee roaster, NYC-B – 1902/12/27:1g
WEBER, Ottmar, un. carp., NYC-M – 1907/09/17:6a
WEBER, P. J., 55, NYC-M – 1887/07/19:1g
WEBER, Paul, 55, carp., NYC-M – 1893/09/26:1d
WEBER, Peter, NYC-Q – 1907/06/28:6a
WEBER, Robert, 52, innkeep, SPD Leipzig – 1899/03/29:2d
WEBER, Rudolf, un. butcher, NYC-M – 1908/05/21:6a
WEBER, Theodor, 38, Mt Vernon, NY – 1912/01/19:2e
WEBER, William H., SP?, NYC-B – 1918/06/29:6a, 30:6a
WEBER, William, 31, tailor, NYC-M – 1899/03/22:3g
WEBER, William, NYC-Q – 1904/11/19:4a
WEBERLING, Carl, mining engineer, + by Apaches – 1882/02/02:2g
WEBERMANN, Rosa, 13, NYC-M – 1904/07/01:3b
WECHE, Anton, 63, NYC-M – 1917/04/21:6a
WECHSUNG, Guenther, druggist, NYC-M – 1889/03/08:1h, 9:1f, 13:1g, 14:2g
WECHTER, Minnie, 3, NYC-M – 1895/03/09:4a

WECK, Carl, 32, nickel galvanoplastic, NYC-M – 1901/03/05:3h
WECK, Otto, 36, Newark, NJ - 1917/12/21:6a
WECKER, Daisy, NYC-M, +@ Genl Slocum – 1904/06/18:3d
WECKERLE, Joseph, NYC-M – 1901/07/03:1d
WECKERLE, M., 76, NYC-M – 1893/09/30:4a
WECKMAN, John A., un. painter, NYC-Bx - 1919/08/02:6a
WECKMANN, John A., un. painter, NYC-Bx – 1919/08/02:6a
WEDDAY, J.O., SP, ed. of Appeal to Reason, + Oklahoma City, OK - 1916/01/20:1f
WEDDE, Johannes, SPD writer, Germany, 10th anniv. Of death – 1900/02/04:7f-g, his = 1890/02/03:2d-e
WEDDINGEN, Otto, NYC? - 1916/08/06:1b
WEDEKAMP, A.'s wife, NYC-M – 1892/04/08:4a
WEDEKIND, Frank, German writer, + Munich/Gy - 1918/04/06:2g
WEDEKIND, Friedrich, Dr. *21 Fb 1816 Bentheim/Gy, '48er, San Francisco 1852-1862?, + in Lenzburg/Switz. – 1888/11/06:2d
WEDEL, Hans Adam von, lawyer & G-A journalist, + British internment camp - 1916/01/19:1e
WEDEL, Joachim von, 30, Bavarian baron, USA 1889, med. student NYC-M – 1890/11/22:1h, 23:1h
WEDEMEYER, Arthur, NYC-M - 1917/05/22:6a
WEDEMEYER, Frederick C., 31, Hudson Heights, NY - 1919/07/17:6a, mem. (spelled Wiedemeyer) 1920/07/15:6a
WEDEMEYER, Meta, 14, NYC-B - 1919/08/22:2b
WEDEMEYER, William W., US Congress, of German parents – 1913/01/04:6c
WEDMEIER, John, 76, NYC-M – 1891/02/03:1g
WEED, Thurlow, politician, Albany, NY – 1882/11/29:1f
WEEGIN, William H., 24, NYC-M - 1919/06/26:6a
WEERTH, Georg, German labor poet, (+ 1856 Havana/Cuba), his life – 1889/07/28:6e-g
WEGA, Louis Palander af, Swedish Polar explorer - 1920/09/15:4d
WEGBECKER, Robert, NYC-B - 1918/11/27:6a
WEGENER % Urff
WEGENER, Charles J., merchant, NYC-M – 1890/09/24:2g
WEGENER, Fritz, 48, un. cigarmaker, NYC-M – 1893/01/29:5c
WEGENER, Fritz, machinist, NYC-M – 1905/03/07:4a
WEGENER, Louise H., b. Stecher, Jersey City Heights, NJ – 1898/06/16:4a
WEGENER, Rosie, b. Boettcher, NYC-B – 1909/01/08:6a
WEGENER, Sophie, b. Meier, 44, fr Altona/Gy, NYC-M – 1893/09/21:4a
WEGMANN, George, 45, Swiss, NYC-B – 1887/08/03:1f
WEGNAR, Minna, NYC-B – 1912/11/04:6a

WEGNER, Ernestine, 32, German actress, + Berlin – 1883/11/20:2e
WEGNER, F., cigarmaker & SPD activist expelled fr Ottensen/Gy, arrived NYC – 1881/06/16:4a
WEGNER, Louis, SLP, NYC-B – 1897/04/13:3d
WEHINGER, Joseph, 21, baker, NYC-M – 1898/03/16:3f
WEHINGER, Joseph, mechanic, NYC-M - 1894/01/08:4a
WEHINGER, Lorenz, NYC-M – 1905/08/29:4a
WEHLAU, J., ship machinist, @1900 dock fire, Hoboken, NJ – 1900/07/03:1c
WEHLE % Stamm
WEHLE, Georg G., SP, un. machinist, ex-pres. Brooklyn Labor Lyceum, *12 Jy 1858 Sychen/Berlin, NYC-B - 1918/02/20:2b, 6a, 21:6a, 22:2a, =23:2d, fam. 24:7a
WEHLE, Madeleine B., b. Menninger, NYC-M – 1886/12/04:3a
WEHMAN, Frederick, soda water manuf., NYC-M – 1907/10/24:1f
WEHMANN % Langreder
WEHMANN, Laura, b. Erdmann, 27, NYC-B – 1892/02/23:4d
WEHMANN, Mrs, SPD Leipzig - 1915/08/29:3b
WEHMEYER, Lina, b. Moll, NYC-B - 1896/03/08:5a
WEHMEYER, William, 52, baker, NYC-B – 1881/09/12:1e
WEHNER, Johann Baptist, 60, machinist, NYC-M – 1885/08/28:1g
WEHNER, John, grocer, NYC-Bx – 1907/04/06:1e
WEHNER, Lena, 11, NYC-M, +@Genl Slocum – 1904/06/23:1c
WEHNER, Louis, NYC-B - 1918/04/05:6a
WEHNERT, Andrew Jr., milk dealer, Paterson, NJ - 1915/12/04: 6c, 10:2e, 12:1f
WEHNINGER, Georg, 57, NYC-B – 1907/06/01:1e
WEHR, Joseph, 75, NYC-Bx – 1912/02/09:6a
WEHRENBERG, Margarethe A., b. Vosbrink, 40, NYC-M – 1890/03/18:4a
WEHRHAHN, Marie, 55, NYC-B – 1910/10/29:6a
WEHRLE, Lina, NYC-M - 1919/04/22:6a, fam. 25:6a
WEHRLIN, John, weaver, Paterson, NJ 1915/04/30:6a
WEIBEL, Annie, NYC-B – 1898/03/01:4b
WEIBEL, Chr., NYC-Q – 1911/09/03:7a
WEIBERT, Henry, NYC-B - 1915/03/11:6a
WEIBLER, Christian, 68, NYC-B – 1891/02/06:2f
WEIBLINGER, Carl, fdr NY Conditor Verein, NYC-M – 1888/04/02:3a
WEIBRECHT, Arnold, 66, smith, USA 1870 fr Stettin/Gy, NYC – 1897/02/28:1c
WEICHAND % Trunk
WEICHERT, Pauline, 31, NYC-M – 1889/09/11:2e
WEICHHAUSER, Henry, 38, NYC-B – 1903/12/28:1e

WEICKERT, E., 50, druggist, NYC-B – 1902/03/17:1e
WEICKUM, Charles, 12, NYC-Q – 1901/02/07:4a
WEID, Michael, Elizabeth, NJ - 1914/05/21:6a
WEIDAUER, Paul, ATB Leipzig/Sax., War 1 - 1914/11/01:3b
WEIDE, Louis, NYC-B - 1919/04/10:6a
WEIDEL, Bruno, un. carp., SP, NYC-Q – 1911/09/01:6a, 2:6a, =4:2c, fam. 5:6a
WEIDEL, Rudolf, 32, NYC-Q - 1914/11/02:6a, 4:6a
WEIDEMANN, Carl, un. brewer, NYC-Bx – 1893/12/16:4a
WEIDEMANN, Margarethe, NYC-Q – 1908/09/26:6a
WEIDEMEYER, William, 27, hay dealer, Hoboken, NJ – 1904/07/11:1a, 12:1f
WEIDENBAUM % Poehland
WEIDENHEIMER, Louis, un. carp., NYC-Bx – 1908/12/01:6a
WEIDENMANN, Caroline, 50, NYC-M, +@ Genl Slocum – 1904/06/17:3c (>Weidman)
WEIDENMUELLER, Adolph, Jersey City Heights, NJ – 1906/10/26:6a, fam. 1 Nv:6a
WEIDENMUELLER, Emma, b. Loeffler, NYC-M - 1920/02/03:8a
WEIDENMUELLER, Emma, NYC – 1912/11/13:6a
WEIDENMUELLER, Wilhelm, 79, NYC-M - 1920/10/03:2a
WEIDER, Ellen, NYC-M, + @ Genl Slocum – 1904/06/17:3c
WEIDER, George P., 64, NYC-M – 1919/11/15:6a
WEIDERMEYER, Henry, tramway driver, NYC-B – 1908/11/08:7c
WEIDERSTRAND, Ally, pianist, then nurse, NYC-M – 1909/05/02:9f
WEIDLER, Henry, NYC-M, + @ Genl Slocum – 1904/06/17:3c
WEIDLER, John H., 28, waiter, NYC-M – 1888/12/18:1e
WEIDMAN, Harriet, NYC-M, + @ Genl Slocum – 1904/06/21:1f (>Weidenmann)
WEIDMANN % Leist
WEIDMANN, Anna, USA 1894, NYC-B – 1900/05/04:1b
WEIDMANN, Charles, 17, NYC-B – 1892/07/05:4e
WEIDMANN, Philip, brewer or cooper, NYC-M – 1901/12/10:4a
WEIDNER, Anna Katharina, b. Oberdorf, 48, NYC-B – 1910/02/26:6a, fam. 2 Mr:6a
WEIDNER, Anton, 63, engineer, NYC-M – 1897/04/25:5d, 26:4a, =28:1g, fam. 2 May:5c
WEIDNER, Fritz, 48, publ. Brooklyn Reform, NYC-B – 1888/09/11:3b, =13:1f
WEIDSCHUTZ, Elizabeth von, 59, NYC-B – 1883/02/03:3a, 5:3a
WEIER, John, NYC-M – 1883/01/03:4c
WEIERICH, George, NYC-M – 1907/02/28:6a

WEIGAND, Carl, NYC-M - 1917/06/01:6a
WEIGAND, Christoph, 61, NYC-M - 1892/06/14:4a
WEIGAND, Friedrich, SPD Frankfurt-Bornheim, War 1 - 1914/11/01:3b
WEIGAND, Kaspar, 22, NYC-M - 1892/09/28:2e
WEIGAND, W., NYC-Q - 1910/11/06:7a
WEIGAND, William, 34, NYC-B - 1893/12/27:2d
WEIGANT, Hattie E., 19, actress, NYC-M - 1892/03/15:1f, 16:1h, 17:4f
WEIGEL, Anna, 35, NYC-M - 1902/08/04:1h
WEIGEL, August, 46, NYC-B - 1890/04/26:4a
WEIGEL, Bertha, b. Kilian, 28, Jersey City, NJ - 1916/10/07:6a, 14:6a
WEIGEL, Elizabeth, b. Mogk, NYC-Q - 1913/12/25:3a
WEIGEL, George, un. carp., NYC-M - 1892/02/23:4a
WEIGEL, John P., chief edit Brauer-Zeitung, SP, + Cincinatti, OH - 1906/08/21:3c
WEIGEL, John, 45, Orange, NJ - 1893/09/25:1g
WEIGEL, Julius F., hotelier, NYC-Q - 1911/07/04:6b
WEIGELE, Max, West Hoboken, NJ - 1904/10/22:1g
WEIGELMANN, Louis, 30, un. painter, NYC-M - 1904/10/25:3c
WEIGELT, Dora, 36, Hoboken, NJ - 1910/03/31:2e
WEIGELT, Karl, 50, MdL for SPD Steinach/Thueringia - 1911/02/12:3e
WEIGERT, Adolf, 40, un. painter, NYC-M - 1917/03/20:6a
WEIGERT, Georg, NYC-M - 1915/06/21:6a
WEIGERT, John, 44, NYC-M - 1905/11/03:4a
WEIGERT, Joseph, un. knife maker, NYC-M - 1903/02/10:4a
WEIGL, Florentina Marie, NYC-B - 1913/04/26:6a
WEIGLER, John, 56, NYC-M - 1900/07/19:1e
WEIGMANN, Charles F., ex-Massilion, OH, Newark, NJ - 1909/05/06:3d
WEIGUNY, Anton, SPO Linz/Austria, tailor & MdR for Linz, + 16 De - 1915/01/15:4d, =17:3c-d
WEIHE, William, union leader, incl. Homestead, + Pittsburg, PA - 1908/08/25:1b
WEIHER, Mrs Geibert, wd of John, un. tailor, NYC-B - 1878/08/16:3c
WEIHMANN, Friedrich Emil, bookbinder & SPD Leipzig/Gy - 1909/08/29:3e, note 5 Sept:3d
WEIKEL, H. E., artist, Mt Carmel, NJ - 1899/01/11:4c
WEIKER, Andreas, 47, NYC-M - 1896/08/29:1g
WEIKERT, Otto, un. butcher, NYC-Bx - 1920/03/09:6a
WEIL % Egner/Wisch, % Glass
WEIL, August, blouse manuf., 50, NYC-M - 1907/10/10:5f, 11:1d
WEIL, Bertha, 1, NYC-M - 1883/12/24:3a
WEIL, Caroline, NYC-B - 1891/02/26:4a
WEIL, Emily, NYC-M - 1892/08/21:5b

WEIL, Felix, 86, NYC-M − 1892/02/28:5e
WEIL, Frank, 50, brewing engineer, NYC-B − 1905/10/22:1g
WEIL, Hermann, machinist, NYC-M − 1896/08/15:4a
WEIL, Isidor, 47, NYC-M − 1891/06/24:4a
WEIL, Jacob, 55, & Rosalie, restaurant owners, NYC-B − 1907/01/29:3b
WEIL, Jean, 65, G-A journalist, * Marburg/Hessen, USA 1867, ed. Brewers' Journal/Brauereizeitung, NYC-Bx - 1915/04/20:2a, 21:6a
WEIL, Lina, NYC-M − 1893/01/22:5b
WEIL, Robert, 35, NYC-M − 1892/07/31:5c
WEIL, S. H., St Louis, MO + NYC-M − 1891/02/03:1g
WEIL, William, 44, inspector at Water Dept., NYC-B − 1900/12/20:1e
WEILAND, Elizabeth, b. Kircher, NYC-M − 1901/08/11:5a
WEILBACH, Peter, NYC-M − 1880/05/06:4b
WEILBACKER, Charles, NYC-M − 1885/03/02:3a
WEILEDER, Bertha, wd Sturmer, 62, NYC-Q - 1920/10/04:6a
WEILENBRONNER % Altmann
WEILER, Charles, NYC-Bx − 1909/10/26:6a
WEILER, John, Jersey City Heights, NJ − 1900/04/06:4a, 7:4a, fam. 12:4a
WEILER, Peter, Newark, NJ, will of − 1880/05/07:4e
WEILIGMANN, Frank, tailor, NYC-B − 1881/11/12:3b
WEIL-KIES, Helena, 64, NYC-M - 1919/07/19:6a
WEILL, Josephine, 55, NYC-M − 1892/12/13:4a
WEILL, Regina, 79, NYC-M − 1907/07/25:3e
WEIMAN, Nicholas, 72, carp., NYC-Q - 1918/12/01:7d
WEIMAN, William, lawyer, NYC − 1900/04/17:2h
WEIMANN, Christine, NYC - 1914/03/30:6a
WEIMANN, Frank, SP, NYC-Bx − 1906/01/18:1h
WEIMANN, Jakob, carp., NYC-M − 1883/02/24:3b
WEIMANN, John, 64, NYC-M − 1912/12/23:6a
WEIMANN, Paul, 30, clerk, Jersey City, NJ − 1907/04/10:3d
WEIMAR, Otto, Newark, NJ − 1910/01/11:6a
WEIMEBERG, Charles, 45, glass worker, NYC-B - 1919/08/17:3e
WEIMER, Joseph, 65, farm laborer, NYC-Q - 1913/07/31:3b-c
WEIMER, Maria, 50, Newark, NJ − 1907/07/13:3c
WEINACHT, Rudolf, un. carp., NYC-M − 1904/04/07:4a
WEINBAUER, Henry, 48, builder, NYC-B − 1880/08/29:5g
WEINBERG, Alfred, 60, piano salesman, NYC-M - 1916/05/08:1a
WEINBERG, Charles, 68, Jersey City, NJ - 1916/06/14:6a
WEINBERG, Louis, sailor, + NYC-Bx Sept. 1893, see Hugo von Weissdorn
WEINBERGER, Bernhard, furnit. dealer, NYC-M - 1914/01/05:1b
WEINBERGER, Georg, 63, SP, * Hessen, USA 1898, NYC-M - 1914/10/15:6a, 16:2d

WEINBERGER, Henry, 41, NYC-Bx – 1910/06/25:6a, fam. 28:6a
WEINBRENNER, Christian, NYC-M – 1891/05/15:4a
WEINDORF, Caroline, b. Kain, NYC-M – 1886/01/26:2g
WEINER, Adam, 68, NYC-B – 1881/12/09:2g
WEINER, Mary, NYC-M – 1903/12/26:2g
WEINER, Rosie, @1911 Triangle Shirtwaist Fire, NYC-M – 1911/03/27:1d
WEINER, Rosie, 65, NYC-B – 1907/08/26:3a
WEINERT, Annie, NYC-M – 1905/05/28:1d, 29:1d
WEINERT, Max, 34, un. butcher, NYC-Bx - 1916/05/12:6a
WEINERT, Sophie, 6, NYC-M – 1905/05/20:4a
WEINERT, Wilhelm, un. cigarmaker, NYC-M - 1895/03/06:4a
WEINERT, Wilhelmine, NYC-M – 1908/05/07:6a
WEINGAERTNER, Elisabeth, 68, NYC-Q – 1891/12/02:2d
WEINGAERTNER, George, 50, NYC-M – 1892/03/27:5d
WEINGART, August, 56, businessman, NYC - 1916/05/25:2g
WEINGARTNER, John, un. butcher, NYC-B - 1919/03/11:6a
WEINHAENDLER, Max, 70, worker, Regensburg, Bavaria – 1913/02/16:3b
WEINHAGEN, Louis, driver, NYC-M – 1892/09/24:1a
WEINHEIMER % Erb
WEINHEIMER, Ludwig Traugott, SP, un. metall worker, NYC-B - 1917/05/05:5f
WEINHOLD, Theodor, Boston, MA, + near Elizabeth, NJ – 1886/06/18:2e
WEINICKE, Bertha, NYC-M – 1880/06/24:1f
WEINKAUF, Albert, 48, un. carp., NYC-M – 1891/01/28:2h, 30:4a
WEINMANN, Camille, 45, un. painter, NYC-M – 1890/02/12:4a
WEINMANN, Charles, un. cigarmaker, NYC-M - 1879/04/06:8a
WEINMANN, Christian, NYC-M – 1904/02/24:4a
WEINMANN, Ferdinand, un. painter, NYC-Bx – 1906/01/19:4a
WEINMANN, Henry, 4, NYC-M – 1881/10/28:3b
WEINMANN, Henry, 62, un. carp., NYC-M – 1906/01/05:4a
WEINMANN, Jakob, 42, un. carp., NYC-M – 1883/11/10:3b
WEINMANN, Joseph, Greenville, NJ – 1911/10/12:6a
WEINMANN, Kathie, 4, NYC-M – 1888/04/03:3b
WEINMANN, Peter, 45, butcher, NYC-B – 1888/01/11:2d
WEINMANN, Walter, 21, NYC – 1908/08/25:1d
WEINMUELLER, F., student, NYC-M – 1881/12/04:5d
WEINOEHL, Wilhelm, 64, goldsmith, SP, fr Hanau to US 1880, NYC-M – 1907/08/30:6a, 1 Se:1e
WEINSCHENK, Margarethe, 21, servant, NYC-M – 1887/04/18:2e
WEINSTEIN, Bertha, 23, fr Russia, NYC-Bx - 1916/05/01:1f
WEINSTEIN, Bertha, NYC-M – 1893/08/28:1e

WEINSTEIN, Charles, member Workers Educ. Assoc., NYC-M - 1915/11/30:6a, 12/01:6a, 2:6a
WEINSTEIN, Henry, 14, jeweler apprentice, NYC-M - 1881/12/31:1f
WEINSTEIN, Morris, 40, tailor, NYC-B - 1913/05/28:3a-b
WEINTRAUB, Joseph, 26, NYC-Q - 1913/05/18:11e
WEINTRAUB, Sally, 17, (s.a. 1911 Triangle Shirtwaist Fire, NYC-M), NYC-M - 1911/03/27:1d
WEINTRAUT, Bertha, @1911 Triangle Shirtwaist fire, NYC-M - 1911/03/26:1b
WEINZEL, Margarethe, NYC-B - 1906/05/03:4b
WEINZETTEL, Alois, SP Wien-Ottakring, War 1 - 1914/11/01:3c
WEIPPERT, Anton, Newark, NJ - 1909/12/24:3c
WEIPPERT, Rudolf, 24, NYC-M - 1896/01/16:4a
WEIPPERT, Rudolf, NYC-M - 1911/01/26:6a
WEIRAUCH, Wilhelm, NYC-Q - 1910/04/29:6a
WEIS, Barbara, 19, servant, NYC-M - 1881/02/13:5f
WEIS, Frederick, 19, Salome, 14, John, 5, Tillie, 47, & Amelia, 10, Louis, 21, NYC-M, + @on Genl Slocum - 1904/06/17:3c, 22:1d
WEIS, Heinrich, NYC-B - 1890/03/18:4a
WEIS, John, un. carp., NYC-M - 1903/11/28:4a
WEIS, Karl, un. butcher, 40, NYC-M - 1911/03/20:6a, 21:6a
WEISBECKER, Henry, 49, SP, New Haven, CT - 1917/05/15:6a, fam. 20:7a
WEISBROD, Catharina, 45, NYC-B - 1904/09/05:3d
WEISBROD, Catherine, 45, NYC-B - 1904/09/05:3d
WEISBROD, Emma Mathilda, 5, NYC-B - 1886/06/16:3a
WEISBROD, John A., typesetter, NYC-B - 1887/02/09:2e, 3c, 10:3d, 11:3d
WEISE, Carolina, NYC-M, + @ Genl Slocum - 1904/06/18:3d
WEISE, Oscar, 44,un. bricklayer,NYC-B - 1913/11/09:7b, 10:6a
WEISE, Richard, un. carp., NYC-B - 1913/02/15:6a
WEISE, Willie, NYC-M, + @ Genl Slocum - 1904/06/18:3d
WEISER, Alex, 49, NYC-M - 1899/09/17:1c
WEISER, Dora, NYC-M - 1905/09/25:4a
WEISER, Frederick, 55, farmer & sausage manuf., Scranton, PA - 1912/07/08:2e
WEISER, Joseph, un. brewer, NYC-M - 1895/03/20:4a
WEISER, Karl, 65, German actor, + Weimar - 1913/07/14:4f
WEISERT, Henry, 40, Jersey City, NJ - 1899/04/07:1d
WEISERT, William H., driver, NYC-B - 1885/05/24:1f
WEISGAL, Emanuel, SP, NYC-M - 1920/09/05:2a
WEISGERBER, Franziska, NYC-M - 1908/05/30:6a
WEISGERBER, Frederick., 65, NYC-B - 1894/01/12:4a

WEISGERBER, Jacob, weaver?, NYC-Q - 1913/06/12:6a
WEISGERBER, William F., 20, NYC-B - 1894/01/21:5d
WEISHARD, Meyer, peddler, NYC-M - 1901/01/17:1f, 18:1h, 19:1g
WEISHAUPT, Max, NYC-B - 1917/12/15:6a
WEISHAUT, Abraham, 71, NYC-M - 1891/07/19:5b
WEISHEIT, Minna, 34, NYC-M - 1899/11/30:4a
WEISING, George, 51, NYC-B - 1918/11/21:5g
WEISMANN, August, Prof., 80, German zoologist - 1914/11/08:11e
WEISMANN, Frederick, 34, druggist, Union Hill, NJ - 1914/09/20:7e
WEISMANN, Frederick, Newark, NJ, +Philadelphia, PA - 1908/10/11:1d
WEISMANN, Henry, 34, NYC-B - 1892/11/13:5b
WEISMANN, Martha, servant, Mt Vernon, NY - 1913/08/02:1d
WEISNACH, Frederick, 22, NYC-B - 1903/08/17:3b
WEISROCK, John, 44, butcher, NYC-B - 1903/09/30:4a, 2 Oct:4a
WEISS, Adolf, un. carp., NYC-B - 1915/10/10:11g
WEISS, Alex, advertising agent for N.Y. Herold, fr Vienna, NYC-M - 1891/07/02:4d, 3:1f
WEISS, Andreas, un. carp., NYC-B - 1888/04/17:2h
WEISS, Anna, NYC-B - 1911/03/19:1b, 21:3b
WEISS, Annie, 5, NYC-M - 1892/11/23:1e
WEISS, August, un. carp., NYC? - 1887/11/10:2g
WEISS, Bertha, b. Schuette, NYC-M - 1891/03/27:4a
WEISS, Carl, un. machinist, NYC-M - 1905/06/18:5a, 19:4a
WEISS, Caspar, 49, un. carp., NYC-B - 1912/10/03:6a
WEISS, Charles, * Eiselhohn/Gy, USA 1872, NYC-M - 1886/03/29:1g, 3b
WEISS, Charles, bookkeeper at Dobler Brewery, Schenectady, NY, + NYC-M - 1903/07/28:3b-c
WEISS, Christian, West New York, NJ - 1901/02/03:5b
WEISS, Christopher, 44, salesman, ex-innkeep, NYC-Q - 1911/09/24:7d
WEISS, Elias, 18, 1911 fr Russia, NYC-M - 1911/04/19:1d
WEISS, Emma, b. Werner, NYC-M - 1889/12/02:4a, 3:4a
WEISS, Frank, 58, NYC-M - 1892/05/10:4a
WEISS, Fritz, 55, NYC-M - 1917/02/15:6a
WEISS, George, 56, tailor, NYC-M - 1881/07/09:4a
WEISS, Guido, Democratic publ. in Frankfurt/Main, Gy, to his 70th birthday - 1892/09/31:2c; + 1899/01/18:2b, 31:2e-g, 19 Fb:12e
WEISS, Gustav, potter, SPD Eberswalde/Gy - 1912/09/15:3d
WEISS, Henry F., exec. Lebanon, PA - 1880/05/14:1b
WEISS, Henry, 43, & wife Annie, Jersey City, NJ - 1905/03/29:1d
WEISS, Henry, NYC-M - 1892/04/17:1f
WEISS, Johanna, NYC-B - 1919/01/26:6a

WEISS, John, 38, smith, USA 1888, NYC-B – 1893/12/27:2e
WEISS, John, Newark, + Trenton, NJ – 1899/06/02:1e
WEISS, John, treasurer of Germania Order, NYC-M – 1890/08/04:4a
WEISS, John, un. carp., NYC-M – 1907/06/20:6a
WEISS, Josef, un. baker & SP activist Vienna – 1908/03/15:3e
WEISS, Joseph, 40, baker, NYC-B – 1898/08/18:1d
WEISS, Julius, NYC-M – 1888/11/27:3b
WEISS, Karl, fr Hungary 1891, typesetter at NYC Plattduetsche Post – 1892/11/18:2e
WEISS, Leopold, fr Budapest, on ship Batavia – 1907/03/05:1f
WEISS, Louis, 56, brewer, NYC-B - 1913/12/27:6a
WEISS, Louis, 82, Ridgefield, NJ – 1907/01/16:6a
WEISS, Louise, 18, NYC-B – 1898/12/24:2e
WEISS, Marcus, SLP, NYC-M – 1891/01/06:4a
WEISS, Mary, 50, & daughter Bertha Fass, 16, NYC-B – 1909/12/07:3a
WEISS, Morris, 6, NYC – 1904/09/07:3c
WEISS, Mrs, and daughter Mrs Fargo, NYC-B, on ship "Mystery" – 1887/07/12:1c-e, 13:2g, 15:2e
WEISS, Otto, 1, NYC-M - 1878/10/19:3a
WEISS, Raymond, un. cornice-maker, NYC-M – 1890/09/29:4a
WEISS, Robert, NYC-Bx – 1911/08/15:6a
WEISS, Samuel, 36, printer, edit. G-A labor media, *Hungary, + Erie, PA – 1897/12/06:1b
WEISS, Wilhelm, 50, mgr American House, Cincinatti, OH – 1912/07/08:2c
WEISSACKER, Sadie, 12, NYC-M – 1899/07/27:4b
WEISSBACH, Henry, NYC-M – 1892/06/24:4a
WEISSBACH, Martha, 57, NYC-M - 1920/05/01:2a
WEISSBACH, Richard, 64, Hoboken, NJ - 1918/10/20:12a
WEISSBECKER, Charles, 54, Hoboken?, NJ – 1908/08/17:3d
WEISSBRODT, George, 37, shoeworker, Newark, NJ – 1900/07/25:4b
WEISSDOM, Hugo von, sailor as "Louis Weinberg," + 29 Sept 1893 NYC-Bx, body fd 6 Oct:2d
WEISSEBORN % Heuschke
WEISSENBERGER, Clara, 4, NYC-M - 1894/10/24:4d
WEISSENBERGER, Rudolf, NYC-B – 1908/12/03:3b
WEISSENBORN % Roemer
WEISSENBORN, Marie, b. Schoenhaus, NYC-M – 1889/02/12:4a
WEISSENBORN, William, 21, Dane, farm laborer, USA 1885?, NYC-B – 1885/04/29:2g
WEISSENFELS, Ferdinand, 60, NYC-M – 1898/12/16:4a, fam. 20:4a,b
WEISSER, Eduard, NYC-M – 1903/04/10:4a, 11:4a

WEISSER, Ellen & Mary NYC-M, +@Genl Slocum – 1904/06/18:3d
WEISSER, Gottlieb, NYC-M – 1906/03/26:4a
WEISSGERBER % Pegenkopf
WEISSGERBER, Heinrich, 68, un. machinist, NYC-Bx – 1911/09/04:6a
WEISSHEIMER, Louise, child, NYC-M - 1878/04/05:3a
WEISSHEIMER, Wendelin, labor poet, SPD Kandern/Loerrach/Gy, 70th birthday – 1908/04/05:3a; + Nuernberg/Gy – 1910/07/03:3a
WEISSKOPF, Conrad, un. carpenter, NYC-M - 1914/02/15:7b
WEISSKOPF, Peter, un. cigar maker, NYC-M – 1891/10/11:5d
WEISSKOPF, Peter, un. cigarmaker, NYC-M - 1894/02/15:4a
WEISSKREUZ, N., teacher at Jewish school, NYC-M – 1890/03/22:2f
WEISSMAN, Adam, butcher, Verona, NJ - 1914/08/09:11a
WEISSMAN, Frederick, 50, merchant, NYC-B - 1919/07/27:2b
WEISSMAN, Samuel, 15, NYC-M – 1900/11/06:3e
WEISSMANN, Elisabeth, Newark, NJ – 1902/03/27:1b
WEISSMUELLER, Maggie, 21, servant, NYC-M – 1892/02/05:1g
WEISSNER, Carrie, NYC-M, +@ Genl Slocum – 1904/06/18:3d
WEISSNER, Louise, 49, NYC-Bx - 1918/03/09:6a
WEISTARD, Leopold, 63, tailor, NYC-B – 1903/03/02:3b
WEITBRECHT, Bertha, NYC-M – 1907/06/23:7b
WEITENDORF, Frederick E., NYC-M – 1891/07/03:4a
WEITLING, Wilhelm, 1808-71, German communist, his life – 1908/08/16:6g, 11a-d; 100th anniv. of birth 5 Oct:4b-c, 7 Fb 1909:6c-d
WEITZ, Henry C., 62, un. typesetter, NYC-M – 1901/03/03:5a
WEITZMANN % Kigner
WEITZMANN, Ida, 19, NYC-M - 1919/07/14:5e
WEITZMANN, Samuel, (Weissmann?) 50, wife Sara, son-in-law David Kignor & daughter Beatrice, on farm near New Brunswick,NJ - 1915/11/28:1g, 1 Dec:6b, 2:2d, 30:6c
WELBERG, Gustav, 29, NYC-B – 1907/03/03:9f
WELD, Theodore, 92,abolitionist,+ Hyde Park,MA – 1895/02/05:3g
WELDON, Thomas, 30, steelworker, Homestead, PA – 1892/07/08:1a
WELDT, Minnie, 22, laundress, NYC-M - 1894/05/31:1g
WELKE, Erno, 16, NYC-B – 1905/05/22:4a
WELKE, Hugo, un. cigarmaker, SP, NYC-B – 1911/08/12:6a
WELKER, Henry A., NYC-M – 1880/06/22:1f
WELKER, Jacob, NYC-M – 1910/08/20:6a
WELKERWITZ, Edward, infant, NYC-B – 1908/08/06:2a
WELLACHER, John, 6, + 17 Apr, NYC-M, inquest – 1882/05/24:4c
WELLENBRINK, Marie A., 51, NYC-Q – 1912/10/31:6a
WELLER, Emil, 23, NYC-M – 1909/09/27:6a
WELLER, Friedrich, un. carp., NYC-M - 1916/01/11:6a

WELLER, Hermann, ATB Kirchberg/Sax., War 1 - 1914/11/01:3b
WELLER, Marie, child, NYC-M - 1887/04/11:3d
WELLER, Philipp, 50, cigarmaker, NYC? - 1896/07/13:1f
WELLES, Leonard, ex-Police Commissar, NYC-B - 1898/02/21:1f
WELLMANN % Bruns
WELLS, William, ex-US general, NYC-M - 1892/05/01:4d
WELSCHER, George, NYC-B - 1903/01/04:5a
WELTER, Elizabeth, 67, NYC-M, + @ Genl Slocum - 1904/06/18:3d
WELTMAN, Th., peddler, NYC-B - 1908/11/09:1g
WELTZ, Louis, machinist, *8 Aug 1865 Hannover/Gy, NYC-M - 1908/06/28:7g
WELZ % Ramm
WELZ, George, NYC-M - 1910/06/02:6a
WEMPNER, Louis, NYC-B - 1908/01/25:6a
WEMSEN, William, NYC-Q - 1915/04/07:6a
WENDEBORN, Carl, fr Schleswig-Holstein?, NYC-M - 1880/08/08:8a
WENDEL % Bartholdi
WENDEL, August, 74, Hoboken, NJ - 1907/02/16:6a
WENDEL, Charles, 48, carp., NYC-M - 1893/11/20:1e, 22:4c
WENDEL, Christian, 72, NYC-M - 1885/02/15:5g
WENDEL, Elize, 49, NYC-M - 1910/09/03:6a
WENDEL, George, 25, SLP, NYC-B - 1882/04/22:1g, 3b, 24:1f
WENDEL, Maria, b. Stockmann, 64, NYC-M - 1881/06/06:3b
WENDEL, William, 55, baker, NYC-M - 1897/07/11:1h
WENDELING, Otto, 50, worker, Union, NJ - 1891/02/17:2f
WENDELSTEIN, Henriette, NYC-Evergreen - 1897/02/25:4a
WENDEN, VON DER % Florence
WENDEROTH, John, 65, piano worker, NYC-M - 1890/06/20:4e
WENDEROTH, Marie, NYC-M - 1916/03/21:6a
WENDESTORF, Henry, NYPD, NYC-B - 1897/06/28:3d-e
WENDING, Ferdinand, 54, carpenter, * Gy, NYC-M 1895/04/22:1g
WENDISCH % Schmitz
WENDISCH, Auguste, b. Kootboth, NYC-M? - 1913/06/09:6a
WENDISCH, Max, 40, bartender, NYC-M - 1911/07/14:2c
WENDLANDT, Erich, SPD Magdeburg, ex-ed. Breslauer Volkswacht - 1910/05/01:3b
WENDLANDT, Paul, NYC-M - 1902/11/18:1g
WENDLER % Hohmann
WENDLER, Heinrich, striking worker, + Nuernberg/Gy - 1907/11/07:3a
WENDLING, Margarethe, NYC-M - 1891/03/31:4a
WENDNAGEL, Gustav, Richmond Hill, S.I. - 1920/11/24:6a
WENDORF + on May 1, inquest - 1904/09/14:1e

WENDRICH, Gretchen, NYC-M – 1900/09/29:1g, & 19 Oct:2h
WENDT % Kamps
WENDT, Anna, b. Loehman, 39, NYC-M – 1890/10/15:4a
WENDT, Friedrich, 39, NYC-M – 1890/03/21:4a
WENDT, John, un. carp., NYC-M? - 1915/12/06:3g,6a
WENDT, W., Jersey City, NJ - 1918/10/17:6a
WENDTLAND, Franz, musician & journalist, & his family, Hoboken, NJ – 1890/07/04:2g, 6:4g, 8:4d
WENDTLAND, Martha, NYC-M – 1904/09/20:4a; mem. 1905/09/17:5b; 1907/09/19:6a; 1908/09/18:6a; 1914/09/18:6a
WENGENMAYER, Peter, 52, typesetter, SPD Munich – 1908/02/09:3a
WENGER, Markus, NYC-M – 1883/01/27:8a
WENGERT, Paul, NYC-Q - 1915/07/10:6a
WENGLER, Joseph, 29, NYC-M – 1891/08/08:4a
WENICKER, Annie, 42, NYC-M – 1880/06/17:1g, 18:4e
WENIGMANN, Franz Joseph, NYC-M – 1890/07/10:4a
WENINGER, Friedrich, 52, SPO, at Neues Wiener Tageblatt - 1914/11/29:3d
WENK, Susanna, NYC-B - 1916/01/09:1d
WENKE, George's wife, 46, & daughter Mildred, 9, Elizabeth, NJ – 1909/05/14:1e, 15:3c
WENNEMACHER, Frederick & Peter, NYC-M – 1911/04/09:7b
WENNERHOLM, Frank, 27, exec. Auburn, NY – 1901/07/17:3c
WENNICK, Andrew, NYC-M – 1891/06/24:4a
WENTZ, Frederick, innkeep, NYC-B – 1900/08/10:2h
WENTZ, Minnie K., ~20, NYC-M – 1910/06/14:1e, 13:2d
WENTZEL, Amalia, NYC-B - 1917/12/24:6a
WENTZLAFF, Paul, innkeep, Hoboken, NJ – 1919/09/03:2f, 4:2a
WENTZLER, August, NYC-Q - 1920/01/20.8a
WENZ % Harter
WENZ, A.'s wife, West Hoboken, NJ – 1903/10/18:5a
WENZ, Charles, 40, un. machinist, NYC-M - 1896/03/10:4a
WENZ, Charles's wife, NYC-M, + @Genl Slocum – 1904/06/17:3c
WENZ, Erasmus, 36, fr Gross-Rinderfeld/Bavaria, Jersey City, NJ – 1893/02/06:4a
WENZ, George, 11, NYC-M, + @ Genl Slocum – 1904/06/18:3c, 3d
WENZ, Julia, 33,& Anna,14, May,12,NYC-M - 1915/10/18:1e,19:6a
WENZ, Mathilde, 51, Jersey City Heights, NJ - 1918/10/25:6a
WENZ, Reinhardt, 40, NYC-B – 1888/01/14:3a
WENZBACH, F., NYC-M – 1893/04/02:5a
WENZEL, Anna, 63, NYC-B – 1896/08/27:4b

WENZEL, Carl, SP, wine dealer & restaurant, fr Thueringen, NYC-M – 1911/05/24:2e
WENZEL, Christine, 76, NYC-B – 1904/05/03:4a
WENZEL, Hartman, 65, NYC-B – 1906/08/07:1e, 8:3a-b
WENZEL, John, NYC-B, exec. Ossining, NY – 1907/11/18:1f, done 19:2a
WENZEL, L., Bayonne, NJ - 1913/12/20:6a
WENZEL, Ottilie H., NYC-M – 1891/03/27:4a
WENZEL, Peter, 55, un. cigar maker, NYC-M – 1891/04/21:4a, 22:4a
WENZEL, Stephan, 58, un. pipemaker, SP, ex-NYC-B, + Los Angeles, CA – 1911/07/20:2c
WENZELBERG, Christoph, 67, un. tailor, NYC-M – 1890/02/26:4a
WENZLER, Gustav, NYC-M – 1897/07/03:4a
WEPNER, Hermann, un. cigarmaker, NYC-B – 1893/12/04:4a
WERDERMANN, Charles, 50, NYC-B – 1909/07/08:6a
WERDERMANN, John A.T., 69, un. tailor, NYC-B - 1894/07/31:4a
WERDMAN, Caroline, 45, NYC-M, + @ Genl Slocum – 1904/06/17:3c
WERFELMANN, Wilhelm Heinrich, NYC-M – 1907/02/07:6a
WERGIN, August, 38, un. carp., SP?, NYC-M – 1901/08/03:4a, fam. 7:4a
WERLE, Anna Marie, 71, NYC-B – 1892/07/25:4a
WERLE, Henry, NYC-B - 1920/03/13:8a, 14:12a
WERLE, Joseph, West New York, NJ - 1916/07/31:6a
WERMUTH, Anna, '48er, then laundress for Emperor, + Vienna – 1909/01/17:20c
WERNBERG, Mary Jane, NYC-M – 1899/12/02:1g, 3:5d
WERNECKE, Franz, NYC-M – 1885/02/11:3b
WERNER % Weiss
WERNER, A., NYC-M - 1914/06/09:6a
WERNER, Alexander, NYC-M - 1918/02/15:6a
WERNER, Alfred, SP, un. brewer, * 26 Jan. 1874 Zwickau/Sax., Newark, NJ - 1914/05/29:2d
WERNER, Andreas, 70, Swiss, NYC-M – 1885/10/16:1g, 17:1f
WERNER, Anton, 58, un. cigarmaker, Hoboken, NJ – 1897/11/17:4a
WERNER, Bernhard, 51, worker, NYC-M – 1889/07/07:5d
WERNER, Christian, Elizabeth, NJ – 1906/07/17:6a
WERNER, Dominian, un. baker, fr Steiermark?, NYC-M - 1918/01/11:6a, 12:6a
WERNER, Elisa, 54, NYC-M – 1891/09/25:4a
WERNER, Fr., 70, worker, Hoboken, NJ – 1889/04/19:2f
WERNER, Franz, 57, wood cutter, NYC-M – 1908/02/05:2c, 6:6a, 7:6a, fam. 9:7a, 10:6a
WERNER, Friedrich, 42, NYC-M – 1891/07/18:4a
WERNER, Friedrich, 53, NYC-Q – 1912/04/04:6a

WERNER, G., NYC-M – 1884/07/15:4d
WERNER, Gabriele E., 49, son Ansel, 23, grandchild Yvonne, 2, NYC-M? – 1912/06/05:1e
WERNER, Georg, un. carp., NYC-M – 1907/03/26:6a
WERNER, Gustav, got married, NYC-B – 1898/05/01:4a
WERNER, Heinrich, 42, un. carp., NYC-M – 1900/02/18:5a, 20:4c, 27:3d
WERNER, Hermann, 40, RR employee & hero, NYC-B - 1917/06/18:6a
WERNER, Isidor, NYC-M – 1907/06/14:6a
WERNER, Jacob, 50, brewer, NYC-M - 1914/10/02:6c
WERNER, Jakob, un. carp., NYC-M – 1903/10/23:4a
WERNER, Johanna, 42, Hoboken, NJ – 1898/07/15:4a
WERNER, John, cigarmaker, NYC - 1913/11/26:2d
WERNER, John, NYC-B – 1908/02/12:6a
WERNER, John, NYC-M – 1896/06/17:4a
WERNER, Joseph, & his son, = Bay Cemetery, near Bayonne, NJ – 1886/07/09:2g
WERNER, Joseph, NYC-M – 1891/07/31:4a
WERNER, Joseph, un. baker, NYC-Bx – 1912/08/30:6a
WERNER, Katie, 19, NYC-M - 1894/03/27:4a
WERNER, Katie, NYC-M – 1900/02/15:4a
WERNER, Louis, NYC-Q - 1914/05/12:6a
WERNER, Louise, NYC-B – 1908/05/01:6a, 2:6a
WERNER, M., NYC-B – 1908/03/24:6a
WERNER, Martin, cooper, NYC-M – 1913/03/05:6a
WERNER, Rosa, & daughter Ruth Woodyard, 19, Rutherford, NJ - 1918/02/16:6b
WERNER, Rose, NYC-M – 1897/01/10:5f
WERNET, Franz, NYC-Bx - 1920/06/04:6a
WERNICKE, Lina, 15, worker fr Russia, NYC-B – 1893/05/15:1c, 16:2d
WERNINGER, Hermann, worker, NYC-M – 1887/05/21:3a, trial of alleged killer 20 Sept:4d, 21:2f, 22:1g, not guilty 23:4a
WERNZ, Annie, 22, NYC-M, + @ Genl Slocum – 1904/06/21:1f
WERPUPP, Ella, 19, Newark, NJ – 1903/02/20:1c, =21:1c, 23:3b
WERSELMANN, Johnnie, 5, NYC – 1913/01/05:7a
WERSHING, Simon, 82, NYC-M – 1892/07/29:4a
WERSING, William, 42, butcher, USA 1860s, NYC – 1881/01/15:1f
WERTER, Ellen, 15, Newark, NJ - 1916/01/03:6a
WERTHEIM, Harry, 27, NYC-M – 1891/04/02:4a
WERTHEIM, Leopold, 70, oil dealer, NYC-M – 1892/02/16:1h
WERTHEIM, Leopold, dry goods merchant, NYC-M – 1903/04/29:1f
WERTHEIMER, baby, NYC-B – 1892/05/08:1h, 10:2d, 13:2f
WERTHEIMER, Dorothea, NYC-M – 1890/10/18:4a

WERTHEIMER, Louis, 42, NYC-B – 1889/09/29:5b
WERTHEIMER, Max, 78, NYC-B – 1892/07/12:4a
WERTHER, Edward, NYC-B – 1898/09/06:1c
WERTHMULLER, Bertha, 51, NYC-Q – 1919/11/15:6a
WERZINGER, John, SP, Waterbury, CT – 1912/07/03:2f
WESCHE, Otto, 13, NYC-M - 1894/07/28:4a
WESCHE, Sophie, 67, NYC-Q - 1920/12/08:6a, 9:6a
WESEL, Isaac, 1, NYC-M - 1878/01/28:3d
WESEL, Johanna, 26, NYC-M – 1891/07/22:4a
WESEL, Martin, NYC-M – 1881/09/11:8a
WESEL, Pauline, NYC-M – 1888/08/13:3a
WESEL, William, 19, NYC-M – 1888/03/10:3a
WESELOWSKI, comrade, 39, SPD Koenigsberg/Gy, alderman, War 1 - 1915/08/29:3a
WESELY, Rudolph, NYC-B - 1917/02/12:6a
WESEMANN, William, NYC-M – 1900/12/13:4a
WESENACK, Pauline, b. Koenig, 63, Hoboken, NJ - 1913/12/10:6a
WESENDONK, Hugo, 83, *Elberfeld/Gy, member 1848 Frankfurt Parl., here fdr German Life Ins., NYC-M – 1900/12/21:1g
WESER, Christine Juliane, b. Salgmanns, NYC-M – 1887/04/14:3c
WESS, Gustav, 56, SLP?, NYC-B – 1897/09/19:5a
WESS, Johanna, NYC-Bx – 1909/02/14:7c
WESSEL % Weber
WESSLER, Joseph, un. moulder, Newark, NJ – 1914/06/23:6a, fam. 28:7c
WEST, James, Negro, lynched Shelbyville, KY – 1911/01/16:1d
WESTCAMP, Lillian, NYC-M - 1916/08/23:1d
WESTENBERG, David, NYC-M – 1908/12/12:6a
WESTENBURGER, Wendolin, Jersey City, NJ - 1894/02/06:4a
WESTER, Charlotte, Newark, NJ - 1919/05/22:6a
WESTERBECKS, Eduard, 49, West Sayville, LI - 1913/08/02:1b
WESTERMANN % Faulhaber; WESTERVELT % Graewe
WESTERVELT, Walter W., teacher, NYC-Bx - 1916/05/24:2a
WESTFALL, William, ?NYC-Q – 1908/02/22:6a
WESTHOVEN, Hugo von, 52, *Erfurt/Gy, USA 1873, SDP, ex-Prussian ofcs, here worker, NYC-M – 1900/12/15:3b, 4a, 16:5a, =17:1h
WESTINGHOUSE, George, 68, US industrialist, NYC-M - 1914/03/13:2c
WESTLEY, Jim, Negro, lynched Hempstead, TX – 1902/10/22:3c
WESTPHAL, Carl, un. cigarmaker, NYC-M – 1908/05/15:6a
WESTPHAL, Henry, NYC-M – 1906/02/12:4a
WESTPHAL, Joseph, 32, NYC-M – 1893/03/29:4a
WESTPHAL, Karl, NYC-M – 1903/08/24:4a, 25:4a
WESTRUM, Maggie, NYC-M – 1890/03/07:4a

WETEKAMP, A., cigarmaker, NYC-M - 1895/01/14:4a
WETJEN, Henry, 56, NYC-B - 1903/02/14:4a
WETSTEIN, Jakob, 61, merchant, '48er, * Krakau/Austrian Poland, NYC-M - 1888/07/06:1f
WETTERAU, Katharina, b. Schlude, Elizabethport, NJ - 1883/05/01:3c
WETTERAUER, Florence, 22, NYC-M - 1915/12/04:2b
WETTERER, Alphons, brewery owner, + Cincinatti, OH - 1916/10/06:1b
WETTERHAHN, Elizabeth, NYC-Bx - 1916/01/09:7a, mem. 1917/01/07:7a, 1918/01/07:6a
WETTERHAHN, John W., 67,un. carp.,Newark, NJ - 1919/03/09:6a
WETTEROTH, Mary, 65, Newark, NJ - 1901/07/04:3b
WETTSTEIN, Henry, un. painter, Swiss?, NYC-M - 1905/02/13:4a, 14:4a, fam. 19:5b
WETZ, Anna, b. Mittelstedt, NYC-B - 1904/11/07:4a
WETZEL, Amanda, NYC-M - 1903/05/26:4a
WETZEL, Caroline, NYC-M - 1909/03/11:6a
WETZEL, Charles O., 60, War 2, NYC-Q - 1914/09/14:1f
WETZEL, Emil, un. carp., NYC-M - 1913/04/14:6a
WETZEL, Frances, b. Conner, 27, NYC-M - 1885/04/04:3c, = in Milwaukee
WETZEL, George, un. carp., Englewood, NJ - 1909/10/22:6a
WETZEL, Hermann, 22, NYC-M? - 1912/09/05:6a
WETZEL, John, 29, un. carp., NYC-B - 1914/03/0X:6a, 10:6a
WETZEL, Leo, 48, un. carp., NYC-M - 1911/01/29:7b, =30:6a, fam. 1 Fb:6a
WETZEL, Louis, grocer, NYC-M - 1903/10/03:3f, =5:1g
WETZEL, Maurice, NYC-B - 1904/04/27:4a
WETZEL, Philip, NYC-M - 1903/11/02:4a
WETZELSBERGER, Heinrich, un. carp., NYC-M - 1888/08/02:3b
WETZLER, Valentin, NYC-M - 1918/08/22:6a
WETZSTEIN, John, NYC-B - 1898/12/09:4a
WEWER, Caroline, b. Petring, 56, @1883 School House Fire, NYC-M
WEWER, Engelberth, un. tailor, NYC-M - 1891/09/19:4a, 22:4a
WEY % Seubert
WEYAND, Leonard, NYC-M - 1910/07/14:6a
WEYER, Frederick's wife, 36, Esther, Marie, Carrie, 9, NYC-M, +@Genl Slocum - 1904/06/18:3d, 22:1d, 25:1d
WEYGAND, Emilie, b. Bossert, 20, Hoboken, NJ - 1891/04/06:4a
WEYGAND, Emrich, NYC-M - 1889/05/09:4a
WEYGANDT, August, 40, painter, W. Hoboken, NJ - 1899/09/28:4a
WEYH, Herman, cigarmaker, NYC-M - 1900/05/17:3d

WEYHRAUCH, Charles, 63, Jersey City, NJ - 1917/04/17:6a
WEYHRAUCH, Charlotte, 9, NYC - 1912/12/08:7a
WEYRAUCH, Pauline, NYC-B - 1896/06/01:4a, fam. 3:4a
WEYRICH, Carl, 83, NYC-M - 1894/01/31:4a
WEYRICH, Ferdinand C., 79, oyster dealer, *Frankfurt/Main, NYC-M - 1906/02/07:3f
WEZEL, Hans, ATB Munich/Bav., War 1 - 1914/11/01:3b
WHEELER, Ruth, 15, stenographer, NYC - 1910/03/28:1e, 1 Apr:1e, 2b-c, 2:3d, 3:6b-c, 5:1c, murderer insane 5:1c, 21:1c,2c, 22:1c, 23:1a-b, 24:1c, 28:1g,
WHIMPLEBERG, Samuel, Dr., NYC-M - 1907/07/13:3e
WHITE, Alexander, un. painter, NYC-M - 1918/12/01:12a
WHITE, Andrew D., 85, ex-US Ambassador to Germany, Ithaca, NY - 1918/11/05:2e
WHITE, Thomas J., NYC-M - 1907/08/03:6a
WHITEHEAD, Louis, Negro, lynched Boyan, TX - 1896/06/12:1b
WHITEHEAD, Meyer, 80, NYC-M - 1890/05/23:4a
WHITMAN, Anna, 62, NYC-M, + @ Genl Slocum - 1904/06/17:3c
WHITNEY, Albert O., importer, War 2, NYC-M - 1915/08/17:2e
WHITRIDGE, Frederick Wallingford, pres. Third Avenue Tramway, NYC-M - 1916/12/31:11c, =3 Ja.17:4c
WICH, Jacob, 51, NYC-M - 1917/05/27:7a
WICH, Wilhelm, 52, brewer, NYC-M - 1917/12/28:6a
WICH, William, 32, lampmaker, NYC-B - 1906/05/03:4b
WICHMAN, Frank,75, Jersey City Heights, NJ - 1896/08/06:4c
WICHMAN, Henry, un. baker, NYC-M - 1919/01/02:6a
WICHMANN % Porth, % Raffa
WICHMANN, Albert, NYC-M - 1906/10/15:6a
WICHMANN, Mrs, 44, NYC-M - 1902/06/10:4a
WICHSER, Friedrich, NYC-M - 1891/07/09:4a
WICHT, Frederick, 30, NYC-M - 1891/04/11:4a
WICHT, Louis, + Newark, NJ, 13 Mr, murd. rec 10 yrs - 1900/04/29:5g
WICHTERICHT, Wilhelm, city official in Cologne/Gy, USA 1859, here city street sweeper, NYC-B - 1879/11/27:1f
WICK, Fritz, NYC-M - 1893/01/14:4a
WICKE, George, NYC-M - 1889/02/15:1g
WICKE, William, 74, textile manuf., NYC, + Lawrence, LI - 1912/12/03:2b
WICKENHAUSEN, John, 23, NYC-M - 1880/06/29:1c
WICKER, Charles, NYC-M, +@ on Genl Slocum - 1904/06/18:3d
WICKERSHEIMER, Philipp, NYC-M - 1910/03/25:6a

WICKERT, Gertrude, b. Preusschoff, 23, NYC – 1912/04/08:6a
WICKHORST % Herrlein
WICKMANN, Augusta, 70, Irvington, NJ – 1903/10/03:3c
WICKS, Emma, 22, NYC-M – 1891/07/23:4a
WIDDER, Paul, NYC-B - 1916/11/06:6a
WIDEMAN, Oliver's wife, lynched Troy, SC – 1902/12/28:1a
WIDMAN, Frieda, widow of a wealthy importer, pres. Germania Club Hilfsverein, NYC-B - 1920/01/10:2d
WIDMAN, Maria, NYC-B – 1911/09/02:6a
WIDMAN, Wilhelm, 35,un. brewer, SP, NYC-B – 1902/07/21:4a, 23:4a-b
WIDMANN, Bernhard, NYC-M - 1916/06/02:6a
WIDMANN, Caroline, Yonkers, NY – 1907/04/10:6a
WIDMER, Jacob, gunsmith, Newark, NJ – 1881/08/30:4c
WIDMER, Samuel, 35, fr Canton Aargau/Switz., surgical instr. maker, NYC-M – 1885/10/02:1g
WIEBER, Gustav, un. machinist, NYC-B - 1914/01/31:6a
WIECH, Nellie, 29, Hoboken, NJ - 1917/10/29:2d
WIECKLER, John, NYC-M – 1902/07/10:4a
WIEDE, Alwin, 67, NYC-Q - 1919/02/02:6a
WIEDEMANN, Bertha, NYC-M – 1899/09/22:4a
WIEDEMANN, F. M. G., Dr., NYC-M – 1892/06/22:4a
WIEDEMANN, George B., NYC-M – 1890/11/30:5c
WIEDEMANN, Paul, NYC-M - 1916/08/20:7a
WIEDEMEYER, Frederick C. see Wedemeyer
WIEDERHOLD, Karl F., NYC-M – 1891/07/17:4a
WIEDERHOLD, B.'s wife, Hamburg, Iowa, innkeep's wife, + by Prohibitionists – 1886/04/24:3a-b
WIEDMAYER, Gottlieb Karl, NYC-M – 1890/07/14:4a
WIEDMER, Emil, NYC-Q – 1907/09/17:3b
WIEDNER, A.M., Aug. 1893, note 1893/11/17:4e
WIEGAND, Emil, NYC-M - 1894/01/21:5d
WIEGAND, Friedrich, NYC-M - 1878/03/30:3b,4d, 4 April:4e
WIEGAND, Harriett, fr Copenhaguen/DK, NYC – 1896/09/28:1a,29:1d
WIEGAND, J., 51, NYC-B - 1914/09/22:6a
WIEGAND, Jacob, 53, un. beer driver, NYC-Bx - 1917/07/14:6a
WIEGEL, Johann, 79, NYC-B – 1892/06/18:4a
WIEGEMANN, Christian, 62, un. cigarmaker, NYC-M - 1915/09/03:6a
WIEGNER, George, NYC-B – 1892/08/14:5c
WIEHN, Christian, ~60, worker, NYC-M – 1880/09/08:1e
WIEHN, Henry, un. piano maker, SLP, NYC-Bx – 1886/04/24:3b
WIEL, Adolf, un. machinist, NYC-B - 1914/08/25:6a
WIELAND, Georg, 52, NYC-Q - 1918/03/01:6a

WIELAND, Jakob, NYC-M – 1890/08/02:4a, fam. 29:4a
WIELAND, M., un. carp., NYC-B – 1908/03/10:6a
WIELAND, Martin, un. carp., NYC-M – 1911/02/26:7c
WIELAND, Otto, NYC-M - 1918/07/19:6a
WIEMANN, Friedrich, 74, NYC-M - 1918/07/26:6a
WIEMANN, Louis, un. cigarmaker, NYC-M – 1887/07/01:4e
WIENER, Isaac, brass worker, NYC-B – 1903/11/16:1g
WIENER, Rosa, 23, notes on her murder – 1909/01/02:3b
WIENGER, John, infant, NYC-M – 1901/07/03:1d
WIERNCAS, John, 16, NYC-Q - 1913/06/29:11a
WIERTELARZ, Alex, 50, printer, SPD Erfurt/Gy – 1912/04/07:3a
WIERTZ, William, machinist, NYC-M – 1909/12/16:6a
WIES, John, 49, NYC-M – 1886/12/16:3b
WIESE, Bertha, 19, servant, NYC-M – 1880/10/05:1e
WIESE, Caroline, 50, NYC-M, +@ Genl Slocum – 1904/06/17:3c
WIESELMAYER, Elisabeth, 34, Jersey City Heights, NJ – 1903/0408:6a
WIESELMAYER, Friedrich, 20, Hoboken, NJ - 1918/05/21:6a
WIESELMAYER, Louise, 24, Hoboken, NJ - 1919/03/14:6a
WIESENECKER, Martin, 68, NYC-B – 1892/08/16:4a
WIESER, Carl, un. machinist, NYC-M – 1911/05/31:6a
WIESER, William, un. typesetter, NYC-B – 1904/03/08:4a
WIESINGER, Franz, 66, un. printer, NYC-B - 1920/06/04:6a
WIESKUS, Clemens, un. machinist, NYC-Bx – 1906/01/23:4a, 24:4a
WIESMANN, Jacob, 52, un. beer driver, NYC-M – 1888/03/20:3a
WIESMER, August, un. carp., NYC-M – 1885/12/03:4b
WIESNER, August, un. carp., NYC-M – 1891/09/21:4a
WIESNER, Eduard, 1st German inhab. Of Milwaukee, his 85th birthday, *
 Leipzig – 1885/07/15:2f
WIESNER, Elise, NYC-M – 1899/07/22:4a, fam. 24:4a
WIESS, Samuel, NYC-M, +@ Genl Slocum – 1904/06/18:3d
WIESSMANN, August, un. carp., NYC-M – 1885/08/15:3d
WIGAND, Otto, 61, West Mt Vernon, NY – 1890/11/30:5c
WIGANT, John, 55, Newark, NJ – 1901/07/04:3b
WIGGER, Bernhard, 14, baker-boy, NYC-M - 1918/04/20:2a
WIJUKER, Susman, un.cigarmaker, NYC-M - 1917/12/01:6a,fam.7:6a
WILBUSCHEWITSCH, Russian revol., + Paris Jan. 26 – 1907/02/16:4d-e
WILCKE, Franz Georg von, 48, USA 1907, brother is in Dresden, +
 Demarest, NJ – 1911/02/25:1d
WILCKENS, Auguste, NYC-M – 1903/07/10:4a, 11:4a
WILCKES, Ferdinand, 65, piano tuner, NYC-B – 1896/12/15:4c
WILCOX, George, mayor of Summit, NJ – 1907/03/21:3e
WILD, Annie, 30, Elizabeth, NJ – 1892/07/08:4f

WILD, Anton, 41, NYC-M – 1896/07/25:4a
WILD, Konrad, un. butcher, NYC-B - 1919/03/11:6a
WILDE, Oscar, English poet – 1900/12/01:1b
WILDE, William, 65, NYC-B – 1881/09/24:3b
WILDENHAIN, Hermann, NYC-Q – 1898/05/10:4a
WILDEROTER, Peter, 48, NYC-B - 1894/01/26:4a
WILDERS, Wilhelm, 48, un. cornice-maker, NYC-M – 1888/04/10:3a
WILDHABER, Otto, un. typesetter, NYC-Bx – 1907/07/12:6a
WILDHAGEN, William, 63, NYC-B - 1917/07/09:6a, fam. 12:6a
WILDING, Frederick, 65, NYC-B – 1912/10/25:3b
WILHELM, Christopher, 50, NYC-Bx - 1916/09/18:2e
WILHELM, Conrad, 74, NYC-Q - 1916/09/20:6c
WILHELM, Eugen, NYC-B – 1919/09/25:6a
WILHELM, Frank, 47, Justice of the Peace & builder, Newark, NJ –
  1909/02/03:1e, 4:2e, 5:2d, 7:1d, 26:3d, 27:2c, 28:7f, 10 Mr:2d, 11:3b,
  19:3c. Mrs on trial 11 Nov:3b, 1 Dc:3a, 7:1f, 8:1b, 20 yrs 25:1f
WILHELM, Heinrich, NYC-M – 1891/07/15:4a
WILHELM, Jacob, NYC-M – 1892/06/24:4a
WILHELM, Jakob, 60, NYC-B – 1903/10/22:4a
WILHELM, John, 52, building manager, NYC-M – 1889/05/11:1e
WILHELM, Katherina, b. Bartholomaeus, 62, NYC-M – 1891/08/11:4a
WILHELM, W., Hoboken, NJ - 1916/11/02:6a
WILHELMSON, Agnes, 25, Swede, NYC-B – 1898/09/09:4a
WILINSKY, Markus, NYC-M – 1891/03/16:4a
WILKE % Gruetter
WILKE, August, 43, mason, NYC-M – 1880/11/09:1e
WILKE, B. bookbinder, kids still in Berlin, NYC-M – 1885/04/09:1f
WILKE, Bernhard, 63, SP, NYC-M - 1918/10/02:2g,6a, fam.5:6a
WILKE, Charles, NYC-M – 1896/08/23:5b
WILKE, Elise, b. Kauschky, 36, NYC-M – 1899/04/13:4a
WILKE, Helen, 49, NYC-B - 1915/12/22:3e
WILKE, Henry, NYC-M – 1903/02/14:4a
WILKE, Johann, 30, * Rheinrod/Gy, became mad on ship fr Gy (not +) –
  1881/07/20:4b
WILKE, Maria, 48, Guttenberg, NJ – 1896/05/10:5a
WILKE, Max's wife, NYC-M – 1887/04/14:3e
WILKENS, Georg, 62, un. brewer, West Hoboken, NJ – 1910/02/11:6a
WILKENS, Johanna, 28, 1890 fr Hannover/Gy, NYC-M – 1897/12/04:1e
WILKENS, John, ice cream parlor, NYC-M – 1890/03/11:3b
WILKESMANN, Abraham, SP?, Jersey City, NJ – 1912/10/22:6a, fam.
  24:6a
WILKESMANN, Abraham's wife, 72, Englewood, NJ - 1914/08/22:6a

WILKESMANN, Caspar August, NYC-M - 1878/08/15:3d
WILKINS, Walter, Negro, lynched Waycross, GA – 1908/06/29:5f
WILKOMM % Honnings
WILKUS, Fr., Newark, NJ – 1919/12/29:6a
WILL, John, 46, silk weaver, NYC-M - 1894/01/08:3b
WILLARD, William A. P., US aviator, + Boston, MA – 1912/07/02:2b
WILLAREDT, Julius, 38, NYC-M – 1883/04/18:3b
WILLBURG, H. S., 30, drug clerk, NYC-M – 1911/06/11:1g
WILLE, Charles, un. carp., SLP, fr Altona/Gy, USA 1880, NYC-M – 1893/07/28:4a, 29:1d, =30:5c, fam. 1 Aug.:4a
WILLEISEN, Franz, un. carp., NYC – 1889/04/04:4a
WILLEM, Anna M., infant, NYC-M - 1879/07/03:4f
WILLEM, Cornelius F. M., 3, NYC-M – 1886/03/06:4f
WILLEM, Cornelius J.M., 16 mo., NYC-M - 1878/04/10:3b
WILLEM, Magdalena, 18, NYC-M – 1880/03/05:3a
WILLEM, Pauline, Dr.,60, born duchess of Wuerttemberg, SPD, + 21.IV = in Breslau/Gy - 1914/05/15:4f, mem. 1915/06/16:4c
WILLENBACHER, Vienna hangman s. 1867, long obit – 1886/04/15:6b-c
WILLENBUCHER, Josephine, 53, NYC-Q – 1909/07/13:2b
WILLERT, Christian, NYC-M – 1897/12/20:4a
WILLERT, Lisette, NYC-M – 1893/04/02:5a
WILLESCHITZ, Marie, 19, NYC-M - 1916/10/24:6a
WILLHARDT, Adam, NYC-B – 1905/04/22:4a
Willi, (first name only), 2, NYC-M – 1883/10/28:5f
WILLIAMS, Andrew, Negro, lynched Houston, MS – 1913/02/08:5f, 9:1b
WILLIAMS, Arthur, Negro, lynched Wilborn, FL – 1898/11/08:3e
WILLIAMS, Augustus, Negro, lynched Amite City, LA – 1897/01/21:1c
WILLIAMS, Bob, Negro, lynched Williamston, SC – 1881/11/07:1d
WILLIAMS, Cleve, Negro, lynched Hemphill, TX – 1908/06/23:1e
WILLIAMS, Edward, exec. Trenton, NJ – 1900/03/10:4a
WILLIAMS, Ernest & Frank, Negroes, lynched Blanchard, LA - 1913/12/17:1d
WILLIAMS, Ferdinand, SP?, West Rutley,NJ - 1913/12/13:6a
WILLIAMS, Frederick, Negro, lynched Hemphill, TX – 1908/06/23:1e
WILLIAMS, George, exec. Ossining, NY – 1912/07/09:1b
WILLIAMS, James, Oneoye Falls, NY, exec. Albany, NY – 1912/09/17:1f
WILLIAMS, Jean, 46, un. carp., NYC-M – 1887/11/05:2g
WILLIAMS, Joe, exec. Bridgeton, NJ – 1902/11/26:1h
WILLIAMS, John, exec. Pittsburg, PA – 1906/09/07:1b
WILLIAMS, John, Negro, lynched Neaples, TX – 1908/05/08:1d
WILLIAMS, M. E., Negro, lynched Tanyipalion, LA – 1905/11/28:3f
WILLIAMS, Oscar, Negro, lynched Griffin, GA – 1897/07/23:3g

WILLIAMS, Thomas M., un. tailor, NYC-M – 1890/10/22:4a
WILLIAMS, Tom, 18, Negro, lynched Sulphur Springs, TX – 1905/08/12:1c
WILLIBALDT, Albert, 27, painter, NYC-B – 1913/02/02:1f
WILLIE, Heinrich, un. cigar maker, NYC-M – 1886/03/18:3e
WILLIE, Norbert, NYC-B – 1911/12/16:6a
WILLIN, Fritz, cooper?, NYC-M – 1885/05/18:3a
WILLIN, Fritz, cooper?, NYC-M – 1885/05/18:3a
WILLING, Albert J., NYC-B – 1891/04/07:4a
WILLIS, Nathan, Negro, lynched near Town Creek, NC – 1897/11/30:1b
WILLKOMMEN, Hugo, NYC-M – 1908/11/10:6a
WILLMANN, Andreas, 59, ex-county superv. & assessor, * Duchy of Baden, '48er, NYC-M - 1878/03/06:2b
WILLMANN, Wilhelm, 34, ship carpenter, USA 1878, NYC-B - 1879/06/26:4d, 28:4c
WILLMS % Steinen, Von Den
WILLMS, Eduard, 26, Newark, NJ – 1899/04/02:5e
WILLMS, Friedrich A., Newark, NJ – 1901/07/27:4a
WILLMS, Hermann, 13, NYC-M – 1905/02/18:4a
WILLMS, Hermann, Newark, NJ – 1906/05/12:4a
WILLNER, Max Eduard, NYC-M – 1897/12/24:4a
WILLNER, Wilhelm, 31, Guttenberg, NJ – 1892/06/26:5c
WILLS, Gustav, +@ Genl Slocum, NYC-M – 1904/06/19:1d
WILLS, Margaretha, b. Sondermann, 26, NYC-B – 1892/07/01:4a
WILLS, Wilhelmine, un. cigarmkr, NYC-M – 1892/07/12:4a
WILLSTAEDT, Charles, 25, fr Zuerich?/Switz., NYC-M – 1887/07/23:2f
WILM, Therese, Yonkers, NY – 1907/10/01:6a
WILM, William H., 60, also "Klos," + Kingston, NY – 1896/06/26:1e
WILNAU, Hannah, NYC-M, +@ on Genl Slocum – 1904/06/18:3d
WILSER, Franz, Yonkers, NY – 1912/09/07:6a
WILSING, Herman F., 36, brewer, NYC-M – 1889/02/17:5c,e
WILSON, C. C., pres. United Wireless Co., + Atlanta, GA jail – 1912/08/27:1d
WILSON, David, exec. Morristown, NJ – 1897/06/04:1d
WILSON, Douglas, ed. Machinist Jnal, + Washington, DC - 1915/05/08:1e
WILSON, George, exec. Albion, NY – 1888/06/28:4f
WILSON, James, Negro, lynched Danville, IL – 1903/07/27:1a, 2b
WILSON, Louise, b. Rausch, 19, NYC-M – 1889/05/21:1h
WILSON, M., Negro, lynched near Silver City, GA – 1899/03/24:1d, 25:1c
WILSON, William, fr Sweden, shoemaker, NYC-M – 1900/12/06:3d
WILSON, William, Standard Oil employee fr Bayonne, NJ - 1913/05/25:1f

WILTJES, William, ship steward, @1900 dock fire, Hoboken, NJ – 1900/07/03:1c
WILZIG, Paul, un. brewer, NYC-M, missing 1897/06/10:1f, 14:1g
WILZIN, Frank, 40, salesman, NYC-M – 1902/10/19:1g
WIMMEL, H., un. cigar maker, NYC-B – 1896/08/19:4a
WIMMER, Sarah, 20, NYC-B – 1911/07/12:3a
WIMMERT, Adolf, NYC-B - 1916/04/24:6a
WIMMERT, Emma, b. Wohlfahrt, 32, NYC-Bx – 1906/04/01:5a
WIN, Frederick, 22, NYC-M, fr Gy, War 2 (dying) - 1916/01/01:2a
WINANS, Caroline, NYC-M - 1878/02/10:4d
WINARSKY, Laura, b. Horn, 30, NYC-M – 1899/04/09:5a
WINARSKY, Therese, Austrian Socialist, + Vienna – 1900/03/11:9h
WINCHEVSKY, Morris, Jewish soc. & writer, 60th birthday, NYC - 1917/03/26:3e
WINCKEL% Gottman
WINCKEL, Elizabeth, b. Gottman, NYC-Q - 1914/06/06:6a
WINCKEL, William, innkeep, in @1880 Turnhalle Fire, NYC-M – 1880/01/06:1a-c, 3a, 7:2d, 8:1g, 3a, 9:1e-f, Winckel +, too 12:1g, 3a, 14:3a, =15:4c
WIND, Ole Wilhelm, carp., fr Denmark, on ship Trent – 1908/08/06:1f
WINDEKNECHT, William, 44, Hoboken, NJ – 1904/07/11:1a, 12:1f
WINDELING, Katharina, b. Schweigert, 56, NYC-M - 1879/11/18:3c
WINDERL, George, 48, NYC-Bx - 1919/05/10:6a
WINDFUHR, Otto, SP, Jersey City Heights, NJ, celebr 25th Wedding anniv. – 1912/10/11:6c
WINDISCH, Henry, machinist, NYC-M – 1910/01/23:7d
WINDLER, Hermann, carp., Jersey City, NJ – 1892/09/01:2e
WINDMUELLER, edit. Texas Post, + Dallas, TX – 1898/06/07:1e
WINDMUELLER, Louis,78, businessman, NYC-Q - 1913/10/02:2d
WINDOLPH, Dorothea, NYC-M - 1917/05/08:6a
WINDOM, William, ex-US Secy of Treasury – 1891/01/31:1h
WINDSPERGER, Max, 23, bartender, NYC-B – 1905/03/23:3c
WINES, Dr., minister & prison reformer, Irvington, NJ - 1879/12/12:2d
WINFIELD, Charles H., 69, ex-NJ State Senator, Jersey City, NJ – 1898/03/10:4c
WINGENFIELD, Antoinette, b. Jaeger, 27, NYC-M – 1888/09/21:3b
WINGERTNER, Kath., NYC-B – 1891/06/25:4a
WINGES, Ambros, un. bricklayer, NYC-M – 1909/08/24:6a
WINKEL, Adam, NYC-B – 1890/10/08:4a
WINKEL, Carrie, b. Voelke, NYC-B - 1917/07/02:6a
WINKEL, Wilhelm, 52, NYC-M - 1895/02/13:4a
WINKEL, Wilhelmine, b. Zierold, 68, NYC-Q - 1916/11/14:6a

WINKELBACH, Arnold, 53, NYC-B – 1880/03/12:4c, 13:4b, 15:3a
WINKELMANN, Hermann, NYC-M – 1904/11/17:2c,h
WINKELMANN, Moritz, mason, NYC-M - 1913/05/09:2c
WINKELMANN, Robert, un. carp., NYC-Bx – 1908/03/05:6a
WINKER, Paula, b. Dreher, NYC-M – 1909/08/21:6a
WINKLER % Fischer
WINKLER, Amelia, 6, Union Hill, NJ – 1902/02/ 12:4b
WINKLER, Charles, NYC-Q - 1917/09/16:7a
WINKLER, Ernst, un. carp., NYC-M - 1915/05/31:6a
WINKLER, Frank, un. carp., NYC-B – 1900/04/16:4a
WINKLER, Friedrich, 60, NYC-B – 1897/09/24:4a
WINKLER, Johanna, b. Bertram, NYC-Bx – 1910/07/02:6a
WINKLER, John A., un. carp., pres. Local 464, NYC-Bx – 1906/01/13:4a
WINKLER, John, 22, typesetter, Hoboken, NJ - 1913/09/24:2c
WINKLER, John, 29, un. cigarmaker, NYC-M – 1884/08/07:3d
WINKLER, John, NYC-M – 1886/07/30:3a
WINKLER, Josef, 53, SP, un. machinist, * Moensheim/Wuertt., USA 1883, NYC-Bx - 1916/01/13:6a
WINKLER, Joseph, 19, NYC-Bx, + Calico, NJ – 1910/01/26:6a
WINKLER, Th., West Hoboken, NJ - 1915/03/02:6a
WINNEN, Jacob, 76, un. cigarmaker, USA 1878, SP, *Rhineland, New Haven, CT – 1912/11/19:3c,6a
WINSCHER, Benedikt, un. carp., NYC – 1882/09/18:3c
WINSTERER, Carl, 65, German opera singer, + Mt Vernon, NY – 1907/11/07:1f
WINTELER, Just, 50, NYC-M – 1902/11/02:4a
WINTER, Andreas, bridge engineer fr Bavaria, + Planueles/Mexico – 1883/09/20:2f
WINTER, Clara Helen, Jersey City, NJ – 1907/03/27:3c
WINTER, F., NYC-B – 1897/11/08:4a
WINTER, Fritz, Dr. 44, alderman, Vienna/Austria - 1920/02/25:4f-g
WINTER, George, un. brewery worker, NYC-M - 1894/12/20:4a
WINTER, Jakob & Louise, NYC-M – 1893/10/18:1h
WINTER, Jakob, NYC-M – 1913/03/06:6a
WINTER, John, 87, & wife, NYC-B – 1900/07/20:4a
WINTER, John, NYC-M – 1910/05/01:7a
WINTER, Joseph, 79, Guttenberg, NJ – 1903/11/26:3c
WINTER, Katherina, 18, fr Osthofen, Hessen, to USA, notice, (not +) – 1885/11/28:2f
WINTER, Robert, 65, SP, un. machinist, NYC-Q - 1919/05/28:6a, fam. 4 June:6a; mem. 1920/05/26:6a
WINTER, Robert, NYC-Q - 1917/06/14:6a

WINTER, Victor, 70, tailor, then innkeep, SP Wiesa/Bohemia – 1907/11/07:3d-e
WINTER, William, 48, innkeep, NYC-B – 1910/10/17:2d
WINTER, William, 86, Kearney, NJ – 1900/08/30:4a
WINTERB?UE, Louis, NYC?, fam. 1891/06/08:4a
WINTERER, Erasmus, 66, un. carp., NYC-B – 1912/03/13:6a
WINTERHOLLER, Michael, 47, SP, saddlemaker, fr Bavaria, Can. 1911, + Winnipeg - 1920/06/17:2f
WINTERLING, John, West New York, NJ - 1915/06/26:6a
WINTERROLL, Walter, 19, Orange, NJ - 1913/10/07:2e
WINTERS, Friederike, dressmaker, * Ritterhude/Hannover, USA 1892, NYC-M - 1895/10/16: 3e
WINTERSTEIN, Marie, b. Protz, NYC-M – 1904/03/06:5b
WINTSCHUREK, Anton, 32, worker at Doelger's Brewery, NYC-M – 1881/01/07:1a, =8:1e-f, 9:5f, 10:2a-b, 4e, inquest 8 Fb:1f, 9:1e-f, 10:1e-f
WINTZ, Louis, NYC-M – 1900/08/19:5a
WINZEN, Charles, NYC-M – 1888/01/03:3a
WIPPEFAHL, H., NYC-M – 1906/03/06:4a
WIRICK, Joseph, 61, NYC-M - 1913/05/07:6a
WIRREN, John, NYC-M – 1904/04/17:5b
WIRSCHING, Alois, 79, *Vienna, invented ticker tape telegraph, NYC-B – 1910/07/16:5e
WIRSING, George, 61, Oradell, NJ – 1910/09/28:6a
WIRSUM, William, un. carp., NYC-M – 1907/12/17:6a
WIRTH, Charles, 61, rest. owner, Boston, MA - 1916/11/21:2g
WIRTH, Ernst, un. sheet metal worker, NYC-M – 1899/07/25:4a
WIRTH, Herman, 32, SP, West Hoboken, NJ - 1916/08/14:6a, =18:5f
WIRTH, Jacob, Jersey City, NJ - 1917/09/30:7a
WIRTH, John, 54, NYC-Q - 1916/11/19:7a
WIRTH, Maria, b. Oerthel, NYC-M – 1883/10/23:3a
WIRTH, Theodor, 38, NYC-Q – 1898/10/26:4a
WIRTHLE, August, 53, NYC-M – 1893/12/31:5c
WIRTZ, August, 62, weaver, Paterson, NJ – 1910/12/30:6a
WIRTZ, Kasper, Yonkers, NY – 1907/02/09:6a
WIRWAY, Johanna, 38, NYC-M, +@ on Genl Slocum – 1904/06/17:3c
WIRZ, comrade, 43, carp., SP Wintherthur/Swtz. – 1908/05/24:3f
WIRZ, Oswald, 49, architect, NYC-M – 1900/10/25:1d
WISCH % Schneider
WISCH, Carl, 39, architect, NYC-M - 1913/07/01:3e
WISCH, Mathilda, b. Weil, wd Egner, 48, NYC-B – 1888/10/24:3a
WISCHER % Schwarz
WISCHER, Hermann, 50, realtor, NYC-B – 1912/06/15:1e, 16:1c

WISCHWESER, Henry, fr Cleveland, OH, + NYC-M – 1888/06/30:4d
WISE, John, Negro, lynched Pembroke, GA – 1902/07/29:4b
WISEMAN, Sadie, student at NJ Industrial School, Trenton – 1899/10/04:1f, =7:4b
WISHARDT, Gottlieb, NYC-M – 1911/11/18:6a
WISHAUSEN, Anna, 27, mgr Economy Photograph Store, NYC-Bx - 1920/12/10:5g
WISIAK, Mary, Elisabeth, NJ – 1919/11/29:8a
WISLER, Pauline, b. Walsch, 27, NYC-M – 1883/03/10:3c
WISNER, Jessie, 21, @1911 Triangle Shirtwaist Fire, NYC-M – 1911/03/27:1d
WISNIEWSKI, Franz, un. carp., NYC-M – 1902/12/28:5b
WISNIEWSKY, Constantin, 54, NYC-B – 1907/12/11:6a
WISNYOWSKY, Kalman, 28, un. carp., NYC-M – 1885/09/03:3a
WISOLSKY, Sonia, 17, @1911 Triangle Shirtwaist Fire, NYC-M – 1911/03/27:1d
WISSEMANN, Heinrich, USA 1857 fr Saxony, grocer, NYC-M – 1885/03/05:4d
WISSHARDT, Sophia, NYC-M – 1911/04/25:6a
WISSIG % Haas
WISSLER, Jacques, 84, lithographer, fr Elsass, USA 1849, Camden, NJ – 1887/11/28:2c
WISSMANN, Ernst, un. bag maker, NYC-M – 1888/05/02:3a
WISSMANN, Georg, 12, NYC-M – 1905/10/16:4a
WISSMANN, Wilhelm, 60, SDP, un. painter fr Silesia, ed. Neue Deutsche Zeitung, USA ~1882, NYC-B – 1904/12/04:1h, 5:4a, =6:1e, fam. 7:4a
WISSMUELLER, Friedrich, 33, un. baker, NYC-M – 1909/12/09:6a
WISTHUBER, Mathias, 82, NYC-B – 1905/09/15:3d
WISTMEYER, Hermann, baker, War 2, Philadelphia, PA - 1917/02/09:2e
WITCHEN, Anna C., 62, NYC-M - 1895/05/30:1g
WITH, Joseph, 36, NYC-M – 1888/05/12:3a
WITHERS, Bush, Negro, lynched Andalusia, AL – 1910/10/05:1b
WITHERS, Edward Bellamy,4, son of below, NYC-B - 1896/01/01:4a
WITHERS, James Joseph, 33, electrician & labor organizer, SLP, *17 June 1861 Ireland, sick, benefit org., NYC-B – 1893/08/06:1h; + Jy 21, NYC-B - 1894/07/22:5a,e; =1894/07/23:1e; family in need 1895/12/20: 3e
WITNEY, Edwin B., judge who perrsecuted Eugene Debs in 1897, NYC – 1911/01/06:1b, 7:4d
WITSMAN, Margarete, 56, NYC-M – 1904/02/03:4a
WITT, Amandus, NYC-Q - 1916/10/20:6a
WITT, Anna, NYC-B – 1900/04/18:4a
WITT, August, Hoboken, NJ – 1891/09/19:4a

WITT, Joseph, NYC-B – 1912/09/30:6a
WITT, Julius, actor at Germania Theater, NYC?, + San Francisco - 1879/12/15:1c
WITT, William C., Yonkers, NY – 1907/01/13:7b
WITTASEK, Johann, etuimaker & SP Vienna – 1913/01/19:3e
WITTCHEN, Margaretha H., NYC-M – 1891/06/24:4a
WITTCHEN, Margaretha, 2, Newark, NJ – 1905/08/02:4a
WITTCHEN, Susanna, 60,servant,US 1859, NYC-M - 1895/04/02:1e
WITTE, John, 11, NYC-M, +@ Genl Slocum – 1904/06/24:1d
WITTE, Paul, 11, NYC-M – 1888/06/21:1b
WITTE, W., 44, NYC-B – 1891/03/12:4c
WITTEKIND, Elise, 57, NYC-Bx - 1914/12/12:6a, fam. 15:6a
WITTEKIND, Georg, 21, NYC-M – 1909/01/01:6a, fam. 5:6a
WITTEKIND, Marie, 47, NYC-Bx - 1915/03/11:6a
WITTEL % Fels
WITTER, Bernhard H., 31, NYC-B – 1887/01/03:2e
WITTERER, Crescentia, b. Seiter, 75, NYC-B – 1891/08/12:4a
WITTERMAIER, Anton, 78, SPD alderman in Budenhausen/Elsass/Gy – 1913/03/30:3b
WITTGES, Lina, 29, NYC-M – 1898/07/06:4a
WITTHAUS, Christian, ship's steward, his family?,@1900 dock fire, Hoboken, NJ – 1900/07/05:1b
WITTHUSEN, A., 50, hatmaker, NYC-B – 1890/07/26:2c
WITTICH, Bernard, un. carp. NYC-B – 1907/03/25:6a
WITTICH, George, 45, Newark, NJ – 1911/07/10:3a
WITTICH, Manfred, SPD Leipzig, ed. of Leipziger Waehler – 1902/07/25:2e-f, 26:2d
WITTIG, Anton, 50, carp., Newark, NJ – 1893/12/24:5c
WITTIG, Friedrich A., 59, NYC-B – 1912/11/20:6a
WITTIG, Silvester, 56, un. carp., NYC-M – 1886/06/23:3b
WITTKE, Catherina, 10, NYC-B – 1910/01/02:1b
WITTKE, Charles, + 29 Aug., corpse found, Elizabeth, NJ – 1908/09/03:3e
WITTKE, Katharina, NYC-Q - 1915/07/21:6a
WITTKOPF % Fagen
WITTLIEB, John, Westchester, NY - 1916/05/07:7b
WITTMANN, Auguste, 2, NYC-M - 1878/11/17:8b
WITTMANN, Karl, Elisabeth, NJ – 1912/05/03:6a
WITTMANN, Michael, NYC-M – 1903/06/20:4a
WITTMAR, Louis, NYC-M – 1896/05/05:4a
WITTMER, Charles, NYC-M – 1901/08/15:4a
WITTMER, Henry, 17, NYC-M – 1893/11/04:4b
WITTMER, Jacob, 49, un. bricklayer, Guttenberg, NJ – 1907/05/09:6a

WITTMER, Jeanette, 87, NYC-B – 1912/12/03:3a
WITTMER, Sybilla, Guttenberg, NJ - 1919/05/30:6a
WITTMER, Wilhelm, Jersey City Heights, NJ – 1911/12/28:6a
WITTNEBERT, John Kasper, 71, NYC-M - 1894/01/10:4a
WITTNER, Margaret, 65, Jersey City, NJ - 1916/05/22:6b
WITTNER, Otto, Dr., SPO Vienna, War 1 - 1915/07/18:3c-d
WITTORS, Mary, 46, NYC-B – 1892/08/08:4a
WITZ, William, 63, innkeep, NYC-M – 1890/01/13:1h
WITZE, August, 70, NYC-M – 1891/07/31:4a
WITZEL, August, 61, NYC-B - 1910/03/23:6a
WITZEL, Georg, 50, NYC-B – 1899/04/11:4a
WITZEL, Joseph, 78, park operator & hotelier at Point View Island, fr Fulda, USA 1859, NYC-Q - 1913/10/26:1d, 30:2a, 31:2d, will 8 Nov:3b
WITZIG, Paul, NYC-M – 1901/04/23:4a
WITZMANN, Charles, un. carp., NYC-M - 1915/12/28:6a
WITZMANN, George, 42, NYC-M - 1915/09/04:6a
WLASAK, A., Newark, NJ – 1912/05/11:6a
WOBBE, Henry & Marvin, NYC-B, + @Genl Slocum – 1904/06/18:3d
WOCHMEYER, Joseph, 28, shoemaker, Cincinatti, OH – 1912/07/14:1c
WOCK, Matthias, 75, Mt Vernon, NY – 1908/10/02:2b
WODENSCHECK, Josephine, NYC-M – 1889/03/13:4a
WOE, Georg, infant, NYC-M – 1897/08/28:1g
WOEHLER, August, barber, NYC-? - 1879/11/16:1f
WOEHLING, John, 35, NYC-M – 1882/07/19:3c
WOEHLKEN, August E., innkeep, NYC-B – 1904/04/17:1c
WOEHLTE, Johanna, NYC-M – 1892/08/05:4a
WOEHRLE, Rosina, 67, NYC-M – 1891/03/30:4a
WOELFLING % Haudy
WOELKY, ..., waiter & SPD fr Altona/Gy, arrived NYC – 1880/11/30:1d-e, 2 Dec:2a-b, 6:1d-e
WOELKY, Charles, 63, innkeep, ex-painter, fr Berlin, SP?, NYC-M – 1913/04/30:5f
WOELL, Richard, 64, carp., NYC-B – 1903/10/30:4b
WOELNS, Annie, 80, NYC-B - 1920/05/18:6c
WOERFEL, Charlotte, 8, NYC-M, +@ Genl Slocum – 1904/06/28:1c
WOERISHOFER, Carl F., 43, NYC-M – 1886/05/11:3c
WOERLEIN, Hans, 70, SPD Nuernberg - 1914/06/11:4d
WOERMANN, Adolph, German shipping mogul, + Hamburg – 1911/05/05:1a
WOERNER, Minna, 57, servant, Jersey City, NJ – 1912/12/31:3a
WOERNER, Susanna, 52, NYC-M - 1916/05/14:7a

WOERRISHOFFER, Carola, 26, treasurer of WTUL, NYC –
    1912/01/14:20e-f
WOERZ, C. J., NYC-M – 1899/01/10:4a
WOERZ, Ernest G.W., 61, pres. Beadleston & Woerz brewery, NYC-M -
    1916/05/10:2e
WOERZ, Frederick, 56, Elizabeth, NJ - 1916/10/28:6a
WOGATSKY, Heinrich, 58, shoemaker, * Grusen/Stolp, Pomerania, USA
    1881, SP, NYC-M – 1906/09/14:1b,6a, 15:6a, 16:7c, =18:6a, fam. 19:6a
WOGATZKY, Brigitta, b. Ketterl, 39, NYC-M – 1886/10/13:3b
WOHL, Francis, infant, NYC-M – 1892/08/08:4f
WOHL, Joseph, 60, cigarmaker, NYC-M – 1901/04/18:3b
WOHLFAHRT % Doepping; % Wimmert
WOHLFAHRT, Martin, 57, NYC-M - 1918/06/29:6a
WOHLFAHRT, Philip, 82, Central Islip, LI – 1911/01/25:1d
WOHLFAHRT, William, 60, book dealer, NYC-M – 1910/02/13:1f
WOHLFARTH, Herman, 49, Jersey City Heights, NJ – 1891/04/01:4a
WOHLFARTH, Kilian, NYC-Bx - 1917/07/03:6a
WOHLFEIL % Mongk
WOHLFEIL, Julius, 57, un. wood carver, NYC-M – 1893/07/04:4a
WOHLFEIL, Julius, 6, NYC-M – 1889/02/22:4a
WOHLFERT, Eva, 35, NYC-M, + @Genl Slocum – 1904/06/29:1c
WOHLGEMUTH, Urs., NYC-B – 1893/11/21:4a
WOHLGEMUTH, William, NYC-B – 1896/09/07:4a
WOHLLEB, William, Jersey City Heights, NJ – 1908/12/12:6a
WOHLLEBEN, George, un. carp., NYC – 1911/10/12:6a
WOHLMANN, Mrs, West Hoboken, NJ – 1899/08/19:4a
WOHLSCHLEGEL, Ursula, 63, NYC-B – 1908/01/28:6a
WOITINECK, Anna, NYC-Bx - 1920/08/17:6a
WOITINEK, Bertha, + 19 Mr 1915 - 1916/03/19:7a
WOITINEK, Joseph, NYC-M - 1920/03/13:8a
WOITSCHEK, Franz, NYC-M – 1890/11/29:4a, fam. 1 Dec:5a
WOJNAKOWSKA, Wanda Lenzarqua, Polish revol. Writer, +Paris/F –
    1911/05/04:4d
WOLBER, Mary Elisabeth, b. Wiertz, 74, Newark, NJ – 1891/06/06:4a
WOLCOTT, Erastus, Dr., 76, physician, close to socialism, + Milwaukee –
    1880/01/29:2b
WOLDENBERG, Ludwig, Dr., publ. Klinische Wochenschrift, + Berlin –
    1881/05/02:1d
WOLF % Gerner, % Hallstein, % Linn, % Ittler, % Zehner
WOLF, A., carpenter, NYC-M – 1882/09/25:3c
WOLF, Adolf, 48, un. painter, SP, NYC-Bx – 1907/08/25:7c, 26:6a
WOLF, Albert E., 60, un. carp., NYC-Bx – 1912/12/08:7a

WOLF, Alex, 74, NYC-M – 1903/05/10:5a
WOLF, Alexander, Dr. med., 63, * Wuerzburg/Gy, NYC-M –
  1885/03/01:1f
WOLF, Anton, 86, NYC-M – 1893/03/29:4a
WOLF, August, businessman, NYC-M – 1893/07/04:4d
WOLF, August, cooper, NYC-B – 1913/02/13:6a
WOLF, Bertha, 2, NYC-M – 1882/03/25:3b
WOLF, Bruno, 51, cashier, pres. Lyra MGV, Hoboken, NJ – 1907/05/28:3b
WOLF, Carl, 47, NYC-M – 1889/09/17:4a
WOLF, Carrie, 12, NYC-M – 1889/09/15:5b
WOLF, Charles, NYC-B - 1918/02/26:6a
WOLF, Charles, stable supervisor, NYC-B – 1907/05/26:11a
WOLF, Conrad, 28, carp., NYC-M – 1900/07/13:3b
WOLF, David, 19, NYC-B – 1887/12/10:2c
WOLF, Emma, cook, NYC-M – 1891/06/06:2g, 7:1f
WOLF, Ernst, 48, NYC-M – 1905/12/22:4a
WOLF, F. August, 52, SLP, NYC-M – 1893/10/10:4a, 11:4a, fam. 15:5b
WOLF, Francis, 63, realtor, NYC-M – 1912/03/02:3a
WOLF, Frank Eduard, Jersey City, NJ - 1918/03/11:6a
WOLF, Franz, 44, stonecutter, NYC-M – 1889/08/13:4a
WOLF, Frieda, 2, NYC-B, +@ Genl Slocum – 1904/06/23:4a
WOLF, Friedrich, NYC-M – 1890/03/30:5b
WOLF, Friedrich's wife, NYC-M – 1904/07/08:4a
WOLF, George Jr., NYC-M – 1896/04/16:1c, 17:3a
WOLF, George, un. carp., NYC-M – 1887/10/04:4e
WOLF, Gustav, 50, SP, un. silkworker, fr Maehrisch-Truebau/Moravia,
  Union Hill,NJ – 1920/02/09:6a-b, 10:4d,7f-g,8a, =12:2e, fam. 13:6a
WOLF, Gustav, 55, upholsterer, NYC-Bx - 1913/08/06:3f
WOLF, Heinrich, NYC-M – 1885/10/03:3d
WOLF, Henry, 54, German-born, NYC-M - 1878/04/12:4e
WOLF, Henry, NYC – 1912/12/04:6a
WOLF, Hermann, NYC-M - 1917/12/28:2d
WOLF, Jacob, 65, horsedealer, NYC-M – 1902/06/18:4b
WOLF, John, 22, West New York, NJ - 1918/07/02:6a
WOLF, John, goldworker, Newark, NJ – 1887/10/19:2e
WOLF, Julius, stoker, @1900 dock fire, Hoboken, NJ –1900/07/03:1c
WOLFF, Lena, 30, NYC-M – 1900/05/13:1e, 25:3b, murderer tried 19
  Jy:1e, 21:1g, 24:1g
WOLF, Louis, 33, SP?, Elizabeth, NJ - 1918/11/08:6a
WOLF, Louis, NYC-M – 1909/11/27:6a
WOLF, Madeline, NYC-B, + @ Genl Slocum – 1904/06/17:3c
WOLF, Magdalena, b. Hartkorn, NYC-M – 1892/07/10:5c

WOLF, Maria Eva, b. Zimmermann, + 10 07 18, mem 1919/07/10:6a
WOLF, Maria, 52, Union Hill, NJ – 1891/03/09:4a
WOLF, Martin, 46, machinist, NYC-M – 1902/02/22:4a
WOLF, Max, NYC-M - 1917/07/22:7a
WOLF, Maximilian, 45, teacher at Blum Street German-English school, Newark, NJ - 1878/02/17:8d
WOLF, Mrs, NYC-Q - 1918/07/13:6a
WOLF, Nathan, ex-teacher of German, War 2, NYC-Bx - 1919/04/28:1d
WOLF, Oscar, NYC-B – 1910/09/17:6a
WOLF, Peter, Newark, NJ – 1908/10/11:7c
WOLF, Rosa, 47, NYC-M - 1917/08/03:6a
WOLF, William, NYC-Q – 1909/12/23:6a
WOLF, Wolfgang, NYC-B – 1881/07/20:3a
WOLFARTH, Oscar, NYC-M – 1907/01/25:6a
WOLFE, V., Union Hill, NJ - 1918/12/15:12a
WOLFERMANN, Franz, brewer/cooper, NYC-M – 1901/01/
WOLFERMANN, Frederick, 52, brewer, NYC-M – 1892/08/13:4a, 14:5c
WOLFERTZ, Hermann, 63, NYC-B – 1904/11/28:3c
WOLFF, Anna Olga, un. cigarmaker?, NYC-B – 1897/11/30:4a
WOLFF, August, cashier, NYC-M - 1879/07/18:4a
WOLFF, Carl H., son of Hermann Wolff in Germany, + 3 Mr Dover,NJ, crem. remains to Gy - 1913/08/26:2c
WOLFF, Eduard, music teacher + Cincinatti, OH – 1887/01/07:5c-d
WOLFF, Elisabeth, b. Sullivan, ~28, NYC-M – 1888/03/23:1a, 24:3a, 28:1d-e
WOLFF, Emma A., b. Gessner, NYC-M – 1881/07/05:3d
WOLFF, Fanny, NYC-M – 1886/05/18:4a
WOLFF, Ferdinand, Berlin banker, with wife on ship Teuton – 1881/09/22:2f,
WOLFF, Frank, innkeep, Newark, NJ – 1900/12/25:1g
WOLFF, Fritz, 77, NYC-M - 1913/10/28:6a
WOLFF, George E., 37, Westfield, LI – 1912/02/09:3e
WOLFF, Gustav, un. waiter, NYC-M – 1890/07/19:4a
WOLFF, Harry, 20, NYC-Bx – 1907/05/25:6a, 27:6a
WOLFF, Heinrich, 51, un. carp., NYC-M – 1885/03/24:3c
WOLFF, Helena, 56, Jersey City, NJ – 1910/09/17:6a
WOLFF, Joseph, farm laborer, Secaucus, NJ – 1896/12/25:3e
WOLFF, Julius, 24, candymaker, NYC-M – 1893/12/17:1h
WOLFF, Julius, 25, NYC-B, sailor, + on SS Mozart – 1885/08/17:4d
WOLFF, Ludwig, NYC-M – 1907/03/17:7c, fam. 31:7c
WOLFF, Marguerite, 70, NYC-B – 1905/08/25:3a

WOLFF, Otto's wife, NYC-B – 1900/10/01:1h, husband rec 19 yrs 1 Dec:4a, 6:4a
WOLFF, Pauline, NYC?, + Boston, MA – 1909/02/17:6a
WOLFF, Wilhelm, German soc., 1809-1864, on him 1903/09/13:13f, 100th anniv. – 1909/07/04:6c-e, 11:19e-g
WOLFF, William J., 50, resort in Adirondacks, NYC-B – 1909/05/15:3b
WOLFF, William, Jersey City Heights, NJ – 1912/03/03:7b, fam. 6:6a
WOLFFSOHN, Paul, NYC-M – 1912/03/11:6a
WOLFHERZ, Ernst, un. machinist, NYC-B - 1914/03/14:6a
WOLFRAM, C. B., 68, publ. N.Y. Herold (German), * Pomerania, USA 1867, NYC-M - 1916/04/04:1f
WOLFRAM, Christian, peddler, Camden, NJ – 1882/06/16:1g
WOLFRAM, Wilhelm J., 5, NYC-M – 1882/11/12:8a
WOLFSHOLL % Scharf
WOLFSOHN, David, Hamburg/Gy, Zionist - 1914/09/18:2c
WOLFSOHN, Louis, 52, SP Haverhill, MA – 1906/01/14:11a
WOLFSTEIN % Rosenbaum
WOLFSTROEMER, Miklos, 14, Ferrer Sunday School pupil, NYC-M - 1918/06/01:6a, 4:6a
WOLGERING, Frank's wife, 40, & 2 teenage daughters, NYC-M – 1905/04/22:1d
WOLKENSTEIN, Anna, b. Laemchen, 32 or 22, NYC-B – 1891/12/01:4a
WOLKENSTEIN, Emanuel, 36, NYC-M – 1887/06/13:3a, fam. 15:3b
WOLKOW, Sedalia, 36, NYC – 1901/09/18:3b
WOLL, Frieda, 2, NYC-B, +@Genl Slocum – 1904/06/22:1d
WOLLAM, Barbara, 100, fr Wuerttemberg, NYC-M – 1883/08/10:3c
WOLLEMANN, Anton, un. carp., NYC-M – 1913/04/04:6a
WOLLENHAUPT, Carl, 3, NYC-M – 1880/10/12:3b
WOLLENHAUPT, Heinrich, un. baker, NYC – 1912/05/27:6a, 28:6a
WOLLENTER, Friedericka, 34, NYC-B – 1893/12/29:4a
WOLLENWEBER, August, 47, NYC-B – 1910/07/10:1b
WOLLMAN, Sebastian, Elizabeth, NJ – 1910/03/27:7b
WOLLMER, Catherine, 58, NYC-B, +@Genl Slocum – 1904/06/22:1d
WOLLNY, Eduard, reporter for N.Y. NYSZ, NYC-M - 1878/02/15:1g
WOLLSTADT, Rosina, 86, NYC-B - 1917/05/16:5f
WOLLWEBER, Frank, 17, NYC-M – 1896/07/31:1h, = 4 Aug:4e
WOLLWEBER, Karl, 40, Yonkers, NY - 1919/02/28:6a
WOLPERS, Conrad, 71, NYC-M – 1906/04/20:4a
WOLPIN, Isaac, 22, wallet maker & SP, fr Russia, NYC-M – 1903/12/25:1g
WOLTER, Albert W., 20, exec. Ossining, NY – 1912/01/29:1e, 30;1c
WOLTER, John, 43, un. carp., NYC-B – 1885/12/17:2g

WOLTER, Otto, 54, un. theater worker, Union Hill, NJ – 1897/07/20:4a,c, 21:4a
WOLTERS, Adolph, 36, chemical eng., NYC-B - 1914/11/15:11e
WOLTERS, Annie, 28, NYC-M – 1880/03/16:4a
WOLTERS, F., 71, NYC-M - 1894/01/21:5d
WOLTERS, John, NYC-M - 1918/08/23:6a
WOLTMANN, Ludwig, German Anthropologist & SPD member – 1907/03/01:4g
WOLVERKEMMER, William, 56, chemical worker, Glendale,NJ - 1915/05/13:2c
WONDRA, Louise, Yonkers, NY – 1906/07/18:6a
WONDROSCH, Anna, 78, NYC-Q - 1914/04/02:6a
WOOD, Elizabeth Orlopp-, 20, NYC-M – 1909/01/03:1g
WOOD, Fernando, colorful ex-NYC mayor, NYC – 1881/02/15:1e, 2d, 17:4c, 18:2a, =21:1g, will 24:4a
WOOD, Josef, exec. Dannemora, NY – 1892/08/03:1g
WOOD, Joseph, exec. Ossining, NY – 1891/07/03:1g, rev. 14:2e, 16:1h
WOOD, Robert F., to be exec. Albany, NY – 1911/04/15:1w
WOOD, William E., NYC-B – 1879/10/16:3a
WOOD, William MacDonald, infant, NYC-B - 1879/10/16:3a
WOODLE, Moritz, 56, capmaker, NYC-M – 1892/07/14:1f, 15:4a
WOODRUFF, Robert, NYC-Q – 1911/08/25:6a
WOODRUFF, Timothy, lt-gov NYS 1897-1903,+ NYC - 191310/13:1f
WOODS, Walter E., 28, NYC-M, +@Genl Slocum – 1904/06/22:1d
WOODWARD, Paul, exec. Camden, NJ – 1903/01/08:3c
WOOLBEIN, Hulda, 28, NYC-B, +@Genl Slocum – 1904/06/22:1d
WOOLWORTH, Frank W., 69, Dept Store Fdr, Glen Cove, LI - 1919/04/09:2e
WORDEN, Salter T., RR labor organizer, to be exec. in Calif. 11 Fb – 1898/02/01:2a
WORKMAN, Jennie, Jersey City, NJ, +@Genl Slocum – 1904/06/18:3c,3d, =21:1e
WORM, Eva, 41, NYC-M – 1892/07/20:4a
WORM, John P., NYC-M - 1920/07/28:6a
WORM, Karl Hermann, SP?, West Hoboken, NJ – 1908/10/13:6a
WORM, Robert, West Hoboken, NJ – 1908/09/22:6a
WORM, William, un. carp., NYC-B – 1913/02/27:6a
WORMER, VAN, Willis, Burton & Fred, Greendale, NY, exec. Dannemora, NY for + uncle @Peter Hallenbeck on Xmas eve 1901 – 1903/09/28:1f-g, done 2 Oct:1f-g,
WORMS % Mook
WORMS, Molly, b. Meyer, 38, NYC-M – 1892/07/27:4a

WORMS, Robert, 47, amusement park owner, NYC-Q – 1919/11/20:6a, 21:1g,6a
WORMSER, Simon, banker, NYC-M - 1895/07/31: 1g
WORTHMANN, Geo., ca. 50, garment worker, NYC-B - 1914/12/04:2e
WORTHMANN, John, 46, grocer, NYC-M – 1885/05/02:1, 3:1g
WORTHMANN, Julia, 19, NYC-M, +@ Genl Slocum – 1904/06/27:1h
WORTMANN, August, fr Liestal/Basel, Switz., + Boston, MA – 1886/02/24:3d
WOSCHE, Christina, NYC-M – 1885/08/21:3a
WOSCHE, Herman A., NYC-M – 1888/09/18:3a
WOSSEL, Richard, NYC-M – 1892/06/09:2g
WOSSNER % Bachmann
WOUTRIDGE, John H., Austrian, USA Army, + Fort Slocum, NY, War 2 – - 1915/07/27:1g
WOYSIK, Gieresko, striker, Bayonne, NJ - 1915/07/24:2d
WOYTISEK, Vincent W., 4, NYC-M – 1883/08/14:3c
WOYTISEK, Vincent, SLP candid. 10th Assembly D., father of + little Vincent, NYC-M – 1883/10/15:4c, 18:2c
WRAGE, John, un. upholst., NYC-B – 1891/05/11:4a
WRAY, Sim, the "honest tramp," NYC-M – 1899/09/12:4b
WREISMER, Philip, 45, NYC-B – 1901/07/03:1e
WRENHAN, Mary, 22, NYC-B – 1880/11/19:1f
WRIGHT, Carroll D., Chief Statis. At US Dept of Labor, very crit obit – 1909/02/24:4a-b
WRIGHT, Christine, 31, portrait painter, NYC-M - 1916/12/14:6c
WRIGHT, Else, b. Lemp, 37, + St Louis, MO - 1920/03/22:2d
WRIGHT, Emma Scott, Dr., 31, homeophat, NYC-B - 1879/11/20:4d
WRIGHT, Louis, Negro, lynched New Madrid, MO – 1902/02/18:3b
WRIGHT, Sophie, educator, + 10 June New Orleans, LA – 1912/06/30:20e
WRIGHT, Wilbur, US airplane pioneer – 1912/05/31:2b
WRISSMANN, Magdalena, NYC-M – 1885/07/02:3c
WROBLESKI, general, among leaders of Paris Commune, + France – 1908/08/22:4d
WROCKLAGE % Boye
WUCHDE, Frank, un. butcher, NYC-B - 1919/01/21:6a
WUCHERER, Annie, 2, NYC-M – 1890/11/13:4a
WUCHERER, Carl, un. printer, NYC-M - 1895/12/29: 5a
WUCHERER, Hugo Emil, infant, NYC-M – 1891/07/09:4a
WUCHERER, Johann, 32, NYC-B – 1890/10/11:4a
WUCHERER, Josephine, b. Zerweck, NYC-M – 1887/03/23:3d, 25:3e
WUCHERPFENNING, Ferdinand, un. mason, NYC-M – 1899/01/22:1h, 5h
WUENSCH, Joseph, NYC-B - 1918/01/15:6a

WUERGH, Alfred, SP, NYC-M - 1918/11/16:6a
WUERSTHOFF, Ludwig, 66, carp., son + @Genl Slocum, NYC-M – 1904/07/03:1g
WUERTH, Michael, NYC-M – 1891/07/23:4a
WUERZBURG, Siegfried, ex-police com., Mt Vernon, NY – 1904/01/08:1g
WUERZBURGER, Henry, 40, NYC-M – 1888/03/29:1d
WUEST, August, bookkeeper, NYC-B – 1903/05/27:4a
WUEST, Gottlieb, NYC-B – 1882/04/12:3a
WUEST, Henry, SP?, NYC-B – 1910/09/21:6a
WUEST, John, 64, NYC-B – 1902/11/18:4a, 19:4a
WUEST, Kath., 40, NYC-M – 1891/07/07:4a
WUEST, Nikolaus, 42, NYC-B – 1910/02/24:6a, 26:6a
WUESTEFELD, Charles W., 20, bank clerk, NYC-M – 1908/08/05:1e
WUESTEHUBE, O., West New York, NJ – 1919/09/23:6a
WUESTEL, Emil, un. carp., NYC-M – 1904/03/25:4a
WUESTEL, Louise, b. Gutenkunst, 62, NYC-M – 1904/03/18:4a
WUESTHOFF, Emilie, Newark, NJ – 1902/01/11:4a
WUETHERICH, F., 48, NYC-B - 1919/06/06:6a
WULF, Hermann, NYC-M – 1883/02/06:1g
WULNISKI, Bernhard, NYC-M – 1892/07/24:5b
WULTERIN, Anton, NYC-Q - 1919/01/26:6a
WULTZEN, Friedrich, NYC-M – 1898/07/20:4a
WUNDERLICH, Anna, 65, NYC-M – 1887/05/03:3e
WUNDERLICH, Bertha, b. Hartmann, NYC-M – 1892/03/18:4a
WUNDERLICH, Henriette, b. Warnecke, 71, NYC-M – 1911/04/10:6a
WUNDERLICH, Joseph, 67, baker, NYC-B – 1903/08/01:3c
WUNDERLICH, W. E., restaurant manager, NYC-M – 1901/12/19:4b
WUNDERLICH, Wilhelm, NYC-M - 1919/01/03:6a
WUNDERLIE, John, Buffalo, NY - 1914/11/18:6a
WUNDSAM, Otto, NYC-M – 1891/04/05:5a
WUNDT, Wilhelm, Prof. Dr., 89, German Psychologist - 1920/09/23:4d
WUNNENBERG, Hilda Theresa, NYC – 1910/07/03:1g
WUNSCH, Chr., un. carp., NYC-B – 1889/09/12:4a
WUNSCHEL, Herman, NYC-M - 1917/02/15:6a
WURM, Theresia, b. Hitz, NYC-B - 1920/11/26:6a
WURMSTICH, Barbara, 37, NYC-M, +@ Genl Slocum – 1904/06/21:1f
WURST, Christian F., 64, NYC-B – 1892/11/07:4a
WURST, Friedrich, 80, NYC-M – 1904/12/24:4a, 25:5a
WURSTER, John, Caldwell, NJ - 1920/10/07:6a
WURSTER, Louis, 45, importer, NYC-SI – 1898/11/06:1h
WURTENBERGER, Mary, Mamie & Lillie, 18, NYC-M, +@ Genl Slocum – 1904/06/17:3c, 18:3c, d, 22:1d

WURTHMANN, John, grocer, 46, NYC-M – 1885/05/02:1g
WURTZ, Friedrich, 44, waiter, NYC-M – 1893/09/25:1g
WURTZ, Friedrich, NYC-Q – 1909/06/09:6a
WURTZ, Georg, NYC-Q – 1905/09/09:4a
WURTZ, Max, Philadelphia – 1885/06/17:1b
WUSCHOSIUS, August, 69, SP?, NYC-M – 1920/11/26:6a
WUSCHOSIUS, Hedwig Lange, 48, NYC – 1913/12/04:6a
WUSTERBARTH, Albert, Meridien, CT – 1896/09/08:1d
WUTTKE, Annie, 9, NYC-M – 1900/11/18:5c
WUTTKE, Max, 56, un. cigarmaker, NYC-Q – 1919/04/08:6a, 9:6a
WYLIE, William Hutt Curzon, British colonial officer in India, + by @Dhingra – 1909/07/03:1a
WYSSMANN, Johanna, b. Brandes, NYC-M – 1917/11/17:6a
WYTZKA, John, NYC – 1913/03/09:7b
WYTZKA, Lucius J., infant, NYC-M – 1882/09/05:3c
WYWIOLEK, Anton, inventor, NYC-M – 1903/10/23:1g
YAMAMOTO, Ichizo, 24, Japanese socialist – 1914/03/19:4d-e
YANOWITZ, Morris, 40, NYC-B – 1906/03/24:3c
YENT, Rahel, smith, Baltimore, MD – 1879/09/10:2e
YERBY, Jim, Negro, lynched Watkinsville, GA – 1905/06/30:1h
YOEKEL, Louis, 27, NYC-Bx – 1890/08/11:4a
YOELLMOKE, Sophia, NYC-M – 1891/03/18:4a
YOERK, Otto, 62, NYC-SI – 1919/01/29:6b
YOKERS, Charles, NYC – 1896/07/11:3f
YONDIR, Baraska & family, Poles, NYC-B – 1915/11/03:1e
YORCK, Bertha, NYC-M, + @ SS Genl Slocum – 1904/06/17:3c
YORCK, Theodor, 45, rising German labor leader, + 1 Jan. 1875 in Hamburg, memoria by Wilhelm Blos – 1900/09/16:7g-h
YORK, Richard, NYC-Bx – 1920/06/13:12a
YOST, Charles, worker, NYC-M – 1901/02/08:1e
YOST, Lulu, 14, Newark, NJ – 1892/08/24:4f
YOUNG, Brigham, Mormon leader, 100th anniv. – 1901/06/28:2e-f
YOUNG, Charles De, publ. San Francisco Chronicle – 1880/04/24:1a, 25:4b, 5b-c, 26:1c,2a, 27:2b, 28:2d-e, 1 May:1d, 5:1b, 11:2b-c
YOUNG, D. M., 45, SP, dying, Newburgh, NY – 1905/12/28:1c
YOUNG, Frank T., alias "Caesar," a "sport," NYC-M – 1904/06/05:1f-g, 6:1g, 7:1b, 9:1g, 14:1g
YOUNG, Friedrich, NYC-M – 1891/03/25:4a
YOUNG, John, exec. Mount Holly, NJ – 1902/03/19:3c
YOUNG, John, NYC-Q – 1918/01/16:6a
YOUNG, Richard, Negro, lynched near Ogeechee, GA – 1902/03/31:1d
YOUNKER, Peter, NYC-Q – 1913/12/27:6a

YUCKER, Bertha, 25, Cleveland, OH – 1900/06/01:1b
YUENGLING, Frederick D., son of the brewer, NYC-M – 1908/09/28:1b
YUENGLING, William G., 36, brewery owner, + Pottsville, PA – 1898/08/09:3e
YULCH, Adam, NYC-M – 1896/08/11:1a
YUNCKER, Theodor, 31, NYC-B – 1919/03/18:6a
YUNG, John, machinist, NYC-M – 1878/02/06:4e
YUNGERMANN, Caroline, 63, NYC-B – 1916/09/28:6b
YUNGINGER, Georg, * 11 Dec 1881, SLP?, Hudson County, NJ – 1899/08/12:3b
YURMAN, Max, 23, striking furrier, killed by police, NYC-M – 1920/07/28:1d, 29:1e, 9000 at funeral 30:1g
ZABEL, Karl, 34, NYC-M – 1896/03/29:5a
ZABEL, R., NYC-Bx – 1909/12/07:6a
ZABORSKY % Klein
ZACHAEL, Ernst, 20, West Hoboken, NJ – 1914/04/16:6a
ZACHAEL, William, 60, West Hoboken, NJ – 1918/09/10:6a
ZACHARIAS, Eduard, 70, textile worker & SP Bruenn/Moravia – 1911/01/01:3b
ZACHELLO, Joseph, exec. Ossining, NY – 1901/08/30:2h
ZACHER, Daniel, Orange, NJ – 1913/03/01:6a
ZACHMANN, Heinrich, NYC-M – 1905/01/29:5g
ZADEK % Romm
ZAENKER, Joseph, 28, NYC-M – 1885/03/07:4a
ZAHL, Charles, sailor, NYC-B – 1898/09/06:1c
ZAHLER, Adam, 56, NYC-M – 1888/08/16:1h
ZAHM, Richard, 37, NYC-Q – 1912/06/22:6a
ZAHN, August, 50, NYC-M – 1891/05/29:4a
ZAHN, August, West New York, NJ – 1914/02/10:6a
ZAHN, Bertha, 22, NYC-M, + @on SS Genl Slocum – 1904/06/22:1d
ZAHN, Christina, NYC-M – 1891/04/11:4a
ZAHN, Georg, 6, NYC-M – 1893/08/12:1f
ZAHN, Theodor, NYC? – 1892/07/18:1g
ZAHN, Valentin, cigar-dealer, + 28 Dec 1904, now his brother John, 26, NYC-B – 1905/05/04:3c
ZAHNLEITER, Conrad, 59, un. bricklayer, NYC-M – 1901/12/17:4a
ZAISER, Emma, NYC-Q – 1908/09/21:6a
ZAISER, Gottlieb, NYC-M – 1890/09/26:4a
ZAISER, Joseph, NYC-Q – 1905/04/12:4a
ZAISER, Willy, child, NYC-M – 1885/01/27:3d
ZALABAK, Carl, NYC-M – 1909/01/24:7b
ZALABAK, Telsie, 28, NYC-M – 1905/11/08:4a, 9:4a

ZALESKY, Vincent, Rev., Polish Natl Church Philadelphia, PA – 1899/11/11:1f
ZAMENHOF, Ludwig, Dr., fdr of Esperanto, + Warsaw, Poland - 1917/04/16:1b
ZANCHE, Doris, NYC-Bx, + @ SS Genl Slocum – 1904/06/17:3c, 18:3d
ZANDER, Bertha, b. Strombach, SP, Newark, NJ – 1908/06/30:6a
ZANDER, Oskar, NYC-M – 1888/02/29:3c
ZANDT, VAN, J., 35, NYC-M - 1894/01/25:4a
ZANGLE, Robert, 14, NYC-B – 1893/06/27:3c
ZANZARA, Santa, exec. Ossining, NY – 1912/07/09:1b
ZAPKE, Heinrich, 48, furrier, USA 1881, NYC-M – 1881/12/27:1f
ZAPP, Peter, 48, NYC-M - 1915/02/26:6a
ZARNFALLER, Sophie, 63, NYC-M – 1890/05/16:4a
ZARNKELLER, Carl, 70, NYC-M – 1891/05/12:4a
ZARTE, Henry, NYC-M – 1899/10/08:5a
ZARTH, Joseph, 54, carp., NYC-M – 1908/07/25:2d, 26:7c
ZARTMANN, Gustav, 63, NYC-B – 1897/06/07:4a
ZARZUELA, Spanish peasant soc., exec. Xerez de la Frontera – 1892/02/11:1a-b, 12:1a, NYC prot. 19:1g
ZAUN, William, 50, NYC-B – 1908/07/09:3b
ZEBE, Alwina, 9, NYC-M – 1885/04/21:3d
ZEBITSCH, Wenzel, SP, musician?, NYC-M, needs help – 1907/01/28:2b
ZEBRIS, Joseph, Rev., 51, Lithuanian RC parish, New Britain, CT - 1915/02/10:1c
ZECH, Albert, NYC? - 1914/02/16:6a
ZECK, John, 54, NYC-M – 1890/09/28:5e
ZEEB, Charles, W. Hoboken, NJ – 1900/12/01:4a
ZEEH, Frederick, un. printer, NYC-B - 1918/01/9:6a
ZEGER, Josef, RR worker, SP Vienna/Austria – 1908/08/09:3e
ZEGER, Louise, 69, NYC-M – 1898/05/03:3d
ZEH, Adam, NYC-M – 1891/04/01:4a
ZEH, David, 66, bookbinder, pro–Most, NYC-M – 1906/02/01:1g, 2:4a
ZEHLEIN, Johann Paul, NYC-B – 1891/07/05:5a
ZEHLER, Hermann, painter, fr Breslau/Gy, NYC? – 1883/12/24:3a
ZEHNER, John H., 50, shoemaker, USA 1870 fr Elsass, NYC-M – 1891/06/02:1c
ZEHNER, Magdalena, b. Wolff, 76, NYC-B - 1914/11/22:7b
ZEHNKE % Gloede
ZEHR, William F., 48, engraver, *NYC, NYC-B - 1913/07/11:3a
ZEHRER, Michael, 65, SPO Dornbirn/Vorarlberg - 1913/06/08:3a
ZEIBIG, Gustav, un. carp., NYC-B – 1899/11/20:3b,4a

ZEIBIG, Richard, 64, un. cigarm., SP, *Leipzig/Gy, NYC-M – 1910/06/25:6a, 26:7c, =27:2d, fam. 28:6a
ZEIDEL, Valentin, striker, @Morewood/PA – 1891/04/03:1b, = 4:1a-b
ZEIDLER % Buettner
ZEIDLER, Arby, NYC-M, +@ SS Genl Slocum – 1904/06/22:1d
ZEIDLER, Julius, NYC-B – 1891/04/09:4a
ZEIDLER, Ludwig, NYC-M – 1897/07/06:4a
ZEIDLITZ, Hermann A., NYC-M - 1894/01/15:4c
ZEIGER, Charles Bruno, 2, NYC-M – 1882/08/20:8a
ZEIGER, Eva B., 62, NYC-B – 1892/10/12:4a
ZEIGER, Henry, tailor, NYC-M - 1894/02/20:4e
ZEIGLING, Frederick, NYC-B – 1893/08/07:1h
ZEIMAN, Georg, driver, Cleveland, OH – 1911/06/11:1c
ZEINER, Christian, 27, dying, NYC-M – 1888/12/07:1f
ZEISE, Walter, 4, NYC-B – 1886/07/08:2e
ZEISER, Marie, NYC-M – 1890/03/21:4a
ZEISS, Rebecca, 50, NYC-M – 1882/02/26:3b
ZEISSER, Josephine, NYC-M - 1895/02/01:3d
ZEISSIG, Johann, 68, Jersey City Heights, NJ – 1899/03/06:4a
ZEITINGER, Joseph, NYC-M – 1889/07/01:4a
ZEITLER, Georg, 30, silk weaver, Paterson, NJ – 1897/01/28:4c
ZEITLER, Hermann, 42, W. Hoboken, NJ – 1912/05/17:6a
ZEITLER, John, 37, cook, NYC-M – 1903/08/23:5b
ZEITLER, Meta, b. Jacobsen, West Hoboken, NJ - 1913/10/16:6a
ZEITZ, Anton, NYC-B - 1918/02/26:6a
ZEITZ, John George, 63, NYC-M – 1891/09/02:4a
ZEITZ, Julie, 76, White Plains, NY – 1890/03/19:4a
ZEIZIG, John, NYC-M - 1894/04/30:1b
ZELBIG, Karl, NYC-B – 1889/10/29:4a
ZELENKA, John, Czech, umbrella maker, NYC-M - 1878/03/22:4e, 23:4d, fam. 21 May:3d
ZELIG, "Big Jack," mobster, NYC-M – 1912/10/06:1d, 7:4a-b, 9:4c-d
ZELINER, Xavier, 86, fr Solothurn/Switz., Hoboken, NJ, note – 1880/06/28:1g
ZELINKA, Carl L., 58, NYC-B – 1908/02/26:6a
ZELL, Margarethe see Mata Hari
ZELL, Stella, 20, & son Adolph, 1, Jersey City Heights, NJ – 1904/07/07:3b
ZELLER, Benedikt, NYC-M – 1906/06/20:6a
ZELLER, Clemens, NYC-M - 1917/01/19:6a
ZELLER, Elisabeth, 18, NYC-M - 1878/11/25:1g
ZELLER, George, NYC-B – 1908/11/11:6a
ZELLER, Gottfried, 43, NYC-Q – 1902/03/02:5a

ZELLER, John, 45, well-digger, NYC-Q – 1905/06/05:1g, 6:3c
ZELLER, Katherina, b. Berg, 25, NYC-M – 1889/02/12:4a
ZELLMANN, Bertha, NYC-B – 1912/04/20:6a
ZELOSKI, Sebastian, 48, laborer, Poland, NYC-Q – 1891/06/17:1f
ZELTLAGER, Sophie, b. Eckert, 68, NYC-M – 1891/08/28:4a
ZELTMANN, Christ, NYC-B - 1916/01/02:11f
ZELTNER, Henry, 67, brewer, NYC-M – 1898/06/11:4a, 12:5a
ZELTNER, Xavier, 86, Polish 1830 vet, NYC-M – 1880/12/06:4a
ZEMAN, Adolf, Prof. Dr., 69, Austrian left-liberal politician, + Vienna 16 Dec 1919 - 1920/01/16:4f
ZEMAN, Frank, un. carp., Winfield, LI – 1912/04/30:6a
ZENK, Bertha, NYC-M, +@SS Genl Slocum – 1904/06/18:3d
ZENNER, Fritz, 24, baker, NYC-M – 1892/02/05:1g, 6:1c-d
ZENTGRAF, John, 47, employee, NYC-B – 1886/07/16:3a
ZENTNER, Joseph, * 14 Oct 1866 Wuerzburg/Gy, NYC-B – 1881/12/14:3a
ZENTNER, Lorenz, NYC-B – 1889/11/01:4a
ZENTSEL, Paul, 41, NYC-Q – 1908/11/21:1b
ZENTUS, Bertha, (or Zenius) 29, NYC-M – 1889/08/29:4a, 31:4a
ZENTZ, Richard, Newark, NJ - 1914/07/11:6a
ZEPP, Adolph, 29, worker, NYC-M – 1903/11/17:1g, 18:4a
ZEPPELIN, Count Ferdinand von, 79, inventor - 1917/03/09:1a
ZERBECK, Annie, child, NYC-M - 1895/03/24:5a
ZERBST, Friedrich, NYC-M – 1890/02/24:4a
ZERDONI, Wilhelm, 50, NYC-Q – 1891/03/09:4a
ZERENER, Josef, 33, SP, fr Hungary, NYC-Bx - 1916/08/14:2b,fam. 16:6a
ZERFUSS, Robert, NYC-M – 1911/03/02:6a, 3:6a
ZERNER, Ernst, NYC-Bx - 1917/07/17:6a
ZERWECK % Wucherer
ZERWECK, Sophie W., b. Metsch, SLP, NYC-Q – 1899/08/02:4a, 3:4a, fam. 5:4a
ZERWECK, William, machinist, NYC-B – 1912/03/15:6a
ZERZER, Frank, 58, NYC-B – 1911/02/18:3b
ZESCH, Clara, Newark, NJ – 1884/08/03:5g
ZESCH, Gustav, small manuf., *Forst/Lausitz, USA 1878, SP, Newark, NJ – 1911/04/11:2f, 6a
ZESTER, John, + 1909, mem. 1910/10/04:6a
ZESTER, Katherina, 65, SP, fr Rheydt/Gy, Paterson, NJ – 1912/01/06:6a, =8:6a
ZETKIN, Clara, #, German Socialist, her current life – 1909/02/28:19d-e
ZETSCHE, Adolf, machinist, Yonkers, NJ – 1910/07/13:6a
ZETT, Mrs, Rockville, CT – 1908/08/05:1f
ZETTWOCH, Dorothy K. Clauer, 63, NYC-M - 1920/04/07:6a

ZEUCHNER, Henry P., 50, chemist, NYC-M – 1909/08/16:1b
ZEUG, Gottlob, NYC-M – 1904/12/20:4a
ZEUN, Maria, 68, NYC-B – 1906/10/24:6a
ZEUNER, Carl, NYC-M – 1883/12/22:3a
ZEYDEL, Hermann, 76, NYC-B – 1891/03/17:4a
ZIBETTI, Frank, Jersey City Heights, NJ – 1919/10/27:6a
ZICK, Friedrich, 71, innkeep, SPD Fuerth/Nuernberg/Gy – 1913/01/13:4d-e
ZICK, Marie, NYC-B - 1913/06/16:6a
ZICKFELD, G., fam. 1889/02/17:5e
ZIEBARTH, Hermann, 45, Newark, NJ – 1901/07/04:3b
ZIECKERT, Gustav, 27, NYC-M – 1891/08/26:4a
ZIEGAST, Helene, b. Hanke, + Oneida, NY – 1892/01/24:4a, fam. 1 Fb:4a
ZIEGELHOFER, Julius, NYC-M - 1915/11/18:6a
ZIEGELMUELLER, L., 57, NYC-B – 1902/06/14:4c
ZIEGELTRUM, George, un. carp., NYC-M – 1911/01/30:6a, 31:6a
ZIEGLER % Rammenstein, % Walter, % Webenbauer
ZIEGLER, August, whose father killed during NYC 12 Sept 1871 Orange Riots, officially took stepfather's surname DILL – 1905/09/29:3c
ZIEGLER, August W., NYC-M - 1917/11/13:6a
ZIEGLER, Bertha, 3, & Willie, 6 months, Jersey City, NJ – 1897/07/14:1f
ZIEGLER, Charles A., SDP, NYC-M – 1903/05/05:4a
ZIEGLER, Clara, 65, German actress, + Munich – 1909/12/21:3d
ZIEGLER, Emily, 19, NYC-M, + @ Genl Slocum – 1904/06/17:3c, 18:3d
ZIEGLER, Frank, NYC-Q - 1915/10/26:6a
ZIEGLER, Franz, 1803-1876, mayor of Brandenburg, who had good heart – 1880/04/23:2c. 100th anniv. Of birth – 1903/02/22:4c-e
ZIEGLER, Frederick, 66, un. baker, NYC-M - 1914/04/16:6a
ZIEGLER, Frederick, un. carp., NYC-M – 1907/04/26:6a
ZIEGLER, Gottlieb, un. carp., NYC-M – 1898/04/16:4a
ZIEGLER, Gustav, 62?, fr Weissenfels/Saale in Gy, NYC-M – 1889/02/14:4a
ZIEGLER, Jakob, 60, NYC – 1883/12/26:4d
ZIEGLER, John, New Brunswick, NJ, + on USS Maine – 1898/02/18:1b
ZIEGLER, Joseph, un. carp., NYC-M – 1901/05/09:4a
ZIEGLER, Kasper, un. carp., NYC-M – 1909/02/06:6a
ZIEGLER, Mathilde, NYC-M – 1907/10/21:6a, fam. 23:6a
ZIEGLER, Theodor, NYC-M – 1912/12/20:6d
ZIEGLER, Wilhelm, cooper, NYC-M - 1913/07/08:6a
ZIEHL, Jacob, 51, NYC-Q - 1916/01/08:6a
ZIEHM, Gustav, un. machinist, NYC-M – 1883/04/28:3a
ZIEHNERT, Emil, NYC-Bx – 1912/01/16:6a
ZIELKE, Wilhelm, NYC-M - 1914/06/19:6a

ZIELLY, Charles, merchant, Ridgewood, NJ – 1899/02/02:1f
ZIEMER, Mr., NYC-M – 1893/02/14:4a
ZIER, Theodor, NYC-Bx – 1911/05/11:6a
ZIERAU, Elizabeth, 69,NYC-B - 1917/09/06:6a, fam. thanks 12:6a
ZIERAU, Frieda, 19, NYC-B – 1904/09/25:5a, 26:4a
ZIERLEN, P., 25, NYC-B – 1893/09/02:4a
ZIERMANN, Friedrich, West New York, NJ - 1917/06/06:6a
ZIEROLD % Winkel; ZIESAT % Sinniger
ZIETEN, Henry Hermann, 64, un. carp., NYC-M – 1909/03/20:6a, 21:7a
ZIETSCH, comrade, SPD Berlin, * 23 Apr 1877 Berlin, porcelain worker, MdR - 1913/07/27:3b
ZIFF, Max, 63, locksmith, Jersey City, NJ – 1888/04/07:2e
ZILLIAKUS, Henry, NYC-M – 1890/03/07:4a
ZILM, Otto, un. cigar maker, SLP, * 4 May 1848 Frankfurt/Oder, USA 1871, NYC-M – 1881/06/05:5f, 6:3b,4d, & son Max 24:3a
ZIMBER, Salome, 70, NYC-M – 1891/03/25:4a
ZIMM, Gustav, 30, NYC-M – 1882/07/09:5e
ZIMM, Louis, 55, super-intendent, NYC-M – 1904/12/13:3d
ZIMMER, Albert, worker, NYC-M? or –Bx – 1892/05/06:1e
ZIMMER, Anna Maria, 65, NYC-M – 1890/02/22:4a
ZIMMER, Anna, b. Koch, NYC? - 1913/12/07:7a
ZIMMER, Charles, 46, carp., NYC-B – 1913/04/05:3a
ZIMMER, comrade, 83, weaver, SPD Mittweida/Saxony – 1909/06/13:3d
ZIMMER, Fritz, 49, un. baker, NYC-M - 1921/11/04:7a
ZIMMER, Fritz, NYC-M – 1910/01/26:6a
ZIMMER, Henry, 72, tailor, then RR worker, NYC-B – 1910/03/13:7f
ZIMMER, Hirsch, 20, 1902 fr Sweden, NYC-M – 1902/09/21:1e
ZIMMER, Jacob, NYC-M – 1893/05/14:5b
ZIMMER, John, cigarmaker, NYC-M - 1879/10/23:1d
ZIMMER, Karl Traugott, NYC-Q – 1904/10/24:4a
ZIMMER, Lena, & husband Adam, 76, dying, NYC-B – 1910/04/06:3a
ZIMMER, Martin, tailor, NYC-B – 1878/06/29:3b
ZIMMER, Mathilde, b. Lerch, NYC-M – 1891/03/19:4a
ZIMMER, Paul, + 4 May, NYC-B = 1913/05/23:2e
ZIMMER, Peter, waiter, NYC-M – 1889/06/22:4a
ZIMMER, William, 56, NYC-Q – 1904/12/19:4a, 20:4a
ZIMMERDINGER, Franz, innkeep, Jersey City, body fd – 1882/06/03:1e
ZIMMERMANN % Knies, % Wolf
ZIMMERMANN, ..., musician, + NYC @Genl Slocum – 1904/06/24:1c
ZIMMERMANN, Adam, 60, NYC-M - 1918/11/16:6a
ZIMMERMANN, Adam, NYC-M – 1900/08/12:1d
ZIMMERMANN, Amalie, b. Schadrack, 63, NYC-B – 1892/06/28:4a

ZIMMERMANN, Andreas, 61, un. carp., NYC-M – 1910/02/18:6a
ZIMMERMANN, August, NYC-M – 1907/08/19:6a
ZIMMERMANN, Augusta, 16, & Hugo, 12, NYC-M, +@Genl Slocum – 1904/06/18:3d
ZIMMERMANN, Carl, 24, NYC-M – 1887/02/16:3b
ZIMMERMANN, Charles, 43, jeweler, NYC-B – 1907/11/22:3c
ZIMMERMANN, Charles, West Newark, NJ - 1913/06/14:6a
ZIMMERMANN, Charlotte, infant, NYC-M – 1883/05/18:1f
ZIMMERMANN, Emma, b. Wasserscheid, NYC-M – 1890/11/21:4a
ZIMMERMANN, Franz, 37, NYC-M – 1881/12/18:5e
ZIMMERMANN, Franz, sculptor & SP Vienna, Austria – 1909/05/23:3f, =30:3f
ZIMMERMANN, Heinrich, NYC-M – 1891/06/29:4a
ZIMMERMANN, John H., 53, NYC-B – 1899/05/22:1e, 26:3g
ZIMMERMANN, Joseph, Newark, NJ + 5 Jy, inquest – 1886/07/12:2g
ZIMMERMANN, Julia, 58, NYC-M – 1882/03/06:3b
ZIMMERMANN, Louis, NYC-M – 1899/06/22:3c, 23:1g
ZIMMERMANN, Ludwig, un. cigar maker, NYC-M – 1880/02/03:3b
ZIMMERMANN, Mabel, 19, Elizabeth, NJ – 1903/10/19:3b
ZIMMERMANN, Marie, fam. NYC? – 1906/04/10:4a
ZIMMERMANN, Mary, b. Nicholson, NYC-M – 1904/11/13:1d
ZIMMERMANN, Max, worker at fireworks manuf., Jersey City, NJ - 1914/10/04:1g
ZIMMERMANN, Paul, 29, cigar maker, SPD, exp. fr Hamburg, arrived NYC – 1881/01/19:1g, 20:4c
ZIMMERMANN, Peter, 57, un. brewer, NYC-M – 1891/06/19:4a, 21:5a
ZIMMERMANN, Peter, 63, barber, NYC-M – 1899/01/13:1e, 14:1g
ZIMMERMANN, Samuel, 18, NYC-M - 1895/04/10:1h
ZIMMERMANN, Walter Erwin, lumber dealer fr Berlin/Gy, War 2 in Springfield, IL - 1915/11/26:1f
ZIMMERMANN, William, 42, lace importer, ex-pres. B'lyn Saengerbd, NYC-B – 1880/04/21:4b, 22:1g, will 7 May:1g
ZIMMERMANN, William, 30, waiter, NYC-B – 1909/12/29:3a
ZIMMERMANN, William, NYC-Bx – 1906/08/25:6a
ZIMMERS, Henry G., 14, and his brother Herbert, 7, NYC-B - 1915/03/14:1g
ZIMPEL, Franz Gustav, 35, spice dealer fr Hamburg/Gy, NYC-M – 1899/03/05:1g
ZINCK, Heinrich, 42, machinist, SPD, expelled fr Altona/Hamburg, arrived NYC – 1880/11/30:1d
ZINCK, Henry, 69, un. mach., NYC-M – 1908/03/16:6a
ZINCK, John, NYC-Bx - 1920/05/29:6a, 30:12a

ZINCK, Michael, NYC-B – 1890/07/02:4a
ZINCK, Ottilie, NYC-M - 1916/10/06:6a
ZING % Koerner
ZINGAL, Joseph, 5, NYC-M - 1918/06/21:2f
ZINGELMANN, August, SPD Hamburg-Bergedorf/Gy – 1901/12/11:2d
ZINGELMANN, Maria, 53, NYC-M – 1899/03/05:5a
ZINGLER % Loeffler
ZINK, Conrad, NYC-Bx - 1913/10/08:6a
ZINK, Georg M., 45, NYC-M – 1892/08/15:4a
ZINK, Johann J., 16, NYC-M – 1897/06/10:4a
ZINK, Johann Joseph, 52, NYC-M - 1879/11/13:3a
ZINK, John, 52, Newark, NJ – 1906/09/30:7d
ZINK, John, Newark, NJ – 1892/02/09:1g
ZINK, John, NYC-B – 1909/07/24:6a
ZINK, Richard, 51, NYC-B - 1901/11/05:2g
ZINN, Auguste, 35, NYC-B – 1893/11/21:4a
ZINN, Bertha, 42, & son John, 5, Edgewater, NJ – 1906/06/08:3d
ZINN, Emil Henry, un. silk weaver, NYC-B – 1906/11/01:6a
ZINN, Lina, 61, NYC-M – 1891/06/29:4a
ZINN, Otto, restaurant owner, NYC-M - 1915/04/06:6a, 7:1e, 16 Jy:2f
ZINSER, Frederick, un. baker, NYC-M – 1907/04/27:6a
ZINSMEISTER, Katharina, b. Ruhl, 25, fr Amoeneburg/Hessen, NYC-M - 1879/03/17:3a
ZINSMEISTER, Mrs M., 33, & daughter, NYC-M - 1913/09/27:6d
ZINTEL, August, decorator, NYC-Bx – 1905/12/21:2e, 22:4a
ZINZ, Franziska, b. Bruegger, 61, NYC-M – 1889/07/28:5b
ZIOR, Henry, 76, USA 1853 fr Darmstadt/Gy, Jersey City, NJ – 1908/10/28:3c
ZIPFEL, Albin, 42, NYC-M – 1891/09/03:4a
ZIPFEL, Caroline, NYC-B - 1894/10/16:4a
ZIPFEL, Herman, 54, NYC-M – 1900/04/09:4a
ZIPFEL, Johanna, NYC-M – 1893/03/17:4a
ZIPPERIAN, Henry, 55, NYC-B – 1911/02/15:6a
ZIPPERICH, George, NYC-M – 1890/01/22:4a
ZIPSE, Louise, 10, & Albert, 1, NYC-M, + @SS Genl Slocum – 1904/06/17:3c, 18:3c
ZIRKEL, George, 36, NYC-B – 1893/07/25:2d, 27:4a
ZIRN, Frank, NYC-M - 1918/05/08:6a
ZIRN, Marie, NYC-Bx – 1907/11/10:6a
ZIRNSTEIN, Gustav, 48, NYC-M – 1892/07/28:4a
ZIRRITH, Joseph M., 21, NYC-B - 1916/01/19:6c
ZISKA, Stanislaus, un. baker, NYC-M - 1918/10/15:6a

ZITSCH, Adam, Elizabeth, NJ - 1920/05/27:7a
ZITTEL, Adam, deli-owner, NYC-Q - 1920/07/03:1f, 10:1b, 1 Aug.:1f
ZITZ, Frederick, 25, NYC-M, + Delaware Water Gap – 1897/08/15:1c
ZITZELSBERGER, Joseph, NYC-B – 1909/04/24:6a
ZLAMEL, Josef, exec. Dannemora, NY – 1896/04/15:1e
ZOBEL, Gustav, SPD Liegnitz/Silesia, teamster, War 1 - 1915/10/03:3c
ZOEBEL, Louis, machinist, NYC – 1906/09/07:6d
ZOEBISCH, Maria H., 68, NYC-B – 1892/03/25:4a
ZOECHLING, Ferdinand, SP Hainfeld/Austria, – 1908/02/16:3d-e
ZOELLER, Barbara, 41, NYC-M – 1893/01/17:4a
ZOELLER, Cecilia, 24, NYC-M – 1891/04/04:4a
ZOELLER, Christina, NYC-B – 1911/05/29:6a
ZOELLER, Joseph, NYC-M – 1904/12/21:4a
ZOELLER, Karl, NYC-B - 1913/11/26:6a
ZOELLER, Margaretha, SP?, NYC-M - 1917/11/19:6a
ZOELLER, Martin, 40, manuf. & local polit., Hoboken, NJ – 1897/07/04:5g
ZOELLNER, Johann Carl Friedr., Dr., German astro-physicist – 1882/05/14:5b-c
ZOELLNER, Rudolph, 40, guard, Hoboken, NJ – 1909/04/21:1g
ZOELLY, Katherina, wd Sikorowsky, 61, member NYC Steirer Arbeiter Liedertafel, + Amsterdam, NY- 1920/04/04:12a
ZOERNER, Heinrich, 51, NYC-B – 1912/07/02:6a
ZOETZEL, Carl, 33, worker, Newark, NJ – 1906/08/01:2e
ZOETZL, Minna, 1, Norwich, NY – 1883/09/09:8a
ZOLA, Emile, French writer & activist, #, + – 1902/09/30:1a-c, 2a-b, 5:2c-d, =6:1h, rd lt 9:4c, 19:7f-h, 9a-b, 20:2e, 21:2d; praise of his widow 4 Apr 1905:2e; mem. 1908/04/12:4f-g
ZOLKI, Marie, + 30 Jan., inquest 1890/03/05:4e, 7:1g
ZOLL, Georg, 4, NYC-M – 1890/01/04:4a
ZOLL, Gottlieb, Jersey City Heights, NJ - 1919/01/21:6a
ZOLLER, Philipp, milkman, NYC-B – 1887/01/07:2d
ZOLLINGER, Frederick, 15, NYC-B – 1907/04/04:6c
ZOLLINGER, John, tailor, NYC-M – 1901/04/06:1c
ZOLLINGER, William, roofer, NYC-M – 1880/06/06:5a
ZOPF, Caspar, un. carp., NYC-M – 1902/12/01:4a
ZORN, Barbara, NYC-Bx – 1892/12/22:4a
ZORN, Lena, NYC-M – 1887/06/03:4e, 9:2f, 14:1g, 15:1g, 21:1e, 22:4e
ZORN, Oscar, NYC-B – 1908/03/17:3b
ZOTT, John, 73, musician, NYC-M - 1917/09/12:5f
ZOWE, Eduard, 54 or 34, NYC-M - 1895/01/09:4a
ZSCHERNITZ, Hermann, 49, innkeep, NYC-M – 1890/08/06:4e
ZSCHOKE, Reinhold, NYC-M – 1890/05/24:4a

ZSCHOKLE, Moritz, 36, un. baker, Jersey City, NJ - 1914/09/08:6a
ZUBEIL, Karl Friedrich, 47, SPD, carpenter & MdR, + Berlin - 1895/06/11:1c
ZUBER, Ed., West Hoboken, NJ - 1915/01/06:6a
ZUBER, Jakob, NYC-M – 1891/04/04:4a
ZUBERER % Cleff; ZUBOFF, Count, (alias name), see Lippmann, Roman
ZUCK % Helmreich
ZUCKER, Isidor, 26, waiter, NYC-M – 1902/04/22:1g
ZUCKER, Mary, NYC-B – 1902/08/26:4a-b
ZUCKER, Morris, 18, NYC-M, + Savannah, GA Fall 1904 – 1905/02/13:1d
ZUCKER, Philip, 18, fr Russia 1912, paperhanger, NYC-M? - 1914/01/13:3g
ZUCKERBERG, Salomon, NYC-M - 1913/08/09:2d
ZUCKERMANN, Morris, 23, fr Russia, NYC-B – 1882/12/05:4b
ZUCKERT % Rohner; ZUCKEYER % Carstens
ZUCKSCHWERT, Georg, un. carp., NYC-M – 1897/11/04:4a, 5:4a
ZUEGNER, Peter J., NYC-M – 1891/07/19:5b
ZUENDORF, Charles, 48, un. brewer, * Koeln/Gy, SDP, USA 1889, NYC-B – 1904/12/23:4a, 24:3d, 4a, 25:5a, fam. 26:4a
ZUFALL, Benjamin, 72, barber, NYC-M – 1902/12/17:1d
ZUGSCHWERT % Peters
ZUILLICH, Lina, b. Gietz, Union Hill, NJ – 1891/06/17:4a
ZUKSCHWERT, Frida, b. Ponty, NYC-M – 1888/02/09:3a
ZUMBUSCH, Ferdinand, 49, NYC-M – 1890/07/02:4a
ZUMPE, Martha, b. Loewenthal, NYC-Bx – 1911/07/06:6a
ZUNDMANN, Elizabeth, 67, NYC-M – 1908/09/02:1d
ZUNGMANN, Hannah, 34, NYC-M – 1891/09/20:5f
ZUR HEIDE, Carl, un. painter, NYC-M – 1904/06/22:4a
ZURCHER, Otto, 65, Swiss,sugar planter in Cuba, + NYC - 1919/01/15:3f
ZURETT, Ida, NYC-M – 1910/06/14:1f
ZUSCH, Ferdinand O., 60, (or Zesch), Rev., German Presbyt. Church, NYC-Q – 1910/11/14:2c
ZUSKA, Joseph, 68, Yonkers, NY - 1920/02/24:6a
ZWANITSCHEK, Louis, 20, NYC-M – 1903/03/03:4a
ZWEBELEIN, John, (misspelled Loebelein on 27th) NYC-B – 1902/12/27:4a, 28:5b, 29:4a
ZWEIG, Joseph, 25, un. waiter, NYC-M - 1894/02/21:4a
ZWEISLER, Barbette, 56, NYC-B - 1917/04/17:6b
ZWEITER, Naomi, NYC-B - 1920/03/01:2a
ZWERGEL, Andreas, NYC-B – 1897/11/20:4a
ZWERLEIN, Alois, 33, SP, pres. Butcher Union #211, USA 1903, - 1913/10/06:6a, 7:3d, 6a, =8:3b

ZWETSCH, Hermann, un. cigar maker, NYC-M – 1900/04/05:4a
ZWICK, Alois, 45, NYC-M – 1899/08/30:3e
ZWICK, Otto, ATB Leipzig/Sax., War 1 - 1914/11/01:3b
ZWICKER, Marie, Coytesville, NJ - 1919/03/16:12a
ZWICKERT, Anthony, 43, NYC-M – 1890/06/20:4a
ZWICKERT, Gustav L., 53, NYC-M – 1893/08/27:5a
ZWILLING, H., NYC-M – 1903/01/04:4a
1880 TURNHALLE FIRE, NYC-M – 1880/01/06:1a-c, 3a, comment 7:2d, =8:1g, 3a, 9:1e-f, common card of thanks 11:8a, manager Winckel +, too 12:1g, 3a, 14:3a, =15:4c, inquest 3 Fb:1g
1883 SCHOOL HOUSE FIRE, NYC-M – 1883/02/21:1b, 2a, over 20 little girls + 22:1d, 22:3c, =23:1g, 24:1g, inquest 28:4c-d, 27:4c-d, 1 Mr:1e-f
1885 MANHATTAN FIRE (4 victims) 4 May 1885:1b, 5:1g, 6:1f, 6:1c-d, 2a, 7:1c, 8:1d, inquest 16:2e-f, 23:2g
1887 CHICAGO HAYMARKET, collective entry for Georg Engel, Adolph Fischer, Louis Lingg, Oscar Nebe, Albert R. Parsons, Michael Schwab, August Spiess.
Police killed workers before the bombs 4 May 1886:1g, 5:1g, 6:1a-c, daily reports on the trial 28 May:4e, 29:2f-g, 2 June:2b, 4:1c, 15:2a-b, 21:2a-b, 22:1a-c, 23:1a-c, 24:1a-c, 25:1a-c, 26:1a-b, 29:1a-d, 30:1a-b, 1 Jy 1886:1a, 2:1a-b, 3:1a-b, 5:1a, 7:1a-b, 8:1e, 9:1g, 10:1a, 13:1a, 14:1a, 15:1a-b, 16:1a-c, 17:1a-c, 20:1a-c, 21:1a-c, 22:1a-e, 23:1a-d, 24:1a-e, 27:1a-d, 2a-b, 28:1a-d, 29:1a-c, 30:1a-c, 31:1a-b, 3 Aug:1a-c, 4:1a-c, 5:1a-c, 6:1a-c, 7:1a-c, 10:1a-d, 11:1a-b, 13:1a-b, 14:1a-b, 18:1a-d, 19:1a-c, 20:1a-c, 2a,c, sent. To death 21:1a-g, comment, collections for appeal begun 21 Aug:2a-c, 4e, 23:2a-b, 24:1a-c, 4e, 25:1a-b, 3b, 28:4b, 30:1a, 1 Sept:2a-b, 4f, 4:1b, 4e, etc, 6:2c, 9:2a, 22:2c, 27:5d, petition 2 Oct:1g, 5:1a-d, 6:2e-f, 7:2f, judge Gary refused appeal 8:1a-d, 2b, 9:1a-d, 12:3d, 18:1a-d, 19:5e, 22:4d, 5 Nov:1b-e, 8:1f-g, 19:1c,4c, German SPD plea for pardon 24 Nov:2d , 30:1c, 2 Dec 1886:4d, 3:2b; 5 Feb. 1887:1f, 3 March:1f, 11:1c, 18:1c, wife of Nebe + 14:1g, 28:5e, 16 Apr:1b, rev. of benefit in Weehawken, NJ 13 June:1d, support the appeal 22 June 1887: 2a, 29:1c, NYC workers protest 20 Sept:1a-c, 21:1b, injunction 7 Sept:2a, 15:1a-c, denied, workers stunned 15:2a, 17:1b-c, protests 22:1c-d, 23:1a, 2a, 24:1a-b, 26:1a-c, Neebe pardoned to 15 yrs 28:1b,meetings in Brooklyn etc 29:2a-b, 3 Oct:3a, 4:4d-e, 5:1b, 8:1c-d, 2a-b, 15:2e, 17:1d, 4d, (daily until) 24:2c, even bourgeois papers begin to doubt 25:2c, appeal to US Supr. Ct 26:1b, 2b-c, 27:2b-c, 28:1a-c, 29:1a-e, 31:1g, crit. Felix Adler (Ethical Culture) & Henry George for supporting exec. 31:2a-b, 4e. No decision yet 1 Nov:1c, 2:2a, US Supr. Ct rejected stay 3 Nov:1a-f, 2a, 4:1a-b, 2a, 5:1a-b, 2a, 7:1a-b, 3a, 4e, 8:1a-b, 2a, 9:1g, 4b, 10:1a-f, 2a-b, NYSZ position crit. 10:2f, Fielden & Schwab pardoned to jail, Lingg +

himself, the other 4 exec. 11:1a-g, 2a-b, "People, Do Not Forgive Them, For They [the capitalists] Knew What They Did!" 12:1a-g, 2a-b,d-g, 4a-c, 150,000 workers followed the corpses, NYC workers grieve, Felix Adler again crit. 14 Nov:1a-g, 2a-b, 4a-c, 15:1c-e, 2a,4f, 17:1c-e, more on = of the 5 at Waldheim Cemetery 19:1g,20:1c, rev. 16 Dec:4e, 19:1c-d, h, 21 Dec:4e, SPD in Germany denounces exec. 24 Nov:2d, NYC memorials 29:1a-c, f, 30:1b, 2 Dec:4a, 3:2c, 14:4e, 31:4a.

Memorial-meeting in NYC 23 Jan 1888:1h, 2b, 4d, Fall-out 18 Fb 1888:1b,notes 28 Mr:4e, 29:2f, collections for families 21 Apr:4d, prep. 1st year memorial 8 Sept:4e, NYC area meetings 9 Nov:4f-e, 10:1e-f, 12:1g, 2e-f; 2nd anniv. In NYC area, Chicago etc 10 Nov 1889:1h, 4a-c, 11:1a-e, 12:1a-e, 13:2a, 17:4a-b; 3rd anniv., NYC, Chicago & Elizabeth, NJ 10 Nov. 1890:2a,11:1c-e, 2a-b, 12:1c-d, 13:1e; 4th anniv., in NYC & Brooklyn 6 Nov 1891:1h, 8:5f, 9:1a-c, 10:1a-b, 11:1d-e, 13:2b; 5th anniv., inaug. grave monuments, # 1893/06/25:1b-c, 26:1f-g, 2 Jy:3f-g, meetings various US cities 12 Nov:5c, 13:1c-d, 15:1d; 10th comm. Haymarket 1896/05/04:2a, Chicago comm. met 11 Nov:1d, 2a, 13:1b,2a 10th anniv. exec., 6 Aug. 1897:2a, NYC 9 Oct:1f, 11:2a-b, 15:3e, rev. 13 Nov:9g; + their persecutors capt Schaack & District Attney Grinnell 1898/06/13:2a, but so does Michael Schwab + 3 Jy 98:4a; 12th anniv. memorial meetings in NYC 12 Nov 1899:5e & in Havanna, Cuba 12 Nov:12b; note 10 May 1900:2d, 15th anniv., mem. in NYC 11 Nov 1902:1c; 20th anniv. mem. meetings - 1907/11/11:4a-b; 23rd anniv., NYC meeting 1910/11/12:1b, 12:2a; 25th anniv., NYC meeting 1912/11/12:2a; 26th anniv. 1913/11/11:4a-b

1891 MOREWOOD, PA Massacre (6 workers + by vigilantes) – 3 Apr 1891:1b, =4:1a-b, 5:1f,4a, murderers fd "not guilty" by jury 24 May:1h
1897 HAZLETON, PA, Massacre, (9 coal-miners killed by Militia) – 1897/09/12:1b, 13:1a-c,h,2a, =14:1f-g,2a, 15:1a-e, 2a, 16:1c-d, 2a,c, 17:1a-b,18:1a-e, #2a-b, 3d,19:1a-g,4a-b,20:1h,2a, 21:1c-d, inquest 24:1b, 24:1h,25:1f, h, 27:1b, 28:1c,2b; 16 Oct:1h, 18:1e, 25:3d, 26:1h; trial 24 Dec:2a, 18 Jan. 1898:2a, 2 Fb:1h, jury frees the killers 10 Mr:1g, 2a, 14 Mr:2a-b, 15:1d; trial over 3 Nov:2a, 7:2c
1900 NORTH GERMAN LLOYD DOCK FIRE, Hoboken, NJ – 1 Jy 1900:1b-c, 2:1g, 3:1c, 12:1f
1904 GENERAL SLOCUM FIRE, NYC (over 900 dead) – 1904/06/16:1c-f, 17:3a-e, 18:3, etc, memorials commented 1904/07/13:3d, 15:3d, 17:4a-c, tablet stolen by vandals 1906/11/11:7d, caught 13:1f, 1 Dec:6a
1911 TRIANGLE SHIRTWAIST FIRE, NYC – 1911/03/26:1b, 27:1d, 28:1b-f, 29:1c, 8 Apr:1c

www.ingramcontent.com/pod-product-compliance
Lightning Source LLC
Chambersburg PA
CBHW071213290426
44108CB00013B/1171